Visual
Basic
SuperBible

SECOND EDITION

Bill Potter
Taylor Maxwell
Bryon Scott

WAITE GROUP PRESS™
Corte Madera, CA

Publisher · Mitchell Waite
Editorial Director· Scott Calamar
Managing Editor · John Crudo
Content Editor · Harry Henderson
Technical Reviewer · Jude Kaider
Production Director · Julianne Ososke
Cover Design · Ted Mader & Associates
Design · Cecile Kaufman
Production · LeeAnn Nelson
Part Opener Art · Zachary Rymland, founder of AZ-TECH, El Cerrito, CA

© 1993 by The Waite Group, Inc.®
Published by Waite Group Press™, 200 Tamal Plaza, Corte Madera, CA 94925.

Waite Group Press is distributed to bookstores and book wholesalers by Publishers Group West, Box 8843, Emeryville, CA 94662, 1-800-788-3123 (in California 1-510-658-3453).

Printed in the United States of America
95 96 • 10 9 8 7 6

Potter, Bill, 1963–
  Visual BASIC superbible / Bill Potter, Taylor Maxwell, Bryon Scott. -- 2nd ed.
    p. cm.
  Rev. ed. of: Visual BSIC superbible / Taylor Maxwell. 1992.
  Includes bibliographical references and index.
  ISBN: 1-878739-50-6: $44.95
  1. Windows (Computer programs) 2. Microsoft Visual BASIC.
I. Maxwell, Taylor. II. Scott, Bryon. III. Maxwell, Taylor.
Visual BASIC superbible. IV. Waite Group. V. Title.
QA76.76.W56M515   1993
005.4'3--dc20   93-43801
                                                                    CIP

DEDICATION

Bill Potter: *For my wife Mary.*

Taylor Maxwell: *For my wife Marcia.*

Bryon Scott: *For my wife JoAnn.*

ACKNOWLEDGMENTS

The authors gratefully acknowledge Mitchell Waite for the opportunity to write this book. We would also like to thank Scott Calamar for his encouragement and all of his help in getting this book published. A huge thanks to John Crudo, the ultimate traffic cop. He successfully navigated this mountain of detail over rocky roads strewn with hard-disk crashes, unanswered e-mail, and hyper-busy schedules.

Harry Henderson gave a number of helpful edits, comments, and suggestions that went beyond the expected and pointed out entire new areas to explore. Jude Kaider provided a thorough and detailed technical review of the second edition, as did Dan Derrick for the first edition.

Noami Lucks and KD Sullivan read every one of the half-million words in the manuscript (and corrected more than a few) on its way from manuscript to finished publication. Stephen Bach had the thankless job of indexing this behemoth, and Julianne Ososke and her production crew turned a disparate batch of files and graphics into the beautiful book you're now holding.

Taylor Maxwell would like to thank his father Taylor H. Maxwell Sr. for all of his help and encouragement. Thanks to all of the people on the MSBasic forum on Compuserve for the wealth of information about Visual Basic that exists there. This book would not have been possible without the support of family and friends including most especially my very loving wife Marcia.

Bryon Scott would like to give special thanks to Bob Traxler, for putting up with a tired and grouchy employee during the course of this project. Finally, thanks to my lovely wife, JoAnn. Without her dedication and support, I would have never been able to accomplish what I have. I love you.

Bill Potter would like to thank all of my friends and family for putting up with my almost maniacal focus during this project. A mere "thanks" doesn't do justice to the huge dose of patience and faith exhibited by my amazing wife, Mary. Now let's follow Bruce and Diana's footsteps: Maui no ka oi, here we come!

ABOUT THE AUTHORS

Bill Potter is President of Potter, Saylor & Associates, a marketing and consulting firm in Seattle, Washington. He's been programming for fifteen years, with the past seven years as a professional. His programming focus is entirely on the Windows environment, with a strong emphasis on Visual Basic. He is a graduate of the University of Michigan.

Taylor Maxwell works in a consulting firm which specializes in Windows and Visual Basic programming solutions. He began his programming career in 1985 and works extensively in the xBase and Basic languages. He is a graduate of Alma College in Alma, Michigan. He is a member of the Association of Shareware Professionals (ASP).

Bryon Scott graduated from Coleman College, a computer trade school, in September of 1986. Since then he has worked for a group of ceramic tile distributors developing in-house inventory control/order processing software. He is currently modifying this software for distribution in the retail market. Bryon uses QuickBASIC, Visual Basic, Microsoft Assembler, and a smattering of C in his programming efforts.

Dear Reader:

What is a book? Is it perpetually fated to be inky words on a paper page? Or can a book simply be something that inspires—feeding your head with ideas and creativity regardless of the medium? The latter, I believe. That's why I'm always pushing our books to a higher plane; using new technology to reinvent the medium.

I wrote my first book in 1973, *Projects in Sights, Sounds, and Sensations*. I like to think of it as our first multimedia book. In the years since then, I've learned that people want to *experience* information, not just passively absorb it—they want interactive MTV in a book. With this in mind, I started my own publishing company and published *Master C*, a book/disk package that turned the PC into a C language instructor. Then we branched out to computer graphics with *Fractal Creations*, which included a color poster, 3-D glasses, and a totally rad fractal generator. Ever since, we've included disks and other goodies with most of our books. *Virtual Reality Creations* is bundled with 3-D Fresnel viewing goggles and *Walkthroughs & Flybys CD* comes with a multimedia CD-ROM. We've made complex multimedia accessible for any PC user with *Ray Tracing Creations, Multimedia Creations, Making Movies on Your PC, Image Lab*, and three books on Fractals.

The Waite Group continues to publish innovative multimedia books on cutting-edge topics, and of course the programming books that make up our heritage. Being a programmer myself, I appreciate clear guidance through a tricky OS, so our books come bundled with disks and CDs loaded with code, utilities, and custom controls.

By 1994, The Waite Group will have published 135 books. Our next step is to develop a new type of book, an interactive, multimedia experience involving the reader on many levels.

With this new book, you'll be trained by a computer-based instructor with infinite patience, run a simulation to visualize the topic, play a game that shows you different aspects of the subject, interact with others on-line, and have instant access to a large database on the subject. For traditionalists, there will be a full-color, paper-based book.

In the meantime, they've wired the White House for hi-tech; the information super highway has been proposed; and computers, communication, entertainment, and information are becoming inseparable. To travel in this Digital Age you'll need guidebooks. The Waite Group offers such guidance for the most important software—your mind.

We hope you enjoy this book. For a color catalog, just fill out and send in the Reader Report Card at the back of the book. You can reach me on CIS as 75146,3515, MCI mail as mwaite, and usenet as mitch@well.sf.ca.us.

Sincerely,

Mitchell Waite

Mitchell Waite

PREFACE

Visual Basic has influenced the way Windows programming languages work and look to such an extent that we now think of its innovations as "normal." Visual Basic 1.0, with its easy to use interface and powerful event-driven programming language spawned a whole series of competitors, add-ons, and companion products. Versions 2.0 and 3.0 of Visual Basic have extended the language to the point where corporate MIS departments and professional programmers regularly use it for robust, critical applications. We've come so far that it's easy to lose sight of Visual Basic's beginnings.

In a way, the story of Visual Basic begins more than 25 years ago at Dartmouth College, more than a decade before the first personal computers came on the market. Professors John G. Kemeny and Thomas E. Kurtz had a problem. At a time when "computers" meant huge mainframes and batches of punched cards, Dartmouth had decided that all of its students would become "computer literate." After all, computers were already making an impact in just about every field of study from physics to linguistics. Students were likely to be using computers throughout their careers in unforeseen ways.

Kemeny and Kurtz believed that to make computers accessible, there had to be a simpler way to program them. The most popular languages of the time, FORTRAN and COBOL, were awkward and tedious to use. Equally important, programming had to become interactive. Instead of submitting hundreds of punched cards and waiting a day or more for results, students should be able to type in a command or simple program and see the results immediately. If students could get immediate feedback, they would feel free to experiment with new commands and features. They could tinker with programs and easily try out new ideas.

To meet these needs, the two Dartmouth professors simplified the FORTRAN language, added some new features, and in 1965 came up with BASIC (the acronym stood for "Beginner's All-purpose Symbolic Instruction Code"). Instead of using punch cards, students sat at teletype terminals that looked something like a typewriter on steroids. They typed in their programs, typed "run," and the results were banged out immediately on the teletype. Thousands of people began to think of computers differently.

The next chapter in our story took place in the mid to late 1970s, when the first true personal computers became available. Machines such as the Apple II, TRS-80, Commodore Pet, Atari 800, and their more obscure brethren proliferated. So too did a tiny company called Microsoft. Before there was an MS-DOS or an IBM PC, Microsoft was known for its BASIC interpreters. Just about every PC had its own version of Microsoft BASIC, usually stored in a ROM chip so that it would be available as soon as you booted up. And while a select group of wizards used assembly language to hand-craft the movement of bytes through the early 8-bit microprocessors, the rest of us turned to BASIC. Very little commercial software was available in the early years of personal computing. We spent many hours typing in BASIC listings from magazines and books, sometimes translating them from one machine's BASIC to another's. And when the IBM PC came out in 1982, Microsoft not only provided its DOS, it also provided the on-board BASIC interpreter, called BASICA. As personal computers continued to penetrate the business world, the demand for software grew. The trickle of explorers on the programming frontier soon became a torrent.

Every frontier needs its maps. One of the first sources of reliable and accessible books on personal computing was Mitchell Waite and The Waite Group. Mitch gave himself and his fellow authors a mandate to show readers how to really put BASIC through its paces. Authors were required to make their books thorough, accurate, and useful. Just as important, they were encouraged to make them fun. An example was The Waite Group's BASIC Programming Primer, first published in 1982. This book offered practical programs for such things as loan amortization and metric conversion, but it also offered a "Micro Space Invaders" game, Tic-Tac-Toe, and (in a later edition) a program that solved Rubik's cubes. With this and other Waite Group books, readers learned to write programs that drew colorful graphics, formatted text, dialed modems, and even played tunes.

But all was not well in the world of BASIC. Early BASICs, such as BASICA, suffered from serious structural problems. First of all, BASICA was interpreted, not compiled. This meant that each program instruction had to be decoded each time it was run, resulting in sluggish performance. And as programs became longer and more complex, programmers began to turn increasingly to the techniques of "structured programming." Unfortunately early BASIC was not well-suited to structured programming. All BASIC variables were "global," meaning that they could be changed willy-nilly from anywhere in the program. And while BASICA had simple subroutines, it did not have the self-contained procedures and modules needed for structured programming.

Microsoft met these concerns in the mid-1980s by coming out with QuickBASIC. This new BASIC was compiled rather than interpreted. It supported procedures and modules, as well as long user-defined functions. Line numbers were no longer needed, and the troublesome GOTO statement could be dispensed with in nearly all cases. Finally, QuickBASIC offered an integrated programming environment (pioneered by Borland's Turbo Pascal). Programmers could now edit, compile, run, debug, and revise programs from the same screen.

The Waite Group provided this second generation of BASIC programmers with such popular guides as the Microsoft QuickBASIC Bible and the Microsoft QuickBASIC Primer Plus. These books served the new, more sophisticated BASIC by integrating principles of structured programming with an even more thorough exploration of the BASIC language. Now readers could write programs to control the new laser printers, and to draw graphics using the more detailed and complex EGA and VGA graphics modes.

The new BASICs, such as QuickBASIC, were powerful and easy to use. Unfortunately, however, programs in the MS-DOS world were often hard to use. Many programs (and DOS itself) required the typing in of precise commands, and text was displayed line by line in a way not unlike teletypes back in the 1960s. Programmers responded to user complaints by designing menus, and eventually dialog boxes and screen windows. The mouse, with its ability to point to, select, and manipulate objects, became increasingly prevalent. But all these improvements in the user interface required tedious coding in each program. Furthermore, there was no standard as to how menus, dialog boxes, and other objects would behave. As a result, users had to relearn the interface each time they used a new program. No wonder they looked enviously at their colleagues' Macintoshes.

Microsoft had decided early on that the character-based PC was reaching a dead end. The result was a massive development project through most of the 1980s. Finally, with Windows 3.0 in 1990, the GUI ("Graphical User Interface") for PCs came of age. Now PC users had a consistent, easy-to-use interface for their applications. Windows has redefined what it means to use a PC.

At first Windows' friendliness did not extend to the programmer. Until very recently, learning to write Windows programs was like a Westerner learning Japanese. The language needed for programming Windows was not merely different, it was different in different ways. Old PC programs were structured hierarchically, with the main program calling subroutines in a predictable order. Graphics, when used at all, were essentially an afterthought.

Windows programs, on the other hand, consisted of a kind of "ecology" of coexisting objects that send and receive "messages" describing their status. These objects, such as menus, windows, buttons, and lists, can be activated at almost any time by the user. While an old DOS program tended to control the user, a Windows program is controlled by the user, usually with the mouse. And in Windows everything you see on the screen, including text, is really a graphical object. Even experienced programmers had to learn to think in a radically different way.

Fortunately Windows provides a tremendous amount of built-in functionality to support the objects that make up a Windows application. But programming in Windows "the old way" required the use of C, a concise but rather cryptic language. It required an expensive, often cumbersome C compiler, plus something called the "Software Development Kit" (SDK). While the SDK offered some tools for creating screen objects, the tools were limited and not well-integrated.

Furthermore, programming Windows required mastery of hundreds of C functions, many requiring numerous arguments. When it cost at least $1000 and several months of study to learn Windows programming, it seemed like the good old days of free and easy experimentation were gone for good.

Finally programming tools began to catch up with Windows. Products such as Borland's Turbo C++ for Windows, Turbo Pascal for Windows, and Microsoft's QuickC for Windows offer a Windows-based programming environment and libraries of predefined objects that considerably simplify Windows programming. But for many of us the best news of all came in 1991 with the release of Microsoft Visual Basic.

Visual Basic marries two powerful ideas. The first is: Use Windows to design Windows programs. Select and customize your menus, windows, dialog boxes, buttons, and other features right on the screen where you can see how they'll look. The user interface, traditionally one of the hardest parts of program to write, becomes a snap. The second idea is: Use the simple but powerful Basic language to specify what will happen when the user selects an object, and get the instant feedback for which BASIC is famous.

And so we've come full circle. BASIC is back, and programming is exciting and fun again. Visual Basic 1.0's revolutionary changes made Windows as friendly for the programmer as it is for the user. Versions 2.0 and 3.0 have added a number of evolutionary changes to both increase the power of the language as well as its ease of use.

We at the Waite Group Press are proud to provide new maps for the third generation of BASIC programmers. Just as BASIC has evolved, so also have we refined our Bibles as reference tools. We have made sure that you can both explore the features and capabilities of Visual Basic and zero in on the answers to your programming questions.

The frontier is wide open again. We're excited to see the tremendous interest and growth in Windows programming created by Visual Basic. We believe that for Windows programmers, the best is yet to come!

INTRODUCTION

Visual Basic 1.0 revolutionized Windows programming, and versions 2.0 and 3.0 bring the language to the forefront of modern programming tools. This second edition of the *Visual Basic SuperBible* has been completely revised to cover all of Visual Basic's new features.

The *Visual Basic SuperBible* will prove invaluable to beginning as well as advanced programmers. Its encyclopedic coverage of the language is designed to be both a ready reference and a study aid.

Chapter 1, *Using the Visual Basic SuperBible*, explains in detail how the book is organized and gives suggestions on how to use it effectively. This brief introduction will simply give a few tips to help you get started.

The *Visual Basic SuperBible* has no additional hardware or system requirements. If you can run Windows, you can run Visual Basic. If you can run Visual Basic, you can run any of the program projects described in this book and provided on the accompanying disk. To get started with the example projects, turn to Appendix G, *Project Disk*.

While the *Visual Basic SuperBible* isn't designed to be a tutorial, you don't have to know much about Visual Basic to use this book effectively. Reading Chapter 2, *Introducing Visual Basic*, and Chapter 3, *Using Objects*, will give you an overview of how Visual Basic works and of what it offers. If you haven't run Microsoft's online Visual Basic tutorial (by choosing Tutorial from the Help menu in Visual Basic), we suggest that you do so, and that you look over the *Microsoft Visual Basic Programmer's Guide* that comes in your Visual Basic package. After you've learned the fundamentals and created a few applications of your own, we recommend that you look at our companion book, *The Waite Group's Visual Basic How-To*. This book provides a wealth of programming techniques for just about any situation you might encounter. See Appendix F, *Further Reading*, for other book suggestions.

If you're currently working on a programming project, you can quickly look up any object, method, statement, or function in the alphabetical "jump table" on the inside cover of this book. To find out what language features are related to a task you want your program to perform, turn toward the Task Jump Table on the inside back cover.

Do you want to learn more about a particular aspect of Visual Basic? Just turn to the table of contents, find the chapter or appendix that deals with your topic, and jump in. Other than the first three chapters, which lay the groundwork for the rest of the book, each chapter is self-contained.

We have used the ⇐ character to indicate program lines that "overflow" onto more than one line in this book. The overflow character means that you should continue to type that line on one line. Do not type the ⇐ symbol or a carriage return.

We hope you will enjoy using this book in your work with Visual Basic. While we were writing this book, hardly a day went past without our being reminded of just how much fun Visual Basic is. Happy programming!

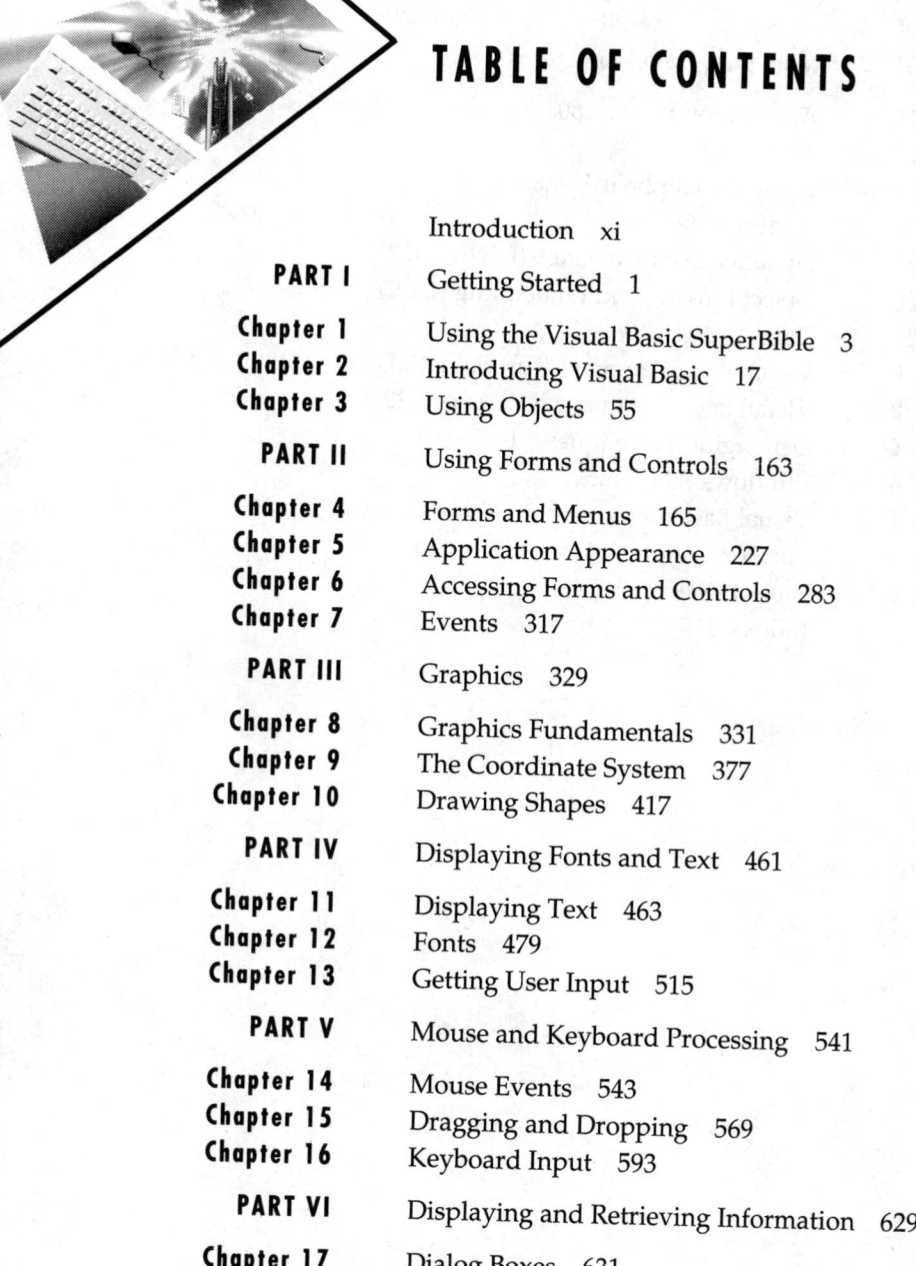

TABLE OF CONTENTS

CONTENTS

PART I

Getting Started

1

USING THE VISUAL BASIC SUPERBIBLE

Visual Basic 1.0 revolutionized Windows programming, and familiarized many BASIC programmers with object-based, event-driven programming. The best-selling first edition of the *Visual Basic SuperBible* has helped tens of thousands of BASIC programmers learn the tricks of using this new language. We've completely rewritten this second edition of the *SuperBible* to cover the immense number of additions and changes in Visual Basic in the two versions since its introduction. Versions 2.0 and 3.0 bring Visual Basic to the forefront of modern programming languages with an amazing array of sophisticated features.

Visual Basic's object-based nature requires a variety of programming perspectives—more so than with its procedural predecessors, such as QuickBASIC. For instance, you may be designing a new application from scratch. You might begin by visualizing the application in your mind's eye as the user will see it. You start work on the screen layouts by selecting the appropriate forms, objects, and controls needed to communicate with the user. You then write the BASIC statements that make up the "engine" of the program: the code that performs calculations, formats text, or draws images.

Another time you might have an existing BASIC program that needs an easy to work with "front end." Here you may work from the inside out. First, you look at the kind of input the application needs, and then you design your screens to provide the most efficient and comfortable way for the user to interact with your program. You may also want to use Visual Basic's powerful form and printer facilities to improve the appearance of the program's output.

Designing a Visual Basic program is an interactive process, and your perspective may well change from "outside in" to "inside out" even during the same project. This means that the kind of information you need from a reference book will also change. You may need to review the characteristics and properties of Visual Basic's built-in objects, explore a particular property, event, or statement in more detail, or match up a desired program function with appropriate Visual Basic techniques.

The *Visual Basic SuperBible* is designed with these shifts of perspective in mind. We combine a detailed, systematic reference with a variety of access methods for getting at the information you need. Wherever you're coming from, we'll make sure you get where you need to go.

HOW THE VISUAL BASIC SUPERBIBLE IS ORGANIZED

The *Visual Basic SuperBible* is a complete, versatile tool for expanding and honing your knowledge of Visual Basic. It combines topical organization by part and chapter with direct access to the elements of Visual Basic alphabetically, by entry name and by programming task. The *Visual Basic SuperBible* is organized into 27 chapters arranged in seven topical parts, plus seven important appendices.

Part 1. Getting Started

Part 1, Getting Started, is your overview of the book and of the Visual Basic language. In this, the first chapter, you will become acquainted with the book's features and different ways to use them. In Chapter 2, Introducing Visual Basic, you will look at the main features of the Visual Basic language and the topics covered in the rest of the book. In Chapter 3, Using Objects, you will see how to create and manipulate each of the objects that make up the "core" of the Visual Basic programming environment and that provide so much built-in functionality.

Part 2. Using Forms and Controls

Part 2, Using Forms and Controls, is devoted to these key building blocks of Visual Basic applications. In Chapter 4, Forms and Menus, you will learn about creating your own forms and menus, and about the new capacity of creating Multiple Document Interface applications. Chapter 5, Application Appearance, explains how to customize the way forms look and behave on the screen. In Chapter 6, Accessing Forms and Controls, and Chapter 7, Events, you will work with code statements that refer to and manipulate forms as the program runs, and learn to manage the events that allow you to respond to changes the user makes. Figure 1-1 shows the techniques of this section applied to a well-designed form.

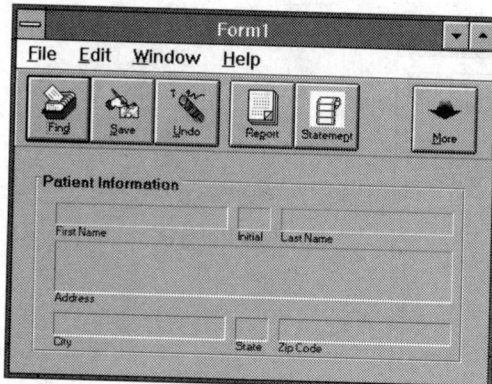

Figure 1-1 Part 2, Using Forms and
Controls, explores these fundamental
Visual Basic building blocks

Part 3. Graphics

Part 3, Graphics, looks at the creation of graphics, which are especially important
in the graphics-based Windows environment. In Chapter 8, Graphics
Fundamentals, you will explore the basics of Visual Basic's graphical methods;
while Chapter 9, The Coordinate System, shows you the meaning of the coordinates and measurement systems used by Visual Basic. In Chapter 10, Drawing

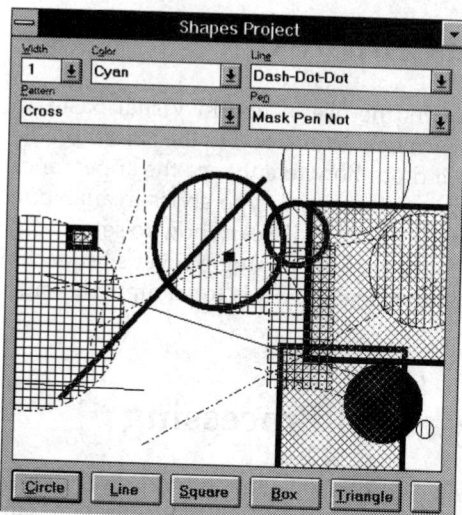

Figure 1-2 Part 3, Graphics, shows
how to create sophisticated graphical
applications

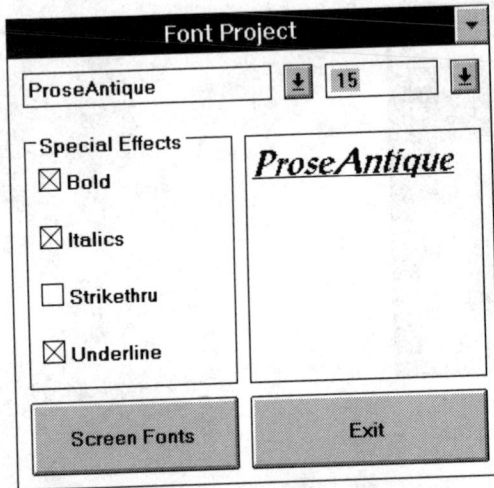

Figure 1-3 Part 4, Displaying Fonts and Text, shows how easy it is to manipulate fonts and text in Visual Basic

Shapes, you will explore the techniques for drawing, coloring, and filling in shapes, using both the graphics methods and the new graphical controls. Figure 1-2 shows the Shapes project of Chapter 10.

Part 4. Displaying Fonts and Text

Part 4, Displaying Fonts and Text, covers the use of text in Visual Basic. In Chapter 11, Displaying Text, you will learn how to add text to the objects on the screen. In Chapter 12, Fonts, you will find out how to enhance the appearance of text output by selecting from the many fonts and type styles available in Windows. In Chapter 13, Getting User Input, you will learn how to set up and use the text box, Visual Basic's answer to the traditional programmer's headache of data entry and editing. Figure 1-3 shows how easy it is to manipulate fonts with Visual Basic.

Part 5. Mouse and Keyboard Processing

Part 5, Mouse and Keyboard Processing, begins with the interaction between Visual Basic applications and the mouse. In Chapter 14, Mouse Events, you will study the events that allow you to track what the user is doing with the mouse and to respond to single-clicks and double-clicks. In Chapter 15, Dragging and Dropping, you will see how you can enable the user to manipulate objects in your

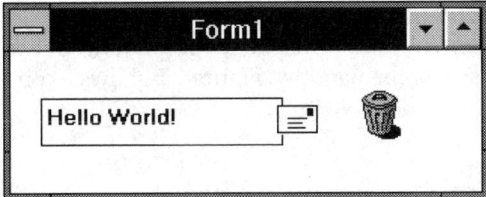

Figure 1-4 Part 5, Mouse and Keyboard Processing, shows how to implement sophisticated activities like drag-and-drop processing in your programs

application by dragging with the mouse. Finally, in Chapter 16, Keyboard Input, you will learn how to provide a complete keyboard interface for your application through direct handling of the keyboard, including special keys and key combinations. Figure 1-4 shows an example from Chapter 15 on how to implement drag-and-drop in your applications.

Part 6. Displaying and Retrieving Information

Part 6, Displaying and Retrieving Information, looks in detail at the various kinds of controls that Visual Basic provides for displaying choices to the user and getting selections or text input. In Chapter 17, Dialog Boxes, you will survey the features you can use in dialog boxes to present information and options, and learn how to use the new common dialog control to perform routine tasks quickly and simply. In Chapter 18, Lists, Combos, and Grids, you will learn how to present selections to the user with general-purpose list boxes, combo boxes, and the versatile new grid control. Chapter 19, File System Controls, covers the special

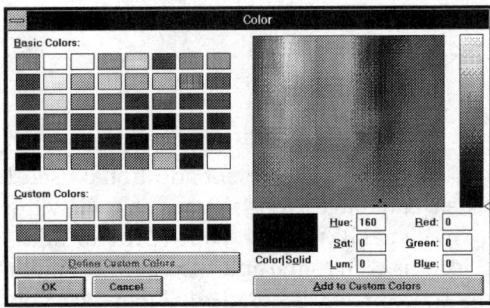

Figure 1-5 Displaying and Retrieving Information (Part 6) is easy with objects like the common dialog box control

boxes that provide for selection of drives, directories, and files. In Chapter 20, Scroll Bars, you will learn how to use scroll bars to display large amounts of text (or large pictures), regardless of the size of the window. Figure 1-5 shows a common dialog box from Chapter 17.

Part 7. Managing Data Flow

Part 7, Managing Data Flow, deals with ways in which a Visual Basic application can transfer or exchange data with the outside world. In Chapter 21, Application Focus, you will see how you can control which application (or part of an application) will receive user input. Your Visual Basic application can also find out the date and time from the system clock; and in Chapter 22, Time, you will learn how to format date and time information and how to set timers that will execute code at specified intervals.

In Chapter 23, Using the Clipboard, you will explore the question of transferring data between applications, showing how your application can use the standard Windows Clipboard for the purpose. In Chapter 24, Printing, you will learn how Visual Basic treats the printer much like a screen form, giving you complete control over the printed page, and you will learn how to place and format text.

In Chapter 25, Dynamic Data Exchange (DDE), you will explore the powerful but rather esoteric Windows feature called Dynamic Data Exchange (DDE). When working with applications that support DDE, your Visual Basic application can interactively update both applications with the latest results from processing. Chapter 26, Object Linking and Embedding (OLE), takes this one step further with the powerful new OLE control. We show you how to manipulate and edit complex objects in their native format using the new OLE 2.0 specification and even use compatible application objects like you'd use Visual Basic custom controls through OLE automation. Finally, Chapter 27, Data Access, introduces you to concepts and techniques of database management using the powerful new data control and its underlying Access database engine. Figure 1-6 shows the sophisticated icon management program created as Chapter 27's project.

Appendices

Finally, the appendices in the *Visual Basic SuperBible* present additional useful information. In Appendix A, Visual Basic Language Tutorial, you can review the statements and functions you use in the Visual Basic code, which provide additional control over the behavior of objects as well as the ability to perform math and process textual data. In Appendix B, Visual Basic Language Reference, you can look up each Visual Basic function or statement in an alphabetical reference. In Appendix C, Debugging Techniques, you will find techniques you can use to test and debug your Visual Basic applications.

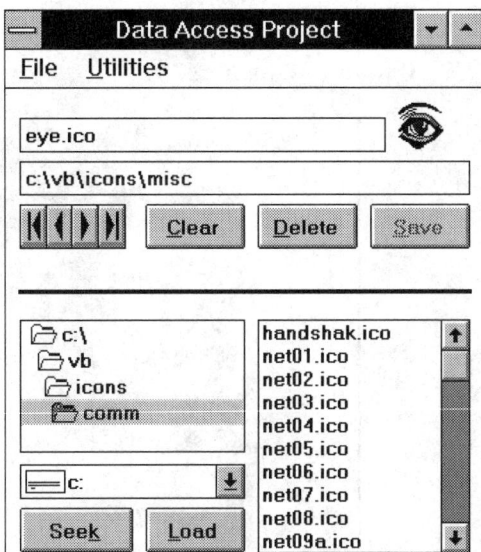

Figure 1-6 Part 7, Managing Data Flow,
explores powerful new features like OLE
and data access

Appendix D, Windows API, introduces you to another esoteric but powerful topic: how to use the Windows API from Visual Basic. The Windows API (Application Program Interface) provides hundreds of functions that can supplement Visual Basic's many built-in capabilities. Appendix E, Professional Edition, gives a brief overview of the features found in the Professional versions of Visual Basic. If you would like to learn more about the BASIC language in Visual Basic, or general concepts of Windows programming, Appendix F, Further Reading, provides a selection of books for your further study. Finally, Appendix G, Project Disk, explains how to use the accompanying disk of example programming projects.

THE EXAMPLE PROJECT DISK

The *Visual Basic SuperBible* comes with a disk containing the projects detailed at the end of each chapter in ready-to-run program files. Appendix G explains the simple steps needed for running these programs. Since you won't have to undertake the tedious and mistake-prone process of typing in all these projects by hand, you will be able to see right away how each project works. Visual Basic is so interactive, you'll be able to easily tinker with the projects and perhaps add your own features—an excellent way to master the techniques you've been reading about!

CONTENTS

xv

Figure 1-7 The Table of Contents contains a detailed outline showing both major and minor topics of each chapter

THE DETAILED OUTLINE

The *Visual Basic SuperBible* also includes a detailed outline (see Figure 1-7). This outline shows each major topic heading within the chapter, and the name of each reference entry included in the chapter. Use this outline to become more familiar with the contents of each chapter, as well as the name of the properties, events, and methods discussed.

WHAT'S IN A CHAPTER?

Each chapter of the *Visual Basic SuperBible* (except for Chapters 1 and 2, which are organized as overviews) begins with a brief introductory narrative that describes the significance of the chapter's topic and gives an overview of the contents. The introductory material often includes tables that concisely summarize the use of the elements of Visual Basic discussed in the chapter.

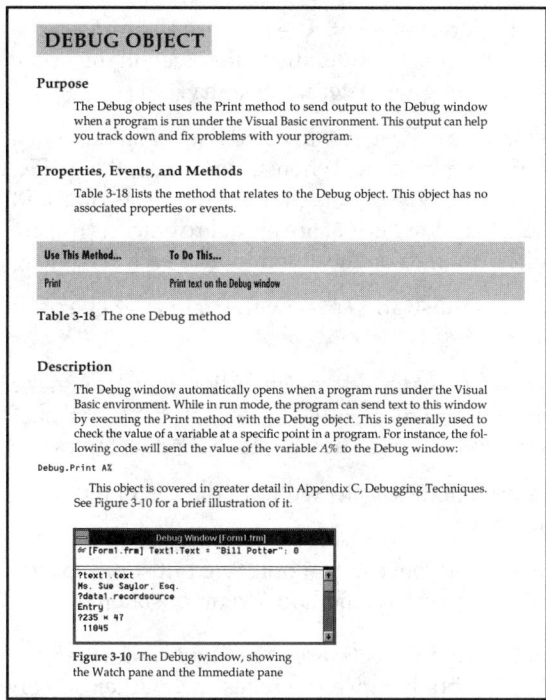

Figure 1-8 Parts of a reference entry

Reference Entries

The bulk of each chapter consists of alphabetical reference entries covering each Visual Basic element related to the chapter topic. For example, Chapter 10, Drawing Shapes, has a reference entry for each property, method, event, function, and statement that directly influences drawing shapes.

The reference entries are designed to put the most concise information first: what this feature does and the rules (syntax) for using it. With the exception of those in Chapter 3, the reference entries in the *Visual Basic SuperBible* follow the format shown in Figure 1-8.

The elements of a reference entry include the following:

▶ The *name* of the object, property, event, or statement being described. The detailed Table of Contents and the Alphabetical Jump Table list the entry by this name.

▶ *Objects affected* lists all the Visual Basic objects, with bullets next to those that can be used with this feature. Properties are often implemented for more than one object. In some cases statements don't affect any objects directly; in such cases this section is omitted. Events (such as mouse or keyboard events) are usually defined for many different objects.

11

➤ The *purpose* of the item is given in a short statement. The purpose is the answer to the question, "What is this used for?" Some considerations involved in the use of the item are summarized, but details are given later in the entry.

➤ The *general syntax* shows the order in which the item name and any arguments must be given when you use the item in program code. Where appropriate, the BASIC data declarations are given to show what type of data (integer, double, string, and so on) is required for each argument. Arguments that are in square brackets ([ ]) are optional. Where needed, a table often expands on the description of each argument.

➤ The *example syntax* provides an actual illustration of how the item might be used in a program, using real arguments.

➤ The bulk of the reference entry is made up of the *description* section, which gives the details of the item's usage and behavior, and relationship to other elements of Visual Basic. For complex items the description is broken down into individual topics.

➤ A description of how this entry is used in the *chapter project* at the end of the chapter reinforces what you've just learned.

➤ Sometimes a *comment* concludes the reference entry, pointing out some special circumstance or "quirk" of the object, property, method, event, or statement.

The reference entries in Chapter 3, Using Objects, are organized somewhat differently from those in the rest of the book. Since the focus in Chapter 3 is on objects, the entry for each object brings together the properties, events, and methods used with that object. These are summarized in tables. Note that each property or event has its own entry elsewhere in the book (to find the entry, use the Alphabetical Jump Table, described later). Each object reference entry consists of the following parts:

➤ The *purpose* briefly states what the object does.

➤ The *appearance* of the object shown in a figure illustrates a typical example of the object, as seen by the user.

➤ The *properties, events, and methods* section uses tables to summarize the properties (characteristics) that the object can have, the events to which the object can respond, and the methods that your program can use to manipulate the object.

➤ Finally, there is a *description* consisting of several paragraphs that summarize the use of the object and the considerations involved in programming.

Chapter Projects

Following the reference entries, each chapter (starting with Chapter 4) concludes with a Visual Basic project that illustrates many of the features discussed in the chapter, as shown in Figure 1-9.

THE FORMS PROJECT

Project Overview

The Forms project demonstrates several important features of Visual Basic forms. This example shows how to use the properties, events, methods, and statements that directly control a form's basic appearance.

This project has four forms: an MDI form, an MDI child, and two dialog boxes. Each form's setup is broken down into three sections: assembly, figure display, and source code. Please refer to the figures to see where the forms' elements should be placed.

Assembling the Project: MDI Form

1. Begin a new project by selecting the File menu and the New project option. Make a new MDI form by selecting File New MDI Form and give it the objects and properties shown in Table 4-25. Properties not listed should be left at their default value. Make sure this form is set as the startup form by going into th Options menu, selecting the Project menu command, and setting the Startup form option for MDIForm1.

Object	Property	Setting
MDIForm	Caption	MDI Form – Forms and Menus Project
	Name	MDIForm1
Picture	Alignment	1 – Align Top
	BackColor	Light Gray, &H00C0C0C0&
	Name	pictToolbar
Picture	Alignment	2 – Align Bottom
	BackColor	Light Gray, &H00C0C0C0&
	Name	pictStatus
Command	Name	Command1

Figure 1-9 Each chapter has a project that ties together all the details of that chapter

Each chapter project is a complete, ready-to-run Visual Basic program. In the interest of space and because of the need to focus on particular aspects of Visual Basic, however, these projects are not full-fledged applications. Each project includes the following elements:

➤ A *project overview* discussing what the project does and what Visual Basic features it illustrates.

➤ *Instructions* for assembling the project, including tables showing what objects to create, which properties to set, and the value to be used for each property.

➤ *Illustrations* showing you the appearance of the forms used in the project, during design and when running.

➤ The *code* entered into Visual Basic for each event, which includes all necessary global values and subroutines.

➤ The *How It Works* section discussing the details of each project and explaining some of the behind-the-scenes tricks and techniques.

Figure 1-10 The Alphabetical Jump Table, at the beginning of the book, lets you look up reference entries fast

HOW TO USE THE VISUAL BASIC SUPERBIBLE

Now that you know the organization of the *Visual Basic SuperBible*, let us look at the many ways that you can best access its wealth of information. You will use one or more of the following methods to find the information you need while developing your Visual Basic programs.

Looking Up Reference Entries

Suppose you are designing your program's user interface and you decide that you need to get a short bit of text from the user (perhaps the user's name). If you know that the InputBox$ function can do the job of asking the user for some text, you can turn to the Alphabetical Jump Table shown in Figure1-10 and skim until you find the entry for InputBox$.

14

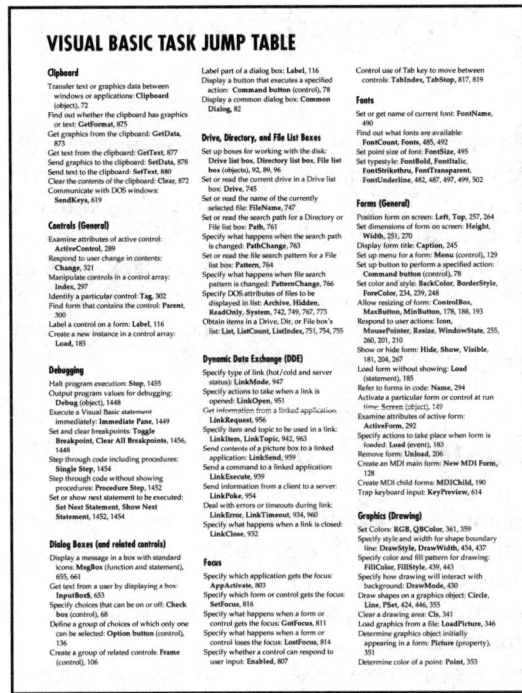

Figure 1-11 The Task Jump Table, at the back of the book, helps you focus on how to do things when you're not sure of the applicable items

The Alphabetical Jump Table, found on the inside front cover of this book, lists all the reference entries in the *Visual Basic SuperBible,* with the page number on which each entry begins. When you know what object, property, event, method, statement, or function you want, and simply desire more information about it, the Alphabetical Jump Table is the fastest way to get to it.

Looking Up Complete Topics

While the Alphabetical Jump Table is the fastest method for finding the reference entry, the index at the end of this book is far more complete. The index gives a complete listing of the page numbers throughout the book where a topic (such as "forms") or a particular item (such as "Change event") is discussed. This lets you learn about a programming topic from many different angles.

Finding Out How to Do Something in Visual Basic

When you're in the midst of developing a program, you often think functionally. That is, you know what you need your program to do, but you may not know exactly how to accomplish it. For example, you may know that you need to get some text from the user, but you're not sure what methods Visual Basic provides for the purpose. This is where the Task Jump Table (on the inside back cover of the book) comes in. This table, shown in Figure 1-11, is organized by programming task. In our example you skim along the table until you find "Text box" and discover the pages where associated methods are discussed.

Reviewing Visual Basic in Depth

If you decide that you want to review an area of Visual Basic programming in depth, simply look at the outline and browse the topic headings there. You can then proceed to read individual reference entries or entire chapters, using the introductory discussion, reference entries, and chapter project to sharpen and complete your understanding of the topic presented.

As you have seen, you can use and benefit from the *Visual Basic SuperBible* in many ways. We recommend that you read chapters 2 and 3 to review your understanding of Visual Basic, and follow up by reading each chapter's introductory discussion. If you find that you aren't sure of your understanding of a particular topic, you may want to study its chapter in depth and perhaps take advantage of the tutorials and advanced programming tips offered in the books discussed in Appendix F.

2 INTRODUCING VISUAL BASIC

WHY VISUAL BASIC?

Visual Basic makes programming Windows applications easy. Visual Basic lets you design the look and feel of an application by visually positioning the user interface objects directly on the screen. It automatically handles all the tricky aspects of responding to events like mouse movements and keyboard input. All that's left is for you to write the core code to make this beautiful interface you've just created actually do something.

Visual Basic lets beginners jump in and create good-looking Windows applications right away. Intermediate programmers will find an amazing amount of power and functionality hiding behind the pretty face, and professional and corporate programmers can take advantage of advanced features like Object Linking and Embedding (OLE) and direct access to the Windows Application Programming Interface (API). Visual Basic offers something for every programmer.

Visual Basic 1.0 revolutionized Windows programming. Bulletin boards and online services now boast thousands of Visual Basic applications created by programmers just like you. Visual Basic versions 2.0 and 3.0 have built on this foundation to further expand the power and versatility of the language. Literally hundreds of new features have moved Visual Basic into the big leagues for Windows program development. This increased power comes packaged in an environment that manages to improve on the fantastic ease of use pioneered by the first edition.

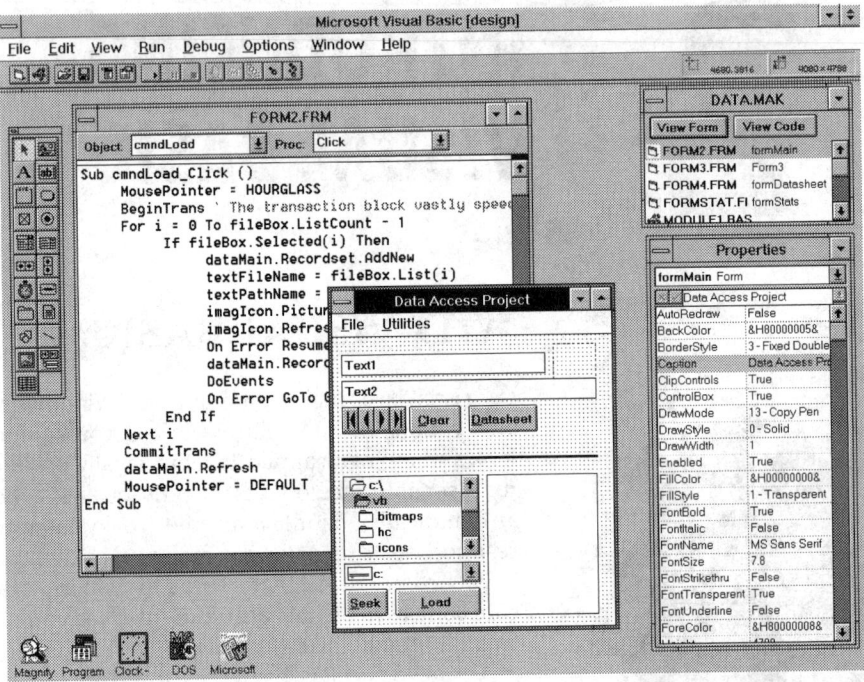

Figure 2-1 Visual Basic's revolutionary design environment

Before Visual Basic the development of Windows applications was a difficult process with a steep learning curve. Programming in C, and using the unwieldy Software Development Kit (SDK) with its thousands of routines and twisted syntax, virtually guaranteed a headache for developers.

Microsoft found a solution to this problem by going back to its oldest roots, which were not in the C language but in BASIC. Virtually every personal computer that came on the market in the late 1970s and early 1980s had a version of Microsoft BASIC. The key advantage of BASIC has always been its interactive nature. Unlike the tedious compile/link/run/debug process used in C, BASIC let you write some code, test it right away, and make changes on the fly.

Microsoft considerably enhanced its original BASIC by developing QuickBASIC, which added a compiler for speed and efficiency while retaining fast interaction. It also added powerful new control structures, flexible data types, and new commands for interacting with DOS and creating graphics. When Microsoft looked for a way to make Windows programming easier and more interactive, it naturally turned to a marriage of BASIC and an interactive, highly visual way of designing programs (see Figure 2-1).

The remainder of this chapter surveys the Visual Basic topics covered in this book. If you are new to Visual Basic, reading this overview will help you grasp the concepts and procedures needed for successful programming. Even if you are

18

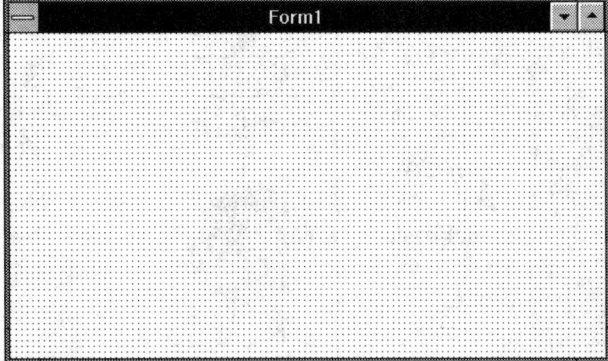

Figure 2-2 Forms are the basis of most Visual Basic programs

an experienced Visual Basic programmer, the overview can help orient you to the organization of the *Visual Basic SuperBible*.

CHAPTER 3: USING OBJECTS

Windows is a multitasking system in which more than one program may be running concurrently. Windows programs must be designed to be event driven—programs don't control the computer, they react to events that the computer makes happen. Event-driven programs have a set of objects that wait for specific events to occur, and then execute program code to react to the event. This lets programs run in the background while other programs wait for an event to occur.

Visual Basic comes with many predefined *objects*. Each of these objects fulfills a specific purpose and reacts to a predefined set of events. Each object has an associated set of properties and methods that allow you to define certain characteristics, like color or size, and to perform actions on the object. Visual Basic objects are not quite the same as those in object-oriented languages like C++, so we refer to Visual Basic as an object-based language rather than an object-oriented language. Reviewing the objects discussed in this chapter will give you a broad picture of Visual Basic's capabilities.

Forms

Forms define a window on the screen. You design an application by placing controls on forms. Most applications have more than one form. This allows you to design a main screen area for your program, as well as one or more custom message or dialog boxes. Figure 2-2 shows a blank form, ready to have controls placed on it. Some applications allow the user to open many documents at once.

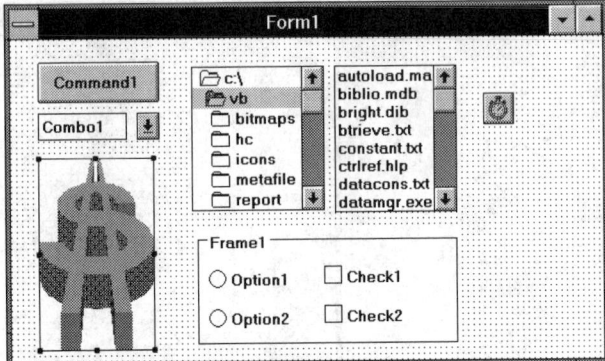

Figure 2-3
Use the
Visual Basic
Toolbox to
create
controls

Figure 2-4 Place controls on a form by clicking on its
icon in the Toolbox and drawing it directly on the form

Visual Basic 2.0 and 3.0 provide full support for the Multiple Document Interface
(MDI), so your applications can have this feature of simultaneously opening
many documents.

Controls

Controls are objects placed on a Visual Basic form. Each control performs a specific function. Visual Basic provides many familiar user-interface controls, such
as command buttons, check boxes, and list boxes. Each control has an icon in the
Visual Basic Toolbox window, as shown in Figure 2-3. You create a control by
clicking on its icon and then drawing the control on a form. Figure 2-4 shows a
form with several controls placed on it.

Object Arrays

An *object array* is a group of the same type of control or form sharing the same
name and events. Although the elements of an object array share the same name,
each is a separate object and is identified by a unique index number. The Name
and Index properties define an object array. The Name property is the same for

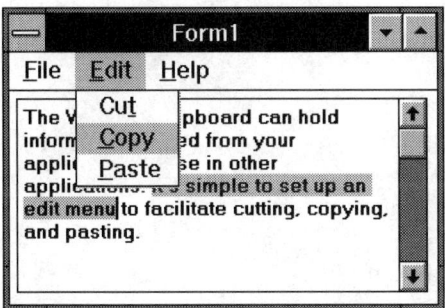

Figure 2-5 Your Visual Basic
program can use the Windows
Clipboard to transfer text or graphics

all elements of the array. The Index property refers to a particular element in the object array. Object arrays let you easily create and manipulate dynamic controls and forms that respond to changing user requirements.

Special Objects

Visual Basic also provides several special objects that are neither forms nor controls. These are the App, Clipboard, Debug, Printer, and Screen objects.

The App object lets your program find out important information about the environment, like the name of the associated help file and the application's path.

The Clipboard object lets your program interact with the Windows Clipboard area. Visual Basic programs can copy text or graphics to and from the Clipboard (see Figure 2-5). Chapter 23, Using the Clipboard, presents detailed information on how to use the Clipboard object.

The Debug object, used only within the Visual Basic environment, can help with the testing and debugging of a program. This object is covered in detail in Appendix C, Debugging Techniques.

The Printer object generates printed output. Since the Windows environment handles the actual printing duties, your Visual Basic program doesn't really send output to the printer. Instead, the Printer object sends that output to the Windows printing routines, which in turn send the data to the printer. Chapter 24, Printing, covers the Printer object in detail.

The Screen object globally references other objects. Your program can use the Screen object to determine which form or control is active, and how many and what types of fonts are available to the system.

The data control, explored in Chapter 27, Data Access, also has several underlying objects. These objects let you interact with the underlying database engine to perform sophisticated database actions.

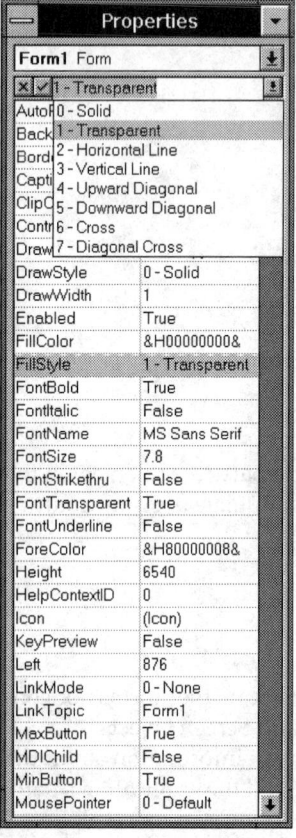

Figure 2-6 The properties box lets you set a control's properties during the design phase

Properties

Properties define the appearance of an object and how it will react to a user's actions. You can set the properties for an object when you design an application. The application can also change most properties while it is running.

Use the *properties box* to set a property during the design phase of a program. This box is a large scrolling list box (see Figure 2-6). The first column lists all the properties that are available at design time for the currently selected object. The second column lists the available settings for the selected property. If there is not a fixed set of values for the current property, you may change the setting by editing the text within the text box portion of the drop-down list.

Most property values can also be read or changed within the program's code while a program is running. Use the following syntax in your program to refer to a property:

```
ObjectName.PropertyName [ = argument]
```

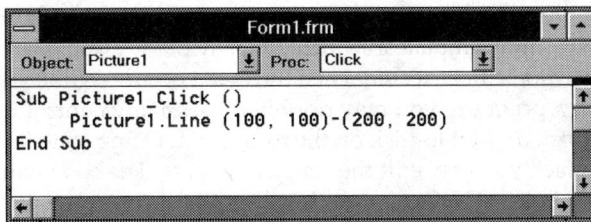

Figure 2-7 The code window lets you attach code to a control's events

Or, if the object is part of an object array, indicate the specific element of the array as follows:

```
ObjectName(Index).PropertyName [ = argument]
```

For instance, if a project has a picture control that has been named Pict1, we could place the value of its Height property in a variable with the following statement:

```
pictureHeight = Pict1.Height
```

Methods

Methods are very much like regular language statements, but they act directly on an object. Each method may have one or more arguments detailing specifically how the method will operate. The syntax for executing a method is

```
ObjectName.MethodName [arguments]
```

Or, if the object is part of an object array, indicate the specific element of the array as follows:

```
ObjectName(Index).MethodName [arguments]
```

The ObjectName specifies which object the method acts on. The MethodName is the method executed. If the method has any arguments, they are specified after the method name. For instance:

```
Pict1.Line (100, 100)-(200, 200)
```

In the above example, the Line method acts on the object named Pict1. This statement draws a line on the object starting at horizontal position 100 and vertical position 100, and ending at horizontal position 200 and vertical position 200.

Events

Events are predefined Visual Basic procedures that trigger when the user or program code performs some sort of action on a control. Each control has its own unique set of events. Each event reacts to a different action.

An event initially has no instructions associated with it. An event starts out as an empty template in which you may place Visual Basic statements, functions, or methods that execute when the event occurs. While you are in the design phase of a program, you may double-click on any control that you have drawn on a form, or double-click on the form itself. Doing so will display a code window in which you may edit the control's events. The code window has two drop-down list boxes. The first, on the left, lists all the controls that reside on the current form. The second, on the right, lists all the events associated with the current control. Figure 2-7 shows the code window with some code associated with the Picture1_Click event.

Each event begins with a Sub statement and an event name, and ends with an End Sub statement. When you first bring up an event in the code window, it will have the following format:

```
Sub ObjectName_EventName([arguments])

End Sub
```

Or, if the object is part of an object array, the Index argument specifies the particular element of the array on which the event occurred:

```
Sub ObjectName_EventName([Index As Integer,] [arguments])

End Sub
```

Events are in the same format as a Visual Basic *sub procedure* definition. A sub procedure consists of a set of BASIC statements that perform a specific function (this is covered in more detail in Appendix A, Visual Basic Language Tutorial). All you have to do is plug in the instructions you wish to execute when the event occurs. To illustrate, let's again use the example of the picture control Pict1. One of the events associated with a picture control is the Click event, which occurs when the user clicks on the picture. In the following event, we instruct the program to draw a line on the Pict1 picture control when the user clicks on it:

```
Sub Pict1_Click()
    Pict1.Line (100, 100)-(200, 200)
End Sub
```

CHAPTER 4: FORMS AND MENUS

Begin designing a Visual Basic program by first setting up the forms that constitute the basis of your application. Some forms will be used as the main screen area for your program, some for dialog boxes, and others to display miscellaneous messages. You have considerable control over the appearance and behavior of forms.

Managing Forms

You can designate one form as the *startup form* for your application. This form automatically loads and displays when your program begins. Any other forms in your project must be loaded into memory by your program's code. This is done with either the Load statement or the Show method. The Load statement merely loads a form into memory; it does not display it. To display a form, use the Show method. If a form is not currently loaded in memory when the Show method executes, it will automatically load.

Any time a form loads into memory, any code within its Load event executes. This event can be used to initialize the form's variables and controls.

Forms can be hidden by using the Hide method on a form. Hiding a form makes it invisible, but does not unload it from memory. Your program can still perform methods on the form and on its controls.

You can use the Unload statement to unload a form from memory. Executing the Unload statement on a form that is currently displayed makes the form disappear from the screen before being erased from memory. Unloading the last form of an application ends the program. Unloading a form initiates the form's QueryUnload and Unload events. You can add code for these events to take care of any cleanup that may need to be done before exiting the form.

Most Windows main windows have a gray control box in the upper-left corner, and Minimize and Maximize buttons in the right-hand corner. You can specify whether the form you are designing has these items by setting the ControlBox, MinButton, and MaxButton properties for the form. You may also specify a title for your form by setting the Caption property.

The menu structure of an application provides easy access to the sometimes dozens of commands available. Visual Basic lets you design a complete menuing system that includes multiple levels of submenus and has the capacity to add pop-up menus.

Forms and the Desktop

When a form displays with the Show method, you may specify its *modal state*. The modal state of a form determines how much control a form has over the rest of the desktop. A form can be *modal* or *modeless*.

When a modal form displays, it retains control of the desktop until it is closed. The user cannot switch to any other window from the same application while a modal form is displayed. This type of form is used primarily for dialog boxes. For instance, when you open a Visual Basic project, an Open Project dialog box appears on the screen. As long as this box is open, you are not permitted to change to any other Visual Basic window. Thus the Open Project window is a modal window.

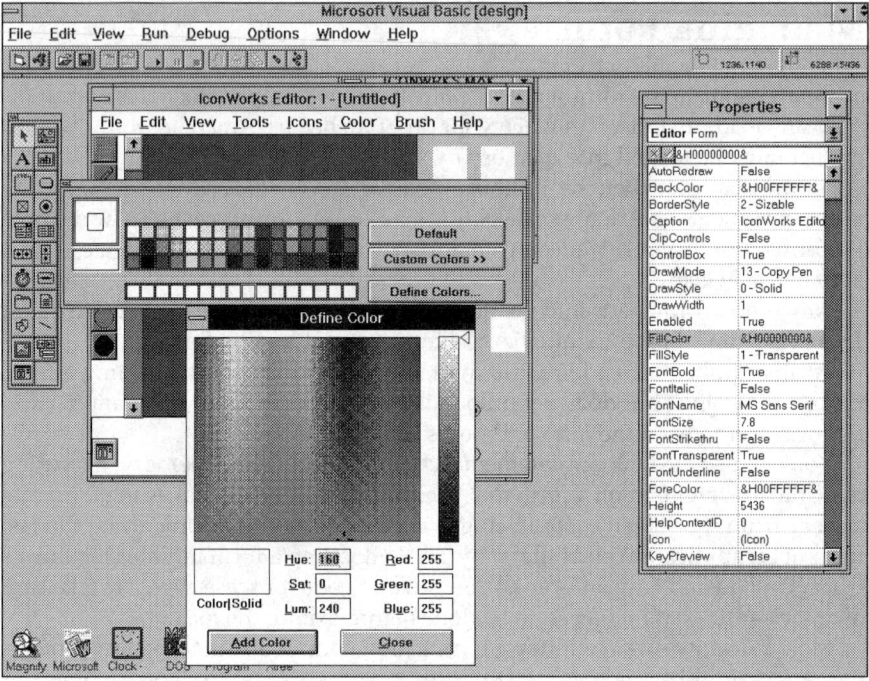

Figure 2-8 Color and other properties make your application's screen distinctive

A modeless form places no restrictions on which window is active. When a modeless form is displayed, the user can switch to any other window on the desktop. Visual Basic's Project window is a modeless window.

Visual Basic 2.0 and 3.0 make programming a *Multiple Document Interface (MDI)* application easy. An MDI program can display many different documents (like spreadsheets, charts, or a word processing document) at the same time. The MDIForm is the main form of the application, and contains all the *child* forms that represent the multiple documents. You can also have regular, non-MDI forms in an MDI application to serve as dialog boxes.

CHAPTER 5: APPLICATION APPEARANCE

You can tailor the appearance of the screen elements to suit your application and the kind of information involved. You determine the appearance of the forms and controls in your application. By setting the appropriate properties, you can specify the label (caption) for a form or control, its dimensions, its foreground and background color, and the kind of border it will have (see Figure 2-8). You can also specify an icon to represent a form when it is minimized, and a pointer to be used when the mouse moves over the form.

CHAPTER 6: ACCESSING FORMS AND CONTROLS

Every form and control has a name that you can use to refer to it in your code. The syntax section of the reference entries for items that refer to a form or control show how to specify the name in your code. For example, the Height property of MyForm can be changed to 100 as follows:

```
MyForm.Height = 100
```

Controls are often scaled to other objects. For example, you can make MyForm the same size as the screen with this code:

```
MyForm.Height = Screen.Height
MyForm.Width = Screen.Width
```

Here you refer to both MyForm and the Screen object, which (among its other properties) tracks the height and width of the display.

You can also refer to controls on a form other than the one in which the code is currently running. Do this by specifying the Name property of the form, followed by an exclamation mark (!) and the Name property of the control:

```
MyForm!Pict1.Height = MyForm!Command1.Height
```

Sometimes you will want to write code procedures that affect more than one form. You do this by creating a module and writing code in its code window. This is particularly useful if the same procedure is to be used with several different forms: any changes to the procedure will only have to be made in one place, and your code is also less bulky.

CHAPTER 7: EVENTS

An *event* is an action recognized by a form or control, such as a mouse click or a keystroke. Event-driven languages like Visual Basic let the user control program flow. The application spends most of its time idle, waiting for the user to act on it. When the user does something (or the system causes an event, like a shutdown message), the program responds to that action. This is the essence of a graphical user interface: create a flexible environment that the user can control.

Each object in Visual Basic has a number of specific events it recognizes. You can make your application respond to events by writing code in an *event procedure*. Much like regular sub procedures, event procedures contain code that performs specific actions. For example, clicking a command button with the mouse triggers its Click event; code you write for this event procedure might confirm that the user wants to end the application. Although each control recognizes a predefined set of events, you determine if they respond to those events by writing code in the event procedures. Each object has its own set of event procedures that are independent of any other objects in the application.

CHAPTER 8: GRAPHICS FUNDAMENTALS

Visual Basic has a powerful array of graphics methods. Many of the instructions that were statements in the classic BASIC languages have been changed into Visual Basic methods, and are now executed directly on a Visual Basic form or picture control.

The most basic graphics operations display a picture or icon on a form, or in a picture or image control. Files that are either a BMP (Windows bitmap), ICO (Windows icon), or WMF (Windows metafile) may be displayed by setting the Picture property to the file name at design time, or with the LoadPicture function at runtime.

Graphics Permanence

Other windows in the workspace can cover graphics that your program generates. When this happens, some sort of system must redraw your graphics when finally uncovered. The AutoRedraw property can do this automatically, or you can manually do it in the Paint event.

If you set the AutoRedraw property of a form or picture box to True, a copy of the screen image of that object is kept in memory. Any graphics methods that act on the object while AutoRedraw is True also act on the memory copy image. If the object gets covered by another window, it uses its memory copy to restore its image when it is uncovered. Using this technique is very convenient, but it takes more memory and is slower.

The Paint event occurs any time a previously covered form or a picture box becomes uncovered, or when one of these objects is resized. This event does not occur when the AutoRedraw property is set to True. If the graphics you have placed on this object are fairly simple and easily redrawn, you may wish to leave the object's AutoRedraw property set to False, and place code in the Paint event to redraw the graphics when needed.

Specifying Color

In Visual Basic a 4-byte integer represents colors. The number indicates a mixture of the three electronic primary colors: blue, green, and red. The first byte of this number is ignored. The second, third, and fourth bytes represent how much blue, red, and green, respectively, will be used in the color mixture. Each color can be assigned a value between 0 and 255 (or 0 to FF in hexadecimal notation), which indicates that color's intensity in the mixture.

You may represent a color by three means. The first method involves using a hexadecimal numeric literal. In this method two hexadecimal digits are used for each byte in the color number. The second method for specifying a color is the RGB function. This function lets you supply a decimal number for each electronic primary color, and returns a color number based on these values. Each primary color is represented by a number between 0 and 255. The third method goes back to the old versions of BASIC. In the QuickBASIC languages, you set the current color by using the COLOR statement to choose one of 16 colors. The QBColor function translates an old QuickBASIC color number (from 0 to 15) to the 4-byte format used by Visual Basic.

```
Pict1.ForeColor = &HFF00FF           'Magenta using Hexadecimal literal
Pict1.ForeColor = RGB(255, 0, 255)   'Magenta using RGB function
Pict1.ForeColor = QBColor(5)         'Magenta using QBColor
```

The final color-related element in Visual Basic is the Point method. This method determines the current color setting at a specific position on a form or picture box. This is useful when you wish to change one color to another. The code fragment below uses the Point and PSet methods to change all points on a form that are blue to red.

```
For x = 0 To ScaleWidth
    For y = 0 to ScaleHeight
        pointColor = Point(x, y)
        If pointColor = &HFF0000 Then PSet (x, y), &H0000FF
    Next y
Next x
```

CHAPTER 9: THE COORDINATE SYSTEM

All the Visual Basic graphics methods use a coordinate system to specify where on the object to perform an action. A coordinate consists of two numbers, separated by a comma. These numbers represent the horizontal (generally called x) and vertical (generally called y) positioning for the method. By default, the upper-left corner of a form or picture box is coordinate 0, 0. You can specify a point by using coordinates that are relative to the upper-left corner. This kind of coordinate is called an *absolute coordinate*.

Each form or picture box has two properties, CurrentX and CurrentY, which indicate where the last graphics method ended its operation on that object. Coordinates in Visual Basic can be specified relative to the current point specified by these properties rather than the upper-left corner. This type of coordinate is called a *relative coordinate*.

Windows supports many different standards for video displays. Each of these standards supports a different number of colors and pixels per screen. For instance, the Hercules Graphics Card (HGC) displays two colors at 720 horizontal pixels by 348 vertical pixels, while the Enhanced Graphics Adapter (EGA) dis-

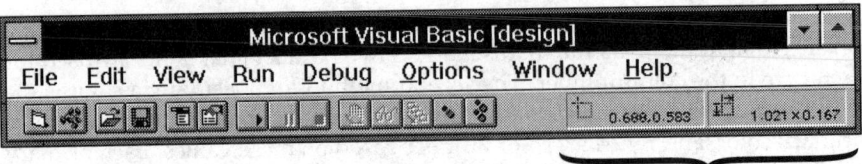

Figure 2-9 The right side of the toolbar displays your current coordinates

plays 16 colors at 640 by 350 pixels. Standard VGA can display 16 colors at 640 by 480 pixels, and modern Super-VGA (SVGA) can display up to 16 million colors at 800 by 600, 1024 by 768, or even 1280 by 1024 pixels! This means you have to be able to specify a screen position in your program without having to know what type of video display your program is running on.

To solve this problem, Visual Basic allows you to set the type of coordinates you are using with the ScaleMode, ScaleHeight, and ScaleWidth properties. These properties determine whether the forms and controls in your programs will be measured in twips, points, pixels, characters, inches, millimeters, or centimeters, or if you're going to use a user-defined system. The right side of the main Visual Basic toolbar shows the coordinates of the top-left corner of a selected object as well as its size. These measurements reflect whatever measurement system you've chosen. Figure 2-9 illustrates this using inches as the measurement.

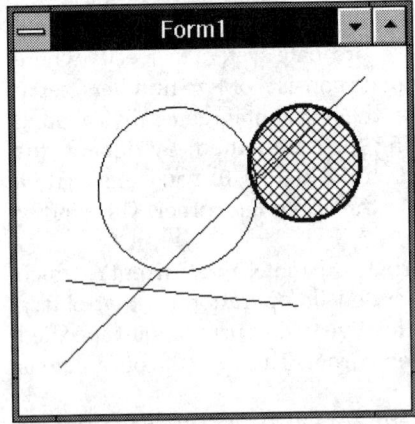

Figure 2-10 Visual Basic's graphics methods make it easy to create graphics applications

30

Figure 2-11 Visual Basic
offers excellent text control

CHAPTER 10: DRAWING SHAPES

You can use two kinds of graphics with Visual Basic. One kind is the bitmap designed pixel by pixel with a paint program such as Windows Paintbrush and stored in bitmap files. The other kind of graphics are lines and curves that can be generated with program statements in traditional BASIC. With Visual Basic you use the Circle and Line methods to draw simple shapes on a form or picture box (see Figure 2-10). Other methods make it easy to control the general appearance of a shape and its boundaries. The FillColor and FillStyle properties determine the color and "texture" of the interior of a shape. Setting the DrawMode property to an appropriate value controls the interaction between new drawings and existing ones.

CHAPTER 11: DISPLAYING TEXT

Windows allows tremendous flexibility in displaying text. With traditional DOS programs, once text was written to the screen it was no longer the concern of the programmer. Visual Basic, however, deals with Windows, where text is part of an object that can be resized by the user. In fact, text drawn on an object such as a form or picture box is really graphics, and is subject to the usual Windows procedures for repainting. Since the font and point size chosen for the form, picture box, or Printer object can vary, you first need to use the TextHeight and TextWidth methods to get the dimensions needed by the string you wish to print. You can then use the Print method to position the string in the output area (see Figure 2-11).

31

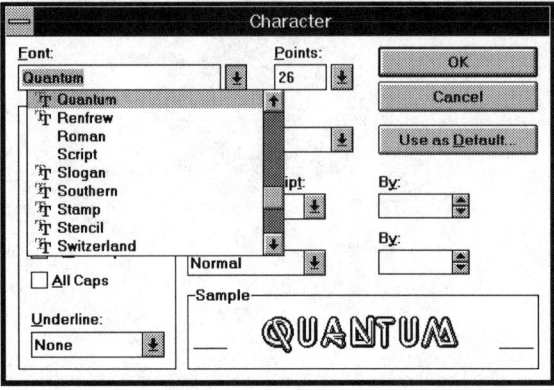

Figure 2-12 Visual Basic can use all of the many fonts available for Windows

CHAPTER 12: FONTS

Windows allows the programs that run under it to work with multiple fonts. Windows comes with several standard fonts, and many third-party fonts are available (see Figure 2-12). Your program can find out how many and what types of fonts are available to it by using the FontCount and Fonts properties with the Screen and Printer objects. The Fonts property is an array of font names available for the specified object, and the FontCount property indicates the number of entries in the Fonts property array.

You may change an object's font type by setting its FontName property to the name of the desired font. The size of the chosen font is controlled with the FontSize property.

You can display special effects on the chosen font by setting the FontBold, FontItalic, FontStrikeThru, FontTransparent, or FontUnderline properties.

CHAPTER 13: GETTING USER INPUT

Most applications have four primary tasks: collecting, processing, storing, and retrieving information. A program may work with many types of information, but the most common is text, or alphanumeric, information. Text consists of letters, numbers, and punctuation that have been typed in from the keyboard by the user. Instead of making you write extensive routines to capture and process the user's keystrokes, Visual Basic provides the text box control. Your programs can use this control to collect alphanumeric information from the user. The text box provides the user with convenient cursor-positioning and editing capabilities (see Figure 2-13).

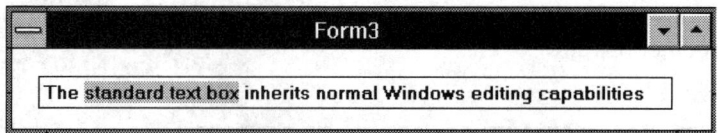

Figure 2-13 The text box provides convenient user input
for your Visual Basic applications

CHAPTER 14: MOUSE EVENTS

The mouse is integral to most Windows applications. The mouse selects items,
initiates actions, and drags items to different areas of the screen. In a Windows
program, mouse support cannot be an afterthought: each of your application's
controls must integrate with the operation of the mouse.

Visual Basic makes handling the mouse easy. Your programs define mouse-
oriented events that specify how a particular mouse action will be handled. These
events tell your program when the user has pressed or released any of the buttons on the mouse, or when the user moves the mouse. You can plug code into
these events to handle the user's mouse actions.

Several mouse operations have a standard meaning when used on specific
objects. For instance, a single mouse click on a command button usually initiates
the action described in its caption. When working with list or combo boxes, a sin-
gle-click signifies that an item is selected, and a double-click usually means the
user wishes to perform an action on the double-clicked item. You should write
your programs with these standard mouse operations in mind. If you don't know
how an object should react to a mouse action, find another Windows program
with a similar object and set up your object's events to emulate that. This ensures
that your Windows applications will have an interface consistent with other
Windows programs. You may also wish to refer to the *Style Guide* that comes
with Visual Basic.

CHAPTER 15: DRAGGING AND DROPPING

Only the mouse can perform the intuitive technique of *dragging*. Dragging
involves grabbing an item with the mouse and moving it to another position on
the screen. Do this by placing the mouse's pointer on top of the item, and pressing and holding down the left (or primary) mouse button. You then drag the item
by moving the mouse pointer to the desired position on the screen, which may
either represent a new position for the item, or may "drop" it onto another object
for further processing. You can place code in the mouse events to perform this
task, or you can set an object up so that Visual Basic automatically handles any
dragging operations on it. Visual Basic has a full set of events and properties that

occur when the user begins dragging an object, or when an object is being dragged over another object.

CHAPTER 16: KEYBOARD INPUT

Keyboard input is handled much like the mouse. Visual Basic has events attached to the keyboard that trigger any time a key is pressed, held down, or released.

The KeyDown event occurs when the user presses or holds down any key on the keyboard. This includes keys that send unprintable characters, such as the (INS) and (DELETE) keys. If the user holds a key down, this event will be called repeatedly for that key.

The KeyPress event occurs when the user presses and then releases any key on the keyboard that generates a printable ASCII character. The printable ASCII characters consist of the uppercase or lowercase letters A through Z, the numbers 0 through 9, and the following punctuation characters: ',./<>?;'[]{}~!@#$%^&*()_+|\'.

The KeyUp event is the inverse of the KeyDown event. It occurs when a user releases any key on the keyboard. Like KeyDown, this event responds to unprintable character codes.

You may also assign special actions to the (ENTER) and (ESC) keys. This is done by creating command buttons on a form and setting their Default and Cancel properties. Setting a command button's Default property to True causes its Click event to occur when the user presses the (ENTER) key. In other words, when the user presses (ENTER), the default action for the command button executes. A similar relationship is held by a button's Cancel property and the (ESC) key.

Finally, Visual Basic has the SendKeys statement, which simulates keyboard input. This statement can be used to send keystrokes to your applications or to other Windows programs. This is useful when you wish to send data to a program that does not support Dynamic Data Exchange (DDE).

CHAPTER 17: DIALOG BOXES

Dialog boxes are another distinctive feature of Windows programs. You can use them to alert the user with important information, allow the user to tailor the operation of the program, or to get information needed to complete an operation. While elaborate operations are best done with forms designed for the purpose, Visual Basic provides a set of three predefined dialog boxes using just single-line functions and statements. These dialog boxes allow your programs to perform simple, no-frills interaction with the user, without having to design a new form for each operation. Two of these dialog boxes, provided by the Input$ and MsgBox functions, return a value based on the user's actions when that dialog box displays. The third, provided by the MsgBox statement, merely displays a

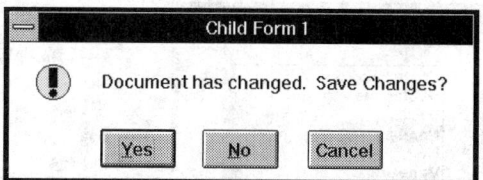

Figure 2-14 Create simple dialog boxes
like this with one line of code

message in a box and returns no value. Figure 2-14 illustrates a typical MsgBox, complete with a predefined icon.

The common dialog control, new to Visual Basic 3.0, allows you to automatically display several of the most commonly used dialog boxes with no additional code or form design. It displays File Open, Save As, Select Font, Choose Color, Print, and Help dialog boxes. These are standard dialog boxes that many commercial applications use. Using the common dialog boxes saves you many hours of work and makes your applications look consistent and professional.

CHAPTER 18: LISTS, COMBOS, AND GRIDS

In many of the programs you write, you will want to present users with a list of items and let them choose one item from the list. Generally, you would want the user to choose from a list in order to reduce typing errors and to help ensure valid data entry.

List and Combo Boxes

A *list box* appears on a form as a box that contains one or more text items. The user can choose an item by clicking on it with the mouse, or by using the ⊕ and ⊕ keys on the keyboard. Selecting an item in the list highlights it. If the area needed to display the list of items exceeds the area defined on the form for the list box, scroll bars are automatically added to the right edge of the box. This allows the user to scroll up and down the list with the mouse or the (PGUP) and (PGDN) keys.

Sometimes you may wish to get text input from a user, but at the same time you want your program to suggest a predefined list of items as possible values. Combo boxes are perfect for this use, and come in both simple and drop-down styles. A *simple combo box* is a single control that has the features of both a text box and a list box. With this control a list box appears directly below an edit area that looks and acts just like a text box control. The user can either type or edit text in this edit area, or select an item from the attached list.

A combo box may also be a *drop-down box*, where the list portion of the box remains hidden until the user clicks on the arrow to open it up. The list then

Figure 2-15 List boxes and
combo boxes let users select
items from a list

drops down from the edit portion of the box, and the user can select an item from
the list. One of these two formats is called the *drop-down list box*. This form of the
combo box control restricts the user to those items that are in its list. The other
format, called the *drop-down combo box*, lets the user type and edit text in its edit
area as well as select an item from its list. The Style property determines the
combo box format.

Specifying Selections for Lists and Combos

When a program begins, the lists provided by these controls are empty. If your
program has any of these controls, the list portion of the control needs to be
loaded with items from which the user can choose. Use the AddItem method to
do this. By default, the AddItem method automatically positions the new entry
in the list. Your program can also specify a particular position in the list if you'd
like direct control over where the entry appears. Setting a list or combo box's
Sorted property to true automatically sorts the list in alphabetical order.

The reverse of the AddItem method is the RemoveItem method, which deletes
entries from a list or a combo box's list. Unlike the AddItem method, your program must specify which particular item in the list to remove. You can also use
the Clear method to clear all entries in a list.

Figure 2-15 shows a list box, a simple combo, and a drop-down combo. All
have their sorted property turned on.

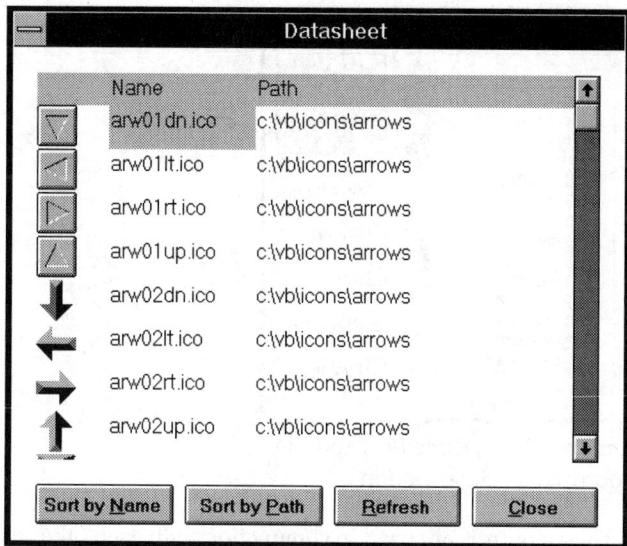

Figure 2-16 The versatile grid control

Grids

Visual Basic 3.0 adds the versatile grid control to its tool chest. This control allows you to set up display structures similar to a spreadsheet. Rows and columns intersect to form individual cells. These cells may have their contents changed independently, and may be selected individually or as a region. You also have the facility to create fixed rows and columns, which would be familiar to spreadsheet users as Row and Column heads (A1, B3, etc). See Figure 2-16 for an example of a grid control.

The most direct way of changing the contents of a cell is with its Text property. The Text property applies to whatever cell is at the intersection of the Rows and Cols properties. If the FillStyle property is 1, then the text is applied to all cells whose CellSelected property is True, regardless of the Rows and Cols settings. Grid cells can also contain graphics; assign a graphic to a grid cell by using the LoadPicture function with the grid's Picture property.

CHAPTER 19: FILE SYSTEM CONTROLS

Most programs have four main tasks: collecting, processing, storing, and retrieving information. The third and fourth tasks, storage and retrieval, are mostly done on floppy or hard disk drives in the form of files. Visual Basic includes three controls that simplify creating code that deals with storage media: the drive, direc-

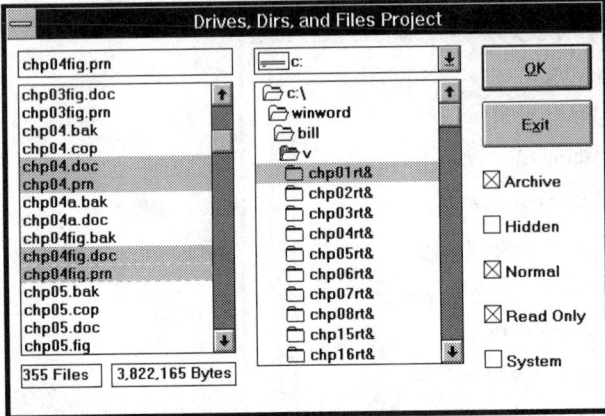

Figure 2-17 You can combine drive, directory, and file lists to give complete control over file selection

tory, and file list boxes. These controls are used in conjunction with each other to provide a visual interface for navigating the DOS file system (see Figure 2-17).

Types of Storage Devices

Virtually every system that runs your programs will have access to at least one disk drive. DOS assigns each drive available to the computer a drive letter that uniquely identifies that drive. A drive can further be identified by its label, an 11-character name optionally assigned to it by the user.

There are generally three types of disk drives. First is the removable floppy-disk drive. Users can insert and remove the disk media from a removable floppy-disk drive at will. This allows the user to save files to a floppy disk, and then use that disk on another computer.

Second, your program can access a fixed hard drive. Fixed drives have the advantage of having a large capacity, but usually cannot be removed from the computer.

Finally, if the computer your program runs on is attached to a network, it may have access to a shared network drive. A network drive is physically located in a separate computer, but the network interface means that information can be stored or retrieved on that drive by remote computers. All network drives are identified by a unique network name. When a remote computer wishes to use a network drive, it specifies that drive's network name, and assigns it a logical drive letter. Once this has been done, programs can access the network drive by the assigned drive letter.

Your programs can let the user choose a source or destination drive for file operations with the drive list box. This control is a drop-down list box whose entries list all the available drive letters on the system. If a listed drive is a fixed hard disk drive, its label, if any, is also listed. If a listed drive is connected through a network, its network name displays along with its logical drive letter.

Navigating the Directory Structure

DOS has a hierarchical file structure. The top of the hierarchy is called the root directory, and it can hold a limited number of files. The root directory can have one or more optional child directories underneath it, which can hold an unlimited number of files. The child directories are called subdirectories, and can in turn have any number of levels of subdirectories.

Navigating through all the possible directories on a disk can be a daunting task, particularly for a novice user. Visual Basic's directory list box provides an intuitive, visual way of directory navigation. The directories of a disk display in a directory list box. The user can then select a directory entry by clicking on it, or change to a directory by double-clicking on it.

Each directory can contain one or more files. The file list box control allows users to choose a particular file within the directory. By manipulating this control's properties, you can limit the displayed files to match a particular file pattern, or list only those files whose status bits (archive, hidden, read only, and system) match a particular setting.

When working in a networked environment, the drives, directories, and files available to a program can change at any time without notice to the program. For that reason it's a good idea to use the Refresh method on a regular basis with these controls. When this method executes, the specified control is refreshed with the most current information.

CHAPTER 20: SCROLL BARS

When the number of items in a list or combo box exceeds the display area for that control, Visual Basic automatically adds scroll bars to the box so the user can quickly scroll through the list with the mouse. You can also instruct Visual Basic to add a horizontal or vertical scroll bar to the edges of a multiple-line text box or an MDI form. In some instances, however, you may need to attach a scroll bar to an object that does not automatically have this capability. Visual Basic provides the vertical and horizontal scroll bar controls to do this.

The scroll bar controls consist of gray bars with arrows at each end. Between the arrows is a small scroll button, or thumb. The position of this thumb represents a value relative to the length of the bar. Each scroll bar has a minimum and a maximum possible value, set by the scroll bar's Min and Max properties. In order to determine the setting of the scroll bar's thumb, your program can examine the bar's Value property. This property is a numeric representation of the thumb's position on the bar in relation to the values of the Min and Max properties.

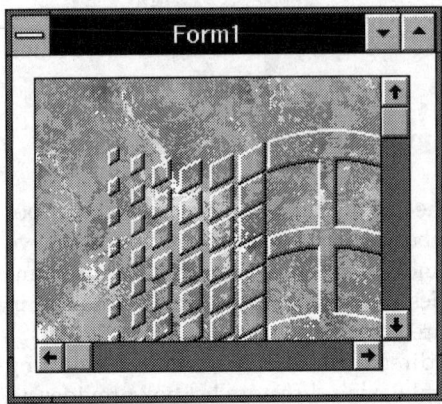

Figure 2-18 Scroll bars allow the user to move an image

Scroll Bars as Positioning Tools

There are two primary purposes for using the scroll bar controls. The first and most obvious purpose is to scroll the contents of a box up or down, or left or right. This is sometimes needed when a box or window is too small to display the entire item that it contains. For instance, if you load a large graphic image from a file into a smaller picture box control, it will not display the entire graphic. If you want to allow the user to view the undisplayed areas of the image, you can attach scroll bars that allow the user to move the image around the picture box (see Figure 2-18).

Scroll Bars as Slider Controls

Scroll bars also provide a visual technique for setting the value of a number, much like the volume and tone controls on some radios. Because the position of the scroll bar's thumb indicates a numeric value relative to the bar's possible minimum and maximum values, the user can set a numeric value by manipulating the scroll bar's thumb. For instance, imagine you're developing a program that can shrink and grow a graphic image. You wish to let the user set the size of the image from 50 to 200 percent of its original size. Instead of making the user type in a percentage in a text box, and then auditing the box to see if the value is in the desired range, you could set up a scroll bar with its Min and Max properties set to 50 and 200, respectively. The user could then set the desired image size by manipulating the scroll bar thumb.

CHAPTER 21: APPLICATION FOCUS

Forms you design for your Visual Basic applications usually contain more than just one control. You don't want to have all of the controls battling each other over which one receives keystrokes, so there must be a system for determining which of the controls will react to the keyboard. In Visual Basic only one control at a time can own the *focus*. The control that can receive keyboard input has the focus. Because Windows can have more than one application running at a time, focus can also refer to the form or program that is the parent of the control with the focus.

Not all forms and controls can receive the focus at all times. When a modal form displays, it restricts the user from selecting any other forms from the same application until it closes. By the same token, no control on any of these other forms can receive the focus as long as the modal form is displayed.

In some cases you might not want a control to receive the focus, even though Visual Basic allows it. You should prevent controls that cannot process input from the keyboard from receiving the focus. For example, a scroll bar can only be controlled by the user with the mouse. Your program should ensure that the scroll bars don't retain the focus. To prevent a control from receiving the focus, set that control's TabStop property to False. Also note that any control that has its Enabled property set to False cannot receive the focus.

The focus can move from one running application to another in two ways. First, the user can click on another application's window or icon with the mouse. Second, you can move the focus to another running program by using the AppActivate statement within your program's code.

The focus can move to another control in one of three ways. First, the user can click on another control with the mouse. If the selected control is eligible to receive the focus, it becomes the active control. Second, the user can cycle through all the eligible controls on a form by pressing the (TAB) key. This moves the focus from one control to another in the order determined by the TabIndex property of all of the controls on the form. Finally, your program can change the focus by using the SetFocus method, which allows your program to directly set the focus to a particular control. A control keeps the focus until the focus is moved to another control. The exception to this rule is the menu control. Just prior to executing any of its events, the menu control returns the focus to the control that owned it before the menu was opened.

Receiving the focus initiates a control's GotFocus event. You can use this event to prepare the control for the user's actions. For instance, you might use the GotFocus event to update the entries in a file list box when it receives the focus.

CHAPTER 22: TIME

Sometimes the virtual world inside the computer must be synchronized with the passage of real time. For example, you may need to perform a communications link up or file transfer at a certain time each day. Much like QuickBASIC, Visual Basic has a Timer function, which uses the system clock to return the number of seconds that have elapsed since midnight. This function can time specific operations. For instance, you can determine how long it takes a fragment of code to execute by assigning the returned value from the Timer function to a variable just prior to the beginning of the code fragment. At the end of the code fragment, you assign the Timer function to another variable. You can then subtract the starting variable from the ending variable to determine the number of seconds that elapsed while the code was running.

QuickBASIC also has an ON TIMER GOSUB statement, which allows a program to repeatedly execute a set of commands at a predefined interval. Visual Basic needs no such statement. Instead, it provides a control called the timer. The timer control's Interval property controls how often its Timer event triggers, allowing you to regularly update a displayed value or run another routine.

Visual Basic automatically provides time information through a variety of functions, statements, and events. You can get the current date and time through a serial number and perform a number of transformations on the time value with built-in date and time functions.

CHAPTER 23: USING THE CLIPBOARD

The Windows Clipboard is an area in memory set aside for programs to use for copying and pasting information. It can be used to store several types of information. First, and most common, is text. Text information consists of any characters that can be represented by an ASCII code. The Clipboard can also store graphic images that are in one of three formats: Windows bitmap, Windows metafile, and device independent bitmap (DIB). Finally, Windows uses the Clipboard area to store information during Dynamic Data Exchange (DDE) conversations (see Chapter 25, Dynamic Data Exchange [DDE]) as well as objects using Object Linking and Embedding (OLE) (see Chapter 26, Object Linking and Embedding). The Clipboard can hold one entry each of all of these types of information. Copying a piece of information replaces any information of the same type previously stored there.

Your Visual Basic programs can access this area by manipulating the Clipboard object. This object has five associated methods with which you can determine what type of data is on the Clipboard, and copy text or graphics to or from the Clipboard. These are GetFormat, GetText, GetData, SetText, and SetData.

Retrieving Information from the Clipboard

Before your program retrieves information from the Clipboard, it needs to determine if the Clipboard contains the desired type of information. Use the

GetFormat method with the Clipboard object to see if the Clipboard contains the kind of information you specified.

Once you've determined that the desired information is available, you can use either the GetText or GetData methods with the Clipboard object to retrieve it. The GetText method retrieves text information, and it can also be used to retrieve DDE information by specifying that format. You can assign the results of this method to any Visual Basic string or variant, or any control property that accepts strings or variants.

The GetData method retrieves graphics. By default, this method returns a Windows bitmap. Optionally, your program can specify which type of graphic information it is requesting, bitmap, metafile, or DIB. You can use this method to assign an image from the Clipboard to the Picture property of a form or picture control.

Sending Information to the Clipboard

The converse of the GetText and GetData methods are the SetText and SetData methods. SetText copies text information to the Clipboard. Like GetText, it can also be used to copy DDE information by specifying that format. SetData copies the image of a Form object or picture control to the Clipboard. With this method, your program supplies the Picture or Image property of the object, and optionally specifies the image format (bitmap, metafile, or DIB).

CHAPTER 24: PRINTING

Windows handles the low-level input and output to devices such as screens and printers. This makes it simpler for you to create programs that print complex forms and graphics than it would be in the DOS environment.

In most languages the printer functions as a sequential output device. Programs write data to a printer one character at a time; and once this is done, there can be no going back. Visual Basic, however, takes a very different approach. It provides a special Printer object to handle printed output.

Instead of outputting data in a character-by-character manner, the Printer object is a page-oriented device. The Printer object sets up in memory the image of a blank printer page. Any methods executed on the Printer object occur on this page in memory and are held there until your program tells the Printer object to start a new page.

You may use any of the methods used for drawing graphics or printing characters on a form or picture on the Printer object. When you execute methods such as Pset, Line, and Circle on the Printer object, their output goes to the current printer page in memory. The only difference between using these methods on the screen and using them with a printer is that most printers can only perform their operations in black and white. With such printers, specifying the color in a graphics method has no effect.

Coordinate Systems on the Printer Object

The size of the printed page will depend on the particular brand and model of printer. The absolute size of each page is measured in twips. A twip is defined as 1/20 point, which is 1440 twips per printed inch. Therefore, if the default printer has its page size defined as 8-1/2 by 11 inches, the size of the Printer object's print page will be 12240 by 15840 twips. Your program can determine the absolute height and width of the printer page by using the Height and Width properties with the Printer object. However, the values returned by these properties do not necessarily reflect the usable page area. This is because every printer has a unique border area around the page in which it cannot print. The actual size of the usable print area can be obtained with the ScaleHeight and ScaleWidth properties of the Printer object.

Controlling the Printer Page

Your program uses the NewPage method to inform the Printer object when it is done printing a page of output. This method ends the output to the current print page in memory and creates a new blank page for subsequent printing. The NewPage method also updates the Page property of the Printer object.

The Page property counts the number of pages that have been printed to the Printer object. Each time your program executes the NewPage method the Page number increments. The Page property is a read-only property; the EndDoc method is the only way to reset it.

The EndDoc method tells the Printer object that your program has completed printing the current document. When it executes, all of the printer pages stored in memory are then sent to the Windows printing routines. Windows handles the task of outputting those pages to the printer. If your program has sent output to the Printer object since the last executed NewPage, EndDoc automatically sends a NewPage.

Printing Forms

Visual Basic also provides a very useful method for printing forms. The PrintForm method is used with a form object, and sends a copy of that form to the printer. Any graphics, text, or controls (with the exception of the menu controls) on that form print out.

CHAPTER 25: DYNAMIC DATA EXCHANGE (DDE)

The *Dynamic Data Exchange (DDE)* protocol developed by Microsoft allows you to establish real-time communication between two Windows applications: DDE allows programs to "talk" to each other. This lets you set up data links between documents created by the same or different applications. Depending on how this link is set up, the changes in the data in one document can automatically update the data in the other. Whenever two applications talk with each other using Dynamic Data Exchange, it is called a DDE conversation. All DDE conversations consist of four elements: the source, the destination, the topic, and the item.

Every DDE conversation involves two applications exchanging information. The conversation starts when one of the two applications requests data from the other. The program that requests the data is called the *destination* application, and the program that supplies the data is called the *source* application. (These used to be called the *client* and the *server*.)

In order for a DDE conversation to occur, both the destination and the source must be running. If the destination requests data from an application that is not currently running, a dialog box appears informing the user of this, and asks if the source application should be executed. When the conversation begins, the destination application can set up the link between the two programs in two ways. An *automatic link* instructs the source application to update the link every time the requested data changes. A *manual link* exchanges information only when the destination requests it. A *notify link* simply notifies the destination application that the data has changed, but does not update the actual data.

When a conversation starts, the destination application informs the source application what particular piece of data it needs using the topic and item. The *topic* of a DDE conversation refers to the general form or document on which the requested data resides. The *item* of a DDE conversation refers to the specific piece of data requested. The source application defines which of its objects are available as DDE topics and DDE items. For instance, in a DDE conversation with a spreadsheet application as the source, the spreadsheet document could be a DDE topic, and the data in a particular cell in that spreadsheet could be a DDE item. If you wish to use another application as a DDE source, you will need to refer to its documentation in order to find out what it defines as a DDE topic and a DDE item.

Your Visual Basic programs can work as both DDE destinations and DDE sources. You can even set up an application to be both source and destination at the same time. Keep in mind, however, that not all Windows programs can perform DDE operations. Before you attempt to create a DDE link between your application and another, make sure the other application has the capabilities needed to participate in a DDE conversation.

CHAPTER 26: OBJECT LINKING AND EMBEDDING (OLE)

Object Linking and Embedding lets your Visual Basic application display and manipulate data from other Windows applications. For example, your application could have a spreadsheet object from Excel, a drawing object from

	B	C	D	E	F	G
2		Win3.1	Win 3.0	Win 3.0	Win 3.1	Win 3.
3		8x6x16	8x6x16	8x6x256	8x6x256	8x6x256
5	Lines	2.9 ms	2.9 ms	4.2 ms	2.1 ms	4.2 n
6	Rectangles	7.3 ms	7.2 ms	22.6 ms	2.8 ms	22.6 n
7	Ellipse	39.4 ms	38.4 ms	72.0 ms	31.4 ms	72.0 n
8	BitBlt	4.2 ms	4.0 ms	4.0 ms	0.5 ms	4.0 n
9	StretchBlt	61.3 ms	60.8 ms	70.3 ms	53.5 ms	70.3 n
10	Scroll	4.6 ms	5.1 ms	5.6 ms	1.9 ms	5.6 n
11	Fill	26.3 ms	25.6 ms	142.0 ms	4.9 ms	142.0 n
13	Total:	146.0 ms	144.0 ms	320.7 ms	97.1 ms	320.7 n

Figure 2-19 An embedded Excel object

CorelDRAW, and a word processor object from AmiPro. Even though you haven't written any code to do all the things these other applications can, your application can still serve as a front end to tie them all together.

Although OLE and DDE are both ways of sharing data between applications, there are some fundamental differences in their approach. OLE temporarily transfers control to the program that originally created the data to do any data manipulation, while DDE functions solely within your Visual Basic application. OLE also displays the data as the original application would, whereas DDE data displays in whatever way you choose to format it. For example, if the original application is a spreadsheet created in Excel, the OLE control displays its contents exactly as it would appear in Excel, complete with row and column headers and gridlines. Figure 2-19 illustrates how an OLE object retains its formatting.

The OLE control lets you create both linked and embedded objects. A *linked* object is really just a placeholder for and pointer to the real data. For example, if you link a drawing into an OLE control, the data for the drawing stays in the original source file. Only an image of the data and a link back to the original data are stored in the OLE control. This makes it possible to access the linked data from several different applications.

An *embedded* object actually stores the data within the OLE control. You can store the contents of the control in a file, and the file contains the name of the application that produced the object originally, the actual data, and an image of the data for display. When you embed an object in an OLE control, only your application can access the data; no other application can read or write the data directly.

OLE 1.0

Visual Basic 2.0 uses the OLE 1.0 specification. This allows for editing the embedded or linked object using the originating program as described above. Double-clicking on the object typically brings up the originating application in its own window and opens the embedded object for editing. Closing the original application either saves the object to disk (for linked objects) or updates the data in your Visual Basic application (for embedded objects.)

OLE 2.0

Visual Basic 3.0 is one of the first applications to support the OLE 2.0 specification. This adds tremendous flexibility to programs that implement it, and paves the way for a true object-oriented environment.

OLE 2.0 supports the normal editing procedure introduced with OLE 1.0—double-click to bring up the originating application in its own window. It also supports *in-place editing*. This allows users to edit the embedded object directly in your application, without explicitly bringing up the originating application. This makes it look as if your application is doing all the work.

OLE 2.0 also introduces *OLE automation*. This exciting development lets you use another application's commands and functions directly from within your Visual Basic application. For instance, you might want to perform some complex financial calculations. You can use a spreadsheet's financial functions to do this using OLE automation rather than having to write your own functions from scratch.

The combination of in-place editing and OLE automation will make for more seamless integration between applications. You can write relatively simple "container" applications that embed many different kinds of objects, and use the power of the originating programs to do the actual manipulation. Documents, rather than programs, will become a user's main focus.

CHAPTER 27: DATA ACCESS

Most programs need to deal with storing and retrieving data. Complex requirements like multiple related tables and index maintenance would require hundreds of lines of code if you tried to do it yourself. Rather than focusing on the application and the user, you end up focusing on trying to create what should really be a tool. Visual Basic 3.0 breaks through this barrier with the data control.

Traditional databases typically don't provide the fine control over the user's computing environment the way Visual Basic does. Even the newest breed of Windows databases fall short on their capacity to mold the user interface. Their strength lies instead in powerful database languages and *data aware* user interface objects that automatically update and display the database's underlying fields.

The data control lets you access a complete database engine through several implicit objects and many methods. It also makes some controls data aware. This means that with very little code, you can place data aware objects like text boxes, check boxes, and picture controls directly on the form and have them automatically synchronize to the external database. The data control visually looks like a set of VCR controls (see Figure 2-20). Clicking on the arrows moves the user to the beginning of the database, back one record, forward one record, and to the end of the database. Data aware controls can be *bound* to underlying fields. A bound control automatically updates the field when its data changes, and automatically displays the field's data when the data control moves from record to record.

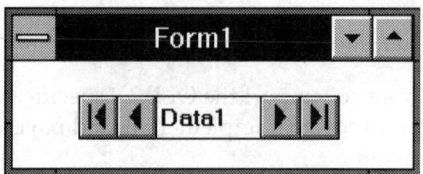

Figure 2-20 The data control provides access to a powerful database engine

Although this set of arrows is the most visible manifestation of the data control, its real power lies in the objects and methods it brings to Visual Basic. Its two implicit objects, Database and Recordset, plus their attendant methods, give you almost all of the power of a dedicated database product like Paradox or Microsoft Access. In fact, the data control is based on the Microsoft Access database engine. If you are familiar with Access, programming with the data control's methods will be very natural. Even if you've never programmed a database before, you'll find the techniques approachable and intuitive. Chapter 27, Data Access, gives a thorough introduction of the basics of database creation and programming.

APPENDIX A: VISUAL BASIC LANGUAGE TUTORIAL

Visual Basic's objects and controls deal mostly with providing you, the programmer, with visual tools for building an intuitive user interface. In most cases, however, these tools cannot perform the actual processing of data, which is the heart of any application. Visual Basic's programming language handles this task.

Microsoft built Visual Basic on the foundation of their very popular QuickBASIC language. In fact, most of the commands in Visual Basic have the same syntax as their QuickBASIC counterparts. The "compatibility boxes" in the reference entries in Appendix A indicate whether a given Visual Basic statement or function has a counterpart in QuickBASIC 4.5 or Microsoft BASIC Professional Development System 7.0. Therefore, if you're already a QuickBASIC programmer, the Visual Basic language will be old hat. If not, don't worry: Visual Basic is a straightforward, easy-to-understand language.

Variables

Any programming language needs a technique for storing and accessing data in the computer's memory. A variable is a symbolic name for a location in memory. In your programs, you can read and write to memory by assigning a value from or to a variable. Smart programmers will assign names to variables that describe the purpose of the data that they represent. This practice makes your programs more readable.

For instance, if you were to set up a variable that will hold the total dollar amount of an invoice, you could name it something ambiguous, such as X. As you are writing the program, that variable name would be fresh in your mind, and you'd have no problem deciphering what it represents. However, if you have to come back many months later to make changes to the program, the meaning of X will not be so fresh in your mind, and you could waste a lot of time just trying to figure out what it means. Instead, give the variable a name that tells you what it represents, such as InvoiceTotal. This variable name is descriptive enough so that when you come back to the program to make modifications, you don't need to trace through the whole program to find out what it represents.

Visual Basic has some rules regarding how you may set up a variable name. These rules help Visual Basic to tell the difference between variables that you set up and other elements of the language. These rules are as follows

1. A variable name may be no longer than 40 characters.

2. The first character of a variable name must be a letter (A through Z). This letter can be uppercase or lowercase.

3. The remaining characters can be letters (A through Z or a through z), numbers (0 through 9), or underscores (_).

4. The last character can be one of these type declaration characters (explained later): %, &, !, #, @, $.

5. The variable name cannot be a Visual Basic reserved word. Reserved words include Visual Basic properties, events, methods, operators, statements, and functions.

Type Declarations

Variables can hold a variety of information. You may wish to store some text, an integer, a date, or even an amount that represents money. A *type declaration* tells Visual Basic what kind of information is stored in a particular variable.

The seven types Visual Basic recognizes are integers (%) like 3 and -27; long integers (&) like 1287543; single-precision numbers (!) like 32.75 or -923.1093; double-precision numbers (#) like 283.3094884953; currency (@) like $28.33 or $1,000,000,000.00; text (or strings) ($) like "this is some text"; and the variant type (no implicit declaration character) that can store any kind of data. The variant type is new to Visual Basic 2.0 and 3.0, and lends considerable flexibility to the language.

You declare variables explicitly with the Dim, ReDim, Static, or Global statements. You can also declare variables implicitly, just by using them in your code using the correct type declaration character. A new feature of Visual Basic 2.0 and 3.0 lets you use the Option Explicit statement to force yourself to explicitly declare all variables. This can be extremely helpful in debugging your program.

Operators

Operators perform an operation with one or more elements. For instance, the plus sign (+) is an arithmetic operator. It adds two or more numeric values. Visual Basic has three types of operators: arithmetic, relational, and logical. Arithmetic operators perform math functions on numeric values. Relational operators are used to compare the values of two items. You can use relational operators to determine if one value is equal to, greater than, or less than another value. Logical operators perform bitwise operations on numeric variables. Each logical operator will change the bit values of a numeric variable in a different way.

Statements and Functions

The core of the Visual Basic language is based on commands, which come in two types: statements and functions. A statement performs a prescribed task without returning any values. A function is similar to a statement in that it also performs a task, but it also returns a value based on the results of the task. You can modify the behavior of a statement or function by supplying arguments to the command. Statements and functions use the information supplied in these arguments to direct them in their task.

APPENDIX B: VISUAL BASIC LANGUAGE REFERENCE

This section provides a concise and complete reference to all the statements and functions in Visual Basic. It starts with a discussion of variable types and operators. Reference entries on each statement and function make up the bulk of the appendix.

APPENDIX C: DEBUGGING TECHNIQUES

Once you've written a Visual Basic program, your job has only begun. Although it can catch your syntax errors, Visual Basic can't know when you've made an error in your programming logic. You find logic errors only by rigorously testing and retesting your completed program. Once you find a logic error, you need to determine the cause of the error and fix it.

The Debug Window

When you start a program while in the Visual Basic environment, your form becomes the window on the desktop with the focus. Another window, called the Debug window, displays underneath your form. Any time your program is running, you may break out of your program and bring the Debug window to the front. Once you've done so, you can type commands into the Immediate pane of this window, and they will execute immediately. Above the Immediate pane lies the Watch pane. This area lets you track the contents of expressions, and can halt the program if a variable or expression reaches a certain value that you've set. The Debug window forms the centerpiece of the debugging environment.

The Debug Object

The Debug object gives your program access to the Debug window while its running. This object can only be accessed in your program while it runs under the Visual Basic environment—it does not affect standalone Visual Basic programs. Its single method, Print, simply makes it print the value of its arguments to the Immediate pane of the Debug window. This allows you to place Print methods at strategic areas in your program that can print the value of certain variables or properties. You can use this in addition to the *Watch* variable feature.

Breakpoints

Most times while you are trying to debug a program, you will have a fairly good idea as to where in your program an error occurs. You may want the program to execute normally until just prior to reaching the area of the suspected error. For this reason Visual Basic lets you set *breakpoints* in your program. Setting a breakpoint makes your program stop at the indicated line. You set a breakpoint by placing the insertion point on the line where you wish to halt program execution and choosing the Toggle Breakpoint option from the Run menu. You can also toggle a breakpoint by pressing the F9 function key.

APPENDIX D: WINDOWS API

When Microsoft first created the Windows operating environment, they included the ability for Windows programs to utilize *Dynamic Link Libraries (DLLs)*—collections of working routines that can be linked to a Windows program. In this respect DLLs are very much like the classic type of linkable library. The difference between the two is that in order to use routines in a classic library, the programmer needs to link the library to the program during the compilation process. A program that uses routines in a DLL, however, is fully compiled without the library. When the program begins, it searches for the appropriate DLL library file, and links to it at runtime—thus the "Dynamic" part of the name. All that is required is for the program to know the name of the DLL file and the syntax needed to execute the routines in the library. Several programs can share the same DLL in memory, considerably reducing the amount of memory needed by the sum of the running applications.

You can access almost all of the Windows Application Program Interface (API) through Dynamic Link Libraries. An API defines the manner in which a program can be written in order to interact with a particular environment. In Windows, programs can access the API by calling routines from certain Dynamic Link Libraries that come with the environment.

Visual Basic provides your programs with the ability to execute routines contained in these DLLs. Before you try to call a DLL, you need to tell Visual Basic about the DLL by placing a Declare statement in the global module of your program (see Appendix A for the syntax of the Declare statement). Once this is done, you can call the DLL routine in the same manner as for any other Visual Basic sub procedure or function.

The API calls are most often used in Visual Basic for performing unusual or behind the scenes kind of tasks. Visual Basic has such a rich set of tools with its default controls and all the third-party add-on tools that the need to use the API is becoming increasingly rare. Sometimes, however, the only way to accomplish a difficult task lies in using direct API calls. This appendix covers the most useful API calls.

APPENDIX E: PROFESSIONAL EDITION

The Professional Edition of Visual Basic ships with even more controls than the Standard Edition. These controls provide access to three-dimensional check boxes, panels, frames, and buttons, as well as animated buttons, communications, masked edit, pen extensions, and a spin button. Appendix E takes you on a quick tour of these controls and gives concrete examples of their use.

Professional Visual Basic also has extensions to the Database objects, and more sophisticated data management add-on programs and controls. One key feature is its ability to connect to SQL databases. SQL, or Structured Query Language, is a de facto standard for complex client-server and mainframe computing.

APPENDIX F: FURTHER READING

There is no limit to exploration and no end to learning. We conclude the *Visual Basic SuperBible* with a description of books from Waite Group Press and other publishers that can help you master various aspects of Visual Basic. You will also find books on QuickBASIC and related languages, since much of the functionality of QuickBASIC is included in Visual Basic. We also include some titles about Windows programming.

APPENDIX G: PROJECT DISK

Almost every chapter in the *SuperBible* concludes with a project illustrating the techniques used in that chapter. The disk included with the book contains every project, complete with all forms and code, just as you see it printed.

Having the example programs on disk saves you valuable time, and much frustration over trying to type them in by hand. This appendix covers the installation and use of the examples.

APPENDIX 3: PROTECK DISK

3

USING OBJECTS

Visual Basic provides many predefined *objects* that inherently perform common tasks. Forms, controls, and menus are all examples of built-in Visual Basic objects that help form the user interface. Some objects are invisible during runtime, but no less important: timers, the Clipboard, and the data control's underlying Database and Recordset are all examples of hidden objects that play a vital role in an application.

Most objects have certain properties that define in detail how they will appear and react to the user. Most objects also have a set of events assigned to them that define what actions to take when they are manipulated by the user. You then add Visual Basic code to specify the appropriate behavior.

These objects are what make Visual Basic a programming "environment" instead of just a programming language. If you were working with a programming language, you would have to write code that defines each object and specifies its behavior and how it acts once it's used—or obtain a library of such objects written by another programmer. In Visual Basic each control is already predefined. The properties and behavior of an object are easily set up without doing any programming. The only coding that you need to do is to define how an object will react to the user's actions.

Note that this use of the word *object* is more restricted than its use in *object-oriented programming*. Visual Basic objects share many similarities with objects in object-oriented programming languages like C++ or Smalltalk. Visual Basic objects are encapsulated (that is, a text box inherently "knows" how to perform text editing), can have multiple instances (more than one text box can appear on a form), but are not polymorphous (an important feature in object-oriented programming, where the programmer can change key aspects of an object and all lower-level objects inherit that change). For this reason we refer to Visual Basic as an object-based language, not an object-oriented language.

This chapter gives an overview of the types of objects in Visual Basic, including the exciting additions

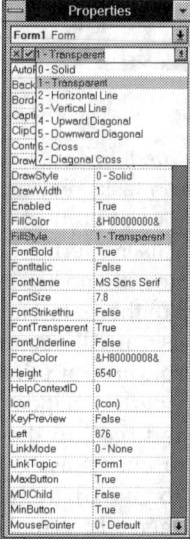

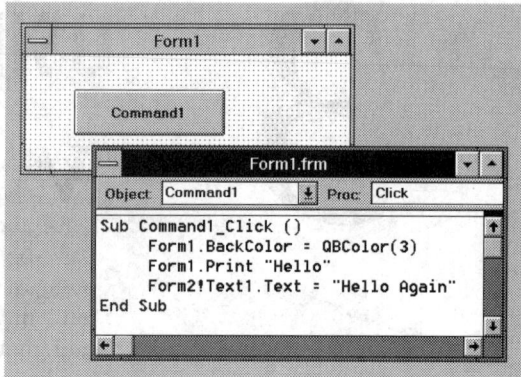

Figure 3-1 Set object properties in the properties box during the design phase

Figure 3-2 React to user actions with event sub procedures

in versions 2.0 and 3.0, such as the OLE, common dialog, and data controls. We also cover how to name and use these objects, and discuss the vital topic of object variables. Finally, each object is summarized with a description of what it is and what it does, including complete tables of all applicable properties, methods, and events.

PROPERTIES, EVENTS, AND METHODS

Each object in Visual Basic has a set of *properties* associated with it. These properties (such as Height, BorderStyle, or Caption) determine the appearance and behavior of an object. You set an object's properties initially when you create your application during the design phase using the properties box illustrated in Figure 3-1. In most cases your program can read or set these properties while it is running. Some properties are read only at runtime, meaning their value can only be set when the program is in its design phase. Other properties cannot be set during the design phase; you must make any changes to the properties in the program's code.

Visual Basic also assigns a set of *events* to each object. These events are Visual Basic sub procedures that occur when the user performs an action with an object. For instance, GotFocus, Click, MouseMove, and LostFocus are events common to many objects. Double-clicking on an object in design phase displays Visual Basic's Code window. From here, you may define the actions to take when a particular event occurs. See Appendix A, Visual Basic Language Tutorial, for an explanation of sub procedures and a description of the statements and functions you can use in Visual Basic code; see Chapter 7, Events, for more information about event procedures. Figure 3-2 shows a command button on a form, with an event sub procedure shown in the code window.

Figure 3-3 Choose control objects from the tool palette

Most objects also have associated *methods*. Methods are commands that perform an action with or on an object. They are used like Visual Basic's statements or functions, but their operations act directly on an object when invoked by code. For example, a list box has the Clear method, which clears it of all entries.

TYPES OF OBJECTS

Visual Basic has several different types of objects. The *form* is one of the most basic objects. A form is a window that contains application code and has other objects placed on it to create the user interface. A form may fill the entire screen, have other forms contained within it, or may be a smaller custom dialog box. Chapter 4, Forms and Menus, discusses these in detail.

The most familiar objects are the standard user interface objects: command buttons, list boxes, menus, and so forth. These objects are commonly referred to as *controls*. A control object is typically drawn directly on the form, except for the menu control, which is created with the menu design window. You draw controls on the form by selecting the type of control from the *tool palette,* illustrated in Figure 3-3, and dragging the mouse on the form where you want to place the control. Details about controls, and their associated properties, events, and methods make up the bulk of this book. See Chapter 4, Forms and Menus, for details about menus, and chapters 5 through 27 on the rest of the controls.

Visual Basic also has five specialized system objects that let you work with an application's environment. These are the App, Clipboard, Debug, Printer, and Screen objects.

The App object lets your program find out important information about the environment, such as the name of the associated help file and the application's path. The Clipboard object lets your program interact with the Windows Clipboard area. Visual Basic programs can copy text or graphics to and from the Clipboard. Chapter 23, Using the Clipboard, presents detailed information on how to use the Clipboard object. The Debug object, used only within the Visual Basic environment, can help with the testing and debugging of a program. This object is covered in detail in Appendix C, Debugging Techniques.

The Printer object generates printed output. Since the Windows environment handles the actual printing duties, your Visual Basic program doesn't really send output to the printer. Instead, the Printer object sends that output to the Windows printing routines, which then send the data to the printer. Chapter 24, Printing, covers the Printer object in detail. The Screen object globally references other objects. Your program can use the Screen object to determine which form or control is active, and how many and what types of fonts are available to the system.

The data control, explored in Chapter 27, Data Access, also has several underlying objects. The two primary objects, Database and Recordset, let you interact with the underlying database engine to perform sophisticated database actions. These two objects, in turn, have properties that expose further objects within them. You may also encounter third-party custom controls that expose objects like the data control does, and the new OLE 2.0 control can expose other application's objects in a very similar manner. See Chapter 26, Object Linking and Embedding (OLE), for more details about using other applications' objects.

NAMING CONVENTIONS

Each Visual Basic object has a name that you use to refer to it in code. Set the name of forms and controls during the design phase with the Name property in the properties box. The name must start with a letter and may be up to 40 characters long. It may contain the underscore character (although this is not recommended, as it makes event procedures harder to read), but may not contain any other punctuation symbols. Each control or form starts with a default name consisting of the object type plus a unique integer. For example, the first text box is named Text1, the second one Text2; the fourth list box created would be named List4.

The default names work well for smaller applications. Most of the code examples in this book keep the default names for simplicity. Larger applications demand intelligent and consistent naming practices to help debug your code. Just as with any variable, you should name an object with something that indicates its purpose: for example, PatientName or ShippingMethods.

You will find it very helpful to start any object name with some sort of abbreviation that indicates what kind of object it is. This will help you as you trace your code, and also has the advantage of grouping like kinds of controls together in the code window (for example, all text box event procedures would be near each other). Microsoft suggests using a three-letter code (such as txt for text box, lst for list box). There are many possible conventions; what is important is that you're consistent. For larger examples and many of the larger projects, this book uses four-letter abbreviations (such as text for text box, list for list box). The examples given in the last paragraph might then be named textPatientName and listShippingMethods. Chapter 6, Accessing Forms and Controls, gives a table of suggested object prefixes.

The system objects (App, Clipboard, Debug, Printer, and Screen) cannot be renamed. You always refer to them by their default name. The data control's two underlying objects (Database and Recordset) also cannot be renamed.

Refer to an object's properties and methods with the *dot operator*. This consists of the object's Name property, a period (.), and the property or method. For example:

```
reponse$ = Text1.Text
Clipboard.Clear
Form1.ScaleHeight = 2700
textPatientName.ForeColor = YELLOW
listShippingMethods.AddItem "Federal Express"
```

Refer to a control on another form with the *exclamation operator*. This consists of the form's Name property, an exclamation point (!), and the name of the control:

```
reponse$ = Form2!Text1.Text
Form3!textPatientName.ForeColor = YELLOW
formShip!listShippingMethods.AddItem "Federal Express"
```

You may also use the dot operator in place of the exclamation. Visual Basic 1.0 used this type of construction exclusively, and Visual Basic 2.0 and 3.0 have retained it to ease compatibility with older applications. The exclamation operator more clearly differentiates between the name of the control you're referencing, and the property or method of that control.

```
Form2.Text1.Text = "Hello"    'Works; not recommended. Kept for compatibility with VB 1.0
Form2!Text1.Text = "Hello"    'Recommended. Clearer distinction between name and property
```

Finally, events are usually named with the Name property of the control, an underscore (_), and the name of the event, as in textPatientName_Click. Forms are the exception; rather than using the name of the form, the event routine uses the keyword 'Form'.

```
Sub Command1_Click ()
    MsgBox "You've just clicked Command1!"
End Sub

Sub textPatientName_GotFocus ()
```

(continued on next page)

(continued from previous page)

```
    textPatientName.BackColor = QBColor(7)
    textPatientName.ForeColor = QBColor(1)
    textPatientName.SelLength = Len(textPatientName.Text)
End Sub

Sub Form_Load ()
    List1.AddItem "Red"
    List1.AddItem "Blue"
    List1.AddItem "Green"
End Sub
```

For more information about naming and referring to objects, see Chapter 6, Accessing Forms and Controls.

OBJECT VARIABLES

You can assign most objects to an object variable. This lets you manipulate the object just as easily as you would with any standard variable, such as a string or integer variable. You can pass objects to sub procedures or functions, create arrays of objects, and shorten and simplify your code.

Declare an object variable just as you would with any standard variable by using the Dim, ReDim, Static, or Global keywords. (For more on these keywords, see Appendix A, Visual Basic Language Tutorial, and Appendix B, Visual Basic Language Reference.) Table 3-1 lists the available control types and the *class name* associated with it. The property box lists the *class name* in the right-hand portion of the top combo box; this is especially helpful for determining the class name of custom controls.

Control Type	Class Name Used in Dim, ReDim, Static, or Global Statements
(any control)	Control
(any form)	Form
(custom controls)	Custom control's class name
Check	CheckBox
Combo	ComboBox
Command	CommandButton
Data	Data
Dir	DirListBox

Control Type	Class Name Used in Dim, ReDim, Static, or Global Statements
Drive	DriveListBox
File	FileListBox
Form	Name property of specific form
Frame	Frame
Grid	Grid
Horizontal Scroll	HScrollBar
Image	Image
Label	Label
Line	Line
List	ListBox
MDIForm	MDIForm
Menu	Menu
OLE	OLE
Option	OptionButton
Picture	PictureBox
Shape	Shape
Text	TextBox
Timer	Timer
Vertical Scroll	VScrollBar

Table 3-1 Class names used for creating object variables

For example, declare a variable that can refer to any text box in your application:

```
Dim myTextBoxVariable As TextBox
```

You can then use this variable just as you would the actual name of the object, and assign an object to it with the Set keyword:

```
Set myTextBoxVariable = Text1
myTextBoxVariable.Text = "Hello"
```

This next example shows how to shorten and simplify your code by using an object variable:

```
Sub Command1_Click ()              ' Without object variable
    newName$ = formPatientInput!textPatientName.Text & " (discharged)"
    formPatientInput!textPatientName.Text = newName$
    formPatientInput!textPatientName.ForeColor = QBColor(3)
End Sub

Sub Command1_Click ()              ' Using object variable to simplify code
    Dim old As TextBox
    Set old = formPatientInput!textPatientName
    newName$ = old & " (discharged)"
    old.Text = newName$
    old.ForeColor = QBColor(3)
End Sub
```

You can also declare an object variable to accept any kind of control with the Control class name. This allows you to write generic functions and sub procedures. For example, this hides or unhides any control that is passed to it:

```
Sub Flip (c As Control)
    c.Visible = Not c.Visible
End Sub
```

Some controls may not have the property or method you're trying to use, which would cause an error. For instance, timers don't have the Visible property. You can check for what kind of control an object variable represents with the If TypeOf *control* Is *classname* construction. Note that TypeOf...Is can only be used in an If statement; you cannot use it in a Select Case block. You also may not combine it with any other conditional tests or operators. The following example shows how to simulate an If TypeOf c Is Not Timer construction by using the If statement's Else block to handle the Not:

```
Sub Flip (c As Control)
    If TypeOf c Is Timer Then        'Timers don't have the visible property
    Else                             'Not a timer, OK to flip visibility
        c.Visible = Not c.Visible
    End If
End Sub
```

You may also use the Is keyword without TypeOf to test to see if two object variables refer to the same object:

```
Sub Test (c As Control, d As Control)
     If c Is d Then MsgBox "Controls are the same!"
End Sub
```

Generic object variables declared with the Control class name are flexible, as they can refer to any type of control, but are slower than specific class name variables. You should use specific object variables whenever possible. Visual Basic can create the reference to a specific variable while your program starts up, while generic object variables need to have the reference created each time they are used.

Form object variables can refer to the generic class of "all forms" by using the Form class name. You may also refer to specific forms by using the form's Name property as its class name, in contrast to regular control variables that can never refer to specific controls. For example,

```
Sub Command1_Click ()
     Dim f As formPatientForm
     f.Caption = "This is still the formPatientForm"
     f!Text1.Text = "Hello"
End Sub
```

INSTANCES

You may have multiple instances of your program running at one time, and multiple instances of forms within a single application. An *instance* means an exact but independent copy of something. For example, two copies of your program can be running at the same time, without interacting or interfering with each other. As another example, a single application can contain multiple copies of a single form; these forms are completely independent. Although they are exact copies of the original "template" form, their data remains separate form the other forms and they each may be manipulated independently.

This is an important concept used in creating Multiple Document Interface (MDI) applications, a subject covered in more detail in Chapter 4, Forms and Menus. In an MDI application, you may have several documents open at one time. For instance, Microsoft Word or Lotus Ami let you have many different files available for editing at once, and it is possible to simultaneously view more than one at a time.

Your Visual Basic program can do this by creating a single document form with all the user interface elements, like command buttons, text boxes, and menu structure, plus all the code that is document specific, like repagination or search and replace, during the design phase. Then each time the user needs to create a new document, your program creates a new instance of the original form. It retains all the code and user interface of the original, but without interacting with any other open documents based on the original form. You may create new instances of forms by using the New keyword in the declaration statement:

```
Sub menuNewDocument_Click ()
    Dim d As New formBlankDocument      'create a new document form
    d.Show                              'and display it
End Sub
```

You may think of the original form as a "template" used to create the other instances. Each instance gets its own copy of data, so you cannot use module-level variables to share information between the various instances; use global-level variables instead.

You usually don't need to know what instance of a form is currently being used. Event code automatically runs in the appropriate instance. Sometimes, however, you need to distinguish among the various instances. The Me keyword lets you refer to the instance in which the code is running:

```
Sub Command1_Click ()
    Me.Hide                ' Hide this form instance
End Sub
```

Chapter 6, Accessing Forms and Controls, gives more examples of using the Me keyword. The keyword Me also plays an important role in the project at the end of Chapter 4, Forms and Menus.

COLLECTIONS

Visual Basic provides several different collections. A *collection* is an ordered set of similarly typed objects. For example, the *Forms collection* consists of all the forms in your application and the *Controls collections* consist of the controls on each form, with each form having its own controls collection. The data control has several other collections: the *TableDefs collection* of each table in a database, the *Fields collection* of each field in a table, and the *Indexes collection* of each index in a table. See Chapter 27, Data Access, for more information on the data collections.

Each collection is like a *zero-based* array of objects. The first member of a zero-based array has an ordinal position (index) of 0, not 1. You don't need to declare the collection, Visual Basic declares them automatically. Each collection has a Count property, which gives the total number of members in the collection (for example, Form1.Controls.Count gives the total number of controls on Form1). Unlike a regular array, you can't use UBound or LBound to determine the bounds, but this is really unnecessary: the lower bound is always 0, and the upper bound is always (Count –1). Although you can't pass a collection to a procedure, you can directly access the properties and methods of the collection member or assign the member to an object variable.

Collections are particularly useful when you want to iterate through all the loaded instances of the objects. For example, the following few lines of code steps through all controls on all forms and puts the controls' Tag property into an array for subsequent use:

```
For i = 0 To Forms.Count -1
    For j = 0 To Forms(i).Controls.Count -1
        TagArray(i, j) = Forms(i).Controls(j).Tag
    Next j
Next i
```

Combining the collections with the TypeOf test lets you perform repeated actions on similar types of controls. This code steps through all controls on all forms, and sets the FontName and ForeColor properties of all text boxes:

```
Dim c As Control
For i = 0 To Forms.Count -1
    For j = 0 To Forms(i).Controls.Count -1
        Set c = Forms(i).Controls(j)
        If TypeOf c Is TextBox Then
            c.FontName = "Arial"
            c.ForeColor = QBColor(2)
        End If
    Next j
Next i
```

OBJECTS SUMMARY

These objects are summarized in Table 3-2. Note that the word "object" is used in two senses in Visual Basic. Each of the items in the table is an "object," as described above, but some objects are also "controls." A control, as the name implies, is an object that the user can use to communicate with or control the application. Objects that are not controls are not directly manipulated by the user.

Use This...		To Do This...
App	Object	Determine environmental settings for the application
Check box	Control	Display a choice that the user can turn on or off
Clipboard	Object	Copy and paste text or graphics to and from the Windows Clipboard
Combo box	Control	Display a list box with a text input area
Command button	Control	Display a button that performs a function when the user clicks on it
Common Dialog	Control	Display Open, Save As, Print, Color, and Font dialog boxes
Data	Control	Connect an application to a database file

(continued on next page)

(continued from previous page)

Use This...		To Do This...
Debug	Object	Get help in the development/debugging process of a program
Directory list box	Control	Allow the user to choose a disk directory from a list box
Drive list box	Control	Allow the user to choose a disk drive from a drop-down list box
File list box	Control	Allow the user to choose a file in a specific directory from a list box
Form	Object	Define a window on the screen on which objects may be placed
Frame	Control	Define an area on a form that can contain several related controls
Grid	Control	Display a series of rows and columns with cells at the intersection
Image	Control	Define an area to display a picture
Label	Control	Place a text label on a form, picture, or frame
Line	Control	Display a horizontal, vertical, or diagonal line
List box	Control	Display a list of items in a box from which the user can choose
MDI Form	Object	Define a window to contain MDI child forms
Menu	Control	Define pull-down menus that appear at the top of a form
OLE	Control	Create linked or embedded objects
Option button	Control	Define a group of choices where only one choice may be selected
Picture box	Control	Define an area on a form for displaying graphics
Printer	Object	Generate output to the printer
Screen	Object	Activate a specific form or control at runtime
Scroll bars	Control	Provide a visual method for setting a value
Shape	Control	Display a graphical control

Use This...		To Do This...
Text box	Control	Define an area on a form for text editing
Timer	Control	Provide a program with timing capabilities

Table 3-2 Visual Basic objects

In this chapter we will explore the purposes and uses of each of these objects. Each entry discusses the object's related properties, events, and methods. An accompanying figure shows each object's appearance on the screen, unless the object is not visible. Also, if the object is covered in a later chapter of this book, you will be directed there for an example of how it is used.

APP OBJECT

Purpose

The App object determines environmental settings for the application, such as the path and file name of the application itself and its associated help files.

Properties, Events, and Methods

Table 3-3 summarizes the properties of the App object; it has no events or methods.

Use This Property...	To Do This...
EXEName	Determine the file name of the application's executable file
HelpFile	Read or set the name of this application's help file
PathName	Read the absolute path of the application's executable file
PrevInstance	Determine if a previous instance of the application is running
Title	Read or set the title of the application as it appears in the Task Manager

Table 3-3 Properties of the App object

Description

Use the App object to set and determine some fundamental information about your application's environment. The PathName property gives the full path, including drive letters, to the directory in which the executable file (*.EXE) resides. The EXEName property gives the actual name of the executable file (without path) even if the user has renamed it after the application was compiled. HelpFile specifies the name of the Help file associated with this application. PrevInstance lets you determine if another instance of your application is already running. If so, you may wish to determine this during the Form_Load event to prevent more than one instance from loading. Finally, the Title property determines the exact title for your application in the Windows Task Manager.

CHECK BOX CONTROL

Purpose

The check box control presents the user with an on/off choice. The user can either select or deselect this control by clicking on it. Your program can determine whether the user has selected this control by examining its properties.

Properties, Events, and Methods

Tables 3-4, 3-5, and 3-6 list the properties, events, and methods that relate to the check box control.

Use This Property...	To Do This...
Alignment	Read or set the alignment of this object
BackColor, ForeColor	Read or set the background and foreground colors of this object
Caption	Assign text to this object
DataChanged	Determine if the value displayed in this object has changed
DataField	Read or set the name of a field in the recordset of the data control
DataSource	Set the name of the data control to which this object is bound
DragIcon	Read or set what displays when this control is dragged
DragMode	Determine whether drag operations are to occur manually or automatically

Use This Property...	To Do This...
Enabled	Read or set whether this object can react to events
FontBold, FontItalic, FontStrikeThru, FontUnderline	Read or set special effects for this object's font
FontName	Read or set the name of this object's font
FontSize	Read or set the size of this object's font
Height	Read or set the height of this object
HelpContextID	Read or set the context number to this object for context-sensitive help
hWnd	Determine a handle to this object
Index	Uniquely identify an element of a control array
Left	Read or set the left edge position of this control on a picture or form
MousePointer	Read or set the shape of the mouse pointer when it's over this object
Name	Set the name used in code to refer to this object
Parent	Read the name of the form to which the control belongs
TabIndex	Read or set the placement of this control within the form's tab order
TabStop	Read or set whether this control is included in the form's tab order
Tag	Read or set text information that is particular to this object
Top	Read or set the coordinate of this control's top edge
Value	Read or set the current state of this control
Visible	Read or set whether this object is visible
Width	Read or set the width of this object

Table 3-4 Properties of the check box control

Use This Event...	To Do This...
Click	React to the user clicking on this object
DragDrop	React to the user dropping another object onto this object
DragOver	React to the user dragging another object over this object
GotFocus	Initiate an action when this object receives the focus
KeyDown	Initiate an action when the user presses or holds a key down
KeyPress	React to the user typing an ASCII character
KeyUp	Initiate an action when the user releases a key on the keyboard
LostFocus	Initiate an action when this object loses the focus

Table 3-5 Events of the check box control

Use This Method...	To Do This...
Drag	Control manual dragging of this object
Move	Change the position of this object
Refresh	Cause this object to be updated immediately
SetFocus	Move the focus to the specified object
ZOrder	Place this object at the front or back of the z-order

Table 3-6 Methods of the check box control

Description

The check box control presents the user with a choice that has only two possible settings. It consists of a small box, which may be checked or empty, and some accompanying text (see Figure 3-4). When the user clicks on this control, the sta-

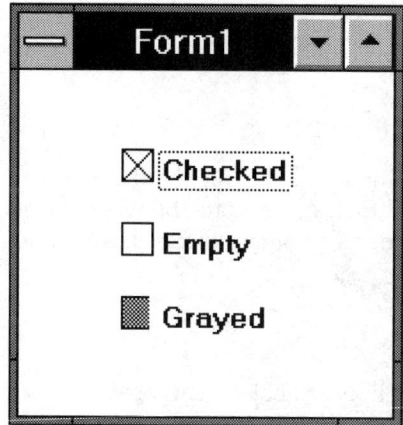

Figure 3-4 The three possible states
of the check box

tus of the box is reversed: if it was checked before the user clicked it, the box will now be empty; if it was empty, it will now be checked. Unlike the option button, the operation of each check box on a form, label, or picture is independent of all other check boxes; changing the status of one check box does not affect other check boxes.

The program can set or read the current status with the Value property. This property has three possible settings. A setting of 0 indicates the box is currently empty. A setting of 1 means the box is currently checked. A setting of 2 indicates the control is grayed. The Value property can only be set to 2 by your program's code. This allows your programs to have an alternate method for indicating that a check box has been selected. However, this does not disable the control. It can still receive the focus, and will still react to the user's activity. If clicked on while in this state, the check box's Value property will be set to 0, and the box will be cleared.

The Caption property defines the text that will accompany the check box. The size and style of this text is defined by the settings of the Font... properties. Including an ampersand (&) underlines the following letter, and the check box may be selected by holding down the (ALT) key and pressing that letter. For instance, if a check box's Caption property is set to &Cash, the displayed text will be "Cash" and the user can select the box by pressing (ALT)-(C). Chapter 21, Application Focus, covers the Caption property in more detail.

Clicking on this control activates its Click event. Use this so your program can react immediately to any changes in the setting of the check box. This event also initiates if the user presses the spacebar while the check box has the focus, or any time the check box's Value property is changed within the program's code.

CLIPBOARD OBJECT

Purpose

The Clipboard object copies and pastes data to and from the Clipboard area of the Windows environment. This enables you to transfer data between most Windows applications as well as between forms or other objects in the same application.

Properties, Events, and Methods

Table 3-7 lists the methods that relate to the Clipboard object. This object has no associated properties or events.

Use This Method...	To Do This...
Clear	Clear the contents of the Clipboard
GetData	Return graphics information from the Clipboard
GetFormat	Return whether or not the Clipboard holds a desired type of data
GetText	Return text information from the Clipboard
SetData	Send graphics information to the Clipboard
SetText	Send text information to the Clipboard

Table 3-7 Methods of the Clipboard object

Description

One of the advantages of the Windows operating environment is that all Windows programs can copy and retrieve text and graphics to and from an area in the environment called the Clipboard. The Clipboard is a temporary holding area for data that has been cut or copied from the current or another program.

This Clipboard area is an element of the operating environment, and as such can be used by any program running in the environment. This means you can cut or copy information from one program and paste it into another. All Windows programs can use the Clipboard area.

The Clipboard can hold three types of items. First, it can hold text. Text is any letters, numbers, or characters that can be represented by an ASCII code. Second, it can hold graphics. Windows lets the user cut and paste pictures as well as text. Last, the Clipboard can hold DDE messages sent from one program to another. For more information on working with DDE messages, see Chapter 25, Dynamic Data Exchange (DDE).

The Clipboard may hold only one of each of type of these data items at a time. When a program copies an item to the Clipboard, it replaces any item of the same type that previously resided there. The GetText and SetText methods retrieve and send text from and to the Clipboard. GetData and SetData are used to retrieve and send graphics from and to the Clipboard. The GetFormat method tests whether a specific type of data is currently being held by the Clipboard.

The Clipboard object is discussed in detail in Chapter 23, Using the Clipboard.

COMBO BOX

Purpose

The combo box control provides three techniques for presenting a list of choices to the user.

Properties, Events, and Methods

Tables 3-8, 3-9, and 3-10 list the properties, events, and methods that relate to the combo box.

Use This Property...	To Do This...
BackColor, ForeColor	Read or set the background and foreground colors of this object
DragIcon	Read or set what displays when this control is dragged
DragMode	Determine whether drag operations are to occur manually or automatically
Enabled	Read or set whether this object can react to events
FontBold, FontItalic, FontStrikeThru, FontUnderline	Read or set special effects for this object's font
FontName	Read or set the name of this object's font

(continued on next page)

(continued from previous page)

Use This Property...	To Do This...
FontSize	Read or set the size of this object's font
Height	Read or set the height of this object
HelpContextID	Read or set the context number to this object for context-sensitive help
hWnd	Determine a handle to this object
Index	Uniquely identify an element of a control array
ItemData	Read or set an index entry associated with the currently selected item
Left	Read or set the left edge placement of this control on a picture or form
List	Read or set the value of a listed item
ListCount	Read the number of items in a list
ListIndex	Read or set the index of the currently selected item in a list
MousePointer	Read or set the shape of the mouse pointer when it's over this object
Name	Set the name used in code to refer to this object
NewIndex	Read the index of the item most recently added to this object
Parent	Read the name of the form to which this control belongs
SelLength	Read or set the number of characters selected in a text box
SelStart	Read or set the starting position of selected text in a text box
SelText	Read or replace the selected text in a text box
Sorted	Read or set whether Visual Basic will automatically sort the list
Style	Read or set the style of this object
TabIndex	Read or set the placement of this control within the form's tab order

Use This Property...	To Do This...
TabStop	Read or set whether this control is part of the form's tab order
Tag	Read or set text information that is particular to this object
Text	Read or set the text contained in this object
Top	Read or set the coordinate of this control's top edge
Visible	Read or set whether this object is visible
Width	Read or set the width of this object

Table 3-8 Properties of the combo box control

Use This Event...	To Do This...
Change	React to a change in a combo box's text property (Style = 0 or 1)
Click	React to the user clicking on this object
DblClick	React to the user double-clicking on this object
DragDrop	React to the user dragging and dropping an object onto this object
DragOver	React to the user dragging another object over this object
DropDown	React to the user clicking on the down scroll arrow of a combo box
GotFocus	Initiate an action when this object receives the focus
KeyDown	Initiate an action when the user presses or holds a key down
KeyPress	React to the user typing an ASCII character
KeyUp	Initiate an action when the user releases a key
LostFocus	Initiate an action when this object loses the focus

Table 3-9 Events of the combo box control

Use This Method...	To Do This...
AddItem	Add an item to this control's list
Clear	Clears the contents of this control
Drag	Control manual dragging of this control
Move	Change the position of this control
Refresh	Cause this object to be updated immediately
RemoveItem	Delete items from a list
SetFocus	Move the focus to this control
ZOrder	Place this object at the front or back of the z-order

Table 3-10 Methods of the combo box control

Description

Combo boxes provide a combination of the list box and the text box objects. All combo boxes have an edit area and a list area. The currently selected item is always displayed in the edit area of a combo box. The list area, when visible, appears below the edit area. The user may choose an item from the list portion of a combo box by clicking on it or by using the ⬆ and ⬇ keys to move the reverse highlight to the desired item and pressing (ENTER). If there are more items in the list than can be displayed in the list portion of the combo box, Visual Basic automatically adds a vertical scroll bar on the right edge of the list. The user can then use this scroll bar to move up or down.

There are three types of combo boxes: the drop-down combo, the simple combo, and the drop-down list box. Setting the Style property determines which type will be used. The Style property can only be set at design time. It is a read-only property at runtime.

Setting the Style property to 0 causes a combo box to become a drop-down combo. The drop-down combo box displays the currently selected item in an edit area similar to a text box (see Figure 3-5). A down scroll arrow displays to the right of the edit area. The list portion of this combo box stays hidden until the user clicks the down scroll arrow. This causes the list of items to drop down. The user may either choose an item from the list, or type an entry in the edit area.

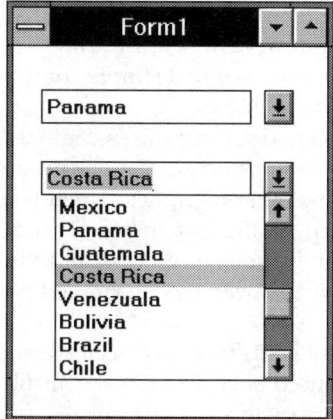

Figure 3-5 The drop-down combo box

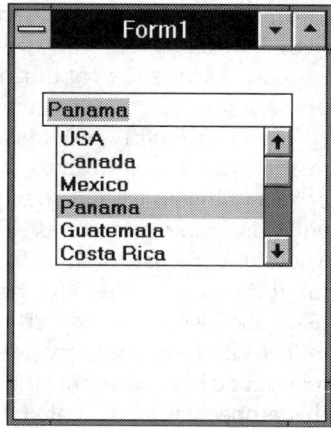

Figure 3-6 The simple combo box

Setting the Style property to 1 causes a combo box to become a simple combo. The simple combo box also has an edit area that displays the currently selected item (see Figure 3-6). The list portion of this combo box is always visible under the edit area. As with the drop-down combo, the user may either choose an item from the list or type an entry in the edit area.

Setting the Style property to 2 causes a combo box to become a drop-down list. The drop-down list box is similar in structure to the drop-down combo box. As with the drop-down combo, the list area stays hidden until the user clicks on the down scroll arrow. However, the user cannot edit the text in the edit area, but can only choose an item from the list portion of the drop-down list (see Figure 3-7).

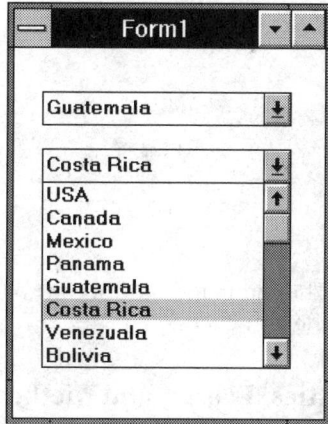

Figure 3-7 The drop-down list box

The Text property reads the text associated with the currently selected list item. If no item is currently selected, this property returns a null string. The Text property can also be set during runtime for the drop-down and simple combo boxes, but is a read-only property with the drop-down list box.

The List property provides a method for reading and setting a list's contents in a manner similar to accessing and assigning values in an array. The List property is followed by an index number in parentheses that identifies which list entry is being referenced. The index numbering of the list is zero-based. Therefore, if a list contains five items, the first item is index number 0, and the highest index number is 4. The number of items in a list can be determined by using the ListCount property.

The ListCount property determines the number of items that have been added to a combo box. Each time the AddItem method is used on a combo box control, this property is incremented. Using the RemoveItem method decrements it.

The ListIndex property returns the index number of the currently selected item in a list. If no item is currently selected, a -1 is returned. If the user enters text in the edit area of the simple or drop-down combo box, and that text does not match a listed item, this property will also return a ListIndex value of -1.

The program may also set the currently selected item of a list by setting this property. When using the ListIndex property to set the currently selected list entry, the program must use an index number that references a currently existing item in the list. For instance, if a list has five items in it, an index number of 0 to 4 must be specified, or an "Invalid property array index" error occurs.

The AddItem and RemoveItem methods add and delete items from a combo box's list, and the new Clear method clears the combo of all items.

This object is discussed in detail in Chapter 18, Lists, Combos, and Grids.

COMMAND BUTTON CONTROL

Purpose

The command button control displays a button that performs a function when the user clicks on it.

Properties, Events, and Methods

Tables 3-11, 3-12, and 3-13 list the properties, events, and methods that relate to the command button control.

Use This Property...	To Do This...
BackColor, ForeColor	Read or set the background and foreground colors of this object
Cancel	Assign a command button's Click event to the (ESC) key
Caption	Assign text to this object
Default	Assign a command button's Click event to the (ENTER) key
DragIcon	Read or set what displays when this control is dragged
DragMode	Determine whether drag operations are to occur manually or automatically
Enabled	Read or set whether this object can react to events
FontBold, FontItalic, FontStrikeThru, FontUnderline	Read or set special effects for this object's font
FontName	Read or set the name of this object's font
FontSize	Read or set the size of this object's font
Height	Read or set the height of this object
HelpContextID	Read or set the context number to this object for context-sensitive help
hWnd	Determine a handle to this object
Index	Uniquely identify an element of a control array
Left	Read or set the left edge placement of this control on a picture or form
MousePointer	Read or set the shape of the mouse pointer when it's over this object
Name	Set the name used in code to refer to this object
Parent	Read the name of the form to which this control belongs
TabIndex	Read or set the placement of this control within the form's tab order
TabStop	Read or set whether this control is part of the form's tab order

(continued on next page)

(continued from previous page)

Use This Property...	To Do This...
Tag	Read or set text information that is particular to this object
Top	Read or set the coordinate of this control's top edge
Value	Determine whether this control is chosen
Visible	Read or set whether this object is visible
Width	Read or set the width of this object

Table 3-11 Properties of the command button control

Use This Event...	To Do This...
Click	React to the user clicking on this object
DragDrop	React to the user dragging and dropping an object onto this object
DragOver	React to the user dragging another object over this object
GotFocus	Initiate an action when this object receives the focus
KeyDown	Initiate an action when the user presses or holds a key down
KeyPress	React to the user typing an ASCII character
KeyUp	Initiate an action when the user releases a key
LostFocus	Initiate an action when this object loses the focus
MouseDown	React to the user pressing any mouse button
MouseMove	React to the user moving the mouse over this object
MouseUp	React to the user releasing any mouse button

Table 3-12 Events of the command button control

Use This Method...	To Do This...
Drag	Control manual dragging of this control
Move	Change the position of this control
Refresh	Cause this object to be updated immediately
SetFocus	Move the focus to this control
ZOrder	Place this object at the front or back of the z-order

Table 3-13 Methods of the command button control

Description

A command button is an object that represents a task to be performed. Pressing the button activates the associated task.

The user can press a button by clicking on it, or by pressing the (ENTER) key or the spacebar while the button has the focus. Doing so initiates the command button's Click event. This event defines the actions to take when the button is pressed.

The Caption property defines the text displayed on the button (see Figure 3-8). The size and style of this text is defined by the settings of the Font... properties. Including an ampersand (&) underlines the following letter, and the button can be selected by holding down the (ALT) key and pressing that letter. For instance, if the button's Caption property is set to &Cash, the displayed text will be "Cash" and the user can select the box by pressing (ALT)-(C).

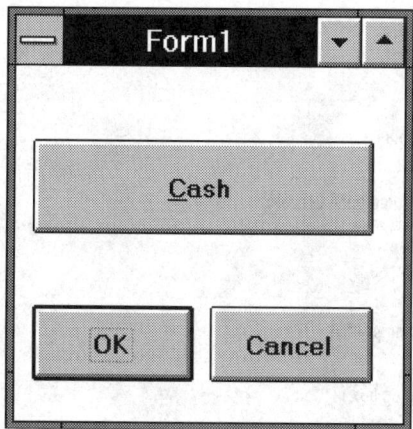

Figure 3-8 Normal, default, and cancel command buttons

In most cases a form has one command button that performs the default action for that form. The Default property allows you to assign that default action to the (ENTER) key so that pressing (ENTER) has the same effect as clicking on the command button. This property can either be set to True (-1) or False (0) by you at design time, or by the application during runtime. Because only one button on a form may be the default, setting this property to True for one button automatically sets it to False for all the other buttons on the same form.

Sometimes it is necessary to give the user a way to back out of, or cancel, an operation. The Cancel property allows the programmer to assign that cancel action to the (ESC) key. This property can either be set to True (-1) or False (0) by you at design time, or by the application during runtime. Because only one button on a form may be the cancel button, setting this property to True for one button automatically sets it to False for all the other buttons on the same form.

The Default and Cancel properties are covered in greater detail in Chapter 16, Keyboard Input.

COMMON DIALOG

Purpose

The common dialog control provides an easy way to produce standard dialog boxes like File Open, File Save, Print, Select Font, and Choose Color.

Properties, Events, and Methods

Table 3-14 lists the properties for the common dialog control. It has no events or methods.

Use This Property...	To Do This...
Action	Specify the type of dialog box to display
CancelError	Determine whether an error is generated upon Cancel
Color	Read or set the selected color
Copies	Read or set the number of copies to be printed
DefaultExt	Set the default extension for the dialog box
DialogTitle	Set the caption of the dialog box's title bar

Use This Property...	To Do This...
FileName	Read or set the path and name of the file to open or save
FileTitle	Read the name of the file to open or save
Filter	Set or read the file filter specification in File Open and Save As
FilterIndex	Set or read the default file filter
Flags	Sets various options for each dialog box
FontBold, FontItalic, FontStrikeThru, FontUnderline	Read or set special effects for this object's font
FontName	Read or set the name of this object's font
FontSize	Read or set the size of this object's font
FromPage, ToPage	Read or set the values of the Print From and To
hDC	Read the Windows device handle for this object
HelpCommand	Set the kind of help requested
HelpContext	Set the context number for context-sensitive help
HelpFile	Set the name of the Help file to display
HelpKey	Set the keyword for the Help file to search for
InitDir	Set the initial file directory
Min, Max	Set the smallest and largest fonts displayed
Min, Max	Set the smallest and largest page numbers to be printed
MaxFileSize	Set the maximum length of the file name given in the FileName property
PrinterDefault	Determine whether changes in Print dialog change default printer settings

Table 3-14 Properties of the common dialog control

Description

The common dialog control gives you easy access to the most commonly used dialog boxes. This saves you from having to re-create standard dialog boxes for every application. The Action property determines which kind of dialog box to display and immediately displays it. There are six styles of dialog box: Open, Save As, Color, Font, Printer, and Help.

The Open dialog box has areas for file name, directories, drives, and default file types. The Save As dialog looks identical to Open, except for its caption. The Color dialog allows the user to select a color from a palette or from a custom color-picker. This is the same box as is used in the Windows Control Panel Desktop color choice. The Font dialog displays a list of all available fonts, and shows an example of the selected font. The Printer box allows the user to choose printers, page defaults, and page print ranges.

The Action setting for Help runs WINHELP.EXE rather than calling up a dialog box. This gives you a simple way to call up your custom help file for your application. The HelpFile, HelpKey, HelpCommand, and HelpContext let you pass the appropriate information to the Help program to pull up general help, context-sensitive help, or the help Search dialog. Custom Help files can be created in the Professional edition of Visual Basic.

The CancelError property sets whether the dialog box returns an error if the user chooses the Cancel button. Your code can then test for this error and take appropriate action.

See Chapter 17, Dialog Boxes, for more information on this versatile control.

DATA CONTROL

Purpose

The data control introduced in version 3.0 lets you access databases and display the information in bound controls. The data control uses the same database engine that powers Microsoft Access. This gives you the capacity to work with databases in a variety of formats, including Access, Btrieve, dBase, Paradox, and SQL.

Properties, Events, and Methods

Tables 3-15, 3-16, and 3-17 list the properties, events, and methods that relate to the data control.

Use This Property...	To Do This...
BackColor, ForeColor	Read or set the background and foreground colors of this object
Caption	Assign text to this object
Connect	Read or set information to open or attach to an external database
Database	Reference the associated Database object
DatabaseName	Read or set the name and location of the database
EditMode	Read the editing state of the current record
Enabled	Read or set whether this object can react to events
Exclusive	Read or set whether database is single user or multiuser
FontBold, FontItalic, FontStrikeThru, FontUnderline	Read or set special effects for this object's font
FontName	Read or set the name of this object's font
FontSize	Read or set the size of this object's font
Height	Read or set the height of this object
Index	Uniquely identify an element of a control array
Left	Read or set the left edge placement of this control on a picture or form
MousePointer	Read or set the shape of the mouse pointer when it's over this object
Name	Set the name used in code to refer to this object
Options	Read or set characteristics of the control's Dynaset
ReadOnly	Determine whether the database is opened for read-only access
Recordset	Access the underlying recordset object
RecordSource	Specify the current table, SQL statement, or QueryDef for the recordset

(continued on next page)

(continued from previous page)

Use This Property...	To Do This...
Tag	Read or set text information that is particular to this object
Top	Read or set the coordinate of this control's top edge
Value	Determine whether this control is chosen
Width	Read or set the width of this object

Table 3-15 Properties of the data control

Use This Event...	To Do This...
DragDrop	React to the user dragging and dropping an object onto this object
DragOver	React to the user dragging another object over this object
Error	React to errors in reading data
MouseDown	React to the user pressing any mouse button
MouseMove	React to the user moving the mouse over this object
MouseUp	React to the user releasing any mouse button
Reposition	React to when a new record becomes current
Validate	Initiate an action before a different record becomes current

Table 3-16 Events of the data control

Use This Method...	To Do This...
Drag	Control manual dragging of this control
Move	Change the position of this control or form
ZOrder	Place this object at the front or back of the z-order

Table 3-17 Methods of the data control

Description

Many applications work with data. The data control lets your application perform sophisticated database manipulation without writing any code at all. The control inherits the capability to create new records, delete old ones, move from record to record, maintain referential integrity, create virtual query tables (called Dynasets or Recordsets), maintain indexes, and immediately update bound controls. (Visual Basic also includes DATAMGR.EXE, a program that lets you create databases compatible with the data control and Access.)

It does all this by using the database engine from Microsoft Access. If you're familiar with Access, you'll find working with the data control very natural. Even if you've never used Access (or any other database), the data control makes working with databases much easier than trying to develop the thousands of lines of code yourself. Many simple database applications can be written with virtually no code other than that for the user interface by using the data control.

To use the data control, set the DatabaseName property to the full path and name of the underlying database. Set the RecordSource property to the name of the table within the database you want to use. Then use any data aware control (text box, check box, image, label, and picture box from the Standard version of Visual Basic, plus the masked edit, 3D panel, and 3D check box from the Professional version) to display and edit the underlying information.

These data aware controls are *bound* to the data control by setting their DataSource, DataField, and DataChanged properties. Once bound, each control automatically displays data from the current record for the field indicated by their DataField property. All bound controls are automatically updated each time the data control moves to a new record. Changes made by the user in a bound control are automatically saved in the database when the data control moves to a new record. Figure 3-9 shows the data control and two bound text boxes.

The data control's Database and Recordset properties actually refer to the control's underlying Database object and Dynaset object. Both of these objects have properties and methods of their own that allow you to manipulate your data. These are discussed more thoroughly in Chapter 27, Data Access.

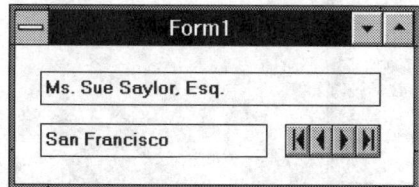

Figure 3-9 The data control lets you easily manipulate external databases

DEBUG OBJECT

Purpose

The Debug object uses the Print method to send output to the Debug window when a program is run under the Visual Basic environment. This output can help you track down and fix problems with your program.

Properties, Events, and Methods

Table 3-18 lists the method that relates to the Debug object. This object has no associated properties or events.

Use This Method...	To Do This...
Print	Print text on the Debug window

Table 3-18 The one Debug method

Description

The Debug window automatically opens when a program runs under the Visual Basic environment. While in run mode, the program can send text to this window by executing the Print method with the Debug object. This is generally used to check the value of a variable at a specific point in a program. For instance, the following code will send the value of the variable $A\%$ to the Debug window:

```
Debug.Print A%
```

This object is covered in greater detail in Appendix C, Debugging Techniques. See Figure 3-10 for a brief illustration of it.

```
┌──────────────────────────────────────┐
│─        Debug Window [Form1.frm]      │
│ ♂ [Form1.frm] Text1.Text = "Bill Potter": 0 │
├──────────────────────────────────────┤
│ ?text1.text                         ▲│
│ Ms. Sue Saylor, Esq.                 │
│ ?data1.recordsource                  │
│ Entry                                │
│ ?235 × 47                            │
│  11045                              ▼│
└──────────────────────────────────────┘
```

Figure 3-10 The Debug window, showing the Watch pane and the Immediate pane

DIRECTORY LIST BOX CONTROL

Purpose

The Directory list box control displays a list box from which the user can navigate through all the directories on the selected disk drive.

Properties, Events, and Methods

Tables 3-19, 3-20, and 3-21 list the properties, events, and methods that relate to the Directory list box control.

Use This Property...	To Do This...
BackColor, ForeColor	Read or set the background and foreground colors of this object
DragIcon	Read or set what displays when this control is dragged
DragMode	Determine whether drag operations are to occur manually or automatically
Enabled	Read or set whether this object can react to events
FontBold, FontItalic, FontStrikeThru, FontUnderline	Read or set special effects for this object's font
FontName	Read or set the name of this object's font
FontSize	Read or set the size of this object's font
Height	Read or set the height of this object
HelpContextID	Read or set the context number to this object for context-sensitive help
hWnd	Determine a handle to this object
Index	Uniquely identify an element of a control array
Left	Read or set the left edge placement of this control on a picture or form
List	Read the value of a listed item

(continued on next page)

(continued from previous page)

Use This Property...	To Do This...
ListCount	Read the number of items in a list
ListIndex	Read or set the index of the currently selected item in a list
MousePointer	Read or set the shape of the mouse pointer when it's over this object
Name	Set the name used in code to refer to this object
Parent	Read the name of the form to which this control belongs
Path	Read or set the currently selected directory path
TabIndex	Read or set the placement of this control within the form's tab order
TabStop	Read or set whether this control is part of the form's tab order
Tag	Read or set text information that is particular to this object
Top	Read or set the coordinate of this control's top edge
Visible	Read or set whether this object is visible
Width	Read or set the width of this object

Table 3-19 Properties of the Directory list box control

Use This Event...	To Do This...
Change	React to the user choosing a new directory, or a change in the Path property
Click	React to the user clicking on this object
DragDrop	React to the user dragging and dropping an object onto this object
DragOver	React to the user dragging another object over this object
GotFocus	Initiate an action when this object receives the focus

Use This Event...	To Do This...
KeyDown	Initiate an action when the user presses or holds a key down
KeyPress	React to the user typing an ASCII character
KeyUp	Initiate an action when the user releases a key
LostFocus	Initiate an action when this object loses the focus
MouseDown	React to the user pressing any mouse button
MouseMove	React to the user moving the mouse over this object
MouseUp	React to the user releasing any mouse button

Table 3-20 Events of the Directory list box control

Use This Method...	To Do This...
Drag	Control manual dragging of this control
Move	Change the position of this control or form
Refresh	Cause this object to be updated immediately
SetFocus	Move the focus to this control
ZOrder	Place this object at the front or back of the z-order

Table 3-21 Methods of the Directory list box control

Description

The Directory list box displays a hierarchical directory tree in a box. Each directory entry displays a small folder icon next to the name of the directory (see Figure 3-11). This object gives the user a method for navigating the DOS file system when used in conjunction with the Drive and File list box objects.

The top of the displayed directory tree represents the root directory of the drive currently selected for that directory box. Each subdirectory that is part of

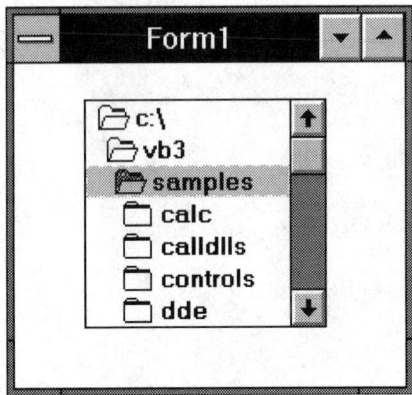

Figure 3-11 The Directory list box

the path to the current directory displays underneath the root. The folder icons for these directories display as open folders. Also displayed are all subdirectories that are one level below the current directory. The folder icons for these directories display as closed.

The user may select a different directory by clicking on its entry in the box. This sets the ListIndex property to the selected directory. However, this does not change the current directory for the list box. To change the current directory, the user must double-click on an entry. This not only changes the ListIndex property for the box, but it also changes the Path property to the new directory. You can also set these properties directly in your code. In that case the directory list box visually reflects these changes.

The Path property sets or reads the current drive and path for the directory list box. Whenever the Path property changes, the directory list box's Change event activates. This event is used so the program can react to the user changing the current directory.

See Chapter 19, File System Controls, for more information on the use of the Directory list box control.

DRIVE LIST BOX CONTROL

Purpose

The Drive list box control displays a drop-down list box that allows the user to choose an available disk drive.

Properties, Events, and Methods

Tables 3-22, 3-23, and 3-24 list the properties, events, and methods that relate to the Drive list box control.

Use This Property...	To Do This...
BackColor, ForeColor	Read or set the background and foreground colors of this object
DragIcon	Read or set what displays when this control is dragged
DragMode	Determine whether drag operations are to occur manually or automatically
Drive	Read or set the current selected drive
Enabled	Read or set whether this object can react to events
FontBold, FontItalic, FontStrikeThru, FontUnderline	Read or set special effects for this object's font
FontName	Read or set the name of this object's font
FontSize	Read or set the size of this object's font
Height	Read or set the height of this object
HelpContextID	Read or set the context number to this object for context-sensitive help
hWnd	Determine a handle to this object
Index	Uniquely identify an element of a control array
Left	Read or set the left edge placement of this control on a picture or form
List	Read the value of a listed item
ListCount	Read the number of items in a list
ListIndex	Read or set the index of the currently selected item in a list
MousePointer	Read or set the shape of the mouse pointer when it's over this object

(continued on next page)

(continued from previous page)

Use This Property...	To Do This...
Name	Set the name used in code to refer to this object
Parent	Read the name of the form to which this control belongs
TabIndex	Read or set the placement of this control within the form's tab order
TabStop	Read or set whether this control is part of the form's tab order
Tag	Read or set text information that is particular to this object
Top	Read or set the coordinate of this control's top edge
Visible	Read or set whether this object is visible
Width	Read or set the width of this object

Table 3-22 Properties of the Drive list box control

Use This Event...	To Do This...
Change	React to the user or code changing the Drive property
DragDrop	React to the user dragging and dropping an object onto this object
DragOver	React to the user dragging another object over this object
GotFocus	Initiate an action when this object receives the focus
KeyDown	Initiate an action when the user presses or holds a key down
KeyPress	React to the user typing an ASCII character
KeyUp	Initiate an action when the user releases a key
LostFocus	Initiate an action when this object loses the focus

Table 3-23 Events of the Drive list box control

Use This Method...	To Do This...
Drag	Control manual dragging of this control
Move	Change the position of this control or form
Refresh	Cause this object to be updated immediately
SetFocus	Move the focus to this control
ZOrder	Place this object at the front or back of the z-order

Table 3-24 Methods of the Drive list box control

Description

The Drive list box, used in conjunction with the Directory and File list boxes, gives the user a way to navigate the DOS file system. It is a drop-down list box in which the current drive displays in the text area (see Figure 3-12). When the user clicks on the down scroll arrow of the box, a list of drives available to the user's system drops down. The user may change the current drive by clicking on one of the listed entries.

When the program starts running, Visual Basic automatically explores the user's system and adds all of the floppy, fixed, and network drives to the list. Drive list items that reflect local fixed disks will also display that disk's label with the drive letter. For network drives, the network name of the drive is also displayed.

The Drive property may be used to set or read the current drive. Changing this property, either by user input or by instructions in the program, activates the Change event.

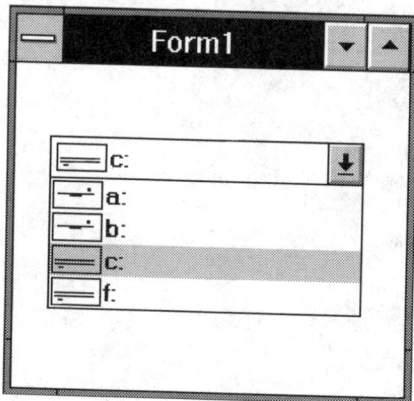

Figure 3-12 The Drive list box

If the program is being run on a network, the Refresh method can be used to update the entries for this control. This will cause the list entries to reflect changes in shared drives.

See Chapter 19, File System Controls, for more information on the Drive list box control.

FILE LIST BOX CONTROL

Purpose

The File list box control displays a list box that lists the files in a specific directory and allows the user to select a file for further operations.

Properties, Events, and Methods

Tables 3-25, 3-26, and 3-27 list the properties, events, and methods that relate to the File list box control.

Use This Property...	To Do This...
Archive	Read or set whether files with their archive bit set will be displayed
BackColor, ForeColor	Read or set the background and foreground colors of this object
DragIcon	Read or set what displays when this control is dragged
DragMode	Determine whether drag operations are to occur manually or automatically
Enabled	Read or set whether this object can react to events
FileName	Read or set the current selected file
FontBold, FontItalic, FontStrikeThru, FontUnderline	Read or set special effects for the font used with this object
FontName	Read or set the name of this object's font
FontSize	Read or set the size of this object's font
Height	Read or set the height of this object

Use This Property...	To Do This...
HelpContextID	Read or set the context number to this object for context-sensitive help
Hidden	Read or set whether files with their hidden bit set will be displayed
hWnd	Determine a handle to this object
Index	Uniquely identify an element of a control array
Left	Read or set the left edge placement of this control on a picture or form
List	Read the value of a listed item
ListCount	Read the number of items in a list
ListIndex	Read or set the index of the currently selected item in a list
MousePointer	Read or set the shape of the mouse pointer when it's over this object
MultiSelect	Determines whether a user can make multiple selections in the list
Name	Set the name used in code to refer to this object
Normal	Read or set whether to display files with system and hidden bits off
Parent	Read the name of the form to which this control belongs
Path	Read or set the currently selected path
Pattern	Read or set the file name pattern
ReadOnly	Read or set whether files with their read-only bits set will be displayed
Selected	Read the selection status of an item in the list
System	Read or set whether files with their system bits set will be displayed
TabIndex	Read or set the placement of this control within the form's tab order
TabStop	Read or set whether this control is part of the form's tab order

(continued on next page)

(continued from previous page)

Use This Property...	To Do This...
Tag	Read or set text information that is particular to this object
Top	Read or set the coordinate of this control's top edge
TopIndex	Read which item in the list appears in the topmost position
Visible	Read or set whether this object is visible
Width	Read or set the width of this object

Table 3-25 Properties of the File list box control

Use This Event...	To Do This...
Click	React to the user clicking on this object
DblClick	React to the user double-clicking on this object
DragDrop	React to the user dragging and dropping an object onto this object
DragOver	React to the user dragging another object over this object
GotFocus	Initiate an action when this object receives the focus
KeyDown	Initiate an action when the user presses or holds a key down
KeyPress	React to the user typing an ASCII character
KeyUp	Initiate an action when the user releases a key
LostFocus	Initiate an action when this object loses the focus
MouseDown	React to the user pressing any mouse button
MouseMove	React to the user moving the mouse over this object
MouseUp	React to the user releasing any mouse button

Use This Event...	To Do This...
PathChange	Initiate an action when the current path of a File list box has changed
PatternChange	Initiate an action when the file pattern of a File list box has changed

Table 3-26 Events of the File list box control

Use This Method...	To Do This...
Drag	Control manual dragging of this control
Move	Change the position of this control or form
Refresh	Cause this object to be updated immediately
SetFocus	Move the focus to this control
ZOrder	Place this object at the front or back of the z-order

Table 3-27 Methods of the File list box control

Description

The File list box, used in conjunction with the drive and directory list boxes, gives the user a way to navigate the DOS file system. This control lists all the files in the directory specified by the control's Path property (see Figure 3-13). The files that

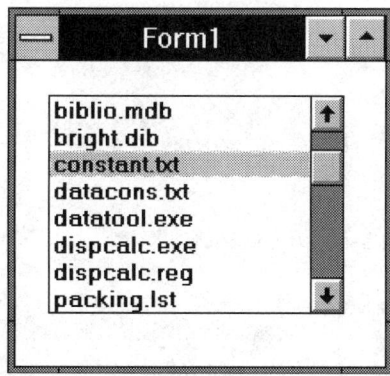

Figure 3-13 The File list box

are displayed are also limited to those whose file names match the control's Pattern property and whose attributes match the Archive, Hidden, ReadOnly, and System properties.

The Path property sets or reads the directory path for the files to be displayed. It is not available during design time. At the start of the program, it defaults to the current default directory. If the Path property changes, the PathChange event will be activated.

The Pattern property defines a subset of files within the directory specified by the Path property. This property consists of any full or partial file name, and can contain the wild card characters * and ? that match file names according to the standard rules for DOS.

The currently selected file in a list box may be read or set by using the FileName property. This property is changed any time the user clicks on a new file name within the file list box.

The File list box control and its related properties, methods, and events are covered in Chapter 19, File System Controls.

FORM OBJECT

Purpose

The Form object defines a visual work area on the Windows desktop on which you can arrange controls. Forms can be used to set up any windows, dialogs, or message boxes that are required for a program.

Properties, Events, and Methods

Tables 3-28, 3-29, and 3-30 list the properties, events, and methods that relate to the Form object.

Use This Property...	To Do This...
ActiveControl	Read which control has the focus
ActiveForm	Read which form is active
AutoReDraw	Read or set whether graphic pictures will be redrawn automatically
BackColor, ForeColor	Read or set the background and foreground colors of this object
BorderStyle	Determine whether this object has a border, and if it does, set its style

Use This Property...	To Do This...
Caption	Assign text to the title bar of this object
ClipControls	Determine whether graphic methods repaint entire object
ControlBox	Determine if this control box displays on a form
Count	Determine the number of loaded forms
CurrentX, CurrentY	Read or set the current graphics position on this object
DrawMode	Read or set the appearance of drawings by graphics methods
DrawStyle	Read or set the style of lines drawn by graphics methods
DrawWidth	Read or set the size of lines drawn by graphics methods
Enabled	Read or set whether this object can react to events
FillColor	Read or set the color used by graphics methods for fill-in effects
FillStyle	Read or set the pattern used by graphics methods for fill-in effects
FontBold, FontItalic, FontStrikeThru, FontName	Read or set the name of this object's font
FontSize	Read or set the size of this object's font
FontTransparent, FontUnderline	Read or set special effects for this object's font
hDC	Read the Windows device context handle for this object
Height	Read or set the height of this object
HelpContextID	Read or set the context number to this object for context-sensitive help
hWnd	Determine a handle to this object
Icon	Read or set the icon used when a form is minimized
Image	Read the Windows device handle for this object's persistent bitmap

(continued on next page)

(continued from previous page)

Use This Property...	To Do This...
KeyPreview	Read or set when form keyboard events are processed
Left	Read or set the left edge placement of this control on a picture or form
LinkMode	Read or set a DDE conversation to hot, cold, or none
LinkTopic	Read or set the topic of a DDE conversation
MaxButton	Read or set whether a Maximize button will appear on a form
MDIChild	Read or set whether a form is an MDIChild form
MinButton	Read or set whether a Minimize button will appear on a form
MousePointer	Read or set the shape of the mouse pointer when it's over this object
Name	Set the name used in code to refer to this object
Picture	Read or assign a graphic image to a picture or form
ScaleHeight	Read or set the number of units that define the height of this object
ScaleLeft	Read or set the coordinates for the left edge of this object
ScaleMode	Read or set the unit of measurement used to place and size objects
ScaleTop	Read or set the coordinates for the top edge of this object
ScaleWidth	Read or set the number of units that define the width of this object
Tag	Read or set text information that is particular to this object
Top	Read or set the coordinate of this control's top edge
Visible	Read or set whether this object is visible
Width	Read or set the width of this object
WindowState	Read or set whether a form is maximized, minimized, or normal

Table 3-28 Properties of the Form object

Use This Event...	To Do This...
Activate	React to when this object becomes activated either by code or by user
Click	React to the user clicking on this object
DblClick	React to the user double-clicking on this object
Deactivate	React to when this object becomes deactivated either by code or by user
DragDrop	React to the user dragging and dropping an object onto this object
DragOver	React to the user dragging another object over this object
GotFocus	Initiate an action when this object receives the focus
KeyDown	Initiate an action when the user presses or holds a key down
KeyPress	React to the user typing an ASCII character
KeyUp	Initiate an action when the user releases a key
LinkClose	React to the termination of a DDE conversation
LinkError	React to an error in a DDE conversation
LinkExecute	React to a DDE Execute command from a DDE client application
LinkOpen	React to the initiation of a DDE conversation
Load	Initiate an action when a form is first loaded into memory
LostFocus	Initiate an action when this object loses the focus
MouseDown	React to the user pressing any mouse button
MouseMove	React to the user moving the mouse over this object
MouseUp	React to the user releasing any mouse button
Paint	Initiate an action when a form or picture needs to be redrawn

(continued on next page)

(continued from previous page)

Use This Method...	To Do This...
QueryUnload	React to an attempt to unload the form
Resize	Initiate an action when a form is first displayed or its size is changed
Unload	Initiate an action when a form is removed from memory

Table 3-29 Events of the Form object

Use This Method...	To Do This...
Circle	Create a circle or ellipse on a form or picture box
Cls	Clear graphics and text that have been drawn on the form at runtime
Hide	Make a form invisible
Line	Draw a line on a form or picture
Move	Change the position of this control or form
Point	Return the color setting of a specified point on a form or picture box
Print	Print text on a form or picture box
PrintForm	Send a copy of a form to the printer
Pset	Set the color of a specified point on a form or picture box
Refresh	Cause this object to be updated immediately
Scale	Define the coordinate system used for the form
SetFocus	Move the focus to this form
Show	Display a previously hidden form
TextHeight	Return the height of text in this object's font

Use This Method...	To Do This...
TextWidth	Return the width of text in this object's font
ZOrder	Place this object at the front or back of the z-order

Table 3-30 Methods of the Form object

Description

A form is a window that you create to use as the screen area for an operation in your program. A program can have one or more forms. Each form represents a window in your program (see Figure 3-14). You can then use Visual Basic's Toolbox to draw controls, such as command buttons, text, and check boxes, on the form (see Figure 3-15). You can create a variety of effects by choosing appropriate controls and manipulating their properties (see Figure 3-16).

Forms define a logical, as well as visual, portion of your program. Each form has its own separate code area. Any procedures entered into a form's code area are local to that form, and cannot be accessed by routines in other forms or code modules. The code portion of a form can contain three types of program code: the General Declarations area, programmer-defined procedures, and object-related events.

A form's General Declarations area declares variables, arrays, and constants. Items declared in this area will be accessible to any program code that also

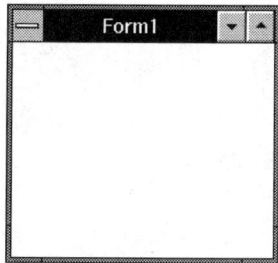

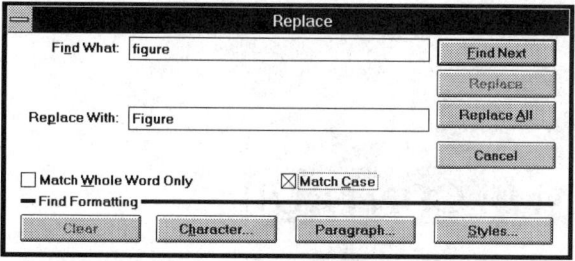

Figure 3-14 A blank form

Figure 3-15 A search and replace dialog box created from a form

> We created this unique form by setting the control box, minimize button, and maximize button to False. We then set the caption to null to get rid of the Title bar, and set the border to single.

Figure 3-16 A simple message box created with a form

105

resides in the code area of the same form. Procedures that are contained in other forms will not be able to use these variables or constants.

Programmer-defined sub procedures and functions are self-contained procedures that you write to handle specific tasks or return certain values. Refer to Appendix A, Visual Basic Language Tutorial, for more on the use of language elements and the definition and use of sub procedures as well as an explanation of *scoping*, or where the variables you create are visible to other procedures.

The program code for each of a form's related events is placed in the form's code area. The event procedures for any controls that have been drawn on a form are also placed in the form's code area.

Each form has a name by which it may be referenced. This name is set at design time, and is specified by the Name property. This property is not available at runtime; however, the name you assign to it at design time is the same name you use to reference the form within your program's code. For more information on referencing forms, see Chapter 6, Accessing Forms and Controls.

The Load and Unload statements load and erase a form from memory at runtime. Loading a form does not automatically display it. This is done with the Show method. If the Unload statement is used on a form, and that form is the only form remaining in memory for that project, the program is ended.

The Show method will display a form that had been previously hidden or not yet displayed. This method also determines if a form is to be modal or modeless. A modal form does not allow any other window on the desktop to receive the focus until it is closed. A modeless form places no restrictions on where the focus goes. A form may be hidden with the Hide method.

Refer to Chapter 4, Forms and Menus, for more information on this object.

FRAME CONTROL

Purpose

The frame control visually groups controls that are functionally related.

Properties, Events, and Methods

Tables 3-31, 3-32, and 3-33 list the properties, events, and methods that relate to the frame control.

Use This Property...	To Do This...
BackColor, ForeColor	Read or set the background and foreground colors of this object
Caption	Assign text to this object
ClipControls	Determine whether graphic methods repaint entire object
DragIcon	Read or set what displays when this control is dragged
DragMode	Determine whether drag operations are to occur manually or automatically
Enabled	Read or set whether this object can react to events
FontBold, FontItalic, FontStrikeThru, FontUnderline	Read or set special effects for this object's font
FontName	Read or set the name of this object's font
FontSize	Read or set the size of this object's font
Height	Read or set the height of this object
HelpContextID	Read or set the context number to this object for context-sensitive help
hWnd	Determine a handle to this object
Index	Uniquely identify an element of a control array
Left	Read or set the left edge placement of this control on a picture or form
MousePointer	Read or set the shape of the mouse pointer when it's over this object
Name	Set the name used in code to refer to this object
Parent	Read the name of the form to which this control belongs
TabIndex	Read or set the placement of this control within the form's tab order
Tag	Read or set text information that is particular to this object
Top	Read or set the coordinate of this control's top edge

(continued on next page)

(continued from previous page)

Use This Property...	To Do This...
Visible	Read or set whether this object is visible
Width	Read or set the width of this object

Table 3-31 Properties of the frame control

Use This Event...	To Do This...
DragDrop	React to the user dragging and dropping an object onto this object
DragOver	React to the user dragging another object over this object

Table 3-32 Events of the frame control

Use This Method...	To Do This...
Click	React to the user clicking on this object
DblClick	React to the user double-clicking on this object
Drag	Control manual dragging of this control
MouseDown	React to the user pressing any mouse button
MouseMove	React to the user moving the mouse over this object
MouseUp	React to the user releasing any mouse button
Move	Change the position of this control or form
Refresh	Cause this object to be updated immediately
ZOrder	Place this object at the front or back of the z-order

Table 3-33 Methods of the frame control

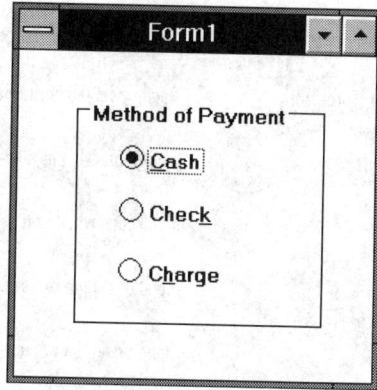

Figure 3-17 The frame control encasing three option buttons

Description

You may draw a frame on a form, and then draw other controls on the frame. This visually groups the controls together. If the frame is moved to a new location on the form, its controls move with it.

When option button controls are placed on a frame (see Figure 3-17), not only are they visually grouped together, but they become logically grouped as well. When several option buttons share a frame, they become mutually exclusive. That is to say, when one button is selected, all the other buttons in the same frame get unselected. This is how you can create "radio buttons."

If you wish to place controls on a frame, the frame must be drawn first. Any controls that are to be within the frame must then be drawn on it. You cannot move an already drawn control onto a frame except by choosing the Edit menu's Cut and Paste commands to paste the control onto the frame.

A title may be displayed at the upper-left corner of the frame by setting its Caption property.

GRID CONTROL

Purpose

The grid control displays a series of rows and columns, with individual cells at the intersections. Although there is no spreadsheet intelligence built in, the grid control is very similar to the way a spreadsheet is laid out.

Properties, Events, and Methods

Tables 3-34, 3-35, and 3-36 list the properties, events, and methods of the grid control.

Use This Property...	To Do This...
BackColor, ForeColor	Read or set the background and foreground colors of this object
BorderStyle	Determine whether this object has a border and, if it does, set its style
CellSelected	Determine whether a cell is currently selected
Clip	Read or set the contents of the cells in a selected region
Col, Row	Read or set the active cell
ColAlignment	Read or set the alignment of a column's data
Cols, Rows	Read or set the total number of columns or rows
ColWidth	Read or set the width of a column
DragIcon	Read or set what displays when this control is dragged
DragMode	Determine whether drag operations are to occur manually or automatically
Enabled	Read or set whether this object can react to events
FillStyle	Read or set how text is assigned to a range of cells
FixedAlignment	Read or set the alignment of data in the fixed cells of a column
FixedCols, FixedRows	Read or set the number of fixed rows or columns on the left and top
FontBold, FontItalic, FontStrikeThru, FontUnderline	Read or set special effects for this object's font
FontName	Read or set the name of this object's font
FontSize	Read or set the size of this object's font
Gridlines	Read or set whether the gridlines are visible
Height	Read or set the height of this object
HelpContextID	Read or set the context number to this object for context-sensitive help

Use This Property...	To Do This...
HighLight	Read or set whether the selected cells appear highlighted
hWnd	Determine a handle to this object
Index	Uniquely identify an element of a control array
Left	Read or set the left edge placement of this control on a picture or form
LeftCol	Read or set the leftmost visible nonfixed column
Name	Set the name used in code to refer to this object
Parent	Read the name of the form to which this control belongs
Picture	Read or assign a graphic image to a cell
RowHeight	Read or set the height of the specified row
ScrollBars	Determine whether scroll bars appear in a multiple-line text box
SelEndCol, SelEndRow, SelStartCol, SelStartRow	Read or set the starting or ending row or column
TabIndex	Read or set the placement of this control within the form's tab order
TabStop	Read or set whether this control is part of the form's tab order
Tag	Read or set text information that is particular to this object
Text	Read or set the text in a cell or a range of cells
Top	Read or set the coordinate of this control's top edge
TopRow	Read or set the topmost nonfixed row
Visible	Read or set whether this object is visible
Width	Read or set the width of this object

Table 3-34 Properties of the grid control

Use This Event...	To Do This...
Click	React to the user clicking on this object
DblClick	React to the user double-clicking on this object
DragDrop	React to the user dragging and dropping an object onto this object
DragOver	React to the user dragging another object over this object
GotFocus	Initiate an action when this object receives the focus
KeyDown	Initiate an action when the user presses or holds a key down
KeyPress	React to the user typing an ASCII character
KeyUp	Initiate an action when the user releases a key
LostFocus	Initiate an action when this object loses the focus
MouseDown	React to the user pressing any mouse button
MouseMove	React to the user moving the mouse over this object
MouseUp	React to the user releasing any mouse button
RowColChange	React to the user changing to a different cell
SelChange	React to the user changing selection to a different range of cells

Table 3-35 Events of the grid control

Use This Method...	To Do This...
AddItem	Add a new row
Drag	Control manual dragging of this control
Move	Change the position of this control or form

Use This Method...	To Do This...
Refresh	Cause this object to be updated immediately
RemoveItem	Remove a row
SetFocus	Move the focus to this control
ZOrder	Place this object at the front or back of the z-order

Table 3-36 Methods of the grid control

Description

The grid control allows you to set up display structures similar to a spreadsheet. Rows and columns intersect to form individual cells. These cells may have their contents changed independently, and may be selected individually or as a region. You also have the facility to create fixed rows and columns, which would be familiar to spreadsheet users as Row and Column heads (A1, B3, etc). For an example of a grid control see Figure 3-18.

Although the grid control looks similar to a spreadsheet, it has no inherent calculation properties. It is merely a collection of cells that you may manipulate with code, and that the user may interact with. One vital difference between the grid control and a spreadsheet is that the user may not directly change the contents of a cell. Your program code can change the contents; so with some additional programming, you can simulate most behaviors of a spreadsheet.

The grid control can be used for any task that requires displaying data in rows and columns. Although a spreadsheet is the most familiar metaphor, there are

%	3 Years	4 Years	5 Years
3.5%	$263.72	$201.20	$163.73
4.0%	$265.72	$203.21	$165.75
4.5%	$267.72	$205.23	$167.79
5.0%	$269.74	$207.26	$169.84
5.5%	$271.76	$209.31	$171.91
6.0%	$273.80	$211.37	$174.00
6.5%	$275.84	$213.43	$176.10
7.0%	$277.89	$215.52	$178.21
7.5%	$279.96	$217.61	$180.34
8.0%	$282.03	$219.72	$182.49
8.5%	$284.11	$221.83	$184.65
9.0%	$286.20	$223.97	$186.83
9.5%	$288.30	$226.11	$189.02
10.0%	$290.40	$228.26	$191.22

Figure 3-18 The grid control

many other possibilities: database tables, general ledger "printouts," and even multiple-column pick lists.

The most direct way of changing the contents of a cell is with its Text property. The Text property applies to whatever cell is at the intersection of the Rows and Cols properties. If the FillStyle property is 1, then the text is applied to all cells whose CellSelected property is True, regardless of the Rows and Cols settings.

IMAGE CONTROL

Purpose

Use the image control to define an area to display a picture. The image control repaints faster and uses less system resources than the picture control, but only has a subset of the picture control's properties.

Properties, Events, and Methods

Tables 3-37, 3-38, and 3-39 list the properties, events, and methods that relate to the image control.

Use This Property...	To Do This...
BorderStyle	Determine whether this object has a border and, if it does, set its style
DataChanged	Determine if the value displayed in this object has changed
DataField	Read or set the name of a field in the recordset of the data control
DataSource	Set the name of the data control to which this object is bound
DragIcon	Read or set what displays when this control is dragged
DragMode	Determine whether drag operations are to occur manually or automatically
Enabled	Read or set whether this object can react to events
Height	Read or set the height of this object
Image	Read the Windows device handle for a picture's persistent bitmap
Index	Uniquely identify an element of a control array

Use This Property...	To Do This...
Left	Read or set the left edge placement of this control on a picture or form
MousePointer	Read or set the shape of the mouse pointer when it's over this object
Name	Set the name used in code to refer to this object
Parent	Read the name of the form to which this control belongs
Picture	Read or assign a graphic image to a picture or form
Stretch	Determine if the picture is resized to fit the control or vice versa
Tag	Read or set text information that is particular to this object
Top	Read or set the coordinate of this control's top edge
Visible	Read or set whether an object is visible
Width	Read or set the width of this object

Table 3-37 Properties of the image control

Use This Event...	To Do This...
Click	React to the user clicking on this object
DblClick	React to the user double-clicking on this object
DragDrop	React to the user dragging and dropping an object onto this object
DragOver	React to the user dragging another object over this object
MouseDown	React to the user pressing any mouse button
MouseMove	React to the user moving the mouse over this object
MouseUp	React to the user releasing any mouse button

Table 3-38 Events of the image control

Use This Method...	To Do This...
Drag	Control manual dragging of this control
Move	Change the position of this control or form
Refresh	Cause this object to be updated immediately
ZOrder	Place this object at the front or back of the z-order

Table 3-39 Methods of the image control

Description

The image control lets you display graphical images without the performance and overhead penalties of the picture box control. The image control repaints faster and uses far fewer system resources than does the picture box. It does this by restricting its properties, events, and methods to those used to display predefined images and eliminating those dealing with creating graphic images. The image control also cannot function as a grouping mechanism for other controls (like a frame) the way a picture box can. It also cannot function in a DDE conversation. For more on the image control, see Chapter 8, Graphics Fundamentals.

LABEL CONTROL

Purpose

The label control labels an area of a frame, form, or picture.

Properties, Events, and Methods

Tables 3-40, 3-41, and 3-42 list the properties, events, and methods that relate to the label control.

Use This Property...	To Do This...
Alignment	Align text to the right, left, or center within the control
AutoSize	Determine whether this control is automatically resized to fit its contents
BackColor, ForeColor	Read or set the background and foreground colors of this object
BackStyle	Determine whether the control's background is opaque or transparent
BorderStyle	Determine whether this object has a border and, if it does, set its style
Caption	Assign text to this object
DataChanged	Determine if the value displayed in this object has changed
DataField	Read or set the name of a field in the recordset of the data control
DataSource	Set the name of the data control to which this object is bound
DragIcon	Read or set what displays when this control is dragged
DragMode	Determine whether drag operations are to occur manually or automatically
Enabled	Read or set whether this object can react to events
FontBold, FontItalic, FontStrikeThru, FontName	Read or set the name of this object's font
FontSize	Read or set the size of this object's font
FontUnderline	Read or set special effects for this object's font
Height	Read or set the height of this object
Index	Uniquely identify an element of a control array
Left	Read or set the left edge placement of this control on a picture or form
LinkItem	Read or set the item in a DDE conversation
LinkMode	Read or set a DDE conversation to hot, cold, or none

(continued on next page)

Use This Property...	To Do This...
LinkTimeout	Read or set the amount of time before a DDE conversation times out
LinkTopic	Read or set the topic of a DDE conversation
MousePointer	Read or set the shape of the mouse pointer when it's over this object
Name	Set the name used in code to refer to this object
Parent	Read the name of the form to which this control belongs
TabIndex	Read or set the placement of this control within the form's tab order
Tag	Read or set text information that is particular to this object
Top	Read or set the coordinate of this control's top edge
Visible	Read or set whether this object is visible
Width	Read or set the width of this object
WordWrap	Determine whether the label expands to fit its contents

Table 3-40 Properties of the label control

Use This Event...	To Do This...
Change	React to a change in the control's Caption property
Click	React to the user clicking on this object
DblClick	React to the user double-clicking on this object
DragDrop	React to the user dragging and dropping an object onto this object
DragOver	React to the user dragging another object over this object
LinkClose	React to the termination of a DDE conversation
LinkError	React to an error in a DDE conversation

Use This Event...	To Do This...
LinkNotify	React to a change in the DDE source data
LinkOpen	React to the initiation of a DDE conversation
MouseDown	React to the user pressing any mouse button
MouseMove	React to the user moving the mouse over this object
MouseUp	React to the user releasing any mouse button

Table 3-41 Events of the label control

Use This Method...	To Do This...
Drag	Control manual dragging of this control
LinkExecute	Send a DDE Execute command to a DDE server application
LinkPoke	Send data from a DDE client to a DDE server
LinkRequest	Ask for data from a DDE server
Move	Change the position of this control or form
Refresh	Cause this object to be updated immediately
ZOrder	Place this object at the front or back of the z-order

Table 3-42 Methods of the label control

Description

The label control places noneditable text on a form, frame, or picture. Most often this control displays a meaningful name that describes the purpose of a text, list, or combo box control. (In Figure 3-19 Find What: and Replace With: are such descriptive labels.)

The text displayed by a label control is defined by its Caption property. At design time this property can be assigned a one-line text string. If needed, at

119

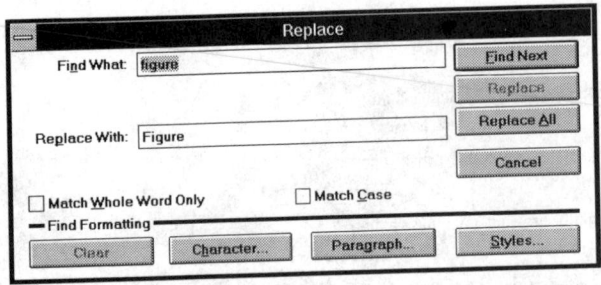

Figure 3-19 The label controls identify the Find What and Replace With boxes

runtime the program's code may assign this property a string that contains carriage return/linefeed pairs to create a multiple-line label. Set the AutoSize and WordWrap properties to display variable length lines or a varying number of lines. See Chapter 21, Application Focus, for more about the Caption property.

LINE CONTROL

Purpose

Use the line control to display a horizontal, vertical, or diagonal line directly on the form.

Properties and Methods

Tables 3-43 and 3-44 list the properties and methods of the line control.

Use This Property...	To Do This...
BorderColor	Read or set the color of the line
BorderStyle	Read or set the style of the line (e.g., solid, dotted, dashed)
BorderWidth	Read or set the width of the line
DrawMode	Read or set the draw mode (e.g., overwrite, inverse, XOR pen)
Index	Uniquely identify an element of a control array
Name	Set the name used in code to refer to this object

Use This Property...	To Do This...
Tag	Read or set text information that is particular to this object
Visible	Read or set whether this object is visible
X1, Y1, X2, Y2	Read or set the coordinates of the endpoints for the line

Table 3-43 Properties of the line control

Use This Method...	To Do This...
Move	Change the position of this object
Refresh	Update this object
ZOrder	Place this object at the front or back of the z-order

Table 3-44 Methods of the line control

Description

The line control draws a line directly on your form during the design phase. This is especially helpful for designing your forms, as you can see the effects immediately. Graphics methods like PSet or Line, in contrast, do not display until run-time and can be difficult to design with. See Chapter 10, Drawing Shapes, for more on the line control.

LIST BOX CONTROL

Purpose

The list box control displays a box with a list of items from which the user may make a selection.

Properties, Events, and Methods

Tables 3-45, 3-46, and 3-47 list the properties, events, and methods that relate to the list box control.

Use This Property...	To Do This...
BackColor, ForeColor	Read or set the background and foreground colors of this object
Columns	Determine how many columns are displayed
DragIcon	Read or set what displays when this control is dragged
DragMode	Determine whether drag operations are to occur manually or automatically
Enabled	Read or set whether this object can react to events
FontBold, FontItalic, FontStrikeThru, FontUnderline	Read or set special effects for this object's font
FontName	Read or set the name of this object's font
FontSize	Read or set the size of this object's font
Height	Read or set the height of this object
HelpContextID	Read or set the context number to this object for context-sensitive help
hWnd	Determine a handle to this object
Index	Uniquely identify an element of a control array
ItemData	Read or set a number associated with the currently selected item
Left	Read or set the left edge placement of this control on a picture or form
List	Read or set the value of a listed item
ListCount	Read the number of items in a list
ListIndex	Read or set the index of the currently selected item in a list
MousePointer	Read or set the shape of the mouse pointer when it's over this object
MultiSelect	Determine whether a user can make multiple selections in the list
Name	Set the name used in code to refer to this object

Use This Property...	To Do This...
NewIndex	Read the index of the item most recently added to this object
Parent	Read the name of the form to which this control belongs
Selected	Read the selection status of an item in the list
Sorted	Read or set whether Visual Basic will automatically sort the list
TabIndex	Read or set the placement of this control within the form's tab order
TabStop	Read or set whether this control is part of the form's tab order
Tag	Read or set text information that is particular to this object
Text	Read the currently selected item
Top	Read or set the coordinate of this control's top edge
TopIndex	Read which item in the list appears in the topmost position
Visible	Read or set whether this object is visible
Width	Read or set the width of this object

Table 3-45 Properties of the list box control

Use This Event...	To Do This...
Click	React to the user clicking on this object
DblClick	React to the user double-clicking on this object
DragDrop	React to the user dragging and dropping an object onto this object
DragOver	React to the user dragging another object over this object
GotFocus	Initiate an action when this object receives the focus
KeyDown	Initiate an action when the user presses or holds a key down

(continued on next page)

(continued from previous page)

Use This Event...	To Do This...
KeyPress	React to the user typing an ASCII character
KeyUp	Initiate an action when the user releases a key
LostFocus	Initiate an action when this object loses the focus
MouseDown	React to the user pressing any mouse button
MouseMove	React to the user moving the mouse over this object
MouseUp	React to the user releasing any mouse button

Table 3-46 Events of the list box control

Use This Method...	To Do This...
AddItem	Add an item to a list box
Clear	Clear the contents of this control
Drag	Control manual dragging of this control
Move	Change the position of this control or form
Refresh	Cause this object to be updated immediately
RemoveItem	Delete items from a list
SetFocus	Move the focus to this control
ZOrder	Place this object at the front or back of the z-order

Table 3-47 Methods of the list box control

Description

The user may choose an item from a list box by clicking on it or by using the ⊕ and ⊕ keys to move the highlight to the desired item (see Figure 3-20). If there

124

are more items in the list than can be displayed in the area defined for the box, Visual Basic will automatically add a vertical scroll bar on the right edge of the list. The user can then use this scroll bar to move up or down in the list.

The List property provides a way to read and set a list's contents in a manner similar to accessing and assigning values in an array. The List property is followed by an index number in parentheses, which identifies which list entry is being referenced. The index numbering of the list is zero-based. Therefore, if a list contains five items, the first item is index number 0 and the highest index number is 4. The number of items in a list can be determined by using the ListCount property.

The ListIndex property returns the index number of the currently selected item in a list. If no item is currently selected, -1 is returned.

The program may also set the ListIndex property directly. When using the ListIndex property to set the currently selected list entry, you must use an index number that references a currently added item in the list. For instance, if a list has five items in it, an index number from 0 to 4 must be specified, or an "Invalid property array index" error will occur.

The AddItem and RemoveItem methods add and delete list entries to and from a list box control. The Clear method clears the entire control of items.

This object is discussed in detail in Chapter 18, Lists, Combos, and Grids.

MDI FORM OBJECT

Purpose

An MDI (Multiple Document Interface) form is a form that acts as a container for other forms, or *child forms*, and serves as the main background form for your application.

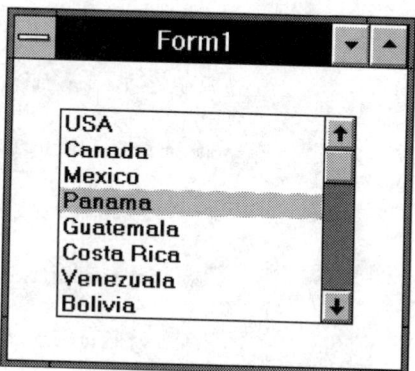

Figure 3-20 The list box

Properties, Events, and Methods

Tables 3-48, 3-49, and 3-50 list the properties, events, and methods of the MDI form.

Use This Property...	To Do This...
ActiveControl	Read which control has the focus
ActiveForm	Read which form is active
Caption	Assign text to the title bar of this object
Enabled	Read or set whether this object can react to events
Height	Read or set the height of this object
HelpContextID	Read or set the context number to this object for context-sensitive help
hWnd	Determine a handle to this object
Icon	Read or set the icon used when a form is minimized
Left	Read or set the left edge placement of this form
LinkMode	Read or set a DDE conversation to hot, cold, or none
LinkTopic	Read or set the topic of a DDE conversation
MousePointer	Read or set the shape of the mouse pointer when it's over this object
Name	Set the name used in code to refer to this object
ScaleHeight	Read or set the number of units that define the height of this object
ScaleWidth	Read or set the number of units that define the width of this object
ScrollBars	Determine whether scroll bars appear in a multiple-line text box
Tag	Read or set text information that is particular to this object
Top	Read or set the coordinate of this control's top edge

Use This Property...	To Do This...
Visible	Read or set whether this object is visible
Width	Read or set the width of this object
WindowState	Read or set whether a form is maximized, minimized, or normal

Table 3-48 Properties of the MDI Form object

Use This Event...	To Do This...
Activate	React to when this object becomes activated either by code or by user
Deactivate	React to when this object becomes deactivated either by code or by user
DragDrop	React to the user dragging and dropping an object onto this object
DragOver	React to the user dragging another object over this object
LinkClose	React to the termination of a DDE conversation
LinkError	React to an error in a DDE conversation
LinkExecute	React to a DDE Execute command from a DDE client application
LinkOpen	React to the initiation of a DDE conversation
Load	Initiate an action when a form is first loaded into memory
QueryUnload	React to an attempt to unload the form
Resize	Initiate an action when a form is first displayed or its size is changed
Unload	Initiate an action when a form is removed from memory

Table 3-49 Events of the MDI Form object

Use This Method...	To Do This...
Arrange	Arrange the windows or icons within this MDI form
Hide	Make a form invisible
Move	Change the position of this control or form
SetFocus	Move the focus to this form
Show	Display a previously hidden form
ZOrder	Place this object at the front or back of the z-order

Table 3-50 Methods of the MDI Form object

Description

A Visual Basic application becomes MDI (Multiple Document Interface) capable by creating an MDI form with the File New MDI Form command. Then flag other forms as children of the main MDI form by setting their MDIChild property to True. Although there may be only one MDI form per Windows application, you may have many kinds of child forms as well as non-MDI forms. For example, Microsoft Excel has both worksheet and chart child forms as well as a host of normal dialog boxes. See Figure 3-21 for an example of how Excel can have many documents of several kinds open at once.

A child's menu bar replaces the MDI form's menu when the child form has the focus. Thus, in the Excel example above, the MDI form may only have the File and Help menu items; the worksheet child form will display File, Edit, Formula, Format, Data, and so on, while the chart child form will display File, Edit, Gallery, Chart, and so forth.

A child form is totally contained within the MDI form. When maximized, the child form takes up the entire client area—that is, the area within the MDI form's borders not taken up with the title bar, menu bar, and any picture controls placed on the top or bottom of the MDI form. When minimized, the child form appears as an icon within the MDI form. Multiple child forms may be open at once, and may be arranged in various ways within the MDI form.

The only control that may be directly placed on an MDI form is the picture control. These would typically be placed at the top and bottom of the form. Once placed, other controls may be placed on top of these picture controls to form toolbars and status bars.

For more information on MDI forms, see Chapter 4, Forms and Menus.

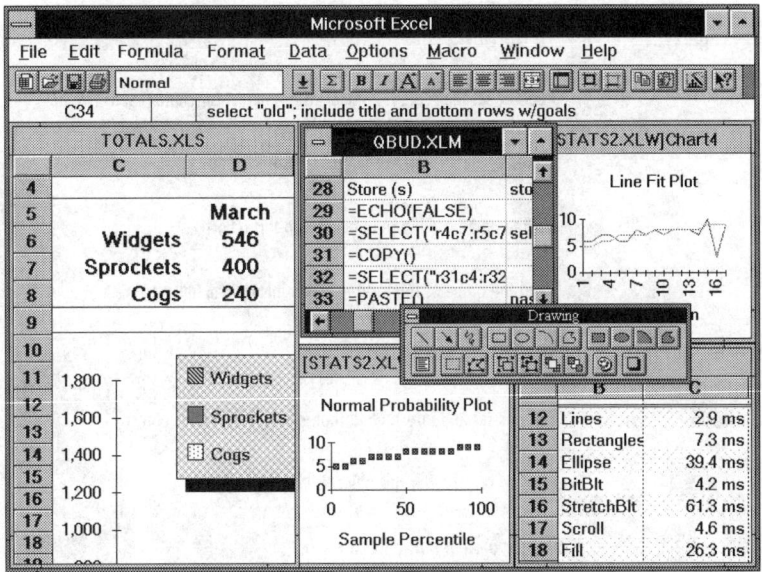

Figure 3-21 The Multiple Document Interface of a commercial application

MENU CONTROL

Purpose

The menu control defines a pull-down menu system for a form.

Properties, Events, and Methods

Tables 3-51 and 3-52 list the properties and events that relate to this object. There are no methods associated with the menu control.

Use This Property...	To Do This...
Caption	Assign text to this object
Checked	Place or remove a check mark from a menu item
Enabled	Read or set whether this object can react to events

(continued on next page)

(continued from previous page)

Use This Property...	To Do This...
HelpContextID	Read or set the context number to this object for context-sensitive help
Index	Uniquely identify an element of a control array
Name	Set the name used in code to refer to this object
Parent	Read the name of the form to which this control belongs
ShortCut	Specify a shortcut key
Tag	Read or set text information that is particular to this object
Visible	Read or set whether this object is visible
WindowList	Display a list of MDI child forms

Table 3-51 Properties of the menu control

Use This Event...	To Do This...
Click	React to the user clicking on this object

Table 3-52 The one menu control event

Description

The major functions performed by most Windows programs are accessible with a pull-down menu system (see Figures 3-22 and 3-23). Visual Basic provides you with the Menu Design window with which you can define a menu system. Each menu may have up to four levels of submenus. Each menu, and each option on each menu, is assigned a Name by which you reference it.

When a user chooses a menu item, that menu's Click event occurs. Code can be placed in this event to perform the task related to the menu or option chosen by the user.

The Enabled property may be set to 0 to disable a particular menu or menu option. Doing so prevents the user from being able to choose that item.

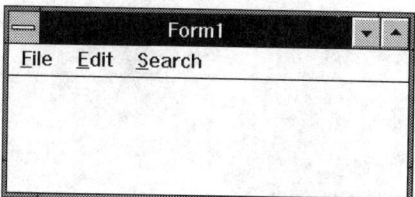

Figure 3-22 A form with File, Edit, and Search menus

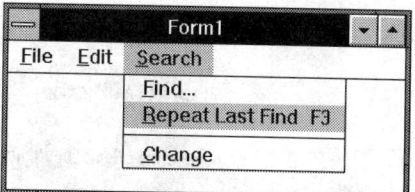

Figure 3-23 The same form with the Search menu open

Disabling a menu effectively disables all options under that menu. A disabled item displays in gray.

The Checked property may have a value of True (-1), meaning checked, or False (0), meaning not checked. When a menu item's Checked property is True, a small check mark will be displayed next to that menu item to show its current setting. For instance, if a menu option turns a particular function on or off, the Checked property may be used to indicate the current status of the function.

In the Menu Design window, if a value is assigned to the Index property for a menu item, that menu item becomes part of a control array. This gives the program the opportunity to dynamically add and delete menu options at runtime, by using the Load and Unload statements (see Chapter 4, Forms and Menus, for more on these statements).

OLE CONTROL

Purpose

The OLE (Object Linking and Embedding) control displays data from many different Windows applications and lets the user of your Visual Basic application edit the data in the original program. Compatible applications even let users edit the data from within your Visual Basic application and may expose features and objects that your Visual Basic program can use much as you'd use a custom control.

Properties, Events, and Methods

Tables 3-53, 3-54, and 3-55 list the properties, events, and methods that relate to the OLE control.

Use This Property...	To Do This...
Action	Perform an OLE action
AppIsRunning	See if the originating application is running
AutoActivate	Determine how an OLE control is activated
AutoVerbMenu	Determine if a menu of the OLE object's verbs is automatically displayed
BackColor, ForeColor	Read or set the background and foreground colors of this object
BorderStyle	Determine whether this object has a border, and if it does, set its style
Class	Read or set the class name of the embedded OLE object
Data	Read a handle to a GDI object containing data in the specified format
DataText	Read or set a string from the OLE object
DisplayType	Read or set if the OLE object displays as an icon or the actual contents
DragIcon	Read or set what displays when this control is dragged
DragMode	Determine whether drag operations are to occur manually or automatically
FileNumber	Read or set the file number used when saving or loading an OLE object
Format	Determine the format used when sending or receiving data
Height	Read or set the height of this object
HelpContextID	Read or set the context number to this object for context-sensitive help
HostName	Read the descriptive name of the application that created the OLE object
hWnd	Determine a handle to this object
Index	Uniquely identify an element of a control array
Left	Read or set the left edge placement of this control on a picture or form

Use This Property...	To Do This...
lpOLEObject	Set the address of the OLE object for API calls
Name	Set the name used in code to refer to this object
Object	Specify an OLE object when using OLE automation
ObjectAcceptFormatsCount	Read the number of formats that can be accepted by the OLE object
ObjectAcceptFormats	Read the list of formats an OLE object can accept
ObjectGetFormatsCount	Read the number of formats that can be returned by the OLE object
ObjectGetFormats	Read the list of formats the OLE object can return
ObjectVerbFlags	Determine the menu state of the object's verbs
ObjectVerbs	List the object's verbs
ObjectVerbsCount	Counts the number of the object's verbs
OleType	Set or determine the type of object (link or embed)
OleTypeAllowed	Determine the types of objects allowed
Parent	Read the name of the form to which this control belongs
PasteOK	Read if the contents of the Clipboard can be pasted into the OLE control
Picture	Read or assign a graphic image to this object
SizeMode	Set or determine how the object reacts to resize
SourceDoc	Set or determine file name of the source document
SourceItem	Set the region or subset of data when creating object
UpdateOptions	Set or determine how OLE control reacts to changes
Verb	Set or determine what action an object performs

(continued on next page)

133

(continued from previous page)

Use This Property...	To Do This...
Tag	Read or set text information that is particular to this object
Top	Read or set the coordinate of this control's top edge
Visible	Read or set whether this object is visible
Width	Read or set the width of this object

Table 3-53 Properties of the OLE control

Use This Event...	To Do This...
Click	React to the user clicking on this object
DblClick	React to the user double-clicking on this object
DragDrop	React to the user dragging and dropping an object onto this object
DragOver	React to the user dragging another object over this object
GotFocus	Initiate an action when this object receives the focus
KeyDown	Initiate an action when the user presses or holds a key down
KeyPress	React to the user typing an ASCII character
KeyUp	Initiate an action when the user releases a key
LostFocus	Initiate an action when this object loses the focus
MouseDown	React to the user pressing any mouse button
MouseMove	React to the user moving the mouse over this object
MouseUp	React to the user releasing any mouse button
Resize	Initiate an action when object is first displayed or its size is changed
Updated	React to a modification in the object's data

Table 3-54 Events of the OLE control

Use This Method...	To Do This...
Drag	Control manual dragging of this control
Move	Change the position of this control or form
Refresh	Cause this object to be updated immediately
SetFocus	Move the focus to this control
ZOrder	Place this object at the front or back of the z-order

Table 3-55 Methods of the OLE control

Description

OLE allows your Visual Basic applications to display and manipulate data from many other Windows programs. For example, your application could have a spreadsheet object from Excel, a drawing object from CorelDRAW, a word processor object from AmiPro, and a music sequencer object from Cakewalk. Even though you haven't written any code to do all the things these other applications can, your application can still serve as a front end to tie them all together.

Although OLE and DDE are both ways of sharing data between applications, there are some fundamental differences in their approach. OLE temporarily transfers control to the program that originally created the data to do any data manipulation, while DDE functions solely within your Visual Basic application. OLE also displays the data as the original application would, whereas DDE data displays in whatever way you choose to format it. For example, if the original application is a spreadsheet created in Excel, the OLE control displays its contents exactly as it would appear in Excel, complete with row and column headers and gridlines (assuming you had those display options turned on in Excel). Figure 3-24 illustrates how an OLE object retains its formatting.

The OLE control lets you create both linked and embedded objects. A linked object is only a placeholder for and pointer to the real data. For example, if you link a drawing into an OLE control, the data for the drawing stays in the original source file. Only an image of the data and a link back to the original data are stored in the OLE control. This makes it possible to access the linked data from several different applications.

An embedded object actually stores the data within the OLE control. You can store the contents of the control in a file, and the file contains the name of the application that produced the object originally, the actual data, and an image of the data for display. When you embed an object in an OLE control, only your application can access the data; no other application can read or write the data directly.

135

	B	C	D	E	F	G
2		**Win3.1**	**Win 3.0**	**Win 3.0**	**Win 3.1**	**Win 3.**
3		8x6x16	8x6x16	8x6x256	8x6x256	8x6x256
5	Lines	2.9 ms	2.9 ms	4.2 ms	2.1 ms	4.2 r
6	Rectangles	7.3 ms	7.2 ms	22.6 ms	2.8 ms	22.6 r
7	Ellipse	39.4 ms	38.4 ms	72.0 ms	31.4 ms	72.0 r
8	BitBlt	4.2 ms	4.0 ms	4.0 ms	0.5 ms	4.0 r
9	StretchBlt	61.3 ms	60.8 ms	70.3 ms	53.5 ms	70.3 r
10	Scroll	4.6 ms	5.1 ms	5.6 ms	1.9 ms	5.6 r
11	Fill	26.3 ms	25.6 ms	142.0 ms	4.9 ms	142.0 r
13	Total:	146.0 ms	144.0 ms	320.7 ms	97.1 ms	320.7 r

Figure 3-24 An embedded Excel object

Visual Basic Version 3.0 is one of the first applications to support the new OLE 2.0 specification. This allows your Visual Basic application to edit another compatible application's object in-place. Rather than starting the other application in its own window, as in OLE 1.0, the other application lets you edit the object within your Visual Basic application. This makes it look as if your application is doing all the work. Some OLE 2.0 compliant applications can even expose a set of objects to your Visual Basic application. This lets you use the other application's features as easily as you would any Visual Basic control.

Refer to Chapter 26, Object Linking and Embedding (OLE), for more information.

OPTION BUTTON CONTROL

Purpose

The option button control provides a technique for presenting a group of choices where only one choice may be selected. In other words, the option button control is used when the selection of one choice excludes the selection of any other related choices.

Properties, Events, and Methods

Tables 3-56, 3-57, and 3-58 list the properties, events, and methods that relate to the option button control.

136

Use This Property...	To Do This...
Alignment	Read or set the alignment of this object
BackColor, ForeColor	Read or set the background and foreground colors of this object
Caption	Assign text to this object
DragIcon	Read or set what displays when this control is dragged
DragMode	Determine whether drag operations are to occur manually or automatically
Enabled	Read or set whether this object can react to events
FontBold, FontItalic, FontStrikeThru, FontUnderline	Read or set special effects for this object's font
FontName	Read or set the name of this object's font
FontSize	Read or set the size of this object's font
Height	Read or set the height of this object
HelpContextID	Read or set the context number to this object for context-sensitive help
hWnd	Determine a handle to this object
Index	Uniquely identify an element of a control array
Left	Read or set the left edge placement of this control on a picture or form
MousePointer	Read or set the shape of the mouse pointer when it's over this object
Name	Set the name used in code to refer to this object
Parent	Read the name of the form to which this control belongs
TabIndex	Read or set the placement of this control within the form's tab order
TabStop	Read or set whether this control is part of the form's tab order
Tag	Read or set text information that is particular to this object

(continued on next page)

(continued from previous page)

Use This Property...	To Do This...
Top	Read or set the coordinate of this control's top edge
Value	Read or set whether the option button is selected
Visible	Read or set whether this object is visible
Width	Read or set the width of this object

Table 3-56 Properties of the option button control

Use This Event...	To Do This...
Click	React to the user clicking on this object
DblClick	React to the user double-clicking on this object
DragDrop	React to the user dragging and dropping an object onto this object
DragOver	React to the user dragging another object over this object
GotFocus	Initiate an action when this object receives the focus
KeyDown	Initiate an action when the user presses or holds a key down
KeyPress	React to the user typing an ASCII character
KeyUp	Initiate an action when the user releases a key
LostFocus	Initiate an action when this object loses the focus
MouseDown	React to the user pressing any mouse button
MouseMove	React to the user moving the mouse over this object
MouseUp	React to the user releasing any mouse button

Table 3-57 Events of the option button control

Use This Method...	To Do This...
Drag	Control manual dragging of this control
Move	Change the position of this control or form
Refresh	Cause this object to be updated immediately
SetFocus	Move the focus to this control
ZOrder	Place this object at the front or back of the z-order

Table 3-58 Methods of the option button control

Description

The option button control consists of a small circle accompanied by text. Generally, the text defines the purpose of the button. Clicking on a button causes the circle to be filled in with a solid dot. This happens regardless of whether or not the circle had already been filled in.

Option buttons generally work in groups (see Figure 3-25). A group of option buttons is created when two or more option buttons are drawn on the same form, frame, or picture. When this is the case, all the option buttons in the same group become mutually exclusive. That is, when one button is clicked, it gets selected and all other buttons in the same group become unselected. Option buttons grouped this way are often called *radio buttons*.

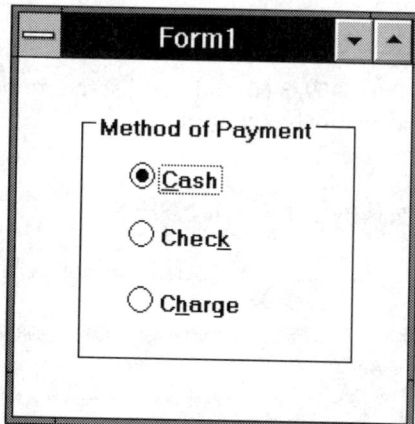

Figure 3-25 Three option buttons grouped together in a frame

139

To create a group of option buttons, first draw the frame or picture on which they will be placed. Then draw the buttons on the frame or picture. To have more than one group of option buttons on the same form, create a frame for each group and then place the buttons in the appropriate frame.

The Caption property defines the text that will accompany the button. The size and style of this text is defined by the settings of the Font... properties. Including an ampersand (&) underlines the following letter, and the check box may be selected by holding down the (ALT) key and pressing that letter. For instance, if a button's Caption property is set to &Cash, the displayed text will be "Cash" and the user can select the button by pressing (ALT)-(C). Chapter 21, Application Focus, covers the caption property in more detail.

The status of an option button control may be set or read by the program's code by using the Value property. This property will be True (-1) if the button is selected and False (0) if not.

When an option button is selected, its Click event triggers. This allows the program to react immediately to the setting of the button.

PICTURE BOX CONTROL

Purpose

The picture box control defines an area on a form, frame, or another picture in which graphics may be displayed. The picture box control can also be used much like the frame control to group together controls that are functionally related based on how they are used in a program.

Properties, Events, and Methods

Tables 3-59, 3-60, and 3-61 list the properties, events, and methods that relate to the picture box control.

Use This Property...	To Do This...
Align	Determine where and how the control appears on a form
AutoReDraw	Read or set whether graphic pictures will be redrawn automatically
AutoSize	Read or set whether the size of a picture is controlled by its source file
BackColor, ForeColor	Read or set the background and foreground colors of this object

Use This Property...	To Do This...
BorderStyle	Determine whether this object has a border and, if it does, set its style
ClipControls	Determine whether graphic methods repaint entire object
CurrentX, CurrentY	Read or set the current graphics position on this object
DataSource	Set the name of the data control to which this object is bound
DataField	Read or set the name of a field in the recordset of the data control
DataChanged	Determine if the value displayed in this object has changed
DragIcon	Read or set what displays when this control is dragged
DragMode	Determine whether drag operations are to occur manually or automatically
DrawMode	Read or set the appearance of drawings by graphics methods
DrawStyle	Read or set the style of lines drawn by graphics methods
DrawWidth	Read or set the size of lines drawn by graphics methods
Enabled	Read or set whether this object can react to events
FillColor	Read or set the color used by graphics methods for fill-in effects
FillStyle	Read or set the pattern used by graphics methods for fill-in effects
FontBold, FontItalic, FontStrikeThru, FontTransparent, FontUnderline	Read or set special effects for this object's font
FontName	Read or set the name of this object's font
FontSize	Read or set the size of this object's font
hDC	Read the Windows device handle for this object
Height	Read or set the height of this object
HelpContextID	Read or set the context number to this object for context-sensitive help

(continued on next page)

(continued from previous page)

Use This Property...	To Do This...
hWnd	Determine a handle to this object
Image	Read the Windows device handle for a picture's persistent bitmap
Index	Uniquely identify an element of a control array
Left	Read or set the left edge placement of this control on a picture or form
LinkItem	Read or set the item in a DDE conversation
LinkMode	Read or set a DDE conversation to hot, cold, or none
LinkTimeout	Read or set the amount of time before a DDE conversation times out
LinkTopic	Read or set the topic of a DDE conversation
MousePointer	Read or set the shape of the mouse pointer when it's over this object
Name	Set the name used in code to refer to this object
Parent	Read the name of the form to which this control belongs
Picture	Read or assign a graphic image to a picture or form
ScaleHeight	Read or set the number of units that define the height of this object
ScaleLeft	Read or set the coordinates for the left edge of this object
ScaleMode	Read or set the unit of measurement used to place and size objects
ScaleTop	Read or set the coordinates for the top edge of this object
ScaleWidth	Read or set the number of units that define the width of this object
TabIndex	Read or set the placement of this control within the form's tab order
TabStop	Read or set whether this control is part of the form's tab order
Tag	Read or set text information that is particular to this object

Use This Property...	To Do This...
Top	Read or set the coordinate of this control's top edge
Visible	Read or set whether an object is visible
Width	Read or set the width of this object

Table 3-59 Properties of the picture box control

Use This Event...	To Do This...
Change	React to a change in the image pointed to by the Picture property
Click	React to the user clicking on this object
DblClick	React to the user double-clicking on this object
DragDrop	React to the user dragging and dropping an object onto this object
DragOver	React to the user dragging another object over this object
GotFocus	Initiate an action when this object receives the focus
KeyDown	Initiate an action when the user presses or holds a key down
KeyPress	React to the user typing an ASCII character
KeyUp	Initiate an action when the user releases a key
LinkClose	React to the termination of a DDE conversation
LinkError	React to an error in a DDE conversation
LinkNotify	React to a change in the DDE source data
LinkOpen	React to the initiation of a DDE conversation
LostFocus	Initiate an action when this object loses the focus

(continued on next page)

(continued from previous page)

Use This Event...	To Do This...
MouseDown	React to the user pressing any mouse button
MouseMove	React to the user moving the mouse over this object
MouseUp	React to the user releasing any mouse button
Paint	Initiate an action when object needs to be redrawn
Resize	Initiate an action when object is first displayed or its size is changed

Table 3-60 Events of the picture box control

Use This Method...	To Do This...
Circle	Create a circle or ellipse on a form or picture box
Cls	Clear graphics and text that have been created at runtime
Drag	Control manual dragging of this control
Line	Draw a line on a form or picture
LinkExecute	Send a DDE Execute command to a DDE server application
LinkPoke	Send data from a DDE client to a DDE server
LinkRequest	Ask for data from a DDE server
LinkSend	Send graphic data to a DDE client
Move	Change the position of this control or form
Point	Return the color setting of a specified point on a form or picture box
Print	Print text on a form or picture box
Pset	Set the color of a specified point on a form or picture box

Use This Method...	To Do This...
Refresh	Cause this object to be updated immediately
Scale	Define the coordinate system used with the picture box control
SetFocus	Move the focus to this control
TextHeight	Return the height of text in this object's font
TextWidth	Return the width of text in this object's font
ZOrder	Place this object at the front or back of the z-order

Table 3-61 Methods of the picture box control

Description

The picture box control is used for two different purposes. Primarily, it displays a graphic image on a form (see Figure 3-26). However, you can also place controls on a picture control in the same manner as placing them on a form or frame. This gives you an alternative to the frame control for grouping together other controls. This is particularly useful when you need to place controls on the client area of an MDI form, as the picture box control is the only standard control that may be placed there.

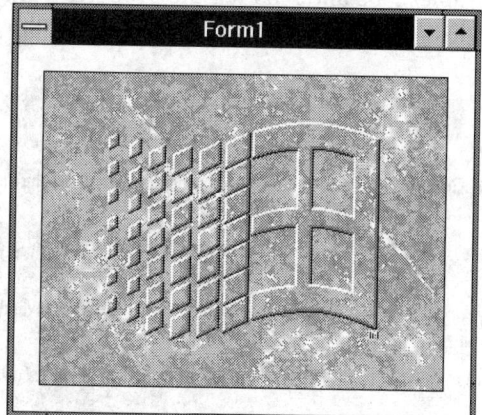

Figure 3-26 The picture box displays graphics

145

The picture property defines the graphic image to be displayed by this control. The picture box control can display icons, Windows bitmaps, and Windows metafiles.

The size of the picture box control defines how much of a graphic image displays. If a graphic image is too large to be displayed within the boundaries of a picture box control, you can use two picture box controls, placing one on top of the other, to simulate scrolling of the image. This technique is demonstrated in Chapter 20, Scroll Bars.

If other controls are drawn on a picture box control, they work in the same manner as if they'd been drawn on a frame control. Because the border can be turned off by using the picture box control's BorderStyle property, this provides a technique for grouping several controls together without displaying a frame around them.

Refer to Chapter 8, Graphics Fundamentals, for more information on this control and its related properties, events, and methods.

PRINTER OBJECT

Purpose

The Printer object generates printed output by assembling pages to be sent to the printer.

Properties, Events, and Methods

Tables 3-62 and 3-63 list the properties and methods that relate to the Printer object. This object has no associated events.

Use This Property...	To Do This...
CurrentX, CurrentY	Read or set the current graphics position on this object
DrawMode	Read or set the appearance of graphics methods
DrawStyle	Read or set the style of lines drawn by graphics methods
DrawWidth	Read or set the size of lines drawn by graphics methods

Use This Property...	To Do This...
FillColor	Read or set the color used by graphics methods for fill-in effects
FillStyle	Read or set the pattern used by graphics methods for fill-in effects
FontBold, FontItalic, FontStrikeThru, FontTransparent, FontUnderline	Read or set special effects for this object's font
FontCount	Read the number of fonts available to the system
FontName	Read or set the name of this object's font
Fonts	Read the names of the fonts available to the system
FontSize	Read or set the size of this object's font
hDC	Read the Windows device handle for this object
Height	Read or set the height of this object
Page	Read the current output page of the Printer object
ScaleHeight	Read or set the number of units that define the height of this object
ScaleLeft	Read or set the coordinates for the left edge of this object
ScaleMode	Read or set the unit of measurement used to place and size objects
ScaleTop	Read or set the coordinates for the top edge of this object
ScaleWidth	Read or set the number of units that define the width of this object
TwipsPerPixelX, TwipsPerPixelY	Read the number of twips per pixel
Width	Read or set the width of this object

Table 3-62 Properties of the Printer object

Use This Method...	To Do This...
Circle	Create a circle or ellipse on the page
EndDoc	End output to the Printer object, and send data to the printer
Line	Draw a line on the page
NewPage	End output to the current printer page and begin a new one
Print	Print text on the page
Pset	Set the color of a specified point on the page
Scale	Define the coordinate system used with the picture box control
TextHeight	Return the height of text in this object's font
TextWidth	Return the width of text in this object's font

Table 3-63 Methods of the Printer object

Description

Many programs need to create some sort of printed output. Because the Windows environment handles all printer output, Visual Basic includes the predefined Printer object. This object sends printer output commands from your programs to the Windows routines that in turn send the output to the printer.

Many other languages treat the printer as a sequential output device. Once an item is written to the printer, the print position advances and there can be no going back. With Visual Basic, however, this is not true.

You can think of the Printer object as a form that cannot be viewed until the Visual Basic program tells Windows to print it. This "form" represents one page of printed output. In most cases, until your program instructs Windows to print it, anything can be done to a page of printer output. This is very advantageous, as it allows the program to move the print position anywhere on a page regardless of where it currently resides. This makes printing graphics and special effects very easy.

The program works one page at a time when creating a printed document. All the output for a specific page is first set up by using many of the same methods that work on a form. These include the Circle, Line, Print, PSet, TextHeight, and TextWidth methods. The program determines where these methods write to a page by specifying coordinates on the page as arguments to the method or by setting the page's CurrentX and CurrentY properties. Each of the properties works in the same manner as when it's used on a form, except that printers incapable of printing in color ignore the color argument.

When the program has finished creating the current page, it can use the NewPage method. This ends the current page, saves it in memory, and clears the Printer object's work area for the next page.

As each page is generated, Visual Basic keeps track of the current page number with the Page property, which is specific to the Printer object. This property can never be set (either at design time or runtime), but it can be read and thereby printed on each page.

The EndDoc method sends all the printer output to the Windows printing routines when all printing is finished. Windows then takes care of the chores associated with sending the output to the printer.

Refer to Chapter 24, Printing, for more information on this object and its uses.

SCREEN OBJECT

Purpose

The Screen object has four basic purposes. First, it defines the physical height and width of the display. Next, it provides access to screen fonts that are available to the system. Third, it references the currently active form or control. Finally, it sets or reads the current shape of the mouse cursor.

Properties, Events, and Methods

Table 3-64 lists the properties that relate to the Screen object. This object has no associated events or methods.

Use This Property...	To Do This...
ActiveControl	Reference the current control with the focus
ActiveForm	Reference the current form with the focus
FontCount	Read the number of fonts available to the system for screen display
Fonts	Read the names of the fonts available to the system for screen display

(continued on next page)

(continued from previous page)

Use This Property...	To Do This...
Height	Read the height of the screen
MousePointer	Read or set the shape of the mouse pointer for all objects
TwipsPerPixelX, TwipsPerPixelY	Read the number of twips per pixel
Width	Read the width of the screen

Table 3-64 Properties of the Screen object

Description

The Height and Width properties of the Screen object define the dimensions of the screen in twips. A twip is defined as 1/20 point, which equates to 1440 twips per printed inch. This gives the Visual Basic program a method for displaying forms and controls in the proper absolute proportions, regardless of the type of display being used. These properties are discussed in Chapter 5, Application Appearance.

The FontCount and Fonts properties are used to determine the number and types of fonts available for display on a form or control on the screen. The use of fonts is covered in Chapter 12, Fonts.

When used with its ActiveControl and ActiveForm properties, the Screen object will reference the control or form that currently has the focus. For more information on referencing forms and controls, see Chapter 6, Accessing Forms and Controls.

Setting the Screen object's MousePointer property overrides the MousePointer property setting for all forms and controls in the program. Setting this property to 0 for the Screen object returns control of this property setting to the individual forms and controls. More discussion on the MousePointer property can be found in Chapter 5, Application Appearance.

SCROLL BARS CONTROL (VERTICAL AND HORIZONTAL)

Purpose

Scroll bars give the user the ability to position text or graphics or set a value by manipulating a visual object. Scroll bars are most commonly used to control the up and down and left to right movement of a graphic view port or list.

Properties, Events, and Methods

Tables 3-65, 3-66, and 3-67 list the properties, events, and methods that relate to this object.

Use This Property...	To Do This...
DragIcon	Read or set what displays when this control is dragged
DragMode	Determine whether drag operations are to occur manually or automatically
Enabled	Read or set whether this object can react to events
Height	Read or set the height of this object
HelpContextID	Read or set the context number to this object for context-sensitive help
hWnd	Determine a handle to this object
Index	Uniquely identify an element of a control array
LargeChange	Read or set the amount of change when a user clicks on the bar
Left	Read or set the left edge placement of this control on a picture or form
Max	Read or set the maximum value possible in a scroll bar
Min	Read or set the minimum value possible in a scroll bar
MousePointer	Read or set the shape of the mouse pointer when it's over this object
Name	Set the name used in code to refer to this object
Parent	Read the name of the form to which this control belongs
SmallChange	Read or set the amount of change when a user clicks on an arrow
TabIndex	Read or set the placement of this control within the form's tab order
TabStop	Read or set whether this control is part of the form's tab order
Tag	Read or set text information that is particular to this object

(continued on next page)

(continued from previous page)

Use This Property...	To Do This...
Top	Read or set the coordinate of this control's top edge
Value	Read or set the current value of this control
Visible	Read or set whether an object is visible
Width	Read or set the width of this object

Table 3-65 Properties of the scroll bars control

Use This Event...	To Do This...
Change	React to a change in the control's Value property
DragDrop	React to the user dragging and dropping an object onto this object
DragOver	React to the user dragging another object over this object
GotFocus	Initiate an action when this object receives the focus
KeyDown	Initiate an action when the user presses or holds a key down
KeyPress	React to the user typing an ASCII character
KeyUp	Initiate an action when the user releases a key
LostFocus	Initiate an action when this object loses the focus
Scroll	Continuously react to a change in the control's Value property

Table 3-66 Events of the scroll bars control

Use This Method...	To Do This...
Drag	Control manual dragging of this control
Move	Change the position of this control or form
Refresh	Cause this object to be updated immediately
SetFocus	Move the focus to this control
ZOrder	Place this object at the front or back of the z-order

Table 3-67 Methods of the scroll bars control

Description

Scroll bars are primarily used to control scrolling of a form, picture, or a list of items. They can also be used as a graphic technique for setting a particular value. For instance, in the Mouse settings of the Windows Control Panel, the user can set the speed of the mouse by manipulating a horizontal scroll bar.

Scroll bars are graphic objects that consist of a bar with arrows at each end and a button (called a thumb) between the arrows (see Figure 3-27). There are two types of scroll bars: vertical and horizontal.

The thumb's position within the scroll bar directly relates to the value represented by the scroll bar. For horizontal scroll bars, the thumb is in the leftmost

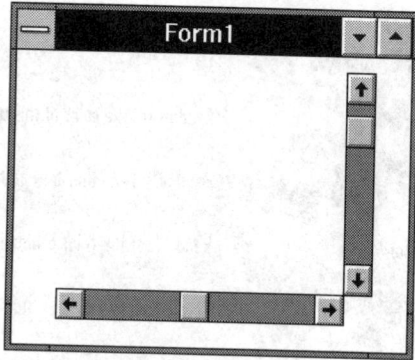

Figure 3-27 Vertical and horizontal scroll bars

position when the value of the scroll bar is at its minimum setting, and at the rightmost when the value is at its maximum. A minimum value on a vertical scroll bar places the thumb at the top, while the maximum value places the thumb at the bottom. Any value in between places the thumb on the bar in a position proportional to the value represented by the bar.

The value represented by the scroll bar can be changed in four ways. First, the user can click on either arrow. This causes the value represented by the scroll bar to be incremented or decremented by a small amount in the direction of the selected arrow. Second, the user may click the scroll bar on one side of the thumb or the other. This causes the scroll bar's value to be affected in a similar manner as with clicking an arrow, but the amount of change is greater. The user can also click and drag the thumb to a specific position on the bar. This causes the value of the Scroll bar to be set according to the position of the thumb. Finally, the value of a scroll bar can be set in the program's code.

The events, methods, and properties that relate to scroll bars are discussed in Chapter 20, Scroll Bars.

SHAPE CONTROL

Purpose

Use the shape control to display a graphical control directly on a form.

Properties and Methods

Tables 3-68 and 3-69 list the properties and methods that relate to the shape control.

Use This Property...	To Do This...
BackColor	Read or set the color of this object
BackStyle	Read or set whether text on this object is opaque or transparent
BorderColor	Read or set the color of the line that surrounds this object
BorderStyle	Read or set the style of the line (e.g., solid, dotted, dashed)
BorderWidth	Read or set the width of the line
DrawMode	Read or set the appearance of drawings by graphics methods

Use This Property...	To Do This...
FillColor	Read or set the color used by graphics methods for fill-in effects
FillStyle	Read or set the pattern used by graphics methods for fill-in effects
Height	Read or set the height of this object
Index	Uniquely identify an element of a control array
Left	Read or set the left edge placement of this control on a picture or form
Name	Set the name used in code to refer to this object
Parent	Read the name of the form to which this control belongs
Shape	Read or set the type of shape
Tag	Read or set text information that is particular to this object
Top	Read or set the coordinate of this control's top edge
Visible	Read or set whether an object is visible
Width	Read or set the width of this object

Table 3-68 Properties of the shape control

Use This Method...	To Do This...
Move	Change the position of this control or form
Refresh	Cause this object to be updated immediately
ZOrder	Place this object at the front or back of the z-order

Table 3-69 Methods of the shape control

Description

The shape control draws a shape (like a circle or rectangle) directly on your form during the design phase. This is especially helpful for designing your forms, as you can see the effects immediately. Graphics methods like PSet or Line, in contrast, do not display until runtime and can be difficult to design with. See Chapter 8, Graphics Fundamentals, for more details.

TEXT BOX CONTROL

Purpose

The text box control is used for displaying and editing text.

Properties, Events, and Methods

Tables 3-70, 3-71, and 3-72 list the properties, events, and methods that relate to the text box control.

Use This Property...	To Do This...
Alignment	Read or set the alignment of this object
BackColor, ForeColor	Read or set the background and foreground colors of this object
BorderStyle	Determine whether this object has a border, and if it does, set its style
DataSource	Set the name of the data control to which this object is bound
DataField	Read or set the name of a field in the recordset of the data control
DataChanged	Determine if the value displayed in this object has changed
DragIcon	Read or set what displays when this control is dragged
DragMode	Determine whether drag operations are to occur manually or automatically
Enabled	Read or set whether this object can react to events

Use This Property...	To Do This...
FontBold, FontItalic, FontStrikeThru, FontUnderline	Read or set special effects for this object's font
FontName	Read or set the name of this object's font
FontSize	Read or set the size of this object's font
Height	Read or set the height of this object
HelpContextID	Read or set the context number to this object for context-sensitive help
HideSelection	Determine whether selected text is highlighted when control loses focus
hWnd	Determine a handle to this object
Index	Uniquely identify an element of a control array
Left	Read or set the left edge placement of this control on a picture or form
LinkItem	Read or set the item in a DDE conversation
LinkMode	Read or set a DDE conversation to hot, cold, or none
LinkTimeout	Read or set the amount of time before a DDE conversation times out
LinkTopic	Read or set the topic of a DDE conversation
MaxLength	Read or set the maximum length of text allowed
MousePointer	Read or set the shape of the mouse pointer when it's over this object
Multiline	Read or set whether a text box can edit multiple lines
Name	Set the name used in code to refer to this object
Parent	Read the name of the form to which this control belongs
PasswordChar	Determine how typed characters appear (used for password entry)
ScrollBars	Determine whether scroll bars appear in a multiple-line text box

(continued on next page)

(continued from previous page)

Use This Property...	To Do This...
SelLength, SelStart, SelText	Read, set, or replace selected text in a text box
TabIndex	Read or set the placement of this control within the form's tab order
TabStop	Read or set whether this control is part of the form's tab order
Tag	Read or set text information that is particular to this object
Text	Read or set the text contained in a text box
Top	Read or set the coordinate of this control's top edge
Visible	Read or set whether an object is visible
Width	Read or set the width of this object

Table 3-70 Properties of the text box control

Use This Event...	To Do This...
Click	React to the user clicking on this object
DblClick	React to the user double-clicking on this object
Change	React to a change in the text box control's Text property
DragDrop	React to the user dragging and dropping an object onto this object
DragOver	React to the user dragging another object over this object
GotFocus	Initiate an action when this object receives the focus
KeyDown	Initiate an action when the user presses or holds a key down
KeyPress	React to the user typing an ASCII character
KeyUp	Initiate an action when the user releases a key

Use This Event...	To Do This...
LinkClose	React to the termination of a DDE conversation
LinkError	React to an error in a DDE conversation
LinkNotify	React to a change in the DDE source data
LinkOpen	React to the initiation of a DDE conversation
LostFocus	Initiate an action when this object loses the focus
MouseDown	React to the user pressing any mouse button
MouseMove	React to the user moving the mouse over this object
MouseUp	React to the user releasing any mouse button

Table 3-71 Events of the text box control

Use This Method...	To Do This...
Drag	Control manual dragging of this control
LinkExecute	Send a DDE Execute command to a DDE server application
LinkPoke	Send data from a DDE client to a DDE server
LinkRequest	Ask for data from a DDE server
Move	Change the position of this control or form
Refresh	Cause this object to be updated immediately
SetFocus	Move the focus to this control
ZOrder	Place this object at the front or back of the z-order

Table 3-72 Methods of the text box control

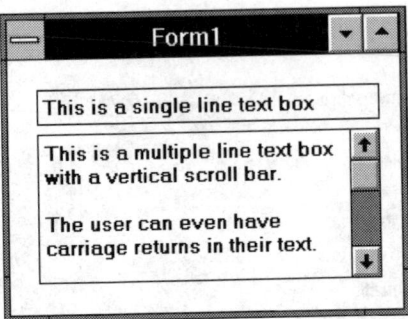

Figure 3-28 Single- and multiple-line
text boxes

Description

The text box control is a rectangle in which the user may enter or edit text. When
a text box control receives the focus, an insertion point appears in the box. The
insertion point is a slim flashing vertical line that indicates where any new text
will be entered within the box. This line can be moved by using the direction keys
or by clicking on the desired position in the text box with the mouse. A Visual
Basic text box automatically inherits all the conventions of a standard Windows
text box, including the ability to cut, copy, and paste to and from the Windows
Clipboard area.

The Text property sets or reads the text that is currently in a text box. The style
and size of the text are determined by the control's font properties.

By default, a text box consists of only one line of text. Setting the MultiLine
property to True (-1) will allow the user to enter more than one line of text (see
Figure 3-28). If you set the MultiLine property to True, you may wish to also set
the ScrollBars property to True. This causes either a horizontal scroll bar, vertical
scroll bar, or both scroll bars to automatically appear at the right of the text box
if the entered text exceeds the screen area defined for the box. See Chapter 13,
Getting User Input, for more information on these properties.

When a text box control has the focus, each keystroke can be intercepted by
the program with the KeyDown, KeyPress, and KeyUp events. This allows a program to create validity checking on edit fields. For instance, if you wish to limit
the number of characters entered in a text box, you could use the KeyPress event
to determine the current length of the text in a text box before allowing the next
keystroke to be added to the text. More information on these events can be found
in Chapter 16, Keyboard Input.

A text box control can be used as a client in a Dynamic Data Exchange.

TIMER CONTROL

Purpose

The timer control runs code at regular intervals.

Properties, Events, and Methods

Tables 3-73 and 3-74 list the properties and events that relate to the timer control. This control has no associated methods.

Use This Property...	To Do This...
Enabled	Read or set whether this object can react to events
Index	Uniquely identify an element of a control array
Interval	Read or set the length of time between each call to a Timer event
Left	Read or set the left edge placement of this control on a picture or form
Name	Set the name used in code to refer to this object
Parent	Read the name of this control's parent form
Tag	Read or set text information that is particular to this object
Top	Read or set the coordinate of this control's top edge

Table 3-73 Properties of the timer control

Use This Event...	To Do This...
Timer	Initiate an action at a regular timed interval

Table 3-74 Events of the timer control

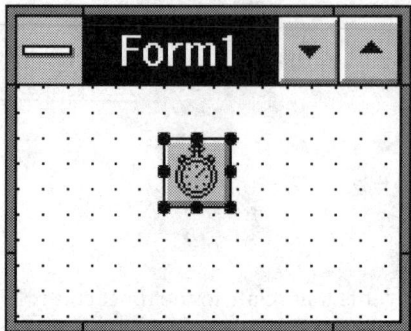

Figure 3-29 The timer control at design time. It is invisible at runtime

Description

The timer control is invisible on a form and cannot be manipulated directly by the user (see Figure 3-29). The main purpose for a timer is to define an activity that is to take place at a regular interval. This is useful for writing routines that are to run in the background of an application with no need for user interaction.

The activity to be performed by the timer is defined by placing code in the control's timer event. The timer control's Interval property specifies how often this event is to be executed. This control, and its properties and events, are covered in Chapter 22, Time.

PART II

Using Forms and Controls

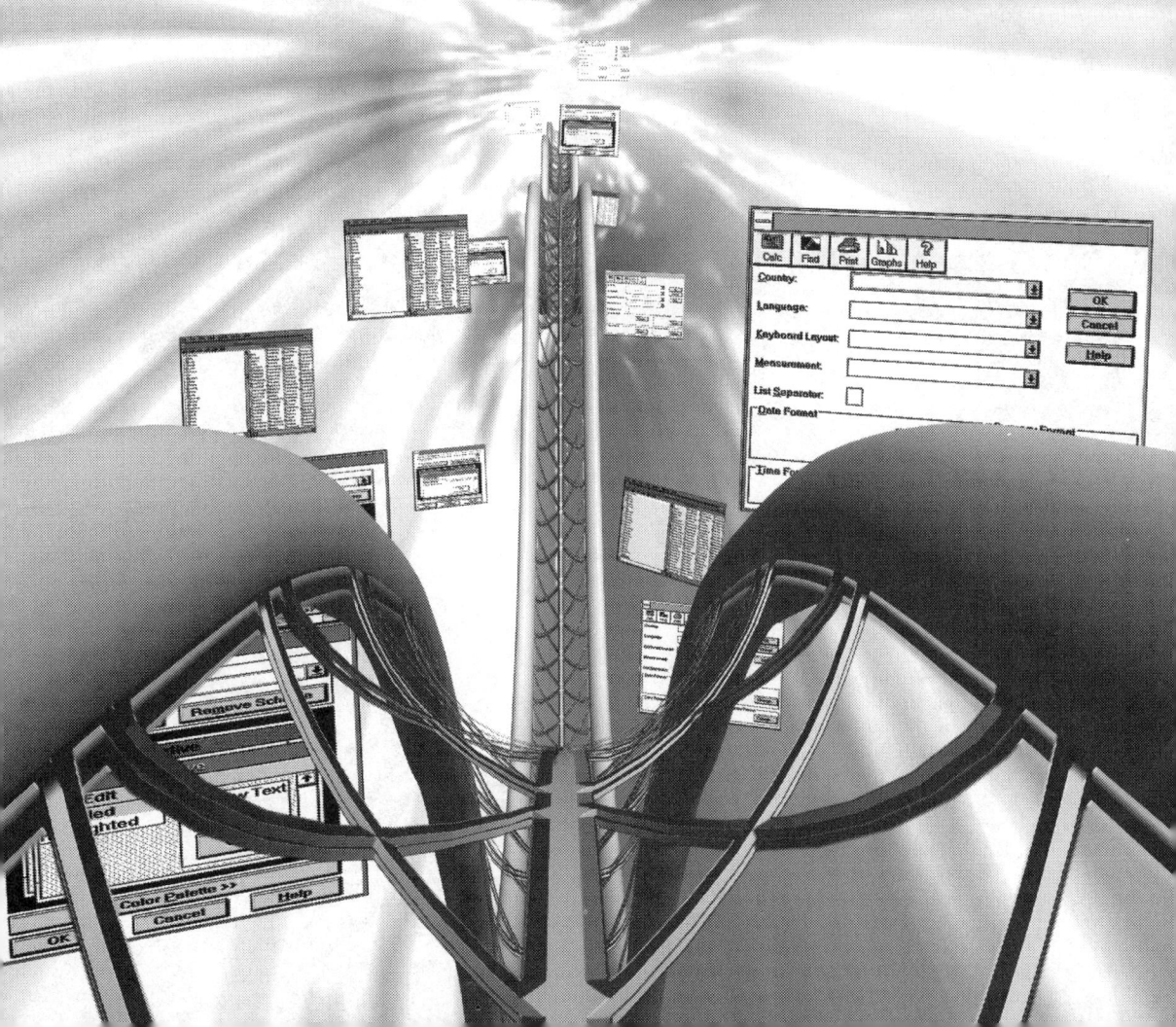

4 FORMS AND MENUS

Designing forms and menus visually and interactively is the heart of Visual Basic programming. Visual Basic 1.0 revolutionized Windows programming by letting you "paint" the entire user interface without writing any code. The newest versions of Visual Basic, versions 2.0 and 3.0, let you easily design even complex structures like a Multiple Document Interface, pop-up menus, and toolbars.

Prior to the release of Microsoft Visual Basic in May of 1991, form setup frequently required several pages of code. This made the process of setting up the forms and menus used by Windows applications a tedious chore. Languages like C need many hundreds of lines of code statements invoking functions with complex syntax to set up an application's forms. Even the familiar "Hello World" window required at least three pages of code. This complexity effectively placed Windows programming out of the reach of most users. Visual Basic replaced this complexity with its elegant simplicity.

This chapter covers the basics of forms and menus. We'll explore the properties, events, methods, and statements used with these two critical elements of the user interface. Later chapters explore all the other controls and interface elements that are placed on forms.

FORMS AND FORM SETUP

Most applications have several different forms that make up the foundation of the user interface. For example, databases have data entry, query, and report forms. A communications program might have a form with a list of phone numbers, and another to alert the user of problems. Many programs allow multiple documents at the same time. For instance, a

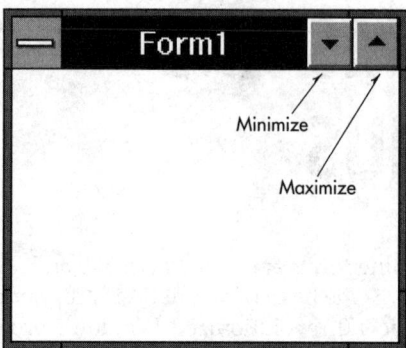

Figure 4-1 Maximize and Minimize
buttons on a form

spreadsheet might allow the user to have several macro sheets, spreadsheets, and charts open at once. The user interacts with each of these forms in specified ways.

Forms must be *loaded* into memory before they can be used. You can *unload* forms from memory when no longer needed; this frees memory for other operations. A loaded form must be explicitly *shown* to be made visible on the screen: the form will be automatically loaded into memory if it's not already present. A form can be *hidden* to make it disappear from screen. Hidden forms still remain in memory, ready for reuse.

Setting up a form requires decisions about five major elements: the Maximize button, the Minimize button, the control box, the border, and the form's MDI (or Multiple Document Interface) status. These elements directly affect the ways the user will be able to manipulate the form. You can attach a menu structure to a form to allow the user to easily choose a variety of program functions. Finally, modern programs often place toolbars and status bars on a form to provide shortcuts for commonly used commands and status information on the program's operation.

Maximize and Minimize Buttons

Like a standard window, a Visual Basic form can be minimized to an icon, restored to its previous size, or maximized to the full screen. To maximize a form, press the Maximize button in the upper-right corner of the form. To minimize a form, press the Minimize button in the upper-right corner of the form. You control whether buttons appear on the form with the MinButton and MaxButton properties; both default to True, thus making them visible. Figure 4-1 shows a window's Minimize button (on the left) and Maximize button (on the right).

Control Box

The control box contains the commands that manipulate the basic appearance and position of the form. Set the form's ControlBox property to True to give a form a control box. The control box is a drop-down menu that Windows activates when the user presses the (ALT) key and space bar ((ALT)-(SPACE)) simultaneously, or clicks on the control box in the upper-left corner of the form. The control box can have a combination of the following commands: Restore, Move, Size, Maximize, Minimize, Close, and Switch To.

The Maximize and Minimize options appear here when their buttons are in the right corner of the form. Choosing one of these command options from the control box has the same effect as pressing the buttons. The Size option lets the user manually change the form's size. The Move option lets the user change the position of the form on the screen without using the mouse. The Close option removes the form from the screen and memory. The Switch To option brings Window's task switch box up on the screen.

Borders

Forms have four possible border styles: none, sizable, fixed single, and fixed double. A form with no border has no Maximize button, Minimize button, or control box. This border style is a popular choice for warning boxes, which do not need these options. Users can change the size of sizable forms, just as the name suggests. Both the fixed single and fixed double borders disable the user's ability to change the form's size with the mouse; however, the user can still minimize and maximize the form. Use the BorderStyle property to specify which kind of border the form will have.

MDI (Multiple Document Interface)

Windows programs such as Excel or Word can open multiple documents at the same time. Each new document (such as a spreadsheet, chart, text file, or formatted word processing file) is contained in and managed within the application. This gives the user the ability to cut and paste between documents, compare versions, or cut up large projects into smaller, more manageable pieces.

This feature is called the *Multiple Document Interface*, or *MDI*, and is available in Visual Basic starting with version 2.0. As you'll see in this chapter, MDI is simply an extension of the object variables discussed in Chapter 3, Using Objects, and is surprisingly easy to manage. You'll learn how to create a complete MDI application, including an MDI-specific Window menu, a toolbar, and a status bar.

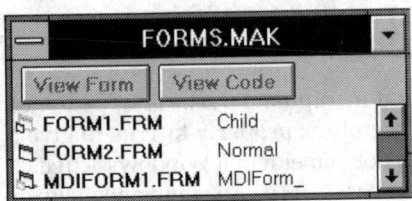

Figure 4-2 The Visual Basic Project window has different icons for normal, MDI, and child forms

A Visual Basic application becomes MDI-capable by creating an MDI form with the File menu's command "New MDI Form." The MDI form functions as a container for multiple *child* forms. Each child form contains a single document type (such as unformatted text or a graphical chart) that you define using whatever controls you place on the child form. Specify other forms as children of the main MDI form by setting their MDIChild property to True in the Properties box. Although there may be only one MDI form per application, you may have many kinds of child forms as well as regular non-MDI forms. For example, Excel has both worksheet and chart child forms as well as a host of normal dialog boxes.

Create new child document forms by creating new instances as discussed in Chapter 3, Using Objects.

Display of Child Forms and Regular, Non-MDI forms

A regular, non-MDI form may display anywhere on the screen. A child form displays completely within the *client area* of the MDI form. The client area is inside the MDI form's borders, not including items like the menu bar, scroll bars, toolbars, or status bars. The user can move and resize the child form, but the child form is restricted to the client area.

When a child form is minimized, its icon appears at the bottom of the client area rather than at the bottom of the desktop as it would for a normal, non-MDI form. A maximized child form fills the entire client area and combines its caption with that of the MDI form and displays it in the MDI form's title bar. A maximized regular, non-MDI form fills the entire screen.

During the design process, child forms are treated like other Visual Basic forms. This lets you move and resize child forms without restriction anywhere on the desktop. You write code, add controls, and set properties, as with any other form. Indeed, they are just a regular form with the one difference of having the MDIChild property set to true.

You can tell if a form is a child form either by looking at the MDIChild property in the Property window, or by looking at the Project window. Child forms have a special icon, as shown in Figure 4-2.

168

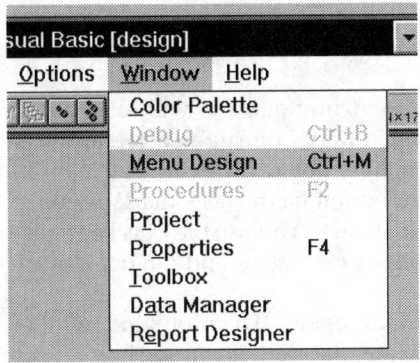

Figure 4-3 How to access the Menu Design dialog box (and a good example of a Windows menu)

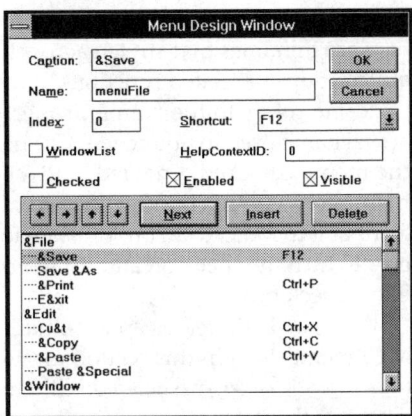

Figure 4-4 The Menu Design dialog box lets you create your own menu structures

MENUS

Most Windows applications have a menu structure. A menu allows the user to access a number of different functions of the program. Typical menu systems have at least two levels: the top level displays on the menu bar, and the second level displays as a drop-down menu. A particular menu structure is always attached to an associated form. Each form may have its own unique menu structure.

Some menu structures have submenus branching off the second level; these allow further refinement of the actions allowed to the user. Visual Basic allows up to four levels of submenus. Be aware that deeply nested menu structures with many sublevels will confound the user and make your program hard to learn. If you find the need to have many choices available to the user, a dialog box would usually make for a clearer implementation.

Creating a Menu Structure

Create menus by clicking on the form you'd like to associate the menu with and choosing Menu Control from the Window menu (shortcut key: (CTRL)-(M)). Figure 4-3 shows how to access the Menu Design box (and incidentally shows what a Windows menu looks like); Figure 4-4 shows the Menu Design window itself.

Caption indicates what text appears on the actual menu, with an ampersand placed in front of a letter indicating an accelerator key. For instance, Visual Basic's Window menu has an ampersand placed in front of the W, which makes it read Window, and makes (ALT)-(W) directly access the menu, as Figure 4-3 illustrates. See Chapter 21, Application Focus, for more details on the Caption property. Entering a hyphen (-) in the Caption places a *separator bar* in that menu position. Separator bars are thin lines that stretch across the width of the open menu to visually separate groups of related functions.

Name refers to the Name property of the menu item, and will serve as the actual name used in your code. Use Index if you want to create an object array for the menu. Checked, Enabled, and Visible simply define the default state of the menu item you're creating. A *checked* menu option has a check mark placed in front of it to indicate an on/off state for a menu item. You use the Checked property to turn the check on and off in your application's code, and can use it much like a check box.

Window List creates an automatic list of all open MDI child windows. See MDI menus later in this section for more details. Shortcut defines a shortcut key (like (CTRL)-(K) or (F1)) associated with this menu entry, and HelpContextID lets you associate the entry with context-sensitive help.

The actual structure of the menu shows as indentation levels in the bottom window. No indentation is a top-level menu that displays on the title bar; each further indentation indicates one deeper level of submenu. You can easily control the level of indentation by highlighting the menu item and clicking on the arrows immediately above the menu dialog's main window.

Using the Menu Structure

A Click event occurs when the user selects a menu item. Place any code you'd like to execute in the Click event procedure. For example,

```
Sub menuPatFileNew_Click ()
    'This routine sets up a new patient
    PatEntry.Show MODAL        'Show the entry dialog
End Sub
```

Pop-Up Menus

Visual Basic 3.0 adds the capability of using *pop-up menus* in your applications. A pop-up menu typically appears when the user clicks the nondefault (usually right) mouse button. Pop-ups are usually context sensitive, and will display options appropriate for the object they are over. For instance, a word processor may pop up a menu listing font choices, sizes, and styles when editing text, and a different menu listing row height or column width adjustments when popped up while editing a table.

Pop-up menus display when you use the PopupMenu method on a form. You specify what menu you want to display, and can give the method optional parameters for exactly where it displays and how it behaves. The menu name you

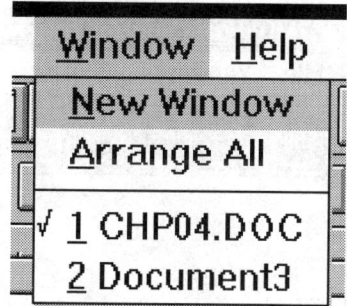

Figure 4-5 MDI forms should have a dedicated Window menu to manage child forms

give can be either an existing menu that appears on a menu bar, or a custom menu designed specifically for that context. The name you give must have at least one sublevel of menus; it is the sublevels that actually display in the pop-up.

You would typically write a pop-up display routine in the MouseDown event, and check to see if the right mouse button is pressed before displaying the menu. The following example shows the menuWindow menu being popped up:

```
Sub Text1_MouseDown (Button As Integer, Shift As Integer, X As Single, Y As Single)
    If Button = RIGHT_BUTTON Then
        PopupMenu menuWindow, 2   'pop up menu, OK to choose item w/right mouse button
    End If
End Sub
```

For more information about MouseDown, see Chapter 14, Mouse Events. For more about the exact usage of the PopupMenu method, see its entry later in this chapter.

MDI Child Form Menus

Child forms display menus slightly differently than non-MDI forms. The child form's menus display on the parent MDI form's menu bar rather than on the child form. If no children are loaded (or the loaded children have no menus), then the MDI form displays its own menu.

Place any menu controls that apply to a child form on the child form. If your application has more than one kind of document, create different child forms to perform the different functions, and supply each child form with its own menu.

An MDI application should have a special Window menu. This typically displays the captions of all child forms and lets the user rearrange the display with commands like Cascade, Tile, and Arrange Icons, as discussed in the Arrange method's entry (see Figure 4-5). Although any menu control on an MDI form or

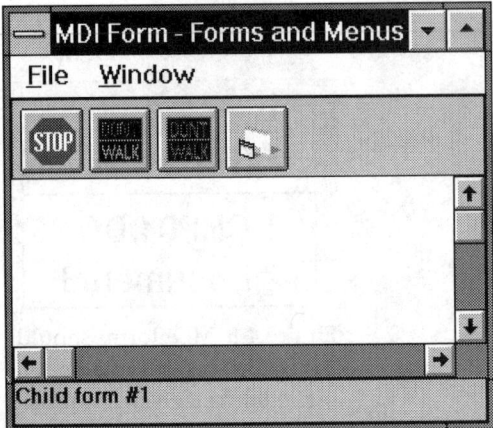

Figure 4-6 Toolbar and status bar made with the picture box control on an MDI form

child form can display the list of child forms, common Windows programming practice puts this list on its own Window menu. To display the list, simply set the WindowList property of that menu control to True. Visual Basic then automatically manages and displays the list of open child forms for you. It displays the captions of each child and places a check mark next to the one that had the focus most recently. The WindowList property applies only to MDI forms and child forms; it has no effect on standard forms.

TOOLBARS AND STATUS BARS

Many Windows applications contain toolbars, ribbon bars, control bars, and status bars. These typically provide easy access to commonly used commands as well as letting you monitor the status of the application.

To create one of these, place a picture box on a regular non-MDI form, or the MDI form if you are creating an MDI application. The picture box will automatically stretch to fill the width of the MDI form. The picture box is the only standard control that may be placed directly on an MDI form, as the MDI form needs the control to support the Align property. (Some third-party controls, such as the 3D panel control that comes with the Professional Edition, also support the Align property.) The Align property for a picture box on an MDI form may be set to the Top (=1) or Bottom (=2).

Place any controls you'd like on the picture box. A toolbar would typically be at the top and use command buttons, animated buttons, image controls, and combo boxes. Status bars would typically be located on the bottom and have labels, picture boxes, and panels. Figure 4-6 shows the Example application for this chapter with these elements noted.

The coding for toolbars is usually very simple, as they most often repeat commands accessible from other areas of your application. When you have several different ways of executing a command (such as by a main menu, a child menu, a toolbar, and a dialog box) you can place the common code in its own sub procedure in a code module. For example,

```
Sub FileClose ()
    ' This procedure is placed in a code module, and is called from several
    ' different areas
    Unload DocumentForm
End Sub

Sub menuMDIFileClose_Click ()
    FileClose
End Sub

Sub menuChildFileClose_Click ()
    FileClose
End Sub

Sub pictToolbarFileClose_Click ()
    FileClose
End Sub

Sub cmndDialogFileClose_Click ()
    FileClose
End Sub
```

SUMMARY OF FORMS AND MENUS

Table 4-1 displays the methods, statements, events, and properties that control the basic setup of a form.

Use or Set This...		To Do This...
Arrange	Method	Arranges MDI child forms within the MDI form
ControlBox	Property	Determine whether the ControlBox appears on a form
Hide	Method	Make a form invisible on the screen
Load	Event	React when a form loads into memory
Load	Statement	Load a form into memory but do not make it visible
MaxButton	Property	Determine whether the form has a Maximize button

(continued on next page)

(continued from previous page)

Use or Set This...		To Do This...
MDIChild	Property	Determine whether a form is a child of the MDI form
MinButton	Property	Determine whether the form has a Minimize button
PopupMenu	Method	Display a pop-up menu
QueryUnload	Event	React before a form is removed from memory
Resize	Event	React when a form's size changes
Show	Method	Make a form visible, and if necessary, load it into memory first
Unload	Event	React when a form is removed from memory
Unload	Statement	Remove a form from memory
WindowState	Property	Read or set whether a form is minimized, maximized, or normal

Table 4-1 Methods, statements, properties, and events dealing with setting up a form

CONSTANT.TXT Values

Many of the properties, events, and methods of this chapter use numeric values as arguments. Using constants rather than the literal value makes your code self-documenting, more readable, and easier to debug.

Microsoft provides a file, CONSTANT.TXT, that has many constant declarations defined for you. For smaller applications it's probably easiest just to type the declarations in yourself. For larger applications you'll find it much easier to read the text file into a new module.

To do this, create a new module by pulling down the File menu and choosing the New Module menu command. Then pull down the File menu again, and choose Load Text. This opens up a dialog box listing all text files in the current directory. CONSTANT.TXT should be in your main Visual Basic directory (default installation would place this in C:\VB). Simply choose CONSTANT.TXT to enter the entire file into your module. These constants will then be available throughout your application.

Table 4-2 lists the value of the constant, the CONSTANT.TXT constant name, and a brief description of what the constant means.

Value	CONSTANT.TXT	Meaning
Arrange method		
0	CASCADE	Cascade all nonminimized MDI child forms
1	TILE_HORIZONTAL	Tile all nonminimized MDI child forms horizontally
2	TILE_VERTICAL	Tile all nonminimized MDI child forms vertically
3	ARRANGE_ICONS	Arrange the icons of all minimized MDI child forms
PopupMenu method		
0	POPUPMENU_LEFTALIGN	(Default) The left side of the pop-up menu is at x
4	POPUPMENU_CENTERALIGN	The pop-up menu is centered at x
8	POPUPMENU_RIGHTALIGN	The right side of the pop-up menu is at x
0	POPUPMENU_LEFTBUTTON	(Default) The pop-up menu responds to the left mouse button only
2	POPUPMENU_RIGHTBUTTON	The pop-up menu responds to both left and right mouse buttons
UnloadMode argument in QueryUnload		
0	FORM_CONTROLMENU	User chose the Close command from the control box
1	FORM_CODE	Unload event invoked in code
2	APP_WINDOWS	Windows is ending
3	APP_TASKMANAGER	Task Manager is closing the application

(continued on next page)

(continued from previous page)

Value	CONSTANT.TXT	Meaning
UnloadMode argument in QueryUnload		
4	FORM_MDIFORM	MDI child form closing because the MDI form is closing
Show method		
0	MODELESS	(Default) Code after the Show method runs normally
1	MODAL	Code after the Show method runs after the form closes
WindowState property		
0	NORMAL	Restores the form to the previous size
1	MINIMIZED	Reduces the form to an icon
2	MAXIMIZED	Fills the screen (or client area for MDI child) with the form

Table 4-2 CONSTANT.TXT values for forms and menus

ARRANGE METHOD

Objects Affected

Check	Clipboard	Combo	Command	CommonDlg
Data	Debug	Dir	Drive	File
Form	Frame	Grid	Image	Label
Line	List	▶ MDI Form	Menu	OLE
Option	Picture	Printer	Screen	Scroll
Shape	Text	Timer		

Purpose

Use the Arrange method on an MDI form to automatically arrange all MDI child forms contained within it. Tables 4-3 and 4-4 summarize the arguments of the Arrange method.

General Syntax

```
[Name.]Arrange setting%
```

Argument	Description
Name	Name property of the MDI form

Table 4-3 Argument of the Arrange method

setting%	CONSTANT.TXT	Meaning
0	CASCADE	Cascade all nonminimized MDI child forms
1	TILE_HORIZONTAL	Tile all nonminimized MDI child forms horizontally
2	TILE_VERTICAL	Tile all nonminimized MDI child forms vertically
3	ARRANGE_ICONS	Arrange the icons of all minimized MDI child forms

Table 4-4 Meanings of the setting% argument in the Arrange method

Example Syntax

```
Sub menuWindow_Click (Index As Integer)
    Select Case Index
        Case 0: MDIForm.Arrange CASCADE
        Case 1: MDIForm.Arrange TILE_HORIZONTAL
        Case 2: MDIForm.Arrange TILE_VERTICAL
        Case 3: MDIForm.Arrange ARRANGE_ICONS
    End Select
End Sub
```

Description

An MDI application should have a special Window menu. This typically displays the captions of all child forms and lets the user rearrange the display with commands like Cascade, Tile, and Arrange Icons using the MDIForm's Arrange method. The Arrange method takes a numerical argument that determines how Windows will arrange the child windows. These arguments are defined in CONSTANT.TXT. See the Forms and Menus Summary at the beginning of this chapter for instructions on how to use CONSTANT.TXT values. Note that only the MDIForm has the Arrange method; regular forms do not.

Common Windows programming practice puts the arrangement choices on their own Window menu, along with a list of all the open child forms. Set the menu's WindowList property to True to have Visual Basic automatically create and track a list of these child forms for you.

Example

The Forms and Menus project at the end of the chapter shows how to build a typical Window menu. It includes all four arrangement methods.

CONTROLBOX PROPERTY

Objects Affected

Check	Clipboard	Combo	Command	CommonDlg
Data	Debug	Dir	Drive	File
▶ Form	Frame	Grid	Image	Label
Line	List	MDI Form	Menu	OLE
Option	Picture	Printer	Screen	Scroll
Shape	Text	Timer		

Purpose

The ControlBox property governs whether a control box appears in the top-left corner of a form. This property is read-only at runtime. Tables 4-5 and 4-6 summarize the meaning of the arguments of the ControlBox property.

General Syntax

```
[form.]ControlBox
```

Argument	Description
form	Name property of the form
	If no name specified, then references the current form's ControlBox property

Table 4-5 Argument of the ControlBox property

Value	Description
True, -1	(Default) Displays the control box
False, 0	Does not display the control box

Table 4-6 Possible values of ControlBox property

Example Syntax

```
Sub SetColor (FormName As Form)
    If FormName.ControlBox=0 Then          'Tests for disabled ControlBox on the form
        FormName.BackColor=RGB(192,192,192) 'Form's background changes to gray
    Else
        FormName.BackColor=RGB(0,128,0)     'Form's background changes to green
    End If
End Sub
```

Description

The ControlBox property manages the user's access to a drop-down command menu that contains options for sizing, closing, or moving the window. The control to access the menu can be selected with the mouse or keyboard. The control box is in a form's upper-left corner, as shown in Figure 4-7. A form's ControlBox property can only be set at design time. Any attempt to change the ControlBox property of a form at runtime will generate an error. You can, however, refer to the ControlBox property at runtime. In the example syntax, a sub procedure named SetColor uses the ControlBox property setting to decide the background color of a form. Figure 4-7 illustrates an opened ControlBox.

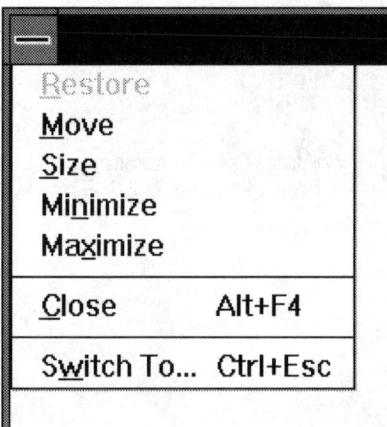

Figure 4-7 An opened control box

BorderStyle, MaxButton, and MinButton Properties

The commands displayed on the control box include the familiar Restore, Move, Size, Minimize, Maximize, Close, and Switch To. Several properties affect the display of the control box when the ControlBox property is True. When the BorderStyle property of the form is 0 (none), the control box will not be displayed. If the MaxButton and MinButton properties of that form are False, then those commands will not appear on the control box. When the BorderStyle property of a form is 1 (fixed single) or 3 (fixed double), Size does not appear in the control box. As long as the ControlBox property of a form is True, both the Restore and Move commands will appear on the control box.

Example

The Forms project at the end of this chapter shows the difference between a form with and without the control box. The Modal dialog box displays without the control box; all the other forms have a control box.

Comments

Notice that the control box can always be seen on a form at design time. It is only at runtime that you can see the effects when a ControlBox property is False. This makes it easier to manipulate the forms while you're designing them.

HIDE METHOD

Objects Affected

Check	Clipboard	Combo	Command	CommonDlg
Data	Debug	Dir	Drive	File
▶ Form	Frame	Grid	Image	Label
Line	List	▶ MDI Form	Menu	OLE
Option	Picture	Printer	Screen	Scroll
Shape	Text	Timer		

Purpose

The Hide method makes an active and visible form disappear from the screen and is the same as setting the form's Visible property to False (0). Table 4-7 summarizes the FormName argument of the Hide method.

General Syntax

```
[form.]Hide
```

Argument	Description
form	Name property of the form

Table 4-7 Argument of the Hide method

Example Syntax

```
Sub Form1_Load ()
    Form2.Hide                          'Hide form2
    Form2.BackColor = RGB(0,255,0)      'Set background color of form2 to light green
    Form2.ForeColor = RGB(0,0,255)      'Set the text color of form2 to blue
    MsgBox "Press OK to see form2"      'Display MsgBox indicating press OK to see form2
    Form2.Show                          'Unhide Form2
End Sub
```

Description

The Hide method reduces clutter by removing a form from the screen without removing it from memory. Any forms not initially needed can be loaded and hidden

181

until desired. The Show method displays a hidden form on the screen. Hidden forms take a little more time to load at program startup, but reduce the load time when needed. For example, a personal information manager might load up the address book, scheduler, and to-do list at program startup. This allows the user to switch quickly between the information found in each form. With this approach each form displays in a fraction of the time necessary to load it.

Hidden forms reside in the operating memory of the computer. A form's Visible property changes to False when the form is hidden with the Hide Method. This method disconnects the form from user input. A hidden form can still respond to coded events and any resulting property changes or DDE (Dynamic Data Exchange) communication. For example, a law firm's client data entry system could begin with the primary name and address form visible and the case detail form hidden. Events could place the information the user enters (such as a name) into the corresponding fields of the hidden data entry form.

The Show Method

The Hide method shares an inverse relationship with the Show method. Hide removes the form from sight and Show restores it. In the example syntax, the two methods work together to make a form invisible while its colors change. After making modifications the Show method restores it to view. This technique also could be used for a warning dialog box that displays different messages depending on the situation.

The Visible Property

When the Hide method makes a form invisible, the Visible property of the form becomes False. The difference between using the Hide method and directly changing the setting of the Visible property lies in the types of objects affected. The Hide method can only be used on a form. In contrast, the Visible property can be used on any of the controls or forms in Visual Basic. This difference can be used in generic functions and procedures to limit an effect to forms, or to apply to all objects.

Example

The Forms project at the end of this section demonstrates the Hide method several times. When the user closes either of the dialog boxes, the Hide event removes the form from the screen. A Hide method expression keeps the form in memory while taking it out of the user's view. In this case the Hide method is better than the Unload statement because it saves time putting the form on screen when needed again.

Comments

A hidden form or control can still have its properties changed or referenced. Forms disappear off the screen as quickly as the computer's processor allows. The amount of available operating memory determines the number of forms that can be hidden.

LOAD EVENT

Objects Affected

Check	Clipboard	Combo	Command	CommonDlg
Data	Debug	Dir	Drive	File
▶ Form	Frame	Grid	Image	Label
Line	List	▶ MDI Form	Menu	OLE
Option	Picture	Printer	Screen	Scroll
Shape	Text	Timer		

Purpose

The Load event specifies what actions occur when a form loads. Table 4-8 summarizes the arguments of the Load event.

General Syntax

```
Sub Form_Load ()
Sub MDIForm_Load ()
```

Argument	Description
Form	'Form' (literal, not the Name property of the form) specifies the normal or MDI child form
MDIForm	'MDIForm' (literal, not the Name property of the MDIForm) specifies the MDI form

Table 4-8 Arguments of the Load event

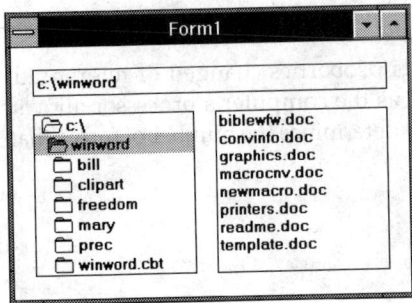

Figure 4-8 Appearance of example syntax in Form_Load event

Example Syntax

```
Sub Form_Load ()
    Dir1.Path = "\WINWORD"          'Sets the initial path to the Winword directory
    File1.Path = Dir1.Path          'Makes File box's path same as Directory box
    File1.FileName = "*.DOC"        'Limits the types of files displayed to the "DOC" extension
    Text1.Text = File1.Path         'Displays current path in the text window
End Sub
```

Description

The Form_Load event procedure initializes the form and any related variables when the form loads. Text boxes may have their initial information inserted. List and combo boxes can be given their lists for the user to choose from. A letter-writing program might prompt the user to select a name from its database. Any option or check box controls may be set to their initial values. The drive, directory, and file boxes get their default Path and FileName properties in the Form_Load event of the example syntax. This relieves the user of the necessity of changing to the correct drive and directory. In the example syntax, the File1 file box displays only files with the DOC extension. Figure 4-8 shows what this form and its controls might look like.

A loaded form is in memory but cannot be seen by the user. A form's Load event takes place in three ways. First, any forms loaded at program startup initiate a Form_Load event. Second, Visual Basic generates a Form_Load event if a form loads using a Load statement. Third, any change or reference made to a property of an "unloaded" control or form loads the form and triggers the Form_Load event. For example, a calculator could have a Form_Load event that changes the Text property of the readout text box to 0. When the user presses a command button labeled Tape, a second form could be loaded below the calculator on the screen. This second form's Load event places the last few calculations made in its display text window.

The Load, Resize, Paint, and GotFocus Events

If more than one event is attached to a particular control, they are processed in the following order: Load, Resize, Paint, and GotFocus. This is an important point to keep in mind if any of the actions that take place in one event depend upon actions in another event. For example, a data entry form for an address book would have problems if the Load event disables the Address1 text box, and the GotFocus event tries to use it.

The Unload Event

The Load event shares an inverse relationship with the Unload event. While the Load event affects the form when opened, the Unload event takes place when it is closed. Both events can depend on each other. For example, the Load event might set up the form to initiate some action. The Unload event could either restore the form to its preloaded settings or process the actions that took place. The address book, for example, might use the Load event to insert into the edit screen the last accessed information. An Unload event might save the information entered into the fields to the database.

Example

The Forms project at the end of the chapter demonstrates the Load event. When the MDI form loads at program startup, the Load event defines the current contents of the program variables and sets up the child forms. This initialization works best here because the Load event is always the first event to be processed when more than one event is called at the same time.

LOAD STATEMENT

Objects Affected

▶ Check	Clipboard	▶ Combo	▶ Command	CommonDlg
▶ Data	Debug	▶ Dir	▶ Drive	▶ File
▶ Form	Frame	▶ Grid	▶ Image	▶ Label
▶ Line	▶ List	▶ MDI Form	Menu	▶ OLE
▶ Option	▶ Picture	Printer	Screen	Scroll
▶ Shape	▶ Text	▶ Timer		

Purpose

The Load statement directly places a form or control into memory without making it visible to the user. Table 4-9 summarizes the meaning of the object argument.

General Syntax

```
Load object
```

Argument	Description
object	Name property of the item to be loaded

Table 4-9 Argument of the Load statement

Example Syntax

```
Sub Form_Load ()                          'Form1's load event
    Load Form2                            'Load form2, but don't display
End Sub

Sub Command1_Click ()                     'Created on Form1
    Form2.Visible = True                  'Display Form2 now
End Sub

Sub Form_Load ()
    optnAuto(0).Caption = "GM"            'existing control created at design time
    optnAuto(0).Top = 200
    Load optnAuto(1)                      'create new control in array at runtime
    optnAuto(1).Caption = "Ford"
    optnAuto(1).Top = 600
    optnAuto(0).Visible = True            'display these option
    optnAuto(1).Visible = True            'buttons on the screen.
End Sub
```

Description

The Load statement loads forms and controls into memory without displaying them. Once a form loads into memory, you can quickly unhide it by changing the Visible property of the form or control to True (-1). While a form is in memory, its properties can be accessed and changed. The second example listed in the example syntax uses the Load statement to create new controls for the optnAuto control array. Figure 4-9 shows this form before running, and Figure 4-10 shows the additional option button created in the code.

The single argument used for this statement is the object. An object argument can be the Name property of a form, control, or control array. A form or control

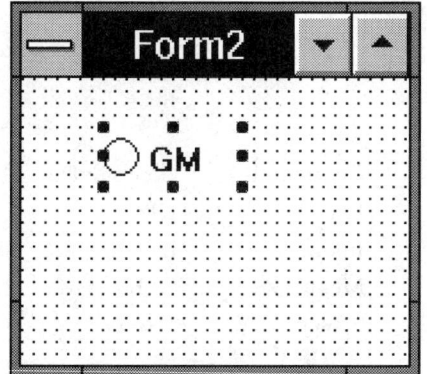

Figure 4-9 Single object forms a "template" for a control array

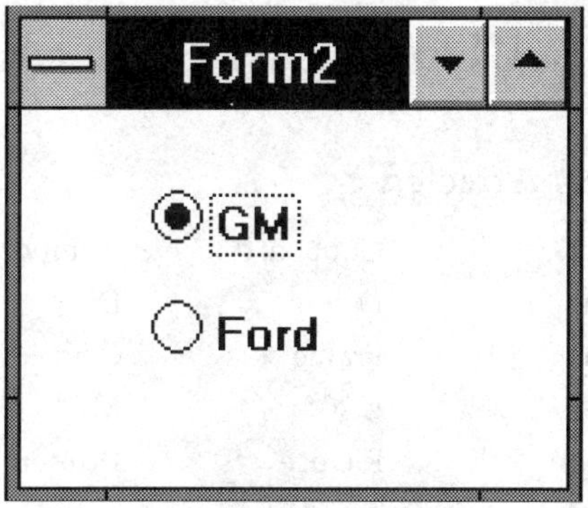

Figure 4-10 Multiple objects in control array Loaded into memory

remains in memory until taken out by an Unload statement or until the program or parent form closes.

The Show Method

The Load statement and the Show method have very similar functions in Visual Basic, but the difference between them is very important. The Load statement does not directly make the controls or forms that it brings into memory visible to the user. The Show method statement both loads the control or form into memory if it hasn't already been loaded and makes it visible to the user. A Load statement allows you to preload a control or form without displaying it. The amount of time required to bring up new screens can be reduced by loading all the necessary forms early.

Example

In the Forms project at the end of this chapter, the Load statement loads the two dialog boxes into memory at program startup. In this case the Load statement is a better choice than a Show method because it does not make the form visible on the screen. This reduces screen clutter and makes it less likely for the user to be confused when confronted with two forms at once.

Comments

Multiple instances of a particular control can be made visible on a form by setting up a control array and giving each control a unique array number. This is useful for standardizing the events for a particular type of control. For example, an option box could be set up and loaded initially with a control array. Each instance of the control array could be made visible and have a different label.

MAXBUTTON PROPERTY

Objects Affected

Check	Clipboard	Combo	Command	CommonDlg
Data	Debug	Dir	Drive	File
▶ Form	Frame	Grid	Image	Label
Line	List	MDI Form	Menu	OLE
Option	Picture	Printer	Screen	Scroll
Shape	Text	Timer		

Purpose

The MaxButton property controls whether the Maximize icon button appears in the top-right corner of a form at runtime. Clicking this button maximizes the form, making it fill the entire screen. The MaxButton property is read-only at runtime. Table 4-10 summarizes the argument of the MaxButton property.

General Syntax

```
[form.]MaxButton
```

Argument	Description
form	Name property of the form
	If no name specified, then references the current form's MaxButton property

Table 4-10 Argument of the MaxButton property

Example Syntax

```
Sub WindowLoad (FormName As Form)
    If FormName.MaxButton = True Then      'Checks for enabled Maximize button
        FormName.WindowState = 2           'Maximizes the specified form
    Else
        FormName.WindowState = 0           'Normalizes the specified form
    End If
End Sub
```

Figure 4-11 The Maximize button of a maximized form. Pressing it would restore the form to its normal size

Figure 4-12 The Maximize button of a normalized form. Pressing it would maximize the form

Description

The MaxButton property of a form controls whether a form displays a Maximize button in the top-right corner. A form's MaxButton property can only be set at design time. Any attempt to change the MaxButton property of a form at runtime generates an error. You can, however, refer to the MaxButton property at runtime. The example syntax uses a form's MaxButton setting to determine whether to maximize or normalize a form. This is a generic procedure that can be used on more than one form of a program. The MaxButton property defaults to True. Note that an MDIForm always has a Maximize button even though it does not have the MaxButton property. Figures 4-11 and 4-12 show what the Maximize buttons of maximized and normalized forms look like.

The BorderStyle and WindowState Properties

The BorderStyle property of a form also affects the appearance of the Maximize control. If the BorderStyle of a form is either 0 (none) or 3 (fixed double), then the Maximize button will not display with either setting. With BorderStyle 3, if the MaxButton property is True, then the Maximize command will appear in the control box of the form even though there is no Maximize button. No matter what the settings of the MaxButton and BorderStyle properties are, you can still maximize a form using the WindowState property, as shown in the example syntax. A form's BorderStyle property has no effect on the form's ability to be maximized.

Example

The Forms project at the end of this chapter shows the difference between a form with and without the Maximize button. The Modal dialog box displays without a Maximize button, while other forms have one.

189

Comments

Remember that the absence of the Maximize button on a form does not prevent the form from being maximized by the user if the maximize option appears in the control box menu.

MDICHILD PROPERTY

Objects Affected

Check	Clipboard	Combo	Command	CommonDlg
Data	Debug	Dir	Drive	File
▶ Form	Frame	Grid	Image	Label
Line	List	MDI Form	Menu	OLE
Option	Picture	Printer	Screen	Scroll
Shape	Text	Timer		

Purpose

The MDIChild property defines whether a form is a regular, non-MDI form or an MDI child form. The MDIChild property is read-only at runtime. Tables 4-11 and 4-12 describe the arguments and settings of the MDIChild property.

General Syntax

```
[Form.]MDIChild
```

Argument	Description
form	Name property of the form

Table 4-11 Argument of the MDIChild property

Setting	Description
True	The form is an MDI child form
False	The form is a normal, non-MDI form

Table 4-12 Settings of the MDIChild Property

190

Example Syntax

```
Sub MDIForm_Load ()
    Dim childForm as New Form1        'Set Form1's MDIChild property to True!
    childForm.Show                    'Display the newly created Child form
    If childForm.MDIChild = True Then
        MsgBox "This is a child form"  'Always true if Form1.MDIChild is True
    End If
End Sub
```

Description

The MDI parent form functions as a container for multiple child forms. Flag other forms as children of the main MDI form by setting their MDIChild property to True. Although there may be only one MDI form per application, you may have many kinds of child forms as well as normal, non-MDI forms. For example, Excel has both worksheet and chart child forms as well as a host of normal dialog boxes.

A regular, non-MDI form may display anywhere on the screen. A child form displays completely within the client area of the MDI form. The client area is inside the MDI form's borders, not including items like the menu bar, scroll bars, toolbars, or status bars. The user can move and resize the child form, but it is restricted to the client area. When a child form is minimized, its icon appears at the bottom of the client area rather than at the bottom of the desktop as it would for a normal, non-MDI form. A maximized child form fills the entire client area and combines its caption with the MDI form's and displays it in the MDI form's title bar. In contrast, a maximized regular, non-MDI form fills the entire screen.

Minimizing the MDI parent form puts its icon at the bottom of the desktop just as with any application. All child forms are contained within the MDI form, so there are no additional icons on the desktop for them.

A regular, non-MDI form's menu (if it has one) displays directly below its title bar. A child form's menus display on the MDI form's menu bar. The only time the MDI form's own menus display is when there are no child forms open. For example, closing all documents in Excel removes most menus and leaves only an abbreviated File menu and Help menu. This is the MDI parent form's menu. Switching between a worksheet and chart changes the menus to reflect the choices available in the two different child forms. See the section on Menus at the beginning of this chapter for more on Menu design.

During the design process, child forms are treated like other Visual Basic forms rather than as child forms. This lets you move and resize child forms without restriction anywhere on the desktop. You write code, add controls, and set properties as with any other form. Indeed, they are just a regular form with the one difference of having the MDIChild property set to True. One of the few exceptions to this is that MDI child forms cannot be modal—they are always modeless.

Create a new MDI child form by declaring it in a Dim statement as in the Example syntax. This creates an MDI child form using Form1 as a template, assuming Form1 has its MDIChild property set to True. The example at the end of this chapter shows a more complete method of creating and tracking MDI child forms. Note that the MDIChild property is read-only at runtime.

Borders, Positioning, and Control

If a child form's borders are sizable (BorderStyle=2), Windows determines the height, width, and position based on the size of the parent MDI form. If a child's borders are fixed (BorderStyle=0, 1, or 3), then it is loaded with the Height and Width of its design time properties.

MDI is fully functional in Windows 3.1. There are some differences when an MDI application is run under Windows 3.0. You can disable the child form's control box, Minimize button, and Maximize button by setting these properties to False. The control box and sizing buttons will still appear on the form even though they won't respond to user clicks. A disabled control box can still drop down (using (ALT) - (-)) but won't have the Close and Next Window commands available.

Loading and Unloading

Loading and unloading child forms is somewhat more involved than with a regular, non-MDI form. Loading a child form automatically loads its parent MDI form. However, loading the parent MDI form does not automatically load any children. If you want to automatically load a blank document into your application, specify the child form as the default startup form.

If a child form's borders are sizable (BorderStyle=2), Windows determines the height, width, and position based on the size of the parent MDI form. The only way to exactly position and size a child form is by using the Top, Left, Width, and Height properties discussed in Chapter 5, Application Appearance, after the form is loaded. If a child's borders are fixed (BorderStyle=0, 1, or 3), then it is loaded with the Height and Width of its design time properties.

A child form unloads whenever it is closed from its control box, an Unload command is performed on it, or its parent MDI form closes. The parent MDI form may be closed for a variety of reasons: it is closed by its control box, within code triggered by a File Exit command, by the Windows Task Manager, or perhaps by Windows shutting down.

Use the QueryUnload event to perform any cleanup necessary before unloading a child form. This event is invoked before any form unloads (in the event of the MDI form or application being closed) and provides a means of stopping the whole unloading process. A typical use for this is to let the user save any changes to a document. The following example uses the Global variable ChangedText to check whether to prompt the user to save before closing:

```
Sub Form_QueryUnload (Cancel As Integer, UnloadMode As Integer)
    If ChangedText Then            ' ChangedText flags changes to this child's data
        Msg = "Document has changed.  Save Changes?"
        SaveChange = MsgBox(Msg, 51) ' Exclamation with Yes/No/Cancel
```

```
        Select Case SaveChange
        Case 2                      ' User chooses cancel; stop unloading process
            Cancel = True
        Case 6                      ' Save the file and continue unloading
            FileSave                ' Save the document!
            Cancel = False
        Case 7                      ' User chooses no save; continue unloading
            Cancel = False
        End Select
    End If
End Sub
```

Example

The Forms project at the end of the chapter uses MDI child forms in addition to normal, non-MDI forms. A button on the main MDI form lets you create multiple instances of the MDI child form.

Comments

Use the QueryUnload event to perform any cleanup necessary before unloading a child form. This event is invoked before any form is unloaded (in the event of the MDI form or application being closed) and provides a means of stopping the whole unloading process. A typical use for this is to let the user save any changes to a document.

MINBUTTON PROPERTY

Objects Affected

Check	Clipboard	Combo	Command	CommonDlg
Data	Debug	Dir	Drive	File
▶ Form	Frame	Grid	Image	Label
Line	List	MDI Form	Menu	OLE
Option	Picture	Printer	Screen	Scroll
Shape	Text	Timer		

Purpose

The MinButton property controls whether the Minimize icon button will appear in the top-right corner of a form at runtime. The MinButton peoperty is read-only at runtime. Table 4-13 summarizes the form argument of the MinButton property.

193

General Syntax

```
[form.]MinButton
```

Argument	Description
form	Name property of the form
	If no name specified, then references the current form's MinButton property

Table 4-13 Argument of the MinButton property

Example Syntax

```
Sub FormSize (FormName As Form)
    If FormName.MinButton = True Then      'Checks for enabled Minimize button
        FormName.WindowState = 1           'Minimizes the specified form
    Else
        FormName.WindowState = 0           'Normalizes the specified form
    End If
End Sub
```

Description

The MinButton property of a form determines whether a form displays its Minimize control button in the top-right corner of the form. A form's MinButton property can only be set at design time. Any attempt to change the MinButton property of a form at runtime will generate an error. You can, however, refer to the MinButton property at runtime. The example above uses the setting of the MinButton property of a form to determine whether the form will appear in normal or minimized size. This function is generic so that it can be used for all of the forms of a program to establish a standard setup.

Figure 4-13 displays how the Minimize button appears on a form. There are two possible settings for the MinButton property, True (-1) and False (0). True is the default value for all forms.

The presence of the MinButton control determines whether the user will be able to use the Minimize button to reduce the size of the form down to the icon symbol designated for it. The MinButton property is a useful tool for removing this ability from the user in cases where this would be inappropriate.

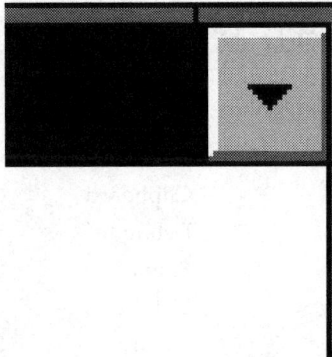

Figure 4-13 The Minimize button. Pressing it would minimize the form

The BorderStyle and WindowState Properties

The BorderStyle property of a form also affects the appearance of the Minimize control. If the BorderStyle of a form is either 0 (none) or 3 (fixed double), then the Minimize button will not be displayed with either setting. As long as the MinButton Property is True and the BorderStyle of the form is 3 (fixed double), the Minimize command will still appear in the control box of a form. No matter what the setting for the MinButton or BorderStyle properties is, a form can still be minimized using the WindowState property, as shown in the example. A form's BorderStyle property has no effect upon the form's ability to be minimized. For example, a form with a MinButton property set to False (0) and a BorderStyle of 3 (fixed double) can still be minimized using this statement:

```
Form.WindowState = 2
```

Example

The Forms project at the end of the chapter demonstrates the differences between forms with and without the Minimize button. The modal dialog box does not have a Minimize button, while all other forms do.

Comments

Remember that the absence of the MinButton on a form does not prevent the user from minimizing a form if the Minimize command appears in the control box menu.

POPUPMENU METHOD

Objects Affected

Check	Clipboard	Combo	Command	CommonDlg
Data	Debug	Dir	Drive	File
▶ Form	Frame	Grid	Image	Label
Line	List	MDI Form	Menu	OLE
Option	Picture	Printer	Screen	Scroll
Shape	Text	Timer		

Purpose

The PopupMenu method displays a *pop-up menu*. These menus can appear anywhere on the form, and are generally context sensitive. Most applications display them when the right mouse button is clicked. Tables 4-14 and 4-15 show the arguments and values for the PopupMenu method.

General Syntax

```
[form.]PopupMenu menuName[, flags%[, x![, y!]]]
```

Arguments	Description
form	Name property of the form
menuName	Name property of the menu to display
flags%	Defines the general location and behavior of the menu
x!, y!	Defines the exact location of the menu

Table 4-14 Arguments of the PopupMenu method

flags%	CONSTANT.TXT	Meaning
0	POPUPMENU_LEFTALIGN	(Default) The left side of the pop-up menu is at x
4	POPUPMENU_CENTERALIGN	The pop-up menu is centered at x
8	POPUPMENU_RIGHTALIGN	The right side of the pop-up menu is at x
0	POPUPMENU_LEFTBUTTON	(Default) The pop-up menu responds to the left mouse button only
2	POPUPMENU_RIGHTBUTTON	The pop-up menu responds to both left and right mouse buttons

Table 4-15 Values for the flags% argument in the PopupMenu method

Example Syntax

```
Sub Text1_MouseDown (Button As Integer, Shift As Integer, X As Single, Y As Single)
    If Button = RIGHT_BUTTON Then
        PopupMenu menuWindow, POPUPMENU_RIGHTBUTTON
    End If
End Sub
```

Description

Visual Basic 3.0 adds the capability of using pop-up menus in your applications. A pop-up menu typically appears when the user clicks the nondefault (usually right) mouse button. Pop-ups are usually context sensitive, and will display options appropriate for the object they are over. For instance, a word processor may pop up a menu listing font choices, sizes, and styles when editing text, and a different menu listing row height or column width adjustments when popped up while editing a table.

Pop-up menus are modal. No code executes, nor can the focus shift from the menu until the user selects a menu item or dismisses the menu with (ESC). If the user selects a menu option, the code in that menu's Click event runs before returning control to the routine that called PopupMenu.

Pop-up menus display when you use the PopupMenu method on a form. You specify what menu you want to display, and can give the method optional parameters for exactly where it displays and how it behaves. The menu name you give can be either an existing menu that appears on a menu bar, or a custom menu designed specifically for that context. The name you give must have at least one sublevel of menus; it is the sublevels that actually display in the pop-up.

Define a custom menu structure for your pop-ups by making a standard menu structure and setting each menu element's Visible property to False. (See the

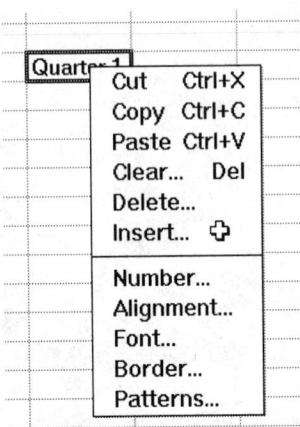

Figure 4-14 Popup menus typically are activated by a right mouse click, and are context sensitive

entry on Menus at the beginning of this chapter for more about defining a menu structure.) This prevents the custom menus from displaying on the menu bar along with the normal menus. PopupMenu ignores the Visible property, and will still display your custom pop-up menus.

You would typically write a pop-up display routine in the MouseDown event, and check to see if the right mouse button is pressed before displaying the menu. The example syntax shows this, and Figure 4-14 illustrates what this example might look like. For more information about MouseDown, see Chapter 14, Mouse Events.

The default position of the pop-up menu is with the menu's top-left corner placed at the current mouse position. You can modify this behavior in both a general way as well as setting very specific placement. The flags% argument specifies left alignment (the default), centered, or right alignment. You can also specify the exact location with the x! and y! arguments. These are in the ScaleMode of the form. For more detail about ScaleMode, see Chapter 9, The Coordinate System. See the Forms and Menus Summary at the beginning of this chapter for instructions on how to use CONSTANT.TXT values.

Pop-ups default to accepting only the left (or default) mouse button clicks just as regular menus do. If you pop the menu up with a right mouse click, as most applications do, it's more convenient for the user to enable either the right or the left mouse buttons for choosing menu items. Specify POPUPMENU_RIGHTBUTTON in the flags argument to allow the menu to respond to either button.

Example

The Forms project at the end of this chapter uses the PopupMenu method to display a pop-up menu that helps manage the MDI child documents.

Comments

PopupMenu is not available in versions earlier than 3.0 The first release of 3.0 properly implements PopupMenu, but does not include the POPUPMENU constants in CONSTANT.TXT. *You must define the POPUPMENU constants yourself* if you are using an early release version of Visual Basic 3.0. Microsoft will most likely fix this omission in later releases.

QUERYUNLOAD EVENT

Objects Affected

Check	Clipboard	Combo	Command	CommonDlg
Data	Debug	Dir	Drive	File
▶ Form	Frame	Grid	Image	Label
Line	List	▶ MDI Form	Menu	OLE
Option	Picture	Printer	Screen	Scroll
Shape	Text	Timer		

Purpose

The QueryUnload event lets you react to an attempt to Unload a form. This allows you to perform any necessary cleanup (like saving unsaved data) and possibly query the user before any form is Unloaded. Tables 4-16 and 4-17 show the arguments and settings for the QueryUnload property.

General Syntax

```
Sub Form_QueryUnload(Cancel as Integer, UnloadMode as Integer)
Sub MDIForm_QueryUnload(Cancel as Integer, UnloadMode as Integer)
```

Argument	Description
Form	'Form' (literal, not the Name property of the form) specifies the normal or MDI child form
MDIForm	'MDIForm' (literal, not the Name property of the MDIForm) specifies the MDI form
Cancel	Set this to True to stop the QueryUnload event for all loaded forms
UnloadMode	Shows the reason for the QueryUnload event

Table 4-16 Arguments of the QueryUnload event

Value	CONSTANT.TXT	Description
0	FORM_CONTROLMENU	User chose the Close command from the control box
1	FORM_CODE	Unload event invoked in code
2	APP_WINDOWS	Windows is ending
3	APP_TASKMANAGER	Task Manager is closing the application
4	FORM_MDIFORM	MDI child form closing because the MDI form is closing

Table 4-17 Values of the UnloadMode argument

Example Syntax

```
Sub Form_QueryUnload (Cancel As Integer, UnloadMode As Integer)
    Dim Msg, SaveChange
    If ChangedText Then              ' Use Global variable to flag changes to document
        Msg = "Document has changed.  Save Changes?"
        SaveChange = MsgBox(Msg, 51) ' Exclamation with Yes/No/Cancel
        Select Case SaveChange
        Case 2                       ' User chooses cancel; stop unloading process
            Cancel = True
        Case 6                       ' Save the file and continue unloading
            FileSave
            Cancel = False
        Case 7                       ' User chooses no save; continue unloading
            Cancel = False
        End Select
    End If
End Sub
```

Description

The Form QueryUnload and MDIForm QueryUnload events specify what actions take place when an attempt is made to close a form. All forms close automatically at the end of the program, and closing an MDI form closes all child forms. An Unload statement can also close a form. Use this event to give the user a final chance to prevent ending the program or to ask about cleanup procedures. In the example syntax, a MsgBox statement in the QueryUnload event asks the user if they want to save files before exiting.

There is an advantage to placing certain routines in a QueryUnload event rather than linking them to a command button or placing them in the Unload event. Using a QueryUnload event provides the user with a safety net that will prevent them from forgetting to save a file or forgetting to enter important infor-

200

mation in a data entry field. In MDI applications, using the QueryUnload event rather than the Unload event gives the user a chance to stop the entire unloading process before any forms are unloaded, which could be important if there are multiple child forms.

The UnloadMode argument gives the reason for the event. You may want to take different actions, depending on the reason that the form is unloading. CON-STANT.TXT defines these values; see the Forms and Menus Summary at the beginning of this chapter for instructions on how to use CONSTANT.TXT values.

Setting 'Cancel' to True will cancel the entire Unload event for all forms. If the user cancels the Unload operation, then all forms remain open as they were before the QueryUnload. Contrast this with putting the same cleanup code in the Unload event: some forms might be unloaded before the user cancels the process. This is particularly critical for MDI applications.

Example

The Forms project at the end of the chapter uses a QueryUnload event for each child form. This event presents a message box asking whether the user wishes to save any changed documents.

Comments

The QueryUnload event occurs first in an MDI form and then in all other forms. If no form cancels the QueryUnload event, all other forms are Unloaded first and then the MDI form is Unloaded last.

RESIZE EVENT

Objects Affected

Check	Clipboard	Combo	Command	CommonDlg
Data	Debug	Dir	Drive	File
▶ Form	Frame	Grid	Image	Label
Line	List	▶ MDI Form	Menu	▶ OLE
Option	▶ Picture	Printer	Screen	Scroll
Shape	Text	Timer		

Purpose

The Resize event specifies what actions take place when the user resizes a form or picture box, or when the form or picture box first becomes visible. This event can be triggered by anything that brings the object into the user's sight or changes its size. Table 4-18 shows the arguments of the Resize event.

General Syntax

```
Sub Form_Resize ()
Sub MDIForm_Resize ()
```

Argument	Description
Form	'Form' (literal, not the Name property of the form) specifies the normal or MDI child form
MDIForm	'MDIForm' (literal, not the Name property of the MDIForm) specifies the MDI form

Table 4-18 Arguments of the Resize event

Example Syntax

```
Sub Form_Load ()
    For i = 1 To 40          'Generates 40 line items in the List1 list box
        List1.AddItem "Line " + Str$(i)
    Next i
End Sub

Sub Form_Resize ()
    List1.Move 25, 25, ScaleWidth-50 ,ScaleHeight-25 'Fill Form1 with List1
End Sub
```

Description

When your program changes the WindowState, Visible, Height, or Width properties of a form, Visual Basic triggers a Resize event. This event is also triggered any time a form loads with the Load or Show statements. The user can also trigger this event by changing the size of the form with the mouse. You can use the Resize event to adjust the position of controls on a form after the form's size has changed. Sometimes changes to the WindowState, Visible, Height, and Width properties make it necessary to adjust the position of controls on the same form. In the syntax example, each time the Form1 form's height or width changes, the Form_Resize event adjusts the height and width of the List1 list box. This makes List1 fill the surface of the form. Figures 4-15 and 4-16 illustrate how this might look.

The ScaleWidth and ScaleHeight Properties

The ScaleWidth and ScaleHeight properties of a form serve as references. Each control's size is a fraction of the values of the ScaleWidth and ScaleHeight properties.

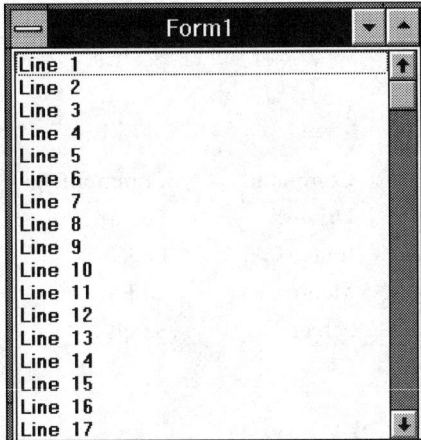

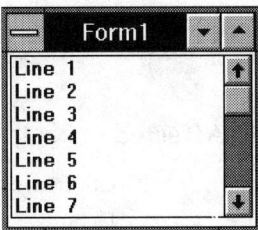

Figure 4-16 Form1 and
List1 made smaller.
Note that List1 still fills
Form1

Figure 4-15 Form1 with List1 list
box filling it after the Resize event

In the example syntax, the Move statement references these properties to change
the size of a control. This is a very basic example of this technique; the Forms project at the end of this chapter shows this process in further detail.

The Load, Paint, and GotFocus Events

If there is more than one event attached to a particular control, they are processed
in the following order: Load, Resize, Paint, and GotFocus. This is an important
point to keep in mind if any of the actions that take place in one event are based
upon actions in another event. For example, a data entry form for an address
book would have problems if the Form_Load event disables the Address1 text
box. If the Form_GotFocus event subsequently attempts to define the Address1
text box's contents, this would create an error.

Example

The Resize event in the Forms project at the end of this chapter controls the size
and placement of the Text1 control within the child form. Whenever the form's
size changes, the Resize event adjusts the size of the text box to completely fill the
internal area of the child form. This shows how a form's controls can be adjusted
to compensate for changes in the form's size.

Comments

The Resize event takes place every time a form loads, resizes, or displays on the
screen.

SHOW METHOD

Objects Affected

Check	Clipboard	Combo	Command	CommonDlg
Data	Debug	Dir	Drive	File
▶ Form	Frame	Grid	Image	Label
Line	List	▶ MDI Form	Menu	OLE
Option	Picture	Printer	Screen	Scroll
Shape	Text	Timer		

Purpose

The Show method loads a form into memory and displays it on the screen. Tables 4-19 and 4-20 summarize the arguments of the Show method.

General Syntax

`[form.]Show [style%]`

Argument	Description
form	Name property of the form
style%	Value representing whether to load the form in modal or modeless format

Table 4-19 Arguments of the Show method

style%	CONSTANT.TXT	Description
0	MODELESS	(Default) Code after the Show method runs normally
1	MODAL	Code after the Show method runs after the form closes

Table 4-20 Possible settings of the style% argument of the Show method

204

Example Syntax

```
Sub Command1_Click ()
     Form1.Show MODELESS        'Display Modeless form
     Text1.Text = ""            'Change text property of Text1 to blank
     Form1.Hide                 'Hide DataForm
     Show MODAL                 'Show current form modally
End Sub
```

Description

The Show method lets you load and display a form on the screen, or display an already loaded form. A form remains in memory until it is removed using an Unload statement or until the program ends. For example, a data entry program could load all of its secondary forms into memory when the program starts. Later the program's main menu could use the Show method to quickly display a form that is needed.

A Show method statement can begin with the Name property of the form. If Show does not specify a form, then the current form appears. A Show method has either a modeless or modal style. The default setting is modeless. Modal forms block the execution of any code until you remove a form from sight. (This also has the effect of preventing the user from changing the focus to another form.) Forms shown in modeless style will allow other code to run.

Modeless vs. Modal Style

A Show method statement has the optional argument style%. This value determines whether the form is to be loaded in modeless (0) or modal (1) style. An MDI form and MDI child forms cannot be modal. If you don't use this argument, the form will be modeless. Modal forms will not permit the execution of any code until they are removed with either a Hide method or an Unload statement. A modal form also prevents the processing of code that follows the modal Show method expression. With this mode you can display a message to the user without specifically interrupting the code. The program will continue where it left off when the modal form is hidden or unloaded. Most forms load using this style. Table 4-20 summarizes the settings of the style% argument. See the Forms and Menus Summary at the beginning of this chapter for instructions on how to use CONSTANT.TXT values.

The Visible Property

Placing a form on the screen with the Show method changes its Visible property to True (-1). The difference between using the Show method and directly changing the setting of the Visible property lies in the types of objects affected. The Show method can only be used on a form. In contrast, the Visible property can be used on any Visual Basic controls or forms. You can use this difference to your advantage in writing generic functions and procedures.

The Load Statement

The Load statement and Show method are very similar, but the difference between them is very important. Load brings controls or forms into memory, but it does not directly make them visible to the user. The Show method makes the control or form visible to the user, loading it if necessary. You can use these functions together to help your program run more smoothly. First, use the Load statement to load your forms into memory at the beginning of the program. Then use the Show method to quickly display the forms.

Many commercial applications display a "splash" screen when first loading to give the user some feedback while they load the more complex screens and code. To duplicate this simply Show a simple form with some nice graphics and then immediately Load the other forms and run any other setup code. Then Hide the splash screen and bring up the main form.

Example

In the Forms project at the end of this chapter, the Show method displays two dialog boxes. The project demonstrates two different modes of operation, modal and modeless. When the form is put on the screen in modeless style, the user's input is not stopped and any events that follow take place without being stopped. In contrast, when the form appears on a screen in modal style, no code that follows will be processed until it is closed.

Comments

The Show method only loads a form if it is not already in memory.

UNLOAD EVENT

Objects Affected

Check	Clipboard	Combo	Command	CommonDlg
Data	Debug	Dir	Drive	File
▶ Form	Frame	Grid	Image	Label
Line	List	▶ MDI Form	Menu	OLE
Option	Picture	Printer	Screen	Scroll
Shape	Text	Timer		

Purpose

The Unload event procedure specifies what actions to take when a form is unloaded. Table 4-21 summarizes the arguments of the Unload event.

General Syntax

```
Sub Form_Unload (Cancel As Integer)
Sub MDIForm_Unload (Cancel As Integer)
```

Argument	Description
Form	'Form' (literal, not the Name property of the form) specifies the normal or MDI child form
MDIForm	'MDIForm' (literal, not the Name property of the MDIForm) specifies the MDI form
Cancel	Set this to True to stop the Unload event

Table 4-21 Arguments of the Unload event

Example Syntax

```
Sub Form_Unload (Cancel As Integer)
    Const YES = 6
    Const MSG = "Are you sure you want to exit?"
    Ans = MsgBox(MSG, 4)            'Ask user if they want to exit
    If Ans = YES Then              'If YES then
        End                        'Terminate program
    Else                           'If NO
        Form1.Show                 'Bring back the main form
    End If
End Sub
```

Description

The Form Unload event specifies what actions take place when a form is closed. All forms close automatically at the end of the program. An Unload statement can also close a form. One use of this event is to reset the information on the form before removing it from memory. Another use of the Unload event can be to give the user a final chance to prevent ending the program. In the example syntax, a MsgBox function in the Unload event asks the user if they really wish to exit.

There is an advantage to placing certain routines in an Unload event rather than linking them to a command button. Using an Unload event provides the user with a safety net that will prevent them from forgetting to save a file or forgetting to enter important information in a data entry field. If save routines are only in command buttons and the user forgets to select the button prior to exiting, the information entered would be lost. In some cases, however, such code might be better attached to an OK button: for example, if you want the user to confirm changes being made to a database.

The Load Event

The Unload event shares an inverse relationship with the Load event. While the Load event affects the form when it is initially opened, the Unload event executes when the form is closed. Both events can depend on each other. For example, the Load event might set up the form to initiate some action. The Unload event could then either restore the form to its preloaded settings or process the actions that took place. An address book might use the Load event to insert the last accessed information into the edit screen. This form's Unload event might ensure that the information entered into the fields is saved to the database.

Example

The Setup project at the end of this section uses an Unload event for the MDI form. This event presents a message box asking whether the user wishes to exit the program.

Comments

The Unload event does not occur when a form is simply hidden.

UNLOAD STATEMENT

Objects Affected

▶ Check	Clipboard	▶ Combo	▶ Command	CommonDlg
▶ Data	Debug	▶ Dir	▶ Drive	▶ File
▶ Form	Frame	▶ Grid	▶ Image	▶ Label
▶ Line	▶ List	▶ MDI Form	Menu	▶ OLE
▶ Option	▶ Picture	Printer	Screen	Scroll
▶ Shape	▶ Text	▶ Timer		

Purpose

The Unload statement removes a form or control from memory. Table 4-22 summarizes the meaning of the object argument of the Unload statement.

208

General Syntax

```
Unload object
```

Argument	Description
object	Name property of the item to be unloaded

Table 4-22 Argument of the Unload statement

Example Syntax

```
Sub Command1_Click
    If Text1.Text = "" Then      'Checks if Text box is blank
        Unload Form2             'Removes Form2 from memory and sight
    Else
        Form2.Hide               'Removes Form2 from sight but leaves in memory
    End If
End Sub
```

Description

The Unload statement unloads forms and controls from both the display and memory. A form remains out of memory unless the program references one of its properties. If this happens, the form will be loaded back into memory, although it won't appear on the screen. Since multiple Load and Unload statements take up processing time, use the corresponding Hide and Show method statements for frequently used forms. In the example syntax, the form is unloaded only if the Text box is blank.

This statement takes an object for its argument. The object can be the Name property of a form, control, or control array. Use the Unload statement to clear forms that are no longer needed. This statement also will reduce the memory being used if a program has a large number of forms. For example, a text editor with a large number of files open simultaneously could use the Unload statement to close files the user no longer needs.

The Hide Method

The Unload statement and Hide method have similar functions in Visual Basic, but the difference between them is very important. Unload removes a form from memory as well as from the user's view. A Hide method statement only takes the form out of view. This difference gives you the flexibility to remove forms that are no longer needed with Unload but to only Hide forms that will be used again.

Example

In the Forms project at the end of the chapter, the Unload statement removes the MDI form from memory. This occurs when the user presses the Quit command button. The Unload statement generates the QueryUnload event and then the Unload event.

Comments

The Unload statement may be used to remove a control of a control array created with the Load statement.

WINDOWSTATE PROPERTY

Objects Affected

Check	Clipboard	Combo	Command	CommonDlg
Data	Debug	Dir	Drive	File
▶ Form	Frame	Grid	Image	Label
Line	List	▶ MDI Form	Menu	OLE
Option	Picture	Printer	Screen	Scroll
Shape	Text	Timer		

Purpose

The WindowState property determines or changes the size of a form window at runtime. You can read and write to this property at runtime. Tables 4-23 and 4-24 summarize the meaning of the form and state% arguments of the WindowState property.

General Syntax

```
[form.]WindowState[ = state%]
```

Argument	Description
form	Name property of the form whose size is being changed
state%	Value indicates what size to make the form

Table 4-23 Arguments of the WindowState property

state%	CONSTANT.TXT	Description
0	NORMAL	Restores the form to the previous size
1	MINIMIZED	Reduces the form to an icon
2	MAXIMIZED	Fills the screen (or client area for MDI child) with the form

Table 4-24 Possible state% settings of the WindowState property

Example Syntax

```
Sub FormLoad (FormName As Form)
      Select Case FormName.MaxButton        'Check the MaxButton property
          Case True
              Form1.WindowState = MAXIMIZED  'Maximize the form
          Case False
              Form1.WindowState = NORMAL     'Normalize the form
      End Select
End Sub
```

Description

The WindowState property determines the appearance of a form on the screen. A form's WindowState property is initialized at design time but can be changed at runtime. This expression begins with the name of the affected form. In the above example, a generic function changes the size of the form based on the MaxButton property.

The state% argument indicates the new size of the form. See the Forms and Menus Summary at the beginning of this chapter for instructions on how to use CONSTANT.TXT values. A value of 2 (MAXIMIZED) will fill the entire screen (or the entire client area for an MDI child form) and 0 (NORMAL) restores the form to the previous size.

A state% value of 1 (MINIMIZED) minimizes the form into an icon. If an icon isn't chosen at design time, the Visual Basic icon appears on the screen. To assign an icon to a form on Visual Basic's programming screen, select the Icon property and double-click on (Icon) at the right-hand side of the properties table. Find the desired icon in the file list box and double-click on its file name to select it. Visual Basic comes with many icons, or you may create your own. See the discussion of the Icon property in Chapter 5, Application Appearance.

The MaxButton and MinButton Properties

The MaxButton and MinButton properties of the same form have no effect on a form's WindowState property. These properties control whether the Maximize

211

and Minimize buttons appear in the top-right corner of a form. The WindowState property can be used to change the size of a form no matter what the setting of the MaxButton and MinButton properties are. For example, a form with both the MaxButton and MinButton properties set to False could still be minimized simply by changing the WindowState property.

The Resize Event

A change in the WindowState property triggers a Resize event. You can use the Resize event in this case to adjust the controls on the screen based on the new size. Use the ScaleWidth, ScaleHeight, ScaleTop, and ScaleLeft properties to specify the size and location of the controls on the screen. For example, a text editor could use the Resize event to adjust the text box to fill the form. This event would take place each time the form size is changed so that the text box always fills the entire form.

Example

The Forms project at the end of this chapter uses the WindowState property to duplicate the actions of the Minimize and Maximize buttons on the modeless dialog box.

Comments

The commands available on the control box of a form have no effect on the WindowState property of a form.

THE FORMS PROJECT

Project Overview

The Forms project demonstrates several important features of Visual Basic forms. This example shows how to use the properties, events, methods, and statements that directly control a form's basic appearance.

This project has four forms: an MDI form, an MDI child, and two dialog boxes. Each form's setup is broken down into three sections: assembly, figure display, and source code. Please refer to the figures to see where the forms' elements should be placed.

Assembling the Project: MDI Form

1. Begin a new project by selecting the File menu and the New project option. Make a new MDI form by selecting File New MDI Form and give it the objects and properties shown in Table 4-25. Properties not listed should be left at their default value. Make sure this form is set as the startup form by going into the Options menu, selecting the Project menu command, and setting the Startup form option for MDIForm1.

Object	Property	Setting
MDIForm	Caption	MDI Form— Forms and Menus Project
	Name	MDIForm1
Picture	Alignment	1—Align Top
	BackColor	Light Gray— &H00C0C0C0&
	Name	pictToolbar
Picture	Alignment	2— Align Bottom
	BackColor	Light Gray— &H00C0C0C0&
	Name	pictStatus
Command	Name	Command1
Command	Name	Command2
Command	Name	Command3
Command	Name	Command4
Picture	AutoSize	-1— True
	BackColor	Light Gray— &H00C0C0C0&
	BorderStyle	0— No Border
	Name	pictQuit

(continued on next page)

(continued from previous page)

Object	Property	Setting	
	Picture	C:\VB\ICONS\TRAFFIC\TRFFC14.ICO	(Stop Sign)
Picture	AutoSize	-1 — True	
	BackColor	Light Gray — &H00C0C0C0&	
	BorderStyle	0 — No Border	
	Name	pictModeless	
	Picture	C:\VB\ICONS\TRAFFIC\TRFFC18A.ICO	(Walk)
Picture	AutoSize	-1 — True	
	BackColor	Light Gray — &H00C0C0C0&	
	BorderStyle	0 — No Border	
	Name	pictModal	
	Picture	C:\VB\ICONS\TRAFFIC\TRFFC18B.ICO	(Don't Walk)
Picture	AutoRedraw	-1 — True	
	AutoSize	-1 — True	
	BackColor	Light Gray — &H00C0C0C0&	
	BorderStyle	0 — No Border	
	Name	pictNewChild	
	Picture	C:\VB\ICONS\COMPUTER\MDICHILD.ICO	(MDI Child)

Table 4-25 Elements of the MDI form

2. Size the objects on the screen, as shown in Figure 4-17. Note that the four command buttons must be placed on pictToolbar. Then draw the four pictures to hold the toolbar icons and move them on top of the command buttons. The command buttons don't really do anything other than give the picture controls some visual

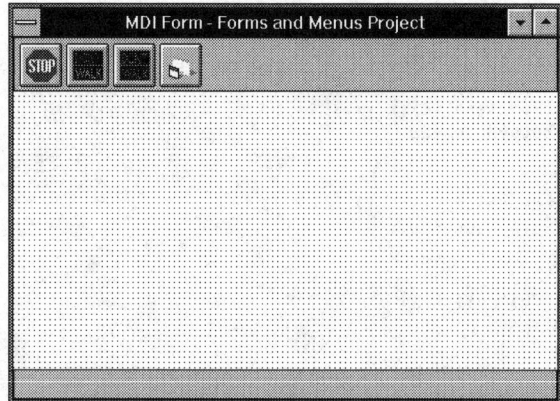

Figure 4-17 MDIForm1 being designed

depth. Give each picture control its icon by selecting Icon (...) in the properties box and selecting the appropriate file name.

3. Enter the following code in the MDIForm_Load event. This initializes the MDI child form document array and the array that tracks changes to the contents of the child form's text box.

```
Sub MDIForm_Load ()
    Load formModal          'load the dialog boxes into memory
    Load formModeless       'to save time later
    'create a new document and an entry in the tracking array
    ReDim Document(0)       'this creates a new child form
    ReDim DocState(0)       'this creates the element to track the child form
    Document(0).Tag = 0     'store the document's index to tracking array
    Document(0).Show        'and display the new child
End Sub
```

4. Enter the following code in the MDIForm_Unload event. This gives the user a final chance to cancel the program's termination.

```
Sub MDIForm_Unload (Cancel As Integer)
    Dim msg, answer
    msg = "Do you really want to quit?"
    answer = MsgBox(msg, 36, "Final Confirmation")  ' yes/no
    If answer = 7 Then
        Cancel = True
    Else
        End
    End If
End Sub
```

5. Enter the following code in the Click events for pictModal, pictModeless, pictNewChild, and pictQuit. These all simply call the appropriate routine in the code module. Note that identical code occurs in the MDI child form's menus.

215

```
Sub pictModal_Click ()
    DisplayModal
End Sub

Sub pictModeless_Click ()
    DisplayModeless
End Sub

Sub pictNewChild_Click ()
    DisplayNewChild
End Sub

Sub pictQuit_Click ()
    Quit
End Sub
```

Assembling the Project: MDI Child Form

1. Create a new form using the specifications in Table 4-26 by selecting the File menu and then choosing New form.

Object	Property	Setting
Form	Caption	Child Form
	MDIChild	True
	Name	formChild
Text	MultiLine	True
	Name	Text1
	ScrollBars	2—Vertical

Table 4-26 Elements of the MDI child form

2. Size the objects on the screen as shown in Figure 4-18. Note that the size of Text1 is immaterial, and that it's important to place its top and left sides directly against the child form's title bar and left border as shown.

3. Create the menu structure shown in Table 4-27 for the form, using the Menu Design window.

216

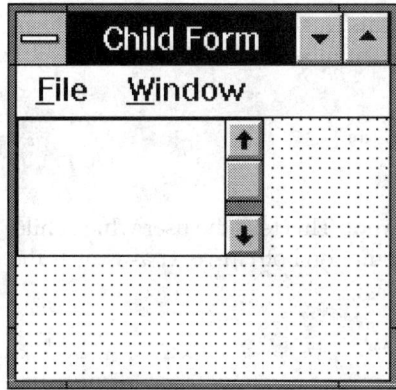

Figure 4-18 MDI child form during the design phase

Name	Caption	Property	Setting
menuFile	&File		
menuFileSave	&Save		
menuFileExit	E&xit		
menuWindow	&Window	WindowList	True
menuWindowArrange	&Cascade	Index	0
menuWindowArrange	Tile &Horizontal	Index	1
menuWindowArrange	Tile &Vertical	Index	2
menuWindowArrange	&Arrange Icons	Index	3
menuWindowArrange		Index	4
menuWindowArrange	&New Child	Index	5
menuWindowArrange	Mo&dal	Index	6
menuWindowArrange	Mode&less	Index	7

Table 4-27 Elements of the child form's menu structure

4. Enter the following code in Form_Activate event. This identifies which child form is currently active by printing the child form's number on the status bar.

```
Sub Form_Activate ()
    MDIForm1!pictStatus.Cls
    MDIForm1!pictStatus.Print "Child form #" & Me.Tag
End Sub
```

5. Enter the following code in the Form_Paint event. This tells the user which child form they're working with. It places this information both in Text1 as well as the child form's title bar.

```
Sub Form_Paint ()
    Text1 = "This is instance # " & Me.Tag
    Me.Caption = "Child Form " & Me.Tag
End Sub
```

6. Place this code in the Form_QueryUnload event. Attempting to Unload the child form triggers this event. It first checks to see if this instance of the child form's Text1 box has changed by looking at the tracking array. If there has been a change, the user is given a chance to "save" the document, continue without saving, or cancel the Unloading process.

```
Sub Form_QueryUnload (Cancel As Integer, UnloadMode As Integer)
    Dim msg, docTitle, saveChange
    If DocState(Me.Tag) Then         ' DocState flags changes to this child's text1
        docTitle = Me.Caption        ' Identifies which document is being saved
        msg = "Document has changed.  Save Changes?"
        saveChange = MsgBox(msg, 51, docTitle)' Exclamation with Yes/No/Cancel
        Select Case saveChange
        Case 2                       ' User chooses cancel; stop unloading process
            Cancel = True
        Case 6                       ' Save the file and continue unloading
            menuFileSave_Click       ' Save the document!
            Cancel = False
        Case 7                       ' User chooses no save; continue unloading
            Cancel = False
        End Select
    End If
End Sub
```

7. Enter this into the Form_Resize event. Resizing the child window (either by maximizing it or by resizing its borders) triggers the Resize event. It makes Text1 completely fill the child's internal area.

```
Sub Form_Resize ()
    'Expand the text box to completely fill
    'Child form's internal area
    Text1.Height = ScaleHeight
    Text1.Width = ScaleWidth
End Sub
```

8. Enter this into the menuFileExit_Click event. This calls the module Quit procedure to shut down the application.

218

```
Sub menuFileExit_Click ()
    Quit
End Sub
```

9. Enter this into the menuFileSave_Click event. This simulates "saving" the document, and then resets the document tracking array to show that it has been saved.

```
Sub menuFileSave_Click ()
    'write whatever code to save the file here...
    DocState(Me.Tag) = False    'and show no changes to text
End Sub
```

10. Enter this into the menuWindowArrange_Click event. The top four menu choices arrange the child forms, while the bottom three choices call the appropriate procedure in the code module to display the various forms. Note that Case 4 is not needed: that menu entry is a separator bar, and separator bars cannot be clicked by the user.

```
Sub menuWindowArrange_Click (Index As Integer)
    Select Case Index
            Case 0: MDIForm1.Arrange CASCADE
            Case 1: MDIForm1.Arrange TILE_HORIZONTAL
            Case 2: MDIForm1.Arrange TILE_VERTICAL
            Case 3: MDIForm1.Arrange ARRANGE_ICONS
            Case 5: DisplayNewChild
            Case 6: DisplayModal
            Case 7: DisplayModeless
    End Select
End Sub
```

11. Enter this into the Text1_Change event. This lets you track whether the "document" has changed for each instance of the child window.

```
Sub Text1_Change ()
    DocState(Me.Tag) = True    'Show that text1 has changed
End Sub
```

12. Enter this code into the Text1_MouseDown event. This lets the user pop up the Window menu by clicking on the text box with the right mouse button. Note how simple it is to create a pop-up menu!

```
Sub Text1_MouseDown (Button As Integer, Shift As Integer, X As Single, Y As Single)
    If Button = RIGHT_BUTTON Then
            PopupMenu menuWindow, 2  'pop up menu, OK to choose item w/right mouse button
    End If
End Sub
```

Assembling the Project: Dialog #1

1. Create a new form using the specifications in Table 4-28 by selecting the File menu and then choosing New form.

Object	Property	Setting
Form	BorderStyle	1—Fixed Single
	Caption	Modal Form
	ControlBox	False
	MaxButton	False
	MinButton	False
	Name	formModal
Command	Caption	OK
	Default	True
	Name	cmndOK
Text	Name	Text1
	Multiline	-1—True
	Text	"This is a modal form. Try clicking on any other form in this project... the focus does not shift. Also notice that the MsgBox hasn't popped up yet."

Table 4-28 Elements of the Modal Dialog form

2. Size the objects on the screen, as shown in Figure 4-19.

3. Enter the following code in the cmndOK_Click event. This simply hides the form.

```
Sub cmndOK_Click ()
      Hide
End Sub
```

Assembling the Project: Dialog #2

1. Create a new form using the specifications in Table 4-29 by selecting the File menu and then choosing New form.

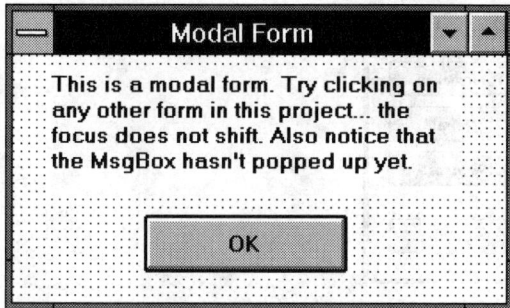

Figure 4-19 Modal dialog box during design

Object	Property	Setting
Form	Caption	Modeless Form
	Name	formModeless
Command	Cancel	True
	Caption	&Close
	Name	cmndClose
Command	Caption	&Minimize
	Name	cmndMinimize
Command	Caption	&Normal
	Name	cmndNormal
Command	Caption	Ma&ximize
	Name	cmndMaximize

Table 4-29 Elements of the Modeless Dialog form

2. Size the objects on the screen, as shown in Figure 4-20.

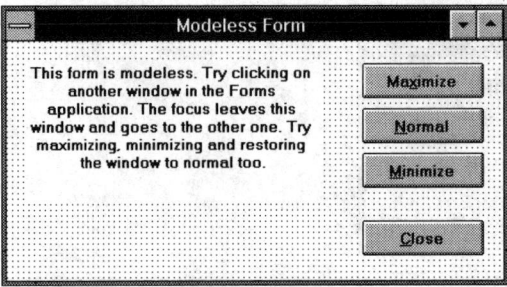

Figure 4-20 Modeless dialog box during design

3. Enter the following code in the cmndClose_Click event. This simply hides the form.

```
Sub cmndClose_Click ()
    Hide
End Sub
```

4. Enter this code in the cmndMaximize_Click event. This duplicates the action of the Maximize button and maximizes the form.

```
Sub cmndMaximize_Click ()
    WindowState = 2
End Sub
```

5. Enter the following code in the cmndMinimize_Click event. This duplicates the action of the Minimize button and minimizes the form.

```
Sub cmndMinimize_Click ()
    WindowState = 1
End Sub
```

6. Enter the following code in the cmndNormal_Click event. This duplicates the action of Restore and restores the form to its size and position before it was minimized or maximized.

```
Sub cmndNormal_Click ()
    WindowState = 0
End Sub
```

Assembling the Project: Global Module

1. Create a new module with the File New Module command and place the following code in the general declarations section. This defines two global arrays. The Document array is actually an array of forms, and is used to create the MDI child forms. The DocState array tracks changes in the child documents' text boxes. It also defines a number of constants taken from CONSTANT.TXT.

222

```
Global Document() As New formChild        'MDI Child forms
Global DocState() As Integer              'Tracks if child form is modified
Global Const CASCADE = 0                  'These arrange child windows
Global Const TILE_HORIZONTAL = 1
Global Const TILE_VERTICAL = 2
Global Const ARRANGE_ICONS = 3

Global Const MODAL = 1                     'Used to display dialog boxes
Global Const MODELESS = 0

Global Const NORMAL = 0                    'These are for windowstates
Global Const MINIMIZE = 1
Global Const MAXIMIZE = 2

Global Const RIGHT_BUTTON = 2             'Mouse button
```

2. Enter the following sub procedures. To enter a sub procedure, go to end of the general procedures section and type in the entire sub procedure starting with the Sub keyword. As soon as you press (ENTER) after typing in the first line, Visual Basic creates a new sub procedure for you that you then type the subsequent code in. This first procedure unloads MDIForm1. Note that we don't want to use End; unloading the form triggers the Unload event, which gives the user one more chance to stop the application's termination.

```
Sub Quit ()
    Unload MDIForm1
End Sub
```

3. This procedure displays the modal dialog box, and follows up with a MsgBox that demonstrates how code stops running after a modal form displays.

```
Sub DisplayModal ()
    formModal.Show MODAL
    MsgBox "This line immediately follows the Show method"
End Sub
```

4. This procedure displays the modeless dialog box, and follows up with a MsgBox that demonstrates how code continues to run after a modeless form displays.

```
Sub DisplayModeless ()
    formModeless.Show MODELESS
    MsgBox "This line immediately follows the Show method"
End Sub
```

5. This code is the magic behind creating a new MDI child form. It first identifies how many documents have been created so far by using UBound on the Document object array. It then makes both the Document and DocState arrays one element larger to make space for the new form. After tagging the new form (so we can easily get the proper index entry to the DocState array), the new child form displays.

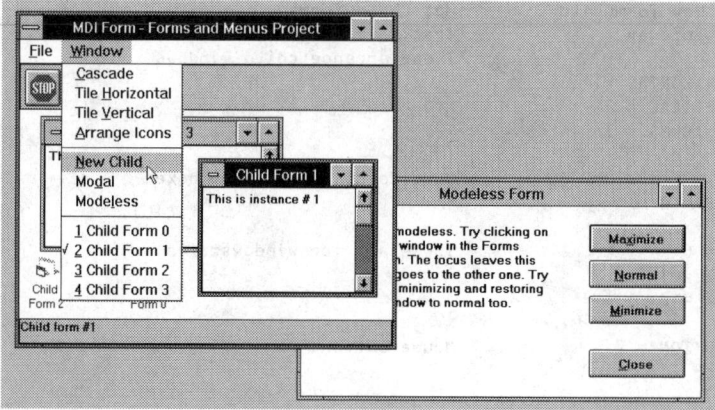

Figure 4-21 The Forms project in action

```
Sub DisplayNewChild ()
    Dim docCount As Integer
    docCount = UBound(Document) 'count # of open documents
    'make space in the tracking array and create a new document
    ReDim Preserve Document(docCount + 1)  'state of the new document
    ReDim Preserve DocState(docCount + 1) 'make the new child document
    Document(docCount + 1).Tag = docCount + 1
    Document(docCount + 1).Show
End Sub
```

How It Works

The Forms project demonstrates some key aspects of Visual Basic forms. The main form is the MDI form. It acts as a container for its child forms. It also has a toolbar with buttons to create more child forms, show a Modal dialog box, and show a Modeless dialog box. To end the project, click on the Stop icon on the toolbar or choose File Exit from the menu.

Clicking on the Modal button brings up a modal dialog box, and clicking on the Modeless button brings up a modeless dialog box. Clicking on the New Child button creates a new child form within the MDI form. The menu system duplicates each of these commands. The Window menu also lets you arrange and choose among the child windows. You can tell what instance the child form is by looking at the child form's title bar. Figure 4-21 illustrates this example project in action.

Modal Dialog Box

The Modal dialog box consists of only a label and an OK button. The Show method in cmndModal_Click shows the form. The first time it is shown, Visual Basic automatically loads it. The design time properties are set to remove the control box and both Minimize and Maximize buttons. Notice how this dialog box retains its focus when you click on other windows of the Forms application. Also note how the MsgBox stating that you've just seen a Modal dialog box comes up only after you close the box, even though the code for it comes immediately after the Show statement. This illustrates how showing a Modal dialog box stops running your code until it is closed or hidden. The OK button Hides this dialog box.

Modeless Dialog Box

The Modeless dialog box consists of a label and four command buttons. The Show method in cmndModeless_Click shows the form. The Close button closes the form with a Hide statement. The other three buttons duplicate the action of the Minimize and Maximize buttons by setting the WindowState appropriately. Notice how clicking on another window of the Forms application sets the focus to wherever you click. Modeless dialog boxes do not need to be closed to lose their focus. Also note how the MsgBox stating that you've just seen a Modeless dialog box comes up immediately after the form is shown, demonstrating how code keeps running after you've shown a modeless form. Both the Modal and Modeless dialog boxes have identical code that shows them and brings up the MsgBox; the only difference in their behavior lies in the value of the single argument given to the Show method.

MDI Form

The MDI form serves as the main form for the project. It contains its child forms, as well as a toolbar that has buttons to quit the project, show the two dialog boxes, and create more child forms. The toolbar is a picture box with its alignment property set to Top. This tells the picture box to automatically readjust its width to completely fill the width of the MDI form. No code is necessary to have it do this. Placing command buttons directly on pictToolbar, and layering four picture controls containing appropriate icons on top of the command buttons, completes our simple toolbox. pictStatus at the bottom of the form creates a simple status bar. Note that a picture box is the only control that may be placed directly in an MDI form.

The Modal and Modeless command buttons simply show their respective dialog boxes and bring up a MsgBox describing what just happened. The New Child button has more involved code that creates a new MDI child form.

MDI children are typically created as a control array. Module1 defines Document as a global array of type Form1—the child form "template." We don't dimension the array when it's declared; this allows us to redimension it when we need a new child form. The global array DocState tracks whether the child forms' Text1 control has changed since the last "save." Although we created a simple array for this example, a typical application would probably define an array of a user type to track multiple states. For example, it may be useful to track changed document, deleted document, cloned document, or even document length.

MDIForm_Load creates the first entry in both arrays. This puts a child document in the MDI form. The child form's Tag property contains the index number of this instance of the child form. This allows us to relate each child instance to its entry in the tracking array.

The New Child button (as well as the New Child entry in the Window menu) creates a new child form. It first checks to see how many instances of the child form exist by reading the UBound of the Document array. (Note that this test fails if there are no documents. A real application should perform additional error checking.) It then creates new entries in the DocState and Document arrays with the ReDim Preserve statements. Preserve tells Visual Basic to keep all the old values in the arrays and just add the new entries to the end of the array. The Show method shows the new child form. Although this simple project doesn't implement this, deleting an instance of a child form would essentially be the reverse of this process.

MDI Child

The MDI child form contains only a text box. The text box has multiline turned on, so it emulates a simple text editor. The Form_Paint event changes the child's title bar and text entry to reflect its particular instance number. This illustrates how some form properties (like Caption) can be changed at runtime. Me acts like an implicit variable that always refers to the form that is currently running code. Visual Basic automatically defines Me, and it acts just like a form variable. See Chapter 3, Using Objects, for more information about Me. Note how we can't put this code in the Form_Load event, as the new instance hasn't been fully created yet!

The Resize event makes Text1 resize itself to completely fill the interior of the child form. Resizing controls to fit a form is a typical use of the Resize event.

QueryUnload checks first to see if this instance's Text1 has changed. The If statement simply looks at the entry in the DocState array indexed by the instance's Tag value. If True, Text1 has changed since the last "save" and an appropriate MsgBox displays. Notice how we access the Caption of the child form to display in the title bar of the MsgBox. The Select statement takes appropriate action depending on the user's response. The menuFileSave subroutine called here simulates saving the document and then setting the DocState entry for this instance to False.

5 APPLICATION APPEARANCE

Poorly designed screens impair the overall usefulness of even the most cleverly written program. A screen with clashing colors annoys users; command buttons placed in haphazard fashion can confuse and frustrate them. Unnecessarily complex control arrangements also create difficulties. Users always notice these kinds of problems, if only on a subconscious level. Such problems reduce the chance that people will bother to work with a program. A user does not see cleverly written code; a user reacts to the way the program looks and behaves. Compare the two functionally equivalent interfaces shown in Figures 5-1 and 5-2. Which would you rather use?

Windows provides menus, dialog boxes, and other objects that operate in a standard way and usually have a common look and feel. The Microsoft Windows environment thus represents an attempt to simplify the operation of computers and computer software. Windows provides a universal interface that a user can theoretically apply to new programs. Well-designed Windows programs are consistent in the way interface

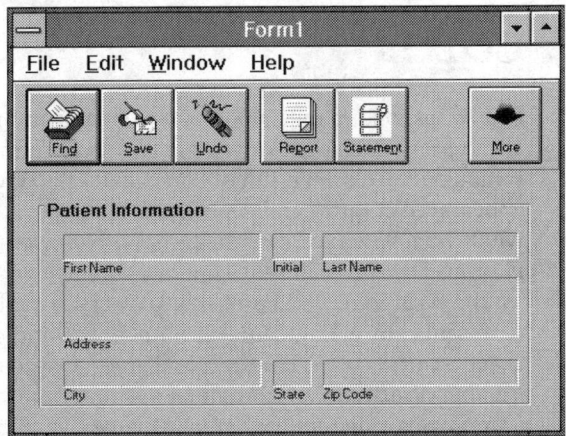

Figure 5-1 Harmonious and effective interface design

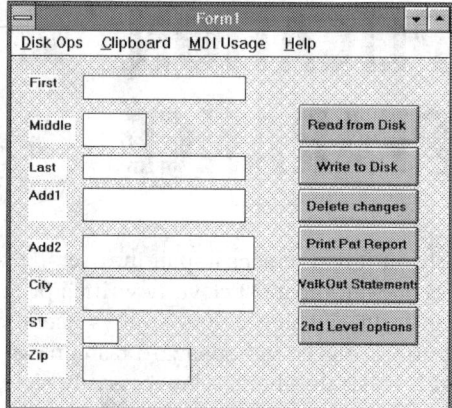

Figure 5-2 Functionally equivalent
to Figure 5-1, yet ineffective

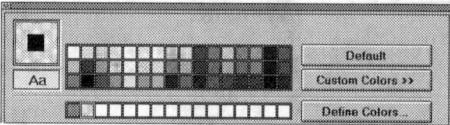

Figure 5-3 The color palette lets you
easily choose colors for your application

elements respond to the user. For example, most menu bars start with "File" and "Edit," and end with "Window" and "Help." Double-clicking an item in most list boxes is the same as single-clicking an item and then clicking on an associated command button.

Hundreds of these conventions, when appropriately applied, make learning Windows programs easy. When you've learned how to use one DOS program, you've learned how to use one DOS program. But when you've learned how to use one Windows program, you've learned much of what you need to know to operate any Windows program.

This chapter covers some of the key elements that make up an application's appearance. Microsoft also provides a wealth of interface design suggestions in the Visual Basic Design Guide application that comes with Visual Basic.

COLOR

People respond to the color of the elements on the screen. For example, red usually represents danger or warning (at least in most Western cultures). Red text stands out on a screen full of black text. This powerful visual tool augments the appearance of forms and controls on the screen. In designing a form interactively with Visual Basic, you can use the on-screen color palette to make color choices (see Figure 5-3).

The BackColor and ForeColor properties control an object's color. Colors are represented by a 4-byte integer number that indicates a mixture of the three electronic primary colors: blue, red, and green. One way to set a color value is to set this number directly. The first byte of this number is ignored. The second, third, and fourth bytes represent how much blue, red, and green, respectively, will be used in the color mixture. Each color can be assigned a value between 0 and 255 (or 0 to FF in hexadecimal notation), which indicates that color's intensity in the mixture. You can also assign a color value with the RGB function. This function lets you supply a decimal number between 0 and 255 for each electronic primary color, and returns a color number based on these values. Still another way to assign a color value uses the QBColor function. This function lets you select one of 16 colors from a palette in a way familiar to QuickBASIC programmers.

APPEARANCE OF SCREEN OBJECTS

Forms have four possible border styles: none, sizable, fixed single, and fixed double. The BorderStyle property of a form determines which type of border appears around it. A form with no border also has no Maximize button, Minimize button, or control box. This border style is a popular choice for warning boxes, which usually do not need these options. The user can change the size of sizable forms with the mouse, just as the name suggests. Both the fixed single and fixed double borders disable the mouse's ability to change their sizes. However, the user can still maximize or minimize the form.

Each object has a height and width. The number representing the object's height and width depends on the type of measurement. A height's value is different if expressed in inches or centimeters (although the object's actual height does not change). For example, objects that are 1 inch in height are also 2.54 centimeter high. Visual Basic determines the height and width of objects with the Height and Width properties of the object in the measurement system set in the ScaleMode property.

Each object on the screen is a certain distance from the edges of another object. A control on a form positions itself in terms of the left and top edges of the form, whereas forms on the screen locate themselves in terms of the left and top edges of the screen. Visual Basic returns the distance from the left and top edges with the Left and Top properties of the object in the measurement system set in the ScaleMode property.

Icons and Pointers

A minimized form becomes an icon that represents the form. This icon reminds the viewer that the form still resides in the operating memory of the computer. Visual Basic lets you modify this icon either at runtime or design time. At design time the properties box provides a list of the icons available. Access this list by selecting the Icon property in the properties box and double-clicking (Icon). Figures 5-4 and 5-5 show what the properties box and list look like in the default Visual Basic setup. For a listing of the icons that shipped with Microsoft Visual Basic, look in the back of the Microsoft Visual Basic Programmer's Guide.

You can also change the icon of the mouse pointer to reflect the current function of the program. Some pointer shapes have become traditional for Windows

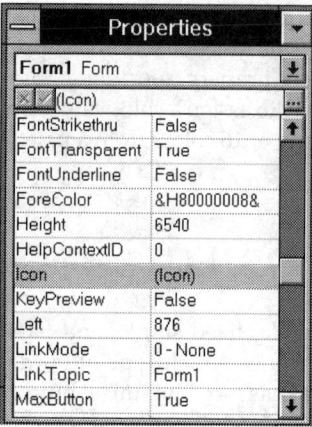

Figure 5-4 Properties box
showing Icon line

programs. When activity takes place in the background such that the user must wait
before continuing work, an hourglass can replace the normal arrow. If the cursor
is over a text box, the cursor can change to an I-beam so the user can manipulate the
text box's contents. In Visual Basic the MousePointer property determines the type
of cursor that appears over an application's forms and controls.

Finally, an object's visibility determines whether or not the user sees it on the
screen. (Don't confuse an invisible object with one that is covered by another window or application.)

APPLICATION APPEARANCE SUMMARY

Table 5-1 summarizes the properties that affect the appearance of forms and controls.

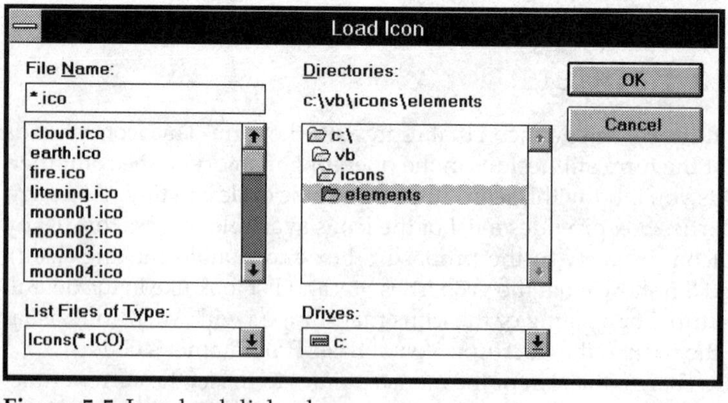

Figure 5-5 Icon load dialog box

Use or Set This...		To Do This...
BackColor	Property	Adjust the background color of a form or control
BackStyle	Property	Determine whether the background of a label or shape is transparent
BorderStyle	Property	Adjust the edges of a form and some controls
Caption	Property	Indicate what text will appear on a form or control
ForeColor	Property	Adjust the color of the text of a form or control
Height	Property	Adjust the vertical size of a form or control
Icon	Property	Determine the icon to display for a minimized form
Left	Property	Adjust the position of a form in relation to the left edge
MousePointer	Property	Determine the icon to display when a mouse is over a form or control
Top	Property	Adjust the position of a form in relation to the top edge
Visible	Property	Determine whether a form is visible to the user
Width	Property	Adjust the horizontal size of a form or control

Table 5-1 Properties dealing with the general appearance of a form or control

CONSTANT.TXT Values

Many of the properties, events, and methods of this chapter use numeric values as arguments. Using constants rather than the literal value makes your code self-documenting, more readable, and easier to debug.

Microsoft provides a file, CONSTANT.TXT, that has many constant declarations defined for you. For smaller applications it's probably easiest just to type the declarations in yourself. For larger applications you'll find it much easier to read the text file into a new module.

To do this, create a new module by pulling down the File menu and choosing the New Module menu command. Then pull down the File menu again, and choose Load Text. This opens up a dialog box listing all text files in the current directory. CONSTANT.TXT should be in your main Visual Basic directory (default installation would place this in C:\VB). Simply choose CONSTANT.TXT to enter the entire file into your module. These constants will then be available throughout your application.

Table 5-2 lists the value of the constant, the CONSTANT.TXT constant name, and a brief description of what the constant means.

Value	CONSTANT.TXT	Meaning
BackColor and ForeColor		
&H0	BLACK	Black
&HFF	RED	Red
&HFF00	GREEN	Green
&HFFFF	YELLOW	Yellow
&HFF0000	BLUE	Blue
&HFF00FF	MAGENTA	Magenta
&HFFFF00	CYAN	Cyan
&HFFFFFF	WHITE	White
BackStyle		
0	TRANSPARENT	Background color and graphics visible behind object
1	SOLID	(Default)—object's BackColor obscures any color or graphics
BorderStyle (forms)		
0	NONE	None (no border, control box, Maximize button, or Minimize button)
1	FIXED_SINGLE	Fixed single (nonsizable, with Maximize or Minimize buttons)

Value	CONSTANT.TXT	Meaning
2	SIZEABLE	(Default) Sizable (sizable border, Maximize and Minimize buttons)
3	FIXED_DOUBLE	Fixed double (nonsizable border, without Minimize or Maximize buttons)
BorderStyle (labels, images, picture boxes, text boxes, OLE)		
0	NONE	None
1	FIXED_SINGLE	Fixed single
BorderStyle (lines and shapes)		
0	TRANSPARENT	Transparent
1	SOLID	Solid
2	DASH	Dash
3	DOT	Dot
4	DASH_DOT	Dash-Dot
5	DASH_DOT_DOT	Dash-Dot-Dot
6	INSIDE_SOLID	Inside Solid
MousePointer		
0	DEFAULT	Default for this control
1	ARROW	Arrow
2	CROSSHAIR	Cross-hair pointer

(continued on next page)

(continued from previous page)

Value	CONSTANT.TXT	Meaning
3	IBEAM	Text entry I-beam
4	ICON_POINTER	Square within a square
5	SIZE_POINTER	Four-directional cross, arrows facing up, down, left, and right
6	SIZE_NE_SW	Two-directional diagonal arrow (Northeast to Southwest)
7	SIZE_N_S	Two-directional up and down arrow (North to South)
8	SIZE_NW_SE	Two-directional diagonal arrow (Northwest to Southeast)
9	SIZE_E_W	Two-directional left and right arrow (East to West)
10	UP_ARROW	Arrow pointing up
11	HOURGLASS	Hourglass
12	NO_DROP	No drop (Circle with line through it)

Table 5-2 CONSTANT.TXT values for application appearance

The following pages investigate these properties in detail. At the end of this section, step-by-step directions describe how to assemble the Appearance project that demonstrates each of these properties.

BACKCOLOR PROPERTY

Objects Affected

- ▶ Check
- Clipboard
- ▶ Combo
- ▶ Command
- CommonDlg
- ▶ Data
- Debug
- ▶ Dir
- ▶ Drive
- ▶ File
- ▶ Form
- ▶ Frame
- ▶ Grid
- Image
- ▶ Label
- Line
- ▶ List
- MDI Form
- Menu
- ▶ OLE
- ▶ Option
- ▶ Picture
- Printer
- Screen
- Scroll
- ▶ Shape
- ▶ Text
- Timer

234

Purpose

The BackColor property defines or determines the background color of a form or control. Table 5-3 summarizes the arguments of the BackColor property, and Table 5-4 lists the values of the color& argument.

General Syntax

```
[form.]BackColor [ = color&]
[form!]Name.BackColor [ = color&]
```

Argument	Description
form	Name property of the form. Changes or references current form if not specified
Name	Name property of the control
color&	Value of the color defined with hexadecimal number, RGB function, or QBColor function

Table 5-3 Arguments of the BackColor property

Color	CONSTANT.TXT	Red Value	Green Value	Blue Value	Hexadecimal	QBColor
Black	BLACK	0	0	0	&H0	0
Red	RED	255	0	0	&HFF	4
Green	GREEN	0	255	0	&HFF00	2
Yellow	YELLOW	0	255	255	&HFFFF	6
Blue	BLUE	0	0	255	&HFF0000	1
Magenta	MAGENTA	255	0	255	&HFF00FF	5
Cyan	CYAN	0	255	255	&HFFFF00	3
White	WHITE	255	255	255	&HFFFFFF	15
Light Gray	n/a	192	192	192	&H00C0C0C0	7
Dark Gray	n/a	128	128	128	&H00808080	8

Table 5-4 Values of common colors in RGB, hexadecimal, and QBColor formats

Example Syntax

```
Sub Form_Resize
    If WindowState = 2 Then              'If the window is maximized
        BackColor = RGB(0, 0, 255)       'Changes the form's background to blue
    Else
        BackColor = RGB(255, 255, 255)  'Changes the form's background to white
    End If
End Sub
```

Description

The BackColor property changes the Windows environment's default settings for the background color of a form or control. (The default setting of the BackColor of a form is the color chosen in the control panel for the Windows background.) Each BackColor property expression begins with the name of the object whose background is being changed. The Name property uniquely identifies a control or form. If no name precedes an expression, the code references or changes the BackColor property of the current form.

The color& argument of a BackColor expression must be a hexadecimal value. Either an explicit hexadecimal number, the RGB function, or the QBColor function defines the hexadecimal value of color&. In the example syntax, the background color of the form changes according to its present size. The background of a maximized form is blue; a normalized form is white.

Setting the Color& Argument

You may set the color& argument in several different ways. Table 5-4 summarizes the settings of the color& argument. The summary section at the beginning of this chapter gives detailed instructions on using the CONSTANT.TXT values.

The most direct method uses the hexadecimal number of the color. A valid hexadecimal value ranges from 0 to 16,777,215 (&HFFFFFF). This is the format that Visual Basic uses if you read the color's property during runtime. Note that the CONSTANT.TXT constants hold these hexadecimal values.

You may also obtain the hexadecimal value of any of the 16 standard Windows colors with the QBColor function by specifying the integer color number as used in Quick BASIC (and other versions of Microsoft BASIC).

The RGB function returns the hexadecimal equivalent given the three arguments red, green, and blue. Each argument ranges from 0 to 255; customized colors result from the adjustment of the values of these three variables. See Appendix A, Visual Basic Language Tutorial, for additional details about the RGB and QBColor functions.

The ForeColor Property

The BackColor and ForeColor properties of a form combine to produce the colors that you see when the form displays. Whenever you change one of these properties, you should consider how the new color combination will work together. If the foreground and background colors clash, it may make your program harder to use and may detract from its usefulness. For example, setting the BackColor property to blue and the ForeColor property to bright red is objectionable to most users.

Example

In the Appearance project at the end of this chapter, the BackColor property of formAppear and formWarning forms is gray (&H00C0C0C0). You will set this property at design time to simplify the process. Notice how the BackColor property of the form has no effect on the setting of the control's background color. Each control has its own separate BackColor property independent of the settings of the form's BackColor property.

Comments

The BackColor property of a form or control is an effective way to highlight certain controls to attract the user's attention or to make something more visible. For instance, to emphasize list boxes on a form with a gray background, set the BackColor property of the list boxes to white.

BACKSTYLE PROPERTY

Objects Affected

Check	Clipboard	Combo	Command	CommonDlg
Data	Debug	Dir	Drive	File
Form	Frame	Grid	Image	▶ Label
Line	List	MDI Form	Menu	OLE
Option	Picture	Printer	Screen	Scroll
▶ Shape	Text	Timer		

Purpose

The BackStyle property determines whether a label or shape's background is opaque or transparent. Tables 5-5 and 5-6 summarize the arguments of the BackStyle property.

General Syntax

```
[form!]Name.BackStyle [ = style%]
```

Argument	Description
form	Name property of the form the control is on
Name	Name property of the shape or label control
style%	Sets the transparency of the background

Table 5-5 Arguments of the BackStyle property

style%	CONSTANT.TXT	Setting
0	TRANSPARENT	Background color and graphics visible behind object
1	SOLID	(Default)—object's BackColor obscures any color or graphics

Table 5-6 Settings of the style% argument in the BackStyle property

Example Syntax

```
Sub Command1_Click ()
    Label1.BackStyle = Abs(Label1.BackStyle - 1)     'Flips transparency of label
    Label1.Caption = Choose(Label1.BackStyle + 1, "Transparent", "Opaque")
End Sub
```

Description

The BackStyle property lets you determine whether to obscure the background when you place a label or shape on top of another object. Setting a label's BackStyle to Transparent (0) lets the background color of its container show through. This may be helpful if you use colored backgrounds, as you don't have to set each label's background color independently. You may also have a need to label a set of graphics. If you leave BackStyle at the default of Solid (1), you run the risk of obscuring the graphics you're trying to label. The Summary section

238

Figure 5-6 Label1 with transparent BackStyle

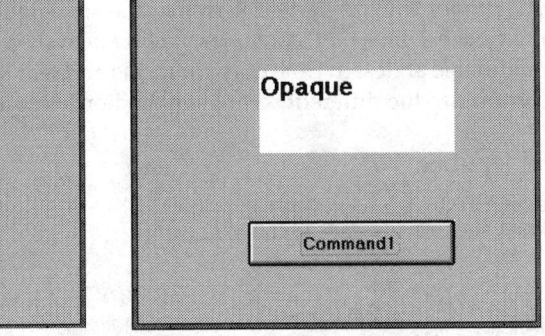

Figure 5-7 Label1 with opaque BackStyle

at the beginning of this chapter gives detailed instructions on how to use the CONSTANT.TXT values.

The example syntax shows how the label obscures the background when its BackStyle property is set to 1, and how it lets the background color of the form show through when its BackStyle property is set to 0. Figures 5-6 and 5-7 show how the example syntax might look.

Example

The Appearance project sets the BackStyle of the labels to Transparent. This makes form design and upkeep easier.

Comment

If the BackStyle property is set to Transparent (0), the BackColor property has no effect.

BORDERSTYLE PROPERTY

Objects Affected

Check	Clipboard	Combo	Command	CommonDlg
Data	Debug	Dir	Drive	File
▶ Form	Frame	▶ Grid	▶ Image	▶ Label
▶ Line	List	MDI Form	Menu	▶ OLE
Option	▶ Picture	Printer	Screen	Scroll
▶ Shape	▶ Text	Timer		

239

Purpose

The BorderStyle property determines the appearance of a border for a form, grid, image, label, line, OLE container, picture box, shape, or text box. This property is modifiable at design time only for forms and text boxes. Tables 5-7 through 5-10 summarize the different settings of the BorderStyle property's arguments.

General Syntax

```
[form.]BorderStyle [ = setting%]
[form!]Name.BorderStyle [ = setting%]
```

Argument	Description
form	Name property of the form
Name	Name property of the text box, label, or picture box
setting%	Value representing the type of border

Table 5-7 Arguments of the BorderStyle property

setting%	CONSTANT.TXT	Description
0	NONE	None (no border, control box, Maximize button, or Minimize button)
1	FIXED_SINGLE	Fixed single (nonsizable, with Maximize or Minimize buttons)
2	SIZEABLE	(Default) Sizable (sizable border, Maximize and Minimize buttons)
3	FIXED_DOUBLE	Fixed double (nonsizable border without Minimize or Maximize buttons)

Table 5-8 Settings for the BorderStyle property of a form

setting%	CONSTANT.TXT	Description	Controls That Default to This Style...
0	NONE	None	label, image
1	FIXED_SINGLE	Fixed single	picture box, text box, OLE

Table 5-9 Settings for the BorderStyle property of labels, images, picture boxes, text boxes, and OLE control

240

setting%	CONSTANT.TXT	Description	Controls That Default to This Style...
0	TRANSPARENT	Transparent	
1	SOLID	Solid	shape, line
2	DASH	Dash	
3	DOT	Dot	
4	DASH_DOT	Dash-Dot	
5	DASH_DOT_DOT	Dash-Dot-Dot	
6	INSIDE_SOLID	Inside Solid	

Table 5-10 Settings for the BorderStyle property of shapes and lines

Example Syntax

```
Sub SetBackground (Name As Form)
    Select Case Name.BorderStyle        'Obtains border of indicated form
        Case NONE                       'No border
            Name.BackColor = BLUE        'Blue Background
            Name.ForeColor = WHITE       'White Text
        Case FIXED_SINGLE               'Fixed Single border
            Name.BackColor = WHITE       'White Background
            Name.ForeColor = BLUE        'Blue Text
        Case SIZEABLE                   'Sizable Border
            Name.BackColor = BLUE        'Blue Background
            Name.ForeColor = YELLOW      'Yellow Text
        Case FIXED_DOUBLE               'Fixed Double Border
            Name.BackColor = CYAN        'Cyan Background
            Name.ForeColor = BLACK       'Black Text
    End Select
End Sub
```

Description

Use the BorderStyle property at design time to set the appearance of the edges of a form, text box, label, or picture box. The border chosen at design time affects a form's control box, Maximize button, and Minimize button at runtime. (At design time the control box, Maximize button, and Minimize button are always visible.) The BorderStyle property of a form also affects the user's ability to change the form's size. When the BorderStyle property of a text box, picture box, or label changes, the single border line around the object appears or disappears.

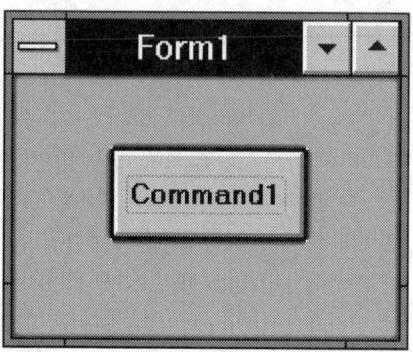

Figure 5-9 BorderStyle 0 gives no border. Note the form's background color set to gray to show the form's size

Figure 5-8 BorderStyle 2 (the default) gives a sizable border

The summary section at the beginning of this chapter explains how to use the CONSTANT.TXT values for the setting% argument.

Forms

BorderStyle applies to both forms and to various controls. The settings for these two groups, although similar, differ enough that we'll cover them separately, discussing forms first.

Sizable Border

The default setting for the BorderStyle property of a form is 2 (sizable). A sizable border has no effect on the display of the control box, Maximize button, and Minimize controls. Figure 5-8 displays how a form with a sizable border appears on the screen. Corresponding values for these properties (ControlBox, MaxButton, MinButton) are True (-1) by default. Changing one of these properties does not affect the other two properties. When a form retains the default border style, the user can change the size of the form at runtime.

No Border

A form with the BorderStyle set to 0 will not have a border or any of the objects normally associated with a border. For this reason the Maximize button, Minimize button, and control box will not appear on the form, regardless of the settings of the ControlBox, MaxButton, or MinButton properties. The title bar of the form will also not appear. When a form's BorderStyle property is 0, the form may not be resized or minimized. You may wish to use this kind of border for warning or informational dialog boxes. For example, this style might be used with an application's first screen ("splash" screen), which quickly displays while

242

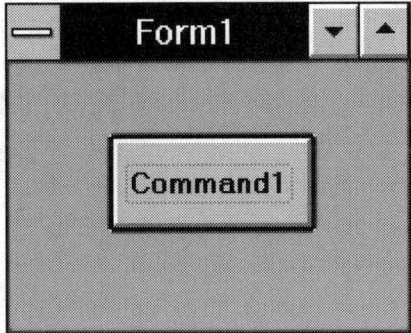

Figure 5-10 BorderStyle 1 gives a single fixed border

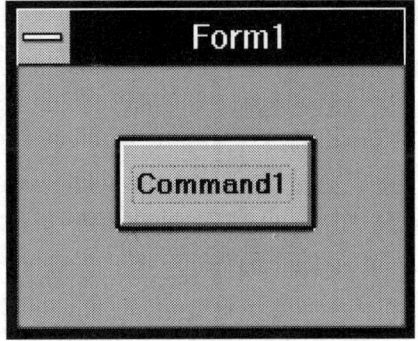

Figure 5-11 BorderStyle 3 gives a double fixed border

the application loads the rest of the forms into memory. Figure 5-9 shows what a form with no border looks like.

Fixed Single Border

If the BorderStyle of a form is 1 (fixed single), then the border is a single line around the form. Figure 5-10 demonstrates the appearance of a form with a fixed single border. The Maximize button, Minimize button, and control box may appear on the form, depending on the setting of the MaxButton, MinButton, and ControlBox properties. A form with this border style may have its size changed only by maximizing or minimizing it. The user maximizes or minimizes this kind of form with either the command options on the control box or the icon buttons.

Fixed Double Border

When a form's BorderStyle property is 3 (fixed double), the border is a thick line around the form. This border does not include the Maximize and Minimize buttons, regardless of the settings of the MaxButton and MinButton properties. A control box appears on the form, provided that the ControlBox property is True. Both the Maximize and Minimize command buttons will be options on the Control Box menu unless the MaxButton and MinButton properties are False. Users may not adjust the size of the form at runtime by dragging the borders with the mouse. Only the WindowState property—or the maximize, minimize, or restore options on the control box—may change the size of a form with this kind of border style. Forms with a menu bar never display as a fixed double border; Visual Basic automatically displays fixed double forms as fixed single forms if there is a menu. Figure 5-11 shows what a form with a fixed double border looks like on the screen.

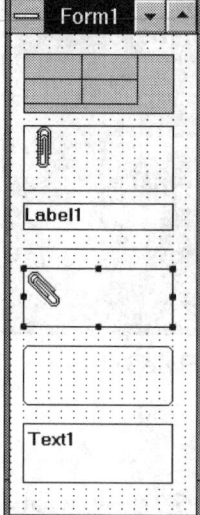

Figure 5-12 Borders around grid, image, label, line, OLE, picture box, shape, and text box

Text Boxes, Labels, and Picture Boxes

Every grid, image, label, line, OLE, picture box, shape, and text box has a BorderStyle property. Figure 5-12 demonstrates the appearance of the border around each of these controls. Unlike the setting of a form's property, the BorderStyle property of a label, text box, or picture box has an effect only if there is a border. This border appears around the indicated control. If the value of this property is True, then a single line appears around the bounds of the label, image, picture box, and text box. A border does not appear around one of these controls with a False (0) BorderStyle property. The line and shape control have a variety of border styles.

Example

In the Appearance project at the end of this chapter, the BorderStyle property removes the border of formWarning. This removes the control box, Maximize button, and Minimize button from the user's view. The BorderStyle property of both the label boxes on the Warning forms remains at the default value of 0. As a result no border appears around either of these labels. FormAppear begins with its border set to fixed single.

Comments

Make sure to choose the correct border for each form in a program. The default sizable setting is not always appropriate. In many cases giving the user the ability to change the size of the form may cause errors. Many forms look bad when maximized—all the controls remain stuck in the upper-left corner, with wide

244

expanses of blank form covering the screen. Strongly consider one of the fixed border styles unless you write special code in the Resize event (covered in Chapter 4, Forms and Menus) to resize and reposition a form's controls.

CAPTION PROPERTY

Objects Affected

▶ Check	Clipboard	Combo	▶ Command	CommonDlg
▶ Data	Debug	Dir	Drive	File
▶ Form	▶ Frame	Grid	Image	▶ Label
Line	List	▶ MDI Form	▶ Menu	OLE
▶ Option	Picture	Printer	Screen	Scroll
Shape	Text	Timer		

Purpose

The Caption property indicates what text displays to label a control or form. A form's Caption property appears in its title bar, between the control box and the Minimize and Maximize buttons. Text in the Caption property of a label, data control, or command button appears on the control. Option buttons or check boxes place the contents of their Caption property to the right of the control. A frame's Caption property displays on the top-right corner of the fame. All of these controls' Caption properties are both read and write at either design time or runtime. Table 5-11 summarizes the arguments of the Caption property.

General Syntax

```
[form.]Caption [ = textstring$]
[form!]Name.Caption [ = textstring$]
```

Argument	Description
form	Name property of the form
Name	Name property of the control
textString$	Text to place in or on the control or form indicated

Table 5-11 Arguments of the Caption property

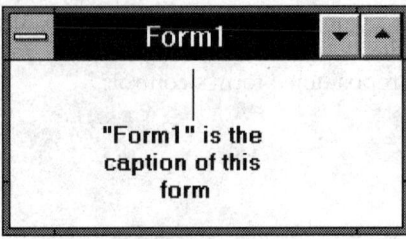

Figure 5-13 Caption property text appears in a form's title bar

Example Syntax

```
Sub Commmand1_Click
    If  Command1.Caption = "Print" Then  'Alternates between displaying the word "Display"
        Command1.Caption = "Display"    'and "Print" each time the user presses Command1
    Else
        Command1.Caption = "Print"
    End If
End Sub
```

Description

The Caption property defines or determines the text that appears on a command button, option box, check box, data control, frame, label, menu, or form. You can set this property at design time with the properties box. You can also set the Caption property of a form or control at runtime. The TextString$ argument contains the string of text to redefine the Caption property with. If the TextString$ argument is blank, then the text on the form or control is blank. In the example, the Caption property of the Command1 command button changes with each clicking of the command button.

Forms

The Caption displays in a form's title bar. The title bar is the region between the control box and the Minimize and Maximize buttons. If the BorderStyle of a form is 0 (no border), then there is no title bar and the Caption property (if any) is ignored. Remember that the Caption property of a form is for visually cueing the user, and not for identifying the form in your code. Figure 5-13 shows how the Caption property appears at the top of Form1.

Labels

Text entered into the Caption property of a label displays on the form in the label's position. A label's Caption property is alterable either at design time or runtime. If the label's AutoSize property is True (-1), then the label's size auto-

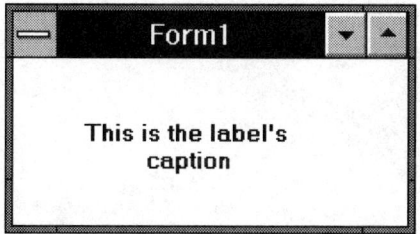

Figure 5-14 Caption property text appears in the label

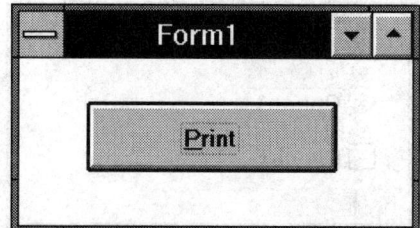

Figure 5-15 Caption property text appears inside a command button. Note the accelerator key P is underlined

matically increases or decreases to fit with each change. For example, the label below a picture box containing a Trashcan icon could change from Delete to Disabled whenever the user turns the delete feature off. In this case the AutoSize property allows the label to expand or contract to accommodate the different word lengths. Figure 5-14 shows where the Caption property of the Label1 label box appears on the label control.

Command Buttons

The Caption property for a command button places the text in the middle of the command button. A command control's Caption property is modifiable either at design time or runtime. You can also use the Caption property to assign an access key to a command button. Place an ampersand (&) before the letter in the caption that you wish to make the access key. For example, the ⓟ key would become the access key for a command button with a Caption property of &Print. The user can then hold down the ⒶⓁⓉ key and press ⓟ to trigger the command button's Click event. This change appears in text on the command button shown with the access letter underlined. If you need to include an ampersand literal within your caption, use double ampersands: For example, "&UPS && Airborne" becomes "UPS & Airborne". Figure 5-15 indicates the location where the Caption property displays on the Command1 command button.

Option Buttons and Check Boxes

Option buttons and check boxes have their Caption property contents placed on the right of the graphic objects. These properties are modifiable at both design time and runtime, but do not possess the AutoSize feature of the label box. Make sure you provide enough space for any changes to the captions of these controls. Figure 5-16 demonstrates the place where the Caption properties of the Option1 option box and Check1 check boxes appear on the screen.

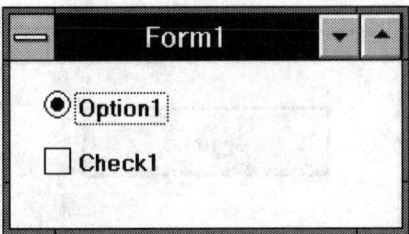

Figure 5-16 Caption property text of option and check boxes appear directly to the side of the box or button

Example

The Appearance project at the end of this chapter uses the Caption property several times. It is set at design time to label various elements used in the program, and the Caption property of formAppear changes to identify what number is being dialed.

Comments

A form's Caption property does not appear when the form's BorderStyle is 0.

FORECOLOR PROPERTY

Objects Affected

▶ Check	Clipboard	▶ Combo	Command	CommonDlg
▶ Data	Debug	▶ Dir	▶ Drive	▶ File
▶ Form	▶ Frame	▶ Grid	Image	▶ Label
Line	▶ List	MDI Form	Menu	▶ OLE
▶ Option	▶ Picture	▶ Printer	Screen	Scroll
Shape	▶ Text	Timer		

Purpose

The ForeColor property reads or sets the foreground color of a form or control. Tables 5-12 and 5-13 list the values of the ForeColor property.

General Syntax

```
[form.]ForeColor [ = color&]
[form!]Name.ForeColor [ = color&]
```

Argument	Description
form	Name property of the form. No name means the current form
Name	Name property of the control
color&	Value of the color defined with hexadecimal number, RBG function, or QBColor function

Table 5-12 Arguments of the ForeColor property

Color	CONSTANT.TXT	Red Value	Green Value	Blue Value	Hexadecimal	QBColor
Black	BLACK	0	0	0	&H0	0
Red	RED	255	0	0	&HFF	4
Green	GREEN	0	255	0	&HFF00	2
Yellow	YELLOW	0	255	255	&HFFFF	6
Blue	BLUE	0	0	255	&HFF0000	1
Magenta	MAGENTA	255	0	255	&HFF00FF	5
Cyan	CYAN	0	255	255	&HFFFF00	3
White	WHITE	255	255	255	&HFFFFFF	15
Light Gray	n/a	192	192	192	&H00C0C0C0	7
Dark Gray	n/a	128	128	128	&H00808080	8

Table 5-13 Values of common colors in RGB, hexadecimal, and QBColor formats

Example Syntax

```
Sub Form_Load ()
    If  ForeColor = RGB(0,0,0) Then
        BackColor = RGB(255,255,255)
    End If
End Sub
```

Description

The ForeColor property changes the Windows environment's default settings for the foreground color of a form or control. (The default setting of the ForeColor of a form is the color chosen in the control panel for the Windows text.) Each ForeColor property expression begins with the name of the object whose foreground is being changed. The Name property uniquely identifies a control or form. If no name precedes an expression, the code references or changes the ForeColor property of the current form.

The color& argument of a ForeColor expression must be a hexadecimal value. Either an explicit hexadecimal number, the RGB function, or the QBColor function defines the hexadecimal value of color&. In the example syntax, the foreground color of the form changes according to its present size. The foreground of a maximized form is blue; a normalized form is white.

Setting the Color& Argument

You may set the color& argument in several different ways. Table 5-13 summarizes the settings of the color& argument. The summary section at the beginning of this chapter gives detailed instructions on using the CONSTANT.TXT values.

The most direct method uses the hexadecimal number of the color. A valid hexadecimal value ranges from 0 to 16,777,215 (&HFFFFFF). This is the format that Visual Basic uses if you read the color's property during runtime. Note that the CONSTANT.TXT constants hold these hexadecimal values.

You may also obtain the hexadecimal value of any of the 16 standard Windows colors with the QBColor function by specifying the integer color number as used in Quick BASIC (and other versions of Microsoft BASIC).

The RGB function returns the hexadecimal equivalent given the three arguments red, green, and blue. Each argument ranges from 0 to 255; customized colors result from the adjustment of the values of these three variables. See Appendix A, Visual Basic Language Tutorial, for additional details about the RGB and QBColor functions.

The BackColor Property

The ForeColor and BackColor properties of a form combine to produce the colors that you see when the form displays. Whenever you change one of these properties, you should consider how the new color combination will work together. If the background and foreground colors clash, it may make your program harder to use and may detract from its usefulness. For example, setting the

ForeColor property to blue and the BackColor property to bright red is objectionable to most users.

Example

In the Appearance project at the end of this chapter, the ForeColor property of the FormAppear and Warning forms changes to blue (&HFF000). This property change occurs at design time for both forms to simplify the process. Modifications are also possible at runtime.

Comments

The ForeColor property of a form or control is an effective means of highlighting certain controls to get the user's attention or to make it easier for the user to see something. For instance, red text on an otherwise black-and-white screen will draw the user's attention.

HEIGHT PROPERTY

Objects Affected

▶ Check	Clipboard	▶ Combo	▶ Command	CommonDlg
▶ Data	Debug	▶ Dir	▶ Drive	▶ File
▶ Form	▶ Frame	▶ Grid	▶ Image	▶ Label
Line	▶ List	▶ MDI Form	Menu	▶ OLE
▶ Option	▶ Picture	▶ Printer	▶ Screen	▶ Scroll
▶ Shape	▶ Text	Timer		

Purpose

The Height property defines or determines the vertical size of a form or control on the screen, form, picture box, or Printer object. Forms, Printer objects, and Screen objects are always measured in twips. A control's size uses the units of measurement set in the ScaleMode property of the current form or picture box. Table 5-14 summarizes the arguments of the Height property, and Table 5-15 outlines measurement types.

General Syntax

```
[form.]Height [ = height!]
[form!]Name.Height [ = height!]
Printer.Height [ = height!]
Screen.Height [ = height!]
```

Argument	Description
form	Name property of the form
Name	Name property of the control
Printer	'Printer' for Printer object
Screen	'Screen' for Screen object
height!	Vertical height of the object

Table 5-14 Arguments of the Height property

Measurement	Size
Twip	1440 twips = 1 inch
Point	72 points = 1 inch
Pixels	Varies depending on system being used
Characters	12 characters horizontally and 6 vertically = 1 inch
Millimeters	254 millimeters = 1 inch
Centimeters	2.54 centimeters = 1 inch

Table 5-15 Possible measurement types in relation to 1 inch

Example Syntax

```
Sub Form_Load
    Form1.Height = (Command1.Height * 5)   'Defines height and width of the form as 5
    Form1.Width = (Command1.Width * 5)     'times the height and width of command button.
End Sub
```

Description

The Height property of an object measures the vertical height of the object. You can enter this value at design time by manually sizing the object with the mouse or by entering the value at the properties box. You can modify the Height property of a

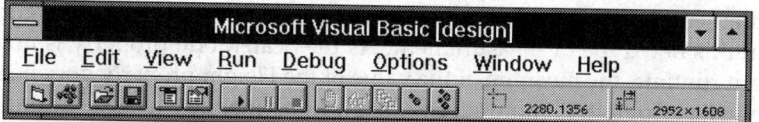

Figure 5-17 The right side of the toolbar shows the Left, Top, Width, and Height properties

control or form either at design time or runtime. In contrast, you can only set the Height properties of the Printer and Screen objects at runtime. A setting must be between 0 and a maximum value specified by the system itself. Visual Basic automatically adjusts itself to the resolution of the screen or printer. You should ensure that your objects are not too large for the most common 640 by 480 and 800 by 600 resolution screens to display.

Left, Top, Width, and Height Properties

When you create a form or control in Visual Basic, the Left, Top, Width, and Height properties display in the far right side of the toolbar. Figure 5-17 shows what the toolbar looks like on the screen.

The first two numbers, separated by a comma, represent the left and top position of the control or form. A form's Height property provides the maximum visible height for the controls placed on it. (Note that it is possible to have a control that is larger than the form it is on; only part of the control would display.) Similarly, the value of the Height property of the screen sets the maximum value of a form's property. This varies from system to system, according to the resolution of the monitor. The width and the height of the object appear to the right of these numbers, separated by an "x." If the object is a control, then the numbers shown are in the units of measurement specified by the ScaleMode property of the current form. A form's Height property is measured in twips. This difference allows for variances in the resolution of screens used for each computer. For example, a system with an 800 by 600 display shows more on the screen than a 640 by 480 display. See Chapter 9, The Coordinate System, for more information.

Screen and Printer

The Height property returns the height of the screen or page available based on the resolution of the computer screen or printer being used. The Height property of the screen and printer objects is not available at design time and is read-only at runtime.

Scale Mode

The ScaleMode property of a form directly controls the meaning of the value of the Height property. When the ScaleMode property changes at design time from one measurement to another, Visual Basic recalculates the value of the Height property in this new type of measurement. As the ScaleMode property is not modifiable at runtime, the meaning of the value of the Height property does not change while the program is running. For example, no matter what size a command box becomes based on changes in the size of the parent form, the Height property will remain the same.

ScaleHeight Property

The ScaleHeight property divides the height of a form, picture box, or Printer object into the number of units set in the property. For example, when a form's ScaleHeight property changes to 100, the height of the form is divided into 100 equal units. (Changing the ScaleHeight property of the form to a new value does not change the actual size of the control.) This unit changes in size as the form's

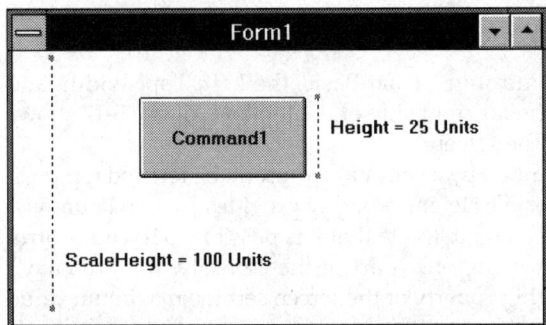

Figure 5-18 Height and ScaleHeight compared at start ...

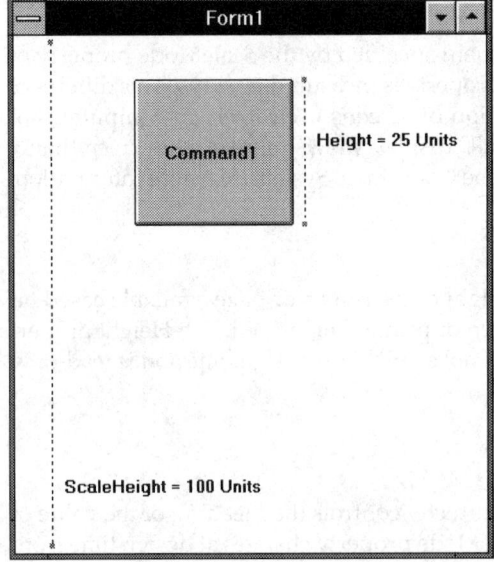

Figure 5-19 ... and after resizing. Note that the Height of the command button is the same number of relative units, although it is physically larger

height changes. Increasing the height of the form thus has the effect of increasing the size of one of these units (the height remains divided into 100 units that are now larger in size). The size of the control adjusts based on the changes in height to the form.

These units define the upper and lower limits of the possible height of controls on this form. For example, a Resize event might adjust the Height property of a command box of a form by triggering a move statement that always ensures that the command box is one-fourth the size of the form. In this example the ScaleHeight property of the form is 100, and the Height property of the Command1 command button is 25 (one-fourth the height of the form). Figures 5-18 and 5-19 display this concept visually.

Example

The Appearance project at the end of this section sets the Height property of the forms and controls at design time. This is done either by dragging the control's edges with the mouse, or by entering the value into the properties box.

ICON PROPERTY

Objects Affected

Check	Clipboard	Combo	Command	CommonDlg
Data	Debug	Dir	Drive	File
▶ Form	Frame	Grid	Image	Label
Line	List	▶ MDI Form	Menu	OLE
Option	Picture	Printer	Screen	Scroll
Shape	Text	Timer		

Purpose

The Icon property defines the icon displayed on the screen when a form is in a minimized window state. This property is only available for a form and the file must be in the standard icon format (*.ICO). Table 5-16 summarizes the argument of the Icon property.

General Syntax

`[form.]Icon`

Argument	Description
form	Name property of the form

Table 5-16 Argument of the Icon property

Example Syntax

```
Sub Form_Resize ()
    If WindowState = 0 Then                              'Checks if form is minimized
        If Form1.Caption = "Dialing Number" Then  'Checks if form reads this text
            Form1.Icon = LoadPicture("\VB\ICONS\COMM\PHONE04.ICO")  'Off Hook phone
        ElseIf Form1.Caption = "Hanging Up" Then  'Checks if form reads this text
            Form1.Icon = LoadPicture("\VB\ICONS\COMM\NET3.ICO")    'knife cutting
        Else
            Form1.Icon = LoadPicture("\VB\ICONS\COMM\PHONE01.ICO")  'regular phone
    End If
End Sub
```

Description

A form's Icon property defines the default icon to display when a form appears minimized on the screen. At creation time a form's Icon property defaults to the Visual Basic Icon. A form's Icon property may be modified either at design time or runtime. In this way you may temporarily change an icon at runtime to reflect changes in the functioning of the program. In the example above, the main form of a communications program's Icon property changes for different functions. An open phone symbol appears for a dialing operation, a knife cutting a cable for a phone hang-up operation, and a phone for an inactive program.

Design Time Setting

At design time you can choose an icon on the properties box. Select the Icon property and click on (Icon). Use the File list box to find the directory containing the icon you want, and then select the icon. Any of the icons included with the Visual Basic package will work well for this property. For a listing of the icons that came with Visual Basic, look in the back of the Microsoft *Visual Basic Programmer's Guide*.

Setting a form's Icon during design time lets Visual Basic make the icon part of the executable file. This relieves you from needing to supply an external icon file with your application.

The LoadPicture Function

Use the LoadPicture function to change the Icon property of a form at runtime. In the example above, the original setting for the form's Icon property is the

PHONE01.ICO icon. This displays if the text on the communications program is neither Dialing Number nor Hanging Up.

Example

In the Appearance project at the end of this chapter, the Icon property of formAppear begins as PHONE01.ICO. This is the icon that appears at the bottom of the screen when the dialer is not running. The Minimize button is on formAppear so that the user may take a look at this default icon.

Pressing timeDial activates the timeDial_Timer, which uses the LoadPicture function to change the Appearance form's Icon property to the PHONE04.ICO icon. The program then minimizes formAppear, and the user sees an icon with the receiver off the hook at the bottom of the computer screen.

After pressing the Cancel command button, the Icon property of formAppear becomes the former icon. This is a graphic means of indicating the completion of the dialing operation. In this way the icons constantly inform the user what operations (if any) are taking place.

Comments

Give every form that can be minimized a different kind of icon rather than leaving the default icon. This enables the user to differentiate between the icons at the bottom of the screen.

LEFT PROPERTY

Objects Affected

▶ Check	Clipboard	▶ Combo	▶ Command	CommonDlg
▶ Data	Debug	▶ Dir	▶ Drive	▶ File
▶ Form	▶ Frame	▶ Grid	▶ Image	▶ Label
Line	▶ List	▶ MDI Form	Menu	▶ OLE
▶ Option	▶ Picture	Printer	Screen	▶ Scroll
▶ Shape	▶ Text	▶ Timer		

Purpose

The Left property defines or determines the distance of a form or control from the left edge of its container. An object's distance is measured in the units indicated by the ScaleMode property of its container. Tables 5-17 and 5-18 summarize the different arguments of the Left property and the possible measurement types.

General Syntax

```
[form.]Left [ = left!]
[form!]Name.Left [ = left!]
```

Argument	Description
form	Name property of the form
Name	Name property of the control
left!	Horizontal left distance of the object

Table 5-17 Arguments of the Left property

Measurement	Converts To...
Twip	1440 twips = 1 inch
Point	72 points = 1 inch
Pixels	Varies depending on system being used
Characters	12 characters horizontally and 6 vertically = 1 inch
Millimeters	254 millimeters = 1 inch
Centimeters	2.54 centimeters = 1 inch

Table 5-18 Possible measurement types in relation to 1 inch

Example Syntax

```
Sub LeftDistance (Ctl As Control, Name As Form)
                          'All of the following values equal one inch
    Select Case Name.ScaleMode 'Based on Control's ScaleMode
        Case 0                 'User-Defined Measurement
            Ctl.Left = Ctl.ScaleLeft     'Distance equals ScaleLeft
        Case 1                'Measure in twips
            Ctl.Left = 1440
        Case 2                'Measure in Points
            Ctl.Left = 72
        Case 3                'Measure in Pixels
            Ctl.Left = 1000
```

```
      Case 4                  'Measure in Characters
          Ctl.Left = 12
      Case 5                  'Measure in Inches
          Ctl.Left = 1
      Case 6                  'Measure in Millimeters
          Ctl.Left = 254
      Case 7                  'Measure in Centimeters
          Ctl.Left = 2.54
   End Select
End Sub
```

Description

The Left property of an object measures the horizontal distance from the left edge of its container, be it a form, screen, or picture box. You can enter this value at design time by manually moving the object with the mouse, or by directly entering the value in the properties box. You can modify the Left property of a control or form either at design time or at runtime. Visual Basic automatically adjusts itself to the resolution of the screen. You should ensure that your objects are not too far from the edges for the most common 640 by 480 and 800 by 600 resolution screens to display.

The example syntax outlines a sub procedure named LeftDistance, which sets a control's distance from the left side of the screen. This change references the ScaleMode property of the form. This shows the use of a generic procedure that applies to more than one control in a program.

Left, Top, Width, and Height Properties

When you create a form or control in Visual Basic, the Left, Top, Width, and Height properties display in the far right side of the toolbar. See the discussion of the toolbar in the Height property entry in this chapter. A form's Left property is measured in twips.

The ScaleMode Property

The ScaleMode property of a form directly controls the meaning of the value of the Left property. When the ScaleMode property changes from one measurement to another at design time, Visual Basic recalculates the value of the Left property in this new type of measurement. As the ScaleMode property is not modifiable at runtime, the meaning of the value of the Left property does not change while the program is running. For example, no matter what size a command box becomes, based on changes in the size of the parent form, the Left property will remain the same.

Example

The Appearance project at the end of this chapter sets the Left property of the forms and controls at design time. This is done either by dragging the control's edges with the mouse, or by entering the value into the properties box.

Comments

Remember that changes to the ScaleLeft property of a form only alter the value of the Left property of a control and not the actual distance.

MOUSEPOINTER PROPERTY

Objects Affected

▸ Check	Clipboard	▸ Combo	▸ Command	CommonDlg
▸ Data	Debug	▸ Dir	▸ Drive	▸ File
▸ Form	▸ Frame	Grid	▸ Image	▸ Label
Line	▸ List	MDI Form	Menu	▸ OLE
▸ Option	▸ Picture	Printer	▸ Screen	▸ Scroll
Shape	▸ Text	Timer		

Purpose

The MousePointer property of a form or control sets which cursor displays when the mouse pointer is over the object. Set this property either at design time or runtime. A mouse pointer can take many forms, including arrow, hourglass, and I-beam. Table 5-19 shows the different arguments of the MousePointer property; Table 5-20 shows the possible values for the MousePointer property.

General Syntax

```
[form.]MousePointer [ = setting%]
[form!]Name.MousePointer [ = setting%]
Screen.MousePointer [ = setting%]
```

Argument	Description
form	Name property of the form
Name	Name property of the control
Screen	'Screen' for Screen object
setting%	Value indicates what style of mouse pointer to use

Table 5-19 Arguments of the Left property

setting%	CONSTANT.TXT	Appearance	Description
0	DEFAULT		Default for this control
1	ARROW		Arrow
2	CROSSHAIR		Cross-hair pointer
3	IBEAM		Text entry I-beam
4	ICON_POINTER		Square within a square
5	SIZE_POINTER		Four-directional cross, arrows facing up, down, left, and right
6	SIZE_NE_SW		Two-directional diagonal arrow (Northeast to Southwest)
7	SIZE_N_S		Two-directional up and down arrow (North to South)
8	SIZE_NW_SE		Two-directional diagonal arrow (Northwest to Southeast)
9	SIZE_E_W		Two-directional left and right arrow (East to West)
10	UP_ARROW		Arrow pointing up
11	HOURGLASS		Hourglass
12	NO_DROP		No drop (Circle with line through it)

Table 5-20 Possible values for the MousePointer property

Example Syntax

```
Sub Command1_GotFocus ()
    Form1.MousePointer = 11      'Changes the MousePointer to an hourglass
End Sub

Sub Command1_LostFocus ()
    Form1.MousePointer = 0       'Changes the MousePointer back to the default
End Sub
```

Description

The MousePointer property determines what cursor to display on the screen when the mouse pointer is over a control or form. Set this property for either the

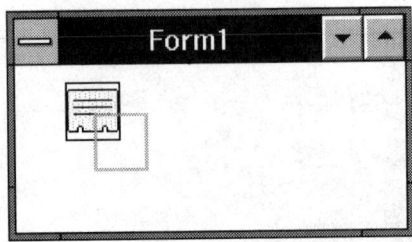
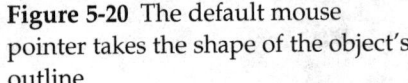

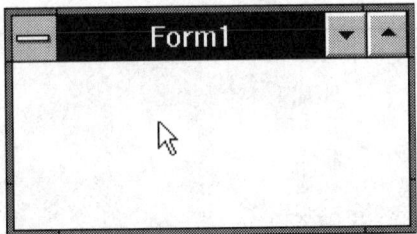

Figure 5-20 The default mouse pointer takes the shape of the object's outline

Figure 5-21 The familiar arrow cursor

entire form or for individual controls. Any form or control may have its MousePointer property changed at runtime. When you modify the Screen object's MousePointer property, the MousePointer property changes for all objects. When you modify a form's MousePointer property, any special settings for individual controls on the form similarly alter. To restore the settings for individual forms or controls, set the MousePointer property of the screen or form to 0. For example, when the user clicks the command button labeled Print, the mouse pointer of the screen becomes an hourglass. The cursor will remain an hourglass until the property restores to the default value of 0. The summary section at the beginning of this chapter explains how to use the CONSTANT.TXT values in your code.

Outline Pointer

Every control begins with the outline of itself as the default mouse pointer. This mouse pointer only appears on the screen during a mouse operation such as a drag operation. You can use this outline to guide the user during a drag operation. Since this property is the default value for a control, it is not necessary to change it for a drag operation. Figure 5-20 shows what the outline mouse pointer looks like.

Arrow Pointer

One of the most familiar mouse pointers is the left-pointing arrow cursor. Figure 5-21 shows how the arrow mouse pointer appears on the screen. This is the cursor most frequently used in Windows to select items and activate programs. When a form's MousePointer property has this value, the user can easily select command buttons, check boxes, and option boxes by placing the arrow's small point directly on the desired object. The horizontal and vertical scroll bars also function well with the arrow mouse pointer.

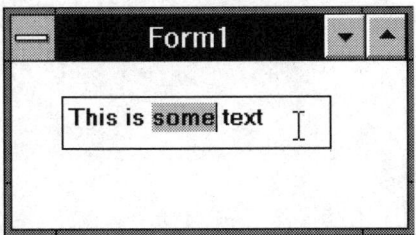

Figure 5-22 The I-beam cursor, particularly useful for text selection

Figure 5-23 The hourglass cursor indicates the user needs to wait

I-Beam Cursor

The I-beam cursor gives the user a guide in selecting and entering text on the screen. Figure 5-22 shows how the I-beam cursor appears over a text box. The I-beam mouse pointer allows easy manipulation of text. Changing to this cursor makes it easier to move in between different characters for editing and selecting text. The I-beam is the best choice for working with text.

Hourglass Cursor

An hourglass is also a familiar symbol to the Windows user (particularly those with older, slower systems!). Figure 5-23 shows an hourglass cursor. This cursor normally reminds the user that the computer is working and cannot process any further commands from the user until it finishes with its current action. When you plan to stop the user from taking further actions, change the MousePointer property of the screen to the hourglass cursor. In this case the cursor will not change, no matter which form or control the mouse pointer moves over.

Sizing Cursors

All of the sizing cursors, which have the values between five and nine, are also familiar to Windows users. Figure 5-24 shows each of these cursors. These cursors appear when the user changes the size of a window on the screen. Each cursor consists of arrows pointing toward the parts of the window that the window's resizing changes.

Example

In the Appearance project at the end of this section, the MousePointer property of the screen changes when the user clicks either timeDial on formAppear or the Redial command button on formWarning. This tells the user that no other actions may take place while the dial operation is under way. The MousePointer property of the screen overrides the settings of the various controls of both the FormAppear and Warning forms. Until the MousePointer property returns to 0, the only MousePointer that displays is the hourglass.

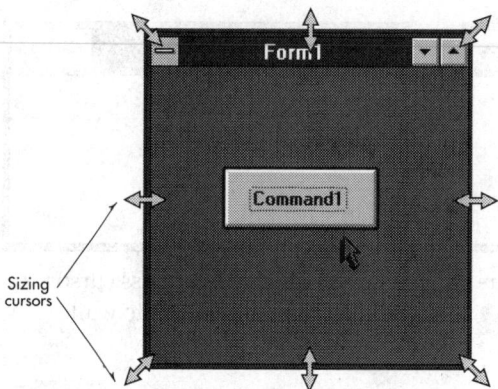

Figure 5-24 The eight sizing cursors

Comments

You may notice other programs using different cursors than Visual Basic allows. For instance, CorelDRAW uses a nifty hourglass that flips itself over as you wait (and with CorelDRAW, you wait a lot—probably the reason why they have an animated hourglass!). Although you may be tempted to add some of these cursors to your Visual Basic applications, the process involves multiple API calls and some tricky coding. For more information on how to do this, see the Waite Group's *Visual Basic How-To, 2nd Edition*.

TOP PROPERTY

Objects Affected

▶ Check	Clipboard	▶ Combo	▶ Command	CommonDlg
▶ Data	Debug	▶ Dir	▶ Drive	▶ File
▶ Form	▶ Frame	▶ Grid	▶ Image	▶ Label
Line	▶ List	▶ MDI Form	Menu	▶ OLE
▶ Option	▶ Picture	Printer	Screen	▶ Scroll
▶ Shape	▶ Text	Timer		

Purpose

The Top property defines or determines the distance of a form or control from the top edge of its container. A control's distance is measured in the units indicated by the ScaleMode property of the container. Forms are always measured in twips. Tables 5-21 and 5-22 summarize the different arguments of the Top property and the possible measurement types.

General Syntax

```
[form.]Top [ = top!]
[form!]Name.Top [ = top!]
```

Argument	Description
form	Name property of the form
Name	Name property of the control
top!	Vertical top distance of the object

Table 5-21 Arguments of the Top property

Measurement	Converts To...
Twip	1440 twips = 1 inch
Point	72 points = 1 inch
Pixels	Varies depending on system being used
Characters	12 characters horizontally and 6 vertically = 1 inch
Millimeters	254 millimeters = 1 inch
Centimeters	2.54 centimeters = 1 inch

Table 5-22 Possible measurement types in relation to 1 inch

Example Syntax

```
Sub ResetForm (Name As Form)
    If Name.ScaleMode <> 0 Then      'Checks if ScaleMode is set to user-defined
        Name.Top = 1                 'Form's distance from top placed at 1
        Name.Left = 1                'Form's distance from left placed at 1
    Else
        Name.Top = Name.ScaleTop     'Form's distance from left and top made equal
        Name.Left = Name.ScaleLeft   'to the value of the ScaleLeft & ScaleTop properties
    End If
End Sub
```

Description

The Top property of an object measures the vertical distance from the top of its container. You can enter this value at design time by manually moving the object with the mouse or by entering the value at the properties box. The Top property of a control or form is modifiable either at design time or runtime. You should ensure that your objects are not too far from the edges for the most common 640 by 480 and 800 by 600 resolution screens to display.

The example syntax outlines a sub function named ResetForm, which sets a form's distance from the left and top sides of the screen. If the ScaleMode property is user-defined, the Left and Top properties are set to the values of the ScaleLeft and ScaleTop properties. This is another excellent example of the use of a generic function to apply to all of the forms in a program.

Left, Top, Width, and Height Properties

When you create a form or control in Visual Basic, the Left, Top, Width, and Height properties display in the far right side of the toolbar. See the discussion of the toolbar in the Height property entry in this chapter. A form's Top property begins with a measurement in twips.

The Scale Mode Property

The ScaleMode property of a form directly controls the meaning of the value of the Top property. When this property changes at design time from one measurement to another, Visual Basic recalculates the value of the Top property in this new type of measurement. As the ScaleMode property is not modifiable at run time, the meaning of the value of the Top property does not change while the program is running. For example, no matter what size a command box becomes based on changes in the size of the parent form, the Top property will remain the same.

Example

In the Appearance project at the end of this chapter, set the Top property of the forms and controls at design time. This is done either by dragging the control's edges with the mouse, or by entering the value into the properties box.

Comments

Remember that changes to the ScaleTop property of a form only alter the value of the Top property of a control and not the actual distance.

VISIBLE PROPERTY

Objects Affected

▶ Check	Clipboard	▶ Combo	▶ Command	CommonDlg
▶ Data	Debug	▶ Dir	▶ Drive	▶ File
▶ Form	▶ Frame	▶ Grid	▶ Image	▶ Label
▶ Line	▶ List	▶ MDI Form	▶ Menu	▶ OLE
▶ Option	▶ Picture	▶ Printer	▶ Screen	▶ Scroll
▶ Shape	▶ Text	Timer		

Purpose

The Visible property defines whether a form or control is visible to the user. Tables 5-23 and 5-24 summarize the arguments of the Visible property.

General Syntax

```
[form.]Visible [ = boolean%]
[form!]Name.Visible [ = boolean%]
```

Argument	Description
form	Name property of the form
Name	Name property of the control
boolean%	Indicates whether the object is visible or invisible to the user

Table 5-23 Arguments of the Visible property

boolean%	Effect
0	False – Makes an object invisible to the user
-1	True – (Default) Makes an object visible to the user

Table 5-24 Available settings for the Visible property

Example Syntax

```
Sub Form_Load ()
    Load "AddressBook"                'Places an invisible form in memory
    Form2.Show                        'Places a visible form in memory
    Form2.Visible = False             'Makes it invisible
End Sub

Sub Change (ControlName As Form, Control)  'Flips the visibility of an object
    If ControlName.Visible = False Then
        ControlName.Visible = True    'Makes indicated control visible
    Else
        ControlName.Visible = False   'Makes indicated control invisible
    End If
End Sub
```

Description

The Visible property lets you show or hide a control or form on the screen. There are two possible settings for the Visible property of a form or control: True (-1) and False (0). A form or control with a False Visible property disappears from the sight of the user. While its Visible property is False, a form or control remains in memory and quickly returns to the screen when needed. When the Visible property of a form or control is True (-1), the form or control is visible to the user. A Show method, Hide method, or Load statement directly affects this value. In the example syntax, the Form_Load event changes the Visible property of Form2 to False.

The Show Method

When a Show method brings a form up on the screen, it automatically sets the Visible property of the form to True. The Show method loads the form into memory if necessary. Setting a form's Visible property directly loads the form into memory if it isn't already there and makes it visible. The main difference is that the Show method has two modes of operation. A form opened with the Modeless Show method will behave in the same way as a form opened by setting the Visible property directly. However, if a form loads with a Modal Show method, then the form has full control of the program until hidden or unloaded from memory. Any code that follows a Modal Show method executes only after the hiding or closing of the modal form. See Chapter 4, Forms and Menus, for more details on modal and modeless forms.

The Hide Method

The Hide method changes the Visible property of a form to False and removes it from view. Unlike the Show method, this element of the language is indistinguishable from the Visible property if applied to a form. Unlike the Hide and Show methods, the Visible property is available for either a form or a control. This makes it flexible for more generic functions. In the example function above, any kind of control or form can be made visible or invisible.

The Load Statement

A Load statement brings a form into memory and sets its Visible property to False. Using this statement differs from setting the Visible property directly in only one way. The Visible property works on both controls and forms and the Load statement will only work on forms. Table 5-25 outlines the different ways that the Hide method, Show method, and Load statement interact with the Visible property.

Element	Effect On	Visible Property	Differences
Show method	Changes	Visible property to True (-1)	Modal mode
Hide method	Changes	Visible property to False (0)	Affects only forms
Load statement	Changes	Visible property to False (0)	Affects only forms

Table 5-25 The effects and differences of various language elements on the Visible property

Example

In the Appearance project at the end of this chapter, the Visible property removes the Results label box from view. This keeps the contents of the Caption property available for reference for the next time the user presses the Redial command button. In this way the Results label box disappears from the user's sight to prevent confusion about what is presently taking place in the program. If the Results label box were not hidden in this fashion, then the user might be confused with the contents of that box when it is no longer needed.

Comments

The Visible property will work on either a form or a control. It is a more flexible element of the language than the Hide and Show methods, which may only be used on forms.

WIDTH PROPERTY

Objects Affected

▶ Check	Clipboard	▶ Combo	▶ Command	CommonDlg
▶ Data	Debug	▶ Dir	▶ Drive	▶ File
▶ Form	▶ Frame	▶ Grid	▶ Image	▶ Label
Line	▶ List	▶ MDI Form	Menu	▶ OLE
▶ Option	▶ Picture	▶ Printer	▶ Screen	▶ Scroll
▶ Shape	▶ Text	Timer		

Purpose

The Width property defines or determines the horizontal size of a form or control on the screen, form, picture box, or Printer object. Forms, Printer objects, and Screen objects are always measured in twips. A control's size uses the units of measure indicated by the ScaleMode property of the current form or picture box. Table 5-26 summarizes the different arguments of the Width property; Table 5-27 summarizes the possible measurement settings of the Width property.

General Syntax

```
[form.]Width [ = width!]
[form!]Name.Width [ = width!]
Printer.Width [ = width!]
Screen.Width [ = width!]
```

Argument	Description
form	Name property of the form
Name	Name property of the control
Printer	'Printer' for Printer object
Screen	'Screen' for Screen object
width!	Horizontal width of the object

Table 5-26 Arguments of the Width property

Measurement	Converts To...
Twip	1440 twips = 1 inch
Point	72 points = 1 inch
Pixels	Varies depending on system being used
Characters	12 characters horizontally and 6 vertically = 1 inch
Millimeters	254 millimeters = 1 inch
Centimeters	2.54 centimeters = 1 inch

Table 5-27 Possible measurement types in relation to 1 inch

Example Syntax

```
Sub Form_Resize
      Form.1.Width = (Picture1.Width * 2)       'Width and height of form made twice the
      Form1.Height = (Picture1.Height * 2)       'size of Picture 1
      Picture1.Top = ((Form1.Height / 2) - ((Picture1.Height) / 2)) 'Picture appears in
      Picture1.Left = ((Form1.Width / 2) - ((Picture1.Width) / 2))  'center of form
End Sub
```

Description

The Width property of an object measures the horizontal width of a form, screen, or picture box. You can enter this value at design time by manually moving the object with the mouse, or by entering the value in the properties box. You can modify the Width property of a control at runtime or design time. In contrast, you can set the Width properties of both the Printer and Screen objects only at runtime. A setting must be between 0 and a maximum value specified by the system itself. Visual Basic automatically adjusts itself to the resolution of the screen or printer. You should ensure that your objects are not too large for the most common 640 by 480 and 800 by 600 resolution screens to display.

In the example syntax, Picture1's Width and Height are set to half of Form1's ScaleWidth and Height. This demonstrates how easily you can resize and move controls. Figure 5-25 shows what this example might look like.

The Left, Top, Width, and Height Properties

When you create a form or control in Visual Basic, the Left, Top, Width, and Height properties display in the far right side of the toolbar. See the discussion

271

Figure 5-25 The example syntax centers Picture1,
no matter what the size or shape of the form

of the toolbar in the Height property entry in this chapter. A form's Width property begins with a value that represents a measurement in twips.

Screen and Printer

The Width property returns the width of the screen or page available based on the resolution of the computer screen and printer being used. With this property, the code determines the amount of usable space available on the printed page or screen. The Width property of the Screen and Printer objects is not available at design time and is read-only at runtime. The value of this property normally serves as a reference and is not changeable at runtime.

ScaleMode

The ScaleMode property of a form directly controls the meaning of the value of the Width property. When the ScaleMode property changes at design time from one measurement to another, Visual Basic recalculates the value of the Width property in this new type of measurement. As the ScaleMode property is not modifiable at runtime, the meaning of the value of the Width property does not change while the program is running. For example, no matter what size a command box becomes, based on changes in the size of the parent form, the Width property will remain the same. See Chapter 9, The Coordinate System, for more information about the ScaleMode property.

The ScaleWidth Property

The ScaleWidth property divides the width of a form, picture box, or Printer object into the number of units set in the property. When a form's ScaleWidth property changes to 100, the width of the form is divided into 100 equal units.

272

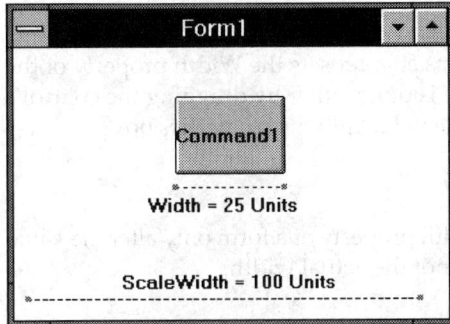

Figure 5-26 Width and ScaleWidth
compared at start ...

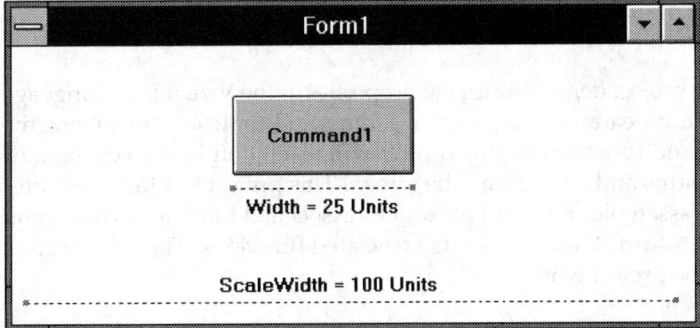

Figure 5-27 ... and after resizing. Note that the Width of the
command button is the same number of relative units,
although it is physically larger

(Changing the ScaleWidth property of the form to a new value does not change
the actual size of the control.)

This unit changes in size as the form's height changes. Increasing the width of
the form has the effect of increasing the size of one of these units. (The width
remains divided into 100 units that are now larger in size.) These units define the
upper and lower limit of the possible width of controls on this form.

With the Move statement, the size of the control adjusts based on the changes in
width to the form. For example, a Resize event might adjust the Width property of
a command box of a form by triggering a move statement that always ensures that
the command box is one-fourth the size of the form. In this example the ScaleWidth
property of the form is 100, and the Width property of the Command1 command
button is 25 (one-fourth the width of the form). Figures 5-26 and 5-27 display this
concept visually.

Example

The Appearance project at the end of this chapter sets the Width property of the forms and controls at design time. This is done either by dragging the control's edges with the mouse or by entering the value into the properties box.

Comments

Remember that changes to the ScaleWidth property of a form only alter the value of the Width property of a control and not the actual width.

THE APPEARANCE PROJECT

Project Overview

The Appearance project demonstrates the properties of the Visual Basic language that influence the appearance of a program's forms and controls. Assembling the different forms and functions of this project will teach you how to change the appearance of forms and controls on the screen. This project has three sections. The first section assembles formAppear and its associated functions. The second section constructs formWarning and its associated functions. The third section discusses how the project works.

Assembling the Project: FormAppear

1. Make a new form (formAppear) with the objects and properties in Table 5-28.

Object	Property	Setting
Form	BorderStyle	1–Fixed single
	Caption	Appearance Project
	Name	formAppear
	Icon	..\VB\ICONS\COMM\PHONE01.ICO
	MaxButton	False
Command	Caption	&Dial
	Name	cmndDial

Object	Property	Setting
	MousePointer	12—No Drop
Command	Caption	E&xit
	Name	cmndExit
ListBox	Name	listPhone
	Sorted	True
Timer	Name	timeDial
	Enabled	False
	Interval	2500

Table 5-28 Settings for formAppear in the Appearance project

2. Size the objects on the screen, as shown in Figure 5-28. Figure 5-29 shows what formAppear will look like when running.

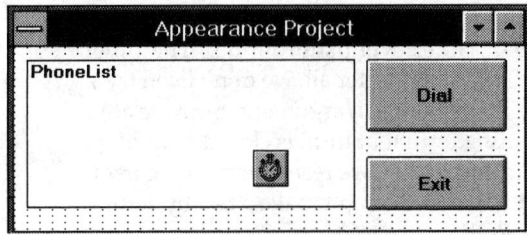

Figure 5-28 FormAppear during design

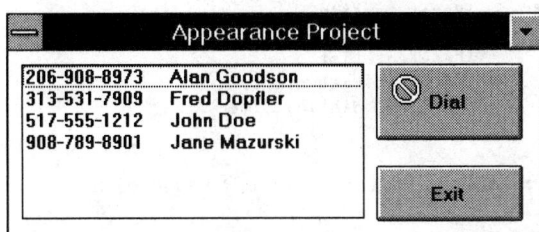

Figure 5-29 FormAppear in action. Note the No Drop cursor; we haven't chosen a name to dial yet

275

3. Enter the following code in the Form_Load event subroutine. This code adds the items to the phone list and disables the timer.

```
Sub Form_Load ()
    timeDial.Enabled = False                              'Make sure dialing timer is disabled
    listPhone.AddItem "517-555-1212    John Doe"          'Fill list box with fake-o numbers
    listPhone.AddItem "908-789-8901    Jane Mazurski"
    listPhone.AddItem "313-531-7909    Fred Dopfler"
    listPhone.AddItem "206-908-8973    Alan Goodson"
End Sub
```

4. Enter the following code in the cmndDial_Click event subroutine. This code executes when the user clicks the cmndDial command button. We first check to make sure we have a number to dial (if the cursor is still NO_DROP, the user hasn't picked a name from the list). Assuming we've got a name to dial, tell the user we're going to be a while by setting the cursor to an hourglass. Set the title bar of formWarning to indicate who we're dialing, change the icon of formAppear to indicate an off-hook phone, and minimize it. Enable the timeDial timer to simulate dialing.

```
Sub cmndDial_Click ()
    If cmndDial.MousePointer <> NO_DROP Then             'Make sure we're supposed to dial
        Screen.MousePointer = HOURGLASS                 'Tell user we've got to wait
        formWarning.Caption = "Dialing " + listPhone.List(listPhone.ListIndex)
        'you might need to change the path in loadpicture to fit your system
        formAppear.Icon = LoadPicture("\VB\ICONS\COMM\PHONE12.ICO")  'Phone Handset
        formAppear.WindowState = MINIMIZED              'Minimize Appear form
        timeDial.Enabled = True                         'Turn on dialing timer
    End If
End Sub
```

5. Enter the following code in the timeDial_Timer event subroutine. The timer delay simulates making a call. When the call "fails" (after all, we don't even try!), display formWarning. Note that because of the MODAL argument, the code after the Show method doesn't continue executing until that form is closed or hidden. When control returns back from the Warning dialog, we reset the mouse cursor, deselect the phone number list box, and flag that we can't make a call by setting timeDial's mouse pointer back to NO_DROP.

```
Sub timeDial_Timer ()
    formWarning.Show MODAL                          'Let the Dialer form take over
    formAppear.Caption = "Appearance Project"        'Reset caption
    Screen.MousePointer = DEFAULT                    'Set cursor to normal
    listPhone.ListIndex = -1                         'Deselect list
    cmndDial.MousePointer = NO_DROP                  'We can't dial now...
    timeDial.Enabled = False                         'Turn off dialing timer
End Sub
```

6. Enter the following code in the cmndExit_Click event subroutine. This closes all forms and exits.

```
Sub cmndExit_Click ()
    End
End Sub
```

276

7. Enter the followingcode in the PhoneList_Click event. This simply resets the Dial button's mouse pointer to the default (which tells the cmndDial_Click event that it's okay to dial now).

```
Sub listPhone_Click ()
    cmndDial.MousePointer = DEFAULT    'We've selected number to dial; OK to push dial button
End Sub
```

Assembling the Project: formWarning

1. Make a new form (formWarning) with the objects and properties in Table 5-29.

Object	Property	Setting
Form	BackColor	&H00C0C0C0& 'light gray
	ForeColor	&H00000000& 'black
	Name	formWarning
	BorderStyle	3 — Fixed Double
Label	Alignment	2 — Centered
	BackStyle	0 — Transparent
	Name	lablDial
Label	Alignment	2 — Centered
	BackStyle	0 — Transparent
	Name	lablResults
Command	Caption	ReDial
	Name	cmndRedial
Command	Caption	Cancel
	Name	cmndCancel

(continued on next page)

(continued from previous page)

Object	Property	Setting
Timer	Name	timeDialing
	Enabled	False
	Interval	1000
Timer	Name	timeResults
	Enabled	False
	Interval	1000

Table 5-29 Settings for formWarning in the Appearance project

2. Size the objects on the screen, as shown in Figure 5-30. Figure 5-31 shows what formWarning looks like when running, and after the user has clicked redial three times.

3. Enter the following code in the cmndCancel_Click event. This resets both labels, unloads the form, resets the main form's icon, and restores the main form from its minimized state.

```
Sub cmndCancel_Click ()
    lablDial.Caption = ""                   'Blank out Dialing label
    lablResults.Caption = ""                'and Results label
    Unload formWarning                      'Unload the form
    'you might need to change the path in loadpicture to fit your system
    formAppear.Icon = LoadPicture("\VB\ICONS\COMM\PHONE01.ICO")
    formAppear.WindowState = NORMAL         'and put back the main form
End Sub
```

4. Enter the following code in the timeResults_Timer event. This simulates making another redial attempt. It redisplays the results label, and makes a choice of what to display next by looking at what it displayed last time. Note that as we continue to get negative "dialing" results, we change the BackStyle from transparent to opaque to add greater emphasis to the label. The cursor goes back to normal now that the program has "called."

```
Sub timeResults_Timer ()
    lablResults.Visible = True              'Display the results box
    Select Case lablResults.Caption         'Determine message based on
                                            '    what we've already done
        Case ""                             'First time through...
            lablResults.Caption = "No Response"
        Case "No Response"                  'Second time through...
            lablResults.Caption = "Sorry, No Response"
```

278

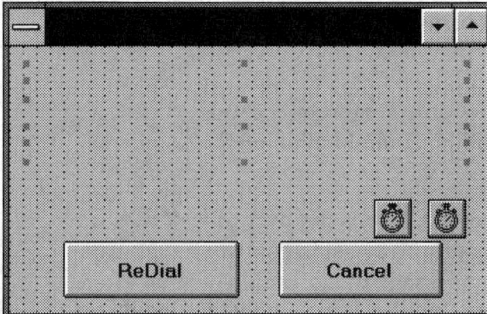

Figure 5-30 formWarning during design
(note the two labels without captions)

Figure 5-31 formWarning in action after the
third click

```
            Case "Sorry, No Response"                     'Third time through...
                lablResults.Caption = "Sorry, Still No Response"
                lablResults.BackStyle = SOLID
                lablResults.BackColor = YELLOW
            Case Else                                      'Pretty persistent, eh?
                lablResults.Caption = "Hey what do you expect? This is a demonstration!"
                lablResults.BackColor = RED
                lablResults.ForeColor = YELLOW
        End Select
        Screen.MousePointer = DEFAULT                      'Done dialing, OK for user to go on
        timeResults.Enabled = False                        'Turn off the results loop
End Sub
```

5. Enter this code into the timeDialing_Timer event. This timer just delays by a second, simulating dialing. It turns itself back off and reenables the timeResults
   timer.

```
Sub timeDialing_Timer ()
    timeDialing.Enabled = False                'Done with dialing delay...
    timeResults.Enabled = True                 'turn on results loop
End Sub
```

279

6. Enter this code into the Form_Load event. It turns on the timeDialing to simulate making a call.

```
Sub Form_Load ()
    timeDialing.Enabled = True              'Simulate a "dialing" delay
    timeResults.Enabled = False             'turn off the results loop
End Sub
```

7. Enter this code into the cmndRedial_Click event. It tells the user to wait by setting the cursor to an hourglass, hides the results box (just in case we have a call that connects?) and displays an appropriate message in lablDial. Note that after the third attempt we add greater emphasis to the label by setting its BackStyle to opaque and making the box red to attract attention.

```
Sub cmndRedial_Click ()
    Screen.MousePointer = HOURGLASS              'Tell user we're going to be a while...
    lablResults.Visible = False                 'Hide the results box (to simulate dialing)
    Select Case lablDial.Caption                'Determine the proper message from what
                                                '   we've already got
        Case ""                                 'First time through...
            lablDial.Caption = "Redialing Number"
        Case "Redialing Number"                 'Second time through...
            lablDial.Caption = "Redialing Number Again!"
        Case Else                               'Third time through...
            lablDial.Caption = "Redialing Number one more time!"
            lablDial.BackStyle = SOLID
            lablDial.BackColor = RED
            lablDial.ForeColor = YELLOW
    End Select
    timeDialing.Enabled = True                  'Set the time to simulate a "dialing" delay
End Sub
```

Assembling the Project: Module1.Bas

1. This module contains a few Global Constants derived from CONSTANT.TXT. For a project of this size, it's probably easiest just to type these in directly to a new module. For a more lengthy application, with many constants, read the CONSTANT.TXT file in directly with the File Load Text command.

```
' Show parameters
Global Const MODAL = 1

' Colors
Global Const RED = &HFF&
Global Const YELLOW = &HFFFF&

' BackStyle
Global Const SOLID = 1

' MousePointer
Global Const DEFAULT = 0
Global Const HOURGLASS = 11
Global Const NO_DROP = 12
```

```
' WindowState
Global Const NORMAL = 0
Global Const MINIMIZED = 1
```

How It Works

The Appearance project opens by displaying a list of phone numbers in a list box on formAppear. When the user selects one of these numbers from the list and presses Dial, formWarning displays on the screen. While formWarning appears on the screen, formAppear is minimized at the bottom of the screen. FormWarning displays the results of the attempt to dial. (Note: This example does not actually dial the number.) Each time the user presses the Redial button on formWarning, new messages appear on the screen. The user presses the Cancel command button to exit formWarning.

Running the Appearance Project

When the user selects a number from the phone list, the mouse pointer for the Dial button changes back to the default pointer from its original value of No Drop. This lets the user click on the dial command button to trigger the cmndDial_Click event. The screen's mouse pointer changes to an hourglass to reflect that the program is busy. Setting the screen's mouse pointer overrides any settings of the other controls.

Next, the Caption property of formWarning is modified to read "Dialing" and show the name and number of the person being dialed. The Caption is displayed in the title bar of formWarning, and is an easy and natural place to show this.

The cmndDial_Click event ends by changing the Icon property of formAppear to a picture of an off-hook phone. It then minimizes formAppear and enables the timeDial timer event. The first command in the timeDial timer shows formWarning. Note that because formWarning displays modally, the code does not continue to run in the timeDialing event until formWarning closes.

At this point the timeDialing_Timer and timeResults_Timer events trigger. The timeResults event makes the Results label box (below the Dial box) visible to the user, and then changes its message based on the current setting. Next, the screen's MousePointer property is restored to the default value of 0, which restores the mouse pointer settings of the controls and forms of the program. In this case the hourglass changes back to the standard arrow.

Each time the user clicks the Redial command button, the screen's mouse pointer changes back to an hourglass and the Dial label box's caption changes. This command button changes the messages on the label boxes to reflect how many times that the Redial command button has been pressed. The Redial routine then triggers the timeDialing_Timer event, which in turn triggers the timeResults_Timer event. Note how we change the appearance of the labels as well as their messages. Setting the BackStyle property to Opaque and setting their BackColor properties attracts attention to the later messages.

When the user clicks the Cancel button, formWarning is unloaded from memory and the Icon property of formAppear changes back to its original setting with a LoadPicture function. This displays a hung-up phone briefly on the bottom of the screen, until formAppear is placed back up on the screen.

Notice that the last portion of the timeDial_Timer event is processed as soon as formWarning is removed. This changes formAppear's Caption property back to the original Appearance project text. To exit the program, press the command button labeled Exit.

6 ACCESSING FORMS AND CONTROLS

Every object in Visual Basic has a unique name that identifies it. You use this name to work with the object's properties, methods, and events. This chapter covers the details of accessing objects directly through the Name property, indirectly through several other useful properties, and gives suggested naming conventions to create clean, self-documenting code.

NAMING CONVENTIONS

Each Visual Basic object has a name that you use to refer to it in code. Set the name of forms and controls during the design phase with the Name property in the properties box. The name must start with a letter and may be up to 40 characters long. It may contain the underscore character (although it is not recommended, as it creates hard to read Event subroutines), but may not contain any other punctuation symbols. Each control or form starts with a default name consisting of the object type plus a unique integer. For example, the first text box is named Text1, the second one Text2; the fourth list box created would be named List4.

For smaller applications the default names work well. Most of the code examples in this book keep the default names for simplicity. Larger applications demand intelligent and consistent naming practices to help debug your code. Just as with any variable, you should name an object with something that indicates its purpose: for example, PatientName or ShippingMethods.

A very helpful practice is to start any object name with some sort of abbreviation that indicates what kind of object it is. This creates self-documenting names, as you can tell at a glance what each object is. This will save time as you trace your code, and also has the advantage of grouping like kinds of controls together in the code window (for example, all text box event procedures would be near each other). Microsoft suggests using a three-letter code (such as txt for text box, lst for list box). There are many possible conventions; what is important is that you're consistent. For larger examples and many of the larger projects, this book uses four-letter abbreviations (such as text for text box, list for list box). The examples given in the last paragraph might then be named textPatientName and listShippingMethods. Table 6-1 lists the prefixes used in this book.

Object	Prefix	Example
Check Box	chek	chekShipNextDay
Combo Box	comb	combStates
Command Button	cmnd	cmndExit
Common Dialog	cdlg	cdlgPrinter
Data	data	dataMain
Dir List Box	dir	dirCurrent
Drive List Box	driv	drivCurrent
File List Box	file	fileCurrent
Form	form	formMain
Frame	fram	framChooseOption
Grid	grid	gridDataSheet
Horizontal Scroll	hsb	hsbPictureView
Image	imag	imagIcon
Label	labl	lablResults
Line	line	lineHorizontal
List Box	list	listContinent

Object	Prefix	Example
MDI Form		not essential, as there can only be one MDI form
Menu	menu	menuWindow
OLE	ole	oleLinkToExcel
Option Button	optn	optnFederalExpress
Picture Box	pict	pictMain
Vertical Scroll	vsb	vsbSliderValue
Shape	shap	shapCircularInfinityWheel
Text Box	text	textMainEntry
Timer	time	timeClockStart

Table 6-1 Use Name prefixes to help create self-documenting code

The system objects (App, Clipboard, Debug, Printer, and Screen) cannot be renamed. You always refer to them by their default name. The data control has two properties (Database and Recordset) that function as system objects; you cannot rename these either, and always refer to them by their default name.

OBJECT PROPERTIES AND METHODS

Refer to an object's properties and methods with the dot operator. This consists of the object's name, a period (.), and the property or method. For example,

```
response$ = Text1.Text
Clipboard.Clear
Form1.ScaleHeight = 2700
textPatientName.ForeColor = YELLOW
ListShippingMethods.AddItem "Federal Express"
```

Refer to a control on another form with the *exclamation operator*. This consists of the form's name, an exclamation point (!), and the name of the control:

```
Form2!Text1.Text = "Hello"
formPatientInput!listShippingMethods.AddItem "Federal Express"
```

You may also use the dot operator in place of the exclamation. Visual Basic 1.0 used this type of construction exclusively, and Visual Basic 2.0 and 3.0 have retained it to ease compatibility issues with older applications. The exclamation operator more clearly differentiates between the name of the control you're referencing, and the property or method of that control.

```
Form2.Text1.Text = "Hello"      'Works; not recommended. Kept for compatibility with VB 1.0
Form2!Text1.Text = "Hello"      'Recommended. Clearer distinction between name and property
```

OBJECT EVENTS

A reference to an event begins with the Name of the object that triggers the event, followed by an underscore (_) and the name of the event:

```
Sub Command1_Click ()
    MsgBox "You've just clicked Command1"
End Sub

Sub textPatientName_GotFocus ()
    textPatientName.BackColor = QBColor(7)
    textPatientName.ForeColor = QBColor(1)
    textPatientName.SelLength = Len(textPatientName.Text)
End Sub
```

Forms are the exception: rather than using the name of the form, the event subroutine uses the keyword 'Form'.

```
Sub Form_Load ()
    List1.AddItem "Red"
    List1.AddItem "Blue"
    List1.AddItem "Green"
End Sub
```

See Chapter 7, Events, for more about event procedures, and Appendix A, Visual Basic Language Tutorial, for information on sub procedures and other language elements.

MODULES

Place code that applies to controls and properties of more than one form in a module. To create a new module, select the New Module command on the Visual Basic File menu (see Figure 6-1). A module includes any functions that refer to or affect the controls or properties of more than one form. In order to create a sub procedure or function in this module, simply type the code into its General Declarations section. Modules allow you to define common behavior for a number of different forms without duplicating code.

286

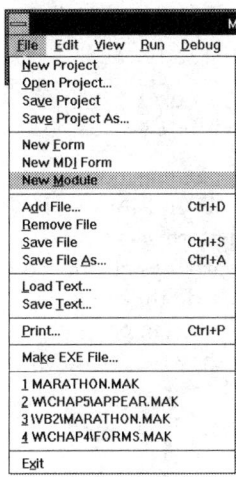

Figure 6-1 How to create a new module

OBJECT ARRAYS

An object array is a group of one or more objects that share the same Name. Each form or control in an array has an index value that distinguishes it from the other controls in the object array. The first object in an object array has an index value of 0. Each new object in the object array receives a successively higher index value. In this way the next object has an index value of 1, the next 2, and so on. This value appears in between parentheses after the Name of the object array. For example, if you have an array of text boxes, you can specify the loading of the "nth" text box as follows:

```
Load TextBoxes(n)
```

A form may also be used in an object array. Do this by declaring a variable to be of type YourForm, and simply dimensioning an array of them. MDI child forms are often created this way. For a more detailed discussion of this, see Chapter 3, Using Objects, and Chapter 4, Forms and Menus. The example at the end of Chapter 4 shows the details of creating an arbitrary and dynamic number of child forms. The following example gives you a quick idea of creating a form array:

```
Dim formNewInfo(10) as New formGetInfoMaster
```

Note that object arrays are different than the collections discussed in Chapter 3.

PARENTS, TAGS, AND ME

In Visual Basic every control is on one of the program's forms. This form is the parent form of the control. Each control has a Parent property at runtime that identifies its parent form. This property enables the code to reference the properties of the parent form without using the parent's Name property.

```
Sub Command1_Click ()
    Text1.Parent.WindowState = 2    'Maximizes the form that Text1 is on
End Sub
```

Sometimes there is a need for special tags on the controls and forms of an application. The Tag property provides a means of identifying forms and controls with descriptive text. Changing a form or control's Tag property has no effect on its appearance or any other property. The Tag property is for identification purposes only. The example project at the end of Chapter 4 uses the tag property to refer back to an index of child forms. As another example of how to use the tag, you may wish to store a text box's value in its Tag so that you can easily "undo" any changes made by the user:

```
Text1.Tag = Text1.Text    'Store old text value
...                        '....intervening code changes value
Text1.Text = Text1.Tag    'Undo changes
```

Sometimes you need to refer to the object where code is currently running. For instance, in an MDI application with multiple child document windows, it may not be clear which child form is making a procedure call or triggering an event. Use the special Me object to refer to the currently running object.

You usually don't need to know what instance of a form is currently being used. Event code runs in the appropriate instance automatically. Sometimes, however, you may need to use a method or property that refers explicitly to a particular instance. The Me keyword lets you refer to the instance in which the code is running. Use Me just as if it were the Name property of the object:

```
Sub Command1_Click ()
    Me.Hide                         'Hide this form instance
End Sub
```

ACTIVE OBJECTS

The *active object* is the currently selected form or control on the screen. Visual Basic identifies the currently active control with the Form or Screen objects' ActiveControl property. Windows displays different colors of title bars and borders for active and inactive forms. (Set these colors in the color section of the Windows control panel.) Use the Screen object's ActiveForm property to refer to the active form if you don't know the name of the active form. This technique can be useful for writing general-purpose procedures to deal with whatever object is active at a particular time. Note that the Me implicit object refers to the form that has had its code run most recently, and may not indicate the active form—for instance, if the user has clicked on a different form's title bar and shifted focus.

288

ACCESSING FORMS AND CONTROLS SUMMARY

Table 6-2 lists the properties that are involved in referencing forms or controls in Visual Basic.

Use or Set This...		To Do This...
ActiveControl	Property	Access the attributes of the active control
ActiveForm	Property	Access the attributes of the active form
Name	Property	Word that identifies an object in code
Index	Property	Identify a control in a control array
Parent	Property	Identify the form that a form is positioned on
Tag	Property	Identify a control or form with a unique text string

Table 6-2 Properties that reference forms and controls

The following pages investigate these properties in detail. At the end of this chapter, step-by-step directions explain how to assemble the Reference project, which illustrates a variety of techniques for referencing objects in code.

ACTIVECONTROL PROPERTY

Objects Affected

Check	Clipboard	Combo	Command	CommonDlg
Data	Debug	Dir	Drive	File
▶ Form	Frame	Grid	Image	Label
Line	List	▶ MDI Form	Menu	OLE
Option	Picture	Printer	▶ Screen	Scroll
Shape	Text	Timer		

Purpose

The ActiveControl property returns the currently active control on the screen or form. The active control is the control that has the focus and will receive subsequent user input. You can examine or change a property of the active control by referring to "Screen.ActiveControl[.property]". Table 6-3 gives the arguments of the ActiveControl property.

General Syntax

```
Screen.ActiveControl[.property|method]
Form.ActiveControl[.property|method]
```

Argument	Description
Screen	'Screen' refers to the Screen object
Form	Name of the form or MDIForm referenced
method	Name of the method used
property	Name of the property referenced

Table 6-3 Arguments of the ActiveControl property

Example Syntax

```
Sub Form_Click ()
    Select Case Screen.ActiveControl.Caption      'Checks active control's Caption property
        Case "Command1"
            Form1.BackColor = RGB(255, 0, 0)      'Changes form's background to red
        Case "Command2"
            Form1.BackColor = RGB(0, 255, 0)      'Changes form's background to green
        Case "Command3"
            Form1.BackColor = RGB(0, 0, 255)      'Changes form's background to blue
    End Select
End Sub

Sub CheckControl ()
    If TypeOf Screen.ActiveControl Is CommandButton Then
        Screen.ActiveControl.Visible = False          'Makes command button invisible
    ElseIf TypeOf Screen.ActiveControl Is TextBox
```

```
        StoredText$ = Screen.ActiveControl.Text        'Stores contents of text box
    End If
End Sub
```

Description

The ActiveControl property substitutes for the name of the control on the screen or form that has the focus. A control has the focus when selected on the screen by the user. This property is only accessible at runtime and will not work at design time. In the example syntax, a Select Case statement determines the background color of the form based on which command button has the focus.

Ineligible Controls

You cannot use the ActiveControl property to reference controls that are ineligible for focus. A control may be ineligible for receiving focus for a number of reasons, such as when the control's Visible property is False. Some controls can never receive the focus, such as the timer and the label controls.

The Tag Property

When none of a control's properties are appropriate for use in an ActiveControl expression, the Tag property can differentiate between the various controls on a form. The Tag property of a control can be assigned a unique text string that you can use to identify the control when necessary. For example, each of the controls on a data entry form can receive a unique Tag property text string in the Form_Load event of the form. This string then identifies the controls. See the Tag property section later in this chapter for more details.

Example

The Reference project at the end of the chapter uses the ActiveControl property at several points in the code to read and set various properties as well as use methods.

Comments

The word Screen or a form Name must appear before ActiveControl or an error occurs.

ACTIVEFORM PROPERTY

Objects Affected

Check	Clipboard	Combo	Command	CommonDlg
Data	Debug	Dir	Drive	File
Form	Frame	Grid	Image	Label
Line	List	▶ MDI Form	Menu	OLE
Option	Picture	Printer	▶ Screen	Scroll
Shape	Text	Timer		

Purpose

The ActiveForm property refers to the currently active form. At runtime you can read the value of this property to determine which form has the focus or to set that form's properties. This property is accessible at runtime only and will not work at design time. Table 6-4 lists the arguments of the ActiveForm property.

General Syntax

```
Screen.ActiveForm[.Property]
Form.ActiveForm[.Property]
```

Argument	Description
Screen	'Screen' refers to the Screen object
Form	Name property of the MDIForm
Property	Name of the property to reference

Table 6-4 Arguments of the ActiveForm property

Example Syntax

```
Sub FormPosition ()
    Screen.ActiveForm.Height = Screen.Height        'Make form's height equal screen
    Screen.ActiveForm.Width = (Screen.Width / 2)    'Make form's width half of screen
    Screen.ActiveForm.Top = 0                       'Place form at top
    Screen.ActiveForm.Left = 0                      'Place form on left margin
End Sub
```

Description

The ActiveForm property returns which form on the screen or within an MDI form has the focus. A form has the focus when it is the selected or active form on the screen; its title bar and border colors are usually different than inactive forms to visually cue the user. (The colors for active and inactive forms are set by the Windows Control Panel.) The example syntax shows the ActiveForm property setting the form's size and position without explicitly referring to the form's Name.

Ineligible Forms

The ActiveForm property cannot reference forms that are ineligible for focus. A form may be ineligible for receiving focus for a number of reasons. When a form's Visible property is False, that control may not have the focus or reference it with the ActiveForm property. In order to change the size of a hidden or invisible form, use an alternate property, such as Name.

The Tag Property

When none of a form's properties are appropriate for use in an ActiveForm expression, the Tag property serves as one possible method for differentiating between the various forms of a program. The Tag property of an object can be assigned a unique text string that you can use to refer to the object when necessary. A Select Case statement might then determine the Tag property of the active form. In this example the active form's background color changes from white to blue.

```
Sub ChangeBackground ()
    Select Case Screen.ActiveForm.Tag                      'Checks Tag Property of form
        Case "Main Form"
            Screen.ActiveForm.BackColor = RGB(255,255,255)  'White background
        Case "Secondary Form"
            Screen.ActiveForm.BackColor = RGB(0,0,255)      'Blue background
    End Select
End Sub
```

Example

In the Reference project at the end of this chapter, the cmndPrint_Click event uses the ActiveForm property to print the letter on the formLetter form. The ActiveForm property determines which form that the GenerateLetter function prints the contents of the letter to. Notice that the ActiveForm is the formLetter form and not the Reference form. Even though the cmndPrint_Click event is a subroutine of the Reference form, the active form is the one currently selected on the screen.

Comments

Either the word Screen or the Name of the MDIForm must precede each ActiveForm property statement or it will not work properly. General procedures using the ActiveForm property should be placed in a module so that form level code can still access these more general routines.

NAME PROPERTY

Objects Affected

▶ Check	Clipboard	▶ Combo	▶ Command	CommonDlg
▶ Data	Debug	▶ Dir	▶ Drive	▶ File
▶ Form	▶ Frame	▶ Grid	▶ Image	▶ Label
▶ Line	▶ List	▶ MDI Form	▶ Menu	▶ OLE
▶ Option	▶ Picture	Printer	Screen	▶ Scroll
▶ Shape	▶ Text	▶ Timer		

Purpose

The Name property identifies each control and form in a program. You then refer to the form or control with its Name in your code. This property is only modifiable at design time; it is not available at runtime. Table 6-5 lists the argument of the Name property.

General Syntax

```
[Name.]Property
```

Argument	Description
Name	Name used to identify the form or control in code

Table 6-5 Argument of the Name property

Example Syntax

```
Sub Form1_Click
    If TextBox(0).Text = "Background is blue" Then        'This subroutine checks the
```

```
        Form1.BackColor = RGB(255,255,255)          'contents of the first part of
        Form1.ForeColor = RGB(0,0,255)              'the TextBox Control array for
        TextBox(0).Text = "Background is white"      'which color to set the
        TextBox(1).Text = "Foreground is blue"       'foreground and background of
    ElseIf TextBox(0).Text = "Background is white" Then 'the form. 'Clicking' the form
        Form1.BackColor = RGB(0,0,255)              'changes background and
        Form1.ForeColor = RGB(255,255,255)          'foreground from blue to white.
        TextBox(0).Text = "Background is blue"
        TextBox(1).Text = "Foreground is white"
    End If
End Sub
```

Description

A form or control's Name property may be up to 40 characters in length and must begin with a letter of the alphabet. It may contain underscores (_), but no other punctuation or spaces. Although you may use a reserved word (like If or Select), this can create confusion and potentially subtle bugs. A newly created object's default Name property is the name of the object type and an integer. For example, the default Name for the first text box is Text1. With each addition of another object of the same type, the integer at the end of the Name increments by 1. For example, the second text box on a form has a default Name property of Text2.

Your code uses an object's Name property to refer to that object. This name is either the default setting or a user-defined choice. The Name of an object normally serves as a part of any expression that directly affects the object.

Using a prefix to indicate the type of control can help make your code be self-documenting and reduce errors. For example, textPatientName refers to a text box, while pictEmployeMugShot refers to a picture control. See Naming Conventions at the beginning of this chapter for more details.

The ActiveControl Property

The ActiveControl property can substitute for the Name of whatever control is currently active (selected). In this case the ActiveControl property identifies the control with the focus. For example, a sub procedure can change the BackColor and ForeColor property of the selected control. This enables the program to visually emphasize the selected control. See ActiveControl for more information.

The ActiveForm Property

The ActiveForm property can substitute for the Name of the active form. For example, a module sub procedure can change the size and position of the currently selected form. This might enable the program to standardize the appearance of the forms that appear on the screen.

Object Arrays

When more than one form or control of the same type has the same Name, these objects are part of an object array. At design time Visual Basic asks if this is what you wish to do in order to prevent the accidental creation of an object array. Any number of objects may belong to an object array, provided that they are the same object type. Each object has a unique index property number in the order of creation, although you may later modify the object's index property in the Property Box. An object array is zero-based; that is, the first object created has an Index of 0, not 1. This number helps to reference that object, and appears in parentheses after the shared Name. For example, the second control of the Assist object array appears as Assist(1).

Object arrays can simplify writing code for similar objects, as they all share the same code. For example, you may have a Validation routine that you'd like to run on every Change event for ten different text boxes. To do this, simply create an object array of textInput(0) to textInput(9) and then put the validation code in the textInput()_Change event.

```
Sub textInput_Change (Index as Integer)
    If textInput(Index).Text = "" Then
        MsgBox "You need to enter some text.  Please retry"
    End If
End Sub
```

Notice that events for object arrays always have the Index argument. This lets you determine which object in the array caused the event. For example, suppose you wanted to place some default text into txtInput(5) and txtInput(7) when they got the focus:

```
Sub textInput_GotFocus (Index as Integer)
    Select Case Index
        Case 5: textInput(Index) = "Seattle"      'Default city
        Case 7: textInput(Index) = "WA"           'Default state
    End Select
End Sub
```

Example

All of the objects of the Reference Project receive names that identify them during the program's operation.

Comment

Visual Basic 1.0 used the CtlName and FormName properties to refer to controls and forms. Visual Basic 2.0 and 3.0 replace these two properties with the single Name property, which refers to both controls and to forms.

INDEX PROPERTY

Objects Affected

▶ Check	Clipboard	▶ Combo	▶ Command	CommonDlg
▶ Data	Debug	▶ Dir	▶ Drive	▶ File
▶ Form	▶ Frame	▶ Grid	▶ Image	▶ Label
▶ Line	▶ List	MDI Form	▶ Menu	▶ OLE
▶ Option	▶ Picture	Printer	Screen	▶ Scroll
▶ Shape	▶ Text	▶ Timer		

Purpose

The Index property determines the referenced element of an object array. When an object is not part of an object array, its Index property has no value. Objects that are part of an object array may have index values of 0 to 32,767. This value may be set at design time and is read-only at runtime. Any reference to an object in an object array must include its Index property value. Table 6-6 lists the arguments of the Index property.

General Syntax

```
[form!]object[(i%)].Index
```

Argument	Description
form	Name property of the parent form
object	Shared Name of the object array
i%	Index value of the form or control

Table 6-6 Arguments of Index property

Example Syntax

```
Sub menuPrinterChoices_Click (Index As Integer)
    Select Case menuPrinterChoices.Index  'see which choice was clicked
        Case 0                            'Control menuPrinterChoices(0)
            textPrinter.Text = "HP LaserJet IIP"
        Case 1                            'Control menuPrinterChoices(1)
```

(continued on next page)

(continued from previous page)

```
                textPrinter.Text = "HP LaserJet II
        Case 2                          'Control menuPrinterChoices(2)
                textPrinter.Text = "HP LaserJet III"
    End Select
End Sub
```

Description

The Index property uniquely identifies an instance of the object within the object array. An Index expression normally consists of the object's Name property followed by the value of the index placed in parentheses. Programs with multiple forms require preceding this with the Name of the form. Forms may also be included in an object array, although the mechanism for doing so differs from creating an object array of controls. See Chapter 3, Using Objects, and Chapter 4, Forms and Menus, for more details on creating form arrays. The Index property may be modified at design time only.

Note that Event sub procedures pass the control's Index value as an argument for use in the subroutine. Using the control's Index property is functionally identical to using the event's Index variable.

Option Buttons, Check Boxes, and Menu Controls

Option buttons, check boxes, and menus can usually be handled most easily as part of an object array. Each control's index property differentiates it from the other controls in the control array, and each control in the array shares the code in common with the other controls. In the example syntax, a Select Case statement uses the Index property of the control array menuPrinterChoices to indicate what name will appear in the text box textPrinter. Note that we could also have used the Index variable passed to the array's event. The following code is functionally equivalent to the example syntax:

```
Sub menuPrinterChoices_Click (Index As Integer)
    Select Case Index               'see which choice was clicked
        Case 0                          'Control menuPrinterChoices(0)
            textPrinter.Text = "HP LaserJet IIP"
        Case 1                          'Control menuPrinterChoices(1)
            textPrinter.Text = "HP LaserJet II
        Case 2                          'Control menuPrinterChoices(2)
            textPrinter.Text = "HP LaserJet III"
    End Select
End Sub
```

The Load and Unload Statements

When used in conjunction with the Load and Unload statements, the Index property of an object array allows the creation of new objects. First, create a single object with an index value of 0. Next, change its Visible property to False (0). At runtime, load a new member of the object array using an unused index value.

When no longer needed, you can disable these objects with the Unload statement. For example, create an option control box with an index value of 0. Each time another option box becomes necessary, load it with the Load statement. This allows your program to dynamically respond to different user needs.

Many programs, for example, place the last four saved files on the bottom of the File menu. When the program starts for the first time, there have been no saved files, so no file names should appear. Each additional file saved adds one more element to the menu.

Creating Multiple Forms in an Array

Forms may also form an object array. To do so simply assign a form to a variable:

```
Dim InputForm(10) as New Form1
```

MDI child forms typically use an object array. You usually don't know how many instances of the form the user will open, so declare the array without explicitly dimensioning it. Each time the user wishes to create a new MDI child form, redimension the array with the Preserve keyword. This creates a new form without affecting the contents of the forms already open.

```
Sub MDIForm_Load()
    Dim InputForm() as New Form1                'Create the form "template"
End Sub

Sub menuFileNew_Click ()
    InputFormCount = UBound(InputForm)          'Count number of child forms open
    ReDim Preserve InputForm(InputFormCount + 1)  'Create new child form
    InputForm(InputFormCount + 1).Show          'Display new child form
End Sub
```

For a much more thorough discussion of creating multiple instances of forms using form arrays, see Chapter 3, Using Objects, and Chapter 4, Menus and Forms.

Example

The Reference project at the end of this chapter sets the Index property for each of the three object arrays in this program. On the Reference form, the object arrays are optnLetter and chekLetter. The formEntry form has the textEntry object array.

The Index property serves as a reference at several points in the Reference project. In the optnLetter_GotFocus event, the Index property determines which part of the code to process. The identification of chekLetter array control to be enabled or disabled includes its Index property in this event subroutine. The chekLetter_Click event use the Index property to indicate exactly which control the user pressed.

Comments

The data control has a completely unrelated Index property associated with the TableDefs collection in addition to this usage of Index. Note that collections (discussed in Chapter 3, Using Objects) also have an index that is completely unrelated to this Index property.

PARENT PROPERTY

Objects Affected

▶ Check	Clipboard	▶ Combo	▶ Command	CommonDlg
▶ Data	Debug	▶ Dir	▶ Drive	▶ File
Form	▶ Frame	▶ Grid	▶ Image	▶ Label
▶ Line	▶ List	MDI Form	▶ Menu	▶ OLE
▶ Option	▶ Picture	Printer	Screen	▶ Scroll
▶ Shape	▶ Text	▶ Timer		

Purpose

Each control belongs to a form. A control's Parent property identifies the control's form. Each Parent property expression must contain the Name of the control being accessed. This property is not available at design time and is read-only at runtime. Using the Parent property lets you design generic subroutines and functions that apply for any control passed to it. Table 6-7 lists the argument of the Parent property.

General Syntax

```
[control.]Parent
```

Argument	Description
control	Name property of the control

Table 6-7 Argument of the Parent property

300

Example Syntax

```
Sub RestorePointer (Source As Control)
    If TypeOf Source Is TextBox Then            'Checks if control is a text box
        Source.Parent.MousePointer = 3          'I-Bar Mouse Pointer
    Else If TypeOf Source Is PictureBox Then    'Checks if control is picture box
        Source.Parent.MousePointer = 4          'Icon Mouse Pointer
    Else                                        'All other controls are given an
        Source.Parent.MousePointer = 1          'Arrow Mouse Pointer
    End If
End Sub
```

Description

The Parent property of a control makes its form's properties and methods available. The Parent property in a subroutine or function can affect the forms of controls on many different forms. Do this with the use of a separate module that holds the function so that any code in any form or module can refer to your generic subroutine or function. In the example syntax for this property, the function RestorePointer changes the MousePointer property of the form to a special type based on the named control in the expression. Note the use of the TypeOf and Is keywords to identify the control type. See Chapter 3, Using Objects, for more information about these two keywords.

The ActiveControl Property

You can create a very general function by combining ActiveControl with the Parent property. The ActiveControl property refers to the control with the focus. Depending on which type of control has the focus, different actions can be taken with the properties and methods of the Parent form. The next example changes the Icon property of the form based on the selected control. This pairing of the ActiveControl and Parent property works best when placed within a separate module so that the function or routine operates on more than one form.

```
Sub ChooseIcon ()
    If TypeOf Screen.ActiveControl Is TextBox Then
        Screen.ActiveControl.Parent.Icon=LoadPicture("C:\VB\ICONS\MISC\FACE02.ICO")
    ElseIf Screen.ActiveControl Is CommandButton Then
        Screen.ActiveControl.Parent.Icon=LoadPicture("C:\VB\ICONS\MISC\FACE01.ICO")
    End If
End Sub

Sub Form_Resize ()
    ChooseIcon
End Sub
```

Example

In the Reference project at the end of this chapter, formEntry's Load event sets the form's caption by using textEntry's Parent property.

Comments

The Parent property works best when placed within an external module, but also works within a form's subroutines.

TAG PROPERTY

Objects Affected

▶ Check   Clipboard   ▶ Combo   ▶ Command   CommonDlg
▶ Data   Debug   ▶ Dir   ▶ Drive   File
▶ Form   ▶ Frame   ▶ Grid   ▶ Image   ▶ Label
▶ Line   ▶ List   ▶ MDI Form   ▶ Menu   ▶ OLE
▶ Option   ▶ Picture   Printer   Screen   ▶ Scroll
▶ Shape   ▶ Text   ▶ Timer

Purpose

The Tag property attaches a text string to a form or control. The other properties of a form or control are unaffected by the text string setting of its Tag property. This property may be changed at either design time or runtime, and has a default empty string. It has various uses, and can be a great problem solver in your code. Table 6-8 lists the arguments of the Tag property.

General Syntax

```
[form.]Tag[ = string$]
[form!]control.Tag[ = string$]
```

Argument	Description
form	Name of the form
control	Name of the control
string$	Contains the identifying string of text

Table 6-8 Arguments of the Tag property

302

Example Syntax

```
Sub Form_Resize ()
     If Form1.Tag = "" Then              'Checks if the form's tag property is blank
          Form1.Tag = "Loaded"           'Changes tag property to "Loaded"
     ElseIf Form1.Tag = "Loaded" Then    'Checks if the form's tag property is "Loaded"
          Form1.Tag = "Changed"          'Changes tag property to "Changed"
     End If
End Sub
```

Description

The Tag property serves as a method for differentiating between the various controls of a form, storing information unique to that form or control, or relating the form or control to something else.

A form or control's Tag property can receive a text string (string$) that refers to anything you want. Visual Basic does not use or modify the Tag, so you have complete flexibility in how you use it. You may wish to store a control's old value in the Tag, an entry that relates it to a variable array's index, or perhaps track a control's state. In the example syntax, the Tag property of a form changes to flag when modifications take place to the size of the form.

Every object has a Tag property (except for the system objects App, Clipboard, Debug, Printer, and Screen). It is the *only* property that all objects have that can be read and written at runtime. This makes it a valuable problem solver, especially when writing generic functions that are supposed to work on more than one type of control.

Example

In the Reference project at the end of this chapter, the Tag property of the textEntry control array contains the appropriate caption to display on the entry form.

Comments

The Tag property of a form or control must be a text string and will not work with a numeric value.

THE REFERENCE PROJECT

Project Overview

The Reference project demonstrates the properties used to access a program's controls and forms. Following the examples of the different forms and subroutines of this project will give you a good understanding of how to reference forms and controls in Visual Basic.

The Reference project consists of three forms: formMain, formLetter, and formEntry. Each of these forms have a section with step-by-step instructions on how to put the form and its controls together. A table lists the different elements of the form's controls, along with a picture of how the form looks with these controls. Then we cover the actual code used on each form. We wrap the project up with the module-level code, and follow that with a complete explanation of the project.

Assembling the Project: Reference Form

1. Make a new form (the Reference form) with the objects and properties in Table 6-9. Notice that all of the CheckBox controls have the same Name property of chekLetter. Similarly, all of the option button controls share the Name property optnLetter. These indicate the controls make up a control array. When you create the second control of the same type and Name, Visual Basic asks if you'd like to create a control array. Answer "yes" to this question.

Object	Property	Setting
Form	BackColor	Light Gray—&H00C0C0C0
	BorderStyle	1—Fixed Single
	Caption	Reference Project
	Name	formMain
Frame	BackColor	Light Gray—&H00C0C0C0
	Caption	Letter Type
	Name	framType
Option	BackColor	Light Gray—&H00C0C0C0
	Caption	&Introduction Letter
	Name	optnLetter
	Index	0

Object	Property	Setting
Option	BackColor	Light Gray—&H00C0C0C0
	Caption	&Acceptance Letter
	Name	optnLetter
	Index	1
Option	BackColor	Light Gray—&H00C0C0C0
	Caption	Ge&neral Letter
	Name	optnLetter
	Index	2
Frame	BackColor	Light Gray—&H00C0C0C0
	Caption	Letter Options
	Name	framOptions
Check	BackColor	Light Gray—&H00C0C0C0
	Caption	&Return Address
	Name	chekLetter
	Index	0
Check	BackColor	Light Gray—&H00C0C0C0
	Caption	A&ddressee
	Name	chekLetter
	Index	1
Check	BackColor	Light Gray—&H00C0C0C0

(continued on next page)

(continued from previous page)

Object	Property	Setting
	Caption	&Greeting
	Name	chekLetter
	Index	2
Check	BackColor	Light Gray—&H00C0C0C0
	Caption	&Body
	Name	chekLetter
	Index	3
Check	BackColor	Light Gray—&H00C0C0C0
	Caption	&Closing
	Name	chekLetter
	Index	4
Check	BackColor	Light Gray—&H00C0C0C0
	Caption	&Enclosure List
	Name	chekLetter
	Index	5
Check	BackColor	Light Gray—&H00C0C0C0
	Caption	Carbon Copy &List
	Name	chekLetter
	Index	6
Command	Caption	&Print Letter

Object	Property	Setting
	Name	cmndPrint
Command	Caption	E&xit
	Name	cmndExit

Table 6-9 Settings for formMain form in the Reference project

2. Size the objects on the screen, as shown in Figure 6-2.

3. Enter the following code in the cmndExit Click event. This simply ends the program when the user clicks on the Exit button.

```
Sub cmndExit_Click ()
    End
End Sub
```

4. Enter the following code in the Form_Load event. This loads the other two forms used in the project so they display more quickly when needed.

```
Sub Form_Load ()
    Load formEntry
    Load formLetter
End Sub
```

5. Enter the following code in the chekLetter_Click event. This routine happens whenever the user changes which letter option they want. It first checks the global variable TypeIndex to see if the Click event was caused by the code in the optnLetter_GotFocus event. The code there checks or grays the check boxes; doing so creates a Click event here, which we need to filter out. If TypeIndex is

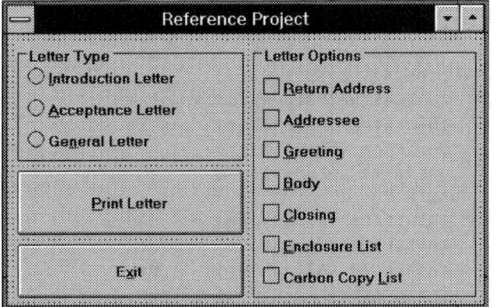

Figure 6-2 What the formMain form should look like when completed

307

different than -1, that means that it's a "real" user-caused click and we need to respond to it. The routine then sets the global variable CurrentIndex to show which option the user chose, and opens up the formEntry form.

```
Sub chekLetter_Click (Index As Integer)
    If TypeIndex <> -1 Then
        CurrentIndex = Index
        formEntry.Show
    End If
End Sub
```

6. Enter this code in the optnLetter_GotFocus event. This event occurs whenever the user changes the letter type. It first highlights the choice in blue, using Screen.ActiveControl to pass the correct name to the HiLite subroutine. It then flags TypeIndex to make sure the chekLetter_Click event doesn't try to handle any check box clicks.

We then use the ActiveControl argument again to check which letter option the user chose. The Select Case statements enable or disable the appropriate check boxes and unhighlight the other letter types. The For Next loop cycles through the check boxes and grays out any that are disabled but checked, and places a check in any that were grayed out previously and are now enabled. The last line of the routine sets the TypeIndex flag to show that we're done manipulating the check boxes with code.

```
Sub optnLetter_Click (Index As Integer)
    HiLite Screen.ActiveControl
    TypeIndex = -1                              'Flag that we're setting type
    Select Case Screen.ActiveControl.Index
        Case 0                                 'Introduction letter
            chekLetter(2).Enabled = False
            chekLetter(3).Enabled = False
            chekLetter(4).Enabled = False
            chekLetter(5).Enabled = False
            chekLetter(6).Enabled = False
            UnHiLite optnLetter(1)
            UnHiLite optnLetter(2)
        Case 1                                 'Acceptance letter
            chekLetter(2).Enabled = True
            chekLetter(3).Enabled = True
            chekLetter(4).Enabled = False
            chekLetter(5).Enabled = False
            chekLetter(6).Enabled = False
            UnHiLite optnLetter(0)
            UnHiLite optnLetter(2)
        Case 2                                 'General letter
            chekLetter(2).Enabled = True
            chekLetter(3).Enabled = True
            chekLetter(4).Enabled = True
            chekLetter(5).Enabled = True
            chekLetter(6).Enabled = True
            UnHiLite optnLetter(0)
            UnHiLite optnLetter(1)
    End Select
```

```
    For X = RTN_ADDRESS To CARBON          'Gray out checked boxes that are now disabled
        If chekLetter(X).Enabled = False And chekLetter(X).Value = CHECKED Then
            chekLetter(X).Value = GRAYED
        End If                              'Check boxes that are grayed out but now enabled
        If chekLetter(X).Enabled = True And chekLetter(X).Value = GRAYED Then
            chekLetter(X).Value = CHECKED
        End If
        DoEvents
    Next X
    TypeIndex = Screen.ActiveControl.Index
End Sub
```

7. Place this code in the cmndPrint Click event. When the user clicks this, we simulate printing the letter by hiding the reference form, generating the letter, and showing the completed letter with the Letter form. Note that because we show the Letter form modally, the rest of the code doesn't run until the user closes that form.

```
Sub cmndPrint_Click ()
    formMain.Hide
    GenerateLetter
    formLetter.Show MODAL
    formLetter.Hide
    formMain.Show
End Sub
```

Assembling the Project: Letter Form

1. Make a new form with the objects and properties in Table 6-10.

Object	Property	Setting
Form	BackColor	White – &H00FFFFFF
	BorderStyle	1 – Fixed Single
	Caption	<blank out caption>
	ControlBox	False
	Name	formLetter
	MaxButton	False
	MinButton	False

(continued on next page)

309

(continued from previous page)

Object	Property	Setting
Command	Cancel	-1—True
	Caption	&Close
	Default	-1—True
	Name	cmndClose
Text	BackColor	Black—&H0
	Name	textShadow
Text	BackColor	White—&H00FFFFFF
	BorderStyle	1—Single
	Name	textPage
Text	BorderStyle	0—None
	FontBold	0—False
	FontName	Times New Roman
	FontSize	7.8
	MultiLine	-1—True
	Name	textPrintOut

Table 6-10 Settings for formLetter Form in the Reference project

2. Size the objects on the screen, as shown in Figure 6-3.

3. Enter the following code in the Close Click event. This just hides the form.

```
Sub cmndClose_Click ()
    formLetter.Hide            'Hide the letter display form
End Sub
```

Figure 6-3 What the formLetter form should look like. Note that textShadow is farthest back, and is covered by textPage, which in turn contains textPrintOut. The illustration shows textPrintOut with a gray outline for clarity

Assembling the Project: formEntry Form

1. Make a new form with the objects and properties in Table 6-11.

Object	Property	Setting
Form	BorderStyle	1—Fixed Single
	ControlBox	False
	Name	formEntry
	MaxButton	False
	MinButton	False
Text	Index	0
	MultiLine	-1—True
	Name	textEntry
	ScrollBar	2—Vertical
	Text	<blank out text>

(continued on next page)

(continued from previous page)

Object	Property	Setting
Command	Caption	&Close
	Name	cmndClose

Table 6-11 Settings for formEntry in the Reference project

Figure 6-4 What the formEntry form
should look like

2. Size the objects on the screen, as shown in Figure 6-4.

3. Enter the following code in the form's Activate event. This event occurs whenever the form receives the focus. It starts by placing the correct text box (as
   defined by CurrentIndex, which the chekLetter check box control array defines)
   at the front of the "stack" of text boxes with the ZOrder method. It then sets the
   title bar of the form by using the tags stored in each text box, and resets the tab
   order correctly.

```
Sub Form_Activate ()
    textEntry(CurrentIndex).ZOrder          'Place the correct Text box in the front of the "stack"
    textEntry(CurrentIndex).Parent.Caption = textEntry(CurrentIndex).Tag  'Label the form
    textEntry(CurrentIndex).TabIndex = 0    'Make the current text box first in the tab order,
    cmndClose.TabIndex = 1                   'And the close button next
End Sub
```

4. Enter the following code in the Form Load event. This first creates an object array
   of text boxes to hold the entries for each letter option. It then sets the tag for each
   of these text boxes to a description of that text box. We use this tag to properly
   identify the formEntry form.

```
Sub Form_Load ()
    For x = ADDRESSEE To CARBON              'We defined the "template" text box
                                             'as textEntry(RTN_ADDRESS)
        Load textEntry(x)                    'Now create all the other text boxes
        textEntry(x).Visible = True          'And make sure they're visible
    Next x
    textEntry(RTN_ADDRESS).Tag = "Return Address"  'The tags of each text box hold descriptive
    textEntry(ADDRESSEE).Tag = "Addressee"   'text that we use to label the data entry
    textEntry(GREETING).Tag = "Greeting"     'Title Bar
```

```
      textEntry(BODY).Tag = "Body Text"
      textEntry(CLOSING).Tag = "Closing"
      textEntry(ENCLOSURE).Tag = "Enclosures"
      textEntry(CARBON).Tag = "Carbon Copies"
End Sub
```

5. Now enter the following code in the form's Paint event. Any time the form repaints itself, we set the focus to the text box so the user may easily make entries. Note that we can't perform this in the Activate event, as the form is only in the process of activating, and isn't yet capable of giving a control the focus.

```
Sub Form_Paint ()
      textEntry(CurrentIndex).SetFocus                'Ready for user to enter text
End Sub
```

6. Enter the following code in the cmndClose Click event. This simply hides the formEntry form.

```
Sub cmndClose_Click ()
      formEntry.Hide                'Hide the entry box; back to reference form
End Sub
```

Assembling the Project: Module

1. Enter the following code into a new module. Start with the general declarations of constants and global variables used throughout the application.

```
Global CurrentIndex As Integer     'Used to track which letter option we're on
Global TypeIndex As Integer        'Used to track if we're actively changing letter type

Global Const RTN_ADDRESS = 0       'These are the seven different letter options
Global Const ADDRESSEE = 1         '        (they are NOT constant.txt values!)
Global Const GREETING = 2
Global Const BODY = 3
Global Const CLOSING = 4
Global Const ENCLOSURE = 5
Global Const CARBON = 6

Global Const MODAL = 1             'Modal Dialog box
Global Const CHECKED = 1          'Checked Check Box
Global Const GRAYED = 2           'Grayed Check Box

Global Const BLACK = &H0          'Colors used in ForeColor property
Global Const BLUE = &HFF0000
```

2. Now create the following subroutines. The GenerateLetter subroutine generates the final letter from the input the user has given. It simply appends each bit of text onto a temporary string, making a few decisions along the way of what to include. Note the syntax of how to refer to the text in each text box, with the form name coming before anything else. The last line of this routine assigns the value of the temporary variable to the final "printout."

```
Sub GenerateLetter ()
```

(continued on next page)

(continued from previous page)

```
        BLANK = Chr$(13) & Chr$(10) & Chr$(13) & Chr$(10)          'Two CR LF combos
        L = ""                                                     'Erase the letter
        L = L & formEntry!textEntry(RTN_ADDRESS).Text & BLANK      'Add return address
        L = L & formEntry!textEntry(ADDRESSEE).Text & BLANK        'Add Addressee
        If formEntry!textEntry(GREETING).Text = "" Then            'If there is no greeting,
            L = L & "To Whom it may concern:" & BLANK              'Add a default greeting
        Else                                                       '...otherwise
            L = L & formEntry!textEntry(GREETING).Text & BLANK     'Add the user's greeting
        End If
        L = L & formEntry!textEntry(BODY).Text & BLANK             'Add body text
        L = L & formEntry!textEntry(CLOSING).Text & BLANK          'Add the closing statement
        If formEntry!textEntry(ENCLOSURE).Text <> "" Then          'If there are enclosures
            L = L & "Encl: " & formEntry!textEntry(ENCLOSURE).Text & BLANK 'Add them
        End If
        If formEntry!textEntry(CARBON).Text <> "" Then             'If there are Carbon Copies
            L = L & "CC:   " & formEntry!textEntry(CC).Text         'Add them
        End If
        formLetter!textPrintOut.Text = L                           'Transfer letter for display
End Sub
```

3. Enter the following code to highlight text by changing its color. Note that this routine is generic, and that it will work with any control that has a ForeColor property.

```
Sub HiLite (controlName As Control)
        controlName.ForeColor = BLUE                    'Make ForeColor text blue
End Sub
```

4. Enter the following code to unhighlight the control by setting its ForeColor property back to the default Black.

```
Sub UnHiLite (controlName As Control)
        controlName.ForeColor = BLACK                   'make ForeColor text back to default Black
End Sub
```

How It Works

The Reference project demonstrates referencing through the creation of different kinds of letters. When the project opens, the user sees a list of the possible types of letters to create: introduction letter, acceptance letter, and general letter. The user chooses the type of letter, and then selects the different letter options to

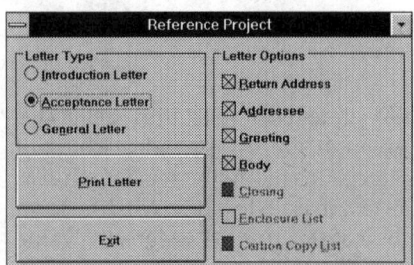

Figure 6-5 Reference form

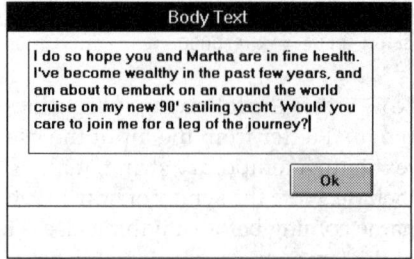

Figure 6-6 Data Entry form

314

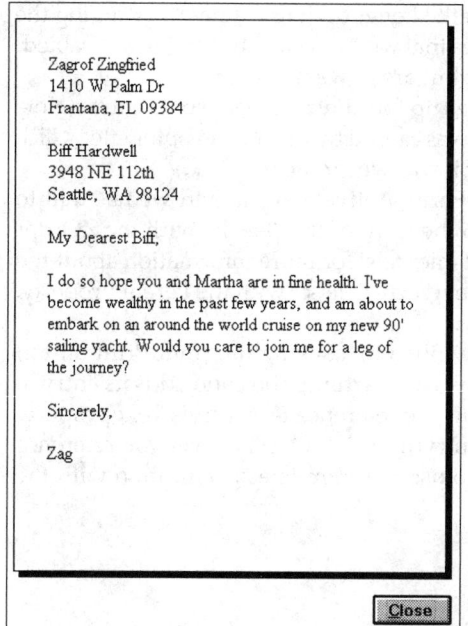

Zagrof Zingfried
1410 W Palm Dr
Frantana, FL 09384

Biff Hardwell
3948 NE 112th
Seattle, WA 98124

My Dearest Biff,

I do so hope you and Martha are in fine health. I've
become wealthy in the past few years, and am about to
embark on an around the world cruise on my new 90'
sailing yacht. Would you care to join me for a leg of
the journey?

Sincerely,

Zag

Figure 6-7 formLetter form showing
final product

include in the letter from the check boxes in the Letter options frame. Each time
the user selects one of these check boxes, Visual Basic asks for the required information. Once the user has selected all of the required options and entered the
information, they press the Print Letter command button to display the letter on
the screen. Figures 6-5, 6-6, and 6-7 show the project in action, with all three
forms displayed.

Each element of the Reference project receives an identification name referenced
throughout the program. Each form has its Name changed from the generic Form1,
Form2, and Form3 to the more descriptive choices of formMain, formLetter, and
formEntry. Likewise, each control takes a more descriptive Name during the
design phase.

When the program starts, formMain displays on the screen, triggering the
Form_Load event. This event loads the other two forms into memory, but does
not display them. The formEntry's Form_Load event creates an object array of
seven textEntry boxes to hold the seven parts of the letter. It uses the original
textEntry box as a "template."

When the user clicks a Letter type option button, the option is highlighted by
the HiLite subroutine. Note that we pass the control argument to the subroutine
using the Screen.ActiveControl. The Name property is not available at runtime, so we can't just give the letter the Name directly (for example, HiLite
optnLetter(Index).Name is illegal). The optnLetter_Click event then enables or

315

disables the appropriate check boxes in the Letter options frame. After setting the check boxes, it grays out the check boxes that were checked but are now disabled, and checks those that were grayed out but are now enabled.

Pressing any of the check boxes brings up formEntry to begin data entry. (Note that we first test to see if the Click event was caused by the code in optnLetter_Click setting and resetting the check boxes; if it was we ignore the click.)

Displaying formEntry triggers the Form_Activate event, and we use that to bring the appropriate textEntry box to the front of the "stack" with the ZOrder method. See Chapter 8, Graphics Fundamentals, for more information about the ZOrder method. The caption of the form gets set with the Parent property. We then set the tab stops appropriately.

After the letter sections are properly filled in, clicking the cmndPrint button "prints" the letter. This just goes through each textEntry box and adds its entry to the end of a temporary string. Note how we reference textEntry's Text property by its complete name, formEntry!textEntry(Index).Text. Whenever you reference a control on another form, you need to use the complete specification with the form's name.

7 EVENTS

Visual Basic is an event-driven language. An event is an action recognized by a form or control, such as a mouse click or a keystroke. Event-driven languages like Visual Basic let the user control program flow. The application spends most of its time idle waiting for the user to act on it. When the user does something (or the system causes an event, like a shutdown message), the program responds to that action. This is the essence of a graphical user interface: create a flexible environment that the user can control.

Contrast this approach with traditional programming methods. A traditional program starts at the beginning and controls all aspects of program flow. The user can certainly give the program input, but cannot alter program flow other than in limited, narrowly defined ways. Traditional programming languages have usually had inflexible user interfaces because of this approach.

Each object in Visual Basic has a number of specific events it recognizes. You can make your application respond to events by writing code in an event procedure. Much like regular sub procedures, event procedures contain code that performs specific actions. For example, clicking a command button with the mouse triggers its Click event; code you write for this event procedure might confirm that the user wants to end the application. Although each control recognizes a predefined set of events, you determine if they respond to those events by writing code in the event procedures. Each object has its own set of event procedures that are independent of any other objects in the application.

Visual Basic recognizes 36 different events. This chapter summarizes those events, and gives details on the one event not covered elsewhere in this book: the Change event.

EVENT PROCEDURES

A reference to an event begins with the Name of the object that triggers the event, followed by an underscore (_) and the name of the event:

```
Sub Command1_Click ()
    MsgBox "You've just clicked Command1"
End Sub

Sub textPatientName_GotFocus ()
    textPatientName.BackColor = QBColor(7)
    textPatientName.ForeColor = QBColor(1)
    textPatientName.SelLength = Len(textPatientName.Text)
End Sub
```

Forms are the exception: rather than using the name of the form, the event subroutine uses the keyword 'Form' (or 'MDIForm' for the main MDI form of an application).

```
Sub Form_Load ()
    List1.AddItem "Red"
    List1.AddItem "Blue"
    List1.AddItem "Green"
End Sub

Sub MDIForm_Load ()
    Form1.Load
    Form2.Load
    Form3.Show
End Sub
```

Many events pass arguments to the procedure that your code can use. For example, the MouseDown event passes information about which mouse button was pressed, which control keys (if any) were held down, and exactly where the mouse is positioned:

```
Sub Picture1_MouseDown (Button As Integer, Shift As Integer, X As Single, Y As Single)
    If Button = LEFT_BUTTON Then                  'Button argument checks which mouse button
        Picture1.Line (x1!, y1!)-(X, Y)           'X and Y are current mouse position
    End If
End Sub
```

Control arrays have just one event procedure for the entire array. This makes it easy to write generic code that applies to related controls that are grouped in the array. Event procedures in control arrays always have an Index argument that determines which control in the array triggered the event. This next example shows a menu control array with four elements. The Select Case uses the Index property to take appropriate action depending on which menu choice the user clicked.

```
Sub menuWindowArrange_Click (Index As Integer)
```

```
        Select Case Index
            Case 0: MDIForm1.Arrange CASCADE
            Case 1: MDIForm1.Arrange TILE_HORIZONTAL
            Case 2: MDIForm1.Arrange TILE_VERTICAL
            Case 3: MDIForm1.Arrange ARRANGE_ICONS
        End Select
End Sub
```

See Appendix A, Visual Basic Language Tutorial, for information on sub procedures and other language elements.

VISUAL BASIC EVENTS

Visual Basic 3.0 has 36 events. Some events are recognized by many objects, some by only a few or even just one object. Almost all events are covered in detail in various chapters throughout this book; the Change event is covered in this chapter. Table 7-1 lists the events, the meaning, and the chapter that they are covered in.

Event	Meaning	Chapter	
Activate	Form just received focus	4	Forms and Menus
Change	Control's value just changed	7	Events
Click	Control just got clicked	14	Mouse Events
DblClick	Control just got double-clicked	14	Mouse Events
Deactivate	Form just lost focus	4	Forms and Menus
DragDrop	Control just got dropped	15	Dragging and Dropping
DragOver	Another control just got dragged over this control	15	Dragging and Dropping
DropDown	User clicked the down arrow on combo box	18	Lists, Combos, and Grids
Error	Externally caused database error	27	Data Access
GotFocus	Control just received the focus	21	Application Focus
KeyDown	User just pressed a key	16	Keyboard Input

(continued on next page)

319

(continued from previous page)

Event	Meaning	Chapter	
KeyPress	User just pressed a key	16	Keyboard Input
KeyUp	User just released a key	16	Keyboard Input
LinkClose	DDE Link just closed	25	Dynamic Data Exchange
LinkError	DDE Link has an error	25	Dynamic Data Exchange
LinkExecute	DDE Link just received an external command	25	Dynamic Data Exchange
LinkNotify	DDE Link data has changed in a Notify style link	25	Dynamic Data Exchange
LinkOpen	DDE Link has just opened	25	Dynamic Data Exchange
Load	Form has just loaded	4	Forms and Menus
LostFocus	Control just lost focus	21	Application Focus
MouseDown	User just pressed mouse button	14	Mouse Events
MouseMove	User just moved mouse	14	Mouse Events
MouseUp	User just released mouse button	14	Mouse Events
Paint	Control just got uncovered	8	Graphics Fundamentals
PathChange	Path property just changed	19	File System Controls
PatternChange	Pattern property just changed	19	File System Controls
QueryUnload	Form is about to unload	4	Forms and Menus
Reposition	Current record just changed	27	Data Access
Resize	Form just changed size	4	Forms and Menus
RowColChange	Grid's active cell just changed	18	Lists, Combos, and Grids
Scroll	Scroll bar thumb just moved	20	Scroll Bars

Event	Meaning	Chapter
SelChange	New cell selected in grid	18 Lists, Combos, and Grids
Timer	Timer interval finished	22 Time
Unload	Form unloading	4 Forms and Menus
Updated	OLE object changed	26 Object Linking and Embedding
Validate	Current record about to change	27 Data Access

Table 7-1 Visual Basic events

CHANGE EVENT

Objects Affected

Check	Clipboard	▶ Combo	Command	CommonDlg
Data	Debug	▶ Dir	▶ Drive	File
Form	Frame	Grid	Image	▶ Label
Line	List	MDI Form	Menu	OLE
Option	▶ Picture	Printer	Screen	▶ Scroll
Shape	▶ Text	Timer		

Purpose

The Change event initiates an action when the user changes the value of an object's primary property, such as by making a selection or entering data. Table 7-2 summarizes the arguments used for the Change event.

General Syntax

```
Sub Name_Change ([Index As Integer])
```

Arguments	Description
Name	Name of the control
Index	An integer that uniquely identifies an element of a control array

Table 7-2 Arguments of the Change event

Example Syntax

```
Global OldText As String

Sub Text1_Change ()
    OldText = Text1.Text      'Update ThisText any time the text in Text1 is changed
End Sub
```

Description

Many of the objects in Visual Basic have a primary property. For instance, the text box control's primary property is the Text property. Use the Change event to respond to any changes in an object's primary property. This event occurs regardless of the manner in which the property is changed: it initiates if the property changes by a user action, the program's code, or DDE events. The Change event doesn't trigger if you assign a value to an object's primary property that is the same as its current setting.

Table 7-3 lists all the objects that use the Change event, and the properties on which it is based.

Use Change with This Object...	To React to a Change in This Property...
Combo	Text
Dir	Path
Drive	Drive
File	Path (use the PathChange event)
File	Pattern (use the PatternChange event)
Label	Caption

Use Change with This Object...	To React to a Change in This Property...
Picture	Picture
Scroll	Value
Text	Text

Table 7-3 Objects that activate the Change event, and their primary properties

Be careful not to code circular Change events. Writing code in one control's Change event that triggers a change in another control's primary property, which in turn changes the original control's primary property, leads to an uncontrollable series of change events that only end when Windows gives an error message after it runs out of stack space. For instance, imagine a program that has two labels, with the following Change events:

```
Sub Label1_Change ()
    Label2.Caption = Str(Val(Label1.Caption) + 1)
End Sub

Sub Label2_Change ()
    Label1.Caption = Str(Val(Label2.Caption) + 1)
End Sub
```

The Label1_Change event modifies the Caption property of the Label2 object. This causes Label2's Change event to occur. That event modifies Label1's Caption property, which will again cause its Change event to occur. As you can see, this will result in both events calling each other endlessly.

Combo Boxes

Changes made to a combo box's Text property trigger its Change event. The Text property only applies when a Combo box's Style property is set to 0 or 1 (dropdown or simple combo); therefore the Change event can only occur with these styles. If a combo box's Style property is set to 2, no Change event could ever be initiated.

Users may change the Text property of a combo box by doing one of two things. First, they can type text directly in the edit portion of a combo box. Since the text changes with each keystroke, the Change event occurs every time the user presses another key. For example, if the user types the word "HELLO," the Change event will be called five times, once for each keystroke. Second, the user can change this property by selecting any of the list entries in the combo box. A list entry is selected any time the user presses the up or down arrow keys, or clicks on one of the entries with the mouse.

Setting the combo box's Text property within a program's code also triggers the Change event. For instance:

```
Combo1.Text = "Hello"
```

In the above line of code, the Text property of a combo box is set to "Hello." After this is performed, Visual Basic initiates the combo box's Change event. When that event has finished, execution will resume at the line following this one. Chapter 18, Lists, Combos, and Grids, contains more detailed information about combo boxes.

Directory, Drive, and File List Boxes

The primary property for the directory list box is the Path property. The Change event will occur any time this property changes. The user may change this property by double-clicking on any entry listed in the directory box. This sets the Path property to the path specified by the entry chosen by the user. Setting the Path property to a new value within a program's code also causes the Change event to occur.

The primary property for the Drive list box is the Drive property. This property can be changed by choosing a new drive letter from the object's drop-down list, or by assigning a value to the property within the program's code.

The File list box has two primary properties: Path and Pattern. Because of this it also has two Change events: PathChange and PatternChange. The PathChange event occurs when the Path property of a File list box has been changed. The PatternChange property occurs when its Pattern property has been modified. Both of these events are explained in detail in Chapter 19, File System Controls.

Label

The primary property for the Label object is the Caption property. The Caption property can be changed by assigning it a string value within your program's code, or as the result of a Dynamic Data Exchange (DDE) operation. Refer to Chapter 5, Application Appearance, Chapter 21, Application Focus, and Chapter 25, Dynamic Data Exchange (DDE), for more about the Caption property and DDE.

Picture Boxes

The primary property for the Picture object is the Picture property. The Picture property can be changed by assigning it a value within your program's code, or as the result of a Dynamic Data Exchange (DDE) operation. Refer to Chapter 8, Graphics Fundamentals, and Chapter 25, Dynamc Data Exchange (DDE), for more on the picture property and DDE.

Scroll Bars

The primary property for the Scroll Bars object is the Value property. This property indicates the relative position of a scroll bar's thumb on the bar. The Value property of a scroll bar can be changed in four ways. First, the user can click on either arrow. This causes the Value property to increment or decrement by the amount indicated by the bar's SmallChange property. Second, clicking the gray area of the scroll bar updates the Value property in a similar manner as clicking an arrow, but with the amount of change indicated by the bar's LargeChange property. Third, the user can click and drag the thumb to a specific position on the bar. This causes the Value property to be set according to the position of the thumb on the bar. Finally, your code can directly set the Value. Chapter 20, Scroll Bars, uses the Change event with the Scroll Bars object in its example project.

Text Boxes

When used with the Text Box object, the Change event occurs when any change is made to the box's Text property. Since the text changes with each keystroke, the Change event occurs every time the user presses a key that generates an ASCII character. For example, if the user types the word "HELLO," the Change event happens five times, once for each keystroke. Assigning a string value to this property within your program will also initiate a Change event. A DDE conversation may also create a change in a text box, causing a Change event.

Chapter 13, Getting User Input, uses the Change event along with the Text Box object.

Comments

Although some objects do not have an associated Change event, you may code your program to react to a change in these objects' primary properties by using other events for the same purpose. For example, the Click event may be used to react to a change in the Check Box, Option Button, and List Box objects.

THE CHANGE PROJECT

Project Overview

The Change project demonstrates the use of the Change event. In this project you will create a form with a text box control and a label control. The text box's Change event will be used to display the number of characters in the box. Although this project uses only one of the controls that have a Change event, the concept behind using the Change event is similar for all other controls.

Assembling the Change Project Form

1. Create a new form (the Change form) and place on it the controls specified in Table 7-4.

Object	Property	Setting
Form	BorderStyle	3—Fixed Double
	Caption	Change Project
	Name	Form1
Text Box	BorderStyle	0—None
	Name	Text1
	Height	1605
	Left	0
	MultiLine	True
	ScrollBars	2—Vertical
	Text	(no text)
Label	BackColor	Light Gray—&H00C0C0C0
	BorderStyle	1—Fixed Single
	Caption	no characters
	Name	Label1

Table 7-4 Property settings for the Change project

2. Check the appearance of your form against Figure 7-1.

3. Enter the following code into the Text1_Change event. In this event the number of characters that reside in the text box is determined with the Len function.

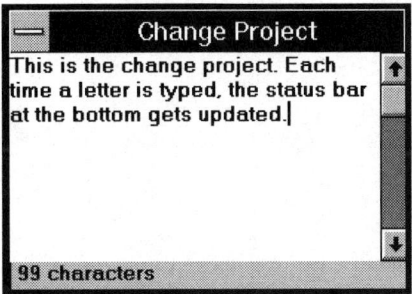

Figure 7-1 The Change project

```
Sub Text1_Change ()
    Dim charCount As Integer
    Dim countMsg As String
    charCount = Len(Text1.Text)
    countMsg = "characters"
    Select Case charCount
    Case 0
        countMsg = " no characters"
    Case 1
        countMsg = " one character"
    Case Else
        countMsg = Format$(CharCount, " ### ")
        countMsg = countMsg + "characters"
    End Select
    Label1.Caption = countMsg
End Sub
```

Running the Change Project

When the user enters some text in the text box, the Change event triggers. The Caption property of Label1 is set in the Text_Change event's code, based on the number of characters found. Because this event occurs any time a change is made to the text in Text1, the label caption gets updated immediately.

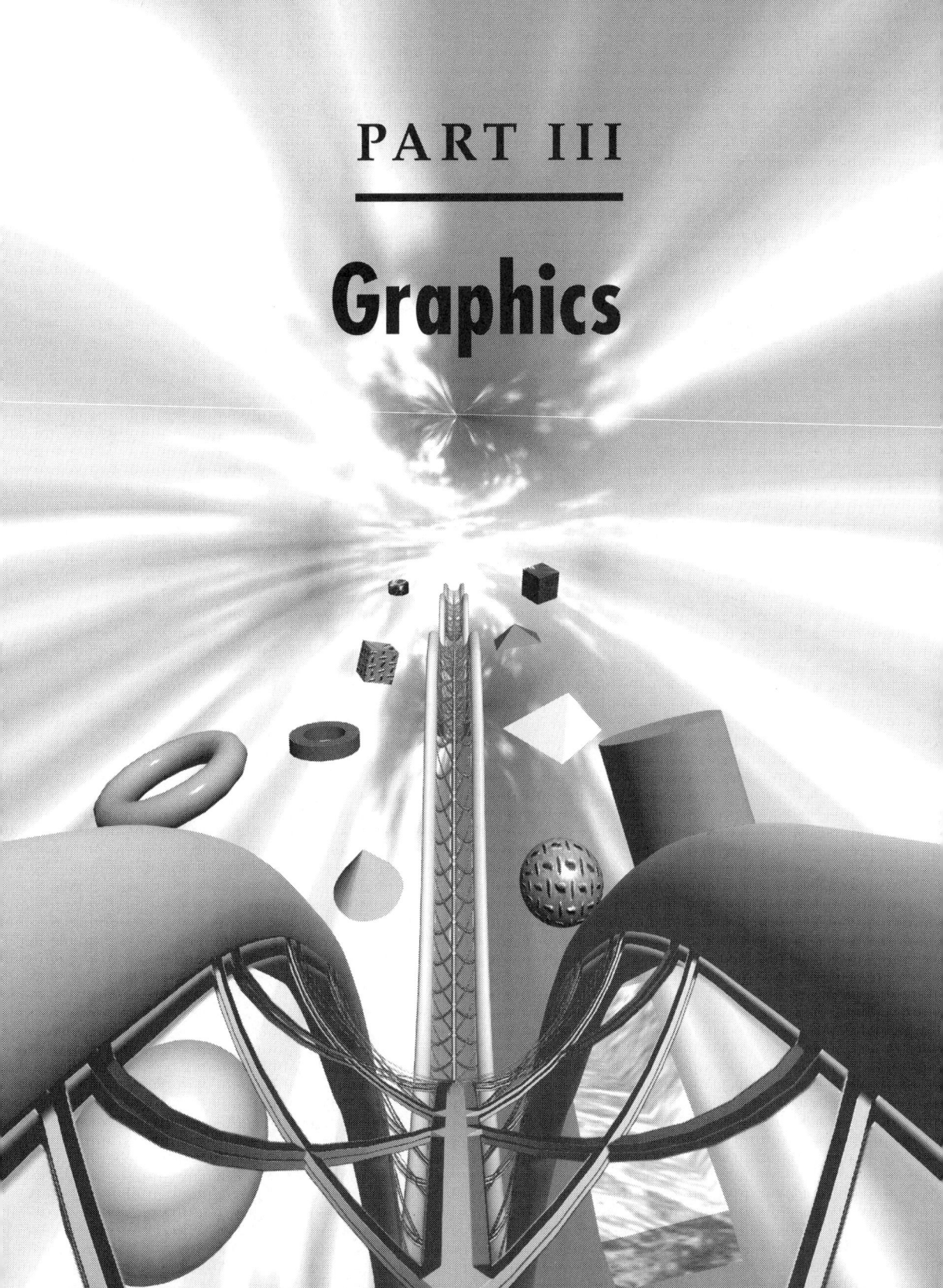

PART III

Graphics

8

GRAPHICS FUNDAMENTALS

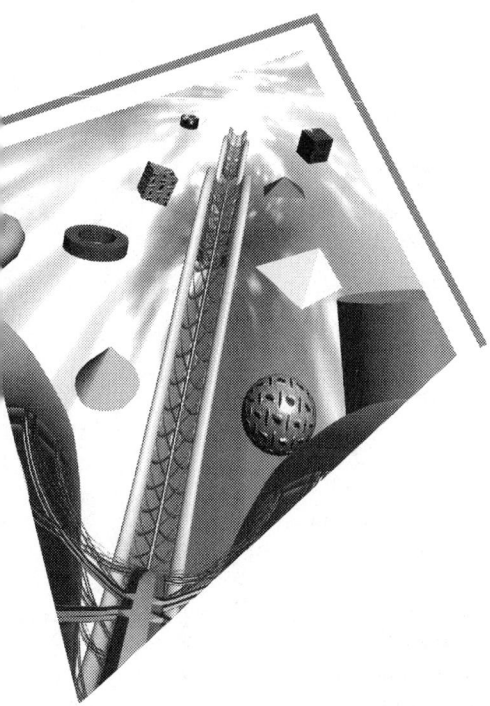

Visual Basic provides a variety of ways to easily create and manipulate graphics. This flexibility makes the process of generating special effects on the screen a simpler task than in many other languages. Users expect and demand graphics of Windows programs. Databases now show pictures instead of just words, spreadsheets have sophisticated drawing functions, and even word processors now support advanced graphics handling.

Graphics elements in Visual Basic applications fall into three main categories: displaying existing graphics, drawing new graphics, and using graphic elements in form design. Forms, picture boxes, and the new image control can all display existing graphics. You can create new graphics by drawing on forms and picture boxes, while the line and shape controls let you easily add graphics elements to forms during design.

This chapter covers the fundamentals of graphics in Visual Basic, focusing on those language elements common to all three graphics categories and providing an overview of how to use graphics in your applications. Chapter 9, The Coordinate System, covers the intricacies of properly specifying position and size; and Chapter 10, Drawing Shapes, goes into detail on how to draw graphics using both the graphics methods and the graphics controls.

GRAPHICS OVERVIEW

Forms, picture boxes, and the new image control can all display existing graphics files. Use the Picture property to load the graphics file. A loaded file may be in icon (*.ICO), Windows metafile (*.WMF), or bitmap (*.BMP) format. To display a file, choose the Picture property in the properties box. Double-click

331

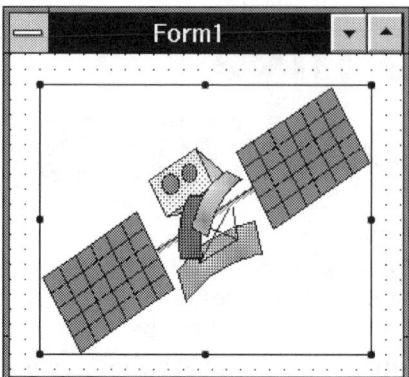

Figure 8-1 Picture box showing a
Windows metafile

on (picture) on the right side of the properties box. Select the file from the File
Open dialog box and press (ENTER) to display it on the screen. Figure 8-1 shows a
picture box displaying the contents of a file.

You normally set the contents of forms, picture boxes, and image controls at
design time. This way, the loaded file becomes a part of the executable file of the
program. You may also load them during runtime, if the picture needs to change
during program execution, by using the LoadPicture function. You can clear an
object of a loaded picture by using LoadPicture with no argument.

Forms and picture boxes handle more complex graphics operations than does
the image control. The image control is like a stripped-down picture box: it can
display existing graphics files, but cannot have the graphics methods used on it
to create new graphics. It uses fewer system resources than does the picture box,
and displays faster.

A variety of graphics methods can act on forms and picture boxes. Drawn
graphics are any shapes produced with the Circle, Line, or PSet graphics methods. The Circle method creates curved objects, including circles, ellipses (ovals),

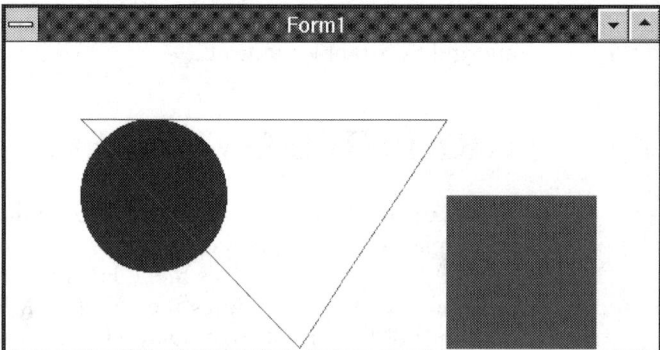

Figure 8-2 Drawn graphics on a form

Figure 8-3 The color palette lets you
pick and create colors

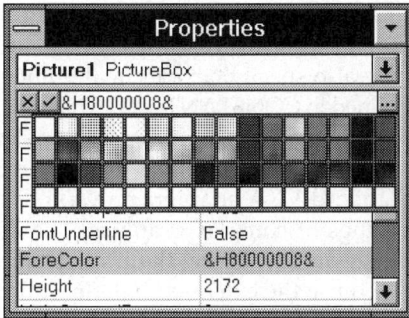

Figure 8-4 This mini-color palette
pops up in the Properties box to help
you quickly set color choices

and arches. The Line method generates lines or box objects, including straight lines, squares, rectangles, and triangles. The PSet method makes spots of varying size and color. Each of these methods produces graphics at runtime. Graphics drawn with these methods can appear on either forms or picture boxes. Use the Cls method to clear the object of any drawn graphics. Figure 8-2 displays a drawn circle, triangle, and box.

You may wish to incorporate graphics elements like lines or rectangles directly in your form design. Although you can use either an existing graphics file or graphics drawn at runtime, the new line and shape controls let you do this more easily. You can draw these controls directly on the form, just as you would with other controls like command buttons and text boxes. This lets you see exactly how the graphics elements look during the design process.

COLOR

Color affects the ways people respond to the elements on the screen. For example, red usually represents danger or warning (at least in most Western cultures). If a warning message is red, and all other text on the screen is black, your user's eye will naturally be drawn to the warning. Color can be a powerful agent in creating a beautiful and effective user interface. Careful and sparing use of color can help increase your user's comprehension and enjoyment; overuse of color elements can create a busy jumble that actually detracts from your application.

Each Visual Basic color has a unique hexadecimal code. Finding a particular color's code involves one of several possible methods. The color palette helps you interactively set color properties at design time. Figure 8-3 shows what the color palette looks like. Double-clicking on a color property setting in the properties box brings up a "mini-palette" that you can use to quickly pick out common colors. Figure 8-4 shows this palette in the ForeColor property.

An object's colors can change at runtime. The RGB and QBColor functions provide the necessary settings for the BackColor and ForeColor properties, and you may also specify hexadecimal numbers directly, or use the constants like those defined in CONSTANT.TXT. Chapter 5, Application Appearance, discusses the use of these functions and properties in detail in the BackColor and ForeColor entries.

Visual Basic, starting with version 2.0, provides support for 256 color palettes. Standard VGA adapters only allow 16 colors, which make for unrealistic renderings of complex graphics. The availability of 256 colors greatly enhances image quality. Visual Basic's implementation of this is really quite simple.

To use the extended palette, simply load a bitmap that contains the palette you'd like into a form, picture box, or image control. This bitmap can be quite small; even a single pixel would suffice. Three palettes ship with Visual Basic: RAINBOW.DIB, PASTEL.DIB, and BRIGHT.DIB. Table 8-1 summarizes this.

Device Independent Bitmap (*.DIB)	Description
RAINBOW.DIB	Standard range of all colors
PASTEL.DIB	Lighter colors, with lots of blues
BRIGHT.DIB	Bright colors

Table 8-1 Standard 256 color palettes that ship with Visual Basic

Once the picture control contains the palette, Windows attempts to match any requested color to the closest available color in the palette. Thus if a line specifies UltraMarine Blue, and the nearest color is Dark Blue, then Dark Blue gets drawn.

Note that there may be many palettes competing for priority. Over 16 million colors are possible, but only 256 can display at any time. The window with the focus generally gets the highest priority from Windows, so its colors are truest. Other windows may look strangely colored if they don't have the focus.

GRAPHICAL LAYERING

Graphical controls and the graphics methods appear on separate layers in a container. Think of a container (say, a form) as having three superimposed transparent layers. The topmost layer, the one closest to the user, contains nongraphical controls like command buttons, check boxes, or file controls. Underneath this is a middle layer containing the graphical controls (Line, Shape, and Image) as well as Labels. Finally, in the back layer, lies the drawing space for the container. All the graphical methods (Line, Circle, Cls, PSet, and so on) apply to this back layer. Objects on the front layers obscure whatever lies behind them. Figure 8-5 illustrates the normal layering arrangement. This means that both graphical and nongraphical controls will obscure graphics methods.

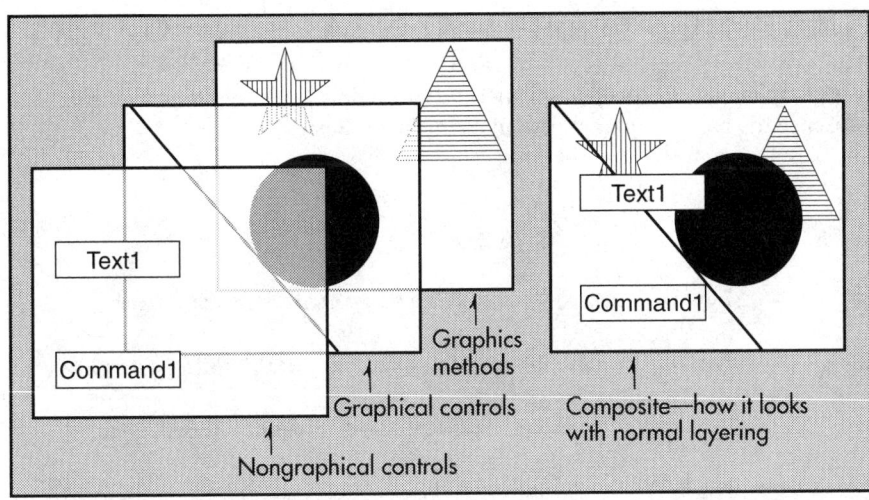

Figure 8-5 Normal layering

This normal layering may change with different settings of the AutoRedraw and ClipControls properties interacting with the Paint Event. Setting AutoRedraw to True always produces normal layering. Although this makes your life simpler, it may also reduce performance due to the large amounts of memory consumed by AutoRedraw. Setting ClipControls to False can speed up the display time for forms. Setting both AutoRedraw and ClipControls to False can have unpredictable results. See Table 8-2 for a summary of layering interactions. As you can see, keeping your graphics methods confined to Paint events always produces predictable, normal layering.

AutoRedraw	ClipControls	Paint Event	Layering Behavior
True	True	n/a	Normal layering
True	False	n/a	Normal layering
False	True	Graphics during Paint	Normal layering
		Graphics out of Paint	Middle and back layers mixed
False	False	Graphics during Paint	Normal layering
		Graphics out of Paint	All three layers mixed

Table 8-2 The possible layering interactions

335

GRAPHICS FUNDAMENTALS SUMMARY

Table 8-3 displays the properties, methods, functions, statements, and events that influence the basic display of graphics in Visual Basic.

Use or Set This...		To Do This...
AutoRedraw	Property	Determine whether a drawn object redisplays after uncovering it
ClipControls	Property	Determine what parts of a newly exposed object are repainted
Cls	Method	Wipe the surface of a picture box or form of all drawn objects
Image	Property	Determine the Microsoft Windows handle name assigned to an object
LoadPicture	Function	Change the graphics contents of a picture box or form
Paint	Event	Trigger when a portion of a form or picture box uncovers
Picture	Property	Determine the graphics object that initially appears in a form or picture box.
Point	Method	Discover the RGB colors of a particular point on a form or picture box
PSet	Method	Change the RGB colors of a particular point on a form or picture box
QBColor	Function	Determine the RGB values of a specified color
RGB	Function	Define the RGB values of an object in an expression
SavePicture	Statement	Save any graphical object on a form or picture box to a specified file name
Stretch	Property	Set or determine how the image control displays graphics
ZOrder	Method	Place an object in front of or in back of other objects

Table 8-3 Methods, properties, events, functions, and statements dealing with graphics

The following pages investigate these items in detail. At the end of this section, step-by-step directions explain how to assemble the Graphics project.

AUTOREDRAW PROPERTY

Objects Affected

Check	Clipboard	Combo	Command	CommonDlg
Data	Debug	Dir	Drive	File
▶ Form	Frame	Grid	Image	Label
Line	List	MDI Form	Menu	OLE
Option	▶ Picture	Printer	Screen	Scroll
Shape	Text	Timer		

Purpose

The AutoRedraw property indicates whether the drawn graphical objects on a form or picture box automatically redisplay when uncovered. Forms with the AutoRedraw property set to True automatically have their graphics redrawn when uncovered by another overlapping window or form, or when resized or restored to normal from being minimized. AutoRedraw may be set at either design time or runtime. Table 8-4 lists the arguments of the AutoRedraw property.

General Syntax

```
[form.]AutoRedraw [ = True | False]
[form!]Name.AutoRedraw [ = True | False]
```

Argument	Description
form	Name of the form
picture box	Name of the picture box
True	False	Value indicating the property's new setting

Table 8-4 Arguments of the AutoRedraw property

Example Syntax

```
Sub Form_Click ()
    ScaleMode = 5          'Displays a circle while the AutoRedraw property is True
    AutoRedraw = True      'and a triangle while AutoRedraw False. If the form is
    FillStyle = 0          'minimized and then restored on the screen, only the circle
```

(continued on next page)

(continued from previous page)

```
    FillColor = RGB(0, 0, 255)   'reappears.
    Circle (1, 1), .5
    AutoRedraw = False
    ForeColor = RGB(255, 0, 0)
    Line (0.5 , 0.5)-(2, 1)
    Line -(2, 2)
    Line -(0.5, 0.5)
End Sub
```

Description

The AutoRedraw property specifies whether a drawn object on a form or picture box redraws after being uncovered on the screen. A drawn object is an object produced with the Circle, Line, or PSet methods. There are two possible settings for this property, True (-1) and False (0).

An AutoRedraw property expression begins with the name of the picture box or form affected. If a Redraw property expression does not begin with the name of the picture box or form, then the active form's property changes. The example syntax provides no name for the object being drawn on, so the circle and triangle appear on the form and the AutoRedraw of the form changes.

The example syntax demonstrates this difference between the two settings of the AutoRedraw property. First, the Circle method draws a circle with the AutoRedraw property set to True (-1). Next, three Line method expressions create a triangle with the AutoRedraw property set to False (0). Figure 8-6 shows what this example should look like. Minimizing and normalizing the form results in erasing the triangle and restoring of the circle. Figure 8-7 shows what Form1 looks like without the triangle.

The Cls Method and BackColor Property

The Cls method and BackColor property of a form or picture box change their effects depending on the setting of the AutoRedraw property. The Cls method and changing the BackColor property will both remove any graphics generated with the AutoRedraw property of the picture box or form set to False (0). Graphics created with the AutoRedraw property set to True (-1) are erased only with a change to the BackColor property; the Cls method does not affect these. This distinction might prove useful when you'd like to have persistent graphics (say, grid lines on a graph) and still retain the capacity to have nonpersistent graphic elements (the actual graph) that could be erased and redrawn at will.

The Paint Event

The Paint event of a form and AutoRedraw property of a form or picture box have similar effects. Both redraw graphic elements with the normalizing, maximizing, or uncovering of a form or picture box. In fact, if the AutoRedraw property was true when the graphics were drawn, no Paint events are needed—Visual Basic handles the redrawing for you.

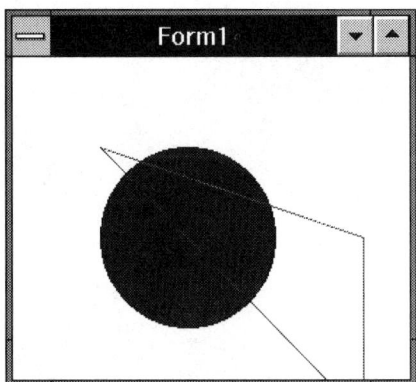

Figure 8-6 Example syntax graphics before minimizing the form

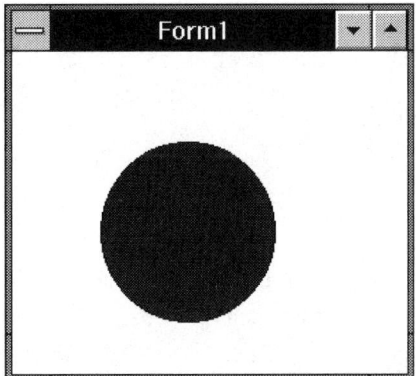

Figure 8-7 Example syntax graphics after minimizing and normalizing the form, showing how object drawn with AutoRedraw = False does not reappear

The ClipControls Property

Normal layering may change with different settings of the AutoRedraw and ClipControls properties interacting with the Paint event. Setting AutoRedraw to True always produces normal layering. Although this makes your life simpler, it may also reduce performance due to the large amounts of memory consumed by AutoRedraw. Setting ClipControls to False can speed up the display time for forms. Setting both AutoRedraw and ClipControls to False can have unpredictable results. See Table 8-2 for a summary of layering interactions.

The Refresh Method

When a form's AutoRedraw property is False, the Refresh method clears whatever graphics are on the screen. If the AutoRedraw property is True, then the Refresh property only removes those elements of the screen generated while the AutoRedraw property was False.

Example

The Graphics project at the end of this chapter adjusts the AutoRedraw property of the image control imagIcon and forms formGraphics and formScreen. The AutoRedraw property of both formGraphics and the image control imagIcon are set to True. This allows any graphics placed on either formGraphics or imagIcon to redisplay after being temporarily obscured. In order to allow periodic removal of the graphics on formScreen, formScreen's AutoRedraw property is False (0).

CLIPCONTROLS PROPERTY

Objects Affected

Check	Clipboard	Combo	Command	CommonDlg
Data	Debug	Dir	Drive	File
▶ Form	▶ Frame	Grid	Image	Label
Line	List	MDI Form	Menu	OLE
Option	▶ Picture	Printer	Screen	Scroll
Shape	Text	Timer		

Purpose

The ClipControls property determines if Windows repaints the entire object, or only newly exposed parts. This property can read and write at both design time and runtime. Tables 8-5 and 8-6 summarize the arguments of the ClipControls property.

General Syntax

```
[form.]ClipControls [ = boolean%]
[form!]Name.ClipControls [ = boolean%]
```

Argument	Description
form	Name property of the form
Name	Name property of the control
boolean%	True/False

Table 8-5 Arguments of the ClipControls property

boolean%	Meaning
True	(Default) Graphics methods in Paint events repaint the entire object; a clipping region is created
False	Graphics methods in Paint events repaint only newly exposed areas; no clipping region created

Table 8-6 Meanings of the boolean% argument in the ClipControls property

340

Example Syntax

```
Sub Command1_Click ()
    Picture1.ClipControls = Not Picture1.ClipControls
End Sub
```

Description

The ClipControls property determines if graphic methods in a Paint event repaint the entire object, or just those parts of the object that are newly exposed. It also determines if a *clipping region* is created for the object. A clipping region is like a mask that Windows keeps in memory that corresponds to the area covered by nongraphical controls like text boxes and command buttons. Setting ClipControls to False can speed up forms display and repainting.

The AutoRedraw Property

Normal layering may change with different settings of the AutoRedraw and ClipControls properties interacting with the Paint event. Setting AutoRedraw to True always produces normal layering. Although this makes your life simpler, it may also reduce performance due to the large amounts of memory consumed by AutoRedraw. Setting ClipControls to False can speed up the display time for forms. Setting both AutoRedraw and ClipControls to False can have unpredictable results. See Table 8-2 for a summary of layering interactions.

Example

The ClipControls property of the forms in the Graphics project are both set to False to increase performance.

CLS METHOD

Objects Affected

Check	Clipboard	Combo	Command	CommonDlg
Data	Debug	Dir	Drive	File
▶ Form	Frame	Grid	Image	Label
Line	List	MDI Form	Menu	OLE
Option	▶ Picture	Printer	Screen	Scroll
Shape	Text	Timer		

Purpose

The Cls method removes drawn graphics or text from an object on the screen. Table 8-7 explains the arguments of the Cls method.

General Syntax

```
[form.]Cls
[form!]Name.Cls
```

Argument	Description
form	Name property of the form
Name	Name property of the picture box; if not specified then acts on current form

Table 8-7 Arguments of the Cls method

Example Syntax

```
Sub Form_Click ()
    FillStyle = 6              'Objects placed on the screen will contain crosshatch lines
    FillColor = QBColor(4)     'Color inside a drawn object will be red
    X = ScaleWidth / 2         'X and Y place the circle in the center of the form
    Y = ScaleHeight / 2
    Radius = ScaleWidth / 4    'Radius defined as one quarter of width of form
    Print "Demo Text"          'Prints this text on screen
    Circle (X, Y), Radius      'Draws Circle
    Select Case AutoRedraw     'Displays message
        Case True
            MsgBox "Effects of Cls with AutoRedraw set to True."
        Case False
            MsgBox "Effects of Cls with AutoRedraw set to False."
    End Select
    AutoRedraw = Not AutoRedraw 'Flip AutoRedraw status
    Cls                        'Clears the form
End Sub
```

Description

The Cls method clears drawn text and graphics on a form or picture box. If a Cls method begins with the Name of a picture box, only the contents of the indicated picture box change. Cls method expressions that begin with no name or the Name of the form only affect the contents of a form. The example syntax doesn't specify a specific named object, so the currently active form is acted on.

This method clears all the objects drawn when AutoRedraw=False off of the indicated form or picture box. The Cls method has no effect on a form's controls and their contents. Loaded pictures do not disappear when the Cls method removes the drawn graphics on a form or picture box. Similarly, a Cls statement directed to the form has no effect on graphics placed on a picture box. Using the Cls method on a picture box has no effect on the graphics on the picture box's form.

The CurrentX and CurrentY Properties

The Cls method changes the CurrentX and CurrentY properties of a form or picture box to 0. Graphics created on a form or picture box with the AutoRedraw property set to True (-1) remain unaffected. In this case the Cls method works well as a means of easily resetting these coordinates.

The Picture Property

The use of the Cls method has no effect on a picture box's Picture property. The Cls method only affects drawn graphics. However, the Cls method clears any drawn graphics within a picture box that also has a loaded picture.

The BackColor Property and AutoRedraw Property

The Cls method and BackColor property of a form or picture box have different effects depending on the setting of the AutoRedraw property. The Cls method and changing the BackColor property will both remove any graphics generated with the AutoRedraw property of the picture box or form set to False (0). Graphics created with the AutoRedraw property at True (-1) are erased only with a change to the BackColor property; the Cls method does not affect these. This distinction might prove useful when you'd like to have persistent graphics (say, gridlines on a graph) and still retain the capacity to have nonpersistent graphic elements (the actual graph lines) that could be erased and redrawn at will.

Example

In the Graphics project at the end of this chapter, the Cls method clears formScreen of all drawn graphics when formScreen is double-clicked.

IMAGE PROPERTY

Objects Affected

Check	Clipboard	Combo	Command	CommonDlg
Data	Debug	Dir	Drive	File
▶ Form	Frame	Grid	Image	Label
Line	List	MDI Form	Menu	OLE
Option	▶ Picture	Printer	Screen	Scroll
Shape	Text	Timer		

Purpose

The Image property defines the value that Microsoft Windows automatically gives to an image on a picture box or form; it serves as a pointer to the memory position that contains the image. Windows sets the value returned by the Image property. It is not available at design time, and is read-only at runtime. Table 8-8 lists the arguments for the Image property.

General Syntax

```
[form].Image
[form!]Name.Image
```

Argument	Description
form	Name property of the affected form
Name	Name property of the affected picture box

Table 8-8 Arguments of the Image property

Example Syntax

```
Sub Command1_Click ()
    AutoRedraw = -1                  'Makes form1's AutoRedraw property True
    FillStyle = 0                    'Defines the object to be drawn as solid
    FillColor = QBColor(4)           'Defines the object to be drawn as red
    ScaleMode = 5                    'Defines dimensions as being measured in inches
    Print "This is a red circle"     'Prints test in top left corner of window
    Circle (1, 1), .5                'Draws a red circle on the form
    FillColor = QBColor(1)           'Defines the object to be drawn as blue
    Circle (3, 1), .5                'Draws a blue circle on the form
    Form2.Show                       'Displays second form on the screen
```

344

```
     Form2.AutoRedraw = -1        'Makes Form2's AutoRedraw property True
     Form2.Picture = Form1.Image 'Gives Form2 the same images as Form1
End Sub
```

Description

The Image property provides the value that Microsoft Windows uses to identify the text and generated graphics on a form or picture box. This value references all of the graphics and text that appear on the object. You can use this in API calls (see Appendix D, Windows API), as well as in saving graphics to disk or transferring graphics images from one control to another.

In the example syntax, the Image property transfers all of the graphics on Form1 to Form2 by setting Form2's Picture property equal to Form1's Image property. This shows that the Image property identifies all of the graphics on a form, not just one individual part of the graphics. As the Windows environment sometimes changes the value returned by the Image property, another variable should never store this value for later reference. Figure 8-8 shows what Form1 and Form2 might look like on the screen.

The Picture Property

The Picture property of a form or picture may be defined as equal to the Image property of another form or picture. This reproduces the same graphics on both

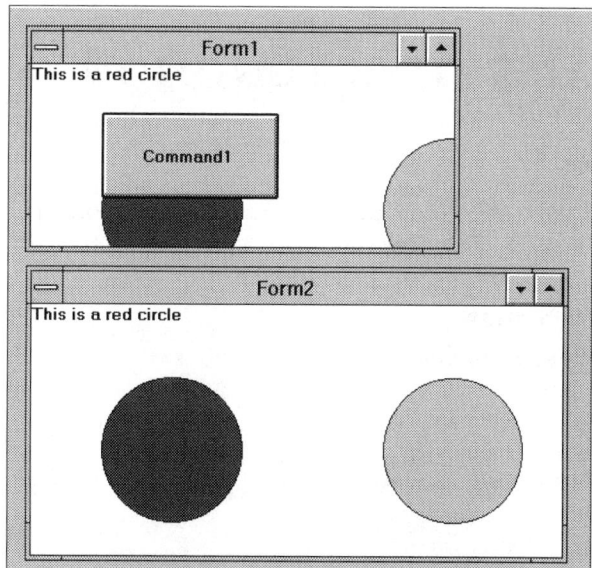

Figure 8-8 The Image property transferred a graphic image of Form1 to Form2

forms and picture boxes. In the example syntax, the Picture property of Form2 is assigned the Image property of Form1, thus making the same graphics appear on both forms. Notice that this change has no effect on the other properties of Form2. As a result the actual image that appears on Form1 appears on Form2 without changes to Form2's ScaleMode, FillColor, and FillStyle properties.

Example

In the Graphics project at the end of this chapter, the Image property serves as a means of saving the current graphics image on the screen. When the user clicks the form, the Form_Click event prompts the user to save the current image to a file. If the user responds "Yes," then the SavePicture statement accesses the Image property of formScreen to determine the Windows handle value. The code then uses this value to save the current contents of the screen to the bitmap file "~TEMP.BMP."

Comments

The Image property of a form or picture box may change during program execution. Do not define variables with this value.

LOADPICTURE FUNCTION

Purpose

The LoadPicture function places pictures in forms, image controls, and picture boxes. Table 8-9 explains the stringexpression$ argument.

General Syntax

```
LoadPicture([stringexpression$])
```

Argument	Description
stringexpression$	path and file name of the graphics file to load

Table 8-9 Argument of LoadPicture function

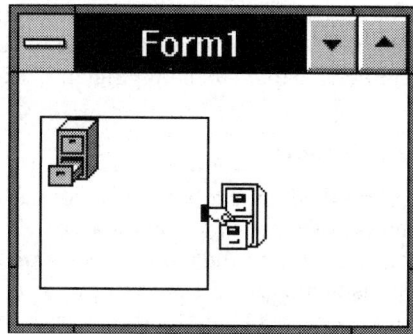

Figure 8-9 The LoadPicture function
lets you change graphics at runtime

Example Syntax

```
Sub Picture1_MouseDown (Button As Integer, Shift As Integer, X As Single, Y As Single)
    Picture1.Picture = LoadPicture("\VB\ICONS\OFFICE\FILES03B.ICO") 'open file cabinet
    Picture1.DragIcon = LoadPicture("\VB\ICONS\OFFICE\FILES04.ICO") 'hand taking file out
    Form1.Icon = LoadPicture("\VB\ICONS\MISC\FACE03.ICO")            'happy face
End Sub
```

Description

The LoadPicture function loads a graphic image into a form, image, or picture box. The loaded picture must be in bitmap (*.BMP), device independent bitmap (*.DIB), icon (*.ICO), run-length encoded (*.RLE), or Windows metafile (*.WMF) format. Stringexpression$ is the name of the picture file, with or without the extension. If the file is in the current search path or the same directory, then the extension is not necessary. In the example syntax, the icons appear with their full paths because none of the icons are in the path and would otherwise generate an error. Use LoadPicture without stringexpression$ (that is, load nothing) to clear the contents of the object.

The Icon, DragIcon, and Picture properties are all definable at runtime with this function. This function overrides the initial setting of these properties.

In the example syntax, the LoadPicture function redefines all three of these properties to signify the beginning of a drag operation. The picture box becomes an open file cabinet to signify the beginning of a drag operation. See Figure 8-9 for a picture of what the example syntax should look like.

The DragIcon Property

Define the DragIcon of a control at runtime with a LoadPicture function similar to the one in the example syntax. This icon displays when a drag operation begins until the drag operation ends. This permits the program to signify to the user the

347

type of operation taking place. For example, the DragIcon changes to an open file folder or a disk to signify when a file or an entire disk copies from one place to another. Chapter 15, Dragging and Dropping, goes into this in more detail.

The Icon Property

Define the Icon property of a control at runtime with a LoadPicture function similar to the one used in the example syntax. This icon represents a minimized form. Changing the Icon property of a form might specify what type of operation is taking place. For example, a communications program might change the icon property of a dialer directory form to a phone off the hook when the dialer dials a number. Chapter 5, Application Appearance, covers the Icon property in more detail.

The Picture Property

The LoadPicture function defines the Picture property of a form, picture box, or image control at runtime in the same way as the example syntax. Either the AutoRedraw of the form or the Picture must be True, or the changes must occur within a Paint event for it to be immediately apparent. For example, the icon displayed in the Picture1 control box does not change unless the AutoRedraw property is True. Note that the grid control also has a Picture property that lets you load graphics images into individual cells.

Example

In the Graphics project at the end of this chapter, the LoadPicture function loads in all the icons to represent the different kinds of screen blankers. The Form_Load event first creates a control array of image controls, then LoadPicture reads in the appropriate icons.

PAINT EVENT

Objects Affected

Check	Clipboard	Combo	Command	CommonDlg
Data	Debug	Dir	Drive	File
▶ Form	Frame	Grid	Image	Label
Line	List	MDI Form	Menu	OLE
Option	▶ Picture	Printer	Screen	Scroll
Shape	Text	Timer		

Purpose

The Paint event defines what actions take place when uncovering a previously obscured part of a form or picture box. Either restoring a minimized form or uncovering an obscured form triggers a Paint event. This event only applies to generated graphics and does not affect the appearance of the controls on a form. Table 8-10 gives the arguments to the Paint event.

General Syntax

```
Sub Form_Paint ()
Sub Name_Paint ([Index As Integer])
```

Argument	Description
Form	'Form' indicates the paint event of the current form
Name	Name property of the affected picture box

Table 8-10 Arguments of the Paint event

Example Syntax

```
Sub Form_Click ()
    Refresh                      'Triggers the Paint event
End Sub

Sub Form_Paint ()
    Static Num As Integer        'Retain value of Num
    X = ScaleWidth / 2           'Define X as half of width of form
    Y = ScaleHeight / 2          'Define Y as half of height of form
    Radius = ScaleWidth / 4      'Define Radius as 1/4 of width of form
    FillStyle = 0                'Objects drawn will be solid
    Num = Num + 1                'Increment the variable Num
    Select Case Num
        Case 1                                 'Num = 1
            FillColor = QBColor(0)                      'FillColor is black
            Circle (X, Y), Radius, , -6.283, -1.571     'Draw part of a circle
        Case 2                                 'Num = 2
            FillColor = QBColor(1)                      'FillColor is blue
            Circle (X, Y), Radius, , -1.571, -3.142     'Draw part of a circle
        Case 3                                 'Num = 3
            FillColor = QBColor(2)                      'FillColor is green
            Circle (X, Y), Radius, , -3.142, -4.713     'Draw part of a circle
        Case 4                                 'Num = 4
            FillColor = QBColor(3)                      'FillColor is cyan
            Circle (X, Y), Radius, , -4.713, -6.283     'Draw part of a circle
        Case 5                                 'Num = 5
            FillColor = QBColor(4)                      'FillColor is red
```

(continued on next page)

(continued from previous page)

```
                Circle (X, Y), Radius          'Draw a red circle
          Case 6                         'Num = 6
             Num = 0                          'Reset Num for the next round
       End Select
End Sub
```

Description

The Paint event may contain actions that place graphics objects on the screen. A Paint event triggers when the form loads, at the uncovering of a form, or when a minimized form changes to normalized or maximized. This event normally reproduces the same graphic image or images on a form or picture box. In some cases however, it can produce a totally new graphics image. In the example syntax, triggering the Paint event by each click on the form produces a new portion of a circle on the screen.

Graphics from the Circle, Line, PSet, and Print Methods

The Paint event directly affects the production of the graphics and text effects produced by the Circle, Line, PSet, and Print methods. With the AutoRedraw property of a form or picture box set to False, the Paint event reproduces any expressions that place graphics or text on the form or picture box. Otherwise, hidden portions of drawn graphics on forms and controls do not reappear when uncovered.

The AutoRedraw Property

The AutoRedraw property and Paint event share similar tasks. Both determine what happens to a form when loaded or uncovered. The example syntax demonstrates one very important difference. A form with its AutoRedraw property set to True (-1) only reproduces the portions of the screens drawn while that property was True. This is in direct contrast to the example syntax showing that the Paint event can process actions that produce entirely different graphics with each triggering of the Paint event.

The ClipControls Property

Normal layering may change with different settings of the AutoRedraw and ClipControls properties interacting with the Paint event. Setting AutoRedraw to True always produces normal layering. Although this makes your life simpler, it may also reduce performance due to the large amounts of memory consumed by AutoRedraw. Setting ClipControls to False can speed up the display time for forms. Setting both AutoRedraw and ClipControls to False can have unpredictable results. See Table 8-2 for a summary of layering interactions.

The Refresh Method

The Refresh method triggers the Paint event of a form. This method represents a means of activating a Paint event when it is necessary without the normal criteria for generating one. In the example syntax, the Refresh method is in the Form_Click event so that the Paint event triggers with each clicking of the form. With this setup, the image on the form changes under the control of the user.

The Load, Resize, Paint, and GotFocus Events

If there is more than one event attached to a particular control, they process in the following order: Load, Resize, Paint, and GotFocus. This is an important point to keep in mind if any of the actions that take place in one event depend on actions in another event. For example, a data entry form for an address book would cause an error if the Load event disables the Address1 text box and the GotFocus event tries to use it.

Example

The Graphics project at the end of this chapter demonstrates the operation of the Paint event as part of formScreen's Click event. When the Form_Click event triggers, the Refresh method activates the Paint event of formScreen.

PICTURE PROPERTY

Objects Affected

Check	Clipboard	Combo	Command	CommonDlg
Data	Debug	Dir	Drive	File
▶ Form	Frame	▶ Grid	▶ Image	Label
Line	List	MDI Form	Menu	▶ OLE
Option	▶ Picture	Printer	Screen	Scroll
Shape	Text	Timer		

Purpose

The Picture property indicates what image appears on a form, grid cell, image control, OLE client, or picture box. This property is definable at either design time or runtime and defaults to display nothing. Table 8-11 summarizes the arguments of the Picture property

General Syntax

```
[form.]Picture [ = picture]
[form!]Name.Picture [ = picture]
```

Argument	Description
Name	Name property of the form, image, OLE client, or picture box
Picture	Picture property setting

Table 8-11 Arguments of the Picture property

Example Syntax

```
Sub Picture1.Click
        Picture1.AutoRedraw = True              'Objects redrawn when uncovered
        X = Picture1.ScaleWidth /2              'X equals width of picture box
        Y = Picture1.ScaleHeight / 2            'Y equals height of picture box
        Radius = Picture1.ScaleWidth /4         'Radius equals picture box's width
        Picture1.FillStyle = 0                  'Solid FillStyle
        Picture1.Fillcolor = QBColor(4)         'Fill color is red
        If Command1.Caption = "Icon" Then       'If the caption is "Icon"
                Picture1.Picture = LoadPicture("\VB\ICONS\MISC\FACE03.ICO") 'smiling face
                Command1.Caption = "Circle"
        ElseIf Command1.Caption = "Circle" Then 'If the caption is "Circle"
                Picture1.Circle (X, Y),Radius       'Draw a circle
                Command1.Caption = "Square"
        ElseIf Command1.Caption = "Square" Then 'If the caption is "Square"
                Picture1.Line(500,500) - Step (1000,1000), , BF  'Draw a square
                Command1.Caption = "Other"
        ElseIf Command1.Caption = "Other" Then  'If the caption is "Other"
                Picture2.Picture = Picture1.Image   'Makes the Picture2 box the same
                Command1.Caption = "Icon"           'as the Picture1 picture box
        End If
End Sub
```

Description

The Picture property determines the graphic image that displays on a form or picture box. A loaded picture must be in bitmap (*.BMP), icon (*.ICO), run-length encoded (*.RLE), or Windows metafile (*.WMF) format. A Picture property contains the full path of the picture file, with or without its extension. If the file is in the current search path or the same directory, then the extension is not necessary. In the example syntax, the picture box displays a circle, a square, or an icon with each clicking of the picture. This demonstrates the full range of graphics that may be displayed on a picture box or form.

The Image Property

In order to place the same picture in one picture box as in another, redefine the Picture property of a picture box with the Image property of another. Microsoft Windows gives every graphic image in Visual Basic a unique value returned by the Image property of a picture box or form. In the example syntax, the Picture property of Picture2 is set to equal the Image property of Picture1. This has reproduced all of the graphic images of Picture1 in the Picture2 picture box.

Example

In the Graphics project at the end of this chapter, the Picture property of the image control imagIcon changes according to the currently selected blanker option on screen.

POINT METHOD

Objects Affected

Check	Clipboard	Combo	Command	CommonDlg
Data	Debug	Dir	Drive	File
▶ Form	Frame	Grid	Image	Label
Line	List	MDI Form	Menu	OLE
Option	▶ Picture	Printer	Screen	Scroll
Shape	Text	Timer		

Purpose

The Point method returns the RGB hexadecimal value of the color of a specified point on a form or picture box. This method only works at runtime. Table 8-12 displays the arguments of the Point method.

General Syntax

```
[form.]Point(x!, y!)
[form!][Name.]Point(x!, y!)
```

Argument	Description
form	Name property of the form
Name	Name of picture box. If not given, defaults to current form
x!	Horizontal coordinate of the point on the object
y!	Vertical coordinate of the point on the object

Table 8-12 Argument of Point method

Example Syntax

```
Sub Form_Click ()
     AutoRedraw = True         'Sets form's AutoRedraw property to True
     FillStyle = 0             'Sets drawn object to solid
     FillColor = QBColor(0)    'Sets drawn object to black
     X = ScaleWidth / 2        'Sets X equal to half of the width of the form
     Y = ScaleHeight / 2       'Sets Y equal to half of the height of the form
     Radius = ScaleWidth / 4   'Sets radius equal to 1/4 of the width of the form
     Circle (X, Y), Radius     'Draws a circle on the form
End Sub

Sub Command1_Click
     BackColor = Point (CurrentX, CurrentY)    'Changes the background color to circle's color
End Sub
```

Description

The Point method returns the color of a place on a form or picture box. Both the x and y coordinates represent values of measurements according to the ScaleMode measurement system of the container. If x! or y! lies outside the bounds of the object, the Point method returns -1.

In the example syntax, the background color of the form changes to match the circle's color when the user presses the command button. The Point method finds the color of the current coordinates on the form in the center of the black circle. This results in changing the background color of the form to black. With no Name provided, the color of the form changes.

The CurrentX and CurrentY Properties

The combination of Point method and the CurrentX and CurrentY properties provides the color of the current coordinates on a form or picture box. The current coordinates begin in the upper-left corner of the form or picture box. Each drawn object changes the coordinates based on where the object appears. As shown in the example syntax, the CurrentX and CurrentY properties directly define the x and y coordinates of the Point method. Since the CurrentX and CurrentY coordinates are already in the center of the drawn circle, the coordinates do not change. This returns the color of the circle in the center of the form.

Example

In the Graphics project at the end of this section, the timeBlanker event uses the Point method to reset the BackColor property of formScreen. This is done with a Point method expression that uses the CurrentX and CurrentY coordinates to determine the color of the current point on the form. Since the BackColor property of the form is already white, the background remains white. Although there is no change to the color of the background of the form, the redefinition of the BackColor of the form has erased all of the graphics images on the screen. If the AutoRedraw property of the form is True, then the graphics image is unaffected.

PSET METHOD

Objects Affected

Check	Clipboard	Combo	Command	CommonDlg
Data	Debug	Dir	Drive	File
▶ Form	Frame	Grid	Image	Label
Line	List	MDI Form	Menu	OLE
Option	▶ Picture	▶ Printer	Screen	Scroll
Shape	Text	Timer		

Purpose

The PSet method sets the color of a point on a form, picture box, or Printer object. The DrawWidth property of the form, picture box, or Printer object determines the size of this point. This method only works at runtime. Table 8-13 lists the arguments of the PSet method.

General Syntax

```
[form.]PSet [ Step ] (x!, y!) [ , color&]
[form!]Name.PSet [ Step ] (x!, y!) [ , color&]
Printer.PSet [ Step ] (x!, y!) [ , color&]
```

Argument	Description
form	Name property of the form
Name	Name of picture box
Printer	'Printer' for Printer object
Step	x and y coordinates measure relative distance from the current coordinates on the object
x!, y!	Horizontal and vertical distance from upper-left corner of the object or the current coordinates
color&	Hexadecimal value representing the created point's color

Table 8-13 Arguments of PSet method

Example Syntax

```
Sub Timer1_Timer ()                     'set timer's interval to something other than zero
    Static Color As Integer             'remember the last color we drew
    If Color <> 15 Then                 'if we haven't run out of QB colors,
        Color = Color + 1               'cycle up to the next color
    Else
        Color = 0                       'back to black
    End If
    X = Int((ScaleWidth - (ScaleWidth / 20)) * Rnd + (ScaleWidth / 20))      'random x
    Y = Int((ScaleHeight - (ScaleHeight / 20)) * Rnd + (ScaleHeight / 20))   'random y
    DrawWidth = 20                      'big dot
    PSet (X, Y), QBColor(Color)         'now plot the big random dot
End Sub
```

Description

The PSet method places a point of color (in RGB hexadecimal format) on a specified point of a form, picture box, or Printer object. If there is no specified object, then the point of color appears on the current form. This method requires both the x! and y! coordinates in single precision.

The Step option makes x! and y! a relative distance from the last plotted point, rather than an absolute coordinate. Without Step, the x! and y! coordinates measure the distance from the upper-left corner of the object. In the example syntax, the PSet method places points with differing colors at absolute, random locations on the screen.

The example syntax uses the QBColor function to redefine the color of the point with each generation of the Timer1 event. A static variable named Color

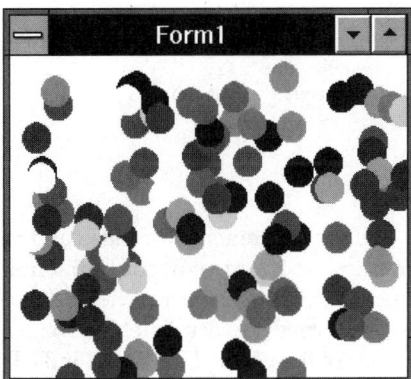

Figure 8-10 The PSet method plots individual points

keeps the last value in the QBColor function between each generation of the Timer1 event. This value increments by one with each execution of the Timer1 event until it reaches 15. See Figure 8-10 for a picture of this example.

The RGB and QBColor Functions

Set the color of a PSet method expression with either the RGB or QBColor functions. For specialized color combinations, use the RGB function. The RGB function provides the ability to set the red, green, and blue elements of a color to produce its hexadecimal value. If one of the standard colors is acceptable, then the QBColor function provides a simple means of setting the color with one value. Set a QBColor function with a value between 0 and 15 as used in Quick BASIC and other versions of Microsoft BASIC. See the BackColor and ForeColor reference entries in Chapter 5, Application Appearance, for more about colors.

The DrawMode and DrawWidth Properties

The PSet method also produces points of varying sizes and colors with changes to DrawMode and DrawWidth properties. These properties control the size and effect of the graphics generated with the PSet method. The next example varies the size of the circles by scaling DrawWidth to a random value. Figure 8-11 shows what this example might look like.

```
Sub Timer1_Timer ()                            'set timer's interval to something other than zero
    Static Color As Integer                    'remember the last color we drew
    If Color <> 15 Then                        'if we haven't run out of QB colors,
        Color = Color + 1                      'cycle up to the next color
    Else
        Color = 0                              'back to black
    End If
    X = Int((ScaleWidth - (ScaleWidth / 20)) * Rnd + (ScaleWidth / 20))        'random x
```

(continued on next page)

(continued from previous page)

```
    Y = Int((ScaleHeight - (ScaleHeight / 20)) * Rnd + (ScaleHeight / 20))  'random y
    DrawMode = Int((16 - (1)) * Rnd + (1))          'random mode and
    DrawWidth = Int((100 - (20)) * Rnd + (20))      'random dot size
    PSet (X, Y), QBColor(Color)            'now plot the truly random dot
End Sub
```

The CurrentX and CurrentY Properties

The CurrentX and CurrentY properties are useful replacements for the x! and y! arguments of the PSet method. These properties return the current horizontal and vertical position on the form, picture box, or Printer object. When a form loads, the default position is in the upper-right corner the form, picture box, or Printer object. This position changes with the use of the Circle, Line, PSet, and Cls methods according to the new coordinates that they set. Using CurrentX and CurrentY lets you continue drawing where the previous graphics method left off.

Example

In the Graphics project at the end of this chapter, the PSet method generates spots of color on the screen with the Spots option selected on formGraphics. A spot of color appears on the screen based on the random setting of the X and Y coordinate variables and the Color variable. The random setting of the DrawWidth property determines the size of the spot. A series of color spots of random size appears on the screen at random locations.

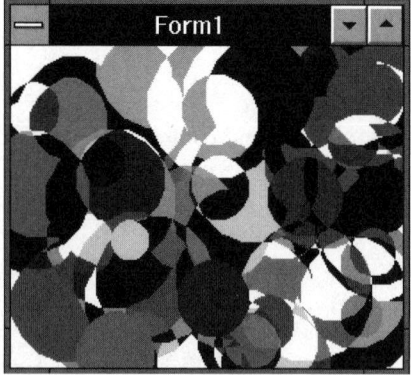

Figure 8-11 What the DrawWidth and DrawMode example should look like: random-sized dots!

QBCOLOR FUNCTION

Purpose

The QBColor function helps define the color of an object on the screen. An object defined with this function is one of 16 possible colors. These colors simulate the 16 standard colors of older DOS-based programming languages. Table 8-14 lists each possible value and the color it defines.

General Syntax

```
QBColor(qbcolor%)
```

qbcolor%	Color
0	Black
1	Blue
2	Green
3	Cyan
4	Red
5	Magenta
6	Yellow
7	White (Light Gray)
8	Gray
9	Light Blue
10	Light Green
11	Light Cyan
12	Light Red

(continued on next page)

qbcolor%	Color
13	Light Magenta
14	Light Yellow
15	Bright White

Table 8-14 List of the colors returned by QBColor

Example Syntax

```
Sub Form_Click ()
    AutoRedraw = True          'Makes sure graphics are drawn immediately
    Cls                        'Clears the screen
    ScaleHeight = 4            'Divides height of form into four parts
    ScaleWidth = 4             'Divides width of form into four parts
    Color = 0                  'Start with black
    For H = 0 To 3             'Draw a grid of 16 colors, 4 high
        For W = 0 To 3         'by 4 wide
            Line (W, H)-(W + 1, H + 1), QBColor(Color), BF
            Color = Color + 1 'next color
        Next W
    Next H
End Sub
```

Description

The QBColor function returns the hexadecimal color code of a specified number. Each number specified in a QBColor function must be between 0 and 15. These numbers represent preset color combinations of RGB values that may be assigned to properties, methods, and statements that use color. In the example syntax, the QBColor function provides the colors of the boxes drawn with the Line method.

Every color is a combination of RGB color values that make up its hexadecimal value. In the example syntax, all 16 of the possible color choices appear in a 16-box grid. Each color displays in numerical order from left to right and top to bottom.

The FillColor, BackColor, and ForeColor Properties

The QBColor function can provide the hexadecimal color for the FillColor, BackColor, and ForeColor properties. In the next example, the background color of a form changes to blue. The code references the new property setting with the next clicking of the form to change the color back to white.

```
Sub Form_Click
    If BackColor = QBColor(15)        'Checks if BackColor is white
        BackColor -=QBColor(1)        'BackColor is blue
    ElseIf BackColor = QBColor(1)     'Checks if BackColor is blue
        BackColor = QBColor(15)       'BackColor is white
    End If
End Sub
```

Example

In the Graphics project at the end of this chapter, the QBColor function sets the BackColor and ForeColor properties of the forms and the color of spots, circles, squares, and lines. The Form_Click and Form_Paint events of formScreen resets its BackColor property to white.

RGB FUNCTION

Purpose

The RGB function provides a means of defining the color of an object on the screen. Each value in an RGB function expression represents the amount of red, green, and blue contained in the displayed color. Table 8-15 lists some common colors with the corresponding red, green, and blue arguments.

General Syntax

```
RGB(red%, green%, blue%)
```

Color	Red Value	Green Value	Blue Value
Black	0	0	0
Red	255	0	0
Green	0	255	0
Yellow	0	255	255
Blue	0	0	255
Magenta	255	0	255

(continued on next page)

(continued from previous page)

Color	Red Value	Green Value	Blue Value
Cyan	0	255	255
White	255	255	255
Light Gray	192	192	192
Dark Gray	128	128	128

Table 8-15 Values of common colors in RGB format

Example Syntax

```
Sub Timer1_Timer ()
    AutoRedraw = True                       'Makes sure graphics are drawn immediately
    Cls                                     'Clears the screen
    ScaleHeight = 4                         'Divides height of form into four parts
    ScaleWidth = 4                          'Divides width of form into four parts
    For H = 0 To 3                          'Draw a grid of 16 colors, 4 high
        For W = 0 To 3                      'by 4 wide
            red = Int(256 * Rnd)            'random red, 0-255
            green = Int(256 * Rnd)          'random green, 0-255
            blue = Int(256 * Rnd)           'random blue, 0-255
            Color = RGB(red, green, blue)   'make the color
            Line (W, H)-(W + 1, H + 1), Color, BF
        Next W
    Next H
End Sub
```

Description

The RGB function returns the hexadecimal value of the combination of three color values. Each of the numbers in a RGB function is between 0 and 255. Thus there are 256x256x256 possible color combinations, or a total of 16,777,216 possible distinct colors. Many video cards do not support this many colors directly. Windows handles this for you by automatically dithering the available onscreen colors to approximate the actual color you specify. See the ForeColor and BackColor entries in Chapter 5, Application Appearance, for more details and a comparison of using the RGB function with QBColor or directly setting the color values with a hexadecimal number or a constant.

In the example syntax, the RGB function defines the color argument of the Line method expression that generates the squares of colors on the screen. Each box has completely random settings for the Red, Green, and Blue components of its color. Make sure the timer interval is set to something other than 0 to make the colors cycle properly.

Example

The Graphics project at the end of this chapter uses the RGB function with the selection of the option box labeled Blank Screen. In this case the timeBlanker event changes the BackColor of the form to black with an RGB function definition.

SAVEPICTURE STATEMENT

Objects Affected

Check	Clipboard	Combo	Command	CommonDlg
Data	Debug	Dir	Drive	File
▶ Form	Frame	Grid	▶ Image	Label
Line	List	MDI Form	Menu	OLE
Option	▶ Picture	Printer	Screen	Scroll
Shape	Text	Timer		

Purpose

The SavePicture statement saves a picture drawn on a picture box, image control, or form to a new file. The picture saves in the same format it was loaded in; image files and drawn graphics are always saved in bitmap (*.BMP) format. Table 8-16 lists the arguments of the SavePicture statement.

General Syntax

```
SavePicture picture, stringexpression$
```

Argument	Description
picture	Picture or Image property of the object
stringexpression$	path and file name of the file to save

Table 8-16 Arguments of SavePicture statement

Example Syntax

```
Sub Command1_Click ()
    AutoRedraw = True        'Ensures that graphics remain on the form
    ScaleWidth = 4           'Draws a square on the screen
    ScaleHeight = 4
```

(continued on next page)

(continued from previous page)

```
      X = 1
      Y = 1
      Line (X, Y)-(X + 2, Y + 2), QBColor(1), BF
      SavePicture Image, "C:\VB\SQUARE.BMP"   'Save the picture
End Sub
```

Description

The SavePicture statement saves the current contents of an image control, picture box, or form to a file. If the picture to save comes from a loaded file, this statement saves the file in its original format. If the picture to save comes from drawn graphics, or is from the image control, then the save format is always a bitmap (*.BMP). The path of the file is optional.

A SavePicture statement's picture argument identifies exactly which graphics to save with the Image property of the form or picture box. The example syntax saves the current contents of the form to the file SQUARE.BMP.

Example

In the Graphics project at the end of this chapter, the SavePicture statement saves the drawn graphics on the screen. Until the user clicks the form with the mouse, the screen either remains black or keeps generating spots, circles, squares, or lines on the screen. Clicking the form displays a message box that asks whether to save the current image on the screen to a file. If the user responds "Yes," then the SavePicture statement uses the Image property of formScreen to determine the Windows handle value. Using this value, SavePicture statement saves the current picture to the bitmap file "~TEMP.BMP".

Comments

The SavePicture statement does not include any of the controls on the form.

STRETCH PROPERTY

Objects Affected

Check	Clipboard	Combo	Command	CommonDlg
Data	Debug	Dir	Drive	File
Form	Frame	Grid	▶ Image	Label
Line	List	MDI Form	Menu	OLE
Option	Picture	Printer	Screen	Scroll
Shape	Text	Timer		

Purpose

The Stretch property determines if the image control stretches to fit the picture, or if the picture stretches to fit the image control. You can read and write with this property at both runtime and design time. Tables 8-17 and 8-18 summarize the arguments of the Stretch property.

General Syntax

```
[form!]Name.Stretch [ = boolean%]
```

Argument	Description
form	Name property of the form
Name	Name property of the image control
boolean%	True/False

Table 8-17 Arguments of the Stretch property

boolean%	Meaning
True	Picture resized to fit the image control
False	(Default) Image control resized to fit the picture

Table 8-18 Meanings of the boolean% argument in the Stretch property

Example Syntax

```
Sub Check1_Click ()
    If Check1.Value = 0 Then
        Image1.Stretch = True
    Else
        Image1.Stretch = False
    End IF
End Sub
```

Description

The Stretch property determines if the image control stretches to fit the picture, or if the picture stretches to fit the image control. If Stretch is True, then resizing the image control also resizes the picture.

Stretching Windows metafiles (*.WMF) does not adversely affect the image quality, as these kinds of images are based on vectors and can be arbitrarily resized. Stretching a bitmap graphic (like a *.BMP) can degrade the image quality. Windows will attempt the smoothest stretch it can, but you will often have moiré patterns and excessive "jaggies" if the stretch is by something other than an exact multiple of the original image size.

Example

The chapter project uses an image control to display an icon of the currently selected blanker type. Stretch is set to True in order to enlarge the small icon.

ZORDER METHOD

Objects Affected

▶ Check	Clipboard	▶ Combo	▶ Command	CommonDlg
▶ Data	Debug	▶ Dir	▶ Drive	▶ File
▶ Form	▶ Frame	▶ Grid	▶ Image	▶ Label
▶ Line	▶ List	▶ MDI Form	Menu	▶ OLE
▶ Option	▶ Picture	Printer	Screen	▶ Scroll
▶ Shape	▶ Text	Timer		

Purpose

The ZOrder method places an object in front of or behind other objects within its graphical level. You can read and write with this method at both design time and runtime. Tables 8-19 and 8-20 summarize the arguments of the ZOrder method.

General Syntax

```
[form.]ZOrder order%
[form!]Name.ZOrder order%
```

Argument	Description
form	Name property of the form
Name	Name property of the control
order%	Bring to front or send to back

Table 8-19 Arguments of the ZOrder method

order%	CONSTANT.TXT	Meaning
0	BRINGTOFRONT	(Default) Place this control or form in front of all others
1	SENDTOBACK	Place this control or form in back of all others

Table 8-20 Meanings of the order% argument in the ZOrder method

Example Syntax

```
Sub Timer1_Timer
    Static I As Integer             'remember what iteration we're on
    Image1(I).ZOrder BRINGTOFRONT   'flip through the image control array stack
    I = I + 1                       'increment which image will display next time...
    If I = 10 Then I = 0            '10 images; reset if cycled through all 10
End Sub
```

Purpose

The ZOrder method lets you control the way in which controls layer. Each object has x and y coordinates (that is, Left and Top); the ZOrder method takes this to the third dimension of a z coordinate. If several different controls or forms overlap each other in the x-y plane, you can use ZOrder to determine which displays in front of the other. You can set the ZOrder of a control at design time by using the Edit menu's Bring To Front or Send To Back commands.

The example syntax rotates through a stack of image controls, using the ZOrder method. If each image control had a slightly different picture in it, this would produce a simple animation.

ZOrder will only change the order of the controls on the layer to which they belong. All graphics controls (shapes, lines, image controls, and labels) exist on the second layer; all nongraphical controls (like command buttons and text boxes) exist on the front layer. The front layer will always obscure the second layer, and both the front and second layers will always obscure the third layer where the graphics methods operate. ZOrder will arrange the controls on each layer but not between layers. See the section on layering at the beginning of this chapter for more details.

The ZOrder method rearranges the display order of MDI child forms. You can control which child is at the front or back of the workspace with ZOrder. You can also apply ZOrder to the MDIForm or any regular form. This arranges the forms on the screen. Thus you can use ZOrder to send a form to the back of the screen without hiding it.

Example

The Graphics project at the end of this chapter uses ZOrder to rotate through a stack of image controls. Each image control contains an icon that represents what kind of screen blanker will run. Clicking on the option buttons chooses the blanker type, and uses the Index argument of the control array to send the appropriate image control to the front of the stack.

THE GRAPHICS PROJECT

Project Overview

The Graphics project demonstrates the properties of the Visual Basic language that affect basic graphics on a form or picture box. Following the examples of the different forms and subroutines of this project will teach you how to change basic graphics on a picture box or form.

The first section deals with the assembly of the controls and subroutines of formGraphics. The next section discusses the construction of the controls and subroutines of formScreen. Each of these sections include step-by-step instructions on how to put together the form and its controls. A section on how the program works follows these two sections. Read this information carefully and use the pictures of the forms as guides in the assembling of this project.

Assembling the Project: formGraphics

1. Make a new form (formGraphics) with the objects and properties listed in Table 8-21. Notice that all of the option box controls have the Name property of optnBlanker. The second control created with the same name generates a message asking you if you wish to create a control array; respond "Yes." If you wish to avoid this, simply change the first control's index property to 0. This creates a control array without the message.

Object	Property	Setting
Form	BorderStyle	1–Fixed Single
	Caption	Graphics Project
	ClipControls	0, False
	ControlBox	False
	Name	formGraphics
	MaxButton	False
	MinButton	True
Frame	Caption	Blanker Options
	Name	framBlanker
Option	Caption	Blank Screen
	Name	optnBlanker
	Index	0
	TabIndex	0
Option	Caption	Color Spots
	Name	optnBlanker
	Index	1
	TabIndex	1
Option	Caption	Circles
	Name	optnBlanker
	Index	2

(continued on next page)

(continued from previous page)

Object	Property	Setting
	TabIndex	2
Option	Caption	Squares
	Name	optnBlanker
	Index	3
	TabIndex	3
Option	Caption	Lines
	Name	optnBlanker
	Index	4
	TabIndex	4
Image	BorderStyle	None
	Index	0
	Name	imagIcon
	Stretch	True
Command	Caption	&Activate
	Name	cmndActivate
Command	Caption	E&xit
	Name	cmndQuit

Table 8-21 Properties and controls of formGraphics in the Graphics project

2. Size the objects on the screen, as shown in Figure 8-12. Note that the image control should be exactly square; set the width equal to the height directly in the properties box.

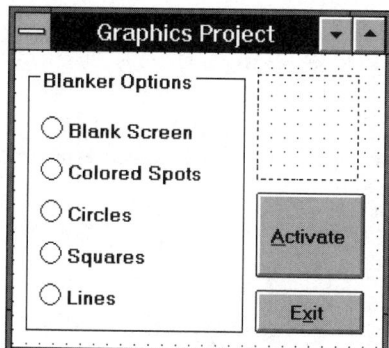

Figure 8-12 What formGraphics
should look like when completed

3. Enter the following code in the cmndActivate_Click event procedure. This code
   triggers when the user presses the command button labeled Activate. This routine hides formGraphics from the user's view, displays formScreen on the screen,
   and activates the timer that does the actual drawing.

```
Sub cmndActivate_Click ()
    formGraphics.Hide
    formScreen.Show
    formScreen!timeBlanker.Enabled = True
End Sub
```

4. Enter the following code in the optnBlanker_GotFocus event procedure. This routine activates when one of the controls of the control array optnBlanker receives
   the focus. The imagIcon control that contains the proper icon is brought to the
   front of the stack using the ZOrder method, the form's Icon property is set to display the same icon, and we place the type of screen blanker in the global variable
   BlankerType.

```
Sub optnBlanker_GotFocus (Index As Integer)
    imagIcon(Index).ZOrder BRINGTOFRONT
    Icon = imagIcon(Index).Picture
    BlankerType = Index
End Sub
```

5. Enter the following code in the cmndQuit_Click event procedure. This code triggers when the user presses the command button labeled Exit. When this is done,
   the End statement closes the program.

```
Sub cmndQuit_Click ()
    End
End Sub
```

6. Enter the following code in the Form_Load event procedure. This creates a control array of the imagIcon controls. Then it reads in the appropriate icons into
   each member of the array using the LoadPicture function.

371

```
Sub Form_Load ()
    For i = 1 To 4              'create a control array of image controls
        Load imagIcon(i)
        imagIcon(i).Visible = True
    Next i
    imagIcon(0).Picture = LoadPicture("\VB\ICONS\ELEMENTS\MOON01.ICO")
    imagIcon(1).Picture = LoadPicture("\VB\ICONS\ELEMENTS\MOON05.ICO")
    imagIcon(2).Picture = LoadPicture("\VB\ICONS\MISC\MISC38.ICO")
    imagIcon(3).Picture = LoadPicture("\VB\ICONS\MISC\MISC36.ICO")
    imagIcon(4).Picture = LoadPicture("\VB\ICONS\MISC\MISC22.ICO")
End Sub
```

Assembling the Project: formScreen

1. Make a new form with the objects and properties listed in Table 8-22.

Object	Property	Setting
Form	AutoRedraw	-1—True
	BorderStyle	0—None
	Caption	""
	ClipControls	0—False
	ControlBox	0—False
	DrawMode	14 'Merge Pen Not
	Name	formScreen
	MaxButton	False
	MinButton	False
Timer	Name	timeBlanker
	Enabled	False
	Interval	1

Table 8-22 Properties and controls of formScreen in the Graphics project

2. Size the objects on the screen as shown in Figure 8-13.

372

Figure 8-13 What formScreen should look like

3. Enter the following code in the timeBlanker event procedure. This routine triggers when the Enabled property of the Blanker timer changes to True and processes at intervals of 1 millisecond. Depending on the selected option box on formGraphics, a blank screen, series of colored spots, circles, squares, or lines appear on the screen. These graphics continue to generate on the screen until the user clicks the form.

```
Sub timeBlanker_Timer ()
    Static Color As Integer 'stores color from previous timer triggering
    X = Int((ScaleWidth - (ScaleWidth / 20)) * Rnd + (ScaleWidth / 20))
    Y = Int((ScaleHeight - (ScaleHeight / 20)) * Rnd + (ScaleHeight / 20))
    DrawWidth = Int((100 - (20)) * Rnd + (20))
    Select Case BlankerType
        Case 0 'Blank screen
            formScreen.BackColor = QBColor(0) ' Black
        Case 1 'Spots
            formScreen.PSet (X, Y), QBColor(Color)
        Case 2 'Circles
            Radius = Int((ScaleWidth / 2 - (ScaleWidth / 20)) * Rnd + (ScaleWidth / 20))
            Circle (X, Y), Radius, QBColor(Color)
        Case 3 'Squares
            X1 = Int((ScaleWidth - (ScaleWidth / 20)) * Rnd + (ScaleWidth / 20))
            Y1 = Int((ScaleHeight - (ScaleHeight / 20)) * Rnd + (ScaleHeight / 20))
            Line (X, Y)-(X1, Y1), QBColor(Color), BF
        Case 4 'Lines
            X1 = Int((ScaleWidth - (ScaleWidth / 20)) * Rnd + (ScaleWidth / 20))
            Y1 = Int((ScaleHeight - (ScaleHeight / 20)) * Rnd + (ScaleHeight / 20))
            Line (X, Y)-(X1, Y1), QBColor(Color)
    End Select
    If BlankerType <> 0 Then
        If Color <> 15 Then
            Color = Color + 1
        Else
            Color = 0
            If Rnd > .6 Then BackColor = Point(CurrentX, CurrentY)
        End If
    End If
End Sub
```

4. Enter the following code in the Form_Click event procedure. This routine processes when the user clicks the form with the mouse. This prompts the user to save the bitmap on the screen. It then clears the form of all drawn graphics, hides itself, and brings up the main control form.

```
Sub Form_Click ()
    timeBlanker.Enabled = False
    Msg$ = "Would you like to save this image?"
    Title$ = "Graphics Project"
    Ans = MsgBox(Msg$, MB_YESNO, Title$)
    If Ans = 6 Then
        MousePointer = HOURGLASS
        SavePicture formScreen.Image, "C:\VB\~TEMP.BMP"
        MousePointer = DEFAULT
    End If
    formScreen.Cls
    formScreen.Hide
    formGraphics.Show
End Sub
```

5. Enter the following code in the Form_Load event procedure. This code triggers when formScreen displays on the screen. This code maximizes the form. Because there is no border or title bar, the drawing surface of the form takes up the entire screen.

```
Sub Form_Load ()
    WindowState = MAXIMIZE
End Sub
```

6. Enter the following code in the Form_Paint event procedure. This code activates whenever the form displays. The Background of formScreen changes to white with this event.

```
Sub Form_Paint ()
    BackColor = RGB(255, 255, 255)' White background
End Sub
```

Assembling the Project: Module

Create a new module by pulling down the File menu and choosing New Module. Type the following declarations and constants into it.

```
Global BlankerType As Integer

Global Const DEFAULT = 0        'mousepointer
Global Const HOURGLASS = 11

Global Const MAXIMIZE = 2       'windowstate

Global Const MB_YESNO = 4       'msgbox
Global Const IDYES = 6

Global Const BRINGTOFRONT = 0   'ZOrder
```

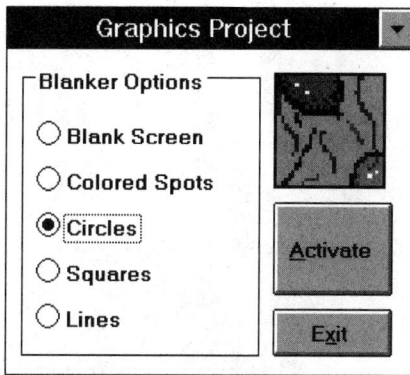

Figure 8-14 The Graphics project in action; note the stretched icon displayed in the image control

How It Works

The Graphics project opens with a configuration form that allows the user to select which kind of blanker to display on the screen (see Figure 8-14). Each time the user selects a new option from the list of options boxes, a new icon appears on the configuration screen. This icon represents the type of blanker chosen by the user. Note that because the Stretch property is set to True, the image control magnifies the small icon and displays it as large as you make the control on the form.

To display the blanker on the screen, the user presses the Activate command button. The chosen graphics continue to display on the screen until the user clicks the screen with the mouse. At this point the system asks the user whether to stop the program, and whether to save the current graphics on the screen. Press the Quit button on the configuration screen to exit.

Startup

The AutoRedraw of the image control imagIcon and forms formGraphics and formScreen receive initial adjustments at design time. The AutoRedraw property of both forms and the image control imagIcon are set to True. This allows any graphics placed on either form or the image control to redisplay every time they are obscured and revealed. We also set formGraphics ClipControls property to False, as we're not going to draw directly on the form and we can save some system overhead this way.

When the program starts, formGraphics displays on the screen. The topmost control of the optnBlanker control array receives the initial focus, triggering the optnBlanker_GotFocus event. This event uses a Select Case statement to set the appropriate icon in imagIcon.

Figure 8-15 The Graphics project lets
you save graphics like this to disk

After determining the icon to display in the image control imagIcon, the Icon property of the Graphics form becomes the same icon. A simple expression makes the Icon property equal to imagIcon.Picture. In this way the Picture property of the image control defines the property of another element of the project.

Running the Graphics Project

Pressing the Activate command button triggers the timeBlanker_Timer event on formScreen. This event displays a series of graphics images on the form in colors defined with the RGB and QBColor functions.

The QBColor function sets the color of each of the spots, circles, squares, and lines that appear on the screen. Each QBColor definition has the variable Color placed in the parentheses that follow the QBColor name. This variable increments by one each time that the Timer event triggers until the value reaches fifteen (15). The value represents a color displayed in the indicated spot, circle, square, or line. At that point the Color variable changes to 0 and the process begins again.

The PSet method draws spots of differing sizes and colors on the screen. Based on the random setting of the x and y coordinate variables and the Color variable, a spot of color appears on the screen. The DrawWidth property determines the size of the spot on the form. In this way a series of spots of random size and color appear on the screen.

Until the user clicks the form with the mouse, the screen keeps generating the indicated graphics. Clicking the form displays a message that asks the user if he or she wishes to save the current image on the screen to a file. If the user responds "Yes," then the SavePicture statement accesses the Image property of formScreen to determine the Windows handle value. Using this value the code saves the current contents of the screen to the bitmap file ~TEMP.BMP. Figure 8-15 shows what this saved screen looks like with the Circles option.

9

THE COORDINATE SYSTEM

Visual Basic's wealth of graphics and text methods require precise positioning on the screen or printer. Windows programs run on systems with very different physical specifications (such as monitor or printer resolutions), so Visual Basic provides a number of ways of specifying and determining exact locations. This chapter covers the details of how to do this.

PHYSICAL DEVICES

The Windows environment supports many video cards and monitors of varying types, resolutions, and manufacture. The most common current resolutions are 640 by 350 pixels (EGA), 640 by 480 (VGA), 800 by 600 (Super VGA), and 1024 by 768 (Super VGA and XGA), and sometimes even higher resolutions, like 1280 by 1024. Windows also supports a huge variety of printers, with resolutions that range from very coarse dot matrix printers all the way through high-resolution Postscript image setters. While Windows does a good job of providing basic functionality with any and all supported video and printer hardware, the possible effects of these differences need to be taken into account for programs that run in Windows.

This enormous variety of monitor and printer types creates the challenge of setting up applications that will work on as many devices as possible. For instance, each monitor type supports a set number of colors that limit the number of colors that your programs can use. EGA cards support the simultaneous display of 16 colors. VGA and super VGA cards can display 16, 256, 32,000, 65,000 or 16 million colors simultaneously. To avoid unpleasant surprises it is often best to let Windows handle graphics operations for you by keeping your graphics code simple.

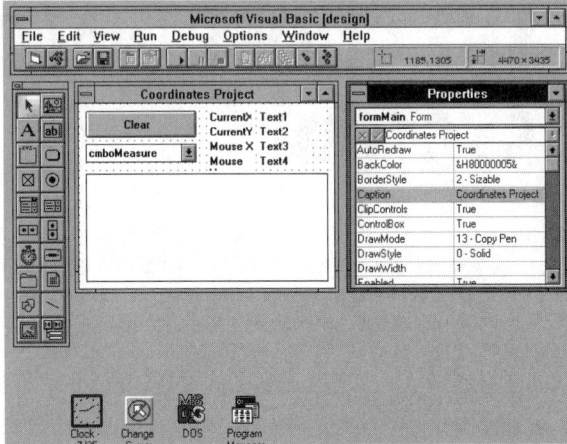

Figure 9-1 Visual Basic design screen on regular VGA 640 by 480 resolution

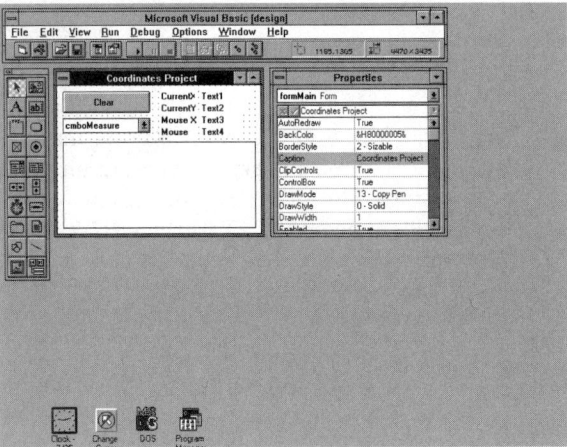

Figure 9-2 Visual Basic design screen on SVGA 800 by 600 resolution

Sometimes you'll need to forego simplicity, and then you'll need to properly consider and account for this variety of display types.

Monitors with different resolutions display the same forms differently. The higher the resolution, the smaller each element displays. Conversely, the higher the resolution the more elements you can fit on a screen. You can also specify different font sizes for some resolutions. For example, 1024 by 768 can use both the regular size fonts as well as a larger, sharper font. Since many monitors are still only capable of displaying 640 by 480 resolution, be careful to ensure that a form will fit on these lower resolution screens. Figures 9-1, 9-2, 9-3, and 9-4 show the differences between the same screen elements displayed at 640 by 480, 800 by 600, 1024 by 768, and 1024 by 768 with big fonts. Notice the difference between Figures 9-3 and 9-4: both are the same resolution (1024 by 768), and no screen elements have moved, but using the larger sized fonts has changed the dimensions of the toolbar and the form!

378

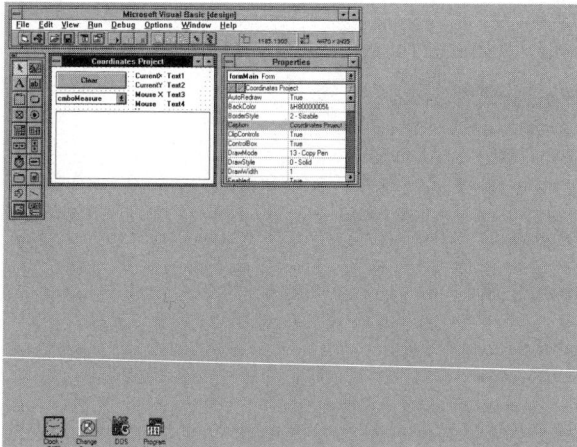

Figure 9-3 Visual Basic design screen on SVGA 1024 by 768 resolution, normal fonts. Note how much more space is available compared to normal VGA resolution

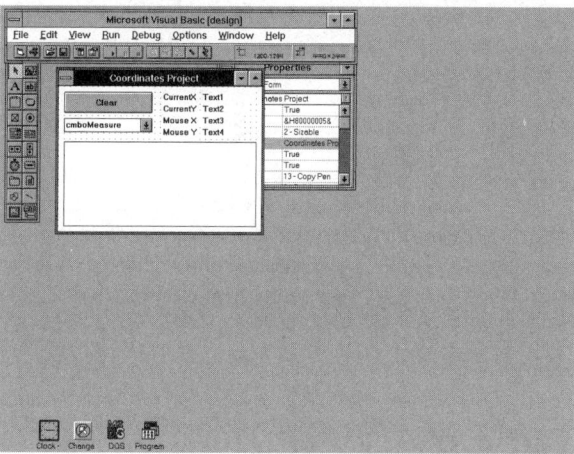

Figure 9-4 Visual Basic design screen on SVGA 1024 by 768 resolution, large fonts. Note how the size of some screen elements (like the tool-bar and the form) have been automatically resized because of the change in font size

MEASUREMENT SYSTEMS

This variety of screen (and printer) resolutions demands some sort of abstraction to make your program device independent. Visual Basic's default measurement system is in twips, with 1440 twips per logical inch. Twips are not always the best unit of measure for every program. For example, a bitmap drawing program works best when the unit of measure is pixels, which measures the very smallest dot on a screen. Word processing applications require precise measurements of text, so the point measure unit works best. Visual Basic provides a number of different measurement systems to satisfy these various measurement needs.

Table 9-1 lists these units of measure. An object's ScaleMode property sets the internal unit of measure. Any object placed on a form, picture box, or Printer object must use the unit of measure defined in its container's ScaleMode property. The default unit of measure for each form, picture box, or Printer object is twips.

Unit of Measure	Description
Twip	1440 twips = 1 inch, 20 twips = 1 point
Point	72 points = 1 inch, 1 point = 20 twips
Pixel	Size of 1 pixel on screen or smallest dot made by printer
Character	x axis: 120 twips = 1 character, y axis: 240 twips = 1 character
Inch	1 inch = 1440 twips, 1 inch = 72 points
Millimeter	254 millimeters = 1 inch, 5.67 twips = 1 millimeter
Centimeter	2.54 centimeters = 1 inch, 567 twips = 1 centimeter
User-defined	Arbitrary; determined by the programmer

Table 9-1 Available units of measure in Visual Basic

A form's coordinates are always measured in twips. Controls use the measurement system of their container. Similarly, graphics drawn on a form or picture box with the Circle, Line, PSet, or Print methods use the form or picture box's unit of measure. The ScaleMode property of a form, picture box, or Printer object determines its internal unit of measure. This is the unit of measure that objects placed on a form, picture box, or Printer object must use.

THE COORDINATE SYSTEM

The coordinate system indicates where an object appears on the screen or the printer. An object's coordinates measure its distance from the top-left corner of the screen, form, picture box, or Printer object. The Left and Top properties contain the coordinates of the object's top-left corner. Figure 9-5 shows the Left and Top properties of a command button. Note how the Visual Basic toolbar indicates the current coordinates.

Each object also has a height and width set by the Height and Width properties. The number representing the same object's height and width of course changes with each new unit of measure. For example, an object 1 inch high would have a Height of 1 if its container's ScaleMode were set to inches; the same object's Height would be 1440 if the container's ScaleMode were set to twips. Note how the status bar displays this information next to the Top and Left coordinates in Figure 9-6.

380

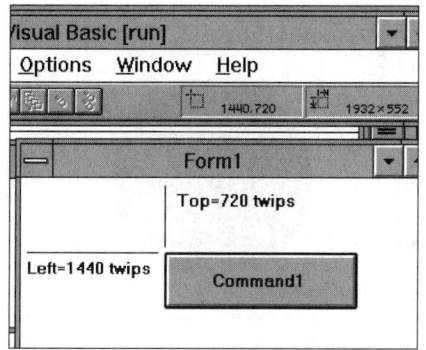

Figure 9-5 Top and Left coordinates of a control. Note the left panel of the toolbar includes this information

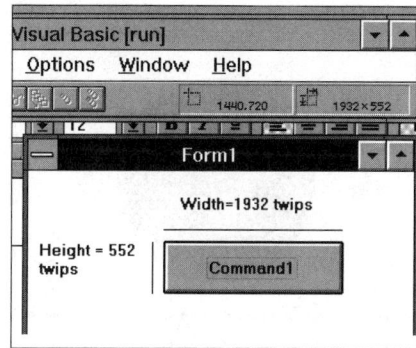

Figure 9-6 Height and Width of a control. Note the right panel of the toolbar includes this information

A form's Height, Width, Left, and Top properties include the borders and title bars. The ScaleHeight, ScaleWidth, ScaleLeft, and ScaleTop properties do not include these parts of a form. These latter properties provide the dimensions of the usable interior surface of a form. Figure 9-7 shows the usable surface of a form with its dimensions set in the ScaleHeight, ScaleWidth, ScaleLeft, and ScaleTop properties. Setting the ScaleLeft and ScaleTop properties to 0 and the ScaleHeight and ScaleWidth properties to 100 divides the form into 100 equal units. An object in the upper-left corner is at the coordinates 0,0. Objects in the lower-right corner have the coordinates 100,100. Notice that these measurements are independent of the actual unit size of the form on the screen. A user-defined coordinate system like this can simplify many procedures.

Changing the settings of the ScaleHeight, ScaleWidth, ScaleLeft, and ScaleTop properties has no effect on an object's size and location. Any modifications only change the scale or unit of measure that objects must use inside this object. Notice that Figures 9-8 and 9-9 are the same size even though the values of the

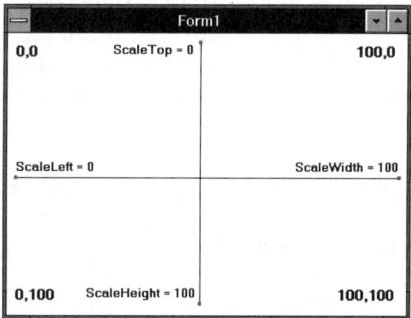

Figure 9-7 ScaleHeight, ScaleWidth, ScaleLeft, and ScaleTop properties

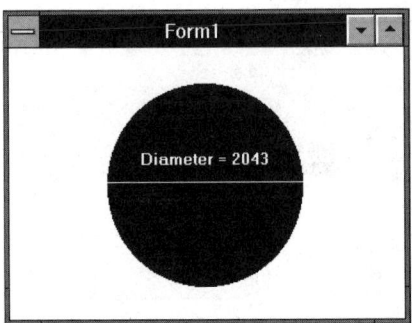

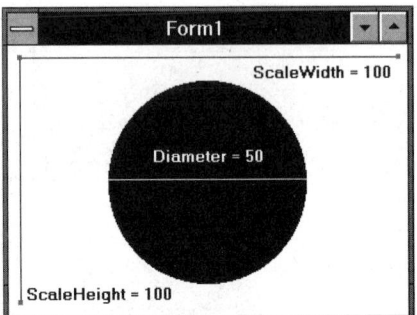

Figure 9-8 Circle drawn on a form using twip measurements

Figure 9-9 Same size circle drawn on a form with custom scale

ScaleHeight and ScaleWidth properties are different. Alterations to these properties change the ScaleMode property to user-defined (0). The values of the ScaleHeight and ScaleWidth properties of a form, picture box, or Printer object represent the new unit of measure. In this way the vertical height and horizontal width of the object divides into 100 units each. Thus it makes sense to use such a custom scale when you are concerned about the *relative* size and position of screen elements rather than their *absolute* physical measurements.

The screen coordinates on a form, picture box, or Printer object begin in the top-left corner. Every time a Circle, PSet, Line, or Print method places graphics or text on an object, these coordinates change. Coordinates measure the distance from the top-left corner of the object using the unit of measure set by the object's ScaleMode property. Using the Circle method changes the current coordinates to the center of the circle. Each Line method modifies the current screen coordinates to the second set of coordinates of the drawn line or box. PSet methods alter the screen coordinates to the center of the drawn spot of color. A Print method expression changes the screen coordinates to the end of the line of text. The CurrentX and CurrentY properties of the form, Printer object, and picture box define exactly where the current screen coordinates presently are on it.

Table 9-2 displays the one method and eleven properties that determine the position of controls and graphics objects on a form, Printer object, or picture box.

Use or Set This...		To Do This...
CurrentX	Property	Set the horizontal position of a drawn object within its container
CurrentY	Property	Set the vertical position of a drawn object within its container

Use or Set This...		To Do This...
Height	Property	Set the vertical length of an object
Left	Property	Set the horizontal distance from the left edge of the container
Scale	Method	Set the limits of the coordinates of a container
ScaleHeight	Property	Set the vertical coordinate of lower-right corner of an object
ScaleLeft	Property	Set the horizontal coordinate of top-left corner of an object
ScaleMode	Property	Determine which unit of measure to use for a container
ScaleTop	Property	Set the vertical coordinate of upper-left corner of an object
ScaleWidth	Property	Set the horizontal coordinate of lower-right corner of an object
Top	Property	Set the vertical distance from the top edge of a container
Width	Property	Set the horizontal length of an object

Table 9-2 Method and properties dealing with the Visual Basic coordinate system

Table 9-2 shows the method and properties that we'll examine in detail in the following pages. The Coordinates project at the end of this chapter provides step-by-step instructions and demonstrates how to use these coordinate system items.

CURRENTX AND CURRENTY PROPERTIES

Objects Affected

Check	Clipboard	Combo	Command	CommonDlg
Data	Debug	Dir	Drive	File
▶ Form	Frame	Grid	Image	Label
Line	List	MDI Form	Menu	OLE
Option	▶ Picture	▶ Printer	Screen	Scroll
Shape	Text	Timer		

Purpose

The CurrentX and CurrentY properties provide the horizontal (CurrentX) and vertical (CurrentY) coordinates on a form, picture box, or Printer object. Table 9-3 describes the arguments of these two properties.

General Syntax

```
[form.]CurrentX [ = x!]
[form!]Name.CurrentX [ = x!]
Printer.CurrentX [ = x!]

[form.]CurrentY [ = y!]
[form!]Name.CurrentY [ = y!]
Printer.CurrentY [ = y!]
```

Arguments	Description
form	Name property of the form
Name	Name property of picture box
Printer	'Printer' identifies Printer object
x!, y!	Current horizontal and vertical positions on the object

Table 9-3 Arguments of CurrentX and CurrentY properties

Example Syntax

```
Sub Form_DblClick ()
    X = CurrentX + 1500        'Defines horizontal and vertical coordinates
    Y = CurrentY + 1500        'the current setting + 1500 units for circle center
    Const PI = 3.14159265      'Define Constant PI
    FillStyle = 0              'Make the color of object drawn solid
    Circle (X, Y), 1000, , -PI / 1, -PI / 2     'Draw a circle with a 90 degree slice removed
End Sub
```

Description

The CurrentX and CurrentY properties indicate the current position on a form, picture box, or Printer object. If no name appears in the expression, the current form's properties are assumed.

These properties begin with the values set in the ScaleLeft and ScaleTop properties of the form, picture box, or Printer object. Any time that a drawn object appears on a form, picture box, or Printer object, the current screen coordinates

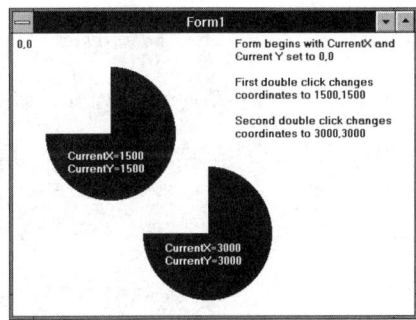

Figure 9-10 The example syntax shows that CurrentX and CurrentY are reset with each use of a graphic method

change. Table 9-4 lists the different methods that affect the values in the CurrentX and CurrentY properties of an object.

The example syntax draws a circle (with a 90-degree slice removed) centered at 1500 units from CurrentX and CurrentY. Each time the user double-clicks the mouse, the program increments x and y based on the CurrentX and CurrentY properties. This causes a second circle to appear 1500 units lower and further to the right of the last circle drawn (remember that we are using twips, the default measure, and that thousands of twips fit on the screen). This demonstrates how the CurrentX and CurrentY properties change with the use of the Circle method. Figure 9-10 shows how these circles might appear on the screen.

Effect of the Circle, Cls, Line, Printer, PSet, and NewPage Methods

The Circle, Cls, EndDoc, Line, NewPage, Print, and PSet methods change the current coordinates on the screen or Printer object. This changes the values in the CurrentX and CurrentY properties of the form, picture box, or Printer object.

For instance, drawing a circle on an object changes the CurrentX and CurrentY properties to the center of the circle. Placing a line on an object moves the CurrentX and CurrentY properties to the second point on the line. Putting a point of color on an object modifies the CurrentX and CurrentY properties to the center of the spot of color. Using the Cls method restores the CurrentX and CurrentY properties to the coordinates of the upper-left corner.

Each print method alters the CurrentX and CurrentY properties to the end of the line of text if the expression ends in semicolon or one character width beyond if the expression ends in a comma. The NewPage method advances to the next page of the Printer object and restores the CurrentX and CurrentY properties to this new page's upper-left corner; the EndDoc method also resets CurrentX and CurrentY to the defaults of 0 and 0. Table 9-4 summarizes the effects of these methods on the CurrentX and CurrentY properties.

Method	Effect on Current Property
Circle	Changes the coordinates inside the container to the center of the circle
Cls	Restores the coordinates within the container to the upper-left corner (0,0)
EndDoc	Terminates a document and resets coordinates to the upper-left corner (0,0)
Line	Changes the coordinates inside the container to the end of the line
NewPage	Advances to next page and resets coordinates to the upper-left corner (0,0)
Print	Changes the coordinates to the next print position in a Printer object
PSet	Places the coordinates of the container to the coordinates of the drawn point

Table 9-4 Effect of various methods on the CurrentX and CurrentY properties

Example

The Coordinates project uses the CurrentX and CurrentY properties to track the last position of a graphics method on pictSurface. It displays these coordinates in two text boxes.

HEIGHT PROPERTY

Objects Affected

- Check
- Clipboard
- ▶ Combo
- ▶ Command
- CommonDlg
- ▶ Data
- Debug
- ▶ Dir
- ▶ Drive
- ▶ File
- ▶ Form
- ▶ Frame
- ▶ Grid
- ▶ Image
- ▶ Label
- Line
- ▶ List
- ▶ MDI Form
- Menu
- ▶ OLE
- ▶ Option
- ▶ Picture
- ▶ Printer
- ▶ Screen
- ▶ Scroll
- ▶ Shape
- ▶ Text
- Timer

Purpose

The Height property reads or sets the vertical size of a form or control on its container. You can read and write with this property at both runtime and design

386

time for most controls and objects; read-only at runtime for the Printer and Screen objects. Table 9-5 summarizes the arguments of the Height property.

General Syntax

```
[form.]Height [ = height!]
[form!]Name.Height [ = height!]
Printer.Height [ = height!]
Screen.Height [ = height!]
```

Argument	Description
form	Name property of the form
Name	Name property of the control
Printer	'Printer' indicates Printer object
Screen	'Screen' indicates Screen object
height!	Vertical height of the object

Table 9-5 Arguments of Height property

Example Syntax

```
Sub Form_Load
    Form1.Height = (Command1.Height * 5)      'Defines height and width of the form as 5
    Form1.Width = (Command1.Width * 5)        'times the height and width of command button.
End Sub
```

Description

The Height property of an object measures the vertical height of a form, screen, or control. You can enter this value at design time by manually sizing the object with the mouse or by entering the value at the properties bar. You can modify the Height property of a control or form either at design time or runtime. The Printer and Screen objects' Height property is set by Windows and is read-only at runtime. A setting must be between 0 and a maximum value specified by the system itself. Visual Basic automatically adjusts itself to the resolution of the screen or printer. You should ensure that your objects are not too large for the most common 640 by 480 and 800 by 600 resolution screens to display. Table 9-6 summarizes the different measurement systems.

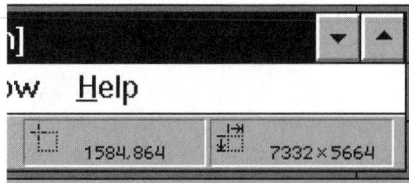

Figure 9-11 Left, Top, Width, and Height display on right side of toolbar

Unit of Measure	Description
Twip	1440 twips = 1 inch, 20 twips = 1 point
Point	72 points = 1 inch, 1 point = 20 twips
Pixel	Size of 1 pixel on screen or smallest dot made by printer
Character	x axis: 120 twips = 1 character, y axis: 240 twips = 1 character
Inch	1 inch = 1440 twips, 1 inch = 72 points
Millimeter	254 millimeters = 1 inch, 5.67 twips = 1 millimeter
Centimeter	2.54 centimeters = 1 inch, 567 twips = 1 centimeter
User-defined	Arbitrary; determined by the programmer

Table 9-6 Available units of measure in Visual Basic

In the example syntax, the Form_Load event defines the height and width of Form1 as five times the height and width of the Command1 command button.

The Left, Top, Width, and Height Properties

When you create a form or control in Visual Basic, the Left, Top, Width, and Height properties display in the far-right side of the toolbar. Figure 9-11 shows what the right end of the toolbar looks like on the screen. The first two numbers, separated by a comma, represent the left and top position of the control or form. The width and the height of the object appear to the right of these numbers, separated by an "x." If the object is a control, then the numbers shown are in the units of measurement specified by the ScaleMode property of its container. The Screen and Printer objects, as well as forms, are always measured in twips.

388

Screen and Printer

When used with the Screen or Printer objects, the Height property returns the height of the screen or page available. Note that these settings are different for different hardware configurations. The Height property of the Screen and Printer objects is not available at design time and is read-only at runtime.

The ScaleMode

The ScaleMode property of a container directly affects the meaning of the value of the Height property for controls placed in that container. When the ScaleMode property changes at design time from one measurement to another, Visual Basic recalculates the value of the Height property in this new type of measurement. Of course, the physical size of the control will remain the same no matter how changes in the ScaleMode of the parent form affect the value of the Height property.

The ScaleHeight Property

The ScaleHeight property divides the height of a form, picture box, or Printer object into the number of units set in the property. For example, when a form's ScaleHeight property changes to 100, the height of the form is divided into 100 equal units. Remember that changing the ScaleHeight property of the form to a new value does not change the actual size of it or any controls on it.

This ScaleHeight unit changes in physical size as the form's height changes: increasing the height of the form increases the size of one of these units. The height remains divided into 100 units that are now larger in size. These units define the upper and lower limits of the possible visible height of controls on this form. For example, a Resize event might adjust the Height property of a command button on a form by triggering a move statement that always ensures that the command box is one-fourth the size of the form. In this example the ScaleHeight property of the form is 100, and the Height property of the Command1 command button is 25 (one-fourth the height of the form). Figure 9-12 displays this concept visually.

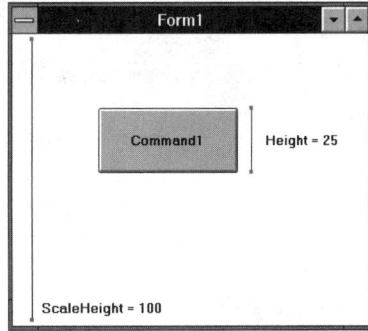

Figure 9-12 Interaction of Scale-Height and Height properties

Example

The Coordinates project at the end of this chapter uses the Height property of pictSurface to resize it when the form resizes.

LEFT PROPERTY

Objects Affected

▶ Check	Clipboard	▶ Combo	▶ Command	CommonDlg
▶ Data	Debug	▶ Dir	▶ Drive	▶ File
▶ Form	▶ Frame	▶ Grid	▶ Image	▶ Label
Line	▶ List	▶ MDI Form	Menu	▶ OLE
▶ Option	▶ Picture	Printer	Screen	▶ Scroll
▶ Shape	▶ Text	▶ Timer		

Purpose

The Left property reads or sets the location of the left side of a form or control on its container. Table 9-7 summarizes the arguments of the Left property.

General Syntax

```
[form.]Left [ = left!]
[form!]Name.Left [ = left!]
```

Argument	Description
form	Name property of the form
Name	Name property of the control
left!	Horizontal left distance of the object

Table 9-7 Arguments of Left property

Example Syntax

```
Sub LeftDistance (Ctl As Control, Frm As Form)
    'All of the following values equal one inch
```

390

```
    Select Case Frm.ScaleMode       'Based on Control's ScaleMode
        Case 0                      'user-defined Measurement
            Ctl.Left = Ctl.ScaleLeft      'Distance equals ScaleLeft
        Case 1                      'Measure in twips
            Ctl.Left = 1440
        Case 2                      'Measure in Points
            Ctl.Left = 72
        Case 3                      'Measure in Pixels
            Ctl.Left = 1000
        Case 4                      'Measure in Characters
            Ctl.Left = 12
        Case 5                      'Measure in Inches
            Ctl.Left = 1
        Case 6                      'Measure in Millimeters
            Ctl.Left = 254
        Case 7                      'Measure in Centimeters
            Ctl.Left = 2.54
    End Select
End Sub
```

Description

The Left property of an object measures the horizontal distance from the left side of its container. You can enter this value at design time by manually moving the object with the mouse or by entering the value at the properties box. You can modify the Left property of a control or form either at design time or runtime. Visual Basic automatically adjusts itself to the resolution of the screen. You should ensure that your objects are not too far from the edges for the most common 640 by 480 and 800 by 600 resolution screens to display.

The example syntax outlines a sub procedure named LeftDistance that can set a control's distance form the left side of its container. The sub procedure references the ScaleMode property of the form to determine what measure to set. This example shows the use of a generic function that applies to more than one control in a program.

Forms are always measured in twips. A control's size uses the units of measurement set in the ScaleMode property of its container. The default unit of measurement is twips. Table 9-8 explains the different measurement systems used by the Left property.

Unit of Measure	Description
Twip	1440 twips = 1 inch, 20 twips = 1 point
Point	72 points = 1 inch, 1 point = 20 twips
Pixel	Size of 1 pixel on screen or smallest dot made by printer

(continued on next page)

(continued from previous page)

Unit of Measure	Description
Character	x axis: 120 twips = 1 character, y axis: 240 twips = 1 character
Inch	1 inch = 1440 twips, 1 inch = 72 points
Millimeter	254 millimeters = 1 inch, 5.67 twips = 1 millimeter
Centimeter	2.54 centimeters = 1 inch, 567 twips = 1 centimeter
User-defined	Arbitrary; determined by the programmer

Table 9-8 Available units of measure in Visual Basic

The Left, Top, Width, and Height Properties

When you create a form or control in Visual Basic, the Left, Top, Width, and Height properties display in the far-right side of the tool bar. Figure 9-11 in the section on the Height property shows what the properties bar looks like on the screen, and explains its layout.

The Scale Mode

The ScaleMode property of a container directly affects the meaning of the value of the Left property for objects placed in that container. When the ScaleMode property changes at design time from one measurement to another, Visual Basic recalculates the value of the Left property in this new type of measurement. For example, changes in the ScaleMode of the parent form change the value of the Left property, but the physical location of the control will remain the same.

Example

In the Coordinates project, the Left property of the pictSurface picture box is adjusted every time the form resizes.

SCALE METHOD

Objects Affected

Check	Clipboard	Combo	Command	CommonDlg
Data	Debug	Dir	Drive	File

▶ Form	Frame	Grid	Image	Label
Line	List	MDI Form	Menu	OLE
Option	▶ Picture	▶ Printer	Screen	Scroll
Shape	Text	Timer		

Purpose

The Scale method defines the boundaries of a form, picture box, or Printer object. This method defines all four of the ScaleHeight, ScaleWidth, ScaleTop, and ScaleLeft properties in one expression instead of four. Table 9-9 lists the definition of each of the coordinates of this method.

General Syntax

```
[form.]Scale [(x1!, y1!) - (x2!, y2!)]
[form!]Name.Scale [(x1!, y1!) - (x2!, y2!)]
Printer.Scale [(x1!, y1!) - (x2!, y2!)]
```

Argument	Description
form	Name property of the form
Name	Name property of a picture box
Printer	'Printer' indicates the Printer object
x1!	Sets ScaleLeft property
y1!	Sets ScaleTop property
x2!	Sets ScaleWidth property
y2!	Sets ScaleHeight property

Table 9-9 Arguments of Scale method

Example Syntax

```
Sub Form1_Resize
    Form1.Scale (0, 0)-(500, 500)      'Defines coordinate system for form
    Text1.Move 0, 0, ScaleWidth, (ScaleHeight/2)    'Text1 window fills upper half of form
    Text2.Move 0, 251, ScaleWidth, (ScaleHeight/2)    'Text2 window fills lower screen
End Sub
```

393

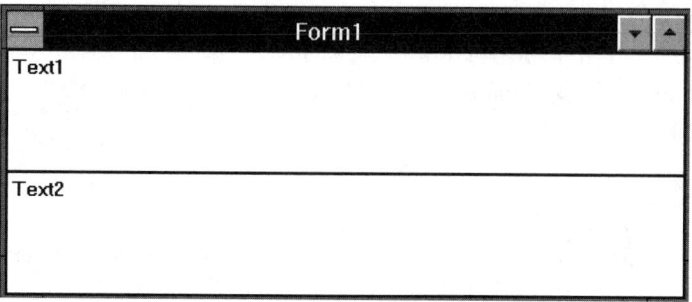

Figure 9-13 The example syntax shows how a Move method uses the relative Scale of the form to resize and reposition two text boxes

Description

The Scale method determines the limits of the coordinates used on a form, picture box, or Printer object. If there is no object name, the coordinate system of the parent form changes. The first set of numbers (x1!, y!) are the horizontal and vertical coordinates of the upper-left corner of the object (ScaleLeft, ScaleTop). The numbers in the next set of numbers (x2!, y2!) represent the lower-right corner of the same object (ScaleWidth, ScaleHeight). This method has no effect on the positioning and size of current controls on the screen; it only affects the relative value of the units used to set positions and sizes.

In the example syntax, the Scale method provides a custom scale that the Form1_Resize event uses to ensure that the Text1 text box remains in the upper half of Form1 and the Text2 text box stays in the lower half. Figure 9-13 shows what these controls should look like on Form1. Note that no matter what the physical size of Form1, this code always places each text box in the right spot.

The CurrentX and CurrentY Properties

The Scale method works well when combined with the CurrentX and CurrentY properties of a form, picture box, or Printer object. Setting a custom scale with the Scale method removes a great deal of confusion that arises from positioning and sizing an object on a form, picture box, or Printer object. For example, working with numbers between 0 and 100 makes it easier to discover the center of an object than numbers like 426 and 2848. This simplifies the process of drawing objects on the screen.

Example

The Coordinates project at the end of this chapter uses the Scale method to create a user-defined scale for the main form. It sets this coordinate system to be (0, 0) - (100, 100) for ease in positioning the picture box.

394

SCALEHEIGHT PROPERTY

Objects Affected

Check	Clipboard	Combo	Command	CommonDlg
Data	Debug	Dir	Drive	File
▶ Form	Frame	Grid	Image	Label
Line	List	▶ MDI Form	Menu	OLE
Option	▶ Picture	▶ Printer	Screen	Scroll
Shape	Text	Timer		

Purpose

The ScaleHeight property reads or sets the usable height of a form, MDIForm, picture box, or Printer object. Usable height excludes the title bar and borders of an object. An object's size is measured in the units indicated by the setting of the ScaleMode property, its container. Table 9-10 lists the arguments of the ScaleHeight property.

General Syntax

```
[form.]ScaleHeight [ = scale!]
[form!]Name.ScaleHeight [ = scale!]
Printer.ScaleHeight [ = scale!]
```

Argument	Description
form	Name property of the form
Name	Name property of the picture box
Printer	'Printer' indicates the Printer object
Scale!	Vertical height of the object

Table 9-10 Arguments of ScaleHeight property

395

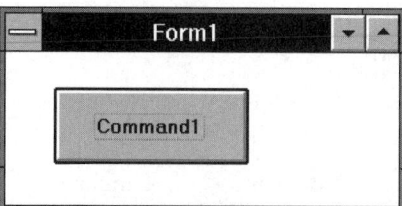

Figure 9-14 Command1 button before form resizes...

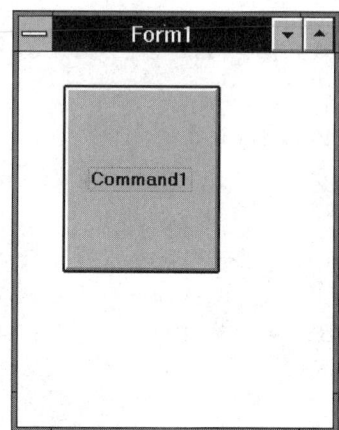

Figure 9-15 ... and after. The example syntax automatically resizes the command button to one-half the size of the form

Example Syntax

```
Sub Form_Resize ()
    ScaleHeight = 100          'Sets the coordinate scale to 100
    ScaleWidth = 100           'for both the height and width
    Command1.Height = 50       'Makes the command button's height 1/2 of height of form
    Command1.Width = 50        'Makes the command button's width 1/2 of width of form
End Sub
```

Description

The ScaleHeight property measures the usable height of a form, picture box, or Printer object, excluding the border or title bar of the object. You can change this value either at design time or runtime (with the exception of the Printer object, which can only be set at runtime). A new value becomes the user-defined proportional measurement of the form, picture box, or Printer object. The height of any control or graphics object is a fraction of the height of the object it is on.

In the example syntax, the Form_Resize event changes the ScaleHeight and ScaleWidth property of Form1 to 100. With this new scale, the Command1 command button's height and width becomes one-quarter that of Form1 by changing them to 25. These settings do not determine the actual size of either the control or the form, but the proportional difference. For this reason the actual size of the Command1 button becomes larger when the form is larger and smaller when the form is smaller. Figures 9-14 and 9-15 show what this example might look like.

396

The ScaleWidth, ScaleTop, and ScaleLeft Properties.

The ScaleHeight, ScaleWidth, ScaleTop, and ScaleLeft properties provide the boundaries of possible settings for objects placed on a form, picture box, or Printer object. Each object's ScaleTop and ScaleLeft properties indicate the coordinates of the upper-left corner. The ScaleWidth and ScaleHeight properties provide the coordinates of the lower-right corner of an object. A visible control or object on a form, picture box, or Printer object must be between the upper and lower boundaries set by these properties. As shown in the example syntax, changes can be specified with the definitions of the size of controls as fractions of the ScaleHeight of the current form. This is very useful for helping ensure that controls are not obscured when a form's size changes. Every time the form's size changes, the controls also change. Figure 9-7 in the section on the Coordinate System in the beginning of this chapter shows the relationship between these properties

Example

The ScaleHeight property appears in the Form_Resize event of the Coordinates project. The pictSurface picture box is resized (using its Height property) by referring to the ScaleHeight property of the form it resides on.

Comments

Remember that the ScaleHeight property does not measure the entire height of a form, picture box, or Printer object. The ScaleHeight property does not include the title bar at the top of a form or the border around an object.

SCALELEFT PROPERTY

Objects Affected

Check	Clipboard	Combo	Command	CommonDlg
Data	Debug	Dir	Drive	File
▶ Form	Frame	Grid	Image	Label
Line	List	MDI Form	Menu	OLE
Option	▶ Picture	▶ Printer	Screen	Scroll
Shape	Text	Timer		

Purpose

The ScaleLeft property sets or determines the left coordinate of the upper-left corner of a form, picture box, or Printer object. Table 9-11 shows the arguments of the ScaleLeft property.

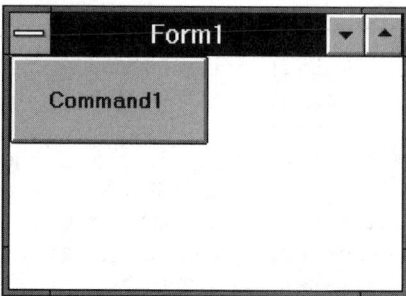

Figure 9-16 Example syntax moves Command1 to the upper-left corner

General Syntax

```
[form.]ScaleLeft [ = scale!]
[form!]Name.ScaleLeft [ = scale!]
Printer.ScaleLeft [ = scale!]
```

Argument	Description
form	Name property of the form
Name	Name property of the picture box
Printer	'Printer' indicates the Printer object
scale!	Left coordinate of an object

Table 9-11 Arguments of ScaleLeft property

Example Syntax

```
Sub Form_Resize ()
     ScaleLeft = 100          'Upper-left corner coordinates
     ScaleTop = 100           'becomes 100,100
     ScaleWidth = 200         'lower-right corner coordinates
     ScaleHeight = 200        'becomes 200,200
     Command1.Move ScaleLeft, ScaleTop 'Move command button to upper-left corner
End Sub
```

Description

The ScaleLeft property reads or sets the lowest usable left coordinate of a form, picture box, or Printer object, excluding the border of the object.

398

In the example syntax, the ScaleLeft property defines the horizontal value of the upper-left corner as 100. The Move method then moves the command button to the upper-left corner. Figure 9-16 shows what this might look like on the screen.

The ScaleWidth, ScaleHeight, and ScaleTop Properties

The ScaleHeight, ScaleWidth, ScaleTop, and ScaleLeft properties provide the boundaries of possible settings for objects placed on a form, picture box, or Printer object. Each object's ScaleTop and ScaleLeft properties indicate the coordinates of the upper-left corner. The ScaleWidth and ScaleHeight properties provide the coordinates of the lower-right corner of an object. A visible control or object on a form, picture box, or Printer object must be between the upper and lower boundaries set by these properties. Figure 9-7 in the section on the Coordinate System in the beginning of this chapter shows the relationship between these properties.

Example

The Coordinates project uses ScaleLeft in several different places. We use formMain's ScaleLeft property to properly size pictSurface when the form is resized, and we set pictSurface's ScaleLeft property as part of setting a user-defined coordinate system.

SCALEMODE PROPERTY

Objects Affected

Check	Clipboard	Combo	Command	CommonDlg
Data	Debug	Dir	Drive	File
▶ Form	Frame	Grid	Image	Label
Line	List	▶ MDI Form	Menu	OLE
Option	▶ Picture	▶ Printer	Screen	Scroll
Shape	Text	Timer		

Purpose

The ScaleMode property indicates what unit of measure to use for the form, picture box, or Printer object. Unless the ScaleMode property is 0 (user-defined), all of the dimensions of the forms, controls, and graphical objects use this measurement. Selecting the user-defined option for this property changes the unit of measure to the range set by the ScaleWidth, ScaleHeight, ScaleTop, and ScaleLeft properties. Tables 9-12 and 9-13 summarize the arguments of the ScaleMode property.

General Syntax

```
[form.]ScaleMode [ = mode%]
[form!]Name.ScaleMode [ = mode%]
[Printer.]ScaleMode [ = mode%]
```

Argument	Description
form	Name property of the form
Name	Name property of the picture box
Printer	'Printer' indicates Printer object
mode%	Current unit of measure

Table 9-12 Arguments of ScaleMode property

mode%	CONSTANT.TXT	Measure Type
0	USER	User-defined. Automatically changed to this setting when the ScaleHeight, ScaleWidth, ScaleLeft, and ScaleTop Properties change
1	TWIPS	(Default) Twip: 1 inch = 1440 twips
2	POINTS	Point: 1 inch = 72 points; 1 point = 20 twips
3	PIXELS	Pixel: smallest point on a monitor or printer determined by its resolution
4	CHARACTERS	Character: horizontal = 12 characters per inch; vertical = 6 lines per inch
5	INCHES	Inch: 1 Inch = 1440 twips; 1 inch = 72 points
6	MILLIMETERS	Millimeter: 1 inch = 254 millimeters; 1 millimeter = 5.67 twips
7	CENTIMETERS	Centimeter: 1 inch = 2.54 centimeters; 1 centimeter = 567 twips

Table 9-13 The different measurement types of the ScaleMode property

400

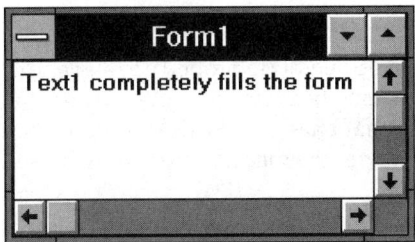

Figure 9-17 Text1 fills Form1 no
matter how Form1 gets resized

Example Syntax

```
Sub Form_Resize ()
     ScaleLeft = 500           'Upper-left corner coordinates becomes
     ScaleTop = 500            '500,500
     ScaleWidth = 1000         'Lower-right corner coordinates becomes
     ScaleHeight = 1000        '1000,1000
     Text1.Move ScaleLeft, ScaleTop, ScaleWidth,ScaleHeight 'Fills screen with text box
End Sub

Sub Form_Load ()
     Form1.ScaleMode = 5       'Defines the form's measure as inches
     Text1.Move 1, 1, 3, 3     'Defines dimensions and position of Text box
End Sub
```

Description

The ScaleMode property defines the measurement unit to use for a form, picture box, or Printer object. If a ScaleMode property expression does not provide the object, then the current form's ScaleMode property changes. ScaleMode property expressions must be one of the values listed in Table 9-13.

The ScaleLeft, ScaleTop, ScaleWidth, and ScaleHeight Properties

In the example syntax, the ScaleMode property of the form affects the size and position of the controls positioned on it. The first example does not even contain a ScaleMode property line in the code. The ScaleMode property automatically changes to 0 (user-defined) when the ScaleLeft, ScaleTop, ScaleWidth, and ScaleHeight properties change. With this example the size and position of the Text1 text box completely fills Form1 no matter what the size (see Figure 9-17).

The Move Method

The second example shows the use of the ScaleMode property to initially adjust the position and shape of the text box on the form. In this case, the ScaleMode property value of 5 sets the unit of measurement to inches. The Move method uses this setting to define the upper-left and lower-right corners of Text1.

401

Example

The Coordinates project changes pictSurface's ScaleMode property to any one of the enumerated types. The cmboMeasure combo box lets the user easily switch ScaleModes. The project makes it obvious that changing ScaleMode does not change the physical size of objects, it just changes the measurement system used for that object.

SCALETOP PROPERTY

Objects Affected

Check	Clipboard	Combo	Command	CommonDlg
Data	Debug	Dir	Drive	File
▶ Form	Frame	Grid	Image	Label
Line	List	MDI Form	Menu	OLE
Option	▶ Picture	▶ Printer	Screen	Scroll
Shape	Text	Timer		

Purpose

The ScaleTop property reads or sets the coordinate of the top of a form, picture box, or Printer object. Table 9-14 shows the arguments of the ScaleTop property.

General Syntax

```
[form.]ScaleTop [ = scale!]
[form!]Name.ScaleTop [ = scale!]
[Printer.]ScaleTop [ = scale!]
```

Argument	Description
form	Name property of the form
Name	Name property of the picture box
Printer	'Printer' indicates Printer object
scale!	Top coordinate of an object

Table 9-14 Arguments of ScaleTop property

Example Syntax

```
Sub Form_Resize ()
     ScaleLeft = 100          'Upper-left corner coordinates
     ScaleTop = 100           'becomes 100,100
     ScaleWidth = 400         'Lower-right corner coordinates
     ScaleHeight = 400        'becomes 400,400
     Command1.Move ScaleLeft * 2, ScaleTop * 2       'Command button changes position
End Sub
```

Description

The ScaleTop property reads or sets the usable top coordinate of a form, picture box, or Printer object, excluding the border or title bar of the object. In the example syntax, the ScaleTop property changes to 100. This change (along with the other Scale property settings) redefines the range of possible coordinates on the form to 100 to 400 for both the horizontal and vertical coordinates.

The ScaleWidth, ScaleHeight, and ScaleLeft Properties

The ScaleHeight, ScaleWidth, ScaleTop, and ScaleLeft properties provide the boundaries of possible settings for objects placed on a form, picture box, or Printer object. Each object's ScaleTop and ScaleLeft properties indicate the coordinates of the upper-left corner. The ScaleWidth and ScaleHeight properties provide the coordinates of the lower-right corner of an object. A visible control or object on a form, picture box, or Printer object must be between the upper and lower boundaries set by these properties. Figure 9-7 in the section on the Coordinate System in the beginning of this chapter shows the relationship between these properties.

Example

The Coordinates project uses pictSurface's ScaleTop property to help define a user-defined coordinate system.

SCALEWIDTH PROPERTY

Objects Affected

Check	Clipboard	Combo	Command	CommonDlg
Data	Debug	Dir	Drive	File
▶ Form	Frame	Grid	Image	Label
Line	List	▶ MDI Form	Menu	OLE
Option	▶ Picture	▶ Printer	Screen	Scroll
Shape	Text	Timer		

403

Purpose

The ScaleWidth property sets or determines the usable width of a form, MDIForm, picture box, or Printer object. Usable width excludes the borders of an object. An object's size is measured in the units indicated by the setting of the ScaleMode property of its container. Table 9-15 lists the arguments of the ScaleWidth property.

General Syntax

```
[form.]ScaleWidth [ = scale!]
[form!]Name.ScaleWidth [ = scale!]
[Printer.]ScaleWidth [ = scale!]
```

Argument	Description
form	Name property of the form or MDIForm
Name	Name property of the picture box
Printer	'Printer' indicates Printer object
scale!	Horizontal size of an object

Table 9-15 Arguments of the ScaleWidth property

Example Syntax

```
Sub Form_Load ()
    ScaleWidth = 100          'Lower-right corner coordinates becomes
    ScaleHeight = 100         '100,100
    List1.Move 0,0,ScaleWidth,ScaleHeight/2  'Centers list box
End Sub
```

Description

The ScaleWidth property measures the usable width of a form, MDIForm, picture box, or Printer object, excluding the border of the object. You can change this value either at design time or runtime. A new value becomes part of the user-defined proportional measurement of the form, picture box, or Printer object. The height of any control or graphics object is a fraction of the height of the object it is on.

In the example syntax, the ScaleWidth property of Form1 changes to 100. This allows the List1 list box to fill the entire width of Form1 when the width portion

404

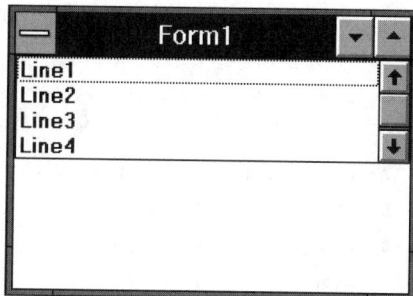

Figure 9-18 Example syntax shows
ScaleWidth used to make List1 fill
entire width of Form1

of the Move method expression moves the list box. Figure 9-18 shows how the
example syntax changes the size of List1.

The ScaleWidth, ScaleTop, and ScaleLeft Properties.

The ScaleWidth, ScaleWidth, ScaleTop, and ScaleLeft properties provide the
boundaries of possible settings for objects placed on a form, MDIForm, picture
box, or Printer object. Each object's ScaleTop and ScaleLeft properties indicate the
coordinates of the upper-left corner. The ScaleWidth and ScaleHeight properties
provide the coordinates of the lower-right corner of an object. A visible control
or object on a form, picture box, or Printer object must be between the upper and
lower boundaries set by these properties. As shown in the example syntax,
changes can be initiated with the definitions of the size of controls as fractions
of the ScaleWidth of the current form. This is very useful for helping ensure that
controls are not obscured when a form's size changes. Every time the form's size
changes, the position and size of the controls also change. Figure 9-7 in the section on the Coordinate System in the beginning of this chapter shows the relationship between these properties.

Example

The Coordinates project uses ScaleWidth in two ways. First, the pictSurface picture box gets resized every time the main form is resized by setting pictSurface's
Width property to be slightly smaller than the form's ScaleWidth. ScaleWidth is
used again to set a user-defined coordinate system for the pictSurface picture box.

405

TOP PROPERTY

Objects Affected

▶ Check	Clipboard	▶ Combo	▶ Command	CommonDlg
▶ Data	Debug	▶ Dir	▶ Drive	▶ File
▶ Form	▶ Frame	▶ Grid	▶ Image	▶ Label
Line	▶ List	▶ MDI Form	Menu	▶ OLE
▶ Option	▶ Picture	Printer	Screen	▶ Scroll
▶ Shape	▶ Text	▶ Timer		

Purpose

The Top property defines or determines the distance of a form or control from the top edge of the form or picture box. A control's distance is measured in the units indicated by the ScaleMode property of its container. The Top property of an object is available at both design time and runtime. Table 9-16 shows the arguments of the Top property.

General Syntax

```
[form.]Top [ = top!]
[form!]Name.Top [ = top!]
```

Argument	Description
form	Name property of the form
Name	Name property of the control
top!	Vertical top distance of the object

Table 9-16 Arguments of Top property

Example Syntax

```
Sub ResetForm (Name As Form)
    If Name.ScaleMode <> 0 Then      'Checks if ScaleMode is set to user-defined
        Name.Top = 1440              'Form's distance from top placed at 1440
        Name.Left = 1440             'Form's distance from left placed at 1440
    Else
        Name.Top = Name.ScaleTop     'Form's distance from left and top made equal
        Name.Left = Name.ScaleLeft   'to the value of the ScaleLeft & ScaleTop
    End If
End Sub
```

406

Description

The Top property of an object measures the vertical distance from the top of a form, screen, or picture box. You can enter this value at design time by manually moving the object with the mouse or by entering the value in the properties box. The Top property of a control or form may be changed either at design time or runtime. Visual Basic automatically adjusts itself to the resolution of the screen. You should ensure that your objects are not too far from the edges for the most common 640 by 480 and 800 by 600 resolution screens to display.

The example syntax outlines a sub procedure named ResetForm that sets a form's distance from the left and top sides of the screen. If the ScaleMode property is "user-defined," the Left and Top properties are set to the values of the ScaleLeft and ScaleTop properties. Otherwise the ResetForm function places the form 1440 twips from the edge of the screen.

The Left, Top, Width, and Height Properties

When you create a form or control in Visual Basic, the Left, Top, Width, and Height properties display in the far-right side of the tool bar. Figures 9-10 and 9-11 in the section on the Height property show what the properties bar looks like on the screen, and explain its layout.

The Scale Mode

The ScaleMode property of a container directly affects the meaning of the value of the Top property for objects placed in that container. When ScaleMode property changes at design time from one measurement to another, Visual Basic recalculates the value of the Top property in this new type of measurement. No matter what the Top property of a control becomes based on changes in the ScaleMode of the parent form, the physical location of the control will remain the same.

Example

The Coordinates project at the end of this chapter uses the pictSurface picture box's Top property to help properly position and size it when the form it's on is resized by the user.

Comments

Remember that changes to the ScaleTop property of a form only alter the value of the Top property of a control and not the actual distance.

WIDTH PROPERTY

Objects Affected

▶ Check	Clipboard	▶ Combo	▶ Command	CommonDlg
▶ Data	Debug	▶ Dir	▶ Drive	▶ File
▶ Form	▶ Frame	▶ Grid	▶ Image	▶ Label
Line	▶ List	▶ MDI Form	Menu	▶ OLE
▶ Option	▶ Picture	▶ Printer	▶ Screen	▶ Scroll
▶ Shape	▶ Text	Timer		

Purpose

The Width property reads or sets the horizontal size of a form or control on the screen, form, picture box, or Printer object. This property is measured in the measurement system defined by the container's ScaleMode property. You can read and write with this property at both runtime and design time for most controls and objects; read-only at runtime for the Printer and Screen objects. Table 9-17 shows the arguments for the Width property.

General Syntax

```
[form.]Width [ = width!]
[form!]Name.Width [ = width!]
Printer.Width [ = width!]
Screen.Width [ = width!]
```

Argument	Description
form	Name property of the form
Name	Name property of the control
Printer	'Printer' indicates the Printer object
Screen	'Screen' indicates the Screen object
width!	Horizontal width of the object

Table 9-17 Arguments of Width property

Example Syntax

```
Sub Form_Load ()
    Form1.Width = (Picture1.Width * 2)      'Width and height of form made twice the size
    Form1.Height = (Picture1.Height * 2)    'of the width and height of picture box.
End Sub
```

Description

The Width property of an object measures its horizontal width. You can enter this value at design time by manually sizing the object with the mouse or by entering the value in the properties box. You can modify the Width property of a control at runtime or design time. The Printer and Screen objects' Width property is set by Windows and is read-only at runtime. A setting must be between 0 and a maximum value specified by the system itself. Visual Basic automatically adjusts itself to the resolution of the screen or printer You should ensure that your objects are not too large for the most common 640 by 480 and 800 by 600 resolution screens to display.

The example syntax sets Form1's Width property to twice the size of the setting of the Picture1 picture box. This demonstrates the ways in which this property can change the measurements of other objects.

The Left, Top, Width, and Height Properties

When you create a form or control in Visual Basic, the Left, Top, Width, and Height properties display in the far-right side of the toolbar. Figure 9-12 in the section on the Height property shows what the properties bar looks like on the screen, and explains its layout. The first two numbers, separated by a comma, represent the left and top position of the control or form. The width and the height of the object appear to the right of these numbers separated by an "x." If the object is a control, then the numbers shown are in the units of measurement specified by the ScaleMode property of its container. The Screen and Printer objects, as well as forms, are always measured in twips.

Screen and Printer

When used with the Screen or Printer objects, the Width property returns the width of the screen or page available. Note that these settings are different for different hardware configurations. The Width property of the Screen and Printer objects is not available at design time and is read-only at runtime.

The ScaleMode

The ScaleMode property of a container directly affects the meaning of the value of the Width property for controls placed in that container. When ScaleMode property changes at design time from one measurement to another, Visual Basic

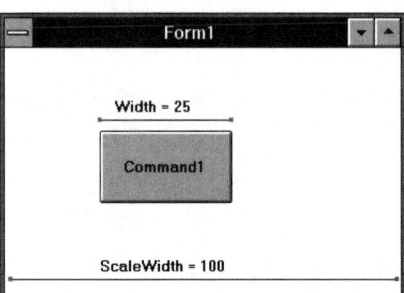

Figure 9-19 Interaction of
ScaleWidth and Width properties

recalculates the value of the Width property in this new type of measurement. No matter what Width a control becomes based on changes in the ScaleMode of the parent form, the physical size of the control will remain the same.

The ScaleWidth Property

The ScaleWidth property divides the Width of a form, picture box, or Printer object into the number of units set in the property. For example, when a form's ScaleWidth property changes to 100, the Width of the form is divided into 100 equal units. Remember that changing the ScaleWidth property of the form to a new value does not change the actual size of it or any controls on it.

This unit changes in size as the form's Width changes. In this way increasing the Width of the form increases the size of one of these units. The Width remains divided into 100 units that are now larger in size. These units define the upper and lower limit of the possible Width of controls on this form. For example, a Resize event might adjust the Width property of a command button on a form by triggering a Move statement that always ensures that the command box is one-fourth the size of the form. In this example the ScaleWidth property of the form is 100, and the Width property of the Command1 command button is 25 (one-fourth the width of the form). Figure 9-19 displays this concept visually.

Example

The Width property of the pictSurface picture box changes when the form is resized to fit the picture box to the width of the form.

Comments

Remember that changes to the ScaleWidth property of a form only alter the value of the Width property of a control and not the actual width.

410

THE COORDINATES PROJECT

Project Overview

The Coordinates project demonstrates the concepts of the coordinate system in Visual Basic. It lets you define your own coordinate system or use one of the predefined ones, and gives you immediate feedback on how these coordinate systems differ.

Assembling the Project: Coordinates Form

1. Make a new form with the objects and properties listed in Table 9-18.

Object	Property	Setting
Form	Caption	"Coordinates Project"
	Name	formMain
Combo	Name	cmboMeasure
Command	Caption	"Clear"
	Name	cmndClear
Label	Caption	"Current X"
Label	Caption	"Current Y"
Label	Caption	"Mouse X"
Label	Caption	"Mouse Y"
Picture	Name	pictSurface
Text	Name	textCurrentX
Text	Name	textCurrentY
Text	Name	textMouseX
Text	Name	textMouseY

Table 9-18 Settings for formMain

411

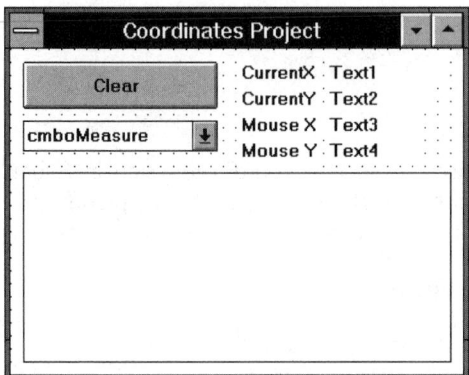

Figure 9-20 formMain during design

2. Size the objects on the screen as shown in Figure 9-20.

3. Enter the following code in the cmndClear_Click event. This simply clears the picture box of all the drawn lines.

```
Sub cmndClear_Click ()
    pictSurface.Cls                          'Clear the picture
End Sub
```

4. Enter the following code in the cmboMeasure_Click event. This triggers when the user chooses a different coordinate system in the combo box. It tests to see if the user wants to specify a user-defined coordinate system. If so, it pops up a dialog box to get the information, then goes on to set the scaling factors appropriately for ScaleTop, ScaleLeft, ScaleHeight, and ScaleWidth for the picture box. If the user chooses one of the standard formats, it sets the Picture1's ScaleMode directly.

```
Sub cmboMeasure_Click ()
    If cmboMeasure.Text = "User Defined" Then          'We need to define coordinate system
        formGetformGetUserDefined.Show 1               'Show modal input box
        pictSurface.ScaleTop = Val(formGetUserDefined!textTop.Text)       'Top
        pictSurface.ScaleLeft = Val(formGetUserDefined!textLeft.Text)     'Left
        pictSurface.ScaleWidth = Val(formGetUserDefined![textWidth].Text)   'Width
        pictSurface.ScaleHeight = Val(formGetUserDefined![textHeight].Text) 'Height
    Else
        pictSurface.ScaleMode = cmboMeasure.ListIndex   'items were added to combo box in
    End If                                              'order, so index is ScaleMode
    textCurrentX.Text = Format$(pictSurface.CurrentX, "####0.00")    'update display
    textCurrentY.Text = Format$(pictSurface.CurrentY, "####0.00")    'when scaleMode changes
End Sub
```

5. Enter the following code in the Form_Load event. This sets up our form, and loads the combo box with the scale mode selections. It then chooses twips as the default starting scale mode.

```
Sub Form_Load ()
    formMain.Scale (0, 0)-(100, 100)         'custom coordinate system for form
```

412

```
cmboMeasure.AddItem "User Defined"        'scaleMode choices into combo box
cmboMeasure.AddItem "Twips"               'note that we add these in the
cmboMeasure.AddItem "Points"              'correct order, so that ListIndex
cmboMeasure.AddItem "Pixels"              'indicates correct ScaleMode
cmboMeasure.AddItem "Characters"
cmboMeasure.AddItem "Inches"
cmboMeasure.AddItem "Millimeters"
cmboMeasure.AddItem "Centimeters"
cmboMeasure.ListIndex = 1                 'set initial ScaleMode to twips
End Sub
```

6. Enter the following code in the Form_Resize event. This triggers any time the form changes size (including startup). This sizes the picture box so it fills the entire bottom part of the form, leaving enough room on top for the controls and a small border on the sides and bottom.

```
Sub Form_Resize ()
    pictSurface.Move 0, 40                              'leave room for controls on top
    pictSurface.Left = formMain.ScaleLeft + 2           'fill rest of form, less a small border
    pictSurface.Width = formMain.ScaleWidth - 4
    pictSurface.Height = formMain.ScaleHeight - 4 - pictSurface.Top
End Sub
```

7. Enter the following code in the pictSurface_MouseDown event. This draws lines on the picture box and updates the text box displays to show our current position. The line drawing can be in either one of two modes: starting to draw a line (first click) or finishing drawing a line (second click). The static variable "drawing" tracks which part of the process we're in, and x1! and y1! remember where the line is supposed to start.

```
Sub pictSurface_MouseDown (Button As Integer, Shift As Integer, X As Single, Y As Single)
    Static drawing As Integer, x1!, y1!                 'drawing is a flag; x1 and y1 are old positions
    If drawing = True Then
        pictSurface.DrawWidth = 1                       'if user's already clicked once,
        pictSurface.Line (x1!, y1!)-(X, Y)              'draw the line
        drawing = False                                 'and get a fresh start next click
    Else
        pictSurface.DrawWidth = 3                       '....otherwise, start the line draw by:
        pictSurface.PSet (X, Y)                         'make a dot where user is starting the line
        x1! = X                                         'remember our starting coordinates
        y1! = Y
        drawing = True                                  'and flag that we're drawing
    End If
    textCurrentX.Text = Format$(pictSurface.CurrentX, "####0.00")    'update display box
    textCurrentY.Text = Format$(pictSurface.CurrentY, "####0.00")    'update display box
End Sub
```

8. Enter the following code in the MouseMove event for pictSurface. This triggers any time the mouse moves when it's over pictSurface. This simply updates the MouseX and MouseY display boxes.

```
Sub pictSurface_MouseMove (Button As Integer, Shift As Integer, X As Single, Y As Single)
    textMouseX.Text = Format$(X, "####0.00")            'update MouseX box
    textMouseY.Text = Format$(Y, "####0.00")            'update MouseY box
End Sub
```

Assembling the Project: Form

1. Make a new form with the objects and properties listed in Table 9-19.

Object	Property	Setting
Form	BorderStyle	3—Fixed Double
	Caption	"User Defined"
Form	Name	formGetUserDefined
Label	Caption	Top
Label	Caption	Left
Label	Caption	Height
Label	Caption	Width
Text	Name	textTop
Text	Name	textLeft
Text	Name	textHeight
Text	Name	textWidth

Table 9-19 Settings for the Coordinates form

2. Size the objects on the screen, as shown in Figure 9-21.

3. Enter the following code in Command1's Click event. This simply hides the form. Note that we only hide it (rather than unload it) because we need to access the information in the text boxes from the other form.

```
Sub Command1_Click ()
    Hide
End Sub
```

How It Works

When the program first starts, the combo box gets filled with an entry for each ScaleMode measurement system. Note that we add these to the combo box in the

414

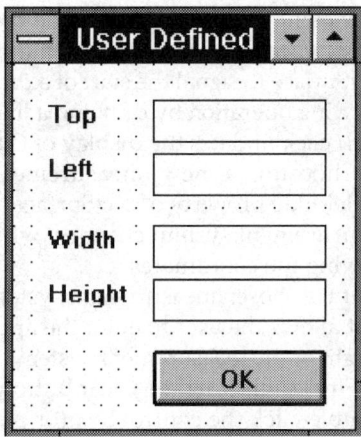

Figure 9-21 formGetUserDefined during design

correct order, so the combo box's ListIndex property refers to the correct ScaleMode setting. The Form_Load also sets a user-defined coordinate system for the form. This lets us easily move and resize the elements on the form in the form's Resize event.

The Resize event triggers when the form first loads, and every time the user resizes the form. This sets the pictSurface picture box's size and position to almost fill the lower half of the form. It uses the form's ScaleLeft, ScaleWidth, and ScaleHeight properties to set its own Left, Width, and Height properties; Top is set to a predetermined spot underneath the controls in the top part of the form.

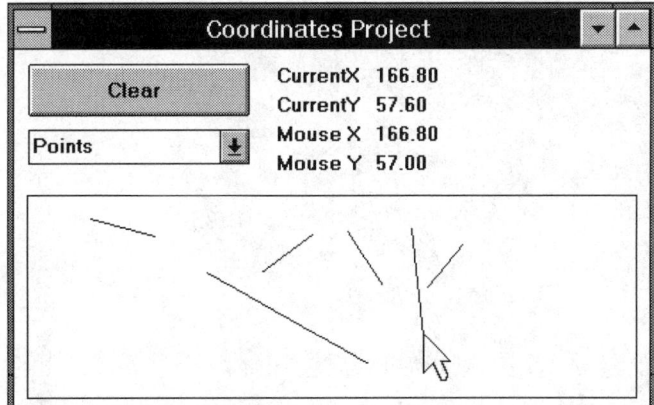

Figure 9-22 The Coordinates project in action

415

Moving the mouse around on pictSurface immediately updates the displays of the current coordinates of the mouse. Clicking the mouse sets a point on pictSurface to signal the start of a drawing operation; the second click finishes the drawing operation by drawing a line connecting the starting and ending points. Each click updates the display of CurrentX and CurrentY.

Choosing a new measurement system in the combo box resets the ScaleMode property of pictSurface. Note how nothing visibly changes; only the measurement system changes, which is illustrated in the four text boxes displaying the coordinates.

If the chosen measurement system is user-defined, then a dialog box pops up that allows the user to enter the appropriate values for the top, left, width, and height of the measurement system.

Finally, clicking the Clear button clears pictSurface to begin a new drawing. Double-click the control box (or pull down the Control Box menu and choose "Close") to end the program. Figure 9-22 shows the project in action.

10

DRAWING SHAPES

Many programs benefit from the use of graphics. Chapter 8, Graphics Fundamentals, covers the basics of using graphical elements, especially for displaying existing graphics files. You'll often need to create your own graphics rather than using existing files. You might need to highlight an area of your form, create animation, graph data, or even set up a complete drawing application. This chapter covers the intricacies of drawing shapes.

Shapes are graphic images drawn on the surface of a form, picture box, or Printer object. Most shapes are drawn using methods. Visual Basic 2.0 introduces two new controls, the shape and line controls, that you can use to draw shapes directly on your form. You can draw with curved lines to produce arcs, circles, and ellipses. Use straight lines to produce lines, squares, rectangles, triangles, and other polygons.

A drawn shape may contain any combination of curved or straight lines. You can define both color and patterns to fill solid (enclosed) shapes. The lines that make up a shape can be solid, dashed, or dotted. You can make the line around a shape any color, or even invisible. When an image appears, it can cover or be covered by the other objects on the screen.

The methods, statements, properties, and functions explained in Chapter 8, Graphics Fundamentals, affect the appearance of shapes on the screen; Chapter 9, The Coordinate System, explains the techniques used in positioning and sizing shapes. Although an understanding of the use of these elements of Visual Basic is not required for this chapter, the concepts discussed in those chapters will prove helpful in giving you a complete picture of how drawn graphics work.

APPEARANCE OF SHAPES

Visual Basic provides several properties for specifying the appearance of shapes on a form, picture box, or Printer object. The Circle method places a curved shape on the indicated portion of a screen. The Line method produces any kind of shape that consists of straight lines. Two controls, the shape and line controls, let you draw graphical controls on your form. Although there are some fundamental differences between the graphics methods and graphical controls, many of the concepts in this chapter apply to both.

Graphical Controls

You'll find the new line and shape controls introduced in Visual Basic 2.0 especially useful for creating graphics at design time. The immediate feedback of seeing the line or shape on your form can save valuable time otherwise spent in tinkering with code for the graphics methods. In many cases you can simply draw the graphic controls with no code whatsoever. Graphic controls also use significantly fewer system resources than the graphics methods, and this improves your program's performance.

Several of the graphics properties (like FillColor and DrawStyle) let you customize the appearance of these controls. Although they are placed on the form at design time, and are normally left where they were placed, you can also manipulate the size and shape of the controls through your program code.

The Shape project at the end of this chapter uses the line and shape controls to dress up the user interface. One shape control serves as a "shadow" behind a picture control to give it more definition, and another shape control lies behind the command buttons to visually group them. This second shape control has two line controls carefully positioned next to it to help create the three-dimensional illusion of being inset, or carved into the form.

Graphics Methods

Graphics methods like Circle and Line offer more flexibility and control than the line and shape controls. You can paint individual pixels, draw partial arcs, and create repetitive graphics (such as gridlines) much more easily with the graphics methods. What you give up in ease of design you make up for in power.

Graphical Layering

Graphical controls and the graphics methods appear on separate layers in a container. Think of a container (say, a form) as having three superimposed trans-

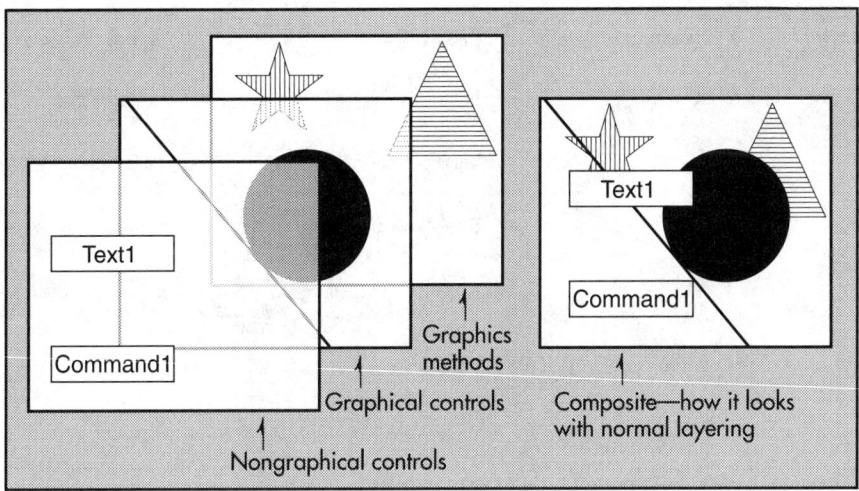

Figure 10-1 Normal layering

parent layers. The topmost layer, the one closest to the user, contains nongraphical controls like command buttons, check boxes, or file controls. Underneath this is a middle layer containing the graphical controls (Line, Shape, and Image) as well as Labels. Finally, in the back layer, lies the drawing space for the container. All the graphical methods (Line, Circle, Cls, PSet, and so on) apply to this back layer. Objects on the front layers obscure whatever lies behind them. Figure 10-1 illustrates the normal layering arrangement. This means that both graphical and nongraphical controls will obscure graphics methods.

This normal layering may change with different settings of the AutoRedraw and ClipControls properties interacting with the Paint event. Setting AutoRedraw to True always produces normal layering. Although this makes your life simpler, it may also reduce performance due to the large amounts of memory consumed by AutoRedraw. Setting ClipControls to False can speed up the display time for forms. Setting both AutoRedraw and ClipControls to False can have unpredictable results. See Table 10-1 for a summary of layering interactions. As you can see, keeping your graphics methods confined to Paint events always produces predictable, normal layering. For more information on AutoRedraw and ClipControls, see Chapter 8, Graphics Fundamentals.

AutoRedraw	ClipControls	Paint Event	Layering Behavior
True	True	n/a	Normal layering
True	False	n/a	Normal layering

(continued on next page)

(continued from previous page)

AutoRedraw	ClipControls	Paint Event	Layering Behavior
False	True	Graphics during Paint	Normal layering
		Graphics out of Paint	Middle and back layers mixed
False	False	Graphics during Paint	Normal layering
		Graphics out of Paint	All three layers mixed

Table 10-1 The possible layering interactions

Drawing Shapes Summary

Once you have a shape, there are a number of ways that you can alter its appearance. The FillColor property determines the color to place within an enclosed shape (or you can make it transparent). You can also use the FillStyle property to specify a pattern to fill a shape; a shape can have both a pattern and a fill color. Setting the DrawMode property of a form or control affects how the shape's colors interact on the screen. This property indicates whether a newly drawn shape covers the existing graphic objects on the screen.

Shapes are also tied to the characteristics of their form or control. Each form or control determines the width of the line around a shape with the DrawWidth property. The DrawStyle property indicates the format of the line that surrounds a shape (solid, dashed, dotted, or even nonexistent). Table 10-2 summarizes these properties and two methods.

Use or Set This...		To Do This...
Circle	Method	Draw a circle, ellipsis, or arc on the form, picture box, or printer
DrawMode	Property	Define the appearance of drawn shapes
DrawStyle	Property	Define the outside line around a shape
DrawWidth	Property	Define the width of the line on the edge of a shape
FillColor	Property	Set the color to fill circles and boxes created with Line and Circle methods

Use or Set This...		To Do This...
FillStyle	Property	Set the pattern to fill circles and boxes
Line	Method	Draw a line, square, or rectangle on a form, picture box, or printer

Table 10-2 Methods and properties dealing with drawing shapes

CONSTANT.TXT Values

Many of the properties, events, and methods of this chapter use numeric values as arguments. Using constants rather than the literal value makes your code self-documenting, more readable, and easier to debug.

Microsoft provides a file, CONSTANT.TXT, that has many constant declarations defined for you. For smaller applications it's probably easiest just to type the declarations in yourself. For larger applications you'll find it much easier to read the text file into a new module.

To do this, create a new module by pulling down the File menu and choosing the New Module menu command. Then pull down the File menu again, and choose Load Text. This opens up a dialog box listing all text files in the current directory. CONSTANT.TXT should be in your main Visual Basic directory (default installation would place this in C:\VB). Simply choose CONSTANT.TXT to enter the entire file into your module. These constants will then be available throughout your application.

Table 10-3 lists the value of the constant, the CONSTANT.TXT constant name, and a brief description of what the constant means.

Value	CONSTANT.TXT	Meaning
DrawMode property		
1	BLACKNESS	All shapes are black
2	NOT_MERGE_PEN	Colors are the inverse of Merge Pen
3	MASK_NOT_PEN	Colors are a mixture of the BackColor and inverse of the FillColor
4	NOT_COPY_PEN	Colors are the inverse of the FillColor
5	MASK_PEN_NOT	Colors are a mixture of the FillColor and the inverse of the BackColor

(continued on next page)

(continued from previous page)

Value	CONSTANT.TXT	Meaning
6	INVERT	Output is inverse of the BackColor property
7	XOR_PEN	Colors are a mixture of the FillColor and BackColor
8	NOT_MASK_PEN	Colors are the inverse of Mask Pen
9	MASK_PEN	Colors are the common ones between the BackColor and FillColor
10	NOT_XOR_PEN	Colors are the inverse of the Xor Pen colors
11	NOP	Output remains unmodified
12	MERGE_NOT_PEN	Colors are a mixture of BackColor and inverse of FillColor
13	COPY_PEN	(Default) FillColor
14	MERGE_PEN_NOT	Colors are a mixture of the FillColor and inverse of BackColor
15	MERGE_PEN	Colors are a mixture of the FillColor and BackColor
16	WHITENESS	All shapes are white

DrawStyle property

Value	CONSTANT.TXT	Meaning
0	SOLID	_____
1	DASH	_ _ _ _ _
2	DOT	. . . .
3	DASH_DOT	_ . _ . _ . _
4	DASH_DOT_DOT	_ . . _ . . _
5	INVISIBLE	
6	INSIDE_SOLID	_____

Value	CONSTANT.TXT	Meaning
FillColor property		
&H0	BLACK	Black
&HFF	RED	Red
&HFF00	GREEN	Green
&HFFFF	YELLOW	Yellow
&HFF0000	BLUE	Blue
&HFF00FF	MAGENTA	Magenta
&HFFFF00	CYAN	Cyan
&HFFFFFF	WHITE	White
FillStyle property		
0	SOLID	Solid fill
1	TRANSPARENT	(Default) Transparent, no fill
2	HORIZONTAL_LINE	Horizontal lines
3	VERTICAL_LINE	Vertical lines
4	UPWARD_DIAGONAL	Upward diagonal lines (from upper left to lower right)
5	DOWNWARD_DIAGONAL	Downward diagonal lines (from lower left to upper right)
6	CROSS	Cross-hatch
7	DIAGONAL	Diagonal cross-hatch

Table 10-3 CONSTANT.TXT values used with drawing shapes

CIRCLE METHOD

Objects Affected

Check	Clipboard	Combo	Command	CommonDlg
Data	Debug	Dir	Drive	File
▶ Form	Frame	Grid	Image	Label
Line	List	MDI Form	Menu	OLE
Option	▶ Picture	▶ Printer	Screen	Scroll
Shape	Text	Timer		

Purpose

The Circle method generates a curved shape on an indicated object on the screen or printer. This method can create a variety of curved objects including circles, ellipses (ovals), and arcs. The object on the screen to be drawn on is a form, picture box, or Printer object. Table 10-4 summarizes the arguments of the Circle method.

General Syntax

```
[form.]Circle [Step] (x!, y!), radius![, [color&][, [start!][, [end!][, aspect!]]]]
[form!]Name.Circle [Step] (x!, y!), radius![, [color&][, [start!][, [end!][, aspect!]]]]
Printer.Circle [Step] (x!, y!), radius![, [color&][, [start!][, [end!][, aspect!]]]]
```

Argument	Description
form	Name property of the form
Name	Name property of the object that the shape is drawn on. If not specified, the form is assumed
Printer	'Printer' indicates the Printer object
Step	If 'Step' is present, makes center coordinates relative to CurrentX and CurrentY
(x!,y!)	The horizontal and vertical coordinates of the shape's center
radius!	The radius (distance from center to edge) of the circle or arc
color&	The RGB color of the outline of the shape; if not specified then use current ForeColor

Argument	Description
start!, end!	Indicates the beginning and ending position, in radians, of a partial circle or arc
aspect!	The aspect ratio of the shape; <1 is horizontal ellipse, =1 is a circle, >1 is vertical ellipse

Table 10-4 Arguments of the Circle method

Example Syntax

```
Sub Command1_Click ()
    'Draws a circle with a slice taken out.
    'This slice grows larger each time the user
    'presses the Command1 command button.

    Static Start As Double           'Defines a static variable
    Cls                              'Clears the form
    Aspect! = 1                      'Aspect = 1:1; a circle
    FillColor = QBColor(7)           'Changes color to white
    FillStyle = 0                    'Makes all objects solid
    X! = ScaleWidth / 2              'Defines x as half ScaleWidth.
    Y! = ScaleHeight / 2             'Defines y as half ScaleHeight.
    R = ScaleWidth / 3               'Defines r as 1/3 ScaleWidth.
    If Abs(Start) > 6.283 Then       'Checks if Start is greater than 6.283.
        Start = 0                    'Defines Start as 0
    End If
    Circle (X!, Y!), R, QBColor(0), Start, -6.283, Aspect!
    Start = Start - .785             'Reduces Start value
End Sub
```

Description

The Circle method produces a curved shape on a form, picture box, or Printer object with several arguments that modify the shape's appearance.

If the keyword Step follows the word Circle, then the x! and y! coordinates are relative to the current values of the CurrentX and CurrentY properties. Omitting the word Step means that x! and y! are relative to the top-left corner of the object. The values of the x! (horizontal) and y! (vertical) coordinates define the position of the center of the shape. The radius! argument defines the curve's radius. All of these measurements are made in the unit of measure defined by the container's ScaleMode property.

The color& argument sets the color of the line that surrounds a curved shape and defaults to the ForeColor property when left blank. Define this argument with either an RGB hexadecimal number, RGB function, or QBColor function. Colors are covered in more detail in the FillColor entry later in this chapter. To skip an argument in the middle of the syntax, include the comma (,) for each argument excluded. Don't end a Circle method with a comma.

425

Using Pi

A circle is a line whose points are all the same distance from a point on a surface. The total length of this line is called the circumference. The distance between the line and the center point is the radius; the distance between each side of the line through the center point is called the diameter and is twice the radius. The ratio of the circumference to the diameter is a number called Pi (π). This is approximately equal to 3.1415926535.

Although most of us have forgotten more of our high school geometry than we can remember, using Pi can make your computations for the Circle method much easier. If you're using the Circle method, define a constant called PI and use the constant in your code. There are also many formulas that use PI, and you'll see a few examples of its use in this chapter. A few formulas are given in Table 10-5.

Formula	Description
2 * Pi * Radius	A circle's circumference
Pi * (Radius)^2	A circle's area
4 * Atn(1)	Finds the value of PI
Degrees * Pi / 180	Radian

Table 10-5 Circle formulas

The start! and end! Arguments

The start! and end! arguments of the Circle method define the dimensions of a partial circle or arc. Each partial circle's start! and end! arguments are expressed in radians. A radian equals (degrees * π / 180). This formula returns a value between 0 and 6.283 representing the degrees of a circle from 0 to 360 degrees. All start! and end! arguments have a value between -2π radians (-6.283) and 2π radians (-6.283). In Visual Basic the 360-degree point on a circle is at the three o'clock position on the circle. Table 10-6 displays the values to use for possible positions on a circle from 45 to 360 at intervals of 45 degrees. Figure 10-2 visually displays these positions on a circle.

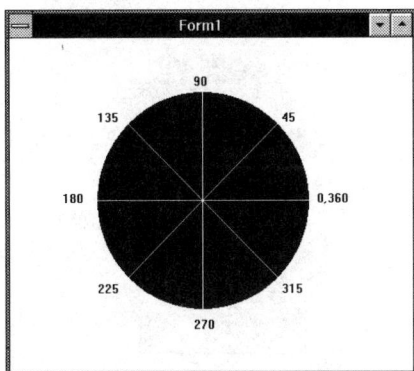

Figure 10-2 Degrees on a circle

Degrees	Approximate Value	Formula
360	6.283	360 * PI/180
315	5.498	315 * PI/180
270	4.712	270 * PI/180
225	3.927	225 * PI/180
180	3.142	180 * PI/180
135	2.356	135 * PI/180
90	1.571	90 * PI/180
45	0.785	45 * PI/180
0	0.000	0 * PI/180

Table 10-6 Approximate values for start! and end! positions on a circle

In the example syntax, the end! argument changes each time that the command button is pressed to reflect a larger and larger slice removed from the circle. Note that the circles drawn by the pressing of the Command1 command button appear behind the button, since drawn graphics are always placed under existing controls. This obscures any parts of the circles that are in the same position as the command button. Figures 10-3 and 10-4 show what these examples might look like.

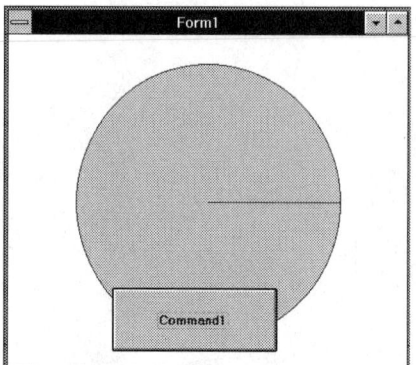

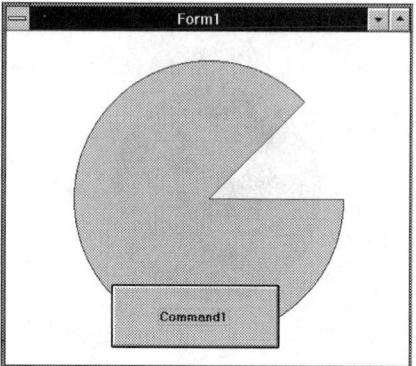

Figure 10-3 Example syntax shows full circle. Note circle is behind command button, demonstrating that in normal layering graphics methods appear behind other interface elements

Figure 10-4 Example syntax shows partial circle after Command1 is pressed

Partial Circles and Arcs

Using the start! and end! arguments in a Circle method produces partial circles. The part of the circle displayed appears between the boundaries of the degrees indicated. When start! and end! are positive, only the outer line on the circumference of the circle is drawn. When the values of the start! and end! arguments are negative numbers, an additional line appears from the center of the circle to the edge of the drawn partial circle. Figure 10-5 displays some example arcs. In the example syntax, the end! argument reduces in size with each pressing of the Command1 command button. This produces a smaller visible portion of the circle on the screen.

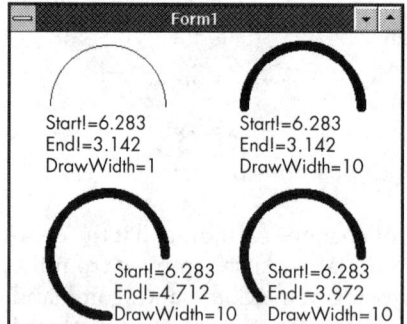

Figure 10-5 The Circle method allows you to draw partial circles, or arcs

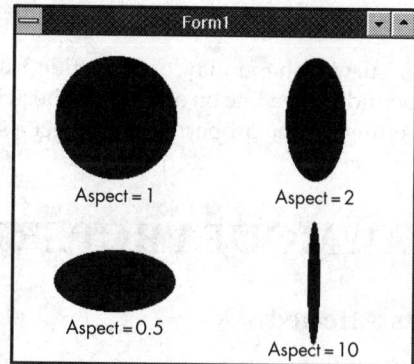

Figure 10-6 The Aspect property lets you create ellipses

Ellipses

The value of the Aspect argument of a Circle method defines the aspect ratio, or whether a circle is a perfect circle or elongated. When the aspect argument is one (1), the horizontal and vertical distances from the edge of the circle to the center are each equal to the radius. If the value is less than one, then the circle is elongated horizontally. Setting the aspect argument to a value greater than one creates a vertical ellipse. A value specified in the aspect argument defines the ratio of difference between the horizontal and vertical dimensions of the circle. Figure 10-6 shows the effects of the aspect on the drawing of a circle.

The FillColor and FillStyle Properties

The FillColor and FillStyle properties affect the contents of a shape drawn with the Circle method. A shape contains the color indicated by the FillColor property of the form, picture box, or Printer object. Depending on the setting of the FillStyle property, the shape contains a solid or pattern form of the color set in the FillColor property.

The DrawWidth Property

The DrawWidth property defines the width of a line that surrounds a shape drawn with the Circle method. If the start! and end! arguments of the Circle method have positive values, then the DrawWidth property defines the width of the line drawn to the center of the circle.

Example

The Shape project at the end of the chapter uses the Circle method to draw circles on the pictSurface picture box. Pressing the cmndDrawCircle command button draws the circle, using the appropriate settings in the combo boxes.

429

Comments

A curved shape may only be filled with a color or pattern when completely bounded by a line on all sides. Otherwise, the shape is empty no matter what the settings of the properties that affect a shape's interior.

DRAWMODE PROPERTY

Objects Affected

Check	Clipboard	Combo	Command	CommonDlg
Data	Debug	Dir	Drive	File
▶ Form	Frame	Grid	Image	Label
▶ Line	List	MDI Form	Menu	OLE
Option	▶ Picture	▶ Printer	Screen	Scroll
▶ Shape	Text	Timer		

Purpose

The DrawMode property determines what happens to a shape's colors when the shape appears on the screen. This property modifies the colors of the FillColor, ForeColor, and BackColor properties of a form, picture box, or Printer object to produce differing results. You can read and write this property at both runtime and design time. Tables 10-7 and 10-8 summarize the arguments of the DrawMode property.

General Syntax

```
[form.]DrawMode [ = mode%]
[form!]Name.DrawMode [ = mode%]
Printer.DrawMode [ = mode%]
```

Argument	Description
form	Name property of form
Name	Name property of the control
Printer	'Printer' indicates Printer object
mode%	Value representing the appearance of new shapes

Table 10-7 Arguments of DrawMode property

430

mode%	CONSTANT.TXT	Effect
1	BLACKNESS	All shapes are black
2	NOT_MERGE_PEN	Colors are the inverse of Merge Pen
3	MASK_NOT_PEN	Colors are a mixture of the BackColor and inverse of the FillColor
4	NOT_COPY_PEN	Colors are the inverse of the FillColor
5	MASK_PEN_NOT	Colors are a mixture of the FillColor and the inverse of the BackColor
6	INVERT	Output is inverse of the BackColor property
7	XOR_PEN	Colors are a mixture of the FillColor and BackColor.
8	NOT_MASK_PEN	Colors are the inverse of Mask Pen
9	MASK_PEN	Colors are the common ones between the BackColor and FillColor
10	NOT_XOR_PEN	Colors are the inverse of the Xor Pen colors
11	NOP	Output remains unmodified
12	MERGE_NOT_PEN	Colors are a mixture of BackColor and inverse of FillColor
13	COPY_PEN	(Default) FillColor
14	MERGE_PEN_NOT	Colors are a mixture of the Fill Color and inverse of BackColor
15	MERGE_PEN	Colors are a mixture of the FillColor and BackColor
16	WHITENESS	All shapes are white

Table 10-8 Possible settings and effects of the DrawMode property

Example Syntax

```
Sub DisplayColor (Num As Integer, Con As Control)
     If Num = 0 Then Con.Text = "Black"
     If Num = 1 Then Con.Text = "Blue"
     If Num = 2 Then Con.Text = "Green"
     If Num = 3 Then Con.Text = "Cyan"
     If Num = 4 Then Con.Text = "Red"
     If Num = 5 Then Con.Text = "Magenta"
     If Num = 6 Then Con.Text = "Yellow"
     If Num = 7 Then Con.Text = "White"
     If Num = 8 Then Con.Text = "Gray"
     If Num = 9 Then Con.Text = "Light Blue"
     If Num = 10 Then Con.Text = "Light Green"
     If Num = 11 Then Con.Text = "Light Cyan"
     If Num = 12 Then Con.Text = "Light Red"
     If Num = 13 Then Con.Text = "Light Magenta"
     If Num = 14 Then Con.Text = "Light Yellow"
     If Num = 15 Then Con.Text = "Bright White"
End Sub
```

```
Sub Form_Click ()
     Static Color As Integer           'Defines temporary variable
     Cls                               'Clears form of graphics
     FillColor = QBColor(Color)        'Defines the color
     FillStyle = 0                     'Graphics are solid
     DrawWidth = 5                     'Drawn lines are 5 pixels in width
     ForeColor = QBColor(1)            'ForeColor is blue
     If DrawMode = 16 Then             'Checks if DrawMode is 16
         DrawMode = 1                  'Changes DrawMode to 1
     Else
         DrawMode = DrawMode + 1       'Increments DrawMode by 1
     End If
     Text1.Text = Str$(DrawMode)       'Display the current DrawMode setting
     DisplayColor Color, Text2         'Calls sub procedure
     X = ScaleWidth / 2                'Defines X as half the width of screen
     Y = ScaleHeight / 2               'Defines Y as half the height of screen
     R = ScaleWidth / 4                'Defines R as 1/4 the width of screen
     Circle (X, Y), R                  'Draws a circle
     If Color = 15 Then                'Checks if Color is 15
         Color = 0                     'Changes Color to black
     Else
         Color = Color + 1             'Increments Color by 1
     End If
     FillColor = QBColor(Color)        'Changes FillColor
     DisplayColor Color, Text3         'Calls sub function DisplayColor
     X = 2 * ScaleWidth / 3            'Defines X as 2/3 the width of screen
     Y = 2 * ScaleHeight / 3           'Defines Y as 2/3 the width of screen
     Circle (X, Y), 1000               'Draws a circle
End Sub
```

Description

The DrawMode property affects the color of shapes drawn on the screen. When
the DrawMode property does not refer to a specific object, the form's DrawMode

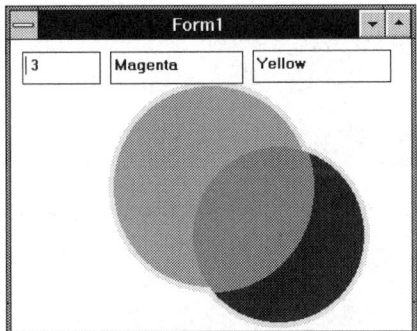

Figure 10-7 Example syntax shows the effects of the DrawMode property

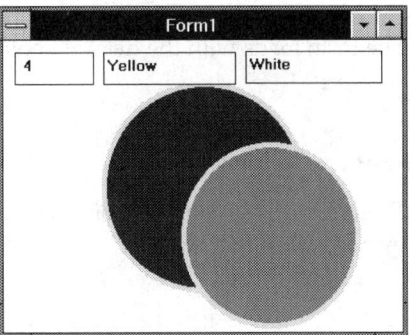

Figure 10-8 Another example of what the example syntax produces

property changes. The mode% argument determines which DrawMode setting subsequent graphics actions take. Each object starts with a default DrawMode property set to 13 (Copy Pen). This setting draws the shape normally. Table 10-8 summarizes the mode% argument's possible values. Notice that each of these values indicates what kind of change to make to a shape's normal colors. The Drawing Shapes Summary at the beginning of this chapter gives the details on how to use the CONSTANT.TXT values.

Visualizing these modes without actually seeing them can be challenging. The example syntax demonstrates each of these settings with each click of the form; this should help you get a feel for how each mode works. Notice that sometimes nothing displays. Try changing the BackColor property to another color and see how this affects each of these settings. As noted earlier the ForeColor and BackColor properties remain unchanged. Although the FillColor property changes, its alteration is independent of the settings of the DrawMode property. Figures 10-7 and 10-8 illustrate two samples created with the example syntax.

Xor Pen

Although each pen has its uses, the Xor Pen can be a particular problem solver for you. If you draw the exact same graphic twice in a row with the Xor Pen, it resets everything back to how it was originally. Thus you can produce simple animation by drawing the object with the Xor Pen, then drawing it again with the Xor Pen in the same position. This erases the graphic. Increment the position and start the process over again to produce the illusion of movement.

Example

In the Shape project at the end of this chapter, the DrawMode property determines how the indicated colors display on the pictSurface picture box. The cmboPickPen combo box lists the possible settings of the DrawMode property. The form loads with the default choice set to Copy Pen.

Comments

This property has no effect on previously drawn shapes, unless they are covered by a newly drawn shape.

DRAWSTYLE PROPERTY

Objects Affected

Check	Clipboard	Combo	Command	CommonDlg
Data	Debug	Dir	Drive	File
▶ Form	Frame	Grid	Image	Label
Line	List	MDI Form	Menu	OLE
Option	▶ Picture	▶ Printer	Screen	Scroll
Shape	Text	Timer		

Purpose

The DrawStyle property controls the appearance of the line surrounding a drawn shape on a form, picture box, or Printer object. An object's DrawStyle property defaults to producing a solid line. Using the other possible settings of the DrawStyle property, the line may change to a dashed line, dotted line, dash-dot line, or dash-dot-dot line. When the DrawStyle property is invisible, the line around a shape does not appear. This property only affects a shape when it is being drawn. Any changes made to this property have no effect on those images that have already been drawn. Table 10-9 summarizes the arguments for the DrawStyle property, and Table 10-10 summarizes the possible values for this property.

General Syntax

```
[form.]DrawStyle [ = style%]
[form!]Name.DrawStyle [ = style%]
Printer.DrawStyle [ = style%]
```

Argument	Description
form	Name property of form
Name	Name property of picture box
Printer	'Printer' indicates the Printer object
style%	Value representing the appearance of lines around shapes

Table 10-9 Arguments of DrawStyle property

style%	CONSTANT.TXT	Example
0	SOLID	_____
1	DASH	_ _ _ _ _ _
2	DOT	....
3	DASH_DOT	_ . _ . _ . _
4	DASH_DOT_DOT	_ . . _ . . _
5	INVISIBLE	
6	INSIDE_SOLID	_____

Table 10-10 Possible settings of the DrawStyle property

Example Syntax

```
Sub Form_Click ()
    If DrawStyle = 7 Then
        DrawStyle = 0
        Exit Sub
    End If
    DrawStyle = DrawStyle + 1      'Increments DrawStyle by one
    X = ScaleWidth / 2             'Defines X as half the width of form
    Y = ScaleHeight / 2            'Defines Y as half the height of form
    C = DrawStyle * 2              'Sets radius to ever increasing sized circles
    R = ScaleWidth / C             'Defines R as a fraction of width of form
    Circle (X, Y), R               'Draws a circle
End Sub
```

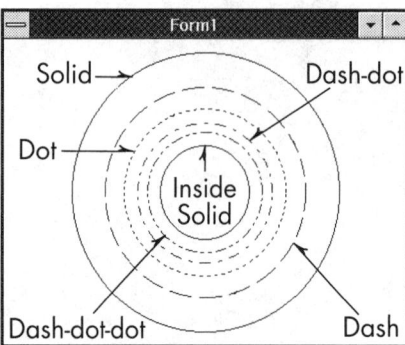

Figure 10-9 Different settings of
DrawStyle property

Description

The DrawStyle property sets the type of line placed around a shape. When a DrawStyle expression does not include an object, the DrawMode property of the current form changes. The style% argument sets the DrawStyle. Each object starts with a default DrawStyle property set to solid (0). With this setting, the line around a shape displays as a solid line. The Drawing Shapes Summary at the beginning of this chapter gives the details on how to use the CONSTANT.TXT values.

The example syntax shows results of each of the possible settings of the style% variable inside the circle. Each of these line patterns display on the screen in successively smaller circles. Figure 10-9 displays what this example might look like on your screen.

The DrawWidth Property

The DrawWidth property defines the thickness of the line around a drawn shape. Changing the value of the DrawWidth property to greater than 1 pixel in width makes the line around the shape solid when the DrawStyle property is a solid line, dash line, dot line, dash-dot line, or dash-dot-dot line (values 0 through 4). When this happens, the actual setting of the DrawStyle property remains unchanged. If the DrawWidth property of the form in the example syntax changes to a value greater than one, the first settings produce four circles with solid lines. This demonstrates the interaction of the DrawWidth and DrawStyle properties.

Example

In the Shape project at the end of this chapter, the DrawStyle property determines how the indicated lines display on the pictSurface picture box. The cmboPickStyle combo box lists the possible settings of the DrawStyle property. The form loads with the default choice set to Solid.

436

Comments

The ForeColor property sets the color of the line around a shape.

DRAWWIDTH PROPERTY

Objects Affected

Check	Clipboard	Combo	Command	CommonDlg
Data	Debug	Dir	Drive	File
▶ Form	Frame	Grid	Image	Label
Line	List	MDI Form	Menu	OLE
Option	▶ Picture	▶ Printer	Screen	Scroll
Shape	Text	Timer		

Purpose

The DrawWidth property sets the width of lines drawn on a form, picture box, or Printer object. A value given to the DrawWidth property represents the thickness of the line in pixels. When this property's value increases, the border around a drawn shape such as a circle or square thickens. Table 10-11 summarizes the arguments of the DrawWidth property.

General Syntax

```
[form.]DrawWidth [ = size%]
[form!]Name.DrawWidth [ = size%]
Printer.DrawWidth [ = size%]
```

Argument	Description
form	Name property of form
Name	Name property of picture box
Printer	'Printer' indicates Printer object
size%	Value representing the width of lines around shapes in pixels

Table 10-11 Arguments of DrawWidth property

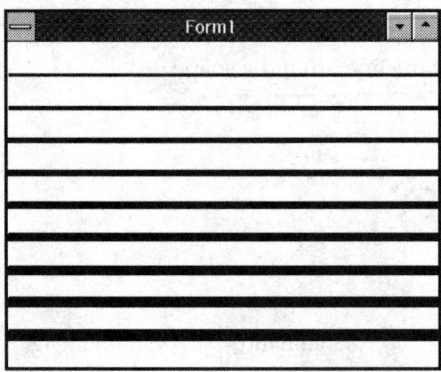

Figure 10-10 DrawWidth property in
the example syntax

Example Syntax

```
Sub Form_Click ()
    Static Y As Integer      'Remember the Y coordinate from click to click...
    CX = ScaleWidth / 500    'Define the horizontal plotting increment
    CY = ScaleHeight / 10    'Define the vertical plotting increment
    DrawWidth = DrawWidth + 1 'Increments DrawWidth
    X = CX                   'Starting point
    Y = Y + CY               'Starting line (incremented up from last click...)
    For L = 1 To 499
        X = X + CX           'Move over by the horizontal plotting increment
        PSet (X, Y)          'Draws a point on a form
    Next L
End Sub
```

Description

The DrawWidth property sets the thickness of a line drawn on a form, picture box, or Printer object. When a DrawWidth property expression doesn't specify an object to act on, the form's DrawWidth property changes. The size% argument sets the DrawWidth. Each object begins with a default DrawWidth property set to one, drawing lines that are 1 pixel thick.

In the example syntax, the DrawWidth property of the form increases by one with each click of the form. Notice that the line created by the PSet method is successively thicker. Figure 10-10 shows what this example might look like on your screen.

The DrawStyle Property

If the DrawWidth property changes to greater than 1, a DrawStyle property of 1, 2, 3, or 4 has no effect on the appearance of a drawn line, which will be solid. With the DrawWidth property set to 1, the DrawStyle property changes the line or lines in

438

a drawn shape from a solid line to dashes, dots, or a combination of the two depending on that property's value. When the DrawWidth property is larger than 4, a line drawn by either the Circle or Line method is solid. This has no effect on the actual setting of the DrawStyle property.

Example

In the Shape project at the end of this chapter, the DrawWidth property determines how the indicated lines display on the pictSurface picture box. The cmboPickWidth combo box lists some of the possible settings of the DrawWidth property.

FILLCOLOR PROPERTY

Objects Affected

Check	Clipboard	Combo	Command	CommonDlg
Data	Debug	Dir	Drive	File
▶ Form	Frame	Grid	Image	Label
Line	List	MDI Form	Menu	OLE
Option	▶ Picture	▶ Printer	Screen	Scroll
▶ Shape	Text	Timer		

Purpose

The FillColor property sets the color of the interior of circles and boxes drawn in a container. Define an object's FillColor property either directly (with a hexadecimal number) or with the QBColor or RGB functions. Any changes made to the FillColor property have no affect on the colors of previously drawn shapes already on the object. This property works in conjunction with the FillStyle property to choose what will fill the interior of circles and boxes. Table 10-12 lists the arguments of the FillColor property, and Table 10-13 lists the values of some common colors.

General Syntax

```
[form.]FillColor [ = color&]
[form!]Name.FillColor [ = color&]
Printer.FillColor [ = color&]
```

Argument	Description
form	Name property of form
Name	Name property of the control
Printer	Printer object
color&	Value representing the interior color of drawn shapes

Table 10-12 Arguments of FillColor property

Color	CONSTANT.TXT	Red Value	Green Value	Blue Value	Hexadecimal	QBColor
Black	BLACK	0	0	0	&H0	0
Red	RED	255	0	0	&HFF	4
Green	GREEN	0	255	0	&HFF00	2
Yellow	YELLOW	0	255	255	&HFFFF	6
Blue	BLUE	0	0	255	&HFF0000	1
Magenta	MAGENTA	255	0	255	&HFF00FF	5
Cyan	CYAN	0	255	255	&HFFFF00	3
White	WHITE	255	255	255	&HFFFFFF	15
Light Gray	n/a	192	192	192	&H00C0C0C0	7
Dark Gray	n/a	128	128	128	&H00808080	8

Table 10-13 Values of common colors in RGB, hexadecimal, and QBColor formats

Example Syntax

```
Sub Form_Click ()
    AutoRedraw = True        'Make sure graphics are drawn immediately
    Cls                      'Clears the form
```

440

```
    ScaleWidth = 4              'Divides the width of the form into four parts
    ScaleHeight = 4             'Divides the height of the form into four parts
    DrawWidth = 5               'Defines thickness as 5 pixels
    FillStyle = 0               'Defines FillStyle as solid
    ForeColor = QBColor(0)      'Defines ForeColor as black (for the box borders)
    Color = 0                   'This will be the FillColor; start with black
    For H = 0 To 3              'Draws 16 colored boxes on the screen with the
        For W = 0 To 3          'FillColor property and Line method.
            FillColor = QBColor(Color)
            Line (W, H)-(W + 1, H + 1), , B
            Color = Color + 1'increment to the next color
        Next W
    Next H
End Sub
```

Description

The FillColor property defines the interior color of drawn circles and boxes on forms, picture boxes, or Printer objects. If a FillColor property expression does not include the object's name, then the current form's FillColor property changes. The FillColor property defaults to black. The *color&* variable refers to the Long value given to the FillColor property. This integer must be in hexadecimal form. You can set this property with either the RGB or QBColor functions, or by directly specifying a hexadecimal number. Table 10-13 lists some common color values; the Forms and Menus Summary at the beginning of this chapter gives instructions on how to use CONSTANT.TXT values.

In the example syntax, the FillColor property changes each time a new box is drawn on the screen, incrementing the value used with the QBColor function by one to get the next color. This results in the division of the form into 16 equal parts, one for each of the 16 possible colors of the QBColor function. Figure 10-11 shows what this example might look like.

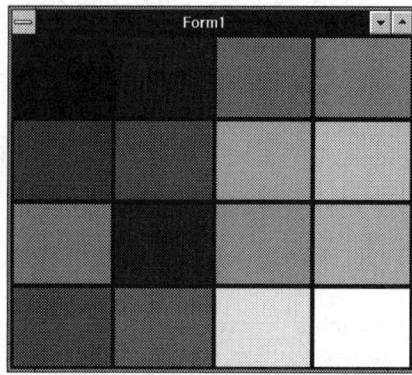

Figure 10-11 Example syntax demonstrates the FillColor property

441

The RGB and QBColor Functions

Both the RGB and QBColor functions provide a means of defining the color of the FillColor property without using the confusing hexadecimal RGB codes. If standard colors like red, green, blue, and cyan are acceptable, then the QBColor function works very well. When you require a special mix of RGB values, the RGB function allows you to specify any one of over 16 million colors. Be careful not to give this property a color that matches the background color of the form or picture box, or else you won't be able to see the graphics shape you've just drawn. Table 10-13 lists the most common settings of the RGB and QBColor functions. In the example syntax, the QBColor function serves as a means of defining the color of each of the boxes as they appear on the screen. Notice that the color of each square is unaffected by the changes made to the FillColor property for the subsequent squares. Once a shape appears on the screen or printer, its attributes are permanent.

The FillStyle Property

The FillStyle property works in conjunction with the FillColor property to define the pattern and color inside drawn circles and boxes. If the FillStyle of a form, picture box, or Printer object is left at the default value of 1 (Transparent), then any drawn objects appear empty. When the FillStyle property is 0 (Solid), the drawn circles and boxes contain the color indicated by the FillColor property. Since the default value of the FillColor property is 0 (Black), the default output is a black circle or box (provided the FillStyle property is set to solid). With the FillStyle property set to a value between two (2) and seven (7) inclusive, the FillColor property determines what color to give the patterns drawn inside the circle or box. In the example syntax, the FillStyle property is 0 to indicate that each of the boxes drawn contain solid styles of the colors indicated by the FillColor property.

Example

In the Shape project at the end of this chapter, the FillColor property determines what color the shapes get filled with on the pictSurface picture box. The cmboPickColor combo box lists some of the possible settings of the FillColor property, and the QBColor function provides the actual color setting. The form loads with the default choice set to Black.

Comments

Remember to change the FillStyle property from the default setting of 1 (Transparent) or the FillColor property has no effect on any shapes drawn with the Line or Circle methods.

FILLSTYLE PROPERTY

Objects Affected

Check	Clipboard	Combo	Command	CommonDlg
Data	Debug	Dir	Drive	File
▶ Form	Frame	▶ Grid	Image	Label
Line	List	MDI Form	Menu	OLE
Option	▶ Picture	▶ Printer	Screen	Scroll
▶ Shape	Text	Timer		

Purpose

The FillStyle property defines the pattern of the interior of a drawn shape on a form, picture box, shape, or Printer object. An object's FillStyle property is a value between 0 and 7 inclusive. This property works in conjunction with the FillColor property to specify what fills the interior of circles and boxes. Tables 10-14 and 10-15 define the arguments used with the FillStyle property.

General Syntax

```
[form.]FillStyle [ = style%]
[form!]Name.FillStyle [ = style%]
Printer.FillStyle [ = style%]
```

Argument	Description
form	Name property of form
Name	Name property of the control
Printer	'Printer' indicates the Printer object
style%	Value representing the style to place in the interior of drawn shapes

Table 10-14 Arguments of FillStyle property

style%	CONSTANT.TXT	Description
0	SOLID	Solid fill
1	TRANSPARENT	(Default) Transparent, no fill
2	HORIZONTAL_LINE	Horizontal lines
3	VERTICAL_LINE	Vertical lines
4	UPWARD_DIAGONAL	Upward diagonal lines (from upper left to lower right)
5	DOWNWARD_DIAGONAL	Downward diagonal lines (from lower left to upper right)
6	CROSS	Cross-hatch
7	DIAGONAL	Diagonal cross-hatch

Table 10-15 List of possible settings of the FillStyle property

Example Syntax

```
Sub Form_Click ()
    AutoRedraw = True            'Makes sure graphics are drawn immediately
    Cls                          'Clears the form
    ScaleWidth = 2               'Divides the width of the form into two parts
    ScaleHeight = 4              'Divides the height of the form into four parts
    FillColor = QBColor(0)       'Defines Color as Black
    FillStyle = 0                'Start with solid fill
    For H = 0 To 3               'Draws 8 patterned boxes on the screen with the
        For W = 0 To 1           'FillColor property and Line method.
            Line (W, H)-(W + 1, H + 1), , B
            If FillStyle = 7 Then Exit Sub   'exit if we've done them all
            FillStyle = FillStyle + 1        'next fill style
        Next W
    Next H
End Sub
```

Description

The FillStyle property defines the interior pattern style of drawn shapes. If a FillStyle property expression does not include the object's name, then the current form's FillStyle property changes. Each form, picture box, and Printer object begins with the FillColor property set to transparent. With its default transparent setting, the FillStyle property prevents the display of the color set in the FillColor

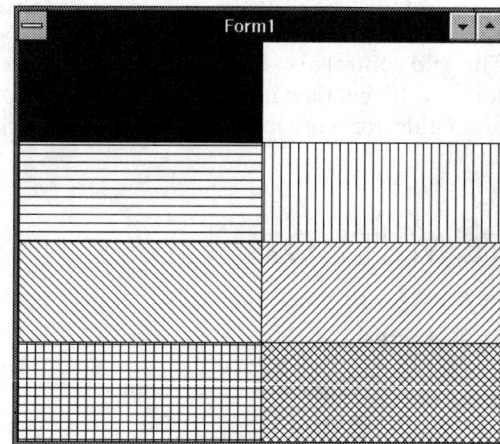

Figure 10-12 The eight possible FillStyles

property. Setting the FillStyle property to 0 produces the solid color indicated by the FillColor property. The other settings, as listed in Table 10-15, give various patterns. See the Forms and Menus Summary at the beginning of this chapter for instructions on how to use CONSTANT.TXT values.

In the example syntax, the FillStyle property increments for each box drawn to display the different possible settings. Figure 10-12 shows each one of the eight possible FillStyles.

The FillColor Property

The FillStyle property works in conjunction with the FillColor property to define the pattern and color inside drawn circles and boxes. If the FillStyle of a form, picture box, or Printer object is left at the default value of 1 (Transparent), then any drawn objects appear empty no matter what the FillColor property is. When the FillStyle property is 0 (Solid), the drawn circles and boxes contain the color indicated by the FillColor property. Since the default value of the FillColor property is 0 (Black), the default output is a black circle or box. With the FillStyle property set to a value between 2 and 7 inclusive, the FillColor property determines what color to give the patterns drawn inside the circle or box.

Example

In the Shape project at the end of this chapter, the FillStyle property determines what style the shapes get filled with on the pictSurface picture box. The cmboPickPattern combo box lists all of the possible settings of the FillStyle property. The form loads with the default choice set to Solid.

445

Comment

The grid control also has a FillStyle property. The grid's use of this property is totally different than its usage as explained above. See Chapter 18, Lists, Combos, and Grids, for more information about the Grid control.

LINE METHOD

Objects Affected

Check	Clipboard	Combo	Command	CommonDlg
Data	Debug	Dir	Drive	File
▸ Form	Frame	Grid	Image	Label
Line	List	MDI Form	Menu	OLE
Option	▸ Picture	▸ Printer	Screen	Scroll
Shape	Text	Timer		

Purpose

The Line method draws a line or box shape on an object on the screen or printer. This method can create a number of shapes, including straight lines, squares, rectangles, polygons, and triangles. The object drawn on must be a form, picture box, or Printer object. Shapes drawn on a form have no effect on the controls placed on the form. Table 10-16 lists the different arguments of the Line method.

General Syntax

```
[form.]Line [[Step] (x1!, y1!)] - [Step] (x2!, y2!) [, [color&], B [F]]]
[form!]Name.Line [[Step] (x1!, y1!)] - [Step] (x2!, y2!) [, [color&], B [F]]]
Printer.Line [[Step] (x1!, y1!)] - [Step] (x2!, y2!) [, [color&], B [F]]]
```

Argument	Description
form	Name property of the form
Name	Name of the picture box
Step	If first 'Step' is present, makes start coordinates relative to CurrentX and CurrentY
x1!, y1!	The horizontal and vertical coordinates of the start of the line

Argument	Description
Step	If second 'Step' is present, makes end coordinates relative to start coordinates
x2!, y2!	The horizontal and vertical coordinates of the end of the line
color&	The RGB color of the outline of the shape; if not specified then use current ForeColor
B	This argument creates a box with the indicated coordinates serving as the opposite corners.
F	If 'B' argument present, then 'F' fills the box with the color specified by the color& argument

Table 10-16 Arguments of the Line method

Example Syntax

```
Sub Picture1_Click ()
    Clr = QBColor(0)                    'Lines will draw in Black
    Picture1.Cls                        'Clear picture
    Picture1.ScaleWidth = 20            'Divides picture's width into 20 parts
    Picture1.ScaleHeight = 20           'Divides picture's height into 20 parts

    Picture1.Line (1, 1)-(4, 4), Clr    'Straight line
    Picture1.Line (10, 1)-(14, 4), Clr, B  'Draws a box.
    Picture1.Line (1, 10)-(4, 14), Clr, BF 'Draws a filled in box

    Picture1.Line (13, 11)-(14, 14), Clr   'Draws a triangle
    Picture1.Line (14, 14)-(11, 13), Clr
    Picture1.Line (11, 13)-(13, 11), Clr

    Picture1.DrawWidth = Picture1.DrawWidth + 1   'Increases the size of the DrawWidth.
End Sub
```

Description

A Line method produces a line or box on a form, picture box, or Printer object. When a Line method expression does not include the object's name, the shape appears on the current form.

The Line method coordinates (x1!, y1!) and (x2!, y2!) represent the positions of the start and end points on a line or the upper-left and lower-right corners of a box. Each of the x1!, x2! coordinates represent the horizontal positions; the y1! and y2! coordinates define the vertical positions. If the Step keyword precedes (x1!, y1!), then the coordinates are relative to the values of the CurrentX and CurrentY properties. If Step precedes (x2!, y2!), then the ending coordinates are relative to the starting coordinates (x1!, y1!). When Step does not appear in either the first or second instance, the appropriate set of coordinates are absolute references relative to the top-left corner of the object.

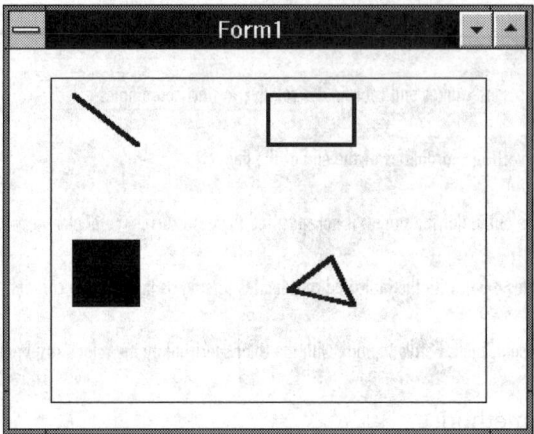

Figure 10-13 Example syntax shows the
Line method in action

The color& argument sets the color of the line surrounding the shape and defaults to the ForeColor property. This argument contains a hexadecimal number that you may specify with an RGB function, a QBColor function, or by directly giving a hexadecimal number. See the entry on FillColor in this chapter for more details about the color& argument.

You may skip an argument in the middle of the syntax, but must include the comma "," for each argument excluded. Don't end a Line method with a comma. Look at the Line method expressions in the example syntax for some examples.

In the example syntax, the Line method draws a line, square, filled-in square, and triangle. Each Line method expression demonstrates the proper operation of this method with different results. The creation of the triangle involves the integration of three different Line method expressions. Figure 10-13 shows what each of these shapes look like on the screen.

The B and F Arguments

When the B and F arguments are in a Line method expression, a box appears instead of a line. In this case the start point (x1!, y1!) coordinates represent the top-left corner of the box and the end point (x2!, y2!) defines the bottom-right corner. If the F argument appears, the interior of the box is the color indicated by the color& argument. With the FillStyle set to the default setting of one (1=transparent), the F argument has no apparent effect; set FillStyle to another setting to see the interior fill. In the example syntax, the B argument and then the B & F arguments produce a square on the picture box. Notice that when the B argument is alone, an unfilled square displays. With both the B and F arguments, a square appears filled with the color specified by the color& argument.

448

Example

In the Shape project at the end of this chapter, the Line method draws lines, squares, rectangles, and triangles on the pictSurface picture box. The command buttons labeled Line, Square, Rectangle, and Triangle all contain Line methods to produce the indicated object on the Draw picture box. When the Line method appears without the B or F arguments in the cmndDrawLine_Click event, a line is drawn between the randomly indicated points. By adding the B argument to the Line method in the cmndDrawRectangle_Click event, a rectangle of varying size and location displays instead of a line. Three Line methods work together in the cmndDrawTriangle_Click event to produce the three sides of the triangle on the Draw picture box.

Comments

The Line method can create polygons or any other type of straight-line shape by making the starting point of one line begin at the same point of another line's end point. If you just need a square or rectangle, it's easier to use the B option.

THE SHAPE PROJECT

Project Overview

The Shape project demonstrates the methods and properties that directly affect the drawing of shapes. Using the Line and Circle methods, the Shape project places circles, lines, squares, rectangles, and triangles on the picture box. By manipulating the settings of the FillColor, FillStyle, DrawMode, DrawStyle, and DrawWidth properties, the Shape project visually displays how these properties affect the interaction between different drawn shapes.

The following pages discuss the assembly and operation of the Shape project. The first section deals with the assembly of the controls on the Shape form. Following this is a discussion that shows and briefly explains the contents of the subroutines of this project. Finally, there is a How It Works guide to the operation of the project. Read this information carefully and use the pictures of the form as guides in the process of assembling the project.

Assembling the Project

1. Make a new form with the objects and properties in Table 10-17. The graphical controls need to be precisely positioned by directly entering their position properties in the properties box.

449

Object	Property	Setting
Form	BorderStyle	1—Fixed Single
	Caption	Shapes Project
	MaxButton	False
Combo	Name	cmboPickWidth
	Style	2—Dropdown List
	TabIndex	1
Combo	Name	cmboPickColor
	Style	2—Dropdown List
	TabIndex	3
Combo	Name	cmboPickLine
	Style	2—Dropdown List
	TabIndex	5
Combo	Name	cmboPickPen
	Style	2—Dropdown List
	TabIndex	7
Combo	Name	cmboPickPattern
	Style	2—Dropdown List
	TabIndex	9
Command	Caption	&Circle
	Name	cmndDrawCircle

Object	Property	Setting
	TabIndex	10
Command	Caption	&Line
	Name	cmndDrawLine
	TabIndex	11
Command	Caption	&Square
	Name	cmndDrawSquare
	TabIndex	12
Command	Caption	&Box
	Name	cmndDrawBox
	TabIndex	13
Command	Caption	&Triangle
	Name	cmndDrawTriangle
	TabIndex	14
Command	Caption	"" {set it to nothing}
	Name	cmndClearScreen
	TabIndex	15
Label	Caption	&Width
	TabIndex	0
Label	Caption	C&olor
	TabIndex	2

(continued on next page)

451

(continued from previous page)

Object	Property	Setting
Label	Caption	Lin&e
	TabIndex	4
Label	Caption	&Pattern
	TabIndex	6
Label	Caption	Pe&n
	TabIndex	8
Picture Box	Height	3660
	Left	120
	Name	pictSurface
	TabIndex	16
	Top	1200
	Width	5385
Shape	BorderColor	&H00FFFFFF&, White
	BorderWidth	2
	Height	615
	Left	135
	Name	Shape1
	Top	5130
	Width	5415
Shape	BorderStyle	0 'Transparent
	FillColor	&H00808080&, Dark Gray

Object	Property	Setting
	FillStyle	0 'Solid
	Height	3645
	Left	225
	Name	Shape2
	Top	1320
	Width	5370
Line	BorderColor	&H00000000&, Black
	BorderWidth	2
	Name	Line1
	X1	135
	X2	135
	Y1	5145
	Y2	5720
Line	BorderColor	&H00000000&, Black
	BorderWidth	2
	Name	Line2
	X1	135
	X2	5517
	Y1	5130
	Y2	5130

Table 10-17 Elements of the Shape form

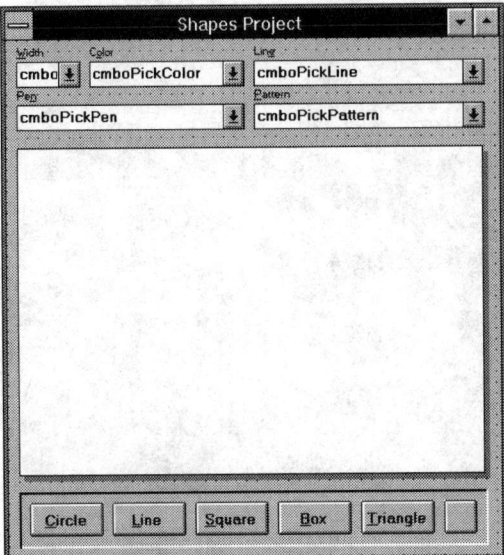

Figure 10-14 What the Shape form should
look like when completed

2. Size the objects on the screen as shown in Figure 10-14.

3. Enter the following code in the cmboPickColor_Click event subroutine. This code
triggers when the user selects a new color in the Color combo box. When this
code activates, the Draw form's FillColor property changes to the new color.

```
Sub cmboPickColor_Click ()
    pictSurface.FillColor = QBColor(cmboPickColor.ListIndex)
End Sub
```

4. Enter the following code in the cmboPickLine_Click event subroutine. When the
user clicks one of the options in the Line combo box, the index value of the chosen option redefines the setting of the DrawStyle property of the pictSurface picture box.

```
Sub cmboPickLine_Click ()
    pictSurface.DrawStyle = cmboPickLine.ListIndex
End Sub
```

5. Enter the following code in the cmboPickPattern_Click event subroutine. When
the user selects an option in the Pattern combo box, the FillStyle property of the
pictSurface picture box changes to the new setting.

```
Sub cmboPickPattern_Click ()
    pictSurface.FillStyle = cmboPickPattern.ListIndex
End Sub
```

454

6. Enter the following code in the cmboPickPen_Click event subroutine. When the user selects an option in the Pen combo box, the DrawMode property of the pictSurface picture box changes to the new setting.

```
Sub cmboPickPen_Click ()
    pictSurface.DrawMode = cmboPickPen.ListIndex + 1
End Sub
```

7. Enter the following code in the cmboPickWidth_Click event subroutine. When the user selects an option in the Width combo box, the DrawWidth property changes to the new setting.

```
Sub cmboPickWidth_Click ()
    pictSurface.DrawWidth = cmboPickWidth.ListIndex + 1
End Sub
```

8. Enter the following code in the cmndDrawBox_Click event subroutine. When the user clicks the Rectangle command button, this code draws a rectangle of random size and location.

```
Sub cmndDrawBox_Click ()
    X1 = Int((75 - (1)) * Rnd + (1))        'Pick starting coordinates
    Y1 = Int((75 - (1)) * Rnd + (1))
    X2 = Int((50 - (1)) * Rnd + (1))        'Pick ending coordinates
    Y2 = Int((50 - (1)) * Rnd + (1))
    pictSurface.Line (X1, Y1)-Step(X2, Y2), , B      'Draw the box
End Sub
```

9. Enter the following code in the cmndDrawCircle_Click event subroutine. When the user clicks the Circle command button, this code draws a circle of random size and location.

```
Sub cmndDrawCircle_Click ()
    X = Int((100 - 1) * Rnd + 1)            'Pick Center coordinates
    Y = Int((100 - 1) * Rnd + 1)
    R = Int((25 - 1) * Rnd + 1)             'Pick Radius
    pictSurface.Circle (X, Y), R            'Draw Circle
End Sub
```

10. Enter the following code in the cmndDrawLine_Click event subroutine. When the user clicks the Line command button, this code draws a line of random length and location.

```
Sub cmndDrawLine_Click ()
    X1 = Int((100 - 1) * Rnd + 1)           'Pick Starting Coordinates
    Y1 = Int((100 - 1) * Rnd + 1)
    X2 = Int((100 - 1) * Rnd + 1)           'Pick Ending Coordinates
    Y2 = Int((100 - 1) * Rnd + 1)
    pictSurface.Line (X1, Y1)-(X2, Y2)      'Draw Box
End Sub
```

11. Enter the following code in the cmndDrawSquare_Click event subroutine. When the user clicks the Square command button, this code draws a square of random size and location.

```
Sub cmndDrawSquare_Click ()
    X1 = Int((50 - 1) * Rnd + 1)          'Pick Starting Coordinates
    Y1 = Int((50 - 1) * Rnd + 1)
    X2 = Int((50 - 1) * Rnd + 1)          'Pick Ending Coordinates
    Y2 = X2
    pictSurface.Line (X1, Y1)-Step(X2, Y2), , B      'Draw Square
End Sub
```

12. Enter the following code in the cmndDrawTriangle_Click event subroutine. When the user clicks the Triangle command button, this code draws a triangle of random size and location.

```
Sub cmndDrawTriangle_Click ()
    X1 = Int((100 - 1) * Rnd + 1)         'Pick one corner
    Y1 = Int((100 - 1) * Rnd + 1)
    X2 = Int((100 - 1) * Rnd + 1)         'Pick another corner
    Y2 = Int((100 - 1) * Rnd + 1)
    X3 = Int((100 - 1) * Rnd + 1)         'Pick third corner
    Y3 = Int((100 - 1) * Rnd + 1)
    pictSurface.Line (X1, Y1)-(X2, Y2)    'Draw Triangle
    pictSurface.Line (X2, Y2)-(X3, Y3)
    pictSurface.Line (X3, Y3)-(X1, Y1)
End Sub
```

13. Enter the following code in the Form_Load event subroutine. This code processes when the program starts. At that time, the code adds the choices to all five of the combo boxes, sets their values to the normal defaults, and sets the default values of the pictSurface picture box.

```
Sub Form_Load ()
    For i = 1 To 10                       'Fill Width pick list with possible widths
        cmboPickWidth.AddItem Str$(i)
    Next i

    cmboPickColor.AddItem "Black"         'Fill Color pick list with possible colors
    cmboPickColor.AddItem "Blue"
    cmboPickColor.AddItem "Green"
    cmboPickColor.AddItem "Cyan"
    cmboPickColor.AddItem "Red"
    cmboPickColor.AddItem "Magenta"
    cmboPickColor.AddItem "Yellow"
    cmboPickColor.AddItem "White"
    cmboPickColor.AddItem "Gray"
    cmboPickColor.AddItem "Light Blue"
    cmboPickColor.AddItem "Light Green"
    cmboPickColor.AddItem "Light Cyan"
    cmboPickColor.AddItem "Light Red"
    cmboPickColor.AddItem "Light Magenta"
    cmboPickColor.AddItem "Light Yellow"
    cmboPickColor.AddItem "Bright White"

    cmboPickPattern.AddItem "Solid"       'Fill Pattern pick list with patterns
    cmboPickPattern.AddItem "Transparent"
```

456

```
cmboPickPattern.AddItem "Horizontal Line"
cmboPickPattern.AddItem "Vertical Line"
cmboPickPattern.AddItem "Upward Diagonal"
cmboPickPattern.AddItem "Downward Diagonal"
cmboPickPattern.AddItem "Cross"
cmboPickPattern.AddItem "Diagonal Cross"

cmboPickPen.AddItem "Blackness"              'Fill Pen pick list with possible pens
cmboPickPen.AddItem "Not Merge Pen"
cmboPickPen.AddItem "Mask Not Pen"
cmboPickPen.AddItem "Not Copy Pen"
cmboPickPen.AddItem "Mask Pen Not"
cmboPickPen.AddItem "Invert"
cmboPickPen.AddItem "Xor Pen"
cmboPickPen.AddItem "Not Mask Pen"
cmboPickPen.AddItem "Mask Pen"
cmboPickPen.AddItem "Not Xor Pen"
cmboPickPen.AddItem "Nop"
cmboPickPen.AddItem "Merge Not Pen"
cmboPickPen.AddItem "Copy Pen"
cmboPickPen.AddItem "Merge Pen Not"
cmboPickPen.AddItem "Merge Pen"
cmboPickPen.AddItem "Whiteness"

cmboPickLine.AddItem "Solid"                 'Fill Line pick list with possible pens
cmboPickLine.AddItem "Dash"
cmboPickLine.AddItem "Dot"
cmboPickLine.AddItem "Dash-Dot"
cmboPickLine.AddItem "Dash-Dot-Dot"
cmboPickLine.AddItem "Invisible"
cmboPickLine.AddItem "Inside Solid"

cmboPickWidth.ListIndex = 0                  '1      (These are all set to defaults)
cmboPickColor.ListIndex = 0                  'Black
cmboPickPattern.ListIndex = 0                'Solid
cmboPickPen.ListIndex = 13                   'Copy Pen
cmboPickLine.ListIndex = 0                   'Solid

pictSurface.ScaleHeight = 100                'Set up an easy custom scale
pictSurface.ScaleWidth = 100
pictSurface.AutoRedraw = True                'Make sure graphics redrawn immediately
End Sub
```

14. Enter the following code in the pictSurface_DblClick event and cmndClearScreen_Click event procedures. This code triggers when the user double-clicks on the picture box or clicks the blank command button. When this happens the pictSurface picture box clears of all the drawn shapes.

```
Sub pictSurface_DblClick ()
    pictSurface.Cls
End Sub

Sub cmndClearScreen_Click ()
    pictSurface.Cls
End Sub
```

How It Works

The Shape project displays a form with a picture box with several command buttons along the form's bottom edge. Each time the user presses one of these command buttons, a graphics image of random size appears in a random location on the picture box. The text on the command button determines what type of graphics appears. For example, a circle appears when the user presses the command button labeled Circle.

To change the way that the graphics get drawn, the user selects a new option in one of the Shape form's combo boxes. These selections represent all the possible settings of the properties that affect the appearance of graphics. The user clearly sees the ways that these properties interact by changing these properties.

The graphic shape and line controls add some pizzazz to the user interface. The Shape2 control serves as a "shadow" behind pictSurface to give it more definition, and Shape1 lies behind the command buttons to visually group them. Notice how the default layering leaves the standard controls like command buttons layered on top of the graphical shape control.

This second shape control has two line controls carefully positioned on the top and left to help create the appearance of being inset, or carved into the form. This illusion is created by setting the shape's border color to white, and then layering the black lines on the top and left. All standard controls (like command buttons) have the "light" coming from the top-left corner, so the black lines create the inset "shadow" and the shape control's white border creates the inset "highlight." Although this is a bit more work than the 3D controls that come with the Professional Version of Visual Basic, it does show that you can create effective user interface touches like these with just the standard controls.

Startup

When the program starts, both the ScaleHeight and ScaleWidth properties of the pictSurface picture box get set to 100. This divides the available space on the pictSurface picture box into 100 equal units. The AutoRedraw property of the pictSurface picture box is True to ensure that layering is normal, and that any graphics are automatically redrawn if obscured (for instance, another form or window opening on top of the Shapes project window).

All the combo boxes get filled with the appropriate value names. Note that we fill the combo boxes so that the name of the value corresponds directly with the ListIndex property. This makes changing the appropriate property very simple. Finally, all the combo boxes get set to the normal default values for the properties they represent.

Running the Shape Project

The actual code after this is easy to follow. The Cick event for each combo box simply sets the appropriate graphic property using the combo box's ListIndex

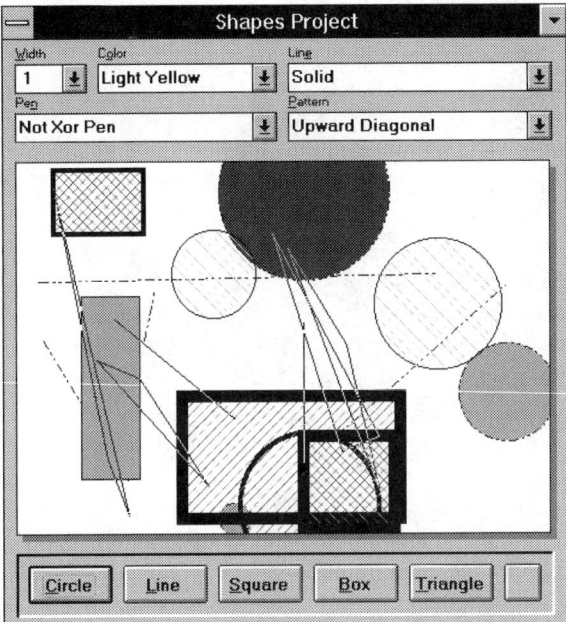

Figure 10-15 The Shapes project in action, showing
the effects of the graphics methods and properties

property. The Click event for each button draws the appropriate shape at a random spot on the picture box, using whatever settings for the graphics properties the user has set with the combo boxes. Figure 10-15 shows how the project looks when running.

PART IV

Displaying
Fonts and Text

11

DISPLAYING TEXT

Windows offers tremendous flexibility in the ways it displays text. Some controls, like text boxes, command buttons, and labels, display text using their Text or Caption properties. Although convenient, these properties don't offer the fine control you can achieve by using Visual Basic's Print method.

The Print method places text directly on a form, picture box, or Printer object. The font properties of these objects define the font, size, and appearance of text strings. Drawing text on an object in this way produces graphics rather than text, and lets you precisely specify placement. After a text string prints on an object, it becomes part of the background of the object and may be saved to a graphics file. Text strings drawn on a form, picture box, or Printer object are not editable. Once a text string is on an object, this text behaves in the same ways as other graphics on the object.

This flexibility lets programs mix a variety of text styles on an object. For example, the word processor used to write this book displays different type faces in different styles and a variety of sizes all at the same time. This ability to display text in the same way it will print is commonly called WYSIWYG (pronounced wizzywig), or *What You See Is What You Get*. Figure 11-1 shows an example of mixing a variety of text styles on the screen. The properties and methods discussed in this chapter are the means of doing this.

DRAWING TEXT IN VISUAL BASIC

Text in Windows can print and display in a variety of fonts and point sizes. You cannot assume that all text will have the same size characters, 80 characters to a line, in the time-honored format of teletypes and text-based DOS programs. Your program must be able to dynamically scale and position text according to the font, size, and object being used.

Displaying Text

Windows offers tremendous flexibility it the ways it displays text. Some controls, like text boxes, command buttons, and labels, display text using their Text or Caption properties. Although convenient, these properties don't offer the fine control you can achieve by using Visual Basic's Print method.

The Print method places text directly on a form, picture box, or printer object. The font properties of these objects define the font, size, and appearance of text strings. Drawing text on an object in this way produces graphics rather than text, and lets you precisely specify placement. After a text string prints on an object, it becomes part of the background of the object and may be saved to a graphics file. Text strings drawn on a form, picture box, or printer object are not editable. Once a text string is on an object, this text behaves in the same way as other graphics on the object.

This flexibility lets programs mix a variety of text styles on an object. For example, the word processor used to write this book displays different type faces in different styles and a variety of sizes all at the same time. This ability to display text in the same way it will print is commonly called WYSIWYG (pronounced wizzywig), or *What You See Is What You Get*. Figure 11-1 shows an example of mixing a variety of text styles on the screen. The properties and methods discussed in this chapter are the means of doing this.

Figure 11-1 The flexible Print method lets you mix a variety of fonts, styles, and sizes to produce WYSIWIG output

Drawing Text in Visual Basic

Text in Windows can print and display in a variety of fonts and point sizes. You cannot assume that all text will have the same size characters, 80 characters to a line, in the time-honored format of

Figure 11-1 The flexible Print method lets you mix a variety of fonts, styles, and sizes to produce WYSIWYG output

Chapter 12, Fonts, discusses several properties that affect the appearance of text strings. An object's FontName property sets the font style to format text strings. The FontSize property of the object sets the size of a text string. With the FontBold, FontStrikeThru, and FontUnderline properties of the object the actual appearance of the text changes to bold, strikethrough, or underline respectively. Using the FontTransparent property of the object can make the text string either overwrite or show the graphics placed under it.

This chapter discusses the methods, properties, and functions that let you precisely position the text on an object after you've determined the font size and style. The TextHeight method returns the amount of vertical space needed to display a specified text string in the current font and size, and the TextWidth method determines the amount of horizontal space necessary to show the text string. Each text string is actually placed on a form, picture box, or Printer object with the Print method. The Spc and Tab functions let you insert a precise number of spaces or print at a specific column. Table 11-1 summarizes the items covered in this chapter.

Use or Set This...		To Do This...
Print	Method	Places a text string or numeric value on the object.
Spc	Function	Insert a given number of spaces
Tab	Function	Move to a specified column position

Use or Set This...		To Do This...
TextHeight	Method	Determine the amount of vertical space needed for an indicated string
TextWidth	Method	Determine the amount of horizontal space needed for an indicated string

Table 11-1 Methods dealing with drawing text

The following pages investigate the methods in Table 11-1 in detail. The Text project at the end of this section includes step-by-step directions to assemble this demonstration of drawing text.

PRINT METHOD

Objects Affected

Check	Clipboard	Combo	Command	CommonDlg
Data	▶ Debug	Dir	Drive	File
▶ Form	Frame	Grid	Image	Label
Line	List	MDI Form	Menu	OLE
Option	▶ Picture	▶ Printer	Screen	Scroll
Shape	Text	Timer		

Purpose

The Print method places text on a form, picture box, or Printer object. Each text string prints at the position on the object indicated by the CurrentX and CurrentY properties (current screen or printer coordinates). Since there is no text wrap feature, any strings that are larger than the space allowed will be cut short on the right. A text string displays on the screen in the font and point size set in the FontName and FontSize property. The form, picture box, or Printer object's ForeColor property determines the text's color. Once a text string prints on an object with the Print method, the content and format of the text cannot be changed.

The Debug object uses the Print method in a very different manner. This can be used to help trace the execution of your programs for debugging purposes. Table 11-2 summarizes the arguments of the Print method.

General Syntax

```
[form.]Print [{Spc(n) | Tab(m)}][expressionlist][{;|,}]
```

(continued on next page)

(continued from previous page)

```
[form!]Name.Print [{Spc(n) | Tab(m)}][expressionlist][{;|,}]
Printer.Print [{Spc(n) | Tab(m)}][expressionlist][{;|,}]
Debug.Print [{Spc(n) | Tab(m)}][expressionlist][{;|,}]
```

Argument	Description
form	Name property of the form
Name	Name property of the picture box
Printer	'Printer' indicates the Printer object
Debug	'Debug' indicates the Debug object
Spc(n)	Insert n number of spaces; multiple use permitted
Tab(m)	Print at column m; multiple use permitted
expressionlist	A number or text string for the Print method to print on the object; multiple use permitted
,	Places the text cursor in the next print zone; multiple use permitted
;	Places the text cursor immediately after the last character; multiple use permitted

Table 11-2 Arguments of the Print method

Example Syntax

```
Sub Timer1_Timer ()
    AutoRedraw = True               'makes sure graphics refresh immediately
    Static Color As Integer         'Color will remember the last used color
    Display$ = "Warning"            'Stores text string
    FontName = "Arial"              'Indicates Arial font
    FontSize = 30                   'Indicates 30pt. font
    X = TextWidth(Display$) / 2     'Defines X as half of Text width
    Y = TextHeight(Display$) / 2    'Defines Y as half of Text height
    CurrentX = (ScaleWidth / 2) - X 'Sets current position so that
    CurrentY = (ScaleHeight / 2) - Y 'the text appears in the center
    If Color = 0 Then               'Alternates the color between black
        Color = 4                   'and red with the triggering of the
    Else                            'timer event
        Color = 0
    End If
    ForeColor = QBColor(Color)
    Print Display$                  'Prints warning on the form.
End Sub
```

Figure 11-2 Example syntax shows
how to precisely position text

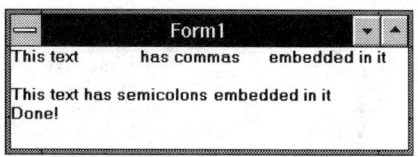

Figure 11-3 Code sample demonstrates difference between commas
and semicolons

Description

The Print method puts a string of text or a numeric value at an object's current
position. Each Print method identifies the object to place the string on by preceding it with the Name property of the form or picture box, or Printer or Debug
for the Printer or Debug objects. If a Print method does not include an object, then
the text prints on the current form. A print method may contain multiple expressions separated by Spc(n), Tab(m), commas, and semicolons.

In the example syntax, the Print method places the text string "Warning" in the
center of the form in the color, point size, and font indicated by the property settings of the form. Notice that the CurrentX and CurrentY properties control the
actual position where the print method puts the text string as modified by the values calculated by the TextHeight and TextWidth methods. Figure 11-2 illustrates
what this example might look like.

Positioning Text with the Commas, Semicolons, Spc(n), and Tab(m)

Print method expressions may have commas and semicolons placed between the
expressions to print, or at the end of the entire expression. If a Print method ends
without a comma or semicolon, the current position is set to the beginning of the
next line. Commas change the current screen or printer coordinates to the next
print zone away from the displayed text on the same line. A print zone is 14 character widths in the current font and point size. Semicolons change the current
screen or printer coordinates to the next character position on the same line
directly after the text. The current screen or printer position determines where the
next text appears on a form, picture box, or Printer or Debug objects. Figure 11-3
shows how the following code example demonstrates the difference between the
comma and semicolon:

```
Sub Form_Click ()
    Print "This text ", "has commas ",      'note the comma at the end of the line
    Print "embedded in it"                  'nothing at end of line; go to next line
    Print                                   'print blank line
    Print "This text "; "has semicolons ";  'note semicolon at the end of the line
    Print "embedded in it"                  'nothing at end of line; go to next line
    Print "Done!"
End Sub
```

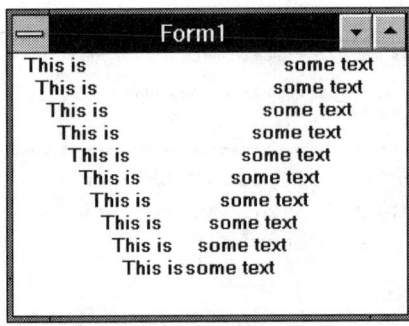

Figure 11-4 Demonstration of the Spc(n) and Tab(m) functions

The Spc(n) and Tab(m) functions let you insert a certain number of spaces in printed expressions, or let you specify what column to print at. Each font's space size is determined by taking the average widths of all characters in that font; each font and size of font will have differently sized spaces. The Spc(n) function places *n* spaces in the printed output. Tab(m) puts the current print position at column *m*, where a column is defined as one space. Thus Spc(n) is relative to the last print position and Tab(m) is relative to the leftmost position on the current line. The following example, illustrated in Figure 11-4, shows the use of the Spc(n) and Tab(m) functions:

```
Sub Form_Click ()
    For j = 1 To 10
        Print Spc(j) "This is" Tab(30 - j) "some text"
    Next j
End Sub
```

Positioning Text with the TextWidth and TextHeight Methods

The TextWidth and TextHeight methods calculate the amount of horizontal and vertical space necessary to display the specified text string in the currently set font and point size. Values returned by these methods use the unit of measure indicated by the ScaleMode property of the form, picture box, or Printer object. These values serve as a reference for positioning the text on the form, picture box, or Printer object. In the example syntax, the TextWidth and TextHeight methods change the current position to print the text in the center of the form.

Positioning Text with the CurrentX, CurrentY, ScaleWidth, and ScaleHeight Properties

The CurrentX and CurrentY properties work well with the ScaleWidth and ScaleHeight properties to determine where a text string prints on a form, picture

468

box, or Printer object. The ScaleWidth and ScaleHeight properties define the units of measurement for the usable horizontal and vertical surface of an object (Height and Width less the borders and title and menu bars). Defining the CurrentX and CurrentY properties as fractions of the ScaleWidth and ScaleHeight properties lets you precisely position the text no matter where the last Print method ended. In the example syntax at the beginning of this item entry, these properties find the center of the form by dividing the ScaleWidth and ScaleHeight properties by half and defining the CurrentX and CurrentY properties with the returned values.

Print Method with the Debug Object

The Print method may also be used with the Debug object. In fact, Print is the only method that can be used with Debug. You can use this method to print the contents of variables or messages on the Immediate pane of the Debug window during the debugging process. Although you have no control over font name, font size, and font color, the semicolon and comma, as well as the Spc(n) and Tab(m) functions, work just as described above. You can also directly type Print methods on the Immediate pane when your program is in Break mode. For more information on the Debug object, see Appendix C, Debugging Techniques.

Example

The Text project at the end of this chapter uses the Print method in both of its examples. The first example demonstrates TextWidth and TextHeight, and the second example demonstrates the Spc() and Tab() functions.

Comments

Visual Basic treats text produced with the Print method as graphics. Displayed text is then subject to the normal effects of graphics operations.

SPC() FUNCTION

Purpose

The Spc() function skips a specified number of spaces in the Print method. Table 11-3 shows the single argument of the Spc() function.

General Syntax

```
Spc(number%)
```

Argument	Meaning
number%	Number of spaces to skip; a 'space' is the average width of all characters in the current font

Table 11-3 Argument of the Spc() function

Example Syntax

```
Sub Command1_Click ()
    Print Spc(10); "Ten spaces in, and now "; Spc(Int(Rnd * 20)); "random!"
End Sub
```

Description

Embed the Spc( ) function in a Print method (or Print # statement) to skip the specified number of spaces, anywhere from 0 to 32767. A *space* is defined as the average width of all characters in the current font, size, and style. Note that the space size will vary depending on your choice of font and appearance. The semicolon is optional. Omitting it results in Visual Basic inserting the semicolon for you.

The Spc( ) always inserts spaces from the last print position. This makes it relative to the last printed character. The Tab( ) function, in contrast, is an absolute position from the leftmost character of the current line. See the Print method entry for an example comparing Spc( ) and Tab( ).

Example

The second example in the Text project at the end of the chapter demonstrates the use of the Spc( ) function. The project inserts a progressively larger number of spaces in a line of text, moving the printed text over each time. It also iterates different sizes of fonts, thus demonstrating that different font sizes have different sized spaces.

TAB() FUNCTION

Purpose

Use the Tab() function to move to a particular character position on the current line. Table 11-4 summarizes the argument of the Tab() function.

470

Argument	Meaning
column%	Number of the column to print at

Table 11-4 Argument of the Tab() function

General Syntax

```
Tab(column%)
```

Example Syntax

```
Sub Command1_Click ()
    For j = 1 To 20
        Print Tab(j); "Test"; Tab(60 - 2 * j); "case"
    Next j
End Sub
```

Description

Embed the Tab() function in a Print method (or Print # statement) to print at the specified column position, anywhere from 0 to 32767. A *column position* is defined as the size of a space, which in turn is defined as the average width of all characters in the current font, size, and style. Note that the space size (and thus the column width) will vary depending on your choice of font and appearance. The leftmost column position is position 1. The semicolon is optional. Omitting it results in Visual Basic inserting the semicolon for you.

The Tab() function is an absolute position from the leftmost character of the current line. The Spc() function, in contrast, inserts spaces from the last print position, making it relative to the last printed character. See the Print method entry for an example comparing Spc() and Tab().

Example

The second example in the Text project at the end of the chapter illustrates the Tab() function. It prints out text both left- and right-justified. The left justification uses just the Tab() function; the right justification uses Tab() to set the initial position which is then modified with the returned value of the TextWidth method.

TEXTHEIGHT AND TEXTWIDTH METHODS

Objects Affected

Check	Clipboard	Combo	Command	CommonDlg
Data	Debug	Dir	Drive	File
▶ Form	Frame	Grid	Image	Label
Line	List	MDI Form	Menu	OLE
Option	▶ Picture	▶ Printer	Screen	Scroll
Shape	Text	Timer		

Purpose

The TextHeight and TextWidth methods help you position text on a form, picture box, or Printer object by telling you what the height and width of the text string would be if displayed using the current font and point size. A value returned by the TextHeight and TextWidth methods represents the size of the text string using the unit of the measure specified in the ScaleMode property. Both of these methods are available at runtime only. Table 11-5 lists the arguments for these properties

General Syntax

```
[form.]TextHeight(expression$)
[form!]Name.TextHeight(expression$)
Print.TextHeight(expression$)

[form.]TextWidth(expression$)
[form!]Name.TextWidth(expression$)
Print.TextWidth(expression$)
```

Argument	Description
form	Name property of the form
Name	Name property of the picture box
Printer	'Printer' indicates the Printer object
expression$	Text string to determine the width or height necessary to display

Table 11-5 Arguments for the TextHeight and Text Width methods

472

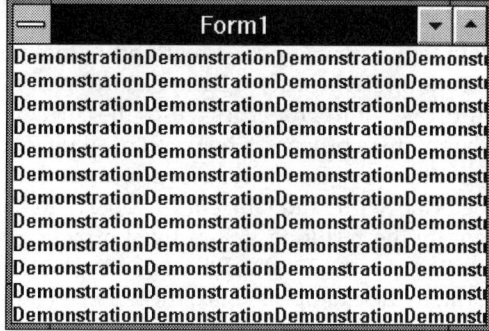

Figure 11-5 Example syntax of TextHeight and TextWidth used to fill the screen

Example Syntax

```
Sub Form_Resize ()
    Cls
    AutoRedraw = True                    'make sure graphics update immediately
    FontName = "Arial"                   'Defines the font.
    FontSize = 8.25                      'Defines the point size.
    Display$ = "Demonstration"           'Defines text variable.
    X = TextWidth(Display$)              'Defines X and Y as the space needed to display
    Y = TextHeight(Display$)             'the Display$ text string.
    EndX = Abs(ScaleWidth / X) + 1       'indicates the number of times that the string
    EndY = Abs(ScaleHeight / Y) + 1      'is displayed horizontally and vertically.
    For H = 1 To EndY                    'Fill the form with the text string.
        For W = 1 To EndX
            Print Display$;
        Next W
        CurrentY = CurrentY + Y          'goto next print line
        CurrentX = 0                     'goto beginning of new line
    Next H
End Sub
```

Description

The TextHeight and TextWidth methods determine the amount of space needed to display the expression$ on an object. An object consists of the Name property of the picture box or form, or Printer for the Printer object. Each expression$ must be a string variable and may not be a numeric value or an error occurs. Note that the Print method can print numeric expressions; convert these to strings with the Str$() function before using them with TextHeight and TextWidth.

In the example syntax, the TextHeight and TextWidth methods are used to calculate the amount of vertical and horizontal space needed to display the text string "Demonstration" such that it is repeated enough times to fill the screen. Figure 11-5 shows what this example might look like on the screen.

Positioning with the CurrentX and CurrentY Properties

Both the CurrentX and CurrentY properties serve as means of determining where a text string appears on a form, picture box, or Printer object. Since the ScaleHeight and ScaleWidth properties return the current height and width of the object, fractions of these properties help you position text on an object. For example, to place the letter T in the center of a form, change the values the CurrentX property to half the ScaleWidth and CurrentY property to half the ScaleHeight property. Then modify the resulting values by subtracting half of the values returned by the TextHeight and TextWidth methods. This places the letter T in the center of the form. In the example syntax, the ScaleHeight and ScaleWidth properties work in conjunction with the TextWidth and TextHeight methods to determine how many times the text appears if printed from top to bottom and left to right. CurrentX and CurrentY are discussed more thoroughly in Chapter 9, The Coordinate System.

Example

Both of the examples in the Text project at the end of the chapter use TextWidth, and the first example uses both TextWidth and TextHeight. They are used to modify the CurrentX and CurrentY positions to properly center or right align text.

THE TEXT PROJECT

Project Overview

The Text project shows how text prints on an form, picture box, or Printer object. These methods calculate the amount of space needed to place the indicated text on the form. This information lets us set exactly where the text appears on the form, and gives the basis for you to do things like creating center and right-aligned tab stops as well as the traditional left-aligned ones.

The following pages discuss the assembly and operation of the Text project. The first section deals with the assembly of the Text form. Next, there is a listing and explanation of the contents of the subroutines of this project. Finally, a How It Works guide to the operation of the project discusses the operation of the code. Please read this information carefully and use the pictures of the form to check your results.

Assembling the Project

1. Make a new form with the objects and properties listed in Table 11-6.

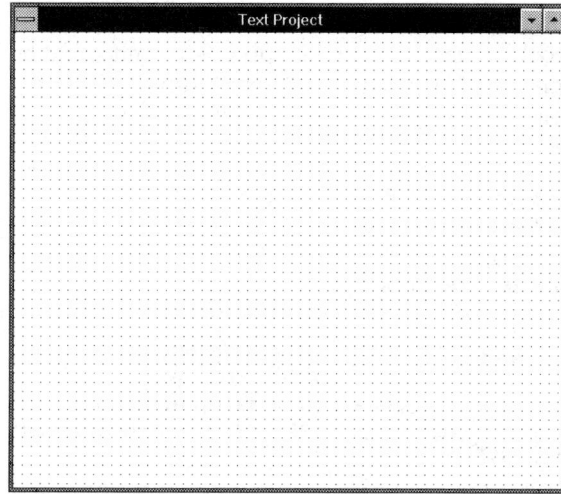

Figure 11-6 The Text project form at design time

Object	Property	Setting
Form	BorderStyle	2–Sizable
	Caption	Text Project

Table 11-6 Elements of the Text form

2. Size the form to approximately this size and shape. Notice how the form should appear with the default text shown in Figure 11-6.

3. Enter the following code in the Form_Click event subroutine. When the user clicks the form, the correct example runs. This routine just alternates between the two examples.

```
Sub Form_Click ()
    Static example As Integer               'track which example to show
    If example = 0 Then example = 1         'start at the first example
    If example = 1 Then
        Example1                            'demonstrate TextHeight and TextWidth
        example = 2                         'next time will be example2
    Else
        Example2                            'demonstrate Spc() and Tab()
        example = 1                         'next time will be example1
    End If
End Sub
```

4. Enter the following code in the general section of the code window. This subroutine places text in the upper-left, center, and bottom-right of the form. Note the use of TextHeight and TextWidth to properly justify the text.

```
Sub Example1 ()
    Const MSG1 = "Top Left"                                'define the text to display
    Const MSG2 = "Center Center"
    Const MSG3 = "Bottom Right"

    Cls                                                    'clear the form
    AutoReDraw = True                                      'graphics automatically repaint
    FontName = "Arial"                                     'select the font
    FontSize = 20                                          'select the font size

    Print MSG1                                             'This goes in upper-left corner

    CurrentX = (ScaleWidth / 2) - (TextWidth(MSG2) / 2)    'position this exactly
    CurrentY = (ScaleHeight / 2) - (TextHeight(MSG2) / 2)  'in the center
    Print MSG2

    CurrentX = ScaleWidth - TextWidth(MSG3)                'position this flush right and
    CurrentY = ScaleHeight - TextHeight(MSG3)              'flush bottom
    Print MSG3
End Sub
```

5. Place this code in the general section in the code window. This example shows the use of the Spc() and Tab() functions. Note how we use TextWidth to help create a right-justified tab stop. The num$ variable lets us build a variable length string to help demonstrate the left and right tab stops.

```
Sub Example2 ()
    Cls                                                     'Clear the form
    AutoReDraw = True                                       'graphics automatically repaint
    FontName = "Times New Roman"                            'Select font
    For size = 8 To 20 Step 4                               'step through font sizes
        num$ = ""                                           'will contain a variable length string
        FontSize = size                                     'Set the font size
        For j = 1 To 5                                       'five examples at each font size
            Print Spc(j); "Space1"; Spc(j * 2); "Space2";   'demonstrate spc()
            num$ = num$ & "*"                               'build up the variable length string
            Print Tab(35); "Left Tab" & num$;               'print at the tab stop
            y = CurrentY                                    'remember what line we're on
            Print Tab(65); "";                              'set the print position to column 65
            CurrentX = CurrentX - TextWidth("Right Tab" & num$)  'right justify at column 65
            CurrentY = y                                    'reset us back to the correct line
            Print "Right Tab" & num$                        'and print the text
        Next j
    Next size
End Sub
```

How It Works

This simple project demonstrates how to use TextHeight and TextWidth to precisely position text. Text always prints with its upper-left corner at CurrentX and CurrentY. For most common operations, this default position works well.

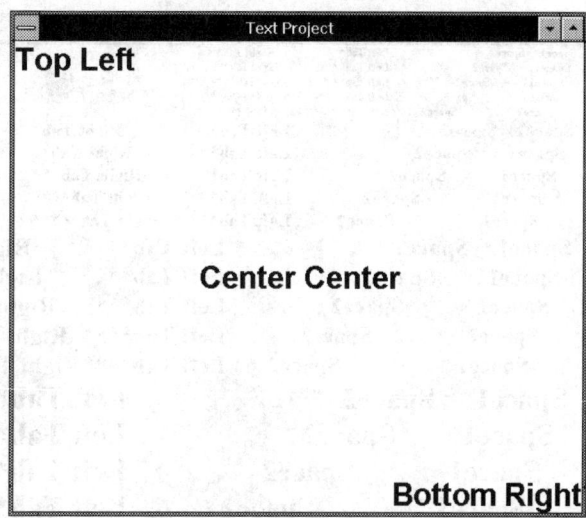

Figure 11-7 Example1 of the Text Project, showing several text alignments using TextHeight and TextWidth

Many applications need more precise positioning than this. The text box control allows for left, center, and right alignment, yet there is no equivalent in the Print method—it is always left-aligned. Although this might seem to make the text box more convenient than the Print method, it doesn't allow for mixing of fonts, sizes, or alignments. TextHeight and TextWidth provide the key for this more precise positioning using the flexible Print method.

Example1 illustrates three common vertical and horizontal positions: left, center, and right; top, middle, and bottom. You could expand the code to allow for multiple fonts, sizes, and alignments to create a full-featured word processor.

Example1 defines the three text strings, calculates the proper position, and prints them. The Top Left setting doesn't need any special calculations, as CurrentX and CurrentY automatically default to 0,0. The Center Center setting simply takes half the ScaleHeight and ScaleWidth of the form, and subtracts half of the TextHeight and TextWidth of the message. This exactly centers the printed text. Likewise, the Bottom Right setting simply subtracts the TextWidth and TextHeight of the message from the ScaleWidth and ScaleHeight of the form to properly position its text. Figure 11-7 illustrates what this example looks like when running.

Notice that Top Left still leaves a little room at the top. This is because TextHeight measures the height of the text including the "leading," or the white space between lines of text. This leading makes TextHeight approximately 120% of the actual height of the text.

Example2 demonstrates the use of the Spc() and Tab() functions. This sub procedure cycles through its example code in several different point sizes. As Figure 11-8 shows, different point sizes have different sizes of the space used in

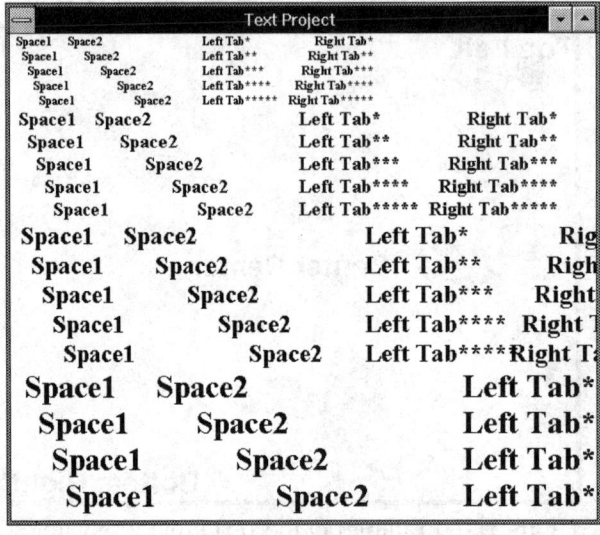

Figure 11-8 Example2 of the Text Project demonstrates the Spc() and Tab() functions

the Spc() and Tab() functions. The only tricky part of this example lies in creating the right tab stop. We use the same idea as in Example1 to right justify the text by subtracting its TextWidth from the CurrentX position. Note how we have to reset CurrentY back to the original line; if we didn't do this, "Right Tab" would print on the next line. Figure 11-8 illustrates this example.

12

FONTS

A specific character style name, or font, determines the overall appearance of text. Windows comes with a standard set of fonts, and you and your users may obtain additional fonts from a variety of sources. Windows makes all installed fonts available transparently to each program.

Most traditional DOS programs do not allow you to see the formatted text on the screen prior to printing it. In the Microsoft Windows environment, however, all fonts displayed on the screen print on any printer almost exactly the same as they are displayed. This WYSIWYG—"What You See Is What You Get"—feature is one of the greatest advantages provided by Windows.

SCREEN AND PRINTER FONTS

There are two general types of fonts in Microsoft Windows: screen and printer fonts. Screen fonts affect the appearance of text on the screen. The Microsoft Windows environment ships with several screen fonts, such as MS Sans Serif, MS Serif, Symbol, and System. Windows may have more screen fonts available if other applications have added them. For instance, Small Fonts and Fences commonly appear on systems with Microsoft application products.

Printer fonts control the look of text output by a printer. A printer font can be either a resident or soft font. Resident fonts are those character styles that are contained in the printer. Soft fonts are typefaces that are located on the computer, and then downloaded to the printer. They allow printers such as the HP Laserjet and Postscript printers to produce a variety of fonts.

Size **Mg**

Figure 12-1 The size of a font

Figure 12-2 Characters in proportionally spaced fonts are different widths

SCALABLE FONTS

An important group of fonts works equally well on the screen and printer. These include the TrueType fonts of Windows 3.1 (Arial, Courier, Times New Roman, and WingDings), a variety of add-on TrueType fonts, and a multitude of other fonts and font technologies from a variety of vendors like Adobe, BitStream, and Agfa.

These newer font technologies can scale their fonts to any arbitrary size. The screen and printer fonts discussed above, in contrast, come in only specific sizes. These older fixed fonts are actually bitmaps representing each character. Although this limits your choice of size, each individual size of bitmap font is often hand-tuned to look as perfect as possible in that particular size.

The newer scalable fonts are actually mathematical descriptions of the outline of each character that is then rasterized (or converted into a bitmap) when needed. This gives Windows the ability to create sharp-looking text at any size on any output device at any resolution. It also makes displayed text look almost exactly the same as printed text.

POINTS AND FONT SIZE

Printing professionals and graphic artists traditionally measure text in points. The point size of a font determines how large or small a text string is on a screen or printed page. Increasing the point size of text makes it larger, decreasing makes it smaller.

The size of a font is the distance between the top of a capital letter and the bottom of a lowercase descender. Figure 12-1 shows this. Note that different fonts have different visual "weights" that may make them look larger or smaller than the actual size indicates. This is simply an optical illusion. Also note that almost all fonts are proportionately spaced, which means that different letters take up different amounts of horizontal space. For instance, a W takes up more space than an I. Figure 12-2 shows this.

There are 72 points per inch, and 20 twips per point. One of the ScaleMode settings (ScaleMode=2) makes the measurement system points. This may be a useful measuring system in text-intensive applications, as you are then measuring in the same units you use to specify text size.

FONTS IN VISUAL BASIC

In Visual Basic the appearance of the text on the screen or the printer can be set to any available font and point size. The FontName and FontSize properties determine the font and size of text on a form, control, or Printer object. The Fonts and FontCount properties provide the number and names of the fonts available for the screen or the printer. Each of the FontBold, FontItalic, FontStrikethru, FontTransparent, and FontUnderline properties add typestyle effects to text on the object.

Table 12-1 displays the properties that affect the appearance of text on a form, control, or Printer object.

Use or Set This...		To Do This...
FontBold	Property	Display a thicker (boldface) font on the printer or screen
FontCount	Property	Return the number of fonts available for the screen or active printer
FontItalic	Property	Display an italic (slanted or cursive) font on the printer or screen
FontName	Property	Set or indicate the name of the current font
Fonts	Property	Return the names of the fonts available for the screen or active printer
FontSize	Property	Set or indicate the point size of the font
FontStrikeThru	Property	Indicate whether text should have a line drawn through it
FontTransparent	Property	Indicate whether text includes the background graphics
FontUnderline	Property	Indicate whether text should have a line drawn under it

Table 12-1 Properties dealing with fonts

The following pages examine the properties in Table 12-1 in detail. The Font project at the end of this chapter pulls all of these items together in a comprehensive demonstration of how to use them.

FONTBOLD PROPERTY

Objects Affected

▶ Check	Clipboard	▶ Combo	▶ Command	▶ CommonDlg
▶ Data	Debug	▶ Dir	▶ Drive	▶ File
▶ Form	▶ Frame	▶ Grid	Image	▶ Label
Line	▶ List	MDI Form	Menu	OLE
▶ Option	▶ Picture	▶ Printer	Screen	Scroll
Shape	▶ Text	Timer		

Purpose

The FontBold property determines whether the text on a form, control, or Printer object appears as boldface type. When it is boldface, the text appears thicker and darker. This property may be modified at either design time or runtime. Any changes made to the FontBold property of a form, picture box, or Printer object only affect the appearance of text drawn after the alteration. A control's FontBold property always changes the appearance of any existing text placed with the control's Caption or Text properties. Tables 12-2 and 12-3 list the arguments and settings of the FontBold property.

General Syntax

```
[form.]FontBold [ = state%]
[form!]Name.FontBold [ = state%]
Printer.FontBold [ = state%]
```

Arguments	Description
form	Name property of the form
Name	Name property of a control
Printer	'Printer' indicates the Printer object
state%	Current setting of FontBold property

Table 12-2 Arguments of FontBold property

state%	Description
True (-1)	Text on the indicated object is bold
False (0)	Text on the indicated object is not bold

Table 12-3 Settings of the state% variable of the FontBold property

Example Syntax

```
Sub Form_Load ()
      AutoRedraw = True              'property is redrawn each time it is uncovered
      FontSize = 8                   'Initial setting of text is 8 pt
      FontName = "Arial"             'Defines name of font
      ForeColor = QBColor(0)         'Black text
      BackColor = QBColor(15)        'White background
      For I = 1 To 10                'Generate the following code 10 times
            FontBold = Not FontBold  'Toggle the FontBold property
            If FontBold = False Then 'Checks if FontBold is False
                  T$ = "Normal"      'Defines text string
                  FontSize = FontSize + 1.8    'Increments point size by 1.8
            Else
                  T$ = "Bold"          'Defines text string
            End If
            Mess$ = "This is " + FontName + " "      'Displays the text on the screen
            Mess$ = Mess$ + Str$(FontSize)
            Mess$ = Mess$ + "pt " + T$
            Print Mess$
      Next I
End Sub
```

Description

The FontBold property affects the appearance of the text on an object. When no object is given, the parent form is assumed to be the object addressed. The FontBold expression ends with a Boolean expression of either True or False. This property defaults to False, meaning that text is not bold, but normal weight text. True can have two possible effects. On forms, picture boxes, and Printer objects, the True setting makes only new text bold. Text on controls (except for the picture box) is immediately affected by changes made to its FontBold property.

In the example syntax, text is printed on the form in both normal and bold format, demonstrating the difference between bold and normal. Figure 12-3 shows approximately what should display on your screen.

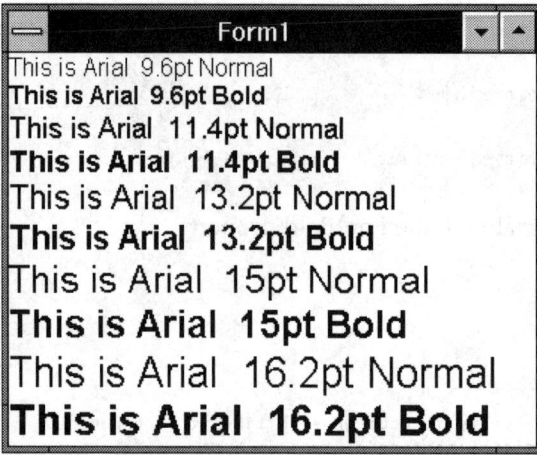

Figure 12-3 Example syntax demonstrates difference between Bold and Normal fonts

FontItalic, FontStrikethru, and FontUnderline

There are three other special effect font properties in Visual Basic. These properties are FontItalic, FontStrikethru, and FontUnderline. More than one of these properties may be set to the same object, combining the indicated effects. For instance, when the FontItalic and FontBold properties are both True, the text on the object is bold italics.

Example

The Font project at the end of this section demonstrates the use of the FontBold property. When the check box labeled Bold is clicked with the mouse, the chekBold_Click event triggers. Each time that this event is processed, the text on the textSample text box is switched from bold to normal and normal to bold.

Comments

Notice that a bold text string needs a larger display space. Be careful to ensure that enough space is provided for bold as well as normal text. See Chapter 11, Displaying Text, for information on font positioning and scaling. Also note that some font families do not include a bold font. If this is the case, setting FontBold to True does not change the displayed or printed font.

FONTCOUNT PROPERTY

Objects Affected

Check	Clipboard	Combo	Command	CommonDlg
Data	Debug	Dir	Drive	File
Form	Frame	Grid	Image	Label
Line	List	MDI Form	Menu	OLE
Option	Picture	▶ Printer	▶ Screen	Scroll
Shape	Text	Timer		

Purpose

The FontCount property indicates the number of printer or screen fonts available, depending on whether you specify the Screen or Printer object. For screen fonts, the value returned encompasses all of the Windows screen fonts as well as scalable fonts. For the printer, the value specifies the number of fonts that may be placed on a Printer object, including all resident and soft fonts as well as scalable fonts. You may only access the FontCount property at runtime, not design time. Used together, the FontCount and Fonts properties produce a list of the names of the possible fonts. Table 12-4 lists the arguments of the FontCount property.

General Syntax

```
Printer.FontCount
Screen.FontCount
```

Arguments	Description
Printer	'Printer' indicates the Printer object
Screen	'Screen' indicates the Screen object

Table 12-4 Arguments of FontCount property

Example Syntax

```
Sub Form_Load ()
    S$ = Str$(Screen.FontCount)        'Finds the current number of
    P$ = Str$(Printer.FontCount)       'screen and printer fonts
    Text1.Text = "There are " + S$ + " Screen fonts"  'Prints number of fonts
    Text2.Text = "There are " + P$ + " Printer fonts"  'Prints number of fonts
End Sub
```

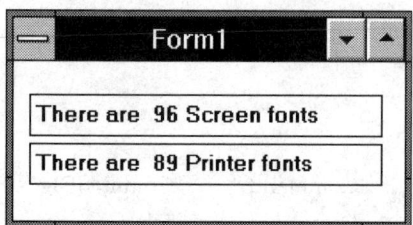

Figure 12-4 Sample screen and printer font count

Description

The FontCount property indicates the number of fonts available for the present configuration. If a FontCount property is preceded by the word Screen, then this property provides the number of screen fonts and scalable fonts. With the word Printer, the value calculated by the FontCount property includes all of the resident and soft fonts as well as scalable fonts. This property, available for reference at run-time only, will only change if fonts are added or removed. Most system configurations result in a different number of available fonts for the screen and printer.

In the example syntax, the FontCount property provides the number of fonts available for the screen and the printer. These numbers are then printed in the Text1 and Text2 text boxes. Figure 12-4 shows what this form might look like on the screen. The actual number of fonts depends on your setup. Notice that the numbers may not match.

The Fonts Property

Using the Fonts and FontCount properties together provides a list of the names of the available fonts. The FontCount property provides the total number of font names that the Fonts property returns. Each value between 0 and (FontCount -1) will provide the name of one of the fonts available for the screen or printer. Remember not to mix the results from both the screen or printer, or the list may not be accurate.

Example

In the Font project at the end of this chapter, the Fonts property generates a list of the fonts available on the system. The FontCount property works with the Fonts property to provide the names of the fonts in string format. At program startup, these properties function together to fill the contents of the cmboFont combo list box. Pressing the command button labeled Display Fonts produces a list of the system fonts on the formFontList form.

Comments

With some configurations a list of screen or printer fonts may include more than one entry for a particular font.

486

FONTITALIC PROPERTY

Objects Affected

▶ Check	Clipboard	▶ Combo	▶ Command	▶ CommonDlg
▶ Data	Debug	▶ Dir	▶ Drive	▶ File
▶ Form	▶ Frame	▶ Grid	Image	▶ Label
Line	▶ List	MDI Form	Menu	OLE
▶ Option	▶ Picture	▶ Printer	Screen	Scroll
Shape	▶ Text	Timer		

Purpose

The FontItalic property specifies whether the text on a form, control, or Printer object appears in italic type. If the FontItalic property is changed to True, then the text becomes either slanted or scriptlike in appearance depending on the font. This property may be modified at either design time or runtime. Any changes made to the FontItalic property of a form, picture box, or Printer object only affect the appearance of text drawn after the change. A control's FontItalic property always changes the appearance of the existing text on it. Tables 12-5 and 12-6 list the arguments and settings of the FontItalic property.

General Syntax

```
[form.]FontItalic [ = state%]
[form!]Name.FontItalic [ = state%]
Printer.FontItalic [ = state%]
```

Arguments	Description
form	Name property of the form
Name	Name property of a control
Printer	'Printer' indicates the Printer object
state%	Current setting of FontItalic property

Table 12-5 Arguments of FontItalic property

state%	Description
True	Text on the indicated object is in italics
False	Text on the indicated object is not in italics

Table 12-6 Settings of the state% variable of the FontItalic property

Example Syntax

```
Sub Form_Load ()
    AutoRedraw = True          'property is redrawn each time it is uncovered
    FontSize = 8               'Initial setting of text is 8 pt
    FontName = "Times New Roman" 'Will use Times font for demo
    ForeColor = QBColor(0)     'Black text
    BackColor = QBColor(15)    'White background
    For I = 1 To 4             'Four iterations of four sizes
        FontBold = False
        FontItalic = False
        PrintMess "Normal"
        FontBold = True
        FontItalic = False
        PrintMess "Bold"
        FontBold = False
        FontItalic = True
        PrintMess "Italics"
        FontBold = True
        FontItalic = True
        PrintMess "Bold Italics"
        FontSize = FontSize + 1.8
    Next I
End Sub

Sub PrintMess (FontStyle As String)
        Mess$ = "This is " + FontName + " " 'Displays the text on the screen
        Mess$ = Mess$ + Str$(FontSize)
        Mess$ = Mess$ + "pt " + FontStyle
        Print Mess$
End Sub
```

Description

The FontItalic property changes the appearance of the text on an object. When no object is given, the parent form is assumed to be the object being addressed. Every FontItalic property statement ends with a Boolean value of either True or False. This property defaults to False, with False meaning that the text placed on the object is displayed or printed normally. True can have two possible effects. On forms, picture boxes, and Printer objects, the True setting only changes new text

Figure 12-5 Example syntax shows normal,
bold, italics, and bold italics

to italics. Existing text, as well as subsequent text on controls (other than the picture box), are immediately affected by changes made to its FontItalic property.

The example syntax provides a listing of the default system's font in normal, italics, bold, and bold italics format. Figure 12-5 shows what this might look like on your system.

The FontBold, FontStrikethru, and FontUnderline Properties

There are three other font typestyle properties in Visual Basic. These properties are FontBold, FontStrikethru, and FontUnderline. More than one of these properties may be set to the same object, combining the effects indicated. For example, when the FontItalic and FontBold properties are both True, the text on the object is bold italics, provided that the font indicated in FontName has a Bold Italics font. Not all typestyles are necessarily available for each font.

Example

The Font project at the end of this chapter demonstrates the FontItalic property. Clicking the check box labeled Italic triggers the chekItalic_Click event. This event changes the setting of the FontItalic property of the textSample text box. Each time this event is processed, the text on the textSample text box is switched between italic and normal.

Comments

Some fonts are unaffected by the FontItalics property, either because there is no italic of the given font, or because the font is inherently italic (like Zapf Chancery).

FONTNAME PROPERTY

Objects Affected

▶ Check	Clipboard	▶ Combo	▶ Command	▶ CommonDlg
▶ Data	Debug	▶ Dir	▶ Drive	▶ File
▶ Form	▶ Frame	▶ Grid	Image	▶ Label
Line	▶ List	MDI Form	Menu	OLE
▶ Option	▶ Picture	▶ Printer	Screen	Scroll
Shape	▶ Text	Timer		

Purpose

The FontName property specifies the name of the current font of a form, control, or Printer object. Any text placed on one of these objects is formatted with the font selected in the object's FontName property. You may access this property at both design time and runtime. Each individual system's configuration controls the default setting of the FontName property. A system's display device and active printing device have a direct effect upon the default setting of the FontName property. Third-party font generators such as the Adobe Type Manager can also affect the default setting of the FontName property. Table 12-7 lists the arguments of the FontName property.

General Syntax

```
[form.]FontName [ = font$]
[form!]Name.FontName [ = font$]
Printer.FontName [ = font$]
```

Arguments	Description
form	Name property of the form
Name	Name property of a control
Printer	'Printer' indicates the Printer object
font$	Text string that represents the name of a specified font

Table 12-7 Arguments of FontName property

490

Example Syntax

```
Sub Form_Load ()
    For I = 0 To (Printer.FontCount - 1)      'Adds each of the font names to
        Combo1.AddItem Printer.Fonts(I)       'the combo list
    Next I
    Combo1.Text = Text1.FontName              'Displays the current font
End Sub

Sub Combo1_Click ()
    Text1.FontName = Combo1.Text              'Changes the current font
    Text2.Text = Combo1.Text                  'Displays the new current font
End Sub
```

Description

The FontName property reads or sets the name of the currently selected font for an object. When no object is given, the parent form is assumed to be the object being addressed. Each object has its own separate font setting that may be different from the choices for the other objects in a program. Change the current font for an object by assigning a text string with a valid font name to the FontName property. This property may also be referenced as a means of obtaining the name of the selected font.

In the example syntax, the fonts provided by the system are included in the Combo1 combo list box (turn on the Sort property of Combo1 to put the fonts in alphabetical order). Notice how the font name chosen in the Combo1 combo list box defines the FontName property of the Text1 text box. Figure 12-6 shows what this example might look like on your screen.

The Fonts and FontCount Properties

The Fonts property gives the exact spelling of the valid font names of a system. The Fonts property uses a number between 0 and (FontCount -1) to provide the font's name. This combination returns a text string that may be utilized to define the FontName property of an object. In the example the Fonts and FontCount properties are accessed to list the available fonts in the Combo1 combo list box. Changing the Sort property to True puts the combo box's list in alphabetical order.

Example

In the Font project at the end of this chapter, the FontName property modifies the appearance of an object's text. Selecting a new font name from the combo list box cmboFont triggers the cmboFont_Click event, which then sets the FontName property of the textSample text box. Pressing the command button labeled Display Fonts changes the FontName property of the pictList picture box for each line of the font list. Each font name on the list appears in the font type named.

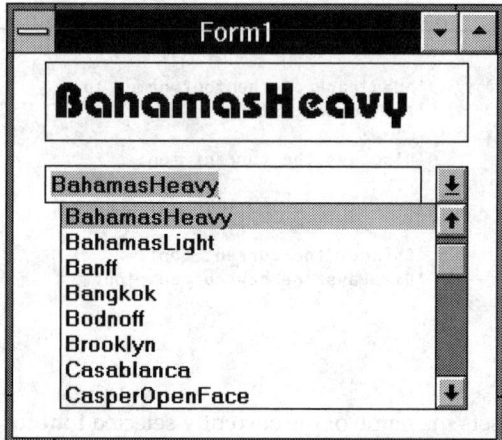

Figure 12-6 Example syntax on the screen;
combo box has all screen fonts loaded in it

Comments

With some system configurations, a list of screen or printer fonts may include
more than one entry for a particular font.

FONTS PROPERTY

Objects Affected

Check	Clipboard	Combo	Command	CommonDlg
Data	Debug	Dir	Drive	File
Form	Frame	Grid	Image	Label
Line	List	MDI Form	Menu	OLE
Option	Picture	▶ Printer	▶ Screen	Scroll
Shape	Text	Timer		

Purpose

The Fonts property provides the name of one of the available fonts of the screen
or printer, depending on which of these objects you specify and which font number you use. Exactly which value stands for which font is determined by the system. This property may change whenever the active printer is changed to another
printing device with different fonts or a new font is added to the system with the

Windows Control Panel. A combination of the FontCount and Fonts properties produces a list of the names of the possible fonts. Table 12-8 lists the arguments of the Fonts property.

General Syntax

```
Printer.Fonts(index%)
Screen.Fonts(index%)
```

Argument	Description
Printer	'Printer' indicates the Printer object
Screen	'Screen' indicates the Screen object
index%	Value that represents a screen or printer font

Table 12-8 Arguments of Fonts property

Example Syntax

```
Sub Form_Load ()
    AutoRedraw = -1                          'Turns on AutoReDraw
    For I = 0 To (Screen.FontCount - 1)      'Displays all of the fonts
        FontName = Screen.Fonts(I)           'Changes font
        Print Screen.Fonts(I)                'Prints the font name
    Next I
End Sub
```

Description

The Fonts property provides the name of an available system font specified by the index number, which must be between 0 and one less than the value of the FontCount property. The FontCount property indicates the total number of fonts available for either the Screen or Printer object. Using Screen with the Fonts property returns all screen and scalable fonts; using Printer returns all soft and resident printer fonts as well as scalable fonts. This property is only available for reference at runtime and will only change if fonts are added to or removed from the system. Most configurations provide a different font name for the same number used with the Screen and Printer objects.

In the example syntax, the Fonts property serves as a means of printing the names of the available screen fonts on the form. A For loop controls the repeated invocation of the Fonts property for each font number from 0 to one less than the value of the FontCount property. These font names are printed in the font indi-

Figure 12-7 Example syntax shows list of available fonts

cated by the font name. Figure 12-7 shows what this list might look like. If the Screen object is changed to Printer, this list may be different.

The FontCount Property

Using the Fonts and FontCount properties together provides a list of the names of the available fonts. The FontCount property returns the total number of fonts available. Each Fonts index value between 0 and (FontCount -1) will provide the name of one of the fonts available for the display or printer. Remember not to mix up the results from both the screen or printer, or the list may not be accurate. In the example, the FontCount property provides the number to use with Fonts to obtain the font name.

Example

In the Font project at the end of this chapter, the Fonts property gives a list of the names of the fonts available on the system. The FontCount property works with the Fonts property to provide the names of the fonts in string format. At program startup, these properties function together to fill the contents of the cmboFont combo list box. Pressing the command button labeled Display Fonts produces a list of the system fonts on the pictList picture box.

Comments

With some system configurations, a list of screen or printer fonts may include more than one entry for a particular font.

FONTSIZE PROPERTY

Objects Affected

▶ Check	Clipboard	▶ Combo	▶ Command	▶ CommonDlg
▶ Data	Debug	▶ Dir	▶ Drive	▶ File
▶ Form	▶ Frame	▶ Grid	Image	▶ Label
Line	▶ List	MDI Form	Menu	OLE
▶ Option	▶ Picture	▶ Printer	Screen	Scroll
Shape	▶ Text	Timer		

Purpose

The FontSize property sets the point size of the current font of a form, control, or Printer object. Any text subsequently placed on one of these objects will be formatted with the point size selected in the object's FontSize property. This property may be accessed at design time or runtime. Each system's configuration controls the default setting of the FontSize property. A system's display device and active printing device have a direct effect upon the default setting of the FontSize property. Third-party font generators such as the Adobe Type Manager can also change the default setting of the FontSize property. Table 12-9 lists the different arguments of the FontSize property.

General Syntax

```
[form.]FontSize [ = points!]
[form!]Name.FontSize [ = points!]
Printer.FontSize [ = points!]
```

Arguments	Description
form	Name property of the form
Name	Name property of a control
Printer	'Printer' indicates the Printer object
points!	Value that represents the size of letters on an object

Table 12-9 Arguments of FontSize property

Example Syntax

```
Sub Form_Click ()
    Text1.Text = "This is " + Str$(Text1.FontSize) + " pt"      'Prints current font size
    Text1.FontSize = Text1.FontSize + 2     'Increments font size
End Sub
```

Description

The FontSize property of an object changes the size of text. When no object is given, the parent form is assumed to be the object being addressed. Define FontSize expressions with a single-precision number up to 2048, which indicates the size of the text in points.

It usually makes no difference in what order you specify FontName, FontBold, FontItalic, FontSize, and so forth. TrueType fonts smaller than 8 points should be handled in a specific order, however. Windows actually uses a different font (internally) for these small TrueType fonts, so specify FontSize first, then FontName, then repeat setting the size again with FontSize.

In the example syntax, the FontSize property of the Text1 text box increments by two each time the form is clicked with the mouse. The text gets progressively larger with each pressing of the mouse.

Text printed on a form, picture box, or printer remains unaffected if the FontSize subsequently changes. (Remember, printed text is actually converted into graphics.) Controls, however, immediately reflect a change in FontSize.

Example

In the Font project at the end of this chapter, the FontSize property modifies the size of an object's text. When a new point size is chosen from the combo box cmboSize, the cmboSize_Click event changes the FontSize property of the textSample text box. This changes the text on the text box to the new size.

Comments

Any changes to the FontSize property of a control immediately affects the existing text on a control. This means all of the text on a control must be the same point size.

FONTSTRIKETHRU PROPERTY

Objects Affected

▶ Check	Clipboard	▶ Combo	▶ Command	▶ CommonDlg
▶ Data	Debug	▶ Dir	▶ Drive	▶ File
▶ Form	▶ Frame	▶ Grid	Image	▶ Label
Line	▶ List	MDI Form	Menu	OLE
▶ Option	▶ Picture	▶ Printer	Screen	Scroll
Shape	▶ Text	Timer		

Purpose

The FontStrikethru property determines if the text on a form, control, or Printer object is formatted with a line through it. Legal documents often use strikethrough text to indicate superseded or eliminated language, or it is used to indicate editorial deletion. This property may be changed at either design time or runtime. Any changes made to the FontStrikethru property of a form, picture box, or Printer object only affect the appearance of text drawn after the change. Changing a control's FontStrikethru property immediately changes all text in that control. Tables 12-10 and 12-11 list the arguments of the FontStrikethru property.

General Syntax

```
[form.]FontStrikethru [ = state%]
[form!]Name.FontStrikethru [ = state%]
Printer.FontStrikethru [ = state%]
```

Arguments	Description
form	Name property of the form
Name	Name property of a control
Printer	'Printer' indicates the Printer object
state%	Current setting of FontStrikethru property

Table 12-10 Arguments of FontStrikethru property

497

state%	Description
True	Text on the indicated object is strikethrough
False	Text on the indicated object is not strikethrough

Table 12-11 Settings of the state% variable of the FontStrikethru property

Example Syntax

```
Sub Form_Click ()
    M$ = "Please Enter your message here"    'Prompt text
    T$ = "Visual Basic SuperBible"           'Title text
    A$ = InputBox$(M$, T$, Text1.Text)       'Text to display
    Text1.FontStrikethru = Not Text1.FontStrikethru 'toggles strikethrough
    Text1.Text = A$
End Sub
```

Description

The FontStrikethru property determines whether to place a horizontal line through the text on an object. If an object name is not provided, the parent form is assumed. Each FontStrikethru property statement ends with a Boolean value of either True or False. False indicates that the text placed on the object is not changed and is displayed normally, with no strikethrough. True can have two possible effects. On forms, picture boxes, and Printer objects, the True setting only places a line through new text. Text on controls (except for picture boxes) is immediately affected by changes made to its FontStrikethru property.

In the example syntax, since a control (text box) is specified, the text immediately reflects the change in the FontStrikethru property. Figure 12-8 displays what this might look like on the screen.

The FontBold, FontItalic, and FontUnderline Properties

Visual Basic provides three other special effects for controlling the appearance of text. These properties are FontBold, FontItalic, and FontUnderline. If more than one of these properties is changed from its default False setting, then the effects are combined.

Example

The Font project at the end of this chapter demonstrates the FontStrikethru property. Clicking the check box labeled Strikethru with the mouse triggers the checkStrikthru_Click event. This event changes the setting of the FontStrikethru

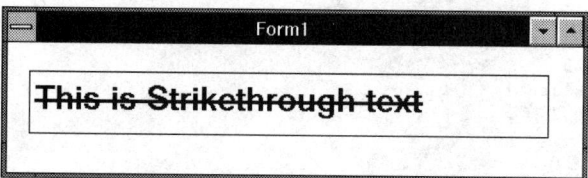

Figure 12-8 Example syntax shows strikethrough text with line through it

property of the textSample text box. Each time that this event is processed, the text on the textSample text box switches from strikethrough to normal and normal to strikethrough.

Comments

Remember that all of the text on a control is affected by any changes to the FontStrikethru property.

FONTTRANSPARENT PROPERTY

Objects Affected

Check	Clipboard	Combo	Command	CommonDlg
Data	Debug	Dir	Drive	File
▶ Form	Frame	Grid	Image	Label
Line	List	MDI Form	Menu	OLE
Option	▶ Picture	▶ Printer	Screen	Scroll
Shape	Text	Timer		

Purpose

The FontTransparent property indicates how the text on a form, picture box, or Printer object interacts with the graphics beneath it. When it is made transparent, the graphics shows through underneath the text. Non-Transparent makes a block of the background color surround the text, obscuring portions of the graphics beneath. This property may be modified at either design time or runtime. Any changes made to the FontTransparent property of a form or Printer object only affect the appearance of text drawn after the change. Tables 12-12 and 12-13 list the arguments of the FontTransparent property.

General Syntax

```
[form.]FontTransparent [ = state%]
[form!]Name.FontTransparent [ = state%]
Printer.FontTransparent [ = state%]
```

Arguments	Description
form	Name property of the form
Name	Name property of the picture box
Printer	'Printer' indicates the Printer object
state%	Current setting of FontTransparent property

Table 12-12 Arguments of FontTransparent property

state%	Description
True	Text on the object lets underlying graphics show through
False	Underlying graphics are obscured by the space around the text

Table 12-13 Settings of the state% variable of the FontTransparent property

Example Syntax

```
Sub Picture1_Click ()
    Picture1.FontName = "Arial"                          'Use Arial font
    Picture1.FontSize = 20                               'Sets the font size to 20
    Picture1.Print "Text on graphics"                    'Prints message on the picture box
    Picture1.FontTransparent = Not Picture1.FontTransparent 'Toggles the setting
End Sub
```

Description

The FontTransparent property determines what happens when graphics and text share the same space on a form or Printer object. If an object name is not provided, the parent form is assumed.

A FontTransparent property statement ends with a Boolean value of either False or True. This property defaults to False, which indicates that the text placed

500

Figure 12-9 Example syntax shows Transparent and Opaque text backgrounds

on the object obscures the underlying graphics. True means that underlying graphics show through the background of the text. Changing this property does not affect any previously placed text.

In the example syntax, the text either obscures or becomes part of the underlying graphics each time the user clicks the form. Figure 12-9 shows what the two options look like.

The FontBold, FontItalic, FontStrikethru, and FontUnderline Properties

Visual Basic provides four other special effects for controlling the appearance of text. These properties are FontBold, FontItalic, FontStrikethru, and FontUnderline. If more than one of these properties is True, then the effects are combined. Note that FontTransparent, unlike the other special effects, cannot be applied to most controls.

Example

The Font project at the end of this chapter demonstrates the FontTransparent property's effects. The Display Fonts command button brings up a form with the pictList picture box on it. A list of all available screen fonts gets drawn on the list over a gray box that was previously drawn on the picture box. Clicking on the picture box toggles the FontTransparent property back and forth to demonstrate its effects.

Comments

The FontTransparent property controls the appearance of the background around the text, not the text itself.

501

FONTUNDERLINE PROPERTY

Objects Affected

▶ Check	Clipboard	▶ Combo	▶ Command	▶ CommonDlg
▶ Data	Debug	▶ Dir	▶ Drive	▶ File
▶ Form	▶ Frame	▶ Grid	Image	▶ Label
Line	▶ List	MDI Form	Menu	OLE
▶ Option	▶ Picture	▶ Printer	Screen	Scroll
Shape	▶ Text	Timer		

Purpose

The FontUnderline property indicates whether the text on a form, control, or Printer object is underlined. When it is underlined, the text has a line placed under it. This property may be modified at either design time or runtime. Any changes made to the FontUnderline property of a form, picture box, or Printer object only affect the appearance of text drawn after the alteration. A control's FontUnderline property always changes the appearance of the text on it. Tables 12-14 and 12-15 summarize the arguments and states of the FontUnderline property.

General Syntax

```
[form.]FontUnderline [ = state%]
[form!]Name.FontUnderline [ = state%]
Printer.FontUnderline [ = state%]
```

Arguments	Description
form	Name property of the form
Name	Name property of a control
Printer	'Printer' indicates the Printer object
state%	Current setting of FontUnderline property

Table 12-14 Arguments of FontUnderline property

Figure 12-10 Example syntax shows underlined text

state%	Description
True	Text on the indicated object is underlined
False	Text on the indicated object is normal

Table 12-15 Settings of the state% variable of the FontUnderline property

Example Syntax

```
Sub Form_Click ()
    M$ = "Please Enter your message here"     'Asks for the word to display in the
    T$ = "Visual Basic SuperBible"            'Text1 text box and displays this
    A$ = InputBox$(M$, T$, Text1.Text)        'text with an underline.
    Text1.FontUnderline = Not Text1.FontUnderline
    Text1.Text = A$
End Sub
```

Description

The FontUnderline property affects whether a line is placed under the text on an object. When no object is given, the parent form is assumed to be the object addressed. Each FontUnderline property expression ends with a Boolean expression of either False or True. This property defaults to False, meaning text displays normally with no underline. True can have two possible effects. On forms, picture boxes, and Printer objects, the True setting only underlines new text. Text on controls is immediately affected by changes made to its FontUnderline property.

In the example syntax, each click of the mouse button changes the FontUnderline property of the Text Box control Text1. Notice that the FontUnderline property affects all of the text entered on the text box. Figure 12-10 shows this.

The FontBold, FontItalic, and FontStrikethru Properties

Visual Basic provides three other special effects for controlling the appearance of text These properties are FontBold, FontItalic, and FontStrikethru. If more than one of these properties is changed from its default False setting, then the effects are combined.

Example

The Font project at the end of this chapter demonstrates the FontUnderline property. Clicking the check box labeled Underline triggers the chekUnderline_Click event. This event changes the setting of the FontUnderline property of the textSample text box. Each time that this event is processed, the text on the textSample text box is switched from underlined to normal and normal to underlined.

Comments

The FontUnderline property places a line under all characters, including blank spaces.

THE FONT PROJECT

Project Overview

The Font project demonstrates the properties that affect the appearance of text in Visual Basic. This example will show the interaction of the properties affecting the text's appearance. By manipulating the different controls of this project, you will see all of the fonts available for your system. Exactly what you will see depends upon what fonts you have installed in your system.

This project has two sections, corresponding to the two forms that comprise the Font project. The first section deals with the assembly of the controls and subroutines of the Font form. The second section explains the formFontList form's subroutine. Each of these sections include step-by-step instructions on how to put the form and its controls together and the different elements of code to enter. After both forms are explained, there is a How It Works guide to the operation of the project. Please read this information carefully and use the pictures of the forms as guides in the process of assembling this project.

Assembling the Project: The Font Project Form

1. Make a new form (the Font form) with the objects and properties shown in Table 12-16.

Object	Property	Setting
Form	BorderStyle	1—Fixed Single
	Caption	Font Project
	MaxButton	False
	Name	formMain
Text box	Name	textSample
	FontBold	False
	FontItalic	False
	FontStrikethru	False
	FontTransparent	False
	FontUnderline	False
Combo	Name	cmboFont
	Sorted	True
Combo	Name	cmboSize
Frame	Caption	Special Effects
	Name	framEffects
Check box	Caption	&Bold
	Name	chekBold
	Value	0—Unchecked
Check box	Caption	&Italic
	Name	chekItalic

(continued on next page)

(continued from previous page)

Object	Property	Setting
	Value	0—Unchecked
Check box	Caption	&StrikeThru
	Name	chekStrikethru
	Value	0—Unchecked
Check box	Caption	&Underline
	Name	chekUnderline
	Value	0—Unchecked
Command	Caption	&Display Fonts
	Name	cmndDisplay
Command	Caption	E&xit
	Name	cmndExit

Table 12-16 Elements of the Font form

2. Size the objects on the screen as shown in Figure 12-11.

3. Enter the following code in the chekBold event subroutine. This code triggers when the user clicks the check box labeled Bold. When the check box has an "X" in it, the text in the text box textSample changes to bold. Otherwise, the text in the text box is normal.

```
Sub chekBold_Click ()
    textSample.FontBold = Not textSample.FontBold
End Sub
```

4. Enter the following code in the chekItalic_Click event subroutine. This code triggers when the user clicks the check box labeled Italic. When there is an "X" in the check box, the text in the text box textSample is changed to italics. Otherwise, the text in the text box is normal.

```
Sub chekItalic_Click ()
    textSample.FontItalic = Not textSample.FontItalic
End Sub
```

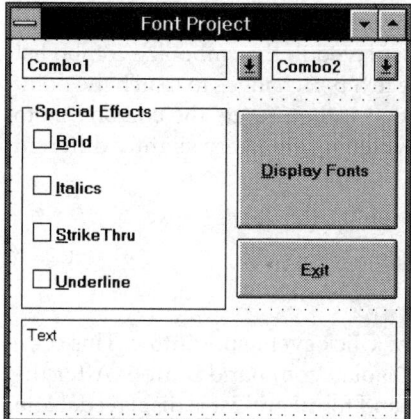

Figure 12-11 What the formMain
form should look like when
completed

5. Enter the following code in the chekStrikethru_Click event subroutine. This code
   triggers when the user clicks the check box labeled Strikethru. When there is an
   "X" in the check box, the text in the text box textSample has a line placed through
   it. Otherwise, the text in the text box is normal.

```
Sub chekStrikethru_Click ()
    textSample.FontStrikethru = Not textSample.FontStrikethru
End Sub
```

6. Enter the following code in the chekUnderline_Click event subroutine. This code
   triggers by the clicking of the check box labeled Underline. When there is an "X"
   in the check box, the text in the text box textSample is underlined. Otherwise, the
   text in the text box is normal.

```
Sub chekUnderline_Click ()
    textSample.FontUnderline = Not textSample.FontUnderline
End Sub
```

7. Enter the following code in the cmboFont_Click event subroutine. This code triggers when the user selects another choice in the combo list box cmboFont. The
   FontName property of the textSample text box is modified to match the font
   selected in the combo list box, and changes the text to the name of the font.

```
Sub cmboFont_Click ()
    textSample.FontName = cmboFont.Text
    textSample.Text = cmboFont.Text
End Sub
```

8. Enter the following code in the cmboSize_Click event subroutine. This code activates when the user changes the number displayed in the cmboSize combo list box. The FontSize property of the textSample text box changes to match the point size indicated in the combo list box. Note that it then resets the combo box to exactly display the correct size of the font, which is often very slightly different than what is specified.

```
Sub cmboSize_Click ()
    textSample.FontSize = Val(cmboSize.Text)
    cmboSize.Text = Str$(textSample.FontSize)
End Sub
```

9. Enter the following code in the cmndDisplay_Click event subroutine. This code activates when the user presses the cmndDisplay command button. After the user presses this button, formMain is hidden and formFontList is displayed. Note that we first Load formFontList; this gives it time to build and print the font list before actually displaying it.

```
Sub cmndDisplay_Click ()
    formMain.Hide              'hide this form
    Load formFontList          'load the font list form, don't display
    formFontList.Show          'and display after the form has had a chance to create list
End Sub
```

10. Enter the following code in the cmndExit_Click event subroutine. This code triggers when the user presses the Exit command button.

```
Sub cmndExit_Click ()
    End
End Sub
```

11. Enter the following code in the Form_Load event subroutine. The Form_Load event is processed at program start up. This code places the names of all of the fonts available in the present system into the cmboFont combo list box. The cmboSize combo list box displays a list of the possible point sizes between 4 and 36.

```
Sub Form_Load ()
    For F = 0 To (Screen.FontCount - 1)      'iterate through all screen fonts
        cmboFont.AddItem Screen.Fonts(F)     'add the font name to the combo box
    Next F
    For P = 4 To 36                          'iterate through some common point sizes
        cmboSize.AddItem Str$(P)             'and add point size to the combo box
    Next P
    cmboFont.Text = textSample.FontName      'set the combo box to the default font
    cmboSize.Text = Str$(textSample.FontSize) 'make combo box read the correct font size
End Sub
```

Assembling the Project: The formFontList Form

1. Make a new form with the objects and properties listed in Table 12-17.

508

Object	Property	Setting
Form	BorderStyle	3—Fixed Double
	Caption	Font List
	Name	formFontList
	ScaleMode	2—Points
Label	Caption	"Transparent"
	Name	lablTransparent
Picture	Name	pictContainer
	ScaleMode	2—Points
Picture	Name	pictList
	ScaleMode	2—Points
VScroll	Name	scrlUpDown

Table 12-17 Elements of the formFontList form

2. Size the objects on the screen as shown in Figure 12-12. Note that pictList must be drawn completely within pictContainer to make it a child of pictContainer.

3. Enter the following code in the cmndClose_Click event subroutine. When the user clicks the mouse button over the formFontList form, the formFontList form is hidden and the formMain form is displayed.

```
Sub cmndClose_Click ()
    formFontList.Hide          'Hide this form
    formMain.Show              'show the main form again
End Sub
```

4. Enter the following code in the Form_Load event subroutine. This code triggers when the formFontList form first loads. This routine first sets the pointer to an hourglass (processing the font list will take a while!). It then sets the dimensions of pictList to completely fill pictContainer, and makes it tall enough to fit the entire font list. Then it sets the scroll bar properties to enable the scrolling of the entire list. It then draws a gray box on pictList to help demonstrate the

509

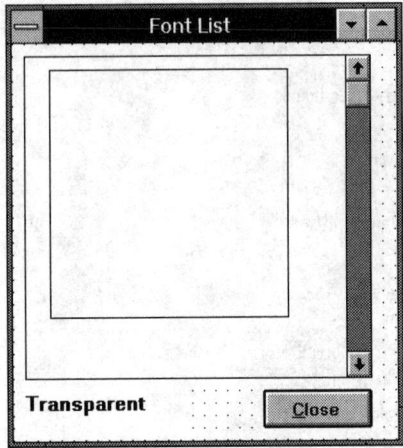

Figure 12-12 What the formFontList
form should look like during design

FontTransparent property later. Finally, it iterates through all screen fonts and
displays them on pictList.

```
Sub Form_Load ()
    Screen.MousePointer = 11                                  'Hourglass
    pictList.FontSize = 18                                    '18 points
    fontsLength = Screen.FontCount * pictList.TextHeight("Test")   'height of entire font list
    pictList.Top = 0                                          'make list flush with container's top
    pictList.Left = 0                                         'make list flush with container's left
    pictList.Width = pictContainer.ScaleWidth                 'make list flush with container's right
    pictList.Height = fontsLength                             'make list as long as entire font list
    scrlUpDown.Min = 0                                        'display top of list
    scrlUpDown.Max = pictList.Height - pictContainer.Height   'length of entire list
    scrlUpDown.LargeChange = scrlUpDown.Max / 50    '1/50th of total list
    scrlUpDown.SmallChange = scrlUpDown.Max / 250   '1/250th of total list
    pictList.Cls                                              'clear the list
    pictList.FillStyle = 0                                    'solid fill
    pictList.FillColor = QBColor(7)                           'light gray
    pictList.AutoRedraw = True                                'repaint automatically when uncovered
    pictList.Line (0, 0)-(pictList.ScaleWidth, pictList.ScaleHeight), QBColor(7), BF
    pictList.CurrentX = 0                                     'reset coordinates to left
    pictList.CurrentY = 0                                     '  ""        ""      top
    For I = 0 To Screen.FontCount - 1                         'iterate through all screen fonts
        pictList.FontName = Screen.Fonts(I)                   'change list's font
        pictList.Print Screen.Fonts(I)                        'and print the name of the font
    Next I
    Screen.MousePointer = 0                                   'set hourglass back to normal
End Sub
```

5. Enter the following code in the pictList_Click event. This event flips the trans-
   parency setting of the list, and resets the label accordingly. It then scrolls to the
   top of the list, and calls the Form_Load procedure to redraw the list.

510

```
Sub pictList_Click ()
    pictList.FontTransparent = Not pictList.FontTransparent 'switch transparency setting
    If pictList.FontTransparent = True Then      'and tell user what the setting is
        lablTransparent = "Transparent"
    Else
        lablTransparent = "Opaque"
    End If
    scrlUpDown.Value = 0                          'go to top of the list
    Form_Load                                     'and redraw the list
End Sub
```

6. Enter the following code in the scrlUpDown_Change event. This event triggers whenever the scroll bar changes value, whether it be by the user moving the thumb, clicking the arrows, clicking the gray areas, or by code setting the value. It scrolls pictList up and down. The pictContainer picture box contains pictList, and clips the much longer pictList.

```
Sub scrlUpDown_Change ()
    pictList.Top = -scrlUpDown.Value          'scroll the list up or down
End Sub
```

How It Works

This program provides a form that allows the user to see how the different fonts of a system look. The text displayed in the textSample text box changes according to the settings of the cmboFont and cmboSize combo list boxes. Each of the check boxes labeled Bold, Italics, Strikethru, and Underline define whether the text appears with these special effects. Pressing the command button labeled Display Fonts produces a list of the available system screen fonts.

When the program loads, the Form_Load event uses the FontCount property to find how many fonts are available in the system. The FontCount property and Fonts property provide the values to place the names of the system's fonts in the cmboFont combo list box. Notice that the Sorted property changes the order that the names appear in this combo box. This is helpful as the list returned by the multiple use of the Fonts property is not in alphabetical order. (You can see the actual order of the fonts in the Display Fonts dialog box brought up by the Display Fonts command button.)

The FontSize property is the default setting of the cmboSize combo list box. This shows the point size of the text in the textSample text box. If this is not done, then the combo list box cmboSize would be initially blank. Notice that many of the values of the FontSize property are fractions.

Running the Program

The settings of the check boxes marked Bold, Italic, Strikethru, and Underline, reflect the appearance of the textSample text box. When a check box is checked, the format of the text in the textSample text box changes. These instructions are contained within the Click event subroutine of each check box.

Figure 12-13 What the main form
will look like when running

Each time that the user selects a new font or point size, the text in the text box
changes to this new setting. This shows the ways in which the point size and font interact with each other. Figure 12-13 shows what the main form looks like when running.

The Fonts, FontCount, and FontName properties are all accessed to display
a list of fonts when the user presses the command button Display Fonts. This list
prints on the pictList on the formFontList form. Each font name appears in the
correct font that it names. For some fonts, such as all-symbol fonts like

Figure 12-14 What the
formFontList form looks like with
FontTransparent set to True

Figure 12-15 What the formFontList form looks like with FontTransparent set to False

WingDings, this makes the font name unreadable. The pictList picture box is contained within the pictContainer picture box. That means that no matter how big pictList is, it will always be clipped at the boundaries of pictContainer. That lets us scroll pictList up and down very easily with the scroll bar scrlUpDown.

The pictList picture box has a gray background drawn on it. Each time pictList is clicked, the FontTransparent property changes and the list is regenerated. When the FontTransparent property is True (as it is initially), the text displays directly on the gray background as Figure 12-14 illustrates. When FontTransparent is false, each font name has an opaque background that obscures the gray background as Figure 12-15 illustrates.

13
GETTING USER INPUT

Visual Basic's text box control lets you easily get text input from the user. The text box control inherits a number of powerful features that make it simple to let your user select, cut, and copy text. The text box also automatically follows Windows conventions with the movement keys like ⬅ and ➡ and the (HOME) and (END) keys. You can tell the text box to automatically create scroll bars for you, and Visual Basic 3.0 even lets you specify a password character to use in a password entry routine.

The text box control lets the user enter or edit text. When a text box control receives the focus, an insertion point appears in the box. The insertion point is a slim flashing vertical line that indicates where any new text will be entered within the box. Although the proper Windows terminology for this line is *caret*, most people commonly refer to it as the *cursor*. This cursor can be moved by using the direction keys, the (HOME) and (END) keys, or by clicking at the desired position in the text box with the mouse pointer. The default behavior for the mouse pointer is to change to an I-beam when over a text box, to facilitate precise positioning. See Chapter 5, Application Appearance, for more about the MousePointer property.

The text box's primary property is the Text property. This property is a string value that contains any text that has been entered into the text box. The value of the Text property can be modified in one of four ways: user input, your program's code, DDE messages, or a change in the record of an underlying database record if the text control has been bound. See Chapter 25, Dynamic Data Exchange, for more information about DDE, and Chapter 27, Data Access, for more about bound controls and databases. Any time the text changes, the text box's Change event occurs (see Chapter 7, Events, for more about the Change event).

515

EDITING IN A TEXT BOX

A Visual Basic text box gives the user full editing capabilities. It automatically inherits all the conventions of a standard Windows text box, including the ability to cut, copy, and paste to and from the Windows Clipboard area. A user can select text for these functions by holding down a (SHIFT) key and pressing (←) or (→), or by clicking and dragging the mouse over the desired text. This highlights the selected text.

Once text has been selected, the user may perform several operations on it. Pressing the (DELETE) key deletes the selected text from the text box. Pressing (SHIFT)-(DELETE) or (CTRL)-(X) will copy the selected text to the Clipboard, and then delete it from the text box. This is commonly called *cutting* text. The user can also *copy* selected text to the Clipboard without deleting it by pressing the (CTRL)-(INS) or (CTRL)-(C) key combinations. Pressing (SHIFT)-(INS) or (CTRL)-(V) will *paste* any text currently stored on the Clipboard into the text box at the position specified by the text box's insertion point. These functions can also be controlled and emulated by your program by using the SelText, SelStart, and SelLength properties. For more information on how to interact with the Windows Clipboard, see Chapter 23, Using the Clipboard.

MultiLine Text Boxes

By default, a text box consists of only one line of text. You may allow the user to enter more than one line of text by setting the MultiLine property to True. If you've set the MultiLine property to True, you may also wish to set the ScrollBars property. This allows you to place scroll bars on the left and bottom edges of the text box. This enables the user to quickly scroll through the text.

Text Boxes and Combo Boxes

The combo box control has two styles, DropDown combo and Simple combo, which include an edit area that is very similar to the text box control. These two styles of combo boxes share the SelLength, SelStart, SelText, and Text properties with the text box control. Refer to Chapter 18, Lists, Combos, and Grids, for more information on these controls.

Getting User Input Summary

Table 13-1 lists the properties that relate to the text box control, and their uses. Each of these properties is explained in detail in this chapter. At the end of the chapter, an example project demonstrates the usage of all of these elements combined.

516

Use or Set This...		To Do This...
MultiLine	Property	Set up a text box to accept multiple-line input
PasswordChar	Property	Set or determine if text box displays actual text or a placeholder
ScrollBars	Property	Set up horizontal or vertical scroll bars (or both) for a text box
SelLength	Property	Set or read the length of the currently selected text (if any)
SelStart	Property	Set or read the starting position of the currently selected text (if any)
SelText	Property	Replace or read the currently selected text string
Text	Property	Set or read the text contained in a text box

Table 13-1 The properties that govern the appearance and behavior of a text box control

CONSTANT.TXT Values

One of the properties in this chapter uses numeric values as arguments. Using constants rather than the literal value makes your code self-documenting, more readable, and easier to debug.

Microsoft provides a file, CONSTANT.TXT, that has many constant declarations defined for you. For smaller applications it's probably easiest just to type the declarations in yourself. For larger applications you'll find it much easier to read the text file into a new module.

To do this, create a new module by pulling down the File menu and choosing the New Module menu command. Then pull down the File menu again, and choose Load Text. This opens up a dialog box listing all text files in the current directory. CONSTANT.TXT should be in your main Visual Basic directory (default installation would place this in C:\VB). Simply choose CONSTANT.TXT to enter the entire file into your module. These constants will then be available throughout your application.

Table 13-2 lists the value of the constant, the CONSTANT.TXT constant name, and a brief description of what the constant means.

Value	CONSTANT.TXT	Effect of Setting
ScrollBars property		
0	NONE	(Default) The text box will have no scroll bars, and text will wrap automatically
1	HORIZONTAL	A horizontal scroll bar appears at the bottom edge of the text box with no word wrapping
2	VERTICAL	A vertical scroll bar appears at the right edge of the text box with automatic word wrapping
3	BOTH	Vertical and horizontal scroll bars with automatic word wrapping

Table 13-2 CONSTANT.TXT values for text input

MULTILINE PROPERTY

Objects Affected

Check	Clipboard	Combo	Command	CommonDlg
Data	Debug	Dir	Drive	File
Form	Frame	Grid	Image	Label
Line	List	MDI Form	Menu	OLE
Option	Picture	Printer	Screen	Scroll
Shape	▶ Text	Timer		

Purpose

The MultiLine property sets up a text box control for entry of multiple lines of text. This property can only be set at design time, although your program can read its value at runtime. Table 13-3 summarizes the arguments of the MultiLine property.

General Syntax

```
[form!]Name.MultiLine
```

518

Arguments	Description
form	Name property of the parent form
Name	Name property of the control

Table 13-3 Arguments of the MultiLine property

Example Syntax

```
Sub Command1_Click ()
    MultiLineStatus = Text1.MultiLine
End Sub
```

Description

By default, this property is set to False (0), causing the associated text box to be a single-line text box. However, you may wish to set this property to True (-1) at design time to create a multiple-line text box. A multiple-line text box allows the user to enter more than one line in the text box.

If the ScrollBars property is set to 0 (none) or 2 (vertical only), a multiple-line text box will automatically wrap text over to the next line when it exceeds the width of the box. If the ScrollBars property is set to 1 (horizontal) or 3 (both horizontal and vertical), it is up to the user to create new lines. If there is no button on the same form with its Default property set to True, the user can create new lines by pressing the (ENTER) key. If there is a default button on the form, the user must use the (CTRL)-(ENTER) key combination to create a new line.

The example syntax reads the value of the MultiLine property for the text box "Text1." It could be used in an If statement to determine whether to format multiline text.

Example

In the TextBox project at the end of this chapter, the edit area of the mini-text editor is a multiple-line text box.

PASSWORDCHAR PROPERTY

Objects Affected

Check	Clipboard	Combo	Command	CommonDlg
Data	Debug	Dir	Drive	File
Form	Frame	Grid	Image	Label
Line	List	MDI Form	Menu	OLE
Option	Picture	Printer	Screen	Scroll
Shape	▶ Text	Timer		

Purpose

Use the PasswordChar property to set up a text box for password entry. This property defaults to displaying typed characters as the actual characters; setting this property to anything other than an empty string will echo the property setting instead of the actual character. This lets you have visual feedback for each character typed without displaying the actual characters. Tables 13-4 and 13-5 summarize the arguments of the PasswordChar property.

General Syntax

`[form!]Name.PasswordChar [ = string$]`

Arguments	Description
form	Name property of the parent form
Name	Name property of the control
string$	Read or set the password character

Table 13-4 Arguments of the PasswordChar property

string$	Meaning
empty string	(Default) Echo typed characters as the actual characters
non-empty string	Echo typed characters as the first character in the string (other characters ignored)

Table 13-5 Meaning of the string$ argument in the PasswordChar property

520

Figure 13-1 The PasswordChar property lets you easily set up password input dialog boxes

Example Syntax

```
Sub Form_Load ()
    Form2.Caption = "Enter Your Password"
    Form2!Text1.PasswordChar = "*"
    Form2.Show MODAL
    If Form2!Text1.Text = Form1.Tag Then
        LoadMainProgram
    Else
        MsgBox "Incorrect Password!"
        End
    End If
End Sub
```

Description

Use the PasswordChar property to convert an ordinary text box into a password entry box. Passwords typically should not be displayed as they are typed in, thus minimizing the risk of prying eyes determining someone's password. Most Windows programs typically use the asterisk (*) character as a placeholder when typing in a password. This gives the user visual feedback as they type each character without displaying the actual character. Figure 13-1 shows what a typical password entry dialog box might look like.

Set the PasswordChar property to a string to make it display the placeholder in the text box. Only the first character of the string is significant; subsequent characters are ignored. The example syntax assigns the asterisk as the placeholder character. Set PasswordChar to an empty string (" ") to disable the password setting and reenable displaying normal text.

The text box will always contain the actual characters, no matter what the PasswordChar property is set to. This lets you check the Text property to determine if the user typed the right password, as the above example shows.

Example

The TextBox project at the end of this chapter uses the PasswordChar property to set up a password entry dialog box. The File New command asks for the password before clearing the editing area.

SCROLLBARS PROPERTY

Objects Affected

Check	Clipboard	Combo	Command	CommonDlg
Data	Debug	Dir	Drive	File
Form	Frame	▶ Grid	Image	Label
Line	List	▶ MDI Form	Menu	OLE
Option	Picture	Printer	Screen	Scroll
Shape	▶ Text	Timer		

Purpose

This property is set at design time to determine what types of scroll bars, if any, will appear at the edges of a text box (or a grid or MDI Form). Scroll bars allow the user to read or position to text that is too wide (or has too many lines) to fit in the window. This property is read-only at runtime. The arguments for the ScrollBars property are summarized in Table 13-6, while Table 13-7 lists the possible values for this property and their effects.

General Syntax

`[form!]Name.ScrollBars`

Arguments	Description
form	Name property of the parent form
Name	Name property of the control

Table 13-6 Arguments of the ScrollBars property

Value	CONSTANT.TXT	Effect of Setting
0	NONE	(Default) The text box will have no scroll bars, and text will wrap automatically
1	HORIZONTAL	A horizontal scroll bar appears at the bottom edge of the text box with no word wrapping
2	VERTICAL	A vertical scroll bar appears at the right edge of the text box with automatic word wrapping
3	BOTH	Vertical and horizontal scroll bars with automatic word wrapping

Table 13-7 Possible settings for the ScrollBars property

Example Syntax

```
Sub Form_Load ()
    ScrollBarStatus = Text1.ScrollBars
End Sub
```

Description

The ScrollBars property is only useful when the MultiLine property is set to True (-1). This property is meaningless for text boxes when the MultiLine property is False. Scroll bars are graphic objects that consist of a bar with arrows at each end and a button (called a thumb) between the arrows. Scroll bars give the user the ability to quickly scroll through text with the mouse. There are two types of scroll bars: vertical and horizontal.

The scroll bar's thumb indicates the relative position of the text box's text. The user can move the thumb by clicking and dragging it, by clicking on the bar itself, or by clicking on one of the arrows at either end of the scroll bar. Moving the button on the scroll bar causes the text within the text box to scroll in proportion to the amount it is moved.

The example syntax stores the current value of the ScrollBars property of form Text1 in the variable ScrollBarStatus. It could be used in an If statement to test for the presence of scroll bars.

If the ScrollBars property is set to 0 (none) or 2 (vertical only), a multiple-line text box will automatically wrap text over to the next line when it exceeds the width of the box. Otherwise, it is up to the user to create new lines. If there is no button on the same form with its Default property set to True, the user can create new lines by hitting the (ENTER) key. If there is a default button on the form, the user must use the (CTRL)-(ENTER) key combination to create a new line.

Example

In the TextBox project at the end of this chapter, the ScrollBars property for the edit portion of the mini-text editor is set to 2 (vertical scroll bars) at design time.

SELLENGTH PROPERTY

Objects Affected

Check	Clipboard	▶ Combo	Command	CommonDlg
Data	Debug	Dir	Drive	File
Form	Frame	Grid	Image	Label
Line	List	MDI Form	Menu	OLE
Option	Picture	Printer	Screen	Scroll
Shape	▶ Text	Timer		

Purpose

Sets or returns the number of selected characters within a text or combo box. Characters can be selected (highlighted) by the user, usually for an editing operation. Your program can also select a portion of the text in the text box. This property can be set and read at runtime only. The arguments for the SelLength property are summarized in Table 13-8.

General Syntax

`[form!]Name.SelLength [ = NumChars&]`

Arguments	Description
form	Name property of the parent form
Name	Name property of the control
NumChars&	Reads or sets the number of selected characters

Table 13-8 Arguments of the SelLength property

Example Syntax

```
Sub Text1_MouseUp (Button As Integer, Shift As Integer, X As Single, Y As Single)
    SaveSelLength = Text1.SelLength        'Save the length of the selected text
    Text2.Text = Str$(SaveSelLength)
End Sub
```

Description

This property is used in conjunction with the SelStart and SelText properties for working with text that has been selected by the user in a text or combo box. A user can select text for these properties by holding down a (SHIFT) key and pressing ← or →, or by clicking and dragging the mouse over the desired text. This highlights the selected text. Your program can then read the settings of these properties in order to perform operations on the selected text. The SelStart property determines the starting point of the selected text within a text or combo box. The SelLength property determines the number of characters selected. SelText is a string property that contains the selected text.

The SelLength property is a long integer that may be used to set or return the number of selected characters in the text. If no characters are selected, this property returns 0.

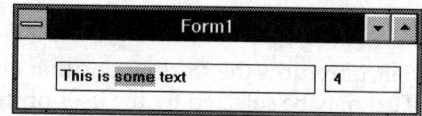

Figure 13-2 Example syntax shows text box with selected text; the other text box shows the SelLength

This property can also be set within a program's code. Doing so has no effect unless the text box has the focus when the property is set. If the text box does have the focus, assigning this property a value causes that number of characters to be selected in the text box, starting at the position indicated by the SelStart property. If the program assigns this property a value that exceeds the length of the text in the text box, only the existing characters are selected, and the SelLength property is adjusted to reflect this. Setting this property to a value less than 0 causes an "Invalid property value" error to occur during runtime.

The example syntax saves the length of the current text selection to a variable for future use. Figure 13-2 shows a text box with selected text.

Example

In the TextBox project at the end of this chapter, the SelLength and SelStart properties are saved in the Text1_KeyDown event. This is done to enable the Undo function of the mini-text editor.

Comments

This property also applies to combo boxes whose Style property has been set to 0 (DropDown Combo) or 1 (Simple Combo). When used on the combo box control, it behaves in the same manner as described above.

SELSTART PROPERTY

Objects Affected

Check	Clipboard	▶ Combo	Command	CommonDlg
Data	Debug	Dir	Drive	File
Form	Frame	Grid	Image	Label
Line	List	MDI Form	Menu	OLE
Option	Picture	Printer	Screen	Scroll
Shape	▶ Text	Timer		

525

Purpose

Sets or returns the starting position of selected text within a text or combo box. Text may be selected by the user or the program, and is highlighted in the text box. If there is no selected text, this property sets or returns the position of the box's insertion point. The arguments for the SelStart property are summarized in Table 13-9.

General Syntax

```
[form!]Name.SelStart [ = StartPos&]
```

Arguments	Description
form	Name property of the parent form
Name	Name property of the control
StartPos&	Reads or sets the character position of the insertion point or the start of selected text

Table 13-9 Arguments of the SelStart property

Example Syntax

```
Sub Text1_MouseUp (Button As Integer, Shift As Integer, X As Single, Y As Single)
    SaveSelStart = Text1.SelStart      'Save the start of the selected text
    Text2.Text = Str$(SaveSelStart)
End Sub
```

Description

This property is used in conjunction with the SelLength and SelText properties for working with text that has been selected in a text or combo box by the user. A user can select text for these properties by holding down a (SHIFT) key and pressing (←) or (→), or by clicking and dragging the mouse over the desired text. This highlights the selected text (see Figure 13-3). Your program can then read the settings of these properties in order to perform operations on the selected text. The SelStart property determines the starting point of the selected text within a text or combo box. SelLength determines the number of characters selected. SelText is a string property that contains the selected text.

The SelStart property is a long integer value that indicates the starting position of the selected characters in a text or combo box. The value of SelStart is zero-based. This means the first selected character is the position after the value of

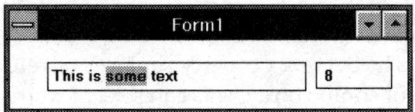

Figure 13-3 Example syntax shows
text box with selected text; the other
text box shows the SelStart

SelStart. For instance, if the value of SelStart is 1, and the value of SelLength is
2, the second and third characters in the text are selected. If there is no text currently selected, SelStart will return the position of the text box's insertion point.

You may set the SelStart property by assigning a long integer value to it. This
value must be a non-negative number, or an "Invalid property value" error will
occur during runtime. If this value is greater than the length of the text in the text
or combo box, SelStart is set to a value equal to the length of the text. Assigning
a value to the SelStart property automatically sets the SelLength property to 0,
and moves the insertion point in the text box to the specified position.

The example syntax saves the starting position of the selected text in a variable
for future use.

Example

In the TextBox project at the end of this chapter, the SelLength and SelStart properties are saved in the Text1_KeyDown event. This is done to enable the Undo
function of the mini-text editor.

Comments

This property also applies to combo boxes whose Style property has been set to 0
(DropDown Combo) or 1 (Simple Combo). When used on the combo box control,
it behaves in the same manner as described above.

SELTEXT PROPERTY

Objects Affected

Check	Clipboard	▶ Combo	Command	CommonDlg
Data	Debug	Dir	Drive	File
Form	Frame	Grid	Image	Label
Line	List	MDI Form	Menu	OLE
Option	Picture	Printer	Screen	Scroll
Shape	▶ Text	Timer		

Purpose

The SelText property replaces or returns the currently selected text within a text or combo box. Users can select text (typically by dragging with the mouse), or text may be selected by program action. The arguments for the SelText property are summarized in Table 13-10.

General Syntax

`[form!]Name.SelText [ = NewText$]`

Arguments	Description
form	Name property of the parent form
Name	Name property of the control
NewText$	A string that can be placed at the text box's insertion point. NewText$ replaces any selected text

Table 13-10 Arguments of the SelText property

Example Syntax

```
Sub Text1_MouseUp (Button As Integer, Shift As Integer, X As Single, Y As Single)
    Clipboard.SetText Text1.SelText     'Save the start of the selected text
    Text2.Text = Text1.SelText
End Sub
```

Description

This property is used in conjunction with the SelLength and SelStart properties for working with text that has been selected in a text or combo box by the user. A user can select text for these properties by holding down a (SHIFT) key and pressing ⊖ or ⊕, or by clicking and dragging the mouse over the desired text. This highlights the selected text. Your program can then read the settings of these properties in order to perform operations on the selected text. The SelStart property determines the starting point of the selected text within a text or combo box. SelLength determines the number of characters selected. SelText is a string property that contains the selected text.

The SelText property returns a string copy of the selected characters from the text or combo box. This string can be used by your programs to cut and paste to the Windows Clipboard. If no characters are currently selected, this property will return a null string.

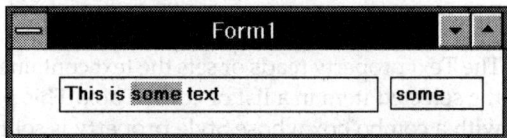

Figure 13-4 Example syntax shows selected
text; the other text box shows SelText

Assigning a string value to this property can cause one of two things to happen. If there is any text selected when the assignment is done, the selected text in the text or combo box is replaced by the assigned text. If no text is selected, the new text is inserted into the text or combo box's text at the box's insertion point.

Figure 13-4 displays a text box with some selected text. In this example the value of the SelStart property would be 8, SelLength would be 4, and SelText would be "some."

The example syntax copies the selected text to the Clipboard by assigning the value of the SelText property of the text box to the SetText method of the Clipboard, and then copies the selected text to Text2.

Comments

This property also applies to combo boxes whose Style property has been set to 0 (DropDown Combo) or 1 (Simple Combo). When used on the combo box control, it behaves in the same manner as described above.

TEXT PROPERTY

Objects Affected

Check	Clipboard	▶ Combo	Command	CommonDlg
Data	Debug	Dir	Drive	File
Form	Frame	▶ Grid	Image	Label
Line	▶ List	MDI Form	Menu	OLE
Option	Picture	Printer	Screen	Scroll
Shape	▶ Text	Timer		

529

Purpose

The Text property reads or sets the text contained in a text box or grid cell, or reads the selected item in a list or combo box. This property can also be set when used with a combo box whose Style property is set to 0 (drop-down combo) or 1 (simple combo). The arguments for the Text property are summarized in Table 13-11.

General Syntax

```
[form.]Name.Text [= TextString$]
```

Arguments	Description
Form	Name property of the parent form
Name	Name property of the control
TextString$	A string that can be assigned to this property, and thereby replaces all text in the text box

Table 13-11 Arguments of the Text property

Example Syntax

```
Command1_Click ()
    Text1.Text = TxtBeforeChange$     'Assigns a string to the text box Text1
    SelectedItem$ = List1.Text        'Assigns the value of a list box's selected item to a string
End Sub
```

Description

The Text property is a string that allows your program to access the contents of the edit area of a text or combo box, or the contents of a grid cell. It also can represent a chosen item in a list box. You can optionally assign a string as the value for this property.

The Text property also allows you to access and manipulate the text inside a text box. This property is a string representation of the contents of the box, and can be manipulated by any of Visual Basic's string functions and statements such as Left$, Mid$, and Right$. Any operations performed on this property are reflected by the text inside a text box.

You may assign a string to the Text property. This replaces the text in the box with the assigned string. The user can also directly edit the text represented by the Text property. Any time a box's Text property is modified, it triggers the box's Change event.

This property can contain a string up to 2048 characters if the MultiLine property is False, and up to approximately 32,000 characters if MultiLine is True. However, assigning large numbers of characters to this property greatly degrades the performance of the box. In other words, the longer the value of the Text property, the slower the text box will react to user input.

The first example syntax assigns a string to the Text property of text box Text1. This text would then appear in the text box. The second example syntax assigns the text in list box List1 to a string for future use.

Combo and List Boxes and the Grid Control

The Text property is also used with the Combo and List box controls. When used on the DropDown (Style = 0) and Simple (Style = 1) combo box styles, this property works in the exact same manner as described above. When used with the List box control or a DropDown list (combo box with Style set to 2), the Text property is read only, and returns the string value of the selected item in the list.

Individual grid cells also have a Text property (although the grid control itself does not). You cannot directly manipulate grid cells, so the Text property needs to be set with your code. You'd typically have a text box accept the input and then assign the text box's Text property to the grid cell's Text property. Refer to Chapter 18, Lists, Combos, and Grids, for more information on these controls.

Example

In the TextBox project at the end of this chapter, a multiline text box is used to edit text. The Text property of this box is manipulated in several procedures. The length of the Text property is determined in the Change event for the text box, so the number of characters typed can be displayed. In the menuFile(0)_Click event, the Text property is set to an empty string. In the Text1_KeyDown event, the value of the Text property is saved in a string variable, so that it can be restored by the user. When the Undo option is chosen from the Edit menu, the EditUndo_Click event occurs. This event assigns the value of the previously saved string variable to the Text property, thereby restoring its original state.

THE TEXTBOX PROJECT

The TextBox Project Overview

The project outlined in the following pages demonstrates the concepts behind the text box control. This project uses each of the properties covered in this chapter, and demonstrates how they work together. By following the examples in this project, you should be able to get a firm grasp on the concepts behind dealing with text boxes.

This project makes use of the KeyDown event. This event occurs when the user presses any key on the keyboard. More information can be found on the KeyDown event in Chapter 16, Keyboard Input. There are also some methods used with Clipboard object in this project. These methods send or receive text from the Clipboard area of Windows. Refer to Chapter 23, Using the Clipboard, for more on this subject.

Assembling the Project: formMain

1. Create a new form (the TextBox form), and place on it the following controls. Use Table 13-12 to set the properties of the form and each control.

Object	Property	Setting
Form	Name	formMain
	Caption	Text Box Project
Label	Name	lablStatus
	Caption	" 0 Characters"
Text box	Name	textDocument
	Text	"" (Null)
	Multiline	True (-1)
	ScrollBars	2—Vertical

Table 13-12 Elements of the TextBox Form

2. Using the Menu Design window, create a menu with the settings in Table 13-13 (choose the Menu Design window option from Visual Basic's Window menu.)

Name	Caption	Property	Setting
menuBar	&File	Index	0
menuFile	&New	Index	0
menuFile		Index	1
menuFile	E&xit	Index	2
menuBar	&Edit	Index	1
menuEdit	&Undo	Index	0
menuEdit		Index	1
menuEdit	Cu&t	Index	2
menuEdit	&Copy	Index	3
menuEdit	&Paste	Index	4
menuEdit	&Delete	Index	5

Table 13-13 Menu settings for the TextBox project

3. Check the appearance of your form with Figure 13-5.

4. Enter the following code into the General Declarations area of the form. Three module-level variables are created for later use in the program. If the user changes the text in the box, these variables save the contents of the text box just prior to the changes. This information can then be used to later restore the text box to its value before the changes were made.

```
Dim TxtBeforeChange As String
Dim PosBeforeChange As Integer
Dim LenBeforeChange As Integer
```

5. Enter the following code into the Form_Resize event. This event occurs when the user changes the size of the form. It adjusts the size of the edit area to match the size of the form.

```
Sub Form_Resize ()
    textDocument.Height = formMain.ScaleHeight - 250
    textDocument.Width = formMain.ScaleWidth
    lablStatus.Top = textDocument.Height
```

(continued on next page)

(continued from previous page)

```
        lablStatus.Height = 250
        lablStatus.Width = formMain.ScaleWidth
End Sub
```

6. Enter the following code in the menuBar_Click event. This event occurs whenever the user clicks on the top-level menu choices (File and Edit), and completes its processing before the menu is actually pulled down. No special processing happens for the File menu, but the Edit menu needs to be set properly depending on if text has been selected or if text is available on the Clipboard. The routine first disables all the menu choices (note that menuEdit(1) is a separator bar). It then checks to see if there is any information stored in the undo buffer TxtBeforeChange. If so, it enables the Undo command. It then checks to see if any text has been selected. If so, the Cut, Copy, and Delete commands are enabled. It then checks the Clipboard to see if there is anything there in text format. If so, the Paste command gets enabled.

```
Sub menuBar_Click (Index As Integer)
    Select Case Index
    Case 0  ' File
    Case 1  ' Edit
        menuEdit(0).Enabled = False      'undo
        menuEdit(2).Enabled = False      'cut
        menuEdit(3).Enabled = False      'copy
        menuEdit(4).Enabled = False      'paste
        menuEdit(5).Enabled = False      'delete
        If Len(TxtBeforeChange) > 0 Then menuEdit(0).Enabled = True 'undo
        If textDocument.SelLength > 0 Then
            menuEdit(2).Enabled = True 'cut
            menuEdit(3).Enabled = True 'copy
            menuEdit(5).Enabled = True 'delete
        End If
        If Clipboard.GetFormat(1) Then menuEdit(4).Enabled = True      'paste
    End Select
End Sub
```

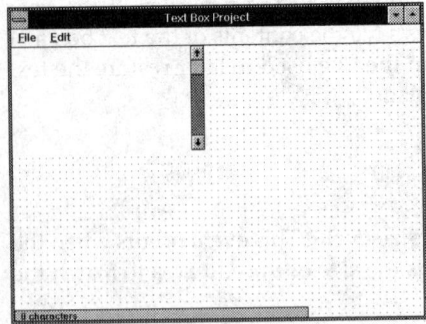

Figure 13-5 How the TextBox project form should look during design

7. Place the following code in the menuEdit_Click command. This event occurs whenever the user chooses a menu choice from the Edit menu. Note that we don't have to worry about inappropriate actions (such as attempting to cut text when there is none selected), because the menuBar_Click routine disables inappropriate menu choices before the menu pulls down.

   The Undo command simply resets the Text, SelStart, and SelLength properties back to their old values as set in the Text_Change event. The Cut command places the selected text on the Clipboard, and then sets the selected text to an empty string to delete it. The Copy command places the selected text on the Clipboard (just like the Cut command) but doesn't do anything to the selected text in the text box. The Paste command places whatever text is on the Clipboard into the selected text in the text box. If no text is selected, it places the new text at the insertion point. Finally, the Delete command sets the selected text to an empty string.

```
Sub menuEdit_Click (Index As Integer)
    Select Case Index
        Case 0 'undo
            textDocument.Text = TxtBeforeChange
            textDocument.SelStart = PosBeforeChange
            textDocument.SelLength = LenBeforeChange
        Case 2 'cut
            Clipboard.SetText textDocument.SelText
            textDocument.SelText = ""
        Case 3 'copy
            Clipboard.SetText textDocument.SelText
        Case 4 'paste
            textDocument.SelText = Clipboard.GetText(1)
        Case 5 'delete
            textDocument.SelText = ""
    End Select
End Sub
```

8. Place the following code in the menuFile_Click event. This event triggers when the user selects a command from the File menu. Note that menuFile(1) is a separator bar. The New command brings up a password protection dialog box before blanking out the text in the text box (to protect the valuable document you're creating?). It first blanks out any old text in the password text box, and then shows the dialog box. Note that we specify Modal in the Show method; this prevents the rest of the code from continuing until the user closes the dialog box. We've set textPassword's PasswordChar property to an asterisk (*) at design time. Once the user closes the dialog box, we check the password to see if it's acceptable. We've made it especially difficult for hackers to break our security here, as the only acceptable password is anything! If the user has somehow managed to divine our devious password strategy, the routine clears textDocument's text for a new document. If the user falls into our trap and simply presses the (ENTER) key in the password box, the routine calls itself again to force another attempt at the password entry. The Exit command ends the program.

535

```
Sub menuFile_Click (Index As Integer)
     Select Case Index
          Case 0 'new
               formPassword!textPassword.Text = ""
               formPassword.Show 1                               'modal
               If formPassword!textPassword.Text <> "" Then      'all passwords work!
                    textDocument.Text = ""
               Else                                              'user didn't even try, so
                    Beep                                         'Bronx cheer
                    menuFile_Click 0                             'bad password, try again
               End If
          Case 2 'exit
               End
     End Select
End Sub
```

9. Enter the following code into the textDocument_Change event. This event deter-
    mines the number of characters in the text box, and displays that information by
    assigning a string to the Caption property of the label control named lablStatus.

```
Sub textDocument_Change ()
     temp = Format$(Len(textDocument.Text), "  ##,###,##0")
     temp = temp + " Character"
     If Len(textDocument.Text) <> 1 Then temp = temp + "s"
     lablStatus.Caption = temp
End Sub
```

10. Enter the following code into the textDocument_KeyDown event. This event
    saves the current settings of the text box before changes are made. The values of
    the Text, SelStart, and SelLength properties are assigned to the variables defined
    in the general declarations area of the form. The Shift argument is tested to deter-
    mine whether the user has pressed the (CTRL) or (ALT) keys. The properties are only
    saved if the Shift argument indicates these have not been pressed. More infor-
    mation can be found on the KeyDown event in Chapter 16, Keyboard Input.

```
Sub textDocument_KeyDown (KeyCode As Integer, Shift As Integer)
     If Shift < 2 Then
          TxtBeforeChange = textDocument.Text
          PosBeforeChange = textDocument.SelStart
          LenBeforeChange = textDocument.SelLength
     End If
End Sub
```

Assembling the Project: Password Form

1. Create a new form (the TextBox form), and place on it the following controls. Use
    Table 13-14 to set the properties of the form and each control.

Figure 13-6 The password entry dialog
box formPassword during design

Object	Property	Setting
Form	Border	3—Fixed Double
	Caption	"Enter Password"
	Name	formPassword
Command	Caption	"OK"
	Default	True
	Name	cmndOK
Text	FontSize	12
	Name	textPassword
	PasswordChar	"*" (asterisk)

Table 13-14 Elements of formPassword

2. Size and position the controls as in Figure 13-6.

3. Enter the following code in the cmndOK_Click event. This simply hides the dialog box. Note that we don't unload it, as the File New routine in the main form needs to access the textPassword's Text property to determine if the user entered the correct password.

```
Sub cmndOK_Click ()
    formPassword.Hide
End Sub
```

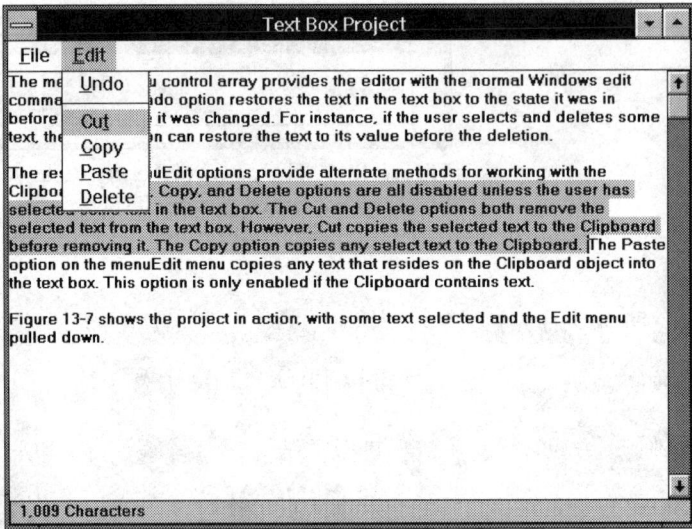

Figure 13-7 The TextBox project in action

How It Works

The program created by this project is a simple text editor. The textDocument control is the text entry area of the form. This control is a multiple-line (MultiLine = True) text box with a vertical scroll bar (ScrollBars = 2) on the right edge of the text area. The user can edit text in this control. Portions of text may be selected with a (SHIFT)-(→) key, or by dragging the mouse over the text. The selected text may be cut with (SHIFT)-(DELETE), or copied with (CTRL)-(INSERT) to the Clipboard, may be deleted (DELETE), or may be replaced by text from the Clipboard with (SHIFT)-(INSERT).

The menuBar control array processes the user's menu clicks before the submenus are pulled down. The File menu doesn't need any further processing, but the Edit menu needs to have its options properly set. The routine first checks to see if any text has been selected; if so, it enables the Cut, Copy, and Delete commands. Paste is enabled if there is any text on the Clipboard, and Undo is enabled if there is anything in the undo variables.

Choosing the New option from the menuFile menu first calls up a password protection dialog box before clearing textDocument. Note that we set the PasswordChar property of the textPassword text box at design time. Choosing Exit causes the program to end.

The menuEdit menu control array provides the editor with the normal Windows edit commands. The Undo option restores the text in the text box to the state it was in before the last time it was changed. For instance, if the user selects and deletes some text, the Undo option can restore the text to its value before the deletion.

The rest of the menuEdit options provide alternative methods for working with the Clipboard. The Cut, Copy, and Delete options are all disabled unless the

538

user has selected some text in the text box. The Cut and Delete options both remove the selected text from the text box. However, Cut copies the selected text to the Clipboard before removing it. The Copy option copies any selected text to the Clipboard. The Paste option on the menuEdit menu copies any text that resides on the Clipboard object into the text box. This option is only enabled if the Clipboard contains text.

Figure 13-7 shows the project in action, with some text selected and the Edit menu pulled down.

PART V

Mouse and Keyboard Processing

14

MOUSE EVENTS

The mouse device is an integral part of the Windows environment. Depending on the application, it allows the user to easily select items (such as buttons or menu options), to move objects (such as icons or the insertion point), to edit text, and to perform drawing functions.

Considered at its most basic level, the mouse can perform three basic tasks. First, moving the mouse changes the position of the mouse pointer on the screen. Second, a button on the mouse can be pressed. And finally, a pressed button on the mouse can be released.

Visual Basic provides five events to handle these three tasks; Click, DblClick, MouseDown, MouseMove, and MouseUp. The Click event is generated when the left button on the mouse has been pressed and then released. The DblClick event occurs when the left button on the mouse has been pressed and then released twice in quick succession. The MouseDown event occurs when any button on the mouse, left, center (on some mice), or right is pressed. The MouseMove event is generated when the mouse is moved. Finally, the MouseUp event occurs when any button on the mouse (left, center, or right) is released. Each of these events are explained in detail within this chapter.

MOUSE EVENTS SUMMARY

Table 14-1 details the five mouse-related events, and their purposes. At the end of this chapter, the Mouse Events project demonstrates the use of all these events combined.

Use This...		To Do This...
Click	Event	React to the user clicking the left mouse button
DblClick	Event	React to the user clicking the left mouse button twice
MouseDown	Event	React to the user pressing any mouse button
MouseMove	Event	React to any mouse movement
MouseUp	Event	React to the user releasing any mouse button

Table 14-1 Events dealing with mouse operations

CONSTANT.TXT Values

Several of the events in this chapter use numeric values as arguments. Using constants rather than the literal value makes your code self-documenting, more readable, and easier to debug.

Microsoft provides a file, CONSTANT.TXT, that has many constant declarations defined for you. For smaller applications it's probably easiest just to type the declarations in yourself. For larger applications you'll find it much easier to read the text file into a new module.

To do this, create a new module by pulling down the File menu and choosing the New Module menu command. Then pull down the File menu again, and choose Load Text. This opens up a dialog box listing all text files in the current directory. CONSTANT.TXT should be in your main Visual Basic directory (default installation would place this in C:\VB). Simply choose CONSTANT.TXT to enter the entire file into your module. These constants will then be available throughout your application.

Table 14-2 lists the value of the constant, the CONSTANT.TXT constant name, and a brief description of what the constant means.

Value	CONSTANT.TXT	Meaning
MouseDown, MouseMove, MouseUp: Button argument		
1	LEFT_BUTTON	Left button was pressed
2	RIGHT_BUTTON	Right button was pressed

Value	CONSTANT.TXT	Meaning
4	MIDDLE_BUTTON	Middle button (if available on mouse) was pressed
MouseDown, MouseMove, MouseUp: Shift argument		
1	SHIFT_MASK	(SHIFT) key was pressed during MouseDown
2	CTRL_MASK	(CTRL) key was pressed during MouseDown
4	ALT_MASK	(ALT) key was pressed during MouseDown

Table 14-2 CONSTANT.TXT values for mouse events

CLICK EVENT

Objects Affected

▶ Check	Clipboard	▶ Combo	▶ Command	CommonDlg
Data	Debug	▶ Dir	Drive	▶ File
▶ Form	▶ Frame	▶ Grid	▶ Image	▶ Label
Line	▶ List	MDI Form	▶ Menu	▶ OLE
▶ Option	▶ Picture	Printer	Screen	Scroll
Shape	▶ Text	Timer		

Purpose

The Click event is called when the user presses and releases the left button on the mouse. This generally selects the control or activates some action associated with it (as in a command button or menu option). Table 14-3 summarizes the arguments of the Click event.

General Syntax

```
Sub Form_Click()
Sub Name_Click([Index As Integer])
```

Arguments	Description
Form	'Form' refers to the parent form of the procedure; not the form's Name property
Name	Name property of the control
Index	Uniquely identifies an element of a control array

Table 14-3 Arguments of the Click event

Example Syntax

```
Sub Form_Click()
    Label1.Caption = "The form has been clicked"
End Sub

Sub Label2_Click(Index As Integer)
    Dim Message As String
    Message = "This is index number "
    Message = Message + Format$(Index, "###")
    Message = Message + " of the Label2 control array."
    Label2(Index).Caption = Message
End Sub
```

Description

The Click event lets you respond to a user clicking once on a control. This normally either selects something or performs an action. For instance, a user will usually click on a command button to activate whatever function is associated with the button. Clicking on a form or any control generally means the user is selecting that form or control. The user might also select individual cells in a grid control, which also generates the Click event.

The Click event is defined in a sub procedure that carries the parent form's name of the control or 'Form', followed by an underscore and Click(). If the referenced control is part of a control array, the word Click is followed by an index variable within parentheses, as in the second syntax example.

The Click event triggers when a user places the mouse pointer over a form or an enabled control, and then presses and releases the left mouse button once. If a control's Enabled property is set to False (0), the Click event passes through to its parent form. Depending on the control, the Click event can also be generated by certain keyboard actions, or by changing the setting of the control's Value property. Table 14-4 lists the actions in addition to a normal mouse click that may activate a Click event.

With This Object...	These Actions Will Activate a Click Event...
All eligible controls	Placing the mouse pointer on the form or control and clicking the left mouse button
Check Box	Pressing the spacebar when the check box has the focus
	Changing the setting of the check box's Value property
Command Button	Pressing the (ENTER) key when the button's Default property is True (-1) and no other button has the focus
	Pressing the (ESC) key when the button has its Cancel property set to True (-1)
	Pressing the spacebar or (ENTER) key when the button has the focus
	Setting the button's Value property to True
Combo Box	Pressing an (↑) or (↓) cursor key on the keyboard when the box has the focus
Directory List Box	Pressing an (↑) or (↓) cursor key on the keyboard when the box has the focus
File List Box	Pressing an (↑) or (↓) cursor key on the keyboard when the box has the focus
List Box	Pressing an (↑) or (↓) cursor key on the keyboard when the box has the focus
Form	Placing the mouse pointer on any disabled control on the form and clicking
Option Button	Giving the focus to an option button whose Value property was previously false
	Setting the button's Value property to true

Table 14-4 Actions (in addition to a normal mouse click) that activate the Click event

The first syntax example simply puts a message in the form's caption when the mouse is clicked on the form. The second example references an array of label controls. The Click event's code inserts the index number of the label that was clicked into the message displayed.

Event Order

With certain objects, clicking the mouse button causes more than one event to occur. On forms, File list boxes, labels, list boxes, and picture boxes, the following events in this order are activated every time the left mouse button is clicked once: MouseDown, MouseUp, Click. For all other eligible controls, only the Click

547

event is activated. See the entry on DblClick for more information on the event order when the left mouse button is clicked more than once.

Control Array

The Index argument is only used if the related control is part of a control array. This Index specifies which element of the array is the one that activated the event. When referencing the control, the element being referenced must be specified by placing the index number between parentheses just after the control name, and before the property name (for example, Name(Index).Property).

Example

In the Mouse Events project at the end of this chapter, the two command buttons cmndClear and cmndExit that use the Click event. The cmndClear_Click event will clear the canvas when the user clicks on the Clear button. The cmndExit_Click event simply ends the program when the user clicks on the Exit button.

The pictColor control array is an array of picture controls that activates the pictColor_Click event when the user clicks on any of the elements in the control array. This event changes the foreground color of the canvas.

Comments

By default, the left mouse button is the one associated with this event. However, Windows lets the user swap the functions of the left and right mouse buttons via the Mouse settings in the Control Panel program. If this has been done, this event will respond to the right mouse button.

DBLCLICK EVENT

Objects Affected

	Check		Clipboard	▶	Combo		Command		CommonDlg
	Data		Debug		Dir		Drive	▶	File
▶	Form	▶	Frame	▶	Grid	▶	Image	▶	Label
	Line	▶	List		MDI Form		Menu	▶	OLE
▶	Option	▶	Picture		Printer		Screen		Scroll
	Shape	▶	Text		Timer				

548

Purpose

The DblClick event responds to the user pressing the left mouse button twice in quick succession, which is known as a *double-click*. A user will usually double-click on a form or control in order to initiate a default action. Depending on the design of the application a double-click on a form or control could be an alternative to clicking on an OK button or pressing (ENTER) to execute the default action. The arguments used in defining a Click event are summarized in Table 14-5.

General Syntax

```
Sub Form_DblClick()
Sub Name_DblClick([Index As Integer])
```

Arguments	Description
Form	'Form' refers to the parent form of the procedure, not the form's Name property
Name	Name property of the control
Index	Uniquely identifies an element of a control array

Table 14-5 Arguments of the DblClick event

Example Syntax

```
Sub Form_DblClick()                        'When the mouse button is pressed twice on the form
    ChangeColors                           'Calls a routine to change the form's colors
End Sub

Sub List1_DblClick(Index As Integer)       'Automatically clicks the proper OK button when a
    cmndOK_Click Index                     'list item is double-clicked on
End Sub
```

Description

The DblClick event is defined in a sub procedure that is named starting with the name of the control or 'Form' for the parent form, followed by an underscore and DblClick(). If the referenced control is part of a control array, the word DblClick is followed by an index variable within parentheses, as in the second syntax example.

The DblClick event occurs when the user presses and releases the left mouse button twice in quick succession. The period of time in which two clicks must occur in order to be considered a double-click is defined in the mouse settings area of the Window's Control Panel. If the mouse is clicked twice, but not in the time defined by the Control Panel, two separate Click events occur.

This event is also activated if the FileName property of a File list box is changed to a name that is the same as that of an existing DOS file.

When used with a combo box, this event is only called if the Style property is set to 1 (Simple Combo), and the double-click occurs when the mouse pointer is over one of the list items.

The first syntax example calls a routine to change the color of the form when the user double-clicks on it (this could be used to highlight the fact that the user has selected the form.) The second example syntax calls the Click event for the OK button whenever any list box in the control array is double-clicked. This makes double-clicking an alternative way for the user to provide the confirmation represented by the OK button.

Event Order

With certain objects, clicking the mouse button causes more than one event to occur. On forms, File list boxes, labels, list boxes, and picture boxes, the following events (in this order) are activated every time the left mouse button is double-clicked: MouseDown, MouseUp, Click, DblClick, MouseUp. For all other eligible controls, the event order is Click, DblClick.

If you have both Click and DblClick event procedures for a single control, the Click procedure always activates before the DblClick procedure unless you create some special trapping code. Windows automatically sends out the Click message immediately after a click to keep performance high—after all, most programs respond to many more clicks than double-clicks. If it waited to see if the user double-clicked before sending out the first Click message, overall performance would suffer.

If you need to ensure that the Click procedure is not processed for double-clicks, follow the instructions given in the Waite Group's *Visual Basic How-To, 2nd Edition*. The basic idea is to have the Click event procedure start up a timer with the interval set to the system's double-click time. (You can obtain the system's double-click time with the API call GetDoubleClickTime.) If the DblClick event triggers before the timer goes off, it was a double-click; if the timer goes off, then it really was a click and the timer's Timer event procedure can then execute the code that would normally have been placed in the Click event. *Visual Basic How-To* gives very specific instructions and a complete example.

Control Array

The Index argument is only used if the related control is part of a control array. This Index specifies which element of the array is the one that activated the event. When referencing the control, the element being referenced must be specified by placing the index number between parentheses just after the control name, and before the property name (for example, Name(Index).Property).

Example

In the Mouse Events project at the end of this chapter, the pictColor control array responds to a double-click by activating the pictColor_DblClick event. This event sets the background color of the canvas.

Comments

By default, the left mouse button is the one associated with this event. However, Windows lets the user swap the functions of the left and right mouse buttons via the Mouse settings in the Control Panel program. If this has been done, this event will respond to the right mouse button.

There is no DblClick event associated with the Directory list box control. However, double-clicking on a path in the directory list box does cause the Path property of the box to change to the selected path.

MOUSEDOWN EVENT

Objects Affected

▶ Check	Clipboard	Combo	▶ Command	CommonDlg
▶ Data	Debug	▶ Dir	Drive	▶ File
▶ Form	▶ Frame	▶ Grid	▶ Image	▶ Label
Line	▶ List	MDI Form	Menu	▶ OLE
▶ Option	▶ Picture	Printer	Screen	Scroll
Shape	▶ Text	Timer		

Purpose

The MouseDown event occurs when any button—left, center, or right—on the mouse is pressed. Unlike the Click event, the MouseDown event can be used to determine not only that a mouse button has been pushed, but which button was pushed. You can also determine whether the (SHIFT), (CTRL), or (ALT) key was being held down when the mouse button was clicked. The arguments for the MouseDown event are summarized in Tables 14-6, 14-7, and 14-8, and explained below.

General Syntax

```
Sub Form_MouseDown(Button As Integer, Shift As Integer, X As Single, Y As Single)
Sub Name_MouseDown([Index As Integer, ]Button As Integer, Shift As Integer, X As Single, Y As Single)
```

Argument	Description
Form	'Form' refers to the parent form of the procedure; not the form's Name property
Name	Name property of the control
Index	Uniquely identifies an element of a control array
Button	Integer variable returning number of button pressed
Shift	Integer variable returning status of (SHIFT), (ALT), and (CTRL) keys at time of button press
X, Y	Single-precision variables returning coordinates of mouse pointer location when button was pushed

Table 14-6 Arguments of the MouseDown event

Button	CONSTANT.TXT	Meaning
1	LEFT_BUTTON	Left button was pressed
2	RIGHT_BUTTON	Right button was pressed
4	MIDDLE_BUTTON	Middle button (if available on mouse) was pressed

Table 14-7 Meanings of the Button values in the MouseDown event

Shift	CONSTANT.TXT	Meaning
1	SHIFT_MASK	(SHIFT) key was pressed during MouseDown
2	CTRL_MASK	(CTRL) key was pressed during MouseDown
4	ALT_MASK	(ALT) key was pressed during MouseDown

Table 14-8 Meanings of the Shift values in the MouseDown event

552

Example Syntax

```
Sub Form_MouseDown(Button As Integer, Shift As Integer, X As Single, Y As Single)
    If Button = LEFT_BUTTON Then          'If the left button is pressed
        StartX = X                        'Save the current coordinates of the mouse pointer
        StartY = Y                        'on the form
    End If
End Sub

Sub Picture_MouseDown(Index As Integer, Button As Integer, Shift As Integer, X As Single, Y
As Single)
    If Shift = SHIFT_MASK Then            'If the shift key is pressed
        StartX(Index) = X                 'Save the current coordinates of the mouse pointer
        StartY(Index) = Y                 'on the picture control
    End If
End Sub
```

Description

The press of a mouse button may indicate selection of an item, pressing a button control, or beginning a drag operation. (Dragging triggers its own event, as discussed in Chapter 15, Dragging and Dropping.) Unlike the Click event, the MouseDown event can be used to determine not only that a mouse button has been pushed, but *which* button was pushed. You can also determine whether the (SHIFT), (CTRL), or (ALT) key was being held down when the mouse button was clicked. This will allow for a variety of different kinds of interactions, with your applications.

The MouseDown event is defined in a sub procedure that is named using the control name or 'Form' for the parent form, and variables representing the button number, shift status, and x and y mouse position coordinates. An Index variable precedes the other variables if the sub procedure is written to handle a control array.

The MouseDown event triggers when the user presses down on any of the three buttons on the mouse. It supplies four arguments that indicate the status of the mouse at the time the event is called.

The integer variable argument Button indicates which button has been pressed. Its value is set to 1 for the left, 2 for the right, and 4 for the center button. The Button argument will indicate the status of only one button at a time.

The integer variable argument Shift indicates the status of the (SHIFT), (ALT), and (CTRL) keys at the time of the event. Each key is assigned a value: 1 for Shift, 2 for Ctrl, and 4 for Alt. When any of these keys is pressed, its value is added to the Shift argument. The easiest way to test the Shift argument is with logical (bitwise) operators. Table 14-9 lists the Boolean constructions to use for checking the status of the buttons and the shift keys.

When the...	This Will Return Nonzero	CONSTANT.TXT Equivalents
(SHIFT) key is pressed	(Shift And 1)	(Shift And SHIFT_MASK)
(CTRL) key is pressed	(Shift And 2)	(Shift And CTRL_MASK)
(ALT) key is pressed	(Shift And 4)	(Shift And ALT_MASK)
Right button is pressed	(Button And 1)	(Button And LEFT_BUTTON)
Left button is pressed	(Button And 2)	(Button And RIGHT_BUTTON)
Center button is pressed	(Button And 4)	(Button And MIDDLE_BUTTON)

Table 14-9 How to test for Shift and Button status

The x and y arguments are single-precision variables that correspond to the mouse pointer's position within the related form or control at the time the event was called. Here, x is the horizontal coordinate, and Y is the vertical coordinate. These arguments use the measurement system defined for the form or control with the ScaleMode, ScaleHeight, ScaleWidth, and other Scale... properties.

Once a mouse button is pressed while the mouse pointer is over a form or control, that form or control "owns" all the successive mouse events until a MouseUp event is processed, even if the mouse pointer leaves the area of the form or object. This could cause some mouse events to receive x and y arguments that are not on the form or control.

The first example syntax saves the current mouse pointer coordinates when the left button (button 1) is pressed. The second example syntax uses an array of picture boxes. When the mouse is clicked with the (SHIFT) key held down on a picture, the current X and Y pointer coordinates are saved in the corresponding elements of the StartX and StartY arrays.

Control Array

The Index argument is only used if the related control is part of a control array. This Index specifies which element of the array is the one that activated the event. When referencing the control, the element being referenced must be specified by placing the index number between parentheses just after the control name, and before the property name (for example, Name(Index).Property).

Example

In the Mouse Events project at the end of this chapter, the pictCanvas picture control initiates the pictCanvas_MouseDown event when the mouse pointer is over it and any button on the mouse is pressed. This event turns on the DrawOn flag, which tells the pictCanvas_MouseMove event to start drawing. It also saves the current coordinates of the mouse pointer for future reference.

Comments

If the program is halted while inside this event, a corresponding MouseUp event may not be called when the mouse button is released. This can happen if a Stop statement is executed or a breakpoint is set inside this event.

MOUSEMOVE EVENT

Objects Affected

▶ Check	Clipboard	Combo	▶ Command	CommonDlg
▶ Data	Debug	▶ Dir	Drive	▶ File
▶ Form	▶ Frame	▶ Grid	▶ Image	▶ Label
Line	▶ List	MDI Form	Menu	▶ OLE
▶ Option	▶ Picture	Printer	Screen	Scroll
Shape	▶ Text	Timer		

Purpose

The MouseMove event defines the actions to take when the user moves the mouse pointer. You can find out where the mouse pointer was when it was moved, what button (if any) was down, and whether the (SHIFT), (CTRL), or (ALT) key was being held down. The arguments and variables for the MouseMove event are summarized in Tables 14-10, 14-11 and 14-12, and are explained below.

General Syntax

```
Sub Form_MouseMove(Button As Integer, Shift As Integer, X As Single, Y As Single)
Sub Name_MouseMove([Index As Integer, ]Button As Integer, Shift As Integer, X As Single, Y As Single)
```

Argument	Description
Form	'Form' refers to the parent form of the procedure, not the form's Name property
Name	Name property of the control

(continued on next page)

(continued from previous page)

Argument	Description
Index	Uniquely identifies an element of a control array
Button	Integer variable returning number of button pressed
Shift	Integer variable returning status of (SHIFT), (ALT), and (CTRL) keys at time of button press
X, Y	Single-precision variables returning coordinates of the current mouse pointer location

Table 14-10 Arguments of the MouseMove event

Button	CONSTANT.TXT	Meaning
1	LEFT_BUTTON	Left button was pressed
2	RIGHT_BUTTON	Right button was pressed
4	MIDDLE_BUTTON	Middle button (if available on mouse) was pressed

Table 14-11 Meanings of the Button values in the MouseMove event

Shift	CONSTANT.TXT	Meaning
1	SHIFT_MASK	(SHIFT) key was pressed during MouseMove
2	CTRL_MASK	(CTRL) key was pressed during MouseMove
4	ALT_MASK	(ALT) key was pressed during MouseMove

Table 14-12 Meanings of the Shift values in the MouseMove event

Example Syntax

```
Sub Form_MouseMove(Button As Integer, Shift As Integer, X As Single, Y As Single)
    If Shift And SHIFT_MASK Then
        Line (LastX, LastY) - (X, Y)
    End If
End Sub
```

```
Sub Picture1_MouseMove(Index As Integer, Button As Integer, Shift As Integer, X As Single, Y As Single)
    If Shift And SHIFT_MASK Then
        Picture1(Index).Line (LastX, LastY) - (X, Y)
    End If
End Sub
```

Description

The MouseMove event is defined in a sub procedure that is named using the control name or 'Form' for the name of the parent form, and variables representing the button number, shift status, and x and y mouse position coordinates. An index variable precedes the other variables if the sub procedure is written to handle a control array.

This event initiates when the user moves the mouse pointer. It supplies four arguments that indicate the status of the mouse at the time the event is called.

The integer argument Button indicates which button has been pressed. Its value is set to 1 for the left, 2 for the right, and 4 for the center button. The Button argument will indicate the status of only one button at a time.

The integer variable argument Shift indicates the status of the (SHIFT), (ALT), or (CTRL) keys at the time of the event. Each key is assigned a value: 1 for (SHIFT), 2 for (CTRL), and 4 for (ALT). When any of these keys is pressed, its value is added to the Shift argument. The easiest way to test the Shift argument is with logical (bitwise) operators. Table 14-9 in the MouseDown event entry goes into detail about handling bitwise operations.

The x and y arguments are single-precision variables that correspond to the mouse pointer's position within the related form or control at the time the event was called. Here, x is the horizontal coordinate and y is the vertical coordinate. These arguments use the measurement system defined for the form or control with the ScaleMode, ScaleHeight, ScaleWidth, and other Scale... properties.

Once a mouse button is pressed while the mouse pointer is over a form or control, that form or control "owns" all the successive mouse events until a MouseUp event is processed, even if the mouse pointer leaves the area of the form or object. This could cause the MouseUp event to receive x and y arguments that are not on the form or control.

The first example syntax checks whether the (SHIFT) key is down when the mouse pointer is moved. If so, a line is drawn from the previously saved pointer position to the current pointer x,y coordinates (that is, where the mouse was at the time the event is triggered). The second example syntax does the same thing except that it is used with an array of picture boxes.

Control Array

The Index argument is only used if the related control is part of a control array. This Index specifies which element of the array is the one that activated the event. When referencing the control, the element being referenced must be specified by placing the index number between parentheses just after the control name, and before the property name (for example, Name(Index).Property).

557

Example

In the Mouse Events project at the end of this chapter, the pictCanvas picture control calls the pictCanvas_MouseMove event whenever the mouse pointer is moved over its surface. If the DrawOn flag is set to true, it will then perform a drawing operation based on which button is pressed and the status of the Shift argument.

Comments

If the program is halted while inside this event, the MouseUp event may not be called when the mouse button is released. This can happen if a Stop statement is executed or a breakpoint is set inside this event.

MOUSEUP EVENT

Objects Affected

▶ Check	Clipboard	Combo	▶ Command	CommonDlg
▶ Data	Debug	▶ Dir	Drive	▶ File
▶ Form	▶ Frame	▶ Grid	▶ Image	▶ Label
Line	▶ List	MDI Form	▶ Menu	▶ OLE
▶ Option	▶ Picture	Printer	Screen	Scroll
Shape	▶ Text	Timer		

Purpose

The MouseUp event occurs when any button—left, center, or right—on the mouse is released. You can also find out where the mouse pointer was when the button was released. You can also determine whether the (SHIFT), (CTRL), or (ALT) key was being held down when the mouse button was released. The arguments and variables for the MouseUp event are summarized in Tables 14-13, 14-14, and 14-15 and explained below.

General Syntax

```
Sub Form_MouseUp(Button As Integer, Shift As Integer, X As Single, Y As Single)
Sub Name_MouseUp([Index As Integer, ]Button As Integer, Shift As Integer, X As Single, Y As Single)
```

Argument	Description
Form	'Form' refers to the parent form of the procedure, not the Form's Name property
Name	Name property of the control
Index	Uniquely identifies an element of a control array
Button	Integer variable returning number of button pressed
Shift	Integer variable returning status of (SHIFT), (ALT), and (CTRL) keys at time of button press
X, Y	Single-precision variables returning coordinates of the mouse pointer location when released

Table 14-13 Arguments of the MouseUp event

Button	CONSTANT.TXT	Meaning
1	LEFT_BUTTON	Left button was pressed
2	RIGHT_BUTTON	Right button was pressed
4	MIDDLE_BUTTON	Middle button (if available on mouse) was pressed

Table 14-14 Meanings of the button values in the MouseUp event

Shift	CONSTANT.TXT	Meaning
1	SHIFT_MASK	(SHIFT) key was pressed during MouseUp
2	CTRL_MASK	(CTRL) key was pressed during MouseUp
4	ALT_MASK	(ALT) key was pressed during MouseUp

Table 14-15 Meanings of the Shift values in the MouseUp event

Example Syntax

```
Sub Form_MouseUp(Button As Integer, Shift As Integer, X As Single, Y As Single)
    If Button = 1 Then              'If the left button was released
        EndX = X                    'Save the current coordinates of the mouse pointer
```

(continued on next page)

559

(continued from previous page)

```
            EndY = Y                    'on the form
        End If
End Sub
Sub Picture_MouseUp(Index As Integer, Button As Integer, Shift As Integer, X As Single, Y As Single)
    If Button = 2 Then                    'If the right button was released
        PopupMenu menuPopPictureEdit  'Pop up a tear-off editing menu on the picture
    End If
End Sub
```

Description

The MouseUp event is defined in a sub procedure that is named using the control name or 'Form' for the parent form, and variables representing the button number, shift status, and x and y mouse position coordinates. An Index variable precedes the other variables if the sub procedure is written to handle a control array.

This event is initiated when the user releases any of the three buttons on the mouse. It supplies four arguments that indicate the status of the mouse at the time the event is called.

The integer variable argument Button indicates which button has been pressed. Its value is set to 1 for the left, 2 for the right, and 4 for the center button. The Button argument will indicate the status of only one button at a time.

The integer variable argument Shift indicates the status of the (SHIFT), (ALT), and (CTRL) keys at the time of the event. Each key is assigned a value: 1 for (SHIFT), 2 for (CTRL), and 4 for (ALT). When any of these keys is pressed, its value is added to the Shift argument. The easiest way to test the Shift argument is with logical (bitwise) operators. Table 14-9 in the MouseDown event entry goes into detail about handling bitwise operations.

The x and y arguments are single-precision variables that correspond to the mouse pointer's position within the related form or control at the time the event was called. Here, x is the horizontal coordinate, and y is the vertical coordinate. These arguments use the measurement system defined for the form or control with the ScaleMode, ScaleHeight, ScaleWidth, and other Scale... properties.

Once a mouse button is pressed while the mouse pointer is over a form or control, that form or control "owns" all the successive mouse events until a MouseUp event is processed. This remains true even if the mouse pointer leaves the area of the form or object. This could cause the MouseUp event to receive x and y arguments that are not on the form or control.

In the first example syntax the current mouse position in the form is saved if the left mouse button was released. The second example shows how easily you can pop up a context-sensitive tear-off menu. Many applications now use the right mouse button as a "properties inspector" to bring up menus of items related to that object. The MouseUp event first checks to see if the right mouse button was released. If so, it brings up a menu (defined with the Menu designer) related to the picture control array. Note that PopupMenu only works in Visual Basic 3.0 or later; for more information on menus, see Chapter 4, Forms and Menus.

Control Array

The Index argument is only used if the related control is part of a control array. This Index specifies which element of the array is the one that activated the event. When referencing the control, the element being referenced must be specified by placing the index number between parentheses just after the control name, and before the property name (for example, Name(Index).Property).

Example

The pictCanvas_MouseUp event in the Mouse Events project at the end of this chapter sets the DrawOn flag to False and clears the coordinates that were saved by the pictCanvas_MouseDown event.

Comments

If the program is halted after a mouse button has been pressed, but before it has been released, this event may not be called when the mouse button is released. This can happen if a Stop statement is executed or a breakpoint is set inside the MouseDown or MouseMove events.

THE MOUSE EVENTS PROJECT

Project Overview

The Mouse Events project demonstrates the use of the five mouse-related events; Click, DblClick, MouseDown, MouseMove, and MouseUp. Each of these events are used at least once in the operation this project. By following the examples in this project, you should be able to learn the principles behind using these events.

Assembling the Project

1. Create a new form (the Mouse form) and place on it the controls specified in Table 14-16. Note there is a group of five picture controls that share the Name of "pictColor". These picture controls are part of a control array. As soon as you create a second picture control with the Name of "pictColor," Visual Basic will ask if you wish to create a control array. Click the Yes button.

Object	Property	Setting
Form	Name	Mouse
	BackColor	Dark Gray—&H00808080&
	Border	1—Fixed Single
	Caption	"Mouse Project"
	MaxButton	0—False
Picture	Name	pictCanvas
	ScaleMode	Twip
Command	Name	cmndClear
	Caption	&Clear
Command	Name	cmndExit
	Caption	E&xit
Label	Name	lablCurrentColor
	Alignment	2—Center
	BorderStyle	1—Fixed Single
	Caption	(bullet symbol: press (ALT)-0183)
	FontName	Symbol
	FontSize	18
Picture	Name	pictColor
	BackColor	Bright White—&HFFFFFF&
	BorderStyle	1—Fixed Single

Object	Property	Setting
	Index	0
Picture	Name	pictColor
	BackColor	Black—&H000000&
	BorderStyle	1—Fixed Single
	Index	1
Picture	Name	pictColor
	BackColor	Red—&H0000FF&
	BorderStyle	1—Fixed Single
	Index	2
Picture	Name	pictColor
	BackColor	Blue—&HFF0000&
	BorderStyle	1—Fixed Single
	Index	3
Picture	Name	pictColor
	BackColor	Bright Yellow—&H00FFFF&
	BorderStyle	1—Fixed Single
	Index	4

Table 14-16 Property settings for the Mouse Events project

2. Check the appearance of your form against Figure 14-1.

3. Enter the following code in the General Declarations area of the Mouse form. These module-level variables are available to all event procedures.

563

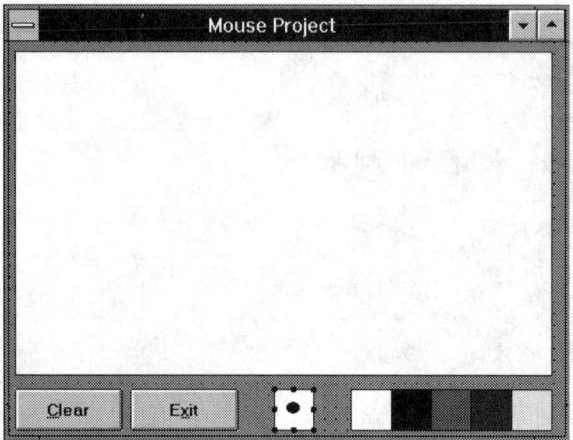

Figure 14-1 What the Mouse form should look like
when complete

```
Dim DrawOn As Integer          'flags if we're in the middle of drawing something

Dim StartX As Single           'remembers the original start coordinates of
Dim StartY As Single           'a drawing operation

Dim LastX As Single            'remembers the last used drawing coordinates
Dim LastY As Single

Dim SaveColor As Single        'remembers the previous color setting changed in the Click event
```

4. Enter the following code in the cmndClear_Click event. This code uses the Cls
   method to clear the pictCanvas picture control when the Clear button is clicked.

```
Sub cmndClear_Click ()
    pictCanvas.Cls                 'clear the canvas
End Sub
```

5. Enter the following code into the cmndExit_Click event. This event ends the program when the Exit button is clicked.

```
Sub cmndExit_Click ()
    End                            'End the program
End Sub
```

6. Enter the following code into the pictCanvas_MouseDown event. This event activates when the user presses down any of the buttons on the mouse while the
   mouse pointer is over the pictCanvas picture control. It sets the DrawOn flag to
   True (-1), and saves the current mouse pointer coordinates. These coordinates are
   later used in the pictCanvas_MouseMove event.

```
Sub pictCanvas_MouseDown (Button As Integer, Shift As Integer, X As Single, Y As Single)
    DrawOn = True                  'flag that we've started drawing
```

564

```
     StartX = X                    'remember our starting coordinates
     StartY = Y
End Sub
```

7. Enter the following code into the pictCanvas_MouseMove event. This event is where the fun stuff happens. When the user moves the mouse pointer across the surface of the pictCanvas picture control, this routine checks to see if the DrawOn flag is set. If so, it then checks to see if the left or right button is currently pressed. If the left button is pressed, it draws a line from the last known position of the mouse pointer to the current position of the mouse pointer, essentially letting the user scribble. If the right button is pressed, it draws a line from the coordinates saved by the pictCanvas_MouseDown event to the current mouse pointer coordinates. This creates a fan-like pattern. If the user is also holding the (SHIFT) key down while pressing the right mouse button, a box is drawn whose opposite corners match the coordinates saved by the pictCanvas_MouseDown event, and the current mouse pointer position. As a last step, this event saves the current mouse pointer position, so it has a reference point for the next time it is called with the left mouse button pressed.

```
Sub pictCanvas_MouseMove (Button As Integer, Shift As Integer, X As Single, Y As Single)
    If DrawOn Then                           'if we've started drawing,
        If Button And LEFT_BUTTON Then       'left button pressed,
            pictCanvas.Line (LastX, LastY)-(X, Y)    'just let the user scribble
        ElseIf Button And RIGHT_BUTTON Then  'right button makes cool guy designs...
            If Shift And SHIFT_MASK Then     'shift button draws a
                pictCanvas.Line (StartX, StartY)-(X, Y), , B   'series of boxes
            End If
            pictCanvas.Line (StartX, StartY)-(X, Y)   'this connects starting point to the current
        End If                               'point, making a "fan" shape
    End If
    LastX = X                                'remember where we left off
    LastY = Y
End Sub
```

8. Enter the following code into the pictCanvas_MouseUp event. This event occurs when the user releases the mouse button. It sets the DrawOn flag to False (0), and zeros out the starting mouse pointer position.

```
Sub pictCanvas_MouseUp (Button As Integer, Shift As Integer, X As Single, Y As Single)
    DrawOn = False               'done drawing now!
    StartX = 0                   'reset starting coordinates
    StartY = 0
End Sub
```

9. Enter the following code into the pictColor_Click event. This event occurs when the user clicks on one of the elements of the pictColor picture control array. This event changes the foreground color of the pictCanvas picture control to the same color as the element that was clicked. The lablCurrentColor ForeColor property is also changed, so the user can see what the current color selections are. This event also happens when the user double-clicks on the element, so it saves the

current ForeColor property for the pictCanvas picture control. This allows us to restore the ForeColor property to its original value if the event was actually activated by a double-click.

```
Sub pictColor_Click (Index As Integer)
    SaveColor = pictCanvas.ForeColor                          'remember ForeColor in case of double-click
    pictCanvas.ForeColor = pictColor(Index).BackColor        'reset the drawing colors
    lablCurrentColor.ForeColor = pictColor(Index).BackColor  'and give the user visual feedback
End Sub
```

10. Enter the following code into the pictColor_DblClick event. This event activates when the user double-clicks one of the elements of the pictColor picture control array. This event changes the background color of the pictCanvas picture control to the same color as the element that was clicked. The lablCurrentColor BackColor property is also changed, so the user can see what the current color selections are. Because this event is triggered after the Click event, we must first restore the ForeColor property of the pictCanvas picture control to its original state.

```
Sub pictColor_DblClick (Index As Integer)
    pictCanvas.ForeColor = SaveColor                         'reset ForeColor changed during Click event
    lablCurrentColor.ForeColor = SaveColor                   'reset visual feedback...
    pictCanvas.BackColor = pictColor(Index).BackColor        'and now change the background color
    lablCurrentColor.BackColor = pictColor(Index).BackColor  'and the visual feedback
End Sub
```

11. Enter the following code in a new module. First, pull down the File menu and select the New Module command. This creates the new module. You can read in the entire CONSTANT.TXT file, as explained in the Summary section at the beginning of this chapter, or simply type in the following constants.

```
' Shift parameter masks
Global Const SHIFT_MASK = 1

' Button parameter masks
Global Const LEFT_BUTTON = 1
Global Const RIGHT_BUTTON = 2
```

How It Works

The application developed in the Mouse Events project is a crude drawing program. When the program starts, the Mouse form appears with a blank canvas. The user can then use the mouse to draw on the canvas.

Pressing and holding down the left mouse button and moving the mouse while the mouse pointer is over the canvas draws a line on the canvas. The pictCanvas_MouseDown event is called first; and because there is a button pressed, it sets the DrawOn flag to True (-1), and saves the current coordinates of the mouse pointer. Then the pictCanvas_MouseMove event is called. In this event a line is drawn from the last known mouse pointer position to the current mouse pointer position. This causes the line to follow the mouse pointer around the canvas until the user releases the left button.

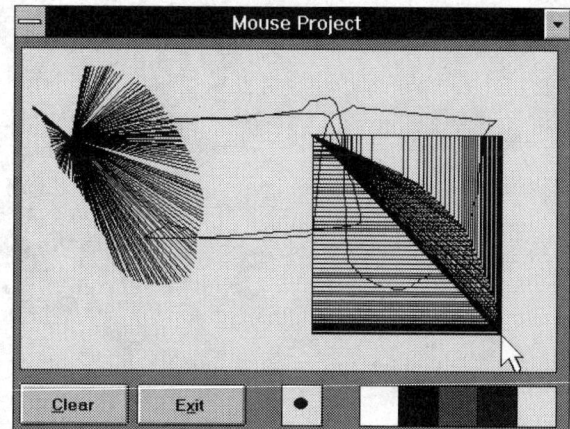

Figure 14-2 The Mouse Events project in action

Pressing and holding down the right mouse button also draws lines on the canvas. The pictCanvas_MouseDown event is called first; and, because there is a button pressed, it sets the DrawOn flag to True (-1), and saves the current coordinates of the mouse pointer. Then the pictCanvas_MouseMove event is called. In this event the coordinates of the saved mouse position are used along with the coordinates of the current mouse pointer position to draw the line. This causes several lines to be drawn, all originating at the same point. This creates a fan-like pattern.

If the (SHIFT) key is held down along with the right mouse button, a box is drawn around each line generated. This creates an interesting effect, as illustrated in Figure 14-2.

When the mouse buttons are released, the pictCanvas_MouseUp event is called. This event turns the DrawOn flag off (sets it to False), and clears the saved mouse position coordinates.

The foreground color of the canvas may be changed by clicking on any of the elements of the pictColor array. This triggers the pictColor_Click event. Because a Click event is always called just prior to the DblClick event, it saves the current foreground color of the canvas before changing it. This allows the DblClick event to restore it, if need be. The pictColor_Click event then changes the foreground color of the canvas to the same color as the background of the pictColor element that was clicked. These changes are also performed on the lablCurrentColor label control. This control displays to the user which colors are currently selected.

The background color of the canvas may be changed by double-clicking on any of the elements of the pictColor array. This causes the pictColor_DblClick event to occur. The first task performed by this event is to restore the foreground color of the canvas. It then sets the background color of the canvas to the same color as the background of the pictColor element that was double-clicked. These changes are also performed on the lablCurrentColor label control. This control displays to the user which colors are currently selected.

15

DRAGGING AND DROPPING

Drag-and-drop is a versatile and exciting Windows feature available to your Visual Basic programs. Dragging means moving a control (such as icon or graphic image) from one position on the screen to another. For example, file managers often allow you to copy or move files between directories by dragging a file name or icon from one directory area to another. Dropping means releasing the dragged control over another control. The file manager example might let you drag a file from one list box and drop it on another to perform an action on it.

To drag a control, select it by pointing at it with your mouse or other pointing device. Press the mouse button (click) on the control and—without releasing the mouse button—move the control to a new location on the screen. When you drag a control, you will see a graphic outline of the control unless you specify otherwise using the DragIcon property. Release the mouse button to drop the control at its new destination.

A drag-and-drop operation involves two possible controls: source and target. The *source* is the control that the user clicks with the mouse. When a drag-and-drop operation ends, the control that the drag icon is over is the *target*. If a drag-and-drop operation does not end over another control, then there is no target control. An example of a drag-and-drop operation including a source and a target is when the user clicks and drags an icon representing a file to the icon symbol of a printer to print a file. The actual printing would involve an event connected with the target. Any kind of action that follows the dropping of the source over the target is part of the target's event procedures.

Drag mode determines how a drag operation begins. There are two settings for drag mode: automatic and manual. In automatic drag mode, dragging operations begin when the user clicks the mouse. This process takes place without the use of any code. Manual drag mode prevents the starting of a drag operation with only the clicking of the mouse. The only way to begin a drag operation on a control with its drag mode set to manual is with a statement in the code of the program.

DRAGGING AND DROPPING SUMMARY

Visual Basic uses several properties, events, and methods to implement dragging. A control's DragMode property indicates its drag mode setting: manual or automatic. The Drag method lets you prepare a control for dragging with a manual DragMode. Each manual drag operation begins and ends with DragMode method expressions. The DragIcon property of the control determines whether the outline of the control or another icon appears on the screen during a drag operation. The DragDrop event contains the actions that take place when a drag operation terminates over a control. The DragOver event contains the actions that take place when the user drags a control over another control.

Table 15-1 displays the Visual Basic properties, events, and methods that determine the means and results of a drag operation.

Use or Set This...		To Do This...
Drag	Method	Begin or end manual dragging
DragDrop	Event	Initiate an action when a dragged control is dropped onto another control
DragIcon	Property	Select the icon to display when the control is part of a drag operation
DragMode	Property	Choose automatic or manual drag mode
DragOver	Event	Initiate an action when a dragged control is over a form or control

Table 15-1 Methods, properties, and events involved in a drag operation

CONSTANT.TXT Values

Several of the properties, events, and methods of this chapter use numeric values as arguments. Using constants rather than the literal value makes your code self-documenting, more readable, and easier to debug.

Microsoft provides a file, CONSTANT.TXT, that has many constant declarations defined for you. For smaller applications it's probably easiest just to type the declarations in yourself. For larger applications you'll find it much easier to read the text file into a new module.

To do this, create a new module by pulling down the File menu and choosing the New Module menu command. Then pull down the File menu again, and choose Load Text. This opens up a dialog box listing all text files in the current directory. CONSTANT.TXT should be in your main Visual Basic directory (default installation would place this in C:\VB). Simply choose CONSTANT.TXT to enter the entire file into your module. These constants will then be available throughout your application.

Table 15-2 lists the value of the constant, the CONSTANT.TXT constant name, and a brief description of what the constant means.

Value	CONSTANT.TXT	Description
Drag method		
0	CANCEL	Cancels a dragging operation
1	BEGIN_DRAG	Begins a dragging operation
2	END_DRAG	Ends a dragging operation
DragMode property		
0	MANUAL	(Default) Drag method is required for a drag operation
1	AUTOMATIC	User pressing the mouse button over a control starts a drag operation
DragOver event		
0	ENTER	Control enters the space above another control
1	LEAVE	Control exits the space above another control
2	OVER	Control is over the space above another control (executes once)

Table 15-2 CONSTANT.TXT values for dragging and dropping

The following pages discuss each of the methods, events, and properties in Table 15-1 in detail. The Drag project at the end of this chapter includes step-by-step directions on how to create a Visual Basic project that uses them all.

DRAG METHOD

Objects Affected

▶ Check	Clipboard	▶ Combo	▶ Command	CommonDlg
▶ Data	Debug	▶ Dir	▶ Drive	▶ File
▶ Form	▶ Frame	▶ Grid	▶ Image	▶ Label
Line	▶ List	MDI Form	Menu	▶ OLE
▶ Option	▶ Picture	Printer	Screen	▶ Scroll
Shape	▶ Text	Timer		

Purpose

The Drag method initiates or ends a dragging operation. With this method you can manipulate controls on the screen when a control's DragMode property is manual. A Drag method statement typically appears in the MouseDown event of the control to be dragged. This has the effect of beginning a drag operation when the user presses the mouse button. Tables 15-3 and 15-4 summarize the arguments and possible values of the Drag method.

General Syntax

```
[form!]Name.Drag [action%]
```

Argument	Description
form	Name property of the parent form
Name	Name property of the control that is affected by the drag operation
action%	Value that indicates what dragging operation to take

Table 15-3 Arguments of the Drag method

action%	CONSTANT.TXT	Description
0	CANCEL	Cancels a dragging operation
1	BEGIN_DRAG	Begins a dragging operation
2	END_DRAG	Ends a dragging operation

Table 15-4 Possible values of the action% argument

Example Syntax

```
Sub Picture1_MouseDown (Button As Integer, Shift As Integer, X As Single, Y As Single)
    Picture1.Drag              'Begins a drag operation.
End Sub

Sub Form_DragDrop (Source As Control, X As Single, Y As Single)
    Source.Move X, Y           'Moves the picture box to the new location.
End Sub
```

Description

A Drag method statement consists of three possible elements. Each Drag method expression begins with the Name property of the control being dragged. This is normally the control whose event contains the Drag method, but it can be any other control. A Drag method ends with a value that represents what type of drag operation to take.

There are three possible settings for the action% parameter: 0, 1, and 2. A value of 0 cancels a dragging operation. This prevents the triggering of any events normally associated with the ending of a drag operation, like DragDrop. Using a value of 1 begins a drag operation. Drag operations end with a value of 2. This triggers the DragDrop event of the form or control that the drag icon is over. The default for action% is 1. Refer to the Dragging and Dropping Summary section at the beginning of this chapter for detailed instructions on how to use the CONSTANT.TXT values.

The DragMode Property

The DragMode property of a control indicates whether the Drag method is necessary to initiate a drag operation. When the DragMode property of a control remains at its default value of 0 (manual), the Drag method is the only way to initiate a drag operation. If the DragMode property changes to 1 (automatic), then the Drag method is not necessary. In this case a drag operation starts when the user presses a mouse button while the mouse pointer is over the control. With the

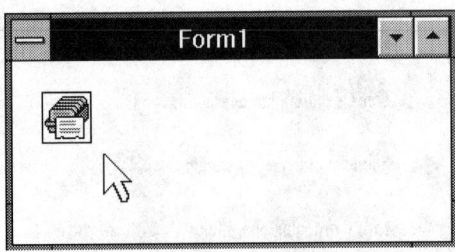

Figure 15-1 Example syntax shows original Picture1 ready to get dragged ...

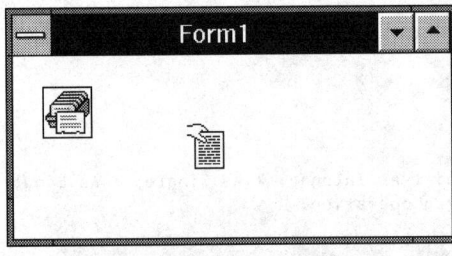

Figure 15-2 ... Picture1 in process of being dragged, showing its DragIcon ...

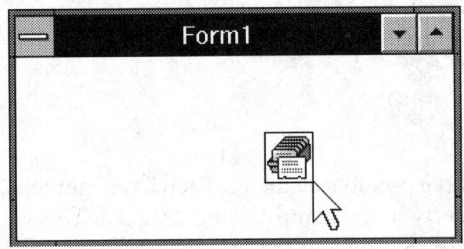

Figure 15-3 ... and Picture1 dropped into a new location

example syntax, the Picture1 picture box's DragMode property remains at its default setting of manual. If you were to change the DragMode property to automatic and remove the Drag method statement from the MouseDown event, the example would work exactly the same.

The DragIcon Property

The DragIcon property sets the icon that appears during a drag operation to show where to move the control. This property's default setting is "none," and a gray outline of the dragged control is used instead. This outline is a guide for where the control appears when the drag operation finishes. In the example syntax, the DragIcon property is a different icon (as set at design time in the Picutre1 DragIcon property) from the one displayed in the Picture1 picture box. Figures 15-1, 15-2, and 15-3 show what a drag operation looks like.

The Move Method

The user can move a control to a new location on the screen with a Move method expression. By placing a Move method expression in the DragDrop event of the

574

form, the control moves to the new location at the end of a drag operation. In the example syntax, the Move method places the Picture1 picture box in a new location on the screen. The x and y values returned by the DragDrop event of the form provide the new coordinates of the Picture1 picture box. Notice that the DragDrop event has Source as Control, so the Name of the control being dragged gets passed to the event handler.

The DragDrop Event

The DragDrop event contains the actions that occur when the user releases the mouse button while the drag icon is over another control or form. This event is unaffected by whether the drag operation began with a Drag method expression or mouse click. In the example syntax, releasing the mouse button over a portion of the form triggers the DragDrop event. Notice that there is no need for another Drag method statement to terminate the drag operation. The user triggers a DragDrop event by releasing the mouse button.

Example

In the Drag project at the end of this chapter, the Drag method is used several times. The Drag method initiates a dragging operation on the selected file in the fileList File list box. In the fileList_Click event, the Drag method processes when the user selects a file. The DragOver event of pictClear demonstrates the setting of action% to 0 (to cancel drag). This drag operation ends when the user clicks on the left mouse button and drags the picture from the pictIcon picture box to the pictClear picture box.

DRAGDROP EVENT

Objects Affected

▶ Check	Clipboard	▶ Combo	▶ Command	CommonDlg
▶ Data	Debug	▶ Dir	▶ Drive	▶ File
▶ Form	▶ Frame	▶ Grid	▶ Image	▶ Label
Line	▶ List	MDI Form	Menu	▶ OLE
▶ Option	▶ Picture	Printer	Screen	▶ Scroll
Shape	▶ Text	Timer		

Purpose

A DragDrop event contains the actions that occur at the completion of a drag-and-drop operation over another control. Drag-and-drop operations terminate with either a Drag method expression or the release of a mouse button. When the user releases the mouse button while the mouse pointer is over a control, this is known as the drop part of a drag-and-drop operation. Table 15-5 summarizes the arguments and variables of the DragDrop event.

General Syntax

```
Sub Form_DragDrop (Source As Control, X As Single, Y As Single)
Sub MDIForm_DragDrop (Source As Control, X As Single, Y As Single)
Sub Name_DragDrop ([Index As Integer,] Source As Control, X As Single, Y As Single)
```

Arguments	Description
Form	'Form' indicates the form
MDIForm	'MDIForm' indicates the MDIForm
Name	Name property of the control that the dragged control is dropped on
Index	Identifies a control in a control array
Source	The control that is dropped over this control
X, Y	Current horizontal (x) and vertical (y) coordinates of the mouse pointer when mouse is released

Table 15-5 Arguments and variables of the DragDrop event

Example Syntax

```
Sub Form_Load ()
    Picture1.Picture = LoadPicture("\VB\ICONS\OFFICE\CRDFLE05.ICO") 'Rolodex w/card
    Picture1.DragMode = 1                    'Sets automatic Drag
    Picture1.DragIcon = LoadPicture("\VB\ICONS\DRAGDROP\DRAG1PG.ICO") 'Hand w/papers
End Sub

Sub Picture2_DragDrop (Source As Control, X As Single, Y As Single)
    Picture2.Picture = Source.Picture        'Picture2 now has Picture1's picture
    Source.Picture = LoadPicture("")         'Blank out the source picture
End Sub
```

Description

A DragDrop event triggers when the user drops a dragged control over another control or form. The x and y coordinates define the location of the dragged control relative to the control being dragged. These coordinates measure the horizontal

576

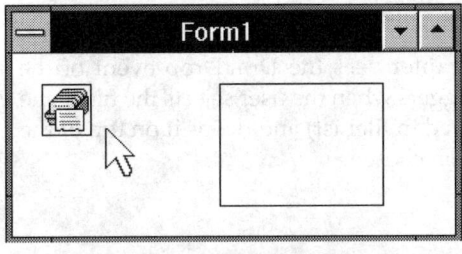

Figure 15-4 Picture1 and Picture2 before the drag-and-drop operation ...

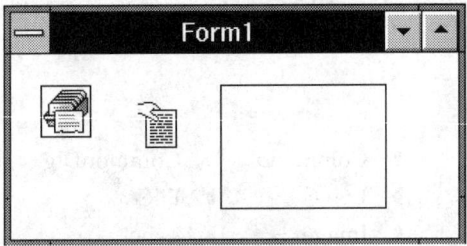

Figure 15-5 ... during the drag-and-drop (note the DragIcon) ...

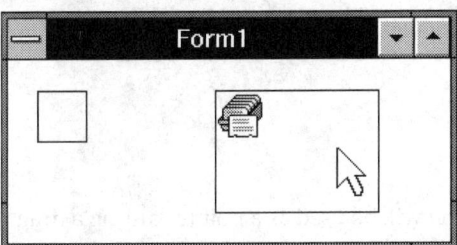

Figure 15-6 ... and after. The example syntax shows how Picture1 and Picture2's contents change during the DragDrop event

and vertical distance in the units defined by the container's ScaleMode property. The Source argument identifies the dragged control that caused the event. Using Source to replace the Name property of the dragged control makes the expression general, so the user can drag-and-drop more than one control over a control.

In the example syntax, an automatic drag operation triggers when the mouse pointer is over the Picture1 picture box (which is the source control) and the user presses the mouse button. The DragDrop event redefines the Picture property of the Picture2 picture box with the Picture property of the dragged control. Figures 15-4, 15-5, and 15-6 illustrate how the contents of the Picture1 transfer over to Picture2.

Control Arrays

If the control designated in a drag-and-drop operation is a member of a control array, then Visual Basic will provide an Index property value. This Index value defines which item of the control array was dropped on the control. This is useful in situations where there is a need to have different actions for different items of the same control array.

Example

The Drag project at the end of this chapter uses the DragDrop event of the Picture1 picture box. This subroutine triggers when the user selects the file name of an icon from the list of icons (displayed in fileList) and drops it on top of the pictIcon picture box that displays the icon chosen.

DRAGICON PROPERTY

Objects Affected

▶ Check	Clipboard	▶ Combo	▶ Command	CommonDlg
▶ Data	Debug	▶ Dir	▶ Drive	▶ File
▶ Form	▶ Frame	▶ Grid	▶ Image	▶ Label
Line	▶ List	MDI Form	Menu	▶ OLE
▶ Option	▶ Picture	Printer	Screen	▶ Scroll
Shape	▶ Text	Timer		

Purpose

The DragIcon property indicates what icon will be used as a pointer during a drag operation. This property is a useful way to indicate what type of drag operation is being initiated. If used with the DragOver and DragDrop events, this property can change the pointer icon during a drag operation. Table 15-6 summarizes the arguments of the DragIcon property, while Table 15-7 shows the possible settings of the DragIcon property.

General Syntax

```
[form.]DragIcon [ = icon]
[form!]Name.DragIcon [ = icon]
```

Argument	Description
form	Name property of the form
Name	Name property of the control
icon	Any valid icon file

Table 15-6 Arguments of the DragIcon property

Icon	Description
None	(Default) Cursor indicated by the MousePointer property, normally the outline of the control
Icon	Any code that returns a legal icon, such as the LoadPicture function

Table 15-7 Possible settings of Icon argument of DragIcon property

Example Syntax

```
Sub Form_Load ()
    Picture1.Picture = LoadPicture("\VB\ICONS\COMPUTER\TRASH01.ICO")
    Picture1.DragMode = 1                    'Sets automatic Drag
    Text1.Text = "Hello World!"
    Text1.DragIcon = LoadPicture("\VB\ICONS\MAIL\MAIL01A.ICO")
    Text1.DragMode = 1                       'Sets automatic Drag
End Sub

Sub Picture1_DragOver (Source As Control, X As Single, Y As Single, State As Integer)
    Select Case State
        Case 0, 2
            Text1.DragIcon = Picture1.Picture
        Case 1
            Text1.DragIcon = LoadPicture("\VB\ICONS\MAIL\MAIL01A.ICO")
    End Select
End Sub

Sub Picture1_DragDrop (Source As Control, X As Single, Y As Single)
    Source.Text = ""            'Blanks the text
    Source.DragIcon = LoadPicture("\VB\ICONS\MAIL\MAIL01A.ICO")
End Sub
```

Description

The DragIcon property identifies what icon to display in place of the mouse pointer during a drag operation. The Name property of the control or form identifies which control's DragIcon property to change. When no name appears, the DragIcon property of the form is changed.

Using Icons

The DragIcon can be specified at both design time and runtime. At design time you select the DragIcon by choosing the DragIcon property in the properties box and clicking on the word (Icon) at the righthand side of the settings bar. To set the DragIcon property at runtime, use the LoadPicture function, including the icon's file name and path.

Figure 15-7 Example syntax shows Text1 and Picture1 before drag-and-drop ...

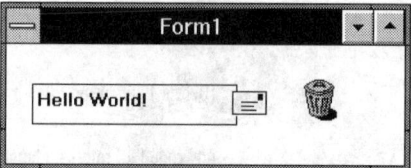

Figure 15-8 ... during the Drag (note the Drag icon) ...

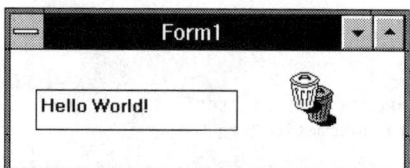

Figure 15-9 ... during the DragOver (note the Drag icon changes again to confirm the ability to drop) ...

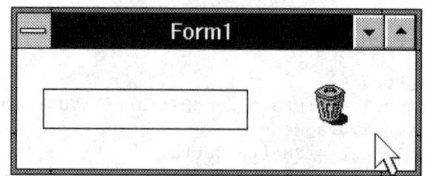

Figure 15-10 ... and after the drop. Note that the code clears Text1 and sets the pointer back to normal

Although the LoadPicture function is the most common way of assigning an icon, you need to distribute the icon files along with your program to use it. A less direct but cleaner way of assigning icons is to use another control's Icon or Picture properties as a temporary storage area. For example, you might create an array of invisible image controls and store the various icons in the image control's Picture property. You could then set the new icon with this code:

```
Sub Picture1_DragOver (Source As Control, X As Single, Y As Single, State As Integer)
    Text1.DragIcon = Image1(State).Picture
End Sub
```

This not only simplifies your code, but also makes the icons a part of the executable file. You don't have to worry about the icons being separated from your application.

In the example syntax, the DragIcon property changes during the DragOver event. The Form_Load sub procedure loads the picture for Picture1 and sets the drag mode to the icon that will be used to indicate that dragging is in progress (the trashcan, in this case). The DragOver event checks that the source control is no longer over the destination. Here, if the source control moves away without being dropped, DragIcon is restored to the original. In the DragDrop event, the DragIcon also changes back to the original, indicating that a drag-and-drop operation has been completed.

In the example syntax, the Drag icon changes to a trashcan when it is over the Picture1 picture box. This graphically shows the user the results of completing the drag-and-drop operation. Notice that when the user drops the control, the text is erased from the Text1 text box. Figures 15-7, 15-8, 15-9, and 15-10 show what the screen looks like before, during, and after the drag-and-drop sequence.

Example

The Drag project at the end of this chapter uses the DragIcon property for the pictIcon picture box and fileList File list box. For the fileList File list box, the DragIcon specifies what icon to use when dragging the icon file to be displayed in the pictIcon picture box. In the pictIcon picture box, the DragIcon property is set at runtime to the icon displayed.

Comments

Even on color displays, the icon for dragging will only be shown in monochrome.

DRAGMODE PROPERTY

Objects Affected

▶ Check	Clipboard	▶ Combo	▶ Command	CommonDlg
▶ Data	Debug	▶ Dir	▶ Drive	▶ File
Form	▶ Frame	▶ Grid	▶ Image	▶ Label
Line	▶ List	MDI Form	Menu	▶ OLE
▶ Option	▶ Picture	Printer	Screen	▶ Scroll
Shape	▶ Text	Timer		

Purpose

The DragMode property of a control indicates whether it may be dragged in a drag operation without the use of a Drag method expression. Every control has an initial setting of manual. This indicates that the control may not normally be dragged. A drag operation may only be begun on a control with a manual setting by using the Drag method. With a control's DragMode property set to automatic, a drag operation automatically begins when the user presses and holds down a mouse button over the control. Tables 15-8 and 15-9 summarize arguments and possible settings of the DragMode property.

General Syntax

`[form!]Name.DragMode [ = mode%]`

Argument	Description
form!	Name property of the form
Name	Name property of the control
mode%	DragMode setting

Table 15-8 Arguments of the DragMode property

mode%	CONSTANT.TXT	Description
0	MANUAL	(Default) Drag method is required for a drag operation
1	AUTOMATIC	User pressing the mouse button over a control starts a drag operation

Table 15-9 Possible settings of the DragMode property

Example Syntax

```
Sub Command1_Click ()
    Command1.Caption = "automatic"   'Changes text on command button
    Command1.DragMode = 1            'Changes DragMode to automatic
End Sub

Sub Form_DragDrop (Source As Control, X As Single, Y As Single)
    Source.Move X, Y                 'Moves the control to the new location
    Command1.Caption = "manual"      'Changes text on command button
    Command1.DragMode = 0            'Changes DragMode to manual
End Sub
```

Description

The DragMode property of a control indicates whether it may be dragged in a drag operation without the use of a Drag method expression. The initial DragMode property value of any newly created control is manual (0). A value of 1 changes the DragMode property to automatic. Controls must use the Drag method unless the DragMode property is changed to automatic. While a control is being dragged, no other mouse actions (Click, Double Click, MouseDown, MouseMove, MouseUp, GotFocus) will function. The CONSTANT.TXT file contains the mode% constants. Refer to the Dragging and Dropping Summary section at the beginning of this chapter for detailed instructions on how to use the CONSTANT.TXT values.

582

In the example syntax, both the manual and automatic DragModes are demonstrated with the Command1 command button. The command button Command1 can only be moved when it reads "automatic." When the user clicks the Command1 command button with the mouse, the DragMode property is changed to automatic. After this property changes, the automatic DragMode enables you to move the command button on the form. Notice that the control cannot be dragged when it reads "manual."

The Drag Method

While the DragMode property of a control is set to manual, the control may not normally be dragged until it is changed to automatic. If the MouseDown event of the control contains a Drag method expression, however, then this will have the same effect as changing the control's DragMode property to automatic.

Example

In the Drag project at the end of this chapter, the majority of the controls remain in manual DragMode. The pictIcon picture box can be changed from manual to automatic DragMode to demonstrate the effects of the modes on dragging icons to the pictClear icon.

DRAGOVER EVENT

Objects Affected

▶ Check	Clipboard	▶ Combo	▶ Command	CommonDlg
▶ Data	Debug	▶ Dir	▶ Drive	▶ File
▶ Form	▶ Frame	▶ Grid	▶ Image	▶ Label
Line	▶ List	MDI Form	Menu	▶ OLE
▶ Option	▶ Picture	Printer	Screen	▶ Scroll
Shape	▶ Text	Timer		

Purpose

A DragOver event contains the actions that take place when a drag operation moves the mouse pointer over a control before the user releases the mouse button. These actions do not necessarily terminate a drag-and-drop operation, but the DragOver event can serve this purpose. Tables 15-10 and 15-11 summarize the arguments and variables of the DragOver event.

General Syntax

```
Sub Form_DragOver (Source As Control, X As Single, Y As Single, State As Integer)
Sub MDIForm_DragOver (Source As Control, X As Single, Y As Single, State As Integer)
Sub Name_DragOver ([Index As Integer,] Source As Control, X As Single, Y As Single, ⇐
State As Integer)
```

Argument	Description
Form	'Form' indicates the form over which the drag-and-drop operation terminates
MDIForm	'MDIForm' indicates the MDIForm over which the drag-and-drop operation terminates
Name	Name property of the control over which the drag-and-drop operation terminates
Index	Identifies a control in a control array
Source	The dragged and dropped control
X, Y	Current horizontal (x) and vertical (y) coordinates of mouse pointer
State	Whether the dragged control is entering, over, or exiting the space above another control

Table 15-10 Arguments and variables of the DragOver event

State	CONSTANT.TXT	Description
0	ENTER	Control enters the space above another control
1	LEAVE	Control exits the space above another control
2	OVER	Control is over the space above another control (executes once)

Table 15-11 Values of the State variable in the DragOver event

Example Syntax

```
Const DRAG_ICO = "\VB2\ICONS\DRAGDROP\DRAG1PG.ICO"      'Hand w/papers
Const DROP_ICO = "\VB2\ICONS\DRAGDROP\DROP1PG.ICO"      'Hand dropping paper

Sub Form_Load ()
```

584

```
        Picture1.Picture = LoadPicture("\VB2\ICONS\OFFICE\CRDFLE05.ICO") 'Rolodex w/card
        Picture1.DragMode = 1                           'Sets automatic Drag
        Picture1.DragIcon = LoadPicture(DRAG_ICO)        'Sets DragIcon property
End Sub

Sub Picture2_DragDrop (Source As Control, X As Single, Y As Single)
        Picture2.BackColor = QBColor(15)                'Changes Background to white
        Picture2.Picture = Picture1.Picture             'Places icon in picture box
        Source.Picture = LoadPicture("")                'Blanks out source
End Sub

Sub Picture2_DragOver (Source As Control, X As Single, Y As Single, State As Integer)
        Select Case State                     'Checks where control is (entering, over, leaving)
           Case 0, 2                        'Checks if the control is over it
                Picture2.BackColor = QBColor(7)         'Changes BackColor to gray
                Source.DragIcon = LoadPicture(DROP_ICO)   'Change to dropping icon
           Case 1                          'Checks if the control is no longer over it
                Picture2.BackColor = QBColor(15)         'Changes BackColor to white
                Source.DragIcon = LoadPicture(DRAG_ICO)   'Changes back to dragging icon
        End Select
End Sub
```

Description

A DragOver event happens when the user drags a control over another control or form. Each DragOver event uses the Name property to indicate exactly which control or form the user drags a control over. The x and y coordinates define the location of the dragged control relative to the control's container. These coordinates measure the horizontal and vertical distance in units defined by the container's ScaleMode property. The Source argument identifies the dragged control that caused the event. Source replaces the Name property of the dragged control in expressions where more than one control can be dropped and dragged to a control.

The DragOver event for Picture2 determines what happens if another control (Picture1 in this case) is dragged over it. Here the background of Picture2 changes to gray while being dragged over (see Figure 15-12), and changes back to white as soon as the dragged control crosses back over Picture2's boundaries. Notice how Picture2's DragOver event also changes the source control's DragIcon as further confirmation of the ability to drop.

The DragDrop event for Picture2 controls what happens if the mouse button is released while another control is over the picture (that is, the other control is being "dropped on" Picture2). When this happens, Picture2's background changes to white and the contents of Picture2 change to those of Picture1, in effect dropping a copy of Picture1 on Picture2. Notice that if the user drops the icon, the DragDrop event must have a line of code that changes the background of the Picture2 picture box to white because the state% argument is never 1 during a drop in a DragOver event—a state of 1 means the control is exiting, so it can't drop!

In the example syntax, the DragOver event triggers up to three separate times. The DragOver event occurs each time the control enters, is over, and exits the space above the Picture2 picture box. Notice how this one event changes the

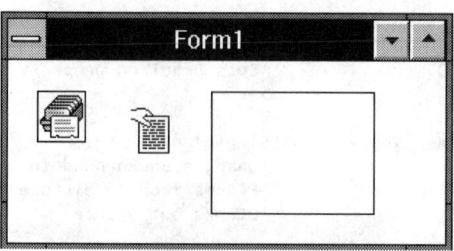

Figure 15-11 Example syntax shows drag operation before DragOver …

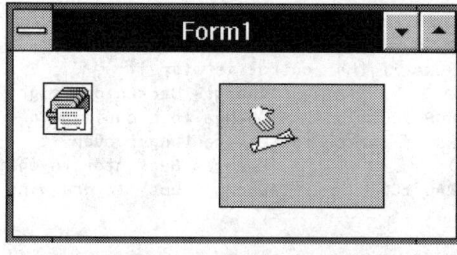

Figure 15-12 … during DragOver (note the changed icon and BackColor) …

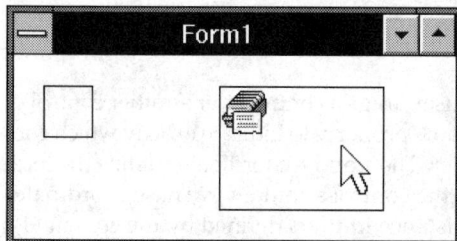

Figure 15-13 … and after the completed DragDrop

appearance of the Picture2 picture box. Figures 15-11, 15-12, and 15-13 display what the screen looks like before, during, and after a DragOver event.

The State Variable

The state% variable returns the three possible ways that a control may be dragged over a control. A control's DragOver event first triggers when a control enters the space above it. When this happens the state% variable returns a value of 0. While a dragged control is over a control or form, the state% variable returns the value of two (2). After a dragged control leaves the space above a control or form, the DragOver event triggers one last time and gives a value of 1. Refer to the Dragging and Dropping Summary section at the beginning of this chapter for detailed instructions on how to use the CONSTANT.TXT values.

Example

In the Drag project at the end of this chapter, the DragOver event clears the icon displayed in the pictIcon picture box. When the user drags that icon over to the pictClear picture box, the state% argument of the DragOver event returns the value of 0. The resulting code changes the Picture property of pictIcon to blank.

THE DRAG PROJECT

Project Overview

This Drag project demonstrates dragging in Visual Basic. This example shows how to use the properties, events, and methods that directly affect dragging.

This project has one form, the formDrag form. The formDrag form's setup is broken down into three sections: assembly, source code, and how it works.

Assembling the Project

1. Make a new form (the Drag form) with the controls and properties listed in Table 15-12.

Control	Property	Setting
Form	BackColor	Light Gray—&H00C0C0
	BorderStyle	1—Fixed Single
	Caption	"Icon View"
	Name	formDrag
	MaxButton	False
Drive	Name	drivList
Directory	Name	dirList
File	Name	fileList
	DragIcon	\VB\ICONS\COMPUTERS\DISK06.ICO
	Pattern	*.ICO
	Tag	fileList
Picture	Name	pictIcon

(continued on next page)

(continued from previous page)

Control	Property	Setting
	DragIcon	\VB\ICONS\COMPUTERS\DISK06.ICO
	DragMode	0—Manual
Picture	BackColor	Light Gray—&H00C0C0
	Name	pictClear
	Picture	\VB\ICONS\COMPUTER\TRASH01.ICO
Command	Caption	&Manual
	Name	cmndMode
Command	Caption	E&xit
	Name	cmndExit

Table 15-12 Elements of the formDrag form

2. Size the controls as shown in Figure 15-14.

3. Enter the following code in the drivList_Change event subroutine. This code triggers when the user chooses another drive in the drivList drive box. When this code changes, the path of the dirList Directory list box changes to display the directories of the new drive chosen.

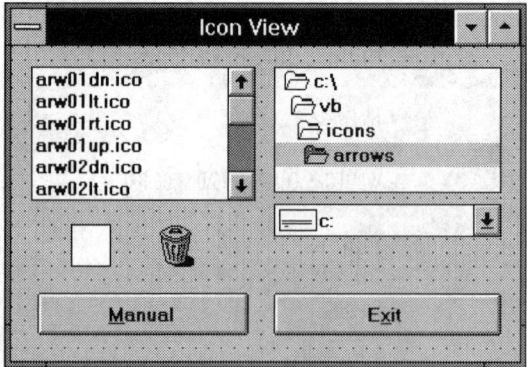

Figure 15-14 The formDrag form

588

```
Sub drivList_Change ()
    dirList.Path = drivList.Drive          'change the dir list's path
End Sub
```

4. Enter the following code in the dirList_Change event subroutine. This code activates when the user selects another directory in the dirList Directory list box. Another way of triggering this code is to change the drive selected in the drivList Drive list box. After this happens, the contents of the fileList are modified to display the icons in the indicated directory.

```
Sub dirList_Change ()
    fileList.Path = dirList.Path           'change the file list's directory
    ChDir fileList.Path                    'change to that directory
    fileList.SetFocus                      'and go to the file list box
End Sub
```

5. Enter this code in the fileList_MouseDown event subroutine. This code activates when the user presses a mouse button over an icon listed in the fileList box. This routine begins a drag operation.

```
Sub fileList_MouseDown (Button As Integer, Shift As Integer, X As Single, Y As Single)
    fileList.Drag BEGIN_DRAG               'starting to drag a file from the file list box
End Sub
```

6. Enter this code in the pictIcon_DragDrop event subroutine. This code triggers when the user releases a mouse button while the drag icon is over the Icon_Display picture box. After checking to make sure that the file dragged is from the fileList File list box, this routine displays the icon.

```
Sub pictIcon_DragDrop (Source As Control, X As Single, Y As Single)
    If Source.Tag = "fileList" Then        'check to make sure it's a new file being dragged
        pictIcon.Picture = LoadPicture(Source.List(Source.ListIndex)) 'show the icon file now
    End If
    pictIcon.DragIcon = pictIcon.Picture   'change to the picture (for the discard drag)
End Sub
```

7. Enter this code in the pictClear_DragOver event subroutine. This code activates when the user drags the Drag icon over the pictClear. When this happens, this routine terminates the drag operation and erases the icon in pictIcon picture box.

```
Sub pictClear_DragOver (Source As Control, X As Single, Y As Single, State As Integer)
    Source.Drag END_DRAG                   'stop dragging now that we've dumped the file
    pictIcon.Picture = LoadPicture()       'blank out the picture (to simulate deletion)
End Sub
```

8. Enter this code in the cmndMode_Click event subroutine. This code triggers when the user presses the cmndMode command button. The caption on the command button alternates between manual to automatic. In this way the caption on the command button indicates the type of drag operation that will take place.

```
Sub cmndMode_Click ()
    If cmndMode.Caption = "&Manual" Then   'Switch modes
        cmndMode.Caption = "&Automatic"    'relabel the command button
```

(continued on next page)

(continued from previous page)

```
        pictIcon.DragMode = AUTOMATIC        'and switch the drag mode
    Else
        cmndMode.Caption = "&Manual"         'relabel the command button
        pictIcon.DragMode = MANUAL           'and switch the drag mode
    End If
End Sub
```

9. Enter this code in the cmndExit_Click event subroutine. This code activates when the user presses the command button labeled Exit. This routine closes down the Drag project.

```
Sub cmndExit_Click ()
    End                            'End the program
End Sub
```

10. Enter the following code in the General Declarations section. These are the CONSTANT.TXT values used in the program.

```
Const BEGIN_DRAG = 1      'drag
Const END_DRAG = 2
Const MANUAL = 0          'DragMode
Const AUTOMATIC = 1
```

How It Works

This project shows a list of the icon files available on a system. The user selects a file from this list and drags it to the pictIcon picture box. When the user releases the mouse button while the dragged icon is over the pictIcon picture box, the icon of that file displays. To erase this icon from the pictIcon picture box, the user drags it to the trashcan. This erases the icon from the pictIcon picture box.

The MouseDown event of the fileList file list box contains a Drag method statement. This is necessary because the DragMode property of the fileList file list is set to manual. This shows that the only way to start a drag operation when the

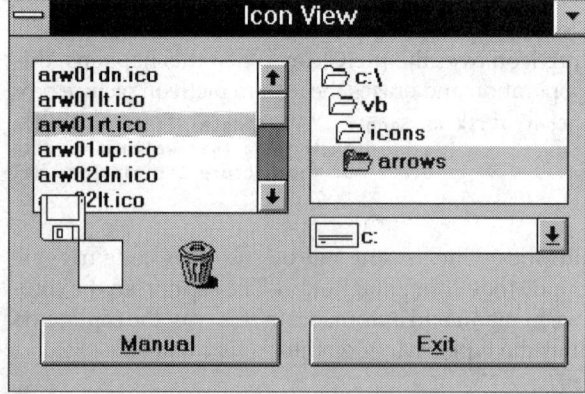

Figure 15-15 Drag operation starts in the MouseDown event of the fileList box

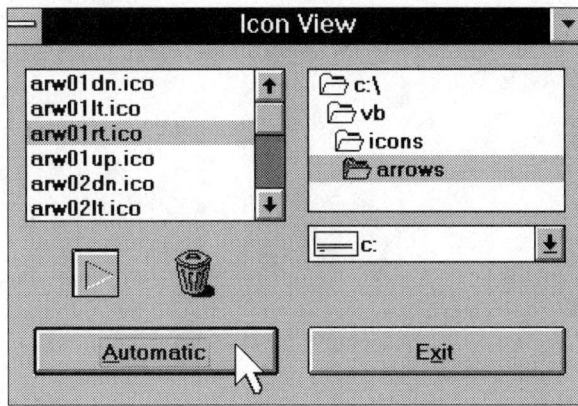

Figure 15-16 The pictIcon picture box filled with the dragged icon. Also note that the cmndMode command button has been clicked to read "Automatic"

DragMode property is set to manual is to use the Drag method. Figure 15-15 shows what the start of a drag operation looks like.

All of the controls in the Drag project start with a default setting of manual (0). When the user presses the cmndMode command button, the pictIcon picture box's DragMode property changes. The text on the command button reflects whether the picture box's property is manual or automatic. The icon displayed in the pictIcon picture box cannot be dragged to the Trashcan icon when the cmndMode command button reads manual. This demonstrates that a drag operation will not work without a Drag method when a control's DragMode is set to manual.

When the user drags a file from the fileList File list box, the box's DragDrop event triggers. The code for this event changes the Picture property of the pictIcon picture box to the icon image in the file that had been dragged to it. This results in the icon from the file displaying in the picture box. Figure 15-16 shows the icon loaded into pictIcon, and how the command button changes its caption when clicked.

The DragOver event is demonstrated while the command button cmndMode reads "Automatic." When the user drags a file to the Clear_Picture picture box, the DragDrop event terminates the drag operation with a Drag method statement. Then the icon displayed in the pictIcon picture box is erased.

16

KEYBOARD INPUT

The keyboard reigns supreme as the main method for entering information into computers. Alternative input devices (like mice) are quite common, and sometimes even required, but most programs use the keyboard to do the bulk of the work. The text box control in Visual Basic can handle keyboard input in most situations, but sometimes you need more direct control over keyboard input—such as when handling special keys and key combinations. For these situations Visual Basic provides a variety of properties, events, and statements that allow you to get down to the nitty-gritty when dealing with the keyboard.

KEYBOARD SHORTCUTS

Even though using the mouse to select objects on the screen is a visually intuitive method, sometimes removing a hand from the keyboard slows the user down. The Default and Cancel properties help keep the user's hands on the keyboard by linking the (ENTER) or (ESC) keys to the Click event of an existing command button. When the Default property of a command button is set to True (-1), pressing the (ENTER) key activates that button's Click event. Similarly, setting the Cancel property of a command button to True lets the user "click" on the button by pressing the (ESC) key. In general, it's a good idea for your application to provide keyboard alternatives to the mouse wherever possible.

Another simple way to provide keyboard shortcuts uses the Caption property of many controls. Placing an ampersand symbol (&) in front of a character in the caption underlines the character and makes it a "speed key." For instance, setting the caption property of a command button to "&Cash" sets the caption to Cash and lets you press the button with (ALT)-(C).

READING THE KEYBOARD

A keyboard can perform only two tasks. First, it can tell a program when a key is currently pressed. Second, it can tell a program when a pressed key is released. Visual Basic has three events for handling these tasks: KeyDown, KeyPress, and KeyUp. The KeyDown event activates every time any key on the keyboard is pressed down. This includes the shift-type keys (SHIFT), (CTRL), and (ALT). The KeyPress event activates when a key corresponding to a valid ASCII character (not a shift key) is pressed and released. The KeyUp event is the inverse of the KeyDown event. It activates when any currently pressed key, including any of the shift keys, is released.

The KeyPreview property of a form, new to versions 2.0 and 3.0, lets you determine whether the form first receives keyboard events or whether the active control does. This lets you build a form-level keyboard handling routine for such things as function key shortcuts.

Finally, Visual Basic provides the SendKeys statement. This statement is used to simulate keyboard activity. It can send keystrokes to the same program that issues the statement, or to any other Windows program that is currently running. This statement can be useful for automatic program testing or (to a limited extent) communication between programs.

Table 16-1 details these elements and their purposes.

Use or Set This...		To Do This...
Cancel	Property	Link the (ESC) key to a command button's Click event
Caption	Property	Link an (ALT)-key combination to a control's Click event
Default	Property	Link the (ENTER) key to a command button's Click event
KeyDown	Event	Intercept a keystroke when it is pressed
KeyPress	Event	Intercept an ASCII character keystroke
KeyPreview	Property	Sets whether the form or active control receives keyboard events first
KeyUp	Event	Intercept a keystroke when it is released
SendKeys	Statement	Simulate keyboard input from within the program

Table 16-1 Properties, events, and statement that deal with the keyboard

CONSTANT.TXT Values

Two of the events in this chapter use numeric values as arguments. Using constants rather than the literal value makes your code self-documenting, more readable, and easier to debug.

Microsoft provides a file, CONSTANT.TXT, that has many constant declarations defined for you. For smaller applications it's probably easiest just to type the declarations in yourself. For larger applications you'll find it much easier to read the text file into a new module.

To do this, create a new module by pulling down the File menu and choosing the New Module menu command. Then pull down the File menu again, and choose Load Text. This opens up a dialog box listing all text files in the current directory. CONSTANT.TXT should be in your main Visual Basic directory (default installation would place this in C:\VB). Simply choose CONSTANT.TXT to enter the entire file into your module. These constants will then be available throughout your application.

Table 16-2 lists the value of the constant, the CONSTANT.TXT constant name, and a brief description of what the constant means.

Value	CONSTANT.TXT	Meaning
KeyDown and KeyUp: KeyCode values		
&H1	KEY_LBUTTON	(uncommon)
&H2	KEY_RBUTTON	(uncommon)
&H3	KEY_CANCEL	(uncommon)
&H4	KEY_MBUTTON	(uncommon)
&H8	KEY_BACK	(BACKSPACE)
&H9	KEY_TAB	(TAB)
&HC	KEY_CLEAR	(CLEAR)
&HD	KEY_RETURN	(RETURN) or (ENTER)
&H10	KEY_SHIFT	(SHIFT)
&H11	KEY_CONTROL	(CTRL)

(continued on next page)

(continued from previous page)

Value	CONSTANT.TXT	Meaning
KeyDown and KeyUp: KeyCode values		
&H12	KEY_MENU	ALT
&H13	KEY_PAUSE	PAUSE
&H14	KEY_CAPITAL	CAPS LOCK
&H1B	KEY_ESCAPE	ESC
&H20	KEY_SPACE	SPACEBAR
&H21	KEY_PRIOR	PGUP
&H22	KEY_NEXT	PGDN
&H23	KEY_END	END
&H24	KEY_HOME	HOME
&H25	KEY_LEFT	←
&H26	KEY_UP	↑
&H27	KEY_RIGHT	→
&H28	KEY_DOWN	↓
&H29	KEY_SELECT	(uncommon)
&H2A	KEY_PRINT	PRTSC
&H2B	KEY_EXECUTE	(uncommon)
&H2C	KEY_SNAPSHOT	(uncommon)
&H2D	KEY_INSERT	INS
&H2E	KEY_DELETE	DEL

Value	CONSTANT.TXT	Meaning
KeyDown and KeyUp: KeyCode values		
&H2F	KEY_HELP	(uncommon)
	KEY_A through KEY_Z are the same as their ASCII equivalents: (A) through (Z)	
	KEY_0 through KEY_9 are the same as their ASCII equivalents: (0) through (9)	
&H60	KEY_NUMPAD0	Numeric pad (0)
&H61	KEY_NUMPAD1	Numeric pad (1)
&H62	KEY_NUMPAD2	Numeric pad (2)
&H63	KEY_NUMPAD3	Numeric pad (3)
&H64	KEY_NUMPAD4	Numeric pad (4)
&H65	KEY_NUMPAD5	Numeric pad (5)
&H66	KEY_NUMPAD6	Numeric pad (6)
&H67	KEY_NUMPAD7	Numeric pad (7)
&H68	KEY_NUMPAD8	Numeric pad (8)
&H69	KEY_NUMPAD9	Numeric pad (9)
&H6A	KEY_MULTIPLY	Numeric pad (*)
&H6B	KEY_ADD	Numeric pad (+)
&H6C	KEY_SEPARATOR	(uncommon)
&H6D	KEY_SUBTRACT	Numeric pad (-)
&H6E	KEY_DECIMAL	Numeric pad (.)
&H6F	KEY_DIVIDE	Numeric pad (/)

(continued on next page)

(continued from previous page)

Value	CONSTANT.TXT	Meaning
KeyDown and KeyUp: KeyCode values		
&H70	KEY_F1	(F1)
&H71	KEY_F2	(F2)
&H72	KEY_F3	(F3)
&H73	KEY_F4	(F4)
&H74	KEY_F5	(F5)
&H75	KEY_F6	(F6)
&H76	KEY_F7	(F7)
&H77	KEY_F8	(F8)
&H78	KEY_F9	(F9)
&H79	KEY_F10	(F10)
&H7A	KEY_F11	(F11)
&H7B	KEY_F12	(F12)
&H7C	KEY_F13	(uncommon)
&H7D	KEY_F14	(uncommon)
&H7E	KEY_F15	(uncommon)
&H7F	KEY_F16	(uncommon)
&H90	KEY_NUMLOCK	Numeric pad (NUM LOCK)
&H91	n/a	(SCROLL LOCK)

Value	CONSTANT.TXT	Meaning
KeyDown and KeyUp: Shift values		
1	SHIFT_MASK	(SHIFT) key was pressed
2	CTRL_MASK	(CTRL) key was pressed
4	ALT_MASK	(ALT) key was pressed

Table 16-2 CONSTANT.TXT entries for keyboard handling

CANCEL PROPERTY

Objects Affected

Check	Clipboard	Combo	▶ Command	CommonDlg
Data	Debug	Dir	Drive	File
Form	Frame	Grid	Image	Label
Line	List	MDI Form	Menu	OLE
Option	Picture	Printer	Screen	Scroll
Shape	Text	Timer		

Purpose

The Cancel property enables the (ESC) key to execute the Click event of a command button. Use the Cancel property when one button on the form is set up to initiate a cancel action, and you want the user to be able to use the (ESC) key as an alternative way to cancel an action. This property can be set at design time, and set or read at runtime. Tables 16-3 and 16-4 summarize the arguments of the Cancel property.

General Syntax

```
[form!]Name.Cancel [ = boolean%]
```

Arguments	Description
form	Name property of the parent form
Name	Name property of the command button
boolean%	True or False

Table 16-3 Arguments of the Cancel property

boolean%	Meaning
True	(ESC) causes Click event
False	(Default) No special handling for (ESC)

Table 16-4 Meanings of the two possible values for the Cancel property

Example Syntax

```
Sub Form_Load ()
     cmndClear.Cancel = True          'Links the Clear button to the Escape key
End Sub
```

Description

Sometimes it is necessary to provide the user with a command button with which to back out of, or cancel, an operation. The Cancel property allows you to assign that cancel action to the (ESC) key. This property can either be set to True (-1), or False (0) by you at design time, or by the application during runtime. Because only one button on a form may be the cancel button, setting this property to True for one button automatically sets it to False for all the other buttons on the same form.

In order to make a button on a form the cancel button, the Cancel, Enabled, and Visible properties must all be set to True (-1). Also, the button's parent form must be the active form on the screen. If all these conditions are met, the cancel button's Click event will trigger when the user presses the (ESC) key.

Although the Click event for the cancel button executes when the user presses the (ESC) key, the cancel button does not receive the focus. Unless the cancel button's Click event sets the focus to another control, it stays at the control that originally had the focus when the (ESC) key was pressed.

600

In the example syntax, the Cancel property of the cmndClear control is set to True (-1). Now if the user presses the (ESC) key, the effect will be the same as clicking on cmndClear, except that the focus will not shift to the button.

Example

In the Keys project at the end of this chapter, the Cancel property of the cmndClear control is set to True (-1) at design time. This setting causes the cmndClear control's Click event to occur if the user presses the (ESC) key.

Comments

The KeyDown, KeyPress, and KeyUp events, which are usually activated when a user presses a key on the keyboard, are bypassed when the (ESC) key is pressed to activate a cancel button's Click event.

CAPTION PROPERTY

Objects Affected

▶ Check	Clipboard	Combo	▶ Command	CommonDlg
▶ Data	Debug	Dir	Drive	File
▶ Form	▶ Frame	Grid	Image	▶ Label
Line	List	▶ MDI Form	▶ Menu	OLE
▶ Option	Picture	Printer	Screen	Scroll
Shape	Text	Timer		

Purpose

The Caption property sets the text displayed in or next to a control. It also sets the text displayed on a Form's title bar. Use an ampersand (&) to underline a letter in a control's caption to create an (ALT) key shortcut for that control. Table 16-5 summarizes the arguments of the Caption property.

General Syntax

```
[form!]Name.Caption [ = text$]
```

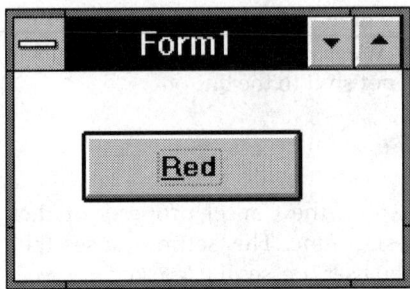

Figure 16-1 Example syntax sets the Caption to "&Red"

Argument	Description
form!	Name property of the parent form
Name	Name of the control
text$	Text to appear in the caption

Table 16-5 Arguments of the Caption property

Example Syntax

```
Sub Command1_Click()
    If Command1.Caption = "&Blue" Then
        Command1.Caption = "&Red"
    Else
        Command1.Caption = "&Blue"
    End If
End Sub
```

Description

Most controls on a form should have a keyboard shortcut to select them. Although the mouse is an intuitive input device, it's oftentimes faster to keep your hands on the keyboard. Providing keyboard shortcuts makes your programs easier to use for experienced typists.

The Caption property of many controls lets you set a keyboard shortcut by simply placing an ampersand symbol (&) in front of the shortcut key letter. For instance, setting a command button's Caption property to "&Red" makes the button read Red and lets the user select it directly by using ⒜ⓁⓉ-Ⓡ. Figure 16-1 shows this example.

Figure 16-2 Example shows how to include an ampersand as a literal character

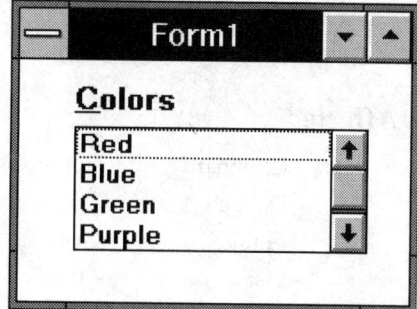

Figure 16-3 Label used to create a shortcut key for the list box, which doesn't have any Caption property

To include an ampersand literal within a control's caption, put two ampersands together. Figure 16-2 shows the following example:

```
Command1.Caption = "Fe&dex && UPS"
```

Some controls don't have a caption property. For these controls, place a label next to the control and set the label's caption to include the shortcut key. Make sure the label's TabIndex is set to one less than the control's. Labels can't receive the focus, so when the user presses the shortcut key combination, the Label passes the focus to the next control in the tab order. Figure 16-3 shows how to create a label for a list box, which doesn't have a Caption property itself.

Example

The Keys project at the end of this chapter sets the command button's Caption properties to include the shortcut key combinations.

Comment

A Form's Caption property sets the text that appears in its Title Bar. It does not have the capacity to include a shortcut key. Placing an ampersand in the Caption does not underline the following letter; it just includes the ampersand as a literal character.

DEFAULT PROPERTY

Objects Affected

Check	Clipboard	Combo	▶ Command	CommonDlg
Data	Debug	Dir	Drive	File
Form	Frame	Grid	Image	Label
Line	List	MDI Form	Menu	OLE
Option	Picture	Printer	Screen	Scroll
Shape	Text	Timer		

Purpose

The Default property enables the (ENTER) key to execute the Click event of a command button. This is used when one button on the form will initiate a default action, and you want the user to be able to press the (ENTER) key as an alternative way to say, "Okay, do it." This property can be set at design time, and set or read at run-time. Tables 16-6 and 16-7 summarize the arguments of the Default property.

General Syntax

```
[form!]Name.Default [ = boolean%]
```

Argument	Description
form!	Name property of the parent form
Name	Name of the command button
boolean%	True or False

Table 16-6 Arguments of the Default property

boolean%	Meaning
True	(ENTER) causes Click event
False	(Default) No special handling for (ENTER)

Table 16-7 Meanings of the two possible values for the Default property

604

Example Syntax

```
Sub Form_Load ()
    OkButton.Default = True          'Links the OkButton to the Enter key
End Sub
```

Description

In most cases a form has one command button that is used to perform the default action for that form. The Default property allows you to assign that default action to the (ENTER) key. This property can either be set to True (-1), or False (0) by you at design time, or by the application during runtime. Because only one button on a form may be the default, setting this property to True for one button automatically sets it to False for all the other buttons on the same form.

In order to make a button on a form the default, the Default, Enabled, and Visible properties must all be set to True (-1). Also, the button's parent form must be the active form on the screen. If all these conditions are met, and no other button currently has the focus, the default button's Click event will execute when the user hits the (ENTER) key.

Although the Click event for the default button executes, the focus is not shifted to the default button when the user presses the (ENTER) key. Unless the default button's Click event sets the focus to another control, it stays at the control that originally had the focus when the (ENTER) key was pressed.

The example syntax sets the Default property of the OK button to -1 (True). Pressing (ENTER) will now be equivalent to clicking on the OK button, except the focus will not shift to the button.

Example

In the Keys project at the end of this chapter, the Default property of the cmndSend control is set to True (-1) at design time. This setting causes the cmndSend control's Click event to occur if the user presses the (ENTER) key.

Comments

The KeyDown, KeyPress, and KeyUp events, which are usually activated when a user presses a key on the keyboard, are bypassed when the (ENTER) key is pressed to activate a default button's Click event.

KEYDOWN EVENT

Objects Affected

▶ Check	Clipboard	▶ Combo	▶ Command	CommonDlg
Data	Debug	▶ Dir	▶ Drive	▶ File
▶ Form	Frame	▶ Grid	Image	Label
Line	▶ List	MDI Form	Menu	▶ OLE
▶ Option	▶ Picture	Printer	Screen	▶ Scroll
Shape	▶ Text	Timer		

Purpose

Use the KeyDown event for low-level keyboard handling. It reports the current status of the keyboard when a key is pressed and this event's control has the focus. The arguments of the KeyDown event are summarized in Table 16-8, 16-9, and 16-10.

General Syntax

```
Sub Form_KeyDown (KeyCode As Integer, Shift As Integer)
Sub Name_KeyDown ([Index As Integer, ] KeyCode As Integer, Shift As Integer)
```

Arguments	Description
Form	'Form' for the parent form
Name	Name of the control
Index	Uniquely identifies an element of a control array
KeyCode	Integer variable returning the scan code of the key pressed
Shift	Integer variable indicating the status of the (CTRL), (ALT), and (SHIFT) keys

Table 16-8 Arguments of the KeyDown event

KeyCode	CONSTANT.TXT	Meaning
&H1	KEY_LBUTTON	(uncommon)
&H2	KEY_RBUTTON	(uncommon)
&H3	KEY_CANCEL	(uncommon)
&H4	KEY_MBUTTON	(uncommon)
&H8	KEY_BACK	BACKSPACE
&H9	KEY_TAB	TAB
&HC	KEY_CLEAR	CLEAR
&HD	KEY_RETURN	RETURN or ENTER
&H10	KEY_SHIFT	SHIFT
&H11	KEY_CONTROL	CTRL
&H12	KEY_MENU	ALT
&H13	KEY_PAUSE	PAUSE
&H14	KEY_CAPITAL	CAPS LOCK
&H1B	KEY_ESCAPE	ESC
&H20	KEY_SPACE	SPACEBAR
&H21	KEY_PRIOR	PGUP
&H22	KEY_NEXT	PGDN
&H23	KEY_END	END
&H24	KEY_HOME	HOME
&H25	KEY_LEFT	←

(continued on next page)

(continued from previous page)

KeyCode	CONSTANT.TXT	Meaning
&H26	KEY_UP	⊕
&H27	KEY_RIGHT	→
&H28	KEY_DOWN	⊕
&H29	KEY_SELECT	(uncommon)
&H2A	KEY_PRINT	PRTSC
&H2B	KEY_EXECUTE	(uncommon)
&H2C	KEY_SNAPSHOT	(uncommon)
&H2D	KEY_INSERT	INS
&H2E	KEY_DELETE	DEL
&H2F	KEY_HELP	(uncommon)
	KEY_A through KEY_Z are the same as their ASCII equivalents: A through Z	
	KEY_0 through KEY_9 are the same as their ASCII equivalents: 0 through 9	
&H60	KEY_NUMPAD0	Numeric pad 0
&H61	KEY_NUMPAD1	Numeric pad 1
&H62	KEY_NUMPAD2	Numeric pad 2
&H63	KEY_NUMPAD3	Numeric pad 3
&H64	KEY_NUMPAD4	Numeric pad 4
&H65	KEY_NUMPAD5	Numeric pad 5
&H66	KEY_NUMPAD6	Numeric pad 6
&H67	KEY_NUMPAD7	Numeric pad 7

KeyCode	CONSTANT.TXT	Meaning
&H68	KEY_NUMPAD8	Numeric pad (8)
&H69	KEY_NUMPAD9	Numeric pad (9)
&H6A	KEY_MULTIPLY	Numeric pad (*)
&H6B	KEY_ADD	Numeric pad (·)
&H6C	KEY_SEPARATOR	(uncommon)
&H6D	KEY_SUBTRACT	Numeric pad (-)
&H6E	KEY_DECIMAL	Numeric pad (.)
&H6F	KEY_DIVIDE	Numeric pad (/)
&H70	KEY_F1	(F1)
&H71	KEY_F2	(F2)
&H72	KEY_F3	(F3)
&H73	KEY_F4	(F4)
&H74	KEY_F5	(F5)
&H75	KEY_F6	(F6)
&H76	KEY_F7	(F7)
&H77	KEY_F8	(F8)
&H78	KEY_F9	(F9)
&H79	KEY_F10	(F10)
&H7A	KEY_F11	(F11)
&H7B	KEY_F12	(F12)

(continued on next page)

(continued from previous page)

KeyCode	CONSTANT.TXT	Meaning
&H7C	KEY_F13	(uncommon)
&H7D	KEY_F14	(uncommon)
&H7E	KEY_F15	(uncommon)
&H7F	KEY_F16	(uncommon)
&H90	KEY_NUMLOCK	Numeric pad (NUM LOCK)
&H91	n/a	(SCROLL LOCK)

Table 16-9 Meanings of the KeyCode values in the KeyDown event

Shift	CONSTANT.TXT	Meaning
1	SHIFT_MASK	(SHIFT) key was pressed
2	CTRL_MASK	(CTRL) key was pressed
4	ALT_MASK	(ALT) key was pressed

Table 16-10 Meanings of the Shift values in the KeyDown event

Example Syntax

```
Sub Form_KeyDown (KeyCode As Integer, Shift As Integer)
    Beep                        'Beep any time a user tries to type on an empty form.
End Sub

Sub Text1_KeyDown (Index As Integer, KeyCode As Integer, Shift As Integer)
    Dim AltOn As Integer
    Dim CtrlOn As Integer
    Dim ShiftOn As Integer
    If Shift And ALT_MASK Then AltOn = 1        'If one of the shift keys
    If Shift And CTRL_MASK Then CtrlOn = 1      'is on, turn on its corresponding
    If Shift And SHIFT_MASK Then ShiftOn = 1    'check box
    Alt_Check.Value = AltOn
    Ctrl_Check.Value = CtrlOn
    Shift_Check.Value = ShiftOn
End Sub
```

610

Description

Each time a user presses a key on the keyboard, including the (SHIFT), (CTRL), or (ALT) keys, the KeyDown event triggers for the control that currently has the focus. Forms also have a KeyDown event, but it will occur only if the form contains no active controls or if the form's KeyPreview property is set to True (-1).

This event lets the program react to the user pressing function keys 1 through @, or any unusual key combinations such as (CTRL)-(SHIFT)-key because it processes all keys, not just character keys. This event supplies two arguments, KeyCode and Shift, that tell the program which key or keys pressed caused the event to occur.

The KeyCode argument supplies a number that uniquely identifies the key pressed. This number corresponds to the physical key on the keyboard, not the character that the key generates. For instance, if the user holds down the (SHIFT) key and presses (A), the KeyCode argument will contain the same value as when the user presses the (A) key alone, even though the character generated will be different. The CONSTANT.TXT file lists the possible values for the KeyCode argument. Note that every key on the keyboard, including arrows and all the gray keys, have a KeyCode associated with them. See the Summary section at the beginning of this chapter for more details on how to use CONSTANT.TXT.

The Shift argument is an integer variable that indicates the status of the (SHIFT), (ALT), and (CTRL) keys at the time the event was called. Each of the three special shift keys is assigned a value: 1 for (SHIFT), 2 for (CTRL), and 4 for (ALT). When any of these keys is pressed, its value is added to the Shift argument. The easiest way to test the Shift argument is with logical (bitwise) operators. Table 16-11 lists logical equations that return a nonzero value if a certain shift key is pressed.

When the...	Will Return Nonzero	If CONSTANT.TXT Is Loaded, Use This
Shift key is pressed	(Shift And 1)	(Shift And SHIFT_MASK)
Ctrl key is pressed	(Shift And 2)	(Shift And CTRL_MASK)
Alt key is pressed	(Shift And 4)	(Shift And ALT_MASK)

Table 16-11 Logical equations for testing the Shift status

Keep in mind that this event is called when any key on the keyboard is pressed. Therefore, if the user presses any (SHIFT) key combination, the event occurs for as many keys as are in the combination. For instance, if the user presses (CTRL)-(SHIFT)-(A), this event will occur three times. The first time, the KeyCode argument will be 11 (the code for the (CTRL) key), and the Shift argument will be 2 (the shift code for (CTRL)). The second time KeyCode will be 10 (the code for the (SHIFT) key), and the

Shift argument will be 3 (the shift code for (CTRL) plus the shift code for (SHIFT)). Finally, on the third call, KeyCode will be 41 (the code for the (A) key), and (SHIFT) will again be 3.

The first example syntax produces a beep whenever a key is pressed. The second example syntax uses the logical relationships in Table 16-11 to store the status of the (ALT), (CTRL), and (SHIFT) keys in variables.

Control Array

The Index argument is only used if the related control is part of a control array. This Index specifies which element of the array is the one that activated the event. When referencing the control, the element being referenced must be specified by placing the index number between parentheses just after the control name and before the property name (for example, Name(Index).Property).

Example

In the Keys project at the end of this chapter, the Key_Down event is used to count the number of times a key is pressed. It is also used to set the values of the check boxes that indicate whether the (ALT), (CTRL), and (SHIFT) keys are pressed.

Comments

Pressing and holding a key down will cause this event to be activated repeatedly until the key is released.

KEYPRESS EVENT

Objects Affected

▶ Check	Clipboard	▶ Combo	▶ Command	CommonDlg
Data	Debug	▶ Dir	▶ Drive	▶ File
▶ Form	Frame	▶ Grid	Image	Label
Line	▶ List	MDI Form	Menu	▶ OLE
▶ Option	▶ Picture	Printer	Screen	▶ Scroll
Shape	▶ Text	Timer		

Purpose

The KeyPress event intercepts ASCII keystrokes when this event's control has the focus. This lets the program audit the user's input, byte by byte. This can be useful for validating data input and alerting the user as soon as an invalid character is entered. Table 16-12 summarizes the arguments of the KeyPress event.

General Syntax

```
Form_KeyPress(KeyAscii As Integer)
Name_KeyPress([Index As Integer], KeyAscii As Integer)
```

Argument	Description
form	'Form' for the parent form
Name	Name of the control
Index	Uniquely identifies an element of a control array
KeyAscii	An integer number representing the ASCII code of the character whose key was pressed

Table 16-12 Arguments of the KeyPress event

Example Syntax

```
Text1_KeyPress(Index As Integer, KeyAscii As Integer)
    Char = Chr$(KeyAscii)           'Change the code to a character
    Char = UCase$(Char)             'Change the character to uppercase
    KeyAscii = Asc(Char)            'Replace the character code
End Sub
```

Description

The object with the focus receives this event every time the user presses a key that corresponds to a valid ASCII character. Visual Basic considers the following as valid ASCII keystrokes, as summarized in Table 16-13:

Valid Character	KeyAscii Code
Any printable keyboard character	ASCII code of the character
(CTRL)-(A) through (CTRL)-(Z)	1 through 26
(ENTER) and (CTRL)-(ENTER)	13 and 10
(BACKSPACE) and (CTRL)-(BACKSPACE)	8 and 127
(TAB)	9

Table 16-13 Possible values for the KeyAscii argument

Define the KeyPress event starting with the name of the affected control and an Index variable (if using a control array). If the value of KeyAscii is modified within this event, the modification is passed on to the control. This allows you to audit the text being entered. For instance, if you only want uppercase letters to be entered in a text box, you can use the KeyPress event for that control to change each character to uppercase as it's entered. This is done in the example syntax by first getting the character code from the KeyAscii event by applying Basic's Chr$ function, then using the Basic UCase$ function to change the character to its uppercase equivalent. Finally, assigning the uppercase character back to the KeyAscii event changes the character just entered to uppercase (if it had been lowercase).

Note that KeyPress does not process keystrokes at as fine a level as KeyDown and KeyUp. It only processes the printable characters, the control characters, and a very few special keystrokes. It does not process function keys, navigation keys, and any modifications of this with the Shift modifiers. It also differentiates between upper- and lowercase printable characters. Thus KeyPress processes "a" as ASCII 97 (lowercase a); KeyDown would process this as Shift=1 and ASCII 65 (the (SHIFT) key, then uppercase (A)) in two separate triggerings of the event.

Control Array

The Index argument is only used if the related control is part of a control array. This Index specifies which element of the array is the one that activated the event. When referencing the control, the element being referenced must be specified by placing the index number between parentheses just after the control name and before the property name (for example, Name(Index).Property).

Example

In the Keys project at the end of this chapter, the KeyPress event is used to change any lowercase input to uppercase.

KEYPREVIEW PROPERTY

Objects Affected

Check	Clipboard	Combo	Command	CommonDlg
Data	Debug	Dir	Drive	File
▶ Form	Frame	Grid	Image	Label
Line	List	MDI Form	Menu	OLE
Option	Picture	Printer	Screen	Scroll
Shape	Text	Timer		

Purpose

Forms normally do not receive the KeyDown, KeyPress, and KeyUp events. Turning the form's KeyPreview property to True makes the form process these events before any active control on the form gets them. This lets you perform form-level keyboard processing for tasks such as function or status key checking. Tables 16-14 and 16-15 give the syntax for KeyPreview.

General Syntax

```
[form.]KeyPreview [ = boolean%]
```

Argument	Description
form	Name property of the parent form
boolean%	True or False

Table 16-14 Arguments of the KeyPreview property

Value	Meaning
True	Form receives keyboard events first, then the active control
False	(Default) Active control receives keyboard events

Table 16-15 The two possible settings for KeyPreview

Example Syntax

```
Sub Form_Load()
    KeyPreview = True           'Set the form-level keyboard event handler to On
End Sub
```

Description

Turn the KeyPreview property to True when you want to have form-level keyboard event handling. This may be useful if you want to check for and process special keys like (F1) through (F12), (INS), (SHIFT), or (SCROLL LOCK) before they get passed to an individual control.

615

KeyPreview defaults to False (0). This means that the form doesn't receive the KeyDown, KeyUp, and KeyPress events. Setting KeyPreview to True (-1) makes the form intercept the keystrokes first. After processing the keystrokes in the form's KeyDown, KeyUp, and KeyPress events, the appropriate event in the active control then triggers, allowing for further, more specific processing at the control level.

If you want the form to capture all keystrokes and disable any control from generating the Key events, set KeyAscii to 0 in the form's KeyPress event and set KeyCode to 0 in the form's KeyDown event. This prevents the Key events from passing through to the controls.

Example

The example project at the end of the chapter uses the form's KeyPreview to check and display the status of the (SHIFT), (CTRL), and (ALT) keys.

Comment

If there are no visible and enabled controls on a form, the form automatically receives all keyboard events, no matter what the setting of KeyPreview.

KEYUP EVENT

Objects Affected

▶ Check	Clipboard	▶ Combo	▶ Command	CommonDlg
Data	Debug	▶ Dir	▶ Drive	▶ File
▶ Form	▶ Frame	▶ Grid	Image	Label
Line	▶ List	MDI Form	Menu	▶ OLE
▶ Option	▶ Picture	Printer	Screen	▶ Scroll
Shape	▶ Text	Timer		

Purpose

The KeyUp event is used for low-level keyboard handling. It reports the current status of the keyboard when a key is released and this event's control has the focus. Tables 16-16, 16-17, and 16-18 summarize the arguments of the KeyUp event.

General Syntax

```
Sub Form_KeyUp (KeyCode As Integer, Shift As Integer)
Sub Name_KeyUp ([Index As Integer, ]KeyCode As Integer, Shift As Integer)
```

Argument	Description
Form	'Form' for the parent form
Name	Name of the control
Index	Uniquely identifies an element of a control array
KeyCode	An integer number representing the scan code of the key released
Shift	An integer number indicating the status of the (CTRL), (ALT), and (SHIFT) keys

Table 16-16 Arguments of the KeyUp event

KeyCode	CONSTANT.TXT	Meaning
See Table 16-9 in the KeyDown entry		

Table 16-17 Meanings of the KeyCode argument in KeyUp are the same as for KeyDown

Shift	CONSTANT.TXT	Meaning
1	SHIFT_MASK	(SHIFT) key was pressed
2	CTRL_MASK	(CTRL) key was pressed
4	ALT_MASK	(ALT) key was pressed

Table 16-18 Meanings of the Shift values in the KeyUp event

Example Syntax

```
Sub Form_KeyUp (KeyCode As Integer, Shift As Integer)
    Beep                        'Beep any time a user tries to type on an empty form.
End Sub

Sub Text1_KeyUp (KeyCode As Integer, Shift As Integer)
    Label1.Caption = Format$(KeyCode, "###")    'Show last key released
End Sub
```

Description

This is the complement to the KeyDown event. Every time a user releases a pressed key on the keyboard, including the (SHIFT), (CTRL), or (ALT) keys, the object that currently has the focus receives this event. Before this event occurs, a KeyDown event will occur at least once, with an identical KeyCode value. Where the KeyDown event may be executed several times when a user holds a key down, the KeyUp event is only executed once per keystroke, when the user releases the key. This makes this event perfect for low-level keyboard handlers when you wish to disable the automatic repetition of keys on the keyboard.

The KeyCode argument returns a number that uniquely identifies the key released. This number corresponds to the physical key on the keyboard, not the character that the key generates. For instance, if the user holds down the (SHIFT) key and then presses and releases (A), the KeyCode argument will contain the same value as when the user presses and releases the (A) key alone, even though the character generated will be different. The CONSTANT.TXT file that comes with Visual Basic lists the possible values for the KeyCode argument. Table 16-9 in the KeyDown item entry lists the KeyCode values and their CONSTANT.TXT equivalents.

The Shift argument is an integer variable that indicates the status of the (SHIFT), (ALT), and (CTRL) keys at the time the event was called. Each shift key is assigned a value: 1 for (SHIFT), 2 for (CTRL), and 4 for (ALT). When any of these keys is pressed, its value is added to the Shift argument. The easiest way to test the Shift argument is with logical (bitwise) operators. See Table 16-11 in the entry for KeyDown for more information on testing the value of the Shift argument.

Keep in mind the KeyUp event is called when any key on the keyboard is released. Therefore, if the user presses and then releases any (SHIFT)-key combination, the event occurs for as many keys as are in the combination. For instance, if the user presses (CTRL)-(SHIFT)-(A), and then releases them in reverse order, the KeyUp event will occur three times. The first time, KeyCode will be 41 (the code for the (A) key), and shift will be 3 (the shift code for (CTRL) plus the shift code for (SHIFT)). The second time KeyCode will be 10 (the code for the (SHIFT) key), and the Shift argument will again be 3. Finally, on the third call, the KeyCode argument will be 11 (the code for the (CTRL) key), and the Shift argument will be 2 (the shift code for (CTRL)).

The first example syntax simply beeps when any key is released. The second example syntax formats the KeyCode for the key just released and displays it by assigning it to the control's Caption property.

Control Array

The Index argument is only used if the related control is part of a control array. This index specifies which element of the array activated the event. When referencing the control, the element being referenced must be specified by placing the index number between parentheses just after the control name, and before the property name (for example, Name(Index).Property).

Example

In the Keys project at the end of this chapter, the Key_Up event is used to count the number of times a key is released. It is also used to set the values of the check boxes indicate whether the (ALT), (CTRL), and (SHIFT) keys were pressed.

Comments

The only time a form receives the KeyUp event is when either its KeyPreview property is set to True, or there are no visible and enabled controls on the form.

SENDKEYS STATEMENT

Purpose

The SendKeys statement allows your program to simulate keyboard input. The keystrokes created by the program go to whatever application is running in the active window. Only Windows programs can receive these characters. This statement is very useful for controlling a program that does not support DDE (Dynamic Data Exchange), and can also be used to test programs automatically with sample input. Table 16-19 summarizes the arguments of the SendKeys statement.

General Syntax

```
SendKeys Keystrokes$[, Pause%]
```

Argument	Description
Keystrokes$	A string of keystrokes and commands that simulate keystrokes
Pause%	A True (-1) or False (0) value indicating whether to wait for the keystrokes to be processed before continuing

Table 16-19 Arguments of the SendKeys statement

Example Syntax

```
Sub Command1_Click ()
    AppActivate "NotePad - (untitled)"        'activate notepad
    SendKeys "This is simulated keyboard input{ENTER}", True
End Sub
```

Description

The Keystrokes$ argument specifies the keyboard characters being sent, and must be a string expression. When used in the Keystrokes$ argument, Visual Basic assigns special meanings to certain characters, as shown in Table 16-20.

Character	Meaning
%	(ALT)-key—the string "%F" generates (ALT)-(F); "%(ABC)" is (ALT)-(A)-(ALT)-(B)-(ALT)-(C)
^	(CTRL)-key—the string "^C" generates (CTRL)-(C); "^(AB)" is (CTRL)-(A)-(CTRL)-(B)
+	(SHIFT)-key—the string "+D" generates (SHIFT)-(D); "+(AB)" is (SHIFT)-(A)-(SHIFT)-(B)
{	Beginning of a special code
}	Ending of a special code
~	(ENTER)-key—same as {Enter}
()	Parentheses group characters that are being SHIFTed, CTRLed, or ALTed
[]	Braces cause an "Illegal function call"; use {[} and {]} if you wish to send them

Table 16-20 Special characters and their meanings with the SendKeys statement

If you wish to send any of the characters that have a special meaning, you need to place braces around the character. For instance, if you wish to send the addition sign, you need to specify this string: "{+}"

Nonprintable keystrokes (such as function keys) may be sent by using one of the symbolic codes listed in Table 16-21.

Nonprintable keystrokes		
{BACKSPACE}	{BKSP} (for backspace)	{BS} (for backspace)
{BREAK}	{CAPSLOCK}	{CLEAR}
{DELETE}	{DEL} (for delete)	{DOWN}
{END}	{ENTER} or ~	{ESCAPE} or {ESC}

{HELP}	{HOME}	{INSERT}
{LEFT}	{NUMLOCK}	{PG DN} (page down)
{PG UP} (page up)	{PRTSC} (print screen)	{RIGHT}
{SCROLLOCK}	{TAB}	{F1} (function key)
{F2} (function key)	{F3} (function key)	{F4} (function key)
{F5} (function key)	{F6} (function key)	{F7} (function key)
{F8} (function key)	{F9} (function key)	{F10} (function key)
{F11} (function key)	{F12} (function key)	{F13} (function key)
{F14} (function key)	{F15} (function key)	{F16} (function key)

Table 16-21 Nonprintable keystroke codes for the SendKeys statement

You may also specify that a character be repeated by placing the character and a number specifying the number of repetitions together inside braces. For instance, in the following examples, the {RIGHT} code and the character "A" are both sent 25 times:

```
SendKeys {Right 25}
SendKeys {A 25}
```

The Pause% argument is a Boolean value that specifies whether or not to wait for the program to process the characters. This only has an effect if the program receiving the keystrokes is not the one issuing the SendKeys statement. If the value of Pause% is True (-1), the next statement in the sending program will not be executed until the receiving program has processed the characters. If Pause% is False (0), or omitted, execution continues as soon as the keystrokes are sent.

The example syntax shows one way to put specified characters into the Notepad application. Notice that the focus must first be set to the Notepad using AppActivate so that the string used with the SendKeys statement is sent there as input. See Chapter 21, Application Focus, for more information about AppActivate.

SendKeys and DOS programs

SendKeys does not work with DOS programs, only Windows programs. If you're running in Windows Enhanced mode, DOS programs can run within a window.

If you try to use SendKeys to send keystrokes to the DOS application, you'll notice that it never receives them. That's because SendKeys doesn't send the keystrokes to the DOS application, it sends them to the DOS box that the application is running in.

Although this is rarely mentioned in any other books or references, you can get around some of the limitations of SendKeys not working with DOS applications. Set the string you'd like to send on to the Clipboard. (See Chapter 23, Using the Clipboard, for more details, on how to do this.) Set the focus to the DOS box your application is running in using AppActivate (see Chapter 21, Application Focus). Then use SendKeys to pull down the DOS box's control menu and use Edit Paste:

```
SendKeys "% ep"
```

This pastes the text into the DOS app. You can use this same idea to Edit Mark and Edit Copy the DOS box's screen onto the Clipboard for parsing and processing by your Visual Basic application. This lets you establish a crude two-way communication between your Windows application and the DOS application.

Example

In the Keys project at the end of this chapter, the cmndSend_Click event uses the SendKeys statement to send text to the Windows NotePad program. The first SendKeys statement sends an (ALT)-(SPACE)-(X) combination to open the NotePad's control box and maximize its window. Then the text in the text box of the Keys project form is sent to the NotePad.

Comments

If the program in the active window is the one sending the keystrokes, it will also be the one receiving the keystrokes. When this is the case, the Pause% argument has no effect. Therefore it is generally a good idea to follow each SendKeys statement with a DoEvents() function call so the program can process the keystrokes.

THE KEYS PROJECT

Project Overview

The Keys project explores the use of the properties, events, and statement covered in this chapter. Each of these is used at least once in the following project. By following the examples here, you should develop a good understanding of the subjects covered in this chapter.

Assembling the Project

1. Create a new form and place the following controls on it. Use Table 16-22 to set the properties of the form and each control.

Object	Property	Setting
Form	BorderStyle	3—Fixed double
	Caption	Keys Project
	KeyPreview	True
	Name	formMain
Check	Caption	&Uppercase
	Name	chekUpper
Command	Caption	Send
	Default	True (-1)
	Name	cmndSend
Command	Caption	Clear
	Cancel	True (-1)
	Name	cmndClear
Command	Caption	E&xit
	Name	cmndExit
Label	Caption	Alt
	Name	lablAlt
	Visible	False
Label	Caption	Ctrl

(continued on next page)

(continued from previous page)

Object	Property	Setting
	Name	lablCtrl
	Visible	False
Label	Caption	Shift
	Name	lablShift
	Visible	False
Label	BorderStyle	1—Fixed single
	Caption	Keys Pressed:
	Name	Label1
Label	BorderStyle	1—Fixed single
	Caption	Keys Released:
	Name	Label2
Label	BorderStyle	1—Fixed single
	Caption	Keys Code:
	Name	Label3
Label	Alignment	1—Right justify
	BorderStyle	1—Fixed single
	Caption	0
	Name	lablKeyDown
Label	Alignment	1—Right justify
	BorderStyle	1—Fixed single

Object	Property	Setting
	Caption	0
	Name	lablKeyUp
Label	Alignment	1 – Right justify
	BorderStyle	1 – Fixed single
	Caption	0
	Name	lablKeyCode
Text	Name	textBox
	ScrollBars	2 – Vertical

Table 16-22 Controls and property settings for the Keys project

2. Check the appearance of your form against Figure 16-4.

3. Enter the following code into the General Declarations area of formMain. This sets up some constants for use with the KeyDown, KeyPressed, and KeyUp events.

```
Const SHIFT_MASK = 1      'for KeyDown and KeyUp
Const CTRL_MASK = 2
Const ALT_MASK = 4
Const CHECKED = 1         'to read status of check box
```

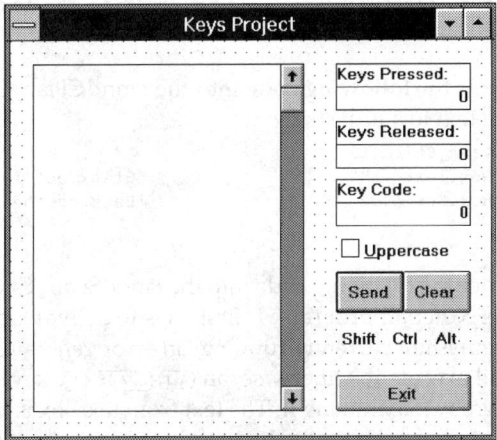

Figure 16-4 The finished Keys form

625

4. Enter the following code into the textBox_KeyDown event. This routine counts the number of keypresses, and displays the key code of the key pressed.

```
Sub textBox_KeyDown (KeyCode As Integer, Shift As Integer)
    Static KeysPressed As Long                      'remembers how many keys pressed

    KeysPressed = KeysPressed + 1                   'count total of keys pressed
    lablKeyDown.Caption = Format$(KeysPressed, "########0")    'and update the display
    lablKeyCode.Caption = Hex$(KeyCode)
End Sub
```

5. Enter the following code into the textBox_KeyUp event. This routine counts the number of key releases.

```
Sub textBox_KeyUp (KeyCode As Integer, Shift As Integer)
    Static KeysReleased                             'Remembers number of keys released

    KeysReleased = KeysReleased + 1                 'count keys released
    lablKeyUp.Caption = Format$(KeysReleased, "########0")    'and update display
End Sub
```

6. Enter the following code into the textBox_KeyPress event. This event converts each character that is typed in the textBox text box to an uppercase character if the chekUpper check box is checked.

```
Sub textBox_KeyPress (KeyAscii As Integer)
    If chekUpper.Value = CHECKED Then    'If caps lock is checked,
        Char = UCase$(Chr$(KeyAscii))    '...then convert the keystroke to uppercase
        KeyAscii = Asc(Char)             '...and change it before it gets to the text box
    End If
End Sub
```

7. Enter the following code into the chekUpper_Click event. This simply sets the focus back to the text entry box.

```
Sub chekUpper_Click ()
    textBox.SetFocus                     'Back to the text box for more entry
End Sub
```

8. Enter the following code into the cmndClear_Click event. This event will clear the text to a null string.

```
Sub cmndClear_Click ()
    textBox.Text = ""                    'Blank out Text box
    textBox.SetFocus                     'Back to the text box for more entry
End Sub
```

9. Enter the following code into the cmndSend_Click event. This event sends text to the Notepad program. It first tries to activate the program. If the Notepad program is not currently running, an error generates, and the error-handling routine will execute it. Otherwise, an (ALT)-(SPACE)-(X) key sequence is sent to the program, thereby maximizing it. The text from textBox is then sent to the Notepad, and the program waits for the Notepad to process it.

```
Sub cmndSend_Click ()
    Dim Tries As Integer                      'Remember how many times tried to start notepad

    On Error GoTo Load_Notepad                'Can't activate? then load it
    AppActivate "Notepad - (untitled)"        'activate notepad
    On Error GoTo 0                           'Successful activation
    SendKeys "%{ }x"                          'Maximize notepad
    SendKeys textBox.Text, True               'send it contents of text box
Exit Sub

Load_NotePad:                                 'Need to load notepad
    If Tries > 0 Then                         'Tried this before and failed, so
        MsgBox "Cannot Load Notepad"          '...tell user they're out of luck
        Exit Sub
    Else                                      'We haven't tried before, so
        Tries = Shell("Notepad")              '...load notepad
    End If
Resume                                        'Go back and activate notepad
End Sub
```

10. Enter the following code in the cmndExit_Click event. This ends the program.

```
Sub cmndExit_Click ()
    End                         'End the program
End Sub
```

How It Works

This project demonstrates each of the ways of handling keyboard input. Figure 16-5 shows what the project looks like when running. Note the text varies from lowercase to uppercase, the number of keys pressed exceeds the keys released, and the (CTRL) indicator is highlighted.

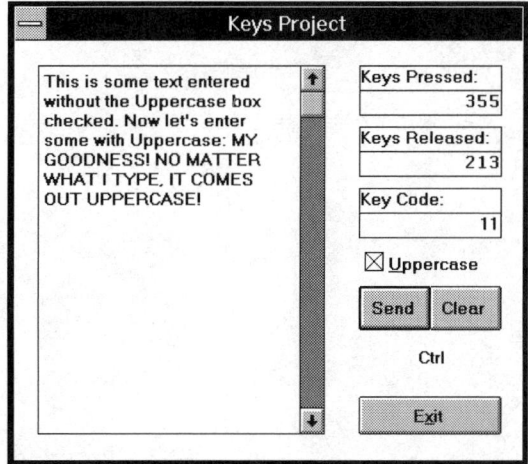

Figure 16-5 The Keys project in action

We first set some properties during the design phase that will assist us in processing the keyboard while running. We set the form's KeyPreview to True to allow us to check for the (SHIFT) key status. We also set the Send button's Default property to True and the Clear button's Cancel property to False to allow (ENTER) and (ESC) to trigger these two buttons. Finally, we set the chekUpper check box's and cmndExit's Caption properties to include a hot-key combination.

All keystrokes are first processed by the form because we set the KeyPreview property to True. The form's KeyDown and KeyUp events checks on the status for the (SHIFT), (CTRL), and (ALT) keys. It then sets the Visible properties of the appropriate labels to show the Shift status to the user.

Once a keystroke gets through the form's keystroke handlers, it then gets processed by textBox's KeyDown handler. This updates the lablKeyDown and lablKeyCode labels. The KeyPressed handler is next. This checks to see if Caps Lock is checked, and if so, makes the text uppercase. Finally, the KeyUp handler updates lablKeyUp's display

The Send button calls up the Notepad application and uses SendKeys to maximize Notepad (using Notepad's control box) and then "types" the text from textBox.

PART VI

Displaying and Retrieving Information

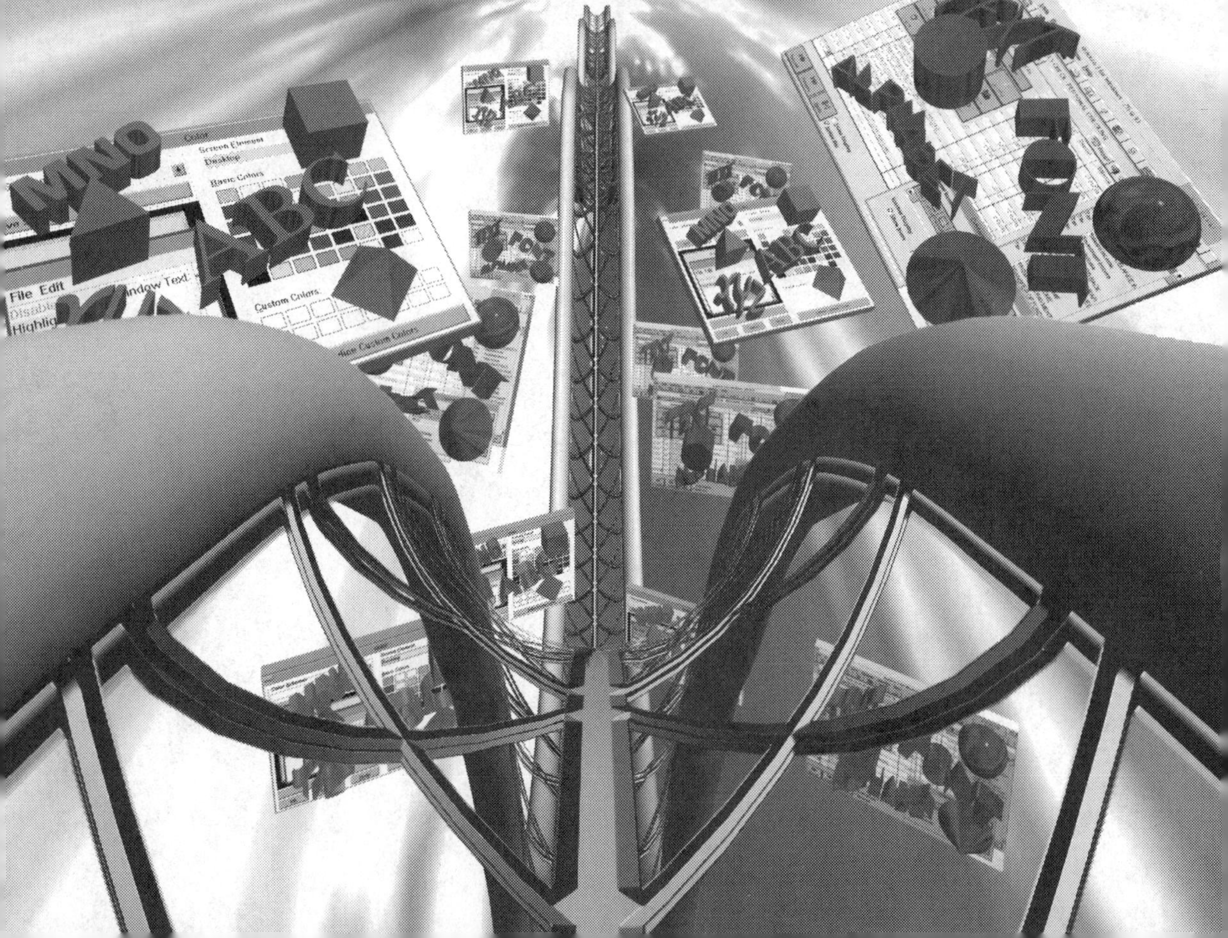

17

DIALOG BOXES

Dialog boxes appear in almost every Windows program. A *dialog box* is a specialized form meant to display or obtain specific information, and is hidden from sight once it has done its work. Some dialog boxes are extremely simple, displaying just a single line of text while the program is performing a lengthy action. Other dialog boxes may be complex, with many controls displaying a variety of information that the user can interact with.

Most applications have one main window, from which the user directs the program. Although the user will spend most of his or her time working within this window, some of a program's tasks require information that is not part of the main window's user interface. The dialog box created to do this may contain one or more objects, such as text boxes or command buttons, with which the user can respond to the program's request or make additional settings.

For instance, within the Visual Basic environment, you load a project onto the desktop by selecting Open Project from the File menu. When you do this, Visual Basic needs to determine which project file you wish to open. In order to get your input, Visual Basic displays a dialog box where you can select a project file. Once you've selected your file, the dialog box disappears and you are returned to the main area of the Visual Basic environment.

Visual Basic supplies several kinds of predefined dialog boxes. These make your programming job easier, as one line of code can call up a completed box to display a message or solicit input. An exciting development in the newest versions of Visual Basic is the ability to use the common dialog boxes. These are complete dialog boxes that let the user do common tasks, such as change printer settings or choose colors. Using a common dialog box can save hours of your time.

TYPES OF DIALOG BOXES

There are five basic styles of dialog boxes. Visual Basic provides four styles of predefined dialog boxes. You can use these with just a few lines of code to perform most basic interactions. The fifth style is a custom dialog box you build yourself. It can be as complex as you like.

The first style is the simple message box. This type of dialog box simply displays a message and waits for the user to close the box by clicking on a button. The simple message dialog box is used to notify the user of certain information. For instance, when a runtime error occurs in a Visual Basic program, a simple message dialog box is displayed telling you which error caused the program to halt. You can use a simple message box when you need to tell the user what has happened, but don't require anything from the user other than the acknowledgment implied in clicking on the OK button.

The second style of dialog box also displays a simple message. However, more than one command button is displayed on the dialog box so the user can make a choice of several options. In most Windows programs, if you attempt to exit a program with unsaved files, this type of dialog box appears and asks if you want to save the files before exiting. Generally, such a dialog box will have Yes, No, and Cancel buttons. How the program acts when the dialog box closes is based on the button that you choose.

The third style is a simple input box. If you need a quick and easy method to enter a single line of text, you can use a single statement to do this.

The fourth style of dialog box is really a whole family of commonly used dialog boxes. Visual Basic 2.0 Professional and 3.0 Standard and Professional feature the common dialog box control. These are fairly complex dialog boxes that let the user choose printer settings, open and save files, change fonts and select and define colors. Many commercial applications use these common dialog boxes. Using common dialog boxes saves you a substantial amount of work and lends your programs a professional appearance, giving your programs a consistency that users have grown to expect.

The fifth style of dialog box is a custom dialog box. These are really just another form, but one designed specifically as a dialog box. If one of the four predefined types don't meet your needs, you'll need to design your own by placing the appropriate controls on a standard form object.

DIALOG BOX SUMMARY

This chapter discusses these functions and statement in detail. At the end of the chapter, the Dialog project demonstrates the use of these elements of Visual Basic. Table 17-1 lists the control, functions, and statement that help create dialog boxes.

Use This...		To Do This...
CommonDlg	Control	Display a custom dialog box
InputBox	Function	Display a box with a message that returns a line of text from the user
MsgBox	Function	Display a message in a box that returns a button choice from the user
MsgBox	Statement	Display a message in a box with just an OK button

Table 17-1 The four built-in styles of dialog boxes

CONSTANT.TXT Values

Many of the properties, functions, and statements of this chapter use numeric values as arguments. Using constants rather than the literal value makes your code self-documenting, more readable, and easier to debug.

Microsoft provides a file, CONSTANT.TXT, that has many constant declarations defined for you. For smaller applications it's probably easiest just to type the declarations in yourself. For larger applications you'll find it much easier to read the text file into a new module.

To do this, create a new module by pulling down the File menu and choosing the New Module menu command. Then pull down the File menu again, and choose Load Text. This opens up a dialog box listing all text files in the current directory. CONSTANT.TXT should be in your main Visual Basic directory (default installation would place this in C:\VB). Simply choose CONSTANT.TXT to enter the entire file into your module. These constants will then be available throughout your application.

Table 17-2 lists the value of the constant, the CONSTANT.TXT constant name, and a brief description of what the constant means.

Value	CONSTANT.TXT	To Do This...
Common Dialog Action property: the six kinds of common dialog boxes		
0	NONE	No action taken
1	DLG_FILE_OPEN	Open a file; lists drives, directories, files, and pattern

(continued on next page)

(continued from previous page)

Value	CONSTANT.TXT	To Do This...
2	DLG_FILE_SAVE	Save a file; lists drives, directories, files, and pattern
3	DLG_COLOR	Set or define colors; shows the color palette and optional color-picker
4	DLG_FONT	Set the font; shows list of fonts and font example
5	DLG_PRINT	Specify print settings; shows the printer options for the selected printer
6	DLG_HELP	Invoke WINHELP.EXE

File Open and Save As flags		
&H200	OFN_ALLOWMULTISELECT	File Name list box allows for multiple selections
&H2000	OFN_CREATEPROMPT	Box will prompt if user wants to create a file that doesn't exist yet
&H400	OFN_EXTENSIONDIFFERENT	Return flag indicates returned extension is different from DefaultExt
&H1000	OFN_FILEMUSTEXIST	Specify that user must enter a file name that already exists
&H4	OFN_HIDEREADONLY	Hide the read-only check box
&H8	OFN_NOCHANGDIR	Force the box to set the current directory to what it was when invoked
&H8000	OFN_NOREADONLYRETURN	Specify returned file cannot be read-only or in a write-protected directory
&H100	OFN_NOVALIDATE	Box will accept invalid characters in the returned file name
&H2	OFN_OVERWRITEPROMPT	Box will prompt user to confirm overwriting an existing file
&H800	OFN_PATHMUSTEXIST	Specify user can only enter valid path names
&H1	OFN_READONLY	Read-only box defaults to checked
&H4000	OFN_SHAREAWARE	Specify that OF_SHARINGVIOLATION error be ignored
&H10	OFN_SHOWHELP	Box will display the Help button

Value	CONSTANT.TXT	To Do This...
Color flags		
&H2	CC_FULLOPEN	Open the dialog box already showing the custom color-picker
&H4	CC_PREVENTFULLOPEN	Disable the Define Custom Colors command button
&H1	CC_RGBINIT	Set the initial value for the dialog box
&H8	CC_SHOWHELP	Make the box display a Help button
Font flags		
&H200	CF_APPLY	Enabls the box's Apply button
&H400	CF_ANSIONLY	Only allow selection of fonts that use the Windows character set
&H3	CF_BOTH	List both printer and screen fonts
&H100	CF_EFFECTS	Enable strikeout, underline, and color effects
&H4000	CF_FIXEDPITCHONLY	Only allow selection of fixed-pitch fonts
&H10000	CF_FORCEFONTEXIST	Make box generate error if user attempts to select a nonexistent font
&H2000	CF_LIMITSIZE	Box will select only sizes between Min and Max
&H1000	CF_NOSIMULATIONS	Box will not allow GDI font simulations
&H800	CF_NOVECTORFONTS	Box will not allow vector fonts
&H2	CF_PRINTERFONTS	List only printer fonts
&H20000	CF_SCALABLEONLY	List only scalable fonts
&H1	CF_SCREENFONTS	List only screen fonts
&H4	CF_SHOWHELP	Box displays a Help button

(continued on next page)

Value	CONSTANT.TXT	To Do This...
&H40000	CF_TTONLY	List only True Type fonts
&H8000	CF_WYSIWYG	List only fonts common to both printer and screen

Print flags		
&H0	PD_ALLPAGES	Set or return the state of the All Pages option button in Print Range
&H10	PD_COLLATE	Set or return the state of the Collate check box
&H80000	PD_DISABLEPRINTTOFILE	Disable the Print To File check box
&H100000	PD_HIDEPRINTTOFILE	Hide the Print To File check box
&H8	PD_NOPAGENUMS	Disable the Print Range option buttons and text boxes
&H80	PD_NOWARNING	Suppress a warning message if there is no default printer
&H4	PD_NOSELECTION	Disable the Selection option button in Print Range
&H2	PD_PAGENUMS	Set or return the state of the Pages option button in Print Range
&H40	PD_PRINTSETUP	Displays the Print Setup dialog box instead of the Print dialog box
&H20	PD_PRINTTOFILE	Set or return the state of the Print To File check box
&H100	PD_RETURNDC	Return a device context for the printer selected in Print Setup
&H200	PD_RETURNIC	Return an information context for the printer selected in Print Setup
&H1	PD_SELECTION	Set or returns the state of the Selection option button in Print Range
&H800	PD_SHOWHELP	Display a Help button
&H40000	PD_USEDEVMODECOPIES	Disable Copies edit box if printer driver doesn't support multiple copies; stores the requested number of copies in the Copies property if the printer driver does support multiple copies

Value	CONSTANT.TXT	To Do This...
HelpCommand		
&H1	HELP_CONTEXT	Display help for a context; use the HelpContext property to specify
&H4	HELP_HELPONHELP	Display help for using the Help application
&H3	HELP_INDEX	Display the Index for a Help file
&H101	HELP_KEY	Display Help for a particular keyword; use HelpKeyword to specify
&H2	HELP_QUIT	Terminate the Help file
&H5	HELP_SETINDEX	Choose a particular index in the Help file; use HelpContext to specify
MsgBox types		
0	MB_OK	(Default) Display an OK button only
1	MB_OKCANCEL	Display OK and Cancel buttons
2	MB_ABORTRETRYIGNORE	Display Abort, Retry, and Ignore buttons
3	MB_YESNOCANCEL	Display Yes, No, and Cancel buttons
4	MB_YESNO	Display Yes and No buttons
5	MB_RETRYCANCEL	Display Retry and Cancel buttons
MsgBox default buttons		
0	MB_DEFBUTTON1	(Default) Sets first button as default
256	MB_DEFBUTTON2	Set second button as default
512	MB_DEFBUTTON3	Set third button as default

(continued on next page)

(continued from previous page)

Value	CONSTANT.TXT	To Do This...
MsgBox icons		
16	MB_ICONSTOP	Red STOP sign
32	MB_ICONQUESTION	Question mark in green circle
48	MB_ICONEXCLAMATION	Exclamation mark in red circle
64	MB_ICONINFORMATION	Letter "i" in a blue circle
MsgBox return values		
1	IDOK	OK
2	IDCANCEL	Cancel
3	IDABORT	Abort
4	IDRETRY	Retry
5	IDIGNORE	Ignore
6	IDYES	Yes
7	IDNO	No

Table 17-2 CONSTANT.TXT values used in dialog boxes

COMMON DIALOG

Purpose

The Common Dialog control provides an easy way to produce standard dialog boxes like File Open, File Save, Print, Select Font, and Choose Color.

Properties, Events, and Methods

Table 17-3 lists the properties for the Common Dialog control. It has no events or methods.

Use This Property...	To Do This...
Action	Specify the type of dialog box to display
CancelError	Determine whether an error is generated upon Cancel
Color	Read or set the selected color
Copies	Read or set the number of copies to be printed
DefaultExt	Set the default extension for the dialog box
DialogTitle	Set the caption of the dialog box's title bar
FileName	Read or set the path and name of the file to open or save
FileTitle	Read the name of the file to open or save
Filter	Read or set the filter for the kinds of files the file list box displays
FilterIndex	Read or set the index number of the Filter for the default pattern
Flags	Set various options for each dialog box
FontBold, FontItalic, FontStrikeThru, FontUnderline	Read or set special effects for this object's font
FontName	Read or set the name of this object's font
FontSize	Read or set the size of this object's font
FromPage, ToPage	Read or set the values of the Print From and To
hDC	Read the Windows device handle for this object
HelpCommand	Set the kind of help requested
HelpContextID	Set the context number for context-sensitive help

(continued on next page)

(continued from previous page)

Use This Property...	To Do This...
HelpFile	Set the name of the Help file to display
HelpKey	Set the keyword for the Help file to search for
InitDir	Read or set the initial directory to use for file open
Max, Min	Set the smallest and largest fonts displayed
Max, Min	Set the smallest and largest page numbers to be printed
MaxFileSize	Sets the maximum length of file name used in the FileName property
PrinterDefault	Determine whether changes in Print dialog change default printer settings

Table 17-3 Properties of the common dialog box control

Description

The common dialog control gives you easy access to the most commonly used dialog boxes. This saves you from having to recreate standard dialog boxes for every application. The Action property determines which kind of dialog box to display and immediately displays it. There are six styles of dialog box: Open, Save As, Color, Font, Printer, and Help.

The Open dialog box has areas for file name, directories, drives, and default file types. The Save As dialog looks identical to Open, except for its caption. The Color dialog allows the user to select a color from a palette or from a custom color-picker. This is the same box as is used in the Window's Control Panel Desktop color choice. The Font dialog displays a list of all available fonts, and shows an example of the selected font. The Printer box allows the user to choose printers, page defaults, and page print ranges.

The Action setting for Help runs WINHELP.EXE rather than calling up a dialog box. This gives you a simple way to call up your custom help file for your application. The HelpFile, HelpKey, HelpCommand, and HelpContextID let you pass the appropriate information to the Help program to pull up general help, context-sensitive help, or the help Search dialog. Custom help files can be created in the Professional edition of Visual Basic.

Common Features

Although each style of common dialog box has unique settings, the general process of using them is the same for all six types. To use a common dialog box

640

in an application, draw a common dialog control on the form. Much like the timer, it will resize itself and is invisible at runtime. You can place it anywhere you want on the form without affecting your application's appearance. A single common dialog control can produce any of the common dialog boxes. You need to make sure to distribute the COMMDLG.DLL file along with your program; place this file in the Windows system directory.

At runtime, set the appropriate values for the kind of dialog box you're about to display. For example, set the default drive, path, and pattern for the Open dialog. Then set the common dialog's Action property to display the correct dialog box. Table 17-4 summarizes the arguments for Action.

Action Setting	CONSTANT.TXT	To Do This...
0	NONE	No action taken
1	DLG_FILE_OPEN	Open a file; lists drives, directories, files, and pattern
2	DLG_FILE_SAVE	Save a file; lists drives, directories, files, and pattern
3	DLG_COLOR	Set or define colors; shows the color palette and optional color-picker
4	DLG_FONT	Set the font; shows list of fonts and font example
5	DLG_PRINT	Specify print settings; shows the printer options for the selected printer
6	DLG_HELP	Invoke WINHELP.EXE

Table 17-4 The six possible kinds of common dialog boxes

The CancelError property lets you trap for whether the user pressed the cancel button. If CancelError is set to True, pressing cancel on the dialog box generates error 32755, defined in CONSTANT.TXT as CDERR_CANCEL. You can then trap this error and take appropriate action. This helps prevent errors if your code tries to assign nothing to a property that needs something; for instance, specifying a null BackColor causes a runtime error. If CancelError is set to False (the default) then no error occurs; the box just closes and returns a null. The following example shows a simple implementation of this idea to prevent attempting to set the ForeColor to a nonexistent color:

```
Sub menuFormatColor_Click ()
    CMDialog1.Color = QBColor(1)           'default color
    CMDialog1.Flags = CC_RGBINIT Or CC_FULLOPEN 'rgb style, open with full color-picker
    CMDialog1.CancelError = True           'trap for the cancel key
    On Error GoTo errCancel                'set the trap
```

(continued on next page)

(continued from previous page)

```
        CMDialog1.Action = DLG_COLOR            'display the color box
        On Error GoTo 0                         'no cancel; turn off error trap
        Text1.Backcolor = CMDialog1.Color       'set the color
Exit Sub                                        'done!

errCancel:                                      'error trap
        If Err <> CDERR_CANCEL Then Stop        'if it wasn't a cancel, then we've got a bug!
End Sub
```

Open and Save As

The Open and Save As dialog boxes let the user open or save a file. They have areas for choosing drives, directories, file names, a list of available files, a list of patterns (file extensions), the option to open the file read-only, and advanced options for opening files on a network. Figure 17-1 shows what the example syntax looks like, and Tables 17-5 and 17-6 summarize the subset of properties and flag settings that apply to the Open and Save As dialog boxes.

Example Syntax

```
Sub Command1_Click ()
        CMDialog1.DefaultExt = "*.BMP"
        CMDialog1.DialogTitle = "Place Graphics File"
        CMDialog1.Filter = "Icons|*.ICO|Bitmaps|*.BMP|Metafiles|*.WMF"
        CMDialog1.FilterIndex = 2
        CMDialog1.Flags = OFN_SHOWHELP
        CMDialog1.Action = DLG_FILE_OPEN
        Picture1.Picture = LoadPicture(CMDialog1.FileName)
End Sub
```

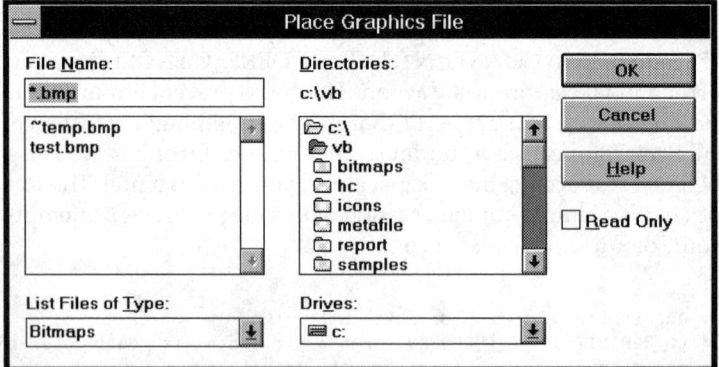

Figure 17-1 Example syntax opens this Open common dialog box

Property	Action
DefaultExt	Sets the default extension for a saved file if no extension given
DialogTitle	Sets the title displayed in the dialog box's title bar
FileName	Sets or returns the full name and path of the file to open or save
FileTitle	Returns the name only (no path) of the file to open or save
Filter	Sets the filter patterns and names for the box's Type combo box
FilterIndex	Sets the default filter
Flags	Sets a variety of options for the dialog box
InitDir	Sets the initial file directory
MaxFileSize	Sets the maximum length of the file name specified by FileName

Table 17-5 Properties particular to the Open and Save As common dialog boxes

Use DefaultExt to set the default extension for a Save As box. For example, a word processing application might default to the extension DOC. If the user enters just the file name with no extension, the DefaultExt is appended to the file name.

The FileName property sets or returns the name and full path of the file to open or save. When the user selects a file and clicks on the box's OK button, the FileName property takes on a value that can be used to save or open the file. Setting this property before the box displays sets the initial name shown in the File Name text box. The FileTitle property is similar, but is read only and returns just the name of the file without any path.

The Filter property lets you define a number of filter patterns to display in the File Type combo box. These patterns determine which files in the current directory will be listed. For example, if the filter is "*.ICO", then only files with that extension get listed. Specify this as a string that follows this format: the description, the pipe symbol (|), then the actual file pattern. For example,

```
description1|filter1|description2|filter2|description3|filter3

Dialog1.Filter = "Icons|*.ico|Bitmaps|*.bmp|Metafiles|*.wmf"
```

FilterIndex can then be used to set the default pattern filter. In the above example, setting the FilterIndex property to 2 makes Bitmaps (*.BMP) the default filter.

The Flags property sets and returns a number of miscellaneous settings for the dialog box. Table 17-6 summarizes these.

Flag	CONSTANT.TXT	Meaning
&H200	OFN_ALLOWMULTISELECT	File Name list box allows for multiple selections
&H2000	OFN_CREATEPROMPT	Box will prompt if user wants to create a file that doesn't exist yet
&H400	OFN_EXTENSIONDIFFERENT	Return flag indicates returned extension is different from DefaultExt
&H1000	OFN_FILEMUSTEXIST	Specifies that user must enter a file name that already exists
&H4	OFN_HIDEREADONLY	Hides the read-only check box
&H8	OFN_NOCHANGDIR	Forces the box to set the current directory to what it was when invoked
&H8000	OFN_NOREADONLYRETURN	Specifies returned file cannot be read-only or in a write-protected directory
&H100	OFN_NOVALIDATE	Box will accept invalid characters in the returned file name
&H2	OFN_OVERWRITEPROMPT	Box will prompt user to confirm overwriting an existing file
&H800	OFN_PATHMUSTEXIST	Specifies user can only enter valid path names
&H1	OFN_READONLY	Read-only box defaults to checked
&H4000	OFN_SHAREAWARE	Specifies that OF_SHARINGVIOLATION error be ignored
&H10	OFN_SHOWHELP	Box will display the Help button

Table 17-6 Settings for Open and Save As flags

The Summary section at the beginning of this chapter explains how to use these CONSTANT.TXT flag values. Make sure CONSTANT.TXT is loaded into a module somewhere in your application to properly use them. Specify multiple flags by using the Or operator. For example, use this line to specify showing the help button, not showing the read only check box, and prompt on overwrite:

```
Dialog1.Flags = OFN_SHOWHELP Or OFN_HIDEREADONLY Or OFN_OVERWRITEPROMPT
```

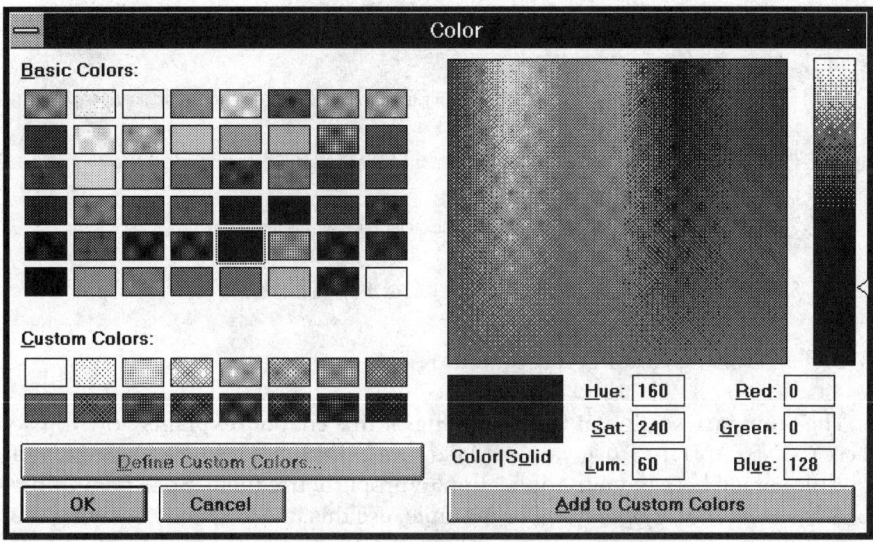

Figure 17-2 Example syntax displays this Color common dialog box

Color

The Color common dialog box lets the user choose a color from a palette or create new colors. It shows the actual palette colors, and when expanded to allow the creation of new colors, shows the whole color gamut and has input boxes for both HSV (Hue, Saturation, Value) and RGB (Red, Green, Blue) values. The example syntax displays the dialog box shown in Figure 17-2; Tables 17-7 and 17-8 summarize the properties and flags particular to the Color common dialog box.

Example Syntax

```
Sub Command1_Click ()
    CMDialog1.Color = QBColor(1)
    CMDialog1.Flags = CC_RGBINIT Or CC_FULLOPEN
    CMDialog1.Action = DLG_COLOR
    Text1.Backcolor = CMDialog1.Color
End Sub
```

Property	Action
Color	Sets or returns the selected color as a long integer; make sure to set the CC_RGBINIT flag too
Flags	Sets or returns a number of dialog box options

Table 17-7 Properties unique to the Color common dialog box

Flag	CONSTANT.TXT	Meaning
&H2	CC_FULLOPEN	Opens the dialog box already showing the custom color-picker
&H4	CC_PREVENTFULLOPEN	Disables the Define Custom Colors command button
&H1	CC_RGBINIT	Sets the initial value for the dialog box
&H8	CC_SHOWHELP	Makes the box display a Help button

Table 17-8 Flags for the Color common dialog box

The Summary section at the beginning of this chapter explains how to use these CONSTANT.TXT flag values. Make sure CONSTANT.TXT is loaded into a module somewhere in your application to properly use them. Specify multiple flags by using the Or operator. For example, use this line to specify showing the Help button, and preventing the user from defining custom colors:

```
CMDialog1.Flags = CC_PREVENTFULLOPEN Or CC_SHOWHELP
```

Fonts

The Font common dialog box lets the user choose a font. It has combo boxes listing the names of all the available fonts, colors, sizes, and styles particular to the system the program is running on. It shows the selected font and attributes in a sample window. The example syntax displays the font box illustrated in Figure 17-3, and Tables 17-9 and 17-10 list the properties and flags particular to the font box.

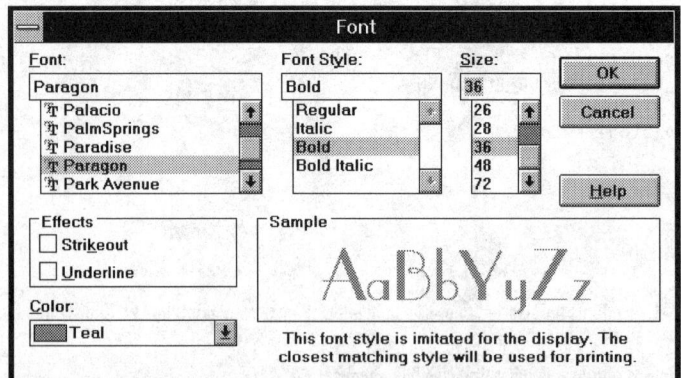

Figure 17-3 Example syntax displays the Font common dialog box

646

Example Syntax

```
Sub Command1_Click ()
    CMDialog1.Flags = CF_BOTH Or CF_SHOWHELP Or CF_EFFECTS Or CF_TTONLY
    CMDialog1.FontBold = Text1.FontBold
    CMDialog1.FontItalic = Text1.FontItalic
    CMDialog1.FontUnderLine = Text1.FontUnderline
    CMDialog1.FontStrikeThru = Text1.FontStrikethru
    CMDialog1.Color = Text1.ForeColor
    CMDialog1.FontName = Text1.FontName
    CMDialog1.FontSize = Text1.FontSize
    CMDialog1.Action = 4                          'Display the Font dialog box
    Text1.FontBold = CMDialog1.FontBold
    Text1.FontItalic = CMDialog1.FontItalic
    Text1.FontStrikethru = CMDialog1.FontStrikeThru
    Text1.FontUnderline = CMDialog1.FontUnderLine
    Text1.ForeColor = CMDialog1.Color
    Text1.FontName = CMDialog1.FontName
    Text1.FontSize = CMDialog1.FontSize
End Sub
```

Property	Action
Color	Sets or returns the color of the font
Flags	Sets or returns a number of options
FontBold	Sets or returns the bold status of the font
FontItalic	Sets or returns the italics status of the font
FontStrikethru	Sets or returns the strikethrough status of the font
FontUnderline	Sets or returns the underline status of the font
FontName	Sets or returns the name of the selected font
FontSize	Sets or returns the size of the selected font
Max	Sets the maximum font size displayed in the Size combo box; set CF_LIMITSIZE first
Min	Sets the minimum font size displayed in the Size combo box; set CF_LIMITSIZE first

Table 17-9 Property settings unique to the Font common dialog box

Some properties need to have flags set before using them. Color, FontBold, FontItalic, FontStrikethru, and FontUnderline all need the CF_EFFECTS flag set. Min and Max need CF_LIMITSIZE set before these take effect. CF_WYSYWIG needs to have both CF_SCREENFONTS and CF_PRINTERFONTS set too. Make sure you set at least one of CF_SCREENFONTS, CF_PRINTERFONTS, or CF_BOTH before calling the dialog box, otherwise the "No Fonts Exist" error occurs. Table 17-10 lists the flags for the Fonts dialog box.

Flag	CONSTANT.TXT	Meaning
&H200	CF_APPLY	Enable the box's Apply button
&H400	CF_ANSIONLY	Only allow selection of fonts that use the Windows character set
&H3	CF_BOTH	List both printer and screen fonts
&H100	CF_EFFECTS	Enable strikeout, underline, and color effects
&H4000	CF_FIXEDPITCHONLY	Only allow selection of fixed-pitch fonts
&H10000	CF_FORCEFONTEXIST	Make box generate error if user attempts to select a nonexistent font
&H2000	CF_LIMITSIZE	Box will select only sizes between Min and Max
&H1000	CF_NOSIMULATIONS	Box will not allow GDI font simulations
&H800	CF_NOVECTORFONTS	Box will not allow vector fonts
&H2	CF_PRINTERFONTS	List only printer fonts
&H20000	CF_SCALABLEONLY	List only scalable fonts
&H1	CF_SCREENFONTS	List only screen fonts
&H4	CF_SHOWHELP	Box displays a help button
&H40000	CF_TTONLY	List only TrueType fonts
&H8000	CF_WYSIWYG	List only fonts common to both printer and screen

Table 17-10 Flags particular to the Font common dialog box

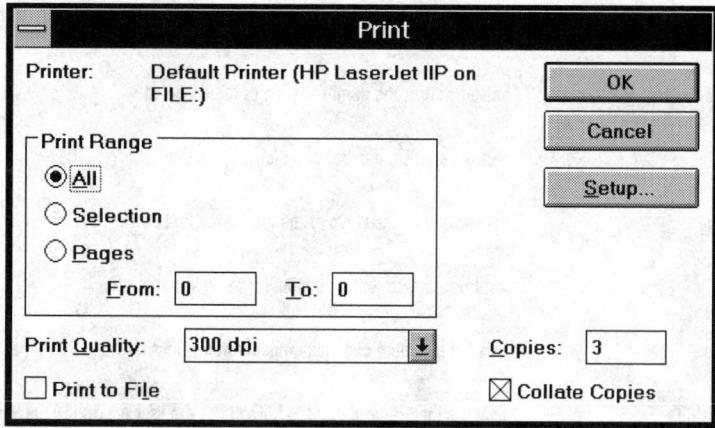

Figure 17-4 Example syntax displays this Print common dialog box

The Summary section at the beginning of this chapter explains how to use these CONSTANT.TXT flag values. Make sure CONSTANT.TXT is loaded into a module somewhere in your application to properly use them. Specify multiple flags by using the Or operator. For example, use this line to specify showing only WYSI-WYG fonts, which require that the fonts be available to both printer and screen:

```
CMDialog1.Flags = CF_WYSIWYG Or CF_PRINTERFONTS Or CF_SCREENFONTS
```

Print

The Print common dialog box lets the user specify how material is to be printed. It has areas that allow for input of page ranges, number of copies, print quality, collation, and print to file, and has command buttons that allow for setting up the current printer or specifying a different printer. Note that the dialog box does not do any actual printing; your code still has to do that. The example syntax displays the Print common dialog box shown in Figure 17-4, and Tables 17-11 and 17-12 show the properties and flags for the Print dialog box.

Example Syntax

```
Sub Command1_Click ()
    CMDialog1.Copies = 3
    CMDialog1.Flags = PD_ALLPAGES Or PD_COLLATE
    CMDialog1.Action = DLG_PRINT
End Sub
```

Property	Action
Copies	Sets or returns the number of copies to be printed
Flags	Sets or returns a number of options
FromPage	Sets or returns the value of the Print From text box
hDC	Returns a device context handle for the selected printer
Max, Min	Sets the minimum and maximum allowed values for the print range
PrinterDefault	Changes the printer default to the settings the user makes in Printer Setup
ToPage	Sets or returns the value of the Print To text box

Table 17-11 Properties particular to the Print common dialog

If the default printer is selected, you can print directly to the Visual Basic Printer object. If the user selects another printer in Print Setup, you need to use the hDC property to make Windows API calls to the GDI and do your printing directly. Setting the PrinterDefault property to True avoids this challenge by always making the user's selection the default printer.

Flag	CONSTANT.TXT	Meaning
&H0	PD_ALLPAGES	Sets or returns the state of the All Pages option button in Print Range
&H10	PD_COLLATE	Sets or returns the state of the Collate check box
&H80000	PD_DISABLEPRINTTOFILE	Disables the Print To File check box
&H100000	PD_HIDEPRINTTOFILE	Hides the Print To File check box
&H8	PD_NOPAGENUMS	Disables the Print Range option buttons and text boxes
&H80	PD_NOWARNING	Suppresses a warning message if there is no default printer
&H4	PD_NOSELECTION	Disables the Selection option button in Print Range
&H2	PD_PAGENUMS	Sets or returns the state of the Pages option button in Print Range

Flag	CONSTANT.TXT	Meaning
&H40	PD_PRINTSETUP	Display the Print Setup dialog box instead of the Print dialog box
&H20	PD_PRINTTOFILE	Sets or returns the state of the Print To File check box
&H100	PD_RETURNDC	Returns a device context for the printer selected in Print Setup
&H200	PD_RETURNIC	Returns an information context for the printer selected in Print Setup
&H1	PD_SELECTION	Sets or returns the state of the Selection option button in Print Range
&H800	PD_SHOWHELP	Displays a Help button
&H40000	PD_USEDEVMODECOPIES	Disables Copies edit box if printer driver doesn't support multiple copies; stores the requested number of copies in the Copies property if the printer driver does support multiple copies

Table 17-12 Flags particular to the Print common dialog box

The Summary section at the beginning of this chapter explains how to use these CONSTANT.TXT flag values. Make sure CONSTANT.TXT is loaded into a module somewhere in your application to properly use them. Specify multiple flags by using the Or operator. For example, use this line to specify showing the Help button, disabling Print To File, and using the device driver's copies setting:

```
CMDialog1.Flags = PD_SHOWHELP Or PD_HIDEPRINTTOFILE Or PD_USEDEVMODECOPIES
```

Help

The Help common dialog box action doesn't really bring up a dialog box. Instead, it calls WINHELP.EXE and passes it the proper parameters for context-sensitive help, keyword searches, or even help on Help. Tables 17-13 and 17-14 show the properties and arguments of the Help settings.

Example Syntax

```
Sub Command1_Click ()
    CMDialog1.HelpFile = "MYAPP.HLP"
    CMDialog1.HelpCommand = HELP_KEY
    CMDialog1.HelpKey = "Graphing"
    CMDialog1.Action = 6
End Sub
```

651

Property	Action
HelpCommand	Specifies the type of help
HelpContext	Specifies the context ID of the Help topic
HelpFile	Specifies the name of the Help file
HelpKey	Specifies the keyword for a keyword search

Table 17-13 The properties that deal with common dialog Help procedures

HelpCommand	CONSTANT.TXT	Meaning
&H1	HELP_CONTEXT	Display Help for a context; use the HelpContext property to specify
&H4	HELP_HELPONHELP	Display Help for using the Help application
&H3	HELP_INDEX	Display the Index for a Help file
&H101	HELP_KEY	Display help for a particular keyword; use HelpKeyword to specify
&H2	HELP_QUIT	Terminate the Help file
&H5	HELP_SETINDEX	Choose a particular index in the Help file; use HelpContext to specify

Table 17-14 Meanings of the values for the HelpCommand property of the Help common dialog box

The Summary section at the beginning of this chapter explains how to use these CONSTANT.TXT values. Make sure CONSTANT.TXT is loaded into a module somewhere in your application to properly use them.

Example

The Dialog project at the end of this chapter focuses almost entirely on displaying each of these common dialog boxes. Each box is brought up by a menu command after having the appropriate properties and flags set correctly.

Comment

You cannot specify where any common dialog box appears on the screen.

INPUTBOX$ FUNCTION

Purpose

The InputBox$ function displays a dialog box with a message and a text box in which the user may enter some text. It returns a string containing the text entered by the user. The InputBox$ function is thus an alternative to designing a form with a text box for simple text input. Table 17-15 summarizes the arguments for the InputBox$ function.

General Syntax

```
InputBox$(Prompt$ [, BoxName$][, DefaultText$][, Left%, Top%])
```

Arguments	Description
Prompt$	Instructions for the user
BoxName$	The title of the dialog box
DefaultText$	Default entry in the dialog's text box
Left%, Top%	Placement of the dialog box on the screen

Table 17-15 Arguments of the InputBox$ function

Example Syntax

```
Sub Command1_Click ()
    Title$ = "Greetings"
    Prompt$ = "What is your name?"
    Default$ = ""
    X% = 2000
    Y% = 4000
    N$ = InputBox$(Prompt$, Title$, Default$, X%, Y%)
End Sub
```

Description

Use the InputBox$ function when you want to get a line of text from the user. InputBox$ displays a dialog box that contains an OK button and a Cancel button, a text box for user input, and the text specified by the Prompt$ argument. The Prompt$ argument may be any string expression of up to approximately 255 characters (the exact number of characters allowed is determined by the width of the characters used). If this string is too long to fit on one line in the dialog box, the text will automatically wrap around to the next line. You may force a new line by inserting a carriage return/line feed pair (Chr$(13) & Chr$(10)) in the prompt string.

The BoxName$ argument specifies the text displayed in the title area of the dialog box. If this argument is not used, the title bar will be empty.

When the dialog box displays, the text specified by the DefaultText$ argument is automatically placed in the dialog's text box. This argument specifies a default entry in the text box; normally, this is what you anticipate will be the most frequently used response. This text is selected, so any new entry will replace it unless the user presses (HOME), (END), (←), or (→), or clicks on the text box with the mouse. If this argument is not used, the text box will be empty when the dialog box initially displays. Note that you can either define an optional argument as an empty string ("") and name it in the function call, or put a comma in place of the omitted argument. For example, the following two lines function identically:

```
N$ = InputBox$("Type your name", "", "", 500, 750)
N$ = InputBox$("Type your name",,, 500, 750)
```

The Left% and Top% arguments specify the position of the dialog box on the screen. They must both be used or both be omitted. These are integer numbers expressed in twips. A twip is a measurement equal to 1/1440 of a printed inch. The Top% argument indicates the distance between the top of the screen and the top of the dialog box. The Left% argument specifies the distance between the left edge of the screen and the left edge of the dialog box. If these arguments are omitted, the

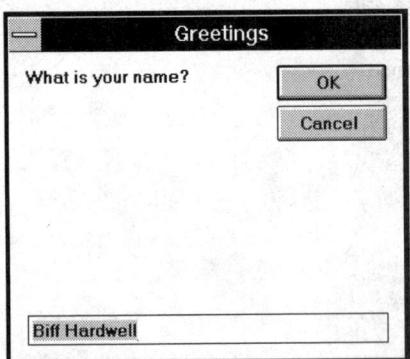

Figure 17-5 Example syntax displays this Input box

box will be centered horizontally, and placed one-third of the way from the top of the screen. See Chapter 5, Application Appearance, for more about screen measurements and positioning objects.

While the dialog box is displayed, the user can type text in its text box. When the user clicks on the OK button, or presses the (ENTER) key, the dialog box will disappear and return the string in the text box. Optionally, the user can click on the Cancel button, or press the (ESC) key. This also makes the dialog box disappear, but the string returned is null ("").

The example syntax displays a dialog box with the title "Greetings" that asks for the user's name, as shown in Figure 17-5.

Example

The Dialog project at the end of this chapter uses an InputBox$ function to get a file name from the user in the error-handling section of the File Open routine.

MSGBOX FUNCTION

Purpose

The MsgBox function displays a dialog box with a message and an optional icon. Your program instructs the function to display one or more sets of predefined command buttons on the dialog box. When the user selects one of these buttons, this function returns a number based on the selected button. The arguments for the MsgBox function are summarized in Tables 17-16, 17-17, 17-18, 17-19, and 17-20.

General Syntax

```
MsgBox(Message$[, Options%][, BoxName$])
```

Arguments	Description
Message$	A string expression containing a message to the user
Options%	An integer value specifying which icon (if any) and button set will be used with the dialog box
BoxName$	A string expression that will be used for the title of the dialog box

Table 17-16 Arguments of the MsgBox function

Button Value	CONSTANT.TXT Value	Meaning of Value
0	MB_OK	(Default) Display an OK button only
1	MB_OKCANCEL	Display OK and Cancel buttons
2	MB_ABORTRETRYIGNORE	Display Abort, Retry, and Ignore buttons
3	MB_YESNOCANCEL	Display Yes, No, and Cancel buttons
4	MB_YESNO	Display Yes and No buttons
5	MB_RETRYCANCEL	Display Retry and Cancel buttons

Table 17-17 Values for the buttons displayed with the MsgBox function and statement

Default Value	CONSTANT.TXT Value	Meaning of Value
0	MB_DEFBUTTON1	(Default) Sets first button as default
256	MB_DEFBUTTON2	Sets second button as default
512	MB_DEFBUTTON3	Sets third button as default

Table 17-18 Values for the default button setting with the MsgBox function and statement

Icon Value	CONSTANT.TXT Value	Displays	Used For
16	MB_ICONSTOP	Red STOP sign	Critical messages
32	MB_ICONQUESTION	Question mark in green circle	Queries
48	MB_ICONEXCLAMATION	Exclamation mark in red circle	Warnings
64	MB_ICONINFORMATION	Letter "i" in a blue circle	Informative messages

Table 17-19 Values for the icons displayed with the MsgBox function and statement

Return Value	CONSTANT.TXT Value	Button That Was Pressed
1	IDOK	OK
2	IDCANCEL	Cancel
3	IDABORT	Abort
4	IDRETRY	Retry
5	IDIGNORE	Ignore
6	IDYES	Yes
7	IDNO	No

Table 17-20 Values returned by the MsgBox function

Example Syntax

```
Sub FileOpen ()
    On Error Goto DinnaOpen
    Open "Zirfgrod.prn" For Input As #1
Exit Sub

DinnaOpen:
    ButtonPressed = MsgBox("Disk Error", MB_ABORTRETRYIGNORE, "Cannot Open File")
    Select Case ButtonPressed
        Case IDABORT, IDIGNORE   'Abort, Ignore
            Exit Sub
        Case IDRETRY             'Retry
            Resume
    End Select
End Sub
```

Description

The MsgBox function displays a message in a dialog box with an optional icon. Your program specifies a set of buttons to display on the dialog box, and the function returns a value that indicates which button the user clicked on. You use this function to get a decision from the user. Figure 17-6 shows a typical use of the MsgBox function.

The Message$ argument specifies the text that prompts the user. This must be a string expression of up to 1024 characters. Any characters past the 1024-character limit will be truncated. The message will automatically word wrap at the

657

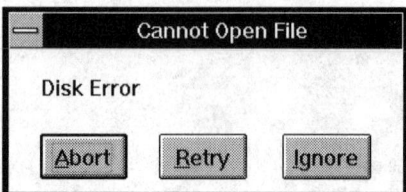

Figure 17-6 Example syntax displays
this MsgBox

right edge of the box. However, this word wrapping requires that spaces appear
somewhere within the text. If no spaces are present, the displayed string is truncated at the 255th character. You may force a new line by inserting a carriage
return/line feed pair (Chr$(13) & Chr$(10)) in the message string.

The Options% argument determines the appearance of the dialog box. The
value of this argument controls three things: the icon displayed (if any) the command buttons displayed, and which command button will be the default. The
Summary section at the beginning of this chapter explains how to use CON-
STANT.TXT values for this argument. Make sure CONSTANT.TXT is loaded
into a module somewhere in your application to properly use them.

Button Types

The MsgBox function has six predefined sets of buttons that may be displayed on
its dialog box. The Options% argument specifies which of these sets are used. Each
set provides a group of possible answers to a specific type of question. For instance,
one set displays Abort, Retry, and Ignore buttons. You can use this set to give the
user a choice of actions to take when the program encounters some sort of hardware error. Another set displays Yes, No, and Cancel buttons. A good use for this
set is to ask the user if he or she wishes to save any open files before exiting a program. Table 17-17 summarizes the six sets of buttons available to the MsgBox function. If no button set is specified, the dialog box displays one OK button.

Default Button

The default button on the dialog box is the button whose value will be returned
if the user presses the (ENTER) key. Normally, the leftmost button on the dialog box
is set as the default button. However, you may change the default to another button by setting the Options% argument to one of the values defined in Table 17-18.
If a dialog box displays a Cancel button, the Cancel button's value will be
returned if the user presses the (ESC) key.

Icon

Placing an icon on the dialog box helps the user understand the nature of the dialog box. For example, suppose the user has instructed your program to delete a

Figure 17-7 MB_ICONSTOP (16); use for critical messages

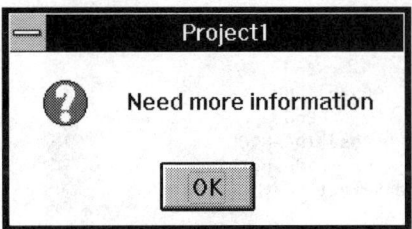

Figure 17-8 MB_ICONQUESTION (32); use for queries

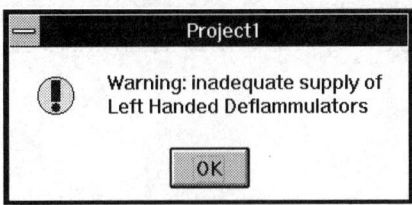

Figure 17-9 MB_ICONEXCLAMA-TION (48); use for warnings

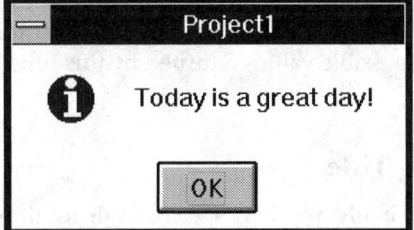

Figure 17-10 MB_ICONINFORMA-TION (64); use for informative messages

file. Knowing that people can make mistakes, you might want to display a message in a dialog box and make the user confirm the action. Displaying the familiar stop sign in the dialog box is a good visual tool to let the user know that a critical operation is about to be performed. Your program uses the Options% argument to specify one of several predefined icons. Table 17-19 summarizes the types of icons available and their values; Figures 17-7 through 17-10 show the actual icons.

Combining the Various Options

You specify a combination of the above settings by using the logical Or operator. For instance, to display a critical error dialog box with Yes, No, and Cancel buttons, and the Cancel button as the default, your code would look something like this (keep in mind that this example uses constants that are declared by placing the CONSTANT.TXT file in the program's global module). Figure 17-11 shows the resulting dialog box.

```
Sub Command1_Click ()
    MB_Options = MB_YESNOCANCEL Or MB_DEFBUTTON3 Or MB_ICONQUESTION
    ButtonPressed = MsgBox("Save open files before exiting?", MB_Options)
    Select Case ButtonPressed
```

(continued on next page)

659

(continued from previous page)

```
        Case IDYES
            SaveFiles
            End
        Case IDNO
            End
        Case IDCANCEL
            'do nothing
    End Select
End Sub
```

Returned Value

When the user chooses a button, the dialog box disappears and the function will return a value indicating which button was chosen. Table 17-20 summarizes the possible values returned by this function.

Dialog Title

Finally, you may specify a title for the dialog box using the boxName$ argument. This argument must be a string expression, and will be displayed in the title area of the dialog box. If this argument is omitted, the name of the project is displayed. For instance, if your project is named "Project1," that is what will be displayed.

Example

The chapter project uses the MsgBox function to ask the user if they wish to Abort, Retry, or Fail after a failed attempt to open a text file. This occurs in the File Open error-handling routine.

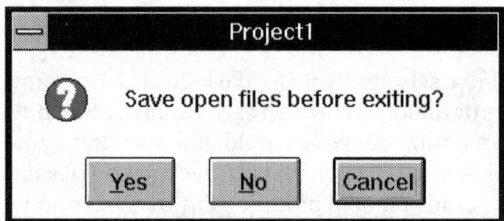

Figure 17-11 Example syntax shows multiple MB constants used to define MsgBox parameters

660

MSGBOX STATEMENT

Purpose

The MsgBox statement displays a dialog box with a message, an OK button, and an optional icon. The only user action is acknowledging the message by clicking on the OK button. No value is returned to the program. Table 17-21 summarizes the arguments of the MsgBox statement; Tables 17-17 through 17-20 in the MsgBox$ function entry summarize the values of the Options% argument.

General Syntax

```
MsgBox Message$[, Options%][, BoxName$]
```

Argument	Description
Message$	A string expression containing a message to the user
Options%	An integer value specifying which icon, if any, and button set will be used with the dialog box
BoxName$	A string expression that will be used for the title of the dialog box

Table 17-21 Arguments of the MsgBox statement

Example Syntax

```
Form_Load ()
    MsgBox "Greetings!", 48
End Sub
```

Description

The MsgBox statement displays a message in a dialog box. The message displayed is specified by the Message$ argument. This must be a string expression up to 1024 characters long. Any characters past the 1024-character limit will be truncated. The message will automatically word wrap at the right edge of the box. However, this word wrapping requires that spaces appear somewhere within the text. If no spaces are present, the displayed string is truncated at the 255th

Figure 17-12 Example syntax shows the MsgBox statement used to produce a simple acknowledgment

character. You may force a new line by inserting a carriage return/line feed pair (Chr$(13) + Chr$(10)) in the message string.

The Options% argument determines the appearance of the dialog box. The value of this argument controls three things: the command buttons to be displayed, which command button will be the default, and which icon (if any) will be displayed. This argument is used in the same manner as the Options% argument of the MsgBox function. Its possible values are defined in Tables 17-17, 17-18, 17-19, and 17-20 in the preceding entry. Just as with the MsgBox function, you can use this argument to define a specific set of buttons to place on the dialog box. However, because the MsgBox statement returns no value, there is no way for your program to determine which button the user chose. Therefore it is useless to specify that any buttons aside from the default OK button be displayed on the MsgBox statement's dialog box.

You may specify a title for the dialog box using the BoxName$ argument. This argument must be a string expression, and will be displayed in the title area of the dialog box. If this argument is omitted, the name of the project is displayed. For instance, if your project is named "Project1," that is what will be displayed.

The example syntax creates a box that displays the message "Greetings" together with the exclamation mark icon, as shown in Figure 17-12.

Example

The File Open error handling routine in the chapter project uses the MsgBox statement to confirm that no text was overwritten during a failed attempt to open a text file.

THE DIALOG PROJECT

Project Overview

This project demonstrates each of the built-in kinds of dialog boxes: MsgBox function, MsgBox statement, InputBox, and each of the common dialog boxes. The main form has a text box to display sample text, and another form serves as a user-defined dialog box.

Assembling the Project: formMain

1. Make a form with the objects and properties listed below in Table 17-22. After placing these controls on the form, start the Menu Designer up using the Window's Menu command. Use Table 17-23 as a guide to set up the menu structure.

Object	Property	Setting
Form	BorderStyle	2–Sizable
	Caption	Dialog Project
	Name	formMain
CMDialog	Name	cdlgBox
Text	Name	textEntry
	Multiline	-1 True
	Scrollbars	2–Vertical

Table 17-22 Property settings for the Dialog project

Name	Caption	Property	Setting
menuBar	&File	Index	0
menuFile	&Open	Index	0

(continued on next page)

(continued from previous page)

Name	Caption	Property	Setting
menuFile	&Save	Index	1
menuFile		Index	2
menuFile	&Print Setup	Index	3
menuFile		Index	4
menuFile	E&xit	Index	5
menuBar	F&ormat	Index	1
menuFormat	&Color	Index	0
menuFormat	&Font	Index	1
menuBar	&Help	Index	2
menuHelp	&VB MsgBox	Index	0
menuHelp	&Search	Index	1
menuHelp	-	Index	2
menuHelp	&About	Index	3

Table 17-23 Menu settings for formMain

2. Size and place the objects as shown in Figure 17-13.

3. Place the following lines in the General Declarations section. These define the constants used throughout the program.

```
'MsgBox constants
 Const MB_ABORTRETRYIGNORE = 2
 Const MB_ICONEXCLAMATION = 48
 Const MB_DEFBUTTON3 = 512
 Const IDABORT = 3
 Const IDRETRY = 4
 Const IDIGNORE = 5

'Common Dialog Control
'Action Property
 Const DLG_FILE_OPEN = 1
```

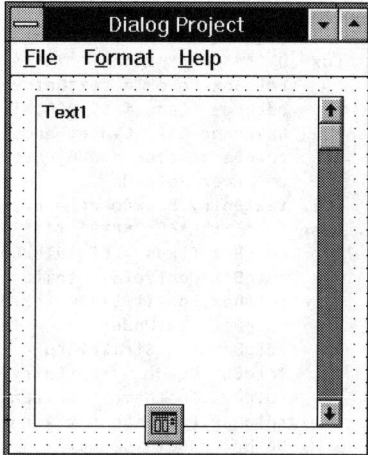

Figure 17-13 The Dialog project during design

```
Const DLG_FILE_SAVE = 2
Const DLG_COLOR = 3
Const DLG_FONT = 4
Const DLG_PRINT = 5
Const DLG_HELP = 6

'Individual flags
Const CC_RGBINIT = &H1&
Const CF_BOTH = &H3&
Const CF_EFFECTS = &H100&
Const PD_ALLPAGES = &H0&
Const HELP_KEY = &H101
Const HELP_PARTIALKEY = &H105
Const HELP_QUIT = &H2
```

4. Place the following code in the menuFormat_Click event. It changes the background color of the text box using the Color common dialog box and changes the font the text displays in. An On Error Goto CancelFormat statement precedes each call to the common dialog box to set an error trap. If the user presses cancel on the common dialog box, the error routine simply does nothing and exits the procedure.

    The Color command first sets the dialog's color to match the current background of Text1, tells it that we're using RGB values to specify colors, and then calls the common dialog box using the Color action constant. All common dialog boxes are modal, so the next line only executes once the user closes the Color dialog box. It sets the background color of Text1 to whatever the user specified.

    The Font command will set all the font attributes for Text1 using the Font common dialog box. It first sets all the font parameters for the dialog box to equal what's already in Text1. After calling the Font dialog box, it then sets all the parameters for Text1 to what the user selects in the dialog box.

665

```
Sub menuFormat_Click (Index As Integer)
    Select Case Index
        Case 0 '**************************** color
            cdlgBox.Color = textEntry.BackColor          'default color
            cdlgBox.Flags = CC_RGBINIT                   'set for rgb values
            On Error GoTo CancelFormat                   'trap for user pressing cancel
            cdlgBox.Action = DLG_COLOR                   'Display color box
            On Error GoTo 0                              'user didn't press cancel
            textEntry.BackColor = cdlgBox.Color          'set the new color
        Case 1 '**************************** font
            cdlgBox.Flags = CF_BOTH Or CF_EFFECTS        'both printer and screen
            cdlgBox.FontBold = textEntry.FontBold        'set the dialog box's default
            cdlgBox.FontItalic = textEntry.FontItalic    'values to what's already in
            cdlgBox.FontUnderLine = textEntry.FontUnderline   'the text box
            cdlgBox.FontStrikeThru = textEntry.FontStrikethru
            cdlgBox.Color = textEntry.ForeColor
            cdlgBox.FontName = textEntry.FontName
            cdlgBox.FontSize = textEntry.FontSize
            On Error GoTo Cancel                         'trap for user pressing cancel
            cdlgBox.Action = DLG_FONT                    'Display the Font dialog box
            On Error GoTo 0                              'user didn't press cancel
            textEntry.FontBold = cdlgBox.FontBold        'set the text box's properties
            textEntry.FontItalic = cdlgBox.FontItalic
            textEntry.FontStrikethru = cdlgBox.FontStrikeThru
            textEntry.FontUnderline = cdlgBox.FontUnderLine
            textEntry.ForeColor = cdlgBox.Color
            textEntry.FontName = cdlgBox.FontName
            textEntry.FontSize = cdlgBox.FontSize
    End Select
Exit Sub

CancelFormat:                                            'user pressed cancel key
    'just exit sub without doing anything
End Sub
```

5. Place the following code in the menuHelp_Click event. The first command calls up the Visual Basic Help file on the MsgBox command by using the common dialog box's HELP_KEY HelpCommand. The Search command uses HELP_PARTIALKEY to bring up the help program's Search dialog box. The About command displays the About custom dialog box.

```
Sub menuHelp_Click (Index As Integer)
    Select Case Index
        Case 0 '********************** VB Help
            cdlgBox.HelpFile = "VB.HLP"                  'we're going to call up VB help
            cdlgBox.HelpCommand = HELP_KEY               'search for a keyword
            cdlgBox.HelpKey = "MsgBox"                   'ask about MsgBox!
            cdlgBox.Action = DLG_HELP                    'do it
        Case 1 '********************** Search
            cdlgBox.HelpFile = "VB.HLP"                  'we're going to call up VB help
            cdlgBox.HelpCommand = HELP_PARTIALKEY        'bring up search box
            cdlgBox.Action = DLG_HELP                    'do it
        Case 2 '(separator bar)
        Case 3 '********************** About
            formAbout.Show 1                             'show about box modally
    End Select
End Sub
```

6. Place the following code in the menuFile_Click event. It calls up the Open common dialog box to read a file into Text1, the Save As common dialog box to simulate saving the file, and the Print common dialog box to set up the printer, and it has the Exit command to Exit the program. The File Open error-handling routine uses the three other predefined dialog boxes. An On Error Goto CancelFile statement precedes each call to the common dialog box to set an error trap. If the user presses cancel on the common dialog box, the error routine simply does nothing and exits the procedure.

The File Open command is the most involved routine. Note how we set the filter to read-only text files (*.TXT) but leave the user the option of reading all files (*.*). We set an error trap before attempting to open the file in case something goes wrong (for example, if the user types in a name by hand in the File Name box for a nonexistent file). If the file opens correctly, the routine reads in up to ten lines of text and assigns the text to Text1 before exiting the subroutine.

If an error occurs while opening the file, the DinnaOpen error handler takes over. It first displays a MsgBox asking the user to Abort, Retry, or Ignore. It uses the answer to select which action to take. If the user Aborts, then the routine displays a warning MsgBox to confirm that the text has not been altered. If Retry, the routine asks the user to type in another file name in an InputBox function. (This, of course, is for demonstrating the InputBox function; a better approach would be to redisplay the Open dialog box.) After getting the user's input, the routine attempts to Resume at the "Open For Input" statement. Ignore simply exits the subroutine.

The Save routine calls up the Save As common dialog box. Note that we don't really save anything to prevent this project from wiping out anything during the demonstration! The default for the Save As dialog box is to warn on overwrite, so experiment with trying to overwrite a file safe in the knowledge that nothing will happen.

The Print routine simply calls up the Print common dialog box and prints the contents of the text box.

The Exit routine first calls the Help common dialog to close down the Help file opened by the Help command. It then ends the program.

```
Sub menuFile_Click (Index As Integer)
    Select Case Index
        Case 0 '***************************** Open
            Dim lines As Integer, newLine As String, bigLine As String
            Dim mbType As Integer, buttonPressed As Integer, Filename As String

            cdlgBox.DialogTitle = "Open Text File"
            cdlgBox.Filter = "Text Files (*.TXT)|*.TXT|All Files (*.*)|*.*"
            cdlgBox.FilterIndex = 1                      'set default to text files
            On Error GoTo CancelFile                     'trap for user pressing cancel
            cdlgBox.Action = DLG_FILE_OPEN               'Show the File Open dialog
            Filename = cdlgBox.Filename                  'store the filename

            On Error GoTo DinnaOpen                      'set error trap
            Open Filename For Input As #1                'open up the file
            On Error GoTo 0                              'successful! turn off trap
```

(continued on next page)

(continued from previous page)

```
                Do While (Not EOF(1)) And Lines < 10          'read in up to 10 lines
                    Line Input #1, newLine                    'get the line
                    bigLine = bigLine & newLine & Chr$(13) & Chr$(10) 'append the line
                    Lines = Lines + 1
                Loop
                textEntry.Text = bigLine                      'assign the line to the text box
                Close                                         'close the text file
        Case 1 '***************************** Save
                cdlgBox.DefaultExt = "TXT"
                cdlgBox.DialogTitle = "Save Text File"
                cdlgBox.Filter = "Text Files (*.TXT)|*.TXT|All Files (*.*)|*.*"
                cdlgBox.FilterIndex = 1
                On Error GoTo CancelFile                      'trap for user pressing cancel
                cdlgBox.Action = DLG_FILE_SAVE                'Show the File Open dialog
                On Error GoTo 0                               'didn't press cancel
                                                              'We're not really going ⇐
                                                              'to write anything

        Case 2 '(separator bar)
        Case 3 '***************************** Print Setup
                cdlgBox.PrinterDefault = True
                cdlgBox.Flags = PD_ALLPAGES
                On Error GoTo CancelFile                      'trap for user pressing cancel
                cdlgBox.Action = DLG_PRINT                    'Display Print dialog box
                On Error GoTo 0                               'user didn't press cancel
                Printer.Print textEntry.Text
        Case 4 '(separator bar)
        Case 5 '***************************** Exit
                cdlgBox.HelpFile = "VB.HLP"                   'we're going to call up VB help
                cdlgBox.HelpCommand = HELP_QUIT               'to close down the help file
                cdlgBox.Action = DLG_HELP                     'do it
                End                                           'end program
        End Select
Exit Sub

CancelFile:                                                   'user pressed cancel key
        Exit Sub

DinnaOpen:                                                    'oops! bad file name
    mbType = MB_ABORTRETRYIGNORE Or MB_DEFBUTTON3 Or MB_ICONEXCLAMATION
    buttonPressed = MsgBox("Disk Error", mbType, "Cannot Open File") 'what to do?
    Select Case buttonPressed
        Case IDABORT                                         'stop the action
            MsgBox "Text is unchanged"                       'confirm nothing happened
            Exit Sub                                         'and leave
        Case IDRETRY                                         'let's do it again!
            Filename = InputBox$("Enter new filename:")      'plug in a new filename by hand
            Resume                                           'and try to open it again
        Case IDIGNORE                                        'no big deal, just ignore it
            Exit Sub                                         'and leave
    End Select
End Sub
```

7. Enter the following code in the Form_Load event. This tells the common dialog
   box to generate a trappable error when the user presses the (CANCEL) key.

```
Sub Form_Load ()
    cdlgBox.CancelError = True          'trap for user pressing cancel
End Sub
```

668

8. Enter the following code in the Form_Resize event. This resizes the text box to take up the entire form when the form changes size.

```
Sub Form_Resize ()
    textEntry.Top = 0                      'make the text box fill the whole form
    textEntry.Left = 0
    textEntry.Height = formMain.ScaleHeight
    textEntry.Width = formMain.ScaleWidth
End Sub
```

Assembling the Project: formMain

1. Make a form with the objects and properties listed in Table 17-24.

Object	Property	Setting
Form	BackColor	&H00C0C0C0—Light Gray
	BorderStyle	3—Fixed Double
	Name	formAbout
Command	Caption	OK
	Default	True
	Name	cmndOK
Label	AutoSize	-1—True
	Caption	Dialog Project
	FontSize	24

Table 17-24 Elements of formAbout

2. Position the controls as shown in Figure 17-14.

3. Enter the following code in the Form_Load event. This occurs when the form first loads. It duplicates the existing label twice, and then moves the copies very slightly out of position. It colors one white (to serve as a highlight) and the other the same light gray as the form. The original label's color was black, and this serves as the "shadow." It then brings the light gray one up, to the top of the

669

Figure 17-14 The formAbout form
during design

stack. The resultant effect looks like the form has been embossed with the words
"Dialog Project." This illustrates why the built-in dialog boxes don't work for all
occasions—think of how much weaker the MsgBox function would be in this
context. The functionality would be identical, but this custom dialog box looks
a lot snazzier.

```
Sub Form_Load ()
        offset = 14                                  'how deep is inset effect
        Load lablProject(1)                          'create two identical
        Load lablProject(2)                          'label copies to create inset
        lablProject(1).ForeColor = QBColor(15)   'White (highlight)
        lablProject(1).Left = lablProject(0).Left - 1.8 * offset
        lablProject(1).Top = lablProject(0).Top - 1.8 * offset
        lablProject(1).Visible = True
        lablProject(2).ForeColor = QBColor(7)    'Light Gray (same as background)
        lablProject(2).Left = lablProject(0).Left - offset
        lablProject(2).Top = lablProject(0).Top - offset
        lablProject(2).Visible = True
        lablProject(2).ZOrder                        'bring to front of stack
End Sub
```

4. Enter the following code in the cmndOK_Click event. This just hides the form.

```
Sub cmndOK_Click ()
      Hide
End Sub
```

How It Works

As you can see, a small amount of code and form design produces the illusion of
a great deal of thought and effort in this project. Using the common dialog boxes
gives this project the air of a commercial application with hardly any effort. Note
that the single common dialog box control brings up all six of the common dialog box types.

The main form calls up each of the six common dialog boxes. Figure 17-15
shows the main form in action, after having set the fonts and colors. The bulk of
the code in each subroutine sets up the dialog box parameters before display, and
then displays the box. As this project demonstrates, using the common dialog

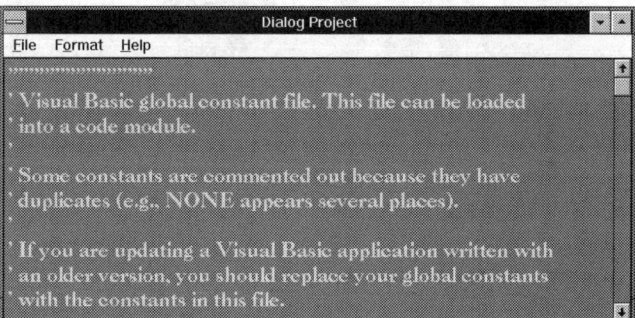

Figure 17-15 The Dialog project in action

boxes with mostly default parameters gives great results. The common dialog boxes have quite a lot of built-in intelligence, and will alter themselves or display warning messages automatically given various user input.

Note that the common dialog box is always modal; that is, your code stops executing until the dialog box closes.

We display the three other types of built-in dialog boxes in the Open errorhandling routine. This shows typical examples of specifying parameters for the MsgBoxes and InputBox before and during the box display. Note how we use the returned button value in the MsgBox function to choose which action to take.

Finally, the Help About command brings up a custom dialog box. Although the functionality is the same as the MsgBox statement (single line of text with an OK button), this dialog box does some tricky formatting the MsgBox statement couldn't do. Figure 17-16 shows the About box with its embossed text.

Figure 17-16 Sometimes you need to use a customized dialog box to get the effect you want

18

LISTS, COMBOS, AND GRIDS

Visual Basic provides several powerful controls for presenting lists from which users can choose options such as colors, styles, fonts, or even data records. Selection lists can even be combined with text input to give the user the choice of selecting a listed item or typing in the name of some other choice. One style of list box, three styles of combo boxes, and the powerful new grid control provide you with a variety of tools for presenting a list of choices or displaying information to the user.

LIST BOXES

The list box contains a list of items that have been defined by the program. The user may choose an item from a list box by clicking on it, or by using the up and down arrow keys to move the highlight bar to the desired item and then pressing (ENTER). If there are more items in the list than can be displayed in the list box, Visual Basic will automatically add a scroll bar on the right edge of the list box. The user can then scroll up and down the list quickly with the mouse or the (PAGEUP) and (PAGEDN) keys.

COMBO BOXES

Combo boxes, as the name implies, provide a combination of the List Box and the Text Box objects. All combo boxes have an edit area and a list area. The currently selected item from the list displays in the edit area of a combo box. The list area appears below the edit area, and when visible, acts in the same manner as a list box. There are three styles of combo boxes: the drop-down combo, the simple combo, and the drop-down list.

The drop-down combo box displays the currently selected item in an edit area similar to that of a text box. A down arrow is displayed to the right of the edit area. The list portion of this combo box stays hidden until the user clicks the down arrow, causing the list of items to drop down. The user may either choose an item from the list, or type an entry in the edit area.

The simple combo box also has an edit area in which the currently selected item is displayed. The list portion of this combo box is always visible under the edit area. As with the drop-down combo, the user may either choose an item from the list or type an entry in the edit area.

The drop-down list box is similar in structure to the drop-down combo box. As with the drop-down combo, the list area stays hidden until the user clicks on the down arrow. However, the user cannot edit the text in the edit area, but can only choose an item from the list portion of the drop-down list.

The types of list and combo boxes are summarized in Table 18-1.

Use This Type of Box...	To Do This...
Simple list box	Present a list of items for selection
Drop-down combo	Let user type in a selection, or open a list from which to make a selection
Simple combo	Let user type in a selection, or select from a list that is always visible
Drop-down list box	Let user accept displayed selection, or open a list for a different selection

Table 18-1 Types of list and combo boxes

GRIDS

The versatile grid control, introduced in Visual Basic 2.0, gives you the power of a two-dimensional list box with many additional features. The grid control allows you to set up display structures similar to a spreadsheet. Rows and columns intersect to form individual cells. These cells may have their contents changed independently, and may be selected individually or as a region. You also have the facility to create fixed rows and columns, which would be familiar to spreadsheet users as Row and Column heads (A1, B3, and so on). Both text and graphics may be placed in the cells.

Although the grid control looks similar to a spreadsheet, it has no inherent calculation properties. It is merely a collection of cells that you may manipulate with code, and that the user may interact with. One vital difference between the grid control and a spreadsheet is that the user may not directly change the contents of a cell. Much like a list box, the grid needs all of its values set by program code.

The grid control can be used for any task that requires displaying data in rows and columns. Although a spreadsheet is the most familiar metaphor, other possibilities include database tables, general ledger "printouts," and even multiple-column pick lists.

USING LISTS AND COMBO BOXES

Lists and combo boxes are quite similar to work with. When you first create a list or combo box, there are no items in the control's list. Items need to be added to a control's list from within your program's code. This is done with the AddItem method. Visual Basic keeps track of how many items have been added to a list, and places that number in the ListCount property. Items may be deleted from a list with the RemoveItem method. When this is done, the ListCount property is automatically updated to reflect that an item has been removed.

The lists of these controls are quite similar to one-dimensional string arrays. Each entry is assigned an index number when it is added to the list. Your program can specify the index number of an item when it is added, or Visual Basic can automatically assign the index number. The string value of each listed entry can be read by your program with the List property. Your program supplies an index number to this property, which returns a string copy of the listed item specified by the index. Note that multicolumn list boxes are still a one-dimensional array. The data snakes from column to column; it does not have different kinds of information in each column. Use the grid control for that.

The idea of using a list or combo box is so your program can determine the user's choice from a list of items. The ListIndex and Text properties are used to determine which item in the list the user has selected. The ListIndex property returns the index number of the selected item, while the Text property returns a string copy of the selected item. The Selected property lets you determine if a list item is selected in a multiple-selection list box.

USING GRIDS

You use a grid control by first dimensioning it with the Rows and Cols properties to set the number of rows and columns in the grid. You can change these properties at will to dynamically resize your grid control. You can then set individual column widths and row heights as well as specify if data is to be left-aligned, right-aligned, or centered.

You can use the AddItem method to add new data to a grid, much like a list or combo box. More commonly, though, you'll either select a region and assign a group of values to the selection with the Clip property, or activate an individual cell with the Row and Col properties to assign its Text or Picture properties.

LISTS, COMBOS, AND GRIDS SUMMARY

Table 18-2 displays the methods, events, and properties that influence the settings and effects of the list, combo box, and grid controls.

Use or Set This...		To Do This...
AddItem	Method	Add items to the list, combo box, or grid
CellSelected	Property	Determine if the grid's active cell is selected
Clear	Method	Clear all items from a list or combo box
Clip	Property	Read or set a selected region in a grid
ColAlignment	Property	Read or set the alignment of a column's data in a grid
Cols, Rows	Property	Read or set the total number of columns or rows in a grid
Columns	Property	Set or return the number of columns in a list box
ColWidth	Property	Read or set the width of a column in a grid
DropDown	Event	Initiate an action when a drop-down box is opened
FixedAlignment	Property	Read or set the alignment of data in the fixed cells of a column in a grid
FixedCols, FixedRows	Property	Read or set the number of grid's fixed rows or columns on the left and top
Gridlines	Property	Read or set whether the gridlines are visible
HighLight	Property	Read or set whether the selected cells appear highlighted in a grid
ItemData	Property	Read or set an associated data item with the list entry
LeftCol	Property	Read or set the leftmost visible nonfixed column in a grid

Use or Set This...		To Do This...
List	Property	Set or return the text in a list entry in a list or combo box
ListCount	Property	Return the number of items in a list or combo box
ListIndex	Property	Set or return the index number of the selected item in a list or combo box
MultiSelect	Property	Set or return if a list box allows for multiple selections
NewIndex	Property	Determine the ListIndex value of the newest added item in a list or combo
RemoveItem	Method	Remove an item from a list, combo box, or grid
RowColChange	Event	React to a new cell becoming active in a grid
RowHeight	Property	Read or set the height of a row in a grid
SelChange	Event	React to a new selection in a grid
Selected	Property	Return the selection status of listed items in a MultiSelect list box
SelEndCol, SelEndRow, SelStartCol, SelStartRow	Property	Read or set the starting or ending row or column in a grid
Sorted	Property	Sort the items in a list or combo box
Style	Property	Set the style of a combo box
Text	Property	Return the selected item in a list, combo box, or grid cell
TopRow	Property	Read or set the topmost nonfixed row in a grid

Table 18-2 Methods, events, and properties dealing with list and combo boxes

CONSTANT.TXT Values

Two of the properties in this chapter use numeric values as arguments. Using constants rather than the literal value makes your code self-documenting, more readable, and easier to debug.

Microsoft provides a file, CONSTANT.TXT, that has many constant declarations defined for you. For smaller applications it's probably easiest just to type the declarations in yourself. For larger applications you'll find it much easier to read the text file into a new module.

To do this, create a new module by pulling down the File menu and choosing the New Module menu command. Then pull down the File menu again, and choose Load Text. This opens up a dialog box listing all text files in the current directory. CONSTANT.TXT should be in your main Visual Basic directory (default installation would place this in C:\VB). Simply choose CONSTANT.TXT to enter the entire file into your module. These constants will then be available throughout your application.

Table 18-3 lists the value of the constant, the CONSTANT.TXT constant name, and a brief description of what the constant means.

Value	CONSTANT.TXT	Meaning
ColAlignment and FixedAlignment		
0	GRID_ALIGNLEFT	(Default) Left-align column data
1	GRID_ALIGNRIGHT	Right-align column data
2	GRID_ALIGNCENTER	Center-align column data

Table 18-3 CONSTANT.TXT values for lists, combos, and grids

The following pages describe the use of the methods, event, and properties that enable you to set up and manage the various types of list, grids, and combo boxes. The ListBox project at the end of the chapter demonstrates how these list management techniques are used together.

ADDITEM METHOD

Objects Affected

Check	Clipboard	▶ Combo	Command	CommonDlg
Data	Debug	Dir	Drive	File
Form	Frame	▶ Grid	Image	Label
Line	▶ List	MDI Form	Menu	OLE
Option	Picture	Printer	Screen	Scroll
Shape	Text	Timer		

678

Purpose

The AddItem method adds an item to the list of a grid, list box, or combo box. Table 18-4 summarizes the arguments of the AddItem method.

General Syntax

```
[form!]Name.AddItem Item$ [, Index%]
```

Argument	Description
form	Name of the control's parent form
Name	Name of the list, combo box, or grid
Item$	A string expression containing the value that is being added to the list
Index%	An optional index number specifying the placement of the new item in the list

Table 18-4 Arguments of the AddItem method

Example Syntax

```
Sub Form_Load ()
    List1.AddItem "Red"        'Add color names to a list box
    List1.AddItem "Blue"
    List1.AddItem "Yellow"
    List1.AddItem "Green"
    List1.AddItem "Purple"
End Sub
```

Description

When the list box and combo box objects first display, no items are assigned to the list. You must use the AddItem method to create list entries. When the AddItem method executes, the value of the string expression specified by the item$ argument is added to the list.

You can specify the exact placement of the new item in the list by providing the index argument. If you supply the index number, Visual Basic will add one to the index number of the item that currently holds the specified index, and all those items that follow it. The new item is then added to the list at the specified index (see Figure 18-1). Supplying an index number inserts the new item at that position in the list. It does not replace the item that is currently at that position.

679

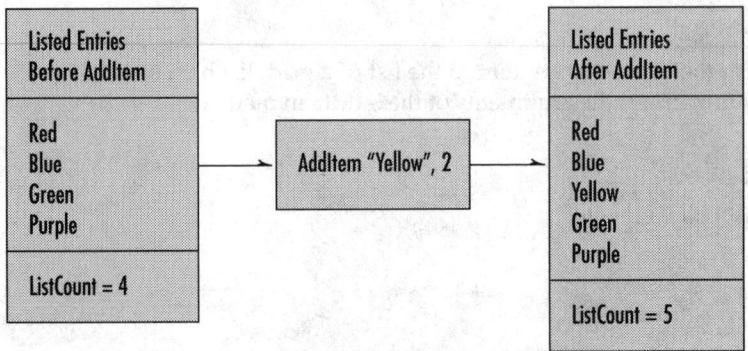

Figure 18-1 Specifying a specific index with the AddItem method

If you supply the index number, it must be no less than 0 and no greater than the value of the ListCount property. If the index specified is not in this range, Visual Basic issues an Illegal function call error.

The index numbering of the list is zero-based. Therefore, if a list contains five items, the first item is index number 0, and the highest index number is 4. Most often, the AddItem method is used in the Form_Load event of the parent form to initialize the list entries. This ensures the list is loaded before the user has access to the list or combo box.

If you omit the index argument, Visual Basic assigns the next available index number to the new item. In other words, if there are five items in the list, the highest index number will be 4. Therefore the next available index number will be 5.

The example syntax adds five color names to a list box. Assuming nothing was added previously, "Red" will have index 0, "Blue" index 1, and so on. Figure 18-2 shows how this list box looks when loaded.

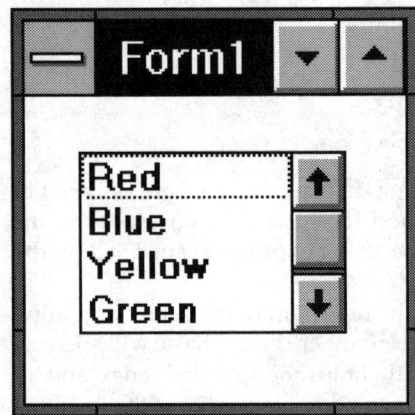

Figure 18-2 Example syntax uses the AddItem method to load the list box

Example

The Form_Load event in the ListBox project uses the AddItem method to initialize several combo boxes with their settings. Each time the user specifies a new financial scenario, the combIncome_DropDown event adds the new scenario to the combo box. Finally, for each new set of values, the NewValues subroutine adds a record of the calculation to the listHistory list box.

Comments

It is not recommended that the index argument of the AddItem method be used with a list or combo box that has the Sorted property set to True. This may cause the sort order of the list to be corrupted.

CELLSELECTED PROPERTY

Objects Affected

Check	Clipboard	Combo	Command	CommonDlg
Data	Debug	Dir	Drive	File
Form	Frame	▶ Grid	Image	Label
Line	List	MDI Form	Menu	OLE
Option	Picture	Printer	Screen	Scroll
Shape	Text	Timer		

Purpose

Use the CellSelected property to determine whether the current cell (as specified by the Row and Col properties) is within the grid's selected region. Not available at design time, read-only at runtime. Table 18-5 summarizes the arguments of the CellSelected property.

General Syntax

`[form!]Name.CellSelected`

Argument	Description
form	Name property of the form
Name	Name property of the grid control

Table 18-5 Arguments of the CellSelected property

Example Syntax

```
Sub Command1_Click ()
    If Grid1.CellSelected Then
        Text1.Text = Grid1.Text
    End If
End Sub
```

Description

Use the CellSelected property to find out if the active cell is selected or not. The active cell is the cell specified by the Row and Col properties. A user can select cells by dragging over them with a mouse, or by pressing a (SHIFT)-(→) combination.

You can use the SelStartCol, SelStartRow, SelEndCol, and SelEndRow properties to determine the boundaries of the selected region.

Example

The ListBox project at the end of this chapter checks the CellSelected property each time the user changes from cell to cell or selects new cells. Routines in both the RowColChange and SelChange events check the value and display a status value in the lablCellSelected label.

CLEAR METHOD

Objects Affected

Check	▶ Clipboard	▶ Combo	Command	CommonDlg
Data	Debug	Dir	Drive	File
Form	Frame	Grid	Image	Label
Line	▶ List	MDI Form	Menu	OLE
Option	Picture	Printer	Screen	Scroll
Shape	Text	Timer		

Purpose

The Clear method clears all the items from a list or combo box in one statement. The Clipboard also has a Clear method, which is discussed in more detail in Chapter 23, Using the Clipboard. Table 18-6 gives the arguments of the Clear method.

682

General Syntax

```
[form!]Name.Clear
```

Argument	Description
form	Name of the parent form
Name	The Name of the combo box or list box

Table 18-6 Arguments of the Clear method

Example Syntax

```
Sub Command1_Click ()
    List1.Clear
End Sub
```

Description

The Clear method gives you an easy way to completely clear a list box or combo box. In Visual Basic 1.0, you had to use the RemoveItem method for each item in a Do loop or For-Next loop; Visual Basic 2.0 and 3.0 let you accomplish the same thing more easily with the Clear method. Using the Clear method also saves time compared to removing each item individually, and will make your application perform better.

Example

The sample project at the end of the chapter uses the Clear method to (surprise!) clear the list box of all items when the user double-clicks on it.

CLIP PROPERTY

Objects Affected

Check	Clipboard	Combo	Command	CommonDlg
Data	Debug	Dir	Drive	File
Form	Frame	▶ Grid	Image	Label
Line	List	MDI Form	Menu	OLE
Option	Picture	Printer	Screen	Scroll
Shape	Text	Timer		

Purpose

Use the Clip property to read or set the contents of the cells in a selected region. This is the most efficient method of reading or setting large areas of a grid control. Not available at design time, read only at runtime. Table 18-7 summarizes the arguments of the Clip property.

General Syntax

```
[form!]Name.Clip [ = expression$]
```

Argument	Description
form	Name property of the form
Name	Name property of the Grid control
expression$	Contains delimited values to place in selected cells

Table 18-7 Arguments of the Clip property

Example Syntax

```
Sub Command1_Click ()
    Grid1.Rows = UBound(Addresses, 1)            '# of rows in array (Option Base 1)
    Grid1.Cols = UBound(Addresses, 2)            '# of columns in array
    Grid1.SelStartCol = 1                        'Select the entire grid
    Grid1.SelStartRow = 1                        'of non-fixed cells
    Grid1.SelEndCol = Grid1.Cols - 1
    Grid1.SelEndRow = Grid1.Rows - 1
    For i = 1 To Grid1.Rows                      'step through each array row
        For j = 1 To Grid1.Cols                  'step through each array column
            data$ = data$ & Addresses(i, j)      'add data value to string
            If j <> Grid1.Cols Then              'if not at end of row,
                data$ = data$ & Chr$(9)          'add item delimiter
            End If
        Next j
        data$ = data$ & Chr$(13)                 'new row; add row delimiter
    Next i
    Grid1.Clip = data$                           'put the data into the grid
End Sub
```

Description

Use the Clip property to read or set large regions of the grid control. The string expression this property uses delimits each entry with a tab character (Chr$(9))

and each row with a carriage return (Chr$(13)). The Clip property uses values like this:

```
value TAB value TAB value CR value TAB value TAB value CR value TAB value TAB value CR
R1C1      R1C2      R1C3      R2C1      R2C2      R2C3      R3C1      R3C2      R3C3
```

The example syntax builds up a string expression from a two-dimensional array. It iterates through each item of the array, adding the data value to the string expression, and adding a tab character if it's not at the end of a row, and a carriage return character if it is at the end of a row.

The Clip property only operates on a selected region. If no cells are selected, it returns a null string; if you attempt to assign a string expression to a grid with no selected cells, the string is ignored. If the selected region is smaller than the number of items in the string expression, extra entries are ignored. If the selected region is larger than the number of items in the string expression, then the unassigned cells get set to a null string.

Example

The ListBox project at the end of this chapter uses the Clip property to save and restore the contents of the grid to a file. Both cmndOpen_Click and cmndSave_Click use the Clip property to do this. cmndSave_Click is the simplest: it just writes the entire Clip property to disk without modification. The cmndOpen_Click event reads in the contents of file one line at a time and reassembles the string by appending each line plus a carriage return. It then assigns the built up string to the Clip property to restore the grid contents.

Comment

The graph control in the Professional Version of Visual Basic uses this same format for its QuickData property. You can assign the contents of a grid to the graph with a single line of code:

```
Graph1.QuickData = Grid1.Clip
```

COL, ROW PROPERTIES

Objects Affected

Check	Clipboard	Combo	Command	CommonDlg
Data	Debug	Dir	Drive	File
Form	Frame	▶ Grid	Image	Label
Line	List	MDI Form	Menu	OLE
Option	Picture	Printer	Screen	Scroll
Shape	Text	Timer		

Purpose

Use the Col and Row properties to determine or set the active cell in a grid. Once an active cell is set, you can use other properties on that cell, such as Text and Picture. Not available at design time, read and write at runtime. Table 18-8 summarizes the arguments of the Col and Row properties.

General Syntax

```
[form!]Name.Col [ = column%]
[form!]Name.Row [ = row%]
```

Argument	Description
form	Name property of the form
Name	Name property of the grid control
column%	Column number of active cell
row%	Row number of active cell

Table 18-8 Arguments of the Col and Row properties

Example Syntax

```
Sub Command1_Click ()
    Grid1.Rows = UBound(Addresses, 1)        '# of rows in array (Option Base 1)
    Grid1.Cols = UBound(Addresses, 2)        '# of columns in array
    For i = 1 To Grid1.Rows                   'step through each nonfixed grid row
        For j = 1 To Grid1.Cols               'step through each nonfixed grid column
            Grid1.Col = j                     'set active cell's column
            Grid1.Row = i                     'set active cell's row
            Grid1.Text = Addresses(i, j)      'place data in cell
        Next j
    Next i
End Sub
```

Description

A grid control consists of a two-dimensional array of cells. Each cell belongs to a specific row and column. The Col and Row properties set the active cell using the column and row numbers. You can use other properties (like Text or Picture) once you've set the active cell.

686

Grids are zero-based; that is, the first column's number is 0 and the first row is 0. The Cols and Rows properties (*not* the same as the Col and Row properties we're discussing here!) set the total number of columns and rows in a grid.

The example syntax steps through each nonfixed row and column of the grid and assigns it the value contained in the array. The Col and Row properties set which cell to update.

Example

The ListBox project at the end of this chapter uses Col and Row many times to both set the active cell and to determine which cell is active. You'll find Col and Row in the Form_Load, gridSheet_RowColChange, and NewValues procedures.

COLALIGNMENT PROPERTY

Objects Affected

Check	Clipboard	Combo	Command	CommonDlg
Data	Debug	Dir	Drive	File
Form	Frame	▶ Grid	Image	Label
Line	List	MDI Form	Menu	OLE
Option	Picture	Printer	Screen	Scroll
Shape	Text	Timer		

Purpose

Use the grid's ColAlignment property to read or set the alignment of a column's data. You can specify left-aligned, right-aligned, or centered. Not available at design time, read and write at runtime. Only available for nonfixed columns; use the FixedAlignment property to set the alignment for fixed columns. Tables 18-9 and 18-10 summarize the arguments of the ColAlignment property.

General Syntax

```
[form!]Name.ColAlignment(column%) [ = alignment%]
```

Argument	Description
form	Name property of the form
Name	Name property of the grid control
column%	Number of the column (starting from the far left, column%=0)
alignment%	Expression indicated left-, right-, or center-aligned

Table 18-9 Arguments of the ColAlignment property

alignment%	CONSTANT.TXT	Meaning
0	GRID_ALIGNLEFT	(Default) Left-align column data
1	GRID_ALIGNRIGHT	Right-align column data
2	GRID_ALIGNCENTER	Center-align column data

Table 18-10 Meanings of the alignment% argument in the grid's ColAlignment property

Example Syntax

```
Sub Form_Load ()
    Combo1.AddItem "Left"
    Combo1.AddItem "Right"
    Combo1.AddItem "Center"
End Sub

Sub Combo1_Click ()
    'Combo has the alignments in the correct order
    Grid1.ColAlignment(Grid1.Col) = Combo1.ListIndex    'set current column's alignment
End Sub
```

Description

Each column in a grid may have its own alignment—left-, right-, or center-aligned. The ColAlignment property lets you read or set the alignment of individual columns. Choose one of the three possible alignments, as summarized in Table 18-10. The Summary section at the beginning of this chapter covers the use of the CONSTANT.TXT values.

688

This property only affects cells in nonfixed rows. A grid may have both fixed and nonfixed rows. Fixed rows are typically used for headings like "1992," "1993," "1994," and so on. Use the FixedAlignment property to set the alignment of cells in fixed rows.

The example syntax uses a combo box that has been filled with the alignment possibilities in the correct order. It uses the combo box's ListIndex property to set the alignment of the column with the active cell.

Example

The Listbox project at the end of this chapter uses a combo box, as in the example syntax above, to set the grid's alignment. The cmboAlign_Click event does this.

COLS, ROWS PROPERTIES

Objects Affected

Check	Clipboard	Combo	Command	CommonDlg
Data	Debug	Dir	Drive	File
Form	Frame	▶ Grid	Image	Label
Line	List	MDI Form	Menu	OLE
Option	Picture	Printer	Screen	Scroll
Shape	Text	Timer		

Purpose

Use the Cols and Rows properties to read or set the total number of columns or rows in a grid. Not available at design time; read and write at runtime. Table 18-11 summarizes the arguments of the Cols and Rows properties.

General Syntax

```
[form!]Name.Cols [ = columns%]
[form!]Name.Rows [ = rows%]
```

Argument	Description
form	Name property of the form
Name	Name property of the grid control

(continued on next page)

(continued from previous page)

Argument	Description
columns%	Number of columns in a grid, including any fixed columns, up to a maximum of 400
rows%	Number of rows in a grid, including any fixed rows, up to a maximum of 2000

Table 18-11 Arguments of the Cols and Rows properties

Example Syntax

```
Sub Command1_Click ()
    Grid1.Rows = UBound(Addresses, 1)       '# of rows in array (Option Base 1)
    Grid1.Cols = UBound(Addresses, 2)       '# of columns in array
    For i = 1 To Grid1.Rows                  'step through each non-fixed grid row
        For j = 1 To Grid1.Cols              'step through each non-fixed grid column
            Grid1.Col = j                    'set active cell's column
            Grid1.Row = i                    'set active cell's row
            Grid1.Text = Addresses(i, j)     'place data in cell
        Next j
    Next i
End Sub
```

Description

Use the Cols and Rows properties to read or set the total number of rows and columns in a grid. The example syntax shows how the grid is set up to include each entry of a two-dimensional array. The Cols and Rows properties set up the grid with enough cells to include the entire array.

The maximum number of columns in a grid is 400; the maximum number of rows is 2000. These totals include any fixed rows or columns. You may dynamically change the number of rows and columns in a grid to account for changes in your data. If you expand a grid's size, all existing values contained in the grid are maintained. If you make a grid smaller, data in the remaining cells remains unaffected; data in the now-nonexistent cells disappears.

Example

The ListBox project at the end of this chapter assigns the Cols and Rows properties in the Form_Load event to initially dimension the grid. It also reads the Cols and Rows properties several times to set the selection range, as in the cmndOpen_Click and cmndClose_Click events.

Comment

The Cols and Rows properties are not the same as the Col and Row properties. Cols and Rows set the total number of columns and rows; Col and Row determine the active cell.

COLUMNS PROPERTY

Objects Affected

Check	Clipboard	Combo	Command	CommonDlg
Data	Debug	Dir	Drive	File
Form	Frame	Grid	Image	Label
Line	▶ List	MDI Form	Menu	OLE
Option	Picture	Printer	Screen	Scroll
Shape	Text	Timer		

Purpose

The Columns property lets you scroll a list box horizontally rather than vertically. Note that the list box is still a one-dimensional array; use the grid control if you need a two-dimensional array. Columns defaults to 0 (vertical scrolling). Numbers greater than 0 make it scroll horizontally, with the number indicating the number of columns. Entries will snake automatically from column to column. Table 18-12 summarizes the arguments of the Columns property.

General Syntax

[form!]Name.Columns [= number%]

Argument	Description
form	Name of the parent form
Name	Name of the list box
number%	Number of columns

Table 18-12 Arguments of the Columns property

Example Syntax

```
Sub Form_Load ()
    numFonts = Screen.FontCount                 'how many fonts?
    numColumns = Int((numFonts + 25) / 25)      'break into reasonable # of columns
    List1.Columns = numColumns                  'make enough columns
    For i = 0 To numFonts                       'and fill list box
        List1.AddItem Screen.Fonts(i)           'horizontally scrolling
```

(continued on next page)

(continued from previous page)

```
        List2.AddItem Screen.Fonts(i)          'vertically scrolling
    Next i
End Sub
```

Description

The Columns property lets you scroll a list box horizontally rather than vertically if you wish. It defaults to 0, meaning you get a familiar vertically scrolling list box. Setting number% to something greater than 0 gives that many columns. The width of each column is automatically set to the width of the list box divided by the number of columns. Items snake from column to column, filling each column in sequence from left to right.

The number of columns may not change from 0 to anything else, or from anything else to 0 at runtime. That is, you can never convert a vertically scrolling list box into a horizontally scrolling list box. However, you may change the number of columns in a horizontally scrolling list box, as the example syntax shows. Figure 18-3 compares a horizontally and vertically scrolling list box.

Example

The ListBox project at the end of this chapter uses vertically scrolling list boxes (columns = 0).

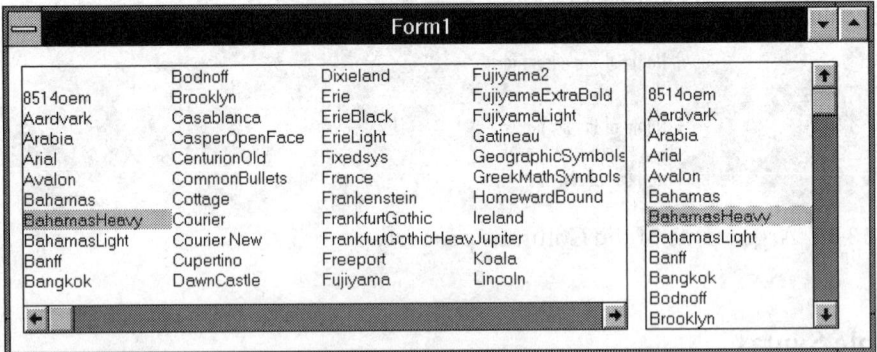

Figure 18-3 Example syntax compares horizontally and vertically scrolling list boxes

692

COLWIDTH AND ROWHEIGHT PROPERTIES

Objects Affected

Check	Clipboard	Combo	Command	CommonDlg
Data	Debug	Dir	Drive	File
Form	Frame	▶ Grid	Image	Label
Line	List	MDI Form	Menu	OLE
Option	Picture	Printer	Screen	Scroll
Shape	Text	Timer		

Purpose

The ColWidth property reads or sets the width of a column in a grid; the RowHeight property reads or sets the height of a row in a grid. Not available at design time, read and write at runtime. Table 18-13 summarizes the arguments of the ColWidth and RowHeight properties.

General Syntax

```
[form!]Name.ColWidth(column%) [ = width&]
[form!]Name.RowHeight(row%) [ = height&]
```

Argument	Description
form	Name property of the form
Name	Name property of the grid control
column%	Number of the column; leftmost column is 0
row%	Number of the row; topmost row is 0
width&	Width of the column in twips
height&	Height of the row in twips

Table 18-13 Arguments of the ColWidth and RowHeight properties

693

Example Syntax

```
Sub Form_Load ()
    Grid1.Rows = 10
    Grid1.Cols = 10
    Grid1.ColWidth(O) = 500
    For i = 1 to Grid1.Rows - 1
        Grid1.RowHeight = 300
    Next i
End Sub
```

Description

Use the ColWidth and RowHeight properties to read or set the width and height of your grid's columns and rows. The user may also adjust the sizes with the mouse by clicking and dragging the gridlines of a fixed row or column.

The sizes are always expressed in twips, with 1440 twips per inch. See Chapter 9, The Coordinate System, for more information about the twips measurement system. You may wish to use the TextHeight and TextWidth properties discussed in Chapter 11, Displaying Text, to help determine the correct settings for the particular font and text you're displaying.

Example

The ListBox project at the end of this chapter uses ColWidth and RowHeight in the Form_Load event to help initialize the grid. The user can also click and drag on the gridlines to manually reset these properties.

DROPDOWN EVENT

Objects Affected

Check	Clipboard	▶ Combo	Command	CommonDlg
Data	Debug	Dir	Drive	File
Form	Frame	Grid	Image	Label
Line	List	MDI Form	Menu	OLE
Option	Picture	Printer	Screen	Scroll
Shape	Text	Timer		

Purpose

The DropDown event specifies what actions will be taken when the user opens the list portion of a drop-down combo box. This provides your program with an opportunity to tailor the list entries based on information that may not have been available at an earlier time, such as the activity the user is performing or preferences previously expressed by the user. Table 18-14 summarizes the arguments of the DropDown event.

General Syntax

```
Sub Name_DropDown([Index As Integer])
```

Argument	Description
Name	Name of the control
Index	A unique number that identifies a specific element in a control array

Table 18-14 Arguments of the DropDown event

Example Syntax

```
Sub Title_DropDown()
    If UserSecurity > 100 then           'If this is a high level user
        If Title.ListCount = 4 then
            Title.AddItem "Manager"      'Add Manager title to list if not yet added
        End if
    End If
End Sub
```

Description

The combo box control used with the DropDown event must be either a drop-down combo box (Style = 0) or drop-down list box (Style = 2). In drop-down boxes, the list portion of the control is not visible until the user opens it by clicking on its scroll arrow. When this happens the control's DropDown event triggers. The code in this event executes before the user can choose from the items in the list.

The example syntax adds an item (the title "Manager") to the list box if the user's security level is high enough. This is an example of how the DropDown event can be used to tailor the choices offered by the program to the circumstances of the user.

Control Array

The index argument is only used if the related control is part of a control array. This index specifies which element of the array is the one that activated the event. When referencing the control, the element being referenced must be specified by placing the index number between parentheses just after the control name, and before the property name (that is, Name(Index).Property).

Example

The ListBox project at the end of this chapter uses the DropDown event to help complete cmboIncome's list. If the user has typed in a new entry that's not already a member of the list, the DropDown event automatically adds that entry to the list.

FIXEDALIGNMENT

Objects Affected

Check	Clipboard	Combo	Command	CommonDlg
Data	Debug	Dir	Drive	File
Form	Frame	▶ Grid	Image	Label
Line	List	MDI Form	Menu	OLE
Option	Picture	Printer	Screen	Scroll
Shape	Text	Timer		

Purpose

Use the FixedAlignment property to read or set the alignment of data in the fixed cells of a grid's column. Not available at design time, read and write at runtime. Tables 18-15 and 18-16 summarize the arguments of the FixedAlignment property.

General Syntax

```
[form!]Name.FixedAlignment(column%) [ = alignment%]
```

Argument	Description
form	Name property of the form
Name	Name property of the grid control
column%	Number of the column (starting from the far left, column%=0)
alignment%	Expression indicating left-, right-, center-aligned; or use ColAlignment setting

Table 18-15 Arguments of the ColAlignment property

alignment%	CONSTANT.TXT	Meaning
0	GRID_ALIGNLEFT	(Default) Left-align column data
1	GRID_ALIGNRIGHT	Right-align column data
2	GRID_ALIGNCENTER	Center-align column data
3	n/a	Use the setting from ColAlignment

Table 18-16 Meanings of the alignment% argument in the grid's FixedAlignment property

Example Syntax

```
Sub Form_Load ()
    Grid1.Rows = 10
    Grid1.Cols = 10
    For i = 0 to Grid1.Cols - 1
        Grid1.ColAlignment(i) = GRID_ALIGNRIGHT
        Grid1.FixedAlignment(i) = GRID_ALIGNCENTER
    Next i
End Sub
```

Description

The FixedAlignment property determines the alignment for grid cells in a fixed column. This alignment may be different from the ColAlignment setting, so the grid's column headings may be aligned differently than the actual data.

The settings are the same as for the ColAlignment property, except for FixedAlignment=3. This setting will make the fixed cells aligned the same as the nonfixed cells.

Example

The ListBox project at the end of this chapter uses the Form_Load event to set the fixed column's alignment to right-aligned.

FIXEDCOLS, FIXEDROWS PROPERTIES

Objects Affected

Check	Clipboard	Combo	Command	CommonDlg
Data	Debug	Dir	Drive	File
Form	Frame	▶ Grid	Image	Label
Line	List	MDI Form	Menu	OLE
Option	Picture	Printer	Screen	Scroll
Shape	Text	Timer		

Purpose

Use the FixedCols and FixedRows properties to read or set the number of fixed rows or columns on the left and top of a grid. Fixed rows and columns are typically used for row and column headings. Not available at design time, read and write at runtime. Table 18-17 summarizes the arguments of the FixedCols and FixedRows properties.

General Syntax

```
[form!]Name.FixedCols [ = columns%]
[form!]Name.FixedRows [ = rows%]
```

Argument	Description
form	Name property of the form
Name	Name property of the grid control
columns%	Number of fixed columns, defaults to 1
rows%	Number of fixed rows, defaults to 1

Table 18-17 Arguments of the FixedCols and FixedRows properties

Example Syntax

```
Sub Form_Load ()
    Grid1.Rows = 10
```

698

```
      Grid1.Cols = 10
      Grid1.FixedRows = 2
      Grid1.FixedCols = 2
End Sub
```

Description

You may wish to give your grid headings for the rows and columns. The FixedCols and FixedRows properties let you define stationary rows and columns to put these headings in. Fixed rows and columns are always visible even if the user scrolls the nonfixed cells away from the edges. This means that heading information you put into the fixed rows and columns is always available to help the user locate their data.

Fixed rows and columns display in gray, and this cannot be changed. They can have their own alignment separate from the nonfixed cells by using the FixedAlignment property. The user may manually change the ColWidth and RowHeight properties by clicking and dragging the gridlines in fixed rows and columns.

You may have any number of fixed rows and columns from 0 to one less than the total number of rows or columns (Rows -1) or (Cols - 1). This means that a grid will always have at least one nonfixed cell. These properties default to 1 fixed row or column.

Example

The ListBox project at the end of this chapter uses the default of one fixed row and column.

GRIDLINES PROPERTY

Objects Affected

Check	Clipboard	Combo	Command	CommonDlg
Data	Debug	Dir	Drive	File
Form	Frame	▶ Grid	Image	Label
Line	List	MDI Form	Menu	OLE
Option	Picture	Printer	Screen	Scroll
Shape	Text	Timer		

Purpose

Use the Gridlines property to read or set whether a grid's gridlines are visible. Gridlines are the light gray lines that visually separate individual cells. Available at design time, read and write at runtime. Tables 18-18 and 18-19 summarize the arguments of the Gridlines property.

General Syntax

```
[form!]Name.Gridlines [ = boolean%]
```

Argument	Description
form	Name property of the form
Name	Name property of the grid control
boolean%	True/False value indicates if gridlines are visible or not

Table 18-18 Arguments of the Gridlines property

boolean%	Meaning
True	(Default) Gridlines are visible between cells
False	Gridlines are not visible between cells

Table 18-19 Meanings of the boolean% argument in the Gridlines property

Example Syntax

```
Sub Check1_Click ()
    Grid1.Gridlines = Not Grid1.Gridlines
End Sub
```

Description

Gridlines are the light gray lines that visually separate cells in the grid. You can use the Gridlines property to turn the lines on and off. The default is to display the gridlines.

Gridlines make it easier for the user to navigate around your grid and give visual feedback for the size and location of individual cells. There may be times, however, when you'd like to display the data without the gridlines. For example, a nicely formatted on-screen report would look better without them.

Example

The cmboGridlines combo box sets the Gridlines property on and off. The combo box is first loaded with the two list items "Gridlines" and "No Gridlines," and its ItemData property is set with the correct value for each choice. The cmboGridlines_Click event then simply assigns the ItemData property to the grid's Gridlines property to set the gridline state.

HIGHLIGHT PROPERTY

Objects Affected

Check	Clipboard	Combo	Command	CommonDlg
Data	Debug	Dir	Drive	File
Form	Frame	▶ Grid	Image	Label
Line	List	MDI Form	Menu	OLE
Option	Picture	Printer	Screen	Scroll
Shape	Text	Timer		

Purpose

The grid's Highlight property reads or sets whether the selected cells appear highlighted. Available at both design time and runtime. Tables 18-20 and 18-21 summarize the arguments of the Highlight property.

General Syntax

```
[form!]Name.Highlight [ = boolean%]
```

Argument	Description
form	Name property of the form
Name	Name property of the grid control
boolean%	True/False value that indicates whether or not selected cells are highlighted

Table 18-20 Arguments of the Highlight property

701

boolean%	Meaning
True	(Default) Selected cells appear highlighted
False	Selected cells do not appear highlighted

Table 18-21 Meanings of the boolean% argument in the Highlight property

Example Syntax

```
Sub menuFileSave ()
     Open "SAVEFILE.TMP" For Output As #1      'file to save grid data in
     Grid1.Highlight = False                    'turn off highlighting
     Grid1.SelStartCol = 0                       'select entire grid
     Grid1.SelStartRow = 0
     Grid1.SelEndCol = Grid1.Cols - 1
     Grid1.SelEndRow = Grid1.Rows - 1
     Print #1, Grid1.Clip                        'Save the data
     Grid1.Highlight = True                      'back to normal
     Close #1
End Sub
```

Description

The Highlight property determines whether selected cells appear highlighted. The default is True, as this gives users visual feedback during a select operation. If Highlight is False, then the user can't tell what cells are selected.

You may want to turn off highlighting when your code manipulates the grid. In the example syntax, the entire grid must be selected for the Clip property to work. Highlighting the grid during the select operation would annoy the user, so we turn off highlighting for the duration of the operation, and then turn it back on when finished.

Example

The cmndOpen and cmndSave click events both call the NoHighlight procedure to turn the gridlines on and off when saving the file. The save routines use the Clip property, which requires that there be a selected range.

ITEMDATA PROPERTY

Purpose

The ItemData property lets you associate a numeric item of data with a displayed value in a list. This can save you the step of having to create an array to hold the data items. Table 18-22 summarizes the arguments of the ItemData property.

General Syntax

```
[form!]Name.ItemData(index%) [ = expression&]
```

Argument	Description
form	Name property of the form
Name	Name property of the list or combo box
index%	Unique identifier of the item's list index position
expression&	Value to associate with the list item

Table 18-22 Arguments of the ItemData property

Example Syntax

```
Sub Form_Load ()
    Combo1.AddItem "No Growth"
    Combo1.ItemData(Combo1.NewIndex) = 0
    Combo1.AddItem "Good Growth"
    Combo1.ItemData(Combo1.NewIndex) = 3
    Combo1.AddItem "Great Growth"
    Combo1.ItemData(Combo1.NewIndex) = 8
End Sub
```

Description

You can use the ItemData property to associate a number with a displayed value in a list. This might save you from having to create an array to store the associated values in. The example syntax associates various numeric growth rates with a displayed description of that growth rate.

Note the use of the NewIndex property in the example syntax. Items in a sorted list may be added anywhere in the list to keep it sorted. The NewIndex property returns the index position of the last added item.

Example

The ListBox project at the end of this chapter uses the ItemData property in two places. First, the cmboGridlines combo box associates the correct gridlines settings (-1 and 0) with the descriptions ("Gridlines" and "No Gridlines"). It also uses ItemData to associate an inflation rate to an income to create a complete scenario.

LEFTCOL, TOPROW PROPERTIES

Objects Affected

Check	Clipboard	Combo	Command	CommonDlg
Data	Debug	Dir	Drive	File
Form	Frame	▶ Grid	Image	Label
Line	List	MDI Form	Menu	OLE
Option	Picture	Printer	Screen	Scroll
Shape	Text	Timer		

Purpose

The LeftCol property reads or sets the leftmost visible nonfixed column in a grid. The TopRow property reads or sets the topmost visible nonfixed row in a grid. These properties let you programatically determine what parts of the grid are visible. Not available at design time, read and write at runtime. Table 18-23 summarizes the arguments of the LeftCol and TopRow properties.

General Syntax

```
[form!]Name.LeftCol [ = column%]
[form!]Name.TopRow [ = row%]
```

Argument	Description
form	Name property of the form
Name	Name property of the grid control

Argument	Description
column%	Column number of leftmost visible nonfixed column
row%	Row number of topmost visible nonfixed row

Table 18-23 Arguments of the LeftCol and TopRow properties

Example Syntax

```
Sub Text1_LostFocus ()
    Grid1.Text = Text1.Text
    Grid1.LeftCol = Grid1.Col
    Grid1.TopRow = Grid1.Row
End Sub
```

Description

Use the LeftCol and TopRow properties to programatically scroll the grid. These properties determine the leftmost and topmost visible column and row. You may have code that alters a cell's data when that cell is not visible. Setting these properties to the row and column of the altered cell brings that cell into view, as in the example syntax.

Fixed rows and columns are always in view, so the LeftCol and TopRow properties only scroll to nonfixed cells.

Example

The NewValues procedure in the ListBox project at the end of this chapter always brings R1C1 back in to view when it finishes recalculating a new scenario.

LIST PROPERTY

Objects Affected

Check	Clipboard	▶ Combo	Command	CommonDlg
Data	Debug	▶ Dir	▶ Drive	▶ File
Form	Frame	Grid	Image	Label
Line	▶ List	MDI Form	Menu	OLE
Option	Picture	Printer	Screen	Scroll
Shape	Text	Timer		

Purpose

The List property has two functions. First, it can set the value of a list entry in a list or combo box—that is, specify an item to be displayed on a list. Second, it can read the current value (contents) of a list entry from a list or combo box. This property cannot be set at design time.

The List property is also used with the Drive, Directory, and File list box controls. For a description of how this property is used with these controls, please refer to Chapter 19, File System Controls.

Table 18-24 summarizes the arguments of the List property.

General Syntax

```
[form!]Name.List(Index%) [= Value$]
```

Argument	Description
form	Name of the control's parent form
Name	Name of the list or combo box
Index%	The index number of the desired list entry
Value$	A string expression that can be assigned to the list entry

Table 18-24 Arguments of the List property

Example Syntax

```
Sub Command1_Click ()
    List1.List(1) = "Hello there"      'Assigns the string to list entry #1
    FirstItem$ = List1.List(0)         'Assigns value of the first listed item to a string
End Sub
```

Description

The List property sets or returns a list's contents in a manner similar to accessing values from and assigning values to an array. The List property begins with the name of the affected list or combo box control. It is followed by an index number in parentheses, which identifies which list entry is being referenced. Optionally, an equals sign and a value can be added to assign the specified value to the list entry.

The index numbering of the list is zero-based. Therefore, if a list contains five items, the first item is index number 0, and the highest index number is 4. The number of items in a list can be determined by using the ListCount property.

706

When using the List property to assign text to a list entry, the program must use an index number that references an item currently in the list. For instance, if a list has five items in it, the program can only use an index number from 0 to 4 when assigning a value to a list entry, or an "Invalid property array index" error will occur. Your program can determine the highest current index number by subtracting 1 from the value of the ListCount property.

When using the List property to read list entries, the contents of the list entry specified by the index are returned. Specifying an index that is out of the range of added entries will return a null string.

In the example code, the first statement assigns the string "Hello there" to item 1 in the list for box List1. Note that 1 is actually the second item in the list. The second statement assigns the value of the first item listed in the list (which is index 0) to the string variable FirstItem$.

Example

The Listbox project at the end of this chapter uses the List property to determine the contents of the combo box's list in the cmboIncome_DropDown event. It uses the value of this property to check if the displayed value equals one of the stored values.

LISTCOUNT PROPERTY

Objects Affected

Check	Clipboard	▶ Combo	Command	CommonDlg
Data	Debug	▶ Dir	▶ Drive	▶ File
Form	Frame	Grid	Image	Label
Line	▶ List	MDI Form	Menu	OLE
Option	Picture	Printer	Screen	Scroll
Shape	Text	Timer		

Purpose

The ListCount property is read at runtime to determine the number of listed items in a list or combo box. This is a read-only property, and cannot be set by the program at design time or runtime.

The ListCount property is also used with the Drive, Directory, and File list box controls. For a description of how this property is used with these controls, please refer to Chapter 19, File System Controls.

Table 18-25 summarizes the arguments of the ListCount property.

General Syntax

```
[form!]Name.ListCount
```

Argument	Description
form	Name of the parent form
Name	Name of the list or combo box

Table 18-25 Arguments of the ListCount property

Example Syntax

```
Sub Command1_Click ()
    For i = 0 to List1.ListCount - 1
        Printer.Print List1.List(i)
    Next i
End Sub
```

Description

The ListCount property returns the number of items in a list. Each time the AddItem method is used on a list control, this property automatically increments. Using the RemoveItem method decrements it.

The ListCount property is most commonly used for bounds checking. When working with a list or combo box, you can check possible Index values against this property to make sure your program does not reference a list entry that does not exist. Keep in mind, however, that the index numbering of a list is zero-based, and that the value of the ListCount property is not the same as the highest index number. In other words, if a list has five items in it, the value of ListCount will be 5, while the highest index number in that list will be 4. Thus you could have a test like this:

```
If Index > MyBox.ListCount - 1      ' Bounds error, index too large for list
```

The example syntax uses a For-Next loop with a maximum value of ListCount - 1 to print out the contents of a list box.

Example

The ListBox project at the end of this chapter uses ListCount in the listHistory_MouseDown event to step through each list item in a MultiSelect list to delete the entries, and in the cmboIncome_DropDown event to help step through the list to see if a displayed entry is already on the list.

708

LISTINDEX PROPERTY

Objects Affected

Check	Clipboard	▶ Combo	Command	CommonDlg
Data	Debug	▶ Dir	▶ Drive	▶ File
Form	Frame	Grid	Image	Label
Line	▶ List	MDI Form	Menu	OLE
Option	Picture	Printer	Screen	Scroll
Shape	Text	Timer		

Purpose

The ListIndex property returns the index number of the selected item in a list. The selected item is the one that has been previously set by the program, or highlighted by the user using the arrow keys or by clicking on the item. Assigning a value to the ListIndex property changes the selected item to the entry at the specified index. This property cannot be set at design time.

The ListIndex property is also used with the Drive, Directory, and File list box controls. For a description of how this property is used with these controls, refer to Chapter 19, File System Controls.

Table 18-26 summarizes the arguments of the ListIndex property.

General Syntax

```
[form!]Name.ListIndex [= Index%]
```

Argument	Description
form	Name of the parent form
Name	Name of the list or combo box
Index%	An index number of an item that is currently in the list

Table 18-26 Arguments of the ListIndex property

Example Syntax

```
Sub Command1_Click ()
    L% = List1.ListIndex          'Assigns to L% the index number of the selected item
```

(continued on next page)

709

(continued from previous page)

```
        List1.ListIndex = 0          'Sets the selected item in List1 to the first entry
End Sub
```

Description

Specify the ListIndex property by beginning with the name of the list box or combo box control to be affected. When read, this property returns the index number of the currently selected item in a list. If no item is currently selected, a -1 is returned. If the user enters text in the edit area of the simple or drop-down combo box, and that text does not match a listed item, this property will also return a ListIndex value of -1.

The program may also change the currently selected item of a list by setting this property. When using the ListIndex property to set the currently selected list entry, the program must use an index number that references an item currently in the list. For instance, if a list has five items in it, an index number from 0 to 4 must be used or an "Invalid property array index" error will occur.

In the first statement of the example syntax, the ListIndex property returns the index number of the currently selected item in List1, and assigns it to the variable L%. The second statement in the example syntax sets the selected item on List1 to the item with the index value 0: that is, the first item on the list.

Example

The Form_Load event sets the ListIndex property of the cmboGridlines, cmboAlign, and cmboInflation combo boxes to their default values. The cmboAlign_Click event reads the ListIndex to set the column alignment, and the cmboGridlines uses the ListIndex to help look up the correct ItemData entry to set the Gridlines property. Finally, the cmboIncome_DropDown event sets the ListIndex property to the newest created entry in the list.

Comments

When used with list and combo boxes, using the statement Name.List(ListIndex) gives the same result as Name.Text.

MULTISELECT PROPERTY

Objects Affected

Check	Clipboard	Combo	Command	CommonDlg
Data	Debug	Dir	Drive	▶ File
Form	Frame	Grid	Image	Label

710

Line	▶ List	MDI Form	Menu	OLE
Option	Picture	Printer	Screen	Scroll
Shape	Text	Timer		

Purpose

The MultiSelect property lets the user choose more than one item at a time from a list box. Its three possible states include no multiple selection allowed, simple multiple selection, and extended multiple selection. Tables 18-27 and 18-28 list the arguments of the MultiSelect property.

General Syntax

`[form!]Name.Multiselect`

Argument	Description
form	Name of the parent form
Name	Name of the list box

Table 18-27 Arguments of the MultiSelect property

Setting	Description
0	(Default). Single selection only, multiple selection not allowed
1	Simple multiple selection. Multiple items selected by clicking or the spacebar
2	Extended multiple selection. Whole domains selected with Shift, individual items with Ctrl

Table 18-28 Possible settings for MultiSelect

Example Syntax

```
Sub ShowList (listBox as Control)
    Select Case listBox.MultiSelect
        Case 0                                      'no multiple selection
            Text1.Text = listBox.Text
        Case 1, 2                                   'multiple selections
            For i = 0 to listBox.ListCount - 1
```

(continued on next page)

711

(continued from previous page)

```
                If listBox.Selected(i) Then
                        bigLine = bigLine & listBox(i).List & Chr$(13) & Chr$(10)
                End If
            Next i
            Text1.Text = bigLine
    End Select
End Sub
```

Description

MultiSelect lets the user choose more than one item from a list box. This lets a user perform batch operations (like moving a group of items) instead of repeating several steps over and over for each item to be operated on.

You'll generally set MultiSelect at design time and write your code to either expect a multiple selection or a single selection. It is possible to read (but not set) MultiSelect at runtime, so you could write a generic procedure that can handle either, as in the above example syntax.

The default setting, 0, means that only single selections may be made in the list box. Selecting a new item deselects any previous item. A setting of 1 means that the user can perform a simple multiple selection. The spacebar, or single mouse click, selects or deselects individual items from the list. The user can scroll up or down through the list with the usual movement keys and the scroll bars. A setting of 2 means the user may use extended multiple selection. (SHIFT) clicking or (SHIFT)-(←) extends the selection from the previously selected item to the current item. (CTRL) clicking selects or deselects individual items in the list. The Selected property is set to True whenever the user selects an item. The example syntax loops through the list entries looking for selected items. Figure 18-4 shows a list with multiple selections.

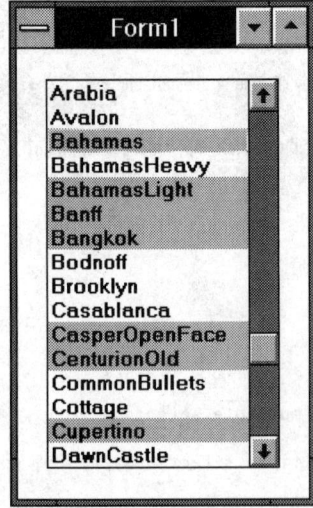

Figure 18-4 The new MultiSelect property lets your list boxes process multiple selections

Example

The ListBox project at the end of this chapter uses a MultiSelect list, listHistory, to keep a record of each scenario used in the calculation. Clicking on the list box with the right mouse button deletes whatever entries are currently highlighted.

NEWINDEX PROPERTY

Purpose

Use the NewIndex property to determine where the newest addition to a sorted list was actually added. Not available at design time, read-only at run-time. Table 18-29 summarizes the arguments of the NewIndex property.

General Syntax

```
[form!]Name.NewIndex
```

Argument	Description
form	Name property of the form
Name	Name property of the list box or combo box control

Table 18-29 Arguments of the NewIndex property

Example Syntax

```
Sub Form_Load ()
    Combo1.AddItem "No Growth"
    Combo1.ItemData(Combo1.NewIndex) = 0
    Combo1.AddItem "Good Growth"
    Combo1.ItemData(Combo1.NewIndex) = 3
    Combo1.AddItem "Great Growth"
    Combo1.ItemData(Combo1.NewIndex) = 8
End Sub
```

Description

Adding items to a sorted list will put that item in an unpredictable position. You can use the NewIndex property to determine where in the list a new item was added. ItemData returns the index number of the last added item, or -1 if there are no items on the list or if an item has been deleted since the last addition.

713

This property is particularly helpful with the ItemData property, as shown above.

Example

The ListBox project at the end of this chapter uses the NewIndex property twice. First, it uses the property much as in the example syntax to set the ItemData property in the cmboIncome_DropDown event. The next line in the event procedure sets ListIndex to equal NewIndex; this selects the newest addition to the list.

REMOVEITEM METHOD

Objects Affected

Check	Clipboard	▶ Combo	Command	CommonDlg
Data	Debug	Dir	Drive	File
Form	Frame	▶ Grid	Image	Label
Line	▶ List	MDI Form	Menu	OLE
Option	Picture	Printer	Screen	Scroll
Shape	Text	Timer		

Purpose

The RemoveItem method deletes an item from the list in a grid, list, or combo box. Table 18-30 summarizes the arguments of the RemoveItem method.

General Syntax

`[form!]Name.RemoveItem Index%`

Argument	Description
form	Name of the parent form
Name	Name of the grid, list, or combo box
Index%	An integer value specifying the index number of the list item to be removed

Table 18-30 Arguments of the RemoveItem method

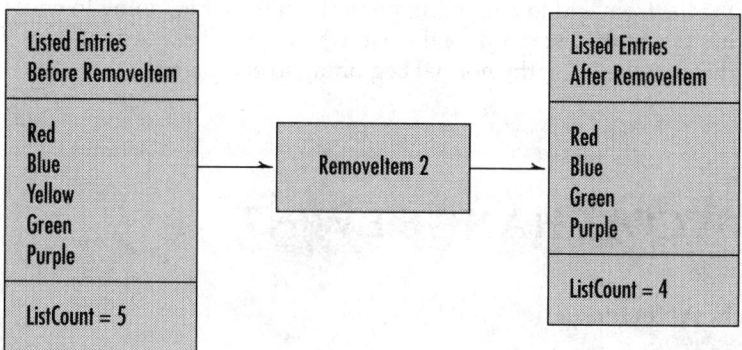

Figure 18-5 Removing an item from a list using the
RemoveItem method

Example Syntax

```
Sub List1_DblClick ()
    L% = List1.ListIndex
    List1.RemoveItem L%
End Sub
```

Description

The RemoveItem method is the complement to the AddItem method. The RemoveItem method deletes from a list or combo box's list the entry indicated by the Index% argument. Begin the specification of the RemoveItem method with the name of the list or combo box to be affected.

When an item is removed from the list, the index number of each entry in the list that followed the removed item is decremented. The ListCount property for the control is also decremented. Figure 18-5 graphically illustrates this process.

Care should be taken when removing items from a list. If your program specifies an index value that is greater than that of the highest current item, Visual Basic will issue an "Illegal function call" error. To be safe, always check the ListCount property before using the RemoveItem method. The index numbering of the list is zero-based. If a list contains five items, the first item has an index of 0, and the highest index number is 4. Therefore the value of supplied index should always be less than the value of the ListCount property.

The example code uses List1's DblClick event to remove the currently selected item from the list.

Example

The listHistory_MouseDown event uses the RemoveItem method to remove highlighted entries from the list. It iterates through the list, checks to see if the item is highlighted, and removes it if it is. Notice that the routine steps through

715

the list from end to beginning rather than from beginning to end: removing an item from the list reorders the list, which would cause problems if we iterated through the list in the normal beginning to end manner.

ROWCOLCHANGE EVENT

Objects Affected

Check	Clipboard	Combo	Command	CommonDlg
Data	Debug	Dir	Drive	File
Form	Frame	▶ Grid	Image	Label
Line	List	MDI Form	Menu	OLE
Option	Picture	Printer	Screen	Scroll
Shape	Text	Timer		

Purpose

Use the RowColChange event to react to the user changing to a different cell. Table 18-31 summarizes the arguments of the RowColChange event.

General Syntax

```
Name_RowColChange ([Index As Integer])
```

Argument	Description
Name	Name property of the grid control
Index	Uniquely identifies member of a control array

Table 18-31 Arguments of the RowColChange event

Example Syntax

```
Sub Grid1_RowColChange ()
    Label1.Caption = "Row " & Grid1.Row & " , Column " & Grid1.Col
End Sub
```

716

Description

Use the RowColChange event to react to the user changing to a different cell. This event triggers both by user actions (such as using the arrow keys or clicking with the mouse) and by program actions, such as setting the Row and Col properties.

The example syntax updates a label that displays the current coordinates. It gets updated every time the active cell changes.

The SelChange event also triggers when a user clicks on a new cell, but does not trigger when the program changes the active cell.

Example

The ListBox project at the end of this chapter uses the RowColChange to update two labels, lablActive to display the active cell, and lablCellSelected to display if the active cell is selected.

SELCHANGE EVENT

Objects Affected

Check	Clipboard	Combo	Command	CommonDlg
Data	Debug	Dir	Drive	File
Form	Frame	▶ Grid	Image	Label
Line	List	MDI Form	Menu	OLE
Option	Picture	Printer	Screen	Scroll
Shape	Text	Timer		

Purpose

Use the SelChange event to react to the user or the program changing the selection to a different range of cells in a grid. Table 18-32 summarizes the arguments of the SelChange event.

General Syntax

```
Name_SelChange ([Index As Integer])
```

Argument	Description
Name	Name property of the grid control
Index	Uniquely identifies member of a control array

Table 18-32 Arguments of the SelChange event

Example Syntax

```
Sub Grid1_SelChange ()
    numRows = Abs(Grid1.SelEndRow - Grid1.SelStartRow)
    numCols = Abs(Grid1.SelEndCol - Grid1.SelStartCol)
    If numRows + numCols > 0 Then
        Label1.Caption = "Selection: " & numRows & " x " & numCols & " cells"
    Else
        Label1.Caption = ""
    End If
End Sub
```

Description

Use the SelChange event to react to a new selection range. This event triggers both by the user selecting cells or by the program using the SelStart... and SelEnd... properties. It triggers multiple times if the user clicks and drags to create a new selection. It does not trigger if the active cell changes because of new settings to the Row and Col properties.

The RowColChange event also triggers if the user clicks on a cell. The RowColChange event does not trigger if the selection changes by program code, and only triggers once if the user clicks and drags to create a new selection.

Example

The ListBox project at the end of this chapter uses the SelChange event to update two labels: lablSelection and lablCellSelected.

SELECTED PROPERTY

Objects Affected

Check	Clipboard	Combo	Command	CommonDlg
Data	Debug	Dir	Drive	▶ File

Form	Frame	Grid	Image	Label
Line	▶ List	MDI Form	Menu	OLE
Option	Picture	Printer	Screen	Scroll
Shape	Text	Timer		

Purpose

The Selected property lets you determine which items in a multiple selection list are selected. This property is an array of True and False values, with one entry for each item in the list. Table 18-33 summarizes the arguments for the Selected property.

General Syntax

```
[form!]Name.Selected(Index%) [= boolean%]
```

Argument	Description
form	Name of the parent form
Name	Name of the list box
Index%	Index in the array; corresponds to ListIndex
boolean%	True (-1) if selected; False (0) if not selected

Table 18-33 Arguments for the Selected property

Example Syntax

```
Sub Command1_Click ()
    For i = 0 to listBox.ListCount - 1
        If listBox.Selected(i) Then
            bigLine = bigLine & listBox(i).List & Chr$(13) & Chr$(10)
        End If
    Next i
    Text1.Text = bigLine
End Sub
```

Description

The Selected property lets you determine which items in a multiple-selection list box are selected. Using ListIndex in a multiple selection will only return the number of the item if the highlight bar is on; not whether or not that item is selected.

The Selected property returns an array of Boolean values with a one-to-one correspondence to the ListIndex property of the list. Stepping through the array, as in the example syntax, is an easy way to check each item for its selected status.

Example

The List Project uses the Selected property to remove multiple items from the listHistory list box in the listHistory_MouseDown event.

SELENDCOL, SELENDROW, SELSTARTCOL, SELSTARTROW PROPERTIES

Objects Affected

Check	Clipboard	Combo	Command	CommonDlg
Data	Debug	Dir	Drive	File
Form	Frame	▶ Grid	Image	Label
Line	List	MDI Form	Menu	OLE
Option	Picture	Printer	Screen	Scroll
Shape	Text	Timer		

Purpose

Use these properties to read or set the grid's starting or ending row or column in a selection. Not available at design time, read and write at runtime. Table 18-34 summarizes the arguments of the Sel... properties.

General Syntax

```
[form!]Name.SelEndCol [ = column%]
[form!]Name.SelEndRow [ = row%]
[form!]Name.SelStartCol [ = column%]
[form!]Name.SelStartRow [ = row%]
```

Argument	Description
form	Name property of the form
Name	Name property of the grid control

720

Argument	Description
column%	Number of the indicated column
row%	Number of the indicated row

Table 18-34 Arguments of the SelEndCol, SelEndRow, SelStartCol, and SelStartRow properties

Example Syntax

```
Sub Command1_Click ()
    Grid1.Rows = UBound(Addresses, 1)          '# of rows in array (Option Base 1)
    Grid1.Cols = UBound(Addresses, 2)          '# of columns in array
    Grid1.SelStartCol = 1                      'Select the entire grid
    Grid1.SelStartRow = 1                      'of non-fixed cells
    Grid1.SelEndCol = Grid1.Cols - 1
    Grid1.SelEndRow = Grid1.Rows - 1
    For i = 1 To Grid1.Rows                     'step through each array row
        For j = 1 To Grid1.Cols                 'step through each array column
            data$ = data$ & Addresses(i, j)     'add data value to string
            If j <> Grid1.Cols Then             'if not at end of row,
                data$ = data$ & Chr$(9)         'add item delimiter
            End If
        Next j
        data$ = data$ & Chr$(13)                'new row; add row delimiter
    Next i
    Grid1.Clip = data$                          'put the data into the grid
End Sub
```

Description

You may wish to read or set the selected region in a grid. Some properties, like Clip, need a region to be selected before they work. The example syntax above selects the entire grid so it can use the Clip property to read the values.

SelStartCol and SelStartRow reads or sets the upper-left corner of a selection; SelEndCol and SelEndRow reads or sets the lower-right corner. There can only be one selected area on the grid, and it must be rectangular and contiguous. Some advanced spreadsheets, like Microsoft Excel, support discontiguous spreadsheet selections.

Example

The Listbox project at the end of this chapter uses these properties to select the entire grid before using the Clip property in the cmndOpen and cmndSave routines. The gridSheet_SelChange event uses the properties to determine the size of a selection, and the cmboAlign_Click event uses them to step through each column in a selection.

SORTED PROPERTY

Objects Affected

Check	Clipboard	▶ Combo	Command	CommonDlg
Data	Debug	Dir	Drive	File
Form	Frame	Grid	Image	Label
Line	▶ List	MDI Form	Menu	OLE
Option	Picture	Printer	Screen	Scroll
Shape	Text	Timer		

Purpose

The Sorted property specifies at design time whether or not the items in the list or combo box are to be automatically sorted by Visual Basic. Table 18-35 summarizes the arguments of the Sorted property.

General Syntax

```
[form!]Name.Sorted
```

Argument	Description
form	Name of the parent form
Name	Name of the list or combo box

Table 18-35 Arguments of the Sorted property

Example Syntax

```
If Combo1.Sorted = True then        'If the items in the Combo box are sorted
    Call BinarySearch(Search$)      'Use a binary search
Else
    Call LinearSearch(Search$)      'Otherwise search one item at a time
End If
```

722

Description

The Sorted property is a great time-saving feature of list and combo boxes. When you set the Sorted property to True (-1), Visual Basic automatically attends to all the chores associated with keeping the list sorted alphabetically. If this property is set to False, no sorting of any kind is performed on the list. This property may only be set at design time, but it may be checked during runtime as a Boolean value.

In order to keep items sorted, Visual Basic changes the index numbers of the items in a list as necessary. Because of this Visual Basic needs absolute control over how the index numbers are assigned when items are added. Therefore using the index argument of the AddItem method is not recommended for a list or combo box that has the Sorted property set to True. You can determine where Visual Basic added the item to the list with the NewIndex property.

The example syntax checks the Sorted property of the box Combo1 to determine whether to do a binary search (which is very fast but works only on a sorted list) or a linear search (which is much slower, but can work on an unsorted list).

Example

The cmboIncome combo box is sorted.

STYLE PROPERTY

Objects Affected

Check	Clipboard	▶ Combo	Command	CommonDlg
Data	Debug	Dir	Drive	File
Form	Frame	Grid	Image	Label
Line	List	MDI Form	Menu	OLE
Option	Picture	Printer	Screen	Scroll
Shape	Text	Timer		

Purpose

The Style property sets the style of a combo box. A combo box can be one of three styles: drop-down combo, simple combo, or drop-down list. Table 18-36 summarizes the arguments of the Style property.

General Syntax

```
[form!]Name.Style
```

Argument	Description
form	Name of the parent form
Name	Name of the list or combo box

Table 18-36 Arguments of the Style property

Example Syntax

```
If Combo1.Style = 0 Then Text1.Text = "Drop down Combo"
If Combo1.Style = 1 Then Text1.Text = "Simple Combo"
If Combo1.Style = 2 Then Text1.Text = "Drop Down List"
```

Description

Three settings are available for the Style property: 0 for drop-down combo, 1 for simple combo, and 2 for drop-down list. This property can only be set at design time, but it may be checked at runtime as an integer value.

Specify the Style property starting with the name of the combo box control to be affected. The example code simply determines what type of combo box Combo1 is, and sets the text accordingly.

Drop-Down Combo Box

The drop-down combo box consists of three areas: the edit area, the down arrow, and the list area. The edit area allows the user to enter text in the same manner as a text box. The down arrow is displayed just to the right, but separated from the edit area. The list area of the drop-down combo box stays hidden from view until the user clicks on the down arrow associated with the box, or when the user presses (ALT)-(↓). Either action causes the list area to drop-down below the edit area. The list area closes as soon as the user selects an item. Because the user can enter text, or choose from a list of items, this style provides a useful tool for data entry fields that may have some often used values, yet cannot be restricted to a limited number of choices. Figure 18-6 shows both a closed and dropped-down combo box.

Simple Combo Box

The simple combo box is much like a drop-down combo box that has its list area always open. Again, its value can be set by user input in the edit area, or by the user clicking on the desired list item. The default setting for the Height property of this object will display only the edit area. Therefore it's a good idea to increase the Height property at design time in order to let the items in the list be viewed. Because the list area of this style is constantly open, it uses more screen space than the drop-down combo box. Figure 18-7 shows a simple combo box.

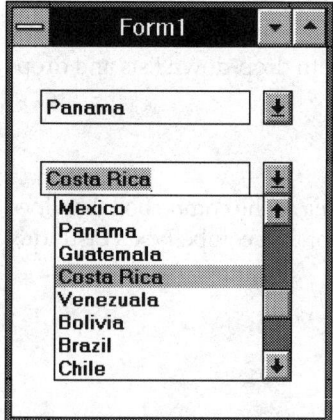

Figure 18-6 Drop-Down combo box closed and dropped-down

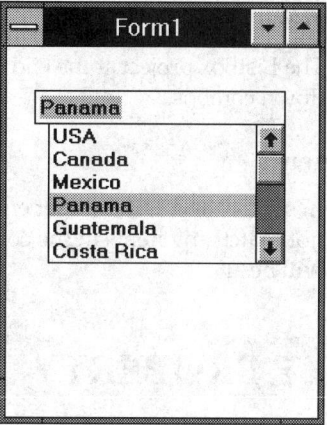

Figure 18-7 Simple combo box is always open

Drop-Down List Box

The drop-down list box is almost identical to the drop-down combo. The major functional difference is that the drop-down list box requires the user to choose an item from the list area. While the selected item appears in the edit area, nothing can be typed there by the user. This style is used for data entry fields that have a limited number of valid values. Figure 18-8 shows both a closed and opened drop-down list box.

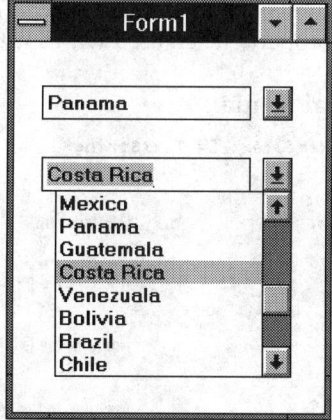

Figure 18-8 Drop-down list box

Example

The ListBox project at the end of this chapter uses both drop-down lists and drop-down combos.

Comments

In styles 0 and 1, if the user enters text in the edit area of the combo box that does not match any items in the control's list, the value of that combo box's ListIndex will be -1.

TEXT PROPERTY

Objects Affected

Check	Clipboard	▶ Combo	Command	CommonDlg
Data	Debug	Dir	Drive	File
Form	Frame	▶ Grid	Image	Label
Line	▶ List	MDI Form	Menu	OLE
Option	Picture	Printer	Screen	Scroll
Shape	▶ Text	Timer		

Purpose

The Text property is used to read the text of the selected item in a list or combo box, or a cell entry in a grid. Additionally, the Text property can be used to set the selected item in combo boxes whose Style property is set to 0 (Drop-Down combo) or 1 (simple combo). Table 18-37 summarizes the arguments of the Text property when used with a list box or combo box.

General Syntax

`[form!]Name.Text [= TextString$]`

Argument	Description
form	Name of the parent form
Name	Name of the list, combo box, or grid control
TextString$	Assigned to the edit area of the drop-down and simple combo box styles or cell of a grid

Table 18-37 Arguments of the Text property when used with a list box or combo box

726

Example Syntax

```
Sub Command1_Click ()
    SelectedItem$ = List1.Text    'Assigns the value of a list box's selected item to a string
    Combo1.Text = "Hello"         'Assigns a string to the edit area of a simple combo box
End Sub
```

Description

When used with list and combo boxes, the Text property returns a string copy of the currently selected item in the control's list. If no item has yet been selected, this property will return a null string.

This is an alternative to using the List and ListIndex properties together. For instance, in most cases the following two lines of code are functionally equivalent:

```
A$ = List1.List(ListIndex)
A$ = List1.Text
```

The only difference between these two examples occurs when the user has not yet selected an item in the list. When this is the case, the first line in the example would generate an error (because ListIndex would have a value of -1). The second line of code would not. Instead, the variable A$ would be assigned a null value.

When used with the grid control, the Text property reads or sets the contents of the active cell. The active cell is set with the Row and Col properties.

In the example syntax the first statement stores the text of the currently selected item for List1 in the string variable SelectedItem$. The second statement assigns the string "Hello" to the selected item in Combo1: This causes the word "Hello" to appear in the edit area of this combo box.

Drop-Down and Simple Combos

As discussed in the introduction to this chapter, the drop-down combo and simple combo box styles allow the user to edit text in the edit area of the control. Because of this, the Text property takes on a somewhat different meaning when used with these combo box styles.

When used on drop-down or simple combo boxes, the Text property is a string representation of the contents of the edit area of the control. By default, this is the selected item from the list; thus in the default case, the Text property has the same meaning as with non-combo list boxes. However, since the user can type text into the edit area of a combo box, the Text property can sometimes contain such an input item, probably not matching any item on the list.

You can manipulate the contents of the edit area by assigning it a value, or by using it as an argument with any of Visual Basic's string functions and statements such as Left$, Mid$, and Right$. Any operations performed on this property are reflected by the text inside the edit area.

You may assign a string to the Text property. This causes the text in the box to be replaced by the assigned string. The user can also directly edit the text represented by the Text property. Any time a combo box's Text property is modified, it causes the combo box's Change event to occur.

Example

The ListBox project at the end of this chapter uses the Text property several times. The cmboIncome_DropDown statement uses it to check the contents of the cmboIncome combo box. The grid's Text property is both read and set in the Form_Load and NewValues procedures.

THE LISTBOX PROJECT

Project Overview

Assembling the Project

1. Assemble the controls summarized on Table 18-38 on a blank form.

Object	Property	Setting
Form	BackColor	&H00C0C0C0&, Light Gray
	BorderStyle	3 'Fixed Double
	Caption	"Lists, Combos, and Grids Project"
	Name	formMain
Combo	Name	cmboInflation
	TabIndex	1
Combo	Name	cmboIncome
	Sorted	-1 'True

Object	Property	Setting
	TabIndex	0
Combo	Name	cmboGridlines
	Style	2 'Dropdown List
Combo	Name	cmboAlign
	Style	2 'Dropdown List
Command	Caption	"&Save"
	Name	cmndSave
Command	Caption	"E&xit"
	Name	cmndExit
Command	Caption	"&Open"
	Name	cmndOpen
Grid	FontBold	0 'False
	Name	gridSheet
	TabIndex	2
Label	BackColor	&H00C0C0C0&—Light Gray
	FontBold	0 'False
	Name	lablCellSelected
Label	BackColor	&H00C0C0C0&—Light Gray
	FontBold	0 'False
	Name	lablSelection

(continued on next page)

(continued from previous page)

Object	Property	Setting
Label	BackColor	&H00C0C0C0&—Light Gray
	FontBold	0 'False
	Name	lablActive
ListBox	FontBold	0—False
	FontName	FixedSys
	MultiSelect	2 'Extended
	Name	listHistory

Table 18-38 Controls for the ListBox project

2. Position and size the controls, as shown on Figure 18-9.

3. Enter the following code in the cmboAlign_Click event. This triggers when the user clicks on a list item, or presses enter after selecting an item. It iterates through each selected column and sets the column alignment.

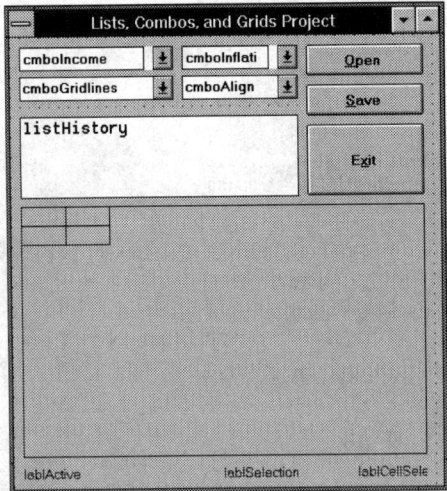

Figure 18-9 The ListBox project during design

```
Sub cmboAlign_Click ()
    For i = gridSheet.SelStartCol To gridSheet.SelEndCol 'iterate through selected columns
        gridSheet.ColAlignment(i) = cmboAlign.ListIndex    'and set alignment
    Next i
End Sub
```

4. Enter the following code in the cmboGrilines_Click event. This turns the gridlines on and off.

```
Sub cmboGridlines_Click ()
    gridSheet.GridLines = cmboGridlines.ItemData(cmboGridlines.ListIndex) 'set gridlines
End Sub
```

5. Enter the following code in the cmboIncome_DropDown event. This first checks to see if the scenario (that is, the income and inflation rate combination) has already been entered into the list. If it has, it just exits the procedure. If not, it adds it to the list, and also adds an entry for the inflation rate in the ItemData property.

```
Sub cmboIncome_DropDown ()
    If InStr(cmboIncome.Text, "  ") Then         'If this is a previously formatted entry
        value = clean(Left$(cmboIncome.Text, InStr(cmboIncome.Text, "  ")))
    Else                                          'otherwise
        value = clean((cmboIncome.Text))          'income value is all there is
    End If
    value = Format$(value, "$###,###,###")        'pretty up the value
    display = value & Space$(12 - Len(value) - Len(cmboInflation.Text)) & cmboInflation.Text
    For i = 0 To cmboIncome.ListCount - 1         'run through the existing list
        If display = cmboIncome.List(i) Then      'if we've already got this scenario,
            Exit Sub                              'leave
        End If
    Next i
    cmboIncome.AddItem display                    'new scenario, so add it to list
    cmboIncome.ItemData(cmboIncome.NewIndex) = cmboInflation.Text 'remember inflation rate
    cmboIncome.ListIndex = cmboIncome.NewIndex    'and set box to this newest entry
End Sub
```

6. Enter the following code in the cmboIncome_GotFocus event. This triggers every time the Income combo box gets the focus, and highlights the text in the combo box's edit area.

```
Sub cmboIncome_GotFocus ()
    cmboIncome.SelLength = Len(cmboIncome.Text)   'highlight the whole entry
End Sub
```

7. Enter the following code in the gridSheet_GotFocus procedure. Whenever the user moves into the Grid control (either by clicking with the mouse or with the tab key) this event recalculates the scenario. It first makes sure the income text is properly formatted by calling the cmboIncome_DropDown event procedure, then it extracts the income and the inflation rate. It then calls NewValues to do the actual computation.

```
Sub gridSheet_GotFocus ()
    cmboIncome_DropDown                           'force the display's update
```

731

```
      bucks = clean(Left$(cmboIncome.Text, InStr(cmboIncome.Text, " "))) 'take income
      inflation = 1 + Val(cmboIncome.ItemData(cmboIncome.ListIndex)) / 100 '& inflation
      NewValues bucks, inflation          'and compute new scenario
End Sub
```

8. Enter the following code in the cmndExit_Click procedure. This simply ends the program.

```
Sub cmndExit_Click ()
      End                    'end the program
End Sub
```

9. Enter the following code in the cmndOpen_Click event procedure. This opens up a data file saved by the cmndSave procedure. It first opens up the data file (providing an error trap in the process). Then it reads in each line of the file. The Clip property used to save the file embeds carriage returns at the end of each row; we need to put the carriage returns back in, as the Line Input statement reads up to, but not including, a carriage return. Once we've read the data in, we turn off the highlighting and select the entire grid so we can use the Clip property to assign the saved values back to the grid. We end by resetting the highlighting and selection.

```
Sub cmndOpen_Click ()
      On Error GoTo badopen                     'set error trap
      Open "chp18.tmp" For Input As #1          'open the data file
      On Error GoTo 0                           'success!
      Do While Not EOF(1)                       'while there's still data,
      Line Input #1, rawdata$                   'get a line
      clipdata$ = clipdata$ & rawdata$ & Chr$(13) 'add the carriage return back in
      Loop
      Close                                     'close data file
      NoHilite True                             'turn off highlighting, select whole grid
      gridSheet.Clip = clipdata$                'and put the saved data in the grid
      NoHilite False                            'turn back highlighting, select whole grid
Exit Sub

badopen:                                        'oops! bad file
      MsgBox "Failed to open"                   'inform user
Exit Sub                                        'and leave

End Sub
```

10. Enter the following code in the cmndSave_Click event. This saves the grid data so the cmndOpen procedure can read it back in. We first open up the save file (setting up an error trap along the way). We then turn off highlighting and select the entire grid. The single Print #1 line is all we need to save the entire contents of the nonfixed grid cells! We then turn on the highlighting and reset the selection.

```
Sub cmndSave_Click ()
      On Error GoTo badsave                     'set error trap
      Open "chp18.tmp" For Output As #1         'open data file
      On Error GoTo 0                           'success!
      NoHilite True                             'turn off highlighting, select entire grid
      Print #1, gridSheet.Clip                  'save the grid's data
      NoHilite False                            'turn on highlighting, select old selection
      Close                                     'close data file
```

```
Exit Sub                                    'done

badsave:                                    'oops! bad file
    MsgBox "Failed to save"                 'inform user
Exit Sub                                    'leave

End Sub
```

11. Enter the following code in the Form_Load procedure. This sets up the grid and the various combo boxes.

```
Sub Form_Load ()
    gridSheet.Rows = 22                                    'dimension grid
    gridSheet.Cols = 5
    gridSheet.RowHeight(0) = gridSheet.RowHeight(1) * 1.3 'make top row a bit bigger
    gridSheet.Row = 0                                      'add in the labels
    gridSheet.Col = 1
    gridSheet.Text = "Yearly"
    gridSheet.Col = 2
    gridSheet.Text = "Monthly"
    gridSheet.Col = 3
    gridSheet.Text = "Weekly"
    gridSheet.Col = 4
    gridSheet.Text = "Hourly"
    For i = 1 To gridSheet.Cols - 1                        'set column widths and alignments
        gridSheet.ColWidth(i) = 950
        gridSheet.ColAlignment(i) = 1                       'right align
        gridSheet.FixedAlignment(i) = 1                     'right align
    Next i
    cmboGridlines.AddItem "No Gridlines"                   'set up gridlines combo box
    cmboGridlines.ItemData(0) = 0                          'associate correct settings
    cmboGridlines.AddItem "Gridlines"                      'with the displayed items
    cmboGridlines.ItemData(1) = -1
    cmboGridlines.ListIndex = 1                            'set the default to "Gridlines"
    cmboALign.AddItem "Left Align"                         'add alignment options in correct order
    cmboALign.AddItem "Right Align"
    cmboALign.AddItem "Center Align"
    cmboALign.ListIndex = 1                                'set default alignment to right align
    For i = 2 To 20                                        'set up inflation box with
        comboInflation.AddItem i                           'inflation rates from 2 to 20
    Next i
    cmboInflation.ListIndex = 4                            'set default inflation rate
    gridSheet_RowColChange                                'force update the active cell label
    cmboIncome.Text = "$50,000"                           'put in default value
    cmboIncome_DropDown                                   'force update the displayed value
End Sub
```

12. Enter the following code in the gridSheet_RowColChange event. This triggers every time the active cell moves. It puts the cell's coordinates in a label beneath the grid control.

```
Sub gridSheet_RowColChange ()
    currentRow$ = "Row " & gridSheet.Row                  'update the label every time
    currentCol$ = "Column " & gridSheet.Col               'a new cell becomes active
    lablActive.Caption = currentRow$ & " " & currentCol$
    If gridSheet.CellSelected Then                        'and figure out if the active
```

(continued on next page)

(continued from previous page)

```
            lablCellSelected.Caption = "[selected]"          'cell is selected
        Else
            lablCellSelected.Caption = ""
        End If
End Sub
```

13. Enter the following code in the gridSheet_SelChange procedure. This triggers any time the user (or code) changes the selection. It first computes and displays the size of the selection, then checks to see if the active cell is selected.

```
Sub gridSheet_SelChange ()
    numRows = Abs(gridSheet.SelEndRow - gridSheet.SelStartRow) + 1 'num selected rows
    numCols = Abs(gridSheet.SelEndCol - gridSheet.SelStartCol) + 1 'num selected columns
    If numCols + numRows = 0 Then                    'if there no selection
        lablSelection.Caption = "(no selection)"     'say so
    Else                                             'otherwise
        lablSelection.Caption = numRows & " x " & numCols 'display selection size
    End If
    If gridSheet.CellSelected Then                   'selection has changed, so the
        lablCellSelected.Caption = "[selected]"      'active cell may or may not be
    Else                                             'selected, so check and update
        lablCellSelected.Caption = ""                'display
    End If
End Sub
```

14. Enter the following code in the listHistory_DblClick event. This deletes all entries from the history list.

```
Sub listHistory_DblClick ()
    listHistory.Clear                'clear all history entries
End Sub
```

15. Enter the following code in the listHistory_MouseDown event. This triggers whenever the user presses a button over the list box. This goes through the list and checks to see if the user has selected any items. It deletes them from the list if it finds any.

```
Sub listHistory_MouseDown (Button As Integer, Shift As Integer, X As Single, Y As Single)
    If Button = 2 Then                               'right mouse button
        For i = (listHistory.ListCount - 1) To 0 Step -1 'step through from last to first
            If listHistory.Selected(i) Then          'if user selected item,
                listHistory.RemoveItem i             'delete it
            End If
        Next i
    End If
End Sub
```

16. Enter the following code in the General Declarations section. This routine is the main engine of the program. It displays the calculated values of taking the amount of income specified in the cmboIncome combo box, and calculating out over 20 years what inflation will do. Once it's finished, it builds a summary statement involving the initial parameters and the result in the tenth year.

```
Sub NewValues (bucks, inflation)
    For years = 1 To 20                      'figure out values for the next 20 years
```

```
        gridSheet.Row = years                   'go to the correct row
        gridSheet.Col = 0                        'go to label column
        gridSheet.Text = Str$(1992 + years)      'and create label
        gridSheet.Col = 1                        'go to yearly income column
        If years = 1 Then                        'first year?
            gridSheet.Text = Format$(Val(bucks), "$###,###,###") 'just give it base figure
        Else                                     'otherwise
            gridSheet.Row = gridSheet.Row - 1    'get last year's data
            oldVal = clean((gridSheet.Text))     'clean it up
            gridSheet.Row = gridSheet.Row + 1    'go back to current year
            gridSheet.Text = Format$(oldVal * inflation, "$###,###,###")
        End If
        newBucks = clean((gridSheet.Text))       'this year's inflated value
        gridSheet.Col = 2                        'Monthly wage
        gridSheet.Text = Format$(newBucks / 12, "$###,###,###")
        gridSheet.Col = 3                        'Weekly wage
        gridSheet.Text = Format$(newBucks / 52, "$###,###,###")
        gridSheet.Col = 4                        'Hourly wage
        gridSheet.Text = Format$(newBucks / 2000, "$###,###,###.00")
    Next years
    gridSheet.Col = 1                            'Yearly wage
    gridSheet.Row = 10                           'for year 10
    year10 = gridSheet.Text
    listHistory.AddItem cmboIncome.Text & Space$(14 - Len(year10)) & year10 'add in history
    gridSheet.TopRow = 1                         'and scroll to the top
    gridSheet.LeftCol = 1                        'left corner of the grid
End Sub
```

17. Add in the following code to the General Declarations section. This procedure
    selects the entire grid so the Clip property in the calling procedure can open or
    save a file. It first determines if we're turning the highlighting on or off. If we're
    turning it off, it stores the current selection in the four static variables for use in
    the next call to the procedure. It then turns off the highlighting and selects the
    entire grid. When it's called to turn on the highlighting again, it restores the pre-
    viously selected area and turns on the highlighting.

```
Sub NoHilite (onOff As Integer)
    Static sCol%, sRow%, eCol%, eRow%            'will remember current selection
    If onOff = True Then                         'turn hilite off
      sCol% = gridSheet.SelStartCol              'remember current selection
      sRow% = gridSheet.SelStartRow
      eCol% = gridSheet.SelEndCol
      eRow% = gridSheet.SelEndRow
      gridSheet.HighLight = False                'turn off highlight
      gridSheet.SelStartCol = 1                  'and select entire grid
      gridSheet.SelStartRow = 1
      gridSheet.SelEndCol = gridSheet.Cols - 1
      gridSheet.SelEndRow = gridSheet.Rows - 1
    Else                                         'back to normal
      gridSheet.SelStartCol = sCol%              'reset old selection
      gridSheet.SelStartRow = sRow%
      gridSheet.SelEndCol = eCol%
      gridSheet.SelEndRow = eRow%
      gridSheet.HighLight = True                 'and turn on highlighting
    End If
End Sub
```

735

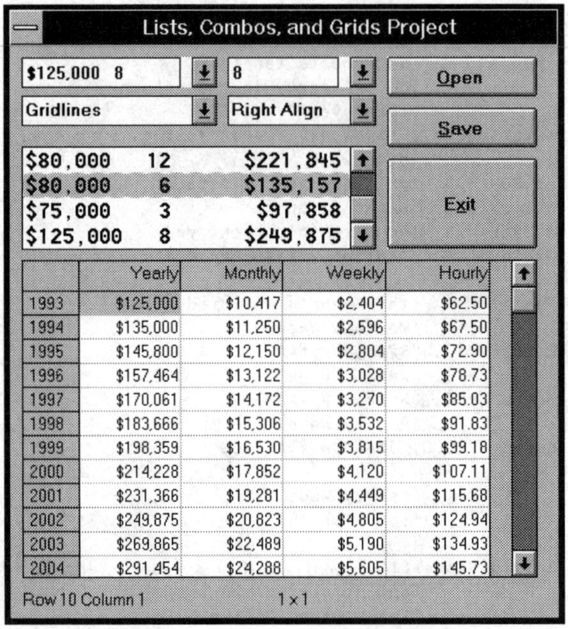

Figure 18-10 The ListBox project in action

18. Add in the following code to the General Declarations section. This routine cleans up a number, removing any extraneous characters (like dollar signs and commas) and then converts the clean string to a number.

```
Function clean (number As Variant) As Single
    'this cleans up a number, removing garbage like commas and dollar signs
    On Error GoTo woops                         'just in case .
    For i = 1 To Len(number)                     'iterate through entire string
    If InStr("1234567890", Mid$(number, i, 1)) = 0 Then    'if character isn't a number,
        Mid$(number, i, 1) = " "                'replace with an inoffensive blank
    End If
    Next i
    clean = Val(number)                          'and make string into a number
Exit Function                                    'done

woops:                                           'something went wrong
    clean = 0                                    'so fake it
Exit Function                                    'and leave

End Function
```

How It Works

This project displays a list of figures showing the effects of inflation on your earning power. You enter a dollar figure in one combo box, and an inflation rate in another. The program then uses a grid control to display how that initial dollar

736

figure grows over time. The grid has columns for yearly, monthly, weekly, and hourly wages needed to stay even. Although the results may prompt you to find ways to increase your income (you mean I have to earn an extra $40,000 just to break even?!), the project does illustrate each of the properties, events, and methods detailed in the chapter. Figure 18-10 shows the project in action

Enter a figure in the top left combo box. It's set to default to $50,000. Set the inflation rate in the next combo box over. After you tab out of this combo box, the grid control gets updated to display the results. You can scroll up and down with the scroll bar, and can move the active cell and select cells. The labels at the bottom of the grid are updated to show cell and selection status.

The large list box contains a history of what "scenarios," or combinations of income and inflation rate, you've displayed. It lists the starting parameters plus the amount of money after ten years you'd need to just break even. You can clear the entire history by double-clicking on it, or you can delete selected lines by selecting them and then clicking with the right mouse button. The list box is set up as a MultiSelect box, so you can select more than one item.

The bottom two combo boxes let you turn the gridlines on and off and set the alignment of selected columns.

The Save command button saves the grid data to a file, and the Open command button retrieves the information from the file. Exit, of course, exits the program.

19

FILE SYSTEM CONTROLS

Windows users will expect your application to provide the same easy access to the file system through point-and-click navigation as the commercial applications they're used to. Visual Basic provides the Drive, Directory, and File list boxes for you to use in providing the interface that lets the user move around the logical structure of the DOS files system. These controls take most of the work out of dealing with selecting drives, directories, and files. This lets you concentrate on the main work of the application.

FILE-ORIENTED LIST BOXES

For the user and the programmer, the list boxes that present the file system work much like the List Box and Combo Box controls described in Chapter 18, Lists, Combos, and Grids. In fact, the file-related list boxes share the List, ListCount, ListIndex, MultiSelect, and Selection properties with the list and combo boxes. These properties are discussed again in this chapter because there are some differences that need to be taken into account when they're used with the file-related list boxes. Here, however, your program does not have to add or remove items from the lists of the file-related list boxes. Visual Basic automatically reads the structure of the disk, builds the lists of directories and files, and updates the list when the user adds or removes files.

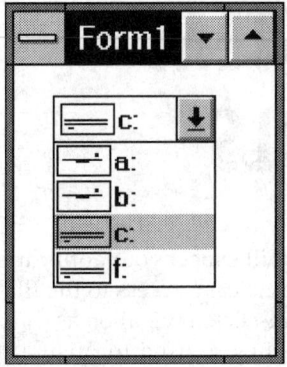

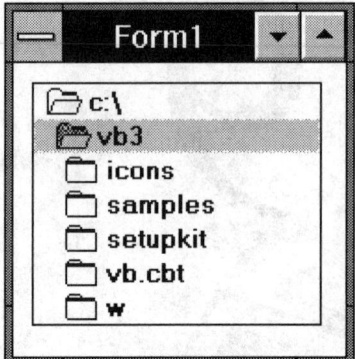

Figure 19-1 The Drive list box

Figure 19-2 The Directory list box

The Drive List Box

The Drive list box is like a drop-down list box that lets the user choose from any of the available drives on the system. Visual Basic automatically explores the user's system, and adds all of the floppy, fixed, and network drives to the list. Drive list items that reflect local fixed disks will also display that disk's label with the drive letter. For network drives, the network name is displayed. Figure 19-1 shows a Drive list box with the drop-down list open.

The Directory List Box

The Directory list box is like a simple list box that lets the user choose a directory on a disk drive. Clicking once on any of the listed directories moves the selection bar; double-clicking on a directory entry changes the current directory for the directory list box. Figure 19-2 shows the Directory list box.

The File List Box and File Attributes

The File list box is like a standard list box, except that it is automatically filled with the available files in the directory. A single click selects each individual file. Visual Basic 2.0 and 3.0 have added the ability to select multiple files if the MultiSelect property is set to either 1 (simple MultiSelect) or 2 (extended MultiSelect). Figure 19-3 shows the File list box.

In the DOS file system, each entry for a file in a directory includes four attributes: archive, hidden, system, and read-only. The File list box has several properties that allow you to select which files are displayed in the box, based on the settings of these bits. These are the Archive, Hidden, Normal, ReadOnly, and System properties.

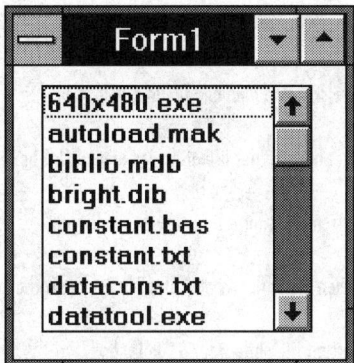

Figure 19-3 The File list box

When the File list box control scans a directory, it selects files for display based on the settings of these properties. If more than one of these properties is set on, then the files selected will reflect a combination of the set properties.

FILE SYSTEM CONTROLS SUMMARY

In this chapter we will be discussing the properties, events, and methods that are specific to these file-related controls. They are summarized in Table 19-1. At the end of the section, the Drive project demonstrates the use of each of these controls and their properties, events, and methods.

Use or Set This...		To Do This...
Archive	Property	Set or read whether archive files are shown in a File list box
Drive	Property	Set or read the current drive selected in a Drive list box
FileName	Property	Set or read the current file selected in a File list box
Hidden	Property	Set or read whether hidden files are shown in a File list box
List	Property	Return an item from a Drive, Directory, or File list box's list
ListCount	Property	Return the number of items in a Drive, Directory, or File list box's list
ListIndex	Property	Return the index of the selected item in a Drive, Directory, or File list

(continued on next page)

(continued from previous page)

Use or Set This...		To Do This...
MultiSelect	Property	Enable the user to select more than one file at a time
Normal	Property	Set or return whether normal files are displayed in a File list box
Path	Property	Set or return the current path for a Directory or File list box
PathChange	Event	Initiate an action when the Path property of a File list box is changed
Pattern	Property	Set or return the current file pattern for a File list box
PatternChange	Event	Initiate an action when a File list box's Pattern property is changed
ReadOnly	Property	Set or return whether read-only files are displayed in a File list box
Refresh	Method	Reset the list entries in a Drive, Directory, or File list box
Selected	Property	Determine which files are selected in a multiple selection
System	Property	Set or return whether System files are displayed in a File list box

Table 19-1 The properties, events, and method that pertain to Drive, Directory, and File list boxes

ARCHIVE PROPERTY

Objects Affected

Check	Clipboard	Combo	Command	CommonDlg
Data	Debug	Dir	Drive	▶ File
Form	Frame	Grid	Image	Label
Line	List	MDI Form	Menu	OLE
Option	Picture	Printer	Screen	Scroll
Shape	Text	Timer		

Purpose

The Archive property sets or returns a value that determines whether or not files with their archive bit set on will be displayed in a File list box. Files with the archive bit set have been copied by the DOS XCOPY or BACKUP commands, or similar programs. Setting this property to false will thus suppress the display of files that have been backed up, which can be helpful for file management. The Archive property can be set at design time, and set or read at runtime. Table 19-2 summarizes the arguments of the Archive property.

General Syntax

```
[form!]Name.Archive [= boolean%]
```

Argument	Description
form	Name of the parent form
Name	Name of the File list box
boolean%	A True (-1) or False (0) indicating whether archive files will be selected or not

Table 19-2 Arguments of the Archive property

Example Syntax

```
Sub ArchiveCheck_Click ()
    File1.Archive = -ArchiveCheck.Value      'CheckBox on the dialog box or form
End Sub

Sub Form_Load ()
    ArchiveBit = Abs(File1.Archive)          'Read the Archive property setting
    ArchiveCheck.Value = ArchiveBit          'Set the check box to reflect it
End Sub
```

Description

The DOS file system sets aside 1 byte in the directory entry of each file for attribute information. Five properties can select files for display in a File list box based on the setting of this attribute byte. These are the Archive, Hidden, Normal, ReadOnly, and System properties. The set of files that are displayed in a File list box is based on the combination of these properties.

One of the bits in the attribute byte is the archive bit. This bit is set on automatically by DOS every time a file is modified. Certain programs (such as

743

XCOPY and BACKUP) can then set this bit off when a file is backed up. This allows the system to make incremental backups based on whether a file has been modified since the last backup.

The Archive property selects files based on the setting of the archive bit. Specify this property by starting with the name of the file list box control to be affected. This property has two possible values: True (-1) or False (0). It defaults to True.

Interaction of the Archive Property and Other Properties

The files selected when the Archive property is True are a subset of the files selected by the Normal property. In other words, setting this property to True has no effect unless the Normal property is set to False. In that case any files whose archive bit is set on, but with no other attribute bits set other than read-only, will be selected for display. However, if a file's archive bit is on, but its hidden or system bits are also set on, it will not be selected unless the Hidden or System properties are also True.

Table 19-3 lists all the possible combinations for the attribute byte, and which of those combinations will be displayed when the Archive property is True. This table lists only the files that will be selected with the archive bit as the basis. Other files may be selected for the same File list box by setting the ReadOnly, Hidden, or System properties.

Attribute Value	Select This File?
Archive	Yes
Archive, Read Only	Yes
— anything else —	Any other combination will not display the file

Table 19-3 Files displayed when the Archive property is True, but System, Hidden, and ReadOnly are False

Example

In the File System Controls project at the end of this chapter, the Archive property is first read in the Form_Load event. The value returned sets the ArchiveCheck check box. In the ArchiveCheck_Click event, this property is set to reflect the status of the check box. When the check box is checked, the Archive property is set to True (-1). This code is also shown in the example syntax. Note that the Abs() function must be used to change the True value (-1) to the value of 1 needed to set a check box. A false (0) value is of course not affected.

DRIVE PROPERTY

Objects Affected

Check	Clipboard	Combo	Command	CommonDlg
Data	Debug	Dir	▶ Drive	File
Form	Frame	Grid	Image	Label
Line	List	MDI Form	Menu	OLE
Option	Picture	Printer	Screen	Scroll
Shape	Text	Timer		

Purpose

The Drive property sets or returns the selected drive for a Drive list box. Directories on the selected drive will be recognized and displayed by an associated Directory list box, and with proper coding can in turn display the files in the current directory on the new drive. This property is also helpful for responding when the user changes the current drive. The arguments for the Drive property are summarized in Table 19-4.

General Syntax

```
[form!]Name.Drive [= drive$]
```

Argument	Description
form	Name of the parent form
Name	Name of the Drive list box
drive$	A string whose first letter is that of a valid DOS drive

Table 19-4 Arguments of the Drive property

Example Syntax

```
Sub Drive1_Change ()
    Dir1.Path = CurDir$(Drive1.Drive)        'Uses the Drive property to set path
End Sub

Sub Command1_Click ()
    Drive1.Drive = "A:\"            'Sets the selected drive for the Drive list
End Sub
```

745

Description

The Drive property can be read at runtime to find out which is the selected drive for a Drive list box. For all types of drives, a 2-byte drive designation string is returned with the letter of the drive followed by a colon (for example, "D:"). When the selected drive is a local fixed disk, the 2-byte drive string is followed by the drive's label, if any. For instance, if the fixed disk "C:" has the label "MASTER," this property will return the string "C: [MASTER]." Network drives return the name of the network connection for this drive. For instance, if the shared drive "\\SERVER\MAIN" is mounted as logical drive "D:", this property will return the string "d: [\\SERVER\MAIN]."

Specify the Drive property by starting with the name of the Drive list box control to be affected. You can set the value for this property by assigning a string with a drive letter to it. Only the first character of the string is used. For instance in the example above, although the supplied string is three characters long, only the character "A" is used to set the Drive property. The balance of the string is ignored. The supplied character must reflect a valid drive on the system, otherwise an error occurs.

When the Drive property sets the selected drive in a Drive list box, it refreshes the list and activates the Drive_Change event. You can include code for this event to do such things as setting a new default path. If this property is not set at design time, it is set to the current default drive as recognized by DOS.

The first sub procedure in the example syntax reacts to a change in the current drive by using the CurDir$ function together with the Drive property to get the current directory for the new drive. This directory path is then used to set the current path for the Dir1 Directory list box. The second example sub procedure simply sets the current drive for drive list box Drive1 to "A:\".

Example

In the File System Controls project at the end of this chapter, the Drive property is set in the Form_Load event to the current drive. In the Drive1_Change event, the Drive property sets the Path property of the Dir1 directory list box control.

Comments

The Refresh method can be used with the Drive list box to update any network drive changes.

FILENAME PROPERTY

Objects Affected

Check	Clipboard	Combo	Command	▶ CommonDlg
Data	Debug	Dir	Drive	▶ File
Form	Frame	Grid	Image	Label
Line	List	MDI Form	Menu	OLE
Option	Picture	Printer	Screen	Scroll
Shape	Text	Timer		

Purpose

The FileName property allows your program to read the currently selected file name for a File list box, or to set a new current file name. This property can only be set or read at runtime. Table 19-5 summarizes the arguments of the FileName property.

General Syntax

```
[form!]Name.FileName [= path$]
```

Argument	Description
form	Name of the parent form
Name	Name of the File list box
path$	A string containing a path or file name pattern

Table 19-5 Arguments of the FileName property

Example Syntax

```
Sub File1_Click ()
    Text1.Text = File1.FileName          'Set the text box to the currently selected file
End Sub

Sub Command1_Click ()
    oldFileName$ = File1.FileName          'Change the selected file
    On Error Resume Next
    File1.FileName = Text1.Text
    If Err > 0 Then MsgBox "Invalid File Name Specified", 48
End Sub
```

747

Description

The FileName property allows your program to read the currently selected file name for a File list box, or to set a new current file name. When you don't specify a path or pattern to set this property, the property returns a string that specifies the name of the currently selected file in the File list box. The string returned does not specify the drive or path of the file. Use the Path property to determine that information. If no file is selected, a null string is returned.

When setting this property in your program, you can use a drive, path, and file name. The file name can contain wildcard characters (* and ?). When your program supplies the drive or path, the File list box's Path property gets changed to the drive and path specified, and a PathChange event occurs. If the supplied file name contains wildcard characters, the file list box's Pattern property gets changed to the file pattern specified and a PatternChange event occurs. This makes the FileName property perfect for allowing the user to change the path and file search pattern by using a text box.

The first sub procedure in the example syntax activates when the user clicks on the File list box. When this happens, the Text property for the text box is set to the currently selected file returned by the FileName property. This makes the selected file name appear in the text box, which is the typical behavior for this control. The second sub procedure, activated when the user clicks on the OK button, sets the FileName property to whatever text is in the text box and then checks for any error involving the file name. This procedure can thus handle the user typing in a file name not on the current list.

Example

In the File System Controls project at the end of this chapter, the FileName property is read to set the Text property of the TextSelected text box control in the File1_PathChange, File1_PatternChange, and File1_Click events. In the cmndOK_Click event, the FileName property is set to the value of the Text property of the TextSelected text box control.

Comments

When setting this property, make sure to check the string you're about to assign to make sure it specifies a valid drive and path. Note that the common dialog box also has a FileName property; the common dialog box is covered in detail in Chapter 17, Dialog Boxes.

HIDDEN PROPERTY

Objects Affected

Check	Clipboard	Combo	Command	CommonDlg
Data	Debug	Dir	Drive	▸ File
Form	Frame	Grid	Image	Label
Line	List	MDI Form	Menu	OLE
Option	Picture	Printer	Screen	Scroll
Shape	Text	Timer		

Purpose

The Hidden property sets or returns a value that determines whether or not files with their hidden bit on will be displayed in a File list box. (Under DOS, hidden files are not normally displayed in directory listings.) This property can be set at design time, and set or read at runtime. Table 19-6 summarizes the arguments of the Hidden property.

General Syntax

```
[form!]Name.Hidden [= boolean%]
```

Argument	Description
form	Name of the parent form
Name	Name of the File list box
boolean%	A True (-1) or False (0) indicating whether hidden files will be selected

Table 19-6 Arguments of the Hidden property

Example Syntax

```
Sub HiddenCheck_Click ()
    File1.Hidden = -HiddenCheck.Value      'Sets the Hidden property of File1 list box
End Sub

Sub Form_Load ()
    HiddenBit = Abs(File1.Hidden)          'Read the Hidden property setting
    chekHidden.Value = HiddenBit           'Set the check box to reflect it
End Sub
```

Description

The DOS file system sets aside 1 byte in the directory entry of each file for attribute information. Five possible properties select files for display in a File list box based on the setting of this attribute byte. These are the Archive, Hidden, Normal, ReadOnly, and System properties. The set of files displayed in a File list box is based on the combination of these properties.

One of the bits in this attribute byte is the hidden bit. This bit hides files from the user. When this bit is set on, the related file is invisible to DIR (except with DIR /A or DIR /A:H in DOS 5.0 or greater), COPY, and most other DOS commands, as well as most programs. This provides a very limited security scheme for certain files.

The Hidden property selects files based on the setting of the hidden attribute bit. Specify this property by beginning with the name of the File Box control to be affected. This property has two possible values: True (-1) or False (0). If this property is not changed at design time, its value will be False (0) when the program begins.

Setting this property to True (-1) selects files with their hidden bit set on to be displayed, regardless of the setting of the archive and read-only bits. However, if a file also has its system bit set on, it will only be displayed if the System property is also set to True. Setting this property to False prevents all files whose hidden bit is set on from being excluded from the File list box, regardless of the settings of the other four attribute properties. Omitting the setting returns the current value of the Hidden property.

Table 19-7 lists all the possible combinations for the attribute byte, and which of those combinations will be displayed when the Hidden property is True. This table only lists those files that will be selected with the hidden bit as the basis. Other files may be selected for the same File list box by setting the Archive, Normal, ReadOnly, or System properties.

Attribute Value	Select This File?
Archive, Hidden	Yes
Archive, Hidden, ReadOnly	Yes
Hidden	Yes
Hidden, ReadOnly	Yes
— anything else —	Any other combination will not display the file

Table 19-7 Displayed files when the Hidden property is True and Archive, ReadOnly, and System are False

Example

In the File System Controls project at the end of this chapter, the Hidden property is first read in the Form_Load event. The value returned sets the HiddenCheck check box. In the HiddenCheck_Click event, this property is set to reflect the status of the check box. When the check box is checked, the Hidden property is set to True (-1). This code is also shown in the example syntax given earlier. Note the Abs() function must be used to change the True value (-1) to the value of 1 needed to set a check box. A False (0) value is, of course, not affected.

LIST PROPERTY

Objects Affected

Check	Clipboard	▶ Combo	Command	CommonDlg
Data	Debug	▶ Dir	▶ Drive	▶ File
Form	Frame	Grid	Image	Label
Line	▶ List	MDI Form	Menu	OLE
Option	Picture	Printer	Screen	Scroll
Shape	Text	Timer		

Purpose

The List property can be used with a Drive, Directory, or File list box to read the name of a drive designation, directory name, or file name, respectively. The designation or name to be read is specified using an index to its position in the list. This property is read-only, and cannot be set at design time or runtime. Table 19-8 summarizes the arguments for the List property.

General Syntax

`[form]Name.List(Index%)`

Argument	Description
form	Name of the parent form
Name	Name of the control
Index%	An integer that identifies a particular list entry

Table 19-8 Arguments of the List property

Example Syntax

```
Sub Command1_Click ()
     ThisFile$ = File1.List(1)        'Puts second file name in list in ThisFile$
End Sub
```

Description

The List property works in the same general way with Drive, Directory, and File list boxes, differing only in the meaning of the item retrieved. (Note that directory boxes use a different index numbering system than other types of list boxes; see below.)

Specify the List property starting with the name of the Drive, Directory, or File list box to be affected. The List property is followed by an index number in parentheses designating the position of the item in the list to be read.

Note that the List property is also used with generic list and combo boxes. See Chapter 18, Lists, Combos, and Grids, for details.

Drive List Boxes

A Drive box's List property can be read at runtime to determine which drives are in the list and thus presumably available for use. The desired list item is specified by referencing the List property with an index number in a manner similar to using an array. The drives are listed in alphabetical order, and the index numbering starts at 0. So if a system has drives A:, B:, C:, and D:, drive A: has an index number of 0, and drive D: has an index number of 3. If the supplied index is greater than the highest list item's index number, a null string is returned.

For all types of drives, a 2-byte drive designation string is returned with the letter of the drive followed by a colon (for example, "D:"). When the listed drive is a local fixed disk, the 2-byte drive string is followed by the drive's label, if any. For instance, if the fixed disk "C:" has the label "MASTER," this property will return the string "C: [MASTER]". Network drives return the name of the network connection for this drive. For instance, if the shared drive \\SERVER\MAIN is mounted as logical drive D:, this property will return the string d: [\\SERVER\MAIN].

Directory List Boxes

A Directory box's List property can be read to determine the names of all the directories that are currently being displayed in the Directory list box. The desired list item is specified by referencing the List property with an index number in a manner similar to using an array.

The current open directory is set to index number -1. The index number is incremented once for each subdirectory under the current directory, and decremented for each parent directory over it. For instance, Figure 19-4 shows three Directory list boxes, all with different current directories in the same directory tree.

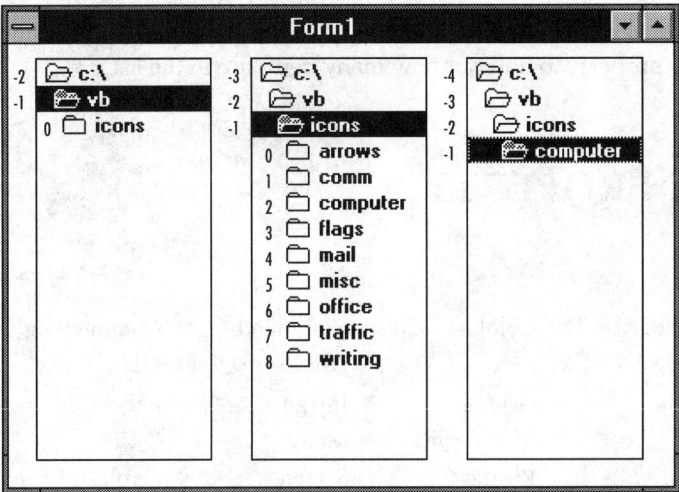

Figure 19-4 Index number assignment for Directory list boxes

In the first Directory box, the range for the index numbers in the list is -2 to 0. The current open directory is "VB," therefore it is assigned an index value of -1. The "C:\" directory is 1 above it, so it's assigned index -2. The "ICONS" directory is assigned index 0, since it is the first subdirectory under the first-level VB directory. The second directory box begins the index assignment at the "icons" directory, giving it an index of -1. The directories "VB" and "C:\" are assigned index numbers -2 and -3, respectively. As you can probably now guess, the range of index numbers in the third Directory box is -4 to -1.

The string returned when the List property is used with the Directory box contains the full path name from the root directory to the directory in the specified list item.

File List Boxes

A File list box's List property can be read at runtime to find out all the files that match the current Archive, Hidden, Normal, Pattern, ReadOnly, and System properties. The file name returned by this property does not include the file's full path. The latter can be obtained using the Path property with the File list box.

The desired list item is specified by referencing the List property with an index number in a manner similar to using an array. The first file in the list is index 0. The last file has an index number equal to the number of files in the list minus 1. If the supplied index is greater than the highest list item's index number, a null string is returned.

The example syntax assigns the name of the second file in the file list to the variable ThisFile$. Notice that the meaning of the index value 1 would be different if a directory list box were used: in that case 1 would mean the second file name listed below the current directory.

Comment

Use the ListCount property to find out how many items are in the list.

LISTCOUNT PROPERTY

Objects Affected

Check	Clipboard	▶ Combo	Command	CommonDlg
Data	Debug	▶ Dir	▶ Drive	▶ File
Form	Frame	Grid	Image	Label
Line	▶ List	MDI Form	Menu	OLE
Option	Picture	Printer	Screen	Scroll
Shape	Text	Timer		

Purpose

The ListCount property is read at runtime to determine the number of listed items in a Drive, Directory, or File list box. This is a read-only property, and cannot be set at design time or runtime. Table 19-9 summarizes the arguments of the ListCount property.

General Syntax

```
[form!]Name.ListCount
```

Argument	Description
form	Name of the parent form
Name	Name of the control

Table 19-9 Arguments of the ListCount property

Example Syntax

```
Form_Load ()
    NumberOfFiles% = File1.ListCount
    NumberOfSubDirs% = Dir1.ListCount
End Sub
```

754

Description

When used with Drive and File list boxes, the ListCount property returns the number of items in the list. When used with a Directory list box, the property returns the number of subdirectories under the current directory entry.

Specify the ListCount property beginning with the name of the Drive, Directory, or File list control to be affected.

The example syntax uses the ListCount property to obtain the number of files and subdirectories, respectively. These numbers are assigned to variables for future use.

Note that the ListCount property is also used with generic list and combo boxes. See Chapter 18, Lists, Combos, and Grids, for details.

Example

The ListCount property is used in several of the events in the File System Controls project at the end of this chapter. In each of these events, the File1.ListCount property updates the Caption property of the lablCount label. This label displays to the user the number of files contained in the File list box.

Comments

The property returns the number of items in a list, not the index number of the last listed item. Because the index numbers in a list are zero-based, the index number of the last listed item is always ListCount - 1.

LISTINDEX PROPERTY

Objects Affected

Check	Clipboard	▶ Combo	Command	CommonDlg
Data	Debug	▶ Dir	▶ Drive	▶ File
Form	Frame	Grid	Image	Label
Line	▶ List	MDI Form	Menu	OLE
Option	Picture	Printer	Screen	Scroll
Shape	Text	Timer		

Purpose

The ListIndex property returns or sets the index number of the selected item in a Drive, Directory, or File list box. This property cannot be set at design time. Table 19-10 summarizes the arguments of the ListIndex property.

General Syntax

```
[form!]Name.ListIndex [= Index%]
```

Argument	Description
form	Name of the parent form
Name	Name of the control
Index%	Identifies a particular entry in the control's list

Table 19-10 Arguments of the ListIndex property

Example Syntax

```
Sub Command1_Click ()
    File1.ListIndex = 0      'Sets the selected item to the first item in the list
    L% = File1.ListIndex     'Assigns L% the index of the selected item in File1
End Sub
```

Description

The ListIndex property can be used to read the index number of the selected item in a Drive, Directory, or File list box. Specifying an index sets the currently selected item to the item in that position on the list, keeping in mind that the first item is referenced with index number 0.

When the program begins, the ListIndex for a drive list box is assigned the value that corresponds to the current default drive. For a Directory list box, the program begins with ListIndex set to -1, indicating the current open directory. For File list boxes, the ListIndex property begins at -1, indicating that no file has been selected yet. When used on a Directory list box, keep in mind that the selected directory can be different from the current directory in the box. Clicking on a directory entry once selects it; double-clicking an entry opens it. In order to determine the current open directory entry, use the List property with a -1 index value.

The ListIndex property can also be assigned a value in order to change the selected item in a Drive, Directory, or File list box. The value assigned to the ListIndex property must be within the range of the list or an "Invalid property array index" error will occur.

The first statement in the example syntax sets the currently selected file in file list box File1 to the first item on the displayed list. The second example statement saves the index number of the currently selected file in File list box File1 in the variable L%.

MULTISELECT PROPERTY

Objects Affected

Check	Clipboard	Combo	Command	CommonDlg
Data	Debug	Dir	Drive	▶ File
Form	Frame	Grid	Image	Label
Line	▶ List	MDI Form	Menu	OLE
Option	Picture	Printer	Screen	Scroll
Shape	Text	Timer		

Purpose

The MultiSelect property lets the user choose more than one file at a time from the File list box. Its three possible states include no multiple select allowed, simple multiple select, and extended multiple select. Tables 19-11 and 19-12 list the arguments and possible settings of the MultiSelect property.

General Syntax

```
[form!]Name.Multiselect
```

Argument	Description
Form	Name of the parent form
Name	Name of the list box

Table 19-11 Arguments of the MultiSelect property

Setting	Description
0	(Default). Single selection only, multiple selection not allowed
1	Simple multiple selection. Multiple items selected by clicking or the spacebar
2	Extended multiple selection. Whole domains selected with Shift, individual items with Ctrl

Table 19-12 Possible settings for MultiSelect

757

Example Syntax

```
Sub DeleteFiles (ListBox as Control)
    Select Case listBox.MultiSelect
        Case 0                                  'no multiple selection
            Kill listBox.FileName
        Case 1, 2                               'multiple selections
            For i = 0 to listBox.ListCount - 1
                If listBox.Selected(i) Then
                    Kill listBox.FileName
                End If
            Next i
    End Select
End Sub
```

Description

MultiSelect lets the user choose more than one item from a list box. This lets a user perform batch operations (like moving or deleting a group of files) instead of repeating several steps over and over for each file to be operated on. Note that a regular list box also has the MultiSelect property; for more details, see Chapter 18, Lists, Combos, and Grids.

You'll generally set MultiSelect at design time and write your code to either expect a multiple selection or a single selection. It is possible to read (but not set) MultiSelect at runtime, so you could write a generic procedure that can handle either, as in the above example syntax.

The default setting, 0, means that only single selections may be made in the list box. Selecting a new file deselects any previous file. A setting of 1 means that the user can perform a simple multiple selection. The spacebar, or single mouse click, selects or deselects individual files from the list. The user can scroll up or down through the list with the usual movement keys and the scroll bars. A setting of 2 means the user may use extended multiple selection. (SHIFT) clicking or (SHIFT)-(↑), (↓), (←), (→) extends the selection from the previously selected file to the current file. (CTRL) clicking selects or deselects individual files in the list.

Example

The File list box in the File System Controls project at the end of this chapter uses MultiSelect to allow for batch operations.

NORMAL PROPERTY

Objects Affected

Check	Clipboard	Combo	Command	CommonDlg
Data	Debug	Dir	Drive	▶ File

Form	Frame	Grid	Image	Label
Line	List	MDI Form	Menu	OLE
Option	Picture	Printer	Screen	Scroll
Shape	Text	Timer		

Purpose

The Normal property sets or returns a value that determines whether or not normal files will be displayed in a File list box. Normal files are those that do not have the hidden or system attribute set. This property can be set at design time, and set or read at runtime. Table 19-13 summarizes the arguments of the Normal property.

General Syntax

```
[form!]Name.Normal [= boolean%]
```

Argument	Description
form	Name of the parent form
Name	Name of the File list box
boolean%	A True (-1) or False (0) indicating whether normal files will be selected

Table 19-13 Arguments of the Normal property

Example Syntax

```
Sub NormalCheck_Click ()
    File1.Normal = -NormalCheck.Value     'Sets the Normal property of File1
End Sub

Sub Form_Load ()
    NormalBit = Abs(File1.Normal)      'Read the Normal property setting
    NormalCheck.Value = NormalBit      'Set the check box to reflect it
End Sub
```

Description

The DOS file system sets aside 1 byte in the directory entry of each file for attribute information. Five properties select files for display in a File list box based on the setting of this attribute byte: the Archive, Hidden, Normal, ReadOnly, and System properties. The set of files displayed in a File list box is based on the combination of these properties. Normal files are defined as all files

759

whose hidden and system bits are not set on, regardless of the settings of the archive and read-only bits.

The Normal property has two possible values: True (-1) or False (0). If the Normal property is not changed at design time, its value will be True (-1) when the program begins.

Setting this property to True selects all files whose hidden and system bits are set off, regardless of the settings of the archive and read-only bits. In essence, this makes normal files a superset of the files selected with the Archive and ReadOnly properties, combined with all files that have no attribute bits set on. When this property is set to False, the File list box excludes any files that have none of the attribute bits set on. Any other files may be selected by setting the other four attribute properties.

Table 19-14 lists all the possible combinations for the attribute byte, and which of those combinations will be selected when the Normal property is True. This table lists only those files that will be selected when the hidden and system bits are off. Other files may be selected by setting the Hidden and System properties.

Attribute Value	Select This File?
none set	Yes
Archive	Yes
Archive, ReadOnly	Yes
ReadOnly	Yes
— anything else —	Any other combination will not display the file

Table 19-14 Displayed files when the Normal property is True and System and Hidden are False

Example

In the File System Controls project at the end of this chapter, the Normal property is first read in the Form_Load event. The value returned sets the NormalCheck check box. In the NormalCheck_Click event, this property is set to reflect the status of the check box. When the check box is checked, the Normal property is set to True (-1). This code is also shown in the example syntax above. Note that the Abs() function must be used to turn a regular True value (-1) into the one value needed to set a check box.

PATH PROPERTY

Objects Affected

Check	Clipboard	Combo	Command	CommonDlg
Data	Debug	▶ Dir	Drive	▶ File
Form	Frame	Grid	Image	Label
Line	List	MDI Form	Menu	OLE
Option	Picture	Printer	Screen	Scroll
Shape	Text	Timer		

Purpose

The Path property sets or reads the currently opened directory path in a Directory list box, or the current directory in a File list box. At design time this property is set to the current default directory, and cannot be changed. However, this property can be set or read at runtime. Table 19-15 summarizes the arguments of the Path property.

General Syntax

```
[form!]Name.Path [= path$]
```

Argument	Description
form	Name of the parent form
Name	Name of the File or Directory list box
path$	A string containing a valid path name

Table 19-15 Arguments of the Path property

Example Syntax

```
Sub Dir1_Change ()              'Read the Dir list box Path to set the
    File1.Path = Dir1.Path      'File list box Path property and
    ChDir Dir1.Path             'change the current directory.
End Sub

Sub File1_PathChange ()
    Dir1.Path = File1.Path      'Change the Dir list box Path to the
    Drive1.Drive = File1.Path   'Path from the File list box
End Sub
```

Description

Specify the Path property by beginning with the name of the Directory or File list box to be affected. To set this property, specify a string containing a valid path name.

The operation of the Path property for Directory list boxes is somewhat different than in File list boxes, so the two controls will be discussed separately.

Directory List Boxes

A user can select a directory entry in a Directory list box by clicking on it. However, this does not open the directory; it merely moves the highlight bar to it and changes the ListIndex property to reflect the selected directory. When a user double-clicks on a directory entry, that entry is opened, and any subdirectories underneath it are displayed.

The Path property returns the directory path of the currently open directory in a Directory list box. The full path is returned, including the drive letter.

You can also assign a string to this property from within your program's code. This string must contain the valid path name of an existing directory on the system on which your program is run. This causes the open directory in the Directory list box to be changed to the path specified in the string.

Any time the Path property of a Directory list box is changed, either by the user or by the program, the Directory list box's Change event is triggered.

File List Boxes

The Path property of the File list box control specifies the directory from which the box is to select its files. Reading this property returns the full path of the File list box's current directory, including the drive letter.

You can change the current directory path for a File list box by assigning a string to this property from within your program's code. This string must contain the valid path name of an existing directory on the system on which your program is run. This causes the current directory of a File list box to be changed to the path specified in the string.

Any time the Path property of a File list box is changed, the File list box's PathChange event is triggered.

Example

The Path property for the File1 list box is set in the Form_Load and Dir1_Change events. For the Dir1 list box, it is set in the Form_Load and File1_PathChange events. Whenever the user changes the path in the Directory list or File list box, the other's property is set to reflect the change. This code is also shown in the example syntax above.

Comments

Some sort of validity checking should be in place to ensure the string being assigned to the Path property is a valid existing drive and path. If the path is not valid, an error will occur.

PATHCHANGE EVENT

Objects Affected

Check	Clipboard	Combo	Command	CommonDlg
Data	Debug	Dir	Drive	▶ File
Form	Frame	Grid	Image	Label
Line	List	MDI Form	Menu	OLE
Option	Picture	Printer	Screen	Scroll
Shape	Text	Timer		

Purpose

The PathChange event specifies the actions to take when the current path of a File list box changes. The arguments for the PathChange event are summarized in Table 19-16.

General Syntax

```
Name_PathChange ([Index As Integer])
```

Argument	Description
Name	Name of the File list box
Index	Uniquely identifies an element of a control array

Table 19-16 Arguments of the PathChange event

Example Syntax

```
Sub File1_PathChange ()
    Dir1.Path = File1.Path          'When the File list box's path is changed,
    Drive1.Drive = File1.Path       'change the path in the Dir & Drive list boxes
End Sub
```

763

Description

The PathChange event activates anytime the current path for a File list box changes. This can happen by assigning a new value to the Path property, or by assigning a value that includes a path to the FileName property of the File list box.

This event is mostly used so the program can change the Path or Drive properties for any Directory or Drive list boxes that are on the same form. The example syntax shows how to update the path for a Drive and a Directory list box when a file box's path is changed somewhere in the code.

Control Array

The index argument is only used if the related control is part of a control array. This index specifies which element of the array is the one that activated the event. When referencing the control, the element being referenced must be specified by placing the index number between parentheses just after the control name, and before the property name (for example, Name(Index).Property).

Example

In the File System Controls project at the end of this chapter, the Path property of the Directory list box control, Dir1, can be changed by the user when a directory entry is clicked on. This causes the Dir1_Change event to occur. In this event, The Path property of Dir1 is assigned to the Path property of the File list box control, File1. This causes the current directory for File1 to be changed to the directory opened by the user. When File1.Path is assigned the value of Dir1.Path, the listed entries in File1 are updated to reflect the files in the opened directory.

Comments

Directory list boxes do not have a PathChange event. This function is covered by using their Change event.

PATTERN PROPERTY

Objects Affected

Check	Clipboard	Combo	Command	CommonDlg
Data	Debug	Dir	Drive ▶	File
Form	Frame	Grid	Image	Label
Line	List	MDI Form	Menu	OLE
Option	Picture	Printer	Screen	Scroll
Shape	Text	Timer		

Purpose

The Pattern property sets or reads the currently selected file-matching pattern in a File list box. Only files that match the Pattern property are displayed in the File list box. This property can be set at design time, and set or read at runtime. Table 19-17 lists the arguments for the Pattern property.

General Syntax

```
[form!]Name.FileName [= pattern$]
```

Argument	Description
form	Name of the parent form
Name	Name of the File list box
pattern$	Full or partial file name pattern

Table 19-17 Arguments of the Pattern property

Example Syntax

```
Sub Text1_LostFocus ()
    File1.Pattern = Text1.Text
End Sub
```

Description

The setting of the Pattern property determines which files will be displayed in the File list box. Begin the specification of this property with the name of the File list box to be affected. Follow the property name with an equal sign and a string containing a valid DOS file pattern. The pattern can have no more than eight characters for a name, a period, and up to three characters for the extension. The wildcard characters (* and ?) can be (and most often are) used in the pattern. The "?" wildcard matches all characters that share the same position in the file name. The "*" wildcard matches all files that share the same pattern up to the position held by it. The Pattern property cannot specify a drive or path. When this property is changed by a program it activates the PatternChange event for that File list box.

When the Pattern property is read, it returns the current pattern setting for the specified File list box.

The example code assigns the string "*.DAT" to the Pattern for the File1 File list box. The list will change to show only those files that end in the .DAT extension. (What is displayed is also subject to the settings of the attribute properties.)

Example

In the File System Controls project at the end of this chapter, the Pattern property for the File1 list box is set at design time to display all the files (*.*).

Comments

Some sort of validity checking should be in place to ensure the string being assigned to the Pattern property is a valid pattern. If the pattern is not valid, an error will occur. Note that you can specify a drive and path as well as pattern by using the FileName property rather than the Pattern property.

PATTERNCHANGE EVENT

Objects Affected

Check	Clipboard	Combo	Command	CommonDlg
Data	Debug	Dir	Drive	▶ File
Form	Frame	Grid	Image	Label
Line	List	MDI Form	Menu	OLE
Option	Picture	Printer	Screen	Scroll
Shape	Text	Timer		

Purpose

The PatternChange event specifies the actions to take when the Pattern property of a File list box changes. The Pattern property specifies a pattern (including DOS wildcards) that specifies which file names will be listed in a file list box. The arguments for the PatternChange event are summarized in Table 19-18.

General Syntax

```
Name_PatternChange ([Index As Integer])
```

Argument	Description
Name	Name of the File list box
Index	Uniquely identifies an element of a control array

Table 19-18 Arguments of the PatternChange property

Example Syntax

```
Sub File1_PatternChange ()
    Pattern.Text = File1.Pattern
End Sub
```

Description

The PatternChange event activates anytime the display pattern for a File list box changes. This happens when a new value is assigned to the Pattern property or the FileName property of the File list box.

The example syntax responds to a change in the file pattern by assigning the new pattern to the text for the Pattern text box, displaying it as the default text in the text entry area.

Control Array

The index argument is only used if the related control is part of a control array. This index specifies which element of the array is the one that activated the event. When referencing the control, the element being referenced must be specified by placing the index number between parentheses just after the control name, and before the property name (for example, Name(Index).Property).

Example

In the File System Controls project at the end of this chapter, the PathChange event for File list box File1 is coded so that it shows the number of matching files in the box's caption, and also updates the display of the selected file in the TextSelected text box.

Comments

Directory list boxes do not have a PathChange event. This function is covered by using the Change event.

READONLY PROPERTY

Objects Affected

Check	Clipboard	Combo	Command	CommonDlg
▶ Data	Debug	Dir	Drive	▶ File
Form	Frame	Grid	Image	Label
Line	List	MDI Form	Menu	OLE

(continued on next page)

(continued from previous page)

Option	Picture	Printer	Screen	Scroll
Shape	Text	Timer		

Purpose

The ReadOnly property sets or returns a value that determines whether or not files with their read-only bit on will be displayed in a File list box. Read-only files cannot be changed or deleted, but only examined. Making files read-only thus offers a measure of protection for important files. The ReadOnly property can be set at design time, and set or read at runtime. The arguments for the ReadOnly property are summarized in Table 19-19.

General Syntax

```
[form!]Name.ReadOnly [= boolean%]
```

Argument	Description
form	Name of the parent form
Name	Name of the File list box
boolean%	A True (-1) or False (0) indicating whether read-only files will be selected

Table 19-19 Arguments of the ReadOnly property

Example Syntax

```
Sub ReadOnlyCheck_Click ()
    File1.ReadOnly = -ReadOnlyCheck.Value       'Sets the ReadOnly property of File1
End Sub

Sub Form_Load ()
    Dim ReadOnlyBit
    ReadOnlyBit = Abs(File1.ReadOnly)           'Read the ReadOnly property setting
    ReadOnlyCheck.Value = ReadOnlyBit           'Set the check box to reflect it
End Sub
```

Description

The DOS file system sets aside 1 byte in the directory entry of each file for attribute information. Five properties can select files for display in a File list box based on the setting of this attribute byte: the Archive, Hidden, Normal, ReadOnly, and System properties. The set of files displayed in a File list box is based on the combination of these properties.

768

One of the bits in this attribute byte is the read-only bit. When this bit is set on, DOS allows the related file to be read from, but not written to or deleted. This prevents users from inadvertently changing or erasing sensitive files.

The ReadOnly property selects files based on the setting of the read-only bit. You can assign a value to the ReadOnly property, or obtain the current value of this attribute.

The ReadOnly property has two possible values: True (-1) or False (0). If the ReadOnly property is not changed at design time, its value will be True (-1) when the program begins.

The files selected when this property is True are a subset of the files selected by the Normal property. In other words, setting this property to True has no effect unless the Normal property is set to False. In that case any files whose read-only bit is set on will be selected for display, regardless of the setting of the archive bit. However, if a file's read-only bit is on, but its hidden or system bits are also set on, it will not be selected unless the Hidden or System properties are also True.

Table 19-20 lists all the possible combinations for the attribute byte, and which of those combinations will be displayed when the ReadOnly property is True. This table lists only the files that will be selected with the ReadOnly bit as the basis. Other files may be selected for the same File list box by setting the Archive, Hidden, or System properties.

Attribute Value	Select This File?
Archive, ReadOnly	Yes
ReadOnly	Yes
— anything else —	Any other combination will not display the file

Table 19-20 Displayed files when the ReadOnly property is True, and Archive, System, and Hidden are False

Example

In the File System Controls project at the end of this chapter, the ReadOnly property is first read in the Form_Load event. The value returned sets the ReadOnlyCheck check box. In the ReadOnlyCheck_Click event, this property is set to reflect the status of the check box. When the check box is checked, the ReadOnly property is set to True (-1). This is also shown in the example syntax. Note that the Abs() function must be used to turn a True (-1) value into the value of 1 needed to set the check box.

Comment

The data control also has a ReadOnly property that is completely different than the file system ReadOnly property discussed here.

REFRESH METHOD

Objects Affected

▶ Check	Clipboard	▶ Combo	▶ Command	CommonDlg
▶ Data	Debug	▶ Dir	▶ Drive	▶ File
▶ Form	▶ Frame	▶ Grid	▶ Image	▶ Label
▶ Line	▶ List	MDI Form	Menu	▶ OLE
▶ Option	▶ Picture	Printer	Screen	▶ Scroll
▶ Shape	▶ Text	Timer		

Purpose

The Refresh method forces any changes affecting a control to be reflected in its status or display immediately. Table 19-21 summarizes the arguments for the Refresh property.

General Syntax

```
[form!]Name.Refresh
```

Argument	Description
form	Name of the parent form
Name	Name of the control

Table 19-21 Arguments of the Refresh method

Example Syntax

```
Sub Timer1_Timer ()
    File1.Refresh            'Refresh the file list box in case of network activity
End Sub
```

770

Description

The Refresh method is useful in two situations. First, because Windows is a multi-tasking program, it is possible to make a change to a control that is not reflected on the screen because background processing is in progress. Using the Refresh method causes any changes to the specified control to be reflected immediately.

Second, the Refresh method can be used to cause the Drive, Directory, and File list boxes to update their lists. These controls only read their information from the disk when the user chooses an item from their list. This can cause problems if the files or directories have changed since the information was read. For instance, if a program uses the File list box to delete a file, unless the Refresh method is invoked, that file name stays in the File list box after the user deletes it. These controls may also need to be refreshed on a regular basis if the user is working in a networked environment, where the file information can change without notice.

Specify the Refresh method by beginning with the name of the control (such as a Drive, Directory, or File list box) to be affected.

In the example syntax, the control File1 (presumably a file list box) is refreshed. Any files that have been added to or deleted from the directory displayed by the file list box (perhaps by another running process on a network) will now be reflected in the file list.

Example

In the File System Controls project at the end of this chapter, the Refresh method is used in the File1_Click event. This causes any changes that have been made to the drive and file information by any other programs to be updated in this program.

Comments

Other than the File-related list boxes, most controls will automatically refresh as fast as needed without using the Refresh method.

SELECTED PROPERTY

Objects Affected

Check	Clipboard	Combo	Command	CommonDlg
Data	Debug	Dir	Drive	▸ File
Form	Frame	Grid	Image	Label
Line	▸ List	MDI Form	Menu	OLE
Option	Picture	Printer	Screen	Scroll
Shape	Text	Timer		

Purpose

The Selected property lets you determine which items in a multiple selection list are selected. This property is an array of True and False values, with one entry for each item in the list. Table 19-22 summarizes the arguments for the Selected property.

General Syntax

```
[form!]Name.Selected(Index%) [= boolean%]
```

Argument	Description
form	Name of the parent form
Name	Name of the list box
Index%	Index in the array; corresponds to ListIndex
boolean%	True (-1) if selected; False (0) if not selected

Table 19-22 Arguments for the Selected property

Example Syntax

```
Sub Command1_Click ()
    For i = 0 to File1.ListCount - 1
        If File1.Selected(i) Then
            Kill File1.FileName
        End If
    Next i
End Sub
```

Description

The Selected property lets you determine which files in a multiple selection list box are selected. Using ListIndex in a multiple selection will only return the number of the file the highlight bar is on; not whether or not that file is selected.

The Selected property returns an array of Boolean values with a one-to-one correspondence to the ListIndex property of the list. Stepping through the array, as in the example syntax, is an easy way to check each file for its selected status.

772

Example

The File System Controls project at the end of the chapter uses the Selected property to move multiple files from a list box to a combo box.

SYSTEM PROPERTY

Objects Affected

Check	Clipboard	Combo	Command	CommonDlg
Data	Debug	Dir	Drive ▶	File
Form	Frame	Grid	Image	Label
Line	List	MDI Form	Menu	OLE
Option	Picture	Printer	Screen	Scroll
Shape	Text	Timer		

Purpose

The System property sets or returns a value that determines whether or not files with their system bit set on will be displayed in a File list box. The System bit is used by DOS to designate files that are of special importance to the system, and thus should be hidden from sight and protected from deletion. The System property can be set at design time, and set or read at runtime. Table 19-23 summarizes the arguments of the System property.

General Syntax

```
[form!]Name.System [= boolean%]
```

Argument	Description
form	Name of the parent form
Name	Name of the File list box
boolean%	A True (-1) or False (0) indicating whether system files will be selected

Table 19-23 Arguments of the System property

Example Syntax

```
Sub SystemCheck_Click ()
    File1.System = -SystemCheck.Value        'Sets the System property of File1
End Sub

Sub Form_Load ()
    Dim SystemBit
    SystemBit = Abs(File1.System)        'Read the System property setting
    SystemCheck.Value = SystemBit        'Set the check box to reflect it
End Sub
```

Description

The DOS file system sets aside 1 byte in the directory entry of each file for attribute information. Five properties can select files for display in a File list box based on the setting of this attribute byte: the Archive, Hidden, Normal, ReadOnly, and System properties. The set of files displayed in a file list box is based on the combination of these properties.

The system attribute bit normally designates a file as one of the DOS kernel or BIOS files. However, this bit can be set for other nonsystem files, such as the Windows permanent swap file or a disk doubler's hidden volume. As with the read-only attribute bit, files with the system bit set cannot be deleted.

The System property selects files based on the setting of the system attribute bit. This property has two possible values: True (-1) or False (0). If the System property is not changed at design time, its value will be False (0) when the program begins.

Setting this property to True (-1) selects files with their system bit set on to be displayed, regardless of the setting of the archive and read-only bits. However, if a file also has its hidden bit set on, it will only be displayed if the Hidden property is also set to True. Setting this property to False prevents all files whose system bit is set on to be excluded from the File list box, regardless of the settings of the other four attribute properties.

Table 19-24 lists all the possible combinations for the attribute byte, and which of those combinations will be displayed when the System property is True. This table only lists those files that will be selected with the system bit as the basis. Other files may be selected for the same File list box by setting the Archive, Hidden, Normal, or ReadOnly properties.

Attribute Value	Select This File?
Archive, ReadOnly, System	Yes
Archive, System	Yes

Attribute Value	Select This File?
ReadOnly, System	Yes
System	Yes
— anything else —	Any other combination will not display the file

Table 19-24 Displayed files when the System property is True, and Archive, ReadOnly, and Hidden are False

Example

In the File System Controls project at the end of this chapter, the System property is first read in the Form_Load event. The value returned sets the SystemCheck check box. In the SystemCheck_Click event, this property is set to reflect the status of the check box. When the check box is checked, the System property is set to True (-1). This code is also shown in the example syntax. Note that the Abs() function must be used to turn the -1 (True) value into the value of 1 needed to set the check box.

THE FILE SYSTEM CONTROLS PROJECT

Project Overview

This project creates a program that lets the user explore the drives, directories, and files on a system. It uses each of the properties and events discussed in this chapter. By following the examples in this project, you should be able to learn the principles of Drive, Directory, and File list boxes.

Assembling the Project

1. Create a new form (the File System Controls form), and place on it the following controls. Use Table 19-25 to set the properties of the form and each control.

Object	Property	Setting
Form	BorderStyle	3–Fixed Double

(continued on next page)

(continued from previous page)

Object	Property	Setting
	Caption	File System Controls Project
	Name	formMain
Check Box	Caption	Archive
	Index	0
	Name	chekAttrib
Check Box	Caption	Hidden
	Index	1
	Name	chekAttrib
Check Box	Caption	Normal
	Index	2
	Name	chekAttrib
Check Box	Caption	Read Only
	Index	3
	Name	chekAttrib
Check Box	Caption	System
	Index	4
	Name	chekAttrib
TextBox	Name	textSelected
	Text	*.*
File List Box	Name	File1

Object	Property	Setting
	Pattern	*.*
Label	Name	lablCount
Label	Name	lablBytes
Drive	Name	Drive1
Directory	Name	Dir1
Command	Caption	&OK
	Default	True (-1)
	Name	cmndOK
Command	Caption	&Refresh
	Name	cmndRefresh
Command	Caption	E&xit
	Name	cmndExit

Table 19-25 Property settings for the File System Controls project

2. Check the appearance of your form against Figure 19-5.

3. Enter the following code into the Form_Load event. This event uses the CurDir$ function to set the starting paths for the Drive1, Dir1, and File1 list boxes. It also reads the default attribute settings from the File1 File list box control, and sets the values of the chekAttrib control array. Check boxes are set on with a value of 1, while the attribute properties of a File list box return a 0 or a -1. Therefore, the Abs() (absolute value) function changes the -1 to a 1.

```
Sub Form_Load ()
    Drive1.Drive = CurDir$
    Dir1.Path = CurDir$
    File1.Path = CurDir$
    chekAttrib(0).Value = Abs(File1.Archive)
    chekAttrib(1).Value = Abs(File1.Hidden)
```

(continued on next page)

(continued from previous page)

```
        chekAttrib(2).Value = Abs(File1.Normal)
        chekAttrib(3).Value = Abs(File1.ReadOnly)
        chekAttrib(4).Value = Abs(File1.System)
        textSelected.Text = ParseFileName()
End Sub
```

4. Enter the following code into the chekAttrib_Click event. This event uses the value of the control array member's check box Value property to set the corresponding attribute property of the File1 File list box. They also update the label lablCount to reflect the number of files displayed in the File1 File list box.

```
Sub chekAttrib_Click (Index As Integer)
    Select Case Index
        Case 0' attrib
            File1.Archive = -chekAttrib(0).Value
        Case 1' hidden
            File1.Hidden = -chekAttrib(1).Value
        Case 2' normal
            File1.Normal = -chekAttrib(2).Value
        Case 3' read only
            File1.ReadOnly = -chekAttrib(3).Value
        Case 4' system
            File1.System = -chekAttrib(4).Value
    End Select
    lablCount.Caption = Format$(File1.ListCount, "##,###") + " Files"
End Sub
```

5. Enter the following code into the Dir1_Change event. This event does two things. First it updates the Path property of the File1 File list box to reflect the change made to this directory's path. If the new path is different from the old, doing this also causes the File1_PathChange event to be activated. Second, it changes the current directory to the one specified by the new path.

```
Sub Dir1_Change ()
    File1.Path = Dir1.Path
    ChDir Dir1.Path
End Sub
```

6. Enter the following code into the File1_Change event. This event first updates the Path property of the Dir1 Directory list box. If the new path is different from the old, doing this also causes the Dir1_Change event to occur. It also sets the Drive property of the Drive1 drive list box. Again, if this changes the current Drive setting, the Drive1_Change event will be activated. The event then updates the text in the TextSelected text box control by making a call to the ParseFileName function. Finally, the number of files displayed in the File1 File list box is updated.

```
Sub File1_PathChange ()
    lablCount.Caption = Format$(File1.ListCount, "##,##0") + " Files"
    textSelected.Text = ParseFileName()
    Dir1.Path = File1.Path
    Drive1.Drive = File1.Path
    lablBytes.Caption = ""
End Sub
```

778

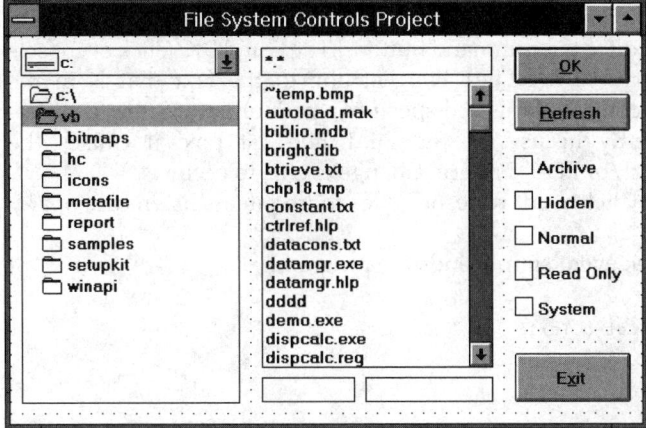

Figure 19-5 The File System Controls project during design

7. Enter the following code into the File1_PatternChange event. This event occurs when the user changes the FileName property by editing the text in the TextSelected text box.

```
Sub File1_PatternChange ()
    lablCount.Caption = Format$(File1.ListCount, "##,##0") + " Files"
    textSelected.Text = ParseFileName()
End Sub
```

8. Enter the following text into the Drive1_Change event. This event sets the Path property of the Dir1 Directory list box. If this changes the current path for the Directory list box, the Dir1_Change event will be initiated.

```
Sub Drive1_Change ()
    Dir1.Path = CurDir$(Drive1.Drive)
End Sub
```

9. Enter the following code into the File1_Click event. Clicking on a file places its name in the TextSelected text box.

```
Sub File1_Click ()
    textSelected.Text = File1.FileName
End Sub
```

10. Enter the following code in the File1_MouseUp event. This steps through the files in the File list box and adds up the total number of bytes for the selected files.

```
Sub File1_MouseUp (Button As Integer, Shift As Integer, X As Single, Y As Single)
    For i = 0 To File1.ListCount - 1
        if Right$(File1.Path,1) = "\" Then
            TempPath$ = File1.Path + "\" + File1.Filename
        else
            TempPath$ = File1.Path + File1.Filename
        end if
        If File1.Selected(i) Then
            bytes = bytes + FileLen(File1.List(i))
        End If
    Next i
    lablBytes.Caption = Format$(bytes, " ###,###,##0") & " Bytes"
End Sub
```

779

11. Enter the following text for the command buttons. The cmndOK_Click event sets the FileName property of the File1 File list box to the text that is in the TextSelected text box control. If this text specifies a path or pattern that is different than that currently in use by the File1 File list box, it causes the File1_PathChange, and/or File1_Pattern_Change events to occur.

The cmndRefresh_Click event refreshes File1 to update its list in case of any background changes.

The cmndExit_Click event simply ends the program.

```
Sub cmndOK_Click ()
    File1.FileName = TextSelected.Text
End Sub

Sub cmndRefresh_Click ()
    File1.Refresh
End Sub

Sub cmndExit_Click ()
    End
End Sub
```

12. Enter the following code in the General Declarations area of the form. Once the first line is complete (Function…) Visual Basic will give this function its own window. This function reads the current File1.Path and File1.FileName properties and, based on these, parses together the full path and file name of the selected file(s).

```
Function ParseFileName () As String
    Dim tempFile As String
    Dim tempDir As String

    tempDir = File1.Path
    tempFile = File1.Pattern
    If tempFile = "" Then tempFile = "*.*"
    If Right$(tempDir, 1) <> "\" Then tempFile = "\" + tempFile
    ParseFileName = tempDir + tempFile
End Function
```

How It Works

This very simple program allows the user to explore the disk drives, directories, and files on the system on which it is run. The user can select drives, directories, and files by clicking or double-clicking on the desired lists. Clicking on the attribute (Archive, Hidden, Normal, Read Only, and System) check boxes causes the selection of the files in the File1 File list box to be limited to those that match the checked boxes.

The selected files for display in the File1 File list box can also be modified by entering a new path or pattern in the TextSelected text box control, and clicking the OK button (or pressing the (ENTER) key, since the Default property of the cmndOK control is set to True). For instance, placing the text "*.EXE" will cause

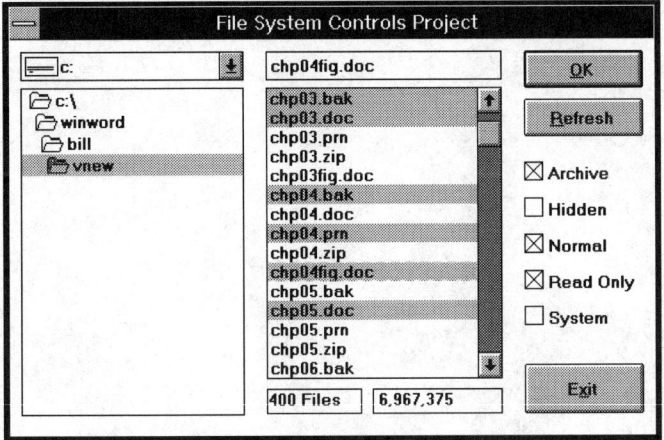

Figure 19-6 The File System Controls project in action

only the files in the selected directory that have an extension of "EXE" to be displayed in the file list box.

Selecting a file or multiple files in File1 also updates the total bytes label. The routine steps through each file in the list box and if it has been selected, it adds the length of the file in bytes to the running total.

Regardless of where a change is made, that change is reflected by all the related controls. For instance, if the current directory is changed by double-clicking on the Dir1 directory list box, the files in the File1 File list box are updated. Figure 19-6 shows the program in action

20

SCROLL BARS

You'll most commonly see scroll bars being used to move through, or *scroll*, long text entries. Clicking on the scroll bar lets you move up and down or left and right through text that is too large to display in the window. It's as though you had a small viewport that could be moved around to view a larger world beyond.

This analogy becomes more compelling when scroll bars control a graphics viewport. Imagine a graphic image of a map that's too large to display in the window. Scrolling would let you "fly" over the map to expose whatever area you wanted.

Scroll bars can also graphically represent numeric values. Let's say that you had a number that represented magnification of your map image. Rather than forcing users to take their hands off the mouse to manually enter numbers for the amount of magnification, you could set up a scroll bar so they could directly manipulate the value. This would also provide a graphic representation of how the present magnification related to the minimum and maximum values. Now they can both fly over their map and dive into it.

Scroll bars are ubiquitous features in Windows programs. Visual Basic, as usual, makes it simple to use these powerful tools in your programs.

OPERATING SCROLL BARS

Scroll bars consist of a bar with arrows at each end and a button (called the *thumb*) between the arrows. There are two types of scroll bars: vertical (VScroll) and horizontal (HScroll). Figure 20-1 illustrates the two kinds of scroll bars.

The thumb's position directly relates to the value represented by the scroll bar. For horizontal scroll bars, the thumb is all the way to the left when the value of the scroll bar is at its minimum setting and

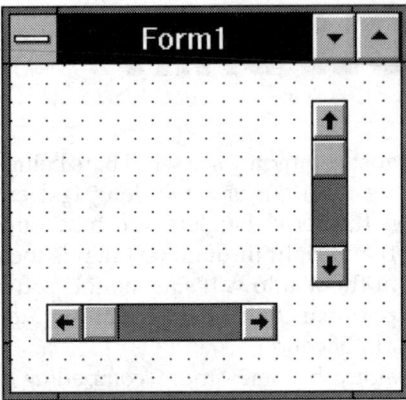

Figure 20-1 Scroll bars can be either
vertical or horizontal

all the way to the right when the value is at its maximum. A minimum value on
a vertical scroll bar places the thumb at the top, while the maximum value places
the thumb at the bottom. Any value in between places the thumb on the bar in
a position proportional to the value represented by the scroll bar.

The value represented by a scroll bar can be changed in four ways. First, the
user can click on either arrow. This causes the value represented by the scroll bar
to increment or decrement by a small amount in the direction of the selected
arrow. Second, the user may click the scroll bar on one side of the thumb or the
other. This causes the scroll bar's value to increment or decrement also, but the
amount of change is greater. The user can also click and drag the thumb to a specific position on the bar. This causes the value of the scroll bar to be set according
to the position of the thumb. Finally, you can set the value of a scroll bar in the
program's code.

SCROLL BARS SUMMARY

Table 20-1 displays the properties that control the operation of scroll bars.

Use or Set This...		To Do This...
LargeChange	Property	Set or return the amount changed when the user clicks on the bar
Max	Property	Set or return the maximum value represented by the scroll bar
Min	Property	Set or return the minimum value represented by the scroll bar

Use or Set This...		To Do This...
SmallChange	Property	Set or return the amount changed when the user clicks on an arrow
Value	Property	Set or return the value represented by the scroll bar

Table 20-1 Properties that affect the operation of a scroll bar

These five properties are explored in the next section. The Scroll Bars project at this end of the chapter puts scroll bars to use in a sample application.

LARGECHANGE PROPERTY

Objects Affected

Check	Clipboard	Combo	Command	CommonDlg
Data	Debug	Dir	Drive	File
Form	Frame	Grid	Image	Label
Line	List	MDI Form	Menu	OLE
Option	Picture	Printer	Screen	▶ Scroll
Shape	Text	Timer		

Purpose

The LargeChange property sets or returns the amount of change that occurs when the user clicks on the bar portion of a scroll bar. This property can be set at design time, and set or read at runtime. Table 20-2 summarizes the arguments of the LargeChange property.

General Syntax

```
[form!]Name.LargeChange [ = amount%]
```

Argument	Description
form	Name of the parent form
Name	Name of the scroll bar control

(continued on next page)

(continued from previous page)

Argument	Description
amount%	An integer value indicating the amount of change made when the user clicks on the bar

Table 20-2 Arguments of the LargeChange property

Example Syntax

```
Sub Form_Load ()
    HScroll2.LargeChange = 100
    Text1.Text = Str$(VScroll1.LargeChange)
End Sub
```

Description

The LargeChange property sets or returns the amount of change that occurs in a scroll bar's value when the user clicks on the bar portion of a scroll bar. Clicking on the bar portion of the scroll bar adjusts the Value property of the scroll bar by whatever amount is defined by the LargeChange property. For instance, if the LargeChange property is set to 100, clicking below the thumb on the bar portion of a vertical scroll bar will add 100 to the scroll bar's Value property.

Any value you assign to this property must be an integer whose value is within the range defined by the Min and Max properties of the same control. If the program tries to assign a value that is not in this range, an "Invalid property value" error occurs.

The first statement in the example syntax sets the LargeChange value for the scroll bar control HScroll2 to 100. This is the amount by which the scroll bar's Value property will change when the user clicks on the bar between the thumb and one of the arrows. The second statement simply displays the LargeChange property of the scroll bar VScroll1 in Text1.

Example

In the Scroll Bars project at the end of this chapter, the LargeChange property is set to 100 at design time. This causes the control Picture2 to be scrolled 100 twips at a time.

Comments

The SmallChange property defines a smaller amount of change for when the user clicks one of the arrows at either end of the bar.

MAX PROPERTY

Objects Affected

Check	Clipboard	Combo	Command	CommonDlg
Data	Debug	Dir	Drive	File
Form	Frame	Grid	Image	Label
Line	List	MDI Form	Menu	OLE
Option	Picture	Printer	Screen	▶ Scroll
Shape	Text	Timer		

Purpose

The Max property sets or returns the maximum value of a scroll bar. This property can be set at design time, and set or read at runtime. Table 20-3 summarizes the arguments of the Max property.

General Syntax

```
[form!]Name.Max [ = value%]
```

Argument	Description
form	Name of the parent form
Name	Name of the scroll bar control
value%	An integer expression indicating the value at the high end of the scroll bar

Table 20-3 Arguments of the Max property

Example Syntax

```
Sub Form_Load ()
    HScroll1.Max = 1000            'Sets the maximum value for the scroll bar to 1000
End Sub
```

787

Description

The Max property defines the value represented by a vertical scroll bar when the thumb is at its bottom position, or by a horizontal scroll bar when its thumb is at its farthest right position. This is an integer value in the range -32,768 to 32,767. Along with the Min property, Max defines the acceptable range of values for a scroll bar. By default, this property is set to 32,767.

One would expect the Max property to always be a value greater than the Min property. However, this is not always true. Visual Basic will accept a Max property that is less than the Min property for the same control. This causes changes to the value of the scroll bar to change opposite the normal manner. For instance, if the Max property is less than the Min property, clicking on the top arrow of a vertical scroll bar would add to the scroll bar's value instead of subtracting.

The example syntax sets the maximum value for scroll bar HScroll1 to 1000. Since this is a horizontal scroll bar, it will have the value 1000 when the thumb is all the way to the right.

Example

In the Scroll Bars project at the end of this chapter, the Max property of the horizontal and vertical scroll bars is set in the Form_Load event. The value placed in the Max property is an arithmetic equation that figures out what values for the Picture2.Top and Picture2.Left properties that would allow the right and bottom edges of the control Picture2 to be displayed.

MIN PROPERTY

Objects Affected

Check	Clipboard	Combo	Command	CommonDlg
Data	Debug	Dir	Drive	File
Form	Frame	Grid	Image	Label
Line	List	MDI Form	Menu	OLE
Option	Picture	Printer	Screen	▶ Scroll
Shape	Text	Timer		

Purpose

The Min property sets or returns the minimum value of a scroll bar. This property can be set at design time, and set or read at runtime. Table 20-4 summarizes the arguments of the Min property.

General Syntax

```
[form!]Name.Min [ = value%]
```

Argument	Description
form	Name of the parent form
Name	Name of the scroll bar control
value%	An integer expression indicating the value at the low end of the scroll bar

Table 20-4 Arguments of the Min property

Example Syntax

```
Sub Form_Load ()
    HScroll1.Min = 100                    'Sets the minimum value for the scroll bar to 100
End Sub
```

Description

The Min property defines the value represented by a vertical scroll bar when the thumb is at its top position, or for a horizontal scroll bar when the thumb is at its farthest left position. This is an integer value that in the range -32,768 to 32,767. Along with the Max property, Min defines the acceptable range of values for a scroll bar. By default, this property is set to 0.

One would expect the Min property to always be a value less than the Max property. However, this is not always true. Visual Basic will accept a Min property that is greater than the Max property for the same control. This causes changes to the value of the scroll bar to change opposite the normal manner. For instance, if the Min property is greater than the Max property, clicking on the top arrow of a vertical scroll bar would add to the scroll bar's value instead of subtracting.

In the example syntax, the minimum value of the horizontal scroll bar HScroll1 is set to 100. This is the value the scroll bar will have when the thumb is all the way to the left.

Example

In the Scroll Bars project at the end of this chapter, the Min property of the horizontal and vertical scroll bars is set to 0 in the Form_Load event.

789

SMALLCHANGE PROPERTY

Objects Affected

Check	Clipboard	Combo	Command	CommonDlg
Data	Debug	Dir	Drive	File
Form	Frame	Grid	Image	Label
Line	List	MDI Form	Menu	OLE
Option	Picture	Printer	Screen ▶	Scroll
Shape	Text	Timer		

Purpose

The SmallChange property sets or returns the amount of change that occurs when the user clicks on one of the arrows at either end of a scroll bar. This property can be set at design time, and set or read at runtime. Table 20-5 summarizes the arguments of the SmallChange property.

General Syntax

```
[form!]Name.SmallChange [ = amount%]
```

Argument	Description
form	Name of the parent form
Name	Name of the scroll bar control
amount%	An integer value indicating the amount of change made when the user clicks on one of the bar's arrows

Table 20-5 Arguments of the SmallChange property

Example Syntax

```
Sub Form_Load ()
    HScroll1.SmallChange = 10        'The value of the will be changed in increments of 10
    L% = VScroll1.SmallChange        'Assigns the SmallChange value to L%
End Sub
```

790

Description

The SmallChange property sets or returns the amount of change that occurs when the user clicks on one of the arrows at either end of a scroll bar. Clicking on one of the arrows adjusts the value of the scroll bar by the amount defined by the SmallChange property.

The SmallChange property is an integer whose range must be between the values defined by the Min and Max properties of the same control. If the program tries to assign a value that is not in this range, an "Invalid property value" error occurs.

In the example syntax the SmallChange property for the HScroll1 scroll bar is set to 10. This is the amount by which the value of the scroll bar will increase or decrease when the user clicks on the arrows at the ends of the scroll bar.

Example

In the Scroll Bars project at the end of this chapter, the SmallChange property is set to 10 at design time. This causes the control Picture2 to be scrolled 10 twips at a time when the user clicks an arrow.

Comments

The LargeChange property defines a larger amount of change for when the user clicks on the scroll bar itself.

VALUE PROPERTY

Objects Affected

▶ Check	Clipboard	Combo	▶ Command	CommonDlg
Data	Debug	Dir	Drive	File
Form	Frame	Grid	Image	Label
Line	List	MDI Form	Menu	OLE
▶ Option	Picture	Printer	Screen	▶ Scroll
Shape	Text	Timer		

Purpose

The Value property sets or returns the value currently represented by a scroll bar. This property can be set at design time, and set or read at runtime. Table 20-6 shows the arguments of the Value property.

General Syntax

```
[form!]Name.Value [ = value%]
```

Argument	Description
form	Name of the parent form
Name	Name of the scroll bar control
value%	An integer expression indicating a position on the scroll bar

Table 20-6 Arguments of the Value property

Example Syntax

```
Sub Form_Load ()
     V% = VScroll1.Value            'Assigns the value from the scroll bar to V%
End Sub
```

Description

The Value property contains a value that is proportional to the current position of the thumb on the scroll bar relative to the values specified by the Min and Max properties. For instance, if the thumb is three-quarters across a horizontal scroll bar, and the Min and Max properties are set to 0 and 100, respectively, the Value property will have a value of 75. Conversely, if the Value property for the same scroll bar is set to 25, the thumb will be moved to a position one-fourth of the distance across the bar.

If the program sets this property, it must be within the range defined by the Min and Max properties, or an "Invalid property value" error will occur. When read, this property returns an integer between the same range. The maximum range for Min and Max is -32,768 to 32,767, so the Value property for a scroll bar control is always within this range.

This property can be changed in four ways. First, the user can click on the arrow at either end of the Scroll Bar. This causes the Value property to be incremented or decremented by the amount defined by the SmallChange property in the direction of the selected arrow. Second, the user may click the scroll bar on one side of the thumb or the other. This also increments or decrements the value, but the amount of change is that defined by the LargeChange property. The user can also click and drag the thumb to a specific position on the bar. This causes the Value of the scroll bar to be set according to the position of the thumb in proportion to the Min and Max properties. Finally, the value of a scroll bar can be set in the program's code.

The example syntax saves the current value of the scroll bar VScroll1 in the integer variable *V%*.

Example

In the Scroll Bars project at the end of this chapter, the Value property is read in the HScroll1_Change and VScroll1_Change events. In these events this property is used to set the position of Picture2.

This property is set by each of the Click events for all the thumbs on the form. By setting the Value property, each of these thumbs positions Picture2 at a different corner.

Comments

The Value property is also used for the check box, command button, and option button controls. For command and option buttons, the possible values for the Value property are True (-1), and False (0), meaning the button is or is not selected. Check boxes can have the values 0 (not checked), 1 (checked), or 2 (grayed). For more information on these items, see the appropriate entry in Chapter 3, Using Objects.

THE SCROLL BARS PROJECT

The Scroll Bars Project

The project outlined in the following pages demonstrates the concepts behind the use of scroll bars. You will learn how to use the LargeChange, Min, Max, SmallChange, and Value properties by experimenting with the project.

Assembling the Project

1. Create a new form (the Scroll Bars form) and place on it the following controls. Use Table 20-7 to set the properties of the form and each control.

    Note: When you create the Picture2 control, first make sure Picture1 has the focus. Then double click on the picture control icon. This creates Picture2 as a child of Picture1, which is necessary for this program to operate correctly.

Object	Property	Setting
Form	Name	Scroll

(continued on next page)

Object	Property	Setting
	Caption	Scroll Bars Project
Picture	Name	Picture1
Picture	Name	Picture2
	AutoSize	True (-1)
	Picture	(Bitmap) WAITE.BMP
Command	Name	cmndBottomLeft
	Caption	Bottom Left
Command	Name	cmndBottomRight
	Caption	Bottom Right
Command	Name	cmndTopLeft
	Caption	Top Left
Command	Name	cmndTopRight
	Caption	Top Right
Horizontal Scroll	Name	HScroll1
	LargeChange	100
	SmallChange	10
Vertical Scroll	Name	VScroll1
	LargeChange	100
	SmallChange	10

Table 20-7 Property settings for the Scroll Bars project

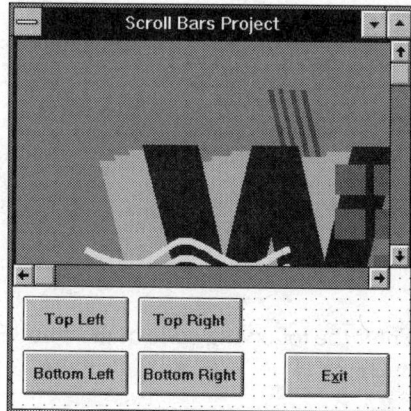

Figure 20-2 How the Scroll Bars
form should look when complete

2. Check the appearance of your form with Figure 20-2.

3. Enter the following code into the HScroll1_Change and VScroll1_Change events. These events set the coordinates for the upper-left corner of Picture2.

```
Sub HScroll1_Change ()
     Picture2.Left = -HScroll1.Value
End Sub

Sub VScroll1_Change ()
     Picture2.Top = -VScroll1.Value
End Sub
```

4. Enter the following code into the Form_Load event. This event sets the minimum and maximum values for the HScroll1 and VScroll1 scroll bar controls.

```
Sub Form_Load ()
    HScroll1.Max = (Picture2.Width - Picture1.Width)
    VScroll1.Max = (Picture2.Height - Picture1.Height)
    HScroll1.Min = 0
    VScroll1.Min = 0
End Sub
```

5. Enter the following code into the Click events for the four thumbs. These routines set the coordinates for the Picture2 picture control. By choosing one of these thumbs, the picture gets set to the respective corner.

```
Sub cmndTopLeft_Click ()
    HScroll1.Value = HScroll1.Min
    VScroll1.Value = VScroll1.Min
End Sub

Sub cmndTopRight_Click ()
    HScroll1.Value = HScroll1.Max
```

(continued on next page)

(continued from previous page)

```
      VScroll1.Value = VScroll1.Min
End Sub

Sub cmndBottomLeft_Click ()
      HScroll1.Value = HScroll1.Min
      VScroll1.Value = VScroll1.Max
End Sub

Sub cmndBottomRight_Click ()
      HScroll1.Value = HScroll1.Max
      VScroll1.Value = VScroll1.Max
End Sub
```

6.   Enter the following code in the cmndExit_Click event. This ends the program.

```
Sub cmndExit_Click ()
      End
End Sub
```

How It Works

This project creates a program that displays the WAITE.BMP bitmap. However, the area for displaying the picture is smaller than the picture itself. Therefore we need to provide a method for the user to "scroll" the picture to the left and right, and up and down.

The picture control Picture1 defines the viewing area for the bitmap. Picture2 is placed as a child of Picture1, with its AutoSize property set to True (-1). Although Picture2 is larger than Picture1, because it is a child the displayed portion of Picture2 cannot overlap the area defined by Picture1.

We can now determine which portion of Picture2 is displayed by changing its Left and Top properties. Initially, the Left and Top properties are set to 0. These

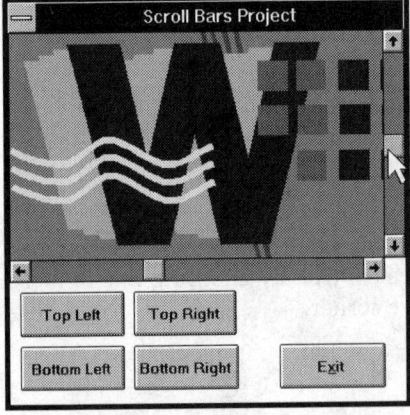

Figure 20-3 The Scroll Bars Project in action

properties are changed in the HScroll1_Change and VScroll1_Change events, which occur whenever the user changes the value of either the horizontal or vertical scroll bars. The minimum and maximum values for the scroll bars are defined in the Form_Load event. In this event the minimum for each bar is set to 0, while the maximum is set to a value that will reflect the Left and Top values of Picture2 when the bottom right-hand corner of the picture is being displayed.

Each of the Click routines set the Value property of the scroll bars. Doing so also causes the Change events for the scroll bars to occur, thereby changing the Top and Left coordinates of Picture2. Figure 20-3 shows the Scroll Bars project in action, with the picture being scrolled by the vertical scroll bar.

PART VII

Managing Data Flow

21

APPLICATION FOCUS

A control or form that is currently active and ready to respond to a mouse click or keypress has the application *focus*. Users should normally be able to set the focus however they wish, giving them the most control over the program.

Some situations, however, make it imperative that you control the focus from within your code. For example, you may wish to validate a user entry in a text box. If the entry is incorrect, your code might display a message giving the correct format and set the focus back to the text box to give the user another try. Another setting in your program might make certain options unavailable: you might have a database application that has both browse mode (for looking at records without changing them) and edit mode (for adding or updating records). A menu command might then toggle between these two modes. Browse mode would disable all the text boxes displaying database values to make sure the user couldn't inadvertently change the data; Edit mode would enable these text boxes to allow editing.

This chapter covers the Visual Basic features that let you both control your application focus and respond to changes in focus.

CHANGING FOCUS

Focus can shift for a number of reasons. First, the user can establish the focus on a control using the (TAB) key or mouse. The user can press the (TAB) (or (SHIFT)-(TAB)) key until the control is graphically outlined. More commonly, the user can click on a control with the mouse to select it. If available, the user can press a speed key combination to automatically select the control, by using an (ALT)-key combination like (ALT)-(C) for a command button with the caption of Cash. Your code can also set focus with the SetFocus method.

Giving a control the focus triggers two events. First, the LostFocus event of the control that previously held the focus triggers. This event lets you perform any final validations before leaving the control. Your code in this event can also use the SetFocus method to selectively move the focus to any other control that's eligible. The GotFocus event of the control receiving the focus then triggers. This event lets you react appropriately to getting the focus. For instance, common programming practice highlights the contents of text boxes when they receive the focus. Note that if the LostFocus event sets the focus programatically, a different control than what the user clicked on or tabbed to might actually get the focus.

FOCUS SUMMARY

Several tools in Visual Basic influence the setting of the focus and its effects. The AppActivate statement gives the focus to another Windows application. A form or control within the application can be given the focus with the SetFocus method. The GotFocus event contains any actions that occur when a form or control receives the focus. Actions in the LostFocus event take place when a form or control loses the focus. A control's Enabled property indicates whether it is eligible or ineligible for receiving the focus. The Caption property of many controls lets you define an (ALT)-key combination to immediately set focus to that control. The TabIndex property determines the order in which the user can access the controls on a form with the (TAB) key. A control's TabStop property indicates whether a control is accessible with the (TAB) key.

Table 21-1 displays the statements, methods, events, and properties that influence the setting and effects of focus in Visual Basic.

Use or Set This...		To Do This...
AppActivate	Statement	Give the focus to another application
Caption	Property	Define an (ALT)-key combination to set focus to this control
Enabled	Property	Indicate whether a control or form can respond to events
GotFocus	Event	Initiate an action when a control or form is given the focus
LostFocus	Event	Initiate an action when a control or form gives up the focus
SetFocus	Method	Give the focus to the indicated control or form

802

Use or Set This...		To Do This...
TabIndex	Property	Set or discover a control's place in the tab order
TabStop	Property	Determine whether a control is accessible with the (TAB) key

Table 21-1 Statement, method, properties, and events dealing with the Focus

We investigate the statements, methods, events, and properties in Table 21-1 in detail in the following pages. You'll find step-by-step directions to assemble the Focus project at the end of the chapter.

APPACTIVATE STATEMENT

Purpose

The AppActivate statement gives a particular application the focus when there are multiple Windows applications on your screen. An application keeps the focus until it is closed or another form or control receives the focus. Table 21-2 summarizes the argument of the AppActivate statement.

General Syntax

```
AppActivate titletext$
```

Argument	Description
titletext$	The text that appears in the title bar of an application

Table 21-2 Argument of AppActivate statement

Example Syntax

```
Sub Command1_Click ()
    On Error GoTo OpenFileMan          'Filemanager not open, open it on error
    AppActivate "File Manager"         'Attempts to give the focus to File Manager
    SendKeys "%( ){Down 4}{Enter}", -1 'SendKeys maximizes File Manager
    MsgBox "File Manager is now active" 'Displays Message with OK button
    SendKeys "%( ){Down 5}{Enter}", -1 'SendKeys directs File Manager to close itself
    SendKeys "{Enter}", -1             'SendKeys sends enter to confirm close
Exit Sub
```

(continued on next page)

803

(continued from previous page)

```
OpenFileMan:
    x = Shell("\WINDOWS\WINFILE.EXE", 2)    'Open File Manager
    Resume                                   'Try activating filemanager again
End Sub
```

Description

The AppActivate statement gives a particular application the focus when there are multiple Windows applications on your screen. This is useful for accessing, controlling, or obtaining information from another active Windows application from your Visual Basic program without using DDE or OLE links. DDE, a means of establishing data links between Windows applications, is discussed in Chapter 25, Dynamic Data Exchange. Chapter 26, Object Linking and Embedding, covers the advanced techniques of exchanging native format data and controlling other applications with OLE automation.

The AppActivate statement has only one argument, titletext$, which specifies what program receives the focus. The titletext$ argument can be a text string between quotation marks or a previously defined text variable. This argument contains only the text found in the program bar at the top of the application that is to receive the focus. In the example syntax, the title bar of the program reads File Manager.

There are several limits to using the AppActivate statement to shift the focus of an application. If the text is not exactly the same as that shown in the application's title bar, an error occurs. While the host program is still in control, all of the commands that are sent to the application with the focus must be done using SendKeys. AppActivate does not establish a DDE connection.

In the example syntax, AppActivate works in conjunction with SendKeys to open the Windows File Manager application. Notice how the SendKeys statement is used to send the specific keystrokes to the File Manager that are needed first to maximize, and then to close, that application. (The SendKeys statement is discussed in Chapter 16, Keyboard Input. In that chapter you will learn how to specify special keys as well as regular ASCII characters.)

Example

The Focus project at the end of this chapter uses the AppActivate statement to activate the Windows Notepad application. Once this application has the focus, a SendKeys statement sends the contents of the letter to the notepad for viewing and editing. After sending the text, AppActivate is used once again to set the focus back to the project application.

Comments

If more than one instance of the same program is in memory, then the AppActivate statement activates one of them at random.

CAPTION PROPERTY

Objects Affected

▶ Check	Clipboard	Combo	▶ Command	CommonDlg
▶ Data	Debug	Dir	Drive	File
▶ Form	▶ Frame	Grid	Image	▶ Label
Line	List	▶ MDI Form	▶ Menu	OLE
▶ Option	Picture	Printer	Screen	Scroll
Shape	Text	Timer		

Purpose

The Caption property sets the text displayed in or next to a control, and provides a quick way of setting focus to that control with an (ALT)-key combination. Table 21-3 summarizes the arguments of the Caption property.

General Syntax

```
[form!]Name.Caption [ = text$]
```

Argument	Description
form	Name property of the parent form
Name	Name of the control
text$	Text to appear in the caption

Table 21-3 Arguments of the Caption property

Example Syntax

```
Sub Command1_Click()
    If Command1.Caption = "&Blue" Then
        Command1.Caption = "&Red"
    Else
        Command1.Caption = "&Blue"
    End If
End Sub
```

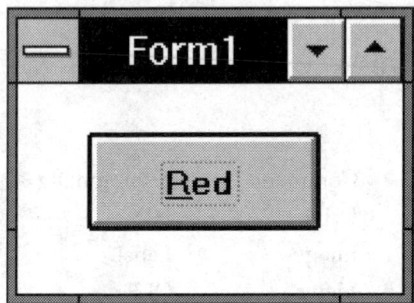

Figure 21-1 The Caption property lets you define (ALT)-key accelerator key combinations like (ALT)-(R)

Description

Most controls on a form should have a keyboard shortcut to select them. Although the mouse is an intuitive input device, it's often faster to keep your hands on the keyboard. Providing keyboard shortcuts makes your programs easier to use for experienced typists.

The Caption property of many controls lets you set a keyboard shortcut by simply placing an ampersand symbol (&) in front of the shortcut key letter. For instance, setting a command button's Caption property to "&Red" makes the button read R̲ed (as illustrated in Figure 21-1) and lets the user select it directly by using (ALT)-(R).

To include an ampersand literal within a control's caption, put two ampersands together, as in the following example:

```
Command1.Caption = "Fe&dex && UPS"
```

Some controls don't have a caption property. For these controls, place a label next to the control and set the label's caption to include the shortcut key. Make sure the label's TabIndex is set to one less than the control's. Labels can't receive the focus, so when the user presses the shortcut key combination, the Label passes the focus to the next control in the tab order.

Example

The Focus project at the end of this chapter sets the Caption properties of the option buttons, labels, and command buttons to include the shortcut key combinations. Each label's TabIndex property is set to one less than the text box it labels to make sure focus automatically goes to the text box when the user presses the (ALT)-key combination for the label.

Comment

A Form's Caption property sets the text that appears in its Title Bar. It does not have the capacity to include a shortcut key. Placing an ampersand in the Caption does not underline the following letter; it just includes the ampersand as a literal character.

ENABLED PROPERTY

Objects Affected

▶ Check	Clipboard	▶ Combo	▶ Command	CommonDlg
▶ Data	Debug	▶ Dir	▶ Drive	▶ File
▶ Form	▶ Frame	▶ Grid	▶ Image	▶ Label
Line	▶ List	▶ MDI Form	▶ Menu	OLE
▶ Option	▶ Picture	Printer	Screen	▶ Scroll
Shape	▶ Text	▶ Timer		

Purpose

Use the Enabled property to specify whether a control can respond to user input. Use this property to make certain controls or forms inaccessible or unchangeable while they are still visible on the screen. Read and write at both design time and runtime. Table 21-4 summarizes the arguments of the Enabled property, and Table 21-5 summarizes its Boolean values.

General Syntax

```
[form.]Enabled [= boolean%]
[form!]Name.Enabled [= boolean%]
```

Argument	Description
form	Name of the form
Name	Name of the control
boolean%	True or False value

Table 21-4 Arguments of the Enabled property

boolean%	Description
0	False—Control or form is disabled
-1	(Default) True—Control or form is enabled

Table 21-5 Boolean values of the Enabled property

Example Syntax

```
Sub textCityStateZip_Change
    Frame1.Enabled = False          'Disables the frame
End Sub

Sub Drive1_Change
    If Text1.Text = Password$ Then  'Disables the drive box when the user has not
        Dir1.Path = Drive1.Drive    'entered the correct password in the text box
        File1.Path = Dir1.Path
    Else
        Drive1.Enabled = False
        File1.Path = Dir1.Path
        Drive1.Drive = "C:"
    End If
End Sub

Sub Check1_Change
    If Check1.Value = 1 Then
        onOff = True
    Else
        onOff = False
    End If
    cmndDelete.Enabled = onOff
    optnConfirm.Enabled = onOff
    menuDelete.Enabled = onOff
    pictTrashcan.Enabled = onOff
End Sub

Sub CommandSnooze_Click
    Timer1.Enabled = Not(Timer1.Enabled)   'toggle timer on and off
End Sub
```

Description

Use the Enabled property to specify whether a control can respond to user input. Use this property to make certain controls or forms inaccessible or unchangeable while they are still visible on the screen.

There are only two possible settings for the Enabled property: True (-1) and False (0). Using a variable makes it possible to control the Enabled property of several controls at once. With this kind of setup, entire groups of controls can be

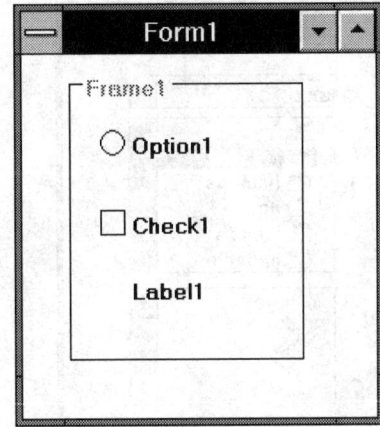

Figure 21-2 Disabling Frame1 effectively disables all the controls contained within it

enabled and disabled by modifying only one variable as the third example above shows. This property can be changed at either design time or runtime.

The Enabled property can be used with both forms and controls. A control that has been disabled will turn gray on a color monitor (it will turn a lighter shade of gray or reverse video on monochrome). For example, the OK button on a data entry form could be disabled until the user finishes an entry session.

A control will not recognize any input when its Enabled property is set to False. Focus may never be given to a disabled control. Mouse events (Click, DblClick, MouseDown, MouseMove, MouseUp, and GotFocus) will not affect a disabled control. No matter what place it has in a form's TabIndex order, the user will be unable to access a control using the (TAB) key.

Forms and Frames

A frame is a grouping of controls within a form. Forms and frames respond to the Enabled property in the same ways. When the Enabled property of a frame or form is False, all of the controls within are also effectively disabled. Even though a control will not respond to user input or mouse events when its parent form or frame is set to False, the actual value of the control's Enabled property remains unchanged. Although you can't set the focus to these controls, they are not dimmed as they would be if their individual Enabled properties were set to False. In the first example syntax, disabling the frame effectively disables all the controls it contains. Figure 21-2 shows what this might look like.

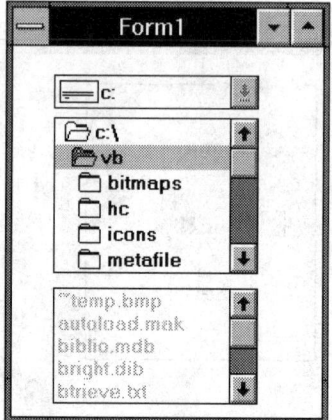

Figure 21-3 Only the File list
box changes appearance
when disabled; the Drive
and Directory list boxes look
the same

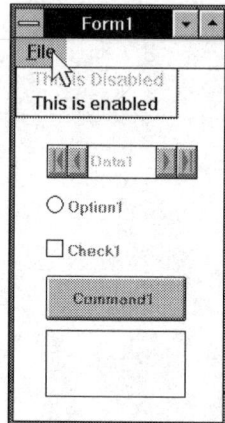

Figure 21-4
Disabled data,
option, check, com-
mand, picture, and
menu controls

Drive, Directory, and File Boxes

Drive, Directory, and File list box controls give the user access to the files in a
computer. If the Enabled property of one of these controls is false, then access to
the files in the computer is restricted. The Drive and Directory list boxes don't
change their appearance, but file names in the File list box appear grayed. Figure
21-3 illustrates disabled Drive, Directory, and File list boxes. In the second sub
procedure in the example syntax, a user without the password cannot access the
files on other drives. When the word Password does not appear in the Text1 text
box, the Drive1 drive box's Enable property is changed to False.

Data, Option, Check, Command, Picture, and Menu

Enabling and disabling the Enabled property of the data, option, check, command button, picture box, or menu controls prevents the user from using these
controls. This removes choices from the user if those choices are inappropriate for
that particular context. Option and check boxes that do not apply to a particular
situation can be disabled by changing their Enable property to False. Command
and menu controls can be turned off so that the user does not initiate inapplica-
ble actions. The third sub procedure in the example syntax restricts the user's
access to the other controls on the form, while the Check1 check box remains
unmarked. Figure 21-4 shows disabled data, option, check, command, picture,
and menu controls.

List, Combo, and Text Boxes

Enabling and disabling the Enabled property of a list, combo, or text box prevents the user from changing the information in these controls. The text on a disabled list, combo, or text box appears gray. It is a lighter gray or reverse video on monochrome monitors.

Timer

The Enabled property of the timer control turns it on and off. This is useful for stopping previously scheduled events from taking place. In the fourth sub procedure in the example syntax, a snooze button for an alarm program postpones or terminates the upcoming alarm from sounding by changing the timer control's Enabled property to False. This change suspends the timer event's operation. Note that a timer can never receive the focus even when it's enabled because it is never visible.

Example

The Focus project at the end of this chapter uses the Option_Click event to enable and disable some of the text boxes, depending on whether the user chose to create a personal or business letter.

Comments

Notice that a control that has the Enabled property set to False cannot be accessed with either the mouse or the keyboard. If you wish to prevent (TAB) key access to a control, then setting the TabStop property will accomplish this without needing to disable the control itself. When the TabStop property of a control is set to False, the control can still be accessed or given the focus using the mouse or the SetFocus method.

GOTFOCUS EVENT

Objects Affected

▶ Check	Clipboard	▶ Combo	▶ Command	CommonDlg
Data	Debug	▶ Dir	▶ Drive	▶ File
▶ Form	Frame	▶ Grid	Image	Label
Line	▶ List	MDI Form	Menu	▶ OLE
▶ Option	▶ Picture	Printer	Screen	▶ Scroll
Shape	▶ Text	Timer		

Purpose

The GotFocus event specifies what actions to take when a control or form receives the focus. A control or form receives the focus either by user action (tab keypress or mouse click) or by code using the SetFocus method. Table 21-6 summarizes the arguments of the GotFocus event.

General Syntax

```
Sub Form_GotFocus ()
Sub Name_GotFocus ([Index As Integer])
```

Argument	Description
Form	'Form' for the form with the focus
Name	Name property of the control with the focus
Index	Index value of the control in a control array

Table 21-6 Arguments of the GotFocus event

Example Syntax

```
Sub Form_GotFocus ()
    Command2.Visible = True         'Command button control made visible
    Text1.Visible = True            'Text control made visible
    Picture1.Visible = True         'Picture control made visible
    Option1(0).Visible = True       'First option control of array made visible
    Option1(1).Visible = True       'Second option control of array made visible
    Command1.Enable = True          'Second command button control enabled
End Sub

Sub Text1_GotFocus (Index As Integer)
    Text1(Index).BackColor = QBColor(15)      'Highlight text box
    Select Case Index
        Case 0: lablStatusBar.Caption = "Enter the Patient's Name"
        Case 1: lablStatusBar.Caption = "Enter the Patient's Address"
        Case 2: lablStatusBar.Caption = "Enter the Patient's Status"
    End Select
End Sub
```

Description

The GotFocus event triggers when the focus shifts to a form or control. A control or form can get the focus in several ways. A user may select a new form or control

812

with the mouse, or by moving through the controls on a form with the (TAB) key, or your code can use the SetFocus method. Begin the specification of the GotFocus event with the name of the form or control to be affected. If you are working with a control array, add an index variable in parentheses at the end of the statement.

Forms and controls can receive the focus with the SetFocus method. A form may only be given the focus when all of the visible controls are disabled using the Enable property. When a form or control receives the focus, you may use the GotFocus event to change the properties of the object with the focus. In the first example, the Enable properties of the controls on Form1 change to True when the form receives the focus.

The first example syntax responds to a form's receiving the focus by making a variety of controls visible. This is done by setting the Visible property of each control to -1 (True). Notice that two of the controls specified are part of an array of option buttons. Another common use of the GotFocus event is to display context-sensitive help messages on a status bar at the bottom of the screen as the user moves from one control or form to another. The second example syntax highlights a text box and displays a message on a status bar.

The Load, Resize, Paint, and GotFocus Events

If more than one event is attached to a particular control, the events are processed in the following order: Load, Resize, Paint, and GotFocus. This is an important point to keep in mind if any of the actions that take place in one event depend on actions in another event. For example, a data entry form for an address book would cause errors if the Load event disables the Address1 text box and the GotFocus event tries to use it.

Control Arrays

If the control with the focus is part of a Control Array, then the index argument indicates which part of the array has the focus. The index number specifies the affected part of the control array and appears between parentheses between the control's Name property and the property in the form of Control(Index%).property.

Example

The Focus project at the end of this chapter uses the GotFocus event of the text boxes to highlight the box with a different background color and then selects all the text in the box for subsequent editing.

Comments

Controls will not function with either of the Enabled and Visible properties set to False. GotFocus will not work unless they are both True. Labels and frames are not eligible to receive the focus.

LOSTFOCUS EVENT

Objects Affected

▶ Check	Clipboard	▶ Combo	▶ Command	CommonDlg
Data	Debug	▶ Dir	▶ Drive	▶ File
▶ Form	Frame	▶ Grid	Image	Label
Line	▶ List	MDI Form	Menu	▶ OLE
▶ Option	▶ Picture	Printer	Screen	▶ Scroll
Shape	▶ Text	Timer		

Purpose

The LostFocus event specifies what actions to take when a control or form loses the focus, either because the user selected another object or the code reassigned the focus. Table 21-7 summarizes the arguments of the LostFocus event.

General Syntax

```
Sub Form_LostFocus ()
Sub Name_LostFocus ([Index As Integer])
```

Argument	Description
form	Name property of the form losing focus
Name	Name property of the control losing focus
Index	Index value of the control in a control array

Table 21-7 Arguments of the LostFocus event

Example Syntax

```
Sub Text1_LostFocus ()
    Command1.ForeColor = H00FF0000&        'Highlight the command button
    Command1.SetFocus                      'Go to the command button
End Sub
```

814

Description

The LostFocus event triggers when the focus changes from the current control or form to another control or form. This could occur in several ways. A user may choose another control with the use of a mouse, or by moving through the controls on a form with the (TAB) key. A SetFocus method can also give the focus to another control.

When a control loses the focus, you may want to change the properties of some other control or form. The LostFocus event can contain actions that may change the appearance of controls or forms to signify that this control has lost the focus. Certain other controls or forms may have their Enabled property changed to True or False. In the example syntax, the color of the text on the Command1 command button changes to blue when the Text1 text box loses the focus, and then focus shifts to the command button.

Control Arrays

If the control with the focus is part of a control array, then the index argument indicates which part of the array has the focus. The index number specifies the affected part of the control array and appears between parentheses between the control's Name property and the property in the form of Control(Index #).property.

Example

The LostFocus event in the text box control array first unhighlights the box. (Each text box is highlighted by its GotFocus event.) Then it checks to see if the user is leaving the first member of the text box array, the contact name box. If so, then it performs some validity checking to make sure there is an honorific (such as Mr., Mrs., Dr.) and then sets some of the other text box's text appropriately.

Comments

As a control will not function with the Enabled and Visible properties set to False, the LostFocus event will not work until they are both True.

SETFOCUS METHOD

Objects Affected

▶ Check	Clipboard	▶ Combo	▶ Command	CommonDlg
Data	Debug	▶ Dir	▶ Drive	▶ File
▶ Form	Frame	▶ Grid	Image	Label
Line	▶ List	MDI Form	Menu	▶ OLE
▶ Option	▶ Picture	Printer	Screen	▶ Scroll
Shape	▶ Text	Timer		

Purpose

The SetFocus method gives the focus to the specified control or form. Table 21-8 summarizes the arguments for the SetFocus method.

General Syntax

```
[form.]SetFocus
[form!]Name.SetFocus
```

Argument	Description
Name	Name property of form or control receiving the focus

Table 21-8 Argument of the SetFocus method

Example Syntax

```
Sub CommandEdit_Click ()
    If CommandSave.Enabled = False Then      'If CommandSave button is disabled
        Text1.SetFocus                        'set the focus to the Text1 box
    Else
        CommandSave.SetFocus                  'Set the focus to the CommandSave button
    End If
End Sub
```

Description

The SetFocus method gives a control or form the focus. The control and form arguments of a SetFocus operation must be the Name property of a form or control.

816

Only those controls and forms with Enabled properties set to True may actually be given the focus. There is no difference in effect between setting the focus in the code or with user input. In the example syntax, the user could also give the focus to the Text1 text box with the mouse or by pressing the (TAB) key. The other way to change the focus is to activate the SetFocus method expression by pressing the CommandEdit command button.

There are several effects of changing the focus with the SetFocus method. Changing the focus to another control or form triggers the LostFocus event for the form or control that loses the focus. The GotFocus event of the form or control that receives the focus triggers when the SetFocus method gives it the focus. In the example syntax, pressing the CommandEdit command button shifts the focus to either the Text1 text box or CommandSave command button depending on whether the CommandSave button is enabled or disabled.

Example

The Focus project at the end of this chapter uses SetFocus twice. First, it sets the focus back to the contact name text box during the text box's LostFocus event if the user did not enter a name in the proper format. Second, the Personal/Business option buttons set the focus to the contact name text box after they've been clicked.

Comments

Labels, frames, and the data control are not eligible to receive the focus.

TABINDEX PROPERTY

Objects Affected

▶ Check	Clipboard	▶ Combo	▶ Command	CommonDlg
Data	Debug	▶ Dir	▶ Drive	▶ File
Form	▶ Frame	▶ Grid	Image	▶ Label
Line	▶ List	MDI Form	Menu	OLE
▶ Option	▶ Picture	Printer	Screen	▶ Scroll
Shape	▶ Text	Timer		

Purpose

The TabIndex property sets the order in which the user can access the controls on a form by pressing the (TAB) key. The control with the lowest TabIndex value (usually 0) is normally the control that receives the focus when the form opens. This property may be modified at either runtime or design time. The arguments of the TabIndex property are summarized in Table 21-9.

General Syntax

```
[form!]Name.TabIndex [= index%]
```

Argument	Description
form	Name property of the form
Name	Name property of the control
index%	Index value of the control in a control array

Table 21-9 Arguments of the TabIndex property

Example Syntax

```
Sub Command1_Click ()              'Changes the tab order of the controls on the form
    Text1.TabIndex = 3             'Run into a new order when the user presses Command1
    Command1.TabIndex = 0          'Run in command button.
    Text2.TabIndex = 1
    Text3.TabIndex = 2
End Sub
```

Description

The TabIndex property can be changed in three possible ways. At design time you may choose to change the order of controls to meet a special need. The TabIndex property of a particular control may also be changed at runtime.

Changing the TabIndex property of a control may cause a change in that property for other controls on the form. For example, if a control with a lower TabIndex property is deleted at design time, then all the controls with higher values will have their TabIndex value reduced by 1. At runtime, altering a control's TabIndex property value to a lower value (for example, changing 2 to 0) changes the TabIndex property value of the other controls to higher values (0 becomes 1, and 1 becomes 2). Changing the TabIndex number of a control to a higher value (such as 0 to 2) reduces the value of the TabIndex property of the other controls (1 becomes 0, and 2 becomes 1).

The TabIndex property of a control can be one of a range of values equal to the number of controls on a form. The first control of a Form has a TabIndex property value of 0. By default, Visual Basic sets the value of each control in the order

818

in which you create the controls. The first control created on a form thus has an initial TabIndex property value of 0.

The example syntax changes the TabIndex (and thus the order of access) of specified controls when the button Command1 is clicked. Note that a control with a TabIndex property of 0 is not always the first control with the focus when the form is opened.

Effects of the Visible, TabStop, and Enabled Properties

Changing the Visible, TabStop, or Enabled property of a control to False has no effect on its TabIndex property value. However, while any of these properties of a control is False, the control is inaccessible with the (TAB) key. In the example syntax, the Command1 command button would not receive the focus when the form loads if any of these properties were False. The command button retains its TabIndex property value of 0, however.

Example

The Focus project at the end of this chapter sets the TabIndex property for each of the controls on the form during the design phase. Special care is taken to make sure the labels precede each of their text boxes to allow the label's (ALT)-key combinations to set the focus to their associated text box.

TABSTOP PROPERTY

Objects Affected

▶ Check	Clipboard	▶ Combo	▶ Command	CommonDlg
Data	Debug	▶ Dir	▶ Drive	▶ File
▶ Form	Frame	▶ Grid	Image	Label
Line	▶ List	MDI Form	Menu	OLE
▶ Option	▶ Picture	Printer	Screen	▶ Scroll
Shape	▶ Text	Timer		

Purpose

The TabStop property indicates whether a control is accessible with the (TAB) key. The TabStop property of a particular control does not affect whether a control can be selected with the mouse or accept user input from the mouse or keyboard. Table 21-10 summarizes the arguments of the TabStop property, and Table 21-11 summarizes its Boolean values.

General Syntax

```
[form!]Name.TabStop [ = boolean%]
```

Argument	Description
form	Name property of the form
Name	Name of control
boolean%	Value represents whether the control is accessible or inaccessible with the (TAB) key

Table 21-10 Arguments of the TabStop property

boolean%	Description
0	False—Control not accessible with the (TAB) key
-1	(Default) True—Control accessible with the (TAB) key

Table 21-11 Boolean values of the TabStop property

Example Syntax

```
Sub Text1.GotFocus ()
    Text2.TabStop = False    'Text2 becomes inaccessible when Text1 receives focus
    Text3.TabStop = True     'and Text3 remains accessible.
End Sub
```

Description

The TabStop property of a control may be either -1 (True) or 0 (False). All controls have this property originally set to True and are accessible with the (TAB) key. If the control's TabStop property is False, then it becomes inaccessible with the (TAB) key. In this case the control can still be given the focus with either the SetFocus method or the mouse. This is different from setting the Enabled property false, which makes the control completely ineligible for the focus.

In the example syntax, the TabStop property of the Text2 and Text3 text boxes changes when the Text1 text box receives the focus. The Text2 text box becomes inaccessible with the (TAB) key and the Text3 text boxes become accessible.

820

Effects of the Visible and Enabled Properties

Changing the Visible or Enabled property of a control to False has no effect on its TabStop property value. While either of these properties of a control is False, however, the control is also inaccessible with the Tab key. Even when a control's TabStop property is False, it can still receive the focus as long as the control is both Enabled and Visible. In the example syntax, both the Text2 and Text3 text boxes remain eligible for the focus by either a mouse click or by the SetFocus method.

Example

The Focus project at the end of this chapter sets the TabStop property of the members of the text box control array when the user chooses a letter type in the Option_Click event. This lets the program direct the natural flow for keyboard input without disabling the text control altogether.

THE FOCUS PROJECT

Project Overview

The Focus project outlined in the following pages demonstrates the concept of Focus in Visual Basic. This example is designed to demonstrate the properties, events, method, and statement that directly affect focus. By following the examples of the different elements of this project, you will learn how to establish and remove focus from controls and forms.

Assembling the Project

1. Make a new form (the Focus form) with the objects and properties listed in Table 21-12.

Object	Property	Setting
Form	BackColor	Light Gray—H00C0C0C0
	BorderStyle	3—Fixed Double
	Caption	Focus

(continued on next page)

(continued from previous page)

Object	Property	Setting
Frame	Caption	Type
Option	Caption	&Business
	Name	Option
	Index	0
	TabIndex	0
Option	Caption	&Personal
	Name	Option
	Index	1
	TabIndex	1
Text	BackColor	Light Gray—H00C0C0C0
	Name	Text
	Index	0, 1, 2, 3, 4, 5
	TabIndex	3, 5, 7, 9, 11, 13
	Text	""
Label	BackStyle	0—Transparent
	BorderStyle	0—None
	Caption	&Name
	Name	Label1
	TabIndex	2
Label	BackStyle	0—Transparent

Object	Property	Setting
	BorderStyle	0—None
	Caption	&Company
	Name	Label3
	TabIndex	4
Label	BackStyle	0—Transparent
	BorderStyle	0—None
	Caption	&Address
	Name	Label2
	TabIndex	6
Label	BackStyle	0—Transparent
	BorderStyle	0—None
	Caption	City, ST, &Zip
	Name	Label4
	TabIndex	8
Label	BackStyle	0—Transparent
	BorderStyle	0—None
	Caption	Saluta&tion
	Name	Label5
	TabIndex	10
Label	BackStyle	0—Transparent

(continued on next page)

(continued from previous page)

Object	Property	Setting
	BorderStyle	0—None
	Caption	&Closing
	Name	Label6
	TabIndex	12
Command	Caption	&Send
	Name	Command1
Command	Caption	E&xit
	Name	Command2

Table 21-12 Objects and properties of the Focus form

2. Size the objects on the screen, as shown in Figure 21-5.

3. Enter the following code in the Command1_Click event. This activates the Notepad using AppActivate to set the focus, and then sends the contents of the text boxes. After finishing sending the text, it reactivates the focus to the Focus project. If it fails to set the focus to the Notepad initially, it attempts to open Notepad using the Shell statement. If it's already tried (and failed) to open Notepad, it gives a warning message and exits.

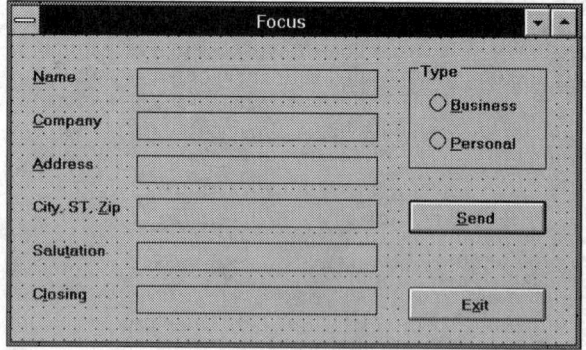

Figure 21-5 The Focus project during design

```
Sub Command1_Click ()
    On Error GoTo OpenNotepad                      'not open yet, so open it
    AppActivate "Notepad - (Untitled)"             'switch focus to notepad
    On Error GoTo 0                                'success!
    For i = 0 To 5                                 'step through each text box
        SendKeys Text(i).Text & Chr$(13), True     'and send it to the notepad
    Next i
    AppActivate "Focus"                            'go back to this project
Exit Sub

OpenNotepad:                                       'need to open the notepad
    If tried Then                                  'if we've already tried, then
        MsgBox "Failed to open notepad"            'no way
        Exit Sub                                   'bye bye
    End If
    tried = True                                   'OK, we're trying now!
    x = Shell("Notepad")                           'attempt to open notepad
    Resume                                         'and start again (AppActivate)
End Sub
```

4. Enter the following code in the Command2_Click event. This simply ends the program.

```
Sub Command2_Click ()
    End
End Sub
```

5. Enter the following code in the Option_Click event. This determines which settings are applicable for business or personal use. If business, (Index = 0), then the Company text box (Text(1)) is enabled along with its label, the Salutation (Text(4)) is removed as a tab stop, and the Closing gets a proper businesslike setting. If personal (Index = 1), then there is no need for a Company entry, so Text(1) is disabled along with its label, the Salutation is put back as a tab stop (in case you want to give a custom greeting), and Salutation is given a somewhat looser setting. Finally, the routine sets the focus to the first text box.

```
Sub Option_Click (Index As Integer)
    If Index = 0 Then '************ Business
        Text(1).Enabled = True      'enable company
        Label3.Enabled = True       'turn on company label
        Text(4).TabStop = False     'make keyboard entry flow past the Salutation
        Text(5).Text = "Sincerely," 'set default closing
    Else                '************ Personal
        Text(1).Enabled = False     'Turn off company box
        Label3.Enabled = False      'and company box label
        Text(4).TabStop = True      'set keyboard flow to include Salutation
        Text(5).Text = "Ciao!"      'Set default closing
    End If
    Text(0).SetFocus                'go to the contact name
End Sub
```

6. Enter the following code in the Text_GotFocus event. This highlights the text box by setting its background white, and selects all the text in it. These are very typical actions to take when a text box is given the focus.

```
Sub Text_GotFocus (Index As Integer)
    Text(Index).BackColor = QBColor(15)              'highlight box with white background
    Text(Index).SelStart = 0                         'select all the text
    Text(Index).SelLength = Len(Text(Index).Text)
End Sub
```

7. Enter the following code in the Text_LostFocus event. This unhighlights the text box by setting its background back to gray, then automatically sets the salutation if we're leaving the Name text box, Text(0). It first sets the text into the variable n for ease in handling the many references to it later. It then looks for a period (.) to isolate the title (for example, Mr. , Mrs. , Ms. , Dr.). If the Company box (Text(1)) is enabled, it tries to set a business-style greeting (for example, Dear Mr. Smith:) by isolating the last name. If there is no period (indicating no title) it beeps and resets the focus to let the user reenter the name with a proper title. If the Company box was not enabled, it implies a personal greeting (for example, Dear John,). It isolates the first name and sets the text. The LostFocus event is often used for this kind of error and validity checking, and updating other controls.

```
Sub Text_LostFocus (Index As Integer)
    Text(Index).BackColor = QBColor(7)            'unhighlight text box
    If Index = 0 Then                             'if editing contact name,
        n = Text(0).Text                          'get the name
        p = InStr(n, ".")                         'find a period (indicating honorific like Mr.,
                                                                  'Mrs., Dr., etc)

        If Text(1).Enabled Then                   'company: business letter requiring formality
            If p = 0 Then                         'and the user hasn't entered honorific, then
                Beep                              'Bronx cheer
                Text(0).SetFocus                  'set focus back to name
            End If
            For i = Len(n) To 1 Step -1           'step backwards to isolate the last name
                If Mid$(n, i, 1) = " " Then Exit For  'found beginning of last word
            Next i
            Text(4).Text = "Dear " & Left$(n, p) & Mid$(n, i) & ":"  '"Dear Mr. Hardwick:"
        Else                                      'personal letter!
            If p = 0 Then                         'if there is no honorific
                i = 1                             'then start at the beginning of the name
            Else                                  'there is an honorific, so
                i = InStr(n, " ") + 1             'start just after the honorific
            End If
            j = InStr(i, n, " ") - i              'isolate the first name
            If j < 1 Then j = Len(n)              'if entered only first name, use entire thing
            Text(4).Text = "Dear " & Mid$(n, i, j) & ","  '"Dear John,"
        End If
    End If
End Sub
```

How It Works

This project illustrates some typical uses for the focus-setting events, methods, and statement. When it first loads, focus is initially set to the Business option button, as it is first in the tab order. That automatically generates a click event for the

826

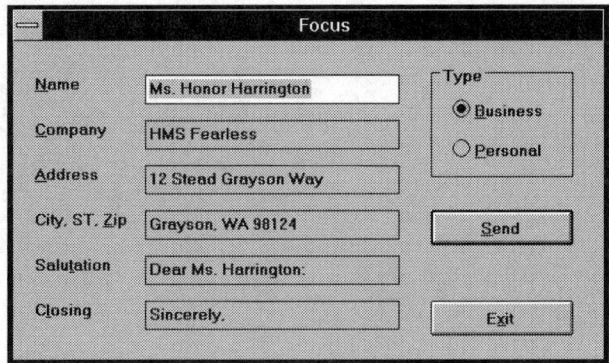

Figure 21-6 The Focus project in action

button, so the text box settings get set for Business use, and focus gets set to Text(0), Name. Note that each label's TabIndex property is set to one less than the TabIndex of the text box it labels. The (ALT)-key combination of the label will thus send the focus to the text box.

All of the text boxes are in a control array. This makes it simple to write the code to highlight and unhighlight the boxes. Highlighting simply sets the background to white, and selects all the text in the box. Many Windows programs default to selecting the text when first entering a text box. Unhighlighting is equally simple; we just set the background back to gray. These are very typical uses for the GotFocus and LostFocus events.

Another typical use for LostFocus is for validity checking. The Text_LostFocus routine checks to see if we're leaving the Text(0) box, Name. If so, we need to verify that the Name includes a title (Mr., Mrs., and so on) if we're doing a business entry. It checks to make sure there is a period in the text, assuming (rather simplistically!) that the period immediately follows the title.

The routine goes further, by automatically setting the Salutation. It parses the text string and isolates the last name (for business use) or the first name (for personal use). It then sets the Salutation appropriately.

Finally, the Send command button (Command1) activates the Notepad and sends the resultant address text to it. If it fails to activate at first, it opens the Notepad application before trying again. Once sent, focus returns to the Focus project. Figure 21-6 shows the Focus project in action.

22

TIME

Some Visual Basic applications need to keep track of time. Visual Basic provides a variety of ways to determine the time at which something happened, or should be made to happen. It also offers a wealth of functions to convert to and from a number of different ways of expressing time.

TIME IN VISUAL BASIC

Visual Basic divides time into units of measure that are familiar to the user, such as the date and time of day. The date uses the month, day, and year to pinpoint a specific date. Each date may be further defined by an exact hour, minute, and second.

Time, Serial Numbers, and the Date Variant

In Visual Basic, the date and time may be expressed with a date variant that can represent both the date and time of day of a specified moment. Visual Basic 1.0 called a more limited version of this date variant a *serial number*. In this serial number, the digits to the left of the decimal point represent the total days elapsed since December 30, 1899. The supplied serial number represents a date in the range between January 1, 100 (-657434) and December 31, 9999 (2958465). For example, the serial number 34931 represents that many days elapsed since December 30, 1899, which works out to August 20, 1995. Note that this range is much larger than the range of dates allowed in Visual Basic 1.0.

The digits to the right of the decimal point represent the total seconds elapsed since 12:00 midnight of the current day, expressed as a decimal fraction of a day. Thus in the serial number 34931.064583333, the time portion corresponds to approximately 1:33 A.M.

Visual Basic 2.0 introduced the Variant variable type. This type of variable can store any of the kinds of variable types, be it a string or any of the numeric types. The date variant is a Variant of type 7. It is stored internally by Visual Basic as a double precision number, much as Visual Basic 1.0 stored its serial numbers. Most of the date and time functions now work with date variants, rather than strings and serial numbers. The great advantage to using date variants is that Visual Basic attempts to automatically convert the arguments and results of the functions to whatever format is appropriate. This makes your code simpler to write, as you don't have to explicitly convert the variable types.

For instance, the Date statement accepts a date variant, and the Date$ statement only accepts a string of the proper format. Both statements do the same thing: change your computer's system date. The Date$ statement accepts only dates expressed as "08-20-94" or "08/24/1994," whereas the Date statement accepts all the formats accepted by the Date$ statement plus expressions like "August 20, 1994", or "20-Aug-94 12:32 am."

The Timer Control

In order for a set of actions to be governed by time, those actions must be connected to a timer control on a Visual Basic form. The timer lets you bypass the normal operation of a program with actions based on time rather than user input. Unless the timer control is disabled, the timer's Timer event triggers each time the amount of time set in the Interval property elapses. Although a Visual Basic application may have as many timer controls as needed, no more than 16 timer controls may be active at any given point. This is a limitation of the Windows environment and not Visual Basic. Timer controls are only visible at design time, not at runtime.

TIME SUMMARY

Visual Basic provides several tools that influence the display and manipulation of time. The Interval property of the timer control indicates how much time must pass before triggering the actions in the Timer event. The Timer event contains the actions that take place when triggered. The Timer function returns the number of seconds that have passed since 12:00 midnight. Obtain the current setting of the time and date in the computer with the Date$ and Time$ functions, and modify them with the Date$ and Time$ statements.

You can convert dates and times with a series of functions: DateSerial, TimeSerial, DateValue, TimeValue, Month, Day, and Year, Hour, Minute, and Second, and CVDate. Table 22-1 displays the statement, property, event, and functions that affect Timing within a Visual Basic application.

Use or Set This...		To Do This...
CVDate	Function	Convert a string or a number to a date variant
Date, Date$	Function	Return the system date set in the computer
Date, Date$	Statement	Set the system date
DateSerial	Function	Return the date variant that represents a date given in integer format
DateValue	Function	Return the date variant of a date given in string format
Day	Function	Return an integer between 1 and 31 that represents the day of the month
Hour	Function	Return an integer between 0 and 23 that represents the hour of the day
Interval	Property	Determine the interval of time before processing the Timer event
Minute	Function	Return an integer between 0 and 59 that represents the minute of the day
Month	Function	Return the integer between 1 and 12 that represents the number of the month
Now	Function	Return a date variant for the current date and time
Second	Function	Return the integer between 0 and 59 that represents the second
Time, Time$	Function	Return the current system time
Time, Time$	Statement	Set the system time
Timer	Event	Determine actions that take place when the Interval has passed
Timer	Function	Return the number of seconds since midnight
TimeSerial	Function	Return the date variant for the indicated time given in numeric format
TimeValue	Function	Convert a time in string format to a date variant
WeekDay	Function	Return an integer between 1 and 7 that represents the day of the week

(continued on next page)

(continued from previous page)

Use or Set This...		To Do This...
Year	Function	Return an integer between 100 and 9999 that represents the year

Table 22-1 The property, event, functions, and statements that affect timing in Visual Basic applications

The following pages investigate the features summarized in Table 22-1 in detail. Step-by-step directions at the end of this section describe how to assemble the Time project.

CVDATE FUNCTION

Purpose

The CVDate function converts a string or numeric expression into a Date Variant. This conversion is more general than other functions like DateValue or TimeSerial, as it accepts either strings or numbers and returns the entire Date Variant. Table 22-2 shows the argument of the CVDate function, and Table 22-3 summarizes how the CVDate handles a variety of inputs.

General Syntax

`CVDate(expression)`

Argument	Description
expression	String or number that can be evaluated as a legal date

Table 22-2 Argument of the CVDate function

Expression is...	The CVDate function returns...
Numeric, -657434 to 2958465	Date
Numeric, out of range	Error 13 (Type Mismatch)

832

Expression is...	The CVDate function returns...
String that looks like a date	Date
String that looks like a number	Date, if number in range; Error 13 if out of range
Other String expression	Error 13 (Type Mismatch)

Table 22-3 CVDate input handling

Example Syntax

```
Sub Form_Load ()
    Dim InDate As String, OutDate As Variant, Msg, NL, TABSTOP
    NL = Chr$(13) + Chr$(10): TABSTOP = Chr$(9)
    Do
        Msg = "Enter any date and time in any format you like."
        InDate = InputBox(Msg)
        If InDate = "" Then Exit Sub
        If Len(Format(InDate, "mm-dd-yy")) <> 8 Or Format(InDate, "mm-dd-yy") = "01-01-00" ⇐
Or (Len(InDate) = 8 And Val(InDate) = 0) Then
            MsgBox "Invalid date!  Try again.", 48
        Else
            OutDate = CVDate(InDate)
            Msg = "You Entered: " + TABSTOP + InDate + NL + NL
            Msg = Msg + "Long Form:    " + TABSTOP + Format(OutDate, "mmmm d, yyyy") + NL
            Msg = Msg + "Long Time:    " + TABSTOP + Format(OutDate, "h:mm:ss am/pm") + NL
            Msg = Msg + "Serial Time: " + TABSTOP + CStr(CDbl(OutDate))
            MsgBox Msg
        End If
    Loop
End Sub
```

Description

The CVDate function converts a variety of input expressions into a valid Date Variant. This saves you from writing more specific code by letting CVDate handle the intricacies of the conversion. The argument must be a string or numeric expression that can be interpreted as a date. If the expression cannot be interpreted as a date, CVDate generates runtime error number 13 (Type Mismatch).

CVDate handles numbers, strings, and strings that look like numbers differently. If the input is numeric, CVDate checks to see if it is within the range of -657434 to 2958465. If it is, it converts it to a date. If not, it generates a runtime error. A string expression that looks like a date (such as "April 1, 1994 11:34 pm" or "12/10/98") is converted into a date. A string expression that looks like a number (such as "3456") is first converted to a number, then validated as for regular numeric input. Finally, any other string expression (such as "Foobar" or "April 1st, 1994 at 11:34 in the morning") generates a runtime error. Table 22-3 summarizes this.

The example above uses the versatile Format function to see if the input is a valid date before passing it to the CVDate function. Format handles a variety of input just as CVDate does, and is more forgiving of input that cannot be interpreted correctly. See Format in Appendix B, Visual Basic Language Reference, for more information about the Format and Format$ functions.

Example

The Time project at the end of this chapter uses the CVDate function to convert a text string the user types in the textThen text box to a legal date. It does this in both the cmndCalculate_Click events and the cmndSet_Click events. The conversion process is surrounded by an error trap to trap any strings that aren't legal dates.

DATE, DATE$ FUNCTIONS

Purpose

The Date$ function returns the current system date as a string, and the Date function returns the current system date as a date variant. Table 22-4 summarizes the return values of the Date$ function.

General Syntax

```
Date$
Date
```

Date	Settings Range
Month (mm)	A number between 01 and 12 inclusive
Day (dd)	A number between 01 and 31 inclusive
Year (yyyy)	A year between 0100 and 9999 inclusive

Table 22-4 Possible returned settings of Date$ function

834

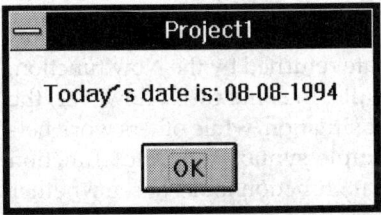

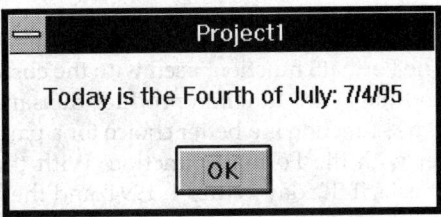

Figure 22-1 The example syntax shows how the Date$ function returns a string that represents the current system date

Figure 22-2 The example syntax shows how the Date function returns a variant that represents the current system date; note the difference in format compared to the Date$ function

Example Syntax

```
Sub Form_Load ()
    Msg$ = "Today's date is: " + Date$
    If Date$ = "07-04-94" Then
        Msg$ = "Today is the Fourth of July:" + Date
    ElseIf Format$(Now,"mm-dd") = "12-25" Then
        Msg$ = "Today is Christmas " + Format$(Now,"mm-dd-yyyy")
    End If
    MsgBox Msg$
End Sub
```

Description

A Date$ function returns a string of ten characters that represents the computer's current system date. The function has no arguments. The character string returned by the Date$ function is presented in the form of mm-dd-yyyy. In this form the mm part of the string stands for the current month, which must be between 01 and 12, for the 12 months of the year. The dd portion of the returned string is the day of the current day of the month and must be between 01 and 31. This string ends with the yyyy that returns the current year between 0100 and 9999. Table 22-4 lists the meaning of the characters returned by the Date$ function.

The Date function returns a date variant that represents the computer's current system date. It functions almost exactly like the Date$ function, except in the type of value it returns. Note that if you put the results of the Date function directly into the Text property of a text box, the text box automatically formats it as m/d/yy. Thus, the Date$ function would return August 20, 1995 as "08-20-1995" and the Date function would look like "8/20/95."

In the example syntax, an If-Then statement checks the current date of the computer to determine which message to display on the screen. Figures 22-1 and 22-2 demonstrate the difference between how the Date$ and Date functions format their return values.

The Format$ Function

The Format$ function, used with the current date returned by the Now function, and the Date$ function produce the same results. In some cases, however, the Date$ function is a better choice for a particular situation, while others work better with the Format$ function. With the example syntax, the Date$ function checks if the day is July 4, 1994, and the Format$ function looks to see whether the day is December 25. Notice that the Date$ function requires less space in the code to display the date, but the Format$ function will work on its date for any year, while the other only operates for the year 1994. This example demonstrates the tradeoff between the flexibility of the Format$ function and the shorter required size of the Date$ function.

Example

The Time project at the end of this chapter uses the Date$ function to display the current system date in the lablNow label. The timeClock_Timer event updates this display several times a second.

Comments

Use the Date$ statement to change the current system date of the computer.

DATE, DATE$ STATEMENTS

Purpose

The Date and Date$ statements allows the user to change the system date of a computer within a Visual Basic application. Table 22-5 summarizes the arguments of the Date$ statement, and Table 22-6 summarizes the possible acceptable contents of the datestring$ argument.

General Syntax

```
Date$ = datestring$
Date = expression$
```

Argument	Description
datestring$	String that represents the date in the form of "mm-dd-yy" or "mm-dd-yyyy"
expression$	String that represents the date (more generalized than datestring$)

Table 22-5 Arguments of Date$ statement

datestring$	Possible Settings
mm	A number between 1 and 12 inclusive
dd	A number between 1 and 31 inclusive
yy	A number between 00 and 99 inclusive
yyyy	A number between 1980 and 2099 inclusive

Table 22-6 Possible acceptable contents of the datestring$ argument

Example Syntax

```
Sub Command1_Click ()
    On Error GoTo BadDate
    Date = Text1.Text
Exit Sub

Bad Date:
    MsgBox "That date is not in an acceptable format!"
Exit Sub

End Sub
```

Description

The Date$ statement allows the user to change the system date of a computer within a Visual Basic application. The Date statement does the same thing, but accepts a much wider variety of formats that it tries to convert to a proper date.

The argument for the Date$ statement must be a string containing a valid date. The valid date formats that the Date$ statement will accept are mm-dd-yy, mm-dd-yyyy, mm/dd/yy, and mm/dd/yyyy. A datestring$ must be a string variable,

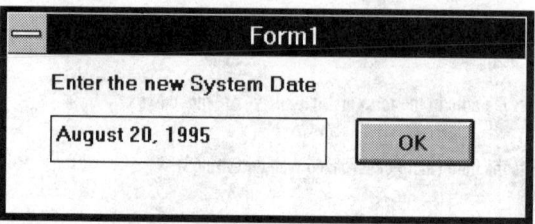

Figure 22-3 The Date statement
accepts a variety of date formats to
set the system date

or the system will generate an error. In this form, the mm part of the string stands for the current month that must be between 0 and 12, for the 12 months of the year. The dd portion of the returned string is the day of the current day of the month and must be between 1 and 31. This string ends with the yyyy that returns the current year, which must be between 1980 and 2099. (Note that this acceptable date range is considerably smaller than what all of the other date functions accept.) Strings that end in yy represent the last two digits of the familiar year, with 1994 being expressed as 94.

The Date statement accepts a wider variety of formats. It accepts variants of variant type 7 (date) and type 8 (string). The Date statement attempts to convert whatever you pass it to a legal date. It recognizes all the string formats that the Date$ format accepts, plus strings that contain unambiguous month names. For instance, "08-20-95", "8/20/1995", "August 20, 1995", "Aug-20-95", and "20/August/95" are all acceptable. You can also use date variants returned by other functions such as the DateSerial function. If the format is not acceptable, the Date statement generates a trappable error.

The example syntax gives the user the opportunity to change the system date with a text box entry. Notice that if the user enters a date in any format other than those shown, the system generates an error that we trap to display an explanatory message box. It's a good idea to always set error traps if you allow your user to manually input dates; the range of acceptable input for statements like Date is quite wide, but not as extensive as what your users will inevitably dream up. Figure 22-3 shows what this might look like.

Example

The Time project at the end of this chapter uses the Date statement to set the system date in the cmndSet_Click event. The user can type any arbitrary date and time in the textThen text box. The cmndSet_Click event first converts the user's input to a valid date with the CVDate function. It then sets the system date. The routine also will reset the system date back to normal if the user presses the button a second time.

Comments

Computers running DOS versions before 3.3 will not permanently change their date; you'll generally need to use a special machine specific setup disk to do this. The chances of your modern windows program running on machines with very old versions of DOS, however, is probably minimal.

Remember that while 31 is the maximum number allowed for the month argument, not all months have 31 days.

DATESERIAL FUNCTION

Purpose

The DateSerial function converts the numeric values of an indicated date to a Visual Basic date variant. Table 22-7 summarizes the arguments for the DateSerial function.

General Syntax

```
DateSerial(year%, month%, day%)
```

Argument	Description
year%	A number or expression that evaluates to between 100 and 9999 inclusive
month%	A number or expression that evaluates to between 1 and 12 inclusive
day%	A number or expression that evaluates to between 1 and 31 inclusive

Table 22-7 Possible arguments for the DateSerial function

Example Syntax

```
Sub Command1_Click ()
    monthsToAdd = Val(Combo1.Text)          'how many months to add to current date
    thisYear = Year(Now())
    thisMonth = Month(Now())
    thisDay = Day(Now())
    On Error GoTo BadDate
    newDate = DateSerial(thisYear, thisMonth + monthsToAdd, thisDay)
    Text1.Text = Format$(newDate, "###,###")
Exit Sub
```

(continued on next page)

(continued from previous page)

```
BadDate:
     MsgBox "The resultant date is not acceptable!"
Exit Sub

End Sub
```

Description

The DateSerial function returns a date variant that represents the month, day, and year of a date on the calendar, as discussed in the introduction to this chapter. Each of the three arguments of this function represents the numeric values of the year, month, and date. The *year%* variable is a number between 100 and 9999 inclusive. Month% stands for the month of a date between 1 and 12, with January being represented by 1 and December by 12. Date% represents the day of a month between 1 and 31. Although the range for the Date% argument goes up to 31, note that many months don't have that many days.

The example syntax adds on a number of months (as determined by Combo1) to the current date, and displays the results in the text box.

The Month, Day, and Year Functions

The Month, Day, and Year functions are the logical choices to use to obtain the variables for a DateSerial function. In the example syntax, each of these functions provides the necessary values of the date entered by the user. Notice how each function only returns the value that represents the month, day, or year, respectively, of the date. Each function ignores all of the other values in the date.

Example

The Time project at the end of this chapter uses the DateSerial function to determine a date given the mouse's coordinates over a picturebox. It scales the mouse's current horizontal position to determine a year, month, and day to use in the DateSerial function.

DATEVALUE FUNCTION

Purpose

The DateValue function converts a date in the form of a string into a Visual Basic date variant. This function changes differently formatted dates to a universal numerical form. Table 22-8 summarizes the argument of the DateValue function, and Table 22-9 summarizes the valid DateValue formats.

840

General Syntax

```
DateValue(datestring$)
```

Argument	Description
datestring$	String that represents a date for the DateValue function to convert

Table 22-8 Argument of DateValue function

datestring$
01/01/1994
01/01/94
January 1, 1994
Jan 1, 1994
01-Jan-1994
01 January 94

Table 22-9 A few examples of valid datestring$ argument values for the DateValue function

Example Syntax

```
Sub Command1_Click ()
Start:
    On Error GoTo NotDate                        'Sets error trap to NotDate.
    If Text1.Text = "" Or Text2.Text = "" Then 'Checks if Text box is blank.
        MsgBox "Please Enter a date in each box."
        Exit Sub
    End If
    FirstDate = DateValue(Text1.Text)            'Finds date variant of entered date.
    EndDate = DateValue(Text2.Text)              'Finds date variant of entered date.
    Text1.Text = Str$(FirstDate)                 'Displays the date variant.
    Text2.Text = Str$(EndDate)                   'Displays the date variant.
    Days = Abs(EndDate - FirstDate)              'Finds number of days between date.
    Label1.Caption = Str$(Days) + " Days"        'Displays the number of days.
Exit Sub                                         'Exits subroutine.
```

(continued on next page)

(continued from previous page)

```
NotDate:
     MsgBox "Please enter a date only"
Exit Sub

End Sub
```

Description

The DateValue function converts a date string to a date variant that represents the month, day, and year of a date on the calendar. There are a number of acceptable date formats for the order of appearance of the month, day, and year in the datestring$. The international section of the WIN.INI file defines the default order of the month, day, and year. If a datestring$ contains the actual name of a month in long or abbreviated form, the DateValue function will also be able to convert it to a date variant. In addition to recognizing 01/01/1994 and 01/01/94, the DateValue function will also be able to convert January 1, 1994, Jan 1, 1994, 01-Jan-1994, and 01 January 94. If the year portion of a datestring$ is omitted, the current year is assumed. All of these combinations will work in the example, so try them out with different date formats for each text box.

In the example syntax, the DateValue function finds the date variant of the two dates that the user enters in the Text1 and Text2 text boxes. The difference between the two date variants provides the number of days that are between the two entered dates. Figure 22-4 shows what this example might look like on the screen.

Example

The Time project at the end of this chapter uses the DateValue function to help build up a representation of the serial number representing the current system time. The timeClock_Timer event triggers several times a second to update the display.

Comments

Although DateValue will not display time information that might be in the text string, invalid time information (such as 89;98) will cause Visual Basic

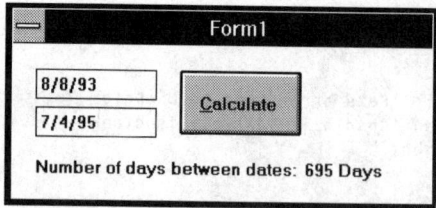

Figure 22-4 The DateValue function converts dates to date variants; you can then easily perform math operations, such as taking the difference between two date variant values

to generate an error. Negative numbers in the date string represent dates prior to December 30, 1899.

HOUR, MINUTE, AND SECOND FUNCTIONS

Purpose

The Hour, Minute, and Second functions convert a number or string to these familiar elements of time. The Hour function returns an integer that is between 0 (12:00AM) and 23 (11:00PM) inclusive. Using the Minute and Second functions returns an integer between 0 and 59 inclusive representing the minute or second portion of the time. Table 2-10 summarizes the argument of the Hour, Minute, and Second functions.

General Syntax

```
Hour(expression)
Minute(expression)
Second(expression)
```

Argument	Description
expression	Variant representing a date and time or a number that can be converted to a serial number

Table 22-10 Argument of the Hour, Minute, and Second functions

Example Syntax

```
Sub Timer1_Timer ()
    Timer1.Interval = 1000              'Sets Interval to 1 Second
    If Hour(Now) > 12 Then              'Checks if time is AM or PM
        DayTime$ = " PM"                'Sets Daytime string to PM
        NormalTime = Hour(Now) - 12     'Changes 24hour to 12hour time
    Else
        DayTime$ = " AM"                'Sets Daytime string to AM
        NormalTime = Hour(Now)          'Finds the current hour
    End If
    Current$ = Str$(NormalTime) + " :"  'Defines variable as the current hour
    Current$ = Current$ + Str$(Minute(Now)) + " :"    'minute, and seconds separated by
    Current$ = Current$ + Str$(Second(Now))           'colons.
    Current$ = Current$ + DayTime$
    Text1.Text = Current$               'Displays the current time in Text1
End Sub
```

Description

The expression argument of an Hour, Minute, or Second function may represent a date and time between January 1, 0100 and December 31, 9999 inclusive. In a date variant, the digit to the right of the decimal point returns the time of the day. Only the right side of the date variant is necessary for the Hour, Minute, and Second functions to produce the time of the day. The part of the date variant on the left side of the decimal point is the date and has no effect on the value returned for the Hour, Minute, and Second functions.

The expression argument may also be any acceptable date and time string expression, such as "12:30 pm" or "August 20, 1995 5:34 AM". See the TimeValue entry for examples of acceptable formats.

In the example syntax, the Hour, Minute, and Second functions work together to display the current time in the Text1 text box on the form. The text AM and PM also follows the time displayed on the screen.

Current Time and the Now Function

The Now function provides the date variant of the current system date and time. When this function is used with the Hour, Minute, and Second functions, the result is a value that defines the hour, minute, and second. In the example syntax, the Now function provides the date variant for the Hour, Minute, and Second functions to display in the text box. Notice that a space is left for the unseen 0 when the number is a single digit.

The Timer Event and Interval Property

When the Timer event and Interval property are used along with the Hour, Minute, Second, and Now functions, the time may be obtained at intervals specified by the Interval property of the timer control. The accuracy of the time displayed on the screen depends on the Interval property. If you watch the seconds change in the example syntax, you will notice that sometimes certain seconds are skipped. In order to keep this problem from happening, reduce the interval to one-half the needed accuracy. For the example, this may be avoided by changing the interval from 1000 milliseconds (1 second) to 500 milliseconds (1/2 second).

Example

The Hour, Minute, and Second functions help display the difference between the current system time and a time the user types in the textThen text box in the cmndCalculate_Click event. Each function converts the present system time and the date represented by the text box and puts the difference in a variable. The variables are then combined for display in the lablDifference label.

INTERVAL PROPERTY

Objects Affected

Check	Clipboard	Combo	Command	CommonDlg
Data	Debug	Dir	Drive	File
Form	Frame	Grid	Image	Label
Line	List	MDI Form	Menu	OLE
Option	Picture	Printer	Screen	Scroll
Shape	Text	▶ Timer		

Purpose

The Interval property of a timer control indicates the length of time to wait before processing the Timer event. This property may be changed either at design time or runtime. Each timer control's Interval property is independent of the Interval properties of other timer controls on the same form. Table 22-11 summarizes the arguments of the Interval property of a timer control, and Table 22-12 summarizes its possible settings.

General Syntax

```
[form!]Name.Interval = milliseconds&
```

Argument	Description
form	Name property of the form
Name	Name property of the timer control being affected
milliseconds&	Amount of time that must pass between the processing of the Timer event (as a long integer)

Table 22-11 Arguments of the Interval property of a timer control

milliseconds&	Effect
0	Disables the timer (default)
1-65,535	Milliseconds between triggerings; 1000 = 1 second

Table 22-12 Possible settings of the Interval property of a timer control

Example Syntax

```
Sub TextUpdateDisplay_LostFocus ()
    Timer1.Interval = Val(TextUpdateDisplay.Text)
End Sub
```

Description

The Interval property of a timer control indicates the length of time to wait before processing the Timer event. The milliseconds& argument may be any number between 0 and 65,535 milliseconds (65.535 seconds). Even though the measurements are in milliseconds, the system measures the passage of time with 18 ticks per second. For this reason the interval cannot be guaranteed to pass exactly on time.

The example syntax uses a text box to set the timer interval, perhaps for a procedure that updates a display in real time (anything from system resources to a stock price!).

The Enabled Property

If the Interval property of a timer control is set to 0, then the timer control is disabled and will not process the Timer event. The Enabled property of a timer control indicates whether the control is active or inactive. When the Enabled property of a timer control is False (0), it is disabled, and the countdown to the next Timer event is suspended. For this reason, if either the Enabled property or the Interval property is disabled in this way, the timer control stays inactive until its Interval property is a non-0 value and the Enabled property is True (-1). In the example syntax, the Enabled property is changed at design time to allow the timer control to activate immediately when the program is started.

The Timer Function

Since the Interval property has a maximum possible length of 65,535 milliseconds (a little more than 65 seconds), the Timer function must be used to generate actions that require longer lengths of time before they are triggered. A timer event could be set up on a form to check the amount of time since midnight with the Timer function until the timer returns an amount that is greater than the time specified for the event to take place.

Example

Both of the timers have their Interval property set during the Time project's design phase. The first timer, timeClock, is set to a quarter second (250 milliseconds) to update the real-time displays. The other timer pauses the display of new times in the pictTheWindsOfTime_MouseMove event for two and a half seconds (2500 milliseconds).

Comments

Although the Interval property of one timer control has no effect on another timer control, Windows has a limit of no more than 16 active timer controls at a time.

NOW FUNCTION

Purpose

The Now function provides the current date and time of the computer's system clock-calendar as a date variant.

General Syntax

```
Now
```

Example Syntax

```
Sub Timer1_Time ()
    Timer1.Interval = 100                              'Sets timer interval.
    Text1.Text = Str$(Now)                             'Displays the date variant
    Text2.Text = Format$(Now,"mmmm-dd-yy hh:mm:ss")    'Displays formatted date and time.
End Sub
```

Description

The Now function has no arguments. The variant returned by the Now function represents the system date and time at the moment that the code runs.

In the example syntax, the Now function serves as a means of displaying the date, time, and date variant on the screen. With this example, the time and date are shown in the Text2 text box and the variant that produces this information, returned by the Now function, is placed in the Text1 text box. Notice that in both cases, the date variant must be converted to a string prior to defining the Text property of the Text1 and Text2 text boxes.

Example

The Now function gives the current system date and time to the Year, Month, Day, Hour, Minute, and Second functions in the cmndCalculate_Click event.

TIME, TIME$ FUNCTIONS

Purpose

The Time$ function returns your computer's current system time when used in a Visual Basic application as a string; the Time function returns the current system time as a date variant. Table 22-13 summarizes the possible returned settings of the Time$ and Time functions.

General Syntax

```
Time$
Time
```

Time	Description
	Returns an eight character string in the form of "hh:mm:ss"
Hour (hh)	A number between 00 and 23 inclusive
Minute (mm)	A number between 00 and 59 inclusive
Second (ss)	A number between 00 and 59 inclusive

Table 22-13 Possible returned values of the Time$ function

Example Syntax

```
Sub Timer1_Timer ()
    Text1.Text = Time$
    Text2.Text = Format$(Now,"hh:mm")
End Sub
```

848

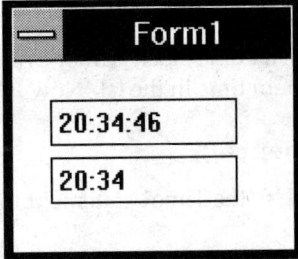

Figure 22-5 The Time$ function (top text box) is a convenient way of displaying the current system time without having to use the Format$ function (bottom text box)

Description

The Time$ function has no arguments. It returns a string of eight characters that represents the computer's current system time in the form of hh:mm:ss. In this form the hh part of the string stands for the current hour and must be between 0 and 23, for the 24 hours of the day. The mm portion of the returned string is the minute of the current day and must be between 00 and 59. This string ends with the ss that returns the current second and must also be between 00 and 59.

The Time function works very similarly, but returns a date variant rather than a string.

The example syntax checks the current time of the computer and displays it in two text boxes. The Time$ function works in the same way as the Format$ function to display the current time in the text boxes. Figure 22-5 shows what this example might look like on the screen.

The Format$ Function

The Format$ function, used with the Now function, and Time$ function produce the same results when the Format function converts the current time to the hh:mm:ss format. In some cases the Time$ function is a better choice for a particular situation, while other applications work better with the Format$ function. In the example syntax, the Time$ and Format$ functions provide the time to display on the screen. Notice that the Time$ function requires less space in the code to display the time. The Format$ function provides a way to display only the hour and minute of the current time. This example demonstrates the tradeoff between the flexibility of the Format$ function and the shorter required size of the Time$ function.

Example

The timeClock_Timer event uses the Time$ function to display the current system time in the lablNow label.

Comments

Use the Time$ statement to change the current system time of the computer.

TIME, TIME$ STATEMENTS

Purpose

The Time and Time$ statements allow the user to change the system time of a computer within a Visual Basic application. Table 22-14 summarizes the arguments of the Time and Time$ statements. Table 22-15 summarizes the possible acceptable contents of the timestring$ argument of a Time$ statement, and Table 22-16 gives examples of some of the acceptable arguments to the Time statement.

General Syntax

```
Time$ = timestring$
Time = expression$
```

Argument	Description
timestring$	Time in string format "hh:mm:ss"
expression$	Acceptable time format (more general than timestring$)

Table 22-14 Arguments of the Time$ statement

timestring$	Possible Settings
hh	A number between 00 and 23 inclusive
mm	A number between 00 and 59 inclusive
ss	A number between 00 and 59 inclusive

Table 22-15 Possible acceptable contents of the TimeString$ of a Time$ statement

expression$
2:21
2:21 pm
14:21
August 12, 1995 12:02 am

Table 22-16 Examples of acceptable time arguments for the Time statement

Example Syntax

```
Sub Command1_Click ()
    h = Val(Text1.Text)
    m = Val(Text2.Text)
    s = Val(Text3.Text)
    If h < 0 or m > 23 Then Beep: Exit Sub
    If m < 0 or m > 59 Then Beep: Exit Sub
    If s < 0 or s > 59 Then Beep: Exit Sub
    Time$ = Str$(h) & ":" & Str$(m) & ":" & Str$(s)
End Sub
```

Description

The Time$ and Time statements set the computer's internal system clock. They function almost identically, but the Time statement accepts a wider variety of time formats.

The valid time formats that the Time$ statement will accept are hh, hh:mm, and hh:mm:ss. The timestring$ argument must be a string variable or the system generates an error. In this form, the hh part of the string stands for the current hour, which must be between 00 and 23. These values represent the 24 hours of the day. The mm portion of the returned string is the minute of the current day, and must be between 00 and 59. This string may end with ss that returns the current seconds. The seconds must be between 0 and 59. For strings that do not end in mm or ss, these settings represent 0.

The Time statement accepts any string that is recognized as a valid time by the TimeValue function. It accepts the same format that the Time$ statement does, plus a wide variety of others. Table 22-16 gives a few examples of acceptable formats for the Time statement.

The example syntax gives the user the opportunity to change the system time by changing the values in three text boxes. Notice that if the user enters an incorrect time, the code beeps and doesn't attempt to change the time. If the time

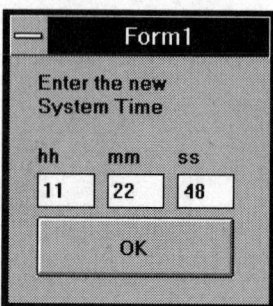

Figure 22-6 The Time$ function lets you change the computer's internal system clock

entered is valid, the Time$ statement changes the system time to the time entered by the user. Figure 22-6 shows what this example might look like on the screen.

Example

The Time statement sets the system time in the cmndSet_Click event. The user can type in any date and time in the textThen text box, and the cmndSet_Click event sets the system date and time to the date in the text box. The routine remembers the original system date and time, and resets them when clicked a second time.

Comments

Computers running DOS versions before 3.3 will not permanently change their time; you'll generally need to use a special machine specific setup disk to do this. The chances of your modern windows program running on machines with very old versions of DOS, however, is probably minimal.

TIMER EVENT

Objects Affected

Check	Clipboard	Combo	Command	CommonDlg
Data	Debug	Dir	Drive	File
Form	Frame	Grid	Image	Label
Line	List	MDI Form	Menu	OLE

Option	Picture	Printer	Screen	Scroll
Shape	Text	▶ Timer		

Purpose

The Timer event contains the actions that take place when a time equal to the interval value of the timer control has elapsed. This event triggers every time that the interval of time elapses until the timer control is disabled. A timer control is disabled by setting its Enabled property to False, by setting its Interval property to 0, or by unloading the form. Table 22-17 summarizes the arguments of the Timer event.

General Syntax

```
Sub Name_Timer ([Index As Integer])
End Sub
```

Argument	Description
Name	Name property of the timer
Index	This argument serves as a reference for the part of a control array

Table 22-17 Arguments of the Timer event

Example Syntax

```
Sub Timer1_Timer ()
    Cls                                      'Clear the form.
    Const PI = 3.14159265                    'Define Constant PI.
    Static Num As Double                     'Define Static Variable
    FillColor = QBColor(1)                   'Sets form's FillColor.
    FillStyle = 0                            'Sets form's FillStyle to solid.
    X% = ScaleWidth / 2                      'Defines as half width of screen.
    Y% = ScaleHeight / 2                     'Defines as half height of screen.
    Radius% = ScaleWidth / 4                 'Defines as 1/4 of width of screen.
    Circle (X%, Y%), Radius%, , Num, -6.283  'Draws partial circle on screen.
    Num = Num - ((2 * PI) / 60)              'Reduces value of variable.
    Text1.Text = Str$(Num)                   'Displays setting of variable.
    If Abs(Num) >= 6.283 Then                'Checks value of variable.
        Num = 0                              'Redefines variable as zero.
        Timer1.Enabled = 0                   'Disables Timer.
        Cls                                  'Clears screen.
    End If
End Sub
```

Description

The Timer event lets you take repeated actions at specific time intervals. You may wish to periodically update a display or check on changeable values.

In the example syntax, the Timer event displays a circle on the screen with a line drawn from the center of the circle to the right edge of the circle. Each time the event runs, it draws a circle with a larger and larger slice removed. When the circle disappears from the screen, the timer control's Enabled property is changed to False, ending the timing.

The Interval Property

The Interval property of a timer control indicates how frequently to process the Timer event. This property is measured in milliseconds and may range in value from 0 to 65,535 (a little more than 65 seconds). No matter what the setting of this property, if the Enabled property is False, the Timer event will not be processed. The example syntax might set the Interval property of the Timer1 control to 1000 during the design phase to process the Timer event at once per second. Setting up the Interval property in this way makes the circle graphically display the amount of time left in the minute since the form first loaded.

The Enabled Property

The Enabled property of a timer control determines whether the control is active or inactive. When the timer control's Enabled property is True, the code processes the Timer event at the intervals specified by the Interval property. While the timer control's property is False, the control remains disabled. If the Interval property is 0, then the Timer event is not processed. In the example syntax, the Enabled property of the timer control must be True to trigger the Timer event at the loading of the form. An If statement sets this property to False when the circle has disappeared off the screen.

Example

The timeClock_Timer event updates the real-time displays of system time and the stopwatch several times a second. The timeMouse_Timer disables the timeMouse timer to reenable mouse movements displaying the resultant date and time in the pictTheWindsOfTime_MouseMove event.

Comment

Timers in a timer control array only trigger a Timer event for the first timer in the array. This makes timer control arrays useless, and are allowed only to be consistent with the rest of Visual Basic controls. Set up each timer as an independent control.

TIMER FUNCTION

Purpose

The Timer function provides the number of seconds that have elapsed since 12:00 midnight. This function may serve as a reference for determining the number of seconds elapsed between two different uses of the Timer function on the same day.

General Syntax

```
Timer
```

Example Syntax

```
Sub Timer1_Timer ()
    Timer1.Interval = 500                        'Sets Timer Interval.
    Static ProgStart As Double                   'Defines static variable.
    Msg$ = " Elapsed seconds since Midnight"     'Defines message.
    Elapsed = Int(Timer)                         'Stores current seconds.
    ST$ = Str$(Elapsed)                          'Converts to text.
    Text1.Text = ST$ + Msg$                      'Displays seconds since midnight.
    If ProgStart = 0 Then                        'If ProgStart has not been set,
        ProgStart = Elapsed                      'sets ProgStart.
    End If
    Msg$ = Str$(Int(Elapsed – ProgStart))        'Stores seconds since startup.
    Msg$ = Msg$ + " Seconds since program start" 'Stores message.
    Text2.Text = Msg$                            'Displays seconds since startup.
End Sub
```

Description

The Timer function returns the value that represents the number of seconds elapsed since midnight. This function has no argument, and returns a value between 0 and 86,400 (the number of seconds in one day). If the day changes (that is, the system clock goes past midnight), the difference between two values gained on different days will not return the true number of seconds elapsed.

The example syntax uses the Timer function to store and display the current number of seconds since midnight and program startup. It finds the difference between the variables produced at program startup and now and then provides the number of elapsed seconds since program startup. Figure 22-7 shows what the example should look like on the screen.

Example

The Time project's timeClock_Timer event uses the Timer function to update the lablStopWatch label. The program's Form_Load event puts the Timer value in

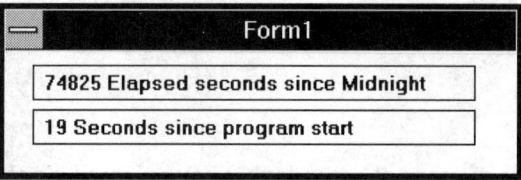

Figure 22-7 The Timer function measures how
many seconds have elapsed since midnight, and
can be used to time program functions

the timeClock's Tag property to use as a baseline. Each triggering of the
timeClock_Timer event then calculates the difference between the baseline and
the current Timer value to determine the number of seconds that has elapsed
since the program first started.

TIMESERIAL FUNCTION

Purpose

The TimeSerial function converts the values of an indicated time to a Visual Basic
date variant. Table 22-18 summarizes the arguments of the TimeSerial function.

General Syntax

```
TimeSerial(hour%, minute%, second%)
```

Argument	Description
hour%	A number or expression that evaluates to a number between 0 and 23 inclusive
minute%	A number or expression that evaluates to a number between 0 and 59 inclusive
second%	A number or expression that evaluates to a number between 0 and 59 inclusive

Table 22-18 Possible arguments for the TimeSerial function

Example Syntax

```
Sub Command1_Click ()
Start:
```

856

```
      On Error GoTo NotTime              'Takes the time entered in Text box 1 and
      If Text1.Text = "" Then GoTo EnterTime   'adds the figures entered in the other text
      BeginTime = TimeValue(Text1.Text)  'boxes to the Hour, Minute, and Second of the
      BeginHour = Hour(BeginTime)        'entered Time to obtain a new time.
      EndHour = Val(Text2.Text)
      BeginMinute = Minute(BeginTime)
      EndMinute = Val(Text3.Text)
      BeginSecond = Second(BeginTime)
      EndSecond = Val(Text4.Text)
      EndTime = TimeSerial(BeginHour + EndHour, BeginMinute + EndMinute, BeginSecond  ⇐
+ EndSecond)
      Label1.Caption = Format$(EndTime, "hh:mm:ss")
      Exit Sub
EnterTime:
      MsgBox "Please Enter a value in each box."
      Exit Sub
NotTime:
      If BeginSecond + EndSecond > 60 Then
          EndSecond = EndSecond - 60
          EndMinute = EndMinute + 1
      ElseIf BeginHour + EndHour > 24 Then
          EndHour = EndHour - 24
      ElseIf BeginMinute + EndMinute > 60 Then
          EndMinute = EndMinute - 60
          EndHour = EndHour + 1
      Else
          MsgBox "Please enter a valid Time."
          Text1.Text = ""
      End If
      Resume Start
End Sub
```

Description

The TimeSerial function returns a date variant that represents the hour, minutes, and seconds of a time on the clock. Each of the three arguments of this function represents the numerical values of time. The hour% argument provides the hour of a day expressed as a two-digit number between 01 and 23 inclusive. The minute% argument stands for the minutes of time between 0 and 59. The second% argument represents the second of a day between 0 and 59.

In the example syntax, the numbers entered into the text boxes below the date increase the hour, minutes, and seconds of the entered time to produce a new time based on the amount specified in each text box.

An error-checking system in the example syntax enforces the limits of each of these arguments.

The Hour, Minute, and Second Functions

The Hour, Minute, and Second functions are the logical choices to use to obtain the variables for the TimeSerial function. The example syntax uses each of these functions to obtain the necessary values of the time entered by the user. Notice that the function only returns the value of the item specified by the function. For example, the Hour function only provides the value of the hour portion of the time.

Example

The Time project at the end of this chapter uses the TimeSerial function to determine a time given the mouse's coordinates over a picturebox. It scales the mouse's current vertical position to determine an hour, minute, and second to use in the TimeSerial function.

TIMEVALUE FUNCTION

Purpose

The TimeValue function converts a time in the form of a string into a Visual Basic date variant. Table 22-19 summarizes the argument of the TimeValue function and Table 22-20 gives some examples of acceptable argument values.

General Syntax

```
TimeValue(timestring$)
```

Argument	Description
timestring$	Text string to convert that is an acceptable time value

Table 22-19 Argument of the TimeValue function

timestring$
3:05
3:05:23
03:05:23
15:05

858

timestring$
3:05 pm
3:05 AM
August 12, 1995 3:05 pm

Table 22-20 Some examples of acceptable timestring$ arguments for the TimeValue function

Example Syntax

```
Sub Command_Click ()
Start:
     On Error GoTo NotTime                      'Sets error trap to NotTime.
     If Text1.Text = "" or Text2.Text = "" Then 'checks to see if text boxes are blank
         MsgBox "Please Enter a Time in each box."
         Exit Sub
     End If
     FirstTime = TimeValue(Text1.Text)          'Finds date variant of entered Time.
     EndTime = TimeValue(Text2.Text)            'Finds date variant of entered Time.
     Text1.Text = Str$(FirstTime)               'Displays the date variant.
     Text2.Text = Str$(EndTime)                 'Displays the date variant.
     T = EndTime - FirstTime                     'Finds the difference between Times.
     Seconds$ = Str$(Int(T * 86400))            'Finds the number of seconds.
     Label1.Caption = Seconds$ + " seconds"      'Displays the number of seconds.
     Exit Sub                                    'Exits subroutine.
NotTime:
     MsgBox "Please enter a Time only"
     Text1.Text = ""
     Text2.Text = ""
     Resume Start
End Sub
```

Description

A TimeValue function converts a time string to a date variant that represents the hour, minutes, and seconds of a time. There are a number of acceptable time formats for the order of appearance of the hour, minutes, and seconds in the timestring$. The time setting of the international section of the WIN.INI defines the default order of the hour, minutes, and seconds.

The example syntax demonstrates how to convert date strings of differing formats to date variants. The TimeValue function is used to find the date variant of the two times that the user enters in the Text1 and Text2 text boxes. When the code finds the difference between the two date variants, the result is the number of days between the two entered times.

859

Example

The Time project at the end of this chapter uses the TimeValue function to help display the current system time during the timeClock_Timer event. It displays a representation of the serial number in the lablSerial label.

WEEKDAY, MONTH, DAY, AND YEAR FUNCTIONS

Purpose

The Weekday, Month, Day, and Year functions convert a date variant to these familiar elements of the date. These values can be used to construct or format a date in the usual terms, such as "Thursday, December 15, 1994." Table 22-21 summarizes the argument of the Weekday, Month, Day, and Year functions.

General Syntax

```
Month(expression$)
Day(expression$)
Minute(expression$)
WeekDay(expression$)
```

Argument	Description
expression$	Date variant to display in month, day, year, or weekday format

Table 22-21 Argument of the Weekday, Month, Day, and Year functions

Example Syntax

```
Sub Form_Load ()
    CMonth% = Month(Now)                    'Stores current month number.
    CDay% = Day(Now)                        'Stores current day number.
    CYear% = Year(Now)                      'Stores current year number.
    Week% = Weekday(Now)                    'Stores current weekday number.
    If CYear% < 2000 Then                   'Checks if current year is less than 2000.
        If CYear% > 1899 Then               'Checks if current year is greater than 1899.
            Yr$ = Format$(CYear%, "yy")     'Stores last two digits of year.
        Else
            Yr$ = Str$(CYear%)              'Stores all four digits of year.
        End If
    End If
    Select Case CMonth%                     'Checks month number to store
        Case 1: M$ = "Q1 - January "
```

860

```
        Case 2: M$ = "Q1 - February "
        Case 3: M$ = "Q1 - March "
        Case 4: M$ = "Q2 - April "
        Case 5: M$ = "Q2 - May "
        Case 6: M$ = "Q2 - June "
        Case 7: M$ = "Q3 - July "
        Case 8: M$ = "Q3 - August "
        Case 9: M$ = "Q3 - September "
        Case 10: M$ = "Q4 - October "
        Case 11: M$ = "Q4 - November "
        Case 12: M$ = "Q4 - December "
    End Select
    Select Case Week%                        'Checks the week number for which week name
        Case 1:  W$ = "Sunday "
        Case 2:  W$ = "Monday "
        Case 3:  W$ = "Tuesday "
        Case 4:  W$ = "Wednesday "
        Case 5:  W$ = "Thursday "
        Case 6:  W$ = "Friday "
        Case 7:  W$ = "Saturday "
    End Select
    Text1.Text = W$ & ", " & M$ &  Str$(CDay%) + ", " + Str$(CYear%)
End Sub
```

Description

The Weekday, Month, Day, and Year functions each take a Visual Basic date variant and return the appropriate numeric value for that element of the date.

The Weekday function returns an integer between 1 (Sunday) and 7 (Saturday). The Month function returns the month as an integer between 1 and 12. January is represented by 1 and December by 12. With the Day function, an integer is returned between 1 and 31 inclusive. Since not every month has 31 days in it, the month of a date variant can reduce the range of possible days. The Year function returns an integer between 100 and 9999 that stands for the year of the date. If the date variant is negative, then it represents a year prior to 1900.

In the example syntax, the date variant produced by the Now function works with each of these functions to find the values that represent the present date stored in the computer. A select case statement determines the month and weekday names using the WeekDay and Year functions. All of this resulting information combines to display the weekday and date in the Text1 textbox.

Example

The Time project at the end of this chapter uses these functions in the cmndCalculate_Click event to help determine the difference between the current system date and a date the user types in the textThen text box. The Year, Month, and Day functions are all used to determine the difference between the two dates. The Weekday function provides the numeric argument for a Choose function that displays the day of the week for the date the user typed in.

THE TIME PROJECT

Project Overview

The Time project outlined in the following pages demonstrates the concept of time in Visual Basic. This example demonstrates the property, event, functions, and statements that directly affect time. By following the examples of the different elements of this project, you will learn how these elements work in Visual Basic.

The following pages discuss the assembly and operation of the Time project. The first section deals with the assembly of the Time form. Next, there is a listing and explanation of the contents of the subroutines of this project. Finally, a guide to the operation of the project discusses the operation of the code. Read this information carefully and use the pictures of the form to check your results.

Assembling the Project

1. Make a new form (the Time form) with the objects and properties listed in Table 22-22.

Object	Property	Setting
Form	BackColor	&H00C0C0C0—Light Gray
	BorderStyle	3—Fixed Double
	Caption	Time Project
Command	Caption	&Calculate
	Default	True
	Name	cmndCalculate
Command	Caption	E&xit
	Name	cmndExit
Command	Caption	&Set System
	Name	cmndSet
Label	BackStyle	0—Transparent

Object	Property	Setting
	Caption	"Now (String)"
Label	BackStyle	0—Transparent
	Caption	"Now (Serial)"
Label	BackStyle	0—Transparent
	Name	lablMrMouse
Label	BackStyle	0—Transparent
	Name	lablNow
Label	BackStyle	0—Transparent
	Name	lablSerial
Label	BackStyle	0—Transparent
	Name	lablDifference
Label	BackColor	&H00000000—Black
	BackStyle	1—Opaque
	FontSize	18
	ForeColor	&H000000FF—Red
	Name	lablStopWatch
Picture	Name	pictTheWindsOfTime
Text	Name	textThen
Timer	Interval	250
	Name	timeClock

(continued on next page)

(continued from previous page)

Object	Property	Setting
Timer	Interval	2500
	Name	timeMouse

Table 22-22 Elements of the Time project form

2. Size and position the elements, as shown in Figure 22-8.

3. Enter the following code in the cmndCalculate_Click event. This calculates the difference between the current system date and time and the value entered by the user in the text box. It first converts the string to a date variant, then calculates the differences. Once the differences have been calculated, it displays the results in the label directly below the text box.

```
Sub cmndCalculate_Click ()
    On Error GoTo BadDate                          'set the trap
    thenDate = CVDate(textThen.Text)               'convert date the user typed in
    On Error GoTo 0                                'success!
    yr = Str$(Year(thenDate) - Year(Now))          'difference in years
    mt = Str$(Month(thenDate) - Month(Now))        'difference in months
    dy = Str$(Day(thenDate) - Day(Now))            'difference in days
    hr = Str$(Hour(thenDate) - Hour(Now))          'difference in hours
    mn = Str$(Minute(thenDate) - Minute(Now))      'difference in minutes
    sc = Str$(Second(thenDate) - Second(Now))      'difference in seconds
    wd = Weekday(thenDate)                         'get new day of week, choose right string
    dow = Choose(wd, "Sunday", "Monday", "Tuesday", "Wednesday", "Thursday", "Friday",
"Saturday")

    msg = yr & " years, " & mt & " months, " & dy & " days; " & Chr$(10) & " "
    msg = msg & hr & " hours, " & mn & " minutes, " & sc & " seconds " & Chr$(10)
    msg = msg & "The day of the week you gave is a " & dow
    lablDifference.Caption = msg
Exit Sub

BadDate:
    Beep
    textThen.SetFocus
Exit Sub

End Sub
```

4. Enter the following code in the cmndExit_Click routine. This ends the program.

```
Sub cmndExit_Click ()
    End                 'Ends the program
End Sub
```

5. Enter the following code in the cmndSet_Click event. This either sets the system clock to the new date and time displayed in the text box, or resets the system time back to the original settings. The two static variables oldTime and newTime will

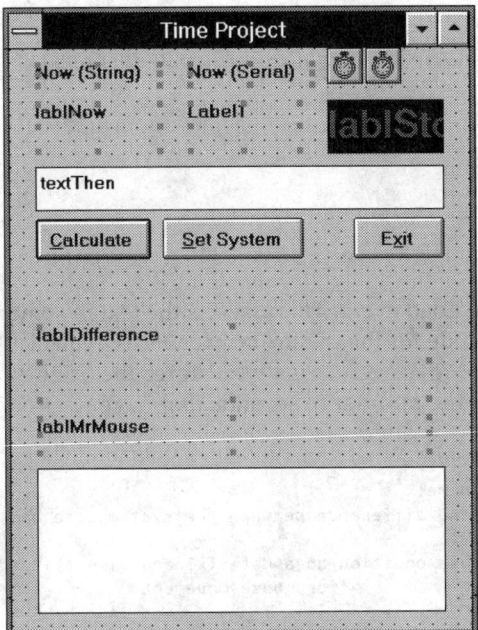

Figure 22-8 The Time project during design

remember the exact time before and after setting the system clock, so we can calculate the difference when resetting. Note although it might appear more elegant
to replace the two sets of Date and Time statements from inside the Select Case
block to one set right after it (after all, we're setting the same variable in both
cases!), that would cause a problem if the user entered an unacceptable date. For
example, if the user enters a legal date for the CVDate function that is before
1980, the Date statement will generate an error. The routine will correctly handle
this error as it is written now. The routine resets the system clock by taking the
elapsed time between the current time and the time it originally finished setting
the system clock, and adding on the original time before it set anything.

```
Sub cmndSet_Click ()
    Static oldTime As Double, newTime As Double    'these allow us to reset the time
    Select Case cmndSet.Caption                     'are we setting or resetting?
        Case "&Set System"                          'set the system clock
            oldTime = Now                           'mark the start of the new time
            On Error GoTo BadSetTime                'set trap
            setTime = CVDate(textThen.Text)         'new date and time
            Date = setTime                          'set the date
            Time = setTime                          'set the time
            On Error GoTo 0                         'successful!
            cmndSet.Caption = "&Reset System"       'now indicate need to reset
        Case "&Reset System"                        'reset time back to where we were
            setTime = oldTime + Now - newTime       'difference between old and new
            Date = setTime                          'set date
            Time = setTime                          'set time
```

(continued on next page)

(continued from previous page)

```
                cmndSet.Caption = "&Set System"        'reset the caption
        End Select
        newTime = Now                                  'the new time after being set
Exit Sub

BadSetTime:
        Beep
        textThen.SetFocus
Exit Sub

End Sub
```

6. Enter the following code in the Form_Load event. This just sets the text in some of the controls. It also sets the ScaleMode for the picture box for ease of calculation in the pictWindsOfTime_MouseMove event. Finally, it stores the original Timer value so that we can calculate the number of seconds that have elapsed since the program began.

```
Sub Form_Load ()
        textThen.Text = "Type a date and time in me!"
        lablDifference.Caption = "I'll display the difference between the system date and the ⇐
date and time you type above."
        lablMrMouse.Caption = "I display the mouse position as a date (x) and time (y)"
        pictTheWindsOfTime.Scale (0, 0)-(1, 1)         'for mouse movement
        pictTheWindsOfTime.Print
        pictTheWindsOfTime.Print "   Click Me!"
        timeClock.Tag = Str$(Timer)                    'remember start time for stopwatch
End Sub
```

7. Enter the following code in the Form_Unload event. This checks to see if the system clock needs to be set back to the original settings, in case the user forgets to do that manually. If so, it resets the clock by calling the cmndSet_Click event procedure before allowing the form to unload.

```
Sub Form_Unload (Cancel As Integer)
        If cmndSet.Caption = "&Reset System" Then      'if we still need to reset the time,
                cmndSet_Click                          'do it before unloading
        End If
End Sub
```

8. Enter the following code in the pictTheWindsOfTime_Click event. This stops mouse movement from wildly updating the label's display for a few seconds. The pictTheWindsOfTime_MouseMove event checks to see if the timer is enabled; if it is, it doesn't update the display.

```
Sub pictTheWindsOfTime_Click ()
        timeMouse.Enabled = True    'stop updating lablMrMouse for a couple of seconds
End Sub
```

9. Enter the following code in the pictTheWindsOfTime_MouseMove event. Every time the user moves the mouse over the picture box, this routine updates the label directly above with a date and time related to the mouse's current position. Moving the mouse horizontally from left to right will gradually increase the date;

866

moving it vertically from top to bottom will gradually increase the time. Note that we first check to see if timeMouse is enabled. If it is, we don't update the display.

```
Sub pictTheWindsOfTime_MouseMove (Button As Integer, Shift As Integer, x As Single, y As Single)
    If timeMouse.Enabled = False Then      'if user hasn't clicked, update lablMrMouse
        yr = 1994                          'keep it to 1994
        mt = Int(x * 12)                   'horizontal mouse position represents the date
        dy = Int(x * 365)
        hr = Int(y * 24)                   'vertical mouse position represents the time
        mn = Int(y * 60 * 24) Mod 60
        sc = Int(y * 60 * 24 * 24) Mod 60
        mouseTime = DateSerial(yr, mt, dy) + TimeSerial(hr, mn, sc)  'put them together
        lablMrMouse.Caption = Format$(mouseTime, "dddd, mmmm d, yyyy   h:mm:ss am/pm")
    End If
End Sub
```

10. Enter the following code in the textThen_GotFocus event. This selects all the text in the text box.

```
Sub textThen_GotFocus ()
    textThen.SelStart = 0                  'select all the text
    textThen.SelLength = Len(textThen.Text)
End Sub
```

11. Enter the following code in the timeMouse_Timer event. This triggers after the timer has counted down the two and a half seconds since it was first enabled, and turns itself off. The pictTheWindsOfTime_MouseMove event checks to see if this timer is enabled before updating the date and time display. If it is enabled, it doesn't update it to give the user a chance to see the display.

```
Sub timeMouse_Timer ()
    timeMouse.Enabled = False       'start updating lablMrMouse again
End Sub
```

12. Enter the following code in the timeClock_Timer event. This triggers several times a second to update the real-time displays of the current date and time and the stopwatch.

```
Sub timeClock_Timer ()
    lablNow.Caption = Date$ & "   " & Time$          'generic functions for right now
    dt = DateValue(Now)                              'extract date serial number
    tm = TimeValue(Now)                              'extract time serial number
    lablSerial = Format$(dt, "00,0000") & Format$(tm, "   .0000000000") 'format as serial
                                                     'numbers, not as date variants!
    startTime = timeClock.Tag                        'this is when program started
    elapsed = Timer - startTime                      'how much time has gone by?
    elapsed = (elapsed \ 60) * 100 + elapsed Mod 60  'time is measured in base 60
    lablStopWatch.Caption = Format$(elapsed, "00:00") 'and update the stopwatch
End Sub
```

How It Works

The Time project does several distinct things. First, it displays the current time in two different formats. The lablNow label displays the current date and time as returned by the Date$ and Time$ functions, and the lablSerial label shows you what this looks like as a serial number. The stopwatch, next to these labels, displays a count of the amount of time the program has been running.

Next, you can type in any date and time you want in the text box. When you press the (ENTER) key, or click on the Calculate button, the difference between the current system date and time and the date and time you entered displays in the label beneath the command buttons.

You can also click on the Set System button to set the system clock to whatever date and time you typed in the text box. Note that you can only set the system clock from 1980 to 2099; even though a far wider range of dates are acceptable to the calculate function, you can't set your system clock to that wide of a range. After you set the clock to some arbitrary time, press the button again (now relabeled as Reset System) to reset the time back to normal. The program will automatically reset the time for you if you forget before exiting.

Finally, you can move the mouse around the picture box to update the label's display of date and time. Moving the mouse horizontally updates the date, and moving it vertically updates the time. Clicking on the picture box starts up a timer that pauses the updates for a few seconds. Although this might seem a somewhat ridiculous use of the mouse at first glance, consider how natural this would be in a program like a personal information manager. You could display a nicely rendered bitmap of a calendar or clock, and derive a date or time setting from the position of the mouse when the user clicks on the bitmap.

Figure 22-9 shows what the project looks like when running.

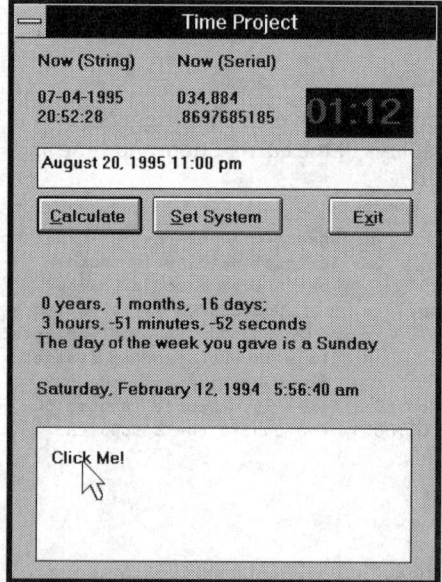

Figure 22-9 The Time 8project in action

23

USING THE CLIPBOARD

A ll Windows programs can access an area of the environment called the Clipboard. The Clipboard is a temporary storage area for text and graphics. Your program can use it to temporarily hold data for use elsewhere in the program, or to share this data with other windows programs.

Windows provides a program called Clipboard that allows the user to view the Clipboard area. This program only lets you view the data in the Clipboard area; it has nothing to do with the process of using the Clipboard from your application. Even though the Clipboard program is not active all the time, the Clipboard area is always accessible as long as Windows is running.

The Clipboard is the simplest way to share data between programs. It lets you exchange text and picture data on a purely manual basis, using the familiar cut-and-paste routines. The next higher level of data exchange uses DDE. This lets you automate the process of exchanging information, even to the point of having the link update in real time as the data changes in the source program. The highest level of information exchange uses OLE. This lets you embed the actual object in its native form within your application, and lets you use the other application's features and functions within your Visual Basic program. For more information on these advanced methods of information exchange, see Chapter 25, Dynamic Data Exchange (DDE), and Chapter 26, Object Linking and Embedding (OLE).

USES OF THE CLIPBOARD

The Clipboard can hold three types of items. First, it can hold text. Text is any combination of letters, numbers, or characters that can be represented by ASCII

869

codes. Second, it can hold graphics. Windows lets the user cut and paste pictures as well as text. However, unlike the case with cutting, copying, and pasting text, each individual program must define how graphics are to be handled. Finally, the Clipboard can hold DDE messages being sent from one program to another, and link information for an OLE object.

The Clipboard is a temporary storage location, and may hold only one item at a time of each of these data types. When a program copies an item to the Clipboard, it replaces any item of the same type that previously resided there. Anything on the Clipboard disappears when you exit Windows, although you can use the Clipboard program to save the Clipboard's contents to a file.

The Windows environment automatically gives the user a way to select text and send it to the Clipboard, and the Visual Basic text box inherits these automatic methods. To select text, hold down the (SHIFT) key and press one of the arrow keys. Alternately, you can click and hold the left mouse button and drag it over the text to be selected. Selected text is highlighted. Once text is selected, press the (CTRL)-(INSERT) or (CTRL)-(C) key combination to copy the text to the Clipboard. Press (SHIFT)-(DEL) or (CTRL)-(X) to send the text to the Clipboard and delete it from the screen. Data that is held in the Clipboard area can be retrieved by pressing the (SHIFT)-(INSERT) or (CTRL)-(V) key combination. Most Windows programs also give menu equivalents to these combinations, usually under the Edit menu.

All of these key combinations and their functions are handled by the Windows environment, so you don't need to program these routines into your Visual Basic application yourself. However, you may want to provide the user with alternative methods for cutting, copying, and pasting data to and from the Clipboard. Visual Basic gives you the tools you will need to clear the Clipboard, copy data or text to it, determine the type of data currently stored on it, or retrieve text or data from it.

CLIPBOARD SUMMARY

The Clear method is the simplest of the Clipboard methods. As you may guess by its name, it clears any data that currently resides on the clipboard. The GetData and GetText methods (used for graphic information and for text, respectively) are used to retrieve information from the Clipboard. These methods must specify the particular type of information that they are requesting. Before either method executes, you can use the GetFormat method to determine whether the desired type of information is currently held on the Clipboard. There are also two methods, SetData (for graphics) and Set Text (for text), which can be used to send information to the Clipboard.

Table 23-1 lists the methods that affect the Clipboard object.

Use or Set This...		To Do This...
Clear	Method	Clear the contents of the Clipboard area
GetData	Method	Retrieve graphic data from the Clipboard area
GetFormat	Method	Return True if the specified data type is stored in the Clipboard area
GetText	Method	Retrieve text from the Clipboard area
SetData	Method	Send graphic data to the Clipboard area
SetText	Method	Send text to the Clipboard area

Table 23-1 Methods that affect the Clipboard object

CONSTANT.TXT Values

Many of the properties, events, and methods of this chapter use numeric values as arguments. Using constants rather than the literal value makes your code self-documenting, more readable, and easier to debug.

Microsoft provides a file, CONSTANT.TXT, that has many constant declarations defined for you. For smaller applications it's probably easiest just to type the declarations in yourself. For larger applications you'll find it much easier to read the text file into a new module.

To do this, create a new module by pulling down the File menu and choosing the New Module menu command. Then pull down the File menu again, and choose Load Text. This opens up a dialog box listing all text files in the current directory. CONSTANT.TXT should be in your main Visual Basic directory (default installation would place this in C:\VB). Simply choose CONSTANT.TXT to enter the entire file into your module. These constants will then be available throughout your application.

Table 23-2 lists the value of the constant, the CONSTANT.TXT constant name, and a brief description of what the constant means.

Constant Name	Value of Constant	Meaning of Constant
CF_LINK	&HBF00	Clipboard holds a DDE link
CF_TEXT	1	Clipboard holds text

(continued on next page)

(continued from previous page)

Constant Name	Value of Constant	Meaning of Constant
CF_BITMAP	2	Clipboard holds a bitmap graphic
CF_METAFILE	3	Clipboard holds a Windows metafile graphic
CF_DIB	8	Clipboard holds a device independent bitmap graphic
CF_PALETTE	9	Clipboard holds a color palette

Table 23-2 Constant declarations in the CONSTANT.TXT file for the Clipboard object

CLEAR METHOD

Objects Affected

Check	▶ Clipboard	▶ Combo	Command	CommonDlg
Data	Debug	Dir	Drive	File
Form	Frame	Grid	Image	Label
Line	▶ List	MDI Form	Menu	OLE
Option	Picture	Printer	Screen	Scroll
Shape	Text	Timer		

Purpose

The Clear method clears the contents of the Clipboard. The Clear method used on list and combo boxes is similar, but with different implications. For more on the Clear method used with list and combo boxes, see Chapter 18, Lists, Combos, and Grids.

General Syntax

```
Clipboard.Clear
```

Example Syntax

```
Sub Command1_Click ()
    Clipboard.Clear
End Sub
```

Description

The Clear method, which has no arguments, clears any and all text and graphics that may be currently stored in the Clipboard area. After this is done, nothing can be retrieved from the Clipboard until some text or graphic information is sent to it.

The example syntax clears the Clipboard. Anything that had been stored in the Clipboard is no longer retrievable.

Example

In the Clipboard project at the end of this chapter, the command button cmndClearClipboard invokes this method to clear the Clipboard.

GETDATA METHOD

Objects Affected

Check	▸ Clipboard	Combo	Command	CommonDlg
Data	Debug	Dir	Drive	File
Form	Frame	Grid	Image	Label
Line	List	MDI Form	Menu	OLE
Option	Picture	Printer	Screen	Scroll
Shape	Text	Timer		

Purpose

Retrieves graphic information (pictures) from the Clipboard area. Table 23-3 summarizes this argument of the GetData method. Table 23-4 details possible values and their meanings.

General Syntax

```
Clipboard.GetData([format%])
```

Argument	Description
format%	An integer expression indicating the desired data format

Table 23-3 Argument of the GetData method

format%	CONSTANT.TXT	Meaning
0 or not specified		(default) Windows attempts to automatically use the correct format
2	CF_BITMAP	Requesting a bitmap graphic
3	CF_METAFILE	Requesting a metafile graphic
8	CF_DIB	Requesting a device independent bitmap graphic
9	CF_PALETTE	Requesting a color palette

Table 23-4 Data formats for the GetData method

Example Syntax

```
Sub Command1_Click ()
    Picture1.Picture = Clipboard.GetData(CF_BITMAP)     'Gets bitmap from the clipboard
End Sub
```

Description

The GetData method copies the specified type of graphic data from the Clipboard into the specified object. The type of data requested is specified by the format% parameter. This parameter is an integer with the value of 2, 3, or 8. The CONSTANT.TXT file holds the values used in the format% argument; see the chapter summary at the beginning of the chapter for details on how to use CONSTANT.TXT.

If the format is not specified, it will default to 0, and Windows will attempt to return the correct format.

The example syntax retrieves a bitmap graphic from the Clipboard and assigns it to the Picture property of Picture1, in essence pasting it into the picture box.

Example

In the Clipboard project at the end of this chapter, the GetData method is used in the menuEdit_Click event. This event copies any bitmap information that may be in the clipboard to the Picture1 picture control.

874

Comments

If no data of the requested type is being stored on the Clipboard, nothing is returned.

GETFORMAT METHOD

Objects Affected

Check	▶ Clipboard	Combo	Command	CommonDlg
Data	Debug	Dir	Drive	File
Form	Frame	Grid	Image	Label
Line	List	MDI Form	Menu	OLE
Option	Picture	Printer	Screen	Scroll
Shape	Text	Timer		

Purpose

The GetFormat method returns an integer value (True or False) indicating whether the requested data type is stored in the Clipboard. Tables 23-5 and 23-6 summarize the arguments of the GetFormat method.

General Syntax

```
Clipboard.GetFormat(format%)
```

Argument	Description
format%	An integer expression indicating the desired data format

Table 23-5 Argument of the GetFormat method

format%	CONSTANT.TXT	Meaning
&HBF00	CF_LINK	Returns True (-1) if a DDE link is stored on the Clipboard
1	CF_TEXT	Returns True (-1) if text is stored on the Clipboard

(continued on next page)

(continued from previous page)

format%	CONSTANT.TXT	Meaning
2	CF_BITMAP	Returns True (-1) if a bitmap graphic is stored on the Clipboard
3	CF_METAFILE	Returns True (-1) if a metafile graphic is stored on the Clipboard
8	CF_DIB	Returns True (-1) if a device independent bitmap graphic is stored on the Clipboard
9	CF_PALETTE	Returns True (-1) if a color palette is stored on the Clipboard

Table 23-6 Data formats for the GetFormat method

Example Syntax

```
Sub Command1_Click ()
    TextStored = GetFormat(CF_TEXT)      'Returns True if text is stored on Clipboard
End Sub
```

Description

The GetFormat method tests the contents of the Clipboard and returns True (-1) if the requested data type is stored on it or False (0) if not. The type of data requested is specified by the format% parameter. This parameter is an integer, and must be one of the values specified in Table 23-6. The CONSTANT.TXT file holds the values used in the format% argument; see the chapter summary at the beginning of the chapter for details on how to use CONSTANT.TXT.

The example syntax determines whether any text is currently residing in the Clipboard. The answer, which will be True (-1) or False (0), is stored in the variable TextStored.

Example

The GetFormat method is used in the menuEditBar_Click and menuEdit_Click events of the Clipboard project at the end of this chapter. The value returned by the GetFormat method is used to determine whether to copy the data from the Clipboard, or to enable the correct menu commands.

876

GETTEXT METHOD

Objects Affected

Check	▶ Clipboard	Combo	Command	CommonDlg
Data	Debug	Dir	Drive	File
Form	Frame	Grid	Image	Label
Line	List	MDI Form	Menu	OLE
Option	Picture	Printer	Screen	Scroll
Shape	Text	Timer		

Purpose

The GetText method retrieves text information from the Clipboard. Tables 23-7 and 23-8 summarize the arguments of the GetText method.

General Syntax

```
Clipboard.GetText([format%])
```

Argument	Description
format%	An integer expression indicating the desired data format

Table 23-7 Argument of the GetText method

format%	CONSTANT.TXT	Meaning
&HBF00	CF_LINK	Requesting a DDE link
1	CF_TEXT	Requesting text information

Table 23-8 Data formats for the GetText method

Example Syntax

```
Sub Command1_Click ()
    Text1.Text = Clipboard.GetText(CF_TEXT) 'Gets text from the Clipboard
End Sub
```

Description

The GetText method copies the specified type of text from the Clipboard into the specified object. The type of data requested is specified by the format% parameter. This parameter is an integer with a value of 1 or &HBF00. Table 23-8 summarizes the data formats for the GetText method. The CONSTANT.TXT file holds the values used in the format% argument; see the chapter summary at the beginning of the chapter for details on how to use CONSTANT.TXT.

The format value CF_LINK (&HBF00) can be used to set up a Dynamic Data Exchange (DDE) link. DDE is discussed in Chapter 25, Dynamic Data Exchange (DDE). If the format is not specified, it will default to 1 (CF_TEXT).

The example syntax copies any text stored on the Clipboard to the text box Text1. Assigning the text returned by the GetText method to the Text property of the text box causes the text to be displayed in the text area of the box.

Example

In the Clipboard project at the end of this chapter, the GetText method is used in the menuEdit_Click event. This event copies any text information that may be in the Clipboard to the Text1 text box control.

Comments

If the requested data type is not present on the Clipboard, a null string is returned.

SETDATA METHOD

Objects Affected

Check	▶ Clipboard	Combo	Command	CommonDlg
Data	Debug	Dir	Drive	File
Form	Frame	Grid	Image	Label
Line	List	MDI Form	Menu	OLE
Option	Picture	Printer	Screen	Scroll
Shape	Text	Timer		

Purpose

The SetData method places graphic information in the clipboard object. Table 23-9 summarizes the arguments of the SetData method, and Table 23-10 gives the meanings of the format% values.

General Syntax

```
Clipboard.SetData graphic%[, format%]
```

Argument	Description
graphic%	An integer number that is the handle of the graphic image (Picture or Image properties)
format%	An integer expression indicating the data format of the graphic image

Table 23-9 Arguments of the SetData method

format%	CONSTANT.TXT	Meaning
0, not specified		Windows will automatically determine the correct format
2	CF_BITMAP	Sending a bitmap graphic
3	CF_METAFILE	Sending a metafile graphic
8	CF_DIB	Sending a device independent bitmap graphic
9	CF_PALETTE	Sending a color palette

Table 23-10 Data formats for the SetData method

Example Syntax

```
Sub Command1_Click()
    AppActivate "CorelDRAW - UNTITLED.CDR"
    Clipboard.SetData Picture1.Picture, CF_BITMAP     'Copies a bitmap to the 1Clipboard
    SendKeys "%ep", True                              'Pastes the bitmap into Corel
    Clipboar1d.SetData Pictur1e2.Picture, CF_METAFILE 'Copies a metafile to the Clipboard
    SendKeys "%ep", True                              'Pastes the metafile into Corel
    Clipboard.SetData Picture3.Picture, CF_DIB        'Copies a device independent bitmap
    SendKeys "%ep", True                              'Pastes the dib into Corel
    Clipboard.SetData Picture4.Picture, CF_PALETTE    'Copies a color palette
    SendKeys "%ep", True                              'Pastes the palette into Corel
End Sub
```

Description

The SetData method is the complement to the GetData method. It copies the specified graphic to the Clipboard in the specified format. You would normally use the Picture or Image properties of the Picture or Image control. The type of data being sent to the Clipboard is specified by the format% parameter. This parameter is an integer with the value of 2, 3, 8, or 9. Table 23-10 details its possible values and their meanings. The CONSTANT.TXT file holds the values used in the format% argument; see the chapter summary at the beginning of the chapter for details on how to use CONSTANT.TXT.

If the format is not specified, it will default to 0, and Windows will attempt to determine the proper format. If a bitmap is placed on the Clipboard, any associated palette is automatically placed along with the bitmap.

The example syntax gives statements showing how the four kinds of graphics listed in Table 23-10 can be copied from a picture box to the Clipboard.

Example

In the Clipboard project at the end of this chapter, this method is used in the menuEdit_Click event. When this event executes, the bitmap in the picture control Picture1 is copied to the Clipboard.

SETTEXT METHOD

Objects Affected

Check	▶ Clipboard	Combo	Command	CommonDlg
Data	Debug	Dir	Drive	File
Form	Frame	Grid	Image	Label
Line	List	MDI Form	Menu	OLE
Option	Picture	Printer	Screen	Scroll
Shape	Text	Timer		

Purpose

The SetText method places text information in the Clipboard object. Tables 23-11 and 23-12 summarize the arguments of the SetText method.

General Syntax

```
Clipboard.SetText Text$[, format%]
```

880

Argument	Description
Text$	A string expression containing the text to be sent to the Clipboard
format%	An integer expression indicating the data format of the text

Table 23-11 Arguments of the SetText method

format%	CONSTANT.TXT	Meaning
&HBF00	CF_LINK	Sending a DDE link
1	CF_TEXT	Sending text information

Table 23-12 Data formats for the SetText method

Example Syntax

```
Sub menuEditCopy_Click ()
     Clipboard.SetText Text1.Text      'Copies the text from the text box to the Clipboard
End Sub
```

Description

The SetText method is the compliment of the GetText method. It copies the specified text information to the Clipboard in the specified format. The type of data being sent to the clipboard is specified by the format% parameter. This parameter is an integer with the value of 1 or &HBF00. Table 23-12 details its possible values and their meanings. The CONSTANT.TXT file holds the values used in the format% argument; see the chapter summary at the beginning of the chapter for details on how to use CONSTANT.TXT.

The format value CF_LINK (&HBF00) can be used to set up a Dynamic Data Exchange (DDE) link. DDE is discussed in Chapter 25, Dynamic Data Exchange (DDE).

If the format is not specified, it will default to 1 (CF_TEXT) as in the example syntax, which copies the text in text box Text1 to the Clipboard.

Example

In the Clipboard project at the end of this chapter, this method is used in the menuEdit_Click event. When this event is executed, the text in the text box control Text1 is copied to the Clipboard.

881

THE CLIPBOARD PROJECT

Project Overview

The project outlined on the following pages demonstrates the use of each of the elements of Visual Basic discussed in this chapter. When you have finished with this project, you should feel comfortable with the concepts behind using the Clear, GetData, GetFormat, GetText, SetData, and SetText methods. This project implements the core functions of a typical Edit menu, and you can easily adapt the techniques detailed here for use in your own programs.

Assembling the Project

1. Create a new form (the clipboard form), and place on it the controls specified in Table 23-13. Use the Menu Design window to create a menu structure for the project, as detailed in Table 23-14.

Object	Property	Setting
Form	BorderStyle	1—Fixed Single
	Caption	Clipboard Project
	Maxbutton	0—False
Picture	AutoRedraw	-1—True
	Name	Picture1
	Picture	(use any .bmp you'd like)
Text	Name	Text1
	MultiLine	-1—True
Command	Name	cmndClearClipboard
	Caption	Clear Clipboard
Command	Name	cmndClearPicture

Object	Property	Setting
	Caption	Clear Picture
Shape	BorderColor	&H00C0C0C0—Light Gray
	BorderWidth	7
	Name	shapPicture
	Visible	0—False
Shape	BorderColor	&H00C0C0C0—Light Gray
	BorderWidth	7
	Name	shapText
	Visible	0—False

Table 23-13 Controls and property settings for the Clipboard project

Name	Caption	Property	Setting
menuFile	&File		
menuExit	E&xit		
menuBarEdit	&Edit		
menuEdit	Cu&t	Index	0
menuEdit	&Copy	Index	1
menuEdit	&Paste	Index	2

Table 23-14 Design parameters for the menu system of the Clipboard project

2. Check the appearance of your form against Figure 23-1. Note that the two Shape controls are exactly the same size and are in the same location as Picture1 and

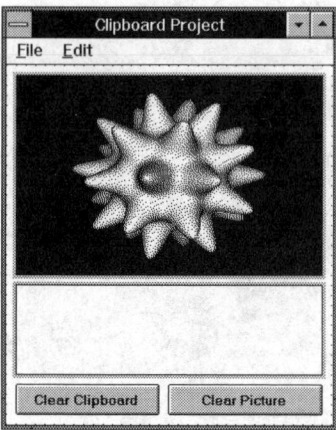

Figure 23-1 The Clipboard project during design

Text1. They are graphical controls, and will automatically place themselves behind the picture and text boxes. (See Chapter 8, Graphics Fundamentals, for a discussion of control layering.) The BorderWidth of 7 makes their borders extend beyond the borders of the controls they're behind.

3. Place the following code in the General Declarations section. You may also choose to load the entire CONSTANT.TXT file in instead. These declarations are for the various Clipboard formats.

```
Const CF_LINK = &HBF00
Const CF_TEXT = 1
Const CF_BITMAP = 2
Const CF_METAFILE = 3
Const CF_DIB = 8
Const CF_PALETTE = 9
```

4. Enter the following code into the cmndClearClipboard_Click event. When the user clicks the cmndClearClipboard button, this event clears the Clipboard of all text and graphic information.

```
Sub cmndClearClipboard_Click ()
    Clipboard.Clear            'clear the clipboard of all data
End Sub
```

5. Enter the following code in the cmndClearPicture_Click event. It queries the user to make sure it's OK to clear the picture, and then does so if the user responds "Yes" to the confirmation MsgBox.

```
Sub cmndClearPicture_Click ()
    If MsgBox("Clear Picture?", 4) = 6 Then    'OK to clear?
        Picture1.Picture = LoadPicture()       'sure, yabetcha, zap the picture
    End If
End Sub
```

884

6. Enter the following code into the Form_Load event. This event activates the Window's Clipboard program, which displays the current contents of the Clipboard area.

```
Sub Form_Load ()
    On Error Resume Next              'if error occurs, it's because clipboard isn't loaded yet
    AppActivate "Clipboard"          'try to activate clipboard
    If Err > 0 Then A% = Shell("CLIPBRD.EXE", 1) 'if activation failed, open clipboard
End Sub
```

7. Enter the following code in the menuBarEdit_Click event. This sets up the Edit menu properly, enabling only those commands that are applicable. It checks to see what control is active, and if it's the text box or picture box, then goes on to check if there is text selected to cut or copy, or if there is information on the Clipboard in the correct format to paste. This provides the correct visual feedback to the user by disabling commands that aren't applicable. It also makes coding in the actual edit commands easier, as no validity checking has to be done—if the command was chosen, then the target control and data must be okay.

```
Sub menuBarEdit_Click ()
    menuEdit(0).Enabled = False                          'Cut
    menuEdit(1).Enabled = False                          'Copy
    menuEdit(2).Enabled = False                          'Paste
    If TypeOf Screen.ActiveControl Is TextBox Then       'on the textbox?
        If Text1.SelText <> "" Then                      'is there text selected?
            menuEdit(0).Enabled = True                   'there is text to cut
            menuEdit(1).Enabled = True                   'there is text to copy
        End If
        If Clipboard.GetFormat(CF_TEXT) Then             'is there text on clipboard?
            menuEdit(2).Enabled = True                   'there is text on clipboard to paste
        End If
    ElseIf TypeOf Screen.ActiveControl Is picturebox Then 'on the picturebox?
        menuEdit(0).Enabled = True                       'OK to cut picture
        menuEdit(1).Enabled = True                       'OK to copy picture
        If Clipboard.GetFormat(CF_BITMAP) Then           'is there a picture on the clipboard?
            menuEdit(2).Enabled = True                   'there is a picture to paste
        End If
    End If
End Sub
```

8. Enter the following code in the menuEdit_Click event. These commands perform the actual edit functions of cutting, copying, and pasting. All three cases first check to see what kind of control they're on. Once that's done, each routine handles things a bit differently. The Cut routine sends the appropriate data (either text or a picture, depending on what control had the focus) to the Clipboard, then clears the data. The Copy routine does the same thing, but without clearing the data. The Paste routine checks to see if the Clipboard has the kind of data needed for the control that has the focus, and if so, copies the clipboard data into the control.

```
Sub menuEdit_Click (Index As Integer)
    Select Case Index
        Case 0 '********************** Cut
            If TypeOf Screen.ActiveControl Is TextBox Then          'on textbox?
```

(continued on next page)

(continued from previous page)

```
                    Clipboard.SetText Text1.SelText              'copy to clipboard
                    Text1.SelText = ""                           'clear selected text
                ElseIf TypeOf Screen.ActiveControl Is picturebox Then  'on picturebox?
                    Clipboard.SetData Picture1.Picture, CF_BITMAP 'copy to clipboard
                    Picture1.Picture = LoadPicture("")           'clear picture
                End If
            Case 1 '********************** Copy
                If TypeOf Screen.ActiveControl Is TextBox Then    'on textbox?
                    Clipboard.SetText Text1.SelText               'copy to clipboard
                ElseIf TypeOf Screen.ActiveControl Is picturebox Then  'on picturebox?
                    Clipboard.SetData Picture1.Picture, CF_BITMAP 'copy to clipboard
                End If
            Case 2 '********************** Paste
                If TypeOf Screen.ActiveControl Is TextBox Then    'on textbox?
                    If Clipboard.GetFormat(CF_TEXT) = True Then   'text to paste?
                        Text1.SelText = Clipboard.GetText(CF_TEXT) 'paste in text
                    End If
                ElseIf TypeOf Screen.ActiveControl Is picturebox Then  'on picturebox?
                    If Clipboard.GetFormat(CF_BITMAP) = True Then 'picture to paste?
                        Picture1.Picture = Clipboard.GetData(CF_BITMAP)   'paste picture
                    End If
                End If
        End Select
End Sub
```

9. Enter the following code in the menuExit routine. This simply ends the
   program.

```
Sub menuExit_Click ()
    End                             'end the program
End Sub
```

10. Enter the following code in the Picture1_DblClick event. This clears the picture
    by calling the cmndClearPicture_Click event discussed above.

```
Sub Picture1_DblClick ()
    cmndClearPicture_Click          'clear the picture
End Sub
```

11. Enter the following code in the appropriate GotFocus and LostFocus routines.
    These make the shapes that lie behind the controls visible or invisible to highlight
    the control that has the focus.

```
Sub Picture1_GotFocus ()
    shapPicture.Visible = True      'highlight the picturebox to show focus
End Sub

Sub Picture1_LostFocus ()
    shapPicture.Visible = False     'unhighlight picturebox to show loss of focus
End Sub

Sub Text1_GotFocus ()
    shapText.Visible = True         'highlight text box to show focus
End Sub

Sub Text1_LostFocus ()
```

```
    shapText.Visible = False        'unhighlight text box to show loss of focus
End Sub
```

How It Works

This program copies graphic and text information to and from the Windows environment Clipboard. When the program begins, the Form_Load event activates the Clipboard viewing program if it is already running. If the Clipboard viewer isn't running, the Form_Load event executes it. (This program works best if the Clipboard viewer and the Clipboard project windows are arranged so that both can be seen at the same time.)

The picture box and text box have Shape controls behind them that are made visible when the appropriate control gets the focus. This makes it obvious where the focus lies.

The command button cmndClearPicture erases the picture in the project window, as does double-clicking on the picture. Clicking the cmndClearClipboard button clears the Clipboard of all text and graphic information.

The Edit menu has the ubiquitous Cut, Copy, and Paste functions. The menuBarEdit_Click routine first sets up the menu to make sure that only the appropriate commands are enabled. For example, if there is no text selected and the text box has the focus, Cut and Copy are disabled. If there is no appropriate information on the Clipboard (either text for the text box, or a bitmap for the picture box), then Paste is disabled.

Once the menu pulls down, the code to add this basic edit functionality is simple. The bulk of the code lies in checking where to cut, copy, or paste; the actual commands to perform these actions only take a couple of lines. The routine first uses the Index property of the control array to see what command was executed. Each command starts by determining what control has the focus. After each routine determines that, it performs the appropriate action, as detailed in Step 8.

Figure 23-2 shows the Clipboard project in action.

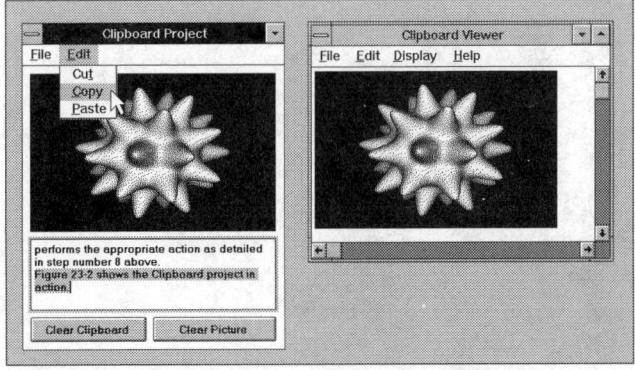

Figure 23-2 The Clipboard project in action

24

PRINTING

Many programs need the capability to create some sort of printed output. Because the Windows environment (rather than individual applications) handles all printer output, Visual Basic provides the predefined Printer object. This object sends printer output commands from your program to the Windows routines, which in turn send the output to the printer.

In other languages (such as QuickBASIC), the printer is usually treated as a sequential output device. Once an item is written to the printer, the print position advances and there can be no going back. With Visual Basic, however, this is not true.

You can think of the Printer object as a form that cannot be viewed until the Visual Basic program tells Windows to print it. This "form" represents one page of printed output. In most cases, until your program instructs Windows to print it, anything can be done to a page of printer output. This allows the program to move the print position anywhere on a page, regardless of where it currently resides. Although printing is one of the most challenging aspects of writing Windows programs, using the Printer object makes outputting graphics and special printing effects to the printer comparatively easy.

COORDINATE SYSTEMS

In order to control the placement of text and graphics on the printer page, the Printer object uses a coordinate system in the same manner as a form. (Coordinates for forms and controls are discussed in Chapter 9, The Coordinate System, which makes good background reading for this chapter.) The only difference between a form's coordinate system and that of the Printer object is that the height and width of the Printer object's page is fixed as long as it represents the same model of printer.

Any point on the printer page can be referred to by specifying that point's position in the format x, y, where x is the horizontal position, and y is the vertical position. The coordinates of the upper-left corner of the printer page can be determined by reading the values of the Printer object's ScaleTop and ScaleLeft properties. Usually, these properties are set to 0 (meaning the upper-left corner is coordinate 0, 0). However, you are allowed to set up your own coordinate system, and in doing so to assign different values to these properties.

The coordinates for the bottom-right corner can be determined by reading the Printer object's ScaleHeight and ScaleWidth properties. These properties return the height and width of the usable page area. The ScaleMode property determines the unit of measurement that is used for the values returned by the ScaleHeight and ScaleWidth properties. It also determines the unit of measurement that is used for the coordinate system of the printer page. By default, the ScaleMode property is set to twips. A twip is equal to 1/1440 of an inch. However, the ScaleMode property can be set to several other types of measurement. Chapter 9, The Coordinate System, covers the ScaleMode settings and measurement systems in detail.

When a method executes on the Printer object, the placement of output on the page is determined by either the coordinates specified in the method, or by the coordinates of the current print position. You can use the CurrentX and CurrentY properties of the Printer object to read or set the current print position on the page. CurrentX represents the horizontal position, while CurrentY represents the vertical position. Again, both of these properties reflect values that represent the unit of measurement specified by the ScaleMode property.

METHODS AND PROPERTIES

Your application works one page at a time when creating a printed document. All the output for a specific page is first set up by using many of the same methods that work on a form. These include the Circle, Line, Print, PSet, TextHeight, and TextWidth methods. (Chapter 10, Drawing Shapes, discusses graphics methods such as Circle and Line. Chapter 11, Displaying Text, discusses methods for scaling text.) Each of these methods works in exactly the same manner as on a form, except for printers that have no color capabilities as is the case with the majority of printers in use today. For noncolor printers, any color parameters are ignored and the output is always black.

Visual Basic keeps track of the current page number via the Page property, which is specific to the Printer object. Each time a new page is generated, the value of this property is incremented. You can use this property to place page numbers on your printed output.

The NewPage method generates a new page. This method ends output to the current page and saves its image in memory. NewPage then increments the value of the Page property and begins a new blank page. When your program has finished generating its printer output, it needs to send the output to the Windows printing routines. The EndDoc method does this. EndDoc sends all the printer pages that have been saved in memory to the Windows printing routines and then clears them from memory. Also, if any methods had been executed on the Printer object since the last NewPage method was executed, EndDoc will automatically generate a new page.

Visual Basic also supplies the PrintForm method. When executed on a form, this method sends a copy of the form to the printer. All graphics, text, and controls (with the exception of the menu control) on the form are printed.

When outputting text to the printer, changing font styles and sizes can be done with the Font... properties. These properties and their uses are covered in detail in Chapter 12, Fonts.

Table 24-1 details the methods and properties that affect the operation of the Printer object.

Use or Set This...		To Do This...
Circle	Method	Generate a circle on the current page
CurrentX	Property	Set or return the current horizontal print position
CurrentY	Property	Set or return the current vertical print position
EndDoc	Method	Send generated output to the Windows printer routines
Line	Method	Generate a line or box on the current page
NewPage	Method	End the current page and start a new blank page
Page	Property	Return the current page number
Print	Method	Generate text output to the current page
PrintForm	Method	Send a copy of a Visual Basic form to the Windows printer routines
PSet	Method	Generate a pixel on the current page
ScaleHeight	Property	Set or return the height of a page in units defined by ScaleMode
ScaleLeft	Property	Set or return the farthest left horizontal position on the printer page
ScaleMode	Property	Set or return the unit of measurement for the coordinate system

(continued on next page)

Use or Set This...		To Do This...
ScaleTop	Property	Set or return the top vertical position on the printer page
ScaleWidth	Property	Set or return the width of a page in units defined by ScaleMode
TextHeight	Method	Calculate the height of text as it would be output to the printer
TextWidth	Method	Calculate the width of text as it would be output to the printer

Table 24-1 Methods and properties that affect the Printer object

The rest of this chapter discusses these methods and properties in detail. At the end of the chapter, the Printer project demonstrates the use of each of these elements of Visual Basic.

Comments

The Printer object is designed to send output to the default printer specified by Windows. Unfortunately, since there can only be one default printer at a time, the only documented way to output to multiple printers simultaneously is by directly accessing the Windows GDI. You can find more information on accessing the GDI directly in any competent book on programming for Windows in C or C++, such as the Waite Group's *Windows API Bible*. The Print common dialog box can return the proper handle to use in your GDI print routines. See Chapter 17, Dialog Boxes, for more on the common dialog box.

As an alternative (if you're willing to jump into undocumented territory), the DOS devices LPT1:, LPT2:, and LPT3: can be opened as a sequential output file, and text can be sent to them by the Print # and Write # statements. This technique will work using Windows 3.1 and Visual Basic 3.0, but there are no guarantees it will continue to perform properly with later versions of these applications. Using this technique could also cause your printer output to conflict with printer output from the Windows print spooler.

CIRCLE METHOD

Objects Affected

Check	Clipboard	Combo	Command	CommonDlg
Data	Debug	Dir	Drive	File

▶ Form   Frame   Grid   Image   Label

   Line   List   MDI Form   Menu   OLE

   Option   ▶ Picture   ▶ Printer   Screen   Scroll

   Shape   Text   Timer

Purpose

The Circle method generates a circle, ellipse, or arc on the current page. The arguments for the Circle method are summarized in Table 24-2.

General Syntax

```
Printer.Circle [Step](XPos!, YPos!), Radius![, Color&][, Start!][, End!][, Aspect!]
```

Argument	Description
Step	'Step' indicates XPos! and YPos! are relative to the current position
XPos!, YPos!	Sets center of the circle on the print page
Radius!	Sets radius of the circle
Start!	Sets arc starting radian
End!	Sets arc ending radian
Color&	Sets print color. Has no effect on black and white printers
Aspect!	Sets shape of graphic (circle or ellipse)

Table 24-2 Arguments of the Circle method

Example Syntax

```
Sub Command1_Click ()
    Printer.Circle (1000, 1000), 800        'Prints a circle with a radius of 800
    Printer.Circle Step (100, 100), 50      'Circle's center is relative to currentX,Y
End Sub
```

Description

You can use the Circle method with the Printer object to print whole circles, portions of circles (arcs), or whole or partial ellipses (flattened circles). The Step,

XPos!, and YPos! parameters specify the center of the circle, ellipse, or arc to print. If the Step keyword is used, XPos! and YPos! indicate a position relative to the current print position (see the entries for CurrentX and CurrentY in this chapter, and in Chapter 9, The Coordinate System). If the Step keyword is omitted, XPos! and YPos! indicate an absolute position on the current print page. In either case the position specified should fall into the range defined by the Printer.ScaleHeight and Printer.ScaleWidth properties.

The Radius! parameter specifies the size of the circle, ellipse, or arc. This value is expressed in the units defined by the Printer.ScaleMode property. By default, this property is set to twips.

When this method is used on a printer without color capabilities, the Color& parameter is ignored. All output occurs in black, regardless of the color specified.

When you want only a partial circle, the Start! and End! parameters define the size and angle of the arc. These parameters are expressed in radians. Visual Basic defines the three o'clock position of a circle as 0 radians. Refer to Chapter 10, Drawing Shapes, for more on the Start! and End! parameters. The Circle method begins drawing at the radian specified by the Start! parameter and stops drawing at the radian defined by the End! parameter.

The Aspect! parameter creates an ellipse. By default, the aspect of the shape is 1, which will create a circle. If Aspect! is greater than 1, or a negative value, a vertical ellipse is created. If Aspect! is between 0 and 1, a horizontal ellipse is drawn.

When finished, the Circle method leaves the CurrentX and CurrentY properties for the Printer object set to the coordinates specified by the Step, XPos!, and YPos! parameters.

If you omit any of the optional parameters, but want to use one or more of the following parameters, use commas to hold the place of the unused parameter. For instance, if you want to specify the aspect, but omit all other optional settings, the statement would read:

```
Printer.Circle (100, 100), 100, , , , 2
```

The first example syntax statement prints a circle at an absolute location (X = 1000, Y = 1000) with a radius of 800. The second example statement centers the circle at a point X = 100, Y = 100, relative to the current print position.

Example

In the Printer project at the end of this chapter, the Circle method is used in the PrintCircle procedure. The menuPrintGraphics_Click event calls this procedure, which occurs when the user clicks the Print Graphics option on the project's File menu. PrintCircle prints the supplied string and then uses the Circle method to draw a circle around it. The placement and radius of the circle are determined using the TextHeight and TextWidth methods and the CurrentX and CurrentY properties.

Comments

This method is covered in greater detail in Chapter 10, Drawing Shapes.

CURRENTX, CURRENTY PROPERTY

Objects Affected

Check	Clipboard	Combo	Command	CommonDlg
Data	Debug	Dir	Drive	File
▶ Form	Frame	Grid	Image	Label
Line	List	MDI Form	Menu	OLE
Option	▶ Picture	▶ Printer	Screen	Scroll
Shape	Text	Timer		

Purpose

The CurrentX and CurrentY properties set or return the current horizontal (x) and vertical (y) print position on the current page. The arguments of the properties are summarized in Table 24-3.

General Syntax

```
Printer.CurrentX [ = hPosition!]
Printer.CurrentY [ = vPosition!]
```

Argument	Description
hPosition!	Sets or returns a horizontal coordinate on the print page
vPosition!	Sets or returns a vertical coordinate on the print page

Table 24-3 Arguments of the CurrentX property

Example Syntax

```
Sub Command1_Click ()
    Printer.CurrentX = Printer.ScaleWidth / 2   'Sets horizontal position to middle of page
    Printer.CurrentY = Printer.ScaleHeight / 2  'Sets vertical position to middle of page
End Sub
```

Description

The CurrentX and CurrentY properties read or set the horizontal (x) and vertical (y) positions on the current print page. They are single-precision values in the range defined by the Printer object's ScaleWidth property. Each of the methods that output to the Printer object can do so in relation to the current print position. The CurrentX property, along with its complementary property, CurrentY, defines that print position.

A Visual Basic program can change the current print position by assigning a value to this property. The value assigned should be between 0 and the value of the Printer.ScaleWidth property. Visual Basic does not check to see if the value being assigned to the CurrentX property is in this range. If it is not, the output will be beyond the boundaries of the printable page, and that method will not appear.

The example statement sets the CurrentX and CurrentY properties to the middle of the page by using the value of the ScaleWidth and ScaleHeight properties. Since the latter represents the width and height of the page, this statement moves the print position to the middle of the printing area.

Example

The CurrentX and CurrentY properties are used throughout the Printer project at the end of this chapter. In most cases, they set the positioning of the next print operation. The graphics printing routines saves the current print position so that it may be restored for the next operation.

Comments

This property is covered in greater detail in Chapter 9, The Coordinate System.

ENDDOC METHOD

Objects Affected

Check	Clipboard	Combo	Command	CommonDlg
Data	Debug	Dir	Drive	File
Form	Frame	Grid	Image	Label
Line	List	MDI Form	Menu	OLE
Option	Picture	▶ Printer	Screen	Scroll
Shape	Text	Timer		

Purpose

The EndDoc method ends the current document and sends output to the Windows printing routines.

General Syntax

```
Printer.EndDoc
```

Example Syntax

```
Sub menuFilePrintNow_Click ()
    Printer.EndDoc
End Sub
```

Description

A *document* in Visual Basic is a set of pages that have been created on the Printer object but not yet sent to the Windows print routines. Remember that, in Visual Basic, printing statements do not result in immediate output to the printer but become part of the current page, which is completed by using the NewPage method. The latter method starts a new page but does not output the previous page.

Use the EndDoc method when you've completed all of the printing for a document. It causes several things to happen. First, if any methods that output to the Printer object have been executed since the last time the NewPage method was used, EndDoc will perform all the same tasks as NewPage. This includes advancing to the next page and setting the CurrentX and CurrentY properties to 0 (top of page). It also sends all output that has been generated by the Printer object to the Windows printing routines. Windows in turn sends this output to the printer (if Print Manager, or another print spooler, is active for this printer, it will intercept the output). EndDoc also sets the value of the Page property back to 1.

The example syntax simply executes the EndDoc method and carries out all applicable procedures discussed above.

Example

The EndDoc method is used in two places in the Printer project at the end of this chapter. First, it is used near the end of the menuPrintGraphics_Click event. When used there, the graphics that have been generated are sent to the Windows printer routines. The EndDoc method in this routine sends the printer a form feed, since a NewPage method hasn't been used yet.

Second, the menuPrintText_Click event uses the EndDoc method soon after a NewPage method executes. It sends all the text that has been generated by this event to the Windows Print Manager.

Comments

Because Visual Basic keeps all output to the Printer object in memory until the EndDoc method is used, it's a good idea to use this method in the middle of large print runs.

LINE METHOD

Objects Affected

Check	Clipboard	Combo	Command	CommonDlg
Data	Debug	Dir	Drive	File
▸ Form	Frame	Grid	Image	Label
Line	List	MDI Form	Menu	OLE
Option	▸ Picture	▸ Printer	Screen	Scroll
Shape	Text	Timer		

Purpose

The Line method generates a line or a box on the current print page. The arguments for the Line method are summarized in Table 24-4.

General Syntax

```
Printer.Line [Step](StartX!, StartY!) - [Step](EndX!, EndY!)[, Color&][, B |, BF]
```

Argument	Description
Step	First 'Step' indicates StartX! and StartY! are relative to the current position
StartX!, StartY!	Coordinates of beginning point of the line
Step	Second 'Step' indicates EndX! and EndY! are relative to StartX! and StartY!
EndX!, EndY!	Coordinates of the end point of the line
Color&	Sets print color; has no effect on black-and-white printers
B	Draws a box with StartX!, StartY! as the upper left corner & EndX!, EndY! as the bottom right

Argument	Description
BF	Draws a box filled with the color specified by Color& (or black if printer has no color ability)

Table 24-4 Arguments of the Line method

Example Syntax

```
Sub Command1_Click ()
    Printer.Line (100, 100)-(200, 200)            'Draws a line with a 45-degree angle
    Printer.Line (100, 100)-(200, 200), , B       'Draws a box whose top left corner is
                                                  'position 100, 100, and bottom right
                                                  'corner is position 200, 200

End Sub
```

Description

The Step, StartX!, and StartY! parameters for the Line method specify the beginning point of the line, or the upper-left corner of the box to be printed. If the first Step keyword is used, StartX! and StartY! indicate a position relative to the current print position (see the entries for CurrentX and CurrentY in this chapter). If the Step keyword is omitted, StartX! and StartY! indicate an absolute position on the current print page. In either case the position specified should fall into the range defined by the Printer.ScaleHeight and Printer.ScaleWidth properties.

The EndX! and EndY! parameters specify the ending point of the line, or the bottom-right corner of the box to be printed. Again, the position specified should fall into the range defined by the Printer.ScaleHeight and Printer.ScaleWidth properties. If the second Step keyword is used before the EndX! and EndY! arguments, then these coordinates are relative to the starting position StartX! and StartY!. If the second Step keyword is omitted, then EndX! and EndY! are absolute coordinates.

When this method is used on a printer without color, the Color& parameter is ignored. All output occurs in black, regardless of the color specified.

The final parameter indicates whether or not a box is drawn and if it is to be filled. If this parameter is omitted, a simple line is generated. If a "B" is specified, an empty box is generated. Finally, if a "BF" is specified, a filled box is generated.

The first statement in the example syntax draws a line between the coordinates 100, 100 and 200, 200. The line moves from upper left to lower right at a 45-degree slope. The second statement uses the same coordinates, but because of the B parameter, the coordinates are considered to be the upper-left and lower-right corners of a box.

Example

The Line method is used in two procedures in the Printer project at the end of this chapter. In the PrintBox procedure, the Line method draws a box around a supplied string. In the PrintLine procedure, the Line method strikes out a line of text. In both cases the placement and dimensions of the box or line are figured using the TextHeight and TextWidth methods and the CurrentX and CurrentY properties.

Comments

This method is covered in greater detail in Chapter 10, Drawing Shapes.

NEWPAGE METHOD

Objects Affected

Check	Clipboard	Combo	Command	CommonDlg
Data	Debug	Dir	Drive	File
Form	Frame	Grid	Image	Label
Line	List	MDI Form	Menu	OLE
Option	Picture	▶ Printer	Screen	Scroll
Shape	Text	Timer		

Purpose

The NewPage method ends output for the current page and sets up the next page for subsequent output.

General Syntax

```
Printer.NewPage
```

Example Syntax

```
Sub CheckForNewAccount (AccountName As String)
    Static oldAccount As String
    If AccountName <> oldAccount Then
        Printer.NewPage
        oldAccount = AccountName
    End If
End Sub
```

Description

The NewPage method, which has no arguments, is the Visual Basic equivalent to issuing a form feed. The current print page is saved and will be output when the program ends or the EndDoc method executes. The work area for the print page is then cleared, and the CurrentX and CurrentY properties are set to 0 to set up a new page. Executing this method also increments the Page property.

   Use this method when all printing on a page is complete. The program can then begin print operations for the next page. If the NewPage method has not been used since the last time data was output to the Printer object, executing the EndDoc method will also cause a new page operation.

   The example syntax executes the NewPage event if the routine receives an AccountName that's different than the one it last processed.

Example

The Printer project at the end of this chapter uses the NewPage method to generate a new page just after a footer has been printed for the menuPrintText_Click event. When this occurs, the current page is saved in memory, the Page property is incremented, and the page work area is cleared. The CurrentX and CurrentY properties are also set to 0.

PAGE PROPERTY

Objects Affected

Check	Clipboard	Combo	Command	CommonDlg
Data	Debug	Dir	Drive	File
Form	Frame	Grid	Image	Label
Line	List	MDI Form	Menu	OLE
Option	Picture	▶ Printer	Screen	Scroll
Shape	Text	Timer		

Purpose

The Page property returns the current page number. You can use this to put the proper page number on each page. Not available at design time, read-only at runtime.

General Syntax

```
Printer.Page
```

Example Syntax

```
Sub PrintLine (lineToPrint As String)
    spaceLeft = Printer.ScaleHeight - Printer.CurrentY
    If spaceLeft < 4 * Printer.TextHeight(lineToPrint) Then
        Printer.Print "Page " & Format$(Printer.Page, "###")
        Printer.NewPage
    End If
    Printer.Print lineToPrint
End Sub
```

Description

Use the Page property to read the current page number that you're printing. You can use the returned value to print the page number on the page.

This property starts at 1 and increments by 1 each time you issue the NewPage method. It also increments if you use the Print method to print text that would not fit on the page; Visual Basic automatically issues a NewPage before printing the text.

Example

The Printer project at the end of this chapter uses the Page property in both the PrintHeader and PrintFooter sub procedures.

PRINT METHOD

Objects Affected

Check	Clipboard	Combo	Command	CommonDlg
Data	Debug	Dir	Drive	File
▶ Form	Frame	Grid	Image	Label
Line	List	MDI Form	Menu	OLE
Option	▶ Picture	▶ Printer	Screen	Scroll
Shape	Text	Timer		

Purpose

The Print method sends text to the Printer object. Table 24-5 summarizes the arguments of the Print method.

General Syntax

```
Printer.Print [{Spc(n) | Tab(m)}][expressionlist][{ ; | , }]
```

Argument	Description
Spc(n)	Precede expressionlist with n spaces from last print position; may be repeated
Tab(m)	Print expressionlist at the mth column; may be repeated
expressionlist	A list of values, string or numeric, that will be printed; may be repeated
;	Set next print position to the next character; may be repeated
,	Set next print position to the next column; may be repeated

Table 24-5 Arguments of the Print method

Example Syntax

```
Sub Command1_Click ()
    Person$ = InputBox$("What is your name?")
    Printer.Print "Hello "; Person$; ", how are you?"
End Sub
```

Description

The Print method prints the text specified by the expressionlist. The expressionlist contains one or more expressions of any data type (Integer, Long, Single, Double, Currency, user defined, String, or Variant). Each expression can be separated by a semicolon or a comma (if neither is used, semicolons are automatically inserted by Visual Basic). Using a semicolon to separate expressions prints each expression as if it were all one concatenated string. Using commas prints the expression that follows a comma at the next print zone. A *print zone* is every 14 columns, where a column is equal to the average width of every character in the current font and font size for the Printer object.

If a comma or semicolon trails the last expression in the list, the CurrentX and CurrentY properties remain at the point following the last character printed. However, if both are omitted from the end of the list, the CurrentX property is set to 0 and CurrentY is set to the next print line. This is the equivalent of doing a carriage return/line feed on a traditional printer.

Each expressionlist may be preceded by the Spc(n) or Tab(m) functions. The Spc(n) function inserts n spaces before the expressionlist, relative to the last print position. The Tab(m) function prints expressionlist m columns from the beginning of the line, where a column is defined as the average width of all the characters in the current font and font size. Thus, Spc(n) is a relative position on the line, and Tab(m) is an absolute position on the line.

If executing a Print method will cause the specified text to be printed below the position defined by Printer.ScaleHeight, a new page is automatically generated. However, if executing a Print method will cause the specified text to be printed beyond the position defined by Printer.ScaleWidth, no new line is generated. The text is merely truncated. Take care not to cause this method to print past position 30,000, as this will cause an "Overflow" to occur. (Note that the exact number that causes an overflow varies depending on the font and font size you're printing with.)

The example syntax sends the literal strings "Hello" and "how are you?" to the print page. (The quote marks themselves are not sent.) Between these items, the contents of the string variable Person$ is also sent. If Person$ had been set to "Bryon," then the resulting output will look something like this:

`Hello Bryon, how are you?`

Notice that any spaces between strings must be included in one or the other of the strings. Semicolons rather than commas are used to separate strings, so that output is not moved to the next print zone.

Example

The Printer project at the end of this chapter uses the Print method quite often. It is most heavily used in the procedures that relate to the menuPrintText_Click event. This event occurs when the user clicks the Print Text option on the File menu of the Printer project. This event reads the file CONSTANT.TXT and uses the Print method to generate a hard copy of the first two pages of the file.

Comments

This method is covered in greater detail in Chapter 11, Displaying Text.

PRINTFORM METHOD

Objects Affected

Check	Clipboard	Combo	Command	CommonDlg
Data	Debug	Dir	Drive	File
Form	Frame	Grid	Image	Label
Line	List	MDI Form	Menu	OLE
Option	Picture	▶ Printer	Screen	Scroll
Shape	Text	Timer		

Purpose

The PrintForm method sends a copy of a Visual Basic form to the Windows printing routines. This can be an easy way to take advantage of Visual Basic's form design capabilities in creating printed forms, and to format printed output so that it is identical to what is shown on the screen. Table 24-6 summarizes the argument of the PrintForm method.

General Syntax

```
[form.]PrintForm
```

Argument	Description
form	Name of the form to be printed

Table 24-6 Argument of the PrintForm method

Example Syntax

```
Sub Command1_Click ()
    AddressForm.PrintForm
End Sub
```

Description

This method allows you to design an output form that can be sent to the printer. The only argument used is the name of the form to be printed. If not explicitly specified, the form with the focus will be printed.

All controls on the form will also be printed, with the exception of the menu controls.

If any graphics have been added to the form, or any picture is on the form, they will only be printed if the AutoReDraw property for that form or picture was set to True (-1) at that time.

Although the form to be printed does have to be loaded into memory when this method executes, it does not need to be visible. This makes it easy to design complicated forms for printing, without having to code complex procedures in your program. You can design an output form in the same manner as a form for the screen. Picture controls can be used for letterhead and other similar features, while labels can be used for any text that will be printed on the form. The Line and Shape graphics controls make it easy to add these elements to your form. When it comes time to print the form, all the program has to do is set the caption property of any labels that represent changed data and execute the PrintForm method. Note that the PrintForm method sends the form directly to the Windows printing routines. It does not use the Printer object or the system of pages and documents used by most other printing techniques.

Although this method makes simple work out of complex form design, it only sends a bitmap of the screen to the printer. A laser printer has a far higher resolution (typically 300 dpi and now even 600 dpi) than a typical screen (typically 72 or 96 dpi). This means that any diagonal or curved lines, and all text, will have visible "jaggies." For the highest quality output, you'll need to use the graphics methods and print directly to the Printer object.

The example syntax sends a copy of AddressForm to the printer.

Example

In the Printer project at the end of this chapter, the menuPrintForm_Click event uses this method. This event activates when the user chooses the Print Form option on the File menu of the Printer project. This event uses the PrintForm method to send a copy of the current form to the printer.

PSET METHOD

Objects Affected

Check	Clipboard	Combo	Command	CommonDlg
Data	Debug	Dir	Drive	File
▶ Form	Frame	Grid	Image	Label
Line	List	MDI Form	Menu	OLE
Option	▶ Picture	▶ Printer	Screen	Scroll
Shape	Text	Timer		

Purpose

The PSet method draws a dot on the current print page. Table 24-7 summarizes the arguments of the PSet method.

General Syntax

```
Printer.PSet [Step](XPos!, YPos!)[, Color&]
```

Argument	Description
Step	Indicates XPos! and YPos! are relative to the current position
XPos!, YPos!	Single-precision expressions indicating the placement of the dot
Color&	Long integer expression indicating print color. Has no effect on black-and-white printers

Table 24-7 Arguments of the PSet method

Example Syntax

```
Sub Shade (Text As String)                'This sub procedure uses the PSet method
    OldX = Form1.CurrentX                 'to shade a line before it is printed
    OldY = Form1.CurrentY                 'Save current coordinates
    NewX = OldX + Form1.TextWidth(Text)
    NewY = OldY + Form1.TextHeight(Text)
    For Y = OldY To NewY Step 50          'For every 50 vertical positions
        For X = OldX To NewX Step 50      'For every 50 horizontal positions
            Form1.PSet (X, Y)             'Print a dot
        Next
    Next
    Form1.CurrentX = OldX
    Form1.CurrentY = OldY
End Sub
```

Description

The PSet method generates a dot on the current print page at the position specified. The Step, XPos!, and YPos! parameters specify where the point is to be generated. If the Step keyword is used, XPos! and YPos! indicate a position relative to the current print position (see the entries for CurrentX and CurrentY in this chapter). If the Step keyword is omitted, XPos! and YPos! indicate an absolute position on the current print page. In either case the position specified should fall into the range defined by the Printer.ScaleHeight and Printer.ScaleWidth properties.

If this method is used on a printer without color capabilities, the Color& parameter is ignored. All output occurs in black, regardless of the color specified.

Example

In the Printer project at the end of this chapter, the PSet method is used in the PrintBox procedure. If PrintBox's Shaded parameter is True, it shades the contents of the box. This shading is done by using the PSet method to generate a dot every 50 positions, horizontally and vertically. This technique is also shown in the example syntax.

Comments

This method is covered in greater detail in Chapter 8, Graphics Fundamentals.

SCALEHEIGHT PROPERTY

Objects Affected

Check	Clipboard	Combo	Command	CommonDlg
Data	Debug	Dir	Drive	File
▶ Form	Frame	Grid	Image	Label
Line	List	▶ MDI Form	Menu	OLE
Option	▶ Picture	▶ Printer	Screen	Scroll
Shape	Text	Timer		

Purpose

The ScaleHeight property sets or returns the height of a printer page in units defined by the ScaleMode property. Table 24-8 summarizes the argument of the ScaleHeight property.

General Syntax

```
Printer.ScaleHeight [ = setting!]
```

Argument	Description
setting!	Sets or returns a programmer-defined coordinate system for the printer page

Table 24-8 Argument of the ScaleHeight property

Example Syntax

```
Sub NewSubject ()
    If (Printer.ScaleHeight - Printer.CurrentY) < 10 Then 'Vertical space on the page
        Printer.NewPage
    End If
End Sub
```

908

Description

The absolute height of a print page can be determined by using the Height property with the Printer object. The print page of most printers has a border in which printing is impossible. The Height property does not take this into account. However, the ScaleHeight property returns the print page's usable height (the height of the area inside the unprintable borders).

The ScaleHeight property is measured in the units defined by the Printer object's ScaleMode property. By default, this property is measured in twips. This, however, can be changed in two ways. First, if the ScaleMode property is changed, ScaleHeight units will reflect the change. Second, you can change the ScaleHeight property explicitly at design time or by the program at runtime. When you explicitly set the ScaleHeight, the ScaleMode property is automatically set to 0 (user-defined scaling). To define your own scale, specify the page height in your own coordinate system using the setting! argument.

The ScaleHeight property is used mainly to help determine the printing position on a page. It can be used in conjunction with the TextHeight method to calculate when an end of a page is going to occur. For instance, in the following code, if the value of SpaceLeft is less than three print lines, a footer is generated:

```
SpaceLeft = Printer.ScaleHeight - Printer.CurrentY      'Vertical space left on page
If SpaceLeft < Printer.TextHeight("Page:") * 3 Then PrintFooter
```

The example syntax uses the same method to determine the amount of vertical space remaining on the page.

Example

In the Printer project at the end of this chapter, the ScaleHeight property is mainly used in the menuPrintText_Click event, where it calculates how close the program is to the bottom of the print page. This determines when to print a footer on the page.

Comments

This property is covered in greater detail in Chapter 9, The Coordinate System.

SCALELEFT PROPERTY

Objects Affected

Check	Clipboard	Combo	Command	CommonDlg
Data	Debug	Dir	Drive	File

(continued on next page)

(continued from previous page)

▶ Form	Frame	Grid	Image	Label
Line	List	MDI Form	Menu	OLE
Option	▶ Picture	▶ Printer	Screen	Scroll
Shape	Text	Timer		

Purpose

The ScaleLeft property sets or returns the leftmost horizontal position on the printer page. This property can be set at design time, and set or read during runtime. Table 24-9 summarizes the argument of the ScaleLeft property.

General Syntax

```
Printer.ScaleLeft [ = setting!]
```

Argument	Description
setting!	Sets or returns a programmer-defined coordinate system for the printer page

Table 24-9 Argument of the ScaleLeft property

Example Syntax

```
Sub NewLine ()
    CurrentX = ScaleLeft          'Set current print position to left edge of page
End Sub
```

Description

The Printer object uses a coordinate system in which any point on a printer page can be specified in the format x, y; where x is the horizontal position, and y is the vertical position. By default, the upper-left corner of the printer page is coordinate 0, 0. However, by using this property along with the ScaleTop property, you can define a custom system in which the coordinates of the upper-left corner have a different value.

Assigning a value to this property does two things. First, the leftmost horizontal position on the printer page will be referred to by the assigned value. Second, if the ScaleMode property has not yet been set to 0 (user defined), setting the ScaleLeft property will also set ScaleMode to 0. The values of the ScaleHeight and ScaleWidth properties still remain the same. See the entries for ScaleHeight, ScaleMode, and ScaleWidth in this chapter, and in Chapter 9, The Coordinate System.

910

The ScaleLeft property can be read to find the coordinate value of the leftmost horizontal position on the printer page. If the value of the ScaleMode property is other than 0 (for example, the coordinate system is not programmer-defined), this property will always return 0.

The example syntax sets the horizontal print position (reflected in the CurrentX property) to the value of the ScaleLeft property. The result is that the print position is moved to the left edge of the page.

Example

The Printer project at the end of this chapter uses the ScaleLeft property in almost every print routine. Each time, it sets CurrentX equal to ScaleLeft, thus moving the print position to the farthest left position on the page.

Comments

This property is covered in greater detail in Chapter 9, The Coordinate System.

SCALEMODE PROPERTY

Objects Affected

Check	Clipboard	Combo	Command	CommonDlg
Data	Debug	Dir	Drive	File
▶ Form	Frame	Grid	Image	Label
Line	List	MDI Form	Menu	OLE
Option	▶ Picture	▶ Printer	Screen	Scroll
Shape	Text	Timer		

Purpose

The ScaleMode property sets the unit of measurement to be used for the Printer object's coordinate system. This property can be both read and set at design time or runtime. Table 24-10 summarizes the setting argument for the ScaleMode property. Table 24-11 shows the possible values for the property.

General Syntax

```
Printer.ScaleMode [ = mode%]
```

Argument	Description
mode%	Sets or returns the coordinate system for the printer page

Table 24-10 Argument of the ScaleMode property

Setting	Unit Used	Description
0	User-defined	User-defined; ScaleHeight and ScaleWidth set by programmer
1	Twip	Equal to 1/1440 inch; 1440 twips per inch; 20 twips per point
2	Point	Equal to 1/72 inch; 72 points per inch
3	Pixel	Smallest dot possible on the printer (different for different printers)
4	Character	Height is 1/6 inch, width is 1/12 inch
5	Inch	Standard inch
6	Millimeter	Metric millimeter
7	Centimeter	Metric centimeter

Table 24-11 Settings for the ScaleMode property

Example Syntax

```
Form_Load ()
    Printer.ScaleMode = 5          'Set the scale mode to inches
End Sub
```

Description

The Printer object's coordinate system specifies the placement of text and graphics methods on the printer page. This placement is specified by supplying the position in the format x, y; where x is the horizontal position and y is the vertical position on the page. The ScaleMode property determines the unit of measurement that the values in x and y represent.

The default for the ScaleMode property is twips, which equate to 1/1440 inch. This is generally adequate; however, Visual Basic allows you to choose from several other units of measurement, as well as define your own system.

The example syntax sets the unit of measurement for the Printer object to inches.

Example

The Printer project at the end of this chapter leaves the Printer's ScaleMode set to the default of twips.

Comments

This property is covered in greater detail in Chapter 9, The Coordinate System.

SCALETOP PROPERTY

Objects Affected

Check	Clipboard	Combo	Command	CommonDlg
Data	Debug	Dir	Drive	File
▶ Form	Frame	Grid	Image	Label
Line	List	MDI Form	Menu	OLE
Option	▶ Picture	▶ Printer	Screen	Scroll
Shape	Text	Timer		

Purpose

The ScaleTop property sets or returns the topmost vertical position on the printer page. This property can be set at design time and set or read during runtime. The setting argument for the ScaleTop property is summarized in Table 24-12.

General Syntax

```
Printer.ScaleTop [ = setting!]
```

Argument	Description
setting!	Sets or returns a programmer-defined coordinate system for the printer page

Table 24-12 Argument of the ScaleTop property

Example Syntax

```
Sub NewCircle ()
    CurrentY = ScaleTop              'Set current print position to top of page
End Sub
```

Description

The Printer object uses a coordinate system in which any point on a printer page can be specified in the format x, y; where x is the horizontal position, and y is the vertical position. By default, the upper-left corner of the printer page is coordinate 0, 0. However, by using this property, along with the ScaleLeft property, you can custom define a system in which the coordinates of the upper-left corner have a different value.

Assigning a value to this property does two things. First, the topmost vertical position on the printer page is set to the assigned value. Second, assigning a value to the ScaleTop property will also set ScaleMode to 0 (programmer-defined coordinate system). The values of the ScaleHeight and ScaleWidth properties remain the same. See the entries for ScaleHeight, ScaleMode, and ScaleWidth in this chapter, and in Chapter 9, The Coordinate System.

The ScaleTop property can also be read by your program to determine the coordinate value of the topmost vertical position on the printer page. If the value of the ScaleMode property is any value other than 0 (that is, the coordinate system is not programmer-defined), this property will always return 0.

The example syntax sets the vertical print position to the value of the ScaleTop property, thus moving the print position to the top of the page.

Example

The Printer project at the end of this chapter uses the ScaleTop property when it checks to see how much room is left on the page in the menuPrintText_Click procedure.

Comments

This property is covered in greater detail in Chapter 9, The Coordinate System.

SCALEWIDTH PROPERTY

Objects Affected

Check	Clipboard	Combo	Command	CommonDlg
Data	Debug	Dir	Drive	File

914

▶ Form	Frame	Grid	Image	Label
Line	List	▶ MDI Form	Menu	OLE
Option	▶ Picture	▶ Printer	Screen	Scroll
Shape	Text	Timer		

Purpose

The ScaleWidth property sets or returns the width of a printer page in units defined by the ScaleMode property. Table 24-13 summarizes the argument of the ScaleWidth property.

General Syntax

```
Printer.ScaleWidth [ = setting!]
```

Argument	Description
setting!	Sets or returns a programmer-defined coordinate system for the printer page

Table 24-13 Argument of the ScaleWidth property

Example Syntax

```
Function SpaceLeft ()
    SpaceLeft = Printer.ScaleWidth - Printer.CurrentX  'Horizontal space left on line
End Function
```

Description

The absolute width of a print page can be determined by using the Width property with the Printer object. The print pages of most printers have a border in which printing is impossible. The Width property does not take this nonprinting border into account. However, the ScaleWidth property returns the print page's usable width (the width of the area inside the unprintable borders).

The ScaleWidth property is measured in the units defined by the Printer object's ScaleMode property. By default, this property is set to twips. This, however, can be changed in two ways. First, if the ScaleMode property is changed, ScaleWidth units will reflect the change. Also, if the ScaleWidth property is set by the program, ScaleMode is automatically set to 0 (user-defined scaling). Finally, you can use the setting argument to set a width value that establishes your own scale for the page measurements.

This property is used mainly to help determine the printing position on a page. It can be used in conjunction with the TextWidth method to calculate when an end of a print line is going to occur. For instance, in the following code, if the value of SpaceLeft is less than the width of the text to be printed, it will advance to the next line.

```
SpaceLeft = Printer.ScaleWidth - Printer.CurrentX   'Horizontal space left on line
If SpaceLeft < Printer.TextWidth(Text$) Then Printer.Print " "
```

The example syntax also uses this technique.

The ScaleWidth and TextWidth properties are also useful for centering or right justifying text on a print page. To right justify text, set the Printer object's CurrentX property to the value of the ScaleWidth minus the TextWidth of the text to be printed. To center text, calculate the same CurrentX value as right justification, and then divide it by 2.

Example

In the Printer project at the end of this chapter, the ScaleWidth property is used in several procedures. Its main task in this program is to provide information so the program can calculate the correct positioning for centering and right justifying text on the page.

Comments

This method is covered in greater detail in Chapter 9, The Coordinate System.

TEXTHEIGHT METHOD

Objects Affected

Check	Clipboard	Combo	Command	CommonDlg
Data	Debug	Dir	Drive	File
▶ Form	Frame	Grid	Image	Label
Line	List	MDI Form	Menu	OLE
Option	▶ Picture	▶ Printer	Screen	Scroll
Shape	Text	Timer		

Purpose

The TextHeight method returns the height of the supplied text as it will be output on the printer. This is helpful for properly positioning and scaling printed output or for adding special effects such as shading and strikeout. The string argument used is summarized in Table 24-14.

916

General Syntax

```
Printer.TextHeight(text$)
```

Argument	Description
text$	A string expression whose text height will be returned

Table 24-14 Argument of the TextHeight method

Example Syntax

```
Sub Shade (Text As String)                    'This sub procedure uses the PSet method
    OldX = Form1.CurrentX                      'to shade a line before it is printed
    OldY = Form1.CurrentY                      'Save current coordinates
    NewX = OldX + Form1.TextWidth(Text)
    NewY = OldY + Form1.TextHeight(Text)       'We need to find out how high to make the shading
    For Y = OldY To NewY Step 50
        For X = OldX To NewX Step 50
            Form1.PSet (X, Y)
        Next X
    Next Y
    Form1.CurrentX = OldX
    Form1.CurrentY = OldY
End Sub
```

Description

The TextHeight method examines the supplied string and returns a value that equals the height of the string as it will be printed in the current font and font size for the Printer object. The number returned is expressed in the format specified by the Printer.ScaleMode property. By default, this property is set to twips.

This method is useful when trying to add special effects to printed text, such as shading and strikeout. It can also be used before a Print method in order to determine whether printing a line of text will cause a new page to be generated. For instance, before using the Print method, the value returned from TextHeight can be added to CurrentY and compared to ScaleHeight. If ScaleHeight is less, the program can anticipate a new page.

The example syntax uses the value returned by the TextHeight method to determine the height of the area to be shaded.

Example

The TextHeight method is used throughout the Printer project at the end of this chapter. In the graphics printing procedures, it helps calculate the coordinates of the graphics that are being printed. In the menuPrintText_Click event, it is used along with the ScaleHeight property to determine when a footer will be printed.

Comments

This method is also covered in Chapter 13, Getting User Input.

TEXTWIDTH METHOD

Objects Affected

Check	Clipboard	Combo	Command	CommonDlg
Data	Debug	Dir	Drive	File
▶ Form	Frame	Grid	Image	Label
Line	List	MDI Form	Menu	OLE
Option	▶ Picture	▶ Printer	Screen	Scroll
Shape	Text	Timer		

Purpose

The TextWidth method returns the width of the supplied text as it will be output on the printer. This is helpful for properly positioning and scaling printed output or for adding special effects such as shading and strikeout. Table 24-15 summarizes the argument of the TextWidth method.

General Syntax

```
Printer.TextWidth(text$)
```

Argument	Description
text$	A string expression whose text width will be returned

Table 24-15 Argument of the TextWidth method

Example Syntax

```
Sub Shade (Text As String)              'This sub procedure uses the PSet method
    OldX = Form1.CurrentX               'to shade a line before it is printed
    OldY = Form1.CurrentY               'Save current coordinates
    NewX = OldX + Form1.TextWidth(Text) 'We need to find out how wide to make the shading
```

```
    NewY = OldY + Form1.TextHeight(Text)
    For Y = OldY To NewY Step 50
        For X = OldX To NewX Step 50
            Form1.PSet (X, Y)
        Next X
    Next Y
    Form1.CurrentX = OldX
    Form1.CurrentY = OldY
End Sub
```

Description

The TextWidth method examines the supplied string arguments and returns a value that equals the width of the string as it will be printed in the current font and font size for the Printer object. The number returned is expressed in the format specified by the Printer.ScaleMode property. By default, this property is set to twips.

This method is useful when trying to add special effects to printed text such as shading and strikeout. It can also be used to determine the correct position for centering or flushing text to the right. For instance, in the example code below, Header$ will be centered on its line while pageNumber$ will be right flushed.

```
CurrentY = Printer.ScaleWidth - Printer.TextWidth(Header$) / 2
Printer.Print Header$
CurrentY = Printer.ScaleWidth - Printer.TextWidth(pageNumber$)
Printer.Print pageNumber$;
```

The example syntax uses the TextWidth method to determine the width of the text area to be shaded.

Example

The TextWidth method is used throughout the Printer project at the end of this chapter. In the graphics printing procedures, it helps calculate the coordinates of the graphics that are being printed. In the menuPrintText_Click event, it is used along with the ScaleWidth property to determine the correct print positioning when the program wishes to center or right justify text.

Comments

This method is also covered in Chapter 13, Getting User Input.

THE PRINTER PROJECT

Project Overview

The following project details the use of the Printer object and its related methods and properties. After you have completed this project, you should have a firm understanding of the concepts behind the Printer object. By following the examples outlined in this project, you will learn how to print Visual Basic forms, output text, and output graphics to the printer.

Assembling the Project

1. Create a new form (the Printer form) and place on it the controls specified in Table 24-16.

Object	Property	Setting
Form	Name	Form1
	Caption	Printer Project
Label	Name	Label1
	Caption	Name:
Label	Name	Label2
	Caption	Address:
Text Box	Name	Text1
Text Box	Name	Text2

Table 24-16 Settings and properties for the Printer project

2. Use the Menu Design window (choose the Menu Design window option from Visual Basic's Window menu) to create a menu with the settings given in Table 24-17.

Name	Caption
menuFile	&File
menuPrintForm	Print &Form
menuPrintGraphics	Print &Graphics

Name	Caption
menuPrintText	Print &Text
menuSeparator	
menuExit	E&it

Table 24-17 Menu settings for the Printer project

3. Check the appearance of your form against Figure 24-1.

4. Enter the following code into the menuPrintGraphics_Click event. This event occurs when the user chooses Print Graphics from the File menu.

```
Sub menuPrintGraphics_Click ()
    Form1.MousePointer = 11                      'hourglass; we're going to be a while
    PrintBox "This text is in a box", False      'print text inside an unshaded box
    PrintBox "This text is in a shaded box", True 'print text inside a shaded box
    PrintLine "This text is crossed out"         'print text with line through the middle
    PrintCircle "This text is in a circle"       'print this text inside a circle
    Printer.EndDoc                               'end printing, send to print routines
    Form1.MousePointer = 0                        'cursor back to normal
    MsgBox "Done Printing Graphics"              'inform the user
End Sub
```

5. Enter the following code into the General Declarations area of the form. This procedure is called from the menuPrintGraphics_Click event. PrintBox prints the supplied string and then uses the Line method to draw a box around it.

   If the Shaded parameter is True, it shades the contents of the box. This shading is done by using the PSet method to generate a dot every 50 positions horizontally and vertically.

   The placement and dimensions of the box are figured using the TextHeight and TextWidth methods and the CurrentX and CurrentY properties.

```
Sub PrintBox (Msg As String, Shaded As Integer)
    leftX = Printer.CurrentX                        'left side of box
    topY = Printer.CurrentY                         'top of box
    rightX = Printer.CurrentX + Printer.TextWidth(Msg) + 200    'a bit wider than the text
    bottomY = Printer.CurrentY + Printer.TextHeight(Msg) + 200  'a bit higher than the text
    Printer.CurrentX = Printer.CurrentX + 100       'indent text in from side of box
    Printer.CurrentY = Printer.CurrentY + 100       'indent text down from top of box
    Printer.Print Msg                               'print the text
    Printer.Line (leftX, topY)-(rightX, bottomY), , B  'draw the box around the text
    If Shaded = True Then                           'supposed to shade?
        For yPos = topY To bottomY Step 50          'go from top to bottom, every 50 dots
            For xPos = leftX To rightX Step 50      'go from left to right, every 50 dots
                Printer.PSet (xPos, yPos)           'and make a dot
            Next
        Next
    End If
```

(continued on next page)

(continued from previous page)

```
        Printer.CurrentX = Printer.ScaleLeft          'go all the way back to the left
        Printer.CurrentY = bottomY + 100               'and go down a bit from where we're at
End Sub
```

6. Enter the following code into the General Declarations area of the form. This procedure is called from the menuPrintGraphics_Click event. PrintLine prints the supplied string and then uses the Line method to strike it out. The placement and length of the strikeout line are figured using the TextHeight and TextWidth methods and the CurrentX and CurrentY properties.

```
Sub PrintLine (Msg As String)
    yPos = (Printer.TextHeight(Msg) / 2) + Printer.CurrentY 'figure out center of text
    xStart = Printer.CurrentX                      'remember where text starts
    xEnd = xStart + Printer.TextWidth(Msg)         'this is where text will end
    Printer.Print Msg                              'print the text
    Printer.Line (xStart, yPos)-(xEnd, yPos)       'and print a line through it
    Printer.CurrentX = Printer.ScaleLeft           'all the way to the left
    Printer.CurrentY = Printer.CurrentY + 100      'and down a bit
End Sub
```

7. Enter the following code into the General Declarations area of the form. This procedure is called from the menuPrintGraphics_Click event. PrintCircle prints the supplied string and then uses the Circle method to draw a circle around it. The placement and radius of the circle are figured using the TextHeight and TextWidth methods and the CurrentX and CurrentY properties.

```
Sub PrintCircle (Msg As String)
    radius = (Printer.TextWidth(Msg) / 2) + 100    'radius a bit bigger than 1/2 the text
    xPos = Printer.CurrentX + radius               'figure out where the center of the
    yPos = Printer.CurrentY + radius               'circle will be
    Printer.CurrentX = Printer.CurrentX + 100      'leave a bit of space horizontally,
    Printer.CurrentY = Printer.CurrentY + radius   'and leave enough room for the circle;
    Printer.Print Msg                              'now print the message
    Printer.Circle (xPos, yPos), radius            'and draw the circle around the message
    Printer.CurrentX = Printer.ScaleLeft           'back to the left side of the page
    Printer.CurrentY = yPos + radius + 100         'and a bit below the bottom of the circle
End Sub
```

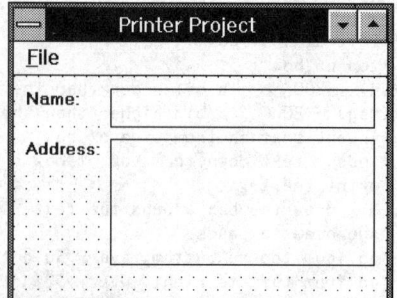

Figure 24-1 The Printer project during design

922

8. Enter the following code in the menuPrintForm_Click event. This event is activated when the user chooses the Print Form option on the File menu of the
Printer project. This event sends a copy of the current form to the printer.

```
Sub menuPrintForm_Click ()
    PrintForm                                    'print the form
End Sub
```

9. Enter the following code into the menuPrintText_Click event. This event occurs
when the user clicks the Print Text option on the File menu of the Printer project.
This event reads and generates the first two pages of the file CONSTANT.TXT.
When the document is finished, the EndDoc statement sends the output to the
Windows printing routines.

Note: The file CONSTANT.TXT must be in the \VB directory on the default
drive, or the Open statement will generate a "File not found" error.

```
Sub menuPrintText_Click ()
    FileNumber = FreeFile                        'get next available file number
    '***** this next line will cause an error if path or file doesn't exist!
    FileName = "\VB\CONSTANT.TXT"
    Open FileName For Input As #FileNumber        'open text file
    Form1.MousePointer = 11                       'hourglass; we're going to be a while
    Do
        If Printer.CurrentX = Printer.ScaleLeft And Printer.CurrentY = 0 Then
            PrintHeader FileName                  'If at beginning of page, print header
        End If
        Line Input #FileNumber, InputLine         'get a new line
        SpaceLeft = Printer.ScaleHeight - Printer.ScaleTop - Printer.CurrentY 'figure out
                                       '         how much space is left at bottom
        Printer.Print InputLine                   'print the line
        If SpaceLeft < (3 * Printer.TextHeight(InputLine)) Then PrintFooter  'if not much
                                       'space left, print footer and start a new page
    Loop Until EOF(FileNumber) Or Printer.Page = 3 'done with file or have printed 3 pages
    Close FileNumber                              'close the file
    Printer.EndDoc                                'send completed document to printer
    Form1.MousePointer = 0                        'cursor back to normal
End Sub
```

10. Enter the following code into the General Declarations area of the form. This procedure is called from the menuPrintText_Click event. It prints a header at the top
line of the page. It uses the ScaleWidth, CurrentX, and CurrentY properties
together with the TextWidth method to center the file name and right-justify the
page number on the top line.

```
Sub PrintHeader (Header As String)
    Printer.CurrentX = Printer.ScaleLeft          'all the way to the left
    Printer.Print Date$;                          'print current system date
    Printer.CurrentX = (Printer.ScaleWidth - Printer.TextWidth(Header)) / 2 'middle
    Printer.Print Header;                         'print header string
    pageNumber = "Page: " + Format$(Printer.Page, "###")     'figure out page number
    Printer.CurrentX = Printer.ScaleWidth - Printer.TextWidth(pageNumber)    'flush right
    Printer.Print pageNumber                      'and print the page number
    Printer.Print " "                             'force a new line
End Sub
```

923

11. Enter the following code into the General Declarations area of the form. This procedure is called from the menuPrintText_Click event. It prints a footer at the bottom line of the page. It uses the ScaleWidth, CurrentX, and CurrentY properties together with the TextWidth method to center the page number. It also uses the NewPage method to end the current page and clear the page work area.

```
Sub PrintFooter ()
    Printer.Print                                   'Print a blank line
    pageNumber = "Page: " + Format$(Printer.Page, "###") 'determine and format page number
    Printer.CurrentX = (Printer.ScaleWidth - Printer.TextWidth(pageNumber)) / 2  'middle
    Printer.Print pageNumber;                       'and print the page number
    Printer.NewPage                                 'start a new page
End Sub
```

12. Enter the following code into the menuExit_Click event. This simply ends the program.

```
Sub menuExit_Click ()
    End                                             'End the program
End Sub
```

How It Works

This example program sets up a simple data entry form that has a menu with four choices: Print Form, Print Graphics, Print Text, and Exit.

The user can print the form by opening the File menu and clicking on the Print Form option. This triggers the menuPrintForm_Click event, which uses the PrintForm method to send a copy of the form, and any text that is visible in the Name and Address text boxes, to the printer.

Choosing the Print Graphics option triggers the menuPrintGraphics_Click event. This event calls three sub procedures that demonstrate the use of the graphics methods on the Printer object.

The first of the three procedures is the PrintBox procedure. This prints a box around the text supplied in one of its arguments by using the Line method. The dimensions and placement of the box are determined using the CurrentX and CurrentY properties along with the TextHeight and TextWidth methods. PrintBox also has the Shaded argument, which indicates whether or not the text inside the box will be shaded. If this argument is True, the PSet method generates a dot every 50 positions inside the box.

The next procedure, PrintLine, prints its supplied text argument, and then proceeds to draw a line through it. Again, the position of the line is determined by the CurrentX and CurrentY properties in conjunction with the TextHeight method. The TextWidth method calculates the length of the strikeout line.

In the last of the three procedures, the PrintCircle method generates a circle with the supplied text argument centered within it. The placement and radius of the circle are figured using the TextHeight and TextWidth methods and the CurrentX and CurrentY properties.

Choosing the Print Text File option triggers the menuPrintText_Click event. This event opens the CONSTANT.TXT file and reads and prints the first two pages. It checks the CurrentX and CurrentY properties to see if they equal ScaleLeft and ScaleTop. If they both do (indicating that the routine is at the top of a new page), it executes the PrintHeader procedure. This procedure prints a header at the top line of the page. It uses the ScaleWidth, CurrentX, and CurrentY properties together with the TextWidth method to center the file name and right justify the page number on the top line. Execution then returns to the menuPrintText_Click event.

The menuPrintText_Click procedure then reads and prints the next line. It then uses the ScaleHeight and TextHeight methods to determine if it is at the bottom of a page. If so, the PrintFooter procedure is called. This procedure prints a centered page number and executes the NewPage method. Doing so increments the Printer.Page property, sets CurrentX and CurrentY equal to ScaleLeft and ScaleTop, and clears the page work area. Upon returning to the menuPrintText_Click event, the Page property is checked. If it equals 3, we have finished printing the first two pages and the procedure ends.

25 DYNAMIC DATA EXCHANGE (DDE)

Dynamic Data Exchange (DDE) is a means of communication between Microsoft Windows applications. This link acts as a conduit for the exchange of data between the connected applications. The data exchanged may either be information, which is copied from one application to another, or commands or keystrokes for the other application to process. Links may not be established with applications that do not support DDE communication. Check your application's documentation to see if it supports DDE.

In a DDE conversation, the application that creates the link is known as the *destination* application, and the application that responds is known as a *source* application. (These used to be referred to as *client* and *server* respectively.) Any application that supports DDE can serve as either a source or a destination. One application can serve as both a destination and a source with several other applications at the same time. Only one active DDE link should be established between a Visual Basic control or form and another application. For example, a link between a Microsoft Excel spreadsheet cell and a text control is acceptable as long as the parent form does not already have a link with the same cell. You might cause an infinite loop of updates if there were more than one link between the same two applications.

ELEMENTS OF A DDE LINK

A DDE conversation between two applications requires an application name, topic, and item. The *application name* is the unique name that identifies the application in Windows. Every DDE link has a *topic*, which indicates what type of data is being addressed

927

by the link. The *item* specifically identifies the data being exchanged by the two applications. Neither the application name nor the topic may be changed once a DDE link has been established, or the DDE connection will be broken. In contrast, the item of a DDE conversation may be changed as many times as necessary.

All of the applications in Windows have a name that identifies them in a DDE link. This name is normally the file name (without the extension) of the executable file used to start the program. The application name of a compiled Visual Basic program is the file name of the executable file. A Visual Basic program running within Visual Basic (for example, during design and testing) has an application name that is the project name without the .MAK extension. Table 25-1 contains the application names of some common Windows applications that support DDE.

Windows Application	File Name	Application Name
Microsoft Excel	EXCEL.EXE	Excel
Microsoft Word	WINWORD.EXE	WinWord
Pioneer Q+E	QE.EXE	QE
Polaris Packrat	PACKRAT.EXE	Packrat
Program Manager (3.1)	PROGMAN.EXE	Progman
Quicken for Windows	QW.EXE	QW

Table 25-1 Application names of common Windows applications

A DDE link also must indicate the topic, or part of the source application, with which to establish the connection. The available topics vary from application to application, but one choice is virtually universal to all DDE supporting applications: System. With the System topic, a DDE link can obtain the other topics that the application supports as well as information about the application, such as the data formats that it supports. In Microsoft Excel, Microsoft Word, and Pioneer Q+E, the path and file name may serve as a topic in a DDE link. Visual Basic applications can define the topic using the LinkTopic property.

The actual data transferred through a DDE link is called the item. In Visual Basic applications, the LinkItem property defines the item. An item in a Visual Basic application may be a text box, label, or picture on a form. When the topic of a DDE link is a spreadsheet, the item may be a cell reference such as R1C1 on an Excel spreadsheet. If a link is established with a WinWord document, the item might be a glossary name.

TYPES OF LINKS

Three basic types of links may be established between two applications: automatic, manual, and notify. An *automatic* link updates the data to the other application every time that the data changes. A *manual* link updates the data only when the data is specifically requested. A *notify* link notifies the other application when the data has changed, but does not send the actual data. A link, whether automatic, manual, or notify, is either a source or a destination link, depending on the direction in which the data passes.

A link may be established between a form or control in a Visual Basic application and another Windows application that supports DDE communication. The destination (initiating application) obtains information from the source (responding application). The type of initially created source link controls when this transfer of information takes place. If this is a manual or notify link, then the transfer takes place only when requested. Data transfers in automatic source links take place every time that the control or form changes.

DDE IN VISUAL BASIC

Visual Basic provides several tools that influence the operation of DDE links with other applications. Any actions tied to the opening or closing of a link appear in the LinkOpen and LinkClose events. The LinkError event provides for actions that take place when problems with links occur. A destination controls a source by sending the source's macro commands through the link with the LinkExecute method. Any actions that need to take place for your Visual Basic application to respond to link execute requests may be placed in the LinkExecute event.

Both the item and the topic of a DDE conversation may be determined with the LinkItem and LinkTopic properties. Whether a DDE link is automatic, manual, or notify may be set with the LinkMode property. When information needs to be moved from the destination to the source (opposite of the normal flow), use the LinkPoke method. Manual DDE links may transfer information manually with the LinkRequest method. Your application is notified of changes in the source data with the LinkNotify event. All of the contents of a Visual Basic application's picture box may be transferred to another application with the LinkSend method. The LinkTimeout property determines how long a control will wait for a response from the other application.

Table 25-2 displays the properties, methods, and events that affect DDE communication with other Windows applications that support this protocol.

929

Use or Set This...		To Do This...
LinkClose	Event	Indicate the actions that take place when a DDE link is closed
LinkError	Event	Indicate the actions that take place when a DDE link produces an error
LinkExecute	Event	Respond to a command sent by the source
LinkExecute	Method	Send a command over the DDE link
LinkItem	Property	Indicate the item to use with a DDE link
LinkMode	Property	Determine whether a control's DDE link is off, automatic, manual, or notify
LinkNotify	Event	Indicate source data has changed
LinkOpen	Event	Indicate the actions that take place when a DDE link is opened
LinkPoke	Method	Send information from the destination to the source
LinkRequest	Method	Ask for and obtain information from another application
LinkSend	Method	Transfer contents of picture box to a connected application
LinkTimeout	Property	Determine the time that a control will wait for a response over a link
LinkTopic	Property	Indicate the topic to use with a DDE link

Table 25-2 Properties, methods, and events dealing with the referencing of forms and controls

CONSTANT.TXT Values

Many of the properties, events, and methods of this chapter use numeric values as arguments. Using constants rather than the literal value makes your code self-documenting, more readable, and easier to debug.

Microsoft provides a file, CONSTANT.TXT, that has many constant declarations defined for you. For smaller applications it's probably easiest just to type the declarations in yourself. For larger applications you'll find it much easier to read the text file into a new module.

To do this, create a new module by pulling down the File menu and choosing the New Module menu command. Then pull down the File menu again and choose Load Text. This opens up a dialog box listing all text files in the current directory. CONSTANT.TXT should be in your main Visual Basic directory (default installation would place this in C:\VB). Simply choose CONSTANT.TXT to enter the entire file into your module. These constants will then be available throughout your application.

Table 25-3 lists the value of the constant, the CONSTANT.TXT constant name, and a brief description of what the constant means.

Value	CONSTANT.TXT	Meaning
LinkErr values		
1	WRONG_FORMAT	The linked application asked for data in an incompatible format
6	DDE_SOURCE_CLOSED	An application attempted a DDE operation after the source form's LinkMode was set to None
7	TOO_MANY_LINKS	There are too many active DDE links established (128 max)
8	DATA_TRANSFER_FAILED	Destination control: automatic link or LinkRequest failed to update control
		Source forms: destination attempted to poke data to a control and failed
11	n/a	There is not enough memory available for a DDE link
LinkMode of text box, picture, or label		
0	NONE	(Default) No DDE link established
1	LINK_AUTOMATIC	The control is updated each time the linked data changes
2	LINK_MANUAL	The control updated only with the LinkRequest method
3	LINK_NOTIFY	The control informed of changes to linked data, but is not updated
LinkMode for forms		
0	NONE	(Default) No DDE links may be established with this form

(continued on next page)

(continued from previous page)

Value	CONSTANT.TXT	Meaning
1	LINK_SOURCE	Source. Permits controls on the form to supply data to the destination application

Table 25-3 CONSTANT.TXT values used in DDE

The following pages investigate the properties, methods, and events in detail. The DDE project at the end of this section includes step-by-step instructions to assemble the project.

LINKCLOSE EVENT

Objects Affected

Check	Clipboard	Combo	Command	CommonDlg
Data	Debug	Dir	Drive	File
▶ Form	Frame	Grid	Image	▶ Label
Line	List	▶ MDI Form	Menu	OLE
Option	▶ Picture	Printer	Screen	Scroll
Shape	▶ Text	Timer		

Purpose

The LinkClose event processes any actions that occur when the DDE link between a form, label, picture box, or text box and another program terminates. Changing the LinkMode property of the object to none (0) terminates a DDE link. Attempting to change the LinkTopic property of an object also closes a DDE link. The LinkClose event contains any of the actions that occur when a link terminates. Table 25-4 summarizes the arguments of the LinkClose event.

General Syntax

```
Sub Form_LinkClose()
Sub Name_LinkClose ([Index As Integer])
```

Argument	Description
Form	'Form' indicates the form

Argument	Description
Name	Name property of control
Index	Identifies control in a control array

Table 25-4 Arguments of the LinkClose event

Example Syntax

```
Sub Form_LinkClose ()
    If LinkMode <> 0 Then                             'Checks if LinkMode is currently at none
        LinkMode = 0                                  'Changes LinkMode to none
        MsgBox "DDE link closed prematurely"          'Displays message on the screen
    Else If LinkMode = 0 Then                         'Checks if LinkMode is currently at none
        MsgBox "DDE Link closed normally"             'Displays normal termination message
    End If
End Sub
```

Description

The LinkClose event contains any actions that occur when a DDE link closes. A DDE link terminates in several ways. Any attempt to modify the topic of a link terminates the link. A form or control's link ends when its LinkMode property changes to 0. Keep each of these possible reasons in mind when setting up a LinkClose event. In the example syntax, the routine checks the current setting of the LinkMode property of the form. The code determines if the link closed with the LinkMode or another method.

The LinkMode Property

Changing the LinkMode property of an object initiates or terminates a link with another application. The LinkClose event triggers when the LinkMode property closes a link. In the example syntax, the LinkClose event checks to determine if a change to the LinkMode property terminated the link.

The LinkTopic Property

The contents of a LinkTopic are part of the unique identifying characteristics of a DDE link. The other characteristics are the application name and topic. A link's topic identifies the element of the other application being linked. Neither of these characteristics may be modified on an active link or the link will close, triggering the LinkClose event. In the example syntax, the routine checks the present setting of the LinkMode property to determine if the link was closed without a change to the LinkMode property. The abnormal message displays if the LinkClose event was triggered by an attempted change of the topic while the link was active.

Control Arrays

When there is a DDE link between a control in a control array and another application, the Index property must be provided. In this case such a link involves a specific control in the control array and does not involve the contents or settings of the other controls in the control array. In order to access all of the controls of a control array, the link must be established with the form that contains the controls.

Example

The DDE project at the end of this chapter uses the LinkClose event to notify the user of the link's changed status. The pictGraphic_LinkClose event changes lablGraphLinkStatus.Caption to read "(unlinked)."

Comments

Since the item of a DDE link is modifiable while the link is active, changes to the item do not trigger the LinkClose event.

LINKERROR EVENT

Objects Affected

Check	Clipboard	Combo	Command	CommonDlg
Data	Debug	Dir	Drive	File
▶ Form	Frame	Grid	Image	▶ Label
Line	List	▶ MDI Form	Menu	OLE
Option	▶ Picture	Printer	Screen	Scroll
Shape	▶ Text	Timer		

Purpose

The LinkError event triggers when a DDE link conversation produces an error. This error can never be caused by Visual Basic code—errors caused by code are normal trappable errors. LinkError events are only triggered as the result of problems with the connected application, the link itself, or the Windows environment. This event returns a value you can use to determine what action to take based upon the error that occurred. Tables 25-5 and 25-6 summarize the valid arguments and values of the LinkError event.

General Syntax

```
Sub Form_LinkError (LinkErr As Integer)
Sub Name_LinkError ([Index As Integer,] LinkErr As Integer)
```

Argument	Effect
Form	'Form' indicates the form
Name	Name property of control
Index	Identifying value of the control in a control array
LinkErr	The LinkErr value returned

Table 25-5 Valid arguments of the LinkError event

LinkErr	CONSTANT.TXT	Problem
1	WRONG_FORMAT	The linked application asked for data in an incompatible format
6	DDE_SOURCE_CLOSED	An application attempted a DDE operation after the source form's LinkMode was set to None
7	TOO_MANY_LINKS	There are too many active DDE links established (128 max)
8	DATA_TRANSFER_FAILED	Destination control: automatic link or LinkRequest failed to update control
		Source forms: destination attempted to poke data to a control and failed
11	n/a	There is not enough memory available for a DDE link

Table 25-6 Causes of the link error values returned in the LinkErr variable. (Missing entries were used in Visual Basic 1.0 but are now obsolete.)

Example Syntax

```
Sub TextBox_LinkError (Index As Integer, LinkErr As Integer)
    Msg$ = "Error in link. (Error #" & Str$(LinkErr) & ")"
    MsgBox Msg$
End Sub
```

Description

The LinkError event provides information about the nature of problems when they occur. The LinkError event contains actions that respond to the problem. Any actions in this event mainly serve as a warning that something is wrong. Table 25-6 lists the possible errors that can trigger this event. In the example syntax, the LinkError event informs the user about what kind of problem has occurred. Since the source application's actions (Excel in this example) cause the error, changes must be made to that application before the link may be successfully processed. Errors of this type typically require recoding in the connected application.

Control Array

When there is a DDE link between a control in a control array and another application, the Index property must be provided. In this case such a link involves a specific control in the control array and does not involve the contents or settings of the other controls in the control array. In order to access all of the controls of a control array, the link must be established with the form that contains the controls.

Example

The DDE project at the end of this chapter uses the LinkError event of three objects—the textBox, pictGraph, and formMain—to call the module-level procedure describeLinkError. This procedure simply produces a message indicating what kind of error occurred.

Comments

The LinkError event LinkErr values have no effect on the value of the Err variable in Err functions.

LINKEXECUTE EVENT

Objects Affected

Check	Clipboard	Combo	Command	CommonDlg
Data	Debug	Dir	Drive	File
▶ Form	Frame	Grid	Image	Label
Line	List	▶ MDI Form	Menu	OLE
Option	Picture	Printer	Screen	Scroll
Shape	Text	Timer		

Purpose

The LinkExecute event contains a Visual Basic application's responses to command strings sent through a DDE link. A LinkExecute event only triggers when the form is the source of a DDE link. The destination application transmits a command through a DDE link to the source application. Forms with no code in the LinkExecute event will ignore any commands sent through the link from the destination application. Table 25-7 summarizes the arguments of the LinkExecute event, and Table 25-8 shows the values of the Cancel return value in the LinkExecute event.

General Syntax

```
Sub Form_LinkExecute (Cmdstr As String, Cancel As Integer)
```

Argument	Effect
Form	'Form' indicates the source form
CmdStr	Contents of the command string transmitted through the link from a destination application
Cancel	Tells destination if command was accepted

Table 25-7 Arguments of the LinkExecute event

Cancel	Meaning
True (-1)	(Default) Set Cancel to True to show destination application that command was rejected
False (0)	Set Cancel to False to show destination application that command was accepted

Table 25-8 Values of the Cancel return value in the LinkExecute event

Example Syntax

```
Sub Form_LinkExecute (CmdStr As String, Cancel As Integer)
    Cancel = False                      'Show that we've accepted command
    Select Case UCase$(CmdStr)          'Format text of cmdstr in all uppercase
        Case "[SETUP]"
            WindowState = 2             'Maximize window
            Cls                         'Clear screen and reset coordinates
            BackColor = QBColor(1)      'Make the background blue
```

(continued on next page)

(continued from previous page)

```
        Case "DATE"
            Print Date$,                    'Prints the date on the form
            Print                           'Puts a space after the date
        Case "TIME"
            Print Time$,                    'Prints the time on the form
            Print                           'Puts a space after the time
        Case "[CLOSE]"
            Hide                            'Hides the current form on the screen
        Case "[SHOW]"
            Form1.Show                      'Displays the form on the screen
        Case Else
            Cancel = True                   'Command not accepted
    End Select
End Sub
```

Description

The LinkExecute event contains a library of possible commands you've created that may be sent to this form through a DDE link. There are two possible arguments for this event, CmdStr and Cancel. Any command sent through a link is stored in the text string CmdStr and may then be accessed to determine what kind of action should take place. When the command string sent does not match any of the criteria listed in a LinkExecute event, change the Cancel variable to True (-1) to indicate that the command was rejected. This informs the sending application that the command was not valid for this application. If your application recognizes and acts on CmdStr, set the Cancel variable to False (0) to indicate the command was accepted.

In the example syntax, the LinkExecute event contains a list of commands that may be sent to its parent form. Any commands that are sent to the form through a DDE link will be checked to see if they match any of the acceptable commands. If a match is made, then the command is processed. Otherwise, the Cancel variable changes to True to inform the sending application that the command was rejected.

Example

The DDE project at the end of this chapter uses the form's LinkExecute method to allow other applications to request information or to end the program. The most important command is Update Graph, which executes a LinkSend method on pictGraph to send it to the requesting application.

Comments

The actions listed in the LinkExecute event of a form have no effect on the use of the LinkExecute method in the same form. The LinkExecute event occurs when your application is the source; your application uses the LinkExecute method when it is the destination.

938

LINKEXECUTE METHOD

Objects Affected

Check	Clipboard	Combo	Command	CommonDlg
Data	Debug	Dir	Drive	File
Form	Frame	Grid	Image	▶ Label
Line	List	MDI Form	Menu	OLE
Option	▶ Picture	Printer	Screen	Scroll
Shape	▶ Text	Timer		

Purpose

The LinkExecute method transmits commands to another application through a DDE link. This method permits the destination application in a DDE link conversation to control the behavior of the source application. Commands sent with the LinkExecute method have the same effect as if the user entered them. Table 25-9 summarizes the arguments of the LinkExecute method.

General Syntax

```
[form!]Name.LinkExecute cmdstr$
```

Argument	Effect
form	Name property of the form
Name	Name property of the text box, picture box, or label control
cmdstrS	Command string for the destination application to send to the source application to process

Table 25-9 Arguments of the LinkExecute method

Example Syntax

```
Sub Form_Load ()
Startup:
    On Error GoTo OpenWinWord            'Sets error trap to open WinWord
    Text1.LinkTimeout = -1               'Turns off Timeout error
    Text1.LinkMode = 0                   'Turn off any existing links
    Text1.LinkTopic = "WinWord|System"   'Sets the Topic for the DDE Link
```

(continued on next page)

(continued from previous page)

```
        Text1.LinkMode = 2                        'Opens a manual link with Winword
        Text1.LinkExecute "[FileClose 2]"         'Closes the current file without saving
        Text1.LinkExecute "[FileNew 0,""Letter""]"   'Opens new file with Letter Template
        AppActivate "Microsoft Word - Document2"     'Gives the focus to Word
        End                                       'Ends program

OpenWinWord:
        If Err = 282 Then                         'Checks if WinWord wasn't in memory
            x = Shell("Winword.exe", 3)           'Start up WinWord
            Resume Startup                        'Try again
        Else
            Error Err                             'Forces display of error message.
        End If
End Sub
```

Description

The LinkExecute method transmits commands to another application through a DDE link. This method lets the destination application in a DDE link conversation control the behavior of the source application. Commands sent with the LinkExecute method have the same effect as if the user entered them. The cmdstr$ argument contains the command you'd like to send over the link. Example syntax contains a routine connected to the Text1 text box that sends a series of commands to Microsoft Word for Windows through a DDE link. These commands open a new file based on the Letter template. When this form opens Word for Windows, the user no longer has to press File, New, and then choose Letter from the list of templates. The program does this automatically and then exits.

The LinkTopic Property

In order for a LinkExecute method to be processed, a link must first be established with the other application. A control or form's LinkTopic property provides the name of the other application along with the topic, which is normally the file name. In this case the System topic is used instead of the file name, because the first command sent by the LinkExecute method closes the open file. As a result the link is maintained with WinWord without being dependent on which document is open at the time. This is a useful technique to use when dealing with multiple documents in DDE-supporting Windows applications.

The LinkTimeout Property

The LinkExecute method requires the proper setting of the LinkTimeout property of the control or form. The LinkTimeout property determines the amount of time that a control will wait for a response from the other application. When the value of the LinkTimeout property is set to -1, the control or form will wait indefinitely (actually about 1 hour 49 minutes), or until the user presses the (ESC) key on the keyboard or the application responds. In the example syntax, the

LinkTimeout property is set to -1 to prevent any delays in execution from generating an error.

The LinkMode Property

The LinkMode property determines what type of link is to be established. Since a form may not serve as a destination in a DDE link, the LinkExecute method requires a link between a control and another application. In some cases the link may only be established with a particular type of control. For example, picture files (*.PCX, *.TIF, and so on) would only be linkable into picture boxes. Some applications may only support a manual link.

Error Trapping

The Err function, Error Statement, and On Error Statement are an important part of the operation of a DDE link subroutine. Through the use of the On Error statement "On Error GoTo OpenWinWord," the code provides for the possibility that WinWord is not loaded when this program runs. If WinWord is not running, an error generates and code in the OpenWinWord section is processed. This routine checks to see if WinWord is not running. If WinWord is not present, then the Shell function loads WinWord into memory. After WinWord loads, the link is established and the LinkExecute command transmits the command strings. An error message displays on the screen when an unanticipated error occurs. Appendix A, Visual Basic Language Tutorial, summarizes these error-related functions and statements.

Example

The DDE project at the end of this chapter uses the LinkExecute method extensively. The heaviest use occurs during the Form_Load event, when the DDE program is first setting up Excel with multiple LinkExecutes.

Comments

Notice that the commands sent in the LinkExecute method in the example are placed between square brackets, and any quotation marks placed within them are double quotation marks. This is a requirement for sending macro commands to Microsoft Word and Excel for Windows. Other applications may have different requirements, much as programs you write that accept LinkExecute events can parse the command string for anything you choose. Consult the other application's documentation (and probably call their tech support!) for the proper formats, commands, and macros it can accept.

LINKITEM PROPERTY

Objects Affected

Check	Clipboard	Combo	Command	CommonDlg
Data	Debug	Dir	Drive	File
Form	Frame	Grid	Image	▶ Label
Line	List	MDI Form	Menu	OLE
Option	▶ Picture	Printer	Screen	Scroll
Shape	▶ Text	Timer		

Purpose

The LinkItem property refers to the data transmitted through a DDE link from the source application to the destination application. This property corresponds to the Item argument of a DDE link and may be changed without closing an active link. When a Visual Basic form is the source in a DDE link, the LinkItem property of the form contains the Name property of the control identified in the item of the DDE link. Table 25-10 summarizes the arguments of the LinkItem property.

General Syntax

`[form!]Name.LinkItem [ = expression$]`

Argument	Description
form	Name property of the form
Name	Name property of the label, picture box, or text box
expression$	Identifies the item of a DDE link

Table 25-10 Arguments of the LinkItem property

Example Syntax

```
Sub Form_Load ()
Startup:
    On Error GoTo OpenQE          'Sets Error trap to OpenQE
    Text1.LinkTimeout = -1        'Turns off Timeout error
    Text1.LinkMode = 0            'Deactivates any existing link
```

```
        Text1.LinkTopic = "QE|System"              'Sets the Topic for DDE link
        Text1.LinkItem = "ALL"                     'Sets the Item for DDE Link
        Text1.LinkMode = 2                         'Opens a manual link with Q+E
        Text1.LinkExecute "[Open('C:\EXCEL\QE\EMP.DBF')]"      'Opens Data file
        Text1.LinkExecute "[Open.Index('C:\EXCEL\QE\EMPLNAME.NDX',TRUE)]"
        Text1.LinkExecute "[SAVE.QUERY.AS('C:\EXCEL\QE\EMP.QEF')]"
        Text1.LinkMode = 0                         'Closes link with Q+E.
        Text1.LinkTopic = "QE|C:\EXCEL\QE\EMP.DBF" 'Changes Topic for DDE link.
        Text1.LinkItem = "C:\EXCEL\QE\EMP.QEF"     'Changes Item for DDE link.
        Text1.LinkMode = 2                         'Opens a manual link with Q+E.
        Text1.LinkExecute "[Open('C:\EXCEL\QE\EMP.QEF')]"      'Opens Query file.
    End                                            'Ends program.
OpenQE:
    If Err = 282 Then                              'Checks if Q+E wasn't in memory
        x = Shell("QE.exe", 3)                     'Start up QE
        Resume Startup                             'try again
    Else
        Error Err                                  'Forces display of error message
    End If
End Sub
```

Description

The LinkItem property refers to the data transmitted through a DDE link from the source application to the destination application. A LinkItem property's expression$ argument contains a string expression in a format acceptable to the application that is being linked with the Visual Basic application. This value must be a string expression and can contain up to 255 characters.

In the example syntax, the LinkItem of the text box Text1 is defined with two text strings. In the first link, the LinkItem is defined as All. This is a Q+E specification for DDE items that means "include the entire database file listed in the topic." In the second link, the LinkItem is defined with the path and name of the Q+E query file EMP.QEF. Notice that the query file still needs to be loaded, even though a link has been established with it.

Details of the DDE link will vary with the application being linked with. For example, links with Microsoft Excel may define the LinkItem property with the location of the cells that contain the appropriate data. In links with Pioneer Q+E, the topic may be the entire database specified in the topic by defining the LinkItem property as All or the appropriate query file name. These settings are used in the following example to display the contents of the EMP.DBF file on the screen.

The LinkTopic Property

The LinkTopic property defines which items may be chosen for a DDE link. The available items also depend on which application you are linking to the Visual Basic application. When the DDE link's topic is set to System, the LinkItem may be set to any available part of the application. In the example syntax, the LinkItem is set at All when the LinkTopic property is System. After the LinkTopic is changed to C:\EXCEL\QE\EMP.DBF, the list of available items is reduced to its query files. For this reason, the newly created query file C:\EXCEL\QE\EMP.QEF is specified.

The LinkMode Property

The LinkMode property determines what type of link is to be established. Since a form may not serve as a destination in a DDE link, the LinkExecute method requires a link between a control and another application. In some cases, the link may only be established with a particular type of control. For example, picture files (*.PCX, *.TIF, and so on) would only be linkable to picture boxes. Some applications may only support a manual link.

Error Trapping

The Err function, Error Statement, and On Error Statement are important parts of the operation of a DDE link subroutine. These error-related functions and statements are summarized in Appendix A, Visual Basic Language Tutorial. Through the use of the On Error Statement "On Error GoTo OpenQE," the code provides for the possibility that Q+E is not loaded when this program runs. If Q+E is not running, an error generates and code in the OpenQE section opens Q+E. If Q+E is not present, then the Shell function loads Q+E into memory. After Q+E has been loaded, the link is established and the LinkExecute transmits the command strings. An error message displays on the screen when an unanticipated error occurs.

Application Items

Each application has its own unique set of items and has its own way of specifying them. You'll need to refer to the other application's documentation to discover what items and formats it supports. Tables 25-11 and 25-12 show some representative applications to give you an idea of what kinds of items you'd expect to be supported. Note that each version of every program is different; newer versions of an application will likely support different (and probably more) topics. DDE is still a young and ill understood protocol. Vendors are constantly changing and adding to their applications' abilities.

WinWord System Items

Three items may be used with the topic System in Microsoft Word for Windows: SysItems, Topics, and Formats. The SysItems item produces a list of the possible items that may be used with the System topic. The Topics item provides a list of the open documents that includes the path names. A Formats item returns a list of all of the Clipboard formats supported by Word for Windows. This is very important information to keep in mind when setting up a link with WinWord. Use Table 25-11 as a reference for obtaining information about Microsoft WinWord.

Item	Description
SysItems	Returns a list of the available items that may be used with the System topic
Topics	Returns a list of available open documents in WinWord
Formats	Returns a list of available Clipboard formats supported by WinWord

Table 25-11 List of possible items for the topic System with Microsoft Word for Windows

Excel System Items

Seven items may be used with the topic System in Microsoft Excel for Windows: SysItems, Topics, Status, Formats, Selection, Protocols, and EditEnvItems. The SysItems item produces a list of the possible items that may be used with the System topic. The Topics item provides a list of the available topics and the path and file names of the open spreadsheets. The Status item returns the text Ready when the Excel application is not busy with an operation of some kind. A Formats item returns a list of all of the Clipboard formats supported by Excel for Windows. The Selection item indicates the reference location of the currently active cell or cells, including the name of the spreadsheet. Protocols items display the types of DDE link protocols that Excel supports, including StdFileEditing and Embedding. The items are summarized in Table 25-12.

Item	Description
SysItems	Returns a list of the available items that may be used with the System topic
Topics	Returns a list of the available topics, which includes the presently open spreadsheets in Excel
Status	Returns the text Ready when Excel is not busy with an operation of some kind
Formats	Returns a list of the Clipboard formats supported by Excel
Selection	Returns the reference of the currently active cell or cells on a spreadsheet
Protocols	Returns the DDE protocols that Excel supports: StdFileEditing and Embedding
EditEnvItems	StdHostNames, StdTargetDevice, and StdDocDimensions

Table 25-12 List of possible items for the topic System with Microsoft Excel for Windows

Q+E System Items

Eight items may be utilized with the topic System in Pioneer Q+E for Windows. They are SysItems, Topics, Formats, Status, LogOn, LogOff, and Sources. The SysItems item produces a list of the items that may be used with the System topic. The Topics item provides a list of the available topics and the path and file names of the open database files. The Formats item returns a list of all of the Clipboard formats supported by Q+E for Windows. The Status item returns the text Ready when Q+E is not busy with an operation of some kind. Both the LogOn and LogOff items provide information about whether Q+E is presently connected to a SQL source. The Sources item returns the database formats that Q+E supports. These items are summarized in Table 25-13.

Item	Description
SysItems	Returns a list of the available items that may be used with the System topic
Topics	Returns a list of the available topics, which includes the presently open files in Q+E
Formats	Returns a list of the Clipboard formats supported by Q+E
Status	Returns the text Ready when Q+E is not processing a DDE link action
LogOn	Returns if Q+E is logged into a SQL source
LogOff	Returns if Q+E is not logged into a SQL source
Sources	Returns the database formats that Q+E supports and can import

Table 25-13 List of possible items for the topic System with Pioneer Q+E for Windows

Example

The DDE project at the end of this chapter uses the LinkItem property to specify what cell in Excel the data is supposed to go in during the Form_Load event.

Comments

The example displayed in this section was written with the version of Q+E 3.0 that is shipped with Microsoft Excel and uses the EMP.DBF and EMPLNAME.NDX files that were shipped with it. This example may not work with other versions of Q+E.

946

LINKMODE PROPERTY

Objects Affected

Check	Clipboard	Combo	Command	CommonDlg
Data	Debug	Dir	Drive	File
Form	Frame	Grid	Image	▶ Label
Line	List	MDI Form	Menu	OLE
Option	▶ Picture	Printer	Screen	Scroll
Shape	▶ Text	Timer		

Purpose

The LinkMode property determines the type of DDE link to establish and then creates this type of link with the application, topic, and item specified in the LinkTopic and LinkItem properties. Available at design time, read and write at runtime. Table 25-14 summarizes the arguments of the LinkMode property. Tables 25-15 and 25-16 summarize the values and effects of the LinkMode property.

General Syntax

```
[form.]LinkMode [ = mode%]
[form!]Name.LinkMode [ = mode%]
```

Argument	Description
form	Name property of the form
Name	Name property of the control
mode%	Current status of the LinkMode property

Table 25-14 Arguments of the LinkMode property

mode%	CONSTANT.TXT	Meaning
0	NONE	(Default) No DDE link established
1	LINK_AUTOMATIC	Automatic. The control is updated each time the linked data changes

(continued on next page)

mode%	CONSTANT.TXT	Meaning
2	LINK_MANUAL	Manual. The control is updated only when the LinkRequest method is used
3	LINK_NOTIFY	Notify. The control is informed of changes to the linked data, but is not updated

Table 25-15 Values and effects of the LinkMode property of a text box, picture box, or label

mode%	CONSTANT.TXT	Meaning
0	NONE	(Default) No DDE links may be established with this form
1	LINK_SOURCE	Source. Permits controls on the form to supply data to the destination application

Table 25-16 Values and effects of the LinkMode property of a form

Example Syntax

```
Sub OptionUpdateStatus_Click (Index as Integer)
Startup:
    On Error GoTo OpenXL                   'Sets Error trap to OpenXL
    Picture1.LinkMode = 0                  'Sets Picture1's LinkMode
    Picture1.LinkTopic = "Excel|Chart1"    'Sets Picture1's Topic
    Picture1.LinkMode = Index              'Opens link (buttons are 1, 2, 3)
    Exit Sub                               'Exits subroutine
OpenXL:
    If Err = 282 Then                      'Checks if Excel wasn't running
        x = Shell("Excel.exe", 3)          'load Excel
        Resume Startup                     'try again
    Else
        Error Err                          'Forces display of error
    End If
End Sub
```

Description

The LinkMode property controls whether a DDE link exists and what type of link it is, if it does exist. This property may be changed at runtime or design time. The value of the LinkMode property determines whether a form may be part of a DDE link. The LinkMode property establishes the presence or absence of an active link as well as the type of the link. When there is no link, the value is 0 (none). An active link may be either automatic (1), manual (2), or notify (3).

The example syntax demonstrates the types of LinkMode links in establishing a link to an Excel spreadsheet, which is shown and updated in the picture box. This example assumes the option button group is indexed as 1, 2, and 3 to correspond to the link modes. Note that depending on the link status, the picture may or may not be updated automatically. For link modes 2 and 3 (manual and notify) other code in another event would have to perform a LinkRequest to update the link.

Using the LinkTopic and LinkItem Properties with Forms

The LinkMode property works with the LinkTopic and LinkItem properties of the form. With a form, the LinkTopic property determines the name for a destination application to use in order to establish a DDE link. A form's LinkItem specifies which control on the form will be connected to the destination application through a DDE link. This property contains the Name property of this indicated control. In this way the source form has some control of the behavior of links that are established by other applications. The LinkTopic property of an active DDE link may not be changed. In contrast, the LinkItem property may be changed as many times as necessary.

Using the LinkTopic and LinkItem Properties with Controls

The LinkMode property functions with the help of the settings of the LinkTopic and LinkItem properties of the same control. With the LinkTopic property, the control, the application name, and topic (usually the file name or System) provide the information needed to establish a DDE link. A control's LinkItem property indicates which part of the source application the control will be connected to.

The LinkError Event

The LinkError event specifies what happens when a destination application initiates an action that generates an error. The LinkError event returns the error in the ErrLink variable which may then be used to specify what the difficulty is. This is the correct method for handling errors generated by applications with their DDE LinkMode properties set to source (1).

Example

The DDE project at the end of this chapter uses LinkMode quite frequently to change modes.

LINKNOTIFY EVENT

Objects Affected

Check	Clipboard	Combo	Command	CommonDlg
Data	Debug	Dir	Drive	File
Form	Frame	Grid	Image	▶ Label
Line	List	MDI Form	Menu	OLE
Option	▶ Picture	Printer	Screen	Scroll
Shape	▶ Text	Timer		

Purpose

The LinkNotify event occurs for links set up as LinkMode 3 (notify) when the source data changes. This lets your code issue a LinkRequest to update the control. Table 25-17 summarizes the arguments of the LinkNotify event.

General Syntax

```
Sub Name_LinkNotify ([Index as Integer])
End Sub
```

Argument	Description
Name	Name of the control
Index	Index number of the control if in a control array

Table 25-17 Arguments of the LinkNotify event

Example Syntax

```
Sub Picture1_LinkNotify ()
    Command1.ForeColor = QBColor(1)                  'Highlight the "Update" button
    StatusBar.Text = "Source chart has been updated. Press 'Update' button to see changes"
End Sub
```

Description

The LinkNotify event lets your code react to changes in the source data for controls with a LinkMode of 3 (notify). You would typically update the control immediately with LinkRequest, ignore the change, or inform the user of the change.

The example syntax takes this last strategy of informing the user of the change. It highlights the command button that contains the LinkRequest code and puts a message on a status bar informing the user of the change.

This technique is most useful for links that transfer substantial amounts of data. For instance, graphics files tend to be quite large and take an appreciable amount of time to update. Letting the user control when to update the destination control might make your application more responsive than trying to automatically update after every change.

Example

The DDE project at the end of this chapter uses the LinkNotify events of both the text box and the picture box to inform the user of the change in the links status. Both routines update the labels immediately to the left of the controls to read "(Data Available)." The user can then select menuLink Update Links to update the links.

LINKOPEN EVENT

Objects Affected

Check	Clipboard	Combo	Command	CommonDlg
Data	Debug	Dir	Drive	File
▶ Form	Frame	Grid	Image	▶ Label
Line	List	▶ MDI Form	Menu	OLE
Option	▶ Picture	Printer	Screen	Scroll
Shape	▶ Text	Timer		

Purpose

The LinkOpen event processes any actions that take place when a DDE link opens between a form, label, picture box, or text box and another program. A link may be opened by either a Visual Basic application or an external application. The LinkOpen event of the form triggers when another application establishes a DDE link. Tables 25-18 and 25-19 summarize the arguments and meanings of the return values for the Cancel argument of the LinkOpen event.

General Syntax

```
Sub Form_LinkOpen (Cancel As Integer)
Sub Name_LinkOpen ([Index As Integer,] Cancel As Integer)
```

Argument	Description
form	'Form' indicates the form
Name	Name property of the control
Index	Index value of the control in a control array with which the link is established
Cancel	Return value, set to False or True to accept or refuse link

Table 25-18 Arguments of the LinkOpen event

Cancel	Meaning
False (0)	(Default) Accept the link
True (-1)	Refuse the link

Table 25-19 Meanings of the return values for the Cancel argument in the LinkOpen event

Example Syntax

```
Sub Command1_Click ()
    Text1.LinkTimeout = -1                  'Turns off Timeout Error
    Text1.LinkMode = 0                      'Deactivate any existing links
    Text1.LinkTopic = "Excel|System"        'Sets Topic
    Text1.LinkMode = 2                      'Opens a Manual link
    Text1.LinkExecute "[File.Close(FALSE)]"   'Closes presently open file in Excel
    Text1.LinkMode = 0                      'Cuts the link with Excel
    End                                     'End Program
End Sub

Sub Text1_LinkOpen (Cancel As Integer)
    If Text1.Text = "No" Then               'Checks the contents of Text box
        Cancel = True                       'Indicates that DDE link is not established
        Exit Sub                            'Exits the subroutine
    Else
```

```
        x = Shell("Excel",3)              'Opens Excel
        Cancel = False                    'Indicates that DDE link is established
    End If
End Sub
```

Description

The LinkOpen event controls whether a link may be created between either a Visual Basic control and another application or another application and a Visual Basic form. Each LinkOpen event returns a value in the Cancel variable that accepts or refuses a DDE link. When the LinkOpen event contains no code or the Cancel variable is 0, the link is accepted. If the Cancel variable is a nonzero value, the link is not established.

In the example syntax, the LinkOpen event of the text box tests whether the Text property contains the word No. As long as the text box does not contain this word, the link is established. Notice that the expressions that are placed after the LinkMode property change are processed after the LinkOpen event executes.

The LinkMode Property

When a DDE link is created by setting the LinkMode property of a picture box, text box, or label to 1 (automatic), 2 (manual), or 3 (notify), the LinkOpen event of that control triggers. Do not place any commands that depend on the link, such as the LinkExecute, LinkRequest, and LinkPoke methods, in the LinkOpen event. The actual link is not set up until the LinkOpen event finishes processing. In cases where the Cancel variable is a nonzero value and the link is not created, any expressions that depend on the link will result in an error. This is why we place Exit Sub after the setting Cancel to True in the example syntax. The code that follows the LinkMode setting would otherwise generate an error.

Access by an External Application

If the LinkMode property of a form is 1 (source), an external application may establish a DDE link with any text box, picture box, or label on the form. Any actions in the LinkOpen event process before the link is established. The Cancel value returned by the LinkOpen event indicates whether the link is accepted or denied. If the Cancel value is 0, the link is permitted. If the Cancel value is a nonzero value, the link is denied.

Example

The DDE project at the end of this chapter uses the LinkOpen event to properly update its display. It updates the lablGraphLinkStatus caption property to "...opening link..." for the duration of the open procedure.

Comments

Any actions that depend on the link must wait until after the LinkOpen event is processed or an error will generate. This is because the link is not actually established with another application until the Cancel value is returned at the end of the LinkOpen event. If the event contains no actions, then the link is established normally. Otherwise, the definition of Cancel as any nonzero value prevents the link.

LINKPOKE METHOD

Objects Affected

Check	Clipboard	Combo	Command	CommonDlg
Data	Debug	Dir	Drive	File
Form	Frame	Grid	Image	▶ Label
Line	List	MDI Form	Menu	OLE
Option	▶ Picture	Printer	Screen	Scroll
Shape	▶ Text	Timer		

Purpose

The LinkPoke method inserts the contents of a Visual Basic destination control into the item specified in the source application. This method temporarily reverses the flow of information. A normal link transfers data from the source to the destination when the link is automatic or the LinkRequest method is utilized. With the LinkPoke method, the destination provides information to the source. This change in the passage of data is only temporary and has no effect on the normal operation of the link either before or after the LinkPoke method. Table 25-20 summarizes the arguments of the LinkPoke method.

General Syntax

`[form!]Name.LinkPoke`

Argument	Description
form	Name property of the form
Name	Name property of the control

Table 25-20 Arguments of the LinkPoke method

954

Example Syntax

```
Sub Command1_Click ()
Startup:
    On Error Goto OpenXL            'Sets Error trap to OpenXL
    Text1.Text = "Data Transferred"  'Defines Text property of Text box
    Text1.LinkTopic = "Excel|Sheet1" 'Defines Topic
    Text1.LinkItem = "R1C1"          'Defines Item (a cell reference)
    Text1.LinkTimeout = -1           'Turns off Timeout error
    Text1.LinkMode = 2               'Opens a manual link
    Text1.LinkPoke                   'Inserts information (Text1.Text) into R1C1
    Text1.LinkMode = 0               'Closes the link
    Exit Sub                         'Exits the subroutine
OpenXL:
    If Err = 282 Then                'Checks if Excel wasn't in memory causing
        x = Shell("Excel.exe", 3)    'the error making it necessary to start
        Resume Startup               'Excel. Returns to the program's beginning
    Else
        Error Err                    'Forces display of error message
    End If
End Sub
```

Description

A LinkPoke method transfers the contents of the control to the item in the linked application identified by the control's LinkItem property. When the specified control is a picture box, the contents of the Picture property are transferred to the item. If the control is a text box, the contents of the Text property are moved to the item. With a label box, the Caption property is transmitted to the item.

The LinkPoke method might be useful if you want to give the other application some data to work on so it could supply the result back to your application. For example, poking sales information into cells on a spreadsheet could set up the spreadsheet to calculate results like quota attainment, variances among sales reps, and so forth. The spreadsheet would then send the results back over the link in the normal manner.

In the example syntax, the LinkPoke method places the contents of the text box Text1 into the Excel spreadsheet's R1C1 cell when the user presses the command button.

The LinkTopic Property

Each LinkPoke method requires that the LinkTopic property contain the name of the application and the topic into which the data is being inserted. The application must support DDE links. The topic is normally the name of the file. In the example syntax, the LinkTopic is defined as "Excel | Sheet1." This indicates that the data will be placed somewhere on Excel's default Sheet1.

The LinkItem Property

The LinkItem property of the control determines the exact destination of the data that the LinkPoke method inserts in the topic. A LinkItem may be changed at runtime so that each LinkPoke method can place data in a new location in the topic. Not setting the LinkItem property of the control generates an error. In the example syntax, the data is placed in the R1C1 cell of the Sheet1 spreadsheet as identified by the LinkItem property of the Text1 text box.

The LinkModeProperty

A LinkPoke method will work when the LinkMode property is set to automatic (1), manual (2), or notify (3). Even though a valid link is established with the LinkMode property, the LinkPoke method will not work unless both the LinkTopic and LinkItem properties are set to valid elements of the other application that may receive the contents of the indicated control. For example, if two Visual Basic applications are linked through a picture box on the destination and a text box on the source, an error will occur.

Example

The LinkPoke method pokes data from the eight text boxes directly into the spreadsheet. Each control array's Change event triggers the LinkPoke method.

LINKREQUEST METHOD

Objects Affected

Check	Clipboard	Combo	Command	CommonDlg
Data	Debug	Dir	Drive	File
Form	Frame	Grid	Image	▶ Label
Line	List	MDI Form	Menu	OLE
Option	▶ Picture	Printer	Screen	Scroll
Shape	▶ Text	Timer		

Purpose

The LinkRequest method updates a manual or notify link between a Visual Basic control and another application. Automatic DDE links between applications do not require this method, as this data is updated automatically. Table 25-21 summarizes the arguments of the LinkRequest method.

General Syntax

```
[form!]Name.LinkRequest
```

Argument	Description
form	Name property of the form
Name	Name property of the control

Table 25-21 Arguments of the LinkRequest method

Example Syntax

```
Sub Command1_Click ()
Startup:
    On Error GoTo OpenWinWord              'Sets error trap to OpenWinWord
    Text1.LinkTimeout = -1                 'Turns off Timeout error
    Text1.LinkMode = 0                     'Deactivates any existing links
    Text1.LinkTopic = "WinWord|System"     'Sets the Topic for the DDE link
    If Text1.Text <> "Text1" Then          'Checks if Text box has default text
        Text1.LinkItem = "SysItems"        'Sets the Item for the DDE link
    ElseIf Text1.LinkItem = "SysItems" Then        'Checks the setting of LinkItem
        Text1.LinkItem = "Topics"          'Sets the Item for the DDE link
    ElseIf Text1.LinkItem = "Topics" Then  'Checks the setting of LinkItem
        Text1.LinkItem = "Formats"         'Sets the Item for the DDE link
    End If
    Text1.LinkMode = 2                     'Opens a manual link with Winword
    Text1.LinkRequest                      'Updates the Text1 text box
    Exit Sub                               'Exits sub
OpenWinWord:
    If Err = 282 Then                      'Checks if WinWord wasn't in memory causing
        x = Shell("Winword.exe", 3)        'the error making it necessary to start
        Resume Startup                     'Winword. Returns to the program's beginning
    Else
        Error Err                          'Forces display of error message
    End If
End Sub
```

Description

A LinkRequest method transfers a source item's contents to a control in a linked application. When the control is a picture box, the Picture property is updated by the item. If the control is a text box, the contents of the Text property change to match the item. With a label box, the Caption property is modified to contain the item's text.

In the example syntax, the LinkRequest method displays a list of the available items for a DDE conversation with the System topic when the user presses the Command1 command button. If the user presses the command button a second time, the LinkRequest method returns the name and path of the open documents in WinWord. When the user presses the Command1 command button a third time, the LinkRequest method returns the clipboard formats supported by Word for Windows.

The LinkTopic Property

The LinkTopic property of a control indicates the topic to use for the DDE link. Each topic serves as a unique identifier along with the name of the application with which the link is being established. This topic may not be changed while the link is active. In the example syntax, the topic is set to System so that the different items available for that topic may be displayed in the text box with the LinkRequest method.

The LinkItem Property

The LinkItem property of the control determines exactly where the LinkRequest method obtains the data to insert into the control. A LinkItem may be changed at runtime so that each time that a LinkRequest method is used, the contents of another source are inserted in the control. Not setting the LinkItem property of the control generates an error. In the example syntax, the LinkItem is changed twice, reflecting the current contents of the Text property of the Text1 text box.

The LinkMode Property

You establish a manual or notify link between a control and another application for two possible reasons. If the other application is only capable of supporting a manual DDE link, then this is the only means of establishing the link. Even if the application supports automatic linking, setting a manual or notify link makes sense if there is a lot of data transmitted. For example, extensive graphics that change constantly can take an appreciable amount of time to update. Letting the user choose when to update (or automatically updating during idle times) makes for a more responsive application than one that tries to keep current at all times.

Example

The LinkRequest method in the menuLink_Click routine updates both the text box's and the picture's links.

Comments

Use the System topic with the items listed in Tables 25-22, 25-23, and 25-24 to discover what items are available for the LinkRequest method to obtain information from.

LINKSEND METHOD

Objects Affected

Check	Clipboard	Combo	Command	CommonDlg
Data	Debug	Dir	Drive	File
Form	Frame	Grid	Image	Label
Line	List	MDI Form	Menu	OLE
Option	▶ Picture	Printer	Screen	Scroll
Shape	Text	Timer		

Purpose

The LinkSend method transfers the contents of a picture box on a form to another application. This method is only useful when the DDE link is established by another application that functions as the destination and your application is the source. This method is necessary for updating the destination application, no matter whether the link created is automatic, manual, or notify. Table 25-22 summarizes the arguments of the LinkSend method.

General Syntax

`[form!]Name.LinkSend`

Argument	Description
form	Name property of the form
Name	Name property of control

Table 25-22 Arguments of the LinkSend method

Example Syntax

```
Sub Form_LinkExecute (CmdStr As String, Cancel As Integer)
    Cancel = False                       'Command was accepted
    Select Case UCase$(cmdStr)           'Makes all of the text of command upper case
        Case "[UPDATE]"                  'Checks if command string is UPDATE
            Picture1.LinkTimeout = -1    'Turns off timeout error
            Picture1.LinkSend            'Updates the contents of other application
        Case Else                        'Otherwise
            Cancel = True                'Command was rejected
    End Select
End Sub
```

Description

The LinkSend method transfers the contents of the picture box control to the linked destination application. All links, even automatic ones, need to have LinkSend to transfer the picture box picture. Without this design, a picture box would try to update an automatic link for each and every pixel changed—a lengthy process! Visual Basic requires you to explicitly notify DDE destinations when your picture box has finished changing.

In the example syntax, the LinkSend method updates the linked application that sends the Update command through the DDE link. The item on the destination application receives the updated picture. This is an important possible use of this method that determines when a picture on another application needs updating.

The LinkExecute Event

The LinkExecute event is an excellent location for the LinkSend method to update the picture on a destination application. In the example syntax, the word UPDATE resets the contents of the picture on the destination application that sends the command. This allows the other application to indicate when the picture on it needs to be updated.

Example

The form's LinkExecute method makes a provision to LinkSend the picture.

LINKTIMEOUT PROPERTY

Objects Affected

Check	Clipboard	Combo	Command	CommonDlg
Data	Debug	Dir	Drive	File
Form	Frame	Grid	Image	▶ Label
Line	List	MDI Form	Menu	OLE
Option	▶ Picture	Printer	Screen	Scroll
Shape	▶ Text	Timer		

Purpose

The LinkTimeout property of a picture box, text box, or label indicates how long a Visual Basic application needs to wait for a response from another application involved in a DDE link. A control's LinkTimeout property only affects the operation of a DDE link in which the control is the destination and the other application is the source. Table 25-23 summarizes the arguments of the LinkTimeout property.

General Syntax

```
[form!]Name.LinkTimeout [ = duration%]
```

Argument	Description
form	Name property of the form
Name	Name property of the picture box, text box, or label control
duration%	The interval specified for the Timeout property in tenths of seconds; default 50 = 5 seconds

Table 25-23 Arguments of the LinkTimeout property

Example Syntax

```
Sub Form_Load ()
Startup:
    On Error GoTo OpenWinWord         'Sets error trap to OpenWinWord
    Label1.LinkTimeout = 100          'Sets Timeout interval to 100 seconds
    Label1.LinkMode = 0               'Deactivate any active link
    Label1.LinkTopic = "WinWord|System" 'Sets the Topic for the DDE link
    Label1.LinkMode = 2               'Opens a manual link with Winword
    Label1.LinkTimeout = -1           'Turns off timeout interval
    Label1.LinkExecute "[FileClose 2]" 'Closes the current file without saving it
    Label1.LinkExecute "[FileOpen]"   'Opens the file open dialog box
    Exit Sub
OpenWinWord:
    If Err = 282 Then                 'Checks if WinWord wasn't in memory causing
        x = Shell("Winword.exe", 3)   'the error making it necessary to start
        Resume Startup                'Winword. Returns to the program's beginning
    Else
        Error Err                     'Forces display of error message.
    End If
End Sub
```

Description

The LinkTimeout property of a picture box, text box, or label sets the length of time that a link remains open without a response from the other application. The control argument of a LinkTimeout property expression contains the Name property of the control.

A control's LinkTimeout property may be adjusted to account for the time that the other application needs to process the commands sent through the link. An error generates if there is no response from the other application in the time specified by the LinkTimeout property of the control.

A control's LinkTimeout property duration% argument defines the amount of time to wait. The duration is measured in tenths of a second, so the default value of 50 represents 5 seconds. The maximum value for duration% is 65535, or about 1 hour 49 minutes. Changing the duration% variable to -1 ensures that the control will wait indefinitely for the other application to respond, or for the user to press (ESC). The example syntax changes the Timeout property of the label control both before and after establishing the link. First, the value is increased from 50 to 100. Next, the Timeout property is modified to -1, disabling the timeout error.

In the example syntax, the Timeout property is initially 100. This routine turns off the timeout error by changing the LinkTimeout property to -1. This prevents the display of any errors created by the opening of the FileOpen dialog box if the Visual Basic application is not closed quickly enough.

The LinkExecute Method

When the LinkExecute method sends commands through the link to the source application, the value of the Timeout property determines how long the destination application will wait for a response from the source application. In cases where the source application needs extra time to process the commands sent to it with the LinkExecute method, increase the LinkTimeout property setting to reflect this need. The example syntax completely disables the LinkTimeout property by setting it to -1. This prevents the timeout error from being generated and allows the processing of the End Statement. This is necessary because WinWord's FileOpen command displays a dialog box that normally prevents the processing of the commands that follow the LinkExecute command.

Example

The Form_Load routine sets the LinkTimeout of the picture box to a high number, just in case the picture takes a long time to evaluate.

Comments

The Timeout property of one control does not affect the Timeout property of another control.

LINKTOPIC PROPERTY

Objects Affected

Check	Clipboard	Combo	Command	CommonDlg
Data	Debug	Dir	Drive	File
Form	Frame	Grid	Image	▶ Label
Line	List	MDI Form	Menu	OLE
Option	▶ Picture	Printer	Screen	Scroll
Shape	▶ Text	Timer		

Purpose

The LinkTopic property defines the application name and subject that uniquely identify a DDE link between a form, picture box, text box, or label and another application. A source form's LinkTopic specifies the topic name that another application must use to create a DDE link with the form. When the control is the destination of a DDE link, the LinkTopic determines the source application and topic of the link. Since a DDE link is uniquely identified by the application name and the topic, the LinkTopic property may not be changed on an active link. Table 25-24 summarizes the arguments of the LinkTopic property, and Tables 25-25 and 25-26 give the meanings of the link$ argument.

General Syntax

```
[form.]LinkTopic [ = link$]
[form!]Name.LinkTopic [ = link$]
```

Argument	Description
form	Name property of the form
Name	Name property of the label, text box, or picture box
link$	Application name and topic of a DDE link

Table 25-24 Arguments of the LinkTopic property

link$	Description
Application Name	The name of the application's executable file without the .EXE extension
Topic	The general location of the data in the application, like the file name

Table 25-25 Two parts of the link$ argument of the LinkTopic property for a destination control

link$	Description
Topic	The application's project file (*.MAK without the extension) from within Visual Basic
	The application's executable file (*.EXE without the extension) when compiled

Table 25-26 Link$ argument of LinkTopic property for a source form

Example Syntax

```
Sub Command1_Click ()
Startup:
    On Error Goto OpenApp
    If Text1.Text = "Winword" Then              'Checks the current contents of textbox
        Text1.LinkTopic = "Winword|System"      'Changes the DDE Link Topic
        App$ = "Winword.exe"                    'Defines App$ Text variable
    ElseIf Text1.Text = "Q+E" Then              'Checks the current contents of textbox
        Text1.LinkTopic = "QE|System"           'Changes the DDE Link Topic
        App$ = "QE.exe"                         'Defines App$ Text variable
    ElseIf Text1.Text = "Excel" Then            'Checks the current contents of textbox
        Text1.LinkTopic = "Excel|System"        'Changes the DDE Link Topic
        App$ = "Excel.exe"                      'Defines App$ Text variable
    Else
        End                                     'Ends Program
    End If
StartLink:
    Text1.LinkItem = "SysItems"                 'Changes the DDE Link Item
    Text1.LinkMode = 2                          'Establishes a link with the application
    Text1.LinkRequest                           'Updates the Text1 text box
OpenApp:
    If Err = 282 Then                           'Checks the err value
        x = Shell(App$, 3)                      'If the application was not in memory, then
        Resume StartLink                        'load the application
    Else
        Error Err                               'Forces display of error message
    End If
End Sub
```

964

Description

The LinkTopic property defines the application name and subject that uniquely identify a DDE link between a form, picture box, text box, or label and another application. There are two possible definitions of the link$ string argument in a LinkTopic property expression. A form's LinkTopic property sets the application name that another application must use to establish a DDE link. The LinkTopic property of a picture box, text box, or label includes the application name and the topic. These two elements are separated from each other by a vertical line (character code 124, the pipe symbol). The LinkTopic must be a string, and there is a limit of 255 characters for the LinkTopic definition.

In the example syntax, the LinkTopic consists of the application name followed by the topic System. This establishes a DDE link with the indicated application that is not dependent on any particular file. Additionally, the other application (WinWord, Excel, or Q+E) may be polled for the acceptable topics for a DDE link.

The LinkItem Property

The LinkItem property of the control determines the exact destination of the general information entered in the LinkTopic property. Unlike the LinkTopic property, the LinkItem property may be changed while a link is active. Some applications will allow the creation of a DDE link without a specific LinkItem. When the System topic is used, the LinkItem may be set to a variety of settings that are dependent upon the application on the other side of the link. The example syntax sets the LinkItem property to SysItems, which returns all of the possible items that may be chosen with the System topic.

The LinkMode Property

A LinkTopic property will work when the LinkMode property is set to automatic (1) or manual (2). Even though the LinkMode property establishes a valid link, the link will not work unless both the LinkTopic and LinkItem properties are set to valid elements of the other application. In the example syntax, the LinkMode property is a manual link so the programmer controls when to update the information to the text box with a LinkRequest method.

The Destination Control

The LinkTopic property identifies the portion of a DDE link that may not be changed without severing the link between the control and another application. An application name is normally the file name of the executable program without the extension. The LinkTopic property of a form identifies a Visual Basic application the Name property as the default setting. Each of the available topics may be obtained by setting the LinkTopic to "System" and the LinkItem to "Topics." Normally, the LinkTopic indicates the path and file name of the data file being accessed through the link.

The Source Form

A form's LinkTopic property determines the name that another application needs to establish a DDE link with this form. This is the name of the Visual Basic project (*.MAK) or executable (*.EXE) file without the extension, as summarized in Table 25-26. This property has no effect on the operation of a link in which one of the controls on the form establishes a DDE link with another application.

Example

The DDE project at the end of this chapter uses the LinkTopic quite extensively. The Form_Load, Form_Unload, and the MenuEdit_Click events all use the LinkTopic property to establish a DDE link.

Comments

Be careful that multiple DDE links between the same application do not create an infinite loop of updates. An example of this problem is if a source form is linked to another application and the text box on the same form is part of a destination link to the same application. An automatic link setup in both directions results in an infinite loop.

THE DDE PROJECT

Project Overview

The DDE project demonstrates each of the properties, methods, and events involved in setting up DDE links between applications. It does this in two distinct ways. First, it links some data entry text boxes on the main form to an Excel worksheet. It then uses Excel to chart the data and update a picture box on the form. This demonstrates a typical use for DDE as a way of setting up powerful front ends for other applications. The second demonstration of DDE is an elaboration of the Edit menu structure first discussed in Chapter 23, Using the Clipboard. You'll see how to put together a complete Edit menu that will let your users establish their own DDE links. You can cut, copy, paste, and paste link both the actual text or graphic information as well as the link information between your Visual Basic application and any other application that supports DDE.

Assembling the Project

1. Create a new form (the DDE form) and place on it the controls shown in Table 25-27.

Object	Property	Setting
Form	BackColor	&H00C0C0C0—Light Gray
	BorderStyle	1—Fixed Single
	Caption	"DDE Project"
	LinkMode	1—Source
	LinkTopic	"formMain"
Text	Alignment	1—Right Justify
	Index	0
	Name	textCogs
Text	Alignment	1—Right Justify
	Index	1
	Name	textCogs
Text	Alignment	1—Right Justify
	Index	2
	Name	textCogs
Text	Alignment	1—Right Justify
	Index	3
	Name	textCogs
Text	Alignment	1—Right Justify
	Index	0
	Name	textSales

(continued on next page)

Object	Property	Setting
Text	Alignment	1 – Right Justify
	Index	1
	Name	textSales
Text	Alignment	1 – Right Justify
	Index	2
	Name	textSales
Text	Alignment	1 – Right Justify
	Index	3
	Name	textSales
Label	Alignment	1 – Right Justify
	BackColor	&H00000000 – Black
	ForeColor	&H00FFFFFF – White
	Index	0
	Name	lablTotal
Label	Alignment	1 – Right Justify
	BackColor	&H00000000 – Black
	ForeColor	&H00FFFFFF – White
	Index	1
	Name	lablTotal
Label	Alignment	1 – Right Justify

Object	Property	Setting
	BackColor	&H00000000—Black
	ForeColor	&H00FFFFFF—White
	Index	2
	Name	lablTotal
Label	Alignment	1—Right Justify
	BackColor	&H00000000—Black
	ForeColor	&H00FFFFFF—White
	Index	3
	Name	lablTotal
Label	Alignment	1—Right Justify
	BackStyle	0—Transparent
	Caption	"Sales"
Label	Alignment	1—Right Justify
	BackStyle	0—Transparent
	Caption	"Cost Of Goods"
Label	Alignment	1—Right Justify
	BackStyle	0—Transparent
	Caption	"Total"
Label	Alignment	1—Right Justify
	BackStyle	0—Transparent

(continued on next page)

Object	Property	Setting
	Caption	"Graph"
Label	Alignment	1—Right Justify
	BackStyle	0—Transparent
	Caption	"Miscellaneous Text"
Label	Alignment	1—Right Justify
	BackStyle	0—Transparent
	FontBold	0—False
	Name	lablGraphLinkStatus
Label	Alignment	1—Right Justify
	BackStyle	0—Transparent
	FontBold	0—False
	Name	lablTextLinkStatus

Table 25-27 Elements of the DDE form

Name	Caption	Property	Setting
menuBar	&File	Index	0
menuFile	E&xit		
menuBar	&Edit	Index	1
menuEdit	Cu&t	Index	0
menuEdit	&Copy	Index	1

Name	Caption	Property	Setting
menuEdit	&Paste	Index	2
menuEdit	Paste &Link	Index	3
menuBar	&Link	Index	2
menuLink	&Automatic	Index	0
menuLink	&Manual	Index	1
menuLink	&Notify	Index	2
menuLink		Index	3
menuLink	&Update Links	Index	4

Table 25-28 Menu design parameters of the DDE project

2. Size and position the controls, as shown in Figure 25-1.

3. Enter the following code in the General Declarations section. This defines the constants used in the program, and then declares a module-level variable that holds the current LinkMode status as set by the Link menu.

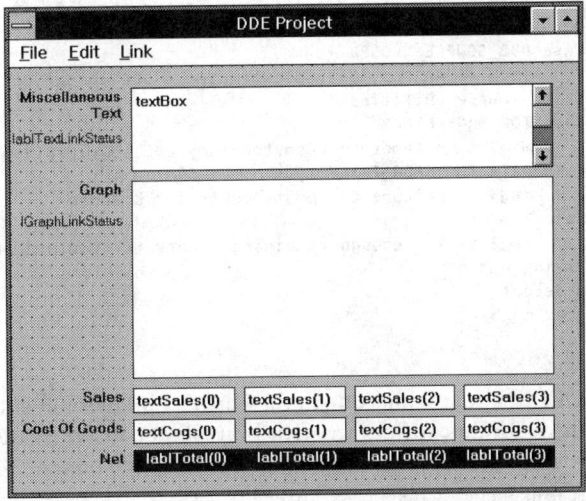

Figure 25-1 The DDE project during design

971

```
' Clipboard formats
Const CF_LINK = &HBF00
Const CF_TEXT = 1
Const CF_BITMAP = 2
Const CF_METAFILE = 3
Const CF_DIB = 8
Const CF_PALETTE = 9
' Link constants
Const NONE = 0
Const LINK_AUTOMATIC = 1
Const LINK_MANUAL = 2
Const LINK_NOTIFY = 3

' link error
Const WRONG_FORMAT = 1
Const DDE_SOURCE_CLOSED = 6
Const TOO_MANY_LINKS = 7
Const DATA_TRANSFER_FAILED = 8

' MousePointer
Const HOURGLASS = 11
Const DEFAULT = 0

Const THISAPPNAME = "CHP25"           'used when establishing links - application name
Const TOPICNAME = "formMain"          'used when establishing links - topic name

Dim MenuLinkModeCheck As Integer      'contains current linkmode setting on the link menu
```

4. Enter the following code in the General Declarations section. This procedure describes any errors that occur during a LinkError event.

```
Sub describeLinkError (linkerror, where)
    Select Case linkerror                           'describe the link error
        Case WRONG_FORMAT
            msg$ = "The linked application asked for data in an incompatible format when ⇐
using the " & where
        Case DDE_SOURCE_CLOSED
            msg$ = "An application attempted a DDE operation after this application ⇐
disabled its source abilities."
        Case TOO_MANY_LINKS
            msg$ = "Attempt to open too many DDE conversations - 128 maximum!"
        Case DATA_TRANSFER_FAILED
            msg$ = "Failure to update control " & where
        Case 11
            msg$ = "Not enough remaining memory to complete DDE link. Close applications ⇐
before trying again"
    End Select
    MsgBox msg$
End Sub
```

5. Enter the following code in the Form's LinkError event. This would occur only if the DDE link suffers an error that is not caused by the program itself. It calls a routine that describes the error in a message box.

```
Sub Form_LinkError (LinkErr As Integer)
    describeLinkError LinkErr, " the form."          'display error message
End Sub
```

972

6. Enter the following code in the Form_LinkExecute event. This event processes any command requests from other applications. (For example, another Visual Basic application you've written could execute a LinkExecute method over the DDE link.) It checks to see what the command is and either updates the other application's graph data, severs the graph link, or ends the program. If it doesn't recognize the command, it tells the other application by setting the Cancel return value to True.

```
Sub Form_LinkExecute (CmdStr As String, Cancel As Integer)
    Cancel = False                          'accept the command
    Select Case CmdStr
        Case "Update Graph"                 'other app wants the graph again
            pictGraph.LinkSend              'give them the graph
        Case "Sever Graph Link"             'other app doesn't want graph at all
            pictGraph.LinkMode = NONE        'cut the link
        Case "End"                          'other app wants this program to end
            End                             'end
        Case Else
            Cancel = True                   'oops! didn't recognize command
    End Select
End Sub
```

7. Enter the following code in the Form_Load event. This happens when the form first loads. It begins by setting up some of the controls' values. Notice the Tag properties for the textBox and pictGraph controls. These values hold the control's Name property for use in the Edit Cut and Edit Copy routines so the correct item can be placed in a source DDE link.

The routine then builds a simple spreadsheet model, listing four Quarters on the top and "Gross Sales," "COGS [cost of goods sold]," and "Net Sales" along the side. The interior of the spreadsheet is filled with the values of the textSales and textCogs text boxes a little later. The last row of the spreadsheet simply subtracts the cost of goods from total sales to find net sales. Note that the spreadsheet is sent to Excel as a tab and carriage-return delimited file. This is an easy way to send lots of information to the spreadsheet and is much easier and more elegant than simply using a LinkExecute command for each value and movement within the spreadsheet. (Note that this delimited format is the same as the grid control's Clip property.) After we build the string, we place it on the Clipboard.

We next execute a series of Excel macro commands with the LinkExecute method. These commands put the spreadsheet data into Excel, format the spreadsheet, and open up a new chart that graphs the data. Note that it doesn't really matter what control uses the method, as all we're doing is sending Excel the method's argument string. Unless you know Excel's macro language, you may have difficulties understanding each command. Refer to the Excel Function Reference guide for details. An easy way to create these LinkExecute arguments is to record a macro in Excel of what you want to do. When you are finished creating the macro, go to the macro sheet and copy the entire macro onto the Clipboard. Paste the macro into Visual Basic and put the LinkExecute method and a quote in front of the macro command and a quote at the end. If there are any quote characters inside the command, as in [ACTIVATE("Sheet1")], then add an extra set of quotes, as in [ACTIVATE(""Sheet1"")]. This trick should work with most macro languages.

Once we've created the spreadsheet and chart, we create some dummy data in the text boxes and create the actual DDE links. Each text box is linked to the appropriate cell in Excel's spreadsheet, and the labels are linked to the SUM formula that gives the Net Sales.

If an error occurred while creating any of these links, it will trigger the error handling routine. This first checks to see if Excel didn't respond to the DDE request, thus implying that it wasn't loaded. If so, the routine checks to see if it's already tried to load Excel. If it hasn't, it loads Excel. If it has, that implies that Excel is probably busy trying to finish loading, so it just gives it some more time with the DoEvents statement.

```
Sub Form_Load ()
    Screen.MousePointer = HOURGLASS
    TextBox.Text = "Type some text here to link to the other app"
    menuLink_Click 0                            'Set default to Automatic link
    TextBox.Tag = "textBox"                     'tags used in links
    pictGraph.Tag = "pictGraph"
    lablTextLinkStatus = "(unlinked)"

    TB = Chr$(9)                                'tab
    CR = Chr$(13) & Chr$(10)                    'carriage return/linefeed

                            'quick little spreadsheet for excel;
                            'tab and carriage return delimited for each cell and row
    s = " " & TB & "Q1" & TB & "Q2" & TB & "Q3" & TB & "Q4" & CR
    s = s & "Gross Sales" & CR
    s = s & "COGS" & CR
    s = s & "Net Sales" & TB & "= SUM(B2 - B3)" & TB & "= SUM(C2 - C3)"
    s = s & TB & "= SUM(D2 - D3)" & TB & "= SUM(E2 - E3)"
    Clipboard.SetText s                         'put spreadsheet data on clipboard

Startup:
    On Error GoTo OpenExcel                     'set trap
    textSales(0).LinkTopic = "Excel|Sheet1"     'blank worksheet
    textSales(0).LinkItem = "R1C1"              'arbitrary; doesn't matter what cell
    textSales(0).LinkMode = LINK_MANUAL         'set up link
    textSales(0).LinkExecute "[ACTIVATE(""Sheet1"")]"       'make sure  on the worksheet
    textSales(0).LinkExecute "[SELECT(""R1C1"")]"           'make Excel select upper left
    textSales(0).LinkExecute "[PASTE]"                      'make Excel paste in clipboard
    textSales(0).LinkExecute "[SELECT(""R1C1:R4C5"")]"      'make Excel select worksheet
    textSales(0).LinkExecute "[COLUMN.WIDTH(,,,3)]"         'make Excel set column widths
    textSales(0).LinkExecute "[SELECT(""R2C2:R4C5"")]"      'make Excel select worksheet
    textSales(0).LinkExecute "[FORMAT.NUMBER(""$#,##0_);($#,##0)"")]"   'currency
    textSales(0).LinkExecute "[SELECT(""R1C1:R4C5"")]"      'make Excel select worksheet
    textSales(0).LinkExecute "[NEW(2,1)]"                   'make Excel create a new chart item
                                            'make Excel format chart as a line chart
    textSales(0).LinkExecute "[FORMAT.MAIN(4,1,,,FALSE,FALSE,FALSE)]"
    textSales(0).LinkExecute "[LEGEND(TRUE)]"              'make Excel give it a legend
    textSales(0).LinkExecute "[SELECT(""Chart"")]"        'make Excel select entire chart
                                            'make Excel format all text on chart as Arial 8 point
```

```
    textSales(0).LinkExecute "[FORMAT.FONT(0,1,FALSE,""Arial"",8,FALSE,FALSE,FALSE,FALSE)]"
    For i = 0 To 3                                'iterate through all members
      textSales(i).LinkTopic = "Excel|Sheet1"     'set their link topics
      textCogs(i).LinkTopic = "Excel|Sheet1"
      lablTotal(i).LinkTopic = "Excel|Sheet1"
      textSales(i).LinkItem = "R2C" & Trim$(Str$(i + 2))      'R2C2, R2C3, R2C4, R2C5
      textCogs(i).LinkItem = "R3C" & Trim$(Str$(i + 2))       'R3C2, R3C3, R3C4, R3C5
      lablTotal(i).LinkItem = "R4C" & Trim$(Str$(i + 2))      'R4C2, R4C3, R4C4, R4C5
      textSales(i).LinkMode = LINK_MANUAL         'establish links
      textCogs(i).LinkMode = LINK_MANUAL
      lablTotal(i).LinkMode = LINK_MANUAL
      textSales(i).Text = Str$((i + 4) * 10000)   'dummy up some data
      textCogs(i).Text = Str$((i + 2) * 8345)     'more dummy data
    Next i
    pictGraph.LinkTimeout = 10000                 'graphics could take a while
    pictGraph.LinkTopic = "Excel|Chart1"          'topic is the new chart
    pictGraph.LinkMode = LINK_NOTIFY              'set up notify link
    pictGraph.LinkRequest                         'immediately update the chart
    lablGraphLinkStatus = "Notify Link"           'set label correctly
    Screen.MousePointer = DEFAULT                 'and we're done
Exit Sub

OpenExcel:                                        'error trap
    If Err = 282 Then                             'if it's not loaded,
      If AlreadyStarted = False Then              'and not waiting for it to finish loading
          X = Shell("EXCEL.EXE", 2)               'then load it!
          AlreadyStarted = True                   'make sure we don't try loading again
      End If
      DoEvents                                    'give it some time to load
      Resume Startup                              'and try the link again
    Else
      Error Err                                   'woops! something else went wrong....
    End If

End Sub
```

8. Enter the following code in the Form_Unload event. This shuts down all the links and sends a command to Excel to shut it down too.

```
Sub Form_Unload (Cancel As Integer)
    For i = 0 To 3                                'iterate through each member
      textSales(i).LinkMode = NONE               'sever the links
      textCogs(i).LinkMode = NONE
      lablTotal(i).LinkMode = NONE
    Next i
    pictGraph.LinkMode = NONE                     'deactivate any existing links
    pictGraph.LinkTopic = "Excel|System"          'talk to excel
    pictGraph.LinkMode = LINK_MANUAL              'set up the link
    pictGraph.LinkExecute "[EXIT]"                'and tell excel to exit
    DoEvents                                       'give it some time to respond
    TextBox.LinkMode = NONE                        'sever link
End Sub
```

9. Enter the following code in the General Declarations section. This code updates the labels that display the link status of the text box and picture box.

```
Sub labelLinkStatus ()
    Select Case pictGraph.LinkMode                      'update the graph label
        Case LINK_AUTOMATIC
            lablGraphLinkStatus.Caption = "Auto Link"
        Case LINK_MANUAL
            lablGraphLinkStatus.Caption = "Manual Link"
        Case LINK_NOTIFY
            lablGraphLinkStatus.Caption = "Notify Link"
        Case Else
            lablGraphLinkStatus.Caption = "(unlinked)"
    End Select
    Select Case TextBox.LinkMode                        'update the text box label
        Case LINK_AUTOMATIC
            lablTextLinkStatus.Caption = "Auto Link"
        Case LINK_MANUAL
            lablTextLinkStatus.Caption = "Manual Link"
        Case LINK_NOTIFY
            lablTextLinkStatus.Caption = "Notify Link"
        Case Else
            lablTextLinkStatus.Caption = "(unlinked)"
    End Select
End Sub
```

10. Enter the following code in the menuBar_Click event. This prepares the menus
    before opening them. Preparing the available menu commands like this helps the
    user by only displaying choices that actually apply. For example, this routine
    checks to see what kind of data is on the Clipboard. If the data would work with
    the control the user is on, it enables the Paste command. The routine systemati-
    cally goes through each possibility for the four menu commands. Doing this
    validity checking here also makes the coding easier in the actual Edit procedures,
    as we can be sure that the menu choice was appropriate given the data and the
    active control.

```
Sub menuBar_Click (Index As Integer)
    Select Case Index
        Case 0 ' ------------ File
        Case 1 ' ------------ Edit
            menuEdit(1).Enabled = False                   'Turn off all menu choices
            menuEdit(2).Enabled = False
            menuEdit(3).Enabled = False
            menuEdit(4).Enabled = False
            If Clipboard.GetFormat(CF_LINK) Then          'if there is link info on clipboard
                linkID = Clipboard.GetText(CF_LINK)       'find out what the link info is
                itemSeparator = InStr(linkID, "!")        'this separates topic from item
                If Left$(linkID, itemSeparator - 1) <> THISAPPNAME & "|" & TOPICNAME Then
                    link = True                           'another app's link; OK for linking
                End If
            End If
            If Clipboard.GetFormat(CF_TEXT) Then Text = True      'there's text on the clipboard
            If Clipboard.GetFormat(CF_BITMAP) Then pict = True    'there's a bitmap on clipboard
            If TypeOf Screen.ActiveControl Is PictureBox Then     'are we on a picture box?
                menuEdit(1).Enabled = True                'OK to cut picture
                menuEdit(2).Enabled = True                'OK to copy picture
                If pict Then                              'if there's a picture on the clipboard
                    menuEdit(3).Enabled = True            'OK to paste clipboard's picture
```

```
                If Link Then                                 'if the picture is linked,
                    menuEdit(4).Enabled = True               'OK to offer Paste Link for picture
                End If
            End If
        End If
        If TypeOf Screen.ActiveControl Is TextBox Then  'if we're on a text box,
            If Screen.ActiveControl.SelText <> "" Then    'and there is some text selected
                menuEdit(1).Enabled = True                'OK to cut text
                menuEdit(2).Enabled = True                'OK to copy text
            End If
            If Text Then                                  'if there's text on the clipboard
                menuEdit(3).Enabled = True                'OK to paste text into text box
                If Link And Screen.ActiveControl.Tag = "textBox" Then  'if there's a link and
                                                          'we're in the top text box,
                    menuEdit(4).Enabled = True            'OK to offer Paste Link for the text
                End If
            End If
        End If
        Case 2 ' ----------- Links
    End Select
End Sub
```

11. Enter the following code in the menuEdit_Click event. This event triggers when the user selects one of the four edit commands: Cut, Copy, Paste, and Paste Link. We know that the menuBar_Click event has only enabled menu commands that are appropriate for this context—for example, if we're on the picture control and Paste Link is enabled, then there is both graphics information and link information on the Clipboard.

Text and graphics use different methods with the Clipboard, so each edit routine first checks to see what kind of control is active: text box or picture box. Each routine then performs normal Clipboard operations, much as in the chapter project for Chapter 23, Using the Clipboard. The next few lines of each routine set up the link status.

Cut and Copy both set the proper link information on the Clipboard after they paste their data. The link information is the application name, the form topic, and the Name property of the control being copied. The Name property cannot be read at runtime, so we use the Tag property instead, having loaded the tag property with the correct name during the Form_Load procedure. The link status line for Paste simply terminates any link if there was one, because a regular paste does not include the link.

The Paste Link command does include the link status. In fact, it never pastes the actual data, letting the link transfer the data instead. It parses the Clipboard's link information to get the topic name and the item and then sets up the link with whatever link mode the user chose on the Link menu.

```
Sub menuEdit_Click (Index As Integer)
    Select Case Index
        Case 0 '********************************************* Cut
            If TypeOf Screen.ActiveControl Is TextBox Then     'on a text box?
                Clipboard.SetText Screen.ActiveControl.Text    'put text on clipboard
                Screen.ActiveControl.SelText = ""              'cut out selected text
```

(continued on next page)

(continued from previous page)

```
        ElseIf TypeOf Screen.ActiveControl Is PictureBox Then 'on a picture box?
            Clipboard.SetData Screen.ActiveControl.Picture      'put picture on clipboard
            Screen.ActiveControl.Picture = LoadPicture("")      'blank out picture
        End If
        itemName = Screen.ActiveControl.Tag                 'Tag has the control's Name
        Clipboard.SetText THISAPPNAME & "|" & TOPICNAME & "!" & itemName, CF_LINK
    Case 1 '********************************************** Copy
        If TypeOf Screen.ActiveControl Is TextBox Then      'on a text box?
            Clipboard.SetText Screen.ActiveControl.Text     'put text on clipboard
        ElseIf TypeOf Screen.ActiveControl Is PictureBox Then 'on a picture box?
            Clipboard.Clear                                 'get rid of any existing junk on clipboard
            Clipboard.SetData Screen.ActiveControl.Picture  'put picture on clipboard
        End If
        itemName = Screen.ActiveControl.Tag                 'Tag has the control's Name
        Clipboard.SetText THISAPPNAME & "|" & TOPICNAME & "!" & itemName, CF_LINK
    Case 3 '********************************************** Paste
        Screen.ActiveControl.LinkMode = NONE                'no link status
        If TypeOf Screen.ActiveControl Is TextBox Then      'on a text box?
            Screen.ActiveControl.SelText = Clipboard.GetText() 'put text from clipboard
        ElseIf TypeOf Screen.ActiveControl Is PictureBox Then 'on a picture box?
            Screen.ActiveControl.Picture = Clipboard.GetData() 'put picture from clipboard
        End If
    Case 4 '********************************************** Paste Link
        linkID = Clipboard.GetText(CF_LINK)          'get link information from clipboard
        itemSeparator = InStr(linkID, "!")           'this separates topic name from item name
        Screen.ActiveControl.LinkMode = NONE         'turn off any existing links
        Screen.ActiveControl.LinkTopic = Left$(linkID, itemSeparator - 1)
        Screen.ActiveControl.LinkItem = Mid$(linkID, itemSeparator + 1)
        Screen.ActiveControl.LinkMode = MenuLinkModeCheck  'link mode to what's on link menu
    End Select
    labelLinkStatus                                        'update labels with correct link status
End Sub
```

12. Enter the following code in the menuFile_Click routine. It ends the program. Note that there is only one command on the menu, so we don't even have to check to see which menu item was clicked.

```
Sub menuFile_Click (Index As Integer)
    End                                          'end the program
End Sub
```

13. Enter the following code in the menuLink_Click routine. This routine triggers whenever the user makes a choice on the Link menu. The first three options, Automatic, Manual, and Notify, are the three possible LinkModes to use when pasting in data. The fourth choice, Update Links, requests new information for both of the controls and then updates their link status labels.

```
Sub menuLink_Click (Index As Integer)
    Select Case Index
    Case 0, 1, 2   'link mode
        menuLink(0).Checked = False                  'turn off all the checkmarks
        menuLink(1).Checked = False
        menuLink(2).Checked = False
        menuLink(Index).Checked = True               'check the one the user clicked
        MenuLinkModeCheck = Index + 1                'and set the correct linkmode
```

```
        Case 4           'update links
            If TextBox.LinkMode <> NONE Then      'if there is a link for text box
              TextBox.LinkRequest                 'update it
            End If
            If pictGraph.LinkMode <> NONE Then    'if there is a link for picture box
              pictGraph.LinkRequest               'update it
            End If
            labelLinkStatus                       'update display of link status labels
      End Select
End Sub
```

14. Enter the following code in the pictGraph_LinkClose event. This triggers as a link is closing down; it simply updates the label caption to indicate the picture box's unlinked status.

```
Sub pictGraph_LinkClose ()
      lablGraphLinkStatus.Caption = "(unlinked)"        'no more link
End Sub
```

15. Enter the following code in the pictGraph_LinkError event. This triggers whenever there is an external DDE error. It calls a routine that displays an appropriate error message.

```
Sub pictGraph_LinkError (LinkErr As Integer)
      describeLinkError LinkErr, "picture box."        'show the error message
End Sub
```

16. Enter the following code in the pictGraph_LinkNotify event. This triggers whenever the LinkMode is set to LINK_NOTIFY (3) and the source data has changed. It changes the link status label's display to notify the user that new data is available.

```
Sub pictGraph_LinkNotify ()
      lablGraphLinkStatus.Caption = "(Data Available)"  'notify user new data available
End Sub
```

17. Enter the following code in the pictGraph_LinkOpen event. This triggers immediately before the link opens. (Note that the link is *not* yet open during this event.) This updates the label to let the user know a link is taking place. Sometimes links can take a while to complete, particularly for large graphics files.

```
Sub pictGraph_LinkOpen (Cancel As Integer)
      lablGraphLinkStatus.Caption = " linking "        'could take a while, eh?
End Sub
```

18. Enter the following code in the textBox_LinkError event. This triggers whenever there is an external DDE error. It calls a routine that displays an appropriate error message.

```
Sub textBox_LinkError (LinkErr As Integer)
      describeLinkError LinkErr, "text box."           'display the error message
End Sub
```

979

19. Enter the following code in the textBox_LinkNotify event. This triggers whenever the LinkMode is set to LINK_NOTIFY (3) and the source data has changed. It changes the link status label's display to notify the user that new data is available.

```
Sub textBox_LinkNotify ()
    LablTextLinkStatus.Caption = "(Data Available)"    'notify user new data available
End Sub
```

20. Enter the following code in the textCogs_Change event. This updates the Excel spreadsheet whenever the text in the text box changes. After updating the display, it requests updated totals information from Excel.

```
Sub textCogs_Change (Index As Integer)
    textCogs(Index).LinkPoke              'give excel the new data
    LablTotal(Index).LinkRequest          'and update the totals
End Sub
```

21. Enter the following code in the textCogs_GotFocus event. This selects the text in the text box.

```
Sub textCogs_GotFocus (Index As Integer)
    textCogs(Index).SelLength = 100       'select all text in the box
End Sub
```

22. Enter the following code in the textSales_Change event. This triggers whenever the text in the text box changes. It updates the Excel spreadsheet with the new data and then requests an update for the totals label.

```
Sub textSales_Change (Index As Integer)
    textSales(Index).LinkPoke             'give excel the new data
    LablTotal(Index).LinkRequest          'and update the totals
End Sub
```

23. Enter the following code in the textSales_GotFocus event. This selects the text in the text box.

```
Sub textSales_GotFocus (Index As Integer)
    textSales(Index).SelLength = 100      'select all text in the box
End Sub
```

How It Works

This program does two distinct things: it serves as a front end for an Excel spreadsheet and chart, and it implements a complete DDE-enabled Edit menu. Figure 25-2 shows the DDE project in action.

The Form_Load event takes care of most of the work for the Excel front end. It creates a small spreadsheet and pastes it into Excel with a LinkExecute method, and then formats the data and creates a chart out of it. The eight text boxes all have Poke methods in their Change events to send any updated data to Excel. The Picture box has a link to the Excel chart, and the Totals labels are also linked to the Excel spreadsheet. Changes to the text boxes are immediately reflected in the labels, but the picture box is set to a Notify link rather than an automatic one.

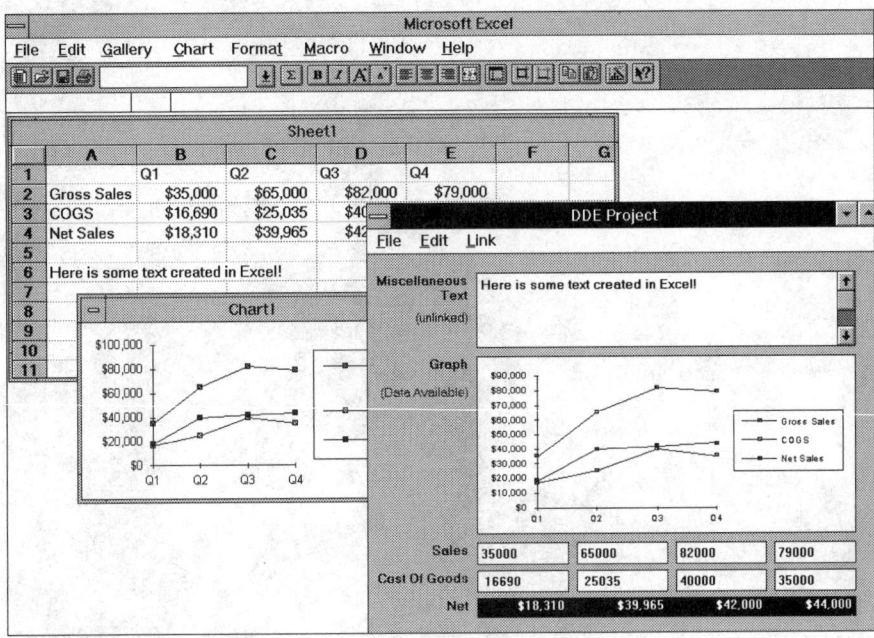

Figure 25-2 The DDE project in action

Choose the Update Links command from the Link menu to update the chart after it's changed.

The DDE-enabled menu is an extension of the chapter project from Chapter 23, Using the Clipboard. Much of the same functionality that applies to a non-DDE Edit menu applies equally well here. The menuBar_Click event determines what menu choices should be available, based on what control the user is on, data selection, and Clipboard contents. Only those choices that are applicable in this context get enabled.

The actual editing routines—copying, cutting, pasting, and linking—are really quite simple, generally only taking up a few lines of code. Using the Clipboard is almost identical to a non-DDE routine. The DDE part simply places the correct link information on the Clipboard (for cut and copy) and puts whatever link information is on the Clipboard into the control (for paste link).

The Link menu contains the three different kinds of links and also has a command that lets you update all the links in the application. Experiment with the different kinds of linking. If you have another DDE-aware application, like Excel, Lotus, Word, WordPerfect, AmiPro, or even Windows Write, you can see link information getting updated instantly across the applications. Try setting up an automatic link with both applications visible. When you change the data in the source application, the data in the project's form updates simultaneously. You can also set up Notify links; watch the labels on the side of the text box and picture change status as the link data changes.

26

OBJECT LINKING AND EMBEDDING (OLE)

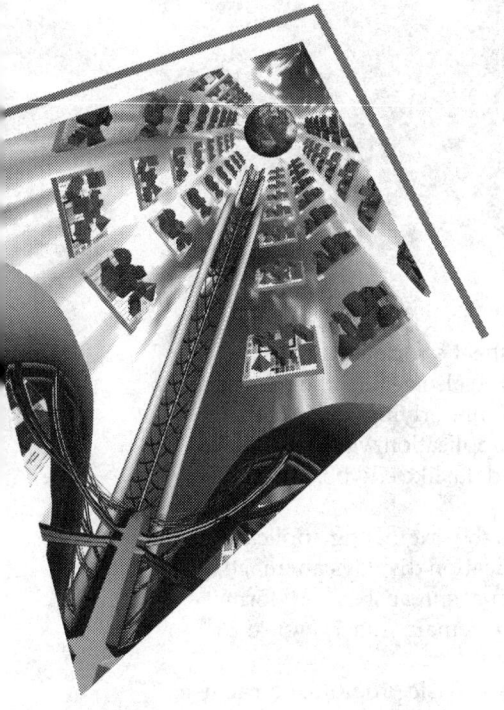

*O*bject Linking and Embedding (OLE) gives your application the power to directly use and manipulate another application's data in its native format. If the other application supports *OLE automation*, you may also be able to use its objects, properties, and methods just as you would a Visual Basic control. OLE 2.0 is one of the most significant new features of Visual Basic 3.0. It's also one of the most important additions to Windows and serves as the basis for creating a true object-oriented environment.

This chapter gives both an overview of OLE and a thorough discussion of every property, event, and function necessary for fully implementing OLE in your applications.

DIFFERENCES BETWEEN DDE AND OLE

Chapter 25, Dynamic Data Exchange (DDE), discussed how to share information between applications. Although there are many similarities between OLE and DDE (both allow you to share data and issue commands between two different applications) there are fundamental differences in how they do it and in how thoroughly the link is implemented.

When you use DDE, you are exchanging unformatted data. Your Visual Basic application needs to take the data and format it properly. For example, you might establish a link to a range of cells on a worksheet. Your application would need to process this data and place it in an appropriate Visual Basic

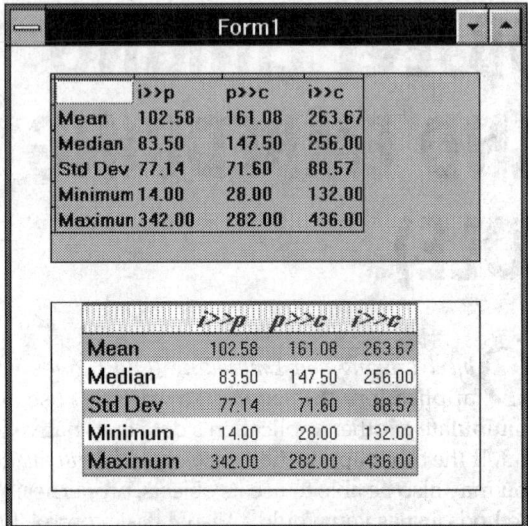

Figure 26-1 DDE exchanges unformatted data.
OLE exchanges fully formatted objects

control, like the grid control. The original spreadsheet's formatting will have nothing to do with what is displayed. In most cases you also get just the "finished product" (e.g., the resultant number) rather than the underlying object (e.g., the formula that calculated the resultant number). Your application would then need to provide all necessary means for manipulating the data, like edit boxes, a menu structure, toolbars, etc.

OLE, in contrast, actually transfers control back to the originating application. In our spreadsheet example, your Visual Basic application displays an image of the spreadsheet data exactly as it appears in the original spreadsheet. All formatting, grid lines, borders, coloring, and font selection remain intact. Figure 26-1 shows this.

When you edit the spreadsheet object in your Visual Basic program, you actually call up the original application and use its menus, toolbars, and other tools to do the editing. The OLE data contains the correct underlying objects (like formulas) so the information remains fully editable. Some applications also support *in-place activation*. This means that instead of the other application taking over the focus, it leaves the object embedded in your application and lets you edit the object in place.

OLE 1.0 AND OLE 2.0

Visual Basic 2.0 implemented the first version of OLE, version 1.0. This OLE specification enables an application to link and embed another application's data in its native format. It also lets the user double-click on the object to edit it; the originating application then loads the object, and the user edits the object in that application.

Visual Basic 3.0 is one of the first applications to support OLE 2.0. This advanced specification lets users link and embed objects just as in the 1.0 specification, but also lets users edit the object totally within the container application. The originating application, rather than starting up and loading the object for editing, actually replaces the container application's menus, toolbars, and palettes with its own. It makes it look as if the container application (i.e., your Visual Basic program) were doing all the work.

OLE 2.0 also opens up the exciting capabilities of OLE automation. This lets your Visual Basic applications use another program's object just as it would a Visual Basic control. For example, you could use a commercial word processor's spell checker rather than having to either write your own or do without spell checking.

OLE 2.0 compliant applications that support in-place activation allow the object's menu system (as provided by the host) to replace the container application's menus. Visual Basic does not support this important feature. This means that applications you write in Visual Basic will allow you to specify in-place activation, but you'll have to create whatever application-specific menus you need, and create the appropriate OLE automation commands for each menu choice. Note that the host toolbars will still automatically appear and "float" above your application if the host application supports them.

Visual Basic 3.0 fully implements OLE 2.0 as a container application (with the exception of the automatic menu replacement noted above). It does not fully implement OLE 2.0 as an originating, or host, application. This means that you cannot write Visual Basic applications that expose their own internal objects, and your application cannot take over another application to perform in-place editing within that application. You'll need to work with one of the C languages to fully implement OLE 2.0 as an originating application—at least until the next release of Visual Basic arrives!

LINKING AND EMBEDDING

Linking lets you use another application's data while leaving it available for other programs. The data remains on disk as a separate file, stored in its normal, native format. It is available for editing by the original application or any other application that can read it. The originating application can save the information to disk. The object in your Visual Basic program contains a link to the proper file (and specific range or set of objects in that file) and an image of what the data looks like for display.

Embedding lets you completely control the data. No other application can directly access the information. The object in your Visual Basic application contains the actual data as well as an image of what the data looks like for display. Although the Visual Basic OLE control contains the actual data, it does not automatically save it to disk. You can use the OLE's Action property to save and retrieve the information. Saving embedded OLE data saves the actual data, the name of the originating application, and an image of what the data looks like.

OLE AUTOMATION

Some OLE 2.0 capable programs allow *OLE automation*. This exposes that application's features to your Visual Basic program as properties and methods. This means that applications that support OLE automation behave almost exactly like Visual Basic custom controls.

CAUTION: Each application will expose its features differently. Refer to that application's documentation to determine the proper syntax. Many of the examples in this chapter use hypothetical sets of properties and methods for hypothetical applications. Your application will be different. OLE automation is still in its infancy, and will rapidly change and mature over the next few years.

For instance, let's assume that a spreadsheet application supports OLE automation. We've embedded a spreadsheet in Ole1, and you'd like to format the data displayed in cell R4C5:

```
Sub Command1_Click ()
    Ole1.Object.Select "R4C5"              'Select cell
    Ole1.Object.Bold True                  'Turn on Bold
    Ole1.Object.Border True, 2, TOP + LEFT 'Make 2 pt border on top & left
End Sub
```

This example uses the originating application (the spreadsheet) to format the information stored in the Ole1 control. See the Object property later in this chapter for more information about how to do this.

You can also use another application's properties and methods without using the OLE control. For example, let's say you want to perform a complex financial calculation that returns the number of periods for a loan. Rather than writing all the code necessary to perform the calculation, you could use the spreadsheet application's NPer function to do it for you. First, create an object that you can then manipulate by declaring a variable of type Object. Then Set that object appropriately with the CreateObject function:

```
Function NumPeriods (rate, payment, presentValue) As Integer
    Dim sheet As Object
    Set sheet = CreateObject("SPREADSHT.WORKSHEET")
    NumPeriods = sheet.NPer(rate, payment, presentValue)
End Function
```

Unlike using the OLE control as in the first example, this example does not display the spreadsheet anywhere, and your Visual Basic application doesn't contain any embedded data. The CreateObject function is covered more thoroughly in its own entry later in this chapter.

Many applications that support OLE automation also have *collections*. A collection is an object that contains zero or more objects of a similar type. For instance, each row in a spreadsheet might be called a Row object, and the collection of all rows on the spreadsheet might be called the Rows collection. Most collections will support the *count* property, which gives the total number of members in the collection. This makes it easy for your application to iterate through an entire collection. This next example takes our hypothetical spreadsheet and places the value of each cell in an array by iterating through the Rows collection:

```
Sub GetValues (worksheetName)
    Dim sheet As Object
    Set sheet = CreateObject("SPREADSHT.WORKSHEET")
    sheet.Activate worksheetName
    rows = sheet.Rows.Count - 1
    cols = sheet.Columns.Count - 1
    ReDim Vals(rows, cols)      'Global level array
    For i = 0 To rows
        For j = 0 To cols
                Vals(i, j) = sheet.Rows(i).Cell(j).Value
        Next j
    Next i
End Function
```

You cannot assume that an application has collections, or that any collections that it does have contain numeric subscripts, or that any subscripts it has are contiguous. You'll need to carefully examine that application's documentation for the details on how to access its objects and collections. See Chapter 3, Using Objects, for more information about collections.

All arguments to OLE automation objects are of the Variant data type, and all returned values are also Variants. Visual Basic will automatically convert a variable to a Variant if you attempt to assign a variable of a different data type to an OLE object argument. See Appendix B, Visual Basic Language Reference, for more details on variable types.

You may notice a similarity between OLE automation and the Data control discussed in Chapter 27, Data Access. The Data control exposes two properties, Database and Recordset, that have many properties and methods and several collections. Although the details on using these differ (for instance, you never have to use the CreateObject function), the principles are very similar.

SUMMARY

Table 26-1 lists the properties, events, and functions particular to the OLE control and to OLE automation.

Use This...		To Do This...
Action	Property	Perform an action on the object
ApplsRunning	Property	See whether the originating application is running
AutoActivate	Property	Determine how the OLE control reacts
AutoVerbMenu	Property	Determine whether the verb menu automatically pops up
Class	Property	Set the class name of the OLE object
CreateObject	Function	Create an object for OLE automation
Data	Property	Transfer data to nonautomation OLE applications
DataText	Property	Transfer text to nonautomation OLE applications
DisplayType	Property	Determine how the object displays
FileNumber	Property	Set the file number to save or load an OLE object
Format	Property	Set the format for Data and DataText transfers
GetObject	Function	Load an object for OLE automation
HostName	Property	Set a user-friendly name for your object
LpOleObject	Property	Read the memory location of the OLE object
Object	Property	Access the OLE control's object for automation
ObjectAcceptFormats	Property	List the formats an object accepts
ObjectAcceptFormatsCount	Property	Count the number of formats an object accepts
ObjectGetFormats	Property	List the formats an object returns
ObjectGetFormatsCount	Property	Count the number of formats an object returns
ObjectVerbFlags	Property	Determine the menu state of the object's verbs

Use This...		To Do This...
ObjectVerbs	Property	List the object's verbs
ObjectVerbsCount	Property	Count the number of the object's verbs
OleType	Property	Set or determine the type of object (link or embed)
OleTypeAllowed	Property	Determine the types of objects allowed
PasteOK	Property	Determine whether the Clipboard can be pasted into OLE
Resize	Event	Respond to a new size of object
SizeMode	Property	Set or determine how the object reacts to resize
SourceDoc	Property	Set or determine the file name of the source document
SourceItem	Property	Set the region or subset of data when creating an object
Updated	Event	React to a linked object's data changing
UpdateOptions	Property	Set or determine how OLE control reacts to changes
Verb	Property	Set or determine what action an object performs

Table 26-1 Properties, events, and functions of OLE

CONSTANT.TXT Values

Many of the properties and events of OLE use numeric values as arguments. Using constants rather than the literal value makes your code self-documenting, more readable, and easier to debug.

Microsoft provides a file, CONSTANT.TXT, that has many constant declarations defined for you. For smaller applications, it's probably easiest just to type the declarations in yourself. For larger applications, you'll find it much easier to read the text file into a new module.

To do this, create a new module by pulling down the File menu and choosing the New Module menu command. Then pull down the File menu again, and choose Load Text. This opens up a dialog box listing all text files in the current directory. CONSTANT.TXT should be in your main Visual Basic directory (default installation would place this in C:\VB). Simply choose CONSTANT.TXT to enter the entire file into your module. These constants will then be available throughout your application.

Table 26-2 lists the value of the constant, the CONSTANT.TXT constant name, and a brief description of what the constant means.

Value	CONSTANT.TXT	Description
Values of the setting% argument in the OLE's Action property		
0	OLE_CREATE_EMBED	Creates an embedded object
1	OLE_CREATE_LINK	Creates a linked object from the contents of a file
2		Reserved for future use
3		Reserved for future use
4	OLE_COPY	Copies the object to the Clipboard
5	OLE_PASTE	Copies data from the Clipboard to an OLE control
6	OLE_UPDATE	Retrieves the current data from the application
7	OLE_ACTIVATE	Opens an OLE object for an operation, such as editing
8		Reserved for future use
9	OLE_CLOSE	Closes an OLE object and terminates the connection
10	OLE_DELETE	Deletes the specified OLE object and frees the memory
11	OLE_SAVE_TO_FILE	Saves an OLE object to a data file
12	OLE_READ_FROM_FILE	Loads an OLE object from a data file
13		Reserved for future use
14	OLE_INSERT_OBJ_DLG	Displays the Insert Object dialog

Value	CONSTANT.TXT	Description
15	OLE_PASTE_SPECIAL_DLG	Displays the Paste Special dialog
16		Reserved for future use
17	OLE_FETCH_VERBS	Updates the list of verbs an object supports
18	OLE_SAVE_TO_OLE1FILE	Saves an object in the OLE1 file format
Meanings of the setting% argument for the AutoActivate property		
0	OLE_ACTIVATE_MANUAL	Not automatically activated
1	OLE_ACTIVATE_GETFOCUS	Automatically activated when receives focus
2	OLE_ACTIVATE_DOUBLECLICK	(Default) Automatically activated when double-clicked
Values of the setting% argument of the DisplayType property		
0	OLE_DISPLAY_CONTENT	(Default) Display actual formatted data
1	OLE_DISPLAY_ICON	Display icon as placeholder
The return values for the ObjectVerbFlags property		
&H0000	VF_ENABLED	The menu item should be enabled
&H0001	VF_GRAYED	The menu item should be grayed
&H0002	VF_DISABLED	The menu item should be disabled (but not grayed)
&H0008	VF_CHECKED	The menu item should be checked
&H0800	VF_SEPARATOR	The menu item is a separator bar

(continued on next page)

(continued from previous page)

Meanings of the values returned by the OleType property

0	OLE_LINKED	Object is linked
1	OLE_EMBEDDED	Object is embedded
3	OLE_NONE	OLE control does not contain an object

Meanings of the values of the OleTypeAllowed property

0	OLE_LINKED	Can only contain a linked object
1	OLE_EMBEDDED	Can only contain an embedded object
2	OLE_EITHER	(Default) Can contain either a linked or embedded object

Meanings of the setting% argument in the SizeMode property

0	OLE_SIZE_CLIP	(Default) Clips the object at OLE control's boundaries
1	OLE_SIZE_STRETCH	Sizes the object to exactly fill the OLE control
2	OLE_SIZE_AUTOSIZE	Resizes the OLE control to fit the object

Meanings of the Code argument in the Updated event

0	OLE_CHANGED	Object's data has changed
1	OLE_SAVED	Object has been saved by the originating application
2	OLE_CLOSED	File containing linked object's data closed by originating application
3	OLE_RENAMED	File containing linked object's data renamed by originating application

Value	CONSTANT.TXT	Description
Meanings of the setting% argument of the UpdateOptions property		
0	OLE_AUTOMATIC	(Default) Object updated each time link data changes
1	OLE_FROZEN	Object updated when originating application saves linked data
2	OLE_MANUAL	Object updated only by Action 6 (OLE_UPDATE)
Verbs that almost all objects support		
0	VERB_PRIMARY	Default verb for object
-1	VERB_SHOW	Open object for editing (in place if supported)
-2	VERB_OPEN	Open object for editing in its own window
-3	VERB_HIDE	Hide the originating application
-4	VERB_INPLACEUIACTIVATE	Leave object open for editing with user interface elements on screen when focus leaves
-5	VERB_INPLACEACTIVATE	Leave object open for editing when focus leaves

Table 26-2 The CONSTANT.TXT values that apply to OLE

The following reference section describes the details of each property, event, and function particular to OLE.

ACTION PROPERTY

Objects Affected

Check	Clipboard	Combo	Command	▶ CommonDlg
Data	Debug	Dir	Drive	File
Form	Frame	Grid	Image	Label

(continued on next page)

(continued from previous page)

Line	List	MDI Form	Menu	▶ OLE
Option	Picture	Printer	Screen	Scroll
Shape	Text	Timer		

Purpose

The Action property determines an action that the OLE control will take. It is not available at design time, and will write only at run time. Tables 26-3 and 26-4 summarize the arguments of the Action property.

General Syntax

`[form!]Name.Action = setting%`

Argument	Meaning
form	Name property of the parent form
Name	Name property of the control
setting%	Value indicating what action to perform

Table 26-3 Arguments of the Action property

setting%	CONSTANT.TXT	Description
0	OLE_CREATE_EMBED	Creates an embedded object
1	OLE_CREATE_LINK	Creates a linked object from the contents of a file
2		Reserved for future use
3		Reserved for future use
4	OLE_COPY	Copies the object to the Clipboard
5	OLE_PASTE	Copies data from the Clipboard to an OLE control
6	OLE_UPDATE	Retrieves the current data from the application

setting%	CONSTANT.TXT	Description
7	OLE_ACTIVATE	Opens an OLE object for an operation, such as editing
8		Reserved for future use
9	OLE_CLOSE	Closes an OLE object and terminates the connection
10	OLE_DELETE	Deletes the specified OLE object and frees the memory
11	OLE_SAVE_TO_FILE	Saves an OLE object to a data file
12	OLE_READ_FROM_FILE	Loads an OLE object from a data file
13		Reserved for future use
14	OLE_INSERT_OBJ_DLG	Displays the Insert Object dialog
15	OLE_PASTE_SPECIAL_DLG	Displays the Paste Special dialog
16		Reserved for future use
17	OLE_FETCH_VERBS	Updates the list of verbs an object supports
18	OLE_SAVE_TO_OLE1FILE	Saves an object in the OLE1 file format

Table 26-4 Values of the setting% argument in the OLE's Action property

Example Syntax

```
Sub menuEditCopy_Click ()
    Ole1.Action = OLE_COPY     'copies object to Clipboard
End Sub
```

Description

Use the Action property to make the OLE control do something with the object. Although Microsoft defines Action as a property, you may find it easier to consider it a method, since it acts on the control. It is similar in concept to the Action property for the Common Dialog box control discussed in Chapter 17, Dialog Boxes. The example syntax shows the Action property being used to copy the OLE control's object to the Clipboard.

There are a number of different actions that you can take. Note that each of these Action constants is defined in CONSTANT.TXT. See the discussion in the Summary section at the beginning of this chapter for details on how to use these constants.

0, OLE_CREATE_EMBED

This creates an embedded object. First set the Class property to the kind of object you'll be embedding (such as a CorelDRAW object, or an Excel Worksheet). The possible values for the Class property vary with each system depending on what applications are installed. Then set the OleTypeAllowed property to either 1 (embedded) or 2 (either linked or embedded). Make sure that the executable file associated with the class name (for example, CORELDRW.EXE) is either currently running or in the system's path.

1, OLE_CREATE_LINK

This creates a linked OLE object from a file. First set the OleTypeAllowed to 0 (linked) or 2 (either linked or embedded). Then set the SourceDoc property to the full path name of the file from which to create the object. You may also specify SourceItem (for example, a spreadsheet range) if the application creating the object supports it. Make sure the executable file associated with SourceDoc is either active or in the system's path.

4, OLE_COPY

This copies the object to the Clipboard. All the data and link information associated with the object are automatically placed on the Clipboard. This makes it simple to implement an Edit Copy command. Both linked and embedded objects may be copied.

5, OLE_PASTE

This copies data from the Clipboard to an OLE control. First set the OleTypeAllowed property properly; 2 (either linked or embedded) gives you the most flexibility. Check to see if the data on the Clipboard can be pasted with the PasteOK property (see PasteOK for details). If it can, then execute the OLE_PASTE action. You can then check on the success of the paste operation by checking the OleType property to make sure it returns either linked (0) or embedded (1); if it returns none (3) you know the paste has failed.

You can actually give your user the most flexibility by displaying the Paste Special dialog box (Action = 15, OLE_PASTE_SPECIAL_DLG) rather than by directly using OLE_PASTE. The dialog box lets your user specify whether they want to link or embed during the paste.

6, OLE_UPDATE

This retrieves the current data from the application that supplied the object. It displays the updated data as a picture in the OLE control. The originating application updates the picture, and it displays in its native format.

7, OLE_ACTIVATE

This opens an OLE object for an operation such as editing, playing a sound file, or some other operation the object's application supports. First set the Verb property to the operation that you want to have happen when the OLE object is activated. There are some verbs that every application supports (like edit), and others that are specific to each originating application. You can access these with the ObjectVerbs property; see Verbs, ObjectVerbs, and ObjectVerbsCount properties for more details. If AutoActivate is set to 2 (Double Click), then double-clicking the OLE control will automatically activate the object with the default verb.

9, OLE_CLOSE

This closes an OLE object and cuts the connection with the originating application. It applies to embedded objects only; linked objects cannot be "closed."

10, OLE_DELETE

This deletes the object and frees the memory used for it. OLE objects are automatically deleted when a form closes or when an object is updated to a new object; this action lets you do this under program control as well.

11, OLE_SAVE_TO_FILE

This saves an OLE object to a data file. First set the FileNumber property to the file number of an open binary file. If the OleType is 0, linked, then only the link information and an image for display is saved to disk. If OleType is 1, embedded, then the actual data is stored along with the name of the originating application and a display image. See the entry for the FileNumber property for an example.

12, OLE_READ_FROM_FILE

This loads an OLE object from a data file created using the OLE_SAVE_TO_FILE Action. First set the FileNumber property to the file number of the open binary file that contains the data. See FileNumber for an example. You should then issue an OLE_UPDATE to synchronize the Ole control with the originating application.

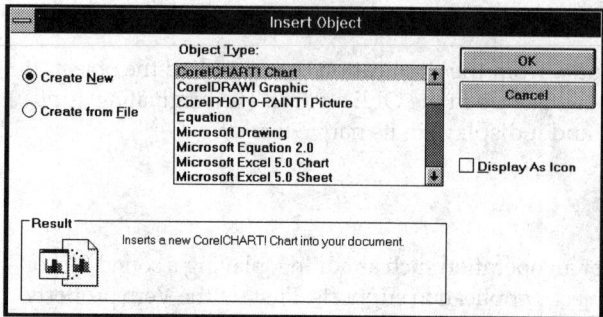

Figure 26-2 The Insert Object dialog box brought up by
Action 14, OLE_INSERT_OBJ_DLG

14, OLE_INSERT_OBJ_DLG

This displays the Insert Object dialog box. This dialog box allows the user to create an OLE object by specifying type (linked or embedded) and the originating
application. Figure 26-2 illustrates what the insert dialog box looks like.

15, OLE_PASTE_SPECIAL_DLG

This displays the Paste Special dialog box. This allows the user to paste an object
from the Clipboard into the Ole control. The user can specify the type of object
(linked or embedded) with the dialog box. Figure 26-3 illustrates what the Paste
special dialog box looks like.

17, OLE_FETCH_VERBS

This updates the list of verbs an object supports. This is useful if the object has
changed since you last determined the verbs, such as after the user pastes a new
object into the OLE control.

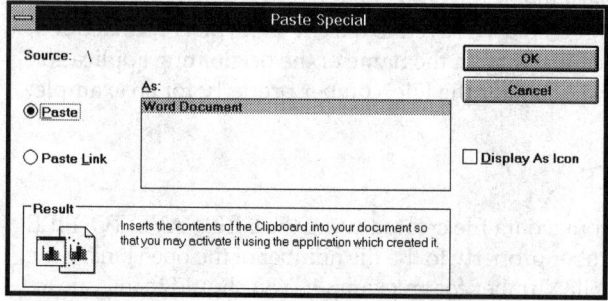

Figure 26-3 The Paste Special dialog box brought up
by Action 15, OLE_PASTE_SPECIAL_DLG

18, OLE_SAVE_TO_OLE1FILE

This saves an object in the older OLE 1.0 file format. OLE 2.0 is a new specification, and many applications may only support OLE 1.0.

Example

The formInfo project at the end of this chapter uses the Action property extensively; virtually every OLE activity features some use of Action.

APPISRUNNING PROPERTY

Objects Affected

Check	Clipboard	Combo	Command	CommonDlg
Data	Debug	Dir	Drive	File
Form	Frame	Grid	Image	Label
Line	List	MDI Form	Menu	▶ OLE
Option	Picture	Printer	Screen	Scroll
Shape	Text	Timer		

Purpose

The AppIsRunning property lets you determine whether the application that created the OLE object is currently running. It is not available at design time, and is read-only at runtime. Table 26-5 summarizes the arguments of the AppIsRunning property.

General Syntax

`[form!]Name.AppIsRunning`

Argument	Meaning
form	Name property of the parent form
Name	Name property of the control

Table 26-5 Arguments of the AppIsRunning property

999

Example Syntax

```
Sub menuEditCopy_Click ()
    If Not Ole1.AppIsRunning Then
        Ole1.Action = OLE_ACTIVATE
    End If
    Ole1.Action = OLE_COPY
End Sub
```

Description

Use the AppIsRunning property to determine whether the application that created the OLE object is currently running. If it is not, you can start it by using the OLE_ACTIVATE action. AppIsRunning returns a Boolean value: True means the application is running, False means it is not. The example syntax first checks to see whether the originating application is running before copying Ole1's object to the Clipboard.

You can set the Verb property before activating an application to control how the host application activates: hidden, exposed, or in-place.

Example

The formInfo project at the end of this chapter checks the AppIsRunning property in the menuEdit_Click event and printInfo procedure before performing additional operations on the OLE object.

AUTOACTIVATE PROPERTY

Objects Affected

Check	Clipboard	Combo	Command	CommonDlg
Data	Debug	Dir	Drive	File
Form	Frame	Grid	Image	Label
Line	List	MDI Form	Menu	▶ OLE
Option	Picture	Printer	Screen	Scroll
Shape	Text	Timer		

Purpose

Use the AutoActivate property to set how an OLE control automatically reacts when double-clicked or given the focus. Tables 26-6 and 26-7 summarize the arguments and values of the AutoActivate property.

General Syntax

```
[form!]Name.AutoActivate [ = setting%]
```

Argument	Meaning
form	Name property of the parent form
Name	Name property of the control
setting%	Value determines the reaction when double-clicked or given focus

Table 26-6 Arguments of the AutoActivate function

setting%	CONSTANT.TXT	Meaning
0	OLE_ACTIVATE_MANUAL	Not automatically activated
1	OLE_ACTIVATE_GETFOCUS	Automatically activated when receives focus
2	OLE_ACTIVATE_DOUBLECLICK	(Default) Automatically activated when double-clicked

Table 26-7 Meanings of the setting% argument for the AutoActivate property

Example Syntax

```
Sub Check1_Click ()
    If Check1.Value = True Then
        Ole1.AutoActivate = OLE_ACTIVATE_DOUBLECLICK
    Else
        Ole1.AutoActivate = OLE_ACTIVATE_GETFOCUS
    End If
End Sub
```

Description

The AutoActivate property determines how an OLE control reacts when it receives the focus or is double-clicked. The default behavior in Visual Basic, and for most other applications, is to activate when double-clicked. Originating applications that support in-place editing might work more naturally if they are activated when the control receives the focus. It might also be appropriate to handle activation manually, and thus turn off AutoActivate. The example syntax shows how the user can control this by turning a check box on and off.

What happens when the application is activated depends on the Verb property. The default for an OLE control's Verb property is to use the originating application's default verb. This may be Edit (for things like spreadsheets and wordprocessors) or something like Play (for a multimedia application). You can also set the verb property yourself, which would change the action taken when activated.

The double-click event does not get passed through to the OLE control if AutoActivate is set to 2, OLE_ACTIVATE_DOUBLECLICK. If you need to activate the object manually when AutoActivate is set to 0, OLE_ACTIVATE_MANUAL, use Action property 7 (OLE_ACTIVATE). Note that each of these AutoActivate constants is defined in CONSTANT.TXT. See the discussion in the Summary section at the beginning of this chapter for details on how to use these constants.

Example

The formInfo project at the end of this chapter leaves AutoActivate set to the default setting of OLE_ACTIVATE_DOUBLECLICK for each of the three OLE containers.

AUTOVERBMENU PROPERTY

Objects Affected

Check	Clipboard	Combo	Command	CommonDlg
Data	Debug	Dir	Drive	File
Form	Frame	Grid	Image	Label
Line	List	MDI Form	Menu ▶ OLE	
Option	Picture	Printer	Screen	Scroll
Shape	Text	Timer		

Purpose

Set the AutoVerbMenu property to True to automatically pop up a menu containing the object's verbs when the user clicks the object with the right mouse button. Table 26-8 lists the arguments of the AutoVerbMenu property.

General Syntax

```
[form!]Name.AutoVerbMenu [ = boolean%]
```

Argument	Meaning
form	Name property of the parent form
Name	Name property of the control
boolean%	True = pop up menu; False = do not pop up menu

Table 26-8 Arguments of the AutoVerbMenu property

Example Syntax

```
Sub Form_Load ()
    Ole1.AutoVerbMenu = True
End Sub
```

Description

Use the AutoVerbMenu property to determine the reaction your OLE object has to being clicked with the right (or nondefault) mouse button. Each OLE object has some commands (or *verbs*) that can execute on it. For example, a sound application might have Edit, Play, Record, Erase, Rewind, and Fast Forward. If AutoVerbMenu is set to True, clicking the OLE object with the right mouse button would then bring up a menu listing each of these verbs. Visual Basic will automatically execute the appropriate action when the user clicks on one of the menu choices. The example syntax turns on AutoVerbMenu when the form loads. Figure 26-4 shows what a typical menu looks like.

Visual Basic automatically updates the AutoVerbMenu before displaying it because the verbs available may change depending on what data the object contains. If AutoActivateMenu is set to True, no Click or MouseDown events from the menu get passed through to the control.

Example

The formInfo project at the end of this chapter uses the Form_Load event to set AutoVerbMenu to True for two of the OLE containers, but sets it to False for the third container (the one that holds the sales talk document). The third container's MouseDown event builds up a custom pop-up menu to show how to gain greater control over what is displayed in the pop-up menu.

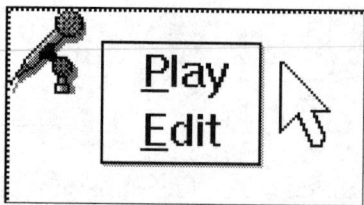

Figure 26-4 Typical menu
brought up by AutoVerbMenu

CLASS PROPERTY

Objects Affected

Check	Clipboard	Combo	Command	CommonDlg
Data	Debug	Dir	Drive	File
Form	Frame	Grid	Image	Label
Line	List	MDI Form	Menu ▶	OLE
Option	Picture	Printer	Screen	Scroll
Shape	Text	Timer		

Purpose

Use the Class property to determine or set the class name of an embedded OLE object. Table 26-9 lists the arguments of the Class property, and Table 26-10 lists some common Class names.

General Syntax

```
[form!]Name.Class [ = className$]           'for OLE 1.0 compliant applications
[form!]Name.Class [ = "appName.objType"]    'for OLE 2.0 compliant applications
```

Argument	Meaning
form	Name property of the parent form
Name	Name property of the control
className$	Class name of the object

Argument	Meaning
appName	Name the originating application is registered as
objType	Type of object the originating application supports

Table 26-9 Arguments of the Class property

className$	Meaning
CDraw	CorelDRAW drawing
CorelChart	CorelChart chart
Equation	MS Equation
ExcelChart	MS Excel Chart
ExcelMacrosheet	MS Excel Macro
ExcelWorksheet	MS Excel Worksheet
MSDraw	MS Draw drawing
MSGraph	MS Graph chart
Package	Object contained by the Package applet
PBrush	MS Paint Brush
PhotoPaint	Corel Paint
SoundRec	MS Sound Recorder WAV file
WordArt	MS Word Art
WordDocument	MS Word for Windows document

Table 26-10 Common class names (OLE 1.0 compliant)

Example Syntax

```
Sub Command1_Click
    Ole1.Class = "ExcelWorksheet"
    Ole1.SourceDoc = "C:\EXCEL\Q1TOTALS.XLS"
    Ole1.SourceItem = "R1C1:R27C14"
    Ole1.Action = OLE_ACTIVATE
End Sub
```

Description

Each OLE object has a *class name* that identifies the program that created it, and if a program can create different kinds of objects, the type of object. For example, Excel can create three different kinds of objects: worksheets, charts, and macros. The example syntax shows how to fully specify a portion of an Excel Worksheet with Class, SourceDoc, and SourceItem before activating it with the Action property.

This property is set automatically whenever you create an object at runtime or design time with the Insert Object or Paste Special dialog boxes, and at runtime when an object gets pasted from the Clipboard.

The class names illustrated in Table 26-10 are all written to the OLE 1.0 specification. OLE 2.0, with its advanced OLE automation features, has an extended naming convention:

```
className$ = "applicationName.objectType"
```

As applications get updated to the OLE 2.0 specification over the next few years, their class names will change from the existing OLE 1.0 standard. Thus, Excel 5.0 has class names like "Excel.Worksheet" rather than "ExcelWorksheet."

You can find out what class names are registered in your system by clicking on the combo box's ellipses (...) for the Class property in the properties box in Visual Basic. Figure 26-5 shows the ellipses about to be clicked by the mouse, and Figure 26-6 shows what the dialog box looks like. You'll note that the class name is a short (sometimes cryptic) abbreviation. The Insert Object dialog brings up a more descriptive, user friendly name. It finds these longer names in the [embedding] section of the WIN.INI file in the Windows directory. If you need to use these longer names in your code, you can access the WIN.INI file with the GetProfileString API call. See Appendix D, Windows API, for a description of this call. Also refer to this book's companion volume *The Waite Group's Visual Basic How To, 2nd Edition*, for an in-depth discussion of this and many other highly useful API calls.

Example

The cmndGraph_Click and cmndReport_Click events both set the Class property before creating embedded OLE objects. The printInfo procedure reads the Class name when it prints out pertinent information about the embedded OLE object. Finally, the Edit Paste routine in the menuEdit_Click event sets the Class property

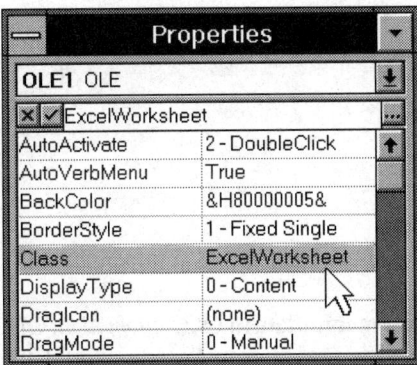

Figure 26-5 The mouse is about to click on the ellipses to bring up the Class names...

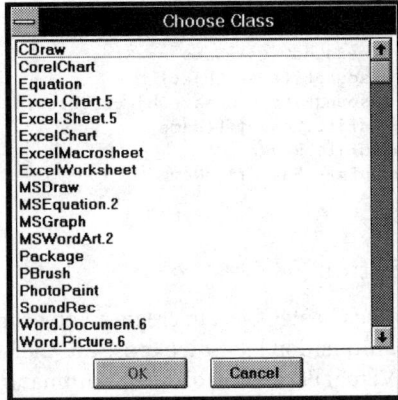

Figure 26-6 ...and here is the Class names dialog box showing all of the OLE registered applications on the system

to "temp" before performing a paste operation. Note that pasting into an OLE object without an existing Class property value generates an error, but the value that is already in the Class property is overwritten by whatever is on the Clipboard. This trick of setting the Class to a meaningless value in the Edit Paste operation makes sure that the paste operation proceeds without error.

CREATEOBJECT FUNCTION

Purpose

The CreateObject function lets you create an OLE object for use in OLE automation. Table 26-11 lists the argument of the CreateObject function.

General Syntax

```
CreateObject(className)
```

Argument	Meaning
className	OLE 2.0 compliant class name, given as "applicationName.objectType"

Table 26-11 Argument of the CreateObject function

Example Syntax

```
Sub ReverseSound (fileName as String)
    Dim soundFile As Object
    Set soundFile = CreateObject("Recorder.WAVFile")
    soundFile.Load fileName
    soundFile.Reverse
    soundFile.Save fileName
End Sub
```

Description

Use CreateObject to create an object that you manipulate in *OLE automation*. OLE automation lets you expose another application's features just as you would any Visual Basic control, like a command button or text box. This makes applications that support OLE automation very similar to Visual Basic custom controls.

The primary difference between a custom control and OLE automation lies fundamentally in distribution: it is easy to distribute Visual Basic custom controls, as they are designed to be distributed as part of Visual Basic programs. An application that supports OLE automation, on the other hand, is generally a full commercial application and legally cannot be distributed without the end user purchasing that application.

As OLE automation matures, and more applications are written to support it, this situation may well change to make distribution of runtime libraries easier. For example, the Access runtime engine supplied with Visual Basic 3.0 functions in many ways like an OLE 2.0 object with full automation. Although this is a hybrid product and isn't implemented exactly like an OLE object, the ease of use and power it brings to Visual Basic give a glimpse into what we can expect in the future. See Chapter 27, Data Access, for more about this control and the objects of the Access 1.1 engine exposed by the data control.

OLE automation also differs from custom controls in that commercial applications that support OLE 2.0 tend to be large and slow to load. You'll incur performance penalties when first creating an OLE automation object (as the host application loads into memory) and will certainly sacrifice larger amounts of disk space than you would with smaller, more optimized custom controls.

Any originating application that supports OLE automation is written to the OLE 2.0 specification, and needs to have the class name given according to that spec. See the entry on the Class property for more information about class name. OLE 2.0 class names are given as

```
applicationName.objectType
```

To use CreateObject, you must first declare a variable of type Object. You can use Dim, ReDim, Global, or Static to declare the variable. After dimensioning the variable, use the Set keyword to assign the object returned by CreateObject to the variable:

```
Global Chart As Object
Set Chart = CreateObject("Spdsheet.Graph")
```

CreateObject will start the originating application (if it isn't already running) and create the object. The object will not display in your Visual Basic program as it would in an OLE control, and depending on what you're doing, may not display in the originating application. For instance, if you're just going to use Word for Window's spell checker, nothing displays in either program. You'll give the spell checking function a word, and it will return a list of suggestions for misspelled words. The data also does not reside in your Visual Basic program unless you create a storage mechanism like an array or a data file to place it in.

Once you've created the object and put it in the object variable, you use whatever properties and methods are appropriate for that object. In the example syntax, we use three methods on a hypothetical Recorder application. We first create the object variable as described above, then we open fileName using the Recorder's Open method, use the Reverse method to reverse the sound wave, and finally use the Save method to save the file.

Example

The formInfo project at the end of this chapter uses OLE automation in two places: cmndGraph_Click and cmndReport_Click. The first use, in cmndGraph_Click, accesses the OLE object through the Object property; see that entry for more about how to use it. The second use, in cmndReport_Click, uses both CreateObject and GetObject interchangeably. Note that the chapter project's example is specific to Word for Windows 6.0 and will not work with any other application unless you modify it.

Comment

Many applications may not support OLE at all, and those that do may not support the advanced feature of OLE automation. Applications that do support OLE automation will have different properties and methods available. You'll need to carefully check that application's documentation for the exact terminology and usage.

Even scouring the host application's documentation may leave you confused and frustrated as you attempt to control the application through OLE automation. One trick that may make it a bit easier is similar to that discussed in Chapter 25, Dynamic Data Exchange. Record a macro in the host application to do what you want. (This trick obviously requires that the host application has a macro language! Applications that support OLE 2.0 will almost always have some sort of macro or programming language.) Edit the macro in the host application, and test it to be sure it works correctly. Once you're satisfied with the macro, copy it to your Visual Basic application and prefix each line with the object name.

For example, recording a macro in Winword 6.0 lets us determine that the following line selects all the text in the document:

```
EditSelectAll
```

Once we've determined this, it's easy to create an OLE automation routine that does the same thing in Visual Basic:

```
Dim wordProc As Object
Set wordProc = CreateObject("Word.Basic")
:
wordProc.EditSelectAll
:
```

DATA PROPERTY

Objects Affected

Check	Clipboard	Combo	Command	CommonDlg
Data	Debug	Dir	Drive	File
Form	Frame	Grid	Image	Label
Line	List	MDI Form	Menu	▶ OLE
Option	Picture	Printer	Screen	Scroll
Shape	Text	Timer		

Purpose

Use the Data property to transfer information to an OLE originating application that does not support OLE automation. There is no guarantee that the application will do anything with this data; most applications ignore it. Table 26-12 summarizes the arguments of the Data property.

General Syntax

```
[form!]Name.Data [ = data&]
```

Argument	Meaning
form	Name property of the parent form
Name	Name property of the control
data&	Handle to a memory or GDI object

Table 26-12 Arguments of the Data property

Example Syntax

```
Sub EditPicture ()
    Ole1.Format = "CF_METAFILEPICT"       'set proper format
    Ole1.Verb = VERB_HIDE                 'make sure the app stays hidden
    Ole1.Action = OLE_ACTIVATE            'activate the OLE app
    If Ole1.AppIsRunning Then             'if it successfully activated,
        Ole1.Data = Picture1.hDC          'give it the GDI handle
        Ole1.Action = OLE_UPDATE          'and update the control's display
    End If
End Sub
```

Description

The Data property lets you pass information back to an originating OLE application that does not support OLE automation. If the application does support automation, using its methods and properties directly offers a much easier and more reliable solution.

You must first set the Format property to indicate the type of data contained in the memory or GDI object. You then activate the object using the Action property, and set the Data property to the handle of the object. You may then wish to use the Action property to update the OLE control and update its display.

The syntax example passes the hDC (device context handle) of the Picture1 control to the OLE control. If the object in the OLE control responds to the Data property, it will display the picture from Picture1.

Very few applications respond to the Data property. With the advent of OLE 2.0, the limited usability of this property will probably fade even more.

Example

The formInfo project at the end of this chapter prints out the value of the Data property handle in the printInfo procedure, but does not pass data to a host with it because no standard, well-known application responds to it.

DATATEXT PROPERTY

Objects Affected

Check	Clipboard	Combo	Command	CommonDlg
Data	Debug	Dir	Drive	File
Form	Frame	Grid	Image	Label
Line	List	MDI Form	Menu	▶ OLE
Option	Picture	Printer	Screen	Scroll
Shape	Text	Timer		

Purpose

Use the DataText property to transfer text to and from an OLE originating application that does not support OLE automation. There is no guarantee that the application will do anything with this data. Table 26-13 summarizes the arguments of the DataText property.

General Syntax

```
[form!]Name.DataText [ = data$]
```

Argument	Meaning
form	Name property of the parent form
Name	Name property of the control
data$	String containing the data to send to the application

Table 26-13 Arguments of the DataText property

Example Syntax

```
Sub Command1_Click ()
    Ole1.Format = "CF_TEXT"                'Set the format to text
    Ole1.SizeMode = OLE_SIZE_AUTOSIZE      'OLE adjusts its size to fit data
    Ole1.Class = "MSGraph"                 'Embed an MS Graph object.
    Ole1.Action = OLE_CREATE_EMBED         'Create the embedded object

    data$ = Grid1.Clip                     'transfer contents of Grid into data$
    Ole1.Verb = VERB_HIDE                  'set up object to hide application
    Ole1.Action = OLE_ACTIVATE             'activate the object
    If Ole1.AppIsRunning Then              'if object successfully activated, then
        Ole1.DataText = data$              'paste in the string data
        Ole1.Action = OLE_UPDATE           'and update the OLE control's display
    End If
End Sub
```

Description

The DataText property lets you send and receive text information from an originating OLE application that does not support OLE automation. If the application does support automation, using its methods and properties directly offers a much easier and more reliable solution. The example syntax shows how to transfer text information to the OLE 1.0 compliant Graph applet that Microsoft ships with their applications.

1012

You must first set the Format property to indicate the type of data contained in the text string. See the entry for Format for more information about acceptable values. You then activate the object using the Action property, and set the DataText property to the string. You may then wish to use the Action property to update the OLE control and update its display.

Many applications respond to the DataText property, unlike the rarity of response to the Data property.

Example

The formInfo project at the end of this chapter passes information to the Graph applet in the cmndGraph_Click event. The data comes from copying spreadsheet information to the Clipboard, then passing the contents of the Clipboard to the OLE object.

DISPLAYTYPE PROPERTY

Objects Affected

Check	Clipboard	Combo	Command	CommonDlg
Data	Debug	Dir	Drive	File
Form	Frame	Grid	Image	Label
Line	List	MDI Form	Menu ▶	OLE
Option	Picture	Printer	Screen	Scroll
Shape	Text	Timer		

Purpose

Use the DisplayType property to set or determine whether an object displays as an icon or as formatted data. Tables 26-14 and 26-15 summarize the arguments of the DisplayType property.

General Syntax

`[form!]Name.DisplayType [ = setting%]`

Argument	Meaning
form	Name property of the parent form

(continued on next page)

(continued from previous page)

Argument	Meaning
Name	Name property of the control
setting%	Value indicates if OLE control displays data or icon

Table 26-14 Arguments of the DisplayType property

setting%	CONSTANT.TXT	Meaning
0	OLE_DISPLAY_CONTENT	(Default) Display actual formatted data
1	OLE_DISPLAY_ICON	Display icon as placeholder

Table 26-15 Values of the setting% argument of the DisplayType property

Example Syntax

```
Sub menuEditPasteSpecial_Click ()
    Ole1.DisplayType = OLE_DISPLAY_ICON
    Ole1.Action = OLE_INSERT_OBJ_DLG
End Sub
```

Description

Use the DisplayType property to determine if an object displays its contents as formatted data or as an icon placeholder. The default setting, formatted data, can sometimes significantly slow down your application if the data consists of detailed graphics. Setting the display type to an icon can improve your application's display performance. You cannot change an object's display type once it is created.

Setting the DisplayType property before calling up the Insert Object or Paste Special dialog boxes sets the Icon check box on the dialog box appropriately. The user can change this setting before closing the dialog box, and the change is reflected in how the object gets created. The example syntax shows how we set the default value of the check box to Icon in the Insert Special dialog box. Figure 26-7 shows the dialog box, and Figures 26-8 and 26-9 show how the two types of displays differ.

Note that each of these DisplayType constants is defined in CONSTANT.TXT. See the discussion in the Summary section at the beginning of this chapter for details on how to use these constants.

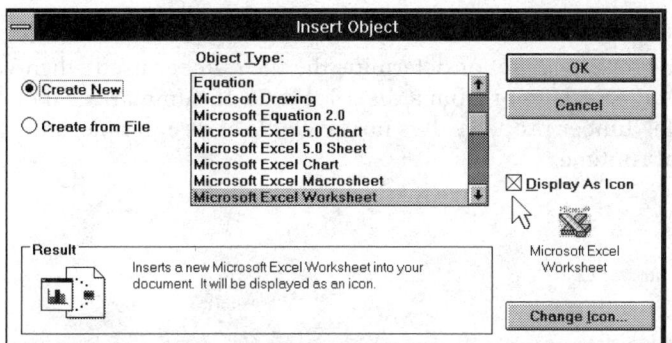

Figure 26-7 The DisplayType property sets the default mode for the Icon check box

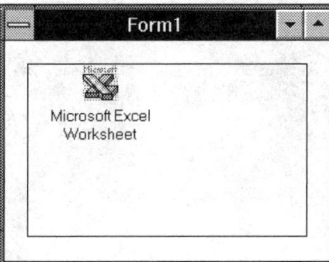

Figure 26-8 Object displayed as icon placeholder

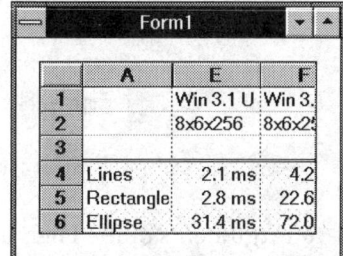

Figure 26-9 Object displayed fully formatted

Example

The Form_Load event in the formInfo project at the end of this chapter sets the DisplayType property of all OLE containers to display the actual contents.

FILENUMBER PROPERTY

Objects Affected

Check	Clipboard	Combo	Command	CommonDlg
Data	Debug	Dir	Drive	File
Form	Frame	Grid	Image	Label
Line	List	MDI Form	Menu	▶ OLE
Option	Picture	Printer	Screen	Scroll
Shape	Text	Timer		

Purpose

Use the FileNumber property to set or determine the file number used when saving or loading OLE objects to or from a disk. Table 26-16 summarizes the arguments of the FileNumber property. It is not available at design time, and will read and write at runtime.

General Syntax

```
[form!]Name.FileNumber [ = number%]
```

Argument	Meaning
form	Name property of the parent form
Name	Name property of the control
number%	Valid file number as used in an Open statement

Table 26-16 Arguments of the FileNumber property

Example Syntax

```
Sub menuSaveObject_Click ()
    fileNum = FreeFile                            'Get a file handle
    Open "SAVEFILE.OLE" For Binary As #fileNum    'Open the file
    Ole1.FileNumber = fileNum                     'Pass file handle to object
    Ole1.Action = OLE_SAVE_TO_FILE                'Save the file to disk
    Close #fileNum                                'Close file
End Sub
```

Description

The FileNumber property lets you pass the file handle of an open binary file to the OLE object. You can then save the file (Action = 11, OLE_SAVE_TO_FILE) or load the file (Action = 12, OLE_READ_FROM_FILE). You may also determine the file handle that was last used with the OLE control, although this is not ordinarily useful information.

Reading and writing files uses almost identical code. The following example reads in a binary file. Note that the only change from the example syntax is that we use Action 12, OLE_READ_FROM_FILE; everything else is identical:

```
Sub menuOpenObject_Click ()
    fileNum = FreeFile                            'Get a file handle
    Open "SAVEFILE.OLE" For Binary As #fileNum    'Open the file
```

1016

```
        Ole1.FileNumber = fileNum              'Pass file handle to object
        Ole1.Action = OLE_READ_FROM_FILE       'Load the file to disk
        Close #fileNum                         'Close file
End Sub
```

Example

The menuFile_Click event in the formInfo project at the end of this chapter sets the FileNumber property for both saving and retrieving the contents of the OLE containers.

FORMAT PROPERTY

Objects Affected

Check	Clipboard	Combo	Command	CommonDlg
Data	Debug	Dir	Drive	File
Form	Frame	Grid	Image	Label
Line	List	MDI Form	Menu	▶ OLE
Option	Picture	Printer	Screen	Scroll
Shape	Text	Timer		

Purpose

Use the Format property to set or determine the kind of data sent to and received from an OLE object using the Data and DataText properties. Table 26-17 summarizes the arguments of the Format property.

General Syntax

`[form!]Name.Format [ = dataType$]`

Argument	Meaning
form	Name property of the parent form
Name	Name property of the control
dataType$	Type of data

Table 26-17 Arguments of the Format property

1017

Example Syntax

```
Sub Command1_Click ()
    Ole1.Format = "CF_TEXT"             'Set the format to text
    Ole1.SizeMode = OLE_SIZE_AUTOSIZE   'OLE adjusts its size to fit data
    Ole1.Class = "MSGraph"              'Embed an MS Graph object.
    Ole1.Action = OLE_CREATE_EMBED      'Create the embedded object

    data$ = Grid1.Clip                  'transfer contents of Grid into data$
    Ole1.Verb = VERB_HIDE               'set up object to hide application
    Ole1.Action = OLE_ACTIVATE          'activate the object
    If Ole1.AppIsRunning Then           'if object successfully activated, then
        Ole1.DataText = data$           'paste in the string data
        Ole1.Action = OLE_UPDATE        'and update the OLE control's display
    End If
End Sub
```

Description

The Format property determines the kind of data sent to or received from the originating OLE application. Both the Data and the DataText properties require that you set the Format property prior to using them. You can use the ObjectGetFormats and ObjectAcceptFormats properties to find out the acceptable formats. Note that some applications accept different formats than they provide. The example syntax sets the Format for the Graph object to CF_TEXT before passing it the data to graph.

Many formats look like the CONSTANT.TXT declarations. Note that they are actual strings, not the values represented in CONSTANT.TXT and that this resemblance is superficial. The example syntax above shows this:

```
Ole1.Format = "CF_TEXT"     'Correct. This string looks like the constant, but
                            'the resemblance is superficial

Ole1.Format = CF_TEXT       'Incorrect! This may look similar, but would
                            'generate an error
```

The first example properly gives the value as a string, and works correctly. The second example uses the CONSTANT.TXT numeric constant and generates an error.

Example

The formInfo project at the end of this chapter sets the format in two places. First, the cmndGraph_Click event sets the Format property before passing information to the MSGraph applet with the DataText property. Second, the printInfo procedure sets the Format before reading the value of the Data property. The printInfo routine also prints out all the available formats.

GETOBJECT FUNCTION

Purpose

GetObject retrieves an object from a file for use in OLE automation. It is not available at design time, and is read-only at runtime. Table 26-18 summarizes the arguments of the GetObject function.

General Syntax

```
GetObject(fileName$[, className])
```

Argument	Meaning
fileName$	File name of the file to use, and an optional topic prefaced by !
className	OLE 2.0 compliant class name in the form "applicationName.objectType"

Table 26-18 Arguments of the GetObject function

Example Syntax

```
Sub Command1_Click ()
    Dim map As Object                                 'declare object variable
    Set map = GetObject("C:\MAPS\USA.CDR!Layer1")     'drawing of the US
    map.Select "Borders"                              'select named range
    map.Copy                                          'copy to clipboard
    Picture1.Picture = Clipboard.GetData()            'paste Clipboard to picture
End Sub
```

Description

Use the GetObject function to retrieve an object for use in OLE automation. You must first declare a variable of type Object using Dim, ReDim, Global, or Static. Then, set the variable to the object returned by the GetObject function. The example syntax shows how to do this with a map of the United States. It then goes on to issue the (hypothetical) automation commands to select just the borders and copy it to the Clipboard. The contents of the Clipboard are then pasted into Picture1.

The fileName$ argument can be an empty string or a full path and file name with an optional range. If it is an empty string, the className argument is required. GetObject then returns the currently active object of the specified type. An error occurs if there is no active object of that type.

If fileName$ is a file name, GetObject starts the originating application if it is not already running and retrieves that particular file. File names can have an optional range argument appended to them after an exclamation point (!) for applications that support retrieving just a part of a file. For instance, many spreadsheets support retrieving either a named range of cells or a range of cells given in the familiar RC style:

```
GetObject("C:\EXCEL\BUDGETS\Q1ACTUAL.XLS!R1C1:R20C10")
```

If you do not specify className, Visual Basic automatically determines the correct application to run from the [Extensions] section of WIN.INI. Some applications, however, support more than one class type for an object. For instance, if the spreadsheet supported class types for the actual worksheet, embedded charts, and the toolbar, you'd need to specify this in the className:

```
GetObject("C:\EXCEL\BUDGETS\Q1ACTUAL.XLS!R1C1:R20C10", "Excel.Worksheet")
```

See the entry for CreateObject for more information about OLE automation.

Example

The formInfo project at the end of this chapter uses both CreateObject and GetObject interchangeably in the cmndReport_Click event.

HOSTNAME PROPERTY

Objects Affected

Check	Clipboard	Combo	Command	CommonDlg
Data	Debug	Dir	Drive	File
Form	Frame	Grid	Image	Label
Line	List	MDI Form	Menu	▶ OLE
Option	Picture	Printer	Screen	Scroll
Shape	Text	Timer		

Purpose

The HostName property sets the user-readable name of your OLE object. This is used by most originating applications to identify the object they're editing. It can read and write at both runtime and design time. Table 26-19 summarizes the arguments of the HostName property.

General Syntax

```
[form!]Name.HostName [ = hostName$]
```

Argument	Meaning
form	Name property of the parent form
Name	Name property of the control
hostName$	Name that identifies the object when edited

Table 26-19 Arguments of the HostName property

Example Syntax

```
Sub Form_Load ()
    Ole1.HostName = "CorelDRAW Extrude Object"
End Sub
```

Description

Use the HostName to give a user-friendly name to an object. This name is then used by most originating applications when they edit the object. For example, assume the object contained in Ole1 in the example syntax is a CorelDRAW object. Editing this object brings up CorelDRAW, and Corel's title bar would display something like "CorelDRAW - Editing CorelDRAW Extrude Object." Most originating applications will also have an Update command on their File menu. This will sometimes indicate the name of the host object, as in "Exit and Return to CorelDRAW Extrude Object." Figure 26-10 shows this.

Not all originating applications make use of the HostName property. Setting the property will not cause an error if the originating application does not support it; the originating application simply ignores it.

Example

The HostName property for each OLE container is initialized in the chapter project's Form_Load event.

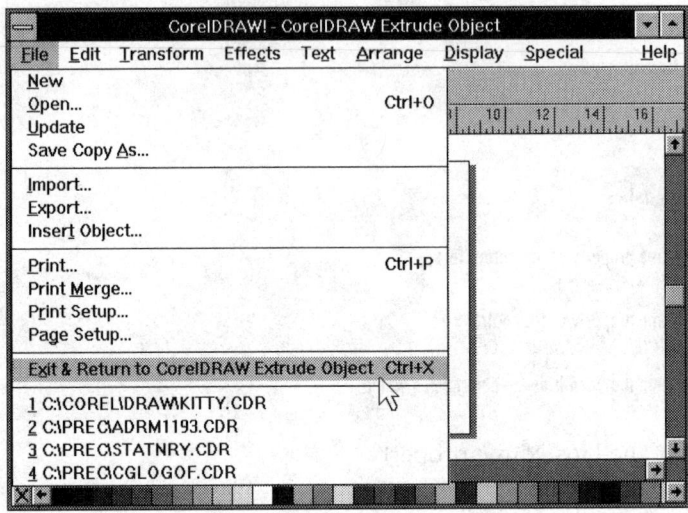

Figure 26-10 The HostName property identifies your object when being edited by the originating application

LPOLEOBJECT PROPERTY

Objects Affected

Check	Clipboard	Combo	Command	CommonDlg
Data	Debug	Dir	Drive	File
Form	Frame	Grid	Image	Label
Line	List	MDI Form	Menu ▶	OLE
Option	Picture	Printer	Screen	Scroll
Shape	Text	Timer		

Purpose

The LpOleObject property gives the memory address of an OLE object. You can then use this address in the OLE API calls. It is not available at design time, and is read-only at runtime. Table 26-20 summarizes the arguments of the LpOleObject property.

General Syntax

```
[form!]Name.LpOleObject
```

Argument	Meaning
form	Name property of the parent form
Name	Name property of the control

Table 26-20 Arguments of the LpOleObject property

Example Syntax

```
Sub Command1_Click
    Dim p As Long
    p = OLE1.LpOleObject
    null = AddRef(p)            'API call using the long pointer
End Sub
```

Description

Many of the OLE 2.0 API calls require a long pointer to the memory position of the object. LpOleObject returns the pointer for use in these API calls. If there is no current object, LpOleObject returns a 0 (zero).

Example

The formInfo project at the end of this chapter prints out the value of the long pointer's address in the printInfo procedure.

OBJECT PROPERTY

Objects Affected

Check	Clipboard	Combo	Command	CommonDlg
Data	Debug	Dir	Drive	File
Form	Frame	Grid	Image	Label
Line	List	MDI Form	Menu	▶ OLE
Option	Picture	Printer	Screen	Scroll
Shape	Text	Timer		

Purpose

The Object property lets you access the underlying object in an OLE control for use in OLE automation. It is not available at design time, and are read-only at runtime. Table 26-21 summarizes the arguments of the Object property.

General Syntax

```
[form!]Name.Object.[property|method] [ = settings]
```

Argument	Meaning
form	Name property of the parent form
Name	Name property of the control
property	Appropriate property of the object
method	Appropriate method of the object
settings	Appropriate arguments for the property or method

Table 26-21 Arguments of the Object property

Example Syntax

```
Sub Command1_Click ()
    Ole1.Object.Bold = True
    Ole1.Object.Insert = "This is some text."
    Ole1.Object.SaveAs "C:\TEMP\TEST.DOC"
End Sub
```

Description

The Object property lets you manipulate the OLE control's object with OLE automation. Contrast this technique with the CreateObject and GetObject functions: the Object property manipulates the object in an OLE control, whereas the functions let you assign an object to an object variable, which you then manipulate

Every originating application that supports OLE automation will have different properties and methods that it makes available. Consult that application's documentation for the details and syntax of what it supports. The example syntax shows the Object property being used to issue the (hypothetical) automation commands to make the font bold, insert some text, and then save the document to a file.

See CreateObject and GetObject for more details on OLE automation.

Example

Both the cmndGraph_Click and cmndReport_Click events in the formInfo project at the end of this chapter use the OLE container's Object property to control the spreadsheet embedded in the container.

OBJECTACCEPTFORMATS PROPERTY

OBJECTACCEPTFORMATSCOUNT PROPERTY

OBJECTGETFORMATS PROPERTY

OBJECTGETFORMATSCOUNT PROPERTY

Objects Affected

Check	Clipboard	Combo	Command	CommonDlg
Data	Debug	Dir	Drive	File
Form	Frame	Grid	Image	Label
Line	List	MDI Form	Menu	▶ OLE
Option	Picture	Printer	Screen	Scroll
Shape	Text	Timer		

Purpose

The ObjectAcceptFormats property returns the list of formats an object can accept. The ObjectGetFormats property returns the list of formats an object returns. Both of these properties return their lists as string arrays. ObjectAcceptsFormatsCount and ObjectGetFormatsCount return the number of members in the appropriate array. These properties are useful for working with the Data and DataText properties for objects that do not implement OLE automation. They are not available at design time, and are read-only at runtime. Table 26-22 lists the arguments of the properties.

General Syntax

```
[form!]Name.ObjectAcceptFormats(Index%)
[form!]Name.ObjectAcceptFormatsCount
[form!]Name.ObjectGetFormats(Index%)
[form!]Name.ObjectGetFormatsCount
```

Argument	Meaning
form	Name property of the parent form
Name	Name property of the control
Index%	Index to a particular member of the array

Table 26-22 Arguments of the ObjectAcceptFormats property

Example Syntax

```
Sub Command1_Click ()
    For i = 0 To Ole1.ObjectAcceptFormatsCount - 1
        List1.AddItem Ole1.ObjectAcceptFormats(i)
    Next i
    For j = 0 to Ole1.ObjectGetFormatsCount - 1
        List2.AddItem Ole1.ObjectGetFormats(j)
    Next j
End Sub
```

Description

ObjectAcceptFormats returns the formats an object can accept; ObjectGetFormats returns the formats an object can return. These format strings are used with the Format property when you use the Data and DataText properties to transfer information. If an application is OLE automation capable, OLE automation offers an easier and more reliable method of exchanging data.

Both properties return the acceptable formats in a zero-based array. This means that the first entry is at index=0, not index=1. The array contains the actual strings that describe the format, and these values can be used directly in the Format property.

ObjectAcceptFormatsCount and ObjectGetFormatsCount return the total number of members in the array. This makes it simple to iterate through the arrays, as we do in the example syntax to add the formats to the list boxes. Note that because the arrays are zero-based, the last member of the array has an index of Count -1.

The example syntax loads two list boxes with the ObjectAcceptFormats and ObjectGetFormats values. Figure 26-11 shows what this example might look like with Excel 5.0.

Example

The formInfo project at the end of this chapter uses these properties in the printInfo routine. This routine iterates through each array and prints out the possible values, much as in the syntax example above.

1026

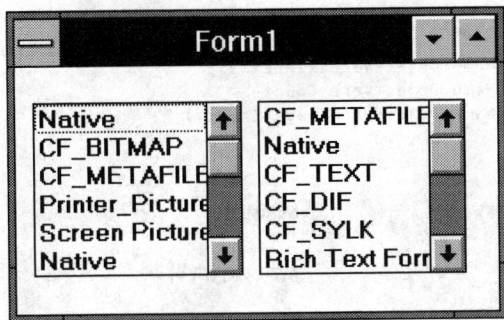

Figure 26-11 ObjectGetFormats and ObjectAcceptFormats help fill these list boxes

OBJECTVERBS PROPERTY

OBJECTVERBSCOUNT PROPERTY

OBJECTVERBFLAGS PROPERTY

Objects Affected

Check	Clipboard	Combo	Command	CommonDlg
Data	Debug	Dir	Drive	File
Form	Frame	Grid	Image	Label
Line	List	MDI Form	Menu ▶ OLE	
Option	Picture	Printer	Screen	Scroll
Shape	Text	Timer		

Purpose

Each object has certain *verbs*, or actions, that apply to it. The ObjectVerbs property returns an array of applicable verbs for an object. The ObjectVerbsCount property returns the total number of verb entries in the ObjectVerbs array. The ObjectVerbFlags property returns the menu state of each item in the ObjectVerbs array. This lets you set up a menu that correctly lists each applicable verb and its state (checked, grayed, etc). They are not available at design time, and are read-only at runtime. Table 26-23 lists the arguments of the three properties and Table 26-24 lists the return values.

General Syntax

```
[form!]Name.ObjectVerbs(Index%)
[form!]Name.ObjectVerbsCount
[form!]Name.ObjectVerbFlags(Index%)
```

Argument	Meaning
form	Name property of the parent form
Name	Name property of the control
Index%	Index to a particular member of the array

Table 26-23 Arguments of the ObjectVerbs, ObjectVerbsCount, and ObjectVerbFlags properties

Value	CONSTANT.TXT	Meaning
&H0000	VF_ENABLED	The menu item should be enabled
&H0001	VF_GRAYED	The menu item should be grayed
&H0002	VF_DISABLED	The menu item should be disabled (but not grayed)
&H0008	VF_CHECKED	The menu item should be checked
&H0800	VF_SEPARATOR	The menu item is a separator bar

Table 26-24 The return values for the ObjectVerbFlags property

Example Syntax

```
Sub Command1_Click ()
    Ole1.Action = OLE_FETCH_VERBS            'update the object's verbs
    For i = 0 To Ole1.ObjectVerbsCount - 1   'step through each verb
        Load menuVerbs(i)                     'create a new menu item
        flag = Ole1.ObjectVerbFlags(i)        'get the flag value
        If flag And VF_SEPARATOR Then
            menuVerbs(i).Caption = "-"         'separator
        Else
```

```
                menuVerbs(i).Caption = Ole1.ObjectVerbs(i)   'actual verb name
        End If
        If flag And VF_ENABLED Then menuVerbs(i).Enabled = True
        If flag And VF_GRAYED Then menuVerbs(i).Enabled = False
        If flag And VF_DISABLED Then menuVerbs(i).Tag = "disabled"
        If flag And VF_CHECKED Then menuVerbs(i).Checked = True
    Next i
End Sub
```

Description

Each object has certain *verbs*, or actions, that apply to it. The ObjectVerbs property returns an array of applicable verbs for an object. The ObjectVerbsCount property returns the total number of verb entries in the ObjectVerbs array.

You can use the ObjectVerbFlags property to determine what state the menu entry for each verb should appear in (checked, grayed, etc). Each object has a number of different actions that can happen to it. For example, a sound application might be able to Play, Record, Rewind, or Reverse a sound. These verbs would then appear in the ObjectVerbs array. Note that each of these ObjectVerbFlags constants is defined in CONSTANT.TXT. See the discussion in the Summary section at the beginning of this chapter for details on how to use these constants.

Not all verbs are applicable at any given time, however. For instance, if there is no sound presently loaded, then the Play, Rewind and Reverse verbs aren't applicable, but the Record verb is. The ObjectVerbFlags property for each verb lets you set the appropriate menu states for each verb. The example syntax shows how to build a menu with the appropriate entries, then set the proper display state for each menu item.

Both the ObjectVerbs and the ObjectVerbFlags arrays are zero-based. This means that the first member in the array has an index=0, not index=1. The last member in the arrays has an index of ObjectVerbsCount -1. The example syntax builds a menu using these arrays, and Figure 26-12 displays what that might look like.

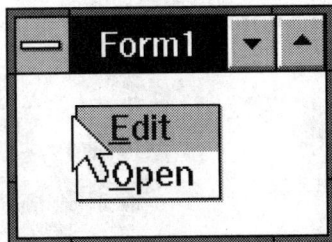

Figure 26-12 The ObjectVerbs and ObjectVerbFlags arrays help build this menu

Make sure you use Action 17, OLE_FETCH_VERBS, before checking the ObjectVerbs or ObjectVerbFlags properties.

Example

The formInfo project at the end of this chapter uses the ObjectVerbsCount and ObjectVerb properties to build a pop-up menu in the OLE_MouseDown event. Two of the containers (the spreadsheet and the graph) have AutoVerbMenu set to True, but the document container has it set to False. The MouseDown event builds a custom pop-up menu with the verbs for the document container. The printInfo routine also uses these properties to print out the available verbs and the menu state of each verb for the selected OLE container.

OLETYPE PROPERTY

Objects Affected

Check	Clipboard	Combo	Command	CommonDlg
Data	Debug	Dir	Drive	File
Form	Frame	Grid	Image	Label
Line	List	MDI Form	Menu	▶ OLE
Option	Picture	Printer	Screen	Scroll
Shape	Text	Timer		

Purpose

Use the OleType property to determine what kind of object (linked, embedded, or none) an OLE control contains. It is not available at design time, and is read-only at runtime. Tables 26-25 and 26-26 summarize the arguments and values of the OleType property.

General Syntax

`[form!]Name.OleType`

Argument	Meaning
form	Name property of the parent form
Name	Name property of the control

Table 26-25 Arguments of the OleType property

Value	CONSTANT.TXT	Meaning
0	OLE_LINKED	Object is linked
1	OLE_EMBEDDED	Object is embedded
3	OLE_NONE	OLE control does not contain an object

Table 26-26 Meanings of the values returned by the OleType property

Example Syntax

```
Sub Command1_Click ()
     Select Case Ole1.OleType
          Case OLE_LINKED: chekLinkStatus.Value = CHECKED
          Case OLE_EMBEDDED: chekLinkStatus.Value = UNCHECKED
          Case OLE_NONE: chekLinkStatus.Value = GRAYED
     End Select
End Sub
```

Description

Use the OleType property to determine what kind of object an OLE control contains. A control may contain a linked object, an embedded object, or no object at all. The example syntax shows how to use this property to set the value of a check box control. Note that each of these OleType constants is defined in CONSTANT.TXT. See the discussion in the Summary section at the beginning of this chapter for details on how to use these constants.

Linking lets you use another application's data while leaving it available for other programs. The data remains on disk as a separate file, stored in its normal, native format. It is available for editing by the original application or any other application that can read it. The originating application can save the information to disk. The object in your Visual Basic program contains a link to the proper file (and specific range or set of objects in that file) and an image of what the data looks like for display. Linked objects have an OleType property of 0 (OLE_LINKED).

Embedding lets you completely control the data. No other application can directly access the information. The object in your Visual Basic application contains the actual data as well as an image of what the data looks like for display. Although the Visual Basic OLE control contains the actual data, it does not automatically save it to disk. You can use the OLE's Action property to save and retrieve the information. Saving embedded OLE data saves the actual data, the name of the originating application, and an image of what the data looks like. Embedded objects have an OleType of 1 (OLE_EMBEDDED). If the control does not contain an object, the OleType property is set to 3 (OLE_NONE).

Example

The formInfo project at the end of this chapter uses the OleType property in several places (such as the menuBar_Click event) to see if there is an object embedded in the container. If the property returns 3 (OLE_NONE), then no object is currently embedded.

OLETYPEALLOWED PROPERTY

Objects Affected

Check	Clipboard	Combo	Command	CommonDlg
Data	Debug	Dir	Drive	File
Form	Frame	Grid	Image	Label
Line	List	MDI Form	Menu	▶ OLE
Option	Picture	Printer	Screen	Scroll
Shape	Text	Timer		

Purpose

Use the OleTypeAllowed property to set what kinds of objects (linked, embedded, or either) may be placed in an OLE control. It will read and write at both run and design time. Tables 26-27 and 26-28 summarize the arguments of the OleTypeAllowed property.

General Syntax

```
[form!]Name.OleTypeAllowed [ = type%]
```

Argument	Meaning
form	Name property of the parent form
Name	Name property of the control
type%	Type of object allowed (linked, embedded, or either)

Table 26-27 Arguments of the OleTypeAllowed property

Value	CONSTANT.TXT	Meaning
0	OLE_LINKED	Can only contain a linked object
1	OLE_EMBEDDED	Can only contain an embedded object
2	OLE_EITHER	(Default) Can contain either a linked or embedded object

Table 26-28 Meanings of the values of the OleTypeAllowed property

Example Syntax

```
Sub Command1_Click ()
    Ole1.OleTypeAllowed = OLE_LINKED
    Ole1.Action = OLE_INSERT_OBJ_DLG
End Sub
```

Description

Use the OleTypeAllowed property to set what kinds of objects (linked, embedded, or either) may be placed in an OLE control. The example syntax sets the OleTypeAllowed property to "linked" before bringing up the Insert Object dialog box. This sets the default property for the Link check box in the dialog. Note that each of these OleTypeAllowed constants is defined in CONSTANT.TXT. See the discussion in the Summary section at the beginning of this chapter for details on how to use these constants.

Linking lets you use another application's data while leaving it available for other programs. The data remains on disk as a separate file, stored in its normal, native format. It is available for editing by the original application or any other application that can read it. The originating application can save the information to disk. The object in your Visual Basic program contains a link to the proper file (and specific range or set of objects in that file) and an image of what the data looks like for display. Linked objects need to have an OleTypeAllowed property of 0 (OLE_LINKED) or 2 (OLE_EITHER).

Embedding lets you completely control the data. No other application can directly access the information. The object in your Visual Basic application contains the actual data as well as an image of what the data looks like for display. Although the Visual Basic OLE control contains the actual data, it does not automatically save it to disk. You can use the OLE's Action property to save and retrieve the information. Saving embedded OLE data saves the actual data, the name of the originating application, and an image of what the data looks like. Embedded objects need to have an OleType of 1 (OLE_EMBEDDED) or 2 (OLE_EITHER).

Example

The formInfo project at the end of this chapter uses the OleTypeAllowed property to set the type of the embedded object in the cmndReport_Click event.

PASTEOK PROPERTY

Objects Affected

Check	Clipboard	Combo	Command	CommonDlg
Data	Debug	Dir	Drive	File
Form	Frame	Grid	Image	Label
Line	List	MDI Form	Menu ▶	OLE
Option	Picture	Printer	Screen	Scroll
Shape	Text	Timer		

Purpose

Use the PasteOK property to determine whether the contents of the Clipboard may be pasted into the OLE control. It is not available at design time, and is read-only at runtime. Table 26-29 summarizes the arguments of the PasteOK property.

General Syntax

```
[form!]Name.PasteOK
```

Argument	Meaning
form	Name property of the parent form
Name	Name property of the control

Table 26-29 Arguments of the PasteOK property

Example Syntax

```
Sub menuEdit_Click ()
    menuEditPaste.Enabled = Ole1.PasteOK 'enables and disables paste command
End Sub
```

Description

Use the PasteOK property to determine whether the contents of the Clipboard may be pasted into the OLE control. If the Clipboard contains an OLE object in the correct format, then PasteOK returns True. If the Clipboard does not contain an OLE object, PasteOK returns False. The example syntax enables and disables an Edit Paste menu command based on the PasteOK return value.

You can paste the object with Action 5 (OLE_PASTE) or Action 15 (OLE_PASTE_SPECIAL_DLG) once you've determined that it's OK to paste. Using the Paste Special dialog box gives you users the most control, as they can choose to link or embed the object.

Example

The formInfo project at the end of this chapter checks the value of the PasteOK property in the menuBar_Click event. If the value is True, the routine then enables the menu controls that allow pasting (Paste and Paste Special).

RESIZE EVENT

Objects Affected

Check	Clipboard	Combo	Command	CommonDlg
Data	Debug	Dir	Drive	File
▶ Form	Frame	Grid	Image	Label
Line	List	▶ MDI Form	Menu	▶ OLE
Option	▶ Picture	Printer	Screen	Scroll
Shape	Text	Timer		

Purpose

Use the OLE control's Resize event to react to a change in the control's size caused by new data when the SizeMode property is set to 2 (AutoSize). Table 26-30 summarizes the arguments of the Resize event.

General Syntax

```
Sub Name_Resize (HeightNew As Integer, WidthNew As Integer)
```

1035

Argument	Meaning
Name	Name property of the control
HeightNew	Optimal height of the control; change this to set new height of control
WidthNew	Optimal width of the control; change this to set new width of control

Table 26-30 Arguments of the SizeMode property

Example Syntax

```
Sub Ole1_Resize (HeightNew As Integer, WidthNew As Integer)
    If HeightNew > 2000 Then
        HeightNew = 2000
    End If
    If WidthNew > 4000 Then
        WidthNew = 4000
    End If
End Sub
```

Description

You can set an OLE control to automatically resize itself when the data it displays changes. Setting the SizeMode property to 2 (AutoSize) will automatically resize the OLE control. You may then want to limit the size of the control to keep it within certain boundaries. The HeightNew and WidthNew arguments in the Resize event contain the optimal height and width (that is, how large the control would need to be to completely display the object). Set these arguments to a different value to force the control into a different size. The example syntax limits the OLE control to no more than 2000 by 4000 twips.

Example

The formInfo project at the end of this chapter uses the Resize event to limit the size of the document OLE container to a maximum size equal to the graph container.

SIZEMODE PROPERTY

Objects Affected

Check	Clipboard	Combo	Command	CommonDlg
Data	Debug	Dir	Drive	File
Form	Frame	Grid	Image	Label
Line	List	MDI Form	Menu	▶ OLE
Option	Picture	Printer	Screen	Scroll
Shape	Text	Timer		

Purpose

The SizeMode property determines how an object is sized within an OLE control. It is not available at design time, and will read and write at runtime. Tables 26-31 and 26-32 summarize the arguments and values of the SizeMode property.

Example Syntax

```
[form!]Name.SizeMode [ = setting%]
```

Argument	Meaning
form	Name property of the parent form
Name	Name property of the control
setting%	Determines the sizing mode: clip, stretch, or AutoSize

Table 26-31 Arguments of the SizeMode property

setting%	CONSTANT.TXT	Meaning
0	OLE_SIZE_CLIP	(Default) Clips the object at OLE control's boundaries
1	OLE_SIZE_STRETCH	Sizes the object to exactly fill the OLE control

(continued on next page)

(continued from previous page)

setting%	CONSTANT.TXT	Meaning
2	OLE_SIZE_AUTOSIZE	Resizes the OLE control to fit the object

Table 26-32 Meanings of the setting% argument in the SizeMode property

Example Syntax

```
Sub List1_Click ()
    Ole1.SizeMode = List1.ListIndex
End Sub
```

Description

The SizeMode property determines how the OLE control sizes and displays the object. The OLE control will almost always be of a different size than the image of the object it displays. You can select whether the control will clip the object's display, size the object to fit the control, or size the control to fit the object. The example syntax sets this property with the index of a list box that has each size mode listed in the correct order. Note that each of these SizeMode constants is defined in CONSTANT.TXT. See the discussion in the Summary section at the beginning of this chapter for details on how to use these constants.

Both the OLE_SIZE_CLIP and OLE_SIZE_STRETCH settings display the object entirely within the OLE control's boundaries, and leave the size of the OLE control unchanged. The clip setting displays the upper-left corner of the object at its actual size, and clips off any part that extends past the control's border. The stretch setting resizes the object to exactly fill the OLE control.

The OLE_SIZE_AUTOSIZE setting resizes the OLE control to match the size of the object. Although you cannot regulate the size of the object, you can set the ultimate size of the OLE control. Resizing the OLE control generates a Resize event, and you can set the Resize event's HeightNew and WidthNew arguments to determine the control's size. This might be helpful if you wanted to let the control expand as much as possible, but not beyond a certain boundary on your form. If you resize the control to a smaller size than the object, then the control clips the object. Figure 26-13 shows the same information displayed in the three modes in three different OLE controls.

Example

The formInfo project at the end of this chapter sets the three OLE containers to the three possible values: the spreadsheet container is set to Clip, the document container is set to AutoSize, and the graph container is set to Stretch.

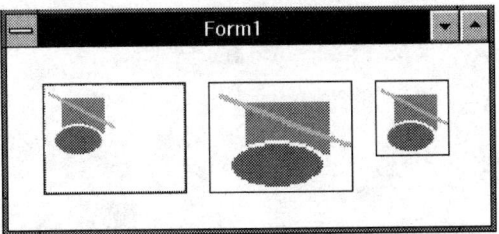

Figure 26-13 The three different OLE display modes: Clip, Stretch, and AutoSize

SOURCEDOC PROPERTY

Objects Affected

Check	Clipboard	Combo	Command	CommonDlg
Data	Debug	Dir	Drive	File
Form	Frame	Grid	Image	Label
Line	List	MDI Form	Menu	▶ OLE
Option	Picture	Printer	Screen	Scroll
Shape	Text	Timer		

SourceDoc

The SourceDoc property sets the file name to use when creating an object, or reads the file name of an existing object. It will read and write at both design and runtime. Table 26-33 summarizes the arguments of the SourceDoc property.

General Syntax

```
[form!]Name.SourceDoc [ = document$]
```

Argument	Meaning
form	Name property of the parent form
Name	Name property of the control
document$	Full path and file name of the document

Table 26-33 Arguments of the SourceDoc property

1039

Example Syntax

```
Sub Form_Load ()
    Ole1.Class = "Excel.Worksheet"
    Ole1.SourceDoc = "C:\DATA\Q1ACTUAL.XLS"
    Ole1.SourceItem = "R1C1:R587C48"
    Ole1.Action = OLE_CREATE_LINK
End Sub
```

Description

The SourceDoc property sets the file name to use when creating an object, or reads the file name and item of an existing object. If the object being created is linked (Action = 1, OLE_CREATE_LINK), then the disk file is linked to the OLE control. If the object is embedded (Action = 0, OLE_CREATE_EMBED), then the disk file is used as a template to create a new object in the OLE control.

SourceDoc has SourceItem concatenated to it after Visual Basic creates the object. The two properties are separated by an exclamation mark (!) or a backslash (\). The originating application controls whether it uses the exclamation or the backslash. Excel uses an exclamation, so after running the example syntax for the Form_Load event, SourceDoc would contain "C:\DATA\Q1ACTUAL.XLS!R1C1:R587C48".

Example

The cmndReport_Click event in the formInfo project at the end of this chapter sets the SourceDoc property when embedding the word processor document.

SOURCEITEM PROPERTY

Objects Affected

Check	Clipboard	Combo	Command	CommonDlg
Data	Debug	Dir	Drive	File
Form	Frame	Grid	Image	Label
Line	List	MDI Form	Menu ▶	OLE
Option	Picture	Printer	Screen	Scroll
Shape	Text	Timer		

Purpose

Use the SourceItem property to specify exactly what data to use when creating a linked object. It will read and write at both design and runtime. Table 26-34 summarizes the arguments of the SourceItem property.

General Syntax

```
[form!]Name.SourceItem [ = item$]
```

Argument	Meaning
form	Name property of the parent form
Name	Name property of the control
item$	Specification for the particular unit of data

Table 26-34 Arguments of the SourceItem property

Example Syntax

```
Sub Form_Load ()
    Ole1.Class = "Excel.Worksheet"
    Ole1.SourceDoc = "C:\DATA\Q1ACTUAL.XLS"
    Ole1.SourceItem = "R1C1:R587C48"
    Ole1.Action = OLE_CREATE_LINK
End Sub
```

Description

The SourceItem property lets you specify exactly what piece or range of data to use for a linked object. It does not apply to embedded objects. Use the SourceDoc property to specify the file in which the item resides. Although you can read SourceItem at runtime, it is useless to do so. Visual Basic concatenates SourceItem to SourceDoc, separating the two with an exclamation (!) or backslash (\). It then sets SourceItem to an empty string (""). See SourceDoc for more details.

The example syntax sets the SourceItem property to a subset of the Q1ACTUAL.XLS worksheet. Excel specifies items in the familiar R1C1 row/column format, so the SourceItem here specifies everything from the top-left corner (row 1, column 1) to the bottom right corner at row 587, column 48.

Excel also supports named ranges, so if the worksheet had a name defined for this region, you could use that instead. For instance, R1C1:R587C48 might be defined as "MarketingExpenses". You could then set SourceItem = "MarketingExpenses". Just as constants make your Visual Basic code self-documenting and easier to debug, named ranges make spreadsheets and other documents easier to work with and change. If the spreadsheet had some rows inserted in this range, R1C1:R587C48 would then be incorrect, but "MarketingExpenses" would still work fine.

Many originating applications let you specify some subset of data to use, but there are as many ways of specifying this as there are applications. You'll need to

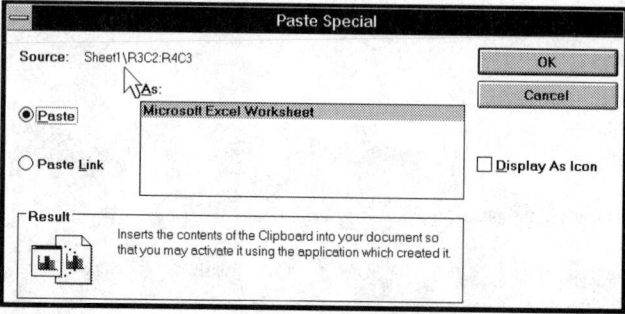

Figure 26-14 Use Paste Special to discover how an undocumented application specifies subsets

carefully read the originating application's documentation to see how it specifies subsets of data, and if it supports named ranges.

You may be able to determine how an application works with subsets even without the documentation's help by using this trick: Select the data you'd like in the originating application, and copy it onto the Clipboard. Then use Paste Special (set the Action property to 14) to paste it into an OLE control in Visual Basic. Look at the Source line in the Paste Special dialog box to see whether the application uses an exclamation (!) or backslash (\), and how it specifies the subset. Figure 26-14 shows how this looks in the property box.

Example

The formInfo project at the end of this chapter doesn't directly set the SourceItem property. It relies on the fact that properly setting the SourceDoc property can correctly specify the SourceItem, as in the cmndReport_Click event.

UPDATED EVENT

Objects Affected

Check	Clipboard	Combo	Command	CommonDlg
Data	Debug	Dir	Drive	File
Form	Frame	Grid	Image	Label
Line	List	MDI Form	Menu	▶ OLE
Option	Picture	Printer	Screen	Scroll
Shape	Text	Timer		

Purpose

Use the Updated event to react to when an object's data changes. Tables 26-35 and 26-36 summarize the arguments of the Updated event.

General Syntax

```
Sub Name_Updated (Code As Integer)
```

Argument	Meaning
Name	Name property of the control
Code	Indicates what action triggered the event

Table 26-35 Arguments of the Updated event

Code	CONSTANT.TXT	Meaning
0	OLE_CHANGED	Object's data has changed
1	OLE_SAVED	Object has been saved by the originating application
2	OLE_CLOSED	File containing linked object's data closed by originating application
3	OLE_RENAMED	File containing linked object's data renamed by originating application

Table 26-36 Meanings of the Code argument in the Updated event

Example Syntax

```
Sub Ole1_Updated (Code As Integer)
    Select Case Code
        Case OLE_CHANGED: NeedToSave = True
        Case OLE_SAVED:   NeedToSave = False
        Case OLE_CLOSED:  NeedToSave = False
        Case OLE_RENAMED: NeedToSave = False
    End Select
End Sub
```

Description

Use the Updated event to react to changes in an OLE control's object. The Code argument lets you take different actions depending on what triggered the event. Note that each of these Code constants is defined in CONSTANT.TXT. See the discussion in the Summary section at the beginning of this chapter for details on how to use these constants.

The example syntax shows a typical use for this event. The Select Case statement sets the global variable NeedToSave when the control is updated. It assumes that the object needs to be saved if it has changed, and doesn't need to be saved if the user has already saved it, closed the application, or renamed it by saving under a different file name.

See Chapter 7, Events, for more about event procedures.

Example

The formInfo project at the end of this chapter uses a global array to track when changes have been made to the OLE containers. The array is flagged in the Update event, and this helps determine whether or not to enable the File Save command.

UPDATEOPTIONS PROPERTY

Objects Affected

Check	Clipboard	Combo	Command	CommonDlg
Data	Debug	Dir	Drive	File
Form	Frame	Grid	Image	Label
Line	List	MDI Form	Menu	▶ OLE
Option	Picture	Printer	Screen	Scroll
Shape	Text	Timer		

Purpose

The UpdateOptions property sets and reads how an OLE control is updated when the linked data changes. It is not available at design time, and will read and write at runtime. Tables 26-37 and 26-38 summarize the arguments of the UpdateOptions property.

General Syntax

```
[form!]Name.UpdateOptions [ = setting%]
```

Argument	Meaning
form	Name property of the parent form
Name	Name property of the control
setting%	Determines how the control is updated: automatic, frozen, or manual

Table 26-37 Arguments of the UpdateOptions property

setting%	CONSTANT.TXT	Meaning
0	OLE_AUTOMATIC	(Default) Object updated each time link data changes
1	OLE_FROZEN	Object updated when originating application saves linked data
2	OLE_MANUAL	Object updated only by Action 6 (OLE_UPDATE)

Table 26-38 Meanings of the setting% argument of the UpdateOptions property

Example Syntax

```
Sub Check1_Click ()
    If Check1.Value = CHECKED Then
        Ole1.UpdateOptions = OLE_AUTOMATIC
    Else
        Ole1.UpdateOptions = OLE_MANUAL
    End If
End Sub
```

Description

Use the UpdateOptions property to determine how the OLE control is updated when its linked data changes. This is only used for linked objects. An embedded object, by definition, cannot have its data changed by external applications. Note that each of these UpdateOptions constants is defined in CONSTANT.TXT. See the discussion in the Summary section at the beginning of this chapter for details on how to use these constants.

This property is most useful for objects that take a long time to display, or that change frequently. For example, assume the object is a graph showing assembly line speed that is updated every three seconds. Setting UpdateOptions to OLE_AUTOMATIC would probably degrade the performance of your application as it tries to keep up with the ever-changing display. It might be smarter to set the property to OLE_MANUAL and have either a user action (like a mouse click) or a timer set to a longer interval update the control.

Each change in the linked data triggers an Updated event. You can then use that event with OLE_MANUAL to fine tune the object's updates. You might have a static variable in the Updated event that counts a certain number of updates before it refreshes the object.

Example

All of the OLE containers in the formInfo project at the end of this chapter are kept to their default value of Automatic.

VERB PROPERTY

Objects Affected

Check	Clipboard	Combo	Command	CommonDlg
Data	Debug	Dir	Drive	File
Form	Frame	Grid	Image	Label
Line	List	MDI Form	Menu	▶ OLE
Option	Picture	Printer	Screen	Scroll
Shape	Text	Timer		

Purpose

Each object can have certain actions performed on it. The *verb* specifies what action to take. It will read and write at both design and runtime. Tables 26-39 and 26-40 summarize the arguments and settings of the Verb property.

General Syntax

`[form!]Name.Verb [ = setting%]`

Argument	Meaning
form	Name property of the parent form
Name	Name property of the control

Argument	Meaning
setting%	Index number of the action to take in the ObjectVerbs list

Table 26-39 Arguments of the Verb property

setting%	CONSTANT.TXT	Meaning
0	VERB_PRIMARY	Default verb for object
-1	VERB_SHOW	Open object for editing (in place if supported)
-2	VERB_OPEN	Open object for editing in its own window
-3	VERB_HIDE	Hide the originating application
-4	VERB_INPLACEUIACTIVATE	Leave object open for editing with user interface elements on screen when focus leaves
-5	VERB_INPLACEACTIVATE	Leave object open for editing when focus leaves

Table 26-40 Verbs that almost all objects support

Example

```
Sub Command1_Click ()
    Ole1.Verb = VERB_HIDE            'set up object to hide application
    Ole1.Action = OLE_ACTIVATE       'activate the object
    If Ole1.AppIsRunning Then         'if object successfully activated, then
        Ole1.Object.Insert "Hello"   'paste string data using automation
        Ole1.Action = OLE_UPDATE     'and update the OLE control's display
    End If
End Sub
```

Description

Objects can have certain actions that can take place with them. These actions are called *verbs*. Each object supports a different set of verbs, and some verbs may or may not be applicable depending on the state of the object. For example, a sound application might have Play, Rewind, and Record as verbs. If the object doesn't contain any sound, then Play and Rewind don't apply, but Record does.

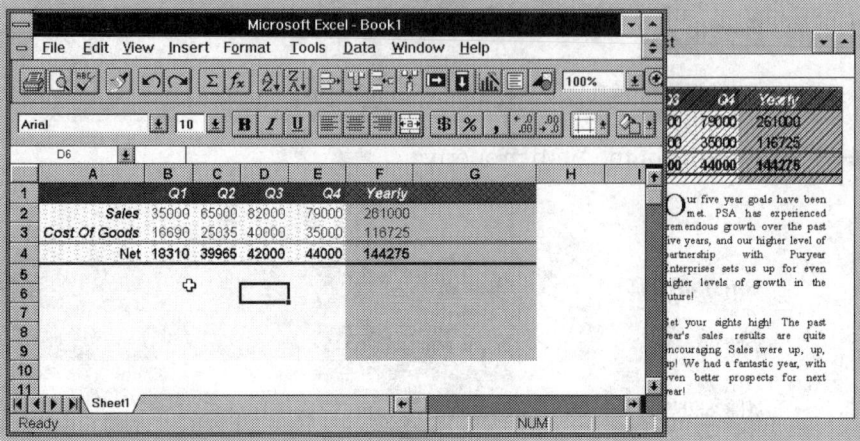

Figure 26-15 The spreadsheet can be edited in the originating application, or…

Verbs can be triggered either manually or automatically. You can trigger a verb manually by using the Action property with OLE_ACTIVATE. You can set an object to activate automatically and trigger the verb by setting the AutoActivate property to either OLE_GETFOCUS or OLE_DOUBLECLICK. The verb would then trigger each time the OLE control got the focus or the user double-clicked on it, depending on the setting you gave to the AutoActivate property.

Almost all objects support the standard verbs shown in Table 26-40. Note that each of these Verb constants is defined in CONSTANT.TXT. See the discussion in the Summary section at the beginning of this chapter for details on how to use these constants.

Each object has a default action that can operate on it. For instance, a sound application might define "Play" as its default verb. A spreadsheet might define "Edit" as its default verb.

Almost all objects can be edited, and there are several different editing values depending on whether the object supports in-place editing and how you want it to respond. The simplest setting is -2, OLE_OPEN. This will always put the object in its own window and shift focus to the originating application, even if the object supports in-place editing. If you specify -1, OLE_SHOW, the object can be edited in-place while it has the focus (assuming the object supports in-place editing). In-place editing leaves the object in the OLE control rather than opening a separate window and places the originating application's user interface elements (such as floating palettes) directly in your application. It looks as if your application is doing all the work. Figure 26-15 shows an object being edited in the originating application, and Figure 26-16 shows the same object being edited in-place.

You can also specify that the object remain active and editable even when it loses focus by using settings -4 and -5. Setting -5, OLE_INPLACEACTIVATE, is just like -1, OLE_SHOW, except that the object is always active and will probably go into edit mode more quickly. Setting -4, OLE_INPLACEUIACTIVATE, leaves

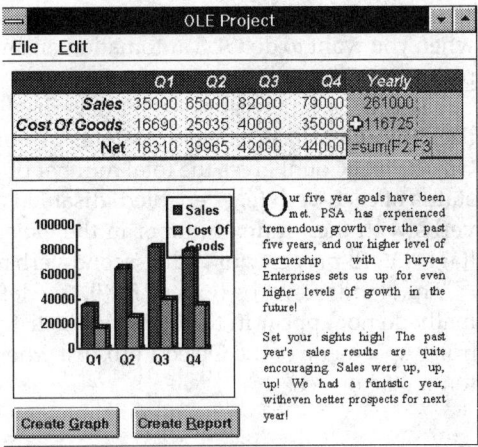

Figure 26-16 …can be edited in-place with
OLE_SHOW

the user interface elements on the screen at all times, even when the object loses focus. Figure 26-17 shows the same spreadsheet object as before with the user interface elements left on the screen.

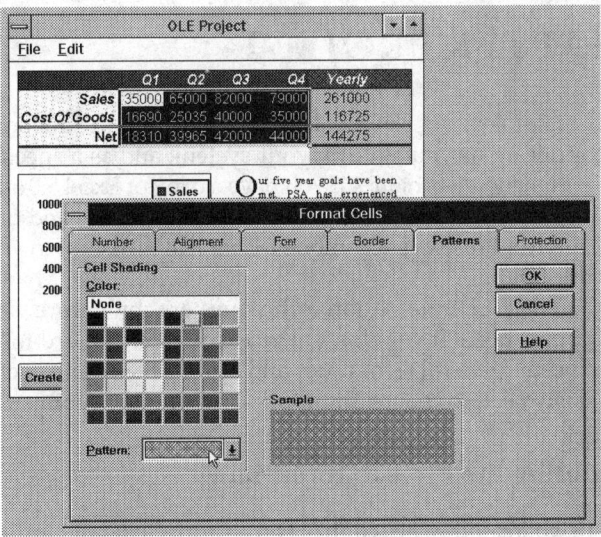

Figure 26-17 OLE_INPLACEUIACTIVATE leaves the originating application's user interface elements on the screen at all times

Option -3, OLE_HIDE, hides the originating application. This might be useful when you want to do OLE automation on an OLE control's object, as in the example syntax.

Many applications support more verbs than just these standard ones. You can use the ObjectVerbs list to get a complete list of supported verbs. ObjectVerbsCount gives the total number of verbs, and ObjectVerbFlags gives the status of each verb (e.g., enabled, disabled, or checked). You then specify these verbs with their index number in the ObjectVerbs array: The first verb would have a Verb property of 1, the second verb a Verb property of 2, and so on.

The standard verbs (except for 0, the default verb) listed in Table 26-40 normally do not appear in the ObjectVerbs list. Setting AutoVerbMenu to True will bring up a menu of the ObjectVerbs list when the user clicks the right mouse button on the object.

Example

The formInfo project at the end of this chapter sets the Verb property many times, and generally to -3 (VERB_HIDE). The Verb property is usually set immediately before activating the OLE object. The menuDOCPop_Click event also sets the Verb property, but lets the index of the chosen menu item (as initially set by the ObjectVerb array in the menuDOC_Click event) control what verb to use.

CHAPTER PROJECT

This project can be used both as a general introduction to OLE no matter what applications you have on your system, and as a specific demonstration of OLE automation techniques if you have a copy of Excel 5.0 and Word for Windows 6.0.

We implement a full OLE aware Edit menu, and demonstrate both OLE file open and file save techniques. This will be useful to you in any application that uses OLE.

The OLE automation techniques are, by nature, specific to individual host applications. If you don't have Excel 5.0 and Word for Windows 6.0, you'll still find the general techniques and approaches quite useful, although you'll obviously need to change the application-specific commands.

Assembling the Project: formMain

1. Place the following controls on a form, as detailed in Table 26-41. After placing the controls on the form, use the Menu Design dialog box to create the menu structure detailed in Table 26-42. Figure 26-18 shows what the completed form should look like.

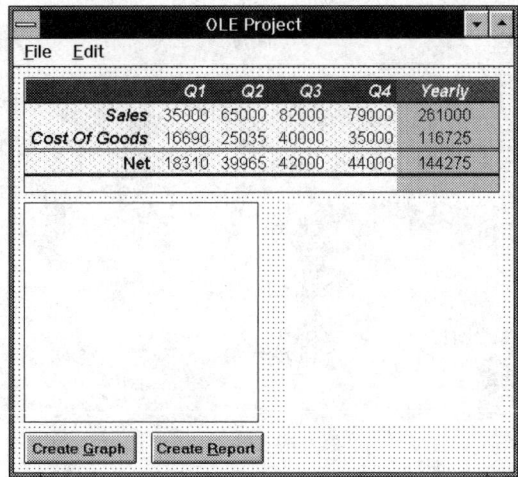

Figure 26-18 The completed formMain during
the design phase

Control	Property	Value
Form	Name	formMain
	BorderStyle	1–Fixed Single
	Caption	"OLE Project"
Command	Name	cmndReport
	Caption	"Create &Report"
Command	Name	cmndGraph
	Caption	"Create &Graph"
OLE	Name	ole
	AutoVerbMenu	0–False
	BorderStyle	0–None

(continued on next page)

(continued from previous page)

Control	Property	Value
	fFFHk	-1–True
	Index	0
OLE	Name	ole
	AutoVerbMenu	0–False
	BorderStyle	1–Fixed Single
	Index	1
OLE	Name	ole
	AutoVerbMenu	0–False
	BorderStyle	1–Fixed Single
	Index	2

Table 26-41 Elements of formMain

Name	Caption	Index
menuBar	&File	0
menuFile	&Open Objects	0
menuFile	&Save Objects	1
menuFile	-	2
menuFile	E&xit	3
menuBar	&Edit	1

Name	Caption	Index
menuEdit	Cu&t	0
menuEdit	&Copy	1
menuEdit	&Paste	2
menuEdit		3
menuEdit	Paste &Special	4
menuEdit	Insert &Object	5
menuEdit		6
menuEdit	&Info	7
menuDoc	(POPUP)	
menuDOCPop	&Generate	0
menuDOCPop	&Copy	1
menuDOCPop		2

Table 26-42 Menu structure for formMain

   2. Enter the following constant definitions into the Declarations section of formMain.

```
Const DOC = 0
Const GRAPH = 1
Const SHEET = 2

Const OLE_CREATE_EMBED = 0
Const OLE_COPY = 4
Const OLE_PASTE = 5
Const OLE_UPDATE = 6
Const OLE_ACTIVATE = 7
Const OLE_CLOSE = 9
Const OLE_DELETE = 10
Const OLE_SAVE_TO_FILE = 11
```

(continued on next page)

1053

(continued from previous page)

```
Const OLE_READ_FROM_FILE = 12
Const OLE_INSERT_OBJ_DLG = 14
Const OLE_PASTE_SPECIAL_DLG = 15
Const OLE_FETCH_VERBS = 17
Const OLE_SAVE_TO_OLE1FILE = 18

Const OLE_DISPLAY_CONTENT = 0

Const OLE_EMBEDDED = 1

Const VERB_PRIMARY = 0
Const VERB_SHOW = -1
Const VERB_OPEN = -2
Const VERB_HIDE = -3
Const VERB_INPLACEUIACTIVATE = -4
Const VERB_INPLACEACTIVATE = -5

Const VF_ENABLED = &H0000
Const VF_GRAYED = &H0001
Const VF_DISABLED = &H0002
Const VF_CHECKED = &H0008
Const VF_SEPARATOR = &H0800

Const DEFAULT = 0
Const HOURGLASS = 11

Dim oleChanged(3) As Integer
```

3. Enter the following code in the cmndGraph_Click event. This reads the information from the spreadsheet object and displays it as a graph object. It first accesses a range of numbers on the spreadsheet through OLE automation by way of the OLE container's Object property. Note that the line that copies the range on to the Clipboard is specific to the spreadsheet host application—Excel 5.0 in this case. Once the data has been placed on the Clipboard, it's easy to create a new object in the graph OLE container and send text to it with the DataText property. The spreadsheet places the information on the Clipboard in the correct format: Each column is tab-delimited, each row is carriage return-delimited.

```
Sub cmndGraph_Click ()

'This routine relies on having Excel 5.0 or greater and MSGraph 1.0 or greater.
'It will bomb unless you have both applications. The general techniques will
'work for OLE automation, but any line commented with ( >> ) is host-application
'specific

    OLE(SHEET).Verb = VERB_HIDE                              'keep app hidden
    OLE(SHEET).Action = OLE_ACTIVATE                         'activate host
    OLE(SHEET).Object.Range("QuarterlyFigures").Copy        ' >> copy to Clipboard
    OLE(SHEET).Action = OLE_CLOSE                            'close host
    AppActivate "OLE Project"                                'back to the project

    quarterlyFigures = Clipboard.GetText()                  'contents of Clipboard

    OLE(GRAPH).Verb = VERB_HIDE                              'keep app hidden
    OLE(GRAPH).Format = "CF_TEXT"                            'we're sending text
```

1054

```
OLE(GRAPH).Class = "MSGraph"                'graph
OLE(GRAPH).Action = OLE_CREATE_EMBED        'embedded object
OLE(GRAPH).Action = OLE_ACTIVATE            'activate host
OLE(GRAPH).DataText = quarterlyFigures      'send it the figures
OLE(GRAPH).Action = OLE_UPDATE              'and update the display

End Sub
```

4. Enter the following code in the cmndReport_Click event. This analyzes the sales trends shown by the sales figures in the spreadsheet object and creates a formatted document using OLE automation. The first few lines access the spreadsheet through the OLE container's Object property with OLE automation. Once the sales figures have been obtained, the routine calculates the overall trend (down, even, or up). It then calls a subroutine that makes up a sales talk based on the results.

The next section formats the document using OLE automation. Winword 6.0 does not support any OLE automation objects other than Word Basic (its macro language), so we restrict ourselves to using it exclusively. First, the routine alternates between the two methods of OLE automation, CreateObject and GetObject. Either method works well in this context, the only difference being that GetObject uses an existing document as a "template" to paste the text into, whereas CreateObject starts fresh with a new document. Once the object is created, a series of Word Basic statements are sent to the host via OLE automation. These format the document with full justification and drop caps, a job well-suited to advanced word processors and obviously easier than attempting the formatting ourselves within Visual Basic.

Finally, we issue a Word Basic command to save the object to disk. Note that the object has never been displayed anywhere, and has up to this point existed only as automation object. We set the OLE container's parameters appropriately to finally display the finished product by reading it in from the disk file.

```
Sub cmndReport_Click ()

'This routine relies on having Excel 5.0 or greater and Winword 6.0 or greater.
'It will bomb unless you have both applications. The general techniques will
'work for OLE automation, but any line commented with ( >> ) is host-application
'specific

    MousePointer = HOURGLASS                    'going to be awhile
    ReDim q(4) As Long                          'four quarter's figures
    Dim wordProc As Object                      'for word processor
    Dim avg1 As Long, avg2 As Long              'quarterly averages
    Static createOrGet As Integer               'two ways of automation

    OLE(SHEET).Verb = VERB_HIDE                 'keep app hidden
    OLE(SHEET).Action = OLE_ACTIVATE            'activate host
    For i = 1 To 4                              'for each of the 4 quarters,
        q(i) = OLE(SHEET).Object.Range("SalesFigures").Cells(1, i).Value
                                                ' >> get the sales total
    Next i
    OLE(SHEET).Action = OLE_CLOSE               'close the host
```

(continued on next page)

(continued from previous page)

```
        AppActivate "OLE Project"                              'the project

      avg1 = (q(1) + q(2)) / 2                                 'first half of year
      avg2 = (q(3) + q(4)) / 2                                 'second half of year
      textToSet = CreateSpiel(avg1, avg2)                      'make up the sales talk

'you can use either CreateObject or GetObject for OLE automation. This block
'alternates between the two methods. CreateObject creates an automation object 'out of
"thin air", while GetObject uses an existing word processor document
'as a "template."

      If createOrGet = False Then                              'use CreateObject?
        Set wordProc = CreateObject("Word.Basic")              'create the object
        wordProc.filenew                                       ' >> create a new document
        createOrGet = True                                     'flip the flag for next time
      Else
        Set wordProc = GetObject(App.Path & "\CHP26A.DOC")     'blank template
        createOrGet = False                                    'flip the flag for next time
      End If
      DoEvents                                                 'give the system some time
      wordProc.FilePageSetup 0, 0, .2, .2, .2, .2, 0, "1.6 in", "10 in"
                                                               ' >> set document margins
      wordProc.Insert textToSet                                ' >> sales talk
      wordProc.EditSelectAll                                   ' >> select entire document
      wordProc.FormatParagraph .1, .1, .1, 8, 0, 0, 3          ' >> paragraph spacing
      wordProc.FormatFont 8                                    ' >> set font to 8 point
      wordProc.StartOfDocument                                 ' >> goto beginning
      wordProc.FormatDropCap 1, , 2, 1                         ' >> format first letter
      wordProc.ParaDown 1                                      ' >> goto next paragraph
      wordProc.FormatDropCap 1, , 2, 1                         ' >> format first letter
      wordProc.FileSaveAs App.Path & "\oledoc.dat"            ' >> save document
      wordProc.FileCloseAll 2                                  ' >> close documents

      OLE(DOC).Class = "Word.Document"                         'set class to Winword 6.0
      OLE(DOC).OLETypeAllowed = OLE_EITHER                     'either linked or embedded
      OLE(DOC).SourceDoc = App.Path & "\oledoc.dat"          'the document we just saved
      OLE(DOC).Action = OLE_CREATE_EMBED                       'an embedded document
      MousePointer = DEFAULT                                   'all done!


End Sub
```

5. Type the following routine into the Declarations section. This function creates a sales talk given two paramaters. It rather simplistically calculates a trend in the two arguments (downward, even, upward) and creates the appropriate text.

```
Function CreateSpiel (a1 As Long, a2 As Long) As String

'create a sales talk, with different verbage dependent on last year's results
      Select Case Sgn(a2 - a1)         'down, even, or upward trend?
          Case -1
              results = "Although sales declined overall for the year, "
              results = results & "we anticipate phenomonal growth next year!"
          Case 0
              results = "Sales were relatively flat throughout the year. "
              results = results & "The strengthening economy will help us set "
              results = results & "new productivity records next year!"
```

```
        Case 1
                results = "Sales were up, up, up! We had a fantastic year, with"
                results = results & "even better prospects for next year!"
        End Select
        spiel = "Our five year goals have been met. "
        spiel = spiel & "PSA has experienced tremendous growth over the past "
        spiel = spiel & "five years, and our higher level of partnership with "
        spiel = spiel & "Puryear Enterprises sets us up for even higher levels "
        spiel = spiel & "of growth in the future!" & Chr$(13)
        spiel = spiel & "Set your sights high! The past year's sales results "
        spiel = spiel & " are quite encouraging. "
        spiel = spiel & results

        CreateSpiel = spiel

End Function
```

6. Type the following code into the Form_Load event This routine sets some of the
    OLE containers' properties.

```
Sub Form_Load ()

    For i = DOC to SHEET                              'for each OLE container,
        OLE(i).HostName = "OLE Project"               'set the host name
        OLE(i).DisplayType = OLE_DISPLAY_CONTENT      'and display type
        If i <> DOC Then                              'SHEET and GRAPH
            OLE(i).AutoVerbMenu = True                'have automatic menus
        Else                                          'but
            OLE(i).AutoVerbMenu = False               'menu created manually
                                                      '(in menuDOC_Click)
        End If
    Next i
    menuFile_Click 0                                  'open objects

End Sub
```

7. Type the following code into the menuBar_Click event. This event triggers when
    the user first pulls down a menu, and it enables the menu options appropriate to
    the context. The File menu checks to see if any of the containers' objects have
    changed, and enables the Save option if they have. The Edit menu checks to see
    if the focus is on an OLE container. If so, then it will enable the Cut, Copy, and
    Info commands if there is an object currently in the container, and will enable the
    Paste and Paste Special commands if there is something on the Clipboard that
    can be pasted.

```
Sub menuBar_Click (Index As Integer)

    Select Case Index
        Case 0 '********** File
            menuFile(1).Enabled = False              'turn off save
            For i = DOC To SHEET                      'go through containers
                If oleChanged(i) = True Then          'if it has changed,
                    menuFile(1).Enabled = True        'then enable File Save
                End If
            Next i
```

(continued on next page)

(*continued from previous page*)

```
            Case 1 '*********** Edit
                For i = 0 To 7                          'iterate through Edit
                                                        'menu commands (except
                                                        'separator bars)
                        If (i <> 3 And i <> 6) Then menuEdit(i).Enabled = False
                                                        'and turn them off
                Next i
                Dim s As Control
                Set s = Screen.ActiveControl            'control that has focus
                If TypeOf s Is OLE Then                  'if it's OLE control,
                    menuEdit(5).Enabled = True           'enable Insert Object
                    If s.OLEType <> 3 Then               'if it's got an object
                        menuEdit(0).Enabled = True       'enable Cut
                        menuEdit(1).Enabled = True       'enable Copy
                        menuEdit(7).Enabled = True       'enable Info
                    End If
                    If s.PasteOK Then                    'if the Clipboard has a
                                                        'pastable object
                        menuEdit(2).Enabled = True       'enable Paste
                        menuEdit(4).Enabled = True       'enable Paste Special
                    End If
                End If
        End Select
End Sub
```

8. Type the following code into the menuDOCPop_Click routine. This event runs when the user chooses a command from the pop-up menu, which is triggered by a right mouse click on the document OLE container. The menu is built in the OLE containers' MouseDown event, and has two static menu choices, a separator bar, and then a variable number of menu commands as determined by the object's verbs. This routine first removes all of the variable menu items (the verbs) to prepare the menu structure for the next time the user right-clicks on the OLE container. It then calls the appropriate routine for the first two choices, and sets the appropriate verb for the variable menu items.

```
Sub menuDOCPop_Click (Index As Integer)

    On Error GoTo noMoreItems               'no more menu items (verbs)
    i = 3                                   'custom menu items begin after
                                            'separator bar
    Do
        Unload menuDOCPop(i)                'get rid of custom menu item
        i = i + 1                           'and go to next one
    Loop

noMoreItems:                               'ok, we've zapped all the verbs!
    On Error GoTo 0

    Select Case Index                       'choose the correct menu item
        Case 0 ' ------- Generate
            cmndReport_Click                'generate the sales talk again
        Case 1 ' ------- Copy
            menuEdit_Click 1                'copy the sales talk to the Clipboard
        Case 2 ' ------- Separator bar
        Case Is > 2                         'if it was a custom item (that is,
                                            'an object verb)
```

```
            OLE(DOC).Verb = Index - 2        'set the verb appropriately
            OLE(DOC).Action = OLE_ACTIVATE   'and perform the verb
    End Select
    Exit Sub

End Sub
```

9. Type the following code into the menuEdit_Click routine. This routine triggers when the user chooses a command from the Edit menu. Note that the menuBar_Click routine only enables commands that are appropriate for the context, so we don't have to perform any additional checks in this routine. For example, we can assume that there is acceptable data already on the Clipboard and that we're on an OLE container that can accept it if either of the Paste commands was selected. As you can see, the code to implement an OLE-aware Edit menu is not very involved. You could also combine this with the DDE aware Edit menu in Chapter 25's project.

```
Sub menuEdit_Click (Index As Integer)

    Dim s As Control
    Set s = Screen.ActiveControl              'control that has focus
    formMain.MousePointer = HOURGLASS         'we're going to be awhile
    Select Case Index
        Case 0 '*********** Cut
            If Not s.AppIsRunning Then        'if host app isn't running,
                s.Verb = VERB_HIDE            'make sure it stays hidden
                s.Action = OLE_ACTIVATE       'and start it up
            End If
            s.Action = OLE_COPY               'copy object to Clipboard
            s.Action = OLE_DELETE             'and get rid of it
        Case 1 '*********** Copy
            If Not s.AppIsRunning Then        'if host app isn't running,
                s.Verb = VERB_HIDE            'make sure it stays hidden
                s.Action = OLE_ACTIVATE       'and start it up
            End If
            s.Action = OLE_COPY               'copy object to Clipboard
        Case 2 '*********** Paste
            s.Class = "temp"                  'if OLE container has never
                                              'been used, class needs to be
                                              'set to something (but
                                              'doesn't really matter what)
            s.Action = OLE_PASTE              'paste the contents of
                                              'Clipboard into container
        Case 3 '*********** (separator bar)
        Case 4 '*********** Paste Special
            s.Action = OLE_PASTE_SPECIAL_DLG  'open Paste Special dialog
        Case 5 '*********** Insert Object
            s.Action = OLE_INSERT_OBJ_DLG     'open Insert Object dialog
        Case 6 ' *********** Separator Bar
        Case 7 ' *********** Info
            printInfo s                       'print info about object
    End Select

    If s.OLEType <> 3 Then                     'object in the OLE container?
        s.Action = OLE_CLOSE                   'close host
        s.Refresh                              'and update display
```

(continued on next page)

```
        End If
        formMain.MousePointer = DEFAULT                    'all done!

End Sub
```

10. Type the following code into the menuFile_Click event. This event triggers when the user chooses a command from the File menu. The Open and Save options are very similar, differing only in what we specify for the OLE Action property. In both cases, we simply open the appropriate file as a Binary file, pass the file number to the OLE containers, and make the OLE container take the appropriate action. This allows the user to both save and open embedded OLE objects without using the host application's save or open functions.

```
Sub menuFile_Click (Index As Integer)

    Select Case Index
        Case 0 ' *********** Open objects
            fileNum = FreeFile                             'get a file handle
            Open App.Path & "\oleobject.dat" For Binary As fileNum    'open
            For i = DOC To SHEET                           'iterate through containers
                OLE(i).FileNumber = fileNum                'set container's file handle
                If OLE(i).OLEType <> 3 Then                'if it's got an object in it,
                    OLE(i).Action = OLE_READ_FROM_FILE 'get object from file
                End If
                oleChanged(i) = False                      'disable saving
            Next i
            Close fileNum                                  'close the file
        Case 1 ' *********** Save objects
            fileNum = FreeFile                             'get a file handle
            Open App.Path & "\oleobject.dat" For Binary As fileNum    'open
            For i = DOC To SHEET                           'iterate through containers
                OLE(i).FileNumber = fileNum                'set the container's file
                If OLE(i).OLEType <> 3 Then                'if it's got an object
                    OLE(i).Action = OLE_SAVE_TO_FILE   'save the object
                End If
                oleChanged(i) = False                      'disable saving
            Next i
            Close fileNum                                  'close the file
Case 2 ' *********** (separator bar)
        Case 3
            End
    End Select

End Sub
```

11. Type the following code into the OLE_MouseDown event. This triggers whenever the user clicks on any of the OLE containers. We first filter the event to recognize only right mouse clicks on the document container (the lower-right OLE control), and check to make sure it's got an object currently in it. If so, we add whatever verbs it supports in its current state to the pop-up menu, and then display the menu.

```
Sub OLE_MouseDown (Index As Integer, Button As Integer, Shift As Integer, X As Single, Y As Single)

    If Button = 2 And Index = DOC And OLE(DOC).OLEType <> 3 Then
                            'right button, on doc, with an object in it:
```

```
    OLE(DOC).Action = OLE_FETCH_VERBS              'update the available verbs
    For i = 1 To OLE(DOC).ObjectVerbsCount - 1     'iterate through each verb
        Load menuDOCPop(2 + i)                     'add a new menu item for verb
        menuDOCPop(2 + i).Caption = OLE(DOC).ObjectVerbs(i) 'and add the verb
    Next i
    PopupMenu menuDOC                              'pop up the menu
  End If

End Sub
```

12. Type the following code into the OLE_Resize event. This event triggers whenever the OLE containers' object changes size. We first filter it to recognize only changes to the document container. If the change occurred in that container, we limit the maximum size the container can assume.

```
Sub OLE_Resize (Index As Integer, HeightNew As Single, WidthNew As Single)
    If Index = DOC Then                            'just for the sales talk,
        If HeightNew > 2772 Then HeightNew = 2772  'don't exceed these
        If WidthNew > 2532 Then WidthNew = 2532    'maximum dimensions
    End If

End Sub
```

13. Type the following code into the OLE_Updated event. This triggers whenever the object in the OLE container gets updated. We check to see if the kind of update is for changed data (Code = 0), and if so, flag the global tracking array so the menuFile_Click event can enable the File Save Objects command.

```
Sub OLE_Updated (Index As Integer, Code As Integer)

    If Code = 0 Then oleChanged(Code) = True       'if object has changed, then
                                                   'flag it to enable saving

End Sub
```

14. Type the following code into the Declarations section of formMain. This routine prints out pertinent information about the current OLE container. It displays a blank form, and prints out some of the underlying details about the object.

```
Sub printInfo (s As Control)

    formInfo.Show                                  'show info form
    formInfo.Cls                                   'wipe it clean
    If Not s.AppIsRunning Then                     'if the host isn't running
        s.Verb = VERB_HIDE                         'make sure it stays hidden
        s.Action = OLE_ACTIVATE                    'and start it up
    End If
    formInfo.Print
    formInfo.Print "  Class:";
    formInfo.Print Tab(20); s.Class                'host class
    formInfo.Print
    formInfo.Print "  Accept Formats:";            'host accepted formats,
    For i = 0 To s.ObjectAcceptFormatsCount - 1    'iterating through each one
        formInfo.Print Tab(20); s.ObjectAcceptFormats(i)
    Next i
    formInfo.Print
    formInfo.Print "  Return Formats:";            'host returned formats,
    For i = 0 To s.ObjectGetFormatsCount - 1       'iterating through each one
```

(continued on next page)

(continued from previous page)

```
        formInfo.Print Tab(20); s.ObjectGetFormats(i)
    Next i
    formInfo.Print
    formInfo.Print "  Verbs:";                        'host verbs,
    For i = 1 To s.ObjectVerbsCount - 1               'iterating through each one
        formInfo.Print Tab(20); s.ObjectVerbs(i); Tab(40);
        Select Case s.ObjectVerbFlags(i)              'and print the menu state
            Case VF_CHECKED: formInfo.Print "Checked"
            Case VF_DISABLED: formInfo.Print "Disabled"
            Case VF_ENABLED: formInfo.Print "Enabled"
            Case VF_GRAYED: formInfo.Print "Grayed"
            Case VF_SEPARATOR: formInfo.Print "Separator"
        End Select
    Next i

    formInfo.Print
    formInfo.Print "  Long Pointer: ";                'memory position of object
    formInfo.Print Tab(20); Hex$(s.LpOleObject)       '(could use with API calls)

    formInfo.Print
    s.Format = "Native"
    formInfo.Print "  Data:";                         'print the GDI handle
    formInfo.Print Tab(20); Hex$(s.Data)

End Sub
```

Assembling the Project: formInfo

1. Create a new form to display the information printed by formMain's Edit Info command. Table 26-43 details the components of the form. Size and position the elements as illustrated in Figure 26-19.

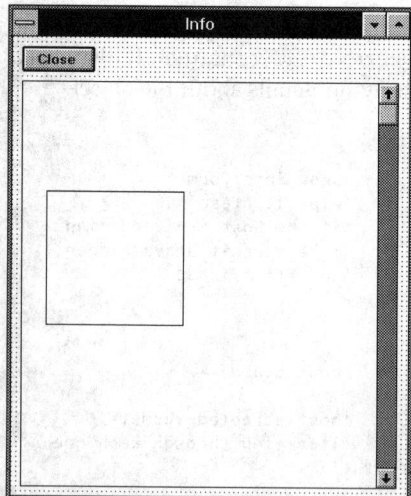

Figure 26-19 formInfo during the design phase

Control	Property	Value
Form	BorderStyle	2–Fixed Double
	Name	formInfo
Command	Cancel	-1–True
	Caption	Close
	Default	-1–True
	Name	cmndClose

Table 26-43 Elements of formInfo

2. Type the following code into the cmndClose_Click event. This hides the form from view.

```
Sub cmndClose_Click ()
    Me.Hide
End Sub
```

How It Works

This project can be used both as a general introduction to OLE no matter what you have on your system, and as a specific demonstration of OLE automation techniques if you have a copy of Excel 5.0 and Word for Windows 6.0.

When the project first opens, it displays an embedded Excel spreadsheet in the top container, and two empty containers on the bottom of the form. Clicking on the Create Graph command button starts a routine that gets the data from the Excel spreadsheet using OLE automation, and then creates a graph using the MSGraph applet that comes with Word for Windows (and other Microsoft applications.) Clicking on the Create Report command button retrieves different data from the Excel spreadsheet, and then creates a formatted document using OLE automation to access the Word for Windows programming language. The formatting routine applies formatting to the document that would be difficult to achieve by just printing the words on a Visual Basic picture box control—the full justification and drop caps would require quite a bit of computation to determine the exact placement of each letter in the report. It is far simpler to use the power of Word for Windows to do the formatting for us.

You can also edit each of these objects by right-clicking the mouse on them and choosing either the Edit or Open command from the pop-up menu. Choosing

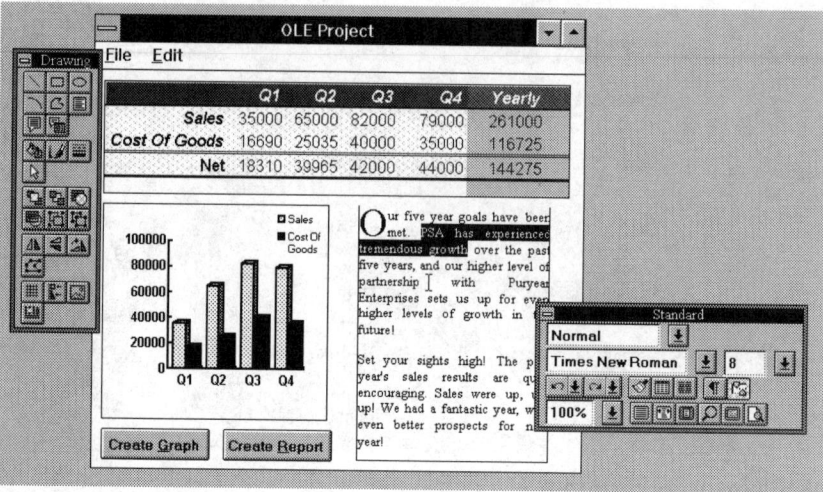

Figure 26-20 The OLE project in action, showing in-place activation

Open will open the document in its own window, with the full power of the host application. Choosing Edit will open the document in-place, letting you edit it without ever appearing to leave the Visual Basic project. This is the real power of OLE—it would be extraordinarily difficult to implement a full- fledged word processor, spreadsheet, or graphic application on your own, but it's very easy to do this by embedding OLE objects. Figure 26-20 shows what the project looks like after creating both the graph and the document. The document is being edited, and you can see Word for Windows floating palettes.

The demonstrations above require Excel 5.0, Winword 6.0, and MSGraph to be available on your system, and will not work without them. This demonstrates the negative side of OLE automation: You cannot distribute a self-contained Visual Basic application, but must rely on the user having a certain specified set of programs.

You'll still find this project useful if you don't have these programs on your system. Notice that the spreadsheet still appears in the top OLE container even without Excel. Remember that OLE containers only display an image of the data unless they're active. What you're seeing is only a picture of what the spreadsheet looks like. Attempting to activate it will generate an error.

Your system will undoubtedly have at least a few OLE applications registered. At a minimum, most users will have at least Paintbrush and Sound, both of which come with Windows 3.1. You can use the Edit menu's Insert Object command to insert either a new object or retrieve an existing file. Try inserting a bitmap using the Paintbrush application. Once you've inserted the object, you can edit it (right-click to bring up the pop-up menu), Cut it, Copy it, or to get Info on it. If you copy it to the Clipboard, you can paste it into another OLE container, or even into another application. Note that most applications will display the title we gave in the HostName property when referring to the object. You can also save the objects and open them using the File menu commands.

27

DATA ACCESS

One of the most exciting developments in Visual Basic 3.0 is its ability to manipulate databases using the powerful Access database engine. This gives you the power of a dedicated relational database with the fine control over the user interface inherent in Visual Basic.

Visual Basic uses the data control to access the database engine. This control lets you specify which database file to attach to, which format (MS Access, dBase, FoxPro, Paradox, or Btrieve) the database is in, and what type of access you need (exclusive or multi-user). It then lets you move around in the database with its built in VCR-style controls. You can perform direct manipulation on the database with your code by using the data control's properties and methods and respond to changes in the database with its events. Finally, controls may be *bound* to the data control. A bound control automatically updates the underlying database record when edited and automatically displays the proper information when the current record changes. Figure 27-1 shows the data control and some controls bound to it.

This chapter covers the data control and the controls bound to it and introduces the events, methods, and properties associated with them.

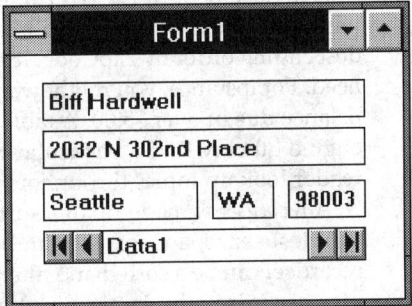

Figure 27-1 The data control and controls bound to it give you effortless access to your databases

1065

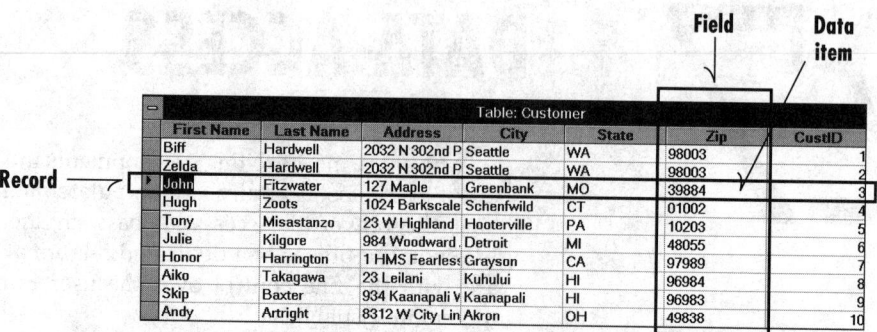

Figure 27-2 Databases are made up of tables containing data items organized by records and fields

DATABASE DESIGN

A *database* is a collection of information stored in an organized way. The Access database engine translates other kinds of database formats (like dBase or Paradox) into its own format. This means that no matter what kind of database you're accessing, you always refer to the structural elements in the same way.

A database is made up of one or more *tables* containing zero or more records. Each record contains one or more *fields*. You can think of a table as being analogous to a spreadsheet, with a record being a row and a field as a column. The intersection of the record and field in a table is called an *item*. The record that the database is operating on is called the *current record*. Figure 27-2 illustrates a typical database table.

A table may be *sorted*, or arranged in a particular order. For example, you may wish to see your data sorted alphabetically by the field CityName, or perhaps in descending order by ZipCode. It may also be *filtered* to show just the records you need. For instance, you might want to see just the records from Wisconsin with a balance due of over $5.00. A table may have various *indexes* that let the database engine quickly find a particular record, much as the index of a book helps the reader look up topics throughout the book.

A *recordset* is made up of a sorted, filtered subset of one or more tables. In its simplest sense, a recordset can be a direct copy of a table. More commonly, a recordset can be a sorted and filtered copy of the table. You can create more complex recordsets by joining multiple tables with a variety of sorts and filters. Changes to a recordset automatically update the underlying table; changes to the underlying table automatically update any recordsets built with that table. The data control operates on a recordset, not the actual table. Figure 27-3 shows a sorted, filtered subset of Figure 27-2's example data.

Last Name	Address	City	State	Zip
Artright	8312 W City Lin	Akron	OH	49838
Baxter	934 Kaanapali V	Kaanapali	HI	96983
Fitzwater	127 Maple	Greenbank	MO	39884
Harrington	1 HMS Fearles:	Grayson	CA	97989
Kilgore	984 Woodward	Detroit	MI	48055
Misastanzo	23 W Highland	Hooterville	PA	10203
Takagawa	23 Leilani	Kuhului	HI	96984

Select Query: Query1

Figure 27-3 Recordsets are made up of sorted, filtered subsets of one or more tables

RELATIONAL DATABASES

Sometimes multiple tables can refer to related information. For instance, you might have an entry for a customer listing the name, city, and state, along with a unique identifier for each customer called CustID. Each customer has a unique value stored in CustID to unambiguously identify that customer, even if multiple customers had the same name (for example, "Smith"). Another table might store individual transaction information on exactly what product each customer bought, the quantity, and the date. The transaction table would also have a CustID field to identify what customer the transaction belonged to.

This kind of shared information is called a *relation*. A *relational database* contains multiple tables with some sort of unambiguous links between the tables. In the Customer table, the CustID is called the *primary key*, as it is the primary means of identifying each particular customer record. In the Transaction table, CustID is called the *foreign key*, as it refers back to another table's primary key. This lets each transaction refer unambiguously to a particular customer. Figure 27-4 illustrates this relationship.

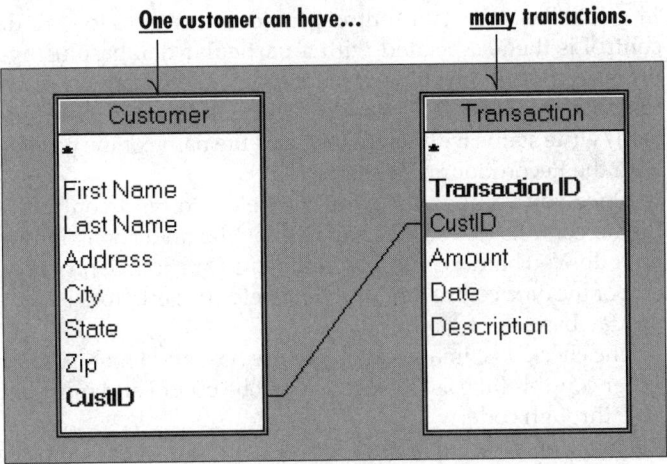

Figure 27-4 Relational databases have multiple related tables

The kind of relation shown in the above example is called a *one-to-many* relation. That is, *one* customer can have *many* transactions, but each transaction can only be associated with one customer. There are also *one-to-one* relations (for example, each Customer record is associated with a single CustomerCredit record) and *many-to-many* relations (for example, many Transactions can refer to many Products).

The action of relating two tables together is called making a *join*. There are several types of joins, including *normal joins, left outer joins, right outer joins,* and *inner joins.*

Visual Basic fully supports the relational database model. It uses *SQL*, or Structured Query Language, as its internal means of operation. SQL is a powerful database metalanguage that is at least nominally compatible between various vendors. You can use SQL statements in setting several recordset properties. For instance, setting a data control's RecordSource property with an SQL statement can provide a sorted, filtered subset of a multiple table join for use as your recordset. SQL also supports *action queries* that perform updates or deletions on a subset of your data. For instance, just one line of code can delete all records from the database that have CityName = "Dallas" and BalanceDue < $5.00.

SQL and the concepts involved in proper database design go well beyond what we can cover in this book. See some of the database books mentioned in the BIBLIO.MDB data file that came with Visual Basic for more on SQL, proper database design, relationships, and joins. The Execute, Find, and RecordSource entries in this chapter discuss the basics of SQL.

VISUAL BASIC'S DATA IMPLEMENTATION

In Visual Basic the data control provides the access to your databases. Each data control is then associated with a particular database using its DatabaseName property. Specify the type of database with the Connect property, multiuser status with the Exclusive property, various options with the Options property, read/write status with ReadOnly, and the name of the particular recordset to use with the RecordSource property.

Once you've done this, you may elect to bind controls to the data control. Bound controls let you edit and display the underlying information with little or no code. You bind a control by setting its DataSource property to the Name property of the data control and the DataField property to the name of the field within the database.

The check box, image, label, picture box, and text box controls may be bound. Other controls (like list boxes) may not be bound and must interact with the database through code.

Once you've set up a form with a data control and some bound controls, you can step through each record of the recordset using the data control's VCR-style

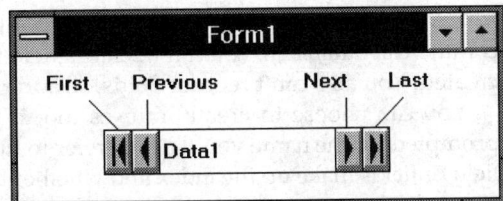

Figure 27-5 The data control's VCR-style buttons let you step through each record

arrow buttons. The four buttons represent First record, Previous record, Next record, and Last record. Figure 27-5 illustrates the data control.

The data control has events, methods, and properties that let you go further than just having the bound controls blindly follow along with the control's movement buttons. The Validate, Error, and Reposition events let you validate user entries, respond to database errors, and write custom database movement routines. A variety of methods let you add new records within your code, delete records, edit and update records, move through the database, start, commit, and undo entire *transactions* (several updates that must be considered as a unit, like a bank's debit and credit into two different accounts), execute SQL action statements on your database, and find out about your database's underlying structure. Finally, the data control's properties let you determine various settings of your database, filter it, sort it, determine which record you're on, set and go to *bookmarks* (individually marked records), and set or update the values of individual items.

DATA MANAGER

Visual Basic ships with a small utility that lets you create Access-compatible databases. With the Data Manager (DATAMGR.EXE), you can create a new database, define the structures of the tables within the database, and create a variety of indexes. Although the functionality is quite limited, it's enough to get the basics done.

To use the Data Manager, double-click on the Datamgr icon in the Visual Basic group in the Program Manager. You can create a new database with File New or open an existing one with File Open. If you're creating a database, you can specify Access 1.0 or 1.1 compatible. (Access 1.0 compatible would only be necessary if you've got an older copy of Microsoft Access that's never been upgraded.) It will then prompt you for the database name.

Once it's created the database, you then use the Table dialog box's New command to create a new table. Give the table a name and then proceed to add in new fields. For each field you can specify the name of the field, the data type, and for some fields (like Text) the actual size of the field. You can add additional tables to your database after you've completed each table.

Be careful to create only the fields you want. Unlike Microsoft Access or other commercial databases, you can't delete a field in the Data Manager once it's been created. You also can't reorder fields, so add them in the order you want them.

You can choose to create indexes too. When you add an index, you'll be prompted for the name you'll use to refer to the index and can then specify what field or fields make up the index and whether the index sorts the fields in ascending or descending order.

DATA ACCESS NOMENCLATURE

The majority of the properties and methods don't really act directly on the data control. Rather, they act on objects of the data control. For instance, you set an item's value by changing the data control's recordset's fields object's value property. The usual Visual Basic naming conventions still hold for data access, but are extended. For example, to set an item's value, you could specify

```
Form1!Data1.Recordset.Fields("CustID").Value = "BAKER23"
```

This translates as: "Set the value of the current record's CustID field, in the recordset associated with the Data1 control on Form1, to 'BAKER23.'" As you can see, the naming conventions allow you to be very specific with what you want done, but at the price of some readability.

You can use alternative, and shorter, syntax to accomplish the same thing. This line is identical in operation to the previous one:

```
Form1!Data1.Recordset!CustID = "BAKER23"
```

The exclamation mark (!) is the separator between the object (Recordset) and the item (CustID). This is similar to the nomenclature of Form1!Text1 = "BAKER23." The exclamation point separates the object (Form1) from the individual item (Text1), and sets Text1's default property, Text. We've mostly avoided using the default property shorthand in this book because of the potential increase in misunderstandings. Thus we would have written this last example as Form1!Text1.Text = "BAKER23" and explicitly given the property we're referencing. In the case of the data control, however, it's actually clearer to use the shorthand method.

PROPERTIES, EVENTS, AND METHODS OF DATA ACCESS

Tables 27-1, 27-2, 27-3 and 27-4 list the properties, events, and methods that relate to data access.

Use This...		To Do This...
Connect	Property	Read or set parameters for connections to external databases
Database	Property	Reference the associated Database object
DatabaseName	Property	Read or set the name and location of the database
DataChanged	Property	Read or set if bound control has new information to save
DataField	Property	Read or set the name of the field a control is bound to
DataSource	Property	Set the Name of the data control this control is bound to
EditMode	Property	Read the editing state of the current record
Error	Event	React to errors in reading data
Exclusive	Property	Read or set whether database is single or multiuser
Options	Property	Read or set characteristics of the control's Dynaset
ReadOnly	Property	Determine whether the Database is opened for read-only access
Recordset	Property	Access the data control's underlying Dynaset object
RecordSource	Property	Determine the source of records for the data control's recordset
Reposition	Event	React to when a new record becomes current
UpdateControls	Method	Make bound controls display the data in the underlying record
UpdateRecord	Method	Save bound controls without triggering the Validate event
Validate	Event	Initiate an action before a different record becomes current

Table 27-1 Properties, methods, and events for the data control and bound controls

Use This...		To Do This...
Attributes	Property	Determines how Visual Basic treats the field
Close	Method	Closes a database
CollatingOrder	Property	Returns the collating (sorting) order
Connect	Property	Returns the string used to connect the database
Count	Property	Returns the number of items in a collection
Execute	Method	Executes an SQL action query
Fields	Collection	Returns the details of the available fields
Indexes	Collection	Returns the details of the available indexes
TableDefs	Collection	Returns the details of the available fields
Transactions	Property	Returns whether a database supports transactions
Updatable	Property	Returns whether a database is updatable

Table 27-2 Properties, methods, and collections for the Database object

Use This...		To Do This...
AddNew	Method	Append a new record to the end of the recordset
AppendChunk	Method	Appends a string to a memo field
BOF	Property	Indicates if current record is at Beginning of File
Bookmark	Property	Sets or returns the pointer to individual records
Bookmarkable	Property	Returns whether a recordset supports bookmarks
Close	Method	Closes a recordset

Use This...		To Do This...
Delete	Method	Deletes the current record
Edit	Method	Opens the current record for editing
EOF	Property	Indicates if current record is at End of File
FieldSize	Method	Returns the size of a memo field
FindFirst	Method	Finds the first occurrence of a searchstring
FindLast	Method	Finds the last occurrence of a searchstring
FindNext	Method	Finds the next occurrence of a searchstring
FindPrevious	Method	Finds the previous occurrence of a searchstring
GetChunk	Method	Gets a string from a memo field
LockEdits	Property	Determine whether record is locked during editing
MoveFirst	Method	Moves to the first record of the recordset
MoveLast	Method	Moves to the last record of the recordset
MoveNext	Method	Moves to the next record of the recordset
MovePrevious	Method	Moves to the previous record of the recordset
NoMatch	Property	Determine whether the Find or Seek methods succeeded
RecordCount	Property	Read the number of records in a recordset
Update	Method	Updates changed records and saves to the database

Table 27-3 Properties and methods of the Recordset object

Use This...		To Do This...
BeginTrans	Statement	Begin a transaction block
CommitTrans	Statement	End a transaction block, commit changes
CompactDatabase	Statement	Compacts a database; can set sort order and encrypt too
FreeLocks	Statement	Suspends processing, makes recordsets current
Rollback	Statement	End a transaction block, do not commit changes

Table 27-4 Statements relating to data access

CONSTANT.TXT and DATACONS.TXT Values

Many of the properties and events of data access use numeric values as arguments. Using constants rather than the literal value makes your code self-documenting, more readable, and easier to debug.

Microsoft provides a file, CONSTANT.TXT, that has many constant declarations defined for you. Data access also uses another text file, DATACONS.TXT, for some of the specialized data constants. For smaller applications it's probably easiest just to type the declarations in yourself. For larger applications you'll find it much easier to read the text file into a new module.

To do this, create a new module by pulling down the File menu and choosing the New Module menu command. Then pull down the File menu again and choose Load Text. This opens up a dialog box listing all text files in the current directory. Both DATACONS.TXT and CONSTANT.TXT should be in your main Visual Basic directory (default installation would place this in C:\VB). Simply choose the appropriate text file to enter the entire file into your module. These constants will then be available throughout your application.

Tables 27-5 and 27-6 list the value of the constant, the constant name, and a brief description of what the constant means.

Value	CONSTANT.TXT	Description
Meanings of the returned values for the EditMode property		
0	DATA_EDITNONE	No editing operation in process

Value	CONSTANT.TXT	Description
1	DATA_EDITMODE	Edit method invoked and current record is in the copy buffer
2	DATA_EDITADD	AddNew method invoked and the current record in the copy buffer is a new record that doesn't yet exist in the database
The meaning of the values for the Response argument in the Error event		
0	DATA_ERRCONTINUE	Continue without displaying error message
1	DATA_ERRDISPLAY	(Default) Display the message

Table 27-5 CONSTANT.TXT values for data access

Value	DATACONS.TXT	Meaning
Meanings of the values of the CollatingOrder property		
0	DB_SORTCASESENSITIVE	Case-sensitive order
1	DB_SORTCASEINSENSITIVE	Case-insensitive order
Meanings of the values of the CollatingOrder property		
256	DB_SORTGENERAL	Sort by EFGPI rules (English, French, German, Portuguese, and Italian)
258	DB_SORTSPANISH	Sort by Spanish rules
259	DB_SORTDUTCH	Sort by Dutch rules
260	DB_SORTSWEDFIN	Sort by Swedish and Finnish rules
261	DB_SORTNORDAN	Sort by Norwegian and Danish rules
262	DB_SORTICELANDIC	Sort by Icelandic rules

(continued on next page)

(continued from previous page)

Value	CONSTANT.TXT	Description
4096	DB_SORTPDXINTL	Sort by Paradox international rules
4097	DB_SORTPDXSWE	Sort by Paradox Swedish and Finnish rules
4098	DB_SORTPDXNOR	Sort by Paradox Norwegian and Danish rules
-1	DB_SORTUNDEFINED	Sort rules are undefined or unknown

Meanings of the options argument for the Execute method

Value	CONSTANT.TXT	Description
1	DB_DENYWRITE	Target tables are locked during update
16	DB_INCONSISTENTUPDATES	(Default) Does not maintain referential integrity
32	DB_CONSISTENTUPDATES	Automatically enforces referential integrity
64	DB_SQLPASSTHROUGH	(Default) Passes SQL statement to remote server

Values for the Attributes property of a member of the Fields collection

Value	CONSTANT.TXT	Description
1	DB_FIXEDFIELD	Field is of fixed length (not Text, Memo, or Binary)
16	DB_AUTOINCRFIELD	Field is a Counter data type, automatically incremented for each new record
32	DB_UPDATABLEFIELD	Field can be modified
512	DB_FIELDODBCGRAPHIC	Contains remote ODBC graphic image

Meanings of the value of the Options expression%

Value	CONSTANT.TXT	Description
1	DB_DENYWRITE	Other users cannot modify recordset
4	DB_READONLY	Cannot modify existing records or add new ones
8	DB_APPENDONLY	Can add new records but not modify existing records

Value	CONSTANT.TXT	Description
16	DB_INCONSISTENTUPDATES	Does not maintain referential integrity
32	DB_CONSISTENTUPDATES	(Default) Automatically enforces referential integrity
64	DB_SQLPASSTHROUGH	Passes SQL statement to remote server

Meanings of the action% argument in the Validate event

Value	CONSTANT.TXT	Description
0	DATA_ACTIONCANCEL	Cancel the operation that triggered the event
1	DATA_ACTIONMOVEFIRST	MoveFirst method
2	DATA_ACTIONMOVEPREVIOUS	MovePrevious method
3	DATA_ACTIONMOVENEXT	MoveNext method
4	DATA_ACTIONMOVELAST	MoveLast method
5	DATA_ACTIONADDNEW	AddNew method
6	DATA_ACTIONUPDATE	Update operation (not UpdateRecord)
7	DATA_ACTIONDELETE	Delete method
8	DATA_ACTIONFIND	Find method
9	DATA_ACTIONBOOKMARK	The Bookmark property has been set
10	DATA_ACTIONCLOSE	The Close method
11	DATA_ACTIONUNLOAD	The form is being unloaded

Values for the Type property for members of the Fields collection

Value	CONSTANT.TXT	Description
1	DB_BOOLEAN	True/False
2	DB_BYTE	Number (TinyInt)

(continued on next page)

(continued from previous page)

Value	CONSTANT.TXT	Description
3	DB_INTEGER	Number (Integer)
4	DB_LONG	Number (Long Integer)
5	DB_CURRENCY	Number (Currency)
6	DB_SINGLE	Number (Single)
7	DB_DOUBLE	Number (Double)
8	DB_DATE	Date/Time
9	DB_BINARY	Binary
10	DB_TEXT	Character, max 64k
11	DB_LONGBINARY	Binary or OLE objects
12	DB_MEMO	Memo

Table 27-6 DATACONS.TXT values for data access

ADDNEW METHOD

Objects Affected

Check	Clipboard	Combo	Command	CommonDlg
▶ Data	Debug	Dir	Drive	File
Form	Frame	Grid	Image	Label
Line	List	MDI Form	Menu	OLE
Option	Picture	Printer	Screen	Scroll
Shape	Text	Timer		

Purpose

The AddNew method appends a new record to the end of the recordset. It actually clears the copy buffer by setting each field in the buffer to null and makes the copy buffer the current record. The data is not actually appended until the Update method executes. Table 27-7 gives the arguments of the AddNew method.

General Syntax

```
[form!]Name.Recordset.AddNew
```

Argument	Description
form	Name property of the form
Name	Name property of the data control
Recordset	'Recordset' indicates the recordset property of the data control

Table 27-7 Arguments of the AddNew method

Example Syntax

```
Sub Command1_Click ()
    Data1.Recordset.AddNew       'add a new record
    Text1.Setfocus               'go to the first field for user input
End Sub
```

Description

Use the AddNew method to create a new record in your database. AddNew actually clears the copy buffer, sets all of its fields to Null, and makes it the current record. After the user has entered all the information, use the Update method to record the changes to the recordset. The *copy buffer* is a memory location reserved by Visual Basic that functions like a temporary "virtual" record.

Using a Move or Find method (or using the data control's movement buttons) automatically updates the record and saves it to the database. Executing another AddNew or an Edit method before updating will clear the copy buffer again without saving its contents.

The new record is added to the end of the recordset, regardless of any sorting. After the update, the record that was current before the AddNew method is again made current. To make the new record current, you must use the MoveLast method. To put the record in the correct sort order, use the Refresh method.

Example

The Data Access project at the end of this chapter uses the AddNew method several times. It creates a new entry for each icon file added to the database in the cmndLoad_Click event; this event also creates a new Log entry for each time the user loads icons. The cmndSeek_Click event also uses AddNew to create a new log entry.

APPENDCHUNK METHOD

Objects Affected

Check	Clipboard	Combo	Command	CommonDlg
▸ Data	Debug	Dir	Drive	File
Form	Frame	Grid	Image	Label
Line	List	MDI Form	Menu	OLE
Option	Picture	Printer	Screen	Scroll
Shape	Text	Timer		

Purpose

Use the AppendChunk method on a member of the Fields collection to append a string to a memo field. This allows you to manipulate memo fields larger than the 64K string-length limit of Visual Basic. Table 27-8 summarizes the arguments of the AppendChunk method.

General Syntax

```
[form!]Name.Recordset.Fields(Index%).AppendChunk(string$)
[form!]Name.Recordset.Fields(Field$).AppendChunk(string$)
[form!]Name.Database.TableDefs(Index%|Table$).Fields[(Index%|Field$)].AppendChunk(string$)
```

Argument	Description
form	Name property of the form
Name	Name property of the data control
Recordset	'Recordset' indicates the recordset property of the data control
Database	'Database' indicates the Database property of the data control
Fields	'Fields' indicates the Fields collection of the recordset or database

Argument	Description
TableDefs	'TableDefs' indicates the TableDefs collection of the database
Index%	The ordinal index position of the member of the collection
Field$	Name of the field (must be memo or long binary)
Table$	Name of the table
string$	Data you wish to append to field

Table 27-8 Arguments of the AppendChunk method

Example Syntax

```
Sub Command1_Click ()
    Data1.Recordset.Edit
    Data1.Recordset!Memo = ""            ' Clear the memo field
    Open "BIGFILE.TXT" For Input As #1   ' Open the external file
    Do While Not EOF(1)                  ' While there's still stuff to get,
        Input #1, in$                    ' Get a line
        Data1.Recordset.Fields("Memo").AppendChunk(in$)  ' Add it to memo field
    Loop
    Data1.Recordset.Update               ' Save the updates
    Close #1                             ' Close the external file
End Sub
```

Description

The AppendChunk method appends a string to a memo field. Strings in Visual Basic are limited to 64K, whereas memo fields may be quite large (many gigabytes for some databases). The AppendChunk lets you build a large memo field from many smaller pieces. Place the information you want to add to the field in the string$ argument. Use the GetChunk method to retrieve the information.

The AppendChunk method will only work with memo and long binary fields.

Example

The cmndLoad_Click event uses the AppendChunk method to build up a record of each file added to the database in the Log table's memo field.

ATTRIBUTES PROPERTY

Objects Affected

Check	Clipboard	Combo	Command	CommonDlg
▶ Data	Debug	Dir	Drive	File
Form	Frame	Grid	Image	Label
Line	List	MDI Form	Menu	OLE
Option	Picture	Printer	Screen	Scroll
Shape	Text	Timer		

Purpose

The Attributes property of each member of a database's TableDefs collection returns information about how the table is attached and if it is a system table. The Attributes property of each member of the Fields collection determines how a field will be treated by Visual Basic. Tables 27-9, 27-10, and 27-11 summarize the arguments of the Attributes property.

General Syntax

```
[form!]Name.Database.TableDefs(Index%|Table$).Attributes

[form!]Name.Recordset.Fields(Index%).Attributes
[form!]Name.Recordset.Fields(Field$).Attributes
[form!]Name.Database.TableDefs(Index%|Table$).Fields[(Index%|Field$)].Attributes
```

Argument	Description
form	Name property of the form
Name	Name property of the data control
Recordset	'Recordset' indicates the recordset property of the data control
Database	'Database' indicates the Database property of the data control
Fields	'Fields' indicates the Fields collection of the recordset or database
TableDefs	'TableDefs' indicates the TableDefs collection of the database

Argument	Description
Index%	The ordinal index position of the member of the collection
Field$	Name of the field (must be memo or long binary)
Table$	Name of the table

Table 27-9 Arguments of the Attributes property

Value	DATACONS.TXT	Meaning
&H00010000	DB_ATTACHEXCLUSIVE	Table is an attached Access table opened for exclusive use
&H00020000	DB_ATTACHSAVEPWD	User ID and password for the Access source table should be saved with the linking information
&H80000002	DB_SYSTEMOBJECT	Table is a system table
&H40000000	DB_ATTACHEDTABLE	Table is an attached table from a non-ODBC database such as Access, dBase, or Paradox
&H20000000	DB_ATTACHEDODBC	Table is an attached table from an ODBC database, such as SQL Server or Oracle

Table 27-10 Values for the Attributes property of a member of the TableDefs collection

Value	DATACONS.TXT	Meaning
1	DB_FIXEDFIELD	Field is of fixed length (not text, memo, or binary)
16	DB_AUTOINCRFIELD	Field is a Counter data type, automatically incremented for each new record
32	DB_UPDATABLEFIELD	Field can be modified
512	DB_FIELDODBCGRAPHIC	Contains remote ODBC graphic image

Table 27-11 Values for the Attributes property of a member of the Fields collection

Example Syntax

```
Sub Command1_Click
    If Data1.Recordset.Fields("Empl").Attributes And DB_UPDATABLEFIELD Then
        ' field can be updated, so put code here
    End If
End Sub
```

Description

The Attributes property of each member of the TableDefs collection gives information on the attached status and shows whether or not the table is a system table. The Attributes property of each member of the Fields collection determines how a field will be treated by Visual Basic.

Note that each of these Attributes constants is defined in DATACONS.TXT. See the discussion in the summary section at the beginning of this chapter for details on how to use these constants. These are bit values, and you need to perform bitwise operations using the AND operator to determine the setting of a given bit. The example syntax shows how to test to see if the Attributes property has the DB_UPDATABLEFIELD flag set.

Example

The PrintStats procedure in the Data Access project at the end of this chapter uses the Attributes property to determine if a table is a system table or not. It skips over the system tables and prints out statistics on the user tables only.

BEGINTRANS STATEMENT

Purpose

The BeginTrans statement begins a block of transactions that need to be completed as a whole. Changes to the database within the block can be recorded permanently to the database or undone without recording them.

General Syntax

```
BeginTrans
```

Example Syntax

```
Sub PostAccounts (debits() As Currency, credits() As Currency)
    BeginTrans
```

```
      Data1.Recordset.MoveFirst
      Do While Not Data1.Recordset.EOF
          Data1.Recordset.Edit
          recNo = Data1.Recordset!ClientID
          Data1.Recordset!Debit = debits(recNo)
          Data1.Recordset!Credit = credits(recNo)
          Data1.Recordset.Update
          Data1.Recordset.MoveNext
      Loop
      CommitTrans
End Sub
```

Description

Transactions are changes to the database that must be made as a whole. Incomplete changes (due to a power outage or unforeseen error) can be avoided by using transactions. For example, most financial operations involve a debit from one account and a corresponding credit to another account. If the transaction failed before completing, one account may have a debit without any corresponding credit.

Use BeginTrans to begin a *transaction block*, or block of statements you would like to group together. You may nest transactions up to five deep. All changes to all databases (not just the one you're working on) are done in a manner that lets you either *commit* them as a block, writing them permanently to disk, or *roll back* and undo all changes since the BeginTrans statement. End a transaction block with CommitTrans or Rollback.

If a database closes before the transaction block ends, no changes are made and an implicit Rollback occurs. In the sample syntax above, a series of debits and credits are posted to the database. Should something unforeseen happen (like someone rebooting the computer), nothing is posted and the database is restored to its state before the BeginTrans statement.

Example

The Data Access project at the end of this chapter uses the BeginTrans statement to start a transaction block in the cmndSeek_Click event. This lets the user cancel the additions to the database if desired and also speeds up processing.

Comment

Transaction blocks can vastly speed up database operations. The Access engine performs all the updates in memory first before writing them to disk. Consider placing any DO...LOOP constructions that update the database inside a transaction block to speed up processing, even if you're not concerned about transactional integrity.

BOF PROPERTY

Objects Affected

Check	Clipboard	Combo	Command	CommonDlg
▶ Data	Debug	Dir	Drive	File
Form	Frame	Grid	Image	Label
Line	List	MDI Form	Menu	OLE
Option	Picture	Printer	Screen	Scroll
Shape	Text	Timer		

Purpose

The BOF property indicates if the current record is set to *beginning of file*, or before the first record. If current record is at beginning of file, BOF returns True; otherwise it returns False. Use this after a Move method to make sure you don't try to move beyond the bounds of your file. Movement beyond BOF generates an error. Tables 27-12 and 27-13 give the arguments of the BOF property.

General Syntax

`[form!]Name.Recordset.BOF`

Argument	Description
form	Name property of the parent form
Name	Name property of the data control
Recordset	'Recordset' indicates the recordset property of the data control

Table 27-12 Arguments of the BOF property

Value	Meaning
True	The current record is before the first record
False	The current record is at or after the first record

Table 27-13 Meanings of the BOF returned values

Example Syntax

```
Sub Data1_Reposition ()
    If Data1.Recordset.BOF Then          ' If we're at the beginning
        Label1.Caption = "Beginning"     ' Tell user where we are
        Command1.Enabled = False         ' Disable "move previous"
    End If
End Sub

Sub Update ()
    Data1.Recordset.MoveLast             ' Go to the end
    Do While Not Data1.Recordset.BOF     ' while still records to process
        Data1.Recordset.Edit             ' edit current record,
        Data1.Recordset!AreaCode = "609" ' set the new field value
        Data1.Recordset.Update           ' save the change
        Data1.Recordset.MovePrevious     ' go to the previous record
    Loop
End Sub
```

Description

The BOF property lets you determine whether the current record is already at the beginning of file marker. Attempting to move before the beginning of file generates an error, so it is important to check this property before attempting additional movement.

The first example syntax shows the BOF property used to update the values in other controls to inform the user as to the current position in the database and to prevent further movement before the beginning of file marker. The second example steps the recordset one record at a time to update a field. It continues to perform the update loop until it reaches the beginning of the file.

Use the EOF property to see if you are at the end of the file.

Example

The Log command on the Utilities menu prints out a log of all additions made to the database. It prints in reverse chronological order (most entries first), so it begins at the end of the log file and goes backwards to the beginning. The BOF property lets us terminate the loop when we reach the beginning.

BOOKMARK PROPERTY

Objects Affected

Check	Clipboard	Combo	Command	CommonDlg
▶ Data	Debug	Dir	Drive	File
Form	Frame	Grid	Image	Label

(continued on next page)

(continued from previous page)

Line	List	MDI Form	Menu	OLE
Option	Picture	Printer	Screen	Scroll
Shape	Text	Timer		

Purpose

The Bookmark property sets or returns the pointer to individual records. This lets you easily return to previous noncontiguous records. Table 27-14 gives the arguments of the Bookmark property.

General Syntax

```
[form!]Name.Recordset.Bookmark [ = string$]
```

Argument	Description
form	Name property of the parent form
Name	Name property of the data control
Recordset	'Recordset' indicates the recordset property of the data control
string$	The unique identifier for the record

Table 27-14 The arguments for the Bookmark property

Example Syntax

```
Global GlobalBookmark() As String

Sub cmndSetBookmark ()
    biggest = UBound(GlobalBookmark)                   'how many bookmarks?
    ReDim Preserve GlobalBookmark(biggest + 1, 1)      'create space for new one
    GlobalBookmark(biggest + 1, 0) = InputBox$("Type name of bookmark")
    GlobalBookmark(biggest + 1, 1) = Data1.Recordset.Bookmark
    List1.AddItem GlobalBookmark(biggest + 1, 0)
End Sub

Sub listJumpToBookmark_DblClick ()
    Data1.Recordset.Bookmark = GlobalBookmark(List1.ListIndex, 1)
End Sub
```

1088

Description

The Bookmark property lets you move to any record that you've previously recorded the bookmark for. This makes it simple to mark where you are, perform some operations that might make a different record current, and then return to where you were before.

Visual Basic creates a bookmark automatically for each record when it creates a recordset. Each bookmark uniquely identifies a record. Note that two recordsets, even created from the same SQL statement, will not have related bookmarks. The bookmarks are essentially random within a recordset and meaningless outside of it. Setting the Bookmark property to a record that has been deleted causes a trappable error.

Only native Access tables may have bookmarks. Use the Bookmarkable property to determine whether a database supports bookmarks.

The example syntax shows one possible use for bookmarks. The bookmarks, and a description of each, are stored in a global array GlobalBookmarks. Setting a bookmark adds a new element to the array, calls up an input box for the description, and assigns the bookmark and the description to the array. List1 gets the new description added to it. Double-clicking on any of the saved bookmarks immediately jumps to that record. List1 cannot be sorted in this example and you would obviously want to remove items from the list for deleted records.

Example

The Data Access project at the end of this chapter uses the Bookmark property to store an entry's bookmark each time a Find method succeeds in the cmndFind_Click event on the Find form. The user may then select each history entry and jump immediately to it. The stored Bookmark property value sets the data control's bookmark, which forces the data control to jump immediately to that record.

BOOKMARKABLE PROPERTY

Objects Affected

Check	Clipboard	Combo	Command	CommonDlg
▶ Data	Debug	Dir	Drive	File
Form	Frame	Grid	Image	Label
Line	List	MDI Form	Menu	OLE
Option	Picture	Printer	Screen	Scroll
Shape	Text	Timer		

Purpose

The Bookmarkable property lets you determine whether a recordset supports bookmarks. Native Access databases do; most other databases do not. Tables 27-15 and 27-16 summarize the arguments for the Bookmarkable property.

General Syntax

```
[form!]Name.Recordset.Bookmarkable
```

Argument	Description
form	Name property of the parent form
Name	Name property of the data control
Recordset	'Recordset' indicates the recordset property of the data control

Table 27-15 Arguments of the Bookmarkable property

Value	Meaning
True	Recordset supports Bookmarks
False	Recordset does not support Bookmarks

Table 27-16 Possible values for the Bookmarkable property

Example Syntax

```
Sub OpenNewDatabase (pathName as String)
    Data1.DatabaseName = pathName
    Data1.Refresh
    If Data1.Recordset.Bookmarkable Then
        cmndMark.Visible = True
        listMarks.Visible = True
    Else
        cmndMark.Visible = False
        listMarks.Visible = False
    End If
End Sub
```

Description

You should check the Bookmarkable property if you've implemented bookmarks in your code and you might connect to non-Access databases. This will tell you if the database you're connected to supports bookmarks. Native Access databases fully support bookmarks, and most other databases do not.

The example syntax sets the two controls associated with bookmarks (the command button that makes the bookmark and the list box that lists them) appropriately for whatever kind of database the routine connects to.

Example

The Data Access project at the end of this chapter checks the Bookmarkable property before attempting to use bookmarks to jump from record to record. It checks this in the cmndFind_Click event on formFind.

CLOSE METHOD

Objects Affected

Check	Clipboard	Combo	Command	CommonDlg
▶ Data	Debug	Dir	Drive	File
Form	Frame	Grid	Image	Label
Line	List	MDI Form	Menu	OLE
Option	Picture	Printer	Screen	Scroll
Shape	Text	Timer		

Purpose

The Close method closes a database or recordset. Closing a database closes all open recordsets based on that database. Table 27-17 lists the arguments of the Close method.

General Syntax

```
[form!]Name.Database.Close
[form!]Name.Recordset.Close
```

Argument	Description
form	Name property of the parent form
Name	Name property of the data control
Database	'Database' indicates the Database property of the data control
Recordset	'Recordset' indicates the Recordset property of the data control

Table 27-17 Arguments of the Close method

Example Syntax

```
Sub Command1_Click ()
    Data1.Recordset.Close
    Data2.Database.Close
End Sub
```

Description

The Close method closes the specified recordset or database. It is possible to open multiple recordsets from a single database by using multiple data controls. Using the Close method on a recordset will close just the recordset you indicate, leaving all the other recordsets based on that database open. Closing the database of any data control will close all recordsets built from that database.

A closed recordset will set all bound controls to Null and will disable the data control's movement buttons. Closing a recordset or database will automatically update any pending AddNew or Edit methods.

Example

The Utilities menu's Compact command uses the Close method to close all the databases prior to compacting them.

COLLATINGORDER PROPERTY

Objects Affected

Check	Clipboard	Combo	Command	CommonDlg
▶ Data	Debug	Dir	Drive	File

Form	Frame	Grid	Image	Label
Line	List	MDI Form	Menu	OLE
Option	Picture	Printer	Screen	Scroll
Shape	Text	Timer		

Purpose

Returns the collating (sorting) order of a database. You can use the value of this property in the InStr and StrComp functions. Tables 27-18 and 27-19 summarize the arguments of the CollatingOrder property.

General Syntax

```
[form!]Name.Database.CollatingOrder
[form!]Name.Recordset.Fields(Index%|fieldName$).CollatingOrder
```

Argument	Description
form	Name property of the parent form
Name	Name property of the data control
Recordset	'Recordset' indicates the Recordset property of the data control
Fields	'Fields' indicates the Fields collection of the recordset
Index%	Ordinal position of the member field within the collection
fieldname$	Name of the field

Table 27-18 Arguments of the CollatingOrder property

Value	DATACONS.TXT	Meaning
0	DB_SORTCASESENSITIVE	Case-sensitive order
1	DB_SORTCASEINSENSITIVE	Case-insensitive order
256	DB_SORTGENERAL	Sort by EFGPI rules (English, French, German, Portuguese, and Italian)

(continued on next page)

(continued from previous page)

Value	DATACONS.TXT	Meaning
258	DB_SORTSPANISH	Sort by Spanish rules
259	DB_SORTDUTCH	Sort by Dutch rules
260	DB_SORTSWEDFIN	Sort by Swedish and Finnish rules
261	DB_SORTNORDAN	Sort by Norwegian and Danish rules
262	DB_SORTICELANDIC	Sort by Icelandic rules
4096	DB_SORTPDXINTL	Sort by Paradox international rules
4097	DB_SORTPDXSWE	Sort by Paradox Swedish and Finnish rules
4098	DB_SORTPDXNOR	Sort by Paradox Norwegian and Danish rules
-1	DB_SORTUNDEFINED	Sort rules are undefined or unknown

Table 27-19 Meanings of the values of the CollatingOrder property

Example Syntax

```
Function CompareStrings(fieldName As String, otherString As Variant) As Variant
    compType = Data1.Recordset.Fields(fieldName).CollatingOrder
    equal = StrComp(Data1.Recordset.Fields(fieldName), otherString, compType)
    CompareStrings = equal
End Function
```

Description

The CollatingOrder property lets you determine how a database or recordset is sorted. It is read-only at runtime. You may set the sort order of a database by using the CompactDatabase statement and setting the *locale* flag to the appropriate setting.

The InStr and StrComp functions can use the property's value directly in their *compare* argument. See Appendix B, Visual Basic Language Reference, for more details on these functions.

Note that each of these Action constants is defined in DATACONS.TXT. See the discussion in the summary section at the beginning of this chapter for details on how to use these constants.

Example

The PrintStats procedure prints out a number of database statistics, including the CollatingOrder property.

COMMITTRANS STATEMENT

Purpose

The CommitTrans statement ends a transaction block. Changes to the database within the block are written permanently to the database.

General Syntax

```
CommitTrans
```

Example Syntax

```
Sub PostAccounts (debits() As Currency, credits() As Currency)
    BeginTrans
    Data1.Recordset.MoveFirst
    Do While Not Data1.Recordset.EOF
        Data1.Recordset.Edit
        recNo = Data1.Recordset!ClientID
        Data1.Recordset!Debit = debits(recNo)
        Data1.Recordset!Credit = credits(recNo)
        Data1.Recordset.Update
        Data1.Recordset.MoveNext
    Loop
    CommitTrans
End Sub
```

Description

Transactions are changes to the database that must be made as a whole. Incomplete changes (due to a power outage or unforeseen error) can be avoided by using transactions. For example, most financial operations involve a debit from one account and a corresponding credit to another account. If the transaction failed before completing, one account may have a debit without any corresponding credit.

Use BeginTrans to begin a *transaction block*, or block of statements you would like to group together. All changes to all databases (not just the one you're working on) are done in a manner that lets you either *commit* them as a block, or *roll back* and undo all changes since the BeginTrans statement. Ending a transaction block with CommitTrans commits all changes permanently to the database.

If a database closes before the transaction block ends, no changes are made and an implicit Rollback occurs. In the sample syntax above, a series of debits and credits are posted to the database. Should something unforeseen happen (like someone rebooting the computer), nothing is posted and the database is restored to its state before the BeginTrans statement. Once the loop finishes, the CommitTrans statement makes the posting transactions permanent.

Example

The cmndSeek_Click event uses a transaction block to give the user the option to accept or cancel mass additions to the database.

COMPACTDATABASE STATEMENT

Purpose

Use the CompactDatabase statement to defragment and shrink the size of your database file. You can also encrypt and decrypt the file, create an Access 1.0 compatible file, and change the collating (sort) order. Tables 27-20, 27-21, and 27-22 summarize the arguments of the CompactDatabase statement.

General Syntax

```
CompactDatabase sourcefile$, destfile$ [, locale$ [, options&]]
```

Argument	Meaning
sourcefile$	Full path and file name of the original file to be compacted
destfile$	Full path and file name of the new compacted file to be created
locale$	Localization information for the destination file; sets collating (sort) order
options&	Determines what version (1.0 or 1.1) to write destination file as, and controls whether to encrypt or decrypt destination

Table 27-20 Meanings of the arguments for the CompactDatabase statement

locale$	DATACONS.TXT	Meaning
;LANGID=0x0809;CP=1252;COUNTRY=0	DB_LANG_GENERAL	English, German, French
;LANGID=0x040A;CP=1252;COUNTRY=0	DB_LANG_SPANISH	Spanish, Italian
;LANGID=0x0413;CP=1252;COUNTRY=0	DB_LANG_DUTCH	Dutch
;LANGID=0x040C;CP=1252;COUNTRY=0	DB_LANG_SWEDFIN	Swedish, Finnish
;LANGID=0x0414;CP=1252;COUNTRY=0	DB_LANG_NORWDAN	Norwegian, Danish
;LANGID=0x040F;CP=1252;COUNTRY=0	DB_LANG_ICELANDIC	Icelandic
;LANGID=0x041D;CP=1252;COUNTRY=0	DB_LANG_NORDIC	Nordic countries

Table 27-21 Values of the locale$ argument in the CompactDatabase statement

options&	DATACONS.TXT	Meaning
1	DB_VERSION10	Create an Access 1.0 compatible database
2	DB_ENCRYPT	Encrypt the database
4	DB_DECRYPT	Decrypt the database

Table 27-22 Values of the option& argument in the CompactDatabase statement

Example Syntax

```
Sub Command1_Click ()
     MousePointer = HOURGLASS
     Data1.Database.Close
     CompactDatabase "C:\DATA\THISFILE.MDB", "C:\DATA\NEWFILE.MDB"
     Name "C:\DATA\THISFILE.MDB", "C:\DATA\THISFILE.BAK"
     Name "C:\DATA\NEWFILE.MDB", "C:\DATA\THISFILE.MDB"
     Data1.Refresh
     MousePointer = NORMAL
End Sub
```

Description

Databases tend to fragment with use as records are added and deleted. Use the CompactDatabase statement to defragment and shrink a database. You can also specify a new sort order, encrypt or decrypt the database, or save it in the older Access 1.0 format.

The CompactDatabase statement creates a new database with the name given in the destfile$ argument. It copies all the security settings from the existing database and then copies each record to the new database. This makes the entire database contiguous on the hard drive (assuming the hard drive itself is defragmented) with each record stored in the most efficient manner possible. Note that sourcefile$ and destfile$ must be different.

You need to close all recordsets built with the database before compacting it. As the example syntax shows, you can then rename the new database after the compaction process.

The locale$ argument can change the collating (sort) order of the new database. The values are most easily given as constants. The DATACONS.TXT contains these values, and the chapter summary section gives details on how to use the DATACONS.TXT file. Note the semicolon (;) at the beginning of the string.

Example

The menuUtils_Click event uses CompactDatabase to compact the database. Compare the size of the database (using the Statistics command) to compare the size of the database before and after compaction.

CONNECT PROPERTY

Objects Affected

Check	Clipboard	Combo	Command	CommonDlg
▶ Data	Debug	Dir	Drive	File
Form	Frame	Grid	Image	Label
Line	List	MDI Form	Menu	OLE
Option	Picture	Printer	Screen	Scroll
Shape	Text	Timer		

Purpose

Use the Connect property to read or set the parameters necessary to attach to an external database or table. This lets you use the Access engine to work with databases from other programs like Paradox or dBase. Tables 27-23 and 27-24 summarize the arguments of the Connect property.

General Syntax

```
[form!]Name.Connect [ = settings$]
[form!]Name.Database.Connect [ = settings$]
[form!]Name.Database.TableDefs(Index%|Table$).Connect [ = settings$]
```

Argument	Description
form	Name property of the parent form
Name	Name property of the data control
Database	'Database' indicates the Database property of the data control
TableDefs	'TableDefs' indicates the TableDef collection of the database
Table$	Name of the table; string variable or literal
Index%	Index number of the table
settings$	Settings unique to that database or table

Table 27-23 Arguments of the Connect property

settings$	Meaning	Set DatabaseName to...	Set RecordSource to...
(none)	MSAccess	drive:\path\file name.MDB	Table name
dBASE III;	dBASE III	drive:\path	File name (*.DBF assumed)
dBASE IV;	dBASE IV	drive:\path	File name (*.DBF assumed)
Paradox;	Paradox	drive:\path	File name (*.DB assumed)
Btrieve;	Btrieve	drive:\path\file name.DDF	Table name
FoxPro 2.0;	FoxPro 2.0	drive:\path	File name (*.DBF assumed)

(continued on next page)

(continued from previous page)

settings$	Meaning	Set DatabaseName to...	Set RecordSource to...
FoxPro 2.5;	FoxPro 2.5	drive:\path	File name (*.DBF assumed)

Table 27-24 Meanings of the settings$ argument of the Connect property

Example Syntax

```
Sub Form_Load ()
    Data1.DatabaseName = "C:\PSI\GHOSTWRITER"    'point to directory
    Data1.RecordSource = "NARRATIV"             'point to table (file name)
    Data1.Connect = "Paradox;"                   'paradox format
End Sub
```

Description

The Connect property lets you specify what kind of database you're connecting to, and can give additional information (like passwords) necessary to open the database or table. Native Access tables (*.MDB) don't need the Connect property; they're considered *internal* databases. All other formats (like Paradox, dBase, Btrieve, FoxBase; and ODBC for the Professional Edition) are considered *external* databases and must specify the Connect property settings. You can open a Microsoft Access database as external if you wish. You might want to do this if the remote database is located on a remote server in a WAN (Wide Area Network).

External databases work much like internal ones. You can use almost all of the properties, events, and methods of the data control without modification.

You need to specify certain settings for the Access engine in either the VB.INI file or your app's *appname*.INI file. These settings control what DLLs to use, time-out settings, page frame sizes, and so forth. The .INI file should normally be stored in the user's WINDOWS directory and have the same name as the executable file, but with an .INI extension. If the .INI file is located elsewhere, or has a different name, you need to specify where to find it with the SetDataAccessOption statement. See Appendix B, Visual Basic Language Reference, for the correct syntax. Failing to provide the .INI file will result in a trappable error.

If you are working with an external MS Access database, you can specify settings like user ID and user password with the SetDefaultWorkspace statement. Appendix B, Visual Basic Language Reference, gives the correct syntax.

You open each database in a similar way, by first setting the DatabaseName and RecordSource properties, as summarized in Table 27-24, and then setting the Connect property using the correct value for the settings$ argument. Note that each value includes a semicolon (;) at the end of the string. The example syntax opens the NARRATIV.DB table in the C:\PSI\GHOSTWRITER directory.

Each database type has specific settings and support file requirements. See the file EXTERNAL.TXT located in your Visual Basic directory for a complete discussion of the details on opening and using each kind of file.

Example

In the Data Access project at the end of this chapter, the database leaves the Connect property blank, as the database is in native Access format. The PrintStats routine (which could easily be transferred to other programs that may access different databases) prints out the Connect string.

COUNT PROPERTY

Objects Affected

Check	Clipboard	Combo	Command	CommonDlg
▶ Data	Debug	Dir	Drive	File
Form	Frame	Grid	Image	Label
Line	List	MDI Form	Menu	OLE
Option	Picture	Printer	Screen	Scroll
Shape	Text	Timer		

Purpose

The Count property returns the number of items in a collection. There are three database collections available in Visual Basic Standard Edition: Tables, Fields, and Indexes. Use the Count property to determine how many of each item are in the collection for use in a loop. Table 27-25 summarizes the arguments of the Count property.

General Syntax

```
[form!]Name.Database.TableDefs.Count                      'number of tables
[form!]Name.Database.TableDefs("tableName").Fields.Count  'number of fields
[form!]Name.Database.TableDefs(tableIndex%).Fields.Count  'number of fields
[form!]Name.Database.TableDefs("tableName").Indexes.Count 'number of indexes
[form!]Name.Database.TableDefs(tableIndex%).Indexes.Count 'number of indexes
```

Argument	Description
form	Name property of the parent form
Name	Name property of the data control
Database	'Database' indicates the Database property of the data control

(continued on next page)

(continued from previous page)

Argument	Description
TableDefs	'TableDefs' indicates the TableDef collection of the database
Fields	'Fields' indicates the Fields collection of the table
Indexes	'Indexes' indicates the Indexes collection of the table
tableName	Name of the table; string variable or literal
tableIndex%	Index number of the table

Table 27-25 Arguments of the Count property

Example Syntax

```
Sub Form_Click ()
    numTables = data1.Database.TableDefs.Count
    For i = 0 To numTables - 1
        If data1.Database.TableDefs(i).Attributes And &H80000002 Then
        Else
            pictP.Print "Table:"; Tab(15); data1.Database.TableDefs(i).Name
            pictP.Print "Fields:  ";
            For j = 0 To data1.Database.TableDefs(i).Fields.Count - 1
                pictP.Print Tab(15); data1.Database.TableDefs(i).Fields(j).Name
            Next j
            pictP.Print "Indexes: ";
            For k = 0 To data1.Database.TableDefs(i).Indexes.Count - 1
                pictP.Print Tab(15); data1.Database.TableDefs(i).Indexes(k).Name
            Next k
            pictP.Print
        End If
    Next i
End Sub
```

Description

Use the Count property to determine how many members of a collection exist. Visual Basic Standard Edition exposes three database collections: Tables, Fields, and Indexes. You can use the Count value for each of these collections to step through the members. For more on collections, see Chapter 3, Using Objects.

As the example syntax shows, there may be more than one table; each table has its associated fields and indexes. The nested loops in the example syntax step through each table in turn and then each member of the Fields and Indexes collections. Figure 27-6 shows an example of what this might produce.

You may refer to a Field or Index collection either by its name in a string variable or literal, or by its ordinal index number as in the example.

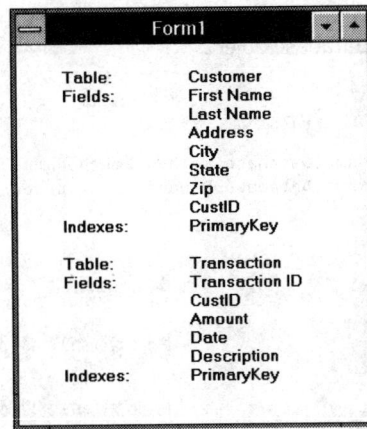

Figure 27-6 The Count property lets you step through a variety of collections to expose the elements of the database

Example

The Data Access project at the end of this chapter uses the Count property several times in the PrintStats sub procedure as it iterates through the TableDefs, Fields, and Indexes collections.

DATABASE PROPERTY

Objects Affected

Check	Clipboard	Combo	Command	CommonDlg
▶ Data	Debug	Dir	Drive	File
Form	Frame	Grid	Image	Label
Line	List	MDI Form	Menu	OLE
Option	Picture	Printer	Screen	Scroll
Shape	Text	Timer		

Purpose

The Database property of a data control references the underlying database object. You may then use the database's collections, properties, and methods. Table 27-26 lists the arguments of the database property, and Table 27-27 lists the collections, properties, and methods most commonly used with the underlying database object.

General Syntax

```
[form!]Name.Database.Method [methodArgs]
[form!]Name.Database.Property [ = propertyValue]
```

Argument	Description
form	Name property of the parent form
Name	Name property of the data control
Database	'Database' indicates the Database property of the data control
Method	An appropriate method for the underlying database object
methodArgs	Arguments for the method
Property	An appropriate property for the underlying database object
propertyValue	Value for the property

Table 27-26 Arguments of the Database property

Use This...		To Do This...
Close	Method	Closes a database
CollatingOrder	Property	Returns the collating (sorting) order
Connect	Property	Returns the string used to connect an external database
Count	Property	Returns the number of items in a collection
Exclusive	Property	Reads or sets whether a database is single or multi-user
Execute	Method	Executes an SQL action query

1104

Use This...		To Do This...
Fields	Collection	Returns the details of the available fields
Indexes	Collection	Returns the details of the available indexes
QueryTimeout	Property	Sets or returns number of seconds before a timeout
TableDefs	Collection	Returns the details of the available fields
Transactions	Property	Returns whether a database supports transactions
Updatable	Property	Returns whether a database is updatable

Table 27-27 Common database collections, methods, and properties

Example Syntax

```
Sub CommitTransactionsNow ()
    If Data1.Database.Transactions Then
        CommitTrans
    Else
        Data1.Database.Close
        MsgBox "Database does not support transactions."
    End If
End Sub
```

Description

Use the Database property to gain access to a data control's underlying Database object. You may then use the Database object's collections, methods, and properties.

The default property for the Database property is the TableDefs collection, so you can omit the TableDefs keyword to shorten your code. This lets you simplify references to items in the TableDefs collection:

```
Data1.Database.TableDefs("Clients").Indexes.Count    'long reference
Data1.Database("Clients").Indexes.Count              'uses default property
```

See the individual entries for the collections, methods, and properties for details about them and more examples of using the Database property.

Example

The Data Access project at the end of this chapter uses the Database property very heavily in the PrintStats routine to access the TableDefs, Fields, and Indexes collections. It also uses it in the cmndClear_Click event to execute an SQL command, and in the Utilities menu Compact command to close the databases before compacting them.

DATABASENAME PROPERTY

Objects Affected

Check	Clipboard	Combo	Command	CommonDlg
▶ Data	Debug	Dir	Drive	File
Form	Frame	Grid	Image	Label
Line	List	MDI Form	Menu	OLE
Option	Picture	Printer	Screen	Scroll
Shape	Text	Timer		

Purpose

The DatabaseName property reads or sets the name and location of the database. Setting the name of a data control's DatabaseName property while your program is running changes the database that control is connected to. You must use the Refresh method to update the control after changing databases. Table 27-28 summarizes the arguments of the DatabaseName property.

General Syntax

```
[form!]Name.DatabaseName [ = pathName$]
```

Argument	Description
form	Name property of the parent form
Name	Name property of the data control
pathName$	Full path and file name of the database

Table 27-28 Arguments of the DatabaseName property

Example Syntax

```
Sub OpenNewDatabase (pathName as String)
     Label1.Caption = "Closing " & Data1.DatabaseName & " database now."
     Data1.DatabaseName = pathName
     Data1.Refresh
     Label1.Caption = "Opened " & Data1.DatabaseName & " database."
End Sub
```

Description

The DatabaseName property lets you set and retrieve the name of the database the data control connects to. Note that the value is a full path, not just the file name. You may set this property at design time in the Properties box DatabaseName entry for the data control.

The pathName$ argument should specify the complete path and file name for Access (*.MDB) and Btrieve (*.DDF) files; dBase, FoxPro, and Paradox files (*.DBF, *.PDX, or *.DB) should only specify the directory of the database file. You may give a fully qualified network name such as \\Server3\Data\Clients.MDB if your network supports it.

Changing this property at runtime implicitly closes any database (and the associated recordset) connected to the control. After closing any existing database, the control connects to the new database. Note that the new database has not been opened; use the Refresh method on it to open it and update the recordset and bound controls.

Remember that changing this property at runtime may well change the names of the fields. If the field names do change, use the DataField properties for any bound controls to change the names of the fields they are bound to.

Example

The Data Access project at the end of this chapter sets the DatabaseName property of the main data control on formMain during the design phase. The FillGrid procedure sets the datasheet's data control's DatabaseName equal to the DatabaseName property of dataMain on the main form.

DATACHANGED PROPERTY

Objects Affected

▶ Check	Clipboard	Combo	Command	CommonDlg
Data	Debug	Dir	Drive	File
Form	Frame	Grid	▶ Image	▶ Label

(continued on next page)

(continued from previous page)

Line	List	MDI Form	Menu	OLE
Option	▶ Picture	Printer	Screen	Scroll
Shape	▶ Text	Timer		

Purpose

The DataChanged property indicates whether the data displayed in a bound control is the same as in the underlying record. If it is True, the data has changed; if you set DataChanged to False, the changed data is not written to the database. Not available at design time, read and write at runtime. Tables 27-29 and 27-30 summarize the arguments of the DataChanged property.

General Syntax

```
[form!]Name.DataChanged [ = boolean%]
```

Argument	Description
form	Name property of the parent form
Name	Name property of the bound control
boolean%	True or False indicates whether data has changed and should be saved

Table 27-29 Arguments of the DataChanged property

boolean%	Meaning
True	Data is different than in underlying record; save changes
False	Data is same as underlying record; do not save any changes

Table 27-30 Meanings of the boolean% argument in the DataChanged property

Example Syntax

```
Sub Data1_Validate (Action As Integer, Save As Integer)
    If textClientID.DataChanged = True Then        'don't change client id!
        If Action <> DATA_ACTIONADDNEW Then        'unless this is a new record
            textClientID.DataChanged = False  'discard changes to id
        End If
    End If
End Sub
```

1108

Description

Use a bound control's DataChanged property to determine if the data displayed in it is the same as the data in the underlying record. If it isn't, the data has been changed either by the user or by some other process like a DDE link or another process in your code. In that case DataChanged is set to True.

You can also set the DataChanged property to either force a save to the underlying record (by setting DataChanged to True), or to prevent any changes from being saved (by setting it to False).

The example syntax shows the data control's Validate event checking the status of a text box that contains an ID code. The Validate event occurs immediately before saving to disk and moving to a new record and is an ideal place to check the DataChanged property. If the ID code has been changed and this is not a new record, the change is discarded and not saved.

Example

The Data Access project's cmndSave_Click event uses the DataChanged property to determine whether it needs to save the displayed data to the record.

DATAFIELD PROPERTY

Objects Affected

▶ Check	Clipboard	Combo	Command	CommonDlg
Data	Debug	Dir	Drive	File
Form	Frame	Grid	▶ Image	▶ Label
Line	List	MDI Form	Menu	OLE
Option	▶ Picture	Printer	Screen	Scroll
Shape	▶ Text	Timer		

Purpose

The DataField property sets or returns the name of the field a bound control is bound to. Both read and write at design time and runtime. Table 27-31 gives the arguments for the DataField property.

General Syntax

```
[form!]Name.DataField [ = fieldName$]
```

Argument	Description
form	Name property of the parent form
Name	Name property of the bound control
fieldNameS	Name of the field in the data control's recordset

Table 27-31 Arguments of the DataField property

Example Syntax

```
Sub SwitchDatabases (pathName as String)
    Data1.DatabaseName = pathName
    Select Case pathName
        Case "C:\DATA\CLIENTS.MDB"
                Text1.DataField = "ClientID"
                Text2.DataField = "ClientName"
                Picture1.DataField = "ClientPhoto"
        Case "C:\DATA\PROSPECT.MDB"
                Text1.DataField = "ProspectID"
                Text2.DataField = "ProspectName"
                Picture1.DataField = "MugShot"
    End Select
    Data1.Refresh
    Label1.Caption = Text1.DataField
    Label2.Caption = Text2.DataField
    Label3.Caption = Picture1.DataField
End Sub
```

Description

Use the DataField property of a bound control to set or return which field it is bound to. A data control has an underlying recordset, as determined by the data control's RecordSource property. The controls bound to the data control must be bound to valid fields within the recordset. The DataField property of the bound control lets you read or set the name of that field at any time.

You may specify this property either at design time or runtime. At design time use the properties box for the bound control. Set the DataSource property first, then the DataField property. When you set the DataSource property, the DataField property will automatically read in the list of available field names in the recordset and let you select one from the drop-down combo box. You may also type in a different name if you know that name will later become valid. At runtime set the DataField property to the name of the field in the recordset. You probably already know the field name if you designed the database, or you may determine the name at runtime with the Fields collection.

1110

You must set the DataSource property for a bound control at design time for the DataField property to have meaning. The DataSource property associates a bound control with a specific data control. The data control, in turn, must have its DatabaseName and RecordSource properties properly set.

A bound control displays the underlying data automatically. It also automatically updates that underlying data if the user edits it in the control.

Example

The Data Access project at the end of this chapter sets the DataField properties for all bound controls at design time. The main form has two text boxes and an image control that are bound to dataMain, and the datasheet form has a hidden image control bound to the hidden data control to help place the icon picture in the grid.

DATASOURCE PROPERTY

Objects Affected

▶ Check	Clipboard	Combo	Command	CommonDlg
Data	Debug	Dir	Drive	File
Form	Frame	Grid	▶ Image	▶ Label
Line	List	MDI Form	Menu	OLE
Option	▶ Picture	Printer	Screen	Scroll
Shape	▶ Text	Timer		

Purpose

The DataSource property sets the Name of the data control this control is bound to. Read and write at design time, not available at runtime. This implies that you may not read or change the DataSource for a control while your program runs.

Description

Each bound control is bound to a particular data control. The DataSource property of the bound control determines to which data control the control is bound. Set this property at design time by specifying the DataSource name in the Properties box. It has a drop-down list of all the available data control Name properties. Choose one of these or type in the Name of a data control you haven't created yet.

Note that although you cannot change the DataSource for a control at runtime, you may change the DataField property to bind the control to different fields in the data control's recordset. You may also change the database the data control uses with the data control's DatabaseName property.

Example

The Data Access project at the end of this chapter sets the DataSource property for all the bound controls at design time to the appropriate data controls.

DELETE METHOD

Objects Affected

Check	Clipboard	Combo	Command	CommonDlg
▶ Data	Debug	Dir	Drive	File
Form	Frame	Grid	Image	Label
Line	List	MDI Form	Menu	OLE
Option	Picture	Printer	Screen	Scroll
Shape	Text	Timer		

Purpose

The Delete method deletes the current record. The deleted record remains current, but any references to it produce an error. Table 27-32 summarizes the arguments of the Delete method.

General Syntax

```
[form!]Name.Recordset.Delete
```

Argument	Description
form	Name property of the parent form
Name	Name property of the data control
Recordset	'Recordset' indicates the recordset property of the data control

Table 27-32 Arguments of the Delete method

1112

Example Syntax

```
Sub Command1_Click ()
    Data1.Recordset.Delete
    Data1.Recordset.MoveNext
End Sub
```

Description

The Delete method deletes the current record. Before you use the Delete method, make sure that a record is current. An error occurs if no record is current (for instance, if you are at the beginning of file marker).

Delete sets the fields in the current record to Null. It leaves the deleted record as the current record, but any references to this record will result in an error. Use a Move or Find method to leave the deleted record. Once you've moved away from the deleted record, you can't move back to it. Note that although the deleted record is only set to Null in the recordset, it is immediately removed from the underlying table of the recordset.

Although you may be tempted to do mass deletions in a DO..LOOP structure, it's usually much faster to use an SQL Execute method. For instance, the following loop deletes all records with the CityName field set to "Dallas":

```
Data1.Recordset.MoveFirst
Do While Not Data1.Recordset.EOF
    If Data1.Recordset!CityName = "Dallas" Then
        Data1.Recordset.Delete
    End If
    Data1.Recordset.MoveNext
Loop
```

The following example accomplishes the same thing with less code, is easier to read, and is much faster than stepping through the entire database:

```
Data1.Database.Execute "DELETE FROM Clients WHERE CityName = 'Dallas'"
```

Use the Delete method to delete individual records, or in cases where a standard query proves unwieldy or impossible. For instance, if you wanted to delete every third client from Dallas, but no more than 20 total, a DO...LOOP structure makes sense.

Example

The cmndDelete_Click event in the Data Access project at the end of this chapter uses the Delete method to delete single entries from the database. Contrast this with the cmndClear_Click event, which uses an SQL Execute method to clear the entire database.

EDIT METHOD

Objects Affected

Check	Clipboard	Combo	Command	CommonDlg
▶ Data	Debug	Dir	Drive	File
Form	Frame	Grid	Image	Label
Line	List	MDI Form	Menu	OLE
Option	Picture	Printer	Screen	Scroll
Shape	Text	Timer		

Purpose

The Edit method copies the current record into the copy buffer for subsequent editing. You must use the Edit method before making changes to a record. Table 27-33 gives the arguments of the Edit method.

General Syntax

```
[form!]Name.Recordset.Edit
```

Argument	Description
form	Name property of the parent form
Name	Name property of the data control
Recordset	'Recordset' indicates the recordset property of the data control

Table 27-33 Arguments of the Edit method

Example Syntax

```
Sub MakeRandom ()
    Data1.Recordset.MoveFirst
    Do While Not Data1.Recordset.EOF
        Data1.Recordset.Edit
        Data1.Recordset!RandomNumber = Rnd
        Data1.Recordset.Update
        Data1.Recordset.MoveNext
    Loop
End Sub
```

Description

Use the Edit method to begin editing a record. Attempting to change an item value generates an error if you don't use the Edit method first. Use the Update method to save the changes to the record.

The Edit method first copies the current record to the copy buffer and then makes the buffer the current record. The *copy buffer* is a memory location reserved by Visual Basic that functions like a temporary "virtual" record. You may change updatable fields in the copy buffer. The Update method saves the copy buffer to the recordset; a Move or Find method also updates the recordset before moving the current record. Using another Edit method before an update erases previous edits and restores the copy buffer to the recordset values. Note that you do not have to explicitly use the Edit or Update methods on bound controls; these automatically edit and update themselves.

During the edit, the record is locked according to the LockEdits property. If LockEdits is True (default), the page the record is on is locked and no other user can access any records on that page. If LockEdits is False, the page is only briefly locked during the update.

You may check to see if a recordset is updatable with the Recordset.Updatable property. Sometimes you may have a recordset with a nonupdatable field (like a counter), yet the rest of the fields are updatable. In this case, Recordset.Updatable returns False, and you can check the individual fields by using the Fields collection. Attempting to edit a nonupdatable field causes an error.

Example

The Data Access project at the end of this chapter uses the Edit method to prepare a Log record for an addition to the memo field. Each record added to the database in the cmndLoad_Click event appends the file name and path name of the entry to the log's memo.

EDITMODE PROPERTY

Objects Affected

Check	Clipboard	Combo	Command	CommonDlg
▶ Data	Debug	Dir	Drive	File
Form	Frame	Grid	Image	Label
Line	List	MDI Form	Menu	OLE
Option	Picture	Printer	Screen	Scroll
Shape	Text	Timer		

Purpose

The EditMode property of a data control lets you read the editing state of the current record. Its return value indicates whether there is no edit in progress, an edit is in progress, or a new record is being added. This property is most useful in the Validate event. Tables 27-34 and 27-35 give the arguments of the EditMode property.

General Syntax

```
[form!]Name.EditMode
```

Argument	Description
form	Name property of the parent form
Name	Name property of the data control

Table 27-34 Arguments of the EditMode property

Value	CONSTANT.TXT	Meaning
0	DATA_EDITNONE	No editing operation in process
1	DATA_EDITMODE	Edit method invoked and current record is in the copy buffer
2	DATA_EDITADD	AddNew method invoked and the current record in the copy buffer is a new record that doesn't yet exist in the database

Table 27-35 Meanings of the returned values for the EditMode property

Example Syntax

```
Sub Data1_Validate (Action As Integer, Save As Integer)
    If Text1.DataChanged Then
        If Data1.EditMode = DATA_EDITMODE Then
            MsgBox "Client ID may only be set when adding a new client!"
            Text1.DataChanged = False
        End If
    End If
End Sub
```

1116

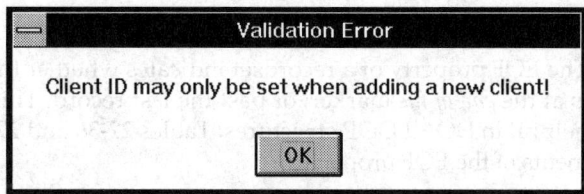

Figure 27-7 The EditMode property lets
you determine if there is an edit in process

Description

Use the data control's EditMode property to determine what the edit status is.
There are three possible states: no editing, normal editing, and adding a new
record. You would typically use this property in the Validate event, as in the
example syntax. This example prevents the user from changing an existing ID
field by checking to see whether the EditMode is editing a current record.
Figure 27-7 shows what this might look like.

Note that each of these Action constants is defined in CONSTANT.TXT. See
the discussion in the summary section at the beginning of this chapter for details
on how to use these constants.

Example

The Data Access project at the end of this chapter uses the EditMode property
in dataMain's Validate event to see if the text box entries have changed because
we're adding a new entry (AddNew). If so, it just saves the record without
renaming the physical disk files. If the text box entries have changed and
EditMode does not indicate AddNew, that implies the user has typed something
in the boxes and the Validate routine attempts to rename the physical disk files.

EOF PROPERTY

Objects Affected

Check	Clipboard	Combo	Command	CommonDlg
▶ Data	Debug	Dir	Drive	File
Form	Frame	Grid	Image	Label
Line	List	MDI Form	Menu	OLE
Option	Picture	Printer	Screen	Scroll
Shape	Text	Timer		

Purpose

The EOF property of a recordset indicates whether the current record position is at the *end of file* marker, or past the last record. This property is particularly helpful in DO...LOOP structures. Tables 27-36 and 27-37 summarize the arguments of the EOF property.

General Syntax

`[form!]Name.Recordset.EOF`

Argument	Description
form	Name property of the parent form
Name	Name property of the data control
Recordset	'Recordset' indicates the recordset property of the data control

Table 27-36 Arguments of the EOF property

Value	Meaning
True	The current record is after the last record, at the end of the file
False	The current record is at or before the last record

Table 27-37 The meanings of the returned values for the EOF property

Example Syntax

```
Sub MakeRandom ()
    Data1.Recordset.MoveFirst
    Do While Not Data1.Recordset.EOF
        Data1.Recordset.Edit
        Data1.Recordset!RandomNumber = Rnd
        Data1.Recordset.Update
        Data1.Recordset.MoveNext
    Loop
End Sub
```

Description

Use the EOF property of a recordset to determine whether you've gone beyond the last record. The EOF property is False for any record in the recordset; using MoveNext at the last record sets EOF to True. Attempting MoveNext again, beyond the end of the file, results in an error. There is no current record when EOF is True.

The example syntax uses EOF in a typical DO...LOOP structure. It steps through each record of the recordset from beginning to end.

Use the BOF property to see whether you are at the beginning of the file.

Example

The Data Access project at the end of this chapter uses the EOF property in the FillGrid procedure. This fills the grid with each record in the database, starting at the first record and proceeding to the end of the file.

ERROR EVENT

Objects Affected

Check	Clipboard	Combo	Command	CommonDlg
▶ Data	Debug	Dir	Drive	File
Form	Frame	Grid	Image	Label
Line	List	MDI Form	Menu	OLE
Option	Picture	Printer	Screen	Scroll
Shape	Text	Timer		

Purpose

The data control's Error event lets you react to errors in reading data that are not caused by your code. Normal runtime errors caused by your code should be handled in a normal error handler with the On Error Goto... construction. Tables 27-38 and 27-39 summarize the arguments of the Error event.

General Syntax

```
Sub Name_Error ([Index As Integer,] DataErr As Integer, Response As
Integer)
```

Argument	Description
Name	Name property of the data control
Index	Index property of a data control in a control array
DataErr	The error number
Response	The kind of response you want to generate

Table 27-38 The arguments of the Error event

Value	CONSTANT.TXT	Meaning
0	DATA_ERRCONTINUE	Continue without displaying error message
1	DATA_ERRDISPLAY	(Default) Display the message

Table 27-39 The meaning of the values for the Response argument in the Error event

Example Syntax

```
Sub Data1_Error (DataError As Integer, Response As Integer)
     If DataError = 3024            'If database file not found
         CMDialog1.Filter = "Datafiles|*.mdb"    'display legal databases
         CMDialog1.DialogTitle = "File not found. Select new datafile:"
         CMDialog1.Action = 1           'Display a File Open dialog
         Data1.DatabaseName = CMDialog1.FileName
         Response = DATA_ERRCONTINUE
     End If
End Sub
```

Description

The Error event lets you respond to data access errors not caused by your code. For instance, the user clicking on the data control's movement buttons, the data control automatically opening a database during Form_Load, or a custom control attempting to use the AddNew or Delete methods when there is no current record all cause errors that are external to your code. Use the Error event to trap these errors.

Errors caused by your code (such as a DO...LOOP moving beyond the end of the file) must be handled by a standard On Error Goto... error handler.

1120

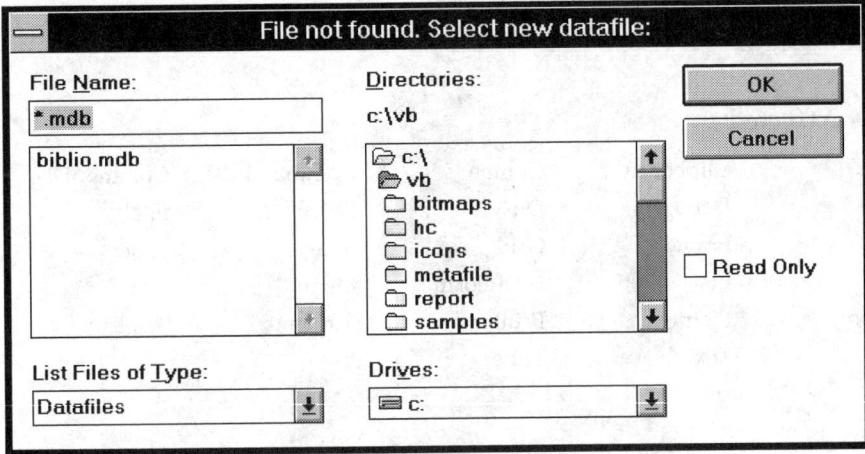

Figure 27-8 The Error event lets you respond to database errors

The example syntax shows how the Error event traps and handles a nonexistent database being specified during the design phase. Form_Load tries to load the database and fails, triggering the Error event. The routine checks to see if the error number is 3024 (database file not found). If so, it sets up a File Open common dialog box and displays it. (See Chapter 17, Dialog Boxes, for more on the common dialog box.) The dialog box's FileName property is then used to open the database. Figure 27-8 shows this example in action.

Note that each of the response Error constants is defined in CONSTANT.TXT. See the discussion in the summary section at the beginning of this chapter for details on how to use these constants.

Example

The Data Access project at the end of this chapter uses dataMain's Error event to trap the "No Current Record" error that occurs when all records are deleted from the database.

Comment

More than 300 data access trappable errors are summarized in the "Trappable Data Access Errors" Help topic. Pull this up by searching for Help on the Error event, clicking on the "See Also" jump topic, and choosing the "Trappable Data Access Errors" Help topic.

EXCLUSIVE PROPERTY

Objects Affected

Check	Clipboard	Combo	Command	CommonDlg
▶ Data	Debug	Dir	Drive	File
Form	Frame	Grid	Image	Label
Line	List	MDI Form	Menu	OLE
Option	Picture	Printer	Screen	Scroll
Shape	Text	Timer		

Purpose

Use the Exclusive property to read or set whether a database is opened for single-user or multiuser access. Read and write at both design time and runtime. Tables 27-40 and 27-41 summarize the arguments of the Exclusive property.

General Syntax

```
[form!]Name.Exclusive [ = boolean%]
```

Argument	Description
form	Name property of the parent form
Name	Name property of the data control
boolean%	True or False indicating multiuser status

Table 27-40 The arguments in the Exclusive property

boolean%	Meaning
True	Single user (exclusive) access. No other process may access the database
False	(Default) Multiuser access. Multiple processes may access the database

Table 27-41 Meanings of the values of the Exclusive property

Example Syntax

```
Sub Form_Load ()
    Data1.DatabaseName = "C:\DATA\ADDRESS.MDB"
    Data1.Exclusive
    Data1.RecordSource = "SELECT * FROM Name ORDER BY Zip"
    Data1.Refresh
End Sub
```

Description

Use the Exclusive property to determine whether a database is opened for single-user or multiuser access. Single-user mode restricts access to the database to just the one application that opened it. (You may have several data controls accessing the same database at the same time, however.) Multiuser mode lets other users on a network or multiple processes and programs on the same machine access the database.

Single-user mode is somewhat faster than multiuser, so set Exclusive=True whenever possible.

Example

The PrintStats routine in the Data Access project at the end of this chapter tests the Exclusive property to determine whether the database is opened in single-user or multiuser mode.

EXECUTE METHOD

Objects Affected

Check	Clipboard	Combo	Command	CommonDlg
▶ Data	Debug	Dir	Drive	File
Form	Frame	Grid	Image	Label
Line	List	MDI Form	Menu	OLE
Option	Picture	Printer	Screen	Scroll
Shape	Text	Timer		

Purpose

The Execute method executes an SQL action query on the data control's underlying Database object. An SQL action query can be easier to code and is almost always significantly faster than a DO…LOOP structure for mass updates or deletions. Tables 27-42 and 27-43 summarize the arguments of the Execute method.

General Syntax

```
[form!]Name.Database.Execute queryName$[, options]
[form!]Name.Database.Execute query$[,options]
[form!]Name.Database.Execute options
```

Argument	Description
form	Name property of the parent form
Name	Name property of the data control
Database	'Database' indicates the Database property of the data control
queryName$	Name of a predefined action query in the database
query$	String or string literal containing valid SQL actions
options	Indicates one or more SQL options

Table 27-42 Arguments of the Execute method

Value	DATACONS.TXT	Meaning
1	DB_DENYWRITE	Target tables are locked during update
16	DB_INCONSISTENTUPDATES	(Default) Does not maintain referential integrity
32	DB_CONSISTENTUPDATES	Automatically enforces referential integrity
64	DB_SQLPASSTHROUGH	(Default) Passes SQL statement to remote server

Table 27-43 Meanings of the options argument for the Execute method

Example Syntax

```
Sub Command1_Click ()
    Data1.Database.Execute "Delete Bad Addresses", DB_CONSISTENTUPDATES
    Data1.Database.Execute "UPDATE Clients SET Amount = 0 WHERE Amount < 5"
End Sub
```

Description

Use the Execute method to execute SQL action queries on your database. An SQL action query is usually easier to write (if you know SQL!) than the equivalent Basic code and almost always runs faster. The Access database engine works internally with SQL and can optimize the query for the most efficient processing.

Note that you cannot create a select query with the Execute method. That is, the Execute method can only update or delete records; it cannot return a recordset. Use an SQL statement in the data control's RecordSource property to return a recordset. An error occurs if you attempt to use the Execute method to select records.

The Execute method can accept either the name of a predefined SQL action query, or a string or string literal that defines an action query. You cannot create a predefined action query with Standard Edition Visual Basic. You may create these in Professional Version using the CreateQueryDef method, or in a database like Microsoft Access. Although you cannot create a predefined query in Standard Edition, you may use one if it already exists in the database.

You can always define your own query at runtime with a string or string literal. The first example line uses a predefined action query (that apparently deletes all records with bad addresses), while the second line uses a query we define on the spot: "Zero the balances for all clients with a balance amount of less than five dollars."

The options argument lets you set several options for the SQL action. An SQL update normally does not lock the affected tables during the update; it normally only locks each record as it updates it. You may wish to lock the entire table with the DB_DENYWRITE option to make sure another user doesn't modify the data you're trying to update. Note that each of these Options constants is defined in DATACONS.TXT. See the discussion in the summary section at the beginning of this chapter for details on how to use these constants.

The Access engine can enforce referential integrity for you. That means that it can restrict itself to updating only the "many" side of a one-to-many relationship. As a practical example, consider two tables, the Client table and the Transactions table. The Client table has information on each client, such as name and address, and has ClientID as the primary key that other tables use to refer to that client. The Transactions table has information on each transaction, such as what was purchased, the date purchased, and the client who purchased it. The client information in the Transactions table uses ClientID to refer back to the Client table; the Client table is the "one" side and the Transactions table is the "many" side of the one-to-many relationship. One client can have lots of transactions, but each transaction was made by only one particular client.

The default setting of DB_INCONSISTENTUPDATES lets your SQL action query update either side of the relationship. You may inadvertently change the ClientIDs in the Client table, thus wreaking complete disaster on the referential integrity of your database. You might end up with Transactions (and potentially many other tables that are joined to the Client table) that point to nonexistent or incorrect clients after such an update. Although there are circumstances that warrant this power, in general this is a foolhardy approach.

The DB_CONSISTENTUPDATES enforces referential integrity by letting you update only the "many" side of a one-to-many relationship. This means that no matter what the query does, it will not affect the "one" side, and will maintain referential integrity for all the other tables that are joined to the "one" table.

The DB_SQLPASSTHROUGH passes your action query through to an external ODBC SQL database rather than having the Access engine perform the query. It is only applicable in the Professional Edition.

Example

The Data Access project at the end of this chapter uses the Execute method to clear the database of all records in the cmndClear_Click event. This SQL action query is vastly faster than deleting each record individually with a DO...LOOP.

FIELDS COLLECTION

Objects Affected

Check	Clipboard	Combo	Command	CommonDlg
▶ Data	Debug	Dir	Drive	File
Form	Frame	Grid	Image	Label
Line	List	MDI Form	Menu	OLE
Option	Picture	Printer	Screen	Scroll
Shape	Text	Timer		

Purpose

The Fields collection returns the details of the available fields in the table or recordset. You use the Fields collection implicitly when you set an item's value, and you may use the collection explicitly to get such information as field name, field data type, field length, and field attributes, as well as to work with long binary and memo fields. Tables 27-44 and 27-45 show the arguments and property of the Fields collection, and Table 27-46 shows the properties and methods of the members within the Fields collection.

General Syntax

```
[form!]Name.Recordset.Fields[(Index|fieldName)].Property|Method
[form!]Name.Database.TableDefs(Index|tableName).Fields[(Index|fieldName)].Property|Method
```

Argument	Description
form	Name property of the parent form
Name	Name property of the data control
Recordset	'Recordset' indicates the recordset property of the data control
Database	'Database' indicates the Database property of the data control
TableDefs	'TableDefs' indicates the TableDefs collection of the database
Fields	'Fields' indicates the Fields collection of the recordset or TableDefs collection
Index	The ordinal index position of the member of the collection
tableName	Name of the table
fieldName	Name of the field
Property	Property of the Fields collection

Table 27-44 Arguments of the Fields collection

Property	Meaning
Count	Number of members in the Fields collection (fields in this table)

Table 27-45 Property of the Fields collection

Property or Method		Meaning
AppendChunk	Method	Appends a string to a long binary or memo field
Attributes	Property	Option bits for this field
CollatingOrder	Property	Collating (sort) order of the field

(continued on next page)

(continued from previous page)

Property or Method		Meaning
FieldSize	Method	Actual size of a long binary or memo field
GetChunk	Method	Gets a portion of a long binary or memo field
Name	Property	Name of the field
OrdinalPosition	Property	Index number in the collection for this field
Size	Property	Maximum size of the field
SourceField	Property	Returns the name of the source field
SourceTable	Property	Returns the name of the source table
Type	Property	Data type of the field
Value	Property	Value of the field

Table 27-46 Properties and methods of the members in a Fields collection

Example Syntax

```
Sub Command1_Click ()
    Print "#","Name","Type"
    For i = 0 to Data1.Recordset.Fields.Count - 1
        Print Data1.Recordset.Fields(i).OrdinalPosition,
        Print Data1.Recordset.Fields(i).Name,
        Select Case Data1.Recordset.Fields(i).Type
            Case 1: Print "Boolean",
            Case 2: Print "Byte",
            Case 3: Print "Integer",
            Case 4: Print "Long",
            Case 5: Print "Currency",
            Case 6: Print "Single",
            Case 7: Print "Double",
            Case 8: Print "Date",
            Case 9: Print "Binary",
            Case 10: Print "Text",
            Case 11: Print "LongBinary",
            Case 12: Print "Memo"
        End Select
    Next i
End Sub
```

1128

Description

The Fields collection lets you access individual properties of each field. You use it implicitly whenever you set the value for a field, and you may wish to use some of its properties explicitly to print out your database structure.

The default property of the Recordset property is the Fields collection; the default property of the Fields collection is the Value property. This lets you simplify the rather lengthy

```
Data1.Recordset.Fields("CityName").Value = "Seattle"
```

to the more manageable

```
Data1.Recordset!CityName = "Seattle"
```

Both lines perform the identical function.

The Fields collection belongs both to the Recordset property of the data control, and to the TableDefs collection of the Database property of the data control. Note that these may give very different results if the RecordSource property of the data control was set using an SQL select query. That query may reorder the fields, create calculated fields, and join multiple tables.

AppendChunk, FieldSize, and GetChunk member properties

The AppendChunk method appends a string to a memo field. Strings in Visual Basic are limited to 64K, whereas memo fields may be quite large (many gigabytes for some databases). AppendChunk lets you build a large memo field from many smaller pieces.

The FieldSize method returns the actual number of bytes in a long binary or memo field. You would typically use this method in conjunction with the GetChunk method. Using it on a field other than a long binary or memo type results in an error. If you assign the value of this method to a variable, make sure it is of type Long or Variant, as binary and memo fields can be quite large.

The GetChunk method gets a portion of a long binary or memo field. These kinds of fields may be quite large (several gigabytes are possible). The GetChunk method lets you get these in "bite-sized chunks" so that you do not exceed Visual Basic's 64K string-length limitations.

See the individual entries on each of these methods for more details and code examples of how to handle large memo fields.

Count property

Use the Count property to determine how many members belong to the collection. Remember that like a list box, this is a zero-based list; that is, the first member has an OrdinalPosition index of 0; the last member has a position of (Count - 1). You can use this number to step through each member of the collection, as in the example syntax.

Attributes member property

The Attributes property of each member determines how a field will be treated by Visual Basic. See the Attributes item entry for more details. These are bit values, and you need to perform bitwise operations using the And operator to determine the setting of a given bit. For example, use this statement to test if the Attributes property has the DB_UPDATABLEFIELD flag set:

```
If Data1.Recordset.Fields("Empl").Attributes And DB_UPDATABLEFIELD Then
    ' field can be updated, so put code here
End If
```

CollatingOrder member property

The CollatingOrder property determines how a field is collated (sorted). You might want to use this value in an InStr or StrComp expression. See the CollatingOrder property entry for more details and an example.

The Name member property

The Name property of the field is the actual name in the recordset or database. You generally use the name to refer to the field both in the implicit and explicit constructions:

```
Data1.Recordset.Fields("CityName").Value = "Seattle"
Data1.Recordset!CityName = "Seattle"
```

Field names may have embedded spaces, unlike Visual Basic variable names. The explicit usage is transparent, as the entire name is in quotes. The implicit usage, with the exclamation mark (!), requires square brackets around the name if the name has spaces in it:

```
Data1.Recordset.Fields("Country of Origin").Value = "South Korea"
Data1.Recordset![Country of Origin] = "South Korea"
```

Field names are generally identical to the names of the fields in the underlying table. However, if the RecordSource for the data control is set using an SQL statement, it is possible to create calculated fields with new names and to rename fields with aliases. Consult one of the books on SQL listed in the BIBLIO.MDB database that comes with Visual Basic for more information on creating calculated fields and aliases; the RecordSource entry has some examples of this.

OrdinalPosition member property

The OrdinalPosition determines where in the collection this member occurs. If you are using a FOR…NEXT construction to step through the collection, your index variable will always equal the OrdinalPosition. This position is determined by the order that the members were added to the collection, or by the order the SQL SELECT statement returns them if the RecordSource was set by an SQL statement.

Size and Type member properties

The Size property determines the maximum size (in bytes) of the field. For fixed length fields, such as Boolean, Byte, Integer, Long, Currency, Single, Double, and Date, the size is the exact length of the field. For variable length fields, such as Text and Memos, this property indicates the maximum allowable length (as set during database design), not the actual length of the data in the field.

The Type property indicates what kind of data is stored in the field. Note that each of these Action constants is defined in DATACONS.TXT. See the discussion in the summary section at the beginning of this chapter for details on how to use these constants. A memo field in a native Access database is limited to 32K, but other databases can support much larger memo fields—up to several gigabytes for some SQL database engines. Table 27-47 summarizes the Size and Type properties.

Value	Size	DATACONS.TXT	Meaning	Value Range
1	1	DB_BOOLEAN	True/False	0 or 1
2	1	DB_BYTE	Number (TinyInt)	0 to 255
3	2	DB_INTEGER	Number (Integer)	-32768 to 32767
4	4	DB_LONG	Number (Long Integer)	-2,147,483,648 to 2,147,483,647
5	8	DB_CURRENCY	Number (Currency)	-922,337,203,685,477.5808 to 922,337,203,685,477.5807
6	4	DB_SINGLE	Number (Single)	+/- 3.402823E38 to +/- 1.401298E-45
7	8	DB_DOUBLE	Number (Double)	+/- 1.79769313486232E308 to +/- 4.94065645841247E-324
8	8	DB_DATE	Date/Time	Jan 1, 100 to Dec 31, 9999
9	0	DB_BINARY	Binary	n/a
10	0	DB_TEXT	Character	0 to 64K characters
11	0	DB_LONGBINARY	Binary or OLE objects	n/a
12	0	DB_MEMO	Memo	32K for Access databases

Table 27-47 Values for the Type property for members of the Fields collection (with size in bytes)

SourceField and SourceTable member properties

The SourceField and SourceTable indicate where a field comes from if the record-set is built from an SQL SELECT statement. It is possible to create calculated fields and join multiple tables with SQL.

Value member property

The Value property sets and returns the value of the field. You most commonly use it implicitly, as the Fields collection is the default property of the Recordset property, and the Value property is the default property of the Fields collection:

```
Data1.Recordset.Fields("CityName").Value = "Seattle"      ' explicit
Data1.Recordset!CityName = "Seattle"                      ' implicit
```

Example

The Data Access project at the end of this chapter prints out a number of details about the Fields collection in the PrintStats routine.

FIELDSIZE METHOD

Objects Affected

Check	Clipboard	Combo	Command	CommonDlg
▶ Data	Debug	Dir	Drive	File
Form	Frame	Grid	Image	Label
Line	List	MDI Form	Menu	OLE
Option	Picture	Printer	Screen	Scroll
Shape	Text	Timer		

Purpose

The FieldSize method returns the actual number of bytes in a long binary or memo field. Table 27-48 summarizes the arguments of the FieldSize method.

General Syntax

```
[form!]Name.Recordset.Fields(Index%).FieldSize
[form!]Name.Recordset.Fields(Field$).FieldSize
[form!]Name.Database.TableDefs(Index%|Table$).Fields[(Index%|Field$)].FieldSize
```

Argument	Description
form	Name property of the form
Name	Name property of the data control
Recordset	'Recordset' indicates the Recordset property of the data control
Database	'Database' indicates the Database property of the data control
Fields	'Fields' indicates the Fields collection of the recordset or database
TableDefs	'TableDefs' indicates the TableDefs collection of the database
Index%	The ordinal index position of the member of the collection
Field$	Name of the field (must be memo or long binary)
Table$	Name of the table

Table 27-48 Arguments of the FieldSize method

Example Syntax

```
Sub Command1_Click ()
    Open "BIGFILE.TXT" For Binary As #1     ' Open the external file
    totalSize = Data1.Recordset.Fields("Memo").FieldSize()
    biteSize = 5000
    numChunks = totalSize \ biteSize
    remChunk = totalSize Mod biteSize
    For i = 0 To numChunks
        If i = numChunks Then biteSize = remChunk
        chunk = Data1.Recordset.Fields("Memo").GetChunk(i * biteSize, biteSize)
        Put #1, , chunk
    Next i
    Close #1                                 ' Close the external file
End Sub
```

Description

The FieldSize method returns the actual number of bytes in a long binary or memo field. You would typically use this method in conjunction with the GetChunk method. Using it on a field other than a long binary or memo type results in an error. If you assign the value of this method to a variable, make sure it is of type Long or Variant, as binary and memo fields can be quite large.

Example

The Utilities menu Log command in the Data Access project at the end of this chapter prints out the Log file's Memo field. It uses the FieldSize method to help determine how many chunks it needs to process, exactly as in the example syntax.

FINDFIRST, FINDLAST, FINDNEXT, FINDPREVIOUS METHODS

Objects Affected

Check	Clipboard	Combo	Command	CommonDlg
▶ Data	Debug	Dir	Drive	File
Form	Frame	Grid	Image	Label
Line	List	MDI Form	Menu	OLE
Option	Picture	Printer	Screen	Scroll
Shape	Text	Timer		

Purpose

The Find methods let you find specific records in your recordset. FindFirst finds the first record, FindNext finds the next one after using a FindFirst or FindLast; FindPrevious finds the previous record after a FindFirst or FindLast, and FindLast finds the last record. Each Find method searches for a specific record as set by its criteria argument and makes it the current record. Table 27-49 lists the arguments of the Find methods.

General Syntax

```
[form!]Name.Recordset.FindFirst criteria$
[form!]Name.Recordset.FindLast criteria$
[form!]Name.Recordset.FindNext criteria$
[form!]Name.Recordset.FindPrevious criteria$
```

Argument	Description
form	Name property of the parent form
Name	Name property of the data control

Argument	Description
Recordset	'Recordset' indicates the recordset property of the data control
criteria$	A valid SQL WHERE clause without the word 'WHERE'

Table 27-49 Arguments of the Find methods

Example Syntax

```
Sub Combo1_DblClick ()
     Data1.Recordset.FindFirst "State = '" & Combo1.Text & "'"
End Sub
```

Description

The Find methods let you search your database for records that meet specific criteria. You can search for the first or last records that meet the criteria with the FindFirst and FindLast methods and then move through subsequent matches using FindNext and FindPrevious. If a Find method fails (if, for example, there is no matching record), the NoMatch property is set to True, and the current record remains the same as it was before the failed Find method.

The Update method automatically triggers to save any pending edits or new records before the Find methods complete the move.

The records in a recordset are ordered by either a table's primary key (if the data control's RecordSource property is set to a table name) or by an SQL ORDER BY statement (if RecordSource is set to an SQL SELECT statement).

The criteria can be any valid SQL WHERE clause, without the 'WHERE' keyword. It can either be a string variable or a string literal. Refer to the books on SQL in the BIBLIO.MDB database that comes with Visual Basic for more information on SQL WHERE clauses; the RecordSource entry in this chapter introduces you to the basics of SQL.

A 'WHERE' clause typically looks quite a bit like the conditional part of an IF...THEN statement. The field you'd like to test goes on the left side of a comparison operator, and the value you're comparing it against goes on the right side of the operator. For instance,

```
If Data1.Recordset!CityName = "Seattle" Then
```

translates to

```
Data1.Recordset.FindFirst "CityName = 'Seattle'"
```

Notice the single quotes (') used to delimit strings within the criteria, as in the word 'Seattle.' This is, of course, due to the criteria itself being enclosed in double quotes ("). The example syntax given at the beginning of this entry uses this same idea to find the first record that matches the text displayed in the Combo1 combo box. It embeds Combo1's Text property inside of a pair of single quotes to complete the criteria string.

You can find embedded text with the Like operator. The SQL LIKE is very similar to the normal Like operator explained in Appendix B, Visual Basic Language Reference. The next two examples find the first record with a last name that has "SMITH" in it (such as "Smith," "Smithson," or "Blacksmithson") and all phone numbers in the 609 area code with a 12 embedded at the 11th character position:

```
Data1.Recordset.FindFirst "LastName LIKE '*SMITH*'"
Data1.Recordset.FindLast "[Phone Number] LIKE '(609) ???-12??'"
```

The Find methods are much more efficient than stepping through each record to update a subset of records. A typical loop using the Move methods to update only records from New York city would have to examine every record in the database:

```
Data1.Recordset.MoveFirst
Do While Not Data1.Recordset.EOF
    If Data1.Recordset!CityName = "New York" Then
        Data1.Recordset.Edit
        Data1.Recordset!Letter = "directmail 0694"
        Data1.Recordset.Update
    End If
    Data1.Recordset.MoveNext
Loop
```

Compare this to using the Find methods to operate only on those records that meet the search criteria. This will operate much more efficiently and quickly:

```
criteria$ = "CityName = 'New York'"
Data1.Recordset.FindFirst criteria$
Do While Not Data1.Recordset.NoMatch
    Data1.Recordset.Edit
    Data1.Recordset!Letter = "directmail 0694"
    Data1.Recordset.Update
    Data1.Recordset.FindNext criteria$
Loop
```

Even though this latter example is more efficient, it doesn't compare to the ease and speed of using an SQL action query with the Execute method:

```
Data1.Database.Execute "UPDATE Prospects SET Letter = 'directmail 0694' WHERE CityName =
'New York'"
```

Use the find methods where an equivalent SQL action query would be cumbersome or impossible, or where you are simply searching for a particular record to display for the user.

Example

The Data Access project at the end of this chapter dedicates an entire dialog box to finding records. The Find methods are all triggered by the cmndFind control array's Click event. The event first builds an SQL WHERE criteria string and then passes that string to the appropriate Find method.

FREELOCKS STATEMENT

Purpose

The FreeLocks statement momentarily suspends data processing to allow recordsets to refresh themselves in a multiuser environment.

General Syntax

```
FreeLocks
```

Example Syntax

```
Sub Command1_Click ()
    Do While Not Data1.EOF
        x = Data1.Recordset!XPos
        y = Data1.Recordset!YPos
        PlotData x, y
        FreeLocks
    Loop
End Sub
```

Description

You can use the FreeLocks statement to allow the database time to free any locked records and update recordsets that may have changed. The Access engine normally does this for you as a background operation when nothing else (including mouse moves) is happening. Intense multiuser and processor-intensive situations might call for manually freeing up the database with FreeLocks. This is somewhat analogous to calling DoEvents to let the Windows environment complete any operations it needs during processor or file-intensive operations.

Example

The FreeLocks statement in the Data Access project at the end of this chapter gets executed after the cmndLoad_Click event is through processing each batch of files. This gives the system some time to refresh itself before the next batch gets processed. Note that this isn't strictly necessary in a single-user environment.

GETCHUNK METHOD

Objects Affected

Check	Clipboard	Combo	Command	CommonDlg
▸ Data	Debug	Dir	Drive	File
Form	Frame	Grid	Image	Label
Line	List	MDI Form	Menu	OLE
Option	Picture	Printer	Screen	Scroll
Shape	Text	Timer		

Purpose

Use the GetChunk method to get a portion of a long binary or memo field. These kinds of fields may well be larger than the 64K limit Visual Basic has on string variables. Table 27-50 summarizes the arguments of the GetChunk method.

General Syntax

```
[form!]Name.Recordset.Fields(Index%).GetChunk(offset%, numbytes%)
[form!]Name.Recordset.Fields(Field$).GetChunk(offset%, numbytes%)
[form!]Name.Database.TableDefs(Index%|Table$).Fields[(Index%|Field$)].GetChunk(offset%,
numbytes%)
```

Argument	Description
form	Name property of the form
Name	Name property of the data control
Recordset	'Recordset' indicates the Recordset property of the data control
Database	'Database' indicates the Database property of the data control
Fields	'Fields' indicates the Fields collection of the recordset or database
TableDefs	'TableDefs' indicates the TableDefs collection of the database
Index%	The ordinal index position of the member of the collection
Field$	Name of the field (must be memo or long binary)

Argument	Description
Table$	Name of the table
offset%	Number of bytes to skip before reading data
numbytes%	Number of bytes to read

Table 27-50 Arguments of the GetChunk method

Example Syntax

```
Sub Command1_Click ()
    Open "BIGFILE.TXT" For Binary As #1     ' Open the external file
    totalSize = Data1.Recordset.Fields("Memo").FieldSize()
    biteSize = 5000
    numChunks = totalSize \ biteSize
    remChunk = totalSize Mod biteSize
    For i = 0 To numChunks
        If i = numChunks Then biteSize = remChunk
        chunk = Data1.Recordset.Fields("Memo").GetChunk(i * biteSize, biteSize)
        Put #1, , chunk
    Next i
    Close #1                                ' Close the external file
End Sub
```

Description

The GetChunk method gets a portion of a long binary or memo field. These kinds of fields may be quite large (several gigabytes are possible). The GetChunk method lets you get these in "bite-sized chunks" so that you do not exceed Visual Basic's 64K string-length limitations. Specify where you want to start reading with the offset% argument and how much you want to read with the numbytes% argument. The example syntax shows how to export the information encoded in the AppendChunk entry.

Example

The Data Access project at the end of this chapter prints out the Log file's Memo field in the menuUtils_Click event. It uses the GetChunk method to grab bite-sized pieces of the Memo field to print out, exactly as in the example syntax.

1139

INDEXES COLLECTION

Objects Affected

Check	Clipboard	Combo	Command	CommonDlg
▶ Data	Debug	Dir	Drive	File
Form	Frame	Grid	Image	Label
Line	List	MDI Form	Menu	OLE
Option	Picture	Printer	Screen	Scroll
Shape	Text	Timer		

Purpose

The Indexes collection lets you access information about a table's indexes. Although this may be useful for mapping a database's structure, index usage is restricted in Visual Basic Standard Edition. Tables 27-51 and 27-52 summarize the arguments and property of the Indexes collection, and Table 27-53 summarizes the properties of the members in the Indexes collection.

General Syntax

```
[form!]Name.Database.TableDefs(Index%|tableName$).Indexes(Index%|fieldName$)].Property
```

Argument	Description
form	Name property of the parent form
Name	Name property of the data control
Recordset	'Recordset' indicates the Recordset property of the data control
Database	'Database' indicates the Database property of the data control
TableDefs	'TableDefs' indicates the TableDefs collection of the database
Indexes	'Indexes' indicates the Indexes collection of the TableDefs collection
Index%	The ordinal index position of the member of the collection
tableName$	Name of the table

Argument	Description
fieldNameS	Name of the field
Property	Property of the Indexes collection

Table 27-51 Arguments of the Indexes collection

Property	Meaning
Count	Number of members in the Fields collection (fields in this table)

Table 27-52 Property of the Indexes collection

Property	Meaning
Fields	The fields that are indexed
Name	Name of the index
Primary	True/False indicates if this is the primary index of table
Unique	True/False indicates if the index is restricted to unique values

Table 27-53 Properties of Indexes collection members

Example Syntax

```
Sub Command1_Click ()
    Print "Name", "Fields", "Primary", "Unique"
    For i = 0 To Data1.Database.TableDefs("Clients").Indexes.Count - 1
        Print Data1.Database.TableDefs("Clients").Indexes(i).Fields,
        Print Data1.Database.TableDefs("Clients").Indexes(i).Name,
        Print Data1.Database.TableDefs("Clients").Indexes(i).Primary,
        Print Data1.Database.TableDefs("Clients").Indexes(i).Unique
    Next i
End Sub
```

1141

Description

The Indexes collection lets you access the settings of the indexes for the tables in your database. Visual Basic Standard Edition has limited support for indexing; you cannot create your own indexes.

Fields

Setting the Fields member property indexes the table by those fields you specify. This property is a string literal or variable up to 254 characters long. Each key field of the index must be a valid field name in the table. Specify multiple-key indexes by separating each field name with a semicolon. *Ascending sorts* (from smallest to largest) are the default and can be explicitly set with the plus sign (+). Designate *descending sorts* (from largest to smallest) with a minus sign (-). The following example sets the table's index to sort first by CityName in ascending order, with "ties" broken by a secondary sort on ZipCode in descending order:

```
Data1.Database.TableDefs("Clients").Indexes(2).Fields = +CityName;-ZipCode
```

Name

The Name member property gives a unique name for the index.

Primary

The Primary member property indicates if the index is the *primary index* of the table. There can only be one primary index per table. Recordsets built on that table default to sorting on that index. If a field or set of fields is specified as the primary index for a table, each value must be unique and non-Null. The field that makes up a primary index is usually the field you use to make joins.

Unique

A *unique index* requires that each item in the field be unique; there may be no duplicates. If a field is designated as unique, the database engine will not allow duplicate records. All primary indexes automatically have their Unique property set to True.

Example

The Data Acces project at the end of this chapter prints out a number of index statistics in the PrintStats routine.

1142

LOCKEDITS PROPERTY

Objects Affected

Check	Clipboard	Combo	Command	CommonDlg
▶ Data	Debug	Dir	Drive	File
Form	Frame	Grid	Image	Label
Line	List	MDI Form	Menu	OLE
Option	Picture	Printer	Screen	Scroll
Shape	Text	Timer		

Purpose

The LockEdits property of a recordset determines whether the page the record is on is locked during editing. The two settings are called *pessimistic locking* (where the page is locked) and *optimistic locking* (where the page is not locked). Read and write at runtime, not available at design time. Tables 27-54 and 27-55 summarize the arguments of the LockEdits property.

General Syntax

```
[form!]Name.Recordset.LockEdits = boolean%
```

Argument	Description
form	Name property of the parent form
Name	Name property of the data control
Recordset	'Recordset' indicates the Recordset property of the data control
boolean%	True or False

Table 27-54 Arguments of the LockEdits property

Value	Meaning
True	(Default, pessimistic locking) Page the record is on is locked during edit

(continued on next page)

(continued from previous page)

Value	Meaning
False	(Optimistic locking) Page is not locked during edit, only during Update

Table 27-55 Meanings of the boolean% value in the LockEdits property

Example Syntax

```
Sub Form_Activate ()
    Data1.Recordset.LockEdits = True
End Sub
```

Description

The LockEdits property of the recordset lets you determine which mode of record locking Visual Basic uses during an edit. Pessimistic locking (the default) locks the page the record is on and prevents other users in a multiuser environment from accessing any of the records on the same page. The number of records on a given page is a function of record size and cannot be easily determined by your program. Optimistic locking does not lock the page during the editing process. It is only briefly locked during the Update method.

Example

The Data Access project at the end of this chapter sets LockEdits to False in the Form_Resize event to help improve speed. Note that it can't be located in the Form_Load event, as the data control has not finished initializing, and you'd get an "Object variable not set" error. The Resize event executes only once in this program, as the main form is set as a fixed border style.

MOVEFIRST, MOVELAST, MOVENEXT, MOVEPREVIOUS METHODS

Objects Affected

Check	Clipboard	Combo	Command	CommonDlg
▶ Data	Debug	Dir	Drive	File
Form	Frame	Grid	Image	Label
Line	List	MDI Form	Menu	OLE
Option	Picture	Printer	Screen	Scroll
Shape	Text	Timer		

1144

Purpose

The Move methods let you navigate through your recordset. These methods are analogous to the movement buttons on the data control. MoveFirst moves to the first record in the recordset; MoveLast moves to the last record. MoveNext moves to the next record, and MovePrevious moves to the previous record. Each Move method makes the new record the current record after finishing the move. Table 27-56 summarizes the arguments of the Move methods.

General Syntax

```
[form!]Name.Recordset.MoveFirst
[form!]Name.Recordset.MoveLast
[form!]Name.Recordset.MoveNext
[form!]Name.Recordset.MovePrevious
```

Argument	Description
form	Name property of the parent form
Name	Name property of the data control
Recordset	'Recordset' indicates the Recordset property of the data control

Table 27-56 Arguments of the Move methods

Example Syntax

```
Sub MakeRandom ()
    Data1.Recordset.MoveFirst
    Do While Not Data1.Recordset.EOF
        Data1.Recordset.Edit
        Data1.Recordset!RandomNumber = Rnd
        Data1.Recordset.Update
        Data1.Recordset.MoveNext
    Loop
End Sub
```

Description

The four buttons on a data control correspond to MoveFirst, MovePrevious, MoveNext, and MoveLast. The Move methods let your code move through the recordset in much the same way.

You typically use the Move methods in some kind of loop, as in the example syntax. The example moves to the first record of the database, then edits each record in turn. After editing each record, the MoveNext goes to the next record.

Moving one record beyond the last record with a MoveNext sets the record-set's EOF property to True. The example syntax checks this value to end the loop when the entire recordset has been traversed. Attempting to MoveNext after the EOF property is True results in an error. Repeated MoveLast methods do not cause an error; they simply leave the last record as the current record. Note that MoveLast places the current record at the last record in the recordset and leaves the EOF property False.

MoveFirst, MovePrevious, and the BOF property function in much the same way. Executing a MovePrevious method at the first record of the recordset changes the recordset's BOF property to True, and an additional attempt to MovePrevious at this point results in an error. Repeated calls to MoveFirst simply leave the first record as the current record.

The movement buttons on the data control never set BOF or EOF to True. For example, clicking on the MoveNext button when the current record is the last record in the recordset does nothing: the last record remains current, and the EOF property remains False.

Using any of the Move methods automatically updates any records currently being edited or added in the copy buffer.

Example

The Move methods are used several times in the Data Access project at the end of this chapter. First, the menuUtils Log routine use them to step through each entry of the log table from last entry to first entry. The FillGrid routine steps through the Icon table from first record to last. The cmndDelete_Click event moves to the previous record after an entry is deleted, and the cmndLoad_Click event uses MoveLast to move to the end of the recordset after each new addition.

NOMATCH PROPERTY

Objects Affected

Check	Clipboard	Combo	Command	CommonDlg
▶ Data	Debug	Dir	Drive	File
Form	Frame	Grid	Image	Label
Line	List	MDI Form	Menu	OLE
Option	Picture	Printer	Screen	Scroll
Shape	Text	Timer		

Purpose

The recordset's NoMatch property determines whether the Find methods succeeded. A False value means the Find method succeeded; a record was found that matched the criteria. A True value means the Find method failed; no record was found that matched the criteria. Not available at design time; read-only at runtime. Table 27-57 summarizes the arguments of the NoMatch property.

General Syntax

```
[form!]Name.Recordset.NoMatch
```

Argument	Description
form	Name property of the parent form
Name	Name property of the data control
Recordset	'Recordset' indicates the Recordset property of the data control

Table 27-57 Arguments of the NoMatch property

Example Syntax

```
criteria$ = "CityName = 'New York'"
Data1.Recordset.FindFirst criteria$
Do Until Data1.Recordset.NoMatch
    Data1.Recordset.Edit
    Data1.Recordset!Letter = "directmail 0694"
    Data1.Recordset.Update
    Data1.Recordset.FindNext criteria$
Loop
```

Description

Use the NoMatch property to determine the success or failure of a Find method. If the last Find method succeeded in finding a match, NoMatch will be False. If the Find method failed to find a match, NoMatch will be True.

The example syntax illustrates a typical use for NoMatch. The DO...LOOP steps through matching records in the recordset. Failure in the FindNext method terminates the loop.

Example

The Data Access project at the end of this chapter tests NoMatch after each Find method in the cmndFind_Click event. If there was no match, the routine disables the appropriate command buttons.

OPTIONS PROPERTY

Objects Affected

Check	Clipboard	Combo	Command	CommonDlg
▶ Data	Debug	Dir	Drive	File
Form	Frame	Grid	Image	Label
Line	List	MDI Form	Menu	OLE
Option	Picture	Printer	Screen	Scroll
Shape	Text	Timer		

Purpose

Use the Options property to read or set characteristics of the control's recordset. Read and write at both design time and runtime. Tables 27-58 and 27-59 summarize the arguments of the Options property.

General Syntax

```
[form!]Name.Options [ = expression%]
```

Argument	Description
form	Name property of the parent form
Name	Name property of the data control
expression%	Bitwise value indicating several settings

Table 27-58 Arguments of the Options property

Value	DATACONS.TXT	Meaning
1	DB_DENYWRITE	Other users cannot modify recordset
4	DB_READONLY	Cannot modify existing records or add new ones
8	DB_APPENDONLY	Can add new records but not modify existing records
16	DB_INCONSISTENTUPDATES	Does not maintain referential integrity
32	DB_CONSISTENTUPDATES	(Default) Automatically enforces referential integrity
64	DB_SQLPASSTHROUGH	Passes SQL statement to remote server

Table 27-59 Meanings of the value of the Options expression%

Example Syntax

```
Sub Form_Load ()
     Data1.Options = DB_READONLY
     Data1.Refresh
End Sub
```

Description

Use the data control's Options property to read or set important properties of the control's underlying recordset. The changes you make will not go into effect until you use the Refresh method on the data control. Note that each of these Options constants is defined in DATACONS.TXT. See the discussion in the summary section at the beginning of this chapter for details on how to use these constants.

These options are individual bits set within the number you read from or assign to the Options property. Use the Or operator to set several options at once; use the And operator to see if an option is set:

```
Data1.Options = DB_READONLY Or DB_SQLPASSTHROUGH
If (Data1.Options And DB_WRITEONLY) Then ....
```

You may want to use the DB_DENYWRITE option in a multiuser environment to lock the entire recordset to make sure another user doesn't modify the data you're accessing. Setting the DB_READONLY option opens the recordset as read-only; you may view existing records but not change existing ones or add new ones. DB_APPENDONLY lets you view existing records and add new ones, but not modify existing ones.

The Access engine can enforce referential integrity for you. That means that it can restrict itself to updating only the "many" side of a one-to-many relationship. As a practical example, consider two tables, the Client table and the Transactions table. The Client table has information on each client, such as name and address, and has ClientID as the primary key that other tables use to refer to that client. The Transactions table has information on each transaction, like what was purchased, the date purchased, and the client who purchased it. The client information in the Transactions table uses ClientID to refer back to the Client table; the Client table is the "one" side and the Transactions table is the "many" side of the one-to-many relationship. One client can have lots of transactions, but each transaction was made by only one particular client.

Setting DB_INCONSISTENTUPDATES lets you update either side of the relationship. You may inadvertently change the ClientIDs in the Client table, thus wreaking complete disaster on the referential integrity of your database. You might end up with Transactions (and potentially many other tables that are joined to the Client table) that point to nonexistent or incorrect clients after such an update. Although there are circumstances that warrant this power, in general this is a foolhardy approach.

The default DB_CONSISTENTUPDATES enforces referential integrity by letting you update only the "many" side of a one-to-many relationship. This means that no matter what the update does, it will not affect the "one" side, and will maintain referential integrity for all the other tables that are joined to the "one" table.

The DB_SQLPASSTHROUGH passes SQL statements and actions through to an external ODBC SQL database rather than having the Access engine perform the query. It is only applicable in the Professional Edition.

Example

The Data Access project at the end of this chapter uses the Options property to set the datasheet's Recordset to read only. It does this in the FillGrid subroutine.

READONLY PROPERTY

Objects Affected

Check	Clipboard	Combo	Command	CommonDlg
▶ Data	Debug	Dir	Drive	File
Form	Frame	Grid	Image	Label
Line	List	MDI Form	Menu	OLE
Option	Picture	Printer	Screen	Scroll
Shape	Text	Timer		

Purpose

The ReadOnly property determines whether the database is opened for read-only access. Note that this affects the database and all resultant recordsets; the Options property deals with individual recordsets. Tables 27-60 and 27-61 list the arguments of the ReadOnly property.

General Syntax

```
[form!]Name.ReadOnly [ = boolean%]
```

Argument	Description
form	Name property of the parent form
Name	Name property of the data control
boolean%	True or False

Table 27-60 Arguments of the ReadOnly property

Value	Meaning
True	The control's database is read-only; no changes are allowed
False	(Default) The control's database is read and write; changes are allowed

Table 27-61 Meanings of the value of boolean% in the ReadOnly property

Example Syntax

```
Sub Form_Load ()
    Data1.ReadOnly = True
    Data1.Refresh
End Sub
```

Description

Use the data control's ReadOnly property to set the read-only status of the database and all recordsets built from that database. The default value of False lets your application both read and write information. Setting the ReadOnly property to True limits your application to only viewing the records and prevents any data from being written.

This property only takes effect for the first instance of the database and is ignored for subsequent instances. Your application may have several data controls all accessing the same database, but with different recordsets. The first call to ReadOnly sets the property for the database as a whole and all associated recordsets. You must close all open instances of the database for a change to the property to take affect. Use the Refresh method to complete the change.

Note that the Options property lets you read and set the ReadOnly property of individual recordsets. You may have a database open with ReadOnly set to False (both reads and writes allowed) but limit write access to individual tables and recordsets within that database by using the Options property.

Example

The Data Access project at the end of this chapter tests the ReadOnly property in the PrintStats routine and then prints out the appropriate setting for the database.

RECORDCOUNT PROPERTY

Objects Affected

Check	Clipboard	Combo	Command	CommonDlg
▶ Data	Debug	Dir	Drive	File
Form	Frame	Grid	Image	Label
Line	List	MDI Form	Menu	OLE
Option	Picture	Printer	Screen	Scroll
Shape	Text	Timer		

Purpose

The RecordCount property returns the number of records in the recordset. Not available at design time, read-only at runtime. Table 27-62 summarizes the arguments of the RecordCount property.

General Syntax

```
[form!]Name.Recordset.RecordCount
```

Argument	Description
form	Name property of the parent form
Recordset	'Recordset' indicates the Recordset property of the data control
Name	Name property of the data control

Table 27-62 Arguments of the RecordCount property

Example Syntax

```
Sub Data1_Validate(Action As Integer, Save As Integer)
    lablStatus.Caption = Str$(Data1.Recordset.RecordCount) & " Total Records"
End Sub
```

Description

Use the recordset's RecordCount property to determine how many records the recordset contains. RecordCount will return 0 for an empty recordset. RecordCount will always return 1 for a nonempty recordset until a Move method is used on the recordset. Once the Move method completes, RecordCount will be accurate and will then return the total number of records. It will automatically track new additions and deletions in a single-user environment. The count may not be accurate in a multiuser environment. Figure 27-9 shows the example syntax, with the label displaying the total number of records in the recordset.

Although you may be tempted to use RecordCount as the target value in a FOR...NEXT loop to step through each record, a Do...Loop construction is generally faster as the database engine doesn't have to count the total number of records before the loop starts. The following two code fragments accomplish the same thing, but the DO...LOOP is preferred.

```
Data1.Recordset.MoveFirst                    'this works, but is a bit
For i = 1 To Data1.Recordset.RecordCount     'slower than the Do Loop
    Data1.Recordset.Edit
    Data1.Recordset!Random = Rnd
    Data1.Recordset.Update
    Data1.Recordset.MoveNext
Next i

Data1.Recordset.MoveFirst                    'This is preferred, as the
Do Until Data1.Recordset.EOF                 'database engine doesn't have
    Data1.Recordset.Edit                     'to go to the end of the
    Data1.Recordset!Random = Rnd             'recordset before starting
    Data1.Recordset.Update                   'the loop
    Data1.Recordset.MoveNext
Loop
```

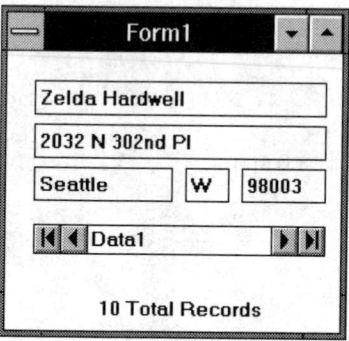

Figure 27-9 The RecordCount property returns the total number of records in a recordset

Example

The Data Access project at the end of this chapter uses the RecordCount property when it sets up the grid in the FillGrid procedure on formDatasheet. The grid needs to have enough rows to fit all the records in the recordset, so we use the RecordCount property to determine how big to make the grid.

RECORDSET PROPERTY

Objects Affected

Check	Clipboard	Combo	Command	CommonDlg
▶ Data	Debug	Dir	Drive	File
Form	Frame	Grid	Image	Label
Line	List	MDI Form	Menu	OLE
Option	Picture	Printer	Screen	Scroll
Shape	Text	Timer		

Purpose

The Recordset property lets you access the data control's underlying recordset. Most methods and properties applicable to Dynasets may then be used with the Recordset. Table 27-63 lists the arguments of the Recordset property, and Table 27-64 lists the properties and methods of the Recordset property.

General Syntax

```
[form!]Name.Recordset.Method [methodArgs]
[form!]Name.Recordset.Property [ = propertyValue]
```

Argument	Description
form	Name property of the parent form
Name	Name property of the data control
Recordset	'Recordset' indicates the Recordset property of the data control
Method	An appropriate method for the underlying Recordset object
methodArgs	Arguments for the method
Property	An appropriate property for the underlying Recordset object
propertyValue	Value for the property

Table 27-63 Arguments of the Recordset property

Use This...		To Do This...
AddNew	Method	Append a new record to the end of the recordset
AppendChunk	Method	Append a string to a memo field
BOF	Property	Indica whether current record is at Beginning of File
Bookmark	Property	Sets or returns the pointer to individual records
Bookmarkable	Property	Indicates whether a recordset supports bookmarks
Close	Method	Close a recordset
Delete	Method	Delete the current record
Edit	Method	Open the current record for editing

(continued on next page)

(continued from previous page)

Use This...		To Do This...
EOF	Property	Indicate whether current record is at End of File
Fields	Collection	Provide access to settings of individual fields
FieldSize	Method	Return the size of a memo field
FindFirst	Method	Find the first occurrence of a searchstring
FindLast	Method	Find the last occurrence of a searchstring
FindNext	Method	Find the next occurrence of a searchstring
FindPrevious	Method	Find the previous occurrence of a searchstring
GetChunk	Method	Get a string from a memo field
LockEdits	Property	Determine whether record is locked during editing
MoveFirst	Method	Move to the first record of the recordset
MoveLast	Method	Move to the last record of the recordset
MoveNext	Method	Move to the next record of the recordset
MovePrevious	Method	Move to the previous record of the recordset
NoMatch	Property	Determine whether the Find or Seek methods succeeded
Update	Method	Update changed records and saves to the database

Table 27-64 Common Recordset methods and properties

Example Syntax

```
Sub PostAccounts (debits() As Currency, credits() As Currency)
    Data1.Recordset.MoveFirst
    Do While Not Data1.Recordset.EOF
        Data1.Recordset.Edit
```

```
            recNo = Data1.Recordset!ClientID
            Data1.Recordset!Debit = debits(recNo)
            Data1.Recordset!Credit = credits(recNo)
            Data1.Recordset.Update
            Data1.Recordset.MoveNext
      Loop
End Sub
```

Description

The Recordset property lets you access the underlying recordset (technically a Dynaset) for the data control. You may then use most of the collections, methods, and properties of a Dynaset to operate on your recordset.

The default property for Recordset is the Fields collection. Combining this with the fact that the default property for the Fields collection is the Value property lets you considerably shorten code that changes an item's value. The following statements have identical results:

```
Data1.Recordset.Fields("CityName").Value = "Dallas"   'long reference
Data1.Recordset!CityName = "Dallas"                    'uses default properties
```

See the individual entries for the collections, methods, and properties for details about them and more examples of using the Recordset property.

Example

The Data Access project at the end of this chapter uses the Recordset property throughout to access the underlying recordset. Each of the cmndClear_Click, cmndDelete_Click, cmndFind_Click, cmndGoto_Click, cmndLoad_Click, cmndSave_Click, cmndSeek_Click, dataMain_Validate, Form_Resize, menuUtils_Click, and FillGrid procedures use the Recordset property.

RECORDSOURCE PROPERTY

Objects Affected

Check	Clipboard	Combo	Command	CommonDlg
▶ Data	Debug	Dir	Drive	File
Form	Frame	Grid	Image	Label
Line	List	MDI Form	Menu	OLE
Option	Picture	Printer	Screen	Scroll
Shape	Text	Timer		

Purpose

The RecordSource property determines the source of records for the data control's recordset. It may be either a table, an SQL SELECT statement, or a predefined SQL query. Table 27-65 summarizes the arguments of the RecordSource property.

General Syntax

```
[form!]Name.RecordSource = tableName$
[form!]Name.RecordSource = queryName$
[form!]Name.RecordSource = sqlSelect$
```

Argument	Description
form	Name property of the parent form
Name	Name property of the data control
tableName$	Name of a valid table within the database
queryName$	Name of a predefined query
sqlSelect$	Valid SQL SELECT statement

Table 27-65 Arguments of the RecordSource property

Example Syntax

```
Sub Form_Load ()
    Data1.RecordSource = "ClientsTable"
    Form2.Data3.RecordSource = "Valid Zip Codes Query"
    c$ = "SELECT ClientName, ClientAddress, ClientZip FROM ClientsTable"
    c$ = c$ & " WHERE ClientZip < 6000 ORDER BY ClientZip"
    Data9.RecordSource = c$
    Data1.Refresh
    Form2.Data3.Refresh
    Data9.Refresh
End Sub
```

Description

Use the RecordSource property to determine what records make up the recordset for a data control. You may use a table name, predefined query, or a valid SQL Select statement as your source.

The simplest and most common source is a table name. You can set the RecordSource in code, as in the example above, or by choosing one of the listed tables in the RecordSource entry in the Properties box at design time. The returned recordset will consist of all records in the table sorted by the table's primary key.

You may also use a predefined query. These may be defined in the Professional Version of Visual Basic or in another database like Microsoft Access. The predefined queries are stored in the database just like the other database objects such as tables and indexes. These predefined queries are simply SQL Select statements.

Finally, you may directly use an SQL Select statement to choose the records. Doing this gives you the most control and power and is highly recommended. SQL is an extremely powerful database "metalanguage" that is at least nominally compatible among different vendors. It lets you pose questions, or *queries*, to the database engine; the engine then performs the actions requested or returns a set of records that match the query. The Execute method lets you perform SQL action queries that update or delete records; setting the RecordSource property with an SQL statement lets you perform an SQL Select query. For more information on SQL, refer to the BIBLIO.MDB datafile that comes with Visual Basic.

SQL Statements

Although SQL can be very complex to master, it's not difficult to use it for many ordinary tasks. An SQL Select statement begins with the SELECT keyword. You then follow this with the names of the fields you'd like returned, in the order you want them returned in. Use the keyword FROM to name the table the fields reside in. For instance, the following example selects the ClientID, ClientName, and ClientAddress fields from the Clients table:

```
Data1.RecordSource = "SELECT ClientID, ClientName, ClientAddress FROM Clients"
```

Use the asterisk (*) to indicate "all available fields in the default order." The following statement retrieves all the fields from the Clients table:

```
Data1.RecordSource = "SELECT * FROM Clients"
```

This gives the same result as simply setting the RecordSource to the Clients table.

Use the WHERE keyword to filter the returned records. The WHERE clause looks much like the conditional part of an IF...THEN statement. Place the field you're comparing to the left of the operator, and the value you're comparing it to on the right side of the operator:

```
Data1.RecordSource = "SELECT * FROM Clients WHERE ClientState = 'WA'"
Data1.RecordSource = "SELECT * FROM Clients WHERE LastName LIKE '*smith*'"
```

Use the ORDER BY keyword to sort the returned records:

```
Data1.RecordSource = "SELECT * FROM Clients ORDER BY ZipCode"
```

You can also create calculated fields with the AS keyword. For example, you have two fields called Quantity and Price in the Transactions table. You just want to return the total amount. A normal Basic statement would look something like Total = Quantity * Price. The SQL statement would read:

```
Data1.RecordSource = "SELECT Quantity * Price AS Total FROM Transactions"
```

This calculated field is called an *alias*. You can bind a control to an alias field just as you would a normal field. You obviously can't update an alias field, so it's best to bind it to a label control that the user can't change.

You might also want to join two tables together. For instance, you might have a Client table, with information on the clients, and a Transactions table that contains information on each transaction a client makes. The two tables are related by the ClientID field in a one-to-many relationship. (Refer to the discussion in the Execute method about this same example.) You might wish to display the client name along with the transaction data. The Transactions table alone won't work; it only contains the transaction data and the ClientID. You'll need to get some fields from the Client table to complete the recordset:

```
c$ = "SELECT * FROM Clients, Transactions "
c$ = c$ & "WHERE Clients.ClientID = Transactions.ClientID"
Data1.RecordSource = c$
```

Finally, consider using SQL statements for creating "pick lists" for your combo and list boxes. Say you wanted to give the user the ability to select a particular client from a list box. You certainly don't expect the user to know what the ClientID is, so you'd like to present the client's first and last names. You'll need to store the ClientID too, as that is the key to accessing the client. The following example should point you in the right direction:

```
Sub PickClientForm_Load ()
    'Get the names of our top clients, sorted by their last name
    c$ = "SELECT FirstName, LastName, ClientID FROM Clients "
    c$ = c$ & "WHERE Code = 'A1' ORDER BY LastName"
    Data1.RecordSource = c$
    Data1.Refresh
    Do While Not Data1.Recordset.EOF          'build the list box with clients
        f$ = Data1.Recordset!FirstName        'list box displays:
        l$ = Data1.Recordset!LastName         'first last
        i = Val(Data1.Recordset!ClientID)     'client ID is an integer
        List1.AddItem f$ & " " & l$           'list not sorted
        List1.ItemData(List1.NewIndex) = i    'store the associated clientID
        Data1.Recordset.MoveNext              'go to next record
    Loop
End Sub

Sub List1_DblClick ()
    i$ = Str$(List1.ItemData(List1.ListIndex)'extract the clientID
```

```
        c$ = "ClientID = '" & i$ & "'"          'build the criteria
        Data1.Recordset.FindFirst c$            'and find the client
End Sub
```

This example builds a list box of all the best clients (WHERE Code = "A1") sorted by the client's last name (ORDER BY LastName). The FirstName and LastName are then added to a list box. If the list box's Sort property is False, the clients will display in order of their last name. This is the same order the record-set is in, which is the order each client is added to the list box. The ClientID gets put in the list box's ItemData property to let us associate the ListItem with the appropriate ClientID. (See Chapter 18, Lists, Combos, and Grids, for more about ItemData.) Figure 27-10 shows what this might look like.

Double-clicking on an entry in the list extracts the ClientID. It then builds the proper criteria string for the subsequent Find method.

Don't be misled by the lack of SQL examples in Visual Basic's written documentation. SQL is the key to writing powerful Visual Basic database programs. You will reap the rewards of your knowledge if you refer to some of the SQL books mentioned in the BIBLIO.MDB database that comes with Visual Basic.

Example

The Data Access project at the end of this chapter sets the RecordSource property with an SQL statement in the Form_Load event and the FillGrid procedures.

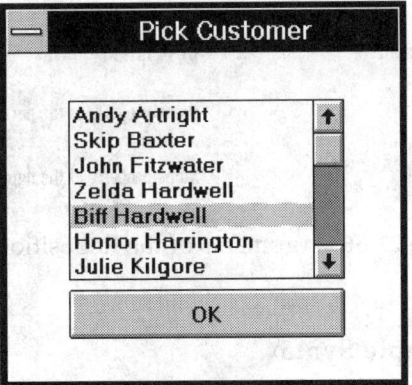

Figure 27-10 A basic knowledge of SQL lets you build pick lists like this from your data

REPOSITION EVENT

Objects Affected

Check	Clipboard	Combo	Command	CommonDlg
▶ Data	Debug	Dir	Drive	File
Form	Frame	Grid	Image	Label
Line	List	MDI Form	Menu	OLE
Option	Picture	Printer	Screen	Scroll
Shape	Text	Timer		

Purpose

The Reposition event lets you react to when a new record becomes current. The Reposition event occurs after a record becomes current; the Validate event occurs before a record becomes current. Use Reposition to update controls on the form based on the values of data fields. Table 27-66 summarizes the arguments of the Reposition event.

General Syntax

```
Sub Name_Reposition ()
```

Argument	Description
form	Name property of the parent form
Name	Name property of the data control

Table 27-66 Arguments of the Reposition event

Example Syntax

```
Sub Data1_Reposition ()
    lablTotal.Caption = Format$(Val(textQ.Text) * Val(textP.Text), "$###0.00")
End Sub
```

Description

A new record becomes current after the user presses the data control's movement buttons, or your code executes a Move or Find method. The Reposition event lets you react to a new record becoming current. The Reposition event occurs after the new record becomes current; use the Validate event to react before the current record is repositioned.

The example syntax shows how a control might be updated based on changes to data. The lablTotal displays a transaction total derived from the bound controls textQ (Quantity) and textP (Price). The total displayed in the lablTotal label gets updated every time a new record becomes current.

Example

The Data Access project at the end of this chapter uses dataMain's Reposition event to disable the cmndSave command button. The assumption is that once we've moved the record there are no changes to be saved, so the command button should be disabled until the user makes an entry in the text boxes.

ROLLBACK STATEMENT

Purpose

Use the RollBack statement to cancel the pending updates in a transaction block. The database is returned to the state it was in when first entering the block.

General Syntax

```
Rollback
```

Example Syntax

```
Sub PostAccounts (debits() As Currency, credits() As Currency)
    BeginTrans
    Data1.Recordset.MoveFirst
    Do While Not Data1.Recordset.EOF
        Data1.Recordset.Edit
        recNo = Data1.Recordset!ClientID
        Data1.Recordset!Debit = debits(recNo)
        Data1.Recordset!Credit = credits(recNo)
        Data1.Recordset.Update
        numRecs = numRecs + 1
        Data1.Recordset.MoveNext
    Loop
    msg$ = Str$(numRecs) & " Records updated." & Chr$(10) & Chr$(13)
    msg$ = msg$ & "Commit posting, or Cancel changes?"
    ans = MsgBox(msg$, 1 + 32, "Confirm Transaction")
    If ans = 2 Then 'Cancel
        RollBack
    Else
```

(continued on next page)

(continued from previous page)

```
        CommitTrans
    End If
End Sub
```

Description

Transactions are changes to the database that must be made as a whole. Incomplete changes (due to a power outage or unforeseen error) can be avoided by using transactions. For example, most financial operations involve a debit from one account and a corresponding credit to another account. If the transaction failed before completing, one account may have a debit without any corresponding credit.

Use BeginTrans to begin a *transaction block*, or block of statements you would like to group together. All changes to all databases (not just the one you're working on) are done in a manner that lets you either *commit* them as a block, or *roll back* and undo all changes since the BeginTrans statement. Ending a transaction block with RollBack cancels all changes to the database and restores the database to the condition it was in when first entering the transaction block.

If a database closes before the transaction block ends, no changes are made and an implicit RollBack occurs. In the sample syntax above, a series of debits and credits are posted to the database. Should something unforeseen happen (like someone rebooting the computer), nothing is posted and the database is restored to its state before the BeginTrans statement. Once the loop finishes, the MsgBox function displays the total number of records updated and asks for confirmation before writing the transactions to disk. If the user presses Cancel, the RollBack statement cancels all the updates. Figure 27-11 shows what this might look like.

Example

The Data Access project at the end of this chapter lets the user cancel any mass additions made with the Seek command. The cmndSeek_Click event displays a message box indicating how many records were added and lets the user confirm or cancel the additions.

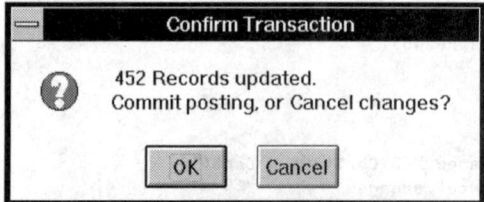

Figure 27-11 The RollBack statement lets you cancel a complete set of changes in a transaction block

TABLEDEFS COLLECTION

Objects Affected

Check	Clipboard	Combo	Command	CommonDlg
▶ Data	Debug	Dir	Drive	File
Form	Frame	Grid	Image	Label
Line	List	MDI Form	Menu	OLE
Option	Picture	Printer	Screen	Scroll
Shape	Text	Timer		

Purpose

The TableDefs collection lets you access the details of the available tables within a database. Tables 27-67 and 27-68 summarize the arguments and property of the TableDefs collection, while Table 27-69 summarizes the properties and collections of the members of the TableDefs collection.

General Syntax

`[form!]Name.Database.TableDefs(Index%|tableName$).Property|Collection`

Argument	Description
form	Name property of the parent form
Name	Name property of the data control
Recordset	'Recordset' indicates the Recordset property of the data control
Database	'Database' indicates the Database property of the data control
TableDefs	'TableDefs' indicates the TableDefs collection of the database
Index%	The ordinal index position of the member of the collection
tableName$	Name of the table
fieldName	Name of the field

Table 27-67 Arguments of the TableDefs collection

1165

Property	Meaning
Count	Number of members in the TableDefs collection (tables in this database)

Table 27-68 Property of the TableDefs collection

Property or Collection		Meaning
Attributes	Property	Reads how Visual Basic treats individual fields
Connect	Property	Read or set parameters for external databases
DateCreated	Property	Contains the date the table was created
Fields	Collection	Collection of all fields within table
Indexes	Collection	Collection of all indexes within table
LastUpdated	Property	Contains the date the table's structure was last modified
Name	Property	Name of the table
Updatable	Property	Reads whether table is updatable
SourceTableName	Property	Reads name of source table in an attached database

Table 27-69 Properties and collections of members of the TableDefs collection

Example Syntax

```
Sub Command1_Click ()
    For i = 0 To Data1.Database.TableDefs.Count - 1
        Print Data1.Database.TableDefs(i).Name,
        Print Data1.Database.TableDefs(i).DateCreated,
        Print Data1.Database.TableDefs(i).Connect
        For j = 0 To Data1.Database.TableDefs(i).Fields.Count - 1
            Print Data1.Database.TableDefs(i).Fields(j).Name,
        Next j
        Print
    Next i
End Sub
```

Description

The TableDefs collection gives you access to individual tables within each database. Each database's TableDefs collection has a single property, Count, that gives the number of members in the collection. The TableDefs collection (like all collections) is zero-based, so the lower bound of the collection is 0 and the upper bound is Count - 1. The Count property represents the number of tables in the database. Each member of the collection (that is, each table in the database) has a variety of properties and two additional collections.

The example syntax steps through each member of the TableDefs collection and prints out some statistics on each table and then lists each field name within the table.

Properties

The Attributes property of each member in the TableDefs collection indicates the characteristics of each table. These characteristics mostly deal with aspects of attached tables. The Attributes entry gives more details about this property.

The DateCreated and LastUpdated properties track the date the table was created and the date the table's structure was last modified. Note that simply updating data within the table does not actually change the table's structure. Visual Basic Standard Edition has no provisions for changing table structure other than through the Datamanager program that comes with Visual Basic. The Professional Edition and other databases, like Microsoft Access, can easily change table structures.

The Name property gives the name of the table, which is set when the table is first designed. The Updatable property returns whether the table's data may be edited, and the SourceTableName gives the name of the table in the original database for attached tables.

Collections

Each member of the TableDefs collection has two collections: the Fields collection and the Indexes collection. The Fields collection lets you access each field within the table, and the Indexes collection lets you access each index within the table. Various properties are available for each member of these collections. See their individual entries for more details.

Each database also has tables reserved by the system for its own use, and these system tables are normally hidden. You can access them through the TableDefs collection, although you can't do much with them.

Example

The PrintStats procedure in the Data Access project at the end of this chapter prints out a wealth of statistics using the TableDefs collection.

TRANSACTIONS PROPERTY

Objects Affected

Check	Clipboard	Combo	Command	CommonDlg
▶ Data	Debug	Dir	Drive	File
Form	Frame	Grid	Image	Label
Line	List	MDI Form	Menu	OLE
Option	Picture	Printer	Screen	Scroll
Shape	Text	Timer		

Purpose

The Transactions property returns whether a database supports transactions. *Transactions* are changes to the database that must be made as a whole. Table 27-70 summarizes the arguments of the Transactions property.

General Syntax

```
[form!]Name.Recordset.Transactions
```

Argument	Description
form	Name property of the parent form
Name	Name property of the data control

Table 27-70 Arguments of the Transactions property

Example Syntax

```
Sub PostAccounts ()
    If Data1.Recordset.Transactions = True Then BeginTrans
    Data1.Database.Execute "queryDefPostDebits"
    Data1.Database.Execute "queryDefPostCredits"
    If Data1.Recordset.Transactions = True Then CommitTrans
End Sub
```

Description

Transactions are changes to the database that must be made as a whole. Incomplete changes (due to a power outage or unforeseen error) can be avoided by using

1168

transactions. For example, most financial operations involve a debit from one account and a corresponding credit to another account. If the transaction failed before completing, one account may have a debit without any corresponding credit.

The recordset's Transactions property returns True when the recordset supports transactions. All native Access databases do, while many external ones (such as Paradox databases) do not.

Use BeginTrans to begin a *transaction block*, or block of statements you would like to group together. All changes to all databases (not just the one you're working on) are done in a manner that lets you either *commit* them as a block, or *roll* back and undo all changes since the BeginTrans statement.

See the individual entries for BeginTrans, CommitTrans, and RollBack for more details.

Example

The cmndSeek_Click event places the procedures that add multiple entries to the database in a transaction block. It tests to see if the database supports transactions when it finishes. If it does support transactions, it queries the user whether to save the additions. If it does not support transactions (which would only be the case if you translated the CHP27.MDB database into another format, like Paradox), then it simply informs the user of the additions without giving the opportunity to cancel them.

UPDATABLE PROPERTY

Objects Affected

Check	Clipboard	Combo	Command	CommonDlg
▶ Data	Debug	Dir	Drive	File
Form	Frame	Grid	Image	Label
Line	List	MDI Form	Menu	OLE
Option	Picture	Printer	Screen	Scroll
Shape	Text	Timer		

Purpose

The Updatable property returns whether or not all fields in a recordset may be updated. Tables 27-71 and 27-72 summarize the arguments of the Updatable property.

General Syntax

```
[form!]Name.Recordset.Updatable
[form!]Name.Database.TableDefs(Index%|Table$).Updatable
```

Argument	Description
form	Name property of the form
Name	Name property of the data control
Recordset	'Recordset' indicates the Recordset property of the data control
Database	'Database' indicates the Database property of the data control
TableDefs	'TableDefs' indicates the TableDefs collection of the database
Index%	The ordinal index position of the member of the collection
Table$	Name of the table

Table 27-71 Arguments of the Updatable property

Return Value	Meaning
True	All fields in the recordset may be updated
False	At least one field in the recordset is not updatable

Table 27-72 Meanings of the returned values of the Updatable property

Example Syntax

```
Sub PrintStats(table$)
    If Data1.Database.TableDefs(table$).Updatable Then
        Print "All fields are updatable"
    Else
        numFields = Data1.Database.TableDefs(table$).Fields.Count
        For i = 0 to numFields - 1
            at = Data1.Database.TableDefs(table$).Fields(i).Attributes
            If at And DB_UPDATABLEFIELD Then
                ud$ = "Updatable"
```

```
            Else
                    ud$ = "Not Updatable"
            End If
            nm$ = Data1.Database.TableDefs(table$).Fields(i).Name
            Print nm$, ud$
        Next i
    End If
End Sub
```

Description

Use the Updatable property to find out if all fields in a recordset are updatable. If there are any fields that may not be edited, the Updatable property returns False. Fields may be uneditable for a number of reasons. For example, counter fields that automatically increment with each new record added to the database are not updatable. Calculated fields created by an SQL alias are also not updatable.

Note that some fields in a recordset may be updatable even if the recordset's Updatable property is False. The example syntax shows a routine that displays the updatable status for the recordset as a whole (if True), or for each individual field in the table (if Updatable is False). See the Attributes property entry for more information about the Attributes property.

Example

The PrintStats procedure in the Data Access project at the end of this chapter checks the Updatable property to report on whether the recordset contains all updatable fields or not.

UPDATE METHOD

Objects Affected

Check	Clipboard	Combo	Command	CommonDlg
▶ Data	Debug	Dir	Drive	File
Form	Frame	Grid	Image	Label
Line	List	MDI Form	Menu	OLE
Option	Picture	Printer	Screen	Scroll
Shape	Text	Timer		

Purpose

Use the Update method to save changed records to the database. Table 27-73 summarizes the arguments of the Update method.

1171

General Syntax

```
[form!]Name.Recordset.Update
```

Argument	Description
form	Name property of the form
Name	Name property of the data control
Recordset	'Recordset' indicates the Recordset property of the data control

Table 27-73 Arguments of the Update method

Example Syntax

```
Sub Command1_Click ()
    Data1.Recordset.MoveFirst
    Do Until Data1.Recordset.EOF
        Data1.Recordset.Edit
        Data1.Recordset!RandomNum = Rnd
        Data1.Recordset.Update
    Loop
End Sub
```

Description

Use the Update method to save changes made to new records being added or existing records being edited. The Update method writes the record in the copy buffer to disk (unless stopped by the Validate event). The *copy buffer* is a memory location reserved by Visual Basic that functions like a temporary "virtual" record. A new record created with the AddNew method is created in the copy buffer, and a record being edited using the Edit method is first copied to the copy buffer before being modified.

The Update method is automatically invoked if an Edit or AddNew method remains pending and the current record changes. For example, using any of the Move methods (or having the user click on one of the data control's movement buttons) will automatically save the record before moving.

Example

The Data Access project at the end of this chapter uses the Update method in the cmndLoad_Click event to update the new Log addition as well as save the new Icon record.

UPDATECONTROLS METHOD

Objects Affected

Check	Clipboard	Combo	Command	CommonDlg
▶ Data	Debug	Dir	Drive	File
Form	Frame	Grid	Image	Label
Line	List	MDI Form	Menu	OLE
Option	Picture	Printer	Screen	Scroll
Shape	Text	Timer		

Purpose

Use the UpdateControls method to make bound controls display the data in the underlying record. This resets any changed data in the controls back to the original values. Table 27-74 summarizes the arguments of the UpdateControls method.

General Syntax

```
[form!]Name.UpdateControls
```

Argument	Description
form	Name property of the form
Name	Name property of the data control

Table 27-74 Arguments of the UpdateControls method

Example Syntax

```
Sub cmndUndo_Click ()
    Data1.UpdateControls
End Sub
```

Description

Use the UpdateControls method to restore bound controls' values to that of the underlying record. This resets them to the state they were in before any changes took place.

The example syntax shows how simple it is to create an "Undo" function for bound controls. This one line restores the original values to all controls bound to the Data1 data control.

Example

The UpdateControls method restores the text box's contents if the user types an invalid file name. This occurs in the error trap section of the dataMain_Validate event.

UPDATERECORD METHOD

Objects Affected

Check	Clipboard	Combo	Command	CommonDlg
▶ Data	Debug	Dir	Drive	File
Form	Frame	Grid	Image	Label
Line	List	MDI Form	Menu	OLE
Option	Picture	Printer	Screen	Scroll
Shape	Text	Timer		

Purpose

Use the UpdateRecord method to save the contents of bound controls without triggering a Validate event. Table 27-75 summarizes the arguments of the UpdateRecord method.

General Syntax

`[form!]Name.UpdateRecord`

Argument	Description
form	Name property of the form
Name	Name property of the data control

Table 27-75 Arguments of the UpdateRecord method

Example Syntax

```
Sub Data1_Validate(Action As Integer, Save As Integer)
    Text1.Text = Format$(Val(Text1.Text), "$###,##0.00", "($###,##0.00")
    Data1.UpdateRecord
End Sub
```

Description

Use the UpdateRecord method to save the contents of bound controls to the database without triggering a Validate event. You would typically use this method in a Validate procedure. You cannot use a regular Update method in a Validate event procedure because the Update would trigger another Validate event, leading to a series of "cascading events" that only ends when Visual Basic runs out of stack space and hangs. Use the UpdateRecord method instead, as it does not trigger the Validate event.

The example syntax shows how the Validate event procedure reformats the contents of one of the bound controls before saving the record with the UpdateRecord method.

Example

The Data Access project's dataMain_Validate event saves the changes to disk if the user types valid file names into the text boxes.

VALIDATE EVENT

Objects Affected

Check	Clipboard	Combo	Command	CommonDlg
▶ Data	Debug	Dir	Drive	File
Form	Frame	Grid	Image	Label
Line	List	MDI Form	Menu	OLE
Option	Picture	Printer	Screen	Scroll
Shape	Text	Timer		

Purpose

Use the Validate event to initiate an action before a different record becomes current. This event typically evaluates data values to make sure they're in the correct format and are in an acceptable range of responses. The Validate event can stop the changes to the database and the movement from the current record if any values are not acceptable. Tables 27-76, 27-77, and 27-78 summarize the arguments of the Validate event.

General Syntax

```
Sub Name_Validate([Index As Integer, ] Action As Integer, Save As Integer)
```

Argument	Description
Name	Name property of the data control
Index	Index property of a data control in a control array
Action	Indicates the action that triggered the event; change action to something else
Save	Indicates whether data has changed; set the kind of response

Table 27-76 Arguments of the Validate event

Action	DATACONS.TXT	Meaning
0	DATA_ACTIONCANCEL	Cancel the operation that triggered the event
1	DATA_ACTIONMOVEFIRST	MoveFirst method
2	DATA_ACTIONMOVEPREVIOUS	MovePrevious method
3	DATA_ACTIONMOVENEXT	MoveNext method
4	DATA_ACTIONMOVELAST	MoveLast method
5	DATA_ACTIONADDNEW	AddNew method
6	DATA_ACTIONUPDATE	Update operation (not UpdateRecord)
7	DATA_ACTIONDELETE	Delete method
8	DATA_ACTIONFIND	Find method
9	DATA_ACTIONBOOKMARK	The Bookmark property has been set

Action	DATACONS.TXT	Meaning
10	DATA_ACTIONCLOSE	The Close method
11	DATA_ACTIONUNLOAD	The form is being unloaded

Table 27-77 Meanings of the Action argument in the Validate event

Save	Meaning
When entering the event:	
True	Data in at least one bound control has changed
False	No data in any bound control has changed
When exiting the event, set Save to do this:	
True	Save the data in the copy buffer to the database
False	Discard changes; do not save to the database

Table 27-78 Meanings of the Save argument in the Validate event

Example Syntax

```
Sub Data1_Validate (Action As Integer, Save As Integer)
    If textClientID.DataChanged = True Then      'don't change client id!
        If Action <> DATA_ACTIONADDNEW Then      'unless this is a new record
            textClientID.DataChanged = False     'discard changes to id
        End If
    End If
    If Val(textNextContact.Text) > 60 Then       'more than 2 months til next call
        MsgBox "You must specify a recontact at least every two months!"
        Action = DATA_ACTIONCANCEL               'cancel move; stay on this record
        Save = False                             'don't save anything yet
        textNextContact.SetFocus                 'and go to recontact field
    End If
End Sub
```

Description

Use the Validate event to verify that the changes the user made to the data are acceptable. You may have fields that require certain limited input or need to fall in a specific range; you may have fields that can change only some of the time. The Validate event lets you test these conditions and react to them.

The Action argument indicates what action caused the Validate event. You may wish to take different actions depending on what triggered it. For example, you may wish to turn off validation routines if the Delete action triggered it and might want to follow up the deletion by deleting all the records on the "many" side of a one-to-many relationship.

You can set the Action argument to determine what happens after the event procedure finishes. If you don't set it, it will finish doing whatever action triggered the event in the first place. If the initial cause of the event was one of the Move methods or an AddNew method, you can change the Action argument to one of the other Move methods or the AddNew method. You can always change an action to 0, DATA_ACTIONCANCEL. This leaves the current record where it is.

The Save argument initially indicates whether any bound controls have been changed. Visual Basic scans each bound control's DataChanged property and sets Save to True if any of them have been changed. You can then set Save at the end of the event procedure to tell Visual Basic if you want to save the changes.

The example syntax checks two items for validity. It first checks to see if the client ID field has been changed. If it has, it disables the change by setting the control's DataChanged property to False unless this is a new record. It next checks to see if a recontact appointment has been set within 60 days of the current date. If it hasn't, it cancels the action (which otherwise would probably have moved off the current record), cancels the save, and then sets the focus back to the field that needs to be changed.

Example

The dataMain_Validate event in the Data Access project at the end of this chapter lets the user rename the physical disk files by typing new file names into the text boxes. If the file names are valid, the physical files get renamed; if invalid, the text boxes are set back to their original values and no changes are made.

THE DATA ACCESS PROJECT

Project Overview

The Data Access project illustrates each of the many properties, methods, events, and statements that deal with database use. The project constructs a database of icons available on the system. It lets you search for individual icons by a fragment of a name or path, as well as by seeing a complete list of the icons, including a picture. It also gives a number of statistics on the inner structure of the database. You will have a strong grasp of the principles of Data Access when you've completed this project.

Assembling the Project: formMain

1. Make a new form (formMain) with the objects and properties in Table 27-79.

Object	Property	Setting
Form	BorderStyle	1 – Fixed Single
	Caption	"Data Access Project"
	Name	formMain
Command	Caption	&Clear
	Name	cmndClear
Command	Caption	&Save
	Name	cmndSave
Command	Caption	&Delete
	Name	cmndDelete
Command	Caption	See&k
	Name	cmndSeek
Command	Caption	&Load
	Name	cmndLoad
Data	DatabaseName	"C:\WAITE\CHP27.MDB"
	RecordSource	"Log"
Data	DatabaseName	"C:\WAITE\CHP27.MDB"

(continued on next page)

(continued from previous page)

Object	Property	Setting
	RecordSource	"Icon"
Dir	Name	dirListBox
Drive	Name	drivListBox
File	MultiSelect	2–Extended
	Name	fileListBox
	Pattern	"*.ICO"
Image	DataField	"Icon"
	DataSource	dataMain
Line	BorderWidth	3
Text	DataField	"FileName"
	DataSource	dataMain
Text	DataField	"PathName"
	DataSource	dataMain

Table 27-79 Elements of formMain

Name	Caption	Property	Setting
menuBar	&File	Index	0
menuFile	E&xit	Index	0
menuBar	&Utilities	Index	1
menuUtils	&Compact	Index	0
menuUtils	&Statistics	Index	1

Name	Caption	Property	Setting
menuUtils	&Log	Index	2
menuUtils	&Find	Index	3
menuUtils	&Datasheet	Index	4

Table 27-80 Elements of the menu structure for formMain

2. Create the menu structure given in Table 27-80 using the menu design window.

3. Size and position the controls, as shown in Figure 27-12.

4. Enter the following code in the General Declarations section. These are module-level variables that track how many records we've loaded in the current transaction block, and whether or not the code should look for all icon files in all subdirectories automatically.

```
Dim Scan As Integer            'tracks if we're recursing or not
Dim TotalLoaded As Integer     'tracks number of new entries
```

5. Enter the following code in the cmndClear_Click event. This clears the entire icon database when the user clicks on the button. Note how simple this is when we use the Execute method to perform an SQL update query. One line deletes every record in the database.

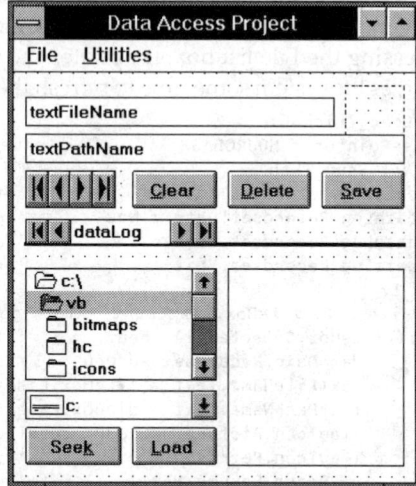

Figure 27-12 FormMain during the design process

1181

An empty recordset causes a "No Current Record" error that you can trap in the Data_Error event. See step 10 for details.

```
Sub cmndClear_Click ()
    MousePointer = HOURGLASS                        'we're going to be a while
    dataMain.Database.Execute "DELETE * FROM Icon"  'delete all records
    dataMain.Refresh                                'update the recordset
    MousePointer = DEFAULT                          'and we're done
End Sub
```

6. Enter the following code in the cmndDelete_Click event. This deletes the current record from the database. After you've deleted a record, no record is current. We use a MovePrevious method to make the record that was before the deleted one current. The line that deletes the actual icon file on the hard drive has been remarked out so you don't have to worry about wiping out your icon files!

```
Sub cmndDelete_Click ()
    Rem *** you could actually enable the delete with this line: ***
    Rem Kill textPathName.Text & "\" & textFileName.Text
    dataMain.Recordset.Delete          'get rid of entry
    dataMain.Recordset.MovePrevious    'and go to a record
End Sub
```

7. Enter the following code in the cmndLoad_Click event. Clicking on the Load command button triggers this. It loads each of the marked items in the File list box into the database. It first checks to see if we're recursing through all the subdirectories (as triggered by the Seek command button). If not, it then creates a new log entry and puts the date and time in it. It then steps through each file in the File list box, and if selected, adds it to the database. It does this by creating a new record, updating the bound controls, and then using the Update method to save the changes. Once the record has been created, it adds another entry into the log's memo field using the AppendChunk method. Once the routine has finished processing the File list box, it updates the log file (if we're not recursing) and then gives the system some time to refresh the recordsets with the FreeLocks statement.

```
Sub cmndLoad_Click ()
    MousePointer = HOURGLASS                      'we're going to be a while
    If Not Scan Then                              'if we're not recursing
        dataLog.Recordset.AddNew                  'start a new log record
        dataLog.Recordset!Date = Now              'and put date and time in it
        dataLog.Recordset.Update                  'save new record
        dataLog.Recordset.Edit                    'prepare current log record for memo
    End If
    For i = 0 To fileBox.ListCount - 1            'go through entire list box
        If fileBox.Selected(i) Then               'if file was selected
            dataMain.Recordset.AddNew             'create a new record for it
            textFileName.Text = fileBox.List(i)      'get file name
            textPathName.Text = dirBox.Path          'get path name
            imagIcon.Picture = LoadPicture(textPathName & "\" & textFileName)
            imagIcon.Refresh                      'force image control to repaint
            On Error Resume Next                  'very first record update causes error
            dataMain.Recordset.Update             'save the new record
            dataMain.Recordset.MoveLast           'and move to it
```

```
        m$ = textPathName.Text & "\" & textFileName.Text & "  added.  "
        dataLog.Recordset.Fields("Memo").AppendChunk (m$) 'make a log entry
        DoEvents                        'give the system time to catch up
        On Error GoTo 0                 'disable trap
        TotalLoaded = TotalLoaded + 1   'remember how many we've loaded
    End If
   Next i                              'go to next file in list box
   If Not Scan Then                    'if we're not recursing
       dataMain.Refresh                'update the recordset
       dataLog.Recordset.Update        'save the log entry
   End If
   FreeLocks                           'let the system refresh databases
   MousePointer = DEFAULT              'we're done
End Sub
```

8. Enter the following code in the cmndSave_Click event. This saves any changes made in the text boxes.

```
Sub cmndSave_Click ()
    fn = textFileName.DataChanged      'file name same as record?
    pn = textPathName.DataChanged      'pathname same as record?
    If fn Or pn Then                   'if either has changed,
        dataMain.Recordset.Update      'Save the record
    Else
        cmndSave.Enabled = False
    End If
End Sub
```

9. Enter the following code in the cmndSeek_Click event. This sets up a process that will look for all icon files in all subdirectories including and below the current one. The module-level variable Scan tells the other routines that we're recursing through all the subdirectories. It places the entire recursion process in a transaction block. This not only lets us cancel the changes at the end, but also vastly speeds up the process. Compare the speed of the Seek procedure with that of the Load procedure. Load does not use a transaction block and is much slower. The actual recursion is done all in the dirBox_Change event. After the procedures have loaded all the icons into the database, the user is given a chance to cancel all the changes. Note how the end of the procedure first checks to see if the database supports transactions. If it doesn't, all transaction statements are ignored (so it doesn't matter that we've already passed through a BeginTrans statement), but we still bring a MsgBox showing the total number of records added.

```
Sub cmndSeek_Click ()
    'this routine recurses through all subdirectories below current one
    MousePointer = HOURGLASS            'we're going to be awhile
    Scan = True                         'tell other procedures to recurse
    TotalLoaded = 0                     'start fresh total
    BeginTrans                          'start a transaction block
    dataLog.Recordset.AddNew            'add a new log entry
    dataLog.Recordset!Date = Now        'and add in the current date and time
    dirBox_Change                       'start the recursion process
    dataLog.Recordset.Update            'all done! save the log entry
    msg$ = Str$(TotalLoaded) & " records loaded." & Chr$(10) & Chr$(13)
```

(continued on next page)

(continued from previous page)

```
        If dataMain.Recordset.Transactions Then 'recordset support transactions?
          msg$ = msg$ & "Write changes to disk?"  'ask user to confirm
          ans = MsgBox(msg$, MB_YESNO + MB_ICONQUESTION, "Confirm Entries")
          If ans = IDYES Then                   'yup, go ahead and add
                CommitTrans                     'save changes to disk
          Else                                  'nope, stop changes
                Rollback                        'cancel all changes
          End If
        Else                                    'transactions NOT supported
          MsgBox msg$, , "Seek completed"       'just inform user
        End If
        dataMain.Refresh                        'regenerate recordset
        dataLog.Refresh                         'regenerate recordset
        MousePointer = DEFAULT                  'we're done
        Scan = False                            'no more recursion
End Sub
```

10. Enter the following code in the dataMain_Error event. This responds to errors not directly caused by code. The "No Current Record" happens whenever the recordset is completely empty (as happens after the cmndClear_Click event). Any other errors are routed through to the Debug pane for subsequent analysis and debugging and are ignored.

```
Sub dataMain_Error (DataErr As Integer, Response As Integer)
    Select Case DataErr
        Case 3021                               'no current record
            Response = 0                        'just ignore it
        Case Else
            Debug.Print DataErr                 'hmm  unanticipated error!
            Response = 0                        'ignore it
    End Select
End Sub
```

11. Enter the following code in the dataMain_Reposition event. This triggers anytime a new record becomes current. If a new record is current, the text boxes will both display the record's underlying data, so the Save command button is disabled.

```
Sub dataMain_Reposition ()
        cmndSave.Enabled = False                'new record, no changes to save!
End Sub
```

12. Enter the following code in the dataMain_Validate event. This occurs immediately before an Update or a Move. This routine renames the physical disk files to match any changes the user has made in the text boxes. The first If statement makes sure that the text boxes have had their data changed (as indicated by the enabled cmndSave) and that this change didn't happen because we're adding a new record. If those conditions are met, it then attempts to rename the physical file. If successful, it updates the database with the UpdateRecord method. If it fails, the error trap beeps, undoes the changes, and returns the user to the text boxes.

```
Sub dataMain_Validate (Action As Integer, Save As Integer)
    If cmndSave.Enabled = True And dataMain.EditMode <> 2 Then   'changed record
```

```
        On Error GoTo badFileName              'set a trap for the renaming process
        fn = dataMain.Recordset!FileName       'get existing file name
        pn = dataMain.Recordset!PathName       'and existing pathname
        Name pn & "\" & fn As textPathName.Text & "\" & textFileName.Text
        dataMain.UpdateRecord                  'aha! success! update the database
      Else
        Select Case Action
                Case 7, 8, 9, 10, 11           'delete, find, bookmark, close, unload
                  Save = False                 'don't bother saving changes
                Case 5, 6                      'addnew, update
                  Save = True                  'yes, save changes
                Case Else
        End Select
      End If
      cmndSave.Enabled = False                 'no more changes to save!
Exit Sub

badFileName:                                   'rename failed
      Beep                                     'enhance the user's mood
      dataMain.UpdateControls                  'undo changes
      textFileName.SetFocus                    'and go back to text box
Exit Sub

End Sub
```

13. Enter the following code in the dirBox_Change event. It starts like almost every other Directory list box Change event by updating the File list box and changing directories. It then sees if it's supposed to recurse through all subdirectories. If so, it selects all icon files in the current directory and loads them. Then it builds a list of all subdirectories in the current directory. It then recursively calls itself for each subdirectory in the list. The dirList array that holds the subdirectories is local for each recursion, so each time it calls itself it starts fresh by loading all the icon files, building a new list of subdirectories, and recursing through them until it hits the bottom of the directory tree. Local variables, as illustrated here, are the key to recursion.

```
Sub dirBox_Change ()
      fileBox.Path = dirBox.Path               'reset file list box
      ChDir dirBox.Path                        'and go to the new directory

      If Scan Then                             'are we recursing?
        'This recursively searches all subdirectories on drive for any *.ico file
        seekPath$ = dirBox.Path                'directory the box is on
        If Right$(seekPath$, 1) <> "\" Then seekPath$ = seekPath$ + "\" 'root
        If Dir$(seekPath$ & "*.ico") <> "" Then        'if there are any icon files
            For i = 0 To fileBox.ListCount - 1         'go through each file
              fileBox.Selected(i) = True       'and select it
            Next i
            cmndLoad_Click                     'load the files into the database
        End If
        numDirs = dirBox.ListCount             'number of subdirectories
        ReDim dirList(numDirs) As String       'make space for each directory entry
        For i = 0 To numDirs - 1               'go through each subdirectory
            dirList(i) = dirBox.List(i)        'and add it to the list
```

(continued on next page)

(continued from previous page)

```
        Next i
        For j = 0 To numDirs - 1        'now for each subdirectory in list,
            DoEvents                    'give the system some time to breathe,
            dirBox.Path = dirList(j)    'recurse down the tree!
        Next j
    End If
End Sub
```

14. Enter the following code in the drivBox_Change event. This just sets a new path in the Directory list box whenever the user changes the drive.

```
Sub drivBox_Change ()
    dirBox.Path = CurDir$(drivBox.Drive) 'set new path
End Sub
```

15. Enter the following code in the Form_Load event. This sets the RecordSource to include all records from the Icon file.

```
Sub Form_Load ()
    dataMain.RecordSource = "SELECT * FROM Icon"        'get all records
End Sub
```

16. Enter the following code in the Form_Resize event. This triggers any time the form is resized. For this particular form, that means just after it finishes loading, as it is a fixed single border form. We set the LockEdits property here to optimistic locking, as that will speed up database operation. Note that we can't do this in the Form_Load routine; the data control hasn't built the recordset until the Form_Load event finishes.

```
Sub Form_Resize ()
    dataMain.Recordset.LockEdits = False 'optimistic locking
End Sub
```

17. Enter the following code in the menuFile_Click event. There is only one element on the File command: Exit. This event procedure ends the program.

```
Sub menuFile_Click (Index As Integer)
    End                                 'end program
End Sub
```

18. Enter the following code in the menuUtils_Click event. This triggers any time the user clicks on one of the Utility menu commands. The first command compacts the database. It closes all databases and then compacts the existing database into a temporary file. Once that succeeds, it deletes the old file and renames the new compacted one. The next command prints out some database statistics using the PrintStats routine. The third command (Case 2), Log, prints out a log of all additions that have been made to the database. It uses the GetChunk method to read in small portions of the Log's memo field and prints them on the Stats form. The Find command simply shows the Find dialog box, and the Datasheet command shows the Datasheet form.

```
Sub menuUtils_Click (Index As Integer)
    Select Case Index
```

1186

```
      Case 0 '********************************* Compact
          MousePointer = HOURGLASS        'we're going to be a while
          dataMain.Database.Close         'close all databases
          dataLog.Database.Close
          formDatasheet!dataGrid.Database.Close
          CompactDatabase App.Path & "\icon.mdb", App.Path & "\~waite27.tmp"
          Kill App.Path & "\icon.mdb"     'get rid of old file
          Name App.Path & "\~waite27.tmp" As App.Path & "\icon.mdb"
          dataMain.Refresh                'open up all databases again
          dataLog.Refresh
          formDatasheet!dataGrid.Refresh
          MousePointer = NORMAL
      Case 1 '********************************* Statistics
          PrintStats                      'prints out the statistics
      Case 2 '********************************* Log
          Dim f As form                   'this just shortens subsequent code
          Set f = formStats
          f.Show                          'show the stats form
          f.Cls                           'clear off any existing text
          dataLog.Recordset.MoveLast      'go to latest log entry
          Do Until dataLog.Recordset.BOF    'at beginning of time yet?
            f.Print
            f.Print dataLog.Recordset!Date    'print date and time of entry
            totalSize = dataLog.Recordset.Fields("Memo").FieldSize()
            biteSize = 2500               'size of our chunks
            numChunks = totalSize \ biteSize   'number of whole chunks
            remChunk = totalSize Mod biteSize  'number of bites remaining
            For i = 0 To numChunks        'go through each chunk
              If i = numChunks Then biteSize = remChunk    'on last chunk?
              chunk = dataLog.Recordset.Fields("Memo").GetChunk(i * biteSize, biteSize)
                                          'eat the chunk
              f.Print chunk               'and print it out
            Next i
            f.Print
            dataLog.Recordset.MovePrevious    'step backwards in time
          Loop
      Case 3 '********************************* Find
          formFind.Show                   'show the find form
      Case 4 '********************************* Datasheet
          MousePointer = HOURGLASS        'we're going to be a while
          formDatasheet.Show              'show the data sheet
          MousePointer = DEFAULT          'ready to roll!
    End Select
End Sub
```

19. Enter the following code in the General Declarations section to create the PrintStats subroutine. This prints out a number of database statistics. It first prints out statistics that apply to the database as a whole, and then goes on to print statistics for each user table in the database.

```
Sub PrintStats ()
    Dim f As formStats                  'This just shortens up subsequent code
    Set f = formStats
    f.Show                              'show the stats form
    f.Cls                              'clear off any existing text
    f.Print
```

(continued on next page)

1187

(continued from previous page)

```
    f.Print , "Database Filename: "; Tab(40); dataMain.DatabaseName
    f.Print , "Database Size:"; Tab(40); FileLen(dataMain.DatabaseName)
    f.Print , "Database User Status:"; Tab(40); Choose(dataMain.Exclusive + 2, "Single ⇐
User", "Multi-User")
    f.Print , "Database Access Mode:"; Tab(40); Choose(dataMain.ReadOnly + 2, "Read ⇐
Only", "Read and Write")
    f.Print , "Database Collating Order"; Tab(40); DataMain.Database.CollatingOrder
    f.Print
    For j = 0 To dataMain.Database.TableDefs.Count - 1
      If (dataMain.Database.TableDefs(j).Attributes And DB_SYSTEMOBJECT) = 0 Then
          f.Print
          f.Print " _____ "
          f.Print
          f.Print , "Table: "; dataMain.Database.TableDefs(j).Name
          f.Print
          f.Print , "Updatable: ";
Choose(dataMain.Database.TableDefs(j).Updatable + 2, "All fields updatable", "Some fields ⇐
not updatable")
          For i = 0 To dataMain.Database.TableDefs(j).Indexes.Count - 1
            f.Print , "Index: "; dataMain.Database.TableDefs(j).Indexes(i).Name,
            f.Print "Fields: "; dataMain.Database.TableDefs(j).Indexes(i).Fields
          Next i
          f.Print
          f.Print , "Field #", "Name", "Type"
          f.Print , "----------------------------------------------------"
          For i = 0 To dataMain.Database.TableDefs(j).Fields.Count - 1
            f.Print , dataMain.Database.TableDefs(j).Fields(i).OrdinalPosition,
            f.Print dataMain.Database.TableDefs(j).Fields(i).Name,
            Select Case dataMain.Database.TableDefs(j).Fields(i).Type
              Case 1: f.Print "Boolean",
              Case 2: f.Print "Byte",
              Case 3: f.Print "Integer",
              Case 4: f.Print "Long",
              Case 5: f.Print "Currency",
              Case 6: f.Print "Single",
              Case 7: f.Print "Double",
              Case 8: f.Print "Date",
              Case 9: f.Print "Binary",
              Case 10: f.Print "Text",
              Case 11: f.Print "LongBinary",
              Case 12: f.Print "Memo",
            End Select
            f.Print
          Next i
      End If
    Next j
End Sub
```

20. Enter the following code in the textFileName_KeyPress and textPathName_KeyPress events. These events enable the Save command button, as a keypress implies that the user has changed the text in the text box.

```
Sub textFileName_KeyPress (KeyAscii As Integer)
    cmndSave.Enabled = True              'user changed entry; enable save button
End Sub
```

```
Sub textPathName_KeyPress (KeyAscii As Integer)
    cmndSave.Enabled = True              'user changed entry; enable save button
End Sub
```

Assembling the Project: formDatasheet

1. Make a new form (formDatasheet) with the objects and properties in Table 27-81.

Object	Property	Setting
Form	BorderStyle	3—Fixed Double
	Caption	"Datasheet"
Command	Caption	&Close
	Name	cmndClose
Command	Caption	&Refresh
	Name	cmndRefresh
Command	Caption	Sort by &Name
	Name	cmndSortByName
Command	Caption	Sort by &Path
	Name	cmndSortByPath
Data	Name	dataGrid
Grid	BorderStyle	0—None
	Cols	3
	FixedCols	0
	FontBold	0—False
	FontName	MS Sans Serif

(continued on next page)

(continued from previous page)

Object	Property	Setting
	FontSize	9.6
	Gridlines	0–False
	Name	gridDatasheet
	Scrollbars	2–Vertical
Image	DataField	Icon
	DataSource	dataGrid
	Name	imagTemp
	Visible	0–False

Table 27-81 Elements of the Datasheet form

2. Size and position the controls, as shown in Figure 27-13.

3. Enter the following code in the cmndClose_Click event. This hides the datatsheet.

```
Sub cmndClose_Click ()
     formDatasheet.Hide                    'hide the form
End Sub
```

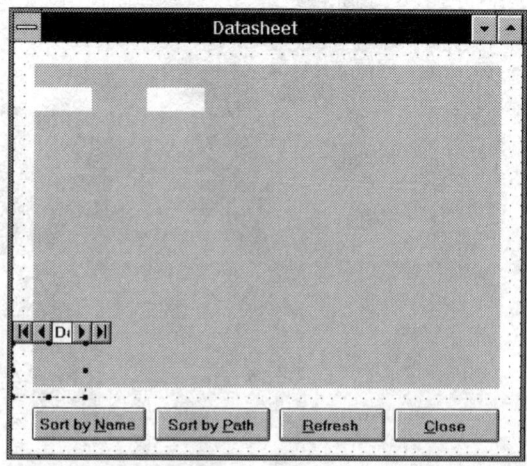

Figure 27-13 The datasheet form during design

1190

4. Enter the following code in the cmndRefresh_Click event. This refills the grid after refreshing the recordset. It does not pass a sort key, so the FillGrid routine uses whatever the existing sort is.

```
Sub cmndRefresh_Click ()
      fillGrid ""                              'fill the grid, use existing sort
End Sub
```

5. Enter the following code in the cmndSortByName_Click event. This refills the grid after refreshing the recordset. It passes the fillGrid routine the name of the field to sort by: "fileName." The fillGrid routine uses this fieldname in an SQL statement.

```
Sub cmndSortByName_Click ()
      fillGrid "fileName"                      'fill the grid, sort by FileName
End Sub
```

6. Enter the following code in the cmndSortByPath_Click event. This refills the grid after refreshing the recordset. It passes the fillGrid routine the name of the field to sort by: "pathName." The fillGrid routine uses this fieldname in an SQL statement.

```
Sub cmndSortByPath_Click ()
      fillGrid "pathName"                      'fill the grid, sort by "PathName"
End Sub
```

7. Enter the following code in the General Declarations section to create the fillGrid subroutine. This routine refreshes the recordset and then fills the grid control with the path name, file name, and picture of the icon. It uses the "sort" argument to determine what field to sort by. This argument is used in the RecordSource property as part of an SQL statement. Notice how the hidden image control imagTemp is used to get the picture from the database for use in the grid control.

```
Sub fillGrid (sort)                            '"sort" is passed by the command buttons

      MousePointer = HOURGLASS                 'we're going to be a long while!
      Static oldSort                           'remember old sort (for "Refresh" button)

      On Error Resume Next
      gridDatasheet.ColWidth(0) = 700
      gridDatasheet.ColWidth(1) = 1400
      gridDatasheet.ColWidth(2) = gridDatasheet.Width - 1500
      gridDatasheet.RowHeight(0) = 300
      gridDatasheet.Row = 0
      gridDatasheet.Col = 1
      gridDatasheet.Text = "Name"
      gridDatasheet.Col = 2
      gridDatasheet.Text = "Path"

      If sort = "" Then                        'refresh button doesn't pass sort
            sort = oldSort
      Else
            oldSort = sort                     'update the sort
      End If
```

(continued on next page)

(continued from previous page)

```
dataGrid.DatabaseName = formMain!dataMain.DatabaseName    'same as main form
dataGrid.RecordSource = "SELECT * FROM Icon ORDER BY " & sort
dataGrid.Options = DB_READONLY          'make sure nothing is changed here
dataGrid.Refresh                        'build the recordset
dataGrid.Recordset.MoveLast             'make sure recordcount is current
gridDatasheet.Rows = dataGrid.Recordset.RecordCount + 1  'make grid big enough
dataGrid.Recordset.MoveFirst            'go to beginning of recordset
Do While Not dataGrid.Recordset.EOF     'and while there are still records,
    i = i + 1                           'go to a new grid row
    gridDatasheet.RowHeight(i) = 410 'set the row height
    gridDatasheet.Row = i               'choose the row
    gridDatasheet.Col = 0               'first column
    gridDatasheet.Picture = imagTemp.Picture        'load the icon
    gridDatasheet.Col = 1               'next column
    gridDatasheet.Text = dataGrid.Recordset!FileName 'load the file name
    gridDatasheet.Col = 2               'next column
    gridDatasheet.Text = dataGrid.Recordset!PathName 'load the pathname
    dataGrid.Recordset.MoveNext         'go to next record
Loop
MousePointer = DEFAULT                   'done!
End Sub
```

8. Enter the following code in the Form_Load event. This fills the grid when the datasheet is first opened.

```
Sub Form_Load ()
    fillGrid "fileName"                 'fill the grid, sort by "FileName"
End Sub
```

Assembling the Project: formFind

1. Make a new form (formFind) with the objects and properties in Table 27-82.

Object	Property	Setting
Form	BorderStyle	3—Fixed Double
	Caption	"Find"
	Name	formFind
Command	Caption	Clear &History
	Name	cmndClearHistory
Command	Caption	&Close

Object	Property	Setting
	Name	cmndClose
Command	Caption	&Goto
	Name	cmndGoto
Command	Caption	OR
	Name	cmndAndOr
Command	Caption	&Previous
	Index	0
	Name	cmndFind
Command	Caption	&Next
	Index	1
	Name	cmndFind
Command	Caption	&First
	Index	2
	Name	cmndFind
Command	Caption	&Last
	Index	3
	Name	cmndFind
List	FontBold	0—False
	Name	listFindHistory
Text	Index	0

(continued on next page)

(continued from previous page)

Object	Property	Setting
	Name	textFind
Text	Index	1
	Name	textFind
Label	Alignment	1 – Right Justify
	Caption	"this in path:"
	FontBold	0 – False
Label	Alignment	1 – Right Justify
	Caption	"Find this in file name:"
	FontBold	0 – False

Table 27-82 Elements of the Find dialog box

2. Size and position the controls, as shown in Figure 27-14.

3. Enter the following code in the General Declarations section. This array will hold bookmarks that correspond to entries in the listFindHistory list box. This lets the user go to an arbitrary set of records that they've used the Find dialog to locate.

```
Dim FindHistory() As String          'module level array to hold bookmarks
```

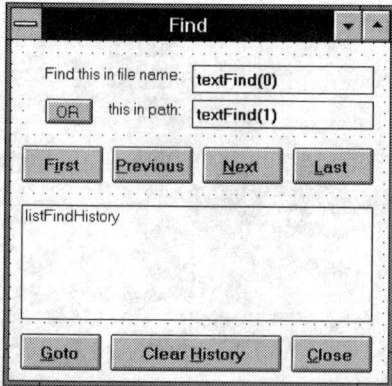

Figure 27-14 The Find dialog box during design

4. Enter the following code in the cmndAndOr_Click event. This event switches the caption back and forth between "OR" and "AND." The caption is used to build an SQL WHERE clause that does the actual finding.

```
Sub cmndAndOr_Click ()
    If cmndAndOr.Caption = "OR" Then    'switch states
        cmndAndOr.Caption = "AND"       '(this caption is used to
    Else                                ' build an SQL WHERE clause)
        cmndAndOr.Caption = "OR"
    End If
End Sub
```

5. Enter the following code in the cmndClearHistory_Click event. This clears out the list box that holds descriptions of previous found records, zeros the bookmark array, and disables the Goto bookmark command button.

```
Sub cmndClearHistory_Click ()
    listFindHistory.Clear          'clear out old history
    ReDim FindHistory(0)           'clear out old bookmarks
    cmndGoto.Enabled = False        'disable goto bookmark
End Sub
```

6. Enter the following code in the cmndClose_Click event. This hides the Find dialog box.

```
Sub cmndClose_Click ()
    formFind.Hide                  'hide this form
    formMain.Show                  'make sure main form is current
End Sub
```

7. Enter the following code in the cmndFind_Click event. This does the actual finding. The four "Find" buttons (Previous, Next, First, Last) are set up as a control array. The only tricky part lies in building the search criteria string. This builds an SQL criteria using both the FileName and the PathName fields. It uses the Like keyword and embeds the actual text to find within asterisks (*). The asterisks work like the DOS asterisk wildcard, and this lets the Find methods find any entries that have the indicated text embedded anywhere in the field. The cmndAndOr button's caption is used to make a logical And/Or connection between the two fields. Building SQL statements like this gives your code tremendous flexibility and power.

The actual Find statements all work similarly. They each first find the record using the criteria string. If Previous or Next fail to find a record (as indicated by the recordset's NoMatch property), then that button is disabled as a visual indicator that there are no more records to be found in that direction. The First and Last routines also disable the Previous or Next buttons, as there are no "previous" or "next" records when you're already at the beginning or the end of the recordset respectively.

If the Find methods find a record, the record description is added to the listFindHistory list box. The record's Bookmark property is then stored in a module-level array so that the user can later skip to any of the previously found

1195

records. Finally, the Goto bookmark command button gets enabled, as there is at least one entry that the user could go to.

```
Sub cmndFind_Click (Index As Integer)
    'build SQL WHERE clause: FileName Like '*name*' AND/OR PathName Like '*path*'
    'this finds any embedded text, not just exact matches
    criteria$ = "FileName Like '*" & textFind(0).Text & "*' " & cmndAndOr.Caption
    criteria$ = criteria$ & " PathName Like '*" & textFind(1).Text & "*'"

    cmndFind(0).Enabled = True          'start by enabling all buttons
    cmndFind(1).Enabled = True
    Select Case Index
        Case 0 'Previous
            formMain!dataMain.Recordset.FindPrevious criteria$
            If formMain!dataMain.Recordset.NoMatch Then cmndFind(0).Enabled = False
        Case 1 'Next
            formMain!dataMain.Recordset.FindNext criteria$
            If formMain!dataMain.Recordset.NoMatch Then cmndFind(1).Enabled = False
        Case 2 'First
            formMain!dataMain.Recordset.FindFirst criteria$
            cmndFind(0).Enabled = False
        Case 3 'Last
            formMain!dataMain.Recordset.FindLast criteria$
            cmndFind(1).Enabled = False
    End Select
    If Not formMain!dataMain.Recordset.NoMatch Then  'if we found a record, then
        item$ = formMain!textPathName.Text & "\" & formMain!textFileName.Text
        listFindHistory.AddItem item$              'add it to the history
        If formMain!dataMain.Recordset.Bookmarkable Then
            ReDim Preserve FindHistory(listFindHistory.ListCount - 1)
            FindHistory(listFindHistory.ListCount - 1) = ⇐
formMain!dataMain.Recordset.Bookmark
            cmndGoto.Enabled = True                 'enable Goto bookmark
        End If
    End If
End Sub
```

8. Enter the following code in the cmndGoto_Click event. This uses the bookmark stored in the FindHistory array to set the Bookmark property of the data control. This makes the data control jump to that record.

```
Sub cmndGoto_Click ()
    book = FindHistory(listFindHistory.ListIndex)    'extract bookmark
    formMain!dataMain.Recordset.Bookmark = book      'and go to it
    formMain!dataMain.UpdateControls                 'make sure display is current
End Sub
```

9. Enter the following code in the Form_Load event. This blanks out any text that is in the text boxes.

```
Sub Form_Load ()
    textFind(0).Text = ""                            'blank out beginning text
    textFind(1).Text = ""
End Sub
```

1196

10. Enter the following code in the listFindHistory_DblClick event. This triggers the cmndGoto_Click event to go to the indicated record.

```
Sub listFindHistory_DblClick ()
    cmndGoto_Click                              'goto bookmark
End Sub
```

11. Enter the following code in the textFind_Change event. If the user changes the criteria, there by definition is no "previous" or "next" record, so those command buttons get disabled.

```
Sub textFind_Change (Index As Integer)
    cmndFind(0).Enabled = False        'changed criteria; no more previous
    cmndFind(1).Enabled = False        'changed criteria; no more next
End Sub
```

12. Enter the following code in the textFind_GotFocus event. This highlights the text in the text box to make it easy for the user to replace old search text.

```
Sub textFind_GotFocus (Index As Integer)
    textFind(Index).SelStart = 0       'start at the beginning of text
    textFind(Index).SelLength = 100    'select all text
End Sub
```

13. Enter the following code in the textFind_LostFocus event. This unhighlights text when the focus shifts away from the text box.

```
Sub textFind_LostFocus (Index As Integer)
    textFind(Index).SelLength = 0      'deselect all text
End Sub
```

Assembling the Project: formStats

1. Make a new form (formStats) with the objects and properties in Table 27-83.

Object	Property	Setting
Form	AutoRedraw	-1—True
	BorderStyle	3—Fixed Double
	Caption	"Database Statistics"
	Name	formStats
Command	Cancel	-1—True

(continued on next page)

(continued from previous page)

Object	Property	Setting
	Caption	"Close"
	Name	cmndClose

Table 27-83 Elements of the Statistics form

2. Size and position the controls, as shown in Figure 27-15.

3. Enter the following code in the cmndClose_Click event. This hides the form.

```
Sub cmndClose_Click ()
     Hide
End Sub
```

Assembling the Project: Global Module

1. Create a new module by pulling down the File menu and choosing the New Module command. Enter the following global constants.

```
Global Const HOURGLASS = 11
Global Const DEFAULT = 0

Global Const MB_YESNO = 4
Global Const MB_ICONQUESTION = 32
Global Const IDYES = 6
Global Const IDNO = 7

Global Const DB_SYSTEMOBJECT = &H80000002
Global Const DB_READONLY = 4
```

How It Works

The Data Access project lets you catalog and manage all of your icon files. The first thing you should do is load some icons into the database. Both the Load and Seek command buttons will do this. Load lets you manually pick the icons from the File list box and will load only the ones you select. (Note that you can select more than one file at a time in the list box.) Seek will select every icon file in your current directory and in all subdirectories beneath the current one. It sets the module-level variable Scan to tell the other procedures to recurse through each subdirectory. Notice how much faster Seek works than Load: the Seek command sets up a transaction block, whereas the Load command processes the files normally. The transaction block dramatically cuts the loading time down.

Once you've got some icons loaded, you can use the data control to step through the database. Each entry will display the file name, the path name, and an image of the icon. You can delete an individual icon by pressing the "Delete" command button. This deletes the icon entry from the database. The line that

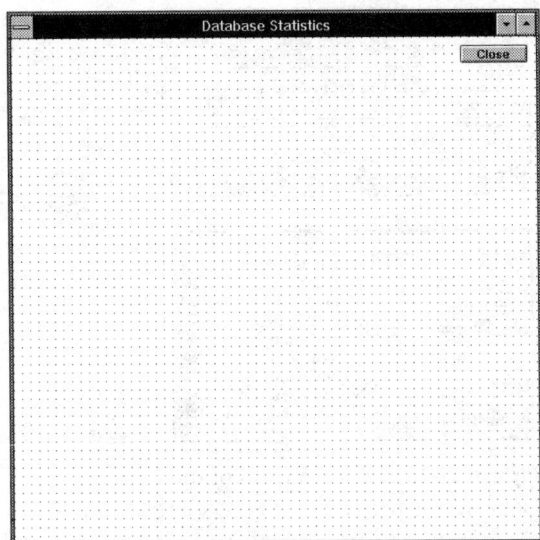

Figure 27-15 The Statistics form during design

would have deleted the actual icon file from your disk has been remarked out, so you don't have to worry about zapping your icon files!

You can also rename any icon file by simply typing in a new file name or path name in the text boxes. This changes the entry in the database, as well as renaming the actual icon file on the disk. This renaming really works, so be sure to rename your icon files back to what they were. All the code for the renaming lies in the Validate event.

You can also clear the entire database with the "Clear" command button. This executes a single SQL command that deletes the entire database. Figure 27-16 shows the main form of the Data Access project in action.

You can bring up a typical datasheet view of the entire database with the Utilities menu command "Datasheet." This calls up the datasheet form and loads the grid control with every record in the database. Notice that the first time you do this, it takes a few seconds for the form to appear as it builds the recordset and loads it into the grid. The grid control is ideal for creating a datasheet view of a database, with records going across as rows and fields going down as columns. Figure 27-17 shows the datasheet.

The data control for the datasheet form has its RecordSource property set by an SQL statement. This makes it simple for us to sort the data. The "Sort by Name" and "Sort by Path" command buttons pass an argument to the FillGrid sub procedure that includes the name of the field to sort by.

The Utilities menu command "Find" brings up another form, the Find dialog box. This lets you locate any icon file in the database. You can type search text in either of the two text boxes. It will find any entry with that text embedded in either the file name or path name. The And/Or command button lets you choose

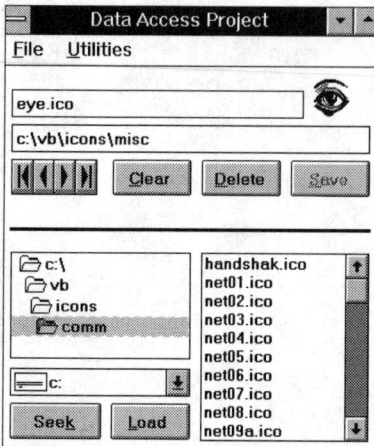

Figure 27-16 The main form of the
Data Access project

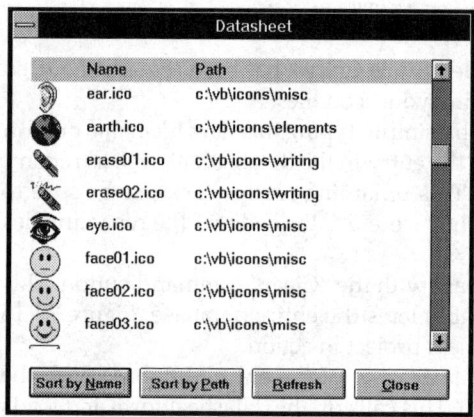

Figure 27-17 The datasheet form of the Data
Access project

whether you want it to find all entries with both the file name text and path name
text, or any entry with either the file name text or the path name text. Figure 27-18
shows the Find form.

The actual finding uses a search string built with the entries from the two text
boxes. Building up SQL statements like this can add tremendous power and flexibility to your database programs.

Each time an entry is found, it gets added to the listFindHistory list box and a
matching entry for the entry's bookmark gets added to FindHistory array. Double-
clicking on any entry (or selecting an entry and clicking on the "Goto" button) will
immediately jump to that record using the bookmark stored in the array.

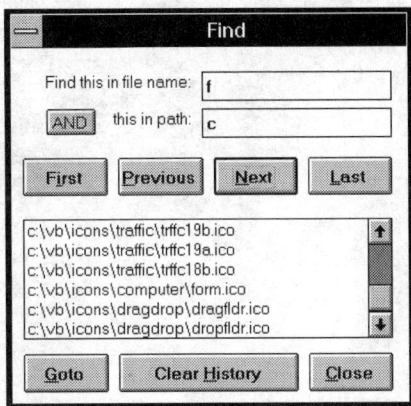

Figure 27-18 The Find form in the
Data Access project lets you search
for embedded text

You can compact the database with the Utilities menu "Compact" command.
This closes the database, compacts it, and then replaces the old file with the
newly compacted one. Use the "Statistics" command to compare the size of the
database before and after compacting.

The "Statistics" command prints out a number of statistics about the database
and each table within the database. Finally, the "Log" command prints out a log
of each time an addition was made to the database. Figure 27-19 shows the
Statistics printout.

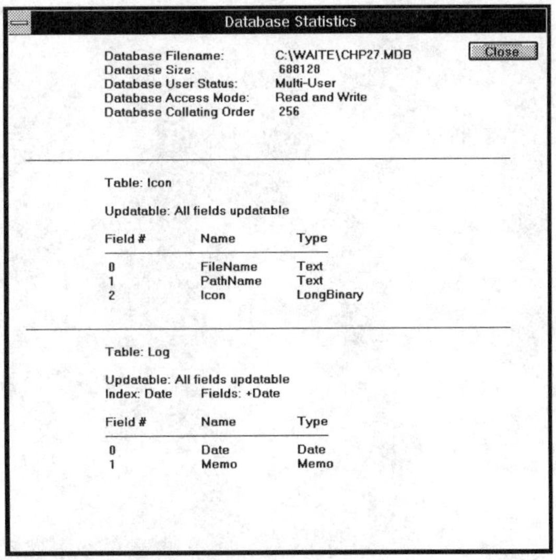

Figure 27-19 The Statistics printout

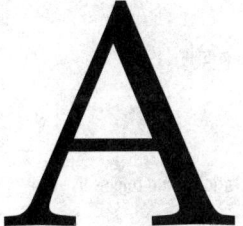

VISUAL BASIC LANGUAGE TUTORIAL

This appendix introduces the key elements of the Visual Basic language and explains some commonly used programming techniques. You'll find the most relevant Visual Basic statements and functions under each topic. This appendix isn't intended to be a complete tutorial in the BASIC language, but it can serve as an introduction for the beginner or as a quick refresher for readers with some BASIC programming experience. For more in-depth coverage of the BASIC language, we suggest that you look at some of the books on BASIC programming listed in Appendix F, Further Reading.

Appendix B, Visual Basic Language Reference, provides a concise alphabetical reference to each statement and function used in Visual Basic. Use that reference to find out more about the exact rules and syntax for using each statement or function, examples of usage, and other details.

VARIABLES

Variables let you temporarily store information. You've seen hundreds of examples of variable usage throughout this book. A variable has both a *name* that you use to refer to it in your code, and a *data type* that indicates what kind of information it stores. Variables also have a *scope* of operation that defines where they're available, and have a *lifetime* that defines how long they retain their value. Table A-1 summarizes the statements used to declare constants and variables.

Use This...		To Do This...
Const	Statement	Assign a permanent value to a name
Dim	Statement	Explicitly declare a local or module-level variable
Global	Statement	Explicitly declare a global-level variable
Static	Statement	Explicitly declare a local or module-level variable that retains its value

Table A-1 Statements used to declare variables and constants

VARIABLE NAMES

A variable's name must start with a letter, may be up to 40 characters long, and must consist of only letters, numbers, and the underscore (_) character. You cannot use a reserved word like For or If. You can use variables *implicitly* by just using them without ever declaring them, as in the following example:

```
Sub Command1_Click ()
    T$ = Text1.Text
    Print LCase$(T$)
End Sub
```

You can also *explicitly* declare a variable before using it. This can dramatically reduce programming errors in large projects. Use the Dim, Static, or Global statements to declare a variable:

```
Sub Command1_Click ()
    Dim T As String
    T = Text1.Text
    Print LCase$(T)
End Sub
```

In Visual Basic 3.0, you can enforce the need to explicitly declare all of your variables by placing the Option Explicit statement in the declarations section of a form or module:

```
Option Explicit        'This forces you to explicitly declare all variables
```

You can also set the Visual Basic environment to automatically add this line to each new project. Do this by pulling down the Environment menu, choosing the options dialog box, and typing "Yes" in the Require Variable Declaration option.

Data Types

Specify the data type of a variable either with a special character appended to the variable name, as in T$, or by a type declaration, as in Dim T As String. Visual Basic supports seven different variable types. Table A-2 lists the type declaration name, the special character, and a description and example of each type.

Type Name	Character	Sample Variable	Description	Example
String	$	msg$	String of characters	Hello, world!
Integer	%	count%	2-byte integer	-3598
Long	&	recordNum&	4-byte integer	39849890
Single	!	xPos!	4-byte floating point	9483.345
Double	#	distanceToGalaxy#	8-byte floating point	829855903.00938994093
Currency	@	nationalDebt@	8-byte, fixed decimal	9389403883.9383
Variant	(none)	littleLegoGuy	any of the above types	

Table A-2 Variable types in Visual Basic

Scope and Lifetime of Variables

Variables have a *scope* of operation and exist for a certain *lifetime*, depending on where and how they are declared. Variables declared in a procedure are *local* to that procedure, and are invisible to any other functions or procedures in the program. You can have variables with identical names declared in different procedures without any interference:

```
Sub Command1_Click ()
    T = Text1.Text          'This variable is local to this procedure
    T = Left$(T, 3)
    Print T
End Sub

Sub Form_Click ()
    T = Now                 'This variable is local to this procedure
    Print Format$(T, "mmmm dd, yyyy")
End Sub
```

These local variables remain in existence only while the procedure executes. They are removed from memory when the procedure ends. If you need to retain the value of a local variable, you can use the Static keyword. This is quite useful for functions that accumulate a value over time, or for variables that flag a particular state:

```
Sub GetTotalWinnings (newAddition)
    Static totalWinnings As Currency, overTheTop As Integer    'retain values

    totalWinnings = totalWinnings + newAddition
    LablWinnings.Caption = Format$(totalWinnings, "$###,###,###")
    If overTheTop = False Then
        If totalWinnings > 1000 Then
            LablOver.Caption = "Over the Top!"
            overTheTop = True
        End If
    Else
        If totalWinnings < 0 Then
            LablOver.Caption = "Busted ."
            overTheTop = False
        End If
    End If
End Sub
```

This example accumulates a running total by adding the newAddition argument to totalWinnings. It also tracks the overTheTop flag to see if the user has already won. The Static declarations for both of these variables lets the procedure retain their values.

Variables declared in the declarations section of a module or form are available to any procedure within that module or form. These variables are called *module-level* variables. Module-level variables remain in existence for the lifetime of the application, and retain their values even if the form is unloaded.

You can also declare *global* variables that are available to any procedure in any form or module. Global variables exist and retain their values throughout the lifetime of the application. Declare these variables in a module's declarations section using the Global keyword rather than the Dim keyword. (Note that you must declare global variables in a code module, and cannot declare them in a form.)

```
Global NumTries As Integer
Global User As String
```

It's good programming practice to keep all of your global declarations in as few modules as possible. Spreading global declarations throughout a large application makes it hard to debug.

Standard programming practice (and most of the examples in this book) uses capitalization to differentiate between local variables and module- or global-level variables. Local variables commonly use a small first letter, and module- or global-level variables use a capital letter:

```
tempString$ = "This is a local variable"
PermString$ = "This is a module (or global) level variable"
```

This is by no means universal, and you may often see different systems (or no system!) used to differentiate between the different scopes of variables.

CONSTANTS

Your code will often contain values or numbers that you refer to, but don't change. You can always refer to these values explicitly by just giving the string or number directly:

```
If T > 7 Then ...
```

You'll find it much easier to debug your code if you replace all literal references to these values with a *symbolic constant*. These are names that contain the value, and make your code much more readable. You can declare a constant with the Const keyword. Constants have scope just as variables do, and the same rules apply for scoping and lifetime. Constants can contain numbers, strings, and dates. You can only assign literal values to them; you cannot use functions like Chr$ or Now. We could rewrite the above example like this:

```
Const MAXTRIES = 7
:
:
If T > MAXTRIES Then
```

This makes it much easier to see what the If...Then statement is testing. Constants make your code self-documenting and actually speed up the development process. Changing the value of a constant requires you to change only the line that it's declared in, rather than search through your entire program for every literal value the constant replaces. Note that it's a common programming practice to make all constants uppercase to distinguish them from variables.

VARIANTS

The default data type of Visual Basic is the *variant*. This special type can contain any of the other types, and automatically converts between them. Visual Basic 2.0 first introduced the variant; Visual Basic 1.0 used the Single data type as its default. Using variants can save you from having to worry about conversion. For example, the following code will automatically convert the number contained in numVar into a string before it performs the concatenation:

```
numVar = 7.2              'variant contains the single precision number 7.2
strVar = "Hello"          'variant contains the string value "Hello"
newVar = strVar & numVar  'variant contains the string value "Hello 7.2"
```

You usually don't have to worry about what data type a variant consists of; all conversions are automatic. There can be a subtle trap when you use the + operator to concatenate strings, as explained in the next section about strings.

Variants can contain two special values that the other data types don't support. Table A-3 shows the keywords used with these special values.

Use This...		To Do This...
IsEmpty	Function	Determine if a variant has had a value assigned to it
IsNull	Function	Determine if a variant contains a Null
Null	Keyword	Assign a Null to a variant

Table A-3 Statements and keywords associated with variants

The first special value is "empty," meaning a variant that has never had anything assigned to it. Note that this is different than 0, an empty string (""), or a Null. You can check for this with the IsEmpty function:

```
If IsEmpty(newVar) Then Print "Variant has never been used"
```

Variants can also contain the Null value. This is a special value that is used with some databases, such as the Access database engine discussed in detail in Chapter 27, Data Access. Nulls have a useful property called *propagation*. This means that if an expression contains a null anywhere, the value of the entire expression is null. Thus, if any of the variants in this next line of code evaluates to Null, then testVar is Null:

```
testVar = var1 + var2 * Trim(var3)
```

You can test for and use the Null value with the IsNull function and the Null keyword:

```
Function getNewName (clientID As Integer)
    On Error Goto BadID

    F = fetchFirstName(clientID)
    L = fetchLastName(clientID)
    fullName = F & " " & L
    If IsNull(fullName) Then
        getNewName = ""
    Else
        getNewName = fullName & "    " & clientID
    End If
Exit Function
```

```
BadID:
    getNewName = Null
Exit Function

End Function
```

You can use the Null value as an error flag in your functions. If you do this consistently, you can ease the burden of error checking somewhat by letting a Null value (indicating an error in a function) propagate through a series of calculations, and only check for the Null at the end of the calculation. Note that Visual Basic will never assign a Null to a variant without you explicitly using the Null keyword, with the one exception of a Null value in a database field. This means that you don't have to write any special Null handling code if you choose not to use Nulls in your program.

Although variants are extremely flexible and useful, they also execute more slowly and take up more memory than the other fundamental data types. For the fastest, most compact code, type each of your variables either implicitly, with the special data-type character, or explicitly in a Dim, Static, or Global statement.

STRINGS

String variables contain strings of characters. For example, "Hello, world!", "John Fitzquattle", and "1234 Main Street" are all strings. Strings that display only numbers, like "1234", are still strings. Some strings contain characters that don't display as letters or numbers, such as a tab character or a carriage return.

Visual Basic has two types of strings: variable length and fixed length. As the names imply, variable-length strings shrink and grow depending on the length of the data that has been assigned to them. Fixed-length strings never change size. If a fixed-length string is assigned a value that is longer than the string, any extra characters are ignored. (Another way to say this is that the string is "truncated" to the number of characters allowed for in the variable.) If it is assigned a value that is shorter than it, the balance of a fixed-length string is padded with spaces.

One of Visual Basic's strongest assets is its string-handling capabilities. Visual Basic has inherited from previous BASIC languages a rich and powerful array of functions and statements designed to make even the most complicated string operations a snap to perform. Table A-4 lists Visual Basic's string-handling commands.

Use This...		To Do This...
Asc	Function	Determine the ASCII value of a string character
Chr$	Function	Translate an ASCII value into a string character

(continued on next page)

(continued from previous page)

Use This...		To Do This...
Format$	Function	Translate a date variant or a number into a formatted string
InStr	Function	Find the position of one string within another
LCase$	Function	Translate all uppercase characters in a string to lowercase
Left$	Function	Return a portion of a string starting from the leftmost character
Len	Function	Determine the length of a string or other variable type
LSet	Function	Left justify a value in a string or a programmer-defined type
LTrim$	Function	Truncate any leading spaces from a string
Mid$	Function	Return a portion of a string by specifying start point and length
Mid$	Statement	Assign a value to a portion of a string
Right$	Function	Return a portion of a string starting from the rightmost character
RSet	Function	Right justify a value in a string or a programmer-defined type
RTrim$	Function	Truncate any following spaces from a string
Space$	Function	Return a specified number of spaces
Str$	Function	Translate a numeric value into an unformatted string
String$	Function	Return a string of characters repeated a specified number of times
Trim$	Function	Truncate any leading or trailing spaces from a string
UCase$	Function	Translate all lowercase characters of a string into uppercase

Table A-4 Functions and statements that affect strings

String Literals and Assigning Values to a String

A string literal consists of an actual string of characters. Create a string by placing the literal within double quotes. For example, this assigns "Hello, world!" to the string variable H$:

```
H$ = "Hello, world!"
```

You can also control how a string will be justified when it is assigned by using the LSet and RSet functions. Justification refers to the alignment of the characters—for example, left justification means that the characters start at the leftmost position, while right justification means that the last character is in the rightmost position. LSet will left justify the source string within the destination string. Conversely, RSet will right justify. Both LSet and RSet treat the destination string as if it were a fixed-length string, regardless of how it was originally declared. Therefore the length of the destination string will never be affected by the LSet or RSet statements. If the destination string is shorter than the source string, any extra characters are truncated. If the destination is longer than the source, it will be padded with spaces. Here are some examples:

```
Dim RString As String * 15    'Define a fixed length string of 15 characters length
LString$ = RString            'Create variable length string LString$ (also 15 characters)
RSet RString = "Hello!"       'Right justify "Hello!" into fixed length string
LSet LString$ = "Hello!"      'Left justify "Hello!" into variable length string
```

In the example above, two string variables are created; one as a fixed-length string, and one as a variable-length string. After being assigned the string literal, the variable RString will have a value of "   Hello!" and LString$ will have a value of "Hello!   ".

Two strings may be combined into one by using string concatenation. You indicate concatenation with the ampersand sign (&):

```
A$ = "Hello"
B$ = "world"
C$ = A$ & ", " & B$
```

In this example the values of A$, the literal string ", ", and B$ are combined and assigned to C$. This sets the value for C$ to "Hello, world".

You may also use the addition sign (+) to concatenate strings. Version 1.0 of Visual Basic used the addition sign exclusively. Its use has been retained in versions 2.0 and 3.0, but is not recommended. It can easily lead to confusion, especially when used with variants. Visual Basic will attempt to convert variants into numbers before combining them, and this can lead to unpredictable results if you use the + operator to attempt concatenation. The following example shows this potential confusion:

```
A = "5"       'variant containing the string literal "5"
B = "6"       'variant containing the string literal "6"
C = A + B     'variants convert to numbers; addition gives C = 11
D = A & B     'variants convert to numbers; concatenation gives D = "56"
```

In this example both A and B are variants holding the strings "5" and "6". The + operator in the third line adds the two numbers represented by A and B because variants automatically attempt to convert their contents to the appropriate format. The & operator in the fourth line correctly assigns the string "56" to D.

Determining the Length of a String

Because strings in Visual Basic can be of variable length, you may sometimes need a way to determine how long a string actually is before processing. The Len function returns the number of characters that are assigned to a string.

```
this$ = "Hello, world!"
StrLen% = Len(this$)
```

In the above example, the variable StrLen% will be assigned a value of 13, which is the length of the string this$. Len also can be used to measure the length (measured in bytes) of any other data type, including programmer-defined data types. For instance:

```
Type PersonType
      Name As String * 10
      SSN As Long
End Type

Dim Person As PersonType
personLen% = Len(Person)
```

This will assign a value of 14 to the variable personLen%, because the programmer-defined type contains a string that is 10 bytes in length, and a long integer that is 4 bytes in length.

Translating a Number into a String

You can translate numbers into strings with the Str$ function. This function translates any numeric value into an unformatted string:

```
X% = 100
Y% = -100
XNum$ = Str$(X%)
YNum$ = Str$(Y%)
```

This example translates the numeric values contained in the integer variables X% and Y% into displayable strings. The Str$ function always reserves a character for the sign of the numeric value it is translating. If the value is positive, the leading character of the returned string will be a space. If it is negative, the leading character will be a minus sign (-). The value of XNum$ in the above example will be " 100" and YNum$ will be "-100".

While the Str$ function presents a workable solution, it does not allow you to easily control the format of the returned string. The Format$ function provides far greater control and flexibility. The Format$ function requires two arguments: the numeric value to be translated and a pattern upon which the format of the returned string will be based. For instance:

```
X! = 234.9
Num1$ = Str$(X!)
Num2$ = Format$(X!, "###.00")
```

In this example Num1$ is assigned the value " 234.9", while Num2$ is assigned the value "234.90".

There are many different formatting options you may apply to the translation of a number with the Format$ function (see Appendix B, Visual Basic Language Reference, for details). This function also translates a date variant number into a readable date or time (see the section on Date and Time later in this appendix).

Finding One String Within Another

Another useful string-related function is Instr. This function will search inside one string for the occurrence of another string pattern. It will then return the position within the source string at which the desired pattern was found. For instance:

```
source$ = "This is a dog."
searchPattern$ = "is"
foundPos% = Instr(source$, searchPattern$)
```

In this example the string variable source$ is searched for the first occurrence of the string pattern "is". FoundPos% is assigned the value 3, because "is" is found at the third character position in Source$ (in the word "This"). You may also specify where in the source string you wish the search to begin by optionally using an argument to indicate a start position:

```
source$ = "This is a dog."
searchPattern$ = "is"
foundPos% = Instr(4, source$, searchPattern$)
```

This example begins its search at the fourth character position in source$. Then foundPos% is assigned the value 6, which is where the next occurrence of the string pattern "is" is found in the word "is. "

If the desired string is not found within the source string, Instr returns 0.

Getting at Parts of a String

Although a string is a self-contained unit, you may wish to get only a portion of it (for example, to change the order of a name or address). Visual Basic has

1213

three functions that allow you to read only a portion of a string. These are the Left$, Mid$, and Right$ functions. As you may guess, the Left$ function returns a number of characters from the left end of a string; Mid$ returns characters from the middle of a string; and Right$ returns characters from the right end of a string. Both the Left$ and Right$ functions require only two arguments: the source string and the number of characters desired. The Mid$ function requires an extra argument that indicates the starting position of the first desired character.

```
fullName$ = "James Thomas Espinoza"
endOfFirstName% = Instr(fullName$, " ")              'Find the first space character
startOfMidName% = endOfFirstName% + 1                'Middle name starts at next character
endOfMidName% = Instr(startOfMidName%, fullName$, " ") 'Find the next space character

firstNameLen% = endOfFirstName% - 1                  'Figure lengths of names
midNameLen% = endOfMidName% - startOfMidName%
lastNameLen% = Len(fullName$) - endOfMidName%

firstName$ = Left$(fullName$, firstNameLen%)         'Extract the names
midName$ = Mid$(fullName$, startOfMidName%%, midNameLen%)
lastName$ = Right$(fullName$, lastNameLen%)
```

This example uses the Left$, Mid$, and Right$ functions to separate the first, middle, and last names from a string containing all three. The separate strings can now be rearranged as desired—for example, you could change a name from "First, Middle, Last" order to "Last, First, Middle" and then alphabetize by last name.

There is also a Mid$ statement. The difference between a statement and a function is that a function returns a value, while a statement does not. The statement form of Mid$ changes the specified portion of an existing string to some other set of characters. Because this is a statement rather than a function, the keyword Mid$ appears to the left of the assignment operator:

```
T$ = "This car is red"
Mid$(T$, 6, 3) = "bat"
```

This example changes the value of T$ to "This bat is red".

Working with the ASCII Character Set

You may sometimes find it useful to be able to determine the ASCII code of a character, or to translate an ASCII code into a character. The Asc and Chr functions handle these duties for you. The Asc function returns the ASCII code for the supplied character. Conversely, the Chr function returns a 1-byte string containing the character that is represented by the supplied ASCII code.

```
Function MakeSecretCode(phrase$) As String
    For i = 1 To Len(phrase$)
        temp = Asc(Mid$(phrase$, i, 1))
```

```
        Mid$(phrase$, i, 1) = Chr$(Abs(temp - 255))
    Next i
End Function
```

In the above example, the function will translate a given phrase into a secret code. It does this by translating each character in the phrase into a different character using a simple transformation, thus effectively scrambling the phrase to casual observers. (Cryptographers would probably laugh at the simplicity of the transformation we use, and could probably break the code in not much more time than it took to write it!)

Comparing Strings

Strings are compared using the same operators (such as =, <, or >) that are used with numbers. With strings, a statement such as:

```
If A$ = B$ Then Print "They are equal"
```

checks to see whether A$ and B$ are equal. But although two strings may seem equal to you, Visual Basic may not agree. For instance:

```
A$ = "Hello"
B$ = "Hello "
If A$ = B$ Then C% = 1 Else C% = 2
```

Even though the strings A$ and B$ are similar, Visual Basic will not consider them equal because B$ has a trailing space while A$ does not. To combat this, Visual Basic has two functions, LTrim$ and RTrim$, which return a copy of a string with extra spaces removed. The LTrim$ function will remove any spaces from the left side of the source string, while RTrim$ removes spaces from the right.

```
A$ = " Hello"
B$ = "Hello "
If LTrim$(A$) = RTrim$(B$) Then Print "Equal!"
```

This example trims the spaces off the beginning and ending of the two strings during the comparison. A$ and B$ are equal after removing the spaces.

Visual Basic 2.0 and 3.0 include the Trim$ function. This combines both LTrim$ and RTrim$, and strips spaces off of both the beginning and ending of a string. The following example shows how Trim$ is equivalent to nesting LTrim$ and RTrim$:

```
A$ = "  Hello  "
If Trim$(A$) = LTrim$(RTrim$(A$)) Then Print "Equal!"
```

Another situation that can interfere with the comparison of two strings is capitalization. If two strings that are otherwise identical are capitalized differently, Visual Basic will not view them as equal.

1215

```
A$ = "HELLO"
B$ = "Hello"
If A$ = B$ Then C% = 1 Else C% = 2
```

In this example A$ and B$ will not be equal because they are capitalized differently. You can change the case of letters within a string with the LCase$ and UCase$ functions. Both functions return a copy of the source string with the case of all letters changed. LCase$ converts the letters to lowercase, while UCase$ converts them to uppercase.

```
A$ = "HELLO"
B$ = "Hello"
If LCase$(A$) = LCase$(B$) Then C% = 1 Else C% = 2
```

In this example A$ and B$ will be equal.

In comparing strings the > (greater than) and < (less than) symbols ask whether one string is later or earlier in the alphabet than the other. For example:

```
If "Dog" > "Cat" Then Print "Greater than"
```

is true because "D" comes after "C" in the alphabet. Note however that comparison is made using the ASCII character sequence. The expression:

```
"Dog < "cat"
```

is actually true, because lowercase letters come after uppercase ones in the ASCII character sequence. Thus you should usually convert strings to all uppercase (with UCase$) or all lowercase (with LCase$) before making any comparisons.

Creating a Series of Characters

Suppose you want to create a string that is 20 bytes long and contains 20 asterisks. To do this, you could assign a string literal of 20 asterisks to a string variable:

```
Asters$ = "********************"
```

While this works, it is not very elegant. What if you need a 200-byte-long string? You certainly wouldn't want to sit and type 200 asterisks! Or suppose, as with printing checks, you need to be able to print a variable number of asterisks following the written amount on demand? A better alternative is to use the String$ function. This function allows you to create strings of repeated characters by supplying two arguments that indicate the number and type of character desired. For example:

```
Asters$ = String$(200, "*")
Fill$ = String$(Remain%, "*")
```

The first line of code assigns 200 asterisks to the variable Asters$, while the second statement uses the value of the variable Remain% to determine how many asterisks will be stored in Fill$.

The Space$ function works in the same manner as the String$ function, except that it always returns spaces.

```
Blanks$ = Space$(100)
```

This line of code assigns 100 spaces to the variable Blank$.

ARITHMETIC AND NUMBERS

One of the primary functions of computers is to relieve the user of the drudgery of having to manually perform mathematical calculations. Visual Basic does a good job of relieving the programmer of these tasks as well. Included in its array of commands are not only the standard math functions, such as addition and subtraction, but several more advanced functions for handling trigonometry, logarithms, and random number generation. Table A-5 lists Visual Basic's arithmetic commands.

Use This...		To Do This...
Abs	Function	Return the absolute value of a numeric expression
Atn	Function	Return the arctangent of a numeric expression
CInt	Function	Translate a numeric expression into integer format
CLng	Function	Translate a numeric expression into long integer format
CSin	Function	Translate a numeric expression into single-precision format
CDbl	Function	Translate a numeric expression into double-precision format
CCur	Function	Translate a numeric expression into currency format
Cos	Function	Return the cosine of a numeric expression
Exp	Function	Raise the natural logarithmic base (e) to the specified power
Fix	Function	Truncate the fractional part of a number and convert it to integer format
Hex$	Function	Return a string that represents a number in hexadecimal (base 16)
Int	Function	Return the largest integer that is less than or equal to a number
Log	Function	Return the natural logarithm of a numeric expression

(continued on next page)

(continued from previous page)

Use This...		To Do This...
OctS	Function	Return a string that represents a number in octal (base 8) notation
Randomize	Statement	Seed the random number generator
Rnd	Function	Return a randomly generated number between 0 and 1
Sgn	Function	Determine the sign of a numeric expression
Sin	Function	Return the sine of a numeric expression
Sqr	Function	Return the square root of a number
Tan	Function	Return the tangent of a number
Val	Function	Return the numeric value of a string

Table A-5 Functions and statements that affect numbers and numeric variables

Working with a Number's Sign

Visual Basic has two functions that work with the sign of a numeric value. First, the Abs function returns a numeric value that is the absolute value of the supplied argument. The absolute value of a number ignores the sign.

```
A% = 5
B% = 10
C% = Abs(A% - B%)
D% = Abs(B% - A%)
```

In this example, the difference between the values in A% and B% are computed by subtracting B% from A%. Because the Abs function is used, this difference will always be a positive value. In other words, both C% and D% will contain the same value: 5.

The second function that deals with the sign of a numeric value is the Sgn function. This function returns the sign of a number.

```
If Sgn(A%) = 1 Then B$ = "A% is a positive value"
If Sgn(A%) = 0 Then B$ = "A% is 0"
If Sgn(A%) = -1 Then B$ = "A% is a negative value"
```

In this example, the value of B$ is set depending on the sign of the variable A%.

1218

Hexadecimal and Octal Notation

By default, numeric values in Visual Basic are decimal (base 10) numbers. However, you can use hexadecimal (base 16) or octal (base 8) notation to specify values. These two forms of notations are sometimes used because they more readily represent the internal organization of computer memory. References to addresses in memory are therefore usually given in hexadecimal. Hexadecimal notation is indicated by preceding a hexadecimal number with the prefix "&H". Octal numbers are preceded by an "&O". For instance:

```
Num1% = &H100     'Assign hexadecimal 100 to Num1% (hexadecimal 100 = decimal 256)
Num2% = &O100     'Assign octal 100 to Num2% (octal 100 = decimal 64)
```

Visual Basic also provides a way to translate decimal numbers for display in hexadecimal or octal format with the Hex$ and Oct$ functions. Each of these functions requires a numeric argument and returns a string that is the value of the argument in the respective notation.

```
HexNum$ = Hex$(256)
OctNum$ = Oct$(64)
```

In this example, the string variable HexNum$ will have a value of "100" and OctNum$ will also have a value of "100."

Converting Between Numeric Types

Visual Basic has five different numeric formats: Integer, Long, Single, Double, and Currency. (See Appendix B for more information on how the different types of numbers can be declared.) Each format is stored in memory in a different manner. There are times in a program when variables of one type must be converted to another type before they can be accurately used. For instance, when a sub procedure is called with arguments, any values passed to the procedure must be of the same type as the sub procedure is expecting. If the value you need to pass is not in the correct format, it must be converted before it is passed. If you assign a value to a variable, Visual Basic will automatically handle any conversion needed. Therefore:

```
B# = 200.22
A! = B#
Call Test(A!)
```

In this example the value is automatically converted to single-precision format before it is assigned to the variable A!. However, if the only reason we are doing this assignment is to pass the value to a sub procedure or function, it adds an extra line of code to your program and it creates an extra variable that is otherwise not needed. A better solution is to use one of the numeric conversion functions: CInt, CLng, CSin, CDbl, or CCur. Each of these functions convert a numeric value from any other

type to the type indicated by the function. Using a conversion function eliminates the extra line of code and the extra variable used in the above example:

```
B# = 200.22
Call Test(CSin(B#))
```

Two more functions are used to convert numeric values. These are the Int and
Fix functions. Like the CInt function, these functions convert a numeric value
(such as a single- or double-precision decimal) to integer format. Both of these
differ slightly from the CInt function in how they treat the fractional portion of
the supplied argument. While CInt will round the fractional portion to the nearest whole number, Int returns the next lowest integer value and Fix simply truncates the fractional portion without doing any rounding, as shown in Table A-6.

Value	Int(Value)	Fix(Value)	Cint(Value)
2.7	2	2	3
2.2	2	2	2
2	2	2	2
-2	-2	-2	-2
-2.2	-3	-2	-2
-2.7	-3	-2	-3

Table A-6 Return values for Fix, Int, and CInt functions

Notice that for a negative number such as -2.7, Fix returns -2 because that is
the next lower integer, while Cint returns -3 because that is the closest integer.
The final conversion function converts a string into a numeric value. This is
done with the Val function. Val accepts one string argument, and if that argument contains a readable number, it will return that number's value. Val does
this by examining the supplied string from left to right. It begins its translation
as soon as it encounters a character that is not a space. The translation ends as
soon as it encounters a non-numeric character. For example:

```
A$ = " 1234 Street"
B$ = " ThisTown, Ca, 92122"
ValA! = Val(A$)
ValB! = Val(B$)
```

In this example, ValA! will be assigned a value of 1234. Because the Val function encounters non-numeric characters before any numeric characters in B$,
ValB! will be assigned a value of 0.

1220

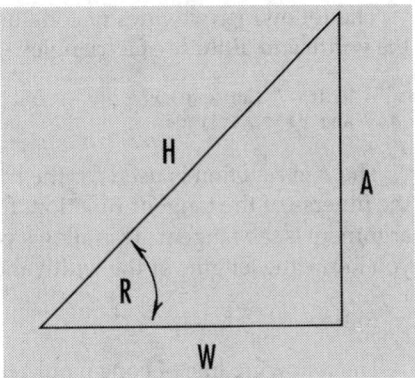

Figure A-1 A right triangle whose width is W, altitude is A, hypotenuse is H, and angle is R

Trigonometric Functions

Trigonometry is a branch of mathematics that involves the measurement of the sides and angles of triangles. Through the use of trigonometric functions, you can determine the length of all sides and the size of all angles in a triangle given limited information.

Trigonometry depends on two concrete facts about a right triangle. First, by definition, the size of one of the angles in a right triangle is always 90 degrees. Second, the sum of all the angles in a triangle is 180 degrees. Using this information, you can determine the measurements of all sides and angles of a right triangle if you know: (a) the length of two of the sides, or (b) the length of one side and the size of one angle (other than the right angle). Figure A-1 shows a right triangle with the parts labeled. We will refer to this triangle throughout the following discussion.

Visual Basic has four trigonometric functions: Tan, Atn , Sin, and Cos. In order to provide the highest accuracy possible, each of these functions treat angle measurements as radians. Therefore, if your angles are measured in units of degrees, you will need to convert your measurements. You can convert degrees to radians with the following function definition:

```
CONST PI = 3.14159265358979
Function Deg2Rad(Degrees)
    Deg2Rad = Degrees * (PI / 180)
End Function
```

The first of the four functions is Tan. This function is based on the trigonometric function tangent. The tangent of an angle is equal to the altitude (A) of the triangle divided by the width (W). Therefore:

```
Tan(R) = A / W   or   W = Tan(R) * A   or   A = W / Tan(R)
```

The following two lines of code use the Tan function to figure the length of the width and altitude of a triangle:

```
Altitude  = Width / Tan(Angle)
Width = Tan(Angle) * Altitude
```

The Atn function is used for the trigonometric arctangent function, which is the inverse of the tangent function. It returns the angle for which the supplied argument is the tangent. This allows you to determine the size of the angle when you know the lengths of the width and altitude:

```
Atn(A / W) = R
```

The following line of code would then determine the angle:

```
Angle = Atn(Altitude / Width)
```

The Sin function is based on the trigonometric sine function. The sine of an angle is equal to the altitude divided by the hypotenuse (the hypotenuse is the side that is opposite the right angle). Therefore:

```
Sin(R) = A / H    or    A = Sin(R) * H    or    H = A / Sin(R)
```

The following two lines of code use the Sin function to figure the length of the hypotenuse and altitude of a triangle:

```
Hypotenuse = Altitude / Sin(Angle)
Altitude = Sin(Angle) * Hypotenuse
```

Finally, the Cos function is used for the trigonometric cosine function. The cosine of an angle is equal to the width divided by the hypotenuse. Therefore:

```
Cos(R) = W / H    or    W = Cos(R) * H    or    H = W / Cos(R)
```

The following two lines of code use the Cos function to figure the length of the hypotenuse and width of a triangle:

```
Hypotenuse = Width / Cos(Angle)
Width = Cos(Angle) * Hypotenuse
```

Your programs can determine the measurements for all sides and angles of a right triangle with only limited information by using these trigonometric functions.

Logarithms

There is a way to reverse the effect of almost every mathematical operation. For example, you can reverse 3 * 4 = 12 as 12 / 4 = 3. This is a fairly simple operation when applied to addition or multiplication; however, when the arithmetic gets a bit more advanced, reversing the operations gets more complicated.

One of the areas where this applies is in exponentiation. You probably know that the formula $X = Y^Z$ means multiply Y by itself the number of times indicated by Z and assign the value to X. So far no problem. But what if you have values for X and Y, and need to determine the value of Z?

This is where logarithms come in. Simply put, a logarithm is the exponent required to raise a certain base number so that it matches the target number. In other words, the logarithm of X is Z, as long as the logarithmic base is agreed upon as being Y.

There are two common types of logarithms: common and natural. Common logarithms have a base of 10. Therefore, using the above equation, Y would equal 10, and Z (the logarithm of X) would be the value needed to raise Z so it matched X. Natural logarithms have a base of approximately 2.71828182845905 (referred to as e). Natural logarithms can be used to calculate the logarithm of a number when the desired base is e, and any desired base through the use of a simple formula.

Visual Basic provides two functions that deal with logarithms: Log and Exp. Both of these functions assume a logarithmic base of e (natural log). The Log function returns the natural logarithm of the supplied numeric value. Exp is the inverse of Log. It raises e to the specified power. The following two lines of code are functionally equivalent:

```
A! = Exp(5)
A! = 2.718282 ^ 5
```

You can use the Log function to return the logarithm of any base. This is done by dividing the natural log of the desired number by the natural log of the desired base. The following function performs this task:

```
Function AnyLog(LogBase, Number)
    AnyLog = Log(Number) / Log(LogBase)
End Function
```

You could also easily write a conversion to a fixed base, as the following example shows:

```
Function Log10(Number)
    Log10 = Log(Number) / Log(10)
End Function
```

This returns the familiar base-10 logarithm.

Random Numbers

In most languages, random number generation is usually left up to the programmer. In Visual Basic, however, this task is handled quite nicely by the Randomize statement and Rnd function.

In computers, random numbers are not truly random. A series of random numbers must start with a seed number on which to base its number generation. This is performed by the Randomize statement. By default, the Randomize statement uses the system timer (which holds the number of seconds elapsed since midnight) as the seed. However, you can optionally specify any other number in the range -32768 to 32767. It's usually best to use the default, as this creates the closest thing to truly random numbers. If you use a specific number as a seed, the series of random numbers generated will always be the same. This may be suitable for some statistical procedures or for debugging, but would not make for good games.

Randomize must be used before the Rnd function is used. Although it can be used several times throughout a program, it is best if it is used only once. The Randomize statement should be placed in the Load event of the main form or module of a program.

The Rnd function returns random numbers (based on the seed provided by the Randomize statement) in a range between 0 and 1. It is often more convenient to return random numbers in some other specified range. The following function assumes that the Randomize statement has already been executed:

```
Function Random(LoVal!, HiVal!)
     Range! = 1 + (HiVal! - LoVal!)
     Random = (Rnd * Range!) + LoVal!
End Function
```

In the above example, the programmer-defined function Random generates a random number that falls into the range defined by the arguments LoVal! and HiVal! You could also use the Int function to produce random integers:

```
Function RandomInt(LoVal%, HiVal%)
     Range% = 1 + (HiVal% - LoVal%)
     RandomInt = Int(Rnd * Range%) + LoVal%
End Function
```

DATE AND TIME

In Visual Basic the date and time may be expressed with a date variant that can represent both the date and time of day of a specified moment. Visual Basic 1.0 called a more limited version of this date variant a *date variant*. In this date variant, the digits to the left of the decimal point represent the total days elapsed since December 30, 1899. The supplied date variant represents a date in the range between January 1, 100 (-657434) and December 31, 9999 (2958465). For example, the date variant 34931 represents that many days elapsed since December 30, 1899, which works out to August 20, 1995. Note that this range is much larger than the range of dates allowed in Visual Basic 1.0.

The digits to the right of the decimal point represent the total seconds elapsed since 12:00 midnight of the current day, expressed as a decimal fraction of a day. Thus in the date variant 34931.064583333, the time portion corresponds to approximately 1:33 AM.

Visual Basic 2.0 introduced the Variant variable type. This type of variable can store any variable type, be it a string or one of the numeric types. The date variant is a Variant of type 7. It is stored internally by Visual Basic as a double-precision number, much as Visual Basic 1.0 stored its date variants. Most of the date and time functions now work with date variants, rather than strings and serial numbers. The great advantage to using date variants is that Visual Basic attempts to automatically convert the arguments and results of the functions to whatever format is appropriate. This makes your code simpler to write, as you don't have to explicitly convert the variable types.

For instance, the Date statement accepts a date variant, and the Date$ statement only accepts a string of the proper format. Both statements do the same thing: change your computer's system date. The Date$ statement accepts only dates expressed as "08-20-94" or "08/24/1994" whereas the Date statement accepts all the formats accepted by the Date$ statement plus expressions like "August 20, 1994" or "20-Aug-94 12:32 am".

Along with the date variant, Visual Basic has functions for retrieving and setting the current system date and time using a string format.

Table A–7 lists Visual Basic date- and time-handling functions.

Use This...		To Do This...
Date$	Function	Return a formatted string representing the current system date
Date$	Statement	Set the current system date
DateSerial	Function	Return a date variant based on supplied day, month, and year values
DateValue	Function	Translate a formatted date string into a date variant
Day	Function	Return the day of the month based on a date variant (1–31)
Format$	Function	Return a formatted date or time string based on a supplied date variant
Hour	Function	Return the hour of the day based on a date variant (0–23)
Minute	Function	Return the minute of the hour based on a date variant (0–59)
Month	Function	Return the month of the year based on a date variant (1–12)

(continued on next page)

(continued from previous page)

Use This...		To Do This...
Now	Function	Return a date variant representing the current system date and time
Second	Function	Return the second of the minute based on a date variant (0–59)
Time$	Function	Return a formatted string representing the current system time
Time$	Statement	Set the current system time
Timer	Function	Return the number of seconds that have elapsed since midnight
TimeSerial	Function	Return a date variant based on the supplied hour, minute, and second
TimeValue	Function	Return a date variant based on a formatted time string
WeekDay	Function	Return the day of the week based on a date variant (1–7)
Year	Function	Return the year based on a date variant (100–9999)

Table A-7 Functions and statements that deal with date and time

Getting the Current Date and Time

The simplest form of date and time handling come from the Date$ and Time$ functions. These functions return the current system date and time in a formatted string. The following lines of code read the current system date and time and assign those values to the Caption property of two labels:

```
Label1.Caption = Date$
Label2.Caption = Time$
```

While the Date$ and Time$ functions return formatted strings, the Now function returns a date variant number that represents the current date and time. As described above, this variant is a double-precision number that holds the date on the left of its decimal point and the time on the right. The following example uses the Now function to retrieve the current system date and time:

```
A# = Now
```

Setting the System Date and Time

Your program can also set the system date and time with the Date$ and Time$ statements. Both of these statements take a formatted string as an argument:

```
Time$ = "12:20:30"          'Set the system time to 12:20:30
Date$ = "01-01-1995"        'Set the system date to Jan 1, 1995
```

Translating Between Formatted Strings and Date Variants

Although the date variant is an efficient method for storing and working with dates and times, the number itself holds little meaning to an end user. We need a way to translate back and forth between the date variant and a readable string.

Translating from a formatted date or time string to the corresponding date variant requires the use of the DateValue and TimeValue functions. Both of these functions take a formatted string as an argument and return a date variant that represents it. Each of these functions returns only the portion of the date variant that pertains to their function. In other words, the value returned by the DateValue function does not have the digits to the right of the decimal that represent time. Conversely, the TimeValue function returns a date variant with no digits to the left of the decimal. The following example is a programmer-defined function that uses the DateValue and TimeValue functions to return a combined date variant.

```
Function DateTimeValue (InDate$, InTime$) As Double
    DateTimeValue# = DateValue(InDate$) + TimeValue(InTime$)
End Function
```

Translating a date variant into a readable string involves the use of the Format$ function. This function requires two arguments: the date variant and an edit pattern. Format$ is a very powerful function that provides several options for formatting the date and time, including the ability to print a full or abbreviated name of the month or day. The examples below use the Format$ function to assign formatted date and time strings to the Caption properties of two label controls:

```
Serial# = Now                                  'Get current system date
Label1.Caption = Format$(Serial#, "mmmm dd, yyyy")   'e.g.; January 24, 1995
Label2.Caption = Format$(Serial#, "hh:mm")     'Display hours and minutes, no seconds
```

See Appendix B, Visual Basic Language Reference, for a detailed explanation of the edit pattern arguments.

Creating a Date Variant from Separate Parts

Sometimes you have all the separate parts of a date or time in numeric format and need to combine these parts into a date variant. For example, imagine your program has three variables that all hold a different piece of date information: YearVal%, MonthVal%, and DayVal%. There may be a need in your program for combining these values into one date variant. This can be done with the DateSerial function. DateSerial requires three integer arguments that specify the year, month, and day and return a date variant that represents those values. The TimeSerial function performs a similar task for date variants using hours, minutes, and seconds.

Extracting Information from a Date Variant

At other times it may be necessary to break a date variant into its component parts—days, month, years, hours, minutes, and seconds. When working with a date variant, you can use the Day (day of month), WeekDay (day of week), Month (month of year), and Year functions. To work with time, Visual Basic includes the Hour, Minute, and Second functions. Each of these functions takes a date variant as an argument and returns a specific piece of data about the date/time represented by the date variant.

The following programmer-defined function uses the Day and WeekDay functions to return a number that corresponds to the week of the month represented by a date variant:

```
Function WeekOfMonth (Serial#) As Integer
    WorkMonth% = Month(Serial#)
    WorkYear% = Year(Serial#)                       'working month and year
    WorkSerial# = DateSerial(WorkYear%, WorkMonth%, 0)   'date variant of first day of month
    FirstWeekDay% = Weekday(FirstDayOfMonth#)       'day the fist day of the month occurs?
    DayOfMonth% = Day(Serial#) + FirstWeekDay%      'how many days into the month?
    Week% = (DayOfMonth% - 1) \ 7                    '0 to 4 depending on DayOfMonth%
    WeekOfMonth = Week% + 1                          'WeekOfMonth = 1 to 5
End Function
```

Performing Math with Dates and Times

The biggest advantage of working with date variants is that they allow you to easily perform math functions on dates and times. This is very useful for applications such as accounting programs that need to figure the number of days between periods. The following example determines the number of days until Christmas:

```
XMasYear% = Year(Now)                    'Get this year
XMasDate# = DateSerial(XMasYear%, 12, 25)   'Get date variant for this year's XMas
If Now > XMasDate# Then                   'Has XMas already passed this year?
```

```
      XMasYear% = XMasYear% + 1                'Next XMas is next year
      XMasDate# = DateSerial(XMasYear%, 12, 25) 'Get date variant for next year's XMas
End If
DaysUntilXMas# = XMasDate# - Now
```

PROCESS CONTROL

One of the reasons computers are more than just advanced calculators is that they have the ability to control the order and flow of the execution of their operations. This control over execution is called process control. Process control can be broken down into three main elements: branching, iteration, and conditional execution.

Branching is the most basic of the process control elements. It involves simply jumping from one area of code to another. In Visual Basic there are two types of branching. The first of the two merely jumps to another part of your program. It does nothing to help you return to your original starting point. The second type saves its place in the program's code before branching. This allows the program to return to where it came from once its task is finished.

Iteration involves the repetition of program instructions. There will be many times in your programs when you will wish to execute a set of instructions a number of times, or continually while (or until) a certain condition exists. Visual Basic provides three techniques for performing iteration.

Conditional execution allows your programs to execute a set of instructions only if a certain condition is true. This gives your programs the ability to make decisions based on the values of data.

Table A-8 lists the statements that perform process control tasks.

Use This...		To Do This...
Do...Loop	Statements	Repeat a group of instructions until or while a condition is True
Exit...	Statement	Exit from a specific block of code
For...Next	Statements	Repeat a group of instructions a specified number of times
Gosub...Return	Statements	Branch to a subroutine then return
Goto	Statement	Branch without return to a portion of code
If...Then...Else...	(Single-line If)	Perform a simple conditional execution of code
If...Then...ElseIf...	(Multiple-line If)	Perform a complex conditional execution of code
On...Gosub	Statements	Branch based on a supplied numeric value, then return

(continued on next page)

(continued from previous page)

Use This...		To Do This...
On...Goto	Statements	Branch based on a supplied numeric value without return
Select Case...	Statements	Perform conditional execution based on the value of one expression
Stop	Statement	Halt execution for debugging
While...Wend	Statements	Repeat a group of instructions while a condition is True

Table A-8 Statements that perform process control

Branching

Visual Basic has two statements that perform branching: Goto and Gosub. The Goto statement branches to the specified label. It does not save its place before branching, so once it has branched, there can be no going back. The Goto statement is generally considered an unstructured command, and its use generally obscures the clarity of your programming. You should use structured programming constructs (like sub procedures, user-defined functions, and loops) rather than resort to the Goto statement.

The Gosub statement also branches to a specified label, but it saves its place before doing so. Your program can then return to its original position in the code by executing a Return statement. You will probably never need to use a Gosub statement in your Visual Basic programs. Sub procedures and user-defined functions offer a more powerful and elegant alternative; Gosub has been retained only for backward compatibility with older BASIC programs.

Both Goto and Gosub must specify a label that exists in the same procedure as the branching instruction. A label is a unique name that ends with a colon. For example:

```
Goto Error:
```

jumps execution to the part of the program that begins with the label Error:
(Visual Basic also allows you to use line numbers instead of labels. Line numbers are a cumbersome feature of early versions of BASIC, and are seldom used today.)

Loops

There are three styles of loop instructions you can use to perform iteration in Visual Basic. These are For...Next, Do...Loop, and While...Wend. Each kind of loop has its own features and is useful in particular circumstances.

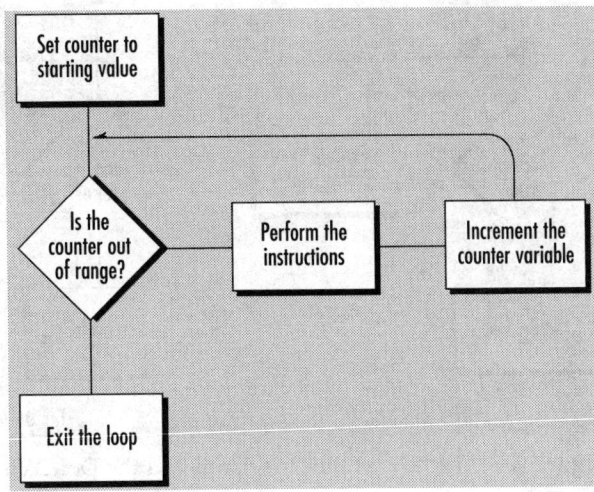

Figure A-2 The flow of a For...Next loop

The For...Next Loop

For...Next loop performs a block of instructions for a set number of times. You specify as arguments to the For statement a starting value, an ending value, and a numeric variable name that will be used as a counter. When the For statement is first encountered, the counter variable is initialized to the starting value. The block of code is then executed until the counter variable exceeds the ending value. Figure A-2 shows the flow of a For...Next loop. The following statements count from 1 to the value of Num%, summing the numbers in between:

```
Total = 0
For N% = 1 To Num%
    Total = Total + N%
Next N%
```

Note that you can specify that the counter be incremented by a number other than 1, by using the Step keyword. You can decrement a counter by using a negative value as the Step value. The following loop counts downward from the value of Num% to 1 by 3's.

```
For N% = Num% To 1 Step -3
```

Varieties of the Do...Loop Structure

The Do...Loop is the most versatile and hence the most useful loop structure in Visual Basic. The statements that comprise a Do...Loop allow you to repeat a block of code as long as a certain condition (which is defined by you) exists, or until a certain condition becomes True. It also lets you specify whether to check the condition at the top or bottom of the loop. This gives you four unique styles of loops: Do While, Do Until, Loop While, and Loop Until.

1231

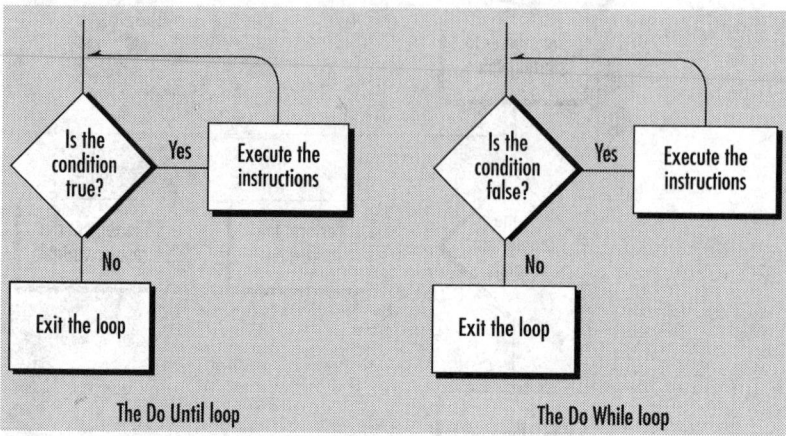

Figure A-3 The flow of the Do...Until and the Do...While loops

Both the Do Until and Do While loops check the condition at the top of the loop. This means that if the exit condition is met before the loop is entered, the instructions within the Do...Loop will not execute. The following are examples of the Do While and Do Until loops:

```
Open "TEST.DAT" For Input As #1
Do Until EOF(1)
     Line Input #1, A$
Loop

Open "TEST.DAT" For Input As #1
Do While Not EOF(1)
     Line Input #1, A$
Loop
```

These two loops are actually equivalent: Both make sure that the end of the file has not been reached before attempting to input any data. Since reading beyond the end of a file generates an error, it is important that checking be done at the top of the loop. Figure A-3 shows the flow of processing in the Loop Until and Loop While loops. Notice that the only difference is that the Loop Until loop checks whether the condition is False, and the Loop While loop checks whether the condition is True.

The Loop Until and Loop While loops check the exit condition at the end of the loop so the statements within the loop are always executed at least once. The following are examples of these styles of loops:

```
Do                                            'This is a Loop Until loop
     Person$ = InputBox$("Please enter your name")   'code within loop will repeat until
     Person$ = Trim$(Person$)                  'user enters something
Loop Until Person$ > ""

Do                                            'This is a Loop While loop
     Person$ = InputBox$("Please enter your name")   'code within loop will repeat as long
     Person$ = Trim$(Person$)                  'as the variable Person$ is empty
Loop While Person$ = ""
```

1232

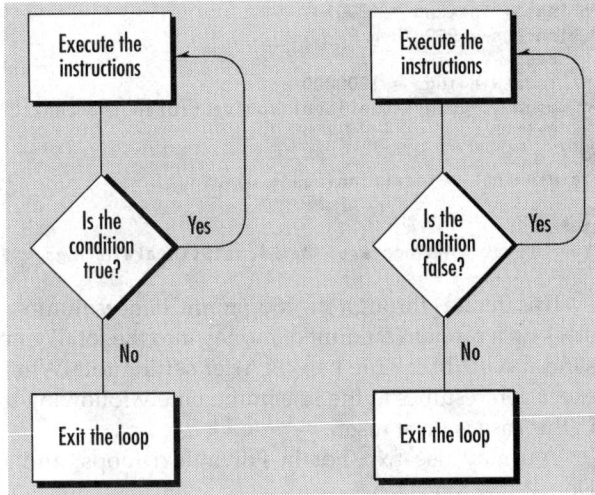

Figure A-4 The flow of the Loop Until and the
Loop While loops

The flow of these loops is illustrated in Figure A-4. Notice that here, too, the
only difference between the loops is that Loop Until checks whether the condition is False, while the Loop While loop checks whether it is True. In both cases,
the code executes once before the check is made, since at least one iteration is
needed for the user to enter the data.

The While...Wend Loop

The final of the three types of loops is the While...Wend loop. This loop structure is left over from older BASIC languages. It performs the same function in
the same manner as the Do While loop discussed above:

```
Open "TEST.DAT" For Input As #1
While Not EOF(1)
     Line Input #1, A$
Wend
```

Exiting Loops

You may have a situation that calls for exiting a loop prematurely. For example,
this loop counts up the winnings in a game. The user has a slight chance of
"breaking the bank," which requires separate handling:

```
msg$ = "Congratulations, you've won!"
For i = 1 to numChances
```

(continued on next page)

(continued from previous page)

```
        winnings = Int(Rnd * 1000)
        If winnings = 999 Then
            Beep
            totalWinnings = 1000000
            msg$ = "Congratulations! You've broken the bank!"
            Exit For
        End If
        totalWinnings = totalWinnings + winnings
Next i
Print msg$
Print "Your total winnings are: "; Format$(totalWinnings, "$###,###,###")
```

This iterates through the loop numChances number of times. It normally just adds up a random amount of money into the totalWinnings. One time in a thousand it will "break the bank." After setting totalWinnings to a million dollars, execution resumes at the line immediately following the Next statement, which in this case is Print msg$.

You may use Exit For in For...Next loops, and Exit Do in Do...Loop or Do...While loops.

Conditional Execution

Conditional execution defines a set of instructions that will only execute if a certain condition (defined by you) is True. In other words, conditional execution allows your program to make decisions and perform specific tasks based on the outcome of these decisions.

The simplest of Visual Basic's decision making statements is the single-line If statement. This statement simply says, If the condition is True, do a task. Optionally, you can also specify a second task for the If statement to perform when the condition is False: If the condition is True, do a task; otherwise do a different task. The following is an example of a single-line If statement:

```
If A = B Then C = True Else C = False
```

The single-line If statement is limited to one line of instructions. In other words, if you need to execute a whole block of instructions based on the outcome of a condition, this statement will not work well. When this is the case, it is better to use a block If statement. This allows you to execute an entire block of code based on the outcome of the If:

```
If GarmentColor = Green Then
    GreenShirts = GreenShirts + 1
    Cost = Cost + 1
Else
    RedShirts = RedShirts + 1
    Cost = Cost + 2
End If
```

The multiple-line If statement lets you group seemingly unrelated tests in the same If statement:

```
If GarmentColor = Green Then
    GreenShirts = GreenShirts + 1
    Cost = Cost + 1
ElseIf GarmentSize = Large Then
    LargeShirts = LargeShirts + 1
End If
```

In this example, the variable GarmentColor is tested to see if it equals the value in Green. If it does, the block of code under the test executes. If it does not, the GarmentSize variable is tested.

If you need to test a single variable for several different values, you can use the Select Case structure. The Select Case structure makes many tests on the same value. Structured programmers prefer to use Select Case rather than a multiple-line If because they feel it is more readable. The following examples show a multiple-line If statement and the equivalent Select Case statement:

```
If ThisColor = Blue Then
    CtrBlue = CtrBlue + 1
ElseIf ThisColor = Red OR ThisColor = Green Then
    CtrNotBlue = CtrNotBlue + 1
Else
    CtrOther = CtrOther + 1
End If

Select Case ThisColor
    Case Blue
        CtrBlue = CtrBlue + 1
    Case Red, Green
        CtrNotBlue% CtrNotBlue% + 1
    Case Else
        CtrOther = CtrOther + 1
End Select
```

Both of the above examples are functionally equivalent. However, the Select Case is clearer and easier to understand.

The final two conditional statements in Visual Basic are the On Goto and On Gosub statements. These statements put a twist on the branching commands Goto and Gosub that we discussed earlier. Instead of specifying one label as the target of the branch operation, you supply these statements with a numeric value and a list of labels. Depending on the value supplied, the program will branch to one of the listed labels:

```
On winner Gosub First, Second, Third
    :
    :
First:
    B$ = "Your horse won!"
    Prize = 1000 * wager
Return

Second:
    B$ = "Your horse placed!"
    Prize = 100 * wager
Return
```

(continued on next page)

(continued from previous page)

```
Third:
    B$ = "Your horse showed!"
    Prize = 10 * wager
Return
```

Note that the On Gosub and On Goto statements automatically assign sequential integers to the specified variable. That is, in the above example, when winner is 1, the instructions at the label First: are executed; when winner is 2, the instructions at Second: are executed; and so on. On Goto works in the same way, except that there is no return from the branch.

These unstructured conditional statements are relics of the past; you should substitute the clearer, more elegantly structured statements instead. The above example done as a Select…Case statement looks like this:

```
Select Case winner
    Case 1
        B$ = "Your horse won!"
        Prize = 1000 * wager
    Case 2
        B$ = "Your horse placed!"
        Prize = 100 * wager
    Case 3
        B$ = "Your horse showed!"
        Prize = 10 * wager
End Select
```

This structure is both clearer and shorter than the unstructured On…Gosub statements.

PROGRAMMER-DEFINED FUNCTIONS AND PROCEDURES

One of the main elements of structured programming involves defining and using self-contained areas of a program called *procedures*. Most often, these procedures perform a single task. Such a procedure can be called any number of times from within a program to perform that task. Coding in this manner provides three distinct advantages. First, once the procedure is coded and debugged, it can be used any number of times without having to recode it. Second, using separate procedures makes a program modular, organizing the code to match the functional structure of the program. This makes it easier to track down and eliminate any logic errors in an application. Finally, because these procedures are entirely self-contained, any variables declared within a procedure become local variables that cannot be changed from outside the procedure. This eliminates any logic errors that might occur if the programmer inadvertently uses the same variable name for two different purposes in different areas of a program.

For many years the BASIC languages did not have the ability to define or use procedures. That is no longer the case. In fact, all of the events that are linked to objects in Visual Basic are procedures. Visual Basic, along with some other modern BASIC languages, includes two types of procedures: functions and sub procedures. Both functions and sub procedures are used to perform specific tasks defined by the programmer. Functions have an added feature in that along with performing their task, they can return a value.

Table A-9 lists the statements used to define and use programmer-defined functions and sub procedures.

Use This...		To Do This...
Call	Statement	Execute a programmer-defined or DLL sub procedure
Declare	Statement	Inform Visual Basic of external DLL procedures
Exit	Statement	Exit a programmer-defined sub procedure or function
Function...End Function	Statements	Define a programmer-defined function
Sub...End Sub	Statements	Define a sub procedure

Table A-9 Statements that control functions and procedures

Scope of Functions and Sub Procedures

Much like variables, functions and sub procedures have a scope. The scope of a function or sub procedure defines that procedure's accessibility to other portions of your program. Functions and sub procedures can be placed in the code area of a form, or inside a module. Any functions or sub procedures that are defined in the code area of a form are local to that form, and cannot be called from another form. Procedures defined in a module are global throughout the application. This means they can be called from any form or module.

Defining and Using Programmer-Defined Sub Procedures

Before a sub procedure can be used, you must define it. You do this with the Sub and End Sub statements. These statements surround the code inside the sub procedure and define the beginning and end of the procedure. Create a sub procedure by typing the Sub keyword followed by the name of the procedure:

```
Sub procedureName
```

Visual Basic will automatically create a new procedure for you, and will terminate the procedure block with the End Sub statement. You can define procedures so that they accept arguments that provide information to act on. The following is an example of a sub procedure that accepts a string argument:

```
Sub printMessage(msg$)
    Cls
    Print msg$
End Sub
```

In this example we have defined a sub procedure that accepts a string. It clears the form and prints the string, then exits. Once the procedure has been designed, it can then be executed by calling it as follows:

```
Call printMessage("Print this!")
```

Alternatively, you can omit the Call keyword and simply have

```
printMessage "Print this!"
```

When you omit the word Call you must also omit the parentheses around the procedure arguments.

Defining and Using Programmer-Defined Functions

As stated above, a function is very similar to a sub procedure. The big difference is that a function returns a value, while a sub procedure does not. Functions are defined in a manner similar to sub procedures. Instead of using Sub and End Sub statements, however, functions are defined with Function and End Function statements. Create a function in the same way as a sub procedure: Simply type in the keyword Function followed by the function name. Visual Basic creates a new function block for you, and ends the block with the End Function statement.

An extra step is also involved in defining a function. Because functions return a value, you need to specify what type of value (single-precision, integer, string, and so on) the function is to return. You also need to tell the function exactly what value to return before exiting. This example shows a function definition:

```
Function BTrim$ (T$)
    T$ = Trim$(T$)
    For i = 1 To Len(T$)
        If Asc(Mid$(T$, i, 1)) = 0 Then
            T$ = Left$(T$, i) & Mid$(T$, i + 1)
        End If
    Next i
    BTrim$ = T$
End Function
```

In this example, we've defined a function that accepts one string argument. Because the function name (BTrim$) ends in a type declaration character ($), we know that it will return a string value. The purpose of this function is to return a copy of its passed argument with both leading and following spaces removed, and without any embedded nulls (ASCII character 0). Notice that the function's code ends with the statement BTrim$ = T$. Assigning a value to the function name (BTrim$) gives the function its return value.

You could also have declared it like this:

```
Function BTrim (T$) As String
```

You would then call the function in your code using just BTrim instead of BTrim$ as in the first example.

THE OPERATING ENVIRONMENT

Regardless of the purpose of the application, chances are it will need to interact with the operating environment in some manner. The operating environment on a computer is the main interface between an application and the hardware present on the system. Because of the existence of the operating environment, your applications will rarely need intimate information about a hardware device in order to use it. Instead, your programs make general requests of the operating environment, and it handles the low-level details of accessing the hardware involved.

Visual Basic provides several useful commands for accessing portions of the operating environment. These commands include the ability to navigate through the DOS file system, to load and execute other applications, and to read and react to special commands and environment variables.

Table A-10 lists the Visual Basic commands that deal with the operating environment.

Use This...		To Do This...
AppActivate	Statement	Give the focus to a running Windows application
Beep	Statement	Sound a tone on the system speaker
ChDir	Statement	Change the current working directory
ChDrive	Statement	Change the default working drive
Command$	Function	Retrieve command-line parameters used to launch the program
CurDir$	Function	Retrieve the current working directory
Dir$	Function	Retrieve a directory entry that matches a specified file name pattern

(continued on next page)

(continued from previous page)

Use This...		To Do This...
Environ$	Function	Retrieve entries from DOS's environment variable table
Kill	Statement	Remove a file from the disk
MkDir	Statement	Create a subdirectory
Name	Statement	Rename a file on the disk
RmDir	Statement	Remove a subdirectory
Shell	Function	Initiate execution of a program

Table A-10 Functions and statements that deal with the operating environment

The DOS File System: Drives, Directories, and Files

In Chapter 19 we discussed how you can use the Visual Basic Drive, Directory, and File list boxes to visually navigate the DOS file system. The Visual Basic language also includes several commands for performing similar tasks from within your program without using those objects. You can use the ChDrive and ChDir statements to change the default drive and working subdirectory. You can also use the CurDir$ function to determine the current default drive and directory.

Visual Basic also has three commands that work with DOS files. The first and most powerful of the three is the Dir$ function. This function returns file names in the current default directory that match a specified pattern, much in the way that the DIR command in DOS does. The following example reads all file names with an extension of "DAT" into a list box:

```
A$ = Dir$("*.DAT")
Do Until Len(A$) = 0          'When A$ is null, all file names have been read
    List1.AddItem A$          'Add the file name to the list box
    A$ = Dir$
Loop
```

The other two commands are the Kill and Name statements. The Kill statement erases files from a disk in a way similar to the DEL command in DOS. The Name statement changes the name of a file (similar to the REN command in DOS, although it is more powerful: Renaming a file with a different directory actually moves the file to that directory).

Command-Line Parameters and Environment Variables

The command line is the text used to launch an application from the Windows environment. It always includes the path and name of the program's executable file. This command line can also include one or more parameters that, when read by the application, direct it to behave in a certain manner on startup. The syntax and meaning of these parameters, sometimes called switches, are defined by the application that reacts to them. You can design your programs to react to command-line switches by reading the string returned by the Command$ function. This function returns all text that appears on the command line following the program's executable file name. You would normally specify this in the Program Manager's File Run dialog box, or in the Command Line item in the Program Item Properties dialog box.

One common use for the Command$ function is to specify the name of a file to automatically load when the program starts up. The following example reads the string returned by the Command$ function, and if a valid file name is specified, calls a procedure to load it:

```
fName$ = Command$                               'Get the command line parameter
If Len(fName$) > 0 Then fName$ = Dir$(fName$)   'If file specified, check to see if exists
If Len(fName$) > 0 Then Call LoadFile(fName$)   'If fName$ is not null, it exists. Load it.
```

Another useful function for obtaining information from the system is the Environ$ function. DOS contains an internal table that holds miscellaneous strings. These strings are called environment variables, and most often hold information regarding the setup of the particular system your program is running on.

Environment variables follow a specific format. The name of the environment variable precedes an equal sign, which is then followed by the value of the variable, as in:

```
variable_name=variable_value
```

For example, this AUTOEXEC.BAT file sets the *TEMP* environment variable to the TEMPDIR subdirectory:

```
@echo off
prompt $p$g
path c:\windows;c:\dos;c:\winword;c:\bat;c:\utils
loadhigh doskey
set temp=c:\tempdir                             << (this line sets environment variable)
cls
```

The Visual Basic Environ$ function lets your programs read these variables in one of two possible ways. First, you can read a variable by specifying its name in the Environ$ function:

```
A$ = Environ$("TEMP")
```

1241

This will copy the value of the *TEMP* variable to the string variable A$. If this example line were run after the above-mentioned AUTOEXEC.BAT file, A$ would contain the string variable "C:\TEMPDIR". (If this variable does not exist, A$ will be given a null value.) Notice that DOS returns environment variables as all uppercase, even if they were typed in as lowercase. The second method for retrieving environment variables involves using a number to indicate the position of the desired variable in the environment table. When this method is used, the variable name as well as its value is returned. This example reads all of a system's environment variables into a list box:

```
Ctr = 1                              'Initialize counter variable
Do
    List1.AddItem Environ$(Ctr)      'Add environment variable name and value into list box
    Ctr = Ctr + 1                    'Point to next environment variable
Loop Until Len(Environ$(Ctr)) = 0    'When Environ$ returns null, all variables have been read
```

Environment variables are set with the DOS SET command. Each computer system will probably have a different set of environment variables with different values. As a matter of fact, it's a fair bet that no two computers have exactly the same group of environment variable settings. However, there are a few environment variables that can be found on most computers. One of these variables is the "*PATH*" variable. This variable lists all drives and directories that should be searched when trying to locate an executable file. Another is the "*COMSPEC*" variable. This variable lists the drive and path in which the DOS command-line processor (COMMAND.COM) can be found. Finally, when Windows starts, it adds its own variable called "*windir*". Unlike all other environment variable names, which are in uppercase letters, this entry is in lowercase. The "*windir*" variable contains the path to the Windows directory.

Executing Other Programs

The Shell function executes other programs. Specify the path and file name of the executable file you wish to run. This file can be a DOS command (such as CHKDSK) or some other program on the disk. You can also specify the status of the program when it begins to control whether the new program will run in windowed or full screen mode, and whether it will immediately receive the focus. Shell automatically searches the DOS path for the executable file. If the file is found and it executes without error, the Shell function will return the Windows task ID of the executing program.

You can also use the AppActivate statement to direct Windows to give the focus to a specific application. This application must already be running before the AppActivate statement executes. (The concept of the application focus is covered in detail in Chapter 21, Application Focus.)

WORKING WITH DATA FILES

Visual Basic puts a complete set of file-manipulation commands at your disposal. In addition to the relational file elements discussed in detail in Chapter 27, Data Access, Visual Basic offers a number of statements and functions for working with nonrelational disk files.

Table A-11 lists the file-related functions and statements in Visual Basic that are not specific to using the Access database engine.

Use This...		To Do This...
Close	Statement	Close an open file
EOF	Function	Determine if the end of a file has been reached
FileAttr	Function	Retrieve system information about an open file
FreeFile	Function	Retrieve an unused file number
Get	Statement	Read data from a binary or random access file
Input	Statement	Read data from a sequential access input file
InputS	Function	Read a specified number of bytes from a file
Line Input	Function	Read one line of data from a sequential access input file
Loc	Function	Retrieve the current location of the file pointer in a file
Lock...UnLock	Statements	Restrict multiple-user access to a portion of a file
LOF	Function	Retrieve the length (in bytes) of an open file
LSet	Statement	Copy data to a record variable
Open	Function	Initiate processing of a file
Print #	Statement	Write undelimited data to a sequential access output file
Put	Statement	Write data to a binary or random access file
Reset	Statement	Close all open files

(continued on next page)

(continued from previous page)

Use This...		To Do This...
Seek	Function	Return the actual position of the file pointer
Seek	Statement	Move the file pointer to a specified position in a file
Type...End Type	Statements	Define a record variable for random access files
Width	Statement	Define the width of a line in a sequential access output file
Write	Statement	Write delimited data to a sequential access output file

Table A-11 Functions and statements for file operations

Opening a File

The Open statement initiates processing on a file. A file must be opened before you can do anything else with it. Using this statement tells Visual Basic the path and name of the file you wish to open, how you wish to process the file, and what number you wish to use in order to refer to this file in subsequent operations. This is an example of a typical open statement:

```
Open "TEST.DAT" For Random As #1 Len = 128
```

This example opens the file TEST.DAT, and specifies that is will be processed in random input/output mode. This file is opened as file number 1. The file number is how this particular file will be referenced by other file operations as long as it is open. No two open files can use the same file number simultaneously. If you wish, you can let Visual Basic keep track of which file numbers are currently in use, and which are available with the FreeFile function. Use the FreeFile function to assign the next available unused file number to a variable. Then you use that variable to reference the file in all subsequent file operations:

```
Dim TestFile As Integer    'Place in the Global module so Testfile can be accessed
                           'from anywhere in the program
  :
  :
TestFile = FreeFile        'Get next available unused file number
Open "TEST.DAT" For Random As #TestFile Len = 128      'Open the file
```

Sequential Access Files

Sequential files are processed from beginning to end in a line-by-line manner. When opened, the file pointer is placed at the beginning of the file (except when opened for Append, which places the pointer at the end of the file). Each read or write moves the file pointer forward. Under normal circumstances the file pointer never goes back; it only moves forward.

Sequential files can be opened in one of three modes: Output, Append, or Input. When you open a sequential output file, Visual Basic searches the specified directory. If the file name you specified in the Open statement does not exist, it will be created. If it does exist, the current file is erased, and a new one is created. You can then write data to the file with the Print # and Write # statements. Both of these statements write ASCII characters to the file. The difference between the two is that the Print # statement does not automatically format the data (although you could add in delimiters yourself), while the Write # statement automatically adds comma delimiters between each value written to the file.

When you open a sequential file for appending, Visual Basic searches the specified directory for the specified file name. If the file is not found, an error occurs. However, if the file is found, the file pointer is placed at the end of the file. From that point on, the file is treated as if it were a sequential output file, and the data you write is added to the file.

When you open a sequential file for input, Visual Basic searches the specified directory for the specified file name. If the file is not found, an error occurs. If the file is found, you may use the Input #, Input$, and Line Input # statements to read data from the file. You must be careful not to read past the end of the file, as this causes an error. You can prevent this by using the EOF function to test for the end of the file. The following example reads a sequential file a line at a time until the end is reached:

```
Open "TEST.DAT" For Input As #TestFile
Do Until EOF(TestFile)
      Line Input #TestFile, A$
Loop
```

Random Access Files

Random access files are both input and output files. Random access files are record based. In other words, they are made up of a group of the same size records. The size of a random access record is defined in the file's Open statement with the Len clause. Unlike sequential files, this type of access mode allows you to move directly to any record position in the file.

Records are read with the Get # statement. The Get # statement allows you to specify which record you wish to read, and a record variable as the target of the operation. Visual Basic will read data from the indicated record and copy it to the record variable. Each time a read is done, a full record is read, regardless of the size of the record variable used. In other words, if you specify a record length of 128 bytes in the Open statement, then 128 bytes will be read with each Get # statement, no matter how large or small the record variable is. Records are most often defined with the Type_End Type structure:

```
                                         'This code appears in the global module
Type NameAndAddress
     First As String * 25               'First name
     Middle As String * 1               'Middle initial
     Last As String * 25                'Last name
     Street As String * 25              'Street name
     City As String * 25                'City name
     State As String * 2                'State abbreviation
     Zip As Long                        'Zip code
     Comment As String * 21             'Comment
End Type

                                         'This code appears in your program
Dim NaddrsRecord As NameAndAddress      'Declare record variable
RecordLen% = Len(NaddrsRecord)          'Get length of record
NaddrsFile% = FreeFile                  'Get a file number
Open "NADDRS.DAT" For Random As #NaddrsFile% Len = RecordLen%    'Open the file
Get #NaddrsFile%, 100, NaddrsRecord
```

This example opens the random file NADDRS.DAT and reads record number 100 into the record variable NaddrsRecord. This record is declared as the user-defined NameAndAddress type. Once you have read a record, you can access its individual parts by referring to the name of the record file and the name of the field you are interested in. For example, NaddrsRecord.Last refers to the last name field, which is a string of 25 characters. (If the actual name is shorter than 25 characters, the remaining characters will be blanks. You can get rid of the blanks with the RTrim$ function.)

The LSet statement can be used to copy the contents of one record variable to another. For example:

```
Dim Person1, Person2 As NameAndAddress
LSet Person1 = Person2
```

copies all the information for Person2 into the Person1 record. Note that if the two records are of different user-defined types only the number of bytes contained in the shorter of the two record types will be copied.

Writing records to a random file is very similar to reading them. Instead of the Get statement, you use the Put statement. Just as in the Get statement, you can specify a record number on which the operation will take place. Again, the record size indicated by the Open statement dictates how many bytes are written to the file.

```
Put #NaddrsFile%, 100, NaddrsRecord
```

This will add a new record to the file at the 100th position, or update the existing contents of the 100th record.

BINARY FILES

Like random files, binary files are also input/output files. However, while random files are record-oriented, binary files are byte-oriented. This means that the records in a binary file can be of variable size. Binary files also use the Get # and Put # statements to read and write to files. Instead of specifying a record position in the file, however, when used on binary files these statements specify a byte position. The length of the read or write is determined by the length of the record variable used.

GETTING INFORMATION ABOUT AN OPEN FILE

Visual Basic provides several commands that report on the current condition of an open file. One of these is the FileAttr function. Depending on which you request, this function returns one of two pieces of information. The first of the two is a code that indicates which mode the file was opened under: Input, Output, Append, Random, or Binary. This function can also return a value that equals the DOS file handle that was assigned to this file by the operating system. This number is sometimes needed in order to access this file from a DLL (Dynamic Link Library). The following example uses both aspects of the FileAttr function:

```
VB_OpenMode% = FileAttr(1, 1)        'get the open mode of file #1
DOS_Handle% = FileAttr(1, 2)         'get the handle number of file #1
```

Another useful function is the LOF (length of file) function. This function returns the length of a file in bytes. It is most useful for determining the end of a binary file or the number of records in a random file. The following example figures the number of 128-byte-length records in a random file that was opened using file number 1:

```
NumberOfRecords& = LOF(1) / 128
```

The Seek function returns a value that indicates the current position of the file pointer. When used on random files, the value returned by this function indicates a record number. With all other file types, this value represents a byte position within the file. You can also use Seek as a statement to move the file pointer to a specific position in a file.

The final function that returns file information is the Loc function. This function is very similar to the Seek function. While the Seek function returns the current position of the file pointer, Loc returns the position of the file pointer at the time of the last read or write. For random files, the value returned is a record number. For binary files, the value is a byte position. For sequential files, the value is the current byte position divided by 128. This makes Loc useless with sequential files.

WORKING IN A NETWORKED ENVIRONMENT

When working in a networked environment, special attention must be paid to how files are accessed. Because several users may have access to the same data in the same file simultaneously, you need to write your programs so they prevent any possible corruption of data. Most often, this is done by restricting multiple accesses to the file or portions of the file at specific times.

To start with, the Open statement has two clauses that control the access to a file, access and lock. The access clause tells the operating system what type of access your program is requesting from the file. You can request read, write, or both read and write privileges. The success or failure of the file open depends on the access you request and any restrictions other users have previously placed on the file.

The lock clause tells the operating system what privileges your program will allow other users once it has opened the file. Your program can specify that other users be allowed full access, or it can restrict read access, write access, or both read and write access.

Requesting access and restricting privileges in the Open statement are file locking measures. In other words, such measures affect the entire file. However, if several users need simultaneous access to a file, you should not restrict access to the entire file. Instead, you should only restrict access to those portions of the file that are currently being worked on by your program. This is done with the Lock and UnLock statements. With the Lock statement, you specify a portion of a file (one or more records for random files, or one or more bytes for binary files) to which no other users may have access. This restriction stays in effect until you reverse it with the UnLock statement.

B

VISUAL BASIC LANGUAGE REFERENCE

This appendix is a complete reference to all the statements and functions that make up the BASIC language used by Visual Basic. We will first review the language elements that you use to construct Visual Basic program statements. These elements include variables, constants, built-in and programmer-defined data types, and operators. The major part of the appendix is an alphabetical reference that consisely describes each of Visual Basic's keywords—both those that form statements (such as Dim and If) and those that represent built-in functions that process data (such as Abs and Format$). Each entry details the purpose and syntax of the statement or function and gives an example of its use and a description of its operation.

If you don't have much experience with BASIC programming, we recommend that you explore one or more of the books listed in Appendix F, Further Reading. If you are familiar with BASIC but want to review some important aspects of the language and learn about some of the special features of Visual Basic's implementation of the BASIC language, we suggest that you read Appendix A, Visual Basic Language Tutorial.

ELEMENTS OF THE VISUAL BASIC LANGUAGE

Visual Basic provides many unique features with its objects, properties, methods, and events. The main purpose of these special features is to provide you with a quick and easy way to give your programs an intuitive graphic user interface. However, these features do not give your programs the tools to do the actual processing tasks that are the core of any application. This appendix describes the Visual Basic language elements that allow you to write complex programs to handle just about any chore.

Variables

Variables are how a programming language refers to the various types of data that can be held in the computer's memory. To use variables successfully, you must know how you can name a variable, what types of data a variable can represent, and how to assign and use the value of a variable.

Variable Names

Visual Basic has some rules regarding how you may set up a variable name. These rules help Visual Basic tell the difference between your variables and other elements of the language. These rules are

1. A variable name may not be longer than 40 characters.

2. The first character of a variable name must be a letter (A through Z). This letter can be uppercase or lowercase.

3. The remaining characters can be letters (A through Z, or a through z), numbers (0 through 9), or underscores (_).

4. The last character can be one of these type declaration characters (explained later): %, &, !, #, @, $, or nothing.

5. The variable name cannot be a Visual Basic reserved word. Reserved words include the names of Visual Basic properties, events, methods, operators, statements, and functions.

    Variable names in Visual Basic are not case-sensitive. That is, Visual Basic makes no distinctions between uppercase and lowercase characters in a variable name. In the code fragment below, all three lines refer to the same variable.

```
invoicetotal = 100
INVOICETOTAL = 100
InvoiceTotal = 100
```

When declaring and using variable names, it is helpful to use a name that can be easily read and describes the purpose of the data that it contains, rather than a cryptic abbreviation such as N or T1. This makes it much easier for you to understand how a program works. Proper use of capitalization can help make variable names more readable. For instance, although the three lines in the example above refer to the same variable, the third format is much easier to read and understand because the first letter of each word in the variable name is capitalized. You can also use the underscore chartacter (_) to help make a variable more readable. For example:

```
Invoice_Total = 100
```

This variable name is made more readable because the underscore character separates different words in the variable name. Underscores, however, have the potential to make your Visual Basic program actually less readable: Visual Basic uses underscores in its event procedures (for example, Command1_Click), so using underscores in your variable names might make your code harder to read.

You can also use proper capitalization to help you identify the scope of a variable. Although Visual Basic does not enforce any particular convention, you will find it convenient to consistently apply capitalization. A common programming practice makes the first letter of a local variable lowercase, the first letter of a module-level or global variable uppercase, and constants all uppercase:

```
invoiceTotal       'local variable
InvoiceTotal       'module-level or global variable
INVOICETOTAL       'constant
```

Variable Types

In most languages variables not only represent the value of data, but the type as well. Each type of variable views its contents in a different way. In Visual Basic there are seven simple variable types: string, integer, long integer, single-precision, double-precision, currency, and variant. String variables represent data as ASCII characters. The five numeric variable types each represent a different method for storing a numeric value. The numeric type you choose determines the range of the values you can place in that variable, and how accurately they can be stored. The variant type can represent any of the other kinds of data, and is the default data type for variables that are not explicitly declared otherwise.

String variables hold text or alphanumeric information. Strings can be of fixed or variable lengths. A fixed-length string is assigned a specific length when it is created, and that length cannot be changed. Variable-length strings continually shrink and grow as values are assigned to them. Theoretically, a string can be up to 65,535 characters long. However, strings require overhead in memory (4 bytes per string) for some control information, so the actual maximum length is a little less than that.

The integer variable type is the simplest kind of numeric data. This variable type requires 2 bytes of memory for storage, and can hold any whole number in the range of from -32768 to +32767. Because integers can only store whole numbers, any fractional portion of a number is rounded off to the nearest whole number when it is assigned to an integer variable.

The long integer variable type is closely related to the integer. The long type, however, uses 4 rather than 2 bytes of storage. Because of this, its range is much greater than the integer variable, allowing you to store whole numbers from -2,147,483,648 to +2,147,483,647.

Both the single-precision and double-precision variable types store numbers that might have a fractional portion. These variables store values in a floating-point number format. Representing numbers in floating-point format is very much like using scientific notation. Like scientific notation, floating-point numbers have a sign, a mantissa, and an exponent. The main difference between the two is that scientific notation is a base 10 system (decimal), and floating-point numbers work on a base 2 (binary) system. The advantage of representing a number in this fashion is that it allows the variables to store a fairly large range of numbers in a limited amount of memory. However, there are disadvantages to using floating-point numbers. Along with the limits on range, a floating-point number is also limited to the number of digits it can represent accurately. As a result of this, rounding floating-point numbers sometimes produces a result that may be insufficiently precise for your application. Finally, math operations on a floating-point number are not as fast as when performed on an integer or long integer variable.

A single-precision variable requires 4 bytes of storage, and has a range of from -3.37E+38 to +3.37E+38. It can accurately hold numbers up to seven digits long. The double-precision variable uses 8 bytes of memory. It can represent numbers from -1.67D+308 to +1.67D+308—a huge range of values, with an accuracy of 16 digits.

The currency variable type is a modified integer. What sets it apart from an integer is that it has an implied decimal point. This allows numbers represented by a currency variable to have up to 4 digits to the right of the decimal point. Because it is stored as an 8-byte integer, math operations are faster on it than on floating-point numbers. The range of a currency variable is from -9.22E+14 to +9.22E+14, and it can accurately represent any number of digits that fall into that range.

Table B-1 lists Visual Basic's variable types, and the range, if any, that can be held in that type.

Variable Type	Type Identifier	Storage Required	Range of Variable
String	$	Length of string + 4	Up to almost 65,535 characters
Integer	%	2 bytes	-32,768 to +32,767
Long	&	4 bytes	-2,147,483,648 to +2,147,483,647

Variable Type	Type Identifier	Storage Required	Range of Variable
Single	!	4 bytes	-3.402823E+38 to -1.401298E+45 and
			+1.401298E-45 to +3.402823E+38
Double	#	8 bytes	-1.797693134862315D+308 to -4.94066D-324 and
			+4.94066D-324 to +1.797693134862315D+308
Currency	@	8 bytes	-922337203685477.5808 to +922337203685477.5807
Variant	(none)	varies	Any of the other data types

Table B-1 Types and ranges of variables in Visual Basic

Variable Scope

When a variable is declared in Visual Basic, the placement of its declaration determines how accessible that variable will be to certain portions of the program. The visibility of a variable to the program is referred to as a variable's scope.

The coding area of Visual Basic is set up in a tiered format. Each tier has associated with it rules that govern how variables declared within it can be accessed. These tiers are set up in a hierarchical manner.

The broadest of these tiers is called the global area. Variables declared in this area are accessible by all portions of a program. As a matter of fact, the sole purpose of the global area is to define items that can be seen by all areas of a program. No procedures or functions may be placed in the global area. When a variable is declared in this area, it is referred to as a "global" variable.

On the next level down are the coding areas of forms and modules. As you already know, a form is the object on which controls can be drawn. Each form has attached to it an area that holds program code. Modules are very much like forms without any visual elements. Instead, modules are simply areas in which to place code. Both forms and modules have an area called the General Declarations area. Variables that are declared in this area are available to any routines that are in the same form or module. These variables cannot be accessed by any routines in a different form or module. Variables declared in this area are called "form-level" or "module-level" variables. Like the global module, the General Declarations area of a form or module is reserved for declaring items. No executable commands may be placed there.

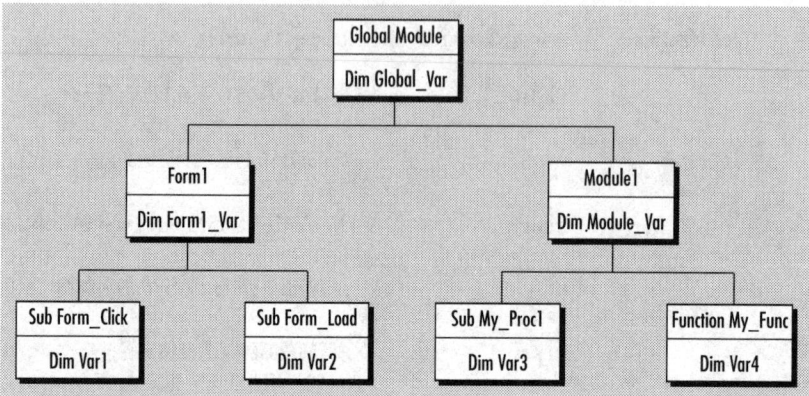

Figure B-1 An example hierarchy chart

The last and lowest-level tier contains Visual Basic procedures. Visual Basic procedures are contained inside a form or module. These include the predefined event procedures that are attached to objects, as well as programmer-defined sub procedures and functions. Because they can only be accessed locally within a procedure, variables that are declared inside a procedure are called "local" variables.

If you have trouble figuring out the scope of a variable, draw yourself a hierarchy chart of your program. Make a box for the global module at the top of the chart, and place one box for each of the forms and modules in your program below it. Draw a line from the global module box to each of the boxes that represent a form or module. Underneath each form and module, place a box for each procedure inside that form or module. Again, draw a line from the form or module box to each of the boxes that represent a procedure inside the form or module. Inside each box, list the variables that have been declared in the area of your program represented by the box. It is now an easy task to examine the scope of the variables in your program. If you have a question about whether a variable can be accessed by a procedure, simply find that procedure's box, and follow the lines upward. Each box you encounter on your way up to the global module will list variables that are available to the procedure in question.

Figure B-1 shows an example hierarchy chart based on a program with two forms and one module, each with at least one procedure.

Declaring Variables

So far we've discussed that you can assign a name and a type to an area of storage and refer to that memory location by its assigned name. The actual practice of assigning a name and type to an area of memory is called "declaring" a variable. In most languages a variable must be declared in a program before it can be used. This is done because most compilers need to know how memory will be set up before it can begin compiling the executable code of a program. Although, like other languages, Visual Basic allows you to formally declare a variable before using it, this is not required. Variables in Visual Basic can be declared either implicitly or explicitly. Implicitly declared variables are variables that have been declared "on the fly"—that is, no code needs to be written to specifically set up a memory location for the variable before it is used in the program. An explicitly declared variable is formally declared before it is used in the program. When you explicitly declare a variable, you include code in your program for the express purpose of informing Visual Basic that memory is to be allocated for a variable.

Implicitly Declared Variables

In order to implicitly declare a variable in Visual Basic, you just use it in a line of code. For instance, in the following line of code, a value is assigned to a numeric variable.

```
MyVar = 1
```

If the variable MyVar had not yet been declared, Visual Basic would create storage for that variable. Because assigning a value to a variable is an executable command, implicitly defined variables can only be defined within a procedure. Therefore all implicit variables are local variables; they cannot be accessed outside of the procedure in which they are used.

By default, when you use a variable that has not been formally declared, Visual Basic assumes that it will be a variant. (Note that Visual Basic 1.0 assumed single precision.) However, there are two ways you can control the type of an implicitly declared variable. First, by appending a type declaration character to the end of the variable name, you can force Visual Basic to use a specific variable type. If you append a type declaration to a variable name, it becomes part of the variable name and must always be used to refer to that variable. For instance, in the code below, three implicit variables are assigned the numeric value of -1. Each one will store this value differently, based on the type declaration character at the end of its variable name.

```
Var1% = -1
Var2! = -1
Var3# = -1
```

In this example, Var1% is an integer variable, Var2! is a single-precision variable, and Var3# is a double-precision variable.

When strings are declared in an implicit manner, they are always declared as variable-length strings. See Table B.2 for a list of the type declaration characters and the variable types with which they are used.

As mentioned previously, if you do not include a type declaration character, Visual Basic assumes an implicit variable is a variant. This can be modified, however, with the DefType statements. This statement is used in the General Declarations area of a form or module to define a range of letters that indicate a specific variable type. If the first letter of an implicit variable falls within this defined range, that variable will be assigned the data type specified by the Deftype statement. For instance:

```
DefInt A-F
```

In the example above, Visual Basic will assign the integer variable type to any variable that is implicitly declared in the same form or module, as long as the first letter of the variable's name falls into the range A through F. Table B-2 lists the six Deftype statements and the variable types with which they are used.

Variable Type	Declaration Character	Deftype Statement
String	$	DefStr
Integer	%	DefInt
Long	&	DefLng
Single	!	DefSng
Double	#	DefDbl
Currency	@	DefCur
Variant	(none)	DefVar

Table B-2 Declaration characters and Deftype statements used to implicitly declare variable types

Because you can declare variables implicitly simply by using them, Visual Basic does not generate an error when it comes across a variable name it has not yet encountered. Instead it allocates storage for that variable and proceeds normally. This can cause logic errors in your programs if you are not careful. One of the most frustrating and hard-to-find bugs that can occur in a Visual Basic program is the one that is caused by the programmer accidently mistyping a variable name. For instance, in the following code fragment, the program is supposed to figure the square root of the number 128, and place it into the variable SqrRoot.

```
ThisNmber = 128          'mis-typed!
SqrRoot = Sqr(ThisNumber) 'Sqr returns the square root of ThisNumber
```

The variable SqrRoot will have the value of 0 assigned to it rather than the expected value of 12 because of the mis-typing in the first assignment.

Explicitly Declared Variables

Visual Basic also allows you to declare variables explicitly. Explicitly declared variables are assigned a variable name and data type before they are used. This is the preferred manner of declaring variables, because it makes your programs more readable. In Visual Basic you explicitly declare variables by using the Dim, Static, or Global statements. These statements have different implications for the visibility of the declared variable.

The Global statement is used when you wish to declare a variable in the global module. These variables are visible to all procedures in the program.

The Dim statement can be used to declare module-level variables in the General Declarations area of a form or module. Module-level variables are accessible to all procedures that are contained in the same form or module as the variable declaration.

The Dim statement can also be used inside a procedure to declare local variables. Local variables are limited in scope to the procedure in which they are declared. They cannot be accessed by other procedures. When the Dim statement is used to declare a local variable, that variable is allocated each time the procedure is entered, and deallocated when it is exited. When Visual Basic begins to execute a procedure, it scans the procedure for Dim statements. If there are any, it will allocate memory for the variables specified by the Dim statement. When Visual Basic is through executing the procedure, it will deallocate any memory that was assigned to a variable in the procedure with the Dim statement. This frees the memory up for other variables. However, it also means that variables declared with the Dim statement do not retain their value between procedure calls. (This sort of variable is sometimes called an "automatic variable.")

The Static statement, like the Dim statement, is used to allocate storage for local variables. Local variables created with the Static statements are often called "static" variables. Unlike local variables that have been declared with the Dim statement, static variables are allocated once, and are not deallocated until the program terminates. This means that static variables retain their value between procedure calls.

To explicitly declare a simple variable, use one of the following syntaxes:

```
Global variable_name As type     'Use this to declare a global variable
Dim variable_name As type        'Use this to declare a module-level, or local variable
Static variable_name As type     'Use this to declare a static local variable
```

In the variable_name parameter, supply a unique name that complies with the rules that apply to variable names listed earlier. Specify the type as Integer, Long, Single, Double, Currency, String, or String * length (for fixed-length strings). For example:

1257

```
Dim IntegerVar As Integer      'Declares an integer variable named IntegerVar
Dim LongVar As Long            'Declares a long integer variable named LongVar
Dim SingleVar As Single        'Declares a single-precision variable named SingleVar
Dim DoubleVar As Double        'Declares a double-precision variable named DoubleVar
Dim CurrencyVar As Currency    'Declares a currency variable named CurrencyVar
Dim StringVar As String        'Declares a variable-length string variable named StringVar
Dim FixedVar As String * 10    'Declares a 10-byte-long fixed-length string named FixedVar
Dim VariantVar As Variant      'Declares a variant variable named VariantVar
```

You can force Visual Basic to make you explicitly declare all variables. This will significantly reduce bugs and make your program far more readable, and is highly recommended for larger projects. Use the Option Explicit statement in any module to force explicit declarations. You can also set Visual Basic's environment to automatically add this statement to all of your programs. Do this by pulling down the Options menu, choosing the Environment command, and setting the Explicit option to Yes.

Constants

Visual Basic allows you to set up a special type of named memory location called a constant. Constants are names that represent unchanging values. Assign them values either in the global module or in the General Declarations area of a form or module. The syntax for declaring a constant is

```
[Global] Const constant_name = value
```

The GLOBAL keyword is used if the constant is being defined in the global module. The constant_name parameter is a unique name you will use in place of the defined value in your program, and follows the same naming rules as for variables. It's common programming practice to make constant names all uppercase.

Constants are used in your programs to give a meaningful name to a value that might otherwise be ambiguous or hard to remember. For instance, colors in Visual Basic are represented by a long integer number. This number represents a mixture of the electronic primary colors: red, green, and blue. You could set the background color of an object by assigning a color's number to its BackColor property:

```
Text1.BackColor = &hFFFF
```

While this works fine, and causes no confusion to Visual Basic, it can cause you a little extra work in deciphering that the hex value FFFF is the color number for yellow. A better, more readable way to do this is to create a constant with a descriptive name, and assign the color number to it:

```
Global Const YELLOW = &hFFFF
```

In the example above, we have created a constant with the name YELLOW, which holds the value of the color number for yellow. We have placed the constant definition in the global module, so we need to precede the Const statement with the GLOBAL keyword. We can then use the constant anywhere in our program:

```
Text1.BackColor = YELLOW
```

Constants can represent string or numeric values.

Microsoft provides a file, CONSTANT.TXT, that has many constant declarations defined for you. For smaller applications, it's probably easiest just to type the declarations in yourself. For larger applications, you'll find it much easier to read the text file into a new module.

To do this, create a new module by pulling down the File menu and choosing the New Module menu command. Then pull down the File menu again, and choose Load Text. This opens up a dialog box listing all text files in the current directory. CONSTANT.TXT should be in your main Visual Basic directory (default installation would place this in C:\VB). Simply choose CONSTANT.TXT to enter the entire file into your module. These constants will then be available throughout your application.

Programmer-Defined Variable Types

Visual Basic provides all the simple variable types needed to write just about any application. For more complex data types, Visual Basic allows you to set up your own variable types in the global module. You can assign meaningful names to these programmer-defined types, and then use them to declare variables anywhere in your program. Programmer-defined variables are set up with the Type...End Type statement:

```
Type NameAndSS
     FirstName As String * 25
     LastName As String * 25
     SocialSecurity As Long
End Type
```

We can then assign this type to variables. This lets us refer to all elements as one variable:

```
Dim Person1 As NameAndSS
Dim Person2 As NameAndSS
Person1.FirstName = "Nick"
Person1.LastName = "Scott"
Person1.SocialSecurity = 427859672
Person1 = Person2
```

As you can see, in the last line of the example, the value of one programmer-defined variable is assigned to another. This copies the contents of all the elements in one programmer-defined variable to the corresponding elements in the other. However, this can only be done when both programmer-defined variables are of the same type. (See the entry for LSet for a way to copy some programmer-defined variables of differing lengths.)

Arrays

The basic function of an array is to store an entire series of the same type of variables and reference them by the same variable name. This is very useful when you are working on several pieces of data that all have the same variable type and purpose.

For example, suppose you need to keep track of an inventory of cars, and you need to separate them by color. You could set up a separate variable for each color, such as RedCars, BlueCars, WhiteCars, and BlackCars. Each of these variables would be declared as an integer. The purpose of each variable is the same: to hold the number of cars that are that color. This presents two problems, however. First, all the cars cannot be referenced by the same name. Therefore, if we need to determine the number of all the cars, we have to add all the variables: AllCars = RedCars + BlueCars + WhiteCars + BlackCars. This makes referring to all the cars an awkward process. Second, if a new color is added, we have to create a new variable to handle it. This means each time a new color is added, you need to modify the program and recompile it.

A better solution is to use an array to hold the data. Using an array allows you to set up one variable name, Cars, that has a separate storage area for each color. Each of these areas is referred to as an element of the array. When you work with an array, you use an index number (called the subscript) to tell Visual Basic which element you are referencing. To create an array, use the Global, Dim, or Static statements. These statements declare an array's name, variable type, and size. For instance:

```
Dim Cars(100) As Integer
Dim Colors(100) As String
```

These statements declare two arrays. The first array, Cars, is an integer array. This array can be used to store the number of cars per color. The second array, Colors, is a string array. It can be used to store the names of each of the possible colors.

The argument inside the parentheses of the array declaration specifies the number of the first and last elements in the array. In the example above, only the number of the last element in the array is specified, so Visual Basic will assume the starting array element is number 0. Therefore both arrays will have 101 elements, numbered from 0 to 100.

The starting element number of an array can be changed in two ways. First, you may place an Option Base statement in the General Declarations area of a form or module. This allows you to set the default starting element number to 0 or 1 when an array is declared. Second, you can specify the starting element in the array declaration:

```
Dim WorkHours(800 To 1700) As String
```

This statement declares an array whose lowest available element is 800, and highest is 1700.

After an array is declared, you need some technique for referencing elements in the array. This is done by specifying the desired element number, or subscript, in parentheses following the array name. For instance, this code fragment assigns a color name to element number 5 of the Colors array:

```
Colors(5) = "Red"
```

Not only can you define the number of elements in an array, but you can also define the number of dimensions. Up to this point, the examples we've used have all been one-dimensional arrays. You can think of one-dimensional arrays in a linear manner. For instance, the Cars array from the example above can be visualized:

```
Cars(0)    Cars(1)    Cars(2)    ...    Cars(98)    Cars(99)    Cars(100)
```

However, Visual Basic allows you to set up multidimensional arrays. Multidimensional arrays have more than one set of subscript elements. For instance, by creating a two-dimensional array, you define that the array has both length and width. This lets us set up data in a tabular format. For example, the following statement sets up a two-dimensional array.

```
Dim Tbl(1 To 5, 1 To 5) As Integer
```

In order to reference an element in a multidimensional array, you need to supply a subscript for each dimension in the array. If you were to visualize the Tbl array, it might look something like this:

```
Tbl(1,1)    Tbl(2,1)    Tbl(3,1)    Tbl(4,1)    Tbl(5,1)
Tbl(1,2)    Tbl(2,2)    Tbl(3,2)    Tbl(4,2)    Tbl(5,2)
Tbl(1,3)    Tbl(2,3)    Tbl(3,3)    Tbl(4,3)    Tbl(5,3)
Tbl(1,4)    Tbl(2,4)    Tbl(3,4)    Tbl(4,4)    Tbl(5,4)
Tbl(1,5)    Tbl(2,5)    Tbl(3,5)    Tbl(4,5)    Tbl(5,5)
```

Adding a third dimension would give the array depth, as well as length and width. However, you do not have to stop at just three dimensions. Visual Basic allows you to create arrays that have as many as 60 dimensions. Although this is a neat feature, your mind can get a little boggled when the number of dimensions in an array exceeds three. Large multidimensional arrays can also consume prodigious amounts of memory.

Dynamic Arrays

Dynamic arrays are arrays that can be allocated and deallocated at runtime. This allows you to make your programs more flexible by creating arrays whose size is determined by factors that are unknown at design time, such as the size of a data file.

Dynamic arrays are allocated using the ReDim statement and deallocated with the Erase statement. The most efficient way to set up a dynamic array is to declare it twice. The first declaration is performed in either the global module with the Global statement, or in the General Declarations area of a form or module with the Dim statement. However, declare the array without any entries inside its parentheses:

```
Dim Cars() As Integer
Dim Colors() As String
```

This tells Visual Basic that you want to declare an array, but you do not yet know how many dimensions or elements it will contain. You can then place the ReDim statement inside a procedure to define the number of dimensions and elements:

```
Sub LoadColors (LastColor As Integer)
    ReDim Colors(LastColor) As String
    ReDim Cars(LastColor) As Integer
    :
    [Place your code here]
    :
End Sub
```

You are not required to use the Global or Dim statements to originally declare a dynamic array. However, when Visual Basic allocates storage for a dynamic array at runtime, the use of these statements allows it to do so faster and more efficiently. Also, the array's scope will reflect the placement of the original declaration (that is, if the array was first declared in the global module, its elements will all be global variables). However, using this method has the disadvantage of limiting a dynamic array to eight dimensions. While eight is usually enough dimensions for any application, some programs will require that an array have more.

If you wish to declare a dynamic array with more than eight dimensions, or wish it to be a local array (not accessible by any other procedure), do not include a Global or Dim statement for the array.

After a dynamic array has been declared, you can again use the ReDim statement any number of times to change the number of elements in the array. Take care when doing this, as redimensioning an array will erase the current contents of the array. The number of dimensions in an array, however, cannot be changed once it has been set.

You can also choose to preserve the contents of a dynamic array rather than erasing them. Use the preserve keyword:

```
Sub LoadColors (LastColor As Integer)
    ReDim Preserve Colors(LastColor) As String
    ReDim Preserve Cars(LastColor) As Integer
    :
    [Place your code here]
    :
End Sub
```

This example preserves the contents of the Colors and Cars arrays during the redimensioning process.

Operators

Operators are symbols that tell Visual Basic to manipulate data in some specified way. For example, the assignment operator (=) can store a value in a variable, while the addition operator (+) adds two quantities together. There are also operators that compare values, returning a True or False value as the result.

The Assignment Operator

In Visual Basic the assignment operator is used to place values into a variable or property. The assignment operator is the equal sign (=). This operator is used by placing a variable or property to the left of the operator, and an expression to the right. This causes the value of the expression to be assigned to the variable or property. For example:

```
Height% = 100
Area! = PI * Radius ^ 2
MyBox.Text = MyPrompt$
```

The first example assigns the numeric literal value 100 to the integer variable Height%. In the second example, the value of the expression PI * Radius ^ 2 is assigned to the single-precision variable Area!. The last example assigns the string MyPrompt$ to the Text property of the object MyBox.

The assignment operator assigns values to both numeric and string variables and properties. If your program assigns a numeric value of one data type to a numeric variable or property of a different data type, Visual Basic will automatically convert the value to the type of the receiving variable or property. For instance, if your program assigns an integer value to a single-precision variable, the value will be converted to a single-precision value before it is assigned to the variable. However, if the value is not within the allowable range for the type of the result data item, an overflow error will occur. For example, your program will cause an error if it assigns a value greater than 32767 or less than -32768 to an integer variable. You cannot assign a string value to a numeric variable or property. This causes a Type Mismatch error. By the same token, you cannot assign a numeric value to a string variable or property. Visual Basic provides the Str$ and Val functions for converting numeric values to strings and strings to numeric values.

Arithmetic Operators

The arithmetic operators perform math functions on numeric values. The familiar addition, subtraction, multiplication, and division operators need no discussion, but there are additional operators that perform other arithmetic functions. The exponentiation operator (^) causes the number on the left of the operator to be raised by the power indicated by the number on the right of the operator. You can change the sign of a numeric value with the negation operator (-). Positive numbers become negative, and negative numbers become positive. The integer division (\) and modulo arithmetic (Mod) operators perform integer math. Integer division divides one value by another, and returns the result with any fractional portion truncated. Modulo arithmetic returns the remainder of an integer division. For instance, in the following code:

```
A% = 5 \ 2
B% = 5 Mod 2
```

The value of A% will be 2 (5 divided by 2 is 2.5, truncate the .5, and you get 2), and the value of B% will be 1 (5 divided by 2 is 2, with a remainder of 1).

Use the & operator to perform string concatenation. This "adds" two strings together. For instance,

```
B$ = "Free"
C$ = "dom"
A$ = B$ & C$
```

The following assignments would leave A$ with a value of "Freedom".

Visual Basic assigns an order of precedence to its arithmetic operators. When more than one operator is used in an expression, the precedence of the operators determines in which order the operations occur. For example:

```
A! = 2 * 4 – 5
```

In this example the variable A! will be assigned a value of 3 because the multiplication operator has a higher precedence than the subtraction operator. Therefore Visual Basic evaluates this expression in this order:

1. Multiply 2 and 4, getting a result of 8.

2. Subtract 5 from the result (8), getting a new result of 3.

3. Assign the new result (3) to A!.

The precedence of an expression can be modified by surrounding an operation with parentheses. This causes the operations inside the parentheses to be executed before any operations outside them. For instance, if we place parentheses around part of the equation used above, a different value will be assigned to the variable:

```
A! = 2 * (4 - 5)
```

In this example Visual Basic evaluates this expression in this order:

1. Subract 5 from 4, getting a result of -1.

2. Multiply that result (-1) by 2, getting a new result of -2.

3. Assign the new result (-2) to A!.

Several sets of parenthesies may be used to control the precedence of a complex expression. The arithmetic operators are listed in Table B-3 in order of precedence.

Use This...	To Perform...	Example
^	Exponentiation	A! = 3^4
-	Negation	A! = -1
*, /	Multiplication and division	A! = B! * C! A! = B! / C!
\	Integer division	A% = B% \ C%
Mod	Modulo arithmetic	A% = B% Mod C%
+, -	Addition and subtraction	A% = B% + C% A% = B% - C%
&	String concatenation	A$ = B$ & C$

Table B-3 Arithmetic operators in order of precedence

Relational Operators

Relational operators are used to compare two expressions and determine their relationship. Using the relational operators, your programs can determine if the values of two expressions are equal, if one is greater than the other, or if one is less than the other. Relational operators all share the same precedence, and unless modified by parentheses, their operations are performed after any arithmetic operations in the same expression. The values in a relational expression are examined from left to right. The relational operators available in Visual Basic are listed in Table B-4.

Use This...	To Test For...	Example	
=	Equality	A% = B%	True if the values of A% and B% are equal
<>	Nonequality	A% <> B%	True if the value of A% is not equal to B%
>	Greater than	A% > B%	True if the value of A% is greater than that of B%
<	Less than	A% < B%	True if the value of A% is less than that of B%
>=	Greater than or equal to	A% >= B%	True if the value of A% is not less than that of B%
<=	Less than or equal to	A% <= B%	True if the value of A% is not greater than that of B%
Like	Compare string with pattern	A$ Like B$	True if the value of A$ matches the pattern in B$
Is	Compare two objects	A Is B	True if A and B refer to the same object

Table B-4 Relational operators

Most commonly, relational operators are used to help your programs make decisions. When used in this fashion, relational operators are very often used in the parameters of an If, Do...Loop, Select Case, or While...Wend statement. For instance, in the following code fragment, the values of two variables are tested for equality:

```
If A% = B% Then Label1.Caption = "A% and B% are equal"
```

In this example, the values of the integer variables A% and B% are compared. If they are equal, the Caption property of a label control is set.

Relational operators return a value that represents the result of the test. If the tested expression is True, a value of -1 is returned. If the expression is False, a value of 0 is returned. You can actually assign the results of a relational test to a numeric variable. For example:

```
C% = (A% = B%)
```

If the values of the integer variables A% and B% are equal, the value of C% will be set to -1. Otherwise C% is assigned a value of 0.

Logical (Bitwise) Operators

If every decision we made were based on only one factor, the world would be a much simpler place to live in. Unfortunately for us and our programs, this is not the case. Each decision made in a lifetime, and in a program, is based on several determining factors. For instance, you could say "If I'm hungry, I'll eat lunch." But what if you don't have the time to eat lunch? This needs to be taken into account, so the decision on when to eat lunch is modified: "If I'm hungry, and I have time, I'll eat lunch." You could have lunch delivered, and that would save you the time you need, so your new decision would be "If I'm hungry, and I have time or the food is delivered, I'll eat lunch." Modifying decisions in this manner is a prime example of how logical operators are used. For instance, you can use logical operators to write a line of code in a program that mirrors our lunch example:

```
If Hungry% = True And (FreeTime% > 30 Or Delivery% = True) Then Call DoLunch
```

Logical operators combine two or more numeric values. Since the result of a relational operation is a numeric value, the most common use for logical operators is to combine relational expressions. This lets you build complex decisions from several simple decisions. Unless modified by parentheses, logical operations occur after all arithmetic and relational operations in the same expression. Like arithmetic operators, logical operators are assigned precedence. It's a good idea to use parentheses liberally when using logical operators. This ensures your program will reflect the exact order of precedence you desire. It also makes your code much more readable. Table B-5 lists the logical operators available in Visual Basic in their order of precedence.

Use This...	For...	Example
Not	Logical negation	If Not (A% = B%)...
And	Logical and	If (A% = B%) And (C% = D%)...
Or	Inclusive or	If (A% = B%) Or (C% = D%)...
Xor	Exclusive or	If (A% = B%) Xor (C% = D%)...
Eqv	Logical equivalence	If (A% = B%) Eqv (C% = D%)...
Imp	Implication	If (A% = B%) Imp (C% = D%)...

Table B-5 Logical operators in order of precedence

Much like relational operators, an expression with logical operators actually returns a numeric value. This value is based on the bit values of the numeric expressions supplied to the logical operator. The logical operators examine these values bit by bit. Based on the settings of the bits, logical operators set a corresponding bit in the result value. Because they actually perform bit operations, logical operators are sometimes referred to as "bitwise" operators.

Logical Negation (the Not Operator)

The logical negation operator, Not, is the only operator that has a single operand. This operator examines each bit in the supplied operand, and sets the corresponding bit in the result value to the exact opposite. In other words, if the bit in the operand is on, the bit in the result will be set off, and vice versa. Table B-6 lists the possible settings of the result bit when the Not operator is used.

Operand Bit	Resulting Bit
1	0
0	1

Table B-6 Truth table for the Not operator

Logical And (the And Operator)

The logical and operator, And, compares the bits of its operands. If both bits are set on, the corresponding bit in the result is set on; otherwise, the result bit is set off. Table B-7 lists the possible settings of the result bit when the And operator is used.

First Operand Bit	Second Operand Bit	Resulting Bit
1	1	1
0	1	0
1	0	0
0	0	0

Table B-7 Truth table for the And operator

Inclusive Or (the Or Operator)

The inclusive or operator, Or, compares the bits of the two operands. If one or both of the bits is on, it sets the corresponding result bit on. The only time the result bit is set off is when both bits in the operands are off. Table B-8 lists the possible settings of the result bit when the Or operator is used.

First Operand Bit	Second Operand Bit	Resulting Bit
1	1	1
0	1	1
1	0	1
0	0	0

Table B-8 Truth table for the Or operator

Exclusive Or (the Xor Operator)

The exclusive or operator, Xor, compares the bits of its two operands. If only one of the two bits is on, it sets the corresponding result bit on. If both bits in the operands are on, or both bits are off, the result bit is set off. Table B-9 lists the possible settings of the result bit when the Xor operator is used.

First Operand Bit	Second Operand Bit	Resulting Bit
1	1	0
0	1	1
1	0	1
0	0	0

Table B-9 Truth table for the Xor operator

Logical Equivalence (the Eqv Operator)

The logical equivalence operator, Eqv, tests the equality of the bits in the two operands. If both bits are on, or both bits are off, the corresponding result bit is set on. If one bit is on and the other is off, the result bit is set off. Table B-10 lists the possible settings of the result bit when the Eqv operator is used.

First Operand Bit	Second Operand Bit	Resulting Bit
1	1	1
0	1	0
1	0	0
0	0	1

Table B-10 Truth table for the Eqv operator

Implication (the Imp Operator)

The implication operator, Imp, is perhaps the strangest one in the bunch. This operator sets its result based on whether the bit in the first operand "implies" the value of the bit in the second operand, according to rules of logic beyond the scope of this book. If the bit in the first operand is on, the implied value for the second operand is also on. However, if the bit in the first operand is off, the implied value for the second operand can be on or off. Therefore the only time this operator sets its result bit to off is when the bit in the first operand is on, and the bit in the second operand is False. Table B-11 lists the possible settings of the result bit when the Imp operator is used.

First Operand Bit	Second Operand Bit	Resulting Bit
1	1	1
0	1	1
1	0	0
0	0	1

Table B-11 Truth table for the Imp operator

AN OVERVIEW OF VISUAL BASIC'S STATEMENTS AND FUNCTIONS

There are three ways to perform tasks in your Visual Basic programs. First, you can use methods to affect a change on a Visual Basic object. Second, you can use operators to return or assign a value, or make a decision based on the value of one or more expressions. Finally, you can use statements and functions to process information. Up to this point, we have covered the methods and operators available in Visual Basic. In the following reference entries, we will explore the statements and functions you can use in your Visual Basic programs.

Statements and functions are very similar. Both perform a specific task in your programs. Depending on the particular statement or function, both can be supplied with, and react to information in the form of passed parameters. The difference between the two is that functions return a value, while statements do not.

For more information on the format of these reference entries, please see Chapter 1, Using the Visual Basic SuperBible.

ABS FUNCTION

See Also: Sgn.

Purpose

The Abs function returns the absolute value of a number.

General Syntax

`Abs(numericExpression)`

Usage

`A = Abs(B)`

This statement places the absolute value of the variable B into the variable A.

Description

Abs returns the unsigned value of the supplied numeric expression. For instance, both Abs(-299) and Abs(299) return the value of 299. A will have the same data type as B. If B is a variant of variant type 8 (string) that can be converted into a number, then A will be a variant of type 5 (double).

APPACTIVATE STATEMENT

See Also: Sendkeys, Shell, and Chapter 21, Application Focus.

Purpose

The AppActivate statement activates a running Windows program, and gives it the current focus. It does not change the windowstate (minimized or maximized) of the program.

General Syntax

```
AppActivate programtitle$
```

Usage

```
AppAcitvate "Paintbrush - (Untitled)"
```

This example will give the Paintbrush application the focus, assuming it is already running, and it has no file loaded. Note that the exact title as it appears in the program's window must be used, although case is disregarded.

Description

This statement is explained in detail in Chapter 21, Application Focus.

ASC FUNCTION

See Also: Chr, Chr$.

Purpose

The Asc function returns the numeric ANSI code of a character.

General Syntax

```
Asc(stringExpression$)
```

Usage

```
A% = Asc("Hello")
```

1272

This example places the value 72 (the ANSI code for the character "H") in the variable A%.

Description

The Asc function returns the numeric ANSI value of the first character in the supplied string.

ATN FUNCTION

See Also: Cos, Sin, Tan, and Appendix A, Visual Basic Language Tutorial (Trigonometric Functions).

Purpose

The Atn function returns the arctangent of a numeric expression.

General Syntax

```
Atn(numericExpression)
```

Usage

```
A! = Atn(B!)
```

This example places the arctangent of the value of B! in the variable A!.

Description

Atn is a trigonometric function that returns the arctangent of the supplied expression. The arctangent is the inverse of tangent. The arctangent of a number gives the size of the angle for which the number is the tangent. The angle returned by the Atn function is in radians. If the supplied numeric expression is an integer, or single-precision variable, the returned value will be single-precision. Otherwise, Atn returns a double-precision value.

BEEP STATEMENT

Purpose

The Beep statement causes the computer's speaker to produce a short tone.

General Syntax

```
Beep
```

Usage

```
If ErrorNumber% > 0 Then Beep
```

This example "beeps" the speaker if the variable ErrorNumber is set.

Description

The Beep statement causes the computer to send a short tone to the speaker. You can control neither the tone nor the duration; however, issuing several beep commands consecutively can create the effect of a longer beep.

The Beep statement won't do anything if sound is turned off in the sound section of the Windows Control Panel application.

BEGINTRANS STATEMENT

See Also: CommitTrans, Rollback, and Chapter 27, Data Access.

Purpose

The BeginTrans statement begins a transaction block during database access.

General Syntax

```
BeginTrans
```

Usage

```
BeginTrans
```

Description

Transactions are changes to the database that must be made as a whole. Incomplete changes (due to a power outage or unforeseen error) can be avoided by using transactions. For example, most financial operations involve a debit from one account and a corresponding credit to another account. If the transaction failed before completing, one account may have a debit without any corresponding credit.

Use BeginTrans to begin a *transaction block,* or block of statements you would like to group together. You may nest transactions up to five deep. All changes to all databases (not just the one you're working on) are done in a manner that

1274

lets you either *commit* them as a block, writing them permanently to disk, or *roll back* and undo all changes since the BeginTrans statement. End a transaction block with CommitTrans or Rollback.

Transactions are only supported for some kinds of databases, and are used only with the Access database engine. See Chapter 27, Data Access, for more details.

CALL STATEMENT

See Also: Declare, Sub.

Purpose

The Call statement executes a Visual Basic sub procedure or a Windows Dynamic Link Library (DLL) procedure.

General Syntax

```
Call procedureName [(argument1[, argument2...]]...)
procedureName [argument1[, argument2 ]] ...
```

Usage

```
Call ManyBeeps (12)
```

This example transfers control to the sub procedure ManyBeeps, and passes the value of 12 to it as an argument.

```
ManyBeeps 12
```

This example transfers control to the sub procedure ManyBeeps, and passes the value of 12 to it as an argument, without using the Call keyword or parentheses.

```
SortArray Colors%()
```

The preceding statement transfers execution to the sub procedure SortArray, and passes the integer array Colors% to the procedure. The Call keyword and parentheses around the argument list have been omitted.

Description

The Call statement transfers control to a Visual Basic sub procedure, or to a procedure in a Windows DLL. The call may be followed by a list of arguments passed to the sub procedure. There are two methods for executing the Call statement. The first requires the use of the Call keyword and parentheses around the group of arguments (if any). The second method allows you to omit the Call keyword, but requires the surrounding parentheses to be omitted as well. In any case, if the argument being passed is an entire array, the array name must be followed by empty parentheses.

If not specified otherwise, variables passed to the sub procedure are passed "by reference." This allows the sub procedure to modify the actual contents of the variable being passed. You can also pass variables "by value," which creates a temporary variable and prevents the routine from changing the value. Do this by either enclosing a passed variable in parentheses or by using the ByVal keyword in the Declare statement for this routine (see the entry for the Declare statement in this appendix).

C<TYPE> (NUMERIC CONVERSION FUNCTIONS)

Purpose

Functions whose names have the form C<Type> convert an expression from any data type into the specified data type. The actual functions used for different data types are given below.

General Syntax

```
CCur(expression)
CDbl(expression)
CInt(expression)
CLng(expression)
CSng(expression)
CStr(expression)
CVar(expression)
```

Usage

```
A@ = CCur(Dbl#)        'Convert from Double to Currency
B# = CDbl(Itg%)        'Convert from Integer to Double
C% = CInt(Lng&)        'Convert from Long to Integer
D& = CLng(Vnt)         'Convert from Variant to Long
E! = CSng(Cnc@)        'Convert from Currency to Single
F$ = CStr(Dbl#)        'Convert from Double to String
G = CVar(Lng&)         'Convert from Long to Variant
```

The above examples demonstrate the use of the seven data type conversion functions.

Description

There are five numeric data type conversion functions, one string conversion function, and one variant conversion function in Visual Basic. These are CCur (convert to currency), CDbl (convert to Double), CInt (convert to Integer), CLng (convert to Long), CSng (convert to single), CStr (convert to string), and CVar (convert to Variant).

Each method converts an expression from any data type to the type specified by the function. You can generally do the same thing, without the explicit use of the conversion functions, by assigning an expression to a variable of the desired data type. The explicit use of the conversion functions can make your code clearer and less prone to inobvious errors. These functions can also be used to ensure the correct data type is being passed to a Visual Basic sub procedure or a Windows Dynamic Link Library (DLL).

With the numeric functions, the numeric expression parameter must be within the range of the resultant data type or Visual Basic will issue an overflow error.

CHDIR STATEMENT

See Also: ChDrive; CurDir, CurDir$; MkDir; RmDir.

Purpose

The ChDir statement changes the current working directory on the specified drive.

General Syntax

```
ChDir path$
```

path$ must be a string in the format of [drive:][\]dir[\subdir][\subdir...]

Usage

```
ChDir "D:\MYDIR"
```

This statement changes the current working (default) directory on drive "D:" to "MYDIR".

```
DirName$ = "\MAIN\MAILBOX"
ChDir DirName$
```

The above statements change the default directory on the default drive to "\MAIN\MAILBOX".

Description

The ChDir statement affects the operation of file-related commands such as Open and Kill. Those commands do not require the drive or path of a file name to be fully specified in order to perform their duties. When the drive and/or directory is not specified, those commands will use the current working, or default, drive and directory. It is thus very important to set the correct working directory before issuing commands that do not specify full path names.

The ChDir statement changes the setting of the default directory. In this statement the path$ parameter must be a valid directory on the drive specified, and may be no longer than 128 characters. If not, Visual Basic will issue a "Path not found error." If no drive is specified in the path parameter, the default drive is used. If a drive other than the current drive is specified, Visual Basic only changes the default directory on that drive; it does not change the default drive to the one in the path parameter. Use the ChDrive statement to change the default drive.

CHDRIVE STATEMENT

See Also: ChDir; CurDir, CurDir$; MkDir; RmDir.

Purpose

The ChDrive statement changes the current default drive.

General Syntax

```
ChDrive Drive$
```

Usage

```
ChDrive "A"
DriveSpec$ = "C:"
ChDrive DriveSpec$
```

Description

The ChDrive statement changes the default working drive for Visual Basic's file-related statements such as Open and Kill. Those commands do not require the drive or path of a file name to be fully specified in order to perform their duties. When the drive and/or directory is not specified, those commands will use the current working, or default, drive and directory.

1278

The ChDrive statement is used to change the current default drive setting. The drive argument must be a string whose first character corresponds to the letter of a valid DOS drive. If the drive argument is a null string, no action is taken.

CHOOSE FUNCTION

See Also: IIf, Switch.

Purpose

Use the Choose function to return a value from a list of arguments.

General Syntax

```
Choose(index%, expression1 [, expression2]...[expression13])
```

Usage

```
Choose(shipType%, "Federal Express", "UPS", "Airborne")
```

If shipType% has the value of 2, this function would then return "UPS".

Description

Use the Choose function to perform simple lookups. You can return any one of 13 different values as indicated by the index% argument. The list is 1 based, not 0 based. Thus, the first element has an index value of 1.

CHR, CHR$ FUNCTIONS

See Also: Asc.

Purpose

The Chr and Chr$ functions return the character that corresponds to the supplied ANSI code.

General Syntax

```
Chr$(AsciiCode%)
Chr(AsciiCode%)
```

Usage

```
CrLf$ = Chr$(13) & Chr$(10)
```

The above example places a carriage return and linefeed in the variable CrLf$.

Description

The Chr$ function is the complement to the Asc function. It returns the character whose ANSI code is specified as its argument. The ANSICode argument must be in the range of from 0 to 255. This function is useful for specifying characters that you cannot type at the keyboard, such as special control codes for the printer. Another good use for this function is generating double quote marks in strings. Because Visual Basic uses double quotes to delimit strings, you cannot include a double quote mark in a string directly. You can, however, use Chr$(34) to produce a double quote mark within a string.

The Chr function works identically but returns a variant instead of a string.

CLOSE STATEMENT

See Also: Open, Reset.

Purpose

Closes an open file channel.

General Syntax

```
Close [#][filenumber%][, [#]filenumber%]
```

Usage

```
Close
```

Closes all open files.

```
Close #1
```

Closes the file opened as file number 1.

```
Close 1, 5, 10
```

Closes the files opened as file number 1, 5 and 10. Notice that the # sign is optional.

Description

The Close statement closes a file that has previously been opened by the Open statement. The Close statement also flushes the buffers associated with the file and writes any remaining data in them to disk. If the file number supplied is not a currently open file, Visual Basic will ignore this statement and continue with the next statement. Although Visual Basic will automatically close all open files at program termination, it is good programming practice to close each open file before the program ends.

Once a file has been closed, the file number cannot be referenced by any other file-related statements (such as Get or Put) until an Open statement has been issued with the file number.

COMMAND, COMMAND$ FUNCTIONS

See Also: Environ, Environ$.

Purpose

The Command and Command$ functions return a variant or string that contains any command-line parameters that were used when Visual Basic or the Visual Basic environment program was started.

General Syntax

```
Command$
Command
```

Usage

```
Params$ = Command$
```

Stores command-line parameters for the current program into the string Params$.

Description

These functions return any text that followed the /CMD parameter on the command line. The string returned by the Visual Basic environment can be modified by choosing the Modify Command$... option from the Run menu. When used with a Visual Basic program, Command$ returns any text that followed the executable file name on the command line. This function is useful for providing a way for the user to set up different options at runtime. (Note that unlike the case with

DOS command-line parameters, the name of the program file is not included in the parameter string.)

Command returns a variant, Command$ returns a string.

COMMITTRANS STATEMENT

See Also: BeginTrans, Rollback, and Chapter 27, Data Access.

Purpose

Use the CommitTrans statement to end a transaction block.

General Syntax

```
CommitTrans
```

Usage

```
CommitTrans
```

Description

Transactions are changes to the database that must be made as a whole. Incomplete changes (due to a power outage or unforeseen error) can be avoided by using transactions. For example, most financial operations involve a debit from one account and a corresponding credit to another account. If the transaction failed before completing, one account may have a debit without any corresponding credit.

Use CommitTrans to end a *transaction block,* or block of statements you would like to group together. You may nest transactions up to five deep. All changes to all databases (not just the one you're working on) are done in a manner that lets you either *commit* them as a block, writing them permanently to disk, or *roll back* and undo all changes since the BeginTrans statement. End a transaction block with CommitTrans or Rollback.

Transactions are only supported for some kinds of databases, and are used only with the Access database engine. See Chapter 27, Data Access, for more details.

COMPACTDATABASE STATEMENT

See Also: RepairDatabase, and Chapter 27, Data Access.

Purpose

Use the CompactDatabase statement to compact, encrypt, or decrypt an Access database.

1282

General Syntax

```
CompactDatabase source$, dest$ [, locale$ [, options&]]
```

Usage

```
CompactDatabase dbFileName$, "~TEMP.TMP"
```

Description

Databases tend to fragment with use as records are added and deleted. Use the CompactDatabase statement to defragment and shrink a database. You can also specify a new sort order, encrypt or decrypt the database, or save it in the older Access 1.0 format.

The CompactDatabase statement creates a new database with the name given in the destfile$ argument. It copies all the security settings from the existing database, and then copies each record to the new database. This makes the entire database contiguous on the hard drive (assuming the hard drive itself is defragmented) with each record stored in the most efficient manner possible. Note that sourcefile$ and destfile$ must be different.

See Chapter 27, Data Access, for more information.

CONST STATEMENT

See Also: Deftype, Dim, Global, ReDim, Static.

Purpose

The Const statement assigns a meaningful symbolic name to a constant value.

General Syntax

```
[Global] Const name = expression [,name = expression]
```

Usage

```
YES = True
NO = False
MAYBE = 999
```

In this example, the Const statement assigns the constant value True to the name "YES," False to the name "NO," and 999 to the name "MAYBE."

Description

The Const statement provides a way for you to set up a symbolic name to represent a constant value. Creating named constants makes for more readable and self-documenting code. Good programmers use constants instead of the literal values. If a program uses the same value in several places, using a constant lets you make changes to the value in only one place when necessary. Visual Basic protects you against inadvertantly changing a constant's value by issuing an error message if any such attempt is made.

A constant must be defined before it is used. If not, Visual Basic generates a "Duplicate definition" error at compile time. It is common to use all capital letters in a constant's name. This makes recognizing constants in a program easier.

If a constant is defined in the global module, the Global keyword may precede the Const statement. This declares the constant as global throughout the project, and may be used by all procedures in all modules. If a constant is defined in the General Declarations area of a module, that constant may be used by all procedures in that module, but is inaccessible to other modules. A Const can also be used within a Visual Basic sub procedure or function, making the constant local to that sub or function.

There are some restrictions on what can be assigned to a constant. A constant may be assigned a numeric or a string literal. A string literal is any string that is bracketed by double quotes. A numeric literal is simply a number, such as 1 or 564.34. Constant assignments may include arithmetic and/or logical operators. The exception to this rule is the exponentiation operator (^), which causes Visual Basic to generate an "Illegal function call" error. Another constant may be used in the assignment of a constant (see the example above), but a variable cannot. A constant cannot be assigned a value from a built-in or programmer-defined function. String concatenation may not be used.

You may specify the data type of the constant by using a type declaration character at the end of the constant name. However, further references to the constant need not include the type declaration character. For instance, in the following code, a constant is set up that specifies the integer data type, yet the declaration character is not used thereafter:

```
Const MAXLOOPS% = 10
x% = 0
Do
     x% = x% + 1
Loop Until x% > MAXLOOPS
```

If no type declaration character is used in the Const statement, Visual Basic will automatically assign a data type to the constant. If you assign a string to a constant, Visual Basic will set the constant up as a string. If the constant is assigned a numeric value, Visual Basic will check the size of the number being assigned to the constant and assign it the simplest possible data type. The data type assigned to a constant is not affected by the use of the DefType statements.

COS FUNCTION

See Also: Atn, Sin, Tan, and Appendix A, Visual Basic Language Tutorial (Trigonometric Functions).

Purpose

The Cos function returns the cosine of an angle.

General Syntax

```
Cos(angle)
```

angle is expressed in radians.

Usage

```
A! = Cos(4.93)
```

The cosine of 4.93 is assigned to the variable A!.

Description

The Cos function determines the cosine of an angle. The function expects the angle to be expressed in radians; therefore, if the angle is in degrees, it must first be converted using the formula radians = degrees * pi/180.

If angle is supplied as an integer or a single-precision value, Cos will return a single-precision value; otherwise it returns a double-precision value.

CREATEOBJECT FUNCTION

See Also: GetObject and Chapter 26, Object Linking and Embedding (OLE).

Purpose

Use the CreateObject function to create an OLE automation object.

General Syntax

```
CreateObject(class$)
```

Usage

```
Dim obj As Object
Set obj = CreateObject("Excel5.WorkSheet")
```

Description

Use CreateObject to create an object that you manipulate in *OLE automation*. OLE automation lets you expose another application's features just as you would any Visual Basic control, like a command button or text box. This makes applications that support OLE automation very similar to Visual Basic custom controls.

To use CreateObject, you must first declare a variable of type Object. You can use Dim, ReDim, Global, or Static to declare the variable. After dimensioning the variable, use the Set keyword to assign the object returned by CreateObject to the variable, as shown in the example given above. Once you've created the object and put it in the object variable, you use whatever properties and methods are appropriate for that object.

See Chapter 26, Object Linking and Embedding (OLE), for more details.

CURDIR, CURDIR$ FUNCTIONS

See Also: ChDir, ChDrive, MkDir, RmDir.

Purpose

The CurDir$ function returns the current default directory for the specified drive.

General Syntax

```
CurDir$[(drive$)]
CurDir[(drive$)]
```

Usage

```
Default$ = CurDir$
A$ = CurDir$("A")
Cdirectory = CurDir("C:")
```

The first example assigns a string containing the default directory path from the default drive to the variable Default$. The second example assigns the default directory on drive A:, while the third example assigns the default directory path on drive C: to the variant C directory.

Description

DOS always maintains a default directory for each drive in the system. The default directory is the one that will be searched first for a file name if no path is specified. The CurDir$ function returns the default directory of the specified drive. If a drive designation is supplied, only the first character is used. The

1286

drive letter can be uppercase or lowercase, and must be a valid drive letter ("A" through n, where n is specified by the Lastdrive parameter in the CONFIG.SYS file, or "E" if not specified). If the letter is not a valid drive, a "Device unavailable" error occurs. If the first character of the drive parameter is not a letter, Visual Basic generates an "Illegal function call" error. If no drive is specified, or the drive parameter is a null string, the default drive is used.

Since the path returned by CurDir$ includes the drive letter, this function is also useful for determining which drive is currently the default drive.

CurDir returns a variant; CurDir$ returns a string.

CVDATE FUNCTION

See Also: C<Type> and Chapter 22, Time.

Purpose

Use the CVDate function to convert a variety of formats into a variant of type 7 (date).

General Syntax

```
CVDate(expression)
```

Usage

```
newDate = CVDate(InputBox$("Enter the new date", "Date"))
```

Description

The CVDate function converts a variety of input expressions into a valid date variant. This saves you from writing more specific code by letting CVDate handle the intricacies of the conversion. The argument must be a string or numeric expression that can be interpreted as a date. If the expression cannot be interpreted as a date, CVDate generates runtime error number 13 (Type Mismatch).

CVDate handles numbers, strings, and strings that look like numbers differently. If the input is numeric, CVDate checks to see if it is within the range of -657434 to 2958465. If it is, it converts it to a date. If not, it generates a runtime error. A string expression that looks like a date (for example, "April 1, 1994, 11:34 pm" or "12/10/98") is converted into a date. A string expression that looks like a number (for example, "3456") is first converted to a number, then validated as for regular numeric input. Finally, any other string expression (such as "Foobar" or "April 1st, 1994 at 11:34 in the morning") generates a runtime error.

See Chapter 22, Time, for more information about the CVDate function.

DATE, DATE$ FUNCTIONS AND STATEMENTS

See Also: DateValue, Now, Time$.

Purpose

The Date and Date$ functions return the current system date, while the Date and Date$ statements set it.

General Syntax

Function:

```
Date$
Date
```

Statement:

```
Date$ = datestring$
Date = dateVariant
```

Usage

```
Today$ = Date$
```

Assigns a string containing the current system date to the variable Today$.

```
Date$ = "01-01-1996"
```

Sets the current system date to January 1, 1996.

Description

Date$ can be used as a function, to return the current system date; or as a statement, to set the current system date. When used as a function, Date$ returns a string with the current system date in the format mm-dd-yyyy. As a statement, the system date may be set by using a string in a valid date format. The valid date string formats are

mm-dd-yyyy
mm/dd/yyyy
mm-dd-yy
mm/dd/yy

The date can be set to any date between January 1, 1980, and December 31, 2099, inclusive. If the date is not in this range, or the format of the date string is not one of those above, Visual Basic issues an "Illegal function call" error.

The Date function returns the current system date as a variant rather than a string. The Date statement sets the system date much as the Date$ statement does, but it accepts a much wider range of date formats. It accepts all formats that the Date$ statement does, and accepts unambiguous dates that contain month names. For instance, "July 4, 1995" or "Aug 20 1993" are both legal arguments for the Date statement.

If the date is set using the Date$ statement, its permanence is dependent on the type of system and version of DOS being used. Generally, if the system has a CMOS memory and is running under DOS 3.3 or greater, the date will be retained in the CMOS. Otherwise, the date may be lost when the system is powered down.

Comments

In the above descriptions, mm refers to the month, dd to the day, yy to a two-digit year, and yyyy to a four-digit year.

DATEADD FUNCTION

See Also: DateDiff, DatePart.

Purpose

Use the DateAdd function to add a specified time interval to a date variant.

General Syntax

```
DateAdd(interval$, number%, dateVar)
```

Usage

```
newDate = DateAdd("m", 3, Now)
```

Description

The DateAdd function returns a date variant obtained by adding the number of intervals you specify to the supplied date. If number% is positive, DateAdd returns a date in the future; if negative, DateAdd returns a date in the past. The example syntax adds three months to the system date. Use Table B-12 to specify the correct interval.

Time	Interval$
Year	yyyy
Quarter	q
Month	m
Day of Year	y
Day	d
Weekday	w
Week	ww
Hour	h
Minute	n
Second	s

Table B-12 Codes used to specify the interval in the DateAdd, DateDiff, and DatePart functions

DATEDIFF FUNCTION

See Also: DateAdd, DatePart.

Purpose

Use the DateDiff function to determine how many time periods lie between two dates.

General Syntax

```
DateDiff(interval$, date1, date2)
```

Usage

```
numWeeks% = DateDiff("ww", lastSaved, Now)
```

Description

The DateDiff lets you find out how many time intervals are in-between two dates. Use the interval$ codes given in Table B-12 in the DateAdd function. The example syntax calculates the number of weeks elapsed between the current system date and the variable lastSaved.

DATEPART FUNCTION

See Also: DateAdd, DateDiff.

Purpose

Use the DatePart function to return a part of date.

General Syntax

```
DatePart(interval$, date)
```

Usage

```
curMonth$ = DatePart("m", Now)
```

Description

The DatePart function returns the specified part of a given date. Use the interval$ codes given in Table B-12 in the DateAdd function. The example syntax returns the name of the current month.

DATESERIAL FUNCTION

See Also: DateValue, Day, Month, Now, Year.

Purpose

The DateSerial function returns a variant of type 7 (date) based on the supplied year, month, and day.

General Syntax

```
DateSerial(year%, month%, day%)
```

Usage

```
MyDate = DateSerial(1921, 02, 26)
```

Places a date variant representing the date February 26, 1921, into the variable MyDate.

Description

The DateSerial function returns a date variant representing a date in the range of from January 1, 100 to December 31, 9999, inclusive. If the date requested is not in this range, Visual Basic issues an "Illegal function call" error. The date variant represents the number of days since December 30, 1899. Therefore, January 01, 1900 has a date variant of 2, while January 1, 1753, has a negative date variant of -53688.

The most useful aspect of this function is its ability to return a date based on the desired date's relation to another date. In other words, if the year, month, and day of January 02, 1996, are plugged into this function, the value 35066 is returned. However, if we subtract 30 from the day parameter,

```
D# = DateSerial(1996, 01, 02 - 30)
```

the value 35036 is returned (30 days before January 2, 1996). The date variant representing the date December 03, 1995 is 35036.

DATEVALUE FUNCTION

See Also: Date, Date$; DateSerial; Day; Month; Now; Weekday; Year.

Purpose

The DateValue function returns a variant of type 7 (date) that represents the date of the supplied string.

General Syntax

```
DateValue(datestring$)
```

Usage

```
D = DateValue("01-01-1996")
```

Assigns a date variant representing the date January 1, 1996, to the variable D.

Description

The DateValue function returns a double-precision date variant representing a date in the range of from January 1, 100 to December 31, 9999, inclusive. If the date requested is not in this range, Visual Basic issues an "Illegal function call" error. The date variant represents the number of days since December 30, 1899. Therefore, January 01, 1900, has a date variant of 2, while January 1, 1753, has a negative date variant of -53688.

DateValue can translate almost any expression that represents an unambiguous date, including strings containing month names. For instance, the following dates can be understood and translated:

August 06, 1995
Aug 06, 1995
06 August, 1995
06 Aug, 1995
8/6/95
08-06-95
08-06-1995

DAY FUNCTION

See Also: DateSerial, DateValue, Now, Weekday.

Purpose

The Day function returns an integer, in the range of 1 to 31, representing the day of the month based on the supplied date variant.

General Syntax

```
Day(dateVariant)
```

Usage

```
Today = DateValue(Date$)
DayOfMonth% = Day(Today)
```

Returns today's day of month from date variant returned by DateValue and Date$ functions.

Description

This function uses a variant of type 7 (date) representing a date to return an integer value representing the day of the month, from 1 to 31, inclusive. The supplied date variant represents the number of days since December 30, 1899. Therefore January 01, 1900, has a value of 2, while January 1, 1753, has a negative value of -53688. The supplied date variant must represent a date in the range of from January 1, 100 to December 31, 9999, inclusive. If the date requested is not in this range, Visual Basic issues an "Illegal function call" error.

DDB FUNCTION

See Also: SLN, SYD.

Purpose

The DDB function returns the depreciation of an asset based on the double-declining balance method.

General Syntax

```
DDB(cost@, salvage@, life%, period%)
```

Usage

```
periodDepreciation = DDB(itemValue, 0, 30, whichPeriod)
```

Description

Use the DDB function to return the proper deprication amount for a given item value at a given point in its lifespan. You can specify the initial cost of the item, the eventual salvage value of the item when finally scrapped, the total lifespan of the item, and which period you want to calculate for. The period must be in the same units as lifespan.

The DDB function uses the double-declining balance method. This places the bulk of the depreciation at the beginning of the lifespan and progressively less at the end.

DECLARE STATEMENT

See Also: Call.

Purpose

The Declare statement informs Visual Basic that you will be using external procedures in Dynamic Link Libraries (DLLs). Declare is also used to specify certain Visual Basic functions for use without parentheses.

General Syntax

```
Declare Sub procname Lib libname$ [Alias aliasname$][(arg-list)]
Declare Function procname [Lib libname$] [Alias aliasname$][(arg-list)][As type]
```

Usage

```
Declare Sub Scramble Lib "Puzzle" (ByVal Pieces As Integer)
```

This example declares the DLL procedure "Scramble" with one integer parameter (to be passed by value to Visual Basic).

```
Declare Function No_Of_Pieces Lib "Puzzle" Alias "_NOP" As Integers
```

This declares the DLL integer function "_NOP" to be referenced as No_Of_Pieces.

```
Declare Function ErrorStatus As Integer
```

This declares a Visual Basic function for use without parentheses.

Description

Use the Declare statement to set up the use of sub procedures and functions contained in a DLL. The Declare statement can only be used in a global module, or in the declarations section of a module or form. DLL routines that are declared in a form's declarations section are available to that form only; otherwise the DLL routines are available to all procedures in all modules.

The procname is the name by which the Visual Basic program will reference the DLL procedure. This name must follow the same rules as a Visual Basic variable name. If the name of the procedure in the DLL does not conform to Visual Basic's naming conventions, you must use the Alias keyword to specify the name of the procedure as it appears in the DLL.

Including a data type declaration character at the end of a function name declares the type of data that function will return. This can also be done by using the As type clause, where type is Integer, Long, Single, Double, Currency, or String.

The libname parameter specifies the DOS filename of the Dynamic Link Library. You must specify the full path name if the library is not in the default directory on the default drive.

Declaring the arguments for an external procedure can sometimes be a tricky process. Several arguments can be declared one after another, separated by commas. The format for declaring arguments is as follows:

```
([ByVal]variablename[As type][,[ByVal]variablename[As type]...])
```

Sometimes a DLL procedure will require that an argument be passed "by value." This means the routine is expecting the value of the argument rather than its address to be pushed onto the stack. You set the ByVal keyword to specify that an argument's value rather than its address is to be provided to the called procedure.

If no type declaration character is used at the end of the argument's variable name, you may use the As type clause to specify the type of variable being passed. Type can be Integer, Long, Single, Double, Currency, String (variable-length only), Variant, Any, Form, Control, or any programmer-defined type. The Any type is used to override data type checking for that argument. The type "Any" cannot be used on arguments that are being passed by value. The Form and Control data types are used only when a form or control is being passed to the external procedure.

An additional use of the Declare statement is to allow your program to call a function that takes no arguments, without having to use empty parentheses in the function call. Thus, in the third example above, your program can now have a statement such as:

```
ErrNo = ErrorStatus
```

rather than:

```
ErrNo = ErrorStatus()
```

This facility is useful mainly in converting older BASIC programs that do not provide parentheses when calling such functions. You can make such declarations only at the module (not global or form) level.

DEF<TYPE> STATEMENT

Purpose

Statements of the form Def<type> can be used to set the default data type for variables and functions in forms and modules. The <type> part of the keyword actually stands for the types specified in the keywords below.

General Syntax

```
DefCur firstletter[-lastletter[, firstletter-[lastletter]]]...
DefDbl firstletter[-lastletter[, firstletter-[lastletter]]]...
DefInt firstletter[-lastletter[, firstletter-[lastletter]]]...
DefLng firstletter[-lastletter[, firstletter-[lastletter]]]...
DefSng firstletter[-lastletter[, firstletter-[lastletter]]]...
DefStr firstletter[-lastletter[, firstletter-[lastletter]]]...
DefVar firstletter[-lastletter[, firstletter-[lastletter]]]...
```

Usage

```
DefCur A-D      'Sets default type to Currency for variables starting with A, B, C, or D
DefDbl E-H      'Sets default type to Double for variables starting with E, F, G, or H
DefInt I-L      'Sets default type to Integer for variables starting with I, J, K, or L
DefLng M-P, Y   'Sets default type to Long for variables starting with M, N, O, P, or Y
DefSng Q-T      'Sets default type to Single for variables starting with Q, R, S, or T
DefStr U-X      'Sets default type to String for variables starting with U, V, W, or X
DefVar Z        'Sets default type to Variant for variables starting with Z
```

Description

The Def<type> statements are used in the declarations section of a form or module. They allow you to define the default data type for variables based on the first letter of the variable's name. The firstletter-lastletter parameters define the range of letters that will be affected by this Def<type> statement. The letter range is not case-sensitive, so g-M is the same as G-M. If the letter range is specified backward (for example, Z-M instead of M-Z), Visual Basic will transpose the letter range in order to process it alphabetically.

The Def<type> statement affects only the module or form in which it appears. Even if it is used in the global module of a program, only those variables defined in the global module are affected.

Once a range has been established with a Def<type> statement, that range cannot be redefined. If a redefinition is attempted, Visual Basic issues a "Duplicate Deftype" error. The use of the Dim, Static, or Global statements for individual variables overrides the type assigned by Def<type>, as does the use of a type declaration character.

DIM STATEMENT

See Also: Global, Option Base, ReDim, Static, Type.

Purpose

The Dim statement allocates storage space for and establishes the data type of Visual Basic variables or arrays in a module or procedure.

General Syntax

For declaring the data type of a simple variable:

```
Dim [Shared] name [As [New] type][, name [As [New] type]]...
```

For declaring an array:

```
Dim [Shared] name[(subscript-range)][As type][, name[(subscript-range)][As type]...
```

Usage

```
Dim A as Integer        'Declares the variable A as an integer
Dim B(100) As Single    'Declares single-precision array B, with 101 elements numbered 0 to 100
Dim C$(-30 to 60)       'Declares string array C$, with 91 elements numbered -30 to +60
```

Description

The Dim statement allocates storage space for and declares data types of both simple and array variables. When the Dim statement is used in the declarations section of a form or module, the variable or array declared by that statement is available to all procedures in that form or module. Using the Dim statement inside a procedure allocates a local simple variable that cannot be seen by any other procedure. Dim cannot be used to allocate storage for an array within a procedure. The Static and ReDim commands are used to do this. To declare a variable or array that is accessible globally (across modules and forms), use the Global statement in the declarations section of the global module, rather than using Dim.

The Dim statement is used along with the As type clause to explicitly declare the data type of a simple variable. For instance,

```
Dim MyVar As Integer
```

creates a storage for an Integer variable named MyVar. This is an alternative method to using the Visual Basic type declaration characters (!, @, #, $, %, &).

1298

This also allows you to assign your own data types (created with the Type statement) to a variable, as in the following code:

```
Type Rolodex
    Name as String * 20
    Number as Long
    Address as String * 100
End Type

Dim Cards as Rolodex
```

The most frequently used purpose for the Dim statement is to allocate storage for an array and to specify its dimensions and range of subscripts. Arrays provide a method for creating an entire series of variables and referencing them by the same variable name. An index number (called the subscript) determines which particular element in an array is being referenced. A more detailed discussion on the concept of arrays can be found in the tutorial in Appendix A.

The dimensions of an array are defined by the entry in the subscript-range portion of the Dim statement. The subscript range follows this format:

```
[lo-element To] hi-element[,[lo-element To] hi-element]...
```

The lo-element parameter lets you define the range of the subscripts as well as the number of elements in the array. If lo-element is not used, the lowest valid subscript will be 0 (unless the default has been changed using Option Base), and the supplied number will be the highest valid subscript. The number of elements allowed in an array depends on the desired data type for that array and available memory. Visual Basic 1.0 allowed approximately 64K of data space for each array, but Visual Basic 2.0 and 3.0 allow for *huge arrays* that can be as large as all available memory. You don't have to do anything special to create huge arrays; Visual Basic handles all the tricky memory management details for you.

Dim initializes all elements of variable-length string arrays to null strings. All other arrays are initialized to 0s (including fixed-length strings and user-defined types).

At times it may be useful to have a multidimensional array. To declare such an array, include as many sets of subscripts as needed, separated by commas.

```
Dim MultiArray (1 To 100, 50 To 60, -100 to 100) As Double
```

The example above declares an array with three dimensions of 100, 11, and 201 elements, respectively. The first dimension can be referenced by subscripts from 1 to 100, the second may have subscripts ranging from 50 to 60, and the third from -100 to +100. Visual Basic allows arrays to have as many as 60 dimensions. Be cautious in declaring arrays of many dimensions; the storage space needed multiplies for each dimension. The above example would create an array with a total of (100 * 11 * 201) = 221,100 elements that needs 1,768,880 bytes to hold it!

Leaving the parentheses empty in a Dim statement declares a dynamic array. The number of dimensions and elements in a dynamic array is defined within a procedure by the ReDim statement. Dynamic arrays are allocated at runtime, and may have the number of elements redefined at any time. However, once set, the number of dimensions in a dynamic array cannot be changed. See the entry for ReDim in this appendix for more discussion of dynamic arrays.

Use the New keyword to create a new object variable. This technique is most commonly used to create a new child form in an MDI application:

```
Dim F As New Form1
```

This example creates a new instance of Form1. All references to F refer to this new instance. F uses Form1 as a "template," and is an exact duplicate of Form1. See the discussion in Chapter 3, Using Objects, and Chapter 4, Forms and Menus, for more about object variables and the use of the New keyword.

The Share keyword does nothing at all; it is retained to maintain compatibility with older versions of BASIC.

DIR, DIR$ FUNCTIONS

See Also: CurDir$, ChDir, ChDrive.

Purpose

The Dir and Dir$ functions return a file name that matches the supplied pattern.

General Syntax

For the first call to Dir$ for a pattern:

```
Dir$(pattern$)
Dir(pattern$)
```

For each successive call for the same pattern:

```
Dir$
Dir
```

Usage

```
temp$ = Dir$("*.DOC")          'Returns the first directory entry that matches "*.DOC"
Do Until temp$ = ""
    i = i + 1                   'increment counter
    docs$(i) = temp$           'store filename
    temp$ = Dir$               'Returns each successive directory entry that matches "*.DOC"
Loop
```

Description

The first time Dir$ is called, the pattern$ parameter must be included, or Visual Basic issues an "Illegal function call" error. Pattern$ refers to a string expression that represents a potential file name. It can include a drive specifier, a file path, and a file name. Wildcard characters (? and *) can be used in the file name, following the usual rules used by DOS. If the drive and/or path is not specified, Dir$ will use the default drive and/or path. When pattern$ is supplied, Dir$ returns the first directory entry that matches the supplied pattern. Dir$ can then be called with no argument to retrieve each successive directory entry that matches the original pattern. The directory entry returned by Dir$ includes only the file name and extension. When all directory entries have been retrieved, Dir$ returns a null string. When this happens, the next call to Dir$ must again supply a pattern or suffer an "Illegal function call" error.

It is not necessary to call Dir$ until a null string is returned before a new pattern is used.

Dir returns a variant; Dir$ returns a string.

Comments

Visual Basic does not check to see if the supplied pattern parameter is a valid DOS file name. If the pattern supplied is not a valid file name, Dir$ just returns a null string. If the pattern specified a drive that does not exist, a "Device unavailable" error will be returned.

DO...LOOP STATEMENTS

See Also: Exit, For...Next, While...Wend.

Purpose

The Do... Loop statements repeat a group of program instructions until a condition is met or while a condition exists.

General Syntax

To test the condition at the top of a loop:

```
Do [{While | Until} condition]
    [statements]
    [Exit Do]
    [statements]
Loop
```

To test the condition at the bottom of the loop:

```
Do
    [statements]
    [Exit Do]
    [statements]
Loop [{While | Until} condition]
```

Usage

```
Do
    A% = MsgBox("Please click Yes button", 3)
Loop Until A% = 6
```

This example repeatedly displays a message box until the user clicks on the "Yes" button.

Description

The Do...Loop statement executes a block of statements while a specified condition is True, or until a condition becomes True. The Microsoft Visual Basic Language Reference documents a "condition" as any expression that can evaluate to a True (-1) or False (0) value. However, the Do...Loop structure considers the condition met if it evaluates to any non-zero numeric value. The condition may be tested at either the beginning or end of the loop. In effect, this provides you with five styles of looping: Do While, Do Until, Loop While, Loop Until, and the infinite Do...Loop.

The Do While...Loop first checks the condition before executing any statements within the statement block. If the condition tests out as a nonzero value, the statement block is executed. When execution reaches the Loop keyword, the program will branch back up to the Do, and the condition will be checked again. The execution of this statement block will repeat until the condition evaluates as a False (0) value.

The Do Until...Loop also first checks the condition before executing any statements within the statement block. If the condition tests out as a False (0) value, the statement block is executed. When execution reaches the Loop keyword, the program will branch back up to the Do, and the condition will be checked again. The execution of this statement block will repeat until the condition evaluates as a Non-False (nonzero) value.

The Do...Loop While will execute all the statements in the block once before checking the condition. When execution reaches the Loop keyword, the condition is checked. If it evaluates as a True (nonzero) value, the program branches back to the Do and the statement block is again executed. The execution of this statement block will repeat until the condition evaluates as a False (0) value.

The Do...Loop Until will execute all the statements in the block once before checking the condition. When execution reaches the Loop keyword, the condition is checked. If it evaluates as a False (0) value, the program branches back to the Do and the statement block is again executed. The execution of this statement block will repeat until the condition evaluates as a Non-False (nonzero) value.

The final style consists of the infinite loop. Because the Do...Loop's conditional statement is optional, you can create a loop that will execute continuously, without end. Generally, this type of loop is used to perform background-oriented tasks. If you write a program with an infinite loop, you should provide a way for the operating system to continue to perform any needed tasks. Most often, this is done with the DoEvents function (see the entry for the DoEvents function in this appendix). Since there is rarely a case in which you would desire to write a true infinite loop, you should provide some sort of trigger that will either end the program, or exit the loop. The most common way to exit an infinite loop is to use the Exit Do statement. This command skips any commands between it and the Loop keyword, exits the loop, and continues execution with the next instruction following the Loop keyword. See the tutorial in Appendix A, Visual Basic Language Tutorial, for further discussion and examples of the Do...Loop constructs.

DOEVENTS FUNCTION AND STATEMENT

Purpose

The DoEvents function temporarily surrenders control to the operating environment (Windows) so that all other programs running in the background may execute any needed tasks. This function returns the number of open windows created by your Visual Basic application. It is most commonly used in idle loops, in conjunction with the SendKeys statement, or during Dynamic Data Exchange conversations. The DoEvents statement does the same thing as the DoEvents function, but does not return a value.

General Syntax

```
DoEvents()          'function
DoEvents            'statement
```

Usage

```
Offset = MaxRow% \ 2
Do While Offset > 0
    Limit = MaxRow% - Offset
    Do
        Switch = False
        For Row = 1 TO Limit
            If SortArray#(Row) > SortArray#(Row + Offset) Then
```

(continued on next page)

(continued from previous page)

```
                    Swap SortArray#(Row), SortArray#(Row + Offset)
                    Switch = Row
              End If
        Next Row
        Limit = Switch - Offset
    Loop While Switch
    Offset = Offset \ 2
    DoEvents                    'Place DoEvents here to give the operating system some time
Loop
```

In this example the DoEvents function is used at the bottom of a loop that controls a sorting algoritm. Since the sort may take a while, we wish to give the operating system a chance to complete some of its tasks while we are sorting.

Description

There are two methods for creating a multitasking environment: preemptive and nonpreemptive. Preemptive environments give each running program a certain amount of processing time. If the program does not complete its task in its allotted time, the operating environment will interrupt it and put it on hold. It will then allow the next program to execute until its allotted time has expired. The operating environment continually performs this switching from program to program, thereby performing multitasking.

Windows is a nonpreemptive environment. Programs that run under Windows wait for events to occur, and when an event happens, the program then executes an event handler to react to it. In Visual Basic all of the events that are related to an object are event handlers. Because they are not actually executing code, several programs can reside together within the Windows environment while waiting for an event to occur. However, once one program begins to execute an event handler, it has full control of the operating environment and prevents other programs from performing any tasks at all until the handler is finished processing. This usually is not a problem, because most event handlers are written to perform their tasks quickly. Even so, some method must be in place so that large and slower processing handlers may temporarily yield to the operating environment and allow other programs to check for events. In Visual Basic the DoEvents function performs this task.

There are three common uses for the DoEvents function. First, this function is used to create an idle loop in your programs. Sometimes your program will have a set of instructions that need to be performed repeatedly in a Do...Loop, For...Next, or While...Wend loop, but you do not wish this loop to monopolize the operating environment. Such a loop is an idle loop. In these cases you may place a DoEvents function somewhere within the loop so other programs in the environment may process any events that have occurred since the loop began (or the last DoEvents was executed). For instance, suppose your program needed to sort a large array. You know that such a sort may take a while, so including a DoEvents function within the sort routine will allow the sort to act as if it is being performed in the background.

1304

Second, DoEvents can be used to pause your program so a SendKeys statement may be processed. Normally, SendKeys is used to send simulated keystrokes to an application. SendKeys has an argument that instructs it to pause until the destination program processes the sent keystrokes. However, this argument is ineffective if the source and destination programs are the same. In this case you can follow the SendKeys statement with a DoEvents function, which will pause processing long enough for the application to process the keystrokes. For more on the SendKeys statement, see Chapter 16, Keyboard Input.

Finally, the DoEvents function can be used during Dynamic Data Exchange (DDE) conversations. As mentioned above, when your Visual Basic program has control of the environment, no other programs can respond to events. Therefore, if your program initiates a DDE conversation with another application, it must allow that application to respond to the DDE events. It is a good practice to follow each DDE Link... operation (or small groups of operations) with a DoEvents function call. For more on DDE, refer to Chapter 25, Dynamic Data Exchange.

The DoEvents statement does exactly the same thing as the DoEvents function, but does not return a value.

Comments

Care should be taken so that the DoEvents function is not called recursively. This means you need to make sure that the event that executes the DoEvents function does not get executed a second time before the DoEvents function returns control to your program. Recursive calls to this function can easily cause Windows to run out of resources. For instance, imagine your application has a command button that performs a time-consuming task when the user clicks on it. You'd probably want to include a DoEvents function call in the routine, so other applications could respond to events while yours performed its task. Your button's Click event might look something like this:

```
Sub Command1_Click ()
    Dim Done As Integer

    Done = FALSE
    Do
        :
        [this is where your code would appear]
        :
        A% = DoEvents()          'Place this here so other programs can do their thing
    Loop Until Done
End Sub
```

At first, it looks as if this routine would perform as wished. However, what happens if the user clicks on the same button while the DoEvents function is executing? Your Visual Basic program would react to the click by again initiating the Command1_Click event, thereby causing two instances of the routine to be executing concurrently.

The best way to prevent this from occurring is to disable the control whose event executes the DoEvents function. For instance, we could add two lines to the above Click event:

```
Sub Command1_Click ()
    Dim Done As Integer

    Command1.Enabled = False    'Disable the button so it cannot execute this event again
    Done = FALSE
    Do
        :
        [this is where your code would appear]
        :
        A% = DoEvents()          'Place this here so other programs can do their thing
    Loop Until Done
    Command1.Enabled = True     'Enable the button so it can now be clicked upon
End Sub
```

In this example the button this event is associated with gets disabled before the time-consuming portion of its task is executed. It stays disabled until the task is complete.

END STATEMENT

See Also: Function, If...Then...Else, Select Case, Stop, Sub, Type.

Purpose

The End statement specifies the end of a program or of a block of statements such as a sub procedure or function.

General Syntax

```
End [Function | If | Select | Sub | Type]
```

Usage

```
Sub Hello
    Print Hello
End Sub
```

Description

The End statement is used to end a program, or, when accompanied by another keyword, to terminate one of several types of statement blocks.

End by itself terminates program execution, closes all files, clears all variables, and erases all forms and modules from memory. Executing the End statement does not trigger the Form_Unload or Form_QueryUnload events.

"End Function" signifies the end of a Function definition. An End Function must terminate every Function block. It is not generally necessary to type this statement in, as Visual Basic automatically adds it when the Function keyword is used.

"End If" terminates a multiple-line If...Then...Else block. If an If...Then...Else statement is in multiple-line format, the End If must be used to terminate the block. Not doing so results in a "Block If without End If" error at compile time.

"End Select" ends a Select Case block. Not using the End Select will generate a "Select Case without End Select" error at compile time.

"End Sub" signifies the end of a sub procedure definition. An End Sub must terminate every Sub block. It is not generally necessary to type this statement in, as Visual Basic automatically adds it when the Sub keyword is used.

"End Type" marks the end of a programmer-defined type definition. End Type must be used with the Type keyword, or a "Statement invalid in Type block" error will result.

ENVIRON, ENVIRON$ FUNCTIONS

See Also: Command, Command$.

Purpose

The Environ$ function returns settings from the operating system's environment table.

General Syntax

```
Environ$({entry-name$ | entry-position%})
Environ({entry-name$ | entry-position%})
```

Usage

```
A$ = Environ$("Path")
```

Places the current path into the variable A$.

```
A$ = Eviron$(1)
```

Places the current setting for the first environment table entry into the variable A$.

Description

DOS maintains a table of strings called "environment variables." Values in the environment table typically store information about such things as the current drive and path, the location of the command processor, or special settings needed by various programs.

The Environ$ function allows the program to read the current setting of the operating system's environment table. Entries in the environment table are set by using the DOS command syntax SET entry-name=entry-value. See a DOS reference manual for more information on the SET command. Environ$ allows you to specify either the name or position of the entry to be retrieved.

If you specify a table entry name, it must match exactly (including capitalization) one of the entry names in the environment table, or a null string is returned. If the supplied string does match an entry name, Environ$ returns only the text assigned to that entry.

You can also specify an entry number as the parameter to Environ$. This number corresponds to the position of an entry in the environment table. For example, if a numeric argument of 2 is used, Environ$ returns the second line in the environment table. If the number specified is 0, Visual Basic generates an "Illegal function call" error. If the number specified is greater than the number of lines in the table, a null string is returned. Using a valid numeric argument causes the entire corresponding entry to be returned in the format entry-name=entry-value.

Environ returns a variant; Environ$ returns a string.

EOF FUNCTION

See Also: Close, Get, Input #, Line Input #, Loc, LOF, Open.

Purpose

The EOF function returns the end of file status of an open file. It is important to check the end of file status so as to avoid reading past the end of a file, which causes an error.

General Syntax

```
EOF(file-number)
```

Usage

```
Do Until EOF(1)
    Line Input #1, A$
Loop
```

Description

For sequential files, the EOF function returns True (-1) if the last Input, or Line Input, statement caused the program to reach the end of the file. For random access and binary files, this function returns True (-1) if the last Get attempted to read a record that was beyond the length of the file.

The file number specified as the argument must be the number used in the Open statement of a currently open file. If not, Visual Basic generates a "Bad file name or number" error.

ERASE STATEMENT

See Also: Dim, ReDim.

Purpose

The Erase statement deallocates space reserved for dynamic arrays. Erase also reinitializes the elements in a fixed array.

General Syntax

```
Erase arrayname [, arrayname]
```

Usage

```
Erase AddressCards
```

Description

Erasing a fixed array merely reinitializes the contents of the array. If the array is a variable-length string array, all the elements are set to zero-length strings. Otherwise, all elements in the array are set to 0.

Erasing a dynamic array actually frees up the memory that the array is using. The program can now use the Dim statement to create a new dynamic array with the same name as the old one. Note that it is not necessary to Erase an array before redeclaring it with ReDim.

ERL FUNCTION

See Also: Err, Error, Error$, On Error Goto, Resume.

Purpose

Returns the line number of the statement that caused an error.

General Syntax

```
Erl
```

Usage

```
BadLine& = Erl
```

Description

The Erl function is useful only if line numbers are used in the program. It does not work with line labels or procedure names. If the line that caused the error does not have a line number, this function will return the number of the line previous to it that does have a number. If no lines in the program have line numbers, 0 is returned. Visual Basic treats line numbers greater than 65,529 as labels; therefore Erl ignores them.

Erl will be set to 0 if a Resume Next, On Error Goto, or On Error Resume Next statement is executed. Also, it is not guaranteed that the value of Erl will remain unchanged when calling a Visual Basic sub procedure or function.

ERR FUNCTION AND STATEMENT

See Also: Erl, Error, Error$, On Error Goto, Resume.

Purpose

As a function, Err returns the error code of the most recent error. As a statement, Err allows you to set the error code.

General Syntax

As a function:

```
Err
```

As a statement:

```
Err = code%
```

Usage

```
Err = 100
```

Set the error code to 100.

```
If Err > 0 Then
    ErrorNumber% = Err
    Call ErrorRoutine(ErrorNumber%)
End if
```

> If an error has occured, save the error number and call an error-handling routine with that number as argument.

Description

> The Err keyword is both a function and a statement. As a function, it returns the error code of the most recent error. As a statement, it allows the program to set the value of the error code. The value of Err is set whenever Visual Basic encounters an error, when the program sets it via the Err statement, or when a Resume Next, On Error Goto, or On Error Resume Next statement is executed. Resume Next, On Error Goto, and On Error Resume Next set the error code to 0. It is not guaranteed the value of Err will remain unchanged when calling a Visual Basic sub procedure or function.

ERROR STATEMENT

> See Also: Erl, Err, Error$, On Error Goto, Resume.

Purpose

> The Error function simulates the occurrence of an error. You can use it as an aid to testing or debugging a program.

General Syntax

```
Error errorcode%
```

Usage

```
Error 5
```

> This generates an "Illegal function call" error.

Description

> The errorcode% specified must be in the range of from 1 to 32,767. This statement is very useful for debugging error-handling routines. Using this statement, you can cause a specific error to occur, and then see if the error-handling code

works properly. You can also use error codes greater than those used by Visual Basic. This allows you to define custom error codes.

ERROR, ERROR$ FUNCTIONS

See Also: Erl, Err, Error, On Error Goto, Resume.

Purpose

The Error and Error$ functions return the error message that corresponds to the supplied error code.

General Syntax

```
Error$[(errorcode%)]
Error[(errorcode%)]
```

Usage

```
Msg$ = Error$(5)
```

This places the text "Illegal function call" into the variable Msg$.

Description

The Error and Error$ functions retrieve Visual Basic's message for a particular error. The errorcode% parameter specifies the desired error message, and must be in the range of from 1 to 32,767. If an error number is not used by Visual Basic, the message "user-defined error" will be returned. If errorcode% is omitted, the message returned will be that of the most recent error. If no error has occurred, Visual Basic returns a null string.

When the errorcode% parameter is used, some of the error messages returned by this function may seem incomplete. This is because they depend on internal variables that are set only when an error has actually occurred. When the error-code% parameter is used, no error has occurred, so the internal variables have not been set. For instance, Error$(382) will return the following message:

```
' ' property cannot be set at runtime
```

Because this error has not occurred, there is no object for it to reference. The single quotes denote the place in the message the object's name would be inserted.
Error returns a variant; Error$ returns a string.

EXIT STATEMENT

See Also: Do...Loop, For...Next, Function, Sub.

Purpose

The Exit statement provides an alternative exit for statement blocks such as a Do...Loop, For...Next, sub, or function.

General Syntax

```
Exit Do
Exit For
Exit Function
Exit Sub
```

Usage

```
Function Fruit$(FruitNo as Integer)
    Dim F as String
    If FruitNo = 0 then Exit Function
    If FruitNo = 1 then F = "Apple"
    If FriutNo = 2 then F = "Grape"
    Fruit$ = F
End Function
```

This example causes the Fruit$() function to terminate if the value of the passed argument FruitNo is 0.

Description

The Exit Do statement exits a Do...Loop and continues execution with the instruction following the Loop instruction. The Exit For statement exits a For...Next loop and continues execution with the instruction following the Next instruction. The Exit Function statement exits a function and continues execution at the instruction following invocation of the function. Similarly the Exit Sub statement exits a sub procedure and continues execution at the instruction following the call to the procedure. The type of Exit used must match the type of statement block it is being used in (for example, Exit Sub cannot be used to exit a For...Next loop).

EXP FUNCTION

See Also: Log.

Purpose

The Exp function raises the natural logarithmic base e to the specified power. (The natural logarithm, which has a base of about 2.718, should not be confused with the common logarithm, whose base is 10.)

General Syntax

```
Exp(power)
```

Usage

```
A! = 14
B! = Exp(A!)
```

Returns a single-precision number that represents the natural logarithmic base raised to the power of 14.

```
C# = 14
D# = Exp(C#)
```

Returns a double-precision number that represents the natural logarithmic base raised to the power of 14.

Description

If the power is supplied as an integer or single-precision number, Exp will return a single-precision value. If any other data type is used, a double-precision number is returned. If supplied as an integer or single-precision number, the power parameter must not exceed 88.02969. If supplied as any other data type, it must not exceed 709.782712893. Doing so will cause an "Overflow" error to occur.

The logarithm of a number is the power to which the logarithmic base must be raised in order to achieve that number. The natural logarithmic base is referred to by the symbol e, and has an approximate value of 2.718282. Exp performs the inverse operation of a natural logarithm. It raises e to the power specified by the power parameter.

FILEATTR FUNCTION

See Also: Open.

Purpose

The FileAttr function returns system information about an open file.

General Syntax

```
FileAttr(filenumber%, infotype%)
```

Usage

```
Open "Test" For Input As #1
VBOpenMode% = FileAttr(1, 1)
DOSHandle% = FileAttr(1, 2)
```

Description

The filenumber% parameter refers to the number that was used when the file was open. If filenumber% does not refer to a currently opened file, Visual Basic issues a "Bad file name or number" error.

The infotype% parameter indicates the type of information that is being requested. If infotype% is 1, FileAttr returns a number that refers to the mode the file was opened under. Table B-13 lists the open modes, and the codes returned.

Open Mode	Return Value
Input	1
Output	2
Random	4
Append	8
Binary	32

Table B-13 Return values for the FileAttr function

When infotype% is 2, FileAttr returns the DOS file handle that has been assigned to this file.

FILECOPY STATEMENT

Purpose

Use the FileCopy statement to copy a file. This is similar to the DOS Copy command.

General Syntax

`FileCopy source$, dest$`

Usage

`FileCopy "~TEMP.TMP", dataFileName`

Description

This command copies a DOS file. The source$ file may be opened for read-only access, but must not be opened for write access. You may specify a drive and directory in either of the file names, but may not specify any wildcards. The example syntax copies the file ~TEMP.TMP to the file name specified by the variable dataFileName.

FILEDATETIME FUNCTION

See Also: GetAttr, FileLen.

Purpose

The FileDateTime function returns a string that indicates the date and time a file was created or last modified.

General Syntax

`FileDateTime(filename$)`

Usage

`lastSaved = CVDate(FileDateTime("DATAFILE.MDB"))`

Description

Use the FileDateTime function to determine when a DOS file was created or last saved. The function returns a string. The example syntax determines when the file DATAFILE.MDB was last modified, and converts the returned string to a date variant. The filename$ argument must be a nonambiguous file, and may not contain wildcards.

FILELEN FUNCTION

See Also: FileDateTime, GetAttr.

Purpose

The FileLen function returns the total length of a file in bytes.

General Syntax

```
FileLen(filename$)
```

Usage

```
totalBytes = totalBytes + FileLen(Dir())
```

Description

Use the FileLen function to determine the size of a DOS file. It returns a long integer indicating the total number of bytes in the file. The example syntax might be used in a Do...Loop to accumulate the total size of a group of files.

FIX FUNCTION

See Also: CInt, Int.

Purpose

The Fix function truncates the fractional part of a numeric expression and returns the rest as an integer.

General Syntax

```
Fix(numericExpression)
```

Usage

```
B! = 54.72
A% = Fix(B!)
```

This assigns the value 54 to the variable A%.

Description

The Fix function returns the whole-number portion of a numericExpression. All digits to the right of the decimal are truncated. No rounding is performed. Use the CInt or CLng functions to convert to an integer with rounding.

The Int function performs the same operation as Fix when the argument is positive, or when there are no digits to the right of the decimal. The difference between the two is how they handle negative values. Int will return the next whole negative number that is less than the argument. Fix returns the next whole negative number that is greater than the argument. Table B-14 compares the effects of Fix versus Int and Cint.

Value	Fix(value)	Int(value)	Cint(value)
2.7	2	2	3
2.2	2	2	2
2	2	2	2
-2	-2	-2	-2
-2.2	-2	-3	-2
-2.7	-2	-3	-3

Table B-14 Return values for Fix, Int, and CInt functions

FOR...NEXT STATEMENTS

See Also: Do...Loop, Exit, While...Wend.

Purpose

The For and Next statements are used to repeat the execution of a block of statements for a specified number of times.

General Syntax

```
For counter = startvalue To endvalue [Step increment]
    [statements]
    [Exit For]
    [statements]
Next [counter][, counter]...
```

Usage

```
A% = 0
For X% = 1 to 10
    A% = A% + X%
Next X%
```

This loop sums the digits from 1 through 10. Each time the loop runs, it adds the next digit in the counter (X%) to the variable A%, which accumulates the total. The final value of A% is thus 1+2+3+4+5+6+7+8+9+10, or 55.

```
For X% = 10 to 1 Step −1
    A% = A% + X%
Next
```

This loop uses the Step keyword with a negative value, so the counter (X%) starts at 10, and decrements on each pass until it reaches 0.

Description

The For...Next loop structure allows you to set up a group of statements that will be executed a specified number of times. The counter parameter counts the iterations of the loop, and must be a simple variable of any numeric data type. It cannot be an array element or a record element. The parameter's startvalue and endvalue indicate the starting and ending values that will be assigned to the counter. They may be any numeric expression of any data type. Increment indicates the amount the counter is changed each time the loop is executed. If not explicitly indicated, increment defaults to one. The variable name of counter can follow the keyword Next, but it is not necessary. If counter is omitted, Visual Basic will match the Next keyword with the most recent For keyword. Your code will generally be clearer and easier to debug if you always explicitly give the name of the counter variable.

When a For...Next loop is encountered, Visual Basic first assigns to the counter the value of startvalue. It then compares counter to endvalue. If increment is positive, and counter is greater than endvalue, the loop is exited. If increment is negative, and counter is less than endvalue, the loop is exited. If counter is within the range indicated by startvalue and endvalue, the statement block between the For and Next keywords is executed. When execution reaches the Next keyword, increment is added to counter. Visual Basic again compares the counter to endvalue. If increment is positive, and counter is greater than endvalue, the loop is exited. If increment is negative, and counter is less than endvalue, the loop is exited. Otherwise the statement block is again executed.

The Exit For statement can also be used inside the statement block to cause the loop to end immediately, and execution then jumps to the statement following the Next keyword.

You can nest several loops within each other. This is useful for setting or getting at the contents of a multidimensional array. Nested loops must be closed in the reverse order in which they were opened. If counter variables are not being used alongside the Next keyword, this is handled automatically, and all you have to do is make sure there is one Next for each For. Visual Basic allows you to use one Next keyword for all the loops by specifying several counter variables. For instance, these two loops are identical:

```
For x% = 1 to 10
    For y% = 1 to 10
        For z% = 1 to 10
            B% = x% + y% + z%
        Next z%
    Next y%
Next x%


For x% = 1 to 10
    For y% = 1 to 10
        For z% = 1 to 10
            B% = x% + y% + z%
Next z%, y%, x%
```

If Visual Basic encounters a For statement, and cannot find a matching Next, it generates a "For without Next" error. If it encounters a Next before encountering a For, a "Next without For" error is issued. This error is also caused when the counter variable alongside the Next keyword does not appear in reverse order of the counter in the For statement. For instance, the following code will generate a "Next without For" message:

```
For t1% = 1 To 10
    For t2% = 1 To 10
        For t3% = 1 To 10
            B% = x% + y% + z%
Next t1%, t2%, t3%
```

FORMAT, FORMAT$ FUNCTIONS

See Also: DateSerial; Now; Str, Str$; TimeSerial.

Purpose

The Format and Format$ functions formats a numeric expression, date variant or string according to a specified pattern.

General Syntax

```
Format$(numericExpression, editPattern$)
```

Usage

```
N! = 545.3
Label1.Caption = Format$(N!, "###.00")
```

> Sets the Caption property of Label1 to "545.30"

```
D# = DateValue("08/22/1964")
Label2.Caption = Format$(D#, "dddd, mmmm dd, yyyy")
```

> Sets the Caption property of Label2 to "Saturday, August 22, 1964"

```
T# = TimeValue("01:02:45")
Label3.Caption = Format$(T#, "h:mm")
```

> Sets the Caption property of Label3 to "1:02"

Description

Any number can be converted to a formatted string. For a number, the edit pattern can have one of four styles. The first style supplies one edit pattern, and all numbers are converted using that pattern. The second style has two edit patterns separated by a semicolon. Non-negative numbers will be formatted according to the first edit pattern, and negative numbers will use the second. The third style has three edit patterns, all separated by semicolons. The first pattern is used to format positive numbers, the second for negative, the third for 0, and the fourth for Null values.

Table B-15 details the numeric formatting characters, and their uses.

Symbol	Effect of Symbol
0	Zero-digit placeholder. If the number has fewer digits than the edit pattern, the empty digits are 0-filled.
#	Null digit place holder. If the number has fewer digits than the edit pattern, the empty digits become null. This placeholder does not blank fill. Therefore, the resultant string may be shorter than the original edit pattern.
%	Percentage place holder. This symbol returns the result of the number multiplied by 100, and appends a % to it.
.	Decimal place holder. Indicates where the decimal point is to be placed in the edit string.

(continued on next page)

Symbol	Effect of Symbol
,	Thousands separator. This is used to separate every three digits to the left of the decimal to make a long number more readable. Two commas adjacent to each other cause the three digits that would be between them to be ignored. The same effect is created when a comma is used just to the left of the decimal place holder.
E-, e-	Returns the number in scientific format. This requires that a digit placeholder (0 or #) be placed to the immediate left of the E or e, or an "Illegal function call" error will occur. An appropriate number of digit place holders should be placed to the right of the - in order to display the exponent. A minus sign will be inserted next to any negative exponents.
E+, e+	Returns the number in scientific notation. Works the same as E- and e-, but a + sign is inserted next to any positive exponents as well as a - sign next to negative exponents.
-, +, $, ( )	These characters will be returned literally and do not affect the format of the number.
\char	This symbol returns the character specified by char. The backslash is not returned.
"string"	Enclosing a string in quotes will return that string literally. Quotation marks can only be inserted into an edit pattern via the use of Chr$(34) and string concatenation.

Table B-15 Numeric format symbols

Date Variants

Date variants can be converted to a string with a variety of date formats. Table B-16 details the date string formatting symbols, and what is returned when a date variant for the date 07/04/1995 is used.

Symbol	Example	Effect of Symbol
/	/	Date separator.
-	-	Date separator.
d	4	Returns the day of the month, omitting any leading 0.
dd	04	Returns the day of the month with a leading 0, if needed.
ddd	Sat	Returns the abbreviated day of the week.

Symbol	Example	Effect of Symbol
dddd	Saturday	Returns the full name of the day of the week.
ddddd	07/04/1995	Returns the full date string in "ShortDate" format specified by WIN.INI.
dddddd	July 04, 1995	Returns the full date string in "Long Date" format specified by WIN.INI.
w		Returns day of week as number (Sunday=1, Saturday=7).
ww		Returns week of year as number (1–53).
m	7	Returns the number of the month of the year, without a leading 0.
mm	07	Returns the number of the month of the year, with a leading 0.
mmm	Jul	Returns the abbreviated name of the month.
mmmm	July	Returns the full name of the month.
q	2	Returns the number of the quarter (1–4).
y		Returns the number of the day of the year (1–366).
yy	95	Returns the 2-digit year.
yyyy	1995	Returns the 4-digit year.
c		Returns date variant as ddddd tttt.

Table B-16 Date variant format symbols

Time Variants

While the whole portion of a date variant represents a date, the fractional part can represent a time, which is stored as a fraction of a day. The time returned will be in 24-hour format unless one of the AM/PM format symbols is used. Time variants can be formatted with the symbols shown in Table B-17 (the examples are based on a time of 1:05:31 AM):

Symbol	Example	Effect of Symbol
:	:	Time separator.
h	1	Returns the hour, without a leading 0.
hh	01	Returns the hour, with a leading 0, if needed.
n	5	Returns the minute, without a leading 0.
nn	05	Returns the minute, with a leading 0.
s	31	Returns the second, without a leading 0.
ss	31	Returns the minute, with a leading 0.
ttttt	01:05:31	Returns the time in the format specified by the entry "sTime" in the WIN.INI file.
c		Returns date variant as ddddd ttttt.
AM/PM, am/pm		Returns "AM" for any hour before noon, and "PM" for any hour after.
A/P, a/p		Returns "A" for any hour before noon, and "P" for any hour after.
AMPM		Uses the AM/PM format specified by the "s1159" and "s2359" entries in the WIN.INI file.

Table B-17 Date variant format symbols

Strings

The Format functions can also format string arguments. Table B-18 summarizes the symbols that control string formatting, with the examples working on the string "Hello".

Symbol	Example	Effect of Symbol
@	Hello	Displays a character, or a space if there is no character.
&	Hello	Displays a character, or nothing if there is no character.

Symbol	Example	Effect of symbol
<	hello	Forces lowercase.
>	HELLO	Forces suppercase.
!	olleH	Forces placeholders to fill from left to right.

Table B-18 String format symbols

FREEFILE FUNCTION

See Also: Open.

Purpose

The FreeFile function returns an unused file number that you can use to open a file.

General Syntax

```
FreeFile
```

Usage

```
FileNo% = FreeFile
Open "Test.Dat" For Random As #FileNo% Len = 32
```

Description

When opening a file, you must supply a number (in the range of from 1 to 255) by which the file will be referenced throughout the program. Visual Basic will issue a "File already open" error if you attempt to open a file using a file number that is assigned to an already open file. FreeFile eliminates the need for you to keep track of which file numbers have and have not been used.

The number returned by the FreeFile function does not change until you open a file with the returned number. Therefore it is a good idea to open a file with the returned number immediately after using this function. For instance:

```
File1% = FreeFile
File2% = FreeFile
Open "file1.dat" For Random As #File1% Len = 128
Open "file2.dat" For Random As #File2% Len = 128
```

In the example code above, Visual Basic will issue a "File already open" error. This will happen because no file was opened after FreeFile was used to assign a value to File1%. Therefore both variables File1% and File2% will have the same value. Instead, always immediately follow the file number assignment with a file Open:

```
File1% = FreeFile
Open "file1.dat" For Random As #File1% Len = 128
File2% = FreeFile
Open "file2.dat" For Random As #File2% Len = 128
```

FREELOCKS STATEMENT

See Also: DoEvents, Chapter 27, Data Access.

Purpose

The FreeLocks statement allows an Access database to release locks on all record pages, thus making any pending changes current in all recordsets in a multiuser environment.

General Syntax

```
FreeLocks
```

Usage

```
FreeLocks
```

Description

You may have an application in a multiuser environment that has especially heavy transaction processing. The Access database engine locks record pages during updates, thus making all records on that page unavailable to any other process. The FreeLocks statement lets you manually force the Access database engine to free all locked pages. This allows all recordsets an opportunity to refresh themselves to show changes caused by other users.

FUNCTION...END FUNCTION STATEMENTS

See Also: End, Exit, Sub.

Purpose

The Function and End Function statements declare and define a Visual Basic procedure that can receive arguments and return a value of a specified data type.

General Syntax

```
[Static] [Private] Function function-name[(arguments)][As type]
    [Static var[,var]...]
    [Dim var[,var]...]
    [statements]
    [function-name = expression]
    [Exit Function]
    [statements]
    [function-name = expression]
End Function
```

Usage

```
Function TrimStr(ByVal I as String) As String
    TrimStr = LTrim(RTrim(I))
End Function

B$ = "  Hello  "
A$ = TrimStr(B$)
```

This function combines the effects of the Visual Basic functions LTrim and RTrim. Because the ByVal keyword is used, the supplied argument is passed by value, and cannot be changed by the function. The result of the function assigns the string "Hello" to the variable A$, with the leading and trailing spaces trimmed off.

Description

Although Visual Basic has many useful predefined functions, it is sometimes necessary to create a custom function that suits a specific need for a program. The Function..End function block allows you to do just that. A call to a programmer-defined function is made in the same manner as a call to a Visual Basic function. The function name can be placed on the right side of an assignment, or can be used as an argument in another function or sub procedure call. The following examples are both correct calls to a function:

```
A$ = TrimStr(B$)
C$ = UCase$(TrimStr(B$))
```

The data type of the returned value must be declared in the function definition. This can be done by appending a data type declaration character (!, @, #, $,
%, &) to the end of the function name. Alternatively, the As type parameter may
be used. Only one of these two methods may be used in a particular function
definition. Return data types may be Integer, Long, Single, Double, Currency,
String, or Variant.

The allocation of local variables (variables that are accessible only to this function) is performed by using either the Dim or Static statements. Variables that are
allocated with the Dim statement are deallocated when the function is exited.
Therefore they do not retain their value between calls to the function. To guarantee that a variable keeps its value between calls, it should be declared with the
Static statement. If you want to have all local variables retain their value between
calls, the function definition should begin with the optional Static keyword.

The Private keyword indicates that the function may be accessed only by
other procedures in the same module. This lets you write general-purpose code
modules with internally used functions (say, for financial modeling or sorting)
without having any conflicts with identically named functions in other modules.
Note that functions in a form are inherently private, because no other procedures can call form procedures.

Arguments may be passed to the function in order to modify its behavior, or to
give it information to act upon. The format for declaring arguments is as follows:

```
([ByVal]variablename[As type][,[ByVal]variablename[As type]...])
```

The variablename indicates the name by which the argument will be referred
to from within the function. It may end in a type declaration character, or the As
type parameter may be used to declare the data type of the incoming argument.
The type may be Integer, Long, Single, Double, Currency, String, Variant, user-
defined, or object (such as Control, ListBox, or Form). By default, the arguments
are passed by reference. This means the address of the variable is passed instead
of the actual value. This allows the Function to make changes to the passed arguments. In order to prevent this from happening, the ByVal keyword may be used
to force the arguments to be passed by value instead. If a function has no arguments, empty parentheses must accompany the function name (unless the function has been declared with the Declare statement).

The function is normally exited when execution reaches the End Function
keywords. However, an alternative exit may be forced by using the Exit
Function statement. This causes the function to be immediately terminated, and
execution returns to the instruction following the call to the function. Before the
function is exited, you may assign a value for it to return. This is done by assigning the desired return value to the function name just prior to exiting the function.

Visual Basic functions can be called recursively. This means that a function
can call itself.

FV FUNCTION

See Also: PV, NPV.

Purpose

Use the FV function to determine the future value of an annuity based on constant payments and a constant interest rate.

General Syntax

```
FV(rate!, numPeriods%, payment@, presentValue@, whenDue%)
```

Usage

```
amountSaved = FV(interestRate / 12, numberMonths, amountInvestedPerMonth, 0, 0)
```

Description

The FV function returns the future value of an annuity given constant payments and a constant interest rate. You can use this funtion either for investments (positive payments) or loans (negative payments). The number of periods should be given in the same units of measure as the interest rate. The whenDue% argument specifies when the payment is due: at the end of the period (0), or at the beginning of the period (1).

The example syntax shows how the FV function can return the total amount of money accrued in an interest-bearing account given a constant revenue stream. In this case, the annual percentage interest rate is divided by 12 to obtain a monthly interest, and the number of periods is given in months. The amount put into the account every month is given by amountInvestedPerMonth. Note that the presentValue@ of the account is given as 0 to indicate this is a new savings account started with a zero balance.

GET STATEMENT

See Also: Lof, Open, Put, Type.

Purpose

The Get statement reads a block of data from a disk file into a predefined record buffer.

General Syntax

```
Get [#]filenumber%,[position&], recordbuffer
```

Usage

```
Type Rolodex
     Name as String * 20
     Number as Long
     Address as String * 100
End Type

Dim PhoneCard as Rolodex
Open "Cards.Dat" For Random As #1 Len = 128
Get #1, 129, PhoneCard
```

> This example opens a file for random access, and reads the 129th record into the user-defined variable PhoneCard. The size of the data read is 128 bytes, as defined by the LEN keyword in the Open statement. Because PhoneCard is only 124 bytes long, and the file was opened for random access, the extra bytes read are discarded.

```
Type Rolodex
     Name as String * 20
     Number as Long
     Address as String * 100
End Type

Dim PhoneCard as Rolodex
Open "Cards.Dat" For Binary As #1
Get #1, 129, PhoneCard
```

> This example opens a file for binary access, and reads the file beginning at the 129th byte. Because the file was opened for binary access, the length of the data read is 124 bytes, as defined by the length of the PhoneCard variable.

Description

The Get statement reads data from a disk file into a previously defined record area. The filenumber% parameter indicates which file is to be read from. This number must be from 1 to 255, and match the number used in the Open statement of a currently open file. If the file number used does not match a currently opened file, a "Bad file name or number" error is generated. The file must have been opened in either Random access or Binary mode. If not, Visual Basic will issue a "Bad file mode" error.

If the position& parameter is omitted, the commas must still be used. If position& specifies an area that is beyond the length of the file, the record buffer will be empty. Visual Basic does no checking to see if a Get is being attempted past

1330

the length of the file. This task is left to you. Use the Lof function to determine the length of an open file.

The recordbuffer parameter refers to the area in which the data from the read will be stored. It can be of any data type. Most often, it is of a type defined by you (using the Type statement) whose fields match those of the file's record structure.

Reading Random Access Files

The position parameter for random access files represents the desired record number. If this parameter is omitted, the next record in the file is read. For instance, if no records have been read, a Get without the position specified will read record number 1. The next Get will read record number 2, etc. The largest possible valid record number is 2,147,483,647.

The variable used for the recordbuffer must be of a length that is less than or equal to the length specified in the Open statement. Using a variable whose length is too long results in a "Bad record length" error.

Reading Binary Files

The position parameter for binary files refers to the byte position in the file where reading is to start. The first byte in the file is position 1, the second is 2, and so on.

The size of the read is determined by the size of the record buffer. This allows a file to have variable record lengths.

GETATTR FUNCTION

See Also: FileDateTime, FileLen.

Purpose

The GetAttr function lets you determine a file, directory, or volume label's attributes.

General Syntax

```
GetAttr(fileName$)
```

Usage

```
If GetAttr(fileName$) And ATTR_HIDDEN Then chekHidden.Value = CHECKED
```

Description

All files, directories, and volumes have an attribute byte associated with them. This information indicates whether the file name is normal, read-only, hidden, system, a volume label, a directory, or has been modified since the last backup. Table B-19 summarizes the return values of the GetAttr function and the CONSTANT.TXT names for the values.

Value	CONSTANT.TXT	Meaning
0	ATTR_NORMAL	Normal file
1	ATTR_READONLY	Read-only file
2	ATTR_HIDDEN	Hidden file
4	ATTR_SYSTEM	System file
8	ATTR_VOLUME	Volume label
16	ATTR_DIRECTORY	DOS directory entry
32	ATTR_ARCHIVE	File has changed since last backup

Table B-19 Meanings of the return values of the GetAttr function

Note that the return value can have several different states set simultaneously—for example, a file can be read-only, system, and hidden. Use the And operator to perform a bitwise test for individual attributes. The example syntax uses the And operator to test whether a file is hidden or not; if it is (GetAttr(fileName$) And ATTR_HIDDEN evaluates to nonzero), then the "hidden" check box gets checked.

GLOBAL STATEMENT

See Also: Const, Dim, Option Base, Static.

Purpose

The Global statement is used in the global module to declare and allocate storage for simple variables and arrays that will be accessible to all modules and forms.

General Syntax

For declaring the data type of a simple variable:

```
Global name [As [New] type][, name [As [New] type]]
```

For declaring an array:

```
Global name[(subscript-range)][As [New] type][, name[(subscript-range)][As [New] type]
```

Usage

```
Global Num1 As Integer, Num2 As Single
```

Declares two variables, Num1 and Num2, as types Integer and Single, respectively.

```
Global MyArray(1 to 100) As Integer
Global YourArray(-10 to 10) As String
```

Declares the arrays MyArray and YourArray. MyArray contains 100 integer elements that can be accessed by using a subscript with a value from 1 to 100. YourArray contains 21 string elements that can be accessed using a subscript with a value of -10 to +10.

Description

Variables declared with the Global statement can be accessed from any form, module, or procedure in a program. This statement must be used in the global module; using it anywhere else generates an "Invalid outside global module" error.

The data type of the variable can be specified by either appending a data type declaration character (!, @, #, $, %, &) to the end of the variable name, or by using the As type clause. The type may be Integer, Long, Single, Double, Currency, String (for variable-length strings), String * length (for fixed-length strings), Variant, a programmer-defined type, or an object.

Arrays may also be declared with the Global statement. Arrays provide a method for creating an entire series of variables, and referencing them by the same variable name. An index number (called the subscript) is used to determine which particular element in an array is being referenced. A more detailed discussion on the concept of arrays can be found in Appendix A, Visual Basic Language Tutorial.

The dimensions of an array are defined by the entry in the subscript-range portion of the Global statement. The subscript range follows this format:

```
[lo-element To] hi-element[,[lo-element To] hi-element]...
```

The lo-element parameter lets you define the range of the subscripts, as well as number of elements in the array. If lo-element is not used, the lowest valid subscript will be 0 (unless the default has been changed using Option Base), and the supplied number will be the highest valid subscript. The number of elements allowed in an array depends on the desired data type for that array. Visual Basic 1.0 allowed approximately 64K of data space for each array, but Visual Basic 2.0 and 3.0 allow for huge arrays of any size up to the amount of available memory. You don't have to do anything special for huge arrays; Visual Basic automatically handles all the complex memory management for you.

Global initializes all elements of variable-length string arrays to zero-length strings. All other arrays are initialized to 0s (including fixed-length strings and programmer-defined types).

At times, it is necessary to have a multidimensional array. To declare such an array, include as many sets of subscripts as needed, separated by commas.

```
Global MultiArray (1 To 100, 50 To 60, -100 to 100) As Integer
```

The example above declares an array with three dimensions of 100, 11, and 201 elements, respectively. The first dimension can be referenced by subscripts from 1 to 100, the second may have subscripts ranging from 50 to 60, and the third, from -100 to +100. Visual Basic allows arrays to have as many as 60 dimensions. Be cautious in declaring arrays of many dimensions; the storage space needed multiplies for each dimension. The above example would create an array with a total of (100 * 11 * 201) = 221,100 elements that needs 1,768,880 bytes to hold it!

Leaving the parentheses empty in a Global statement declares a dynamic array. The number of dimensions and elements in a dynamic array is then defined within a procedure by the ReDim statement. Dynamic arrays are allocated at runtime, and may have the number of elements redefined at any time. However, once set, the number of dimensions in a dynamic array cannot be changed. See the entry for ReDim in this appendix for more on dynamic arrays.

GOSUB...RETURN STATEMENTS

See Also: On...Gosub, Sub.

Purpose

The Gosub statement directs the program to branch to a subroutine. Within the subroutine, the Return statement returns execution to the main program. The subroutine must be contained within the same Visual Basic function or sub procedure as the initiating Gosub.

1334

General Syntax

```
Gosub {linelabel | linenumber}
{linelabel: | linenumber}
    :
    [statement-block]
    :
Return
```

Usage

```
Gosub DoIt
  .. [intervening code here]
[Exit Sub]

DoIt:
    A$ = "Now I've done it!"
Return
```

When the Gosub is executed, the program branches to the label "DoIt:". When the Return executes, the program will return to the instruction following the Gosub.

Description

The Gosub statement is left over from earlier days, when the BASIC languages did not have sub procedures or functions. It has been retained in Visual Basic to provide a bit of backward compatibility. The Gosub causes execution to branch to the specified line label or number. The program will then execute from there until it reaches a Return statement. It will then return to the instruction following the Gosub. The specified line label or number must reside in the same procedure, or Visual Basic issues a "Label not defined" error.

Because a subroutine is not a self-contained procedure like a sub or a function, there is the possibility that execution can just fall into it. For instance, in the following code, the program will begin executing a subroutine without a Gosub:

```
Sub Test(A As Integer)
    If A > 100 then Gosub SquareIt
    SquareIt:
        A = A ^ 2
    Return
End Sub
```

In this example, the program will fall into the subroutine SquareIt even when the test in the If statement is false. Doing so causes execution to reach a Return statement without having executed a Gosub. Visual Basic issues a "Return without gosub" error when this happens. To prevent this, place an Exit statement before any subroutines in a procedure:

```
Sub Test(A As Integer)
    If A > 100 then Gosub SquareIt
    Exit Sub
    SquareIt:
        A = A ^ 2
    Return
End Sub
```

It is generally good practice to avoid the use of Gosub...Return. Whenever possible, use the Function and Sub definitions instead.

GOTO STATEMENT

Purpose

The Goto statement branches unconditionally, and without return, to a line number or label in a procedure.

General Syntax

```
GoTo {linenumber | linelabel}
```

Usage

```
GoTo BadPractice
```
Branches to the label "BadPractice."

Description

The GoTo statement is another relic of early versions of BASIC. The GoTo statement sends execution to the line number or label specified. The line number or label must be in the same procedure as the GoTo. Execution continues at the line specified, and no return address is saved.

GoTo is a highly unstructured command, and should be used with caution, if at all. It is much better programming practice to use the Do...Loop, For...Next, Function, or Sub statements.

HEX, HEX$ FUNCTIONS

See Also: Oct, Oct$.

Purpose

The Hex and Hex$ functions convert a decimal numeric expression to a variant or string that represents the value of the numeric expression in hexadecimal format.

General Syntax

```
Hex$(numericExpression)
Hex(numericExpression)
```

Usage

```
A% = 140
B$ = Hex$(A%)
```

Places a string with the hexidecimal value "8C" into the variable B$.

Description

Hexadecimal notation is a way of counting using 16 digits. The digits in hexadecimal include 0 through 9, and A through F. Hexadecimal "A" equals a decimal 10, "B" equals 11, and so on. Hexadecimal is often used to display memory addresses because it easily converts back and forth from binary. The Hex$ function provides a method of converting a decimal number into hexadecimal.

The supplied numericExpression is rounded to the nearest whole number before conversion is begun. If numericExpression is an integer, the string returned by Hex$ will be 4 or fewer bytes long. Otherwise the return string can be up to 8 bytes long.

Hex returns a variant; Hex$ returns a string.

HOUR FUNCTION

See Also: Now, TimeSerial, TimeValue.

Purpose

The Hour function returns the hour of the day as an integer from 0 (Midnight) to 23 (11 pm), based on the supplied date variant.

General Syntax

```
Hour(dateVariant)
```

Usage

```
A% = Hour(Now)
```

This example uses the Now function to get the current hour of the day.

Description

The hour is returned as an integer in the range of from 0 (12 midnight) to 23 (11 pm).

IF...THEN...ELSE STATEMENTS

See Also: If...Then...ElseIf...End If, Select Case, Iif.

Purpose

The If...Then...and Else statements provide a structure for one-line conditional execution.

General Syntax

```
If condition Then action1 [Else action2]
```

Usage

```
If A% > B% Then C% = A% Else C% = B%
```

This example places the higher of the values A% and B% into the variable C%

Description

Your program will need to make many decisions and, based on those decisions, take one course of action or another. One of the ways you can instruct your program to make such a decision is with the If... statement. Visual Basic has two styles of the If... statement. The style described in this entry involves a simple one-line format, and is generally used where only one or two instructions depend on the condition being tested. There is also a muliple-line If... statement, which is described in the next entry, as well as an Immedite If... function, described in the entry following the mulitple-line If statement.

In the single-line If... statement, the value of the condition determines if an action is to take place. If the condition evaluates to nonzero, the statement(s) in action1 will execute. If the condition evaluates to 0, execution will continue with the next instruction, unless the Else keyword has been used. In that case the statement(s) specified in action2 will be executed.

The condition can be any expression that evaluates to a zero or nonzero value. You can also test the type of an object by using the following syntax in place of condition:

```
TypeOf objectname Is objecttype
```

where objectname is the object being tested, and objecttype is any of the objects listed in Chapter 3, Using Objects. For instance, in the following code, if the tested object is a text box control, the object's ForeColor property is set:

```
Sub ChangeColor (ThisObject As Control)
    If TypeOf ThisObject is TextBox Then ThisObject.ForeColor = RED
End Sub
```

More than one statement may be specified for action1 or action2, as long as the statements are separated by colons. However, this is not suggested practice. The multiple-line If... construct handles this type of task much better.

IF...THEN...ELSEIF...END IF STATEMENTS

See Also: If...Then...Else, Select Case, IIf.

Purpose

The If...Then...ElseIf...and End If statements provide a multiple-line structure for conditional execution.

General Syntax

```
If condition-1 Then
    :
    [actions-1]
    :
[ElseIf condition-2 Then]
    :
    [actions-2]
    :
[ElseIf condition-n Then]
    :
    [actions-n]
    :
[Else]
    :
    [else-actions]
    :
End If
```

Usage

```
If PlantType$ = "Tree" Then
    Message$ = "Is this an Oak, or an Elm?"
    PlantName$ = InputBox$(Message$)
```

(continued on next page)

(continued from previous page)

```
ElseIf PlantHeight% > 80 Then
    Message$ = "Only trees grow this high"
    MsgBox Message$
Else
    Message$ = "What kind of a plant is this?"
    PlantType$ = InputBox$(Message$)
End If
```

Description

The multiple-line If... statement provides two functions. First, it allows conditional execution of several statements. Second, it also allows you to test several different values in the same construct, with each successive condition dependent on the result of the previous conditions.

If condition-1 evaluates to nonzero, the instructions in statement-block-1 will be executed. Visual Basic will then pick up execution at the instruction following the End If clause.

The ElseIf keyword can be used to test more than one condition. Each ElseIf condition is tested only if all the conditions above it have tested false. You may use as many ElseIf conditions as needed.

You may also use the optional Else keyword. The statement block following this keyword will be executed if none of the preceding conditions evaluate as nonzero.

The condition-? parameters can be any expression that evaluates to a zero or nonzero value. You can also test the type of an object by using the following syntax in place of condition-?:

```
TypeOf objectname is objecttype
```

where objectname is the object being tested, and objecttype is any of the objects listed in Chapter 3, Using Objects. For instance, in the following code, if the tested object is a text box control, the object's ForeColor and BackColor properties are set:

```
Sub ChangeColor (ThisObject Has Control)
    If TypeOf ThisObject is TextBox Then
        ThisObject.ForeColor = RED
        ThisObject.BackColor = BLACK
    End If
End Sub
```

Nesting of If... statements is allowed, and can be a very useful tool. Be careful to avoid nesting too many If... statements, as this makes following the logic of a program difficult. The Select Case statement is a better alternative when more than three separate conditions involving the same expression are to be tested. Also, care must be taken to ensure that each multiple-line If has a matching End If.

Visual Basic issues a "Block If without End If" error when there is a missing End If. An "End If without Block If" error is generated when an End If is encountered and cannot be matched to an initiating If.

IIF FUNCTION

See Also: If...Then...Else, Select Case, Choose, Switch.

Purpose

The IIf (Immediate If) function evaluates an expression and returns one of two supplied values.

General syntax

```
IIf(expression, valueIfTrue, valueIfFalse)
```

Usage

```
Text1.ForeColor=IIf(Val(Text1.Text) <0,QBColor(3), QBColor(0))
```

Description

The IIf function is a shorthand way of evaluating an expression and returning one of two values. It evaluates the expression given as the first argument and returns either the second argument if the expression evaluates to True, or the third argument if the expression evaluates to False. The example syntax shows how IIf sets the ForeColor of a text box depending on the text box's value.

You can also use a regular If... statement to do the same thing. IIf is briefer, although a block If... statement is more readable:

```
If Val(Text1.Text) < 0 Then
      Text1.ForeColor = QBColor(3)
Else
      Text1.ForeColor = QBColor(0)
End If
```

IIf always evaluates both of the returned values, so you should make sure that any expressions you use are valid. For example,

```
quota = IIf(totalSales > 100000, 1.1 * totalSales, 1.5 * totalSales / (years - 1)
```

works fine if years is older than 1, but fails with a "Divide by Zero" error if years=1.

1341

INPUT # STATEMENT

See Also: Input, Input$; Line Input#; Write #.

Purpose

The Input # statement reads data from a sequential access file into variables.

General Syntax

```
Input #filenumber, var1[, var2]
```

Usage

```
SeqFile% = FreeFile
Open "TEST.DAT" For Input As #SeqFile%
Input #SeqFile%, A$, B%
```

This example reads data from "TEST.DAT" into the variables A$ and B%.

Description

The Input # statement reads a sequential file, one variable at a time. The filenumber parameter refers to the number the file was opened with. If the filenumber supplied is not an open file, Visual Basic issues a "Bad file name or number" error. As shown in the preceding example, the FreeFile function can be used to obtain a valid file number for use in opening a file.

The Input # statement assigns the data read from the file to the variables that are specified, one after another, in the statement. The type of variables specified should match the type of data being read. How Visual Basic reads the file is based on the data type of the next variable to be read.

If the next variable to be read is numeric, Visual Basic reads until it reaches a space. This is assumed to be the start of the number. It then reads the file until a comma, a carriage return, a linefeed, the end of file marker, or another space is encountered. If the data that it has read is numeric, the variable is assigned the value of the numeric data. Otherwise the variable is assigned the value of 0.

If the next variable to be read is a string, the file is read until a nonspace character is encountered. This becomes the start of the string. The file is then read until a comma, a carriage return, a linefeed, the end of file marker, or another space is encountered.

Trying to read past the end of a sequential file results in an "Input past end of file" error. This can be prevented by using the EOF function.

INPUT, INPUT$ FUNCTIONS

See Also: Input #.

Purpose

The Input$ function reads a string of characters from a file, assigning no special meaning to carriage returns and line feeds.

General Syntax

```
Input$(inputlength%,[#]filenumber%)
```

Usage

```
A$ = Input$(100, 1)
```

Reads 100 characters from the file opened as number 1.

Description

The Input$ function returns a string of the length specified by inputlength% from a data file. The file can be opened under Input, Random, or Binary mode. If it is a Random file, the maximum inputlength% is the record length specified in the Open statement with the Len parameter. For Input and Binary files, the maximum length is 32,767 bytes. However, any attempt to read past the length of the file will cause an "Input past end of file" error to occur. You should therefore use the Lof function or some other means to check for the end of the file before reading.

Input$ assigns no special meaning to commas, quotes, spaces, carriage returns, or linefeeds, so the string returned may contain these characters.

Input returns a variant; Input$ returns a string.

INPUTBOX, INPUTBOX$ FUNCTIONS

See Also: MsgBox, MsgBox$.

Purpose

The InputBox and InputBox$ functions display a dialog box with the specified text, and accept user input.

General Syntax

```
InputBox$(msg$[, [title$][, [default$][, xpos%, ypos%]]])
InputBox(msg$[, [title$][, [default$][, xpos%, ypos%]]])
```

Usage

```
UserInput$ = InputBox$("Enter some text",,"This is some text")
```

Description

The InputBox and InputBox$ functions display a dialog box in which the contents of the string title$ are displayed in the box's title bar, and the string default$ is displayed in the box's text area, usually representing a prompt to the user. The argument xpos% represents the distance of the left side of the dialog box from the left side of the screen, in twips. The ypos% argument represents the distance of the top of the box from the top of the screen, in twips. For more details on the InputBox$ function, see Chapter 17, Dialog Boxes.

InputBox returns a variant; InputBox$ returns a string.

INSTR FUNCTION

Purpose

The Instr function returns the position of an occurrence of a search string within another string being searched.

General Syntax

```
InStr([startpos&], string1$, string2$)
```

Usage

```
B$ = "Good Bye"
A% = InStr(B$, "Bye")
C% = InStr(7, B$, "Bye")
```

The first example assigns the value 6 to the variable A% because the string "Bye" can be found at the sixth byte position in B$. The second example starts the search at byte position 7, therefore "Bye" cannot be found. The variable C% is assigned a value of 0.

Description

The parameter string1$ is the string that will be searched. String2$ is the string that is being searched for. If string2$ is found within string1$, Instr returns the byte position where the beginning of the search string is found. If the string cannot be found, a 0 is returned. You can optionally use the startpos& parameter. This specifies the position in string1$ where you wish the search to start. This is useful for searching one string for multiple occurrences of another. If string2$ is a null string, InStr returns the value of startpos& (or 0, if startpos& was not specified).

INT FUNCTION

See Also: C<Type>, Fix.

Purpose

The Int function returns the largest integer that is less than or equal to the supplied numeric expression.

General Syntax

```
Int(numericExpression)
```

Usage

```
A% = Int(-2.86)
B% = Int(2.86)
```

These statements place the value -3 in the variable A%, and the value 2 in the variable B%.

Description

The Int function essentially rounds a numeric expression to the nearest integer. Int performs the same operation as Fix when the argument is positive, or when there are no digits to the right of the decimal. The difference between the two is how they handle negative values with fractions. Int will return the next whole negative number that is less than the argument. Fix returns the next whole negative number that is greater than the argument. Table B-20 compares the effects of Int, Fix, and Cint.

Value	Int(Value)	Fix(Value)	Cint(Value)
2.7	2	2	3
2.2	2	2	2
2	2	2	2
-2	-2	-2	-2
-2.2	-3	-2	-2
-2.7	-3	-2	-3

Table B-20 Return values for Fix, Int, and CInt functions

IPMT FUNCTION

See Also: Pmt, PPmt, Rate.

Purpose

The IPmt function returns the interest portion of a payment on an annuity given constant payments and constant interest rate.

General Syntax

```
IPmt(rate!, currentPeriod%, numberTotalPeriods%, presentValue@, futureValue@, whenDue%)
```

Usage

```
interest = IPmt(intRate/12, this month, 360, loanAmount, 0, 0)
```

Description

Use the IPmt function to return the interest portion of an annuity payment. The function assumes that payments and interest rates remain constant for the life of the annuity.

Make sure that the interest rate and numberTotalPeriods% are in the same units—for example, months or years. The presentValue@ is the current value of the loan (or starting value of an annuity), and futureValue@ is the value of the loan or annuity when complete. Loans will generally have a futureValue@ of $0, while a savings program would have a positive amount, such as $100,000 for a retirement fund. The whenDue% argument specifies when payments are due: 0 if due at the end of the period, and 1 if the payment is due at the beginning of the period.

The example syntax gives the interest portion of a 30-year home mortgage (numberTotalPeriod% =30*12=360).

IRR FUNCTION

See Also: MIRR, Rate.

Purpose

Use the IRR function to return the Internal Rate of Return for a series of periodic payments and receipts.

General Syntax

```
IRR(valuesArray( ), guess!)
```

Usage

```
money(0) = -500000          'first year startup costs
money(1) = -250000          'second year operation costs
money(2) = 0                'third year breakeven
money(3) = 100000           'fourth year profit
money(4) = 300000
money(5) = 500000
money(6) = 2000000          'seventh year cashout
return = IRR(money(), 0.20) * 100
```

Description

The IRR function can provide the overall rate of return for an investment that has a varying payment and receipt schedule. The valuesArray() argument is a one-dimensional array holding the monetary values; it must have at least one negative amount (the payment) and one positive amount (the receipt). As the example syntax shows, you can provide a varying cashflow stream for the function to evaluate. The IRR function uses the guess! argument as its starting point in an iterative process that refines the returned value to within 0.00001 percent. If guess! is too different than the actual return, IRR may fail to derive a final figure within 20 iterations and will fail.

IRR evaluates a varying cashflow, while the annuity functions (Pmt, IPmt, FV, NPv, etc.) only work with a steady stream of payments.

The example syntax shows how IRR can derive the return for a business startup that loses substantial amounts of money in the beginning but pays off handsomely in the end. This "internal rate of return" is analogous to the APR of loan.

ISDATE, ISEMPTY, ISNULL, ISNUMERIC FUNCTIONS

Purpose

Use the Is... functions to determine if a Variant argument contains the specified data type.

General Syntax

```
IsDate(variant)
IsEmpty(variant)
IsNull(variant)
IsNumeric(variant)
```

Usage

```
If IsNull(Text1.Text) Then
      Print ""
Else
      Print Text1.Text
End If
```

Description

Variants can hold a variety of different data types, and can also hold special values that other variables cannot. Use the Is... functions to determine the data type or special contents of a variant argument.

IsDate evaluates the argument and returns True if the argument could be formatted as a date or time. See DateSerial and TimeSerial for examples of acceptable formats.

IsEmpty tests the variant argument and returns True if it has not yet been initialized. Note that this is not the same as having a value of 0 (for numeric types), and empty string (""), or Null. It will only return True if the variant has never had a value assigned to it.

IsNull evaluates the variant expression and returns True if any part of the expression has the special value of Null. You can set a variant to Null with the

Null keyword, and some databases return the value of Null for fields that have never had any data input. Nulls propagate, so if any part of an expression evaluates to Null, the entire expression will evaluate to Null.

IsNumeric examines the variant expression and returns True if it could be converted to a numeric value.

KILL STATEMENT

See Also: Name, Open.

Purpose

The Kill statement deletes the specified file from the disk.

General Syntax

```
Kill filename$
```

Usage

```
FileName$ = File1.List(File1.ListIndex)
Kill FileName$
```

This example erases the file that is currently selected in the FileListBox named File1.

Description

The Kill statement erases files from a fixed or floppy disk device. The filename$ parameter specifies the path and file name of the file(s) to be deleted. It may contain the wildcard characters "?" and "*". The "?" wildcard is used to match any single character, and the "*" matches a full file name or extension. If the drive or path are not specified in the filename$ parameter, the default drive and/or path is used. If the file does not exist on the specified path, or the path itself does not exist, Visual Basic will issue a "File not found" error.

Great care should be taken when using this statement. It is a destructive command that can, if not handled properly, cause you grief. Improper use of the Kill statement can cause your programs to inadvertently delete needed files. To prevent this from happening, when debugging a program that uses this statement, we suggest that you preface this statement with a MsgBox$ function that confirms the action. Then, when you are sure the program is deleting the correct file (or files), remove the MsgBox$ function if desired.

LBOUND FUNCTION

See Also: UBound.

Purpose

The LBound function returns the value of the smallest usable subscript for the specified dimension of an array.

General Syntax

```
LBound(arrayname[, dimension%])
```

Usage

```
Dim Flowers%(1 To 100, -50 To 50)
A% = LBound(Flowers%, 2)
```

The value -50 is assigned to the variable A%, because that is the smallest subscript available in the second dimension of the array Flowers%.

Description

If the dimension parameter is not specified, the lower bound for the first dimension is returned. LBound is useful in conjunction with UBound for figuring out how many elements a dynamic array has. The number of elements can be found by subtracting the value returned by LBound from the value returned from UBound and adding one.

LCASE, LCASE$ FUNCTIONS

See Also: UCase, UCase$.

Purpose

The LCase and LCase$ functions return a copy of a variant or a string in which all uppercase alphabetic characters have been converted to lowercase.

General Syntax

```
LCase$(expression$)
LCase(expression$)
```

Usage

```
C1$ = Command$
C2$ = LCase$(C1$)
```

This example retrieves the command-line parameters that were used to start the program, and converts the entries to lowercase.

Description

The expression$ parameter can be a fixed- or variable-length string, a string constant, a literal string, the result of any function that returns a string, or any other string expression. The UCase$ function works the same as LCase$, but it converts lowercase to uppercase.

This function is very useful for making a non-case-sensitive comparison of two strings. This is helpful when an internal variable is being compared to a user's string input. By using LCase$ (or UCase$), the program can all but ignore the case of the string that has been entered by the user.

LCase returns a variant; LCase$ returns a string.

LEFT, LEFT$ FUNCTIONS

See Also: Mid, Mid$; Right, Right$.

Purpose

The Left and Left$ functions return a portion of a variant or a string, starting at the first character, of the length specified.

General Syntax

```
Left$(expression$, length&)
```

Usage

```
B$ = "Hello, Dolly!"
C$ = Left$(B$, 5)
```

The above example assigns the leftmost five characters from B$ to the variable C$, giving it a value of "Hello".

Description

The expression$ parameter can be a fixed- or variable-length string, a string constant, a literal string, the result of any function that returns a string, or any other string expression.

The length& parameter refers to the number of characters to copy. This value may be in the range of from 0 to 65,535. If the length specified is greater than or equal to the full length of the source string, Left$ returns an exact copy of the source string. If the length is 0, a null string is returned. If length& has a value of less than 0, or greater than 65,535, an "Illegal function call" error is generated.

Left returns a variant; Left$ returns a string.

LEN FUNCTION

Purpose

The Len function returns the storage length of a variable. It is most commonly used to find the length of a string.

General Syntax

```
Len(variable-name)
```

Usage

```
A$ = "Hello"
StrLen% = Len(A$)
```

Because the string "Hello" is 5 bytes long, this places the value 5 into the variable StrLen%.

```
Type UserType
    A1 As String * 10
    A2 As Integer
    A3 As Single
End Type

Dim Test As UserType
TestLen% = Len(Test)
```

This places the length of the programmer-defined variable Test into the variable TestLen%. The value of TestLen% becomes 16; 10 bytes for Test.A1 (Fixed-length string), 2 bytes for Test.A2 (Integer), and 4 bytes for Test.A3 (Single-precision).

Description

This function returns the amount of data space needed to store a particular variable. Any type of variable may be used, including user-defined variables. Most commonly, Len is used to get the length of a variable-length string so it can be processed with a loop.

LET STATEMENT

See Also: LSet, RSet, Set.

Purpose

The optional Let statement assigns a value to a variable.

General Syntax

```
[Let] variablename = expression
```

Usage

```
Let A% = 100
B! = Day(Now)
```

Description

The Let keyword is required in some older versions of BASIC to begin a statement that assigns a value to a variable. The Let keyword is optional in Visual Basic, and rarely used. The data type of variablename must be a string or variant if expression is a string expression. If expression is numeric, and not of the same data type as variablename, Visual Basic will automatically convert the expression to the type indicated by the variable. If expression is a variant, and variablename is numeric, Visual Basic attempts to convert the variant to a number. The expression being assigned a numeric variable must fall into that variable's range, or an "Overflow" error will occur.

Record variables created with the Type...End Type structure can only use the Let statement if the record variable is being assigned the value of another record variable of the same type. Use the LSet statement to assign a value to a record variable from a different record type.

LINE INPUT # STATEMENT

See Also: Input #, Print #.

Purpose

The Line Input # statement reads from a sequential file until a carriage return/linefeed pair or the end of the file is reached.

General Syntax

```
Line Input #filenumber%, variable
```

Usage

```
SeqFile% = FreeFile
Open "Notes.Txt" For Input As #SeqFile%
Line Input #SeqFile%, A$
```

This example reads one line of data from "Test.Dat" into the variable A$.

Description

The filenumber% parameter must be the file number of a currently open file that was opened under the Input mode. If the file number does not match that of a currently open file, Visual Basic issues a "Bad file name or number" error. (The FreeFile function is handy for obtaining a guaranteed legitimate file number that can be used without worrying about its actual value.)

The variable parameter must be a string variable or variant. This should normally be a variable-length string. If a fixed-length string is used, and the length of the data read is shorter than the string, the balance of the variable will be filled with spaces. If the read length is longer than the string, any characters read beyond the length of the string are lost.

Unlike the Input # statement, Line Input # treats commas, spaces, and quotes no differently than any other characters. This makes it useful for reading ASCII files. A read ends when a carriage return/linefeed pair is encountered, resulting in reading one complete line of text. The carriage return/linefeed pair is then skipped, and the next read continues from the first character after them. A read also ends when the end of the file is reached.

LOAD STATEMENT

See Also: Unload.

Purpose

The Load statement loads a form into memory, or a control into a previously created control array.

General Syntax

For a form:

```
Load form-name
```

For a control:

```
Load control-name(index)
```

Usage

```
Load Form1
```

Loads a form into memory without displaying it.

```
Load Text1(1)
```

Loads a text box into a control array.

Description

This statement loads a form or control into memory. Form-name or control-name represent the name of the form or control to be loaded. If a control is an element of a control array, the index value must be supplied in parentheses following the array name.

Since Visual Basic automatically loads any form or control referenced in code (for example, by the Show method), the Load statement is normally only needed when you want to load a form into memory without showing it. (Sometimes Load is used in order to change one or more properties of a form without immediately displaying the form.)

When a form is loaded, Visual Basic sets all of its properties to their initial (default) values and then executes the Load event procedure for the form.

For more details about the loading and initialization of forms, see Chapter 4, Setting Up Forms, and Chapter 6, Using Forms and Controls in Program Code.

LOADPICTURE FUNCTION

See Also: SavePicture, and Chapter 8, Graphics Fundamentals.

Purpose

Loads a *.BMP, *.ICO, *.RLE or *.WMF picture from a disk file into, or erases it from, a form, picture box, or image control.

General Syntax

To load a picture into a form or picture box:

```
LoadPicture(picturefile$)
```

To clear a picture from a form or picture box:

```
LoadPicture
```

Usage

```
Form1.Picture = LoadPicture("CHESS.BMP")
```

This example loads the Chess.Bmp bitmap file into the current form.

```
PictureBox1.Picture = LoadPicture("POINT13.ICO")
```

This example loads the icon file Point13.ICO into the picture box named PictureBox1.

```
PictureBox1.Picture = LoadPicture
```

This example clears any picture that has been loaded in the picture box named PictureBox1.

Description

The LoadPicture statement loads a picture from a specified disk file into a specified form or picture box. The picture file must be in .BMP (bitmap), .ICO (icon), .RLE (run-length encoded), or .WMF (Windows metafile) format.

1356

The LoadPicture function is explained in detail in Chapter 8, Graphics Fundamentals.

LOC FUNCTION

See Also: EOF, LOF, Open.

Purpose

The Loc function returns the current position of the pointer for an open file, which indicates where the next read or write operation will occur. The meaning of the number returned depends on the mode under which the file was opened.

General Syntax

```
Loc(filenumber%)
```

Usage

```
A% = Loc(1)
```

This example places a number representing the current position in the file opened as #1 in the variable A%.

Description

The filenumber% parameter must be the file number of a currently open file. If the file number does not match that of a currently open file, Visual Basic issues a "Bad file name or number" error.

Visual Basic defaults to a 128-byte file buffer for sequential files. When a read or write is done to a sequential file, it does so 128 bytes at a time. Internally, this is much like reading and writing records with 128-byte lengths. The value returned by the Loc function for a sequential file is the result of the current byte position divided by 128 (which is the "record number" of the last internal read or write). You can open sequential files with a different size of buffer by using the Len= parameter in the Open statement. This does not change the result of Loc; it always divides by 128 no matter what the physical size of the buffer.

For random access files, this function returns the record number of the last Get or Put statement. If no Get or Put statement has yet been executed, the Loc function returns a 0.

Because binary files are byte-oriented, the number returned corresponds to the last byte read or written to the file. Again, if no read or write has been performed, Loc returns a 0.

LOCK...UNLOCK STATEMENTS

See Also: Get, Put.

Purpose

The Lock statement restricts multiuser access to a specified area of a file. The UnLock statement releases the restrictions placed on an area of a file by a previously issued Lock statement. This only applies to files opened with the Open statement; it does not apply to Access databases.

General Syntax

```
Lock [#]filenumber%[,startpos&][ To endpos&]
   :
[statements]
   :
UnLock [#]filenumber%[,startpos&][ To endpos&]
```

Usage

```
Lock #1
   :
UnLock #1
```

This example restricts other users from access to the entire file. When processing of the file is finished, the restrictions are released with the UnLock statement.

```
Open "TEST.DAT" For Random As #1 Len = 32
Lock #1, 100
   :
UnLock #1, 100
```

This example locks and unlocks access to the 100th record in the random access file TEST.DAT.

```
Open "TEST.DAT" For Binary As #1
Lock #1, 10 To 20
   :
UnLock #1, 10 To 20
```

This example locks and unlocks access to byte positions 10 through 20 of the binary file TEST.DAT.

```
Open "TEST.DAT" For Binary As #1
Lock #1, To 300
   :
UnLock #1, To 300
```

This example locks and unlocks access to byte positions 1 through 300 of the binary file TEST.DAT.

Description

The Lock and UnLock statements are used for controlling multiuser access to files in a networked or multitasking environment. Because more than one user may have access to the same file simultaneously, such environments present special problems when it comes to maintaining data integrity. For instance, let us suppose two users, Bob and Mary, are on a network working on the same file. Bob reads a record from the file, and a copy of its contents are placed in the memory of his computer. If the program that Bob is using does not restrict access to the record, Mary can also read the record into her own computer's memory. This in itself causes no problems. However, if Bob updates the record, and then Mary also updates the record, Mary's update will be written over Bob's. By using the Lock and UnLock statements, Bob's program could restrict Mary's access to the record until Bob is finished with it. This ensures that when Mary reads the record, it will reflect any changes Bob has made to it.

The filenumber% parameter must be the file number of a currently open file. If the file number does not match that of a currently open file, Visual Basic issues a "Bad file name or number" error.

The area within the file to be locked may be specified with the startpos& and endpos& parameters. If endpos& is omitted, the TO keyword must also be omitted. This will cause the statement to affect only the position specified by startpos&. If the startpos& parameter is not used, the range affected will be from the beginning of the file to the position specified by endpos&. If both parameters ar omitted, the entire file is affected.

When used on a file that has been opened under Random mode, Lock and UnLock affect the records that fall into the range specified by startpos& and endpos&.

For files opened under the Binary mode, these statements affect a range of bytes specified by the startpos& and endpos& parameters.

When used on a file opened under Input or Output modes, the Lock and UnLock statements restrict access to the entire file. If a range has been specified, it is ignored.

Use the UnLock statement to release the restrictions placed on a file by the Lock statement. The parameters in the UnLock statement must match the parameters in the related Lock statement exactly. Not doing so will result in a "Permission Denied" error. Failing to unlock the locked portions of a file before closing it can cause unpredictable results.

When a Lock is placed on a file, the specified portion of the file is not accessible to any other process. This includes other programs that are running on the same computer. If a Visual Basic program tries to read a portion of a file that has been locked by a different process, a "Permission denied" error will occur. This error will also occur if the program attempts to lock a portion of a file that has already been locked by another process.

Comments

The Lock and UnLock statements depend on the operating system to take care of the details involved with restricting access to files. These capabilities are provided by running SHARE.EXE under a DOS version 3.1 or higher.

LOF FUNCTION

See Also: EOF, Loc.

Purpose

The LOF function returns the number of bytes equal to the length of an open file.

General Syntax

```
LOF([#]filenumber%)
```

Usage

```
Function NumberOfRecords(FileNo%, RecordLength%) As Long
    Dim FileLength As Integer
    FileLength = LOF(FileNo%)
    NumberOfRecords = FileLength \ RecordLength%
End Function
```

This example uses the LOF function to calculate the number of records in a random access file.

Description

This function returns the number of bytes in a file, regardless of the mode under which it was opened.

The filenumber% parameter must be the file number of a currently open file. If the file number does not match that of a currently open file, Visual Basic issues a "Bad file name or number" error.

LOG FUNCTION

See Also: Exp.

Purpose

The Log function returns the natural logarithm of a numeric expression. The natural logarithm, which has a base of approximately 2.718282, should not be confused with the common logarithm, whose base is 10

General Syntax

```
Log(numericExpression)
```

Usage

```
A! = 14
B! = Log(A!)
```

Returns a single-precision number that represents the natural logarithm for 14.

```
C# = 14
D# = Log(C#)
```

Returns a double-precision number that represents the natural logarithm for 14.

Description

The logarithm of a number is the power to which the logarithmic base must be raised in order to achieve that number. The natural logarithmic base is referred to by the symbol e, and has an approximate value of 2.718282.

The supplied numeric expression may be of any numeric format. It must be a nonzero number. If the expression is zero, an "Illegal function call" error will occur.

By default, this function returns a single-precision number. However, if the supplied numericExpression is in double-precision format, the function will return a double-precision number.

Exp performs the inverse operation of a natural logarithm. It raises e to the power specified by the power parameter. Appendix A covers these statements in more detail and gives examples of how to calculate logs using logarithmic bases other than e.

LSET STATEMENT

See Also: Let; RSet; LTrim, LTrim$.

Purpose

The LSet statement copies one string or user-defined type to another, starting from the left and working to the right. It can also be used to left justify the contents of a string variable.

General Syntax

```
LSet resultvariable = sourcevariable
```

Usage

```
Type NameAndAddress1
     Name As String * 20
     Number As Long
     Address As String * 75
End Type

Type NameAndAddress2
     Name As String * 20
     Number As Long
     Street As String * 25
     City As String * 25
     State As String * 20
     Zip As String * 5
End Type

Dim PhoneCard1 As NameAndAddress1
Dim PhoneCard2 As NameAndAddress2

LSet PhoneCard2 = PhoneCard1
```

Description

The LSet statement assigns to resultvariable the value of sourcevariable. Both variables may be fixed- or variable-length strings, or a programmer-defined variable type. The assignment performed by the LSet is done byte by byte from the left of sourcevariable to the right. The assignment cannot change the length of resultvariable. If resultvariable is shorter than sourcevariable, the characters that are beyond the length of resultvariable are truncated. If resultvariable is longer than sourcevariable, spaces are used to fill out the balance of resultvariable.

As can be seen in the example above, this statement allows you to assign one programmer-defined type a value from a different programmer-defined type.

However, it does not allow a programmer-defined type to be assigned to a variable- or fixed-length string. Nor does it allow assignment of different user-defined types when one of those types contains a variable-length string.

The LSet statement can also be used with a single variable as both source and result. For example:

```
A$ = "It starts with two spaces"
LSet A$ = "It starts with two spaces"
```

In this case the text in A$ is left justified: that is, the two spaces at the beginning of the string are removed, the text is moved to the left, and two spaces are added on at the end of the string. The length of the string does not change. This effect is similar to that obtained with the LTrim$ function, except that LTrim$ does not pad the string on the right. The RSet statement performs the same function, except the copy is executed from right to left.

LTRIM, LTRIM$ FUNCTIONS

See Also: RTrim, RTrim$; Trim, Trim$; and Appendix A.

Purpose

The LTrim and LTrim$ functions return a copy of a string with any leading spaces removed.

General Syntax

```
LTrim$(stringExpression$)
LTrim(stringExpression$)
```

Usage

```
A$ = LTrim$("  Good Bye  ")
```
This example assigns the value "Good Bye " to the variable A$.

Description

This is the complement of the RTrim$ function. It returns a copy of the supplied string expression without any leading spaces.

The stringExpression$ parameter can be a fixed- or variable-length string, a string constant, a literal string, the result of any function that returns a string, any other string expression, or a variant that can evaluate to a string.

LTrim returns a variant; LTrim$ returns a string.

MID, MID$ FUNCTIONS

See Also: Left, Left$; Right, Right$.

Purpose

The Mid and Mid$ functions return the specified portion of a string expression.

General Syntax

```
Mid$(stringExpression$, start&[, length&])
Mid(stringExpression$, start&[, length&])
```

Usage

```
A$ = "Good bye, Dolly"
B$ = Mid$(A$, 6, 3)
C$ = Mid$(A$, 11)
```

This uses the Mid$ function to assign the value "bye" to the variable B$. In the second example, the length parameter is omitted, so the string returned starts where indicated and continues for the balance of the length of A$. Therefore, the variable C$ is assigned the value "Dolly."

Description

This function returns the specified substring of a string expression. The stringExpression$ parameter designates the source string and can be a fixed- or variable-length string, a string constant, a literal string, the result of any function that returns a string, or a variant that can evaluate to a string.

The start& parameter specifies the byte position within the source string where the copy will begin. This parameter must be in the range of from 1 to 65535. If not, an "Illegal function call" will occur. If this parameter is greater than the length of the source string, the returned string will be null.

The length& parameter is used to specify how many bytes will be copied. This is an optional parameter. If it is not used, the function will return all the characters from start& to the end of the source string. The length& parameter has a range of from 0 to 65535. If it is not in this range, an "Illegal function call" will occur. If a 0 is specified, a null string is returned. If it specifies a length beyond the end of the source string, only the characters up to the length of the string are returned.

Mid returns a variant; Mid$ returns a string.

MID, MID$ STATEMENTS

See Also: Left, Left$; Right, Right$.

Purpose

The Mid and Mid$ statements replace the specified characters of one string with another string.

General Syntax

```
Mid$(result-string$, start&[, length&]) = stringExpression$
Mid(result-string$, start&[, length&]) = stringExpression$
```

Usage

```
A$ = "Hello, Dolly"
Mid$(A$, 1, 5) = "Oh my"
Mid$(A$, 8) = "Beck"
```

The first example replaces the "Hello" in A$ with "Oh my." The second example starts at the eighth byte position and replaces whatever text is there with "Beck." Because the length is not specified, the replace is effective for the length of "Beck." This makes A$'s final value "Oh my, Becky."

Description

This statement copies the supplied string expression into the specified string. The result-string$ parameter must be a variable- or fixed-length string, or a variant that can evaluate to a string. This is the string that will receive the characters being copied.

The start& parameter specifies where in the result string the characters are to be placed. This parameter must be greater than 0, and cannot exceed the length of the result string. If it is not in this range, an "Illegal function call" will result.

The length& parameter is optional, and it specifies how many characters will be replaced. If this parameter is omitted, the length will default to the size of stringExpression$. Regardless of the value in length&, and the length of stringExpression$, the copy never goes beyond the original length of result-string$.

The stringExpression$ parameter specifies the source of the copy. It can be a fixed- or variable-length string, a string constant, a literal string, the result of any function that returns a string, or a variant that can evaluate to a string.

MINUTE FUNCTION

See Also: Now, TimeSerial, TimeValue.

Purpose

The Minute function returns an integer (with a value of from 0 to 59) that represents the minute of the hour specified by the supplied date variant.

General Syntax

```
Minute(dateVariant)
```

Usage

```
A% = Minute(Now)
```

Places the current minute of the hour in the variable A%.

Description

The minute is returned as an integer in the range of from 0 to 59.

A date variant can represent any time of the day. Its fractional part corresponds to the specified time in proportion to a whole day. Therefore a date variant for 12:00 noon has a value of 0.5 (one-half of a day), while 6 PM has a value of 0.75 (three-quarters of a day). It is created by using the Now, TimeValue, or TimeSerial functions.

Date and time parts of date variants can be combined, because the date part of the date variant is stored on the left side of the decimal point, and the time part of the date variant is stored on the right.

MIRR FUNCTION

See Also: IRR, Rate.

Purpose

The MIRR function returns the Modified Internal Rate of Return for a varying series of cashflows.

General Syntax

```
MIRR(values( ), financeInterestRate!, reinvestmentInternalRate!)
```

Usage

```
money(0) = -500000          'first year startup costs
money(1) = -250000          'second year operation costs
money(2) = 0                'third year breakeven
money(3) = 100000           'fourth year profit
money(4) = 300000
money(5) = 500000
money(6) = 2000000          'seventh year cashout
financeRate = 0.1           'ten percent charged to borrow money
return = MIRR(money(), financeRate, reinvestRate) * 100
```

Description

The MIRR function returns the Modified Internal Rate of Return for a varying series of cashflows. The MIRR differs from the IRR in that it accounts for the finance charges associated with borrowing the initial investment (or the "opportunity cost" of not being able to invest the money in other ventures) as well as the interest earned on reinvestment of returns.

The values array can have a varying cashflow, but must have at least one negative value (the investment) and one positive value (the return).

The example syntax shows how to calculate the MIRR given a cashflow of high startup costs financed at 10% APR and reinvesting the payouts at 8% APR.

MKDIR STATEMENT

See Also: ChDir, RmDir.

Purpose

The MkDir statement creates a subdirectory on the specified drive.

General Syntax

```
MkDir dirname$
```

dirname$ must be in the format of [drive:][\]dir[\subdir][\subdir]...

Usage

```
MkDir "TEST"
```

Creates the subdirectory "TEST" underneath the default directory on the default drive.

```
MkDir "\TEST"
```

Creates the subdirectory "TEST" underneath the root directory of the default drive.

```
MkDir "D:\TEST"
```

Creates the subdirectory "TEST" underneath the root directory of drive D:

Description

This statement works much like the DOS command of the same name. However, unlike the DOS command, the Visual Basic statement cannot be shortened to MD.

MkDir creates the subdirectory specified by the dir-name$ parameter. Unless the full path name is specified, the new subdirectory is created on the default drive, under the default directory. If a full path name is not indicated, and dir-name$ matches a file or directory that resides on the default drive and directory, a "Path file access error" will occur.

Comments

Care should be taken when using this statement. Visual Basic allows you to include spaces in the dir-name$ parameter. This will create a subdirectory that cannot be removed by any means other than another Visual Basic or QuickBASIC program.

MONTH FUNCTION

See Also: DateSerial, DateValue, Now.

Purpose

The Month function returns an integer between 1 and 12 representing the month of the year, based on the supplied date variant.

General Syntax

```
Month(dateVariant)
```

Usage

```
A% = Month(Now)
```

This places the value of the current month into the integer variable A%.

Description

This function uses a date variant representing a date to return an integer value, between 1 and 12, representing the month of the year. The supplied date variant represents the number of days since December 30, 1899. Therefore, January 01, 1900, has a date variant of 2, while January 1, 1753, has a date variant of -53688. The supplied date variant must represent a date in the range of from January 1, 100, and December 31, 9999, inclusive. If the date requested is not in this range, Visual Basic issues an "Illegal function call" error.

MSGBOX FUNCTION AND STATEMENT

See Also: InputBox, InputBox$.

Purpose

The MsgBox statement displays a user-defined message in a window with a desired set of command buttons. If used as a function, MsgBox displays the message and also returns an integer that signifies the selected button.

General Syntax

```
MsgBox(message$[, boxtype%][, windowtitle$])
```

Usage

```
MsgBox("Hello World")
```

Displays a window that says "Hello World" and waits for the user to click the OK button.

Description

The MsgBox statement or function displays the message in message$ in a dialog box. If supplied, windowtitle$ will be placed on the title bar of the dialog box; boxtype% is the sum of up to three values in Table B-21. The values in Table B-21 actually fall into three groups: those that display one or more buttons, those that display a specified icon, and those that determine which button will be considered the default. Thus a boxtype% value of 2 + 16 + 0, or 18, would result in the Abort, Retry, and Ignore buttons being displayed, the "Critical Message" icon being shown in the box, and the "Abort" button being the default action.

When used as a function, MsgBox returns an integer that indicates which button was pressed, as shown in Table B-22.

Value	Effect
0	Displays OK button
1	Displays OK and Cancel buttons
2	Displays Abort, Retry, and Ignore buttons
4	Displays Yes and No buttons
5	Displays Retry and Cancel buttons
16	Displays "Critical Message" icon
32	Displays "Warning Query" icon
64	Displays "Information Message" icon
0	First button is default
256	Second button is default
512	Third button is default

Table B-21 Values that can be summed in boxtype%

Return Value	Meaning
1	OK button was pressed
2	Cancel button was pressed
3	Abort button was pressed
4	Retry button was pressed

Return Value	Meaning
5	Ignore button was pressed
6	Yes button was pressed
7	No button was pressed

Table B-22 Meaning of return values of MsgBox function

Further discussion and examples of use of the MsgBox statement and function can be found in Chapter 17, Dialog Boxes.

NAME STATEMENT

See Also: Kill.

Purpose

The Name statement renames a file or directory, or moves a file to another directory.

General Syntax

```
Name oldname As newname
```

Usage

```
Name "TEST_1.DAT" As "TEST_2.DAT"
```

This example changes the name of the file TEST_1.DAT in the default directory to TEST_2.DAT.

Description

The Name statement is very similar to the RENAME (REN) command in DOS. However, unlike the DOS RENAME, this statement allows the program to rename subdirectories as well as files.

The parameters oldname and newname specify the original and the new path and name of the file. The file specified by oldname must exist. If it does not, a "File not found" error will occur. Conversely, the file specified by newname must not exist or a "File already exists" error is issued. If the drive is specified, the same drive must be used in both oldname and newname, or a "Rename across disks" error will occur. However, Visual Basic does not require the paths of the two parameters to match. This creates the useful side effect of being able to move files from one directory to another. For instance,

```
Name "C:\TEMP\TEST1.DAT" As "C:\TEST1.DAT"
```

will move the file "TEST1.DAT" from the "C:\TEMP" subdirectory to the root directory.

This statement cannot be used if the file specified by either oldname or new-name is currently open. Doing so causes a "File already open" error.

NOW FUNCTION

See Also: Day, Hour, Minute, Month, Second, WeekDay, Year.

Purpose

The Now function returns a date variant that corresponds to the current date and time.

General Syntax

```
Now
```

Usage

```
A = Now
```

Places the date variant for the current system date and time into the variable A.

Description

This function returns a date variant that is a combined date and time representing the current system time. The whole part of the number represents the date and corresponds to the number of days since December 30, 1899. Therefore, January 01, 1900, has a date variant of 2, while January 1, 1753, has a date variant of -53688.

The fractional part represents the time. This fraction corresponds to the current time in proportion to a whole day. Therefore, a date variant for 12:00 noon has a value of 0.5 (one-half of a day), while 6 PM has a value of 0.75 (three-quarters of a day).

NPER FUNCTION

See Also: IPmt, Pmt, PPmt, Rate.

Purpose

The NPer function calculates the number of periods for an annuity assuming constant payments and interest rate.

General Syntax

```
NPer(interestRate!, periodicPayment@, presentValue@, futureValue@, whenDue%)
```

Usage

```
numMonths = NPer(0.0975/12, 350.00, -12000, 0, 0)
```

Description

Use the NPer function to determine how many payments must be made on a loan to pay it off, or how many deposits must be made to achieve a savings goal. It assumes the payments are constant and periodic, and the interest rate does not vary. Make sure the interest rate is given in the same units as the number of payments.

The example syntax determines the number of monthly payments necessary to pay off a $12,000 loan (note the negative sign) at 9.75% APR.

NPV FUNCTION

See Also: IRR, FV, MIRR, PV.

Purpose

The NPV function returns the net present value of a varying series of periodic cashflows (both negative and positive) at a given discount rate.

General Syntax

```
NPV(discountRate!, valuesArray( ) )
```

Usage

```
money(0) = -500000          'first year startup costs
money(1) = -250000          'second year operation costs
money(2) = 0                'third year breakeven
money(3) = 100000           'fourth year profit
money(4) = 300000
money(5) = 500000
money(6) = 2000000          'seventh year cashout
financeRate = 0.1           'ten percent APR
return = NPV(financeRate, money() )
```

Description

Use the NPV function to determine the net present value of a series of varying cashflows. Note that this differs from the PV function in that the payments can vary over time. The values array must have at least one negative and one positive number.

OCT, OCT$ FUNCTIONS

See Also: Hex, Hex$.

Purpose

The Oct and Oct$ functions return a variant or string that represents the supplied numeric expression in Octal notation (base 8).

General Syntax

```
Oct$(numericExpression)
Oct(numericExpression)
```

Usage

```
Octal$ = Oct$(100)
```

This places the octal number 144 into the string variable Octal$.

Description

Octal notation is a method of counting using only eight digits. This is sometimes used to work with memory addresses because it converts back and forth from binary more easily than decimal, although hexadecimal is more commonly used for this purpose. The Oct$ function provides a method of converting a decimal number into octal.

The supplied numericExpression is rounded to the nearest whole number before conversion begins. It cannot exceed the range defined by the long integer data type. If numericExpression is an integer, the string returned by Oct$ will be 4 or fewer bytes long. Otherwise, the return string can be up to 11 bytes long.

Oct returns a variant; Oct$ returns a string.

ON ERROR... STATEMENT

See Also: Erl; Err; Error, Error$; Resume.

Purpose

The On Error statement tells the program what to do if an error occurs.

General Syntax

To enable an error-handling routine:

```
On Error GoTo error-handler
error-handler
    :
    [statements]
Resume [{[0] | Next | {line-number | line-label} }]
```

To cause the Err flag to be set, and then continue with the next statement:

```
On Error Resume Next
```

To give Visual Basic control of error handling:

```
On Error GoTo 0
```

Usage

```
On Error GoTo ErrorTrap
```

This example tells Visual Basic to branch to the label "ErrorTrap" when an error occurs.

```
On Error Resume Next
```

This causes Visual Basic to do little more than set the value of Err, and then resume execution at the next instruction after the statement that caused the error.

```
On Error GoTo 0
```

This deactivates the current error handler and returns all error handling to Visual Basic.

Description

The On Error... statement involves setting up a routine that will be processed when an error occurs. The routine is specified by the error handler parameter. This parameter can be a line number or a line label. Because Visual Basic does not allow a GoTo to jump out of a procedure, the line number or label must reside within the same procedure as the On Error... statement. If this is not the case, Visual Basic will issue a "Label not defined" error at compile time. The error-handling routine should only be exited by using the Resume statement.

The Resume statement is used at the end of the error-handling routine after all the error-handling tasks have been performed. There are three variations on the Resume statement.

The first involves using the Resume statement with no parameters, or a parameter of 0. This causes execution to resume at the statement that caused the error.

Second, the Resume Next statement may be used. This causes execution to pick up at the instruction following the statement that caused the error.

Finally, the Resume keyword may be followed by a line number or line label. This causes execution to continue at the specified line. This is a very unstructured approach, that can lead to "spaghetti code." This variation of the Resume statement should be avoided if possible.

Care should be taken so that the error-handling code is not entered inadvertently. Doing so will cause the Resume statement to be executed when no error has occurred. If this happens, Visual Basic will generate a "Resume without error." This can be prevented by placing an Exit Sub or Exit Function just prior to the error handler.

The On Error Resume Next Statement

This style of the On Error... statement merely sets an error code, and returns control to the statement following the instruction that caused the error. This error code may be obtained with the Err function. Using this style of error processing assumes the program will be checking for errors at strategic places. Failing to do such checking can cause hard to find logic errors in a program. Generally, this type of error processing is used with file input or output. Each time an input or output operation is performed, the Err is checked and reacted upon.

The On Error GoTo 0 Statement

This statement returns control of error handling to Visual Basic. The same effect is achieved when a procedure with an enabled error handler is exited.

Comments

The Local keyword has no effect in Visual Basic. It is only used to provide backward compatibility to earlier versions of the BASIC language.

ON...GOSUB STATEMENT

See Also: On...GoTo, Select Case.

Purpose

The On...GoSub statement transfers execution to a subroutine, based on the value of a numeric expression. When the RETURN keyword is encountered, execution returns to the instruction following the On...GoSub.

General Syntax

```
On numericExpression GoSub line1[, line2][, line3] [, line255]
```

Usage

```
A% = WeekDay(Now)
On A% GoSub Sunday, Monday, Tuesday, Wednesday, Thursday, Friday, Saturday
```

This example executes a different subroutine based on the current day of the week.

Description

This statement has been kept for backward compatibility to earlier BASIC languages. The Select Case statement can perform the same functions, and is much more flexible than On...GoSub.

The numericExpression parameter must be an integer between 0 and 255. If it does not fall into this range, an "Illegal function call" will occur. This parameter determines which routine will be executed.

The line-? parameters are the line labels or numbers of the routines that will be executed. Up to 255 routines may be listed. One or more routines may be listed several times. Line numbers and labels may be mixed in the list.

If numericExpression equals 1, the first routine listed is executed. If it equals 2, the second is executed, and so on. If the value of numericExpression is 0, or greater than the number of routines listed, no routines are executed, and the On ...GoSub statement is ignored.

ON...GOTO STATEMENT

See Also: On...GoSub, Select Case.

Purpose

The On...GoTo statement transfers execution to a line number or label, based on the value of a numeric expression. Execution does not return from the new location.

General Syntax

```
On numericExpression GoTo line1[, line2][, line3] [, line255]
```

Usage

```
A% = WeekDay(Now)
On A% GoTo Sunday, Monday, Tuesday, Wednesday, Thursday, Friday, Saturday
```

This example transfers execution to a different label based on the current day of the week.

Description

This statement has been kept for backward compatibility to earlier BASIC languages. The Select Case can perform the same functions, and is much more flexible and structured than On...GoTo. Because there is no return from a GoTo, it is not good programming practice to use this statement.

The numericExpression parameter must be an integer between 0 and 255. If it does not fall into this range, an "Illegal function call" will occur. This parameter determines to which line number or label execution will be transferred.

The line-? parameters are the line labels or numbers to where execution will be transferred. There may be up to 255 line labels or numbers listed. One or more label or line number may be listed several times. Line numbers and labels may be mixed in the list.

If numericExpression equals 1, execution is transferred to the first label or line number listed. If it equals 2, execution is transferred to the second, and so on. If the value of numericExpression is 0, or greater than the number of labels listed, the On GoTo... statement is ignored.

OPEN STATEMENT

See Also: Close; FreeFile; Get; Input, Input$; Line Input #, Put.

Purpose

The Open statement enables input and output operations on a file.

General Syntax

```
Open filename$ [For mode] [Access access] [locktype] As [#]filenumber [Len=recordlength]
```

Usage

```
Type RecordType
    Type NameAndAddress_1
    Name As String * 20
    Number As Long
    Address As String * 75
End Type

Dim TestRec As RecordType
TestFile% = FreeFile
Open "Test.Dat" For Random Access Read Write Shared As #TestFile% Len = Len(TestRec)
```

This example opens a random access file for reading and writing. The Shared lock parameter allows the file to be opened by other processes. It is opened under the filenumber specified by TestFile%. The LEN keyword is used along with the Len function to define the length of each record.

```
Open "Test.Txt" For Input As #1
```

This statement opens the file Test.Txt for sequential input.

Description

Before any input or output operations may be performed on a file, it must first be opened. Opening a file causes Visual Basic to allocate a buffer area for the file. Because physically reading from and writing to a file is a slow process, this buffer area is set up, and acts as a way station for the file's data. Visual Basic generally reads large blocks of data from a file into this buffer area. When a Get, Input #, Line Input #, or Put statement is executed, the I/O is done from the buffer, not the disk. This reduces the number of physical reads and writes, thereby speeding up file access.

The filename$ parameter can be any type of string expression that contains a valid DOS file name. The drive and path may be specified explicitly. However, if left out, the default drive and/or directory is used.

The For Clause

There are five different types of files in Visual Basic. Each type behaves a little differently. The type of file being opened is specified by the mode parameter. This parameter must be one of the following: Output, Append, Input, Random, or Binary.

Specifying Output creates the specified file, and gets it ready for sequential output. This mode is generally used to write ASCII text files. If a file with the specified name already exists, it is erased, and a new file is created. This mode only allows data to be written to the file via the Print #, and Write # statements. Each write moves the file pointer to the end of the file. Trying to read data from a file opened under this mode causes a "Bad file mode" error to occur.

Specifying Append also causes the specified file to be opened for sequential output. As with the Output mode, if the file does not exist, it will be created. However, unlike the Output mode, if the file already exists it is not erased, but the file pointer is placed at the end of the file. This mode only allows data to be written to the file via the Print # and Write # statements. Each write moves the file pointer to the end of the file. Trying to read data from a file opened under this mode causes an "Input past end" error to occur. This mode is generally used to add material to ASCII text files.

Opening a file under Input mode opens a sequential file for reading only. As with Output and Append, this mode is mostly used for processing ASCII text files. When opened, the file pointer is placed at the beginning of the file. Reads are performed via the Input #, Input$, and Line Input # instructions. Each read moves the file pointer forward in the file. No writing may be done to a file opened under this mode, or a "Bad file mode" error will occur.

Random is the default file mode. This mode allows both input and output of fixed-length records. Reads and writes are performed by the Get and Put statements, respectively. The position of the file pointer may be set in several ways. First, the desired record number may be specified in the Get and Put statements. Second, the file pointer may be set using the Seek statement. Finally, if neither of the two previous methods are used, the file pointer is set to the next record after the most recent operation on this file. This mode is used for files whose records are all of the same or a similar format, and which all have the same length. The structure of the records is defined by using the Type...End Type statement.

Binary mode also allows both input and output. However, instead of requiring fixed-length records, reads and writes may be done at any byte position in the file, for any length. This allows the file to have variable-length records. The Get and Put statements are used for reading and writing to the file, and can optionally specify the starting byte position. The Seek statement can also be used to move the file pointer to a desired byte position in the file.

The Access Clause

When one works in a multiuser or multitasking environment, several processes may have access to the same files. In such an environment, when an Open is performed on a file, it is possible that access to that file has been restricted by another process. Because of this, each process must request specific privileges, which define the tasks that need to be performed when it opens a file. The Access clause is used to request the desired privileges for a file. The entry for access must be one of the following keywords; Read, Write, or Read Write.

Access Read requests read-only access to a file. If the open is successful, only read operations may be performed on it. If a write is attempted, a "Permission denied" error will occur. Files opened under Input, Random, or Binary modes may use this access method. A "Syntax error" is generated if this method is used on a file opened under Output or Append mode.

Access Write requests write-only access. If the open is successful, only write operations may be performed on it. If a read is attempted, a "Permission denied" error will occur. Files opened under Output, Random, and Binary modes may use this access method. Any other modes cause an error to occur.

Access Read Write requests both read and write access to a file. Files opened under Append, Random, and Binary modes may use this access method. Any other modes cause an error to occur.

If the requested access to a file has been restricted by another process, the Open statement will fail, and a "Permission denied" error will occur. The Access clause is only effective when used on a system that is running DOS version 3.1 or higher, and its related SHARE.EXE program. If the DOS version is earlier than 3.1, DOS will issue a "Feature unavailable" error.

The Locktype Parameter

The locktype parameter is the flip side of the Access clause. This parameter specifies what privileges will be granted to other processes that try to open the file after this open has occurred. By default, when a file is opened, all access to that file by other processes is restricted. However, the default does allow the current process to reopen the file at a subsequent time. This can be changed by setting the locktype parameter to Shared, Lock Read, Lock Write, or Lock Read Write.

Using the Shared keyword places no restrictions on the file. It allows other processes to open it for reading or writing.

Lock Read restricts other processes from opening this file with read access. This type of lock can only be used if no other processes currently have read access to the file. If there are other processes that have read access to the file, this Open issues a "Permission denied" error.

Lock Write restricts other processes from opening this file with write access. This type of lock can only be used if no other processes currently have write access to the file. If there are other processes that have write access to the file, this Open issues a "Permission denied" error.

Lock Read Write restricts other processes from opening this file with read or write access. This type of lock can only be used if no other processes currently have read or write access to the file. If there are other processes that have read or write access to the file, this Open issues a "Permission denied" error. Unlike the default locking scheme, this lock prohibits even the current program from opening this file again.

The Filenumber Parameter

A numericExpression between 1 and 255 must be supplied in the filenumber parameter. This is the number that will be used by the Input #, Input$, Line Input #, Get, Put, and other file related statements to reference this file. Only one file at a time can use a particular file number. The best method for keeping track of unused file numbers is to let Visual Basic do it for you via the FreeFile function. Not only does this save you the headache of having to remember which filenumbers are and are not in use, but it also forces the file number to be placed in a variable. If a descriptive variable name is used, it makes the program much more readable.

The Len Clause

For files opened under Random mode, the recordlength parameter defines the number of bytes that are read or written to the file with each Get or Put statement. If this is omitted, the record length will default to 128 bytes.

For files opened under Input, Append, or Output modes, this parameter defines the size of the read/write buffer. By default, sequential files use a 512-byte buffer. Making the buffer larger will increase the speed of the I/O operations on the file, but will take more memory.

Files opened under Binary mode ignore the Len clause.

In any case, the length specified by the Len clause may be no more than 32767 bytes.

OPTION BASE STATEMENT

See Also: Dim, Global, ReDim.

Purpose

The Option Base statement defines the default lower bound value of an array.

General Syntax

```
Option Base {0 | 1}
```

Usage

```
Option Base 1
```

This sets the default value of 1 for the lower bound of any arrays that are defined within the same form or module.

Description

The lowest subscript for arrays created using the Dim, Global, or ReDim statements default to 0. The Option Base statement allows you to change the default lowest subscript from 0 to 1. This statement can only be used in the global module, or in the declarations portion of any module or form. The statement only affects arrays in the same module or form. If it is used, it must appear before any arrays are defined in that module or form. It does not affect arrays within user-defined types (although Microsoft says this will no longer be true in future versions of Visual Basic).

Note that the To clause offers much more control, as you can specify both lower and upper bounds for an array.

OPTION COMPARE STATEMENT

See Also: StrComp.

Purpose

Use the Option Compare statement to control how string comparisons are made.

General Syntax

```
Option Compare (Binary | Text)
```

Usage

```
Option Compare Text
```

Description

Visual Basic defaults to using a binary comparison method when comparing two strings. Binary comparisons are case-sensitive, so "A" does not equal "a". The relative order of characters is determined by their order in the ANSI character set.

Text comparisons are case-insensitive, so "A" does equal "a". Furthermore, the relative order of characters is determined by the international section of WIN.INI.

Place the Option Compare statement in the declarations section of a form or module to control comparisons for code in that form or module.

OPTION EXPLICIT STATEMENT

Purpose

Use the Option Explicit statement to require explicit declaration of all variables.

General Syntax

```
Option Explicit
```

Usage

```
Option Explicit
```

Description

Placing an Option Explicit statement in the declarations section of a form or module forces explicit declaration of all variables in that form or module. Attempting to use an undeclared variable results in an error. This makes debugging your code much easier, and helps enforce the good programming style of declaring and commenting each variable.

You can have Visual Basic add Option Explicit to each form and module automatically by pulling down the Options menu, choosing the environment command, and then setting the Require Variable Declarations option to Yes.

PARTITION FUNCTION

Purpose

The Partition function returns a string indicating which partition a given number falls within in a calculated series of ranges.

General Syntax

```
Partition(number&, startRange&, endRange&, interval&)
```

Usage

```
daysPerBin = 7
startDate = CLng(DateValue("10/28/1995"))
endDate = startDate = (daysPerBin * 7)

SELECT Format$("mmm dd", Partition([leadDate], startDate, endDate, daysPerBin)) AS ⇐
DateGroupings,
        Count([leadDate]) AS NumberOfLeads FROM individualLeads
        GROUP BY Partition([leadDate], startDate, endDate, daysPerBin)
        ORDER BY Partition([leadDate], startDate, endDate, daysPerBin),
        Count([leadDate]):
```

Description

Use the Partition function to return a string calculated by indicating which partition a given number falls within in a calculated series of ranges. This would most commonly be used to generate a histogram, where a continuous or near-continuous set of values is separated into district "bins" or partitions. Each value is evaluated and assigned to the proper bin for either counting, summation, or for use in another expression.

The number& argument is the value being compared. The startRange& and endRange& arguments give the limits of the partitions, and the interval& argument determines how large each partition is.

The example syntax shows how the Partition function works in an SQL statement to count the number of leads in each given date range. The arguments are set to start at October 28, 1995 and end seven weeks later, with each partition one week in width. The output might look something like Table B-23.

DateGroupings	NumberOfLeads
Oct 28 : Nov 02	22
Nov 03 : Nov 09	49

(continued on next page)

(continued from previous page)

DateGroupings	NumberOfLeads
Nov 10 : Nov 16	165
Nov 17 : Nov 23	54
Nov 24 : Nov 30	30
	10
	3

Table B-23 Example output of the Partition function used in an SQL statement

Note how the partition function builds each string, placing the starting value for each partition to the left of the colon and the ending value for the partition on the right side of the colon. Partition will pad shorter strings with leading spaces so that all string values (before and after the colon) are the same length; sorts will work correctly with no additional processing.

The startRange& value must be equal to or greater than 0, and the endRange& argument cannot be less than startRange&. interval& must be equal to or greater than 1.

PMT FUNCTION

See Also: IPmt, NPer, PPmt, Rate.

Purpose

Use the Pmt function to return the total payment amount (principal and interest) on an annuity assuming constant periodic payments and constant interest rate.

General Syntax

```
Pmt(interestRate!, numberOfPayments%, presentValue@, futureValue@, whenDue%)
```

Usage

```
totalPayment = Pmt(intRate/12, numPayments, -mortgage, 0, 0)
```

1386

Description

Use the Pmt function to determine the total payment (both interest and principal) on an annuity. The annuity can either be a loan (negative presentValue@) or an investment (positive presentValue@).

The function assumes a steady stream of unchanging payments, and a nonvarying interest rate. The whenDue% argument determines when the payments are made: 0 indicates at the end of the payment period, and 1 if at the beginning of the payment period. Make sure that the interestRate! and numberOfPayments% arguments are in the same units.

PPMT FUNCTION

See Also: IPmt, NPer, Pmt, Rate.

Purpose

The PPmt function returns the amount of principal payment for an annuity assuming constant periodic payments and an unvarying interest rate.

General Syntax

```
PPmt(interestRate!, whichPeriod%, totalPeriods%, presentValue@, futureValue@, whenDue%)
```

Usage

```
pinicipal = PPmt(intRate/12, period, 360, mortageAmount, 0, 0)
```

Description

Use PPmt to get the amount of principal paid on a loan or investment for a particular period. The function assumes that payments are periodic and unvarying, and that the interest rate remains constant.

The example syntax uses the PPmt function to get the principal on a 30-year (30 years * 12 months = 360) home mortgage. The amount borrowed is given the mortgageAmount argument, the interest rate in the intRate, and the particular period by the period argument. This example might be in a For...Next loop to step through each period and print out a principal payment table.

Make sure that the interest rate and the number of periods are in the same units. The example syntax takes a yearly interest rate and divides it by 12 to put it in the same units (months) as the periods arguments.

PRINT # STATEMENT

See Also: Input, Input #, Write #.

Purpose

The Print # statement writes unformatted data to a sequential file that has been opened under Output or Append modes.

General Syntax

```
Print #filenumber, [[{Spc(n)|Tab(m)}]expression[{;|,}]...]
```

Usage

```
Print #1, "Hello world"
```

This example writes the string literal "Hello world" to the file opened under file number 1. A carriage return/line feed pair is then written to the file.

```
Print #1, 100, A$;
```

This example writes the number 100, and the value of A$ to the file. The comma after the number 100 causes A$ to be written at the next print zone. The semicolon after A$ causes Visual Basic to suppress the printing of the carriage return/linefeed pair.

Description

This statement prints one or more numeric or string expressions to the file indicated by the supplied file number. This is most commonly used to output ASCII text files. If the file number does not match that of a currently open file, Visual Basic issues a "Bad file name or number" error. Also, the file must have been opened under either the Output, or Append modes, or a "Bad file mode" error occurs.

More than one expression may be written at a time. The expressions may be separated by either semicolons or commas. If a semicolon is used, the next expression is written at the very next byte position in the file. If a comma is used, the expression is written at the next print zone. Print zones occur at every 14th byte position in the record.

By default, the Print # statement appends a carriage return/linefeed pair to the end of each record written. This can be suppressed by placing a semicolon after the last expression in the Print # statement.

The Spc and Tab functions can be used to insert n spaces or to write at the mth column. See the entries for these two functions, and Chapter 11, Displaying Text, for more information.

1388

You can have multiple uses of Spc, Tab, and expression. For instance,

```
Print #1, Spc(2); "Hello"; Tab(20); A$; B$; Spc(2); "Seattle", C, Tab(50); E$
```

PUT STATEMENT

See Also: Get, Lof, Open, Type.

Purpose

The Put statement writes data to a file that has been opened under Random or Binary mode.

General Syntax

```
Put [#]filenumber%,[position&], variablename
```

Usage

```
Type Rolodex
     Name as String * 20
     Number as Long
     Address as String * 100
End Type

Dim PhoneCard as Rolodex
Open "CARDS.DAT" For Random As #1 Len = Len(PhoneCard)
     :
     :
     :
Put #1, 129, PhoneCard
```

This example writes the data that is in the record variable PhoneCard to the 129th record in CARDS.DAT.

Description

The Put statement is used to write data to a disk file from a previously defined record variable. The filenumber% parameter indicates the file to which the data is to be written. This number must be from 1 to 255, and match the number used in the Open statement of a currently open file. If the file number used does not match a currently opened file, a "Bad file name or number" error is generated. The file must have been opened in either Random or Binary mode. If not, Visual Basic will issue a "Bad file mode" error.

If the position parameter is omitted, the commas must still be used. If position specifies an area that is beyond the length of the file, the file length is extended to that position. Visual Basic does no checking to see if a Put is being attempted past the current length of the file. This task is left to you. Use the Lof function to determine the length of an open file.

The recordbuffer parameter refers to a variable that contains the data that will be written to the file. It can be of any data type. Most often, it is of a type defined by you (using the Type statement) whose fields match those of the file's record structure.

Positioning in Random Access Files

The position& parameter for random access files specifies the desired record number. If this parameter is omitted, the write occurs at the position currently pointed to by the file pointer. When a Random file is opened, this pointer is set to 1. Each Get or Put sets the file pointer to the next record after the Get or Put. This file pointer may be read using the Seek function, or set by using the Seek statement. The largest valid record number may be 2,147,483,647.

The variable used for the recordbuffer must be of a length that is less than or equal to the length specified in the Open statement. Using a variable whose length is too long results in a "Bad record length" error. If the recordbuffer is a variable length string, a 2-byte string descriptor is also written; therefore these 2 bytes should be accounted for in the length. If the recordbuffer is shorter than the length specified in the Open statement, only the bytes in the variable will be written.

Positioning in Binary Files

The position& parameter for binary files refers to the byte position in the file where writing is to start. The first byte in the file is position 1, the second is 2, and so on. If this parameter is omitted, the write occurs at the position currently pointed to by the file pointer. When a Binary file is opened, this pointer is set to 1. Each Get or Put sets the file pointer to the next byte position after the Get or Put. This file pointer may be read using the Seek function, or set by using the Seek statement.

The size of the write is determined by the size of the record buffer. This allows a file to have variable record lengths.

PV FUNCTION

See Also: FV, IRR, MIRR, NPV.

Purpose

Use the PV function to derive the present value of an annuity assuming a constant stream of periodic payments and an unvarying interest rate.

General Syntax

```
PV(interestRate!, totalPeriods%, payment@, futureValue@, whenDue%)
```

Usage

```
presentValue = PV(intRate!, 360, payout@, 0, 0)
```

Description

The PV function returns the present value of an annuity. It assumes a steady stream of unvarying payments and an unvarying interest rate. The annuity may be either a loan (negative present value) or an investment (positive present value).

　　The example syntax calculates how much money you could borrow at a given interest rate given a monthly payment of payout@.

QBCOLOR FUNCTION

See Also: RGB.

Purpose

The QBColor function converts a color code used in other versions of BASIC to the long integer RGB code used by Visual Basic. The RGB color code is returned in long integer format.

General Syntax

```
QBColor(color-number%)
```

Usage

```
Red = QBColor(4)
```

This places Visual Basic's RGB color number for red into the variable Red.

Description

The QBColor function provides a method of translating the numeric representations for colors from older BASICs to the format used by Visual Basic. This number can then be used to set the foreground or background properties of an object. The supplied color-number% must be a number between 0 and 15. Table B-24 shows the valid color numbers, and the colors they represent.

QuickBASIC	Visual Basic	Color
00	00	Black
01	8388608	Blue
02	32768	Green
03	8421376	Cyan
04	128	Red
05	8388736	Magenta
06	32896	Yellow (actually looks more like brown)
07	12632256	White (looks more like light gray)
08	8421504	Gray
09	16711680	Bright Blue
10	65280	Bright Green
11	16776960	Bright Cyan
12	255	Bright Red
13	16711935	Bright Magenta
14	65535	Bright Yellow
15	16777215	Bright White

Table B-24 Color codes for QBColor

RANDOMIZE STATEMENT

See Also: Rnd, Timer.

Purpose

The Randomize statement seeds the random number generator, allowing the generation of a new sequence of random numbers.

General Syntax

```
Randomize [seed]
```

Usage

```
Function RndInt(LoNum As Integer, HiNum As Integer) As Integer
    Static Seeded As Integer
    Dim Range As Integer
    If Seeded = False Then        'Seed the random number generator if it has not
        Randomize                 'yet been done.
        Seeded = True
    End If
    Range = HiNum - LoNum + 1
    RndInt = Int(Range * Rnd + LoNum)
End Function
```

This example is a function that uses the Randomize statement and Rnd function to return an integer in the range specified by the integer parameters LoNum and HiNum. No parameter is used for the Randomize statement, so the value from the Timer function is automatically used for the seed.

Description

The Randomize statement seeds the random number generator. Random numbers can then be returned by the Rnd function. If this statement is not executed before the Rnd function, each time the program is run the numbers generated will be the same. The seed% parameter should be a number in the range of from -32767 to 32767. If it is omitted, Visual Basic will automatically use the value returned by the Timer function as the seed. This default is usually best for applications that require an unpredictable random number sequence. Seeding with a specific integer may be helpful for returning a repeatable set of "random" numbers during debugging.

RATE FUNCTION

See Also: IPmt, NPer, Pmt, PPmt.

Purpose

The Rate function returns the interest rate of an annuity given a constant periodic series of cash payments and an unvarying interest rate.

General Syntax

```
Rate(totalPeriods%, payment@, presentValue@, futureValue@, whenDue%, guess!)
```

Usage

```
intRate = Rate(360, 600, -100000, 0, 0.1) * 12
```

Description

Use the Rate function to determine the interest rate of a loan or investment given the total number of payments, the payment, and the starting and ending values of the loan. It assumes that payments will be made regularly, and both payments and interest rate remain unchanging.

The example calculates the interest rate on a 30-year $100,000 loan given a $600 payment. Note that we need to multiply the result of the Rate function by the number of months per year to derive the yearly interest rate. Loans have negative present values, and investments have positive values.

The whenDue% argument determines when the payment is made: at the end of each period (0) or at the beginning. Rate is an iterative function, and uses the guess! argument to begin its iterative process. If guess! is too far away from the actual interest rate, the function may not converge.

REDIM STATEMENT

See Also: Dim, Erase, Global, Option Base.

Purpose

The ReDim statement defines the number of dimensions and elements in an array, and allocates or reallocates storage.

General Syntax

```
ReDim [Preserve] name[(suscript-range)][As type][, name[(subscript-range)[As type]]...
```

Usage

```
ReDim MyArray(1 To 100) As Integer
ReDim YourArray(-10 To 10) As String
```

Declares the arrays MyArray and YourArray. MyArray contains 100 integer elements that can be accessed by using a subscript with a value of from 1 to 100. YourArray contains 21 string elements that can be accessed using a subscript with a value of from -10 to +10.

Description

The ReDim statement is used in procedure-level code to perform one of two tasks. First, it can be used to declare and allocate storage for a local dynamic array. The elements in this array may only be accessed within the procedure defined. The ReDim statement can also be used to declare the dimensions and number of elements for a dynamic array that has been declared in the global module, or in the declarations section of the current module or form. Dynamic arrays that are originally declared in the global modules are accessible across all forms and modules. Dynamic arrays that are originally declared in the declarations area of a form or module are accessible only to the procedures within that form or module.

Arrays provide a method for creating an entire series of variables and referencing them by the same variable name. An index number (called the subscript) is used to determine which particular element in an array is being referenced. A more detailed discussion on the concept of arrays can be found in Appendix A, Visual Basic Language Tutorial.

The dimensions of an array are defined by the entry in the subscript-range portion of the ReDim statement. The subscript range follows this format:

```
[lo-element To] hi-element[,[lo-element To] hi-element]...
```

The lo-element parameter lets you define the range of the subscripts, as well as the number of elements in the array. If lo-element is not used, the lowest valid subscript will be 0 (unless the default has been changed using Option Base), and the supplied number will be the highest valid subscript. The number of elements allowed in an array is dependent on the desired data type for that array and the available memory. Visual Basic 1.0 allowed approximately 64K of data space for each array declared, but Visual Basic 2.0 and 3.0 automatically allow for *huge arrays* without any additional coding. These large arrays can be as large as memory will allow.

ReDim initializes all elements of variable-length string arrays to null strings. All other arrays are initialized to 0s (including fixed-length strings and user - efined types). Using the Preserve keyword keeps the old values intact rather than resetting them.

At times, it is necessary to have a multidimensional array. To declare such an array, include as many sets of subscripts as needed, separated by commas.

```
ReDim MultiArray (1 To 100, 50 To 60, -100 to 100) As Double
```

The example above declares an array with three dimensions of 100, 11, and 201 elements, respectively. The first dimension can be referenced by subscripts from 1 to 100, the second may have subscripts ranging of from 50 to 60, and the third from -100 to +100. Visual Basic allows arrays to have as many as 60 dimensions. Storage space multiplies across each dimension, so be cautious when defining multidimensional arrays. MultiArray would contain 100*11*201*8 bytes, or 1,768,880 bytes!

ReDim allows the program to change the number of elements in an array at will. However, once the number of dimensions has been declared, it cannot be changed. For instance, when the following declaration is used,

```
ReDim TestArray(100, 200)
```

the array TestArray is set up with two dimensions of 101 and 201 elements, respectively. A later ReDim statement can change the number of elements defined for each of the two dimensions, but this array must now always have only two dimensions. Along the same lines, a ReDim statement cannot change the data type that has been assigned to an array.

The Erase statement can be used to deallocate a dynamic array. This causes any memory that was being used by the array to be freed. If an array is erased, it may not be referred to or a "Subscript out of range" error will occur.

REM STATEMENT

Purpose

The Rem statement allows you to insert comments in a program.

General Syntax

```
Rem comment
' comment
```

Usage

```
Rem This is a comment. The compiler will ignore it.
A% = 20                 'This is a comment on the same line as an instruction.
```

Description

Good programming practice involves the use of comments throughout a program to help explain the logic of the program. When the Rem statement is used, all the text to the right of the statement is ignored by the compiler. The single quote (') character is equivalent to using the Rem statement with a preceding colon. For instance:

```
A% = B% + C% : Rem The rem statement on this line needs a colon to separate it
D% = A% ^ 2              'But this line does not need a colon
```

The Rem statement may also be used to temporarily disable certain program instructions. This is sometimes useful in debugging a program. For instance:

```
Do
    A% = A% + 1
    Rem Debug.Print A%    'Remove the "Rem" on this line to send output to the immediate pane
Loop Until A% = 10
```

In the code above, if the Rem is removed, the value of the variable A% will be printed in the immediate pane of the Debug window. Placing the Rem statement before the instruction causes the compiler to ignore the entire line, thereby disabling it.

REPAIRDATABASE STATEMENT

See Also: CompactDatabase.

Purpose

Use the RepairDatabase statement to repair a corrupted Access database.

General Syntax

```
RepairDatabase(filename$)
```

Usage

```
fname$ = Data1.DatabaseName
Data1.Database.Close
RepairDatabase(fname$)
```

Description

The RepairDatabase statement will repair a corrupt Access database. A database may become corrupt if the physical media has a defect, or if the computer crashes during an update.

The database must be closed before the repair operation can begin. Any data that cannot be salvaged is discarded.

RESET STATEMENT

See Also: Close, End.

Purpose

The Reset statement writes all data residing in open file buffers to the appropriate disk files, and then closes all open disk files.

General Syntax

```
Reset
```

Usage

```
Reset
```

Description

This performs the same task as using the Close statement with no parameters.

RESUME STATEMENT

See Also: On Error...

Purpose

The Resume statement releases control from an error-handling routine.

General Syntax

```
Resume [{[0] | Next | {line-number | line-label} }]
```

Usage

```
Resume
```

Resumes execution at the instruction that caused the error.

```
Resume Next
```

Resumes execution at the instruction after the one that caused the error.

```
Resume TopOfLoop
```

Resumes execution at the label "TopOfLoop."

Description

The Resume statement is used at the end of an error-handling routine that was initiated by the On Error... statement. There are three variations on the Resume statement.

The first involves using the Resume statement with no parameters, or a parameter of 0. This causes execution to resume at the statement that caused the error. Of course, if the conditions that caused the error have not been corrected, control will jump back to the error-handling routine, creating a kind of endless loop.

Second, the Resume Next statement may be used. This causes execution to pick up at the instruction following the statement that caused the error.

Finally, the Resume keyword may be followed by a line number or line label. This causes execution to continue at the specified line. This is a very unstructured approach, which can lead to "spaghetti code." This variation of the Resume statement should be avoided if possible.

For more information on error handling, see the entry for the On Error... statement, and Appendix C, Debugging Techniques.

RETURN STATEMENT

See Also: GoSub, On...GoSub.

Purpose

The Return statement returns control to the next instruction following the originating GoSub or On...GoSub statement.

General Syntax

```
Return
```

Usage

```
Gosub DoIt
:
Exit Sub
:
:
DoIt:
    A$ = "Now I've done it!"
Return
```

When the Gosub is executed, the program branches to the label "DoIt:". When the Return is executed, the program will return to the instruction following the Gosub.

Description

The Return statement is covered in more detail under the entry for the GoSub statement.

RGB FUNCTION

See Also: QBColor.

Purpose

The RGB function returns a long integer representing the RGB value of a color.

General Syntax

```
RGB(red%, green%, blue%)
```

Usage

```
Form1.BackColor = RGB(100, 200, 50)
```

This sets the BackColor property of Form1.

Description

The parameters red%, green%, and blue% have a value of between 1 and 255, which represents the intensity of each color. If the number supplied for one of these parameters is below 1, an "Illegal function call" error occurs. If a number greater than 255 is used, the value 255 is assumed.

The RGB function mixes the given color values to return a number that represents the color mix. See Chapter 5, Application Appearance, for more details.

RIGHT, RIGHT$ FUNCTIONS

See Also: Left, Left$; Mid, Mid$.

Purpose

The Right and Right$ functions return a portion of a string, starting at the last character and working to the left for the length specified.

General Syntax

```
Right$(expression$, length&)
```

Usage

```
B$ = "Hello, Dolly!"
C$ = Right$(B$, 6)
```

The above example assigns the rightmost six characters from B$ to the variable C$, giving it a value of "Dolly!".

Description

The expression$ parameter can be a fixed- or variable-length string, a string constant, a literal string, the result of any function that returns a string, or any other string expression.

The length& parameter refers to the number of characters to copy. This value may be in the range of 0 to 65,535. If the length specified is greater than or equal to the full length of the source string, Right$ returns an exact copy of the source string. If the length is 0, a null string is returned. If length& has a value of less than 0, or greater than 65,535, an "Illegal function call" error is generated.

Right returns a variant; Right$ returns a string.

RMDIR STATEMENT

See Also: CurDir, CurDir$; MkDir.

Purpose

The RmDir statement removes a subdirectory from a disk.

General Syntax

```
RmDir dirname$
```

dirname$ must be in the format of [drive:][\]dir[\subdir][\subdir]...

Usage

```
RmDir "Test"
```

Removes the subdirectory "Test" underneath the default directory on the default drive.

```
RmDir "\Test"
```

Removes the subdirectory "Test" underneath the root directory of the default drive.

```
RmDir "D:\Test"
```

Removes the subdirectory "Test" underneath the root directory of drive D:.

Description

This statement works much like the DOS command of the same name. However, unlike the DOS command, the Visual Basic statement cannot be shortened to RD.

RmDir removes the subdirectory specified by the dir-name$ parameter. If the drive and/or full path name are not specified in dir-name$, the default drive and/or path are used. If the directory to be removed does not exist, a "Path not found" error will occur. The directory specified must be an empty directory, with no child subdirectories. Attempting to remove a directory that is not empty will also generate a "Path not found" error.

RND FUNCTION

See Also: Randomize.

Purpose

The Rnd function returns a single-precision random number between 0 and 1.

General Syntax

```
Rnd[(numericExpression#)]
```

Usage

```
Function RndInt(LoNum As Integer, HiNum As Integer) As Integer
        Static Seeded As Integer
        Dim Range As Integer
        If Seeded = False Then              'Seed the random number generator if it has not
                Randomize                   'yet been done.
                Seeded = True
        End If
        Range = HiNum - LoNum +1
        RndInt = Int(Range * Rnd + LoNum)
End Function
```

This example is a function that uses the Randomize statement and Rnd function to return an integer in the range specified by the integer parameters LoNum and HiNum.

Description

The Randomize statement should be used before the first time the Rnd function is called. This seeds the random number generator. If this is not done, the numbers returned by the Rnd function will be the same every time the program is run.

The numericExpression# tells the Rnd function what to return. If numericExpression# is omitted, or has a value greater than 0, the next random number is returned. If numericExpression# has a value of 0, the previous random number generated is returned. If numericExpression# has a negative value, the same number is returned for any given numericExpression# for use in debugging your application.

The preceding example shows how to convert the value returned by Rnd to a random integer within a specified range.

ROLLBACK STATEMENT

See Also: BeginTrans, CommitTrans, and Chapter 27, Data Access..

Purpose

Use the Rollback statement to discard any changes made to a database in a transaction block.

General Syntax

```
RollBack
```

Usage

```
RollBack
```

Description

Transactions are changes to the database that must be made as a whole. Incomplete changes (due to a power outage or unforseen error) can be avoided by using transactions. For example, most financial operations involve a debit from one account and a corresponding credit to another account. If the transaction failed before completing, one account may have a debit without any corresponding credit. Use RollBack to end a transaction block and discard any changes made since the beginning of the transaction block.

Use BeginTrans to begin a *transaction block,* or block of statements you would like to group together. You may nest transactions up to five deep. All changes to all databases (not just the one you're working on) are done in a manner that lets you either *commit* them as a block, writing them permanently to disk, or *roll back* and undo all changes since the BeginTrans statement. End a transaction block with CommitTrans or RollBack.

Transactions are only supported for some kinds of databases, and are used only with the Access database engine. See Chapter 27, Data Access, for more details.

RSET STATEMENT

See Also: Let, LSet.

Purpose

The RSet statement copies one string into another, byte by byte, starting at the rightmost character in the source string and working to the left.

General Syntax

```
RSet resultvariable = sourcevariable
```

Usage

```
Dim NumberBuffer As String * 12
A% = 2003.45
B$ = Format$(A%, "#,###,###.#0")
RSet NumberBuffer = B$
Label1.Caption = NumberBuffer
```

This example uses RSet to right justify the string representation of a number in a label object.

Description

This statement assigns to resultvariable the value of sourcevariable. Both variables may be fixed- or variable-length strings. The assignment performed by the RSet is done byte by byte from the right of sourcevariable to the left. The assignment cannot change the length of resultvariable. If resultvariable is shorter than sourcevariable, the characters that are beyond the length of resultvariable are not copied. If resultvariable is longer than sourcevariable, spaces are used to fill out the balance of resultvariable.

RTRIM, RTRIM$ FUNCTIONS

See Also: LTrim, LTrim$; Trim, Trim$.

Purpose

The RTrim and RTrim$ functions return a copy of a string with any following spaces removed.

General Syntax

```
RTrim$(stringExpression$)
RTrim(stringExpression$)
```

Usage

```
A$ = RTrim$("Good Bye   ")
```

This example assigns the value "Good Bye" to the variable A$.

Description

This is the complement of the LTrim$ function. It returns a copy of the supplied string expression without any following spaces.

The stringExpression$ parameter can be a fixed- or variable-length string, a string constant, a literal string, the result of any function that returns a string, or any other string expression.

RTrim returns a variant; RTrim$ returns a string.

SAVEPICTURE STATEMENT

See Also: LoadPicture.

Purpose

The SavePicture statement saves a *.BMP, *.ICO, or *.WMF picture from a form or picture box to a disk file or image object.

General Syntax

```
SavePicture object-name, picturefile$
```

Usage

```
SavePicture Form1.Picture "CHESS.BMP"
```

This example saves the bitmap from Form1's picture property to the file CHESS.BMP.

Description

The object-name parameter must be the picture or image property of the form or control whose picture is to be saved. The string picturefile$ specifies the name of the file into which the picture is to be saved. It should include the appropriate extension (.BMP for bitmaps, .ICO for icons, or .WMF for Windows metafiles). This function is explained in more detail in Chapter 8, Graphics Fundamentals.

SECOND FUNCTION

See Also: Now, TimeSerial, TimeValue.

Purpose

The Second function returns an integer (with a value from 0 to 59) that represents the second of the minute specified by the supplied date variant.

General Syntax

```
Second(dateVariant)
```

Usage

```
A% = Second(Now)
```

Places the current second of the minute in the variable A%.

Description

The second is returned as an integer in the range of from 0 to 59.

A date variant can represent any time of the day. The time portion of it is a fraction that corresponds to the specified time in proportion to a whole day. Therefore a date variant for 12:00 noon has a value of 0.5 (one-half of a day), while 6 PM has a value of 0.75 (three-quarters of a day). It is created by using the Now, TimeValue, or TimeSerial functions.

Date variants and time variants can be combined, because the date variant is stored on the left side of the decimal point, and the date variant is stored on the right.

SEEK FUNCTION AND STATEMENT

See Also: Get, Open, Put.

Purpose

As a function, Seek returns the current position of the file pointer for any open file. As a statement, Seek moves the file pointer to the specified position in any open file.

General Syntax

As a function:

```
Seek(filenumber%)
```

As a statement:

```
Seek [#]filenumber%, position&
```

Usage

```
Open "TEST.DAT" For Random As #1 Len = 32
Get #1, 25, TestRec
CurrentRec& = Seek(1)
Seek #1, 100
```

This example first uses the Seek function to save the position of the file pointer after the file is read. This assigns the value 26 (the next record after the Get statement is executed) to the variable CurrentRec&. The Seek statement is then used to move the file pointer to record number 100.

Description

The filenumber% parameter indicates the file to which Seek is referring. This number must be from 1 to 255, and match the number used in the Open statement of a currently open file. If the file number used does not match a currently opened file, a "Bad file name or number" error is generated.

The Seek Function

For files opened under Random mode, this function returns the current record number. For all other files, the number returned is the current byte position of the file pointer. The position is returned as a long integer, greater than or equal to 1.

The Seek Statement

For files opened under Random mode, this statement moves the file pointer to the record number specified by the position& parameter. For all other files, the position& parameter specifies the byte position to move the file pointer to. The position specified must be a number between 1 and 2,147,483,647.

SELECT CASE STATEMENT

See Also: If...Else, If...Else...End If, IIf, Choose Switch.

Purpose

The Select Case statement provides a convenient and readable way to base execution on which of several values or conditions an expression satisfies.

General Syntax

```
Seclect Case expression
      Case [condition[, condition][, condition]...]
         :
         [statements]
         :
      [Case condition[, condition][, condition]...]
         :
         [statements]
         :
      [Case condition[, condition][, condition]...]
         :
         [statements]
         :
      [Case Else]
         :
         [statements]
         :
End Select
```

The condition parameters may be in one of the following formats:

```
To test for equality:
```

```
[Is =] expression
```

To test a range of values:

```
Lo-expression To hi-expression
```

To test a relation:

```
Is > expression
Is < expression
Is >= expression
Is <= expression
Is <> expression
```

Usage

```
ThisMonth = Month(Now)
Select Case ThisMonth
    Case 2
        DaysThisMonth = 28
    Case 4, 6, 9, 11
        DaysThisMonth = 30
    Case Else
        DaysThisMonth = 31
End Select
```

This example assigns the number of days for the current month to the variable DaysThisMonth.

```
Select Case UCase$(Fruit$)
    Case "APPLE" To "ORANGE"
        FileIndex$ = "A_TO_O.IDX"
    Case Is > "ORANGE"
        FileIndex$ = "O_TO_Z.IDX"
End Select
```

This example sets up the value of a string based on the value of the variable Fruit$. The UCase$ function is used so we can ignore the alphabetic case of the value in Fruit$.

Description

The Select Case structure provides you with a method for testing one expression for one or more possible values. Although similar, it offers several enhancements over the If...Then...Else If...Else...End If structure.

The Select Case structure consists of four elements. First, the Select Case clause defines the expression that is being tested. This expression may be any string or numeric variable or expression, literal, constant, or result of a Visual Basic or user-defined function.

One or more Case clauses can follow the Select Case clause. The condition parameters of the clause define the test, or group of tests, against the expression in the Select Case clause. The condition parameters can test for a single value, a range of values, or a relation to a value. If the expression in the Select Case clause is numeric, all the condition parameters must be numeric. If the expression in the Select Case clause is a string, all the condition parameters must be strings. As long as those two rules are observed, the condition parameters may be a variable, constant, literal, or the result of a Visual Basic or user-defined function. Several condition parameters may appear in the same Case clause. Each Case clause is followed by a block of statements. This block is executed if any of the condition parameters evaluates to True. After a block is executed, the program will branch to the instruction following the End Select clause. This means that only the block for the first "true" expression found will be executed.

The optional Case Else clause allows you to define a block of instructions that will be executed if none of the conditions in any of the Case condition clauses is true.

The End Select clause defines the end if the structure. When a block of statements under any of the Case condition clauses is finished executing, the program will branch to the instruction following this clause.

SENDKEYS STATEMENT

See Also: DoEvents.

Purpose

The SendKeys statement simulates keyboard input to the active window of your Visual Basic application or of another Windows application. It can be used as a simple way to control other programs that do not support the more powerful and flexible features of Dynamic Data Exchange (DDE).

General Syntax

```
SendKeys keystrokes$[, wait%]
```

Usage

```
SendKeys "This input is coming from Visual Basic's SendKeys statement"
```

This example sends the specified string literal to the program in the active window.

Description

The keystrokes$ parameter represents the actual keystrokes to be sent to the application that has the active window. These keys are received just as if they had been typed by the user. The optional wait% parameter is used only when keystrokes are to be sent to an application other than your Visual Basic application. If set to True (-1), wait% ensures that the keystrokes are processed by the receiving application before the SendKeys statement returns control to your Visual Basic procedure. If False (the default), wait% specifies that SendKeys will resume execution at the next statement as soon as the keystrokes have been sent.

For more details, including an explanation of how to specify nonprinting and other special characters as keystrokes, see Chapter 16, Keyboard Input.

SET STATEMENT

See Also: Let, Chapter 3, Using Objects.

Purpose

The Set keyword assigns an object to a variable.

General Syntax

```
Set objectVariableName = [New] objectExpression
Set objectVariableName = Nothing
```

Usage

```
Set childMDIForm(idx) = New formChildtemplate
```

Description

Visual Basic allows you to create variables that refer to objects such as forms, controls, and OLE automation objects. The Set keyword performs the actual assignment.

Set normally creates a reference to the actual object. This means that any change to the object is immediately reflected in all variables that refer to that object. For example, var1 and var2 both refer to the same text box:

```
Dim var1 As TextBox, var2 As TextBox
Set var1 = Text1
Set var2 = Text1
var1.Text = "Hello"
Print var2.Text
```

The Print statement would print "Hello" because var1 and var2 refer to the same object. Note that this behavior is different than what you may expect from regular variables.

You can create an entirely new object by using the New keyword. This would make the object variable refer to the copy of the object, and changes to that object are not reflected in any other copies. This is commonly done when creating MDI child forms. See Chapter 3, Using Objects, and Chapter 4, Forms and Menus, for more information and examples.

You must explicitly declare the object variable (using Dim, Global, ReDim, or Static) to be of the correct type.

SETATTR STATEMENT

See Also: GetAttr.

Purpose

The SetAttr statement sets the attribite information for DOS files.

General Syntax

```
SetAttr fileName$, attrbuteBits%
```

Usage

```
SetAttr "MYFILE.TMP", ATTR_READONLY + ATTR_SYSTEM
```

Description

All files, directories, and volumes have an attribute byte associated with them. This information indicates whether the file name is normal, read-only, hidden, system, a volume label, a directory, or has been modified since the last backup. You can add the values to set multiple bits, as the usage example shows. Table B-25 summerizes the bit values of the SetAttr function and the CONSTANT.TXT names for the values.

Value	CONSTANT.TXT	Meaning
0	ATTR_NORMAL	Normal file
1	ATTR_READONLY	Read-only file
2	ATTR_HIDDEN	Hidden file
4	ATTR_SYSTEM	System file
8	ATTR_VOLUME	Volume label
16	ATTR_DIRECTORY	DOS directory entry
32	ATTR_ARCHIVE	File has changed since last backup

Table B-25 Meanings of the bit values of the SetAttr function

1412

SETDATAACCESSOPTION

Purpose

The SetSataAccessOption sets the path and file name of an initialization file for non-Access format databases.

General Syntax

```
SetDataAccessOption option%, value
```

Usage

```
SetDataAccessOption 1, "C:\DATA\PDOXFILE.INI"
```

Description

SetDataAccessOption in version 3.0 of Visual Basic sets just one option: the path and file name of an INI file for non-Access databases. Future versions of Visual Basic may add more options.

The option% argument should be set to 1 to set the path for the INI file. The value argument should be a string listing the file name (if it is in the current directory) or the entire path and file name. Your application must use an INI file if it uses databases in any other format than the native Access database.

SETDEFAULTWORKSPACE STATEMENT

Purpose

SetDefaultWorkspace sets the user-ID and passwords for security-enabled Access databases.

General Syntax

```
SetDefaultWorkspace userName$, password$
```

Usage

```
SetDefaultWorkspace userName$, password$
```

Description

Use the SetDefaultWorkspace statement to set the user name and password for a secure Access database. This statement must be the first data access statement used. If this statement does not execute before a data control is initialized or any other data access statement (except for SetDataAccessOption) executes, the user name is set to "Admin" and the password is set to an empty string (""). Further attempts to set the user name and password are ignored. All databases should be set to recognize the same user name and password, as they cannot be once set without first exiting the program.

SGN FUNCTION

See Also: Abs.

Purpose

The Sgn function evaluates a numericExpression and returns a value based on whether the numericExpression is negative, positive, or 0.

General Syntax

```
Sgn(numericExpression)
```

Usage

```
A% = Sgn(100)
```

This example sets the variable A% to 1, indicating the numericExpression evaluated was positive.

```
B% = Sgn(0)
```

This example sets the variable B% to 0, indicating the numericExpression evaluated was 0.

```
C% = Sgn(-100)
```

This example sets the variable C% to -1, indicating the numericExpression evaluated was negative.

Description

The Sgn function evaluates the supplied numericExpression, and returns a -1 if it is negative, 1 if it is positive, and 0 if it equals 0.

1414

SHELL FUNCTION

See Also: AppActivate.

Purpose

The Shell function runs a specified *.EXE, *.COM. *.BAT, or *.PIF program.

General Syntax

```
Shell(program-name$[, mode%])
```

Usage

```
A% = Shell("WINWORD.EXE")
```

This example loads and runs the program file WINWORD.EXE. It assumes the file is in the default directory, or in a directory specified by the path statement. Since the mode is not specified, it uses the default mode of 2 (minimized with focus).

```
B% = Shell("C:\WORD\WINWORD.EXE", 3)
```

This example explicitly declares the drive and path of the program file. The program is executed in mode 3 (maximized with focus).

Description

The Shell function loads an executable file into the Windows environment, and returns the task ID number that Windows assigns to each running program. The program-name$ parameter must be a string expression that contains a valid executable file name. If the desired program file is not in the default directory on the default drive, or in a directory in the DOS PATH, the drive and path must be specified, or a "File not found" error will occur. Specifying a file that does not have an extension of EXE, COM, BAT, or PIF will cause an "Illegal function call" error.

The mode% parameter determines how the program will be loaded into the Windows environment. It specifies the window style, and whether the program is to receive the focus immediately. Table B-26 details the settings for mode%.

Mode Value	Window Style	Focus
1	Normal	New program receives focus
2	Minimized	New program receives focus

(continued on next page)

(continued from previous page)

Mode Value	Window Style	Focus
3	Maximized	New program receives focus
4	Normal	Current program retains focus
7	Minimized	Current program retains focus

Table B-26 Shell function values for the mode% parameter

This parameter is optional. If omitted, the new program will be loaded as if mode 2 were specified. The full effect of the mode% parameter can only be taken advantage of by Windows programs. For DOS programs, the mode values 1, 2, and 4 work the same as mode 3.

You could run the DOS command processor by specifying the program "COMMAND.COM."

SIN FUNCTION

See Also: Atn, Cos, Tan.

Purpose

The Sin function returns the sine of an angle.

General Syntax

```
Sin(angle)
```

Usage

```
A! = Sin(4.93)
```

The sine of 4.93 is assigned to the variable A!.

Description

Sin is used to determine the sine of an angle. The function expects the angle to be expressed in radians; therefore, if the angle is in degrees, it must be converted using the formula radians = degrees * pi/180.

If the angle is supplied as an integer or a single-precision value, Sin will return a single-precision value; otherwise it returns a double-precision value.

1416

SLN FUNCTION

See Also: DDB, SYD.

Purpose

Use the SLN function to return the straight-line depreciation of an asset.

General Syntax

```
SLN(initialCost@, salvageValue@, lifeSpan%)
```

Usage

```
yearlyDepreciation=SLN(50000, 2500, 10)
```

Description

The SLN function returns the depreciation value for an asset. You provide the initial cost of the item, the eventual salvage value (what it is worth after its useful life span) and the total life span. SLN will return a single value representing the average depreciation.

SPACE, SPACE$ FUNCTIONS

See Also: Spc; String, String$.

Purpose

The Space and Space$ functions return a string containing the specified number of spaces.

General Syntax

```
Space$(number-of-spaces&)
Space(number-of-spaces&)
```

Usage

```
A$ = Space$(5)
```

Gives the variable A$ the value of " " (five spaces).

Description

This function returns a string of the specified number of spaces (ASCII character 32). The number-of-spaces& parameter can be of any numeric type, but it must be a value from 0 to 65535. If it is not in this range, an "Illegal function call" will occur.

Space returns a variant; Space$ returns a string.

SPC FUNCTION

See Also: Space, Space$; Tab.

Purpose

The Spc function generates spaces for output with the Print method and Print # statement. Unlike Space$, this function respects any settings placed on a file with the Width # statement.

General Syntax

```
Spc(number-of-spaces%)
```

Usage

```
Print #1, "This bracket -> [" Spc(10) "] <- and this bracket are 10 spaces apart"
```

This example writes the text from the string literals with 10 spaces inserted between the brackets.

Description

This function is used for formatting a print line. The number-of-spaces% parameter must be a numericExpression in the range of 0 to 32767.

The fundamental difference between this function and the Space$ function is how it behaves when used on a file whose print line width has been defined with the Width # statement. While the Space$ function ignores the defined width, the Spc function does not. This makes the behavior of the Spc function dependent on three factors: the number of spaces requested, the current print position, and the defined width of the print line. This function can react to these factors in one of three ways. First, if the print position plus the number of spaces requested is less than the width of the print line, the number of spaces requested is generated. Second, if the number-of-spaces% parameter is greater than the width defined for the print line, then the spaces generated are equal to the number of spaces requested modulo (MOD) the width of the print line. Finally, if the print position plus the number of spaces requested is greater than the defined width of the print line, spaces will be printed as far as the defined width on the current line, and the balance of the requested spaces will be printed on the next line. Table B-27 gives examples of the Spc function's behavior when a print line is defined by the Width # statement as being 80 characters long.

Print Position	Spaces Requested	Generated Output
01	50	50 spaces
40	50	40 spaces, carriage return/linefeed pair, 0 spaces
01	100	20 spaces (100 MOD 80)
75	100	5 spaces, carriage return/linefeed pair, 15 spaces (100 MOD 80 returns 20 spaces. As many as possible are printed on the current line, and the balance are printed on the next)

Table B-27 Spaces generated by the Spc function

SQR FUNCTION

Purpose

The Sqr function returns the square root of a number.

General Syntax

```
Sqr(numericExpression)
```

Usage

```
A! = Sqr(72)
```

This example places the square root of 72 into the variable A!, giving it a value of 8.485281.

Description

This function requires that numericExpression be a non-negative number of any numeric data type. If numericExpression is a double-precision value, this function will return a double-precision value. Using any other data type causes Sqr to return a single-precision value.

STATIC STATEMENT

See Also: Dim, Global, Option Base, ReDim, Type.

Purpose

The Static statement allocates storage for permanent Visual Basic variables or arrays in a procedure. Variables declared with the Static statement do not lose their value between procedure calls.

General Syntax

For declaring the data type of a simple variable:

```
Static name [As type][, name [As type]]...
```

For declaring an array:

```
Static name[(suscript-range)][As type][, name[(subscript-range)][As type]...
```

Usage

```
Static A as Integer      'Declares the variable A as an integer
Static B(100) As Single  'Declares single-precision array B, with 101 elements from 0 to 100
Static C$(-30 to 60)     'Declares string array C$, with 91 elements numbered -30 to +60
```

Description

The Static statement is used to declare storage and data types for simple and array variables within a Visual Basic sub or function. It allocates a local simple variable, or a local array, which cannot be seen by any other procedure. If you wish to declare a variable or array that is accessible globally (across modules and forms), use the Global statement in the declarations section of the global module instead. Variables that are declared with the Static statement do not get deallocated when the procedure that defined them is exited. Therefore their value is retained between procedure calls.

The Static statement can be used along with the As type clause to explicitly declare the data type of a simple variable. For instance,

```
Static MyVar As Integer
```

creates a storage for an Integer variable named MyVar. This is an alternative method to using the Visual Basic type declaration characters (!, @, #, $, %, &). This also allows you to assign your own data types (created with the Type statement) to a variable, as in the following code:
This code would appear in the global module:

```
Type Rolodex
    Name as String * 20
    Number as Long
    Address as String * 100
End Type
```

This code would appear in the desired procedure:

```
Static Cards as Rolodex
```

Static can also be used to allocate storage for, and define the parameters of, a local array. Arrays provide a method for creating an entire series of variables and referencing them by the same variable name. An index number (called the subscript) is used to determine which particular element in an array is being referenced. A more detailed discussion on the concept of arrays can be found in Appendix A, Language Tutorial.

The dimensions of an array are defined by the entry in the subscript-range portion of the Static statement. The subscript range follows this format:

```
[lo-element To] hi-element[,[lo-element To] hi-element]...
```

The lo-element parameter lets you define the range of the subscripts, as well as the number of elements in the array. If lo-element is not used, the lowest valid subscript will be 0 (unless the default has been changed using Option Base), and the supplied number will be the highest valid subscript. The number of elements allowed in an array is dependent on the desired data type for that array and the available memory. Visual Basic 1.0 allowed approximately 64K of data space for each array declared, but Visual Basic 2.0 and 3.0 automatically allow for *huge arrays* without any additional coding. These large arrays can be as large as memory will allow.

Sometimes, it is necessary to have a multidimensional array. To declare such an array, include as many sets of subscripts as needed, separated by commas.

```
Static MultiArray (1 To 100, 50 To 60, -100 to 100) As Double
```

The example above declares an array with three dimensions of 100, 11, and 201 elements, respectively. The first dimension can be referenced by subscripts from 1 to 100, the second may have subscripts ranging from 50 to 60, and the third from -100 to +100. Visual Basic allows arrays to have as many as 60 dimensions. Storage space multiplies across each dimension, so be cautious when defining multidimensional arrays. MultiArray would contain 100*11*201*8 bytes, or 1,768,880 bytes!

Visual Basic's Sub and Function statements allow for an optional Static keyword. This causes all variables inside that procedure to be declared as static variables, regardless of whether the variable is declared implicitly, with ReDim or with the Static statement.

STOP STATEMENT

See Also: End.

Purpose

The Stop statement stops program execution without closing files or clearing variables. If encountered while in the Visual Basic environment, the Code window is opened and gets the focus. If encountered in a compiled Visual Basic program, the application is unloaded from memory.

General Syntax

```
Stop
```

Usage

```
Debug.Print A%
Stop
```

The example prints the value of the integer variable A% in the Immediate window, and then stops execution.

Description

The Stop statement is used for purposes of debugging a program. It is sometimes advantageous to be able to view the value of a variable, or step through code one statement at a time, while a program is running. This statement allows you to do just that. When the Stop statement is encountered, all program execution is halted. You can then make use of the debugging features of Visual Basic, such as the Immediate window, or several of the options on the Run menu.

STR, STR$ FUNCTIONS

See Also: Val.

Purpose

The Str and Str$ functions convert a numeric expression to a string.

General Syntax

```
Str$(numericExpression)
```

Usage

```
A$ = Str$(100)
B$ = Str$(-100)
```

The value of A$ becomes " 100." A leading space precedes the number where the positive sign is implied. The value of B$ will be "-100." It has no leading space because the negative sign is explicit.

Description

This function returns a string that is an unformatted representation of numericExpression. If formatting is desired, use the Format$ function instead. When a number is converted to a string, the first space of the string is reserved for the sign of the numeric expression. If the numeric expression is positive, the sign is implied, and the string representation of the number is preceded by a space. If it is negative, the string representation of the number is preceded by a minus (-) sign.

Str returns a variant; Str$ returns a string.

STRCOMP FUNCTION

Purpose

StrComp compare two strings.

General Syntax

```
StrComp(string1$, string2$ [, compareType%])
```

Usage

```
hilo=StrComp(in$, old$)
```

Description

StrComp compares two strings, and returns one of four values (see Table B-28):

Condition	Value
string1$<string2$	-1
string1$=string2$	0
string1$>string2$	1
Either string is Null	Null

Table B-28 Returned values of the StrComp function

You can use the compareType% argument to set how comparisons are made. 0 make string comparison case-sensitive (for example, "A" does not equal "a") and 1 makes it case-insensitive ("A" equals "a").

STRING, STRING$ FUNCTIONS

See Also: Space, Space$.

Purpose

The String and String$ functions return a string containing the specified number of the requested character.

General Syntax

```
String$(number-of-characters&, ascii-code%)
String$(number-of-characters&, character$)
String(number-of-characters&, ascii-code%)
String(number-of-characters&, character$)
```

Usage

```
A$ = String$(10, "*")
B$ = String$(10, 42)
```

Because 42 is the ASCII code for the asterisk character, both of these statements return the same value: *"**********"*.

Description

This function returns a string of the requested character, for the length specified by number-of-characters&. The number-of-characters& parameter must be in the range of 0 to 65535, or an "Illegal function call" will occur. You may specify which character to have returned either by supplying the ASCII code of the desired character or by supplying a string whose first character is the desired character.

String returns a variant; String$ returns a string.

SUB...END SUB STATEMENTS

See Also: Call, End, Exit, Function.

Purpose

The Sub and End Sub statements declare and define a Visual Basic Sub procedure, and its parameters, if any.

General Syntax

```
[Static] [Private] Sub sub-name[(arguments)]
    [Static var[,var]...]
    [Dim var[,var]...]
    [ReDim var[,var]...]
    [statements]
    [Exit Static]
    [statements]
End Sub
```

Usage

```
Sub SwapInt(Num1 As Integer, Num2 As Integer)
    Dim Temp As Integer
    Temp = Num1
    Num1 = Num2
    Num2 = Temp
End Sub
```

This example defines a procedure that swaps the values of two integer variables.

Description

The most common use of a Visual Basic sub procedure is to define the actions of a task that will be performed more than once. This reduces the amount of code necessary in a program, because the same task does not have to be recoded. Visual Basic sub procedures can also be used to break a large task down into several smaller tasks. This makes debugging a program easier, because each particular task is isolated. All of the events caused by Visual Basic controls are sub procedures. A sub procedure is executed when Visual Basic encounters a Call statement. The use of the Call keyword is optional. For instance, these two lines will execute identically:

```
Call SwapInt(A%, B%)
SwapInt A%, B%
```

(Notice that when Call is omitted the parentheses around the procedure arguments must also be omitted.) The allocation of local variables (variables that are accessible only to this procedure) is performed by using the Dim, ReDim, or Static statements. Variables that are originally allocated within the procedure using Dim or ReDim statements are de-allocated when the procedure is exited. Therefore, they do not retain their value between calls to the procedure. To guarantee that a variable keeps its value between calls, it should be declared with the Static statement. If it is desired to have all local variables retain their value between calls, the procedure definition should begin with the optional Static keyword.

Arguments may be passed to the procedure in order to modify its behavior, or to give it information to act on. The format for declaring arguments is as follows:

```
([ByVal]variablename[As type][,[ByVal]variablename[As type]...])
```

The variablename indicates the name that the argument will be referred to within the procedure. It may end in a type declaration character, or the As type parameter may be used to declare the data type of the incoming argument. The type may be Integer, Long, Single, Double, Currency, or String. By default, the arguments are passed by reference. This means the address of the variable is passed instead of the actual value. This allows the procedure to make changes to the passed arguments. In order to prevent this from happening, the ByVal keyword may be used to force the arguments to be passed by value instead.

If the expected argument being passed to the procedure is an entire array, the argument is declared as an array by including an empty set of parentheses at the end of the variable name.

1426

The procedure is normally exited when execution reaches the End Sub keywords. However, an alternative exit may be forced by using the Exit Sub statement. This causes the procedure to be immediately terminated, and execution returns to the instruction following the call to the procedure.

Visual Basic procedures can be called recursively. This means that a procedure can call itself. A recursive Sub should not specify the Static keyword in the procedure definition.

The Private keyword makes the subroutine accessible only from within the same form or module in which the procedure is declared. This lets you code general purpose routines (such as sorts or financial analysis routines) without concern that a procedure name will interfere with one in the main program.

SWITCH FUNCTION

See Also: Choose, IIf, Select Case.

Purpose

The Switch function evaluates up to seven expressions and returns a value you specify for each expression.

General Syntax

```
Switch(expression1, value [, expression2, value2 [, . . . expression7, value7] ] )
```

Usage

```
result$ = Switch(horse1 < horse2, "Win", horse3 > default, "Lose", horse7=horse5, "Draw")
```

Description

Switch is similar to the Choose function, but lets you evaluate more complex expressions. You can evaluate up to seven different expressions. Each expression has an associated value that it returns. The function works left to right and returns the value associated with the first expression that evaluates to True. If no expression evaluates to True, the function returns to Null. All expressions are evaluated, so be sure that each expression is legal.

SYD FUNCTION

See Also: DDB, SLN.

Purpose

The SYD function returns the sum-of-years' digits depreciation of an asset.

General Syntax

```
SYD(initialCost@, salvageValue@, lifeSpan%, period%)
```

Usage

```
For i=1 to 10
      Print SYD(10000, 800, 10, i)
Next i
```

Description

This function returns the depreciation value for a given period using the sum-of-years' digits algorithm. This gives a weighted depreciation schedule, with a greater amount of depreciation in the beginning than that of the SLN depreciation.

You provide the initial cost of the item, the salvage value (what it could be sold for at the end of its life span), the total amount of time it will be in service, and the particular period you need. Note that different periods will yeild different depreciation results.

TAB FUNCTION

See Also: Print #, Spc.

Purpose

The Tab function sets the print position for the Print method or Print # statement.

General Syntax

```
Tab(column%)
```

Usage

```
Print #1, Tab(10) "Hello"
```

This prints the string "Hello" in the tenth column of the current line.

Description

The Tab function is used along with the Print method or Print # statement to set the print position to a specific column in a line.

If the value specified by column% is less than the current print position, column% becomes the new print position. If the current print position is greater than column%, the print position advances to the next line, and then gets set to column%.

If used on a sequential file, the setting of the file's width (via the Width # statement) can affect the behavior of the Tab function. If the value of column% is greater than the width defined for the file, the print position will be calculated as column% modulo (MOD) width.

The print positions on a form are based on the average width of each character in the form's font.

TAN FUNCTION

See Also: Atn, Cos, Sin.

Purpose

The Tan function returns the tangent of an angle.

General Syntax

```
Tan(angle)
```

angle is expressed in radians.

Usage

```
A! = Tan(4.93)
```

The tangent of 4.93 is assigned to the variable A!.

Description

Tan is used to determine the tangent of an angle. The function expects the angle to be expressed in radians; therefore, if the angle is in degrees it must be converted using the formula radians = degrees * pi/180.

If the angle is supplied as an integer or a single-precision value, Tan will return a single-precision value; otherwise it returns a double-precision value.

TIME$ FUNCTION AND STATEMENT

See Also: Date, Date$; Now; TimeValue.

Purpose

The Time$ function returns the current system time. The Time$ statement is used to set the system time.

General Syntax

Function:

```
Time$
```

Statement:

```
Time$ = time-string$
```

Usage

```
T$ = Time$
```

Assigns a string containing the current system date to the variable Today$.

```
Time$ = "12:30:56"
```

Sets the current system time.

Description

Time$ can be used as a function, to return the current system time, or as a statement, to set the current system time. When used as a function, Time$ returns a string with the current system time in the format hh:mm:ss. As a statement, the system time may be set by using a string in the same format (specifying the seconds is optional).

When using Time$ as a statement, if the format of the time string is not in the correct format, Visual Basic issues an "Illegal function call" error.

If the time is set using the Time$ statement, its permanence depends on the type of system and version of DOS being used. Generally, if the system has a CMOS memory and is running under DOS 3.3 or greater, the date will be retained in the CMOS. Otherwise, the date may be lost when the system is powered down.

Comments

In the above descriptions, hh refers to the hour, and must be in military format (that is, 01 to 23), mm refers to the minute (00 to 59), and ss to the second (00 to 59).

TIMER FUNCTION

See Also: Randomize.

Purpose

The Timer function returns the number of seconds since midnight.

General Syntax

```
Timer
```

Usage

```
StartTime! = Timer
Call TestProc
EndTime! = Timer
TimeElapsed! = EndTime! - StartTime!
```

This example uses the Timer function to time how long it takes the procedure TestProc to execute.

Description

This function is useful for timing how long it takes certain tasks to be performed. It returns a double-precision number that represents the number of seconds that have elapsed since midnight.

TIMESERIAL FUNCTION

See Also: Now, TimeValue.

Purpose

The TimeSerial function returns a date variant based on the integer hour, minutes, and seconds arguments.

General Syntax

```
TimeSerial(hour%, minutes%, seconds%)
```

Usage

```
A = TimeSerial(10, 04, 05)
```

Places a date variant for 10:04:05 in the variable A.

Description

A date variant can represent any time of the day. The fractional part corresponds to the specified time in proportion to a whole day. Therefore a date variant for 12:00 noon has a value of 0.5 (one-half of a day), while 6 PM has a value of 0.75 (three-quarters of a day). The Now and TimeValue functions can also create a date variant.

The most useful aspect of this function is its ability to return a date variant based on the desired time's relation to another time. For instance, the following two statements return the same value:

```
TimeSerial(12, 00 - 15, 00)
TimeSerial(11, 45, 00)
```

The times specified by the arguments must combine to indicate a time between 00:00:00 and 23:59:59, or an "Illegal function call" will occur.

Date variants and time variants can be combined, because the date variant is stored on the left side of the decimal point, and the date variant is stored on the right.

TIMEVALUE FUNCTION

See Also: Now, TimeSerial.

Purpose

The TimeValue function returns a date variant based on the supplied string.

General Syntax

```
TimeValue(time-string$)
```

Usage

```
A = TimeValue(Time$)
```

Places a date variant for the current system time in the variable A.

Description

This function returns a date variant based on the supplied string. TimeValue can translate any time string that is in the same format as the string returned by the Time$ function. It can also translate a time string that includes the "AM" or "PM," such as "1:00AM." If the supplied string includes a recognizable date, the date text is ignored.

TRIM, TRIM$ FUNCTIONS

See Also: LTrim, LTrim$; RTrim. RTrim$.

Purpose

The Trim and Trim$ functions remove leading and trailing spaces from a string.

General Syntax

```
Trim$(stringExpression$)
Trim(stringExpression)
```

Usage

```
clean$=Trim$(InputBox("Enter your name"))
```

Description

Trim and Trim$ serves as a combination of LTrim and RTrim, removing all spaces from beginning and ending of strings.
Trim returns a Variant, Trim$ returns a string.

TYPE...END TYPE STATEMENTS

See Also: Dim, Global, ReDim, Static.

Purpose

The Type and End Type statements declare a programmer-defined variable or record structure.

General Syntax

```
Type type-name
    element As type
    [element As type]
        :
        :
End Type
```

Usage

```
Type PhoneCards
    Name As String * 20
    Number As Long
    Address As String * 100
End Type

Dim Cards As PhoneCards
```

Description

The Type...End Type structure is used in the global module to declare pro-grammer-defined variables, and record variables. Such "custom" variables are generally used to keep several related simple variables together, so they can be addressed by one variable name.

The type-name parameter gives a name to this data type. This name will be used to declare the type of a variable in a later Dim, Global, ReDim, or Static statement.

Each element in the programmer-defined type is then defined. An element is defined by placing the element name followed by an As type clause. The type may be Integer, Long, Single, Double, Currency, String (for a variable-length string), String * length (for a fixed-length string), Variant, or any other user-defined type. An element can only be declared as a user-defined type if the referenced user-defined type has already been declared. An element can be declared as an array using the standard declaration syntax for arrays. (Note that Visual Basic 1.0 did not allow arrays within user-defined types.)

The End Type keyword ends the type definition. Within a program, element names are referred to by placing a period between the name of the variable and the element name. For instance, in order to assign a value to the "Name" element of the "Card" variable in the example above, the following syntax would be used:

```
Cards.Name = "Marika E. Scott"
```

UBOUND FUNCTION

See Also: LBound.

Purpose

The UBound function returns the value of the largest usable subscript for the specified dimension of an array.

General Syntax

```
UBound(arrayname[, dimension%])
```

Usage

```
Dim Flowers%(1 To 100, -50 To 50)
A% = UBound(Flowers%, 2)
```

The value 50 is assigned to the variable A%, because that is the largest subscript available in the second dimension of the array Flowers%.

Description

If the dimension parameter is not specified, the upper bound for the first dimension is returned. UBound is useful in conjunction with LBound for figuring out how many elements a dynamic array has. The number of elements can be found by subtracting the value returned by LBound from the value returned from UBound, and adding one.

UCASE, UCASE$ FUNCTION

See Also: LCase, LCase$.

Purpose

The UCase and UCase$ functions return a copy of a string in which all lowercase alphabetic characters have been converted to uppercase.

General Syntax

```
UCase$(expression$)
UCase(expression$)
```

Usage

```
C1$ = Command$
C2$ = UCase$(C1$)
```

This example retrieves the command-line parameters that were used to start the program, and converts the entries to uppercase.

Description

The expression$ parameter can be a fixed- or variable-length string, a string constant, a literal string, the result of any function that returns a string, or any other string expression. The LCase$ function works the same as UCase$, but it converts uppercase to lowercase.

This function is very useful for making a non-case-sensitive comparison of two strings. This is helpful when an internal variable is being compared to a user's string input. By using UCase$ (or LCase$), the program can ignore the case of the string that has been input by the user.

UCase returns a variant; UCase$ returns a string.

UNLOAD STATEMENT

See Also: Load.

Purpose

The Unload statement unloads a form from memory, or a control from a control array.

General Syntax

```
UnLoad form-name
UnLoad control-name(index)
```

Usage

```
UnLoad Form1
```

Unloads a form from memory.

```
UnLoad Text1(1)
```

Unloads a text box from a control array.

1436

Description

The form-name or control-name represents the name of the form or control to be unloaded from memory. If a control is part of a control array, the appropriate index value must be supplied in parentheses, following the name of the array. This statement is explained in more detail in Chapter 3, Using Objects.

VAL FUNCTION

See Also: Str, Str$.

Purpose

The Val function returns the numeric value of the supplied string expression.

General Syntax

```
Val(stringExpression$)
```

Usage

```
A! = Val("123")
B! = Val("1 2 3")
C! = Val(" 123doggy")
D! = Val("G")
```

The first three lines assign a value of 123 to their respective variables. The fourth example returns 0.

Description

The Val function is the complement to the Str$ function. It translates the supplied string expression into a double-precision number. Translation begins at the left of the string and works toward the right. Spaces are ignored. Translation ends at the first non-numeric character or at the end of the string, whichever comes first. The first period encountered in a string is translated as a decimal point, but a second period causes the translation to end. Dollar signs and commas are not recognized as numeric characters.

This function is useful for translating the string representation of hexadecimal or octal values into numeric values. For instance, the following code assigns the value of 255 to the variable A%:

```
B$ = Hex$(255)            'Gives B$ the value "FF"
A% = Val("&H" + B$)       'Same as Val("&HFF") which equals 255
```

VARTYPE FUNCTION

Purpose

The VarType function returns a value indicating how data is stored in a variant.

General Syntax

```
VarType(variant)
```

Usage

```
If VarType(inputString)=V_DATE Then Print inputString
```

Description

Varients can hold a variety of different data types. Use the VarType function to examine a variant and determine how it is storing data. Table B-29 lists the returned values and the CONSTANT.TXT constants for VarType:

Value	CONSTANT.TXT	Meaning
0	V_EMPTY	Empty (never used)
1	V_NULL	Null
2	V_INTEGER	Integer
3	V_LONG	Long
4	V_SINGLE	Single
5	V_DOUBLE	Double
6	V_CURRENCY	Currency
7	V_DATE	Date
8	V_STRING	String

Table B-29 Return values of the VarType function

WEEKDAY FUNCTION

See Also: DateSerial, DateValue, Day, Now.

Purpose

The WeekDay function returns an integer representing the day of the week based on the supplied date variant.

General Syntax

```
WeekDay(dateVariant)
```

Usage

```
DayOfWeek% = WeekDay(Now)
```

Returns today's day of week.

Description

This function evaluates the supplied date variant and returns an integer value representing the day of the week. Sunday returns a value of 1, while Saturday returns a value of 7. The supplied date variant represents the number of days since December 30, 1899. Therefore, January 01, 1900 has a date variant of 2, while January 1, 1753 has a date variant of -53,688. The supplied date variant must represent a date in the range of from January 1, 100 to December 31, 9999, inclusive. If the date requested is not in this range, Visual Basic issues an "Illegal function call" error.

WHILE...WEND STATEMENTS

See Also: Do...Loop.

Purpose

The While and Wend statements repeat a block of instructions while a condition exists.

General Syntax

```
While condition
    :
    [statements]
    :
Wend
```

Usage

```
HiElement = UBound(SortArray$)
Sorting = True
While Sorting = True
    Sorting = False
    For I = 2 To HiElement
        J = I - 1
        If SortArray$(J) > SortArray$(I) Then
            Sorting = True
            Temp$ = SortArray$(I)
            SortArray$(I) = SortArray$(J)
            SortArray$(J) = Temp$
        End IF
    Next
Wend
```

This example uses the While...Wend structure to bubble sort an array.

Description

The specified condition is tested. If it is true, the statements in the body of the loop are executed, and the condition is checked again. Since the condition is checked first, the body is never executed if the condition starts out being false. The While...Wend structure works in the same way as the Do Until...Loop structure. It has been retained for compatibility to earlier BASIC languages.

There must be one Wend for every While, and vice-versa. If there is not a one-for-one ratio of While's and Wend's, a "While without Wend" or "Wend without While" error will occur.

WIDTH # STATEMENT

See Also: Print #, Spc, Tab.

Purpose

The Width # statement defines the width of a sequential file's output line.

General Syntax

```
Width #filenumber, width%
```

Usage

```
Width #1, 80
```

Sets the output line width for file number 1 to 80 columns.

Description

When printing to an ASCII text file, it is sometimes necessary to define a maximum output length for each line. This statement defines the width of an output line. The filenumber parameter must be the number of a currently open file that was opened in either Output or Append modes.

The width parameter can be a value of from 0 to 255 columns. Specifying a column width of 0 sets an infinite output width. The default width for a file when it is open is 0.

WRITE # STATEMENT

See Also: Print #.

Purpose

The Write # statement formats and writes data to a sequential file that has been opened in Output or Append modes.

General Syntax

```
Write #filenumber[, var1][, var2][, var3]..
```

Usage

```
Write #1, A$, B%, C!, D#
```

Writes the specified variables to the file opened under number 1. Double quotes placed around the value in A$, and a comma is written to the file to delimit each variable written. A newline character is written after the value in D# is written.

Description

This statement writes a comma-delimited list of the supplied variables to the indicated file. Double quotes are placed around any strings, and a newline character is written to the file after each write is finished. If no variables are indicated, only the newline character is written to the file.

YEAR FUNCTION

See Also: DateSerial, DateValue, Now, Weekday.

Purpose

The Year function returns an integer representing a year from 100 to 9999, based on the supplied date variant.

General Syntax

```
Year(dateVariant)
```

Usage

```
ThisYear% = Day(Now)
```

Returns the current year.

Description

This function uses a double-precision date variant representing a date to return an integer value representing a year from 100 to 9999. The supplied date variant represents the number of days since December 30, 1899. Therefore January 01, 1900, has a date variant of 2, while January 1, 1753, has a date variant of -53,688. The supplied date variant must represent a date in the range of January 1, 100 to December 31, 9999, inclusive. If the date requested is not in this range, Visual Basic issues an "Illegal function call" error.

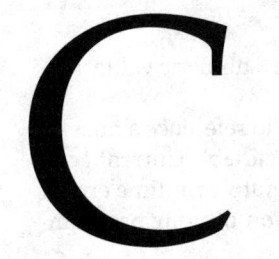

APPENDIX C

DEBUGGING TECHNIQUES

In this appendix you will learn how to deal with bugs, or programming errors. Visual Basic provides several useful facilities for finding and fixing bugs, and versions 2.0 and 3.0 have added several more powerful tools to help the debugging process.

PROGRAMMING ERRORS

There are basically three kinds of programming errors: compilation errors, runtime errors, and logic errors. Of the three, compilation errors are by far the easiest to fix. A compilation error is usually the result of incorrect syntax, such as an incorrect or missing keyword, a missing parenthesis, or a function call that is missing an argument. Visual Basic prevents most syntax errors from becoming compilation errors. It does this by checking the code as you type it, and beeping and displaying an error message as soon as a syntax error is detected. It is, after all, much easier to fix an error at the time you make it than to have to go back and find the errors later. (If you do want to be able to enter all your code before dealing with errors, you can go to the Environment menu and turn syntax checking off.)

Some compilation errors might not be the result of syntax errors. For example, your program may allocate an object that is larger than the limits defined by Visual Basic. Again, you will receive an explanatory error message.

RUNTIME ERRORS

Runtime errors are usually fairly easy to fix. One common kind of runtime error is the type mismatch, when the kind of data you supply as a sub procedure or func-

1443

tion argument is different from the kind that the procedure or function expects. For example, the statement

```
N$ = Str$(A$)
```

will cause a runtime error because the Str$ function expects a numeric value, not a string.

Another common runtime error is caused by an attempt to reference a nonexistent array element. If MyArray has 100 elements, and the variable Current gets set to 101, then a reference to MyArray(Current) will generate a runtime error. This kind of error sometimes requires a closer examination of your program logic, such as the boundaries defined in a loop.

LOGIC ERRORS

A sometimes sad reality of computers is that they always do what you tell them, even if it's not what you wanted. This is the basis for logic errors. A logic error is caused when a portion of an application, although free of syntax and compilation errors, is not performing in a desired manner. Logic errors are the hardest kind of error to fix, because Visual Basic cannot detect them, and thus cannot give you a helpful error message. You must examine the symptoms, make a diagnosis, fix the problem, and then test your code to make sure you really *have* fixed the problem. The process of locating and repairing logic errors is called *debugging*.

The design of a program determines the amount of debugging it will need. When designing an application, remember the five Ps: Proper planning prevents poor performance. An application that is well planned from the outset will be much less likely to encounter unexpected results than one that is designed "on the fly." The more complicated an application, the more chance of a logic error, and the more planning you will need to do.

Even the best-planned project is destined to have some logic errors. Visual Basic provides several tools for ferreting out these errors. Visual Basic versions 2.0 and 3.0 have added a number of powerful features to the debugging suite, like the ability to *watch* variables, set *watchpoints*, and *trace* the execution of a program. You can also set *breakpoints*, which allow you to halt execution at a specified point in the program. This allows you to use the Immediate Pane, or to "step through" the program's code, one line at a time. Visual Basic also features the Debug object, which allows a program to print directly to the Immediate pane.

Table C-1 details the tools available to you for debugging your Visual Basic programs.

1444

Use This...		To Do This...
Break	Command	Halt program execution
Calls	Command	Display a list of all active procedure calls
Clear All	Command	Cancel any breakpoints that have been set in the program
Debug	Object	Send debug information directly to the Immediate pane
Immediate Pane	Object	Execute Visual Basic functions, statements, and methods in real time
Instant Watch	Command	Check the value of an expression
Procedure Step	Command	Step through code, treating sub and function calls as a single step
Set Next Statement	Command	Set the next executing statement to a different line of code
Show Next	Command	Display the next executing statement in the code window
Single Step	Command	Step through code, branching into sub and function calls
Stop	Statement	Halt execution from within the program's code
Toggle Breakpoint	Command	Set a breakpoint in a program on or off
Watch	Command	Set or edit a watch expression

Table C-1 Tools used to debug a Visual Basic program

PROGRAM MODES

At any given time, Visual Basic is in one of three modes: design mode, run mode, or break mode. As the name suggests, design mode is used for creating screen objects and writing code. When you type in code in design mode, Visual Basic traps syntax errors and gives you appropriate feedback. The debugging tools and features discussed in this appendix are not available in design mode, except for setting breakpoints. A breakpoint is a place in the code where execution will automatically stop. You can set a breakpoint by selecting Toggle Breakpoint from the Run menu, or by pressing (F9).

Once you run a program (such as by selecting Start or Restart from the Run menu), Visual Basic is said to be in *run mode*. During run mode, if a runtime error occurs, the program will stop and an appropriate error message will be given. You can also suspend program execution by selecting Break from the Run menu (or pressing the (CTRL) - (BREAK) key combination). Note that the Run menu will not be available if the program is waiting for input (such as in a dialog box).

When you have executed a break, the program is said to be in break mode. All of the debugging tools described in this chapter are available in break mode. In addition, you can use the Immediate pane to examine data or make changes to code in the code window. You can step through code (executing one statement at a time), continue execution of the program at the next statement, or restart the program from the beginning.

BREAK

Purpose

The Break command begins the debugging process. It is used while a program is in run mode to temporarily halt execution so that the program's code and the values of its variables may be examined or modified.

Selection

The Break command can be selected from the Run menu, or can be executed by pressing the (CTRL) and (BREAK) keys simultaneously.

Description

The Break command makes all of Visual Basic's debugging commands available. While your program is in run mode, you may select this command to halt the program. When you do this, Visual Basic goes into break mode, and both the Code and Immediate panes appear. If the program was inactive (waiting for an event to occur), the Immediate pane is given the focus. However, if your program was executing code, the Code window is given the focus, and a box is placed around the next line of code to be executed.

While in break mode, you can perform any of the other Debug commands (Toggle Breakpoint, Procedure Step, Set Next Statement, and so on), and you may enter Visual Basic commands into the Immediate pane. You can even make changes to your code, thereby changing the way your program executes. In most cases after making a change, you can cause the program to continue where it left off, without having to restart it from the beginning. However, some changes will require that the program be restarted. Visual Basic will inform you of this when

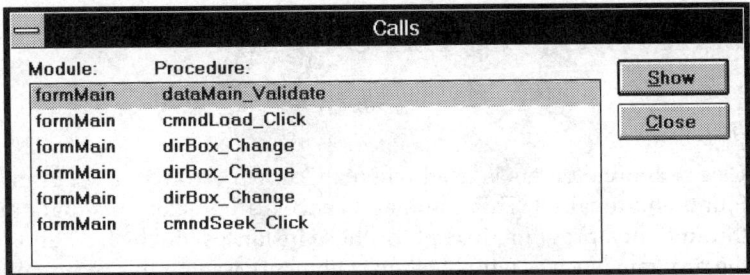

Figure C-1 The Calls dialog box lets you trace active procedures

you make such a change, and allow you to choose whether you wish to continue with the change and restart the program from the beginning, or to undo the change.

There are three ways to exit the break mode. First, you can choose the Continue option from the Run menu (or press the (F5) key). This allows the program to continue at the statement that is surrounded by the box indicating that it is to be the next command to be executed. Second, you can choose the Restart option (or press (SHIFT)-(F5)) from the Run menu. This causes the program to restart from the beginning. Finally, you can choose the End option from the Run menu. This causes the program to terminate, and you are returned to design mode.

CALLS COMMAND

Purpose

The Calls command displays all current procedure calls in the Calls dialog box.

Selection

Select the Calls command from the Debug menu.

Description

Complex programs can often have many procedures running at the same time. You can display a list of all active procedures (procedures that were started but have not yet ended) to help trace program execution. This can be particularly helpful in nested procedures, where one procedure calls another, and that one calls yet another.

The Calls dialog box places the most recent procedure at the top of the list, and works backward through all procedures to the bottom of the list. Figure C-1 shows the Calls dialog box.

CLEAR ALL BREAKPOINTS

Purpose

Clear All Breakpoints is used when all known errors in a program have been found and repaired. This command cancels all breakpoints that have been set throughout a program. Except for those instances in which a halt is coded into the program (such as with the Stop statement), issuing this command allows the program to proceed with no further interruptions.

Selection

Execute this command by choosing the Clear All Breakpoints option from the Run menu.

Description

Breakpoints are placed in your code with the Toggle Breakpoint command. These are used to halt program execution at specified points in your program. The Clear All Breakpoints command searches your program and cancels any breakpoints that have been set.

DEBUG OBJECT

Purpose

The Debug object sends output directly to the Immediate pane.

Selection

The Debug object can only be accessed from within the code of your program. The syntax for using the Debug object is

```
Debug.Print [expression-list]
```

Description

The Debug object is used with the Print method to send output directly to the Immediate pane (for information on the Print method, see Chapter 11, Displaying Text). This object provides an alternative technique for setting up "watch" variables. A watch variable is a variable whose value is displayed each

1448

time it is changed. The use of watch variables is a very helpful technique, because it allows the programmer to see exactly what is being assigned to a variable and when its value changes. Visual Basic provides a direct way of setting watch variables (see the Watch Variables entry for how to do this).

If you need to do more than simply watch the value of a single variable, printing to the Debug object might still make sense. For instance, in the following code fragment, we want to keep tabs on the values of a two-dimensional array:

```
Sub Button1_Click ()
    :
    :
    For i = 1 to 4
        For j = 1 to 4
            Debug.Print watchedArray(i, j);
        Next j
        Debug.Print
    Next i
    :
    :
End Sub
```

In this example the values held by watchedArray will be displayed each time you click on the Command button named Button1. This would have been much harder to do with watch variables.

THE IMMEDIATE PANE

Purpose

Use the Immediate pane to execute Visual Basic functions, statements, and methods in real time, and as an output area for the Debug object.

Selection

This window automatically appears during runtime. It can be selected by clicking the left mouse button while the mouse pointer is over the window. This window can also be selected by choosing the Immediate Pane option from Visual Basic's Window menu, or by pressing (CTRL)-(B). However, real-time commands can only be entered into this window while the Visual Basic environment is in break mode.

Description

When you start a program while in the Visual Basic environment, your form appears as the window on the desktop that has the focus. Underneath your form, another window, called the Immediate pane, is displayed. When a program is halted due to a Break command, a breakpoint, the execution of a Stop statement, or the occurrence of an untrapped error, this window becomes accessible to you. Before the Immediate pane can be used, it must be given the focus. If you have issued a Break command while your program was idle (waiting for an event), the Immediate pane will automatically be given the focus. Otherwise you must give it the focus by selecting it with one of the procedures described above.

While in the Immediate pane, you may enter any valid Visual Basic commands. This includes reading and setting the values of any variables that are accessible from the section of the program where execution was halted. In other words, variables that are accessible to the Immediate pane are those that have been declared: (1) in the global module, (2) in the General Declarations area of the form with the focus, and (3) in the procedure in which execution was halted. For instance, given the following code:

```
Global GlobalVar As Integer    'This variable is declared in the global routine
Dim ModuleVar As Integer       'This variable is declared in the General Declarations area

Sub Button1_Click ()
    Dim ThisVar1 As Integer
    ThisVar1 = Int(34.54)     'There is a breakpoint at this line
End Sub

Sub Button2_Click ()
    Dim ThisVar2 As Integer
    ThisVar2 = Sqr(254)
End Sub
```

When Visual Basic encounters the line in Button1_Click where the breakpoint is set, execution will halt, and the Immediate pane will be given the focus. At that time, you would be able to read and set the values of the variables GlobalVar, ModuleVar, and ThisVar1. However, you would not be able to access ThisVar2, because it is defined in a different procedure from that where execution was halted.

You can examine variable contents by printing them out with the Print keyword. Type in Print and whatever variable list you'd like to examine. You might wish to abbreviate the keyword Print with a question mark (?) when examining the contents of variables. This can save quite a bit of typing in a lengthy debugging session!

The Immediate pane is also used as an output area for the Debug object. This allows you to display information about how a program is running by strategically placing Debug.Print commands in your code. See the entry for the Debug object in this chapter. Figure C-2 illustrates the Debug window with the Immediate pane on the bottom.

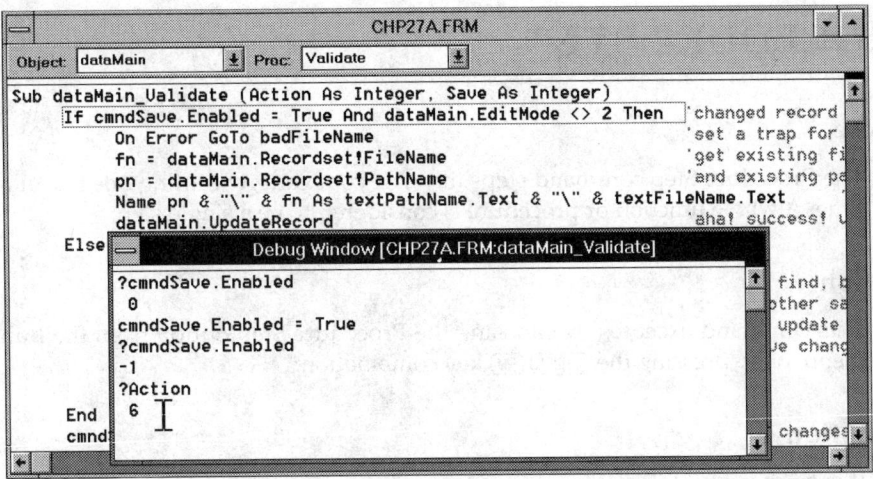

Figure C-2 The Immediate pane of the Debug window lets you display information and type in immediate commands

INSTANT WATCH

Purpose

Use the Instant Watch command to check the value of an expression during break mode.

Selection

Select an expression in the Code window or in the Immediate pane, and choose the Instant Watch command from the Debug menu. You may also press (SHIFT)-(F9).

Description

Use the Instant Watch command to check the value of an expression for which you have not defined a regular watch expression. Select an expression in the Code window or in the Immediate pane, and then choose Instant Watch from the Debug menu. The results of the expression are displayed in the dialog box. You can press the Add Watch button to add this expression as a regular watch expression.

PROCEDURE STEP

Purpose

The Procedure Step command steps through your code, executing one line at a time. A whole function or procedure is considered to be a single step.

Selection

This command executes by choosing the Procedure Step option from the Run menu, or by pressing the (SHIFT)-(F8) key combination.

Description

It is often useful to be able to execute your program one line at a time, so that you may see exactly which steps are taken throughout the program's execution. This helps you determine where bugs in your program may occur. Portions of your code that you are stepping through may include several calls to functions or procedures that you have written. If you have already debugged these functions and procedures, and know they work correctly, there is no reason for you to have to step through each line in those functions or procedures when they are called. When this is the case, you can use the Procedure Step command. This command will step through code one line at a time. However, when a Procedure Step encounters a function or procedure call, it will execute the entire function or procedure as one step. This saves you the hassle of stepping through all the lines of code in that procedure or function.

Comment

If you want to step through every program statement, including code in procedures or functions, use the Single Step command rather than Procedure Step.

SET NEXT STATEMENT

Purpose

The Set Next Statement command is used while in break mode to inform Visual Basic which is the next line of code to execute.

Selection

This command executes by selecting the Set Next Statement option from the Run menu.

Description

When Visual Basic enters break mode, it places a box around the statement that is to be executed next. You can use the Set Next Statement command to move this box to a different line of code. However, the line of code you choose must reside in the same procedure or function as the original next statement. You set the next statement to be executed by placing the insertion point on the desired line of code, and then selecting the Set Next Statement command.

There are two situations in which this command is most commonly used. First, because Visual Basic allows you to change your code while in break mode, you may wish to immediately test how the changes will execute. This can be done by setting up the first line of your change to be the next statement to be executed. You can then use the Procedure Step or Single Step commands to test how the new coding changes will work.

The second common use for this command is to recover from an untrapped error. Any time an error occurs that you have not trapped in your program's code, the program halts, Visual Basic displays an error message, and the Immediate pane is displayed. Sometimes this can happen because of a variable not being set to the correct value. For instance, in the following code fragment, an attempt is made to open a file:

```
FileNumber = Free_File
Open "TEST.DAT" For Random As #FileNumber
```

In this example it seems as though the programmer who wrote this intended to get a free file number from Visual Basic's FreeFile function. Unfortunately, however, our programmer mistyped the function name, and included an underscore. As a result, Visual Basic creates a variable called Free_File and assigns it the default value of 0. When Visual Basic encounters the line that assigns a value to the variable FileNumber, the assigned value will also be 0. This will cause the Open statement on the next line to issue a "Bad file name or number" error.

When this happens you can fix the code immediately, by changing the line above the file open. The new code fragment would look like this:

```
FileNumber = FreeFile
Open "TEST.DAT" For Random As #FileNumber
```

You would then use the Set Next Statement command to inform Visual Basic to continue execution at the line where the FileNumber variable is assigned a value from the FreeFile function. Not only have you fixed the error, but you have also saved yourself from having to restart the program from the beginning.

SHOW NEXT STATEMENT

Purpose

The Show Next Statement command locates the next statement that will be executed, and displays it in the Code window.

Selection

This command executes by selecting the Show Next Statement option from the Run menu.

Description

Visual Basic allows you to edit your program's code while in break mode. When Visual Basic enters break mode, the currently executing procedure is displayed in the Code window. However, you can edit other procedures in the program while in break mode. Doing so causes the current procedure to be replaced in the Code window by the procedure you wish to edit. If you need to edit several procedures, it might happen that you forget in which procedure execution was halted. The Show Next Statement command provides a technique for you to quickly set the focus to the Code window where the program halt occurred. When this command executes, Visual Basic locates the line of code that is to be the next executed statement, and loads its procedure into the Code window. The next line to be executed will be displayed in the center of the window, with a box around it.

SINGLE STEP

Purpose

The Single Step command steps through your code one line at a time. When a function or procedure call is encountered, this command will load the function or procedure into the Code window, and execute its statements one line at a time.

Selection

This command executes by choosing the Single Step option from Visual Basic's Run menu, or by pressing (F8).

Description

It is often useful to be able to execute your program one line at a time, so that you may view exactly which steps are taken throughout the program's execu-

1454

tion. This helps you determine where bugs in your program may occur. Portions of your code that you are stepping through may include several calls to functions or procedures that you have written. If you have not yet debugged these functions and procedures, you may wish to step through each line of code in those functions and procedures when they are called. When this is the case, you can use the Single Step command. This command will step through code one line at a time. When a Single Step encounters a function or procedure call, it will load that function or procedure into the Code window, and execute that function's or procedure's code one line at a time. When execution reaches an Exit Function, End Function, Exit Sub, or End Sub statement, it will load into the Code window the parent function or procedure that made the call to the current function or procedure, and continue execution there a step at a time.

Comment

If you want to step through a main program but not step through the procedures or functions that it calls, use the Procedure Step command instead of Single Step.

STOP STATEMENT

Purpose

The Stop statement halts execution of a program.

Selection

The Stop statement is placed in your code. The syntax for this statement is simply:

```
Stop
```

Description

The Stop statement is used much like a breakpoint in your code. Unlike a breakpoint, which marks a particular line of code, this command is placed inside your code as an executable statement. The effect of a Stop statement is exactly the same as if you had issued a Break command while executing the line of code with the Stop statement on it. When this command executes, Visual Basic is placed into break mode. Both the Code and Immediate panes appear, and the Code window will have the focus. Although it will have already been executed, the line of code with the Stop statement will be surrounded with a box, indicating it is the next statement to be executed. However, performing Single Step or Procedure Step at this time will not execute the Stop statement again; it will just set the next statement to the line following the Stop statement.

Most commonly, the Stop statement halts execution when a condition becomes True. For instance, imagine you have a variable in your program that can be set to True or False. For some reason, you may wish to examine the program when that variable becomes False. Using the following line of code, you can cause the program to halt when this is the case:

```
If ThisVar = False Then Stop
```

This sets a conditional breakpoint in a program. You must be careful if you use the Stop statement in the debugging of your program. If you do not remove all Stop statements in your program before creating an .EXE file, they will be compiled into the executable version of your program. Then if the executable program comes across a Stop statement, it will terminate, and a "Stop statement encountered" message will be displayed. This is a guaranteed way to make the user of the program very unhappy. Therefore, if you ever place a Stop statement in your program, always do a global search for the word "Stop" and remove every Stop statement before creating an .EXE file.

TOGGLE BREAKPOINT

Purpose

The Toggle Breakpoint command sets or clears a flag that marks a point in the program where execution will be halted. This command works like a toggle switch. If a line of code is not yet a breakpoint, choosing this command makes it one; otherwise, it cancels the breakpoint for this line of code.

Selection

This command can be selected by choosing the Toggle Breakpoint option from Visual Basic's Run menu, or by pressing (F9).

Description

A breakpoint is a line of code in your program where you wish execution to be halted. The effect of a breakpoint is exactly the same as if you had issued a Break command while executing the line of code just prior to the breakpoint. In other words, the program is halted before the line with the breakpoint executes. When a breakpoint is encountered, Visual Basic is placed into break mode. Both the Code and Immediate panes appear, and the Code window will have the focus. The line of code with the breakpoint will be surrounded with a box, indicating it is the next statement to be executed.

Breakpoints are used to halt program execution just prior to a portion of code that you wish to step through, or to examine before it executes. A breakpoint can also be used to check the results of a particular routine after it has executed.

WATCH COMMAND

Purpose

Use the Watch command to add, delete, or edit a *watch expression.* Watch statements let you monitor expressions during program execution.

Selection

Add a new watch statement using the Debug menu's Add Watch command. Edit or delete existing watch statements with the Debug menu's Edit Watch command.

Description

Watch expressions help you discover problems that occur only when a variable or property assumes a certain value. Setting watch expressions lets you monitor the behavior of a variable or of an expression throughout a procedure.

Visual Basic automatically monitors each watch expression for you, and updates their values every time the program enters break mode. These values are displayed in the top of the Debug window in the Watch pane (directly above the Immediate pane).

You can also set watch expressions to halt program execution when an expression reaches a certain value. This can be a handy adjunct to setting breakpoints. Breakpoints always halt execution whenever program flow executes that statement; watch expressions can let program flow execute a statement repeatedly (as in a loop) and only halt when the condition you specify is met.

Use the Add Watch dialog box to add a new watch expression. You can enter any valid expression (variable, property, function call, or a complex expression combining all of these) into the Expression text box. Use the Context settings to indicate what the scope of expression will be—local, module level, or global. The Watch Type group lets you set what action to take when the expression is evaluated. You can have Visual Basic display the results of the expression (Watch Expression), break when the expression evaluates to True (Break when Expression is True), or break any time the expression changes value (Break when Expression has Changed). Figure C-3 illustrates the Add Watch dialog box.

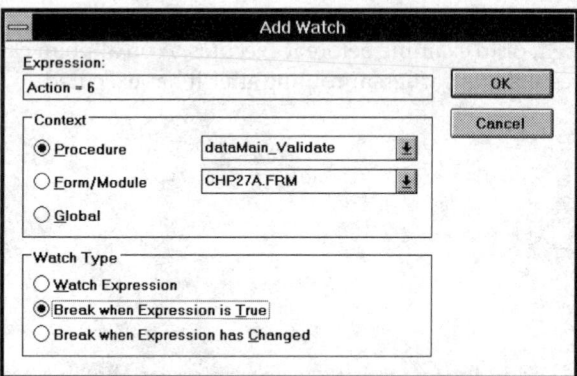

Figure C-3 The Add Watch dialog box lets you add new watch expressions

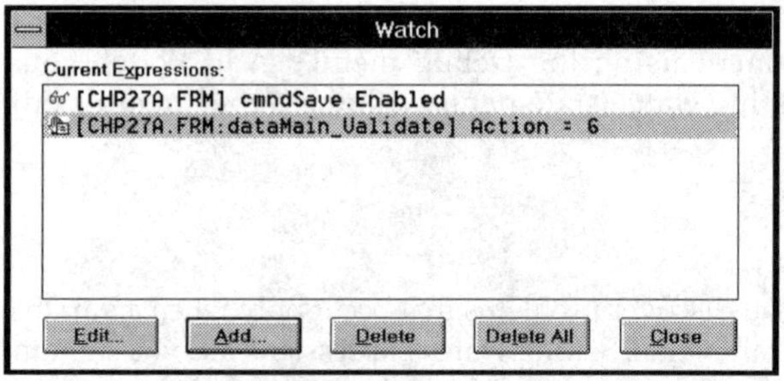

Figure C-4 The Edit Watch dialog box lets you edit or delete existing watch expressions

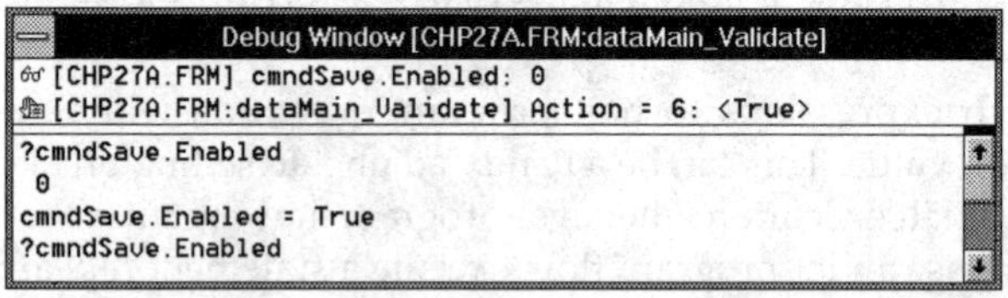

Figure C-5 The Watch pane lets you see the results of your watch expressions

Use the Edit Watch dialog box to edit or delete existing watch expressions. Select whatever expression you'd like (either with the mouse or arrow keys) and choose Edit to change the expression or Delete to delete it. You can also choose Delete All to delete all current watch expressions. Pressing the Add command button brings up the Add Watch dialog box. Figure C-4 shows the Edit Watch dialog box.

The results of the watch expressions are displayed in the Watch pane of the Debug window. Figure C-5 illustrates the Watch pane.

1458

APPENDIX

D

WINDOWS API

The Microsoft Windows environment defines more than 500 separate functions that programs can use to interact directly with the operating environment. Traditional Windows program development involves making calls to many of these functions, usually from programs written in the C language.

Visual Basic provides built-in features that make it unnecessary to use the API functions in most applications. There may be times, however, when you want to accomplish something that is not directly supplied by Visual Basic. For example, the project at the end of this appendix demonstrates how you can read and write the profile strings in *.INI files. Visual Basic lets you access any API function directly from your program, putting all of the power of Windows at your disposal.

VISUAL BASIC AND WINDOWS API FUNCTIONS

In order to make an API function available to a Visual Basic application, the function must be declared in the General Declarations section of a form or module. The exact syntax of the code that declares an API function varies for each function. There are several possible sources for each API function that must be identified properly. These sources include the files KERNEL.EXE, GDI.EXE, USER.EXE, COMM.DRV, MOUSE.DRV, KEYBOARD.DRV, and SOUND.DRV. Unfortunately the *Windows Programmer's Reference* does not list them. This information is provided in the following section, along with the syntax to use in Visual Basic applications.

We do not have room in this book to go into details in the reference entries for API functions, and can only provide a brief summary of syntax, arguments, and values used. You can find a complete list of the Windows API functions in The Waite Group's Windows API Bible (Waite Group Press, 1992). This reference manual is essential for expanding the capabilities of the Visual Basic language. See Appendix F for other books relating to Windows programming and the API.

APPLICATION-EXECUTION FUNCTIONS

LoadModule

This function loads and activates the application named in the lpModuleName argument. If the application is already loaded, then a new version is created. Tables D-1 and D-2 list the arguments and fields of LoadModule.

```
Declare Function LoadModule Lib "Kernel" (ByVal lpModuleName As String, lpParameterBlock
As PARAMETERBLOCK) As Integer
```

Argument	Description
lpModuleName	Null-terminated string containing the file and path of the application to run
lpParameterBlock	Points to a data structure that consists of four possible fields

Table D-1 Arguments of LoadModule

Field	Description
wEnvSeg	Segment Address (0 means copy it)
lpCmdLine	Null-Terminated Command string
lpCmdShow	Appearance of application when loaded
dwReserved	Null

Table D-2 Fields of LoadModule

1460

WinExec

This function executes the Windows or non-Windows application named in the lpCmdLine parameter. Tables D-3 and D-4 list the arguments and returned values of WinExec.

```
Declare Function WinExec Lib "Kernel" (ByVal lpCmdLine As String, nCmdShow As Integer) As
Integer
```

Argument	Description
lpCmdLine	Null-terminated string containing the file and path of the application to run
nCmdShow	Specifies how a Windows application is to be shown. See ShowWindow for possible values

Table D-3 Arguments of WinExec

Returned Value	Meaning
0	Out of memory
2	File not found
3	Path not found
5	Attempt to dynamically link to a task
6	Library requires separate data segments for each task
10	Incorrect Windows version
11	Invalid EXE file
12	OS/2 application
13	DOS 4.0 application
14	Unknown EXE type
15	Attempt to load a Windows application for an earlier version of Windows

(continued on next page)

(continued from previous page)

Returned Value	Meaning
16	Attempt to load an additional instance of an .EXE file
17	Attempt to load a second instance of an application in a large-frame EMS mode
18	Attempt to load a protected-mode application in real mode

Table D-4 Returned Values of WinExec

WinHelp

This function starts the Windows Help application with the Help file identified in the lpHelpFile argument. Table D-5 lists the arguments of WinHelp.

```
Declare Function WinHelp Lib "User" (ByVal hWnd As Integer, ByVal lpHelpFile As String,
ByVal wCommand As Integer, dwData As Any) As Integer
```

Argument	Description
hWnd	Identifies window that requested help
lpHelpFile	Null-terminated string containing the file and path of the Help file
wCommand	Indentifies the type of help requested with one of the folllowing values
dwData	Identifies the context or keyword of the help requested

Table D-5 Arguments of WinHelp

CONSTANT.TXT Variables for WinHelp

HELP_CONTEXT	Help for a particular context
HELP_HELPONHELP	Displays help for using Help
HELP_INDEX	Displays the index for the Help file
HELP_KEY	Displays help for a particular keyword

HELP_MULTIKEY	Displays help for a keyword of an alternate keyword table
HELP_QUIT	Informs the help application that the help file is no longer being used
HELP_SETINDEX	Sets the dwData argument as the current index

CONSTANT.TXT Global Constant Definitions

```
Global Const HELP_CONTEXT = &H1
Global Const HELP_QUIT = &H2
Global Const HELP_INDEX = &H3
Global Const HELP_HELPONHELP = &H4
Global Const HELP_SETINDEX = &H5
Global Const HELP_KEY = &H101
Global Const HELP_MULTIKEY = &H201
```

ATOM-MANAGEMENT FUNCTIONS

AddAtom

This function adds the character string in the lpString argument to the atom table. Table D-6 lists the argument of AddAtom.

```
Declare Function AddAtom Lib "Kernel" (ByVal lpString As String) As Integer
```

Argument	Description
lpString	Null-terminated character string

Table D-6 Argument of AddAtom

DeleteAtom

This function deletes the atom identified by the nAtom argument. Table D-7 lists the argument of DeleteAtom.

```
Declare Function DeleteAtom Lib "Kernel" (ByVal nAtom As Integer) As Integer
```

Argument	Description
nAtom	Identifies the atom and character string to be deleted

Table D- 7 Argument of DeleteAtom

FindAtom

This function finds the atom table for the character string in the lpString argument. Table D-8 lists the argument of FindAtom.

```
Declare Function FindAtom Lib "Kernel" (ByVal lpString As String) As Integer
```

Argument	Description
lpString	Identifies the character string to search for

Table D-8 Argument of FindAtom

GetAtomHandle

This function provides the handle of the string in the atom identified by the wAtom argument. Table D-9 lists the argument of GetAtomHandle.

```
Declare Function GetAtomHandle Lib "Kernel" (ByVal wAtom As Integer) As Integer
```

Argument	Description
wAtom	Integer that identifies the atom whose handle is retrieved

Table D-9 Argument of GetAtomHandle

GetAtomName

This function returns the character string of the nAtom parameter. Table D-10 lists the arguments of GetAtomName.

```
Declare Function GetAtomName Lib "Kernel" (ByVal nAtom As Integer, ByVal lpBuffer As
String, ByVal nSize As Integer) As Integer
```

1464

Argument	Description
nAtom	Identifies the character string to obtain
lpbuffer	Indicates the buffer to put the returned character string in
nSize	Maximum size of the buffer

Table D-10 Arguments of GetAtomName

GlobalAddAtom

This function creates a global atom for a character string identified by the lpString parameter. Table D-11 lists the argument of GlobalAddAtom.

```
Declare Function GlobalAddAtom Lib "Kernel" (ByVal lpString As String) As Integer
```

Argument	Description
lpString	Null-terminated character string to create the atom for

Table D-11 Argument of GlobalAddAtom

GlobalDeleteAtom

This function reduces the reference count of a global atom by 1. If the atom's count is 0, then this removes the string from the atom table. Table D-12 lists the argument of GlobalDeleteAtom.

```
Declare Function GlobalDeleteAtom Lib "Kernel" (ByVal nAtom As Integer) As Integer
```

Argument	Description
nAtom	Specifies the atom affected by this function

Table D-12 Argument of GlobalDeleteAtom

1465

GlobalFindAtom

This function searches for the global atom connected with a character string. Table D-13 lists the argument of GlobalFindAtom.

```
Declare Function GlobalFindAtom Lib "Kernel" (ByVal lpString As String) As Integer
```

Argument	Description
lpString	Null-terminated character string to search for

Table D-13 Argument of GlobalFindAtom

GlobalGetAtomName

This function copies the character string connected with the atom into a buffer. Table D-14 lists the arguments of GlobalGetAtomName.

```
Declare Function GlobalGetAtomName Lib "Kernel" (ByVal nAtom As Integer, ByVal lpbuffer As
String, ByVal nSize As Integer) As Integer
```

Argument	Description
nAtom	Identifies the character string
lpBuffer	Buffer to put the character string into
nSize	Maximum size of the buffer

Table D-14 Arguments of GlobalGetAtomName

InitAtomTable

This function sets up an atom hash table. Table D-15 lists the argument of InitAtomTable.

```
Declare Function InitAtomTable Lib "Kernel" (ByVal nSize As Integer) As Integer
```

Argument	Description
nSize	Indicates the size of the atom hash table

Table D-15 Argument of InitAtomTable

COMMUNICATIONS FUNCTIONS

BuildCommDCB

This function translates the string in the lpDef argument into an appropriate device-control block code. These codes are then placed in the DCB data structure identified by the lpDCB argument Table D-16 lists the argument of BuildCommandDCB.

```
Declare Function BuildCommDCB Lib "User" (ByVal lpDef As String, lpDCB As DCB) As Integer
```

Argument	Description
lpDef	DCB control structure

Table D-16 Argument of BuildCommDCB

ClearCommBreak

This function resets the communication break state of a communications device identified by the nCid argument. Table D-17 lists the argument of ClearCommandBreak.

```
Declare Function ClearCommBreak Lib "User" (ByVal nCid As Integer) As Integer
```

Argument	Description
nCid	Communications device

Table D-17 Argument of ClearCommBreak

CloseComm

This function closes the communications device identified by the nCid argument. Table D-18 lists the argument of CloseComm.

```
Declare Function CloseComm Lib "User" (ByVal nCid As Integer) As Integer
```

Argument	Description
nCid	Communications device

Table D-18 Argument of CloseComm

EscapeCommFunction

This function instructs the communications device identified by the nCid argument to carry out the function in the nFunc argument. Table D-19 lists the arguments of EscapeCommFunction, and Table D-20 lists the function names and meanings.

```
Declare Function EscapeCommFunction Lib "User" (ByVal nCid As Integer, ByVal nFunc As
Integer) As Integer
```

Argument	Description
nCid	Communications device
nFunc	Function for the communications device to carry out

Table D-19 Arguments of EscapeCommFunction

Name	Meaning
CLRDTR	Clears the data-terminal ready (DTR) signal
CLRRTS	Clears the request-to-send (RTS) signal
RESETDEV	Resets the device if possible

Name	Meaning
SETDTR	Sends the data-terminal-ready (DTR) signal
SETRTS	Sends the request-to-send (RTS) signal
SETXOFF	Communications device acts as if an XOFF character is received
SETXON	Communications device acts as if an XON character is received

Table D-20 Function names and their meanings

FlushComm

This function removes all characters from the transmit and receive queue of the communications device identified by the nCid argument. The nQueue argument indicates which queue to flush. Table D-21 lists the arguments of FlushComm.

```
Declare Function FlushComm Lib "User" (ByVal nCid As Integer, ByVal nQueue As Integer) As
Integer
```

Argument	Description
nCid	Communications device
nQueue	Indicates whether to flush the transmit (0) or receive queue (1)

Table D-21 Arguments of FlushComm

GetCommEventMask

This function obtains the current value of an event and then clears it. The returned value indicates whether the event has taken place. Table D-22 lists the arguments of GetCommEventMask.

```
Declare Function GetCommEventMask Lib "User" (ByVal nCid As Integer, ByVal nEvtMask As
Integer) As Integer
```

Argument	Description
nCid	Communications device to examine
nEnvtMask	Indicates which events are enabled

Table D-22 Arguments of GetCommEventMask

GetCommState

This function fills the buffer identified by the lpDCB argument with the device control block. Table D-23 lists the arguments of GetCommState.

```
Declare Function GetCommState Lib "User" (ByVal nCid As Integer, lpDCB as DCB) As Integer
```

Argument	Description
nCid	Communications device to examine
lpDCB	DCB data structure that receives the current device control block

Table D-23 Arguments of GetCommState

OpenComm

This function activates a commications device and gives it an nCid handle. Table D-24 lists the arguments of OpenComm.

```
Declare Function OpenComm Lib "User" (ByVal lpComName As String, ByVal wInQueue As
Integer, ByVal wOutQueue As Integer) As Integer
```

Argument	Description
lpCommName	Indicates a string that contains COMn or LPTn
wInQueue	Indicates the size of the receive queue
wOutQueue	Indicates the size of the transmit queue

Table D-24 Arguments of OpenComm

ReadComm

This function takes the bytes from the communications device identified in the nCid argument and places them in the buffer set in the lpBuf. Table D-25 lists the arguments of ReadComm.

```
Declare Function ReadComm Lib "User" (ByVal nCid As Integer, ByVal lpBuf As String, ByVal
nSize As Integer) As Integer
```

Argument	Description
nCid	Communications device to read
lpBuf	Buffer to place the received characters into
nSize	Indicates the number of characters to be read

Table D-25 Arguments of ReadComm

SetCommBreak

This function changes the communications device identified by the nCid argument to break state. Table D-26 lists the argument of SetCommBreak.

```
Declare Function SetCommBreak Lib "User" (ByVal nCid As Integer) As Integer
```

Argument	Description
nCid	Communications device to affect

Table D-26 Argument of SetCommBreak

SetCommEventMask

This function activates and obtains the event mask of an identified nCid communications device. Tables D-27 and D-28 lists the arguments and event descriptions of SetCommEventMask.

```
Declare Function SetCommEventMask Lib "User" (ByVal nCid as Integer, nEvtMask as Integer)
As Long
```

Argument	Description
nCid	Communications device
nEvtMask	Indicates which events in the table below to activate

Table D-27 Arguments of SetCommEventMask

Event	Description
EV_BREAK	Determines when a break is found on input
EV-CTS	Determines when the clear-to-send (CTS) signal alters state
EV-DSR	Determines when the data-set-read (DSR) signal alters state
EV_ERR	Determines when a line-status error occurs
EV_PERR	Determines when a printer error is found on a parallel device
EV_RING	Determines when a ring indicator is detected
EV_RLSD	Determines when the receive-line-signal-detect (RLSD) signal alters state
EV_RXCHAR	Determines when characters are accepted and moved to the receive queue
EV_RXFLAG	Determines when the event character is accepted and put into the receive queue
EV_TXEMPTY	Determines when the last character in the transmit queue is sent

Table D-28 Event Descriptions for SetCommEventMask

SetCommState

This function changes the state of a communications device to the setting indicated by the device control block in the lpDCB argument. Table D-29 lists the argument of SetCommState.

```
Declare Function SetCommState Lib "User" ()
```

Argument	Description
lpDCB	Points to the DCB data structure that contains the communications setting

Table D-29 Argument of SetCommState

TransmitCommChar

This function places the character identified in the cChar argument at the head of the transmit queue of the communications device specified in the nCid argument. Table D-30 lists the arguments of TransmitCommChar.

```
Declare Function TransmitCommChar Lib "User" (ByVal nCid As Integer, ByVal cChar As
Integer) As Integer
```

Argument	Description
nCid	Communications device
cChar	Contains the character to transmit

Table D-30 Arguments of TransmitCommChar

UngetCommChar

This function places the character in the cChar argument into the receive queue of the nCid communications device. Table D-31 lists the arguments of UngetCommChar.

```
Declare Function UngetCommChar Lib "User" (ByVal nCid As Integer, ByVal cChar As Integer)
As Integer
```

Argument	Description
nCid	Communications device
cChar	Determines the character to place in the receive queue

Table D-31 Arguments of UngetCommChar

WriteComm

This function transfers the characters in the lpBuf buffer to the nCid communications device. Table D-32 lists the arguments of WriteComm.

```
Declare Function WriteComm Lib "User" (ByVal nCid As Integer, ByVal lpBuf As String, ByVal
nSize As Integer) As Integer
```

Argument	Description
nCid	Communications device
lpBuf	Identifies the buffer that holds the characters to be sent
nSize	Indicates the number of characters to transmit

Table D-32 Arguments of WriteComm

Communications Variables in CONSTANT.TXT

```
Global Const SETXOFF = 1
Global Const SETXON = 2
Global Const SETRTS = 3
Global Const CLRRTS = 4
Global Const SETDTR = 5
Global Const CLRDTR = 6
Global Const RESETDEV = 7
Global Const LPTx = &H80
Global Const EV_RXCHAR = &H1
Global Const EV_RXFLAG = &H2
Global Const EV_TXEMPTY = &H4
Global Const EV_CTS = &H8
Global Const EV_DSR = &H10
Global Const EV_RLSD = &H20
Global Const EV_BREAK = &H40
Global Const EV_ERR = &H80
Global Const EV_RING = &H100
Global Const EV_PERR = &H200
Global Const NOPARITY = 0
Global Const ODDPARITY = 1
Global Const EVENPARITY = 2
Global Const MARKPARITY = 3
Global Const SPACEPARITY = 4
Global Const ONESTOPBIT = 0
Global Const ONE5STOPBITS = 1
Global Const TWOSTOPBITS = 2
Global Const IGNORE = 0
Global Const INFINITE = &HFFFF
Global Const CE_RXOVER = &H1
Global Const CE_OVERRUN = &H2
```

```
Global Const CE_RXPARITY = &H4
Global Const CE_FRAME = &H8
Global Const CE_BREAK = &H10
Global Const CE_CTSTO = &H20
Global Const CE_DSRTO = &H40
Global Const CE_RLSDTO = &H80
Global Const CE_TXFULL = &H100
Global Const CE_PTO = &H200
Global Const CE_IOE = &H400
Global Const CE_DNS = &H800
Global Const CE_OOP = &H1000
Global Const CE_MODE = &H8000
Global Const IE_BADID = (-1)
Global Const IE_OPEN = (-2)
Global Const IE_NOPEN = (-3)
Global Const IE_MEMORY = (-4)
Global Const IE_DEFAULT = (-5)
Global Const IE_HARDWARE = (-10)
Global Const IE_BYTESIZE = (-11)
Global Const IE_BAUDRATE = (-12)
Global Const EV_RXCHAR = &H1
Global Const EV_RXFLAG = &H2
Global Const EV_TXEMPTY = &H4
Global Const EV_CTS = &H8
Global Const EV_DSR = &H10
Global Const EV_RLSD = &H20
Global Const EV_BREAK = &H40
Global Const EV_ERR = &H80
Global Const EV_RING = &H100
Global Const EV_PERR = &H200
Global Const SETXOFF = 1
Global Const SETXON = 2
Global Const SETRTS = 3
Global Const CLRRTS = 4
Global Const SETDTR = 5
Global Const CLRDTR = 6
Global Const RESETDEV = 7
Global Const LPTx = &H80
```

DEBUGGING FUNCTIONS

DebugBreak

This function sends a break to the debugger.

```
Declare Sub DebugBreak Lib "Kernel" ()
```

FatalExit

This function shows Windows' current state on the debugging monitor and asks the user for instructions. You are prompted with three options: Abort, Break, or

Ignore. Choose one of these options according to Table D- 33. Table D-33 lists the argument of FatalExit, and Table D-34 lists the responses to FatalExit.

```
Declare Sub FatalExit Lib "Kernel" (ByVal Code As Integer)
```

Argument	Description
Code	The error code to show on the screen

Table D-33 Argument of FatalExit

Response	Description
A (Abort)	Terminates Windows
B (Break)	Emulates a non-maskable interrupt (NMI) to access the debugger
I (Ignore)	Ignores the message

Table D-34 Responses to FatalExit function

OutputDebugString

This function transmits a debugging message to the debugger. Table D-35 lists the argument of OutputDebugString.

```
Declare Sub OutputDebugString Lib "Kernel" (ByVal lpOutputString As String)
```

Argument	Description
lpOutputString	Null-terminated string

Table D-35 Arguments of OutputDebugString

ValidateCodeSegments

This function discovers if any code segments were changed by random memory overwrites.

```
Declare Sub ValidateCodeSegments Lib "Kernel" ()
```

ValidateFreeSpaces

This function looks through free segments of memory for valid contents.

```
Declare Function ValidateFreeSpaces Lib "Kernel" () As Long
```

FILE I/O FUNCTIONS

GetDriveType

This function indicates if a disk drive is removable, fixed, or remote. Table D-36 lists the argument of GetDriveType. Table D-37 shows the possible returned values.

```
Declare Function GetDriveType Lib "Kernel" (ByVal nDrive As Integer) As Integer
```

Argument	Description
nDrive	Indicates which drive is to be checked by this function where Drive A is 0, Drive B is one (1), Drive C is two (2), and so on

Table D-36 Argument of GetDriveType

Returned Value	Description
DRIVE_REMOVEABLE	The disk is removable
DRIVE_FIXED	The disk cannot be removed
DRIVE_REMOTE	The disk is a network drive

Table D-37 Returned value of GetDriveType

1477

GetSystemDirectory

This function provides the path of the Windows System subdirectory. The System subdirectory contains the Windows libraries, drives, and screen font files.Table D-38 lists the arguments of GetSystemDirectory.

```
Declare Function GetSystemDirectory Lib "Kernel" (ByVal lpBuffer As String, ByVal nSize As
Integer) As Integer
```

Argument	Description
lpBuffer	Points to the buffer that will receive the returned pathname string
nSize	Maximum size of the buffer

Table D-38 Arguments of GetSystemDirectory

GetTempDrive

This function provides the letter of the optimal drive for temporary files. Table D-39 lists the argument of GetTempDrive.

```
Declare Function GetTempDrive Lib "Kernel" (ByVal cDriveLetter as Integer) As Integer
```

Argument	Description
cDriveLetter	The disk drive letter

Table D-39 Argument of GetTempDrive

GetTempFileName

This function creates a temporary file name. Table D-40 lists the arguments of GetTempFileName.

```
Declare Function GetTempFileName Lib "Kernel" (ByVal cDriveLetter as Integer, ByVal
lpPrefixString As String, ByVal wUnique As Integer, ByVal lpTempFileName As String) As
Integer
```

Argument	Description
cDriveLetter	Indicates the suggested drive (0 means the default drive)
lpPrefixString	Temporary file's prefix file name
wUnique	Unique identifying integer
lpTempFileName	Buffer that receives the temporary file name

Table D-40 Arguments of GetTempFileName

GetWindowsDirectory

This function provides the path of the Windows directory. The Windows directory contains windows applications, initialization, and help files. Table D-41 lists the arguments of GetWindowsDirectory.

```
Declare Function GetWindowsDirectory Lib "Kernel" (ByVal lpBuffer As String, ByVal nSize
As Integer) As Integer
```

Argument	Description
lpBuffer	The buffer that will receive the path
nSize	Maximum size of the buffer

Table D-41 Arguments of GetWindowsDirectory

_lclose

This function closes the file indicated in the hFile argument. Table D-42 lists the argument of _lclose.

```
Declare Function lclose Lib "Kernel" Alias "_lclose" (ByVal hFile As Integer) As Integer
```

Argument	Description
hFile	The MS-DOS handle of the file to be closed

Table D-42 Argument of _lclose

_lcreat

This function creates a file or opens and truncates an existing file. Tables D-43 and D-44 list the arguments and values of _lcreate.

```
Declare Function lcreat Lib "Kernel" Alias "_lcreat" (ByVal lpPathName As String, ByVal
iAttribute As Integer) As Integer
```

Argument	Description
lpPathName	Name of the file to open
iAttribute	File attributes with one of the values in the next table

Table D-43 Arguments of _lcreate

Value	Description
0	Normal—can be read and written
1	Read-only—cannot be opened for write
2	Hidden—invisible to directory search
3	System—invisible to directory search

Table D-44 Values of _lcreate

_llseek

This function positions the pointer to a previously opened file named in the hFile argument. Tables D-45 and D-46 lists the arguments and values of _llseek.

```
Declare Function llseek Lib "Kernel" Alias "_llseek" (ByVal hFile As Integer, ByVal
lOffset As Long, ByVal iOrigin As Integer) As Long
```

Argument	Description
hFile	MS-DOS handle for the file
lOffset	Number of bytes to move the pointer
iOrigin	Starting position and direction of the pointer. This must be one of the values in the following table

Table D-45 Arguments of _llseek

Value	Description
0	Place the file pointer lOffset bytes from the beginning of the file
1	Place the file pointer lOffset bytes from the current position of the file
2	Place the file pointer lOffset bytes from the end of the file

Table D-46 Values of _llseek

_lopen

This function opens an existing file named in the lpPathName argument. Tables D-47 and D-48 list the argument and values of _lopen.

```
Declare Function lopen Lib "Kernel" Alias "_lopen" (ByVal lpPathName As String, ByVal
iReadWrite As Integer) As Integer
```

Argument	Description
lpPathName	Name and path of the file
iReadWrite	Indicates whether to open the file with read or write access. This must be one of the following values

Table D-47 Arguments of _lopen

1481

Value	Description
OF_READ	Read-only
OF_READWRITE	Read and write
OF_SHARE_COMPAT	Compatibility mode
OF_SHARE_DENY_NONE	Allows other processes read-write access to the file
OF_SHARE_DENY_READ	Refuses other processes read access to the file
OF_SHARE_DENY_WRITE	Refuses other processes write access to the file
OF_SHARE_EXCLUSIVE	Exculsive mode
OF_WRITE	Write only

Table D-48 Values of _lopen

_lread

This function reads the data from a file named in the hFile argument. Table D-49 lists the arguments of _lread.

```
Declare Function lread Lib "Kernel" Alias "_lread" (ByVal hFile As Integer, ByVal lpBuffer
As String, ByVal wBytes As Integer) As Integer
```

Argument	Description
hFile	MS-DOS handle of the file to read
lpBuffer	Buffer to receive the read data
wBytes	Number of bytes to read from the file

Table D-49 Arguments of _lread

_lwrite

This function writes data to the file named in the hFile argument. Table D-50 lists the arguments of _lwrite.

```
Declare Function lwrite Lib "Kernel" Alias "_lwrite" (ByVal hFile As Integer, ByVal
lpBuffer As String, ByVal wBytes As Integer) As Integer
```

Argument	Description
hFile	MS-DOS file handle of the file to be read
lpBuffer	Buffer holding the data to be written
wBytes	Number of bytes to be written to the file

Table D-50 Arguments of _lwrite

OpenFile

This function creates, opens, reopens, or deletes the file named in the lpFileName argument.Table D-51 lists the arguments of OpenFile; Table D-52 lists the values.

```
Declare Function OpenFile Lib "Kernel" (ByVal lpFileName As String, lpReOpenBuff As
OFSTRUCT, ByVal wStyle As Integer) As Integer
```

Argument	Description
lpFileName	Name of the file to open
lpReOpenBuff	OFSTRUCT data structure that will receive the information about the file when it is opened
wStyle	The action to take. This must be a combination of the values in the following table

Table D-51 Arguments of OpenFile

Value	Description
OF_CANCEL	Puts a cancel button in the OF_PROMPT dialog box
OF_CREATE	Creates a new file
OF_DELETE	Deletes the file
OF_EXIST	Checks if the file exists
OF_PARSE	Puts information about file in the OFSTRUCT data structure
OF_PROMPT	Displays a dialog box if Windows could not find the file
OF_READ	Read-only file
OF_READWRITE	Read-write file
OF_REOPEN	Opens file with information in re-open buffer
OF_SHARE-COMPAT	Compatibility mode
OF_SHARE_DENY_NONE	Other processes may have read and write access to the file
OF_SHARE_DENY_READ	Refuses other processes read access
OF_SHARE_DENY_WRITE	Refuses other processes write access
OF_SHARE_EXCLUSIVE	Exclusive mode
OF_VERIFY	Checks the date and time of the file
OF_WRITE	Write only

Table D-52 Values of OpenFile

SetHandleCount

This function modifies the number of handles available to a task. Table D-53 lists the argument of SetHandleCount.

```
Declare Function SetHandleCount Lib "Kernel" (ByVal wNumber As Integer) As Integer
```

Argument	Description
wNumber	Number of file handles

Table D-53 Argument of SetHandleCount

File Variable Definitions

```
Global Const DRIVE_REMOVABLE = 2
Global Const DRIVE_FIXED = 3
Global Const DRIVE_REMOTE = 4
Global Const OF_READ = &H0
Global Const OF_WRITE = &H1
Global Const OF_READWRITE = &H2
Global Const OF_SHARE_COMPAT = &H0
Global Const OF_SHARE_EXCLUSIVE = &H10
Global Const OF_SHARE_DENY_WRITE = &H20
Global Const OF_SHARE_DENY_READ = &H30
Global Const OF_SHARE_DENY_NONE = &H40
Global Const OF_PARSE = &H100
Global Const OF_DELETE = &H200
Global Const OF_VERIFY = &H400
Global Const OF_CANCEL = &H800
Global Const OF_CREATE = &H1000
Global Const OF_PROMPT = &H2000
Global Const OF_EXIST = &H4000
Global Const OF_REOPEN = &H8000
```

INITIALIZATION-FILE FUNCTIONS

GetPrivateProfileInt

This function provides the integer value of a section from an initialization file. Table D-54 lists the arguments of GetPrivateProfileInt.

```
Declare Function GetPrivateProfileInt Lib "Kernel" (ByVal lpApplicationName As String,
ByVal lpKeyName As String, ByVal nDefault As Integer, ByVal lpFileName As String) As
Integer
```

Argument	Description
lpApplicationName	Windows Application name that appears in the initialization file
lpKeyName	Key Name

(continued on next page)

(continued from previous page)

Argument	Description
nDefault	Default value of the key
lpFileName	Name and path of the Initialization file

Table D-54 Arguments of GetPrivateProfileInt

GetPrivateProfileString

This function provides a character string from an initialization file and places it in a buffer. Table D-55 lists the arguments of GetPrivateProfileString.

```
Declare Function GetPrivateProfileString Lib "Kernel" (ByVal lpApplicationName As String,
ByVal lpKeyName As String, ByVal lpDefault As String, ByVal lpReturnedString As String,
ByVal nSize As Integer, ByVal lpFileName As String) As Integer
```

Argument	Description
lpApplicationName	Windows Application name that appears in the initialization file
lpKeyName	KeyName
lpDefault	Default value of the key
lpReturnedString	Buffer that will receive the string
nSize	Maximum number of characters to be transmitted to the buffer
lpFileName	Name and path of the initialization file

Table D-55 Arguments of GetPrivateProfileString

GetProfileInt

This function provides the value of an integer key from the Windows initialization file, WIN.INI. Table D-56 lists the arguments of GetProfileInt.

```
Declare Function GetProfileInt Lib "Kernel" (ByVal lpAppName As String, ByVal lpKeyName As
String, ByVal nDefault As Integer) As Integer
```

Argument	Description
lpAppName	Windows Application name that appears in the Windows initialization file
lpKeyName	KeyName
nDefault	Default value of the key

Table D-56 Arguments of GetProfileInt

GetProfileString

This function provides a character string from the Windows initialization file, WIN.INI, and places it in a buffer. Table D-57 lists the arguments of GetProfileString.

```
Declare Function GetProfileString Lib "Kernel" (ByVal lpAppName As String, ByVal lpKeyName
As String, ByVal lpDefault As String, ByVal lpReturnedString As String, ByVal nSize As
Integer) As Integer
```

Argument	Description
lpAppName	Application name
lpKeyName	KeyName
lpDefault	Default value of the string
lpReturnedString	Buffer that will receive the character string
nSize	Number of characters to be transmitted to the buffer

Table D- 57 Arguments of GetProfileString

WritePrivateProfileString

This function writes the string in the lpString argument under the heading in the specified initialization file. Table D-58 lists the arguments of WritePrivateProfileString.

1487

```
Declare Function WritePrivateProfileString Lib "Kernel" (ByVal lpApplicationName As
String, ByVal lpKeyName As String, ByVal lpString As String, ByVal lplFileName As String)
As Integer
```

Argument	Description
lpApplicationName	Application heading in initialization file
lpKeyName	KeyName
lpString	String to place under the KeyName in the initialization file
lpFileName	Name and path of the initialization file

Table D-58 Arguments of WritePrivateProfileString

WriteProfileString

This function writes the string in the lpString argument under the heading in the Windows initialization file, WIN.INI. Table D-59 lists the arguments of WriteProfileString.

```
Declare Function WriteProfileString Lib "Kernel" (ByVal lpApplicationName As String, ByVal
lpKeyName As String, ByVal lpString As String) As Integer
```

Argument	Description
lpApplicationName	Application heading in the WIN.INI file
lpKeyName	KeyName
lpString	String to place under the KeyName in the initialization file

Table D-59 Arguments of WriteProfileString

1488

MEMORY-MANAGEMENT FUNCTIONS

GetFreeSpace

This function obtains the numbers of bytes available in the global heap. Table D-60 lists the argument of GetFreeSpace.

```
Declare Function GetFreeSpace Lib "Kernel" (ByVal wFlags As Integer) As Long
```

Argument	Description
wFlags	Indicates whether to scan the heap above or below the EMS bank line

Table D-60 Argument of GetFreeSpace

GetWinFlags

This function provides the memory configuration of the current system.

```
Declare Function GetWinFlags Lib "Kernel" () As Long
```

Values in CONSTANT.TXT

Returned Value	Description
WF_80x87	System contains a math coprocessor
WF_CPU086	8086 CPU
WF_CPU186	80186 CPU
WF_CPU286	80286 CPU
WF_CPU386	80386 CPU
WF_CPU486	80486 CPU
WF_ENHANCED	Enhanced 386 Mode

(continued on next page)

(continued from previous page)

Returned Value	Description
WF_LARGEFRAME	Windows running in EMS large-frame memory
WF_PMODE	Windows running in protected mode
WF_SMALLFRAME	Windows running in EMS small-frame memory
WF_STANDARD	Standard mode

GlobalAlloc

This function allocates the number of bytes of memory set in the dwBytes argument. Table D-61 lists the arguments of GlobalAlloc; Table D-62 lists the values.

```
Declare Function GlobalAlloc Lib "Kernel" (ByVal wFlags As Integer, ByVal dwBytes As Long)
As Integer
```

Argument	Description
wFlags	Sets up one or more flags that indicate how to allocate the memory (see Table D-62)
dwBytes	Indicates the number of bytes to be allocated

Table D-61 Arguments of GlobalAlloc

Value	Meaning
GMEM_DDESHARE	Allocates shareable memory for Dynamic Data Exchange
GMEM_DISCARDABLE	Allocates discardable memory
GMEM_FIXED	Allocates shareable memory
LMEM_MOVEABLE	Allocates moveable memory
GMEM_NOCOMPACT	Will not compact or discard to satisfy allocation request
GMEM_NODISCARD	Will not discard to satisfy allocation request

Value	Meaning
GMEM_NOT_BANKED	Allocates non-banked memory
GMEM_NOTIFY	Initiates notification routine if memory object is not discarded
GMEM_ZEROINIT	Initializes memory to 0

Table D-62 Values of GlobalAlloc

GlobalCompact

This function provides the number of free bytes of global memory indicated in the dwMinFree argument. The GlobalCompact function will compact or discard memory if necessary. Table D-63 lists the argument of GlobalCompact.

```
Declare Function GlobalCompact Lib "Kernel" (ByVal dwMinFree As Long) As Long
```

Argument	Description
dwMinFree	Number of free bytes needed

Table D-63 Argument of GlobalCompact

GlobalFlags

This function provides the information about the global memory block in the hMem argument. Table D-64 lists the argument of GlobalFlags; Table D-65 lists the values.

```
Declare Function GlobalFlags Lib "Kernel" (ByVal hMem As Integer) As Integer
```

Argument	Description
hMem	The global memory block

Table D-64 Argument of GlobalFlags

Value	Description
GMEM_DDESHARE	The block can be shared in Dynamic Data Exchange (DDE)
GMEM_DISCARDABLE	This block may be discarded
GMEM_DISCARDED	This block has been discarded
GMEM_NOT_BANKED	This block cannot be banked

Table D-65 Values of GlobalFlags

GlobalFree

This function frees the memory block named in the hMem argument. Table D-66 lists the argument of GlobalFree.

```
Declare Function GlobalFree Lib "Kernel" (ByVal hMem As Integer) As Integer
```

Argument	Description
hMem	The global memory block to free

Table D-66 Argument of GlobalFree

GlobalHandle

This function provides the handle of the global memory object with the segment address indicated in the wMem argument. Table D-67 lists the argument of GlobalHandle.

```
Declare Function GlobalHandle Lib "Kernel" (ByVal wMem As Integer) As Long
```

Argument	Description
wMem	The segment address or selector of the global memory object

Table D-67 Argument of GlobalHandle

GlobalLock

This function provides the pointer to the global memory object in the hMem argument. Table D-68 lists the argument of GlobalLock.

```
Declare Function GlobalLock Lib "Kernel" (ByVal hMem As Integer) As Long
```

Argument	Description
hMem	The global memory block to be locked

Table D-68 Argument of GlobalLock

GlobalLRUNewest

This function places the global memory object in the hMem argument into the newest and least recently used (LRU) position in memory. Table D-69 lists the argument of GlobalLRUNewest.

```
Declare Function GlobalLRUNewest Lib "Kernel" (ByVal hMem As Integer) As Integer
```

Argument	Description
hMem	The global memory object to be moved

Table D-69 Argument of GlobalLRUNewest

GlobalLRUOldest

This function places the global memory object in the hMem argument in the oldest least recently used (LRU) position in memory. Table D-70 lists the argument of GlobalLRUOldest.

```
Declare Function GlobalLRUOldest Lib "Kernel" (ByVal hMem As Integer) As Integer
```

Argument	Description
hMem	The global memory object to be moved

Table D-70 Argument of GlobalLRUOldest

GlobalReAlloc

This function increases or decreases the number of bytes of the global memory block in the hMem argument to the amount set in the dwBytes argument. Table D-71 lists the arguments of GlobalReAlloc; Table D-72 lists the values.

```
Declare Function GlobalReAlloc Lib "Kernel" (ByVal hMem As Integer, ByVal dwBytes As Long,
ByVal wFlags As Integer) As Integer
```

Argument	Description
hMem	The global memory block to reallocate
dwBytes	New size of the global memory block
wFlags	The value of this argument indicates how to reallocate the global memory block according to the next table

Table D-71 Arguments of GlobalReAlloc

Value	Description
GMEM_DISCARDABLE	Memory may be discarded
GMEM_MODIFY	Memory flags are modified but the global memory is not reallocated
GMEM_MOVEABLE	Memory is moveable
GMEM_NOCOMPACT	Memory may not be compacted or discarded
GMEM_NODISCARD	Memory may not be discarded
GMEM_ZEROINIT	If the block is increased in size, additional memory is initialized to 0

Table D-72 Values of GlobalReAlloc

GlobalSize

This function finds the current size in bytes of the global memory block named in the hMem argument. Table D-73 lists the argument of GlobalSize.

```
Declare Function GlobalSize Lib "Kernel" (ByVal hMem As Integer) As Long
```

Argument	Description
hMem	The global memory block

Table D-73 Argument of GlobalSize

GlobalUnlock

This function unlocks the global memory block named in the hMem argument. Table D-74 lists the argument of GlobalUnlock.

```
Declare Function GlobalUnlock Lib "Kernel" (ByVal hMem As Integer) As Integer
```

Argument	Description
hMem	The global memory block to be unlocked

Table D-74 Argument of GlobalUnlock

GlobalUnwire

This function unlocks the global memory segment that was locked with the GlobalWire function. Table D-75 lists the argument of GlobalUnwire.

```
Declare Function GlobalUnWire Lib "Kernel" (ByVal hMem As Integer) As Integer
```

Argument	Description
hMem	The segment to unlock

Table D-75 Argument of GlobalUnwire

GlobalWire

This function places a segment in low memory and locks it. Table D-76 lists the arguments of GlobalWire.

```
Declare Function GlobalWire Lib "Kernel" (ByVal hMem As Integer) As Long
```

Argument	Description
hMem	The segment to lock

Table D-76 Argument of GlobalWire

LimitEMSPages

This function places a limit on the amount of expanded memory that Windows will assign to an application. Table D-77 lists the argument of LimitEMSPages.

```
Declare Sub LimitEmsPages Lib "Kernel" (ByVal dwKbytes As Long)
```

Argument	Description
dwkbytes	The amount of kilobytes of expanded memory that applications may have access to

Table D-77 Argument of LimitEMSPages

LocalAlloc

This function allocates a number of bytes of memory set in the dwBytes argument. Table D-78 lists the arguments of LocalAlloc; Table D-79 lists the values.

```
Declare Function LocalAlloc Lib "Kernel" (ByVal wFlags As Integer, ByVal wBytes As
Integer) As Integer
```

Argument	Description
wFlags	Sets up one or more flags that indicate how to allocate the memory (see Table D-79)
dwBytes	Indicates the number of bytes to be allocated

Table D-78 Arguments of LocalAlloc

Value	Meaning
LMEM_DISCARDABLE	Allocates discardable memory
LMEM_FIXED	Allocates shareable memory
LMEM_MODIFY	Modifies the LMEM_DISCARDABLE flag
LMEM_MOVEABLE	Allocates moveable memory
LMEM_NOCOMPACT	Will not compact or discard to satisfy allocation request
LMEM_NODISCARD	Will not discard to satisfy allocation request
LMEM_ZEROINIT	Initializes memory to 0

Table D-79 Values of LocalAlloc

LocalCompact

This function provides the number of free bytes of memory indicated in the dwMinFree argument. The LocalCompact function will compact or discard memory if this is necessary. Table D-80 lists the argument of LocalCompact.

```
Declare Function LocalCompact Lib "Kernel" (ByVal wMinFree As Integer) As Integer
```

Argument	Description
dwMinFree	Number of free bytes needed

Table D-80 Argument of LocalCompact

LocalFlags

This function provides information about the local memory block in the hMem argument. Table D-81 lists the argument of LocalFlags; Table D-82 lists the values.

```
Declare Function LocalFlags Lib "Kernel" (ByVal hMem As Integer) As Integer
```

1497

Argument	Description
hMem	The local memory block

Table D-81 Argument of LocalFlags

Value	Description
LMEM_DISCARDABLE	This block may be discarded
LMEM_DISCARDED	This block has been discarded

Table D-82 Values of LocalFlags

LocalFree

This function frees the local memory block named in the hMem argument. Table D-83 lists the argument of LocalFree.

```
Declare Function LocalFree Lib "Kernel" (ByVal hMem As Integer) As Integer
```

Argument	Description
hMem	The local memory block to free

Table D-83 Argument of LocalFree

LocalHandle

This function provides the handle of the local memory object with the segment address indicated in the wMem argument. Table D-84 lists the argument of LocalHandle.

```
Declare Function LocalHandle Lib "Kernel" (ByVal wMem As Integer) As Integer
```

Argument	Description
wMem	The segment address or selector of the global memory object

Table D-84 Argument of LocalHandle

LocalInit

This function initializes a local heap in the segment set in the wSegment argument. Table D-85 lists the arguments of LocalInit.

```
Declare Function LocalInit Lib "Kernel" (ByVal wSegment As Integer, ByVal pStart As
Integer, ByVal pEnd As Integer) As Integer
```

Argument	Description
wSegment	The segment address of the segment that contains the local heap
pStart	The starting address of the local heap
pEnd	The ending address of the local heap

Table D-85 Arguments of LocalInit

LocalLock

This function provides the pointer to the local memory object in the hMem argument. Table D-86 lists the argument of LocalLock.

```
Declare Function LocalLock Lib "Kernel" (ByVal hMem As Integer) As Integer '(returns a
near pointer)
```

Argument	Description
hMem	The local memory block to be locked

Table D-86 Argument of LocalLock

LocalReAlloc

This function increases or decreases the number of bytes of the local memory block in the hMem argument to the amount set in the dwBytes argument. Table D-87 lists the arguments of LocalReAlloc; Table D-88 lists the values.

```
Declare Function LocalReAlloc Lib "Kernel" (ByVal hMem As Integer, ByVal wBytes As
Integer, ByVal wFlags As Integer) As Integer
```

Argument	Description
hMem	The local memory block to reallocate
dwBytes	New size of the local memory block
wFlags	The value of this argument indicates how to reallocate the local memory block according to Table D-88

Table D-87 Arguments of LocalReAlloc

Value	Description
LMEM_DISCARDABLE	Memory may be discarded
LMEM_MODIFY	Memory flags are modified but the local memory is not reallocated
LMEM_MOVEABLE	Memory is moveable
LMEM_NOCOMPACT	Memory may not be compacted or discarded
LMEM_NODISCARD	Memory may not be discarded
LMEM_ZEROINIT	If the block is increased in size, additional memory is initialized to 0

Table D-88 Values of LocalReAlloc

LocalShrink

This function shrinks the heap named in the hSeg argument to the size in the wSize argument. Table D-89 lists the arguments of LocalShrink.

```
Declare Function LocalShrink Lib "Kernel" (ByVal hSeg As Integer, ByVal wSize As Integer)
As Integer
```

Argument	Description
hSeg	The segment that contains the local heap
wSize	The desired size for the local heap

Table D-89 Arguments of LocalShrink

LocalSize

This function finds the current size in bytes of the local memory block named in the hMem argument. Table D-90 lists the argument of LocalSize.

```
Declare Function LocalSize Lib "Kernel" (ByVal hMem As Integer) As Integer
```

Argument	Description
hMem	The local memory block

Table D-90 Argument of LocalSize

LocalUnlock

This function unlocks the local memory block named in the hMem argument. Table D-91 lists the argument of LocalUnlock.

```
Declare Function LocalUnlock Lib "Kernel" (ByVal hMem As Integer) As Integer
```

Argument	Description
hMem	The local memory block to be unlocked

Table D-91 Argument of LocalUnlock

Locksegment

This function locks the segment identified by its address in the wSegment argument. Table D-92 lists the argument of Locksegment.

```
Declare Function LockSegment Lib "Kernel" (ByVal wSegment As Integer) As Integer
```

Argument	Description
wSegment	The address of the segment to be locked

Table D-92 Argument of Locksegment

SetSwapAreaSize

This function raises the amount of memory that an application may utilize for its code segments. Table D-93 lists the argument of SetSwapAreaSize.

```
Declare Function SetSwapAreaSize Lib "Kernel" (ByVal rsSize As Integer) As Long
```

Argument	Description
rsSize	The number of 16-byte paragraphs asked for by the application for use as a code segment

Table D-93 Argument of SetSwapAreaSize

SwitchStackBack

This function determines the current stack of the task's data segment.

```
Declare Sub SwitchStackBack Lib "Kernel" ()
```

SwitchStackTo

This function changes the stack of a current task to another data segment. Table D-94 lists the arguments of SwitchStackTo.

```
Declare Sub SwitchStackTo Lib "Kernel" (ByVal wStackSegment As Integer, ByVal
wStackPointer As Integer, ByVal wStackTop As Integer)
```

Argument	Description
wStackSegment	Data segment that will contain the stack
wStackPointer	The offset of the beginning of the stack
wStackTop	The offset of the top of the stack from the beginning of the stack

Table D-94 Arguments of SwitchStackTo

UnlockSegment

This function unlocks a specified data segment. Table D-95 lists the argument of UnlockSegment.

```
Declare Function UnlockSegment Lib "Kernel" (ByVal wSegment As Integer) As Integer
```

Argument	Description
wSegment	The segment address

Table D-95 Argument of UnlockSegment

Memory Management Definitions in CONSTANT.TXT

```
Global Const WF_PMODE = &H1
Global Const WF_CPU286 = &H2
Global Const WF_CPU386 = &H4
Global Const WF_CPU486 = &H8
Global Const WF_STANDARD = &H10
Global Const WF_WIN286 = &H10
Global Const WF_ENHANCED = &H20
Global Const WF_WIN386 = &H20
Global Const WF_CPU086 = &H40
Global Const WF_CPU186 = &H80
Global Const WF_LARGEFRAME = &H100
Global Const WF_SMALLFRAME = &H200
Global Const WF_80x87 = &H400
Global Const GMEM_FIXED = &H0
Global Const GMEM_MOVEABLE = &H2
Global Const GMEM_NOCOMPACT = &H10
Global Const GMEM_NODISCARD = &H20
Global Const GMEM_ZEROINIT = &H40
Global Const GMEM_MODIFY = &H80
Global Const GMEM_DISCARDABLE = &H100
```

(continued on next page)

(continued from previous page)

```
Global Const GMEM_NOT_BANKED = &H1000
Global Const GMEM_SHARE = &H2000
Global Const GMEM_DDESHARE = &H2000
Global Const GMEM_NOTIFY = &H4000
Global Const GMEM_LOWER = GMEM_NOT_BANKED
Global Const GHND = (GMEM_MOVEABLE Or GMEM_ZEROINIT)
Global Const GPTR = (GMEM_FIXED Or GMEM_ZEROINIT)
Global Const GMEM_DISCARDED = &H4000
Global Const GMEM_LOCKCOUNT = &HFF
Global Const LMEM_FIXED = &H0
Global Const LMEM_MOVEABLE = &H2
Global Const LMEM_NOCOMPACT = &H10
Global Const LMEM_NODISCARD = &H20
Global Const LMEM_ZEROINIT = &H40
Global Const LMEM_MODIFY = &H80
Global Const LMEM_DISCARDABLE = &HF00
Global Const LHND = (LMEM_MOVEABLE+LMEM_ZEROINIT)
Global Const LPTR = (LMEM_FIXED+LMEM_ZEROINIT)
Global Const NONZEROLHND = (LMEM_MOVEABLE)
Global Const NONZEROLPTR = (LMEM_FIXED)
Global Const LNOTIFY_OUTOFMEM = 0
Global Const LNOTIFY_MOVE = 1

Global Const LNOTIFY_DISCARD = 2
```

MODULE-MANAGEMENT FUNCTIONS

FreeLibrary

This function reduces the reference count of the loaded library module. Table D-96 lists the argument of FreeLibrary.

```
Declare Sub FreeLibrary Lib "Kernel" (ByVal hLibModule As Integer)
```

Argument	Description
hLibModule	The loaded library module

Table D-96 Argument of FreeLibrary

FreeModule

This function reduces the reference count of the loaded module by one. Table D-97 lists the argument of FreeModule.

```
Declare Sub FreeModule Lib "Kernel" (ByVal hModule As Integer)
```

Argument	Description
hModule	The loaded module

Table D-97 Argument of FreeModule

GetInstanceData

This function tramsmits data from another instance of an application into the data area of the present instance. Table D-98 lists the arguments of GetInstanceData.

```
Declare Function GetInstanceData Lib "Kernel" (ByVal hInstance As Integer, ByVal pData As
Integer, ByVal nCount As Integer) As Integer
```

Argument	Description
hInstance	Previous call of the application
pData	Buffer in the present instance
nCount	Number of bytes to transmit

Table D-98 Arguments of GetInstanceData

GetModuleFileName

This function finds the full path name of the executable file from which a module is loaded. Table D-99 lists the arguments of GetModuleFileName.

```
Declare Function GetModuleFileName Lib "Kernel" (ByVal hModule As Integer, ByVal
lpFilename As String, ByVal nSize As Integer) As Integer
```

Argument	Description
hModule	The module or instance of the module
lpFileName	The buffer to receive the file name
nSize	The maximum number of characters to transmit

Table D-99 Arguments of GetModuleFileName

GetModuleHandle

This function obtains the handle of the module named in the lpModuleName argument. Table D-100 lists the argument of GetModuleHandle.

```
Declare Function GetModuleHandle Lib "Kernel" (ByVal lpModuleName As String) As Integer
```

Argument	Description
lpModuleName	Name of the module

Table D-100 Argument of GetModuleHandle

GetModuleUsage

This function provides the reference count of an indicated module. Table D-101 lists the argument of GetModuleUsage.

```
Declare Function GetModuleUsage Lib "Kernel" (ByVal hModule As Integer) As Integer
```

Argument	Description
hModule	The Module or instance of the module

Table D-101 Argument of GetModuleUsage

GetVersion

This function returns the current version of Windows.

```
Declare Function GetVersion Lib "Kernel" () As Integer
```

LoadLibrary

This function loads the library module indicated by the lpLibFileName argument. Table D-102 lists the argument of LoadLibrary.

```
Declare Function LoadLibrary Lib "Kernel" (ByVal lpLibFileName As String) As Integer
```

Argument	Description
lpLibFileName	The name of the library to load

Table D-102 Argument of LoadLibrary

OPTIMIZATION-TOOL FUNCTIONS

ProfClear

This function removes all of the samples in the sampling buffer when the Microsoft Windows Profiler is running.

```
Declare Sub ProfClear Lib "User" ()
```

ProfFinish

This function stops sampling and flushes the output buffer to disk when the Microsoft Windows Profiler is running.

```
Declare Sub ProfFinish Lib "User" ()
```

ProfFlush

This function flushes the sampling buffer to disk when the Microsoft Windows Profiler is running.

```
Declare Sub ProfFlush Lib "User" ()
```

ProfInsChk

This function checks if the Microsoft Windows Profile is running.

```
Declare Function ProfInsChk Lib "User" () As Integer
```

ProfSampRate

This function determines the rate of code sampling when Microsoft Windows is running. Table D-103 lists the arguments of ProfSampRate; Table D-104 lists the values.

```
Declare Sub ProfSampRate Lib "User" (ByVal nRate286 As Integer, ByVal nRate386 As Integer)
```

Argument	Description
nRate286	Indicates the sampling rate of Profiler when the application is running in standard or real mode
nRate386	Indicates the sampling rate of Profiler when the application is running in 386 enhanced mode

Table D-103 Arguments of ProfSampRate

Value	Sampling Rate
1	1.22.070 microseconds
2	244.141 microseconds
3	488.281 microseconds
4	976.562 microseconds
5	1.953125 milliseconds
6	3.90625 milliseconds
7	7.8125 milliseconds
8	15.625 milliseconds
9	31.25 milliseconds
10	62.5 milliseconds
11	125 milliseconds
12	250 milliseconds
13	500 milliseconds

Table D-104 Values of ProfSampRate

ProfSetup

This function specifies the size of the output buffer when the Microsoft Windows Profiler is running under 386 enhanced mode. Table D-105 lists the arguments of ProfSetup.

```
Declare Sub ProfSetup Lib "User" (ByVal nBufferSize As Integer, ByVal nSamples As Integer)
```

Argument	Description
nBufferSize	Size of the ouput buffer in kilobytes
nSamples	How much sampling data Profiler writes to disk (0 indicates unlimited)

Table D-105 Arguments of ProfSetup

ProfStart

This function starts sampling when running Microsoft Windows Profiler.

```
Declare Sub ProfStart Lib "User" ()
```

ProfStop

This function stops sampling when running Microsoft Windows Profiler.

```
Declare Sub ProfStop Lib "User" ()
```

SwapRecording

If Microsoft Windows Swap is running, then this function begins or ends analyzing swapping behavior. Table D-106 lists the arguments of SwapRecording; Table D-107 lists the values.

```
Declare Sub SwapRecording Lib "Kernel" (ByVal wFlag As Integer)
```

Argument	Description
wFlag	Indicates whether to start or stop the Swap analysis

Table D-106 Argument of SwapRecording

Value	Description
0	Tells Swap to stop analyzing
1	Stores Swap calls, discards swap returns
2	Stores Swap calls, records a large amount of data

Table D-107 Values of SwapRecording

RESOURCE-MANAGEMENT FUNCTIONS

AccessResource

This function returns the DOS file handle for the file indentified by the hInstance and hResInfo arguments. Table D-108 lists the arguments of AccessResource.

```
Declare Function AccessResource Lib "Kernel" (ByVal hInstance As Integer, ByVal hResInfo
As Integer) As Integer
```

Argument	Description
hInstance	Executable file that contains the resource
hResInfo	Identifies the resource (handle created with FindResource)

Table D-108 Arguments of AccessResource

AllocResource

This function identifies the global memory block to allocate for a resource. Table D-109 lists the arguments of AllocResource.

```
Declare Function AllocResource Lib "Kernel" (ByVal hInstance As Integer, ByVal hResInfo As
Integer, ByVal dwSize As Long) As Integer
```

Argument	Description
hInstance	Executable file that contains the resource
hResInfo	Indentifies a resource
dwSize	Minimum size in bytes

Table D-109 Arguments of AllocResource

FindResource

This function returns the location of a resource file. Table D-110 lists the arguments of FindResource; Table D-111 lists the values.

```
Declare Function FindResource Lib "Kernel" (ByVal hInstance As Integer, ByVal lpName As
String, ByVal lpType As Any) As Integer
```

Argument	Description
hInstance	Executable file that contains the resource
lpName	Null-terminated string that represents the name of the resource
lpType	Null-terminated string that stands for the type of resource. Table D-111 contains predefined types

Table D-110 Arguments of FindResource

Value	Description
RT_ACCELERATOR	Accelerator table
RT_BITMAP	Bitmap resource
RT_DIALOG	Dialog box
RT_FONT	Font resource
RT_FONTDIR	Font directory resource

(continued on next page)

1511

(continued from previous page)

Value	Description
RT_MENU	Menu resource
RT_RCDATA	User-defined resource

Table D-111 Values of FindResource

FreeResource

This function returns a Boolean value that indicates whether a resource is successfully removed from memory. Table D-112 lists the argument of FreeResource.

```
Declare Function FreeResource Lib "Kernel" (ByVal hResData As Integer) As Integer
```

Argument	Type	Description
hResData	Handle	Identifies the resource to be removed from memory

Table D-112 Argument of FreeResource

LoadAccelerators

This function returns a Boolean value that indicates whether an accelerator table is successfully loaded. Table D-113 lists the arguments of LoadAccelerators.

```
Declare Function LoadAccelerators Lib "User" (ByVal hInstance As Integer, ByVal
lpTableName As String) As Integer
```

Argument	Type	Description
hInstance	Handle	Executable file that contains an accelerator table
lpTableName	String	Null-terminated string that names an accelerator table

Table D-113 Arguments of LoadAccelerators

1512

LoadBitmap

This function loads the bitmap resource named by the lpBitmapName contained within the executable file named in hInstance. Table D-114 lists the arguments of LoadBitmap.

```
Declare Function LoadBitmap Lib "User" (ByVal hInstance As Integer, ByVal lpBitmapName As
Any) As Integer
```

Argument	Type	Description
hInstance	Handle	Executable file that contains the bitmap
lpBitmapName	String	Null-terminated string that names a bitmap

Table D-114 Arguments of LoadBitmap

LoadCursor

This function loads the cursor resource named by the lpCursorName contained within the executable file named in hInstance. Table D-115 lists the arguments of LoadCursor, Table D-116 lists the values.

```
Declare Function LoadCursor Lib "User" (ByVal hInstance As Integer, ByVal lpCursorName As
Any) As Integer
```

Argument	Type	Description
hInstance	Handle	Executable file that contains the cursor resource
lpCursorName	String	Null-terminated string that names the cursor resource

Table D-115 Arguments of LoadCursor

Value	Description
IDC_ARROW	Default arrow cursor
IDC_CROSS	Crosshair cursor

(continued on next page)

(continued from previous page)

Value	Description
IDC_IBEAM	Text I-beam cursor
IDC_ICON	Empty icon
IDC_SIZE	Square with a smaller square inside its lower-right corner
IDC_SIZENESW	Double-pointed cursor with arrows pointing northeast and southwest
IDC_SIZENS	Double-pointed cursor with arrows pointing north and south
IDC_SIZENWSE	Double-pointed cursor with arrows pointing northwest and southeast
IDC_SIZEWE	Double-pointed cursor with arrows pointing west and east
IDC_UPARROW	Vertical arrow cursor
IDC_WAIT	Hourglass cursor

Table D-116 Values of LoadCursor

LoadIcon

This function loads the icon resource named by the lpIconName contained within the executable file indicated in hInstance. Table D-117 lists the arguments of LoadIcon; Table D-118 lists the values.

```
Declare Function LoadIcon Lib "User" (ByVal hInstance As Integer, ByVal lpIconName As Any)
As Integer
```

Argument	Description
hInstance	Executable file that contains the icon resource
lpIconName	Null-terminated string that names the icon resource

Table D-117 Arguments of LoadIcon

Value	Description
IDI_APPLICATION	Default application icon
IDI_ASTERISK	Asterisk
IDI_EXCLAMATION	Exclamation point
IDI_HAND	Hand-shaped icon
IDI_QUESTION	Question mark

Table D-118 Values of LoadIcon

LoadMenu

This function loads the menu resource named by the lpMenuName contained within the executable file indicated in hInstance. Table D-119 lists the arguments of LoadMenu.

```
Declare Function LoadMenu Lib "User" (ByVal hInstance As Integer, ByVal lpString As
String) As Integer
```

Argument	Description
hInstance	Executable file that contains the menu resource
lpMenuName	Null-terminated string that names the menu resource

Table D-119 Arguments of LoadMenu

LoadResource

This function loads the resource identified by the hResInfo argument. Table D-120 lists the arguments of LoadResource.

```
Declare Function LoadResource Lib "Kernel" (ByVal hInstance As Integer, ByVal hResInfo As
Integer) As Integer
```

Argument	Description
hInstance	Executable file that contains the resource
hResInfo	Identifies the desired resource

Table D-120 Arguments of LoadResource

LoadString

This function loads the sting resource identified in the wID argument. Table D-121 lists the arguments of LoadString.

```
Declare Function LoadString Lib "User" (ByVal hInstance As Integer, ByVal wID As Integer,
ByVal lpBuffer As Any, ByVal nBufferMax As Integer) As Integer
```

Argument	Description
hInstance	Executable file that contains the resource
wID	Indicates the integer identifier of the string
lpBuffer	Buffer to receive the string
nBufferMax	Maximum size of the buffer

Table D-121 Arguments of LoadString

LockResource

This function retrieves the absolute memory address of the resource identified in the hResData argument. Table D-122 lists the argument of LockResource.

```
Declare Function LockResource Lib "Kernel" (ByVal hResData As Integer) As Long
```

Argument	Description
hResData	Identifies the desired resource

Table D-122 Argument of LockResource

SetResourceHandler

This function sets up a function to load resources. Table D-123 lists the arguments of SetResourceHandler.

```
Declare Function SetResourceHandler Lib "Kernel" (ByVal hInstance As Integer, ByVal lpType
As Any, ByVal lpLoadFunc As Any) As Integer
```

Argument	Description
hInstance	Executable file that contains the resource
lpType	A short integer that indicates a resource type
lpLoadFunc	The procedure-instance address of the application-supplied callback function

Table D-123 Arguments of SetResourceHandler

SizeofResource

This function determines the size in bytes of the resource identified in the hInstance argument. Table D-124 lists the arguments of SizeofResource.

```
Declare Function SizeofResource Lib "Kernel" (ByVal hInstance As Integer, ByVal hResInfo
As Integer) As Integer
```

Argument	Description
hInstance	Executable file that contains the resource
hResInfo	Identifies the desired resource

Table D-124 Arguments of SizeofResource

UnlockResource

This function unlocks the resource named in the hResData argument. Table D-125 lists the argument of UnlockResource.

```
Declare Function UnlockResource Lib "Kernel" Alias "GlobalUnlock" (ByVal hMem As Integer)
As Integer
```

Argument	Description
hResData	This identifies the global memory block to be unlocked

Table D-125 Argument of UnlockResource

Resources Definitions in CONSTANT.TXT

```
Global Const RT_CURSOR = 1&
Global Const RT_BITMAP = 2&
Global Const RT_ICON = 3&
Global Const RT_MENU = 4&
Global Const RT_DIALOG = 5&
Global Const RT_STRING = 6&
Global Const RT_FONTDIR = 7&
Global Const RT_FONT = 8&
Global Const RT_ACCELERATOR = 9&
Global Const RT_RCDATA = 10&
Global Const IDC_ARROW = 32512&
Global Const IDC_IBEAM = 32513&
Global Const IDC_WAIT = 32514&
Global Const IDC_CROSS = 32515&
Global Const IDC_UPARROW = 32516&
Global Const IDC_SIZE = 32640&
Global Const IDC_ICON = 32641&
Global Const IDC_SIZENWSE = 32642&
Global Const IDC_SIZENESW = 32643&
Global Const IDC_SIZEWE = 32644&
Global Const IDC_SIZENS = 32645&
Global Const IDI_APPLICATION = 32512&
Global Const IDI_HAND = 32513&
Global Const IDI_QUESTION = 32514&
Global Const IDI_EXCLAMATION = 32515&
Global Const IDI_ASTERISK = 32516&
```

SEGMENT FUNCTIONS

AllocDStoCSAlias

This function accepts a data-segment selector and provides a code-segment selector. Table D-126 lists the argument of AllocDStoCSAlias.

```
Declare Function AllocDStoCSAlias Lib "Kernel" (ByVal wSelector As Integer) As Integer
```

Argument	Description
wSelector	The data-segment selector

Table D-126 Argument of AllocDstoCSAIias

AllocSelector

This function sets up a new selector. Table D-127 lists the arguments of AllocSelector.

```
Declare Function AllocSelector Lib "Kernel" (ByVal wSelector As Integer) As Integer
```

Argument	Description
hInstance	Executable file that contains the resource
hResInfo	The indicated resource
dwSize	Identifies the size in bytes to allocate for a resource

Table D-127 Arguments of AllocSelector

ChangeSelector

This function creates a temporary code selector that corresponds to a specific data selector. Table D-128 lists the arguments of ChangeSelector.

```
Declare Function ChangeSelector Lib "Kernel" (ByVal wDestSelector As Integer, ByVal wSourceSelector As Integer) As Integer
```

Argument	Description
wDestSelector	A previously allocated selector
wSource	The selector to change

Table D-128 Arguments of ChangeSelector

FreeSelector

This function frees a previously allocated selector. Table D-129 lists the argument of FreeSelector.

```
Declare Function FreeSelector Lib "Kernel" (ByVal wSelector As Integer) As Integer
```

Argument	Description
wSelector	The selector to be freed

Table D-129 Argument of FreeSelector

GlobalFix

This function stops a global memory block from moving in linear memory. Table D-130 lists the argument of GlobalFix.

```
Declare Sub GlobalFix Lib "Kernel" (ByVal hMem As Integer)
```

Argument	Description
hMem	The global memory block

Table D-130 Argument of GlobalFix

GlobalPageLock

This function page-locks the memory connected with a global selector and increases its page-lock count. Table D-131 lists the argument of GlobalPageLock.

```
Declare Function GlobalPageLock Lib "Kernel" (ByVal wSelector As Integer) As Integer
```

Argument	Description
wSelector	The memory selector to be page-locked

Table D-131 Argument of GlobalPageLock

GlobalPageUnlock

This function reduces the page-lock count for a block of memory. Table D-132 lists the argument of GlobalPageUnlock.

```
Declare Function GlobalPageUnlock Lib "Kernel" (ByVal wSelector As Integer) As Integer
```

Argument	Description
wSelector	The memory selector to be page-unlocked

Table D-132 Argument of GlobalPageUnlock

GlobalUnfix

This function unlocks a global memory block. Table D-133 lists the argument of GlobalUnfix.

```
Declare Function GlobalUnfix Lib "Kernel" (ByVal hMem As Integer) As Integer
```

Argument	Description
hMem	The global memory block to be unlocked

Table D-133 Argument of GlobalUnfix

LockSegment

This function locks a segment in memory. Table D-134 lists the argument of LockSegment.

```
Declare Function LockSegment Lib "Kernel" (ByVal wSegment As Integer) As Integer
```

Argument	Description
wSegment	Address of the segment to be locked

Table D-134 Argument of LockSegment

UnlockSegment

This function unlocks a segment of memory. Table D-135 lists the argument of UnlockSegment.

```
Declare Function UnlockSegment Lib "Kernel" (ByVal wSegment As Integer) As Integer
```

Argument	Description
wSegment	Address of the segment to be unlocked

Table D-135 Argument of UnlockSegment

SOUND FUNCTIONS

CloseSound

This function closes access to the sound device and makes it available for other applications.

```
Declare Sub CloseSound Lib "Sound" ()
```

CountVoiceNotes

This function returns the number of notes in the nVoice queue. Table D-136 lists the argument of CountVoiceNotes.

```
Declare Function CountVoiceNotes Lib "Sound" (ByVal nVoice As Integer) As Integer
```

Argument	Description
nVoice	The voice queue to be counted (first voice is one)

Table D-136 Argument of CountVoiceNotes

GetThresholdEvent

This function obtains a flag that identifies a threshold event.

```
Declare Function GetThresholdEvent Lib "Sound" () As Integer
```

GetThresholdStatus

This function obtains the status of the threshold event for each voice.

```
Declare Function GetThresholdStatus Lib "Sound" () As Integer
```

OpenSound

This function opens the sound device and prevents any other applications from utilizing it.

```
Declare Function OpenSound Lib "Sound" () As Integer
```

SetSoundNoise

This function determines the source (nSource) and duration of the noise hardware of the sound device. Table D-137 lists the arguments of SetSoundNoise; Table D-138 lists the values.

```
Declare Function SetSoundNoise Lib "Sound" (ByVal nSource As Integer, ByVal nDuration As
Integer) As Integer
```

Argument	Description
nSource	Noise source can be any of the values in Table D-138
nDuration	Duration of the noise

Table D-137 Arguments of SetSoundNoise

Value	Description
S_PERIOD512	Frequency N/512
S_PERIOD1024	Frequency N/1024
S_PERIOD2048	Frequency N/2048
S_PERIODVOICE	Frequency from voice channel

(continued on next page)

(continued from previous page)

Value	Description
S_WHITE512	Frequency N/512
S_WHITE1024	Frequency N/1024
S_WHITE2048	Frequency N/2048
S_WHITEVOICE	Frequency from voice channel

Table D-138 Values of SetSoundNoise

SetVoiceAccent

This function puts an accent in the voice queue. An accent consists of a combination of tempo (nTempo), volume (nVolume), mode (nMode), and pitch (nPitch). Table D-139 lists the arguments of SetVoiceAccent; Table D-140 lists the descriptions of nMode values; and Table D-141 lists returned values.

```
Declare Function SetVoiceAccent Lib "Sound" (ByVal nVoice As Integer, ByVal nTempo As
Integer, ByVal nVolume As Integer, ByVal nMode As Integer, ByVal nPitch As Integer) As
Integer
```

Argument	Description
nVoice	Voice queue (first voice queue is one)
nTempo	Number of quarter notes played per minute (32-255, Default 120)
nVolume	Volume level (0 low to 255 high)
nMode	One of the values in Table D-140
nPitch	Pitch of the notes played (0 to 83)

Table D-139 Arguments of SetVoiceAccent

nMod Values	Description
S_LEGATO	Note is of full duration and blends with next note
S_NORMAL	Note is of full duration and stops before next note
S_STACCATO	Note is only partially held creating a stop between it and the next note

Table D-140 Descriptions of nMode Values

Returned Values	Description
S_SERDMD	Invalid mode
S_SERDTP	Invalid tempo
S_SERDVL	Invalid volume
S_SERQFUL	Queue full

Table D-141 Descriptions of returned values

SetVoiceEnvelope

This function puts the Voice envelope (wave shape and repeat counts) in the voice queue. Table D-142 lists the arguments of SetVoiceEnvelope.

```
Declare Function SetVoiceEnvelope Lib "Sound" (ByVal nVoice As Integer, ByVal nShape As
Integer, ByVal nRepeat As Integer) As Integer
```

Argument	Description
nVoice	Voice queue
nShape	Index to OEM wave-shape table
nRepeat	Number of times to repeat the wave shape during one note

Table D-142 Arguments of SetVoiceEnvelope

SetVoiceNote

This function places a note in the voice queue with the qualities indicated in the nValue, nLength, and nCdots arguments. Table D-142 lists the arguments of SetVoiceNote; Table D-143 lists returned values.

```
Declare Function SetVoiceNote Lib "Sound" (ByVal nVoice As Integer, ByVal nValue As
Integer, ByVal nLength As Integer, ByVal nCdots As Integer) As Integer
```

Argument	Description
nVoice	Voice queue
nValue	Contains a value between 1 and 84 representing the seven octaves
nLength	Reciprocal of the duration of the note. 1 is whole note, 2 is half note, and 4 is quarter note
nCdots	Duration of note in dots

Table D-143 Arguments of SetVoiceNote

Returned Value	Description
S_SERDCC	Dot count incorrect
S_SERDLN	Note length incorrect
S_SERDNT	Note incorrect
S_SERQFUL	Full queue

Table D-144 Description of returned values

SetVoiceQueueSize

This function sets up a queue named nVoice in the size indicated by the nBytes argument. The default value is 192 bytes. Table D-145 lists the arguments of SetVoiceQueueSize; Table D-146 lists returned values.

```
Declare Function SetVoiceQueueSize Lib "Sound" (ByVal nVoice As Integer, ByVal nBytes As
Integer) As Integer
```

Argument	Description
nVoice	Voice queue
nBytes	Number of bytes in the queue

Table D-145 Arguments of SetVoiceQueueSize

Returned Values	Description
S_SERMACT	Active music
S_SEROFM	Not enough memory

Table D-146 Description of returned values

SetVoiceSound

This function stores the sound frequency and duration in the voice queue named by the nVoice argument. Table D-147 lists the arguments of SetVoiceSound.

```
Declare Function SetVoiceSound Lib "Sound" (ByVal nVoice As Integer, ByVal lFrequency As
Long, ByVal nDuration As Integer) As Integer
```

Argument	Description
nVoice	Voice queue
lFrequency	Frequency of the sound
nDuration	Duration of the sound (measured in clock ticks)

Table D-147 Arguments of SetVoiceSound

SetVoiceThreshold

This function determines the voice threshold of a voice queue named in the nVoice argument. When the number of notes in the queue falls below the number in the nNotes argument, the threshold flag is set. Table D-148 lists the arguments of SetVoiceThreshold.

```
Declare Function SetVoiceThreshold Lib "Sound" (ByVal nVoice As Integer, ByVal nNotes As
Integer) As Integer
```

Argument	Description
nVoice	Voice queue
nNotes	Threshold level in number of notes

Table D-148 Arguments of SetVoiceThreshold

StartSound

This function starts to play each voice queue. The contents of the voice queues are not erased by this function and can be played any number of times.

```
Declare Function StartSound Lib "Sound" () As Integer
```

StopSound

This function stops the playing of the voice queues. The contents of each voice queue are flushed and the sound driver is turned off.

```
Declare Function StopSound Lib "Sound" () As Integer
```

SyncAllVoices

This function places a sync mark in each queue. The sync mark has the effect of turning off the voice until sync marks are found in all of the other queues.

```
Declare Function SyncAllVoices Lib "Sound" () As Integer
```

WaitSoundState

This function pauses until the sound driver enters the state indicated in the nState argument. Table D-149 lists the arguments of WaitSoundState.

```
Declare Function WaitSoundState Lib "Sound" (ByVal nState As Integer) As Integer
```

Value	Description
S_ALLTHRESHOLD	Each voice queue is at threshold
S_QUEUEEMPTY	Each voice queue is empty and its sound drivers are off
S_THRESHOLD	Voice queue reaches threshold and restores voice

Table D-149 Values for WaitSoundState

Sound Declarations in CONSTANT.TXT

```
Global Const S_QUEUEEMPTY = 0
Global Const S_THRESHOLD = 1
Global Const S_ALLTHRESHOLD = 2
Global Const S_NORMAL = 0
Global Const S_LEGATO = 1
Global Const S_STACCATO = 2
Global Const S_PERIOD512 = 0
Global Const S_PERIOD1024 = 1
Global Const S_PERIOD2048 = 2
Global Const S_PERIODVOICE = 3
Global Const S_WHITE512 = 4
Global Const S_WHITE1024 = 5
Global Const S_WHITE2048 = 6
Global Const S_WHITEVOICE = 7
Global Const S_SERDVNA = (-1)
Global Const S_SEROFM = (-2)
Global Const S_SERMACT = (-3)
Global Const S_SERQFUL = (-4)
Global Const S_SERBDNT = (-5)
Global Const S_SERDLN = (-6)
Global Const S_SERDCC = (-7)
Global Const S_SERDTP = (-8)
Global Const S_SERDVL = (-9)
Global Const S_SERDMD = (-10)
Global Const S_SERDSH = (-11)
Global Const S_SERDPT = (-12)
Global Const S_SERDFQ = (-13)
Global Const S_SERDDR = (-14)
Global Const S_SERDSR = (-15)
Global Const S_SERDST = (-16)
```

STRING-MANUIPULATION FUNCTIONS

AnsiLower

This function converts the character string named in the lpString argument into lowercase. Table D-150 lists the argument of AnsiLower.

```
Declare Function AnsiLower Lib "User" (ByVal lpString As String) As Long
```

Argument	Description
lpString	Character string to convert

Table D-150 Argument of AnsiLower

AnsiLowerBuff

This function converts a character string in a buffer named in the lpString to lowercase. Table D-151 lists the arguments of AnsiLowerBuff.

```
Declare Function AnsiLowerBuff Lib "User" (ByVal lpString As String, ByVal aWORD As
Integer) As Integer
```

Argument	Description
lpString	Buffer containing the character string
nLength	Number of characters in the buffer (0 represents 64K)

Table D-151 Arguments of AnsiLowerBuff

AnsiNext

This function changes the pointer in a character string to the next character. Table D-152 lists the argument of AnsiNext.

```
Declare Function AnsiNext Lib "User" (ByVal lpString As String) As Long
```

Argument	Description
lpCurrentChar	Indicates a character in a string

Table D-152 Argument of AnsiNext

AnsiPrev

This function changes the pointer in a character string to the previous character. Table D-153 lists the arguments of AnsiPrev.

```
Declare Function AnsiPrev Lib "User" (ByVal lpString As String, ByVal lpString As String)
As Long
```

Argument	Description
lpStart	Points to the start of the string
lpCurrentChar	Indicates a character in a string

Table D-153 Arguments of AnsiPrev

AnsiToOem

This function changes the string named in the lpAnsiStr argument from the ANSI character set to an OEM-defined character set. Table D-154 lists the arguments of AnsiToOem.

```
Declare Function AnsiToOem Lib "Keyboard" (ByVal lpAnsiStr As String, ByVal lpOemStr As
String) As Integer
```

Argument	Description
lpAnsiStr	String to convert
lpOemStr	Indicates the place to put the newly converted string

Table D-154 Arguments of AnsiToOem

AnsiToOemBuff

This function converts the string in the buffer named in the lpAnsiStr argument from the ANSI character set to an OEM-defined character set. Table D-155 lists the arguments of AnsiToOemBuff.

```
Declare Sub AnsiToOemBuff Lib "Keyboard" (ByVal lpAnsiStr As String, ByVal lpOemStr As
String, ByVal nLength As Integer)
```

Argument	Description
lpAnsiStr	Buffer that holds the character string to convert
lpOemStr	Buffer to put the converted character string into
nLength	Number of characters in the buffer that holds the string to convert

Table D-155 Arguments of AnsiToOemBuff

AnsiUpper

This function changes the character string in the lpString argument to uppercase. Table D-156 lists the argument of AnsiUpper.

```
Declare Function AnsiUpper Lib "User" (ByVal lpString As String) As String
```

Argument	Description
lpString	Character string to be converted

Table D-156 Argument of AnsiUpper

AnsiUpperBuff

This function converts a character string in a buffer named in the lpString to uppercase. Table D-157 lists the arguments of AnsiUpperBuff.

```
Declare Function AnsiUpperBuff Lib "User" (ByVal lpString As String, ByVal aWORD As
Integer) As Integer
```

1532

Argument	Description
lpString	Buffer holding the character string to convert
nLength	Number of characters in the buffer (0 means 64K)

Table D-157 Arguments of AnsiUpperBuff

IsCharAlpha

This function indicates whether the character in the cChar argument is an alphabetical character. Table D-158 lists the argument of IsCharAlpha.

```
Declare Function IsCharAlpha Lib "User" (ByVal cChar As Integer) As Integer
```

Argument	Description
cChar	Character to be checked

Table D-158 Argument of IsCharAlpha

IsCharAlphaNumeric

This function indicates whether a character is alphabetical or numerical. If the return value is True, then the character is alphanumeric. Table D-159 lists the argument of IsCharAlphaNumeric.

```
Declare Function IsCharAlphaNumeric Lib "User" (ByVal cChar As Integer) As Integer
```

Argument	Description
cChar	Character to be tested

Table D-159 Argument of IsCharAlphaNumeric

IsCharLower

This function indicates if a character is lowercase. If the return value is True, then the character is lowercase. Table D-160 lists the argument of IsCharLower.

```
Declare Function IsCharLower Lib "User" (ByVal cChar As Integer) As Integer
```

1533

Argument	Description
cChar	Character to be tested

Table D-160 Argument of IsCharLower

IsCharUpper

This function indicates if a character is uppercase. If the return value is True, then the character is uppercase. Table D-161 lists the argument of IsCharUpper.

```
Declare Function IsCharUpper Lib "User" (ByVal cChar As Integer) As Integer
```

Argument	Description
cChar	Character to be tested

Table D-161 Argument of IsCharUpper

OemToAnsi

This function converts the string in the lpOemStr argument from the OEM-defined character set to the ANSI character set. Table D-162 lists the arguments of OemToAnsi.

```
Declare Function OemToAnsi Lib "Keyboard" (ByVal lpOemStr As String, ByVal lpAnsiStr As
String) As Integer
```

Argument	Description
lpOemStr	Character string to convert
lpAnsiStr	Indicates where to place the newly converted string

Table D-162 Arguments of OemToAnsi

OemToAnsiBuff

This function converts the string in the buffer named in the lpOemStr from the OEM-defined character set to the ANSI character set. Table D-163 lists the arguments of OemToAnsiBuff.

```
Declare Sub OemToAnsiBuff Lib "Keyboard" (ByVal lpOemStr As String, ByVal lpAnsiStr As
String, ByVal nLength as Integer)
```

Argument	Description
lpOemStr	Buffer which contains the string to convert
lpAnsiStr	Location to place the newly converted string
nLength	Number of characters in the lpOemStr buffer

Table D-163 Arguments of OemToAnsiBuff

ToAscii

This function converts the virtual-key code in the wVirtKey argument and the keyboard state set in the lpKeyState argument to ANSI character or characters. Table D-164 lists the arguments of ToAscii.

```
Declare Function ToAscii Lib "Keyboard" (ByVal wVirtKey As Integer, ByVal wScanCode As
Integer, lpKeyState As Any, lpChar As Any, Byval wFlags As Integer) As Integer
```

Argument	Description
wVirtKey	Virtual-key code to be translated
wScanCode	Raw scan code of the key to be converted
lpKeyState	Indicates an array of 256 bytes that identifies the state of the keys on the keyboard
lpChar	Buffer that will receive the ANSI characters
wFlags	Bit 0 flag's menu display

Table D-164 Arguments of ToAscii

TASK FUNCTIONS

Catch

This function makes a copy of the current execution environment and places it in a buffer. Table D-165 lists the argument of Catch.

```
Declare Function Catch Lib "Kernel" (lpCatchBuf As Any) As Integer
```

Argument	Description
lpCatchBuf	Indicates the CATCHBUF structure that will accept the execution environment

Table D-165 Argument of Catch

ExitWindows

This function generates a normal Windows shutdown. Table D-166 lists the arguments of ExitWindows.

```
Declare Function ExitWindows Lib "User" (ByVal dwReserved As Long, wReturnCode) As Integer
```

Argument	Description
dwReserved	Reserved (should be 0)
wReturnCode	Return value to pass to DOS

Table D-166 Arguments of ExitWindows

GetCurrentPDB

This function provides the current DOS Program Data Base (PDB)

```
Declare Function GetCurrentPDB Lib "Kernel" () As Integer
```

GetCurrentTask

This function provides the task handle of the present task.

```
Declare Function GetCurrentTask Lib "Kernel" () As Integer
```

GetDOSEnvironment

This function returns the environment string of the present task.

```
Declare Function GetDOSEnvironment Lib "Kernel" () As Long
```

GetNumTasks

This function provides the number of tasks presently running.

```
Declare Function GetNumTasks Lib "Kernel" () As Integer
```

SetErrorMode

This function determines if Windows controls DOS Function 24H errors or permits the application to control them. Table D-167 lists the argument of SetErrorMode.

```
Declare Function SetErrorMode Lib "Kernel" (ByVal wMode As Integer) As Integer
```

Argument	Description
wMode	Error mode flag

Table D-167 Argument of SetErrorMode

Throw

This function returns the execution environment to the indicated values. Table D-168 lists the arguments of Throw.

```
Declare Sub Throw Lib "Kernel" (lpCatchBuf As Any, ByVal nThrowBack As Integer)
```

Argument	Description
lpCatchBuf	Indicates an array that contains the execution environment
nThrowBack	Indicates the value to be given to the Catch function

Table D-168 Arguments of Throw

Yield

This function stops the present task and begins a waiting task.

```
Declare Sub Yield Lib "Kernel" ()
```

THE API PROJECT

Project Overview

The API project demonstrates how to incorporate Windows API calls into a Visual Basic application. You will learn how to use API calls in Visual Basic applications with an easy and useful set of functions that let you read and write to the WIN.INI file.

Assembling the Project

1. Make a new form with the objects and properties in Table D-169.

Object	Property	Setting
Form	Name	Form1

Table D-169 Settings for the Reference form in the Reference project

2. Enter the following code in the General Declarations section. This code defines the API functions to be used in the API project.

```
Declare Function GetProfileInt Lib "Kernel" (ByVal lpAppName$, ByVal lpKeyName$, ByVal ⇐
    nDefault%) As Integer
Declare Function GetProfileString Lib "Kernel" (ByVal lpAppName$, ByVal lpKeyName$, ByVal
    lpDefault$, ByVal lpReturnedString$, ByVal nSize%) As Integer
Declare Function WriteProfileString Lib "Kernel" (ByVal lpApplicationName$, ByVal ⇐
    lpKeyName$, ByVal lpString$) As Integer

Const APPNAME = "Waite Group - Appendix D"
Dim MyColor As Integer
```

3. Enter the following code in the Form_Load event subroutine. This code triggers at program startup. This code reads the appropriate setup values from the WIN.INI file. It sets the form's size, position, and background color to the last saved values. Note how we carefully declare each variable to exactly match the types given in the declarations in step 2. The GetProfileString function places the

return value in the temp variable. (The value of the function, which is assigned to junk, is *not* the value of the string; rather, it is the length of the string passed to the temp variable.) Notice how we initialize the temp variable to be 16 null characters (ASCII 0) long. This properly sets it up for use as a buffer.

```
Sub Form_Load ()

    Dim temp As String * 16
    Dim junk As Integer

    temp = String$(16, 0)
    junk = GetProfileString(APPNAME, "Left", "1000", temp, 16)
    Me.Left = Val(temp)

    temp = String$(16, 0)
    junk = GetProfileString(APPNAME, "Top", "1000", temp, 16)
    Me.Top = Val(temp)

    temp = String$(16, 0)
    junk = GetProfileString(APPNAME, "Width", "5000", temp, 16)
    Me.Width = Val(temp)

    temp = String$(16, 0)
    junk = GetProfileString(APPNAME, "Height", "3000", temp, 16)
    Me.Height = Val(temp)

    Me.BackColor = QBColor(GetProfileInt(APPNAME, "Color", 1))

End Sub
```

4. Enter the following code in the Form_Unload event subroutine. This code triggers when the form is unloaded from memory and saves the settings of the form's size, position, and background color.

```
Sub Form_Unload (Cancel As Integer)

    Dim junk As Integer

    junk = WriteProfileString(APPNAME, "Left", Str$(Me.Left))
    junk = WriteProfileString(APPNAME, "Top", Str$(Me.Top))
    junk = WriteProfileString(APPNAME, "Width", Str$(Me.Width))
    junk = WriteProfileString(APPNAME, "Height", Str$(Me.Height))
    junk = WriteProfileString(APPNAME, "Color", Str$(MyColor))

End Sub
```

5. Enter the following code in the Form_Click event. This increments the form's background color.

1539

```
Sub Form_Click ()
    MyColor = (MyColor + 1) Mod 15
    Me.BackColor = QBColor(MyColor)

End Sub
```

How It Works

This project demonstrates the use of API calls with a simple but useful set of functions. Many programs need to save certain settings from session to session. The Windows API provides several functions that save you from having to write tedious ASCII file parsing routines.

These functions read and write to *.INI files. The three functions illustrated in this project (WriteProfileString, GetProfileString, and GetProfileInt) all read from and write to the WIN.INI file. This file is in the Windows directory and serves as a "master" initialization file for many applications. You may also wish to use three related functions to read and write to a separate, private INI file: WritePrivateProfileString, GetPrivateProfileString, and GetPrivateProfileInt.

All INI files share a common format. They are all ASCII text, and can be edited and viewed by simple text editors and utilities as well as by Windows programs. Each INI file can have multiple sections, with many different named parameters in each section. Each section has a header enclosed in square brackets, and the section continues until the end of the file or until a new section header is encountered. Each parameter is identified by a keyword, followed by an equal sign. The actual data lies to the right of the equal sign. The following listing shows the individual section written and read by this chapter's project:

```
[Waite Group - Appendix D]
Left= 6108
Top= 5040
Width= 1056
Height= 2436
Color= 3
```

The section header [Waite Group—Appendix D] uniquely identifies this section within the much larger WIN.INI file. The five parameters specify the position, size, and background color of the application's form.

When you start the application for the first time, there is no section in your WIN.INI file. The Form_Load event attempts to read the parameters from the file, and not finding the section at all, returns the default values set in the GetProfileString statements.

Once the form is open, click on it to color the background, resize it, and reposition it. Close it by double-clicking on its control box (or by pressing (ALT)-(F4)). Start the application again, and notice how it retains the size, position, and color you last gave it. This happens because the Form_Unload event saves the settings to the WIN.INI file. When the form loads again during program startup, it can successfully read the last saved parameters.

1540

VISUAL BASIC PROFESSIONAL EDITION CONTROLS

Visual Basic Professional Edition ships with a number of custom controls. These controls range from the simple, such as the 3D check box, to the amazingly sophisticated, such as the graph control. Taking advantage of these additional controls will give your programs a more polished look and will slash development time.

There is not enough space to cover these controls in the same detail we used for the Standard Edition controls. This appendix covers each control in enough detail to let the intermediate or advanced programmer begin experimenting with it, although you may wish to supplement this coverage by referring to the online help for precise details on some of the arguments and return values.

Each control's special properties (those that are particular to that control) are discussed, and make up the bulk of the entry. Some regular properties that have a bearing on how the control is used are mentioned in the description section, but most regular properties are the same as for Standard Edition controls and are discussed in more detail in the body of the book.

You'll need to add these Professional Edition controls to your project before you can use them. To load a custom control, choose Visual Basic's File... Add command, and choose the appropriate VBX file. These files are normally installed into your Windows System subdirectory. If you distribute a program that uses a custom control, make sure to include the VBX along with your executable. The Setup wizard will automatically include the appropriate VBX's for you if you use it to create a distribution set.

Table E-1 summarizes the Professional Edition controls.

Control	Purpose	VBX file
3D Controls		
3D check box	Three-dimensional check box	THREED.VBX
3D command button	Three-dimensional command button	THREED.VBX
3D frame	Three-dimensional frame	THREED.VBX
3D group push button	Three-dimensional button (for tool bars)	THREED.VBX
3D option button	Three-dimensional option button	THREED.VBX
3D panel	Three-dimensional grouping rectangle	THREED.VBX
Enhanced Controls		
Animated button	Animated and multistate buttons	ANIBUTON.VBX
Spin button	Increment and decrement other values	SPIN.VBX
Masked edit	Format and validate user input	MSMASKED.VBX
Picture clip	Efficiently store and access many bitmaps	PICCLIP.VBX
Outline	Hierarchical (outline style) list boxes	MSOUTLIN.VBX
Graph	Graph numeric data	GRAPH.VBX
Gauge	Analog style gauges	GAUGE.VBX

Control	Purpose	VBX file
Hardware and Communications		
Key status	Read and modify keyboard state	KEYSTAT.VBX
Communications	Serial communications	MSCOMM.VBX
MAPI Session	Open a session to Microsoft Mail server	MSMAPI.VBX
MAPI Messages	Communicate with a Microsoft Mail server	MSMAPI.VBX
Multimedia MCI	Play and manipulate multimedia devices	MCI.VBX
Pen edit (freeform)	Get pen user input	PENCNTRL.VBX
Pen edit (comb)	Get pen user input, restricted entry	PENCNTRL.VBX
Pen keyboard	Display onscreen keyboard	PENCNTRL.VBX

Table E-1 Professional Edition controls

3D CONTROLS

Several controls in the Professional Edition add a custom three-dimensional look to your programs. These controls add properties that control their three-dimensional look as well as adding other useful properties.

3D CHECK BOX

Purpose

The 3D check box performs the same function as the normal check box control. It presents the user with an on/off choice. The user can either select or deselect this control by clicking on it. Your program can determine whether the user has selected this control by examining its properties. It has extended property attributes that control the 3D effect of the check box and caption text.

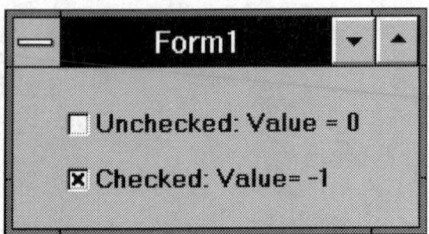

Figure E-1 The two possible states of the 3D check box

Description

The 3D check box control presents the user with a choice that has only two possible settings. It consists of a small box, which may be checked or empty, and some accompanying text (see Figure E-1). Note that the check box appears to be recessed into the form. Make sure you set the form's background to light gray to match the background of the 3D check box.

The status of the box is reversed when the user clicks on this control: If it was checked before the user clicked it, the box will now be empty; If it was empty, it will now be checked. Unlike the option button, the operation of each check box on a form, label, or picture is independent of all other check boxes; changing the status of one check box does not affect other check boxes.

The program can set or read the current status with the Value property. This property has three possible settings. A setting of 0 indicates the box is currently empty. A setting of 1 means the box is currently checked. A setting of 2 indicates the control is grayed. The Value property can only be set to 2 by your program's code. This allows your programs to have an alternative method for indicating that a check box has been selected. However, this does not disable the control. It can still receive the focus, and will still react to the user's activity. If clicked on while in this state, the check box's Value property will be set to 0, and the box will be cleared.

The Caption property defines the text that will accompany the check box. The size and style of this text is defined by the settings of the Font... properties. Including an ampersand (&) underlines the following letter, and the check box may be selected by holding down the (ALT) key and pressing that letter. For instance, if a check box's Caption property is set to &Cash, the displayed text will be "Cash" and the user can select the box by pressing (ALT)-(C). Chapter 21, Application Focus, covers the Caption property in more detail.

Clicking on this control activates its Click event. Use this so your program can react immediately to any changes in the setting of the check box. This event also initiates if the user presses the spacebar while the check box has the focus, or any time the check box's Value property is changed within the program's code.

Special Properties

The text in the Caption property may be displayed with a three-dimensional effect. Table E-2 lists the possible values of the Font3D option.

Value	Description
0	(Default) No 3D effect. Text is displayed normally
1	Raised with light shading
2	Raised with heavy shading
3	Inset with light shading
4	Inset with heavy shading

Table E-2 Possible values of the Font3D property in the 3D check box control

Note that Font3D only affects the text caption; the check box itself is always displayed as inset.

3D COMMAND BUTTON

Purpose

The 3D command button control displays a button that performs a function when the user clicks on it. The 3D control differs from the normal one in that it can display 3D text, a bitmap or an icon, and has an adjustable bevel width to further refine the 3D look.

Description

A command button represents a task to be performed. Pressing the button activates the associated task. The 3D command button does almost everything a normal command button does, but gives you much more control over the appearance of the button. It has a beveled border you can control, as well as being able to display three-dimensional text and bitmaps.

The user can press a button by clicking on it, or by pressing the (ENTER) key or the spacebar while the button has the focus. Doing so initiates the command button's Click event. This event defines the actions to take when the button is pressed.

1545

The Caption property defines the text displayed on the button. The size and style of this text is defined by the settings of the Font... properties. Including an ampersand (&) underlines the following letter, and the button can be selected by holding down the (ALT) key and pressing that letter. For instance, if the button's Caption property is set to &Cash, the displayed text will be "Cash" and the user can select the button by pressing (ALT)-(C).

Unlike the normal command button, the 3D command button does not have the Cancel or Default properties. If you want to make your buttons all 3D but still need to have the functionality of Cancel and Default, you'll need to write a form-level keyboard handler. Place appropriate code in the form's KeyPress event to scan for ASCII characters 27 ((ESC)) and 13 ((ENTER)). This gives you the ability to use the 3D button without sacrificing the ability to trap the (ESC) and (ENTER) keys. The Default and Cancel properties are covered in greater detail in Chapter 16, Keyboard Input.

Note that the 3D command button has the MouseDown, MouseMove, and MouseUp events even though the Microsoft documentation omits them.

Special Properties

The 3D command button has several properties to control its appearance.

The AutoSize property lets you control how the button or an embedded picture are sized. Setting the button's Picture property displays a bitmap in the button, centered and aligned on the top edge. If the Caption property has text in it, the AutoSize property is ignored, and the button is whatever size you make it. If the Caption property is set to an empty string, the AutoSize property can either do nothing (AutoSize = 0), size the picture to equal the size of the button (AutoSize = 1), or size the button to equal the size of the picture (AutoSize = 2). Table E-3 summarizes the settings of the AutoSize property.

Value	Description
0	(Default) No automatic sizing of either the button or the picture
1	Picture resizes to fit the command button (only with no Caption)
2	Command button resizes to fit the picture (only with no Caption)

Table E-3 Meanings of the values of the AutoSize property for the 3D command button

The BevelWidth property lets you set the width of the bevel that surrounds the command button. This helps determine the depth of the three-dimensional shadows. You can set it from 0 (flat) to 10 (highest). The default bevel is 2. Figure E-2 demonstrates several BevelWidth settings.

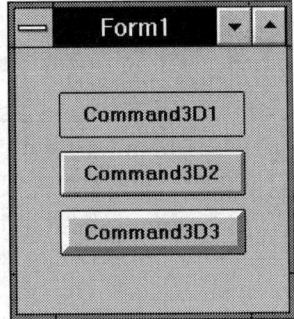

Figure E-2 The BevelWidth property lets you control how beveled the 3D command button looks

The Font3D property controls how caption text displays. You can leave it flat (normal), raise it, or inset it. Table E-4 summarizes the possible settings of the Font3D property.

Value	Description
0	(Default) No 3D effect. Text is displayed normally
1	Raised with light shading
2	Raised with heavy shading
3	Inset with light shading
4	Inset with heavy shading

Table E-4 Possible values of the Font3D property in the 3D check box control

The Outline property lets you control whether you want a one-pixel black border around the 3D command button. The default of True puts a border around it; False removes the border. Figure E-3 shows what the two settings look like.

The Picture property lets you display an icon or bitmap in the 3D command button. You can combine text set with the Caption property and a picture set with the Picture property. The picture displays flush against the top of the button, and

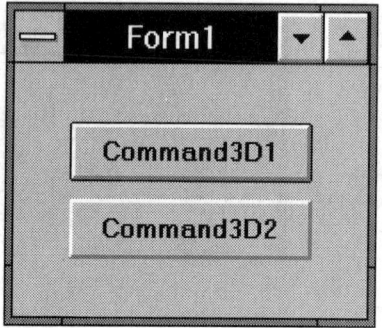
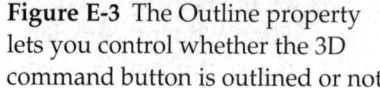

Figure E-3 The Outline property lets you control whether the 3D command button is outlined or not

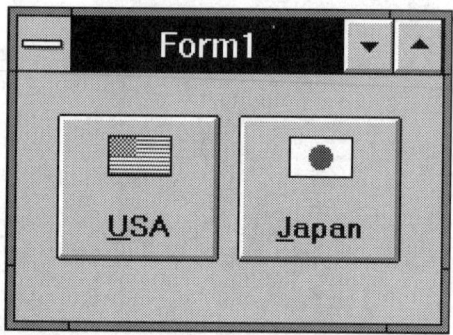

Figure E-4 The 3D command button can have pictures displayed on its face with the Picture property

is centered between the left and right sides. You have no control over exact picture placement, so you may need to add a bit of a light gray border to your bitmap to get it placed correctly on the button face. The animated button control (discussed later) offers more control over picture placement. The AutoSize property lets you resize the picture to the size of the button, the button to the size of the picture, or leave the sizing normal. Figure E-4 shows some examples of command buttons with pictures.

If you load the picture into the button at design time, the bitmap becomes part of the executable file. You can also load a picture in during runtime with the LoadPicture function, or by setting the 3D command button's Picture property with the value of another control's Picture or Image property. The PictureClip control (discussed later) is a particularly handy way of including lots of pictures in your executable file for later assignment.

The RoundedCorners Property lets you display the button as sharp cornered (RoundedCorners = False), or as the default rounded (RoundedCorners = True). A rounded corner simply has the four corner pixels removed from the outline to give the illusion of a smoother corner. Note that this only has an effect if the Outline property is True.

3D FRAME CONTROL

Purpose

The frame control visually groups functionally related controls. The 3D frame control adds additional properties that affect the frame's appearance. It can appear either raised or inset, and the text caption can also appear raised or inset.

Description

You may draw a frame on a form, and then draw other controls on the frame. This visually groups the controls together. If the frame is moved to a new location on the form, its controls move with it. The 3D frame emulates a normal frame while giving more control over the appearance of the caption text and the frame itself.

When option button controls are placed on a frame, not only are they visually grouped together, but they become logically grouped as well. When several option buttons share a frame, they become mutually exclusive. That is to say, when one button is selected, all the other buttons in the same frame get unselected. This is how you can create "radio buttons."

If you wish to place controls on a frame, the frame must be drawn first. Any controls that are to be within the frame must then be drawn on it. You cannot move an already drawn control onto a frame except by choosing the Edit menu's Cut and Paste commands to paste the control onto the frame.

A title may be displayed at the upper left-hand corner of the frame by setting its Caption property.

Microsoft omits the mouse events (Click, DblClick, MouseDown, MouseMove, and MouseUp) from their documentation, but the 3D frame control does have them.

Special Properties

The Alignment property lets you control where the 3D frame's caption appears. The default value of 0 left justifies the caption text, just as in a normal frame. Setting the Alignment property to 1 right justifies the text, and 2 centers it.

The Font3D property lets you control how the caption text appears — normal, raised, or inset. Table E-5 summarizes the settings of the Font3D property.

Value	Description
0	(Default) No 3D effect. Text is displayed normally
1	Raised with light shading
2	Raised with heavy shading
3	Inset with light shading
4	Inset with heavy shading

Table E-5 Possible values of the Font3D property in the 3D check box control

The ShadowColor and ShadowStyle properties let you control how the frame itself appears. You can leave ShadowColor at the default of 0 for a subtle dark gray shadow, or set it to 1 for a more distinct black shadow. Leaving ShadowStyle at the default of 0 gives an inset frame; a ShadowStyle of 1 makes it raised.

3D GROUP PUSH BUTTON

Purpose

The 3D group push button control lets you emulate the buttons on toolbars. There is no standard Visual Basic control that does quite the same thing. You can display a variety of icons in the button depending on its state (down, up, or disabled). You can also make it part of a button group where only one button can be down, such as in a typical word processor's left-center-right-justify alignment button group.

Description

You can use the 3D group push buttons to create toolbars. Most recent programs have some sort of toolbar available that makes common commands available on a set of buttons. Icons represent what each button does. Some sets of buttons need to be mutually exclusive, with one button automatically popping up when another member of the button group is pressed (as in a radio button group).

The control's Click event lets you react to the user pressing the button. This triggers when the user clicks on it with the mouse. Note that the group buttons cannot be made part of the tab order, so there is no keyboard equivalent.

Special Properties

The AutoSize property lets you control how the button or an embedded picture are sized. Setting the button's Picture property displays a bitmap in the button, centered and aligned on the top edge. The AutoSize property can either do nothing (AutoSize = 0), size the picture to equal the size of the button (AutoSize = 1), or size the button to equal the size of the picture (AutoSize = 2). Table E-6 summarizes the settings of the AutoSize property.

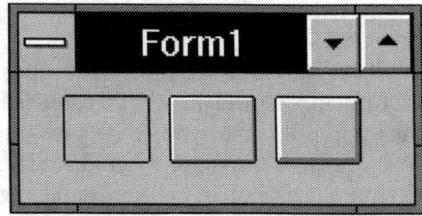

Figure E-5 The BevelWidth property lets you control how beveled the 3D command button looks

Value	Description
0	(Default) No automatic sizing of either the button or the picture
1	Picture resizes to fit the group button
2	Group button resizes to fit the picture

Table E-6 Meanings of the values of the AutoSize property for the 3D command button

The BevelWidth property lets you set the width of the bevel that surrounds the button. This helps determine the depth of the three-dimensional shadows. You can set it from 0 (flat) to 2 (highest). The default bevel is 2. Figure E-5 demonstrates several BevelWidth settings. If the BevelWidth is set to 0, you should create the bevels yourself directly in the bitmap.

The GroupNumber property lets you arrange buttons into logical groups, much as you would with option buttons arranged in a frame as radio buttons. Pushing one button of a logical group sets all other buttons of the group back to the "up" position. Set the GroupNumber property of all buttons in a logical group to the same number, from 1 to 99. Set the GroupNumber to 0 to remove a button from any logical group.

If you want to create a group of buttons that can have all of its members up, set the GroupAllowAllUp. This allows the user to click on the one button that's down to return it to the "up" position; no member of the group would be selected then.

The Outline property determines if a one-pixel wide border will be drawn around the button. Leave it at the default value of True to outline the button; set it to False to remove the black outline. The RoundedCorners property determines if the corners of the outline are sharp (RoundedCorners = False) or rounded

(RoundedCorners = True; default). RoundedCorners has no effect if the Outline property is False.

There are three Picture... properties that determine what bitmap to display: PictureUp, PictureDn, and PictureDisabled. Load each of these properties with the appropriate bitmap to reflect what the button should look like in the up state, when pressed down, or when disabled. You can load the bitmap at design time to store the bitmap in the executable file. You can also load it at runtime with the LoadPicture function, or by assigning the Picture property of another control to the appropriate Picture... property of the button.

If you don't load a picture in the PictureDn property, the PictureDnChange property determines what displays when the button is pressed down. The value determines how Visual Basic modifies the bitmap in the PictureUp property, as shown in Table E-7:

Value	Description
0	PictureUp unchanged
1	(Default) Dither PictureUp; this makes it a lighter shade of gray
2	Invert PictureUp

Table E-7 Meanings of the values of the PictureDnChange property

3D OPTION BUTTON

Purpose

The 3D option button performs the same function as the normal option button control. It presents the user with an on/off choice. The user can either select or deselect this control by clicking on it. Common programming practice puts the option button in a group with other option buttons, and makes only one button in the group selectable. Selecting one button automatically deselects all other buttons in the group. It has extended property attributes that control the 3D effect of the check box and caption text.

Description

The 3D option button control consists of a small recessed circle accompanied by text. Clicking on a button causes the circle to be filled in with a solid dot. The 3D option button works exactly like the normal option button, but is recessed to give it a 3D look. You can also control the three-dimensional look of the Caption property text.

Option buttons generally work in groups. A group of option buttons is created when two or more option buttons are drawn on the same form, frame, or picture. When this is the case, all the option buttons in the same group become mutually exclusive. That is, when one button is clicked, it gets selected and all other buttons in the same group become unselected. Option buttons grouped this way are often called *radio buttons*.

To create a group of option buttons, first draw the frame or picture on which they will be placed. Then draw the buttons on the frame or picture. To have more than one group of option buttons on the same form, create a frame for each group and then place the buttons in the appropriate frame.

The Caption property defines the text that will accompany the button. The size and style of this text is defined by the settings of the Font... properties. Including an ampersand (&) underlines the following letter, and the check box may be selected by holding down the (ALT) key and pressing that letter. For instance, if a button's Caption property is set to &Cash, the displayed text will be "Cash" and the user can select the button by pressing (ALT)-(C). Chapter 21, Application Focus, covers the caption property in more detail.

The status of an option button control may be set or read by the program's code by using the Value property. This property will be True (-1) if the button is selected and False (0) if not.

When an option button is selected, its Click event triggers. This allows the program to react immediately to the setting of the button.

Special Properties

The text in the Caption property may be displayed with a three-dimensional effect. Table E-8 lists the possible values of the Font3D option.

Value	Description
0	(Default) No 3D effect. Text is displayed normally
1	Raised with light shading
2	Raised with heavy shading
3	Inset with light shading
4	Inset with heavy shading

Table E-8 Possible values of the Font3D property in the 3D option button control

Note that Font3D only affects the text caption; the option button itself is always displayed as inset.

3D PANEL

Purpose

The 3D panel displays normal or three-dimensional text on a three-dimensional background. This control is extremely versatile. It can group other controls, like a frame; can make non-three-dimensional controls like text boxes or list boxes look 3D; and can be placed directly on an MDI form to create status bars or toolbars. It also has several properties that make it easy to create status bars that use a dynamically sized color bar to indicate progress.

Description

The 3D panel control is a rectangular area, much like the shape control in the Standard version of Visual Basic. It has four properties (InnerBevel, OuterBevel, BevelWidth, and BorderWidth) that control its three-dimensional appearance. Setting these four properties appropriately gives a wide variety of effects, including a raised panel, inset panel, raised border, and inset border.

The control has a Caption property to display text (much as a label does), and can be bound to a data control. This lets the data control automatically update the text displayed in the panel. Note that the text is set with the Caption property, and is read-only; the panel does not function like a text box.

The 3D panel control can group other controls much as a frame control does. To do this, draw the 3D panel control on your form, and then draw the other controls directly on the panel. All controls drawn on the panel are grouped together. Moving the panel will move all the controls with it. Option buttons grouped together will automatically function as radio buttons.

The control is also one of the few that has the Align property. Only controls with this property may be placed directly on an MDI form. You would typically place a control with the Align property on the MDI form to create a status bar at the bottom or a tool bar at the top. Chapter 4, Forms and Menus, goes into more detail about this. The chapter project for Chapter 4 used a Picture control to make the toolbar; you could use a 3D panel instead to make it look better.

Although Microsoft leaves these events out of their documentation for the 3D panel, it does respond to all the mouse events of Click, DblClick, MouseDown, MouseMove, and MouseUp.

Special Properties

The Alignment property of the 3D panel controls how Caption text displays. It offers much more control than just the standard left/center/right. Table E-9 summarizes the possible values of the Alignment property.

Value	Meaning
0	Left justified at top of panel
1	Left justified in middle of panel
2	Left justified at bottom of panel
3	Right justified at top of panel
4	Right justified in middle of panel
5	Right justified at bottom of panel
6	Centered at top of panel
7	Centered in middle of panel
8	Centered at bottom of panel

Table E-9 Meanings of the values of the Alignment property for the 3D panel control

The AutoSize property determines if the panel is sized to fit its contents. A setting of 0 (default) means no automatic sizing happens. A setting of 1 automatically sizes the panel width (within the inner bevel) to fit the length of the caption. This will always display the caption as a single line regardless of its length. A setting of 2 automatically sizes the panel height (within the inner bevel) to fit the caption. The panel width remains constant. Setting 3 sizes child controls to fit the panel. This can give normal controls (like a text box or list box) a three-dimensional look. Draw the 3D panel first, set its AutoSize property to 3, and then draw the child control on the panel. The child control will automatically size itself to fit within the inner bevel. Figure E-6 illustrates this.

The BevelInner property defaults to 0 (flat), and can be set to 1 (inset) or 2 (raised). The BevelOuter property defaults to 2 (raised), and can be set to 0 (flat) or 1 (inset). The BevelWidth property controls how wide the inner and outer bevels are, which dictates how deeply they're inset or how high they're raised. Legal values are between 0 and 30; the most effective three-dimensional illusion

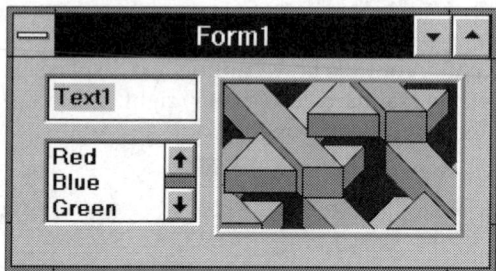

Figure E-6 Setting the AutoSize property to 3 makes a child control size itself to fit the 3D panel; this gives a three-dimensional look to the child control.

is from 1 to 6. The BorderWidth property determines how much space to leave between the inner and outer bevels. Legal values are between 0 and 30. The ShadowColor property sets the color of the bevel shadows. Leave it at the default of 0 to have dark gray shadows for a subtle look; set it to 1 for black shadows and a more distinct look. Figure E-7 gives some examples of the 3D panel control.

The 3D panel can also be used as a status or progress indicator. The FloodType property determines if and how the panel is used as a status indicator. Table E-10 lists the possible values of the FloodType property. Note that setting the FloodType property to anything other than 0 disables the display of the Caption property.

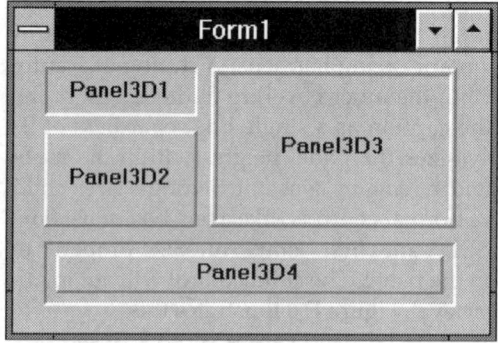

Figure E-7 The 3D panel control can have a variety of looks

Value	Meaning
0	(Default) No status indicator; panel displays caption only
1	Left to right status bar
2	Right to left status bar
3	Top to bottom status bar
4	Bottom to top status bar
5	Widening circle

Table E-10 Meanings of the values of the FloodType property for the 3D panel control

Set the FloodColor property to a valid color number (either directly with a hexadecimal number, with the RGB function, or with the QBColor function) and then use the FloodPercent property to set what percentage of the 3D panel is colored. FloodPercent values range from 0 to 100, with 0 meaning no fill and 100 meaning all filled. The 3D panel is filled within the inner bevel. Leaving the FloodShowPct property at the default of True displays the percentage as text in the center of the panel; setting it to False disables the text percent display. Figure E-8 shows a variety of status indicators created with the 3D panel.

The text in the Caption property may be displayed with a three-dimensional effect. Table E-11 lists the possible values of the Font3D option.

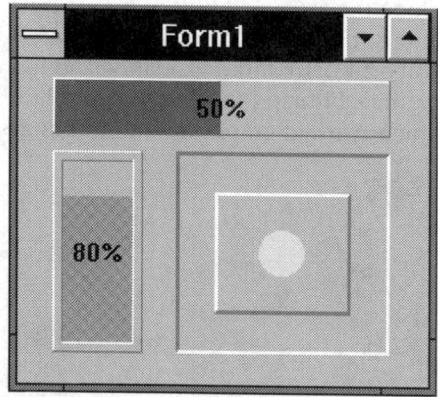

Figure E-8 The 3D panel's Flood... properties let you easily create status indicators

Value	Description
0	(Default) No 3D effect. Text is displayed normally
1	Raised with light shading
2	Raised with heavy shading
3	Inset with light shading
4	Inset with heavy shading

Table E-11 Possible values of the Font3D property in the 3D panel control

Note that Font3D only affects the text caption; the panel itself displays as whatever the Bevel... properties indicate.

The Outline property determines if a one-pixel wide border will be drawn around the panel (outside of the outer bevel). Leave it at the default value of False to remove the black outline; set it to True to outline the panel. The RoundedCorners property determines if the corners of the outline are sharp (RoundedCorners = False) or rounded (RoundedCorners = True; default). RoundedCorners has no effect if the Outline property is False.

ENHANCED CONTROLS

These controls are similar to ones in Visual Basic, Standard Edition, but are enhanced in a variety of ways. They include the animated button for creating animated and multi-state command buttons, the spin control for easy incrementing and decrementing, the masked edit control for input validation and formatting, the picture clip control to hold multiple bitmaps, the outline control for hierarchical list boxes, the graph control for advanced graphing, and the gauge control for analog gauges.

ANIMATED BUTTON

Purpose

Use the animated button control to create a variety of visual effects that would be difficult to achieve with ordinary command buttons. You can have an animated button that displays multiple bitmaps like a short movie; multi-state but-

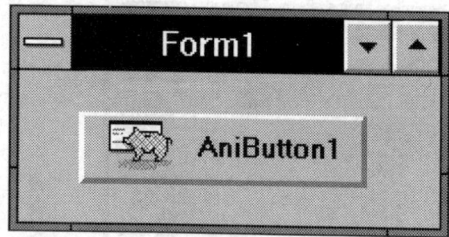

Figure E-9 Animated buttons offer
tremendous control over bitmap display

tons that change their bitmap once for each click; animated or multi-state check
boxes; and even an ordinary one-state command button that displays a bitmap.

Description

The animated button emulates many of the same functions as the normal command button, but offers tremendous control over the display of bitmaps on its
face. Figure E-9 illustrates a typical animated button. It lacks several properties
of the normal command button, however, and you may need to do some additional programming to get around these limitations.

The user can press an animated button by clicking on it, or by pressing the
spacebar while the button has the focus, but cannot do so by pressing the (ENTER)
key as with a normal command button. The animated button does respond to
the KeyPress event, so you could write an event handler that looks for the (ENTER)
keystroke and then calls the button's Click event.

Unlike the normal command button, the animated button does not have the
Cancel or Default properties. If you need to have the functionality of Cancel and
Default, place a keyboard handler in the KeyPress event of the form the button
is on that looks for ASCII 27 ((ESC)) and ASCII 13 ((ENTER)). This gives you the control over the appearance of all your visible buttons without sacrificing the ability
to trap the (ESC) and (ENTER) keys. The Default and Cancel properties are covered
in greater detail in Chapter 16, Keyboard Input.

The Caption property defines the text displayed on the button. The size and
style of this text is defined by the settings of the Font... properties. Including an
ampersand (&) underlines the following letter, and the button can be selected by
holding down the (ALT) key and pressing that letter. For instance, if the button's
Caption property is set to &Cash, the displayed text will be "Cash" and the user
can select the box by pressing (ALT)-(C).

Note that the animated button does not have the normal mouse handling
events MouseDown, MouseMove, and MouseUp.

1559

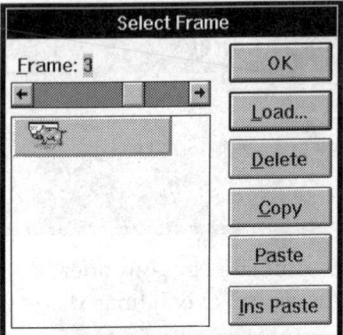

Figure E-10 The Select Frame
dialog box lets you load
pictures into the animated
button control.

Special Properties

Use the Select Frame dialog box to load and manipulate images in the animated button. Bring this dialog box up by either double-clicking on the animated button control with the *right* mouse button, or by clicking on the ellipses (...) by the Frame property in the properties box. The box lets you step through each frame and load an image, delete the current image, insert a new image into the frame sequence, or copy images from frame to frame. Figure E-10 illustrates the Select Frame dialog box.

Use the Load... button on the Select Frame dialog box to load an image into the animated button. The button accepts images in the bitmap (*.BMP) and icon (*.ICO) formats. Note that the button lacks the three-dimensional borders of a normal command button, so you may want to include some sort of border directly in the images. Each image is loaded into the Picture property of the button and stored in a special format. The Picture property actually functions like an array, with the Frame property serving as its index. Each frame has an associated image.

Use the Cycle property to control how the button cycles when clicked. This property determines if the button is an animated, multi-state, or two state button. A setting of 0 (the default) makes it an animated button. It will play one-half of the frame sequence when clicked, and then play the second half of the frame sequence when released. The button then returns to the first frame for the next click.

A setting of 1 makes the button multi-state. Each click jumps to the next frame in the frame sequence and increments the Value property by 1. Clicking the button when it's on the last frame loops it back to the first frame. You can define as many frames (or button states) as you wish.

A setting of 2 makes the button an animated two state button. A click will play half the frame sequence and then stop; it also sets the Value property to 2. A second click will play the second half of the frame sequence and return to frame 1; the value property will be set back to 1.

Experiment with the ClearFirst property to get the smoothest animation. The default value of False draws each new frame directly on top of the old frame; this tends to give the best results. You may notice some "tearing" of the image if there are large changes from frame to frame. Set the ClearFirst property to True to eliminate the tearing. This will clear the button face before drawing a new image. Although this eliminates the tearing, it will cause flickering.

The Speed property sets the delay, in milliseconds, between frames. Enter any integer value between 0 and 32,767. The default of 0 animates as rapidly as possible; larger numbers slow down the animation effect. You'll probably want to keep the number below 100 for best performance.

Use the PictDrawMode property to control how the image is drawn within the control. The default value of 0 positions the image according to the values of the PictureXpos and PictureYpos properties, and places the caption according to the TextPosition property. A setting of 1 automatically sizes the animated button to fit the largest image frame. A setting of 2 automatically sizes the image to fit the control. The caption appears as if the TextPosition property were set to 0, or the top of the image.

The PictureXpos, PictureYpos, TextXpos, TextYpos, and TextPosition properties control the image and text placement. PictureXpos and PictureYpos are set on a 0 to 100 scale, with 0,0 being the top-left corner and 100,100 being the bottom-right corner. The default of 50,50 places the image or text in the center of the control. The TextXpos and TextYpos properties are also on a 0 to 100 scale, but the properties place the text within the caption area (rather than in the button as a whole). The TextPosition property sets where the caption area is. A TextPos setting of 0 (the default) makes the entire button face the caption area; any text will overlay the image. 1 will place the caption to the right of the image; 2 places it to the left; 3 places it above the image, and 4 places it below the image.

The ClickFilter property lets you determine what part of the animated button responds to mouse clicks. The default setting of 0 detects mouse clicks on any part of the control. A setting of 1 will only recognize clicks that occur on the image or caption; 2 will recognize clicks on the image; 3 will recognize clicks only on the caption. You can also "click" the control with your code by setting the SpecialOp property to 1. This will make the button behave exactly as if the user clicked it.

The HideFocus property lets you turn off the dotted line that normally appears around the caption of controls that have the focus. The default value of False leaves the dotted line; a value of True turns it off. You may want to do this if the dotted line hinders animation appearance.

SPIN BUTTON

Purpose

Use the spin button to increment and decrement values in other controls. They function like a scroll bar with just the arrows on the ends and no scroll bar or thumb.

Description

The spin button control looks like two arrows: either left and right, or up and down. Clicking on the arrows generates SpinUp or SpinDown events that let you change a value in another control. A typical use would be to place a spin control next to a text box, and have the Spin... events increment and decrement numeric values in the text box. This lets the user set values without having to remove their hands from the mouse. Figure E-11 illustrates a typical spin control.

Special Properties

The SpinUp and SpinDown events let you react to the user clicking on the spin button arrows. If the user holds down the mouse button on an arrow, a constant series of Spin... events triggers. You would typically update the value of another control during these events. Note that you should use the other control's Refresh method to make sure it gets updated during the spinning. The following code sample increments a text box:

```
Sub Spin1_SpinUp ()
    newMonth = (Month(CVDate(Text1.Text) + 1) Mod 12    'add one month
    newDate = DateSerial(99, newMonth, 1)               'make it a date
    Text1.Text = Format$(newDate, "mmmm")               'long month name
    Text1.Refresh                                       'update the control
End Sub
```

This cycles the text box through each of the 12 months of the year when the user clicks (or clicks and holds) the spin arrow. Note that there is no starting and ending values to the spin control as you'd have with the scroll bar's Min and Max properties. Your code needs to stop the incrementing or decrementing, or wrap the values around back to the beginning as in the above example.

Set the delay between Spin... events with the Delay property. The default of 250 milliseconds (or 1/4 of a second) is normally about right, but you may wish to either speed up or slow down the control depending on the range of values you'd like to step through. Legal values are between 0 and 32,767 milliseconds.

The other special properties determine the button's appearance. The BorderColor property accepts a legal hexadecimal color value (as returned by the

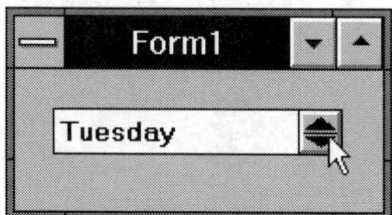

Figure E-11 The spin control
lets you easily increment and
decrement values

RGB or QBColor functions) and sets the color of the border around the control.
The BorderThickness property sets the thickness of the border. The default value
of 1 gives a flat control with a one-pixel border. Values larger than 1 give a three-
dimensional border of that many pixels, and a value of 0 gives no border.

The LightColor property sets the color of the highlight on the top and left
edges of the control; the ShadeColor property sets the color of the highlight on
the right and bottom edges of the control. Setting LightColor to a lighter shade
than ShadeColor makes the control appear raised; setting it to a darker shade
makes it appear recessed. The TdThickness property controls the width of the
shading in pixels. The default value of 0 gives no borders (and thus a flat looking
control). Larger values make for more of a three-dimensional look.

You can also set the ShadowBackColor and ShadowForecolor properties to
control how the control's shadow looks. The ShadowBackColor is normally set
to the same color as the surrounding area, and the ShadowForeColor is usually
set to a darker shade of the same color. The ShadowThickness property controls
how big the shadow is. The default of 0 gives no shadow, larger values make the
control appear to be floating above the surface of the form.

Finally, the SpinOrientation property sets whether the spin button is vertical
or horizontal. The default setting of 0 gives a vertical button, with up and down
arrows. A setting of 1 gives a horizontal button with left and right arrows.

MASKED EDIT

Purpose

The masked edit control functions like a text box, but with enhanced capabilities
of masking and validating input. This gives you the power to easily enforce formatting rules for user input.

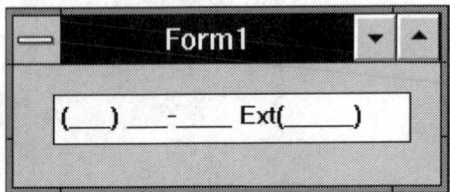

Figure E-12 The masked edit control lets
you validate and format user input

Description

The masked edit control looks and acts like a text box. It shares most properties
of a text box, including the ability to be bound to a data control, but doesn't
include any DDE links.

   The masked edit control lets you specify an input pattern format (specified like
the Format function's pattern string) that formats the user input for you. It also
has a Mask property that either automatically adds literals to the input, or forces
input to be of a specified type (such as numeric). The control also triggers a
ValidationError event when it receives invalid input to let you react to improper
input. Figure E-12 illustrates a typical masked edit control.

Special Properties

The primary purpose of the masked input control is to format and validate user
input. Specify the format of the input text with the Format property. This takes a
pattern string exactly as specified for the Format function; see Appendix B,
Visual Basic Language Reference, for specifications. For example, set the Format
property to "dd-mmm-yy". When the user enters something like "7/4/95", the
masked input control automatically reformats it to "07-Jul-95".

   The Mask property lets you mask out any unwanted characters. If you leave
the Mask property at its default of a null string, no masking takes place. If you
specify a mask and the user enters an invalid character (as determined by the
mask), the control rejects the character and triggers the ValidationError event.
Table E-12 summarizes the characters that make up a mask.

Character	Meaning
#	Any numeric digit (0 through 9)
.	Decimal point; treated as a literal
,	Thousands separator; treated as a literal

Character	Meaning
:	Time separator; treated as a literal
/	Date separator; treated as a literal
\	Treat the next character as a literal
&	Character placeholder (ANSI 32-126 and 128-255)
A	Alphanumeric placeholder (A-Z, a-z, 0-9)
?	Letter placeholder (A-Z, a-z)
Literal	Any other characters display as themselves

Table E-12 Acceptable characters for the Mask property of the masked edit control

All available spaces in the mask are marked by underscore characters in the text box as an aid to the user. If the FontUnderline property is left at its default of False, the underscore disappears when a character is typed in that position. If FontUnderline is set to True, then the underscore stays in place.

Set the AutoTab property to True to automatically tab to the next control in the tab order when the user fills the entire mask. The default is False, meaning the user would tab out of the control normally.

The ClipMode property determines what gets copied or cut to the windows Clipboard. If left at its default of 0, then all characters, including literals, are copied onto the Clipboard. If set to 1, then only the actual formatted entry, without the literals, gets copied.

The ClipText property returns the actual formatted text of the control without the literals. The FormattedText property returns the actual formatted text of the control including the literals. The SelText property returns or sets the selected text in the control. If ClipMode is True, then SelText ignores the literals; if ClipMode is False, then SelText includes all literals.

The MaxLength property sets or returns the maximum length of text allowed. The default value is the maximum of 64 characters, and can be set anywhere from 1 to 64. If the user attempts to enter characters past the maximum allowed, the control generates a beep.

The PromptChar property lets you specify a prompt character for password entry (just as in the normal text box.) The PromptInclude property specifies whether the prompt characters are included in the Text property. The default setting of True means the Text property will contain the prompt characters.

PICTURE CLIP

Purpose

Use the picture clip control to hold a number of smaller bitmaps. This is a much more efficient use of system resources than using many different picture controls. You can "clip" individual bitmaps out of the picture clip control for assignment to other objects like toolbar buttons or normal picture boxes.

Description

The picture clip control is invisible at runtime, and has no events or methods. You assign to it one bitmap that contains all the smaller bitmaps you want to store (*.BMP only.)

You can then retrieve these bitmaps either by absolute x, y positioning for irregularly shaped bitmaps, or by treating the bitmaps as an array for regularly sized bitmaps like toolbar button faces.

Using the picture clip control is much more efficient than loading the bitmaps at runtime or having an array of image or picture controls.

Special Properties

Load a picture into the picture clip control either at design time or at runtime. The Picture property holds the picture just as with the normal picture control. Construct your bitmap from the component parts so that the final bitmap you assign to the picture clip control contains all of the bitmaps you need. You can do this assembly with any paint program that lets you save in the *.BMP format, such as the Paintbrush utility that comes with Windows.

If you have irregularly sized bitmaps, be sure to note the pixel coordinates of each bitmap's corners. If you're using an array of similarly sized bitmaps, note the size of them and load the picture array from left to right, top to bottom.

The ClipX, ClipY, ClipWidth, and ClipHeight properties set the region to clip. Each parameter is given in pixels. The Clip property returns a bitmap from the control as specified by the Clip... properties. Assign the Clip property to your control just as you would with a LoadPicture function. Make sure the ScaleMode of the destination control is set to 3-Pixels.

If you need the resultant bitmap to be of a different size than the source bitmap stored in the picture clip control, set the size (in pixels) you need with the StretchX and StretchY properties. Subsequently assigning the bitmap with the Clip property will then stretch the bitmap to fit the dimensions you specified.

If you'll be using the control to store similarly sized bitmaps, you can make things quite a bit easier by using the Cols, Rows, and GraphicCell properties. Specify the number of bitmaps from left to right with the Cols property, and from top to bottom with the Rows property. This will divide the control's "surface" into a matrix of evenly spaced cells. You can then assign the individual bitmap by using the GraphicCell(Index%) property. Specify Index% by counting from the first cell in the top-left corner (cell number 0) from left to right and top to bottom. For example,

```
For i = 0 to numToolbarButtons
     grpToolBar(i).PictureUp = pclButtons(i * 3)
     grpToolBar(i).PictureDn = pclButtons(i * 3 + 1)
     grpToolBar(i).PictureDisabled = pclButtons(i * 3 + 2)
Next i
```

This example assumes the picture clip bitmap is arranged as a regular array of toolbar button faces, ordered in the same order as the toolbar buttons. Each row contains the bitmaps appropriate for one button, arranged as the bitmap for the button's "up" state, "down" state, and "disabled" state.

OUTLINE

Purpose

Use the outline control to create hierarchical list boxes. A typical example of this kind of list box is the directory file box, which lists all top level directories and lets you "drill down" through subdirectories. The outline control can look just like the directory box, but can also have different bitmaps assigned as symbols, and offers quite a bit of control and flexibility in formatting the appearance and specifying its actions.

Description

The outline control is an enhanced list box. It can display a hierarchical list of items, starting with a few major items and progressing down an outline tree to individual items.

The outline consists of five elements. The tree lines are vertical and horizontal lines that link items with their subordinate items in the tree structure. Each subordinate item is indented one additional level to the right. Plus/minus pictures let you hide or display subordinate trees. Type pictures indicate the state of an item, and text consists of a string displayed for each item. Figure E-13 illustrates a typical outline control with each of these five elements.

The outline control works much the same as a list box, but has enhanced indexing procedures and several new properties to work with the hierarchy. The familiar AddItem and RemoveItem methods are somewhat modified to accommodate placing and removing items within the hierarchy.

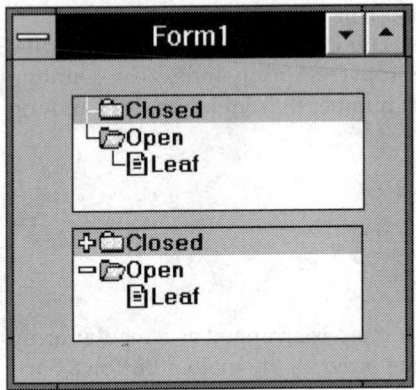

Figure E-13 The outline control lets you set up hierarchical list boxes

Each item in the list has an associated index number, just as in a normal list box. The array is still a one-dimensional, zero-based array ranging from 0 to (ListCount - 1). The outline control has the same List, ListCount, ListIndex, and Index properties that the list box does. Other properties (like PictureType) use each element's Index to set a variety of other settings for each item.

Special Properties

The Style property determines what items display in the outline control. Table E-13 summarizes the possible styles.

Value	Meaning
0	Text only
1	Picture and text
2	(Default) Plus/minus and text
3	Plus/minus, picture, and text
4	Tree lines and text
5	Tree lines, picture and text

Table E-13 Meanings of the values of the Style property for the outline control

Each item can have one of three pictures displayed next to it in Styles 1, 3, and 5. The PictureClosed property typically represents an item that is not displaying any subitems. The PictureOpen property typically represents an item that is displaying its subitems. The PictureLeaf property typically represents an individual item with no subitems. You can load a picture in to each Picture... property either at design time (so the bitmap becomes a part of the executable file) or at runtime with the LoadPicture function. Use the PictureType property array to set the type of picture to display next to each list item. Set PictureType to 0 to use the PictureClosed picture, to 1 to use the PictureOpen picture, and to 2 to use the PictureLeaf picture.

Two additional pictures, PictureMinus and PicturePlus, let you further differentiate between items in the list. You would typically use PictureMinus to indicate an item that can have its subordinate tree collapsed, and the PicturePlus to indicate an item that has available subordinate items to expand. Each item automatically displays the correct picture; there is no property array as there is with the PictureType property.

The Expand event triggers whenever a subordinate item is expanded, and the Collapse event triggers whenever a subordinate item is collapsed. The PictureClick event triggers when a type picture gets clicked, and the PictureDblClick event triggers when a type picture gets double-clicked.

Each item's indentation level is controlled by the Indent property array. Each item's Index property controls where it appears in the list, and the value of its Indent property determines where it appears in the hierarchy. A subordinate item's Indent property must be exactly 1 greater than its parent's, or you will generate a Bad Outline Indentation error. Unlike a normal list box, you can specify an Index value greater than the number of members already in the list. The outline control will generate the necessary additional items and will adjust the ListCount property.

The AddItem method is enhanced to allow for automatic assignment of the indentation level. If the index argument is specified and refers to an item that already exists, the new item is added to the list with the same indentation level as the existing item. If the index argument refers to a nonexistent item, then the indentation level for the new item is set to 0. If the index argument is not specified, the item is added to the end of the first subordinate level branching off of the currently selected item.

The RemoveItem method removes not only the specified item, but any subordinate items as well.

You can determine if an item has subordinate items by examining the read only HasItems property array. You can determine whether an item is currently visible (that is, displayed in an expanded tree) by examining the read only IsItemVisible property array.

Get the fully qualified name of an item with the read only FullPath property array. The fully qualified name is a concatenation of each parent item, separated by the PathSeparator character, and ending with the item given by the index argument to the FullPath property. You'd typically use this in a directory list box to get the full path name of a file. The PathSeparator property defaults to the backslash (\ ) character.

GRAPH

Purpose

The graph control gives you a flexible way of graphing numeric data. It has a wealth of chart types and many variations. It is more flexible and much faster than using an OLE object like MSGraph.

Description

The graph control is a rectangular object that displays a number of different graph types. It can display two- and three-dimensional graphs in area, bar, pie, gantt, line, polar, scatter, or high-low-close styles. It lets you set a variety of other properties to control chart items like axes, gridlines, legends, colors, patterns, and labels. Figure E-14 shows several of the available chart types.

It will display a random set of values during design time to aid you in setting its many properties correctly. This lets you interactively set the properties and immediately see what the effect is. There are so many variations possible with the control that this is probably the best way to approach designing a graph.

Almost all of the chart properties can be set during runtime. This lets you easily create an application and give the user total control over how they want their graph to appear. It will also dynamically update itself during run time if the data values change.

You can also print graphs at the highest resolution of your printer. Rather than printing chunky bitmap graphics, the graph control can automatically send the Printer object vector objects for the highest quality printing.

Data values and many property values are given in two-dimensional arrays. The array indices are controlled through two properties: ThisSet and ThisPoint. ThisSet controls which set of points you're referring to, and ThisPoint identifies the individual element within that set.

Special Properties

Send data to or retrieve data from the graph control either value by value with the GraphData property, or all at once with the QuickData property.

The GraphData property will set or return the value of the graph data for the individaul data point specified by the ThisSet and ThisPoint properties. These

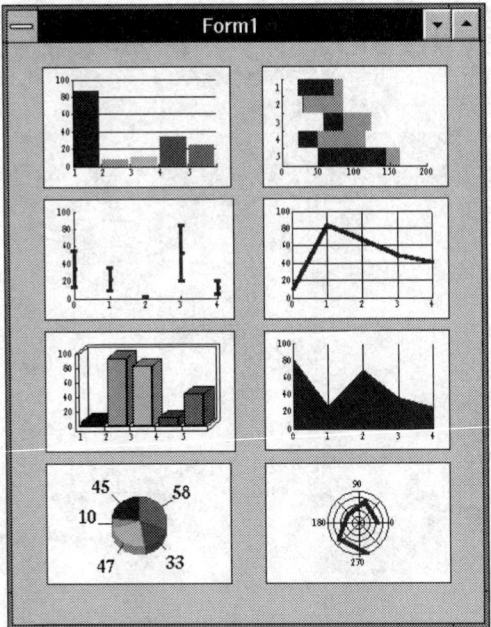

Figure E-14 The versatile graph control
lets you easily graph numeric data

serve as indices into the graph's implied two-dimensional array. You could do this in a nested For...Next or Do...Loop structure, incrementing ThisSet and ThisPoint for each data point. You can also leave the AutoInc property at its default value of True to automatically increment the values of ThisSet and ThisPoint. Each time you assign a value to the graph, the point automatically increments.

The QuickData property lets you send or receive data for the entire graph in one operation. It separates each data value with a Tab character (Chr$(9)), and each set of data with a carriage return (Chr$(13)). Note that this is the same format that the grid control's Clip property returns, and is also the same format most spreadsheets place on the window's Clipboard. This lets you set a graph's data in one line:

```
Graph1.QuickData = Grid1.Clip
```

Set the type of graph with the GraphType property. It defaults to 3 (2D bar chart). Each type of graph can produce a wealth of styles, as given by the GraphStyles property. Table E-14 summarizes the different graph types.

Value	Meaning
0	None
1	2D pie
2	3D pie
3	(Default) 2D bar
4	3D bar
5	Gantt
6	Line
7	Log/Lin
8	Area
9	Scatter
10	Polar
11	High Low Close

Table E-14 Types of graphs the graph control produces

You can turn labels on and off with the Labels property. The default setting of 0 leaves the graph unlabeled. Setting it to 1 labels both the x and y axes. A setting of 2 labels just the x axis, a setting of 3 labels just the y axis. The LabelEvery property determines the interval between labels. The default value of 1 labels every value, but you can set it to a higher integer to label every nth value. For example, if the data values range from 0 to 100, and you set LabelEvery to 25, then labels would appear for 0, 25, 50, 75, and 100.

The Ticks property controls whether tick marks are displayed. The default value of 0 turns off tick marks. Setting the value to 1 turns tick marks on for both x and y axes. Setting it to 2 turns tick marks on for the x axis only, setting it to 3 turns tick marks on for the y axis only. The TickEvery property determines the interval between tick marks on the x axis. The default value of 1 places a tick mark for every value, but you can set it to a higher integer to mark every nth value. For example, if the data values range for 0 to 100, and you set TickEvery to 25, then tick marks would appear for 0, 25, 50, 75, and 100. The YAxisTicks property sets the total number of tick marks that appear on the y axis. The default value of 1 gives a single tick mark at the end of the axis; you can set it to display up to 100 evenly spaced tick marks.

The LegendText property lets you enter text to use as a legend. This is an array value, so the value of ThisPoint or ThisSet determines where to place the text in the array. You can also set the LegendStyle property to control whether to display the legend text in monochrome (0, default), or color (1).

Use the Palette property to select a palette for the colors displayed in the graph. The default value of 0 gives solid colors. Setting this property to 1 dithers the solid colors to give a softer, pastel look. A setting of 2 gives a dithered grayscale graph.

The ColorData property selects colors for each set of data. This is an array value, so you can specify a different color for each set. The colors are specified by an integer from 0 to 15. Each number corresponds to the same color as given to the QBColor function. Thus, 0 is black, 4 is red, and 15 is white.

Set the background color of the graph with the Background property, and the color of all titles, labels, legends, and axes with the Foreground property using the same 0 to 15 scale as the ColorData property. You can set the SeeThru property to True if you want the background to be clear. This lets you superimpose the graph on top of another control, like a picture box or image control.

The PatternData property selects a variety of patterns for solid fills or line styles for patterned lines. This is an array property, so each set can have a different pattern. Lines are normally drawn one pixel thick, but you can set the ThickLines property to True to produce 3-pixel thick lines. If DrawStyle is set to 0 (Monochrome), then the PatternData property determines the actual thickness.

The SymbolData property lets you specify symbols used in line, log/lin, scatter, and polar graphs. There are 10 symbols, enumerated from 0 to 9. This is an array property, so you can specify a different symbol for each set.

GAUGE

Purpose

Use the gauge control to create controls that graphically display single numeric values. You can specify a background bitmap to use. The gauge control can produce a variety of linear filled styles or needle styles. The gauge accepts a number for its value and displays the fill or needle superimposed over the background bitmap.

Description

The gauge control accepts a single numeric value and displays it either as a needle in a circle or semicircle, or as a linear fill either vertically or horizontally. You

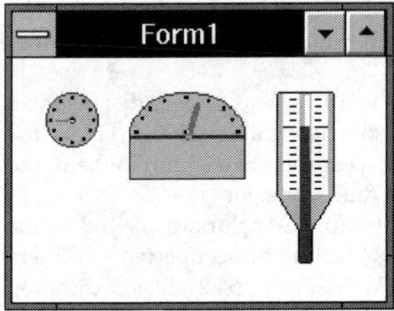

Figure E-15 The gauge control lets you emulate analog gauges

can place a bitmap in the background of the control to give the illusion of a physical gauge, thermometer, dial, or other analog device. Figure E-15 shows a typical gauge.

Use the Picture property to set the bitmap. If you do this in the design phase, the bitmap becomes part of the executable file. You can also load it at runtime either with the LoadPicture function or by assigning another control's Picture property to the gauge's Picture property. Visual Basic ships with several gauge bitmaps in the \VB\BITMAPS\GAUGE directory.

The Min and Max properties set the minimum and maximum values the gauge will accept. Both properties will accept values from 0 to 32,767. Min defaults to 0, Max defaults to 100. Set the Value property to change the gauge's display within the boundaries of the Min and Max values.

Special Properties

Use the Style property to specify what kind of gauge to create. The default Style of 0 gives a horizontal linear gauge, and a setting of 1 gives a vertical linear fill. A setting of 2 gives a semicircular needle gauge, and a setting of 3 gives a full circle gauge. (Note that the Microsoft documentation inadvertently omits the vertical linear style.)

Setting the Value property with the linear fill styles fills the gauge with the appropriate percentage of BackColor and ForeColor. Needle gauges behave somewhat differently. The semicircle gauge (Style = 2) places the base of the needle in the bottom center of the control. When Value is equal to Min, the needle points directly to the left (at the 9 o'clock position). As Value increases, the needle swings clockwise. When Value is equal to Max, the needle points directly to the right (at the 3 o'clock position). The full circle gauge (Style = 3) behaves similarly. The needle base is placed in the center of the control (as given by the Inner... properties). Both Min and Max are all the way to the left (at the 9 o'clock position). As Value increases, the needle swings clockwise around the entire circle.

The InnerBottom, InnerLeft, InnerRight, and InnerTop properties determine the portion of the gauge that displays the linear fill or the needle. All four properties are set in pixels, and all must be greater than 0. All properties are given relative to the appropriate control border. For example, if InnerLeft were set to 100, then the gauge's left display area would be 100 pixels in from the left side of the control. Likewise, if the InnerBottom property were set to 10, then the gauge's display area would start 10 pixels from the bottom of the control.

The Foreground and Background properties determine the colors the gauge displays for linear fill styles. Set these with any appropriate hexadecimal number (as given by the RGB or QBColor functions). The Background property erases the gauge's display area with its color, and the Foreground property draws in that percentage of the gauge given by the Min, Max, and Value properties. The displayable area is given by the Inner... properties.

Use the NeedleWidth property to set the width of the needle in pixels. It defaults to 0, and can accept any integer up to 32,767. Good values will range from 1 to around 25.

HARDWARE AND COMMUNICATIONS CONTROLS

Professional Edition adds a number of controls that make working with hardware and communications easier. These controls include Key Status to monitor and change the state of the keyboard, Communications for serial communications, the two MAPI controls for e-mail, the Multimedia MCI control for multimedia devices, and three pen controls.

KEY STATUS

Purpose

Use the key status control to determine and modify the (CAPS LOCK), (NUM LOCK), (INS), and (SCROLL LOCK) key states.

Description

The keystate control looks like a small command button. It displays the key name with a red OFF or a green ON depending on the key state. If the key is in the ON state, then the button looks like it's been pushed in. Clicking the button with the mouse will toggle the key state. You'd most commonly use these on a status bar at the bottom of the screen. Figure E-16 shows the keystate control.

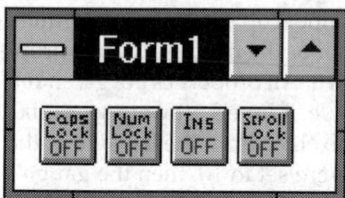

Figure E-16 The keystate control lets you read and set the state of the special keyboard keys

If AutoSize is True, the button is always the same size and cannot be resized. If AutoSize is False, then the Height and Width properties set the button's size.

The Value property sets or returns the current status for the key associated with the button. False indicates the key status is off, and True indicates the key status is on. The Change event triggers when the Value property changes.

Special Properties

The Style property determines which key the button is associated with. The default value of 0 associates it with the (CAPS LOCK), a setting of 1 with (NUM LOCK), a setting of 2 with (INS), and a setting of 3 with (SCROLL LOCK).

The TimerInterval property determines how often the buttons get updated. The default value is 1000 milliseconds (1 second.) Larger values introduce less of a burden on the system, but will lead to delays in updating the button displays. All buttons share the same TimerInterval; setting it for one button sets it for all.

COMMUNICATIONS

Purpose

Use the communications control to manipulate the serial port or serial communications devices such as modems. Each serial port you want to use needs its own communications control. You can set a variety of communications parameters such as baud rate and parity as well as send and receive data.

Description

The communications control is invisible at runtime. Almost all of its properties are special properties pertaining to serial communications.

1576

Special Properties

Start using the communications control by setting the communications port with the CommPort property. You can set it to any value from 1 to 99, but it returns an error if the port does not exist. Most machines only have 2 comm ports; some have 4.

Once you've set the port, use the Settings property to set the baud rate, parity, data bit, and stop bit parameters. The Settings property accepts and returns a string value in the format "BBBB, P, D, S", where BBBB is the baud rate, P is the parity, D is the number of data bits, and S is the number of stop bits. For example,

```
MSComm1.Settings = "2400, N, 8, 1"
```

sets the port to 2400 baud, no parity, eight data bits, and one stop bit.

Set PortOpen to True to open the port. At the end of your communications session, set PortOpen to False to close the port. The communications control will automatically close the port upon termination of your program if you haven't already done so.

The InBufferSize property determines the total number of characters that can be in the buffer. It defaults to 1024 characters, and can range up to 32K. The InBufferCount property returns the total number of characters waiting in the buffer to be removed. You can set InBufferCount to 0 to clear the contents of the buffer.

The InputLen property determines how many characters to remove from the buffer at one time. Its default value of 0 removes all available characters. You may want to set InputLen to some other value if your communications device works with fixed-length strings. The default of 0 works best for most uses.

The Input property removes the characters from the input buffer. It will remove as many characters as the InputLen is set for, or all available characters if InputLen is 0. You can check the InBufferCount property before using the Input property; if InBufferCount is nonzero, then there are characters to input.

Write characters to the output buffer with the Output property. Simply assign whatever string you'd like to send, and the Output property will place the string in the output buffer to await transmission.

The OutBufferSize property determines the size of the output buffer. Its default size is 512 bytes, and you can set it up to 32K. The OutBufferCount property will return the total number of characters awaiting transmission in the output buffer. Set the OutBufferCount property to 0 to flush the output buffer.

You can detect when activity occurs on the serial port with the CommEvent property. The communications control's OnComm event fires each time the CommEvent property changes. There are a number of error values and events this property returns, as shown by Table E-15.

Value	CONSTANT.TXT	Meaning
1	MSCOMM_EV_SEND	Fewer characters in the transmit buffer than SThreshold
2	MSCOMM_EV_RECEIVE	Received RThreshold number of characters
3	MSCOMM_EV_CTS	Change in the Clear To Send line
4	MSCOMM_EV_DSR	Change in the Data Set Ready line from -1 to 0
5	MSCOMM_EV_CD	Change in the Carrier Detect Line
6	MSCOMM_EV_RING	Ring detected
7	MSCOMM_EV_EOF	End of file character (ASCII 26) detected
1001	MSCOMM_ER_BREAK	Break signal received
1002	MSCOMM_ER_CTSTO	Clear To Send timeout
1003	MSCOMM_ER_DSRTO	Data Set Ready timeout
1004	MSCOMM_ER_FRAME	Framing error
1006	MSCOMM_ER_OVERRUN	Port overrun; set the Interval property lower
1007	MSCOMM_ER_CDTO	Carrier Detect Timeout
1008	MSCOMM_ER_RXOVER	Receive buffer overflow
1009	MSCOMM_ER_RXPARITY	Parity error
1010	MSCOMM_ER_TXFULL	Transmit buffer full

Table E-15 Meanings of the values of the CommEvent property for the communications control

You can send a break with the Break property. Most communications devices do not need the break signal, and those that do only need it for a short time. Set Break to True to begin sending the break signal, and back to False to clear it. Do this with a Do...Loop. Store the time of the beginning of the break signal in a variable before entering the loop, and check the difference between the static variable and the present time each time through the loop. When the duration exceeds your specified minimum (probably around one-tenth second), break out of the loop and set Break back to False. Make sure you've got a DoEvents statement inside the loop to allow the system time to process concurrent processes.

Read the CDHolding property to see if the carrier is still detected. Modems set the carrier detect line when they are online. Occasionally querying this property is especially important for a host application (such as a bulletin board) because the client can hang up at any time. If no carrier is detected, you can then close and reinitialize the communications port. The CDTimeout property determines the maximum number of milliseconds to wait before signaling a timeout if the carrier is dropped. The OnComm event would then trigger, and your code could then check the CommEvent and CDHolding properties to confirm that the carrier was lost.

Read the CTSHolding property to determine whether or not you can transmit data. Modems set the Clear To Send line to indicate that they can accept characters for transmission, which the CTSHolding property then queries. The CTSTimeout property sets the number of milliseconds to wait for the Clear To Send signal before generating an OnComm event.

Read the DSRHolding property to determine the state of the Data Set Ready line. Modems send this signal to the computer to indicate they are ready to operate. The DSRTimeout property sets the number of milliseconds to wait for the DSR signal before generating an OnComm event.

You can set the handshaking protocol with the Handshaking property. This sets how the two serial devices determine when to send characters to each other. The default value of 0 gives no handshaking. A setting of 1 gives XON/XOFF handshaking, which is very common. A setting of 2 gives RTS/CTS, and 3 gives XON/XOFF and RTS/CTS.

The SThreshold property sets the number of characters that can be in the output buffer before the OnComm event triggers. The default value of 0 disables generating any OnComm events.

The RThreshold property sets the number of characters that can be in the input buffer before the OnComm event triggers. The default value of 0 disables generating any OnComm events.

The Interval property sets the number of milliseconds for polling the communications hardware under Windows 3.0. This has no effect in Windows 3.1.

You can set the NullDiscard property to determine whether or not nulls (ASCII 0) are transferred from the port to the input buffer. The default value of False transfers the nulls; True discards them.

Set the ParityReplace property to specify the character to replace invalid characters in the input stream. The control knows when it's received an invalid character by checking the parity of the transmitted byte. If it received an invalid character, it replaces the invalid character with the character specified by the ParityReplace property. The default value is a question mark (?). Set ParityReplace to a null string (" ") to disable parity checking.

MAPI SESSION

Purpose

Use the MAPI session control to sign on and establish a MAPI session. MAPI services are provided by Microsoft Mail. Once you've established a MAPI session, you can use the MAPI messages control to perform a variety of e-mail functions.

Description

The MAPI session control is invisible at runtime, and almost all of its properties are special ones dealing with logging on to and establishing a session with the Microsoft Mail server.

Once you've successfully established a session, you can pass the MAPI session control's SessionID property to the MAPI messages control to mail-enable your application.

Special Properties

Begin by setting the UserName and Password properties. Both properties accept strings. You may wish to provide the user with a dialog box to ask for their user name and password. You can use the Password property of a text box to hide the password as it's being typed. You can then use the values of the text boxes to set the UserName and Password properties of the MAPI session control.

The Action property starts or ends a MAPI session. This property is much like the Action property for the common dialog box or the OLE control. You may want to think of it as a method, rather than a property, as it makes the control take action. Set it to 1 to establish a MAPI session after having set the UserName and Password. Set it to 2 to terminate a MAPI session.

Once the session has been established, the MAPI session control's SessionID property contains a long integer that gives a unique messaging handle. You use this SessionID to pass to the MAPI messages control.

The DownloadMail property specifies whether to download new messages from the mail server to the user's in-box. The default value of True will download all new messages; a progress indicator will show the progress of the transfer while it takes place. A value of False prevents the forced downloading.

The LogonUI property specifies whether or not to use a dialog box during log-on. The default value of True displays a dialog box to prompt new users for their user name and password. A False value disables the dialog box. You'll still need to provide the UserName and Password properties proper values to successfully log on.

You can have multiple mail sessions if you wish. The default value of the NewSession property, False, will prevent multiple sessions. Set this value to True to establish multiple mail sessions. Each session will have its own unique SessionID, so be sure to store the old value before establishing a new connection.

MAPI MESSAGES

Purpose

Use the MAPI messages control to perform messaging system functions like creating e-mail, sending and receiving messages, and accessing mail attachments (including OLE objects.)

Description

The MAPI messages control communicates with the Microsoft Mail server. Its actions and properties let you mail-enable your Visual Basic application. You can perform almost all normal e-mail functions using the MAPI messages control.

The MAPI messages control needs the SessionID property value returned by the MAPI session control. Make sure you first establish a session with that control, and pass the SessionID to the MAPI messages control.

There can be multiple messages, and each message can have multiple recipients and multiple attachments. These are arranged as a one-dimensional array to let you access each individual element.

The MAPI messages control has two buffers: a *compose* buffer where messages are created and edited, and a *read* buffer that contains an array of messages sent to the user.

The control is invisible at runtime, and most of its properties are special properties dealing with the e-mail functions.

Special Properties

Set the SessionID property of the MAPI messages control to equal the value returned by the SessionID of the MAPI session control. This associates the messages control with the correct mail session.

The core functionality of the MAPI messages control is accessed through its Action property. This is similar to the Action property of the common dialog box and the OLE control. You may prefer to think of it more as a method rather than a property, as it makes the control do something. Table E-16 summarizes the possible settings for the Action property.

Value	CONSTANT.TXT	Meaning
1	MESSAGE_FETCH	Creates a message set from the Inbox
2	MESSAGE_SENDDLG	Brings up the send dialog box
3	MESSAGE_SEND	Sends a message without the dialog box
4	MESSAGE_SAVEMSG	Saves the message in the compose buffer
5	MESSAGE_COPY	Copies the current message to the compose buffer
6	MESSAGE_COMPOSE	Clears the compose buffer and begins a new message
7	MESSAGE_REPLY	Composes a reply to the current message
8	MESSAGE_REPLYALL	Composes a reply to all recipients of the current message
9	MESSAGE_FORWARD	Copies current message to compose buffer and adds FW: to the subject line
10	MESSAGE_DELETE	Deletes all components of the current message
11	MESSAGE_SHOWADBOOK	Displays the Address Book dialog box
12	MESSAGE_SHOWDETAILS	Displays the message details dialog box
13	MESSAGE_RESOLVENAME	Searches the address book for a match of the current recipient
14	RECIPIENT_DELETE	Deletes the current recipient
15	ATTACHMENT_DELETE	Deletes the current attachment

Table E-16 Meanings of the values of the Action property for the MAPI messages control

Address Book

You can set a number of properties that define how the Address Book dialog box looks when displayed. Set the AddressCaption property with a string to specify the caption that appears at the top of the dialog box.

The AddressEditFieldCount property determines how many edit fields appear on the dialog box. Its values range from 0 to 4. A setting of 0 means no edits are allowed; the dialog box will be used for browsing only. The default setting of 1 means only the To: edit box should be displayed. A setting of 2 brings up both To: and CC: (carbon copy); a setting of 3 brings up To:, CC:, and BCC: (blind carbon copy); a setting of 4 brings up only those edit controls supported by the messaging system.

If the AddressEditFieldCount is set to 1, then assigning a string to the AddressLabel property displays that string rather than "To:". This has no effect if AddressEditFieldCount is set to anything other than 1.

The default value of the AddressModifiable property (False) means that the user may not modify their personal address book. Set this to True if you want them to be able to modify it.

You display the Address Book dialog box by setting the Action property to 11.

Set the AddressResolveUI property to True to display a dialog box that displays similar names to the recipient when the Action property is set to 13 (MESSAGE_RESOLVENAME). It defaults to False, which means that an error occurs if there is no exact match.

Attachments

Each message can have a number of attachments. The AttachmentCount property lets you read the total number of attachments. The AttachmentIndex property serves as an index into the array of attachments. It is a zero-based array, so it extends from 0 to (AttachmentCount - 1). Setting the AttachmentIndex property makes that attachment current. Setting the AttachmentIndex property to a larger number than AttachmentCount will create a new attachment if there is something in the compose buffer (MsgIndex = -1).

The AttachmentName property lets you read the file name of the current attachment. If the attachment is an OLE object, AttachmentName will contain the class name of the object. See Chapter 26, Object Linking and Embedding, for more information about class names. You can set this property only if you are creating a new attachment.

The AttachmentPathName property lets you read the full path name of the attachment. You can set this property only when you are creating a new attachment.

Read or specify the position of the attachment with the AttachmentPosition property. This position is specified by a long integer that is the character position at which the attachment is placed (or will be placed if you're creating a new attachment). This property is read-only unless you're creating a new attachment.

The AttachmentType property specifies the kind of attachment. A value of 0 indicates a data file (which could be almost any disk file: spreadsheet, word processing document, database, graphics image, and so forth). A setting of 1 indicates an embedded OLE object, and a setting of 2 indicates a static OLE object. This property is read only unless you're creating a new attachment.

Retrieving Messages

Set the kind of message with the FetchMessageType property. Its default value of an empty string will fetch all Interpersonal messages. The FetchSorted property specifies how the incoming message set will be sorted: The default value of False sorts them according to the settings in the user's Inbox, while a value of True sorts them in ascending order by time and date received. The FetchUnreadOnly property's default value of True will retrieve only those messages that have not yet been read. Set this to False to retrieve all messages of the proper type. To actually get the messages, set the Action property to 1 (MESSAGE_FETCH.)

Messages

There may be a number of messages available in the Inbox. The MsgCount property returns the total number of messages present in the message set (as returned by the Fetch... properties after setting the Action property to MESSAGE_FETCH). The MsgIndex property lets you step through each message. It is a zero-based array, so its values range from 0 to (MsgCount - 1). The MsgIndex may also be -1, which indicates that the current message is in the compose buffer and needs to be sent.

Each message belongs to a *thread*, or a connected series of messages about a particular subject. A message may be the start of a thread, or may be down the chain as a reply (or a reply to a reply to a reply...). The MsgConversationID property lets you read to which thread a message belongs, or set the thread for a message being composed (when MsgIndex = -1.) All messages belonging to the same thread have the same MsgConversationID.

The MsgNoteText property is the actual body text of a message. It consists of a string, and is thus limited to about 64K. Each paragraph on an incoming message is terminated with a carriage return/linefeed pair (ASCII 13 and ASCII 10); outgoing messages can use a carriage return, a linefeed, or a carriage return/linefeed pair.

The MsgReceiptRequested property defaults to False, and will be set to True if a receipt has been requested. The MsgSubject property contains the subject (a short summary) of the message. The MsgType property specifies the type of the current message. It defaults to Interpersonal Mail (IPM). Many systems don't recognize anything other than IPM and may ignore the setting of this property. Both of these properties are read-only for existing messages, and can be set for messages being composed (MsgIndex = -1).

The MsgDateReceived property lets you read when the current message was received. The MsgID property lets you read the specific ID code for the message. The ID code is a unique 64 character string that the system generates for each new message. The MsgOrigAddress property lets you read the mail address of the current message, while the MsgOrigDisplayName property retrieves the name of the originator of the current message. The MsgRead property indicates whether or not the message has been read. It is True if it has been, and False if it has not. The MsgSent property specifies whether the current message has been sent to the system mail server yet; it is True if it has and False if it has not. All of these properties are read-only, and are automatically set by the system.

Recipients

Each message may have multiple recipients. The RecipCount property returns the total number of recipients for the current message. The RecipIndex property lets you step through each recipient in the array. The array is zero-based, so it ranges from 0 to (RecipCount - 1). If you're creating a new message (MsgIndex = -1), you can create a new recipient by setting a RecipIndex greater than RecipCount.

The RecipAddress property reads or sets the e-mail address of the recipient. The RecipDisplayName reads or sets the name of the recipient. The RecipType property reads or sets the type of the current recipient. A 0 means the message originator; a 1 means the recipient is the primary recipient; a 2 means the recipient is a copy recipient; a 3 means the recipient is a blind copy recipient. Each of these properties is read-only unless you are composing a new message (MsgIndex = -1).

MULTIMEDIA MCI

Purpose

The MCI control lets you control and manipulate multimedia devices. The Multimedia Control Interface (MCI) of Windows lets you manipulate a wide variety of media: CD-ROM, audio CD, laserdisk, sound boards, MIDI (Musical Instrument Digital Interface) devices, video tape, and more. The MCI control lets you record and playback through these various devices without having to get involved with any device dependent code.

Description

The MCI control has a number of buttons that will appear familiar to anyone who has used a VCR or audio equipment. These are buttons for Back (rewind), Step (forward), Play, Pause, Prev (rewind to beginning of selection), Next (forward to beginning of next selection), Stop, Record, and Eject. Figure E-17 illustrates the default setup of the MCI control.

You can keep the buttons visible, or hide them if you'd like to have greater control over the user interface. The buttons can automatically enable and disable themselves to respond to changing conditions, so it makes it easier to get your application up and running quickly if you keep them visible.

Figure E-17 The MCI control lets you
manipulate Mulitmedia devices such as
CD-ROMS and sequencers

The MCI control needs to explicitly open a multimedia device with the Open command. As it does this, it queries the device about some of its capabilities, and can report on these for you. The capabilities of the device are a combination of the physical device and the software drivers.

After the device is opened, you can play the device's media, go to specific parts of the selection, and for some devices, record new parts or eject the media. When you're finished using the device, you should use the Close command.

Special Properties

The Command property lets you issue MCI commands to the device, and is the heart of the MCI control. Pass a string argument to the property, as given by the Value column in Table E-17.

Value	Meaning
Open	Open a device
Close	Close a device
Play	Play a device
Pause	Pause playing or recording, or start again if paused
Stop	Stop playing or recording
Back	Step backward
Step	Step forward
Prev	Go to beginning of current track
Next	Go to beginning of next track

Value	Meaning
Seek	Seek a position (as given by the To property)
Record	Record (between From and To)
Eject	Eject the media
Sound	Play a sound
Save	Save an open file

Table E-17 Possible commands in the MCI control's Command property

The command will be issued immediately, and any errors will immediately appear in the Error and ErrorMessage property.

Once you've opened the device by issuing an Open command, you can determine the device's capabilities with the four read-only Can... properties. CanEject reports True if the device has physical media that can be ejected, CanPlay reports True if the device is capable of playing something, CanRecord reports True if the device is capable of recording new information, and CanStep reports True if the device is capable of stepping frame by frame.

If you leave the AutoEnable property at the default value of True, the MCI buttons will automatically enable and disable themselves according to the device's capabilities and current status. For example, it would automatically disable the record button if playing an audio CD, and would disable the play button while recording a new MIDI track.

If you set the AutoEnable property to False, you can enable and disable individual buttons with the *Button*Enabled properties. Substitute Back, Step, Play, Pause, Prev, Next , Stop, Record, and Eject for *Button* to specify that particular button. For example, to disable the Play button,

```
MMControl1.PlayButton.Enabled = False
```

Setting AutoEnable to True supersedes the individual *Button*Enabled properties. You can disable the entire control for user manipulation with the control's Enabled property. (You could still manipulate it with code, however.)

You can also make individual buttons invisible with the *Button*Visible properties. All buttons default to a *Button*Visible of True. You can make all buttons invisible with the control's Visible property. This would let you design an alternative user interface, or perhaps eliminate the user interface altogether if all you wanted to do was something simple like play some sounds. You can also control the orientation of the buttons with the Orientation property. The default value of 0 leaves the buttons arranged horizontally, while a setting of 1 will arrange them vertically.

Many MCI commands take an indeterminate amount of time to complete. Playing a MIDI file, for example, can take as long as the file is long, or as short as the user's quickness on the Stop button. Set the Notify property to True immediately before issuing an MCI command that you'd like to track. When the task is completed, the MCI control's Done event triggers. You can then test the NotifyMessage and NotifyValue properties to determine the status. NotifyValue will be set to 1 if the command was completed successfully, to 2 if the command was superseded by another command, 4 if aborted by the user, and 8 if the command failed. Note that you need to set the Notify property *immediately* before the MCI command you want to be notified of.

You can specify where in the track to play or record with the From and To properties. These values are given in the units set by the TimeFormat property. The TimeFormat can be set to 0 for milliseconds; 1 for hours, minutes, and seconds; 2 for minutes, seconds, and frames; 3 for frames; 4 for 24-frame SMPTE; 5 for 25-frame SMPTE; 6 for 30-frame SMPTE; 7 for 30-frame drop SMPTE; 8 for bytes; 9 for samples; and 10 for tracks, minutes, seconds, and frames.

The From and To properties can also be set for when you're recording. Setting the RecordMode to 0 will insert new material (pushing old material further down the track), while RecordMode set to 1 will overwrite old material. Setting From and To with RecordMode 1 will give you "punch-in recording" familiar to anyone who's worked in a recording studio.

Several read-only properties let you find out current settings. The Length property returns the length of the media in an open MCI device. The Start property returns the starting position of the media. The Position property returns the current position of the media. The Mode property returns what mode the device is in: 524 for not open, 525 for stopped, 526 for playing, 527 for recording, 528 for seeking, 529 for paused, and 530 for ready (stopped).

Some media supports multiple tracks. Use the Track property to specify which track to work with. The read-only TrackLength property returns the length of the current track, while the read-only TrackPosition property returns the current position of the current track. The read-only Tracks property gives the total number of tracks in the media.

Set the UpdateInterval property for the number of milliseconds between StatusUpdate events. The StatusUpdate event would typically have code to refresh label controls with the values of the current setting properties like Start, Length, and Position. You could, of course, use a timer control to do the same thing, but it's more convenient to use the built-in event in the MCI control.

The FileName property specifies a file to open or save to. The Shareable property determines if multiple programs can share the same MCI device. If True, then more than one application can access the device. The Silent property determines whether or not to play associated sounds (for instance, a video sound track). Set Silent to True to cut out any associated sound.

The read-only UsesWindows property tells you if the MCI device needs a window for output (for example, Video for Windows). It will be set to True if it does. Use the hWndDisplay property to pass a window handle to the MCI control.

PEN EDIT

Purpose

Use the pen edit control as an enhanced text box for pen computing. It comes in two versions: the HEdit control is a text box control with some pen enhancements, and the BEdit control is a text box with comb or box guides for individual characters. The BEdit style of box can increase character recognition rates. Both controls *require* Microsoft Windows for Pen Computing; they won't even load into your form without it.

Description

The HEdit control looks the same as a standard text control, and in most respects operates like one. It cannot be bound to a data control, and cannot participate in a DDE link.

The BEdit control adds graphic elements to help differentiate characters. These elements come in two styles: boxes and combs. Boxes consist of a square for each character, while a comb looks like the bottom half of a box. Either style can be contiguous (one character box or comb butts up against the next one) or separated. A number of properties set the appearance and spacing of these elements.

Both controls can also be set to accept input beyond their borders if the input started within the border. This is vital in pen computing, as it is very common for a user to draw outside the lines.

The control also passes ink to, and receives character text from the handwriting recognition engine built into the operating system. The control comes with a function to help convert between the C style of pointer and normal Visual Basic variables for use with the recognition functions.

Special Properties

The most important set of properties for these controls involve character recognition. When the user writes on the control, the data type is ink — a special form of bitmap that the Pen operating system recognizes. Use the OnTap and DelayRecog properties to determine when to begin character recognition. If DelayRecog is True, no recognition occurs until explicitly asked for. If DelayRecog is False, then the system evaluates the value of OnTap. If OnTap is True, the system waits for a pen tap to begin recognition. If OnTap is False, the system starts recognition right away. The OnTap property defaults to False, as does DelayRecog.

When the recognition engine has finished analyzing the ink, it triggers the RcResult event. This event has an argument that the recognition engine passes to it; the result contains a set of symbols that describe the possible results, a handle to the ink, and its best guess at what the symbols mean. Use the

CPointerToVBType function to convert the RcResult argument into something Visual Basic can deal with. Setting the CharSet property can greatly increase recognition results, as it restricts recognition to a smaller number of possibilities.

Ink has several properties that determine how it looks and acts. The InkColor property sets the color of the ink with a valid hexadecimal number (as returned by the RGB or QBColor functions). The InkDataMode property specifies how new ink interacts with existing ink. The default setting of 0 replaces any old ink, and a setting of 1 merges new ink with old ink. The InkDataString property sets or returns a compressed string containing the ink data. The InkWidth property sets the width of the ink that gets drawn. The default value of -1 sets the ink width to equal the default setting in the Windows Control Panel. Legal ink widths range from 0 to 15. The hInk property returns a handle to an ink structure for use with advanced API calls.

The InflateBottom, InflateLeft, InflateRight, and InflateTop properties let you set how much space (in pixels) to allow your user to have to draw ink outside the control. Note that the user must start drawing the ink inside the control, and that DelayRecog cannot be set True.

The CombBase property determines the distance (in pixels) from the top of the character cell down to the baseline. The CombColor property lets you specify the color of the comb or box. The CombEndHeight and CombHeight properties set the height of the comb. CombNumCols and CombNumRows determines the total number of input columns and rows to display. Set the distance between individual character areas with the CombSpacing property. The CombStyle property determines the style of the character cells: The default value of 0 gives a comb, while a value of 1 gives boxes. The CombEndMark property determines whether the end-of-text marker is displayed.

PEN INK-ON-BITMAP

Purpose

The pen ink-on-bitmap control enhances a normal picture box for pen awareness. The control enables the user to draw and erase ink on top of a bitmap. The control has facilities for saving the ink.

Description

The control looks like a picture control, and shares many properties with the normal picture control. Its pen enhancements deal with manipulating the special data type called ink.

Special Properties

You can control the color of the ink with the InkColor property. Set this with a valid hexadecimal, as returned by the RGB or QBColor functions. The InkWidth property sets or returns the number of pixels an ink line uses. A setting of -1 (the default) uses the Control Panel's value for ink width. A setting of 0 means that no ink is displayed.

The InkDataMode property lets you control how new ink appears. The default value of 0 means that new ink erases any old ink; a value of 1 merges the new ink with the old ink.

The InkingMode property lets you set how the pen behaves. A setting of 0 means that both the pen tip and the barrel button are disabled, so no drawing can take place. A value of 1 means that the pen tip draws ink, but the barrel button is disabled. A setting of 2 means that the pen tip erases old ink; the barrel button is disabled. Finally, a setting of 3 (the default) means that the pen tip draws ink, and if the barrel button is depressed, the pen tip will erase.

The InkDataString property sets or returns a string that contains the ink data in a compressed format. The InkPicture property returns a handle to the bitmap that contains the ink. The Image property returns a handle to a bitmap containing both the background bitmap and the ink; it's a combination of the Picture and InkPicture properties. The Picture property contains the background bitmap. The hDC property returns a handle to the device context of the control, while the hInk property returns a handle to the ink structure. These might be necessary in some pen-centric API calls.

You can erase all ink in the control by setting the EraseInk property to True.
The IOB event triggers whenever the contents of the control have changed.

PEN KEYBOARD

Purpose

Use the pen keyboard control to display a "virtual keyboard" during pen computing.

Description

The pen keyboard control appears on the form as a special command button with a bitmap of a keyboard displayed on its face. The user can press the button to bring up the keyboard.

The virtual keyboard displays in a normal Windows dialog box. It has the keys of a normal 101-key keyboard. The user can tap on a key with the pen to emulate typing. The keyboard itself never really gets the focus; all keystrokes are sent to the calling application.

Special Properties

Bring up the keyboard dialog box by setting the SKBVisible property to True. You can check on the keyboard's visible status with the SKBVisibleStatus property. Note that the control's Visible property has no effect on the keyboard; it only makes the command button visible and invisible.

Set the position of the keyboard with the SKBLeft and SKBTop properties. These are measured in the ScaleMode of the control's container, and are measured relative to the container's borders. You can read the current position of the keyboard (useful if the user has moved it since you initially placed it) with the SKBLeft Status and SKBRightStatus properties.

The SKBMin property determines if the onscreen keyboard is minimized when the keyboard command button is activated. The default value of False means that it is not; True means that it is. The SKBMinStatus property lets you read the current status of the keyboard: True means the keyboard is minimized, False means that it is not.

The SKBType property determines what style of keyboard to display. The default value of 0 brings up a full keyboard; a setting of 1 brings up a basic keyboard without the number pad, and a setting of 2 brings up a number pad only. The SKBTypeStatus property returns the type of keyboard currently displayed, using the same values as for SKBType.

The SKBChange event triggers whenever the user moves, minimizes, or closes the onscreen keyboard.

FURTHER READING

APPENDIX

F

If you want to learn more about Visual Basic and explore advanced programming techniques, there are three kinds of books you should consider. First, of course, are books written specifically about Visual Basic, such as the one you are reading now and our companion volume, *The Waite Group's Visual Basic How-To, 2nd Edition*. Besides books, you might want to check out the MSBASIC forum on CompuServe (go msbasic at the prompt). There you will find hundreds of Visual Basic applications written by your fellow programmers.

Second, since Visual Basic is intimately involved with the Windows environment, you may want to learn more about the general concepts of Windows programming. While our Visual Basic books show you all you really need to know about Windows to write a Visual Basic application, you may want to explore such matters as the Windows Application Program Interface (API), the creation of dynamic link libraries (DLLs), and Dynamic Data Exchange (DDE) in more detail.

Finally, since Visual Basic incorporates a version of the BASIC language, you will find that many books on BASIC have useful routines that can be adapted to Visual Basic. In general, routines that deal with calculation, string formatting, data file management, sorting, and other hardware-independent matters will easily translate into Visual Basic, particularly if they are written in QuickBASIC or QBasic. Routines dealing with the screen and graphics, the printer, the speaker, the serial port, and other devices probably won't be as useful. This is because Visual Basic and the Windows environment handle devices differently than conventional DOS programs do. The best way to extend Visual Basic in these areas is through the use of the API, as shown in Appendix D, Windows API.

The brief reading list that follows cannot attempt to be complete, since numerous new titles appear each month. Nevertheless, the titles we describe have proven reliable and useful to us in writing this book and in our other work with Visual Basic and with Windows.

Master C++. Rex Woollard, Robert Lafore, Harry Henderson (Waite Group Press, 1992). This package consists of an interactive disk-based tutor and a reference book. Instant and precise feedback on your answers to each question enables you to proceed without confusion. Unlike a book, the software can make sure you've mastered each concept before introducing the next one. If Visual Basic has whetted your appetite for Windows programming, the popular C++ language is probably your best next step. Once you've mastered C++, you can move into the mainstream of Windows programming with the other Windows titles, described below.

Programming Windows. Charles Petzold (Microsoft Press, 1990, 2nd edition). This is Microsoft's "official" guide to Windows programming. It is a thorough exploration of Windows features with numerous short, easy-to-understand examples. The programs are in C, and reflect the older style of Windows programming with the Microsoft SDK, but they can easily be transferred to the friendlier Turbo C++ and QuickC for Windows environments. This would be a good book to use in tandem with the *Windows Programming Primer Plus* below.

The Waite Group's Microsoft QuickBASIC Bible. Mitchell Waite, Robert Arnson, Christy Gemmell, Harry Henderson (Microsoft Press, 1990). This book is structured much like the one you are reading, but it deals with Microsoft's popular QuickBASIC, Visual Basic's immediate ancestor. Since Visual Basic shares so many statements and functions with QuickBASIC, the reference entries in the *QuickBASIC Bible* can supplement those in Appendix B. The tutorials that introduce each chapter can also provide useful programming techniques.

The Waite Group's Microsoft QuickBASIC Primer Plus. Stephen Prata with Harry Henderson (Microsoft Press, 1990). This book is the primer companion to the *Microsoft QuickBASIC Bible.* The chapters in the first three parts, dealing with the structure, data types, flow control, and file management of QuickBASIC, are fully applicable to Visual Basic. We especially recommend this book if you come to Visual Basic without any prior experience with the BASIC language.

The Waite Group's Visual Basic How-To, Second Edition. Zane Thomas, Robert Arnson, Mitchell Waite (Waite Group Press, 1993). As you know, Visual Basic makes many programming tasks much easier than ever before. But Visual Basic 3's wealth of features sometimes makes it hard to know just where to begin. This book presents hundreds of programming problems and situations with complete steps for solving them in Visual Basic. With this book in hand, you can quickly implement the standard features used by nearly every program, then move on to the touches that make your application unique.

The Waite Group's Windows API Bible and *Windows API New Testament.* James L. Conger (Waite Group Press, 1992 and 1993, respectively). As you know, Appendix C of the *Visual Basic SuperBible* introduces the Windows API and briefly summarizes the many API functions. The *Windows API Bible* goes far beyond that in providing a complete reference for the programmer who needs to use many of the more than 600 original API calls; Windows API New Testament covers the over 400 functions that have been added since the release of Windows 3.1. The API functions are grouped into logical categories, each of which is introduced by a tutorial. The reference entry for each function fully describes the syntax and gives usage and program examples. All of the Windows messages are also explained in context, and the new features of Windows 3.1 are included.

Windows Programming Primer Plus. James L. Conger (Waite Group Press, 1992). This book is a very accessible way to learn more about the fundamental structure and concepts of Windows "from the ground up." It follows in the tradition of other Waite Group primers, such as *C Primer Plus,* and features a step-by-step, always friendly approach. The book broadens your programming horizons by showing you how to program Windows in C or C++ using the new easy to use Turbo C++ for Windows and Quick C for Windows environments, which are much like Visual Basic in their integrated, graphical approach to programming. C and C++ can give you a more direct access to the Windows environment than is usually possible in Visual Basic. The new features of Windows 3.1 are included. (This book is compatible with C++ but does not discuss features specific to C++. A beginning knowledge of C is recommended, but the author is careful to explain the more advanced C programming techniques.)

Windows Programming Made Easy. James L. Conger (Waite Group Press, 1993). This is a friendly guide to Windows programming essentials. Although it is based on C, Windows' "native language," *Windows Programming Made Easy* provides an easy-to-follow, accelerated approach to writing Windows applications by limiting coverage to only the essential principles and techniques. Master teacher Robert Lafore uses to-the-point explanations and hands-on examples to show you fundamentals like memory management, programming the GUI, and handling files. (Some limited familiarity with C is assumed in this book.)

PROJECT DISK

G

This book includes a Project Disk containing the source code for the chapter projects. The files can be copied to your hard disk or used directly from the floppy drive. In either case, you should make a copy of the Project Disk to work with and store the original in a safe place. *In order to run all of the projects in this book, you must have Visual Basic 3.0.*

This appendix explains how to install the Project Disk files to your hard disk. The instructions assume that your floppy drive is designated as the A: drive and your hard disk is C:. If your system arrangement differs from this, simply substitute the correct letter in the following DOS commands.

COPYING THE DISK

You'll need a second high-density 3.5-inch floppy disk. At the DOS prompt type

```
DISKCOPY A:  A: ENTER
```

then follow the instructions on screen. Throughout the process, you'll be instructed to insert either the "Source" or "Target" disk. The original Project Disk is the Source and the other floppy is the Target. Once finished, store the original and work with the copy. That will protect the original data.

COPYING THE FILES

If you want to copy the source code to your hard disk, make a new directory on the hard disk before transferring the files. At the DOS prompt type

```
MD  C:\VBSB2E  ENTER
```

to create a directory named VBSB2E on your C: drive. Once done, copy the files from the disk to the new directory. At the DOS prompt type

```
COPY  A:*.*  C:\VBSB2E    ENTER
```

The project files copy into the new directory.

PROGRAM SOURCE CODE

The project files follow a standard naming scheme to make it easy to manage the files. Each project file starts with CHPxx for its name, and follows the standard Visual Basic conventions for the extensions (for example, .FRM for a form, .MAK for the make file, and .BAS for a module). If there are several different files of the same type, the name has an A, B, C, or D appended to the name. For example, the most complex project in the book, Chapter 27, Data Access, comes with these files:

```
CHP27.BAS
CHP27A.FRM
CHP27B.FRM
CHP27C.FRM
CHP27D.FRM
CHP27A.FRX
CHP27B.FRX
CHP27C.FRX
CHP27D.FRX
CHP27.LDB
CHP27.MAK
CHP27.MDB
```

The chapter project files are all saved in ASCII format, so you can examine them using any editor or word processor. Open a chapter project by selecting File Open in Visual Basic, and select the appropriate .MAK file. The make file will automatically load each of the appropriate forms for you. You're now ready to experiment!

All the files have been tested. If you get an error message after transferring the programs from one location to another, go into Visual Basic's File menu. From there, select the Add File... option, point to relocated files, and double-click. This will re-link the files in their new positions. Remember to save the project after re-linking it.

The READ.ME File

The Project Disk includes a file (READ.ME) that provides additional details and updates about the programs in this book. To view this file, insert the Project Disk into the floppy drive and type

```
TYPE  A:READ.ME | MORE      ENTER
```

INDEX

Books have a substantial influence on the destruction of the forests of the Earth. For example, it takes 17 trees to produce one ton of paper. A first printing of 30,000 copies of a typical 480 page book consumes 108,000 pounds of paper which will require 918 trees!

Waite Group Press™ is against the clear-cutting of forests and supports reforestation of the Pacific Northwest of the United States and Canada, where most of this paper comes from. As a publisher with several hundred thousand books sold each year, we feel an obligation to give back to the planet. We will therefore support and contribute a percentage of our proceeds to organizations which seek to preserve the forests of planet Earth.

This is a legal agreement between you, the end user and purchaser, and The Waite Group®, Inc., and the authors of the programs contained in the disk. By opening the sealed disk package, you are agreeing to be bound by the terms of this Agreement. If you do not agree with the terms of this Agreement, promptly return the unopened disk package and the accompanying items (including the related book and other written material) to the place you obtained them for a refund.

SOFTWARE LICENSE

1. The Waite Group, Inc. grants you the right to use one copy of the enclosed software programs (the programs) on a single computer system (whether a single CPU, part of a licensed network, or a terminal connected to a single CPU). Each concurrent user of the program must have exclusive use of the related Waite Group, Inc. written materials.

2. The program, including the copyrights in each program, is owned by the respective author and the copyright in the entire work is owned by The Waite Group, Inc. and they are therefore protected under the copyright laws of the United States and other nations, under international treaties. You may make only one copy of the disk containing the programs exclusively for backup or archival purposes, or you may transfer the programs to one hard disk drive, using the original for backup or archival purposes. You may make no other copies of the programs, and you may make no copies of all or any part of the related Waite Group, Inc. written materials.

3. You may not rent or lease the programs, but you may transfer ownership of the programs and related written materials (including any and all updates and earlier versions) if you keep no copies of either, and if you make sure the transferee agrees to the terms of this license.

4. You may not decompile, reverse engineer, disassemble, copy, create a derivative work, or otherwise use the programs except as stated in this Agreement.

GOVERNING LAW

This Agreement is governed by the laws of the State of California.

SOFTWARE LICENSE AGREEMENT

VISUAL BASIC TASK JUMP TABLE

Clipboard

Transfer text or graphics data between windows or applications: **Clipboard** (object), 72

Find out whether the clipboard has graphics or text: **GetFormat**, 875

Get graphics from the clipboard: **GetData**, 873

Get text from the clipboard: **GetText**, 877

Send graphics to the clipboard: **SetData**, 878

Send text to the clipboard: **SetText**, 880

Clear the contents of the clipboard: **Clear**, 872

Communicate with DOS windows: **SendKeys**, 619

Controls (General)

Examine attributes of active control: **ActiveControl**, 289

Respond to user change in contents: **Change**, 321

Manipulate controls in a control array: **Index**, 297

Identify a particular control: **Tag**, 302

Find form that contains the control: **Parent**, 300

Label a control on a form: **Label**, 116

Create a new instance in a control array: **Load**, 185

Debugging

Halt program execution: **Stop**, 1455

Output program values for debugging: **Debug** (object), 1448

Execute a Visual Basic statement immediately: **Immediate Pane**, 1449

Set and clear breakpoints: **Toggle Breakpoint, Clear All Breakpoints**, 1456, 1448

Step through code including procedures: **Single Step**, 1454

Step through code without showing procedures: **Procedure Step**, 1452

Set or show next statement to be executed: **Set Next Statement, Show Next Statement**, 1452, 1454

Dialog Boxes (and related controls)

Display a message in a box with standard icons: **MsgBox** (function and statement), 655, 661

Get text from a user by displaying a box: **InputBox$**, 653

Specify choices that can be on or off: **Check box** (control), 68

Define a group of choices of which only one can be selected: **Option button** (control), 136

Create a group of related controls: **Frame** (control), 106

Label part of a dialog box: **Label**, 116

Display a button that executes a specified action: **Command button** (control), 78

Display a common dialog box: **Common Dialog**, 82

Drive, Directory, and File List Boxes

Set up boxes for working with the disk: **Drive list box, Directory list box, File list box** (objects), 92, 89, 96

Set or read the current drive in a Drive list box: **Drive**, 745

Set or read the name of the currently selected file: **FileName**, 747

Set or read the search path for a Directory or File list box: **Path**, 761

Specify what happens when the search path is changed: **PathChange**, 763

Set or read the file search pattern for a File list box: **Pattern**, 764

Specify what happens when file search pattern is changed: **PatternChange**, 766

Specify DOS attributes of files to be displayed in list: **Archive, Hidden, ReadOnly, System**, 742, 749, 767, 773

Obtain items in a Drive, Dir, or File box's list: **List, ListCount, ListIndex**, 751, 754, 755

Dynamic Data Exchange (DDE)

Specify type of link (hot/cold and server status): **LinkMode**, 947

Specify actions to take when a link is opened: **LinkOpen**, 951

Get information from a linked application: **LinkRequest**, 956

Specify item and topic to be used in a link: **LinkItem, LinkTopic**, 942, 963

Send contents of a picture box to a linked application: **LinkSend**, 959

Send a command to a linked application: **LinkExecute**, 939

Send information from a client to a server: **LinkPoke**, 954

Deal with errors or timeouts during link: **LinkError, LinkTimeout**, 934, 960

Specify what happens when a link is closed: **LinkClose**, 932

Focus

Specify which application gets the focus: **AppActivate**, 803

Specify which form or control gets the focus: **SetFocus**, 816

Specify what happens when a form or control gets the focus: **GotFocus**, 811

Specify what happens when a form or control loses the focus: **LostFocus**, 814

Specify whether a control can respond to user input: **Enabled**, 807

Control use of Tab key to move between controls: **TabIndex, TabStop**, 817, 819

Fonts

Set or get name of current font: **FontName**, 490

Find out what fonts are available: **FontCount, Fonts**, 485, 492

Set point size of font: **FontSize**, 495

Set typestyle: **FontBold, FontItalic, FontStrikethru, FontTransparent, FontUnderline**, 482, 487, 497, 499, 502

Forms (General)

Position form on screen: **Left, Top**, 257, 264

Set dimensions of form on screen: **Height, Width**, 251, 270

Display form title: **Caption**, 245

Set up menu for a form: **Menu** (control), 129

Set up button to perform a specified action: **Command button** (control), 78

Set color and style: **BackColor, BorderStyle, ForeColor**, 234, 239, 248

Allow resizing of form: **ControlBox, MaxButton, MinButton**, 178, 188, 193

Respond to user actions: **Icon, MousePointer, Resize, WindowState**, 255, 260, 201, 210

Show or hide form: **Hide, Show, Visible**, 181, 204, 267

Load form without showing: **Load** (statement), 185

Refer to forms in code: **Name**, 294

Activate a particular form or control at run time: **Screen** (object), 149

Examine attributes of active form: **ActiveForm**, 292

Specify actions to take place when form is loaded: **Load** (event), 183

Remove form: **Unload**, 206

Create an MDI main form: **New MDI Form**, 128

Create MDI child forms: **MDIChild**, 190

Trap keyboard input: **KeyPreview**, 614

Graphics (Drawing)

Set Colors: **RGB, QBColor**, 361, 359

Specify style and width for shape boundary line: **DrawStyle, DrawWidth**, 434, 437

Specify color and fill pattern for drawing: **FillColor, FillStyle**, 439, 443

Specify how drawing will interact with background: **DrawMode**, 430

Draw shapes on a graphics object: **Circle, Line, PSet**, 424, 446, 355

Clear a drawing area: **Cls**, 341

Load graphics from a file: **LoadPicture**, 346

Determine graphics object initially appearing in a form: **Picture** (property), 351

Determine color of a point: **Point**, 353

SATISFACTION REPORT CARD

Please fill out this card if you wish to know of future updates to
***Visual Basic SuperBible, Second Edition,* or to receive our catalog.**

Company Name:

Division/Department: **Mail Stop:**

Last Name: **First Name:**   **Middle Initial:**

Street Address:

City: **State:**   **Zip:**

Daytime telephone: ( )

Date product was acquired: Month   **Day**   **Year**   **Your Occupation:**

Overall, how would you rate *Visual Basic SuperBible, Second Edition*?
- ☐ Excellent
- ☐ Very Good
- ☐ Good
- ☐ Fair
- ☐ Below Average
- ☐ Poor

What did you like MOST about this book?

What did you like LEAST about this book?

Please describe any problems you may have encountered with installing or using the disk:

How did you use this book (problem-solver, tutorial, reference...)?

What is your level of computer expertise?
- ☐ New
- ☐ Dabbler
- ☐ Hacker
- ☐ Power User
- ☐ Programmer
- ☐ Experienced Professional

What computer languages are you familiar with?

Please describe your computer hardware:

Computer _____ Hard disk _____
Disk drive(s) _____ CD ROM _____
Video card _____ Monitor _____
Printer _____ Peripherals _____
Sound card _____ Other _____

Where did you buy this book?
- ☐ Bookstore (name):
- ☐ Discount store (name):
- ☐ Computer store (name):
- ☐ Catalog (name):
- ☐ Direct from WGP
- ☐ Other

What price did you pay for this book?

What influenced your purchase of this book?
- ☐ Recommendation
- ☐ Advertisement
- ☐ Magazine review
- ☐ Store display
- ☐ Mailing
- ☐ Book's format
- ☐ Reputation of Waite Group Press
- ☐ Other

How many computer books do you buy each year?

How many other Waite Group books do you own?

What is your favorite Waite Group book?

Is there any program or subject you would like to see Waite Group Press cover in a similar approach?

Additional comments?

Send to: **Waite Group Press, Inc.**
             200 Tamal Plaza
             Corte Madera, CA 94925

☐ **Check here for a free Waite Group catalog**

Visual Basic SuperBible, Second Edition

BEFORE YOU OPEN THE DISK OR CD-ROM PACKAGE ON THE FACING PAGE, CAREFULLY READ THE LICENSE AGREEMENT.

Opening this package indicates that you agree to abide by the license agreement found in the back of this book. If you do not agree with it, promptly return the unopened disk package (including the related book) to the place you obtained them for a refund.